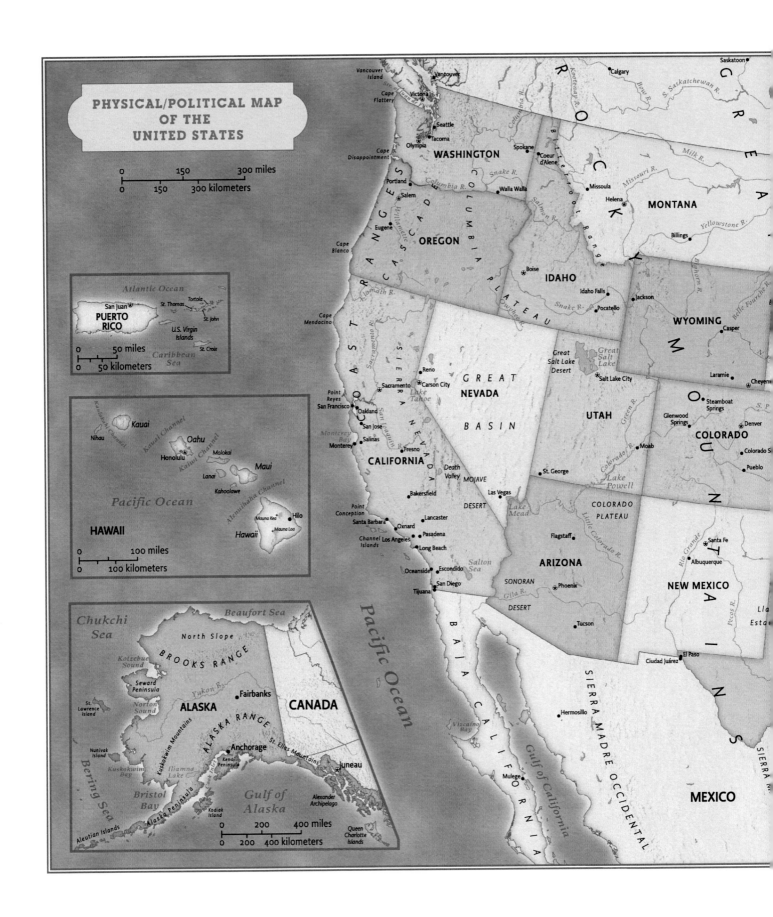

PHYSICAL/POLITICAL MAP
OF THE
UNITED STATES

PRAISE FOR ERIC FONER'S *GIVE ME LIBERTY!*

"The book is inviting to students . . . well-organized and easy to read . . . I love the way Dr. Foner writes! The textbook comes alive with his scholarship and teaching experience."
—Marianne Leeper, *Trinity Valley Community College*

"I find that Foner strikes the perfect balance between political, legal, social, and cultural history. . . . [*Give Me Liberty!*] includes the most current or most relevant scholarship."
—David Anderson, *Louisiana Tech University*

"Often, history textbooks can seem to be disjointed retellings of facts and concepts that remind one of an encyclopedia. [Foner's] freedom theme ties the material together well, which isn't always easy with this kind of broad textbook. I do think it's effective in tying the social and political together."
—James Karmel, *Harford Community College*

"Foner's textbook is superb. It is well informed, elegantly written, and offers a kind of narrative and interpretive coherence that is rare among textbooks."
—Jeffrey Adler, *University of Florida*

"The theme of freedom is very clearly and adeptly integrated. . . . *Give Me Liberty!* provides a good model for students on how to investigate and carry through a theme in their own writings."
—Jim Dudlo, *Brookhaven College, Dallas Community College District*

"*Give Me Liberty!* offers a nice, comprehensive coverage of American history. I feel that equal weight is given to various topics. 'Voices of Freedom' is actually one of the major features of the book that prompted me to adopt the text. I am not aware of any other text on the market that has this superb feature. . . . [A] splendid approach."
—Jonathan A. Noyalas, *Lord Fairfax Community College*

"I've had a number of students in the last year comment on how easy the text is to use with the integrated focus questions and terms."
—Lauren Braun-Strumfels, *Raritan Valley Community College*

"*Give Me Liberty!* is visually appealing in many different ways. The manner in which the illustrations, maps, and pedagogical components are incorporated . . . makes the text more accessible and much less intimidating."
—Kent McGaughy, *Houston Community College–NW Campus*

"I appreciate the book's terrifically accessible writing as well as its clear statement of themes. It has a wonderfully seamless and authoritative quality to its writing. I plan to continue to offer it to my students for many years to come."
—Beverly Gage, *Yale University*

GIVE ME LIBERTY!

AN AMERICAN HISTORY

Fourth Edition

GIVE ME LIBERTY!

AN AMERICAN HISTORY

Fourth Edition

ERIC FONER

W · W · NORTON & COMPANY
NEW YORK · LONDON

W. W. Norton & Company has been independent since its founding in 1923, when William Warder Norton and Mary D. Herter Norton first published lectures delivered at the People's Institute, the adult education division of New York City's Cooper Union. The firm soon expanded its program beyond the Institute, publishing books by celebrated academics from America and abroad. By mid-century, the two major pillars of Norton's publishing program—trade books and college texts—were firmly established. In the 1950s, the Norton family transferred control of the company to its employees, and today—with a staff of 400 and a comparable number of trade, college, and professional titles published each year—W. W. Norton & Company stands as the largest and oldest publishing house owned wholly by its employees.

Fourth Edition

Editor: Steve Forman
Associate Editor: Justin Cahill
Editorial Assistant: Penelope Lin
Managing Editor, College: Marian Johnson
Managing Editor, College Digital Media: Kim Yi
Copy Editor: Ellen Lohman
Marketing Manager: Sarah England
Media Editors: Steve Hoge, Tacy Quinn
Assistant Editor, Media: Stefani Wallace
Production Manager: Sean Mintus
Art Director: Hope Miller Goodell
Designer: Chin-Yee Lai
Photo Editor: Stephanie Romeo
Photo Research: Donna Ranieri
Composition and Layout: Jouve
Manufacturing: Transcontinental

Library of Congress Cataloging-in-Publication Data

Foner, Eric.
    Give me liberty! : An American history / Eric Foner.—Fourth edition.
        pages cm
    Includes bibliographical references and index.
    ISBN 978-0-393-92026-0 (hardcover)
    1. United States—History. 2. United States—Politics and government. 3. Democracy—United States—History. 4. Liberty—History. I. Title.
E178.F66 2014
973—dc23
                                                                    2013029664
ISBN: 978-0-393-92026-0

W. W. Norton & Company, Inc., 500 Fifth Avenue, New York, N.Y. 10110
                        www.wwnorton.com

W. W. Norton & Company Ltd., Castle House, 75/76 Wells Street, London W1T 3QT

1 2 3 4 5 6 7 8 9 0

ABOUT THE AUTHOR

ERIC FONER is DeWitt Clinton Professor of History at Columbia University, where he earned his B.A. and Ph.D. In his teaching and scholarship, he focuses on the Civil War and Reconstruction, slavery, and nineteenth-century America. Professor Foner's publications include *Free Soil, Free Labor, Free Men: The Ideology of the Republican Party before the Civil War*; *Tom Paine and Revolutionary America*; *Nothing but Freedom: Emancipation and Its Legacy*; *Reconstruction: America's Unfinished Revolution, 1863–1877*; *The Story of American Freedom*; and *Forever Free: The Story of Emancipation and Reconstruction*. His history of Reconstruction won the *Los Angeles Times* Book Award for History, the Bancroft Prize, and the Parkman Prize. He has served as president of the Organization of American Historians and the American Historical Association. In 2006 he received the Presidential Award for Outstanding Teaching from Columbia University. His most recent book is *The Fiery Trial: Abraham Lincoln and American Slavery*, winner of the Bancroft and Lincoln Prizes and the Pulitzer Prize for History.

CONTENTS

ABOUT THE AUTHOR ... vii
LIST OF MAPS, TABLES, AND FIGURES ... xxxiii
DEDICATION ... xxxvii
PREFACE ... xxxix
ACKNOWLEDGMENTS ... xlv

PART 1: AMERICAN COLONIES TO 1763

1. A NEW WORLD ... 4

THE FIRST AMERICANS ... 6
The Settling of the Americas ... 6 ⋆ Indian Societies of the
Americas ... 8 ⋆ Mound Builders of the Mississippi River Valley ... 9 ⋆
Western Indians ... 10 ⋆ Indians of Eastern North America ... 10 ⋆ Native
American Religion ... 12 ⋆ Land and Property ... 12 ⋆ Gender
Relations ... 14 ⋆ European Views of the Indians ... 14

INDIAN FREEDOM, EUROPEAN FREEDOM ... 15
Indian Freedom ... 15 ⋆ Christian Liberty ... 16 ⋆ Freedom and
Authority ... 17 ⋆ Liberty and Liberties ... 17

THE EXPANSION OF EUROPE ... 18
Chinese and Portuguese Navigation ... 18 ⋆ Portugal and West
Africa ... 19 ⋆ Freedom and Slavery in Africa ... 20 ⋆ The Voyages of
Columbus ... 20

CONTACT ... 21
Columbus in the New World ... 21 ⋆ Exploration and Conquest ... 23 ⋆
The Demographic Disaster ... 24

THE SPANISH EMPIRE ... 24
Governing Spanish America ... 25 ⋆ Colonists in Spanish
America ... 25 ⋆ Colonists and Indians ... 26 ⋆ Justifications for
Conquest ... 27 ⋆ Spreading the Faith ... 28 ⋆ Piety and Profit ... 29 ⋆
Las Casas's Complaint ... 29 ⋆ Reforming the Empire ... 30 ⋆ Exploring
North America ... 31 ⋆ Spanish Florida ... 33 ⋆ Spain in the
Southwest ... 33 ⋆ The Pueblo Revolt ... 34

THE FRENCH AND DUTCH EMPIRES ... 35
French Colonization ... 35

Voices of Freedom: *From* Bartolomé de las Casas, *History of the Indies*
(1528), and *From* "Declaration of Josephe" (December 19, 1681) ... 36

New France and the Indians ... 38 ⋆ The Dutch Empire ... 41 ⋆ Dutch Freedom ... 41 ⋆ Freedom in New Netherland ... 41 ⋆ The Dutch and Religious Toleration ... 42 ⋆ Settling New Netherland ... 43 ⋆ New Netherland and the Indians ... 44

REVIEW ... 47

2. BEGINNINGS OF ENGLISH AMERICA, 1607-1660 ... 48

ENGLAND AND THE NEW WORLD ... 50
Unifying the English Nation ... 50 ⋆ England and Ireland ... 50 ⋆ England and North America ... 51 ⋆ Spreading Protestantism ... 52 ⋆ The Social Crisis ... 52 ⋆ Masterless Men ... 53

THE COMING OF THE ENGLISH ... 54
English Emigrants ... 54 ⋆ Indentured Servants ... 55 ⋆ Land and Liberty ... 55 ⋆ Englishmen and Indians ... 56 ⋆ The Transformation of Indian Life ... 57 ⋆ Changes in the Land ... 58

SETTLING THE CHESAPEAKE ... 58
The Jamestown Colony ... 58 ⋆ From Company to Society ... 59 ⋆ Powhatan and Pocahontas ... 59 ⋆ The Uprising of 1622 ... 60 ⋆ A Tobacco Colony ... 61 ⋆ Women and the Family ... 62 ⋆ The Maryland Experiment ... 63 ⋆ Religion in Maryland ... 64

THE NEW ENGLAND WAY ... 64
The Rise of Puritanism ... 64 ⋆ Moral Liberty ... 65 ⋆ The Pilgrims at Plymouth ... 66 ⋆ The Great Migration ... 67 ⋆ The Puritan Family ... 68 ⋆ Government and Society in Massachusetts ... 68 ⋆ Church and State in Puritan Massachusetts ... 70

NEW ENGLANDERS DIVIDED ... 70
Roger Williams ... 71 ⋆ Rhode Island and Connecticut ... 71 ⋆ The Trials of Anne Hutchinson ... 72 ⋆ Puritans and Indians ... 73

Voices of Freedom: From "The Trial of Anne Hutchinson" (1637), and From John Winthrop, Speech to the Massachusetts General Court (July 3, 1645) ... 74

The Pequot War ... 76 ⋆ The New England Economy ... 77 ⋆ The Merchant Elite ... 78 ⋆ The Half-Way Covenant ... 78

RELIGION, POLITICS, AND FREEDOM ... 79
The Rights of Englishmen ... 79 ⋆ The English Civil War ... 80 ⋆ England's Debate over Freedom ... 80 ⋆ English Liberty ... 81 ⋆ The Civil War and English America ... 82 ⋆ The Crisis in Maryland ... 82 ⋆ Cromwell and the Empire ... 83

REVIEW ... 85

3. CREATING ANGLO-AMERICA, 1660-1750 ... 86

GLOBAL COMPETITION AND THE EXPANSION OF ENGLAND'S EMPIRE ... 88

The Mercantilist System ... 88 * The Conquest of New Netherland ... 88 * New York and the Rights of Englishmen and Englishwomen ... 90 * New York and the Indians ... 90 * The Charter of Liberties ... 91 * The Founding of Carolina ... 91 * The Holy Experiment ... 92 * Quaker Liberty ... 93 * Land in Pennsylvania ... 94

ORIGINS OF AMERICAN SLAVERY ... 94

Englishmen and Africans ... 94 * Slavery in History ... 95 * Slavery in the West Indies ... 95 * Slavery and the Law ... 97 * The Rise of Chesapeake Slavery ... 98 * Bacon's Rebellion: Land and Labor in Virginia ... 99 * The End of the Rebellion, and Its Consequences ... 100 * A Slave Society ... 100 * Notions of Freedom ... 101

COLONIES IN CRISIS ... 101

The Glorious Revolution ... 102 * The Glorious Revolution in America ... 103 * The Maryland Uprising ... 103 * Leisler's Rebellion ... 104 * Changes in New England ... 104 * The Prosecution of Witches ... 105 * The Salem Witch Trials ... 105

THE GROWTH OF COLONIAL AMERICA ... 106

A Diverse Population ... 107 * Attracting Settlers ... 107 * The German Migration ... 109 * Religious Diversity ... 110 * Indian Life in Transition ... 111

Voices of Freedom: *From* Letter by a Swiss-German Immigrant to Pennsylvania (August 23, 1769), and *From* Memorial against Non-English Immigration (December 1727) ... 112

Regional Diversity ... 114 * The Consumer Revolution ... 115 * Colonial Cities ... 115 * Colonial Artisans ... 116 * An Atlantic World ... 116

SOCIAL CLASSES IN THE COLONIES ... 118

The Colonial Elite ... 118 * Anglicization ... 119 * The South Carolina Aristocracy ... 119 * Poverty in the Colonies ... 120 * The Middle Ranks ... 121 * Women and the Household Economy ... 122 * North America at Mid-Century ... 123

REVIEW ... 125

4. SLAVERY, FREEDOM, AND THE STRUGGLE FOR EMPIRE TO 1763 ... 126

SLAVERY AND EMPIRE ... 128

Atlantic Trade ... 128 * Africa and the Slave Trade ... 130 * The Middle Passage ... 130 * Chesapeake Slavery ... 132 * Freedom and Slavery in the Chesapeake ... 133 * Indian Slavery in Early Carolina ... 133 * The

Rice Kingdom ... 134 * The Georgia Experiment ... 134 * Slavery in the North ... 135

SLAVE CULTURES AND SLAVE RESISTANCE ... 136

Becoming African-American ... 136 * African Religion in Colonial America ... 136 * African-American Cultures ... 137 * Resistance to Slavery ... 138 * The Crisis of 1739–1741 ... 139

AN EMPIRE OF FREEDOM ... 140

British Patriotism ... 140 * The British Constitution ... 140 * The Language of Liberty ... 141 * Republican Liberty ... 141 * Liberal Freedom ... 142

THE PUBLIC SPHERE ... 143

The Right to Vote ... 144 * Political Cultures ... 144 * Colonial Government ... 145 * The Rise of the Assemblies ... 146 * Politics in Public ... 146 * The Colonial Press ... 147 * Freedom of Expression and Its Limits ... 148 * The Trial of Zenger ... 148 * The American Enlightenment ... 149

THE GREAT AWAKENING ... 150

Religious Revivals ... 150 * The Preaching of Whitefield ... 151 * The Awakening's Impact ... 151

IMPERIAL RIVALRIES ... 152

Spanish North America ... 152 * The Spanish in California ... 154 * The French Empire ... 155

BATTLE FOR THE CONTINENT ... 156

The Middle Ground ... 156 * The Seven Years' War ... 157 * A World Transformed ... 158 * Pontiac's Rebellion ... 160 * The Proclamation Line ... 160 * Pennsylvania and the Indians ... 161

Voices of Freedom: *From* Pontiac, *Speeches* (1762 and 1763), and *From The Interesting Narrative of the Life of Olaudah Equiano, or Gustavus Vassa, the African* (1789) ... 162

Colonial Identities ... 164

REVIEW ... 166

PART 2: A NEW NATION, 1763 –1840

5. THE AMERICAN REVOLUTION, 1763-1783 ... 170

THE CRISIS BEGINS ... 171

Consolidating the Empire ... 172 * Taxing the Colonies ... 173 * The Stamp Act Crisis ... 173 * Taxation and Representation ... 174 * Liberty and Resistance ... 175 * Politics in the Streets ... 176 * The Regulators ... 176 * The Tenant Uprising ... 178

THE ROAD TO REVOLUTION ... 178

The Townshend Crisis ... 178 * Homespun Virtue ... 179 * The Boston Massacre ... 179 * Wilkes and Liberty ... 181 * The Tea Act ... 181 * The Intolerable Acts ... 181

THE COMING OF INDEPENDENCE ... 182

The Continental Congress ... 182 * The Continental Association ... 183 * The Sweets of Liberty ... 183 * The Outbreak of War ... 184 * Independence? ... 185 * Common Sense ... 186 * Paine's Impact ... 187 * The Declaration of Independence ... 187

Voices of Freedom: From Thomas Paine, Common Sense (1776), and From Jonathan Boucher, A View of the Causes and Consequences of the American Revolution (1775) ... 188

The Declaration and American Freedom ... 190 * An Asylum for Mankind ... 191 * The Global Declaration of Independence ... 192

SECURING INDEPENDENCE ... 193

The Balance of Power ... 193 * Blacks in the Revolution ... 193 * The First Years of the War ... 194 * The Battle of Saratoga ... 195 * The War in the South ... 197 * Victory at Last ... 199

REVIEW ... 203

6. THE REVOLUTION WITHIN ... 204

DEMOCRATIZING FREEDOM ... 206

The Dream of Equality ... 206 * Expanding the Political Nation ... 206 * The Revolution in Pennsylvania ... 207 * The New Constitutions ... 208 * The Right to Vote ... 209 * Democratizing Government ... 209

TOWARD RELIGIOUS TOLERATION ... 210

Catholic Americans ... 211 * The Founders and Religion ... 211 * Separating Church and State ... 212 * Jefferson and Religious Liberty ... 213 * The Revolution and the Churches ... 214 * Christian Republicanism ... 215

DEFINING ECONOMIC FREEDOM ... 215

Toward Free Labor ... 215 * The Soul of a Republic ... 216 * The Politics of Inflation ... 217 * The Debate over Free Trade ... 218

THE LIMITS OF LIBERTY ... 218

Colonial Loyalists ... 218 * Loyalists' Plight ... 219 * The Indians' Revolution ... 221 * White Freedom, Indian Freedom ... 222

SLAVERY AND THE REVOLUTION ... 223

The Language of Slavery and Freedom ... 223 * Obstacles to Abolition ... 224 * The Cause of General Liberty ... 225 * Petitions for Freedom ... 225 * British Emancipators ... 226 * Voluntary Emancipations ... 228 * Abolition in the North ... 228 * Free Black Communities ... 229

Voices of Freedom: *From* Abigail Adams to John Adams, Braintree, Mass. (March 31, 1776), and *From* Petitions of Slaves to the Massachusetts Legislature (1773 and 1777) ... 230

DAUGHTERS OF LIBERTY ... 232
Revolutionary Women ... 232 * Gender and Politics ... 232 * Republican Motherhood ... 234 * The Arduous Struggle for Liberty ... 235

REVIEW ... 237

7. FOUNDING A NATION, 1783-1791 ... 238

AMERICA UNDER THE CONFEDERATION ... 240
The Articles of Confederation ... 240 * Congress and the West ... 242 * Settlers and the West ... 242 * The Land Ordinances ... 243 * The Confederation's Weaknesses ... 245 * Shays's Rebellion ... 246 * Nationalists of the 1780s ... 246

A NEW CONSTITUTION ... 247
The Structure of Government ... 248 * The Limits of Democracy ... 249 * The Division and Separation of Powers ... 250 * The Debate over Slavery ... 251 * Slavery in the Constitution ... 251 * The Final Document ... 253

THE RATIFICATION DEBATE AND THE ORIGIN OF THE BILL OF RIGHTS ... 254
The Federalist ... 254 * "Extend the Sphere" ... 255 * The Anti-Federalists ... 256 * The Bill of Rights ... 257

Voices of Freedom: *From* David Ramsay, *The History of the American Revolution* (1789), and *From* James Winthrop, Anti-Federalist Essay Signed "Agrippa" (1787) ... 260

"WE THE PEOPLE" ... 263
National Identity ... 263 * Indians in the New Nation ... 263 * Blacks and the Republic ... 266 * Jefferson, Slavery, and Race ... 268 * Principles of Freedom ... 269

REVIEW ... 271

8. SECURING THE REPUBLIC, 1791-1815 ... 272

POLITICS IN AN AGE OF PASSION ... 273
Hamilton's Program ... 274 * The Emergence of Opposition ... 274 * The Jefferson-Hamilton Bargain ... 275 * The Impact of the French Revolution ... 276 * Political Parties ... 277 * The Whiskey Rebellion ... 278 * The Republican Party ... 279 * An Expanding Political Sphere ... 279 * The Democratic-Republican Societies ... 280 * The Rights of Women ... 281 * Women and the Republic ... 281

Voices of Freedom: *From* Judith Sargent Murray, "On the Equality of the Sexes" (1790), and *From* Address of the Democratic-Republican Society of Pennsylvania (December 18, 1794) ... 282

THE ADAMS PRESIDENCY ... 284

The Election of 1796 ... 284 * The "Reign of Witches" ... 285 * The Virginia and Kentucky Revolutions ... 286 * The "Revolution of 1800" ... 287 * Slavery and Politics ... 288 * The Haitian Revolution ... 288 * Gabriel's Rebellion ... 289

JEFFERSON IN POWER ... 290

Judicial Review ... 291 * The Louisiana Purchase ... 292 * Lewis and Clark ... 294 * Incorporating Louisiana ... 294 * The Barbary Wars ... 295 * The Embargo ... 296 * Madison and Pressure for War ... 297

THE "SECOND WAR OF INDEPENDENCE" ... 297

The Indian Response ... 298 * Tecumseh's Vision ... 298 * The War of 1812 ... 299 * The War's Aftermath ... 302 * The End of the Federalist Party ... 303

REVIEW ... 305

9. THE MARKET REVOLUTION, 1800-1840 ... 306

A NEW ECONOMY ... 308

Roads and Steamboats ... 309 * The Erie Canal ... 309 * Railroads and the Telegraph ... 311 * The Rise of the West ... 312 * The Cotton Kingdom ... 315 * The Unfree Westward Movement ... 317

MARKET SOCIETY ... 318

Commercial Farmers ... 318 * The Growth of Cities ... 319 * The Factory System ... 319 * The Industrial Worker ... 323 * The "Mill Girls" ... 323 * The Growth of Immigration ... 324 * Irish and German Newcomers ... 324 * The Rise of Nativism ... 326 * The Transformation of Law ... 327

THE FREE INDIVIDUAL ... 328

The West and Freedom ... 329 * The Transcendentalists ... 330 * Individualism ... 330

Voices of Freedom: *From* Ralph Waldo Emerson, "The American Scholar" (1837), and *From* "Factory Life as It Is, by an Operative" (1845) ... 332

The Second Great Awakening ... 334 * The Awakening's Impact ... 335 * The Emergence of Mormonism ... 336

THE LIMITS OF PROSPERITY ... 337

Liberty and Prosperity ... 337 * Race and Opportunity ... 338 * The Cult of Domesticity ... 339 * Women and Work ... 340 * The Early Labor Movement ... 341 * The "Liberty of Living" ... 342

REVIEW ... 345

10. DEMOCRACY IN AMERICA, 1815–1840 ... 346

THE TRIUMPH OF DEMOCRACY ... 348

Property and Democracy ... 348 * The Dorr War ... 348 * Tocqueville on
Democracy ... 349 * The Information Revolution ... 350 * The Limits of
Democracy ... 351 * A Racial Democracy ... 352 * Race and Class ... 353

NATIONALISM AND ITS DISCONTENTS ... 353

The American System ... 353 * Banks and Money ... 355 * The Panic of ...
1819 ... 355 * The Politics of the Panic ... 356 * The Missouri Controversy
... 356 * The Slavery Question ... 358

NATION, SECTION, AND PARTY ... 359

The United States and the Latin American Wars of Independence ... 359 *
The Monroe Doctrine ... 360 * The Election of 1824 ... 361

Voices of Freedom: *From* President James Monroe, Annual Message
to Congress (1823), and *From* John C. Calhoun, "A Disquisition on
Government" (ca. 1845) ... 362

The Nationalism of John Quincy Adams ... 364 * "Liberty Is
Power" ... 365 * Martin Van Buren and the Democratic Party ... 365 *
The Election of 1828 ... 366

THE AGE OF JACKSON ... 367

The Party System ... 367 * Democrats and Whigs ... 368 * Public and
Private Freedom ... 369 * Politics and Morality ... 370 * South Carolina
and Nullification ... 371 * Calhoun's Political Theory ... 371 * The
Nullification Crisis ... 373 * Indian Removal ... 374 * The Supreme Court
and the Indians ... 374

THE BANK WAR AND AFTER ... 377

Biddle's Bank ... 377 * The Pet Banks and the Economy ... 379 *
The Panic of 1837 ... 380 * Van Buren in Office ... 380 * The Election
of 1840 ... 381 * His Accidency ... 382

REVIEW ... 384

PART 3: SLAVERY, FREEDOM, AND THE CRISIS OF THE UNION, 1840–1877

11. THE PECULIAR INSTITUTION ... 388

THE OLD SOUTH ... 390

Cotton Is King ... 390 * The Second Middle Passage ... 391 * Slavery and
the Nation ... 391 * The Southern Economy ... 393 * Plain Folk of the Old
South ... 394 * The Planter Class ... 395 * The Paternalist Ethos ... 396 *

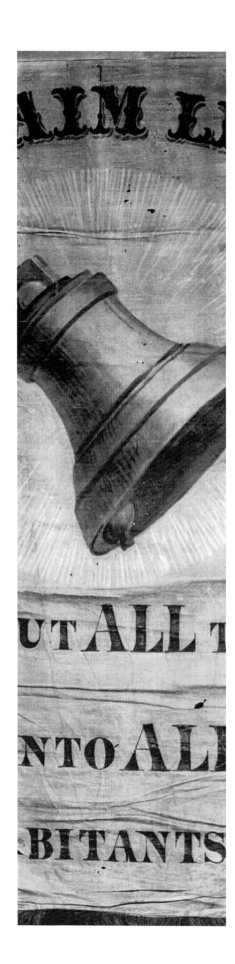

The Code of Honor ... 396 * The Proslavery Argument ... 398 * Abolition
in the Americas ... 399 * Slavery and Liberty ... 400 * Slavery and
Civilization ... 400

LIFE UNDER SLAVERY ... 401
Slaves and the Law ... 401 * Conditions of Slave Life ... 402 * Free Blacks
in the Old South ... 403

Voices of Freedom: *From* Letter by Joseph Taper to Joseph Long
(1840), and *From* "Slavery and the Bible" (1850) ... 404

The Upper and Lower South ... 407 * Slave Labor ... 408 * Gang Labor and
Task Labor ... 408 * Slavery in the Cities ... 410 * Maintaining Order ... 410

SLAVE CULTURE ... 411
The Slave Family ... 412 * The Threat of Sale ... 412 * Gender Roles
among Slaves ... 413 * Slave Religion ... 413 * The Gospel of Freedom ...
414 * The Desire for Liberty ... 415

RESISTANCE TO SLAVERY ... 416
Forms of Resistance ... 416 * Fugitive Slaves ... 418 * The *Amistad* ... 419 *
Slave Revolts ... 419 * Nat Turner's Rebellion ... 420

REVIEW ... 423

12. AN AGE OF REFORM, 1820–1840 ... 424

THE REFORM IMPULSE ... 425
Utopian Communities ... 426 * The Shakers ... 426 * Oneida ... 427 *
Worldly Communities ... 428 * The Owenites ... 429 * Religion and
Reform ... 430 * The Temperance Movement ... 431 * Critics of
Reform ... 431 * Reformers and Freedom ... 432 * The Invention of the
Asylum ... 433 * The Common School ... 433

THE CRUSADE AGAINST SLAVERY ... 435
Colonization ... 435 * Blacks and Colonization ... 435 * Militant Abolitionism
... 436 * The Emergence of Garrison ... 437 * Spreading the Abolitionist
Message ... 437 * Slavery and Moral Suasion ... 439 * Abolitionists and the
Idea of Freedom ... 439 * A New Vision of America ... 440

BLACK AND WHITE ABOLITIONISM ... 441
Black Abolitionists ... 441 * Abolitionism and Race ... 442 * Slavery and
American Freedom ... 443 * Gentlemen of Property and Standing ... 443 *
Slavery and Civil Liberties ... 445

THE ORIGINS OF FEMINISM ... 446
The Rise of the Public Woman ... 446 * Women and Free Speech ... 447 *
Women's Rights ... 448 * Feminism and Freedom ... 449

Voices of Freedom: *From* Angelina Grimké, Letter in *The Liberator*
(August 2, 1837), and *From* Frederick Douglass, Speech on July 5, 1852,
Rochester, New York ... 450

Women and Work ... 452 * The Slavery of Sex ... 453 * "Social Freedom" ... 453 * The Abolitionist Schism ... 454

REVIEW ... 457

13. A HOUSE DIVIDED, 1840–1861 ... 458

FRUITS OF MANIFEST DESTINY ... 459

Continental Expansion ... 459 * The Mexican Frontier: New Mexico and California ... 460 * The Texas Revolt ... 460 * The Election of 1844 ... 463 * The Road to War ... 464 * The War and Its Critics ... 465 * Combat in Mexico ... 466 * Race and Manifest Destiny ... 468 * Redefining Race ... 469 * Gold-Rush California ... 469 * California and the Boundaries of Freedom ... 470 * The Other Gold Rush ... 471 * Opening Japan ... 471

A DOSE OF ARSENIC ... 473

The Wilmot Proviso ... 473 * The Free Soil Appeal ... 474 * Crisis and Compromise ... 474 * The Great Debate ... 475 * The Fugitive Slave Issue ... 475 * Douglas and Popular Sovereignty ... 477 * The Kansas-Nebraska Act ... 478

THE RISE OF THE REPUBLICAN PARTY ... 479

The Northern Economy ... 479 * The Rise and Fall of the Know-Nothings ... 481 * The Free Labor Ideology ... 483 * Bleeding Kansas and the Election of 1856 ... 484

THE EMERGENCE OF LINCOLN ... 485

The Dred Scott Decision ... 485 * The Decision's Aftermath ... 486 * Lincoln and Slavery ... 486 * The Lincoln-Douglas Campaign ... 487 * John Brown at Harpers Ferry ... 489

Voices of Freedom: *From* The Lincoln-Douglas Debates (1858) ... 490

The Rise of Southern Nationalism ... 492 * The Democratic Split ... 493 * The Nomination of Lincoln ... 494 * The Election of 1860 ... 494

THE IMPENDING CRISIS ... 495

The Secession Movement ... 495 * The Secession Crisis ... 496 * And the War Came ... 497

REVIEW ... 501

14. A NEW BIRTH OF FREEDOM: THE CIVIL WAR, 1861–1865 ... 502

THE FIRST MODERN WAR ... 503

The Two Combatants ... 504 * The Technology of War ... 504 * The Public and the War ... 506 * Mobilizing Resources ... 507 * Military

Strategies ... 508 * The War Begins ... 509 * The War in the East,
1862 ... 509 * The War in the West ... 511

THE COMING OF EMANCIPATION ... 511

Slavery and the War ... 511 * The Unraveling of Slavery ... 513 *
Steps toward Emancipation ... 513 * Lincoln's Decision ... 514 *
The Emancipation Proclamation ... 516 * Enlisting Black Troops ... 517 *
The Black Soldier ... 518

THE SECOND AMERICAN REVOLUTION ... 519

Liberty and Union ... 520 * Lincoln's Vision ... 520 * From Union to
Nation ... 521 * The War and American Religion ... 522 * Liberty in
Wartime ... 523 * The North's Transformation ... 524 * Government and
the Economy ... 524 * The War and Native Americans ... 525

Voices of Freedom: *From* Letter of Thomas F. Drayton (April 17, 1861),
and *From* Abraham Lincoln, Address at Sanitary Fair, Baltimore
(April 18, 1864) ... 526

A New Financial System ... 528 * Women and the War ... 528 *
The Divided North ... 530

THE CONFEDERATE NATION ... 531

Leadership and Government ... 531 * The Inner Civil War ... 532 *
Economic Problems ... 533 * Southern Unionists ... 534 * Women and the
Confederacy ... 535 * Black Soldiers for the Confederacy ... 535

TURNING POINTS ... 536

Gettysburg and Vicksburg ... 536 * 1864 ... 537

REHEARSALS FOR RECONSTRUCTION AND
THE END OF THE WAR ... 539

The Sea Islands Experiment ... 539 * Wartime Reconstruction in the
West ... 540 * The Politics of Wartime Reconstruction ... 541 * Victory
at Last ... 541 * The War and the World ... 543 * The War in American
History ... 544

REVIEW ... 547

15. "WHAT IS FREEDOM?": RECONSTRUCTION,
1865-1877 ... 548

THE MEANING OF FREEDOM ... 550

Blacks and the Meaning of Freedom ... 550 * Families in Freedom ... 550 *
Church and School ... 551 * Political Freedom ... 551 * Land, Labor, and
Freedom ... 552 * Masters without Slaves ... 553 * The Free Labor Vision
... 554 * The Freedmen's Bureau ... 555 * The Failure of Land Reform
... 556 * Toward a New South ... 556 * The White Farmer ... 557 *
The Urban South ... 558 * The Aftermath of Slavery ... 559

Voices of Freedom: *From* Petition of Committee in Behalf of the Freedmen to Andrew Johnson (1865), and *From* A Sharecropping Contract (1866) ... 560

THE MAKING OF RADICAL RECONSTRUCTION ... 562
Andrew Johnson ... 562 * The Failure of Presidential Reconstruction ... 563 * The Black Codes ... 563 * The Radical Republicans ... 564 * The Origins of Civil Rights ... 565 * The Fourteenth Amendment ... 566 * The Reconstruction Act ... 566 * Impeachment and the Election of Grant ... 567 * The Fifteenth Amendment ... 568 * The "Great Constitutional Revolution" ... 569 * Boundaries of Freedom ... 570 * The Rights of Women ... 570 * Feminists and Radicals ... 571

RADICAL RECONSTRUCTION IN THE SOUTH ... 572
"The Tocsin of Freedom" ... 572 * The Black Officeholder ... 573 * Carpetbaggers and Scalawags ... 574 * Southern Republicans in Power ... 575 * The Quest for Prosperity ... 576

THE OVERTHROW OF RECONSTRUCTION ... 577
Reconstruction's Opponents ... 577 * "A Reign of Terror" ... 577 * The Liberal Republicans ... 579 * The North's Retreat ... 580 * The Triumph of the Redeemers ... 582 * The Disputed Election and Bargain of 1877 ... 582 * The End of Reconstruction ... 583

REVIEW ... 585

PART 4: TOWARD A GLOBAL PRESENCE, 1870-1920

16. AMERICA'S GILDED AGE, 1870-1890 ... 588

THE SECOND INDUSTRIAL REVOLUTION ... 589
The Industrial Economy ... 590 * Railroads and the National Market ... 591 * The Spirit of Innovation ... 592 * Competition and Consolidation ... 593 * The Rise of Andrew Carnegie ... 594 * The Triumph of John D. Rockefeller ... 597 * Workers' Freedom in an Industrial Age ... 598 * *Sunshine and Shadow:* Increasing Wealth and Poverty ... 599

THE TRANSFORMATION OF THE WEST ... 600
A Diverse Region ... 601 * Farming on the Middle Border ... 602 * Bonanza Farms ... 603 * The Cowboy and the Corporate West ... 604 * Conflict on the Mormon Frontier ... 605 * The Subjugation of the Plains Indians ... 605

Voices of Freedom: *From* Ira Steward, "A Second Declaration of Independence" (1879), and *From* Andrew Carnegie, "Wealth" (1889) ... 606

"Let Me Be a Free Man" ... 608 * Remaking Indian Life ... 610 * The Dawes Act ... 611 * Indian Citizenship ... 612 * The Ghost Dance and Wounded Knee ... 613 * Settler Societies and Global Wests ... 614

POLITICS IN A GILDED AGE ... 615

The Corruption of Politics ... 615 * The Politics of Dead Center ... 616 * Government and the Economy ... 617 * Reform Legislation ... 618 * Political Conflict in the States ... 619

FREEDOM IN THE GILDED AGE ... 620

The Social Problem ... 620 * Freedom, Inequality, and Democracy ... 620 * Social Darwinism in America ... 621 * Liberty of Contract ... 622 * The Courts and Freedom ... 623

LABOR AND THE REPUBLIC ... 624

"The Overwhelming Labor Question" ... 624 * The Knights of Labor and the "Conditions Essential to Liberty" ... 625 * Middle-Class Reformers ... 626 * *Progress and Poverty* ... 627 * *The Cooperative Commonwealth* ... 627 * Bellamy's Utopia ... 627 * Protestants and Moral Reform ... 628 * A Social Gospel ... 629 * The Haymarket Affair ... 629 * Labor and Politics ... 631

REVIEW ... 633

17. FREEDOM'S BOUNDARIES, AT HOME AND ABROAD, 1890–1900 ... 634

THE POPULIST CHALLENGE ... 636

The Farmers' Revolt ... 636 * The People's Party ... 637 * The Populist Platform ... 638 * The Populist Coalition ... 638 * The Government and Labor ... 641 * Populism and Labor ... 642 * Bryan and Free Silver ... 642 * The Campaign of 1896 ... 643

THE SEGREGATED SOUTH ... 645

The Redeemers in Power ... 645 * The Failure of the New South Dream ... 645 * Black Life in the South ... 646 * The Kansas Exodus ... 647 * The Decline of Black Politics ... 648 * The Elimination of Black Voting ... 648 * The Law of Segregation ... 649 * Segregation and White Domination ... 650 * The Rise of Lynching ... 651 * Politics, Religion, and Memory ... 652

REDRAWING THE BOUNDARIES ... 653

The New Immigration and the New Nativism ... 654 * Chinese Exclusion and Chinese Rights ... 654 * The Emergence of Booker T. Washington ... 656 * The Rise of the AFL ... 656 * The Women's Era ... 657

BECOMING A WORLD POWER ... 659

The New Imperialism ... 659 * American Expansionism ... 660 * The Lure of Empire ... 660 * The "Splendid Little War" ... 661 * Roosevelt at San Juan Hill ... 662 * An American Empire ... 664 * The Philippine War ... 666

Voices of Freedom: *From* Josiah Strong, *Our Country* (1885), and *From* "Aguinaldo's Case against the United States" (1899) ... 668

Citizens or Subjects? ... 670 * Drawing the Global Color Line ... 671 * "Republic or Empire?" ... 671

REVIEW ... 675

18. THE PROGRESSIVE ERA, 1900-1916 ... 676

AN URBAN AGE AND A CONSUMER SOCIETY ... 678

Farms and Cities ... 678 * The Muckrakers ... 680 * Immigration as a Global Process ... 680 * The Immigrant Quest for Freedom ... 682 * Consumer Freedom ... 683 * The Working Woman ... 684 * The Rise of Fordism ... 685 * The Promise of Abundance ... 686 * An American Standard of Living ... 687

VARIETIES OF PROGRESSIVISM ... 688

Industrial Freedom ... 688 * The Socialist Presence ... 689 * The Gospel of Debs ... 690 * AFL and IWW ... 691 * The New Immigrants on Strike ... 691

Voices of Freedom: *From* Charlotte Perkins Gilman, *Women and Economics* (1898), and *From* John Mitchell, "A Workingman's Conception of Industrial Liberty" (1910) ... 692

Labor and Civil Liberties ... 695 * The New Feminism ... 695 * The Rise of Personal Freedom ... 696 * The Birth-Control Movement ... 697 * Native American Progressivism ... 698

THE POLITICS OF PROGRESSIVISM ... 698

Effective Freedom ... 698 * State and Local Reforms ... 699 * Progressive Democracy ... 700 * Government by Expert ... 701 * Jane Addams and Hull House ... 701 * "Spearheads for Reform" ... 702 * The Campaign for Woman Suffrage ... 703 * Maternalist Reform ... 704 * The Idea of Economic Citizenship ... 705

THE PROGRESSIVE PRESIDENTS ... 705

Theodore Roosevelt ... 706 * Roosevelt and Economic Regulation ... 706 * John Muir and the Spirituality of Nature ... 707 * The Conservation Movement ... 707 * Taft in Office ... 708 * The Election of 1912 ... 709 * New Freedom and New Nationalism ... 710 * Wilson's First Term ... 710 * The Expanding Role of Government ... 711

REVIEW ... 713

19. SAFE FOR DEMOCRACY: THE UNITED STATES AND WORLD WAR I, 1916-1920 ... 714

AN ERA OF INTERVENTION ... 716

"I Took the Canal Zone" ... 717 * The Roosevelt Corollary ... 718 * Moral Imperialism ... 719 * Wilson and Mexico ... 720

AMERICA AND THE GREAT WAR ... 721
Neutrality and Preparedness ... 722 * The Road to War ... 723 *
The Fourteen Points ... 724

THE WAR AT HOME ... 726
The Progressives' War ... 726 * The Wartime State ... 726 * The
Propaganda War ... 727 * "The Great Cause of Freedom" ... 728 *
The Coming of Woman Suffrage ... 728 * Prohibition ... 730 * Liberty in
Wartime ... 731 * The Espionage Act ... 732 * Coercive Patriotism ... 733

WHO IS AN AMERICAN? ... 734
The "Race Problem" ... 734 * Americanization and Pluralism ... 734

Voices of Freedom: From Eugene V. Debs, Speech to the Jury before
Sentencing under the Espionage Act (1918), and From W. E. B. Du Bois,
"Returning Soldiers," The Crisis (1919) ... 736

The Anti-German Crusade ... 738 * Toward Immigration Restriction ... 739 *
Groups Apart: Mexicans, Puerto Ricans, and Asian-Americans ... 739 * The
Color Line ... 740 * Roosevelt, Wilson, and Race ... 741 * W. E. B. Du Bois
and the Revival of Black Protest ... 742 * Closing Ranks ... 743 * The Great
Migration and the "Promised Land" ... 743 * Racial Violence, North and
South ... 744 * The Rise of Garveyism ... 745

1919 ... 746
A Worldwide Upsurge ... 746 * Upheaval in America ... 746 * The Great
Steel Strike ... 747 * The Red Scare ... 748 * Wilson at Versailles ... 748 *
The Wilsonian Moment ... 749 * The Seeds of Wars to Come ... 752 *
The Treaty Debate ... 753

REVIEW ... 755

PART 5: DEPRESSION AND WARS, 1920-1953

20. FROM BUSINESS CULTURE TO GREAT DEPRESSION: THE TWENTIES, 1920-1932 ... 758

THE BUSINESS OF AMERICA ... 760
A Decade of Prosperity ... 760 * A New Society ... 761 * The Limits of
Prosperity ... 762 * The Farmers' Plight ... 763 * The Image of Business ...
764 * The Decline of Labor ... 765 * The Equal Rights Amendment ... 766 *
Women's Freedom ... 767

BUSINESS AND GOVERNMENT ... 769
The Retreat from Progressivism ... 769 * The Republican Era ... 769 *
Corruption in Government ... 770 * The Election of 1924 ... 770 *
Economic Diplomacy ... 771

Voices of Freedom: *From* André Siegfried, "The Gulf Between," *Atlantic Monthly* (March 1928), and *From* Majority Opinion, Justice James C. McReynolds, in *Meyer v. Nebraska* (1923) ... 772

THE BIRTH OF CIVIL LIBERTIES ... 774

The "Free Mob" ... 775 * A "Clear and Present Danger" ... 776 * The Court and Civil Liberties ... 776

THE CULTURE WARS ... 777

The Fundamentalist Revolt ... 777 * The Scopes Trial ... 779 * The Second Klan ... 780 * Closing the Golden Door ... 781 * Race and the Law ... 783 * Pluralism and Liberty ... 784 * Promoting Tolerance ... 785 * The Emergence of Harlem ... 786 * The Harlem Renaissance ... 787

THE GREAT DEPRESSION ... 788

The Election of 1928 ... 788 * The Coming of the Depression ... 789 * Americans and the Depression ... 791 * Resignation and Protest ... 792 * Hoover's Response ... 792 * The Worsening Economic Outlook ... 794 * Freedom in the Modern World ... 795

REVIEW ... 797

21. THE NEW DEAL, 1932–1940 ... 798

THE FIRST NEW DEAL ... 800

FDR and the Election of 1932 ... 800 * The Coming of the New Deal ... 802 * The Banking Crisis ... 803 * The NRA ... 804 * Government Jobs ... 805 * Public-Works Projects ... 806 * The New Deal and Agriculture ... 807 * The New Deal and Housing ... 808 * The Court and the New Deal ... 810

THE GRASSROOTS REVOLT ... 810

Labor's Great Upheaval ... 810 * The Rise of the CIO ... 812 * Labor and Politics ... 813 * Voices of Protest ... 814 * Religion on the Radio ... 815

THE SECOND NEW DEAL ... 815

The WPA and the Wagner Act ... 816 * The American Welfare State ... 817 * The Social Security System ... 818

A RECKONING WITH LIBERTY ... 818

FDR and the Idea of Freedom ... 819

Voices of Freedom: *From* Franklin D. Roosevelt, "Fireside Chat" (1934), and *From* John Steinbeck, *The Harvest Gypsies: On the Road to the Grapes of Wrath* (1938) ... 820

The Election of 1936 ... 822 * The Court Fight ... 823 * The End of the Second New Deal ... 824

THE LIMITS OF CHANGE ... 824

The New Deal and American Women ... 825 * The Southern Veto ... 826 * The Stigma of Welfare ... 827 * The Indian New Deal ... 827 * The New

Deal and Mexican-Americans ... 828 * Last Hired, First Fired ... 829 *
A New Deal for Blacks ... 829 * Federal Discrimination ... 830

A NEW CONCEPTION OF AMERICA ... 831

The Heyday of American Communism ... 831 * Redefining the People ...
832 * Promoting Diversity ... 833 * Challenging the Color Line ... 834 *
Labor and Civil Liberties ... 835 * The End of the New Deal ... 836 *
The New Deal in American History ... 837

REVIEW ... 839

22. FIGHTING FOR THE FOUR FREEDOMS: WORLD WAR II, 1941-1945 ... 840

FIGHTING WORLD WAR II ... 842

Good Neighbors ... 842 * The Road to War ... 844 * Isolationism ... 844 *
War in Europe ... 845 * Toward Intervention ... 846 * Pearl Harbor ... 847 *
The War in the Pacific ... 848 * The War in Europe ... 849

THE HOME FRONT ... 852

Mobilizing for War ... 852 * Business and the War ... 853 * Labor in
Wartime ... 855 * Fighting for the Four Freedoms ... 855 * Freedom
from Want ... 856 * The Office of War Information ... 857 * The Fifth
Freedom ... 858 * Women at Work ... 859 * The Pull of Tradition ... 860

VISIONS OF POSTWAR FREEDOM ... 860

Toward an American Century ... 860 * "The Way of Life of Free Men" ...
861 * An Economic Bill of Rights ... 862 * *The Road to Serfdom* ... 863

THE AMERICAN DILEMMA ... 863

Patriotic Assimilation ... 864 * The *Bracero* Program ... 865 * Mexican-
American Rights ... 865 * Indians during the War ... 866 * Asian-
Americans in Wartime ... 866 * Japanese-American Internment ... 867 *
Blacks and the War ... 869 * Blacks and Military Service ... 869 * Birth
of the Civil Rights Movement ... 870 * The Double-V ... 871 * *What the
Negro Wants* ... 871

Voices of Freedom: *From* Henry R. Luce, *The American Century*
(1941), and *From* Charles H. Wesley, "The Negro Has Always Wanted
the Four Freedoms," in *What the Negro Wants* (1944) ... 872

An American Dilemma ... 874 * Black Internationalism ... 875

THE END OF THE WAR ... 876

"The Most Terrible Weapon" ... 876 * The Dawn of the Atomic Age ...
877 * The Nature of the War ... 878 * Planning the Postwar World ... 878 *
Yalta and Bretton Woods ... 879 * The United Nations ... 880 * Peace, but
Not Harmony ... 880

REVIEW ... 883

23. THE UNITED STATES AND THE COLD WAR, 1945-1953 ... 884

ORIGINS OF THE COLD WAR ... 886

The Two Powers ... 886 * The Roots of Containment ... 887 * The Iron Curtain ... 887 * The Truman Doctrine ... 887 * The Marshall Plan ... 889 * The Reconstruction of Japan ... 890 * The Berlin Blockade and NATO ... 890 * The Growing Communist Challenge ... 891 * The Korean War ... 891 * Cold War Critics ... 895 * Imperialism and Decolonization ... 896

THE COLD WAR AND THE IDEA OF FREEDOM ... 896

The Cultural Cold War ... 897 * Freedom and Totalitarianism ... 897 * The Rise of Human Rights ... 898 * Ambiguities of Human Rights ... 899

THE TRUMAN PRESIDENCY ... 901

The Fair Deal ... 901 * The Postwar Strike Wave ... 901 * The Republican Resurgence ... 902 * Postwar Civil Rights ... 902 * *To Secure These Rights* ... 904 * The Dixiecrat and Wallace Revolts ... 904 * The 1948 Campaign ... 905

THE ANTICOMMUNIST CRUSADE ... 906

Loyalty and Disloyalty ... 907 * The Spy Trials ... 908 * McCarthy and McCarthyism ... 909 * An Atmosphere of Fear ... 909 * The Uses of Anticommunism ... 910 * Anticommunist Policies ... 911

Voices of Freedom: *From* Will Herberg, *Protestant, Catholic, Jew* (1955), and *From* Henry Steele Commager, "Who Is Loyal to America?" in *Harper's* (September 1947) ... 912

The Cold War and Organized Labor ... 914 * Cold War Civil Rights ... 914

REVIEW ... 917

PART 6: WHAT KIND OF NATION? 1953-2012

24. AN AFFLUENT SOCIETY, 1953-1960 ... 922

THE GOLDEN AGE ... 924

A Changing Economy ... 924 * A Suburban Nation ... 925 * The Growth of the West ... 926 * A Consumer Culture ... 927 * The TV World ... 928 * A New Ford ... 929 * Women at Work and at Home ... 931 * A Segregated Landscape ... 932 * Public Housing and Urban Renewal ... 933 * The Divided Society ... 933 * Religion and Anticommunism ... 934 * Selling Free Enterprise ... 935 * People's Capitalism ... 936 * The Libertarian Conservatives ... 937 * The New Conservatism ... 937

THE EISENHOWER ERA ... 938

Ike and Nixon ... 938 * The 1952 Campaign ... 939 * Modern Republicanism ... 940 * The Social Contract ... 941 * Massive Retaliation ... 941 * Ike and the Russians ... 942 * The Emergence of the Third World ... 943 * The Cold War in the Third World ... 944 * Origins of the Vietnam War ... 945 * Mass Society and Its Critics ... 946 * Rebels without a Cause ... 947 * The Beats ... 948

THE FREEDOM MOVEMENT ... 949

Origins of the Movement ... 949

Voices of Freedom: From Martin Luther King Jr., Speech at Montgomery, Alabama (December 5, 1955), and From The Southern Manifesto (1956) ... 950

The Legal Assault on Segregation ... 952 * The Brown Case ... 953 * The Montgomery Bus Boycott ... 954 * The Daybreak of Freedom ... 955 * The Leadership of King ... 956 * Massive Resistance ... 956 * Eisenhower and Civil Rights ... 957 * The World Views the United States ... 958

THE ELECTION OF 1960 ... 959

Kennedy and Nixon ... 959 * The End of the 1950s ... 960

REVIEW ... 963

25. THE SIXTIES, 1960-1968 ... 964

THE CIVIL RIGHTS REVOLUTION ... 966

The Rising Tide of Protest ... 966 * Birmingham ... 966 * The March on Washington ... 968

THE KENNEDY YEARS ... 969

Kennedy and the World ... 969 * The Missile Crisis ... 970 * Kennedy and Civil Rights ... 971

LYNDON JOHNSON'S PRESIDENCY ... 972

The Civil Rights Act of 1964 ... 972 * Freedom Summer ... 973 * The 1964 Election ... 974 * The Conservative Sixties ... 975 * The Voting Rights Act ... 976 * Immigration Reform ... 976 * The Great Society ... 977 * The War on Poverty ... 977 * Freedom and Equality ... 978

THE CHANGING BLACK MOVEMENT ... 979

The Ghetto Uprisings ... 979 * Malcolm X ... 981 * The Rise of Black Power ... 981

VIETNAM AND THE NEW LEFT ... 982

Old and New Lefts ... 982 * The Fading Consensus ... 983 * The Rise of the SDS ... 984 * America and Vietnam ... 985 * Lyndon Johnson's War ... 986

Voices of Freedom: From Young Americans for Freedom, The Sharon Statement (September 1960), and From Tom Hayden and Others, The Port Huron Statement (June 1962) ... 988

The Antiwar Movement ... 990 * The Counterculture ... 991 * Personal Liberation and the Free Individual ... 992 * Faith and the Counterculture ... 992

THE NEW MOVEMENTS AND THE RIGHTS REVOLUTION ... 994

The Feminine Mystique ... 994 * Women's Liberation ... 995 * Personal Freedom ... 996 * Gay Liberation ... 997 * Latino Activism ... 997 * Red Power ... 998 * *Silent Spring* ... 998 * The New Environmentalism ... 999 * The Rights Revolution ... 1000 * Policing the States ... 1001 * The Right to Privacy ... 1002

1968 ... 1002

A Year of Turmoil ... 1002 * The Global 1968 ... 1004 * Nixon's Comeback ... 1005 * The Legacy of the Sixties ... 1005

REVIEW ... 1007

26. THE TRIUMPH OF CONSERVATISM, 1969-1988 ... 1008

PRESIDENT NIXON ... 1009

Nixon's Domestic Policies ... 1010 * Nixon and Welfare ... 1010 * Nixon and Race ... 1011 * The Burger Court ... 1012 * The Court and Affirmative Action ... 1013 * The Continuing Sexual Revolution ... 1013 * Nixon and Détente ... 1014

VIETNAM AND WATERGATE ... 1016

Nixon and Vietnam ... 1016 * The End of the Vietnam War ... 1017 * Watergate ... 1018 * Nixon's Fall ... 1019

THE END OF THE GOLDEN AGE ... 1020

The Decline of Manufacturing ... 1020 * Stagflation ... 1020 * The Beleaguered Social Compact ... 1021 * Labor on the Defensive ... 1022 * Ford as President ... 1023 * The Carter Administration ... 1023 * Carter and the Economic Crisis ... 1024 * The Emergence of Human Rights Politics ... 1025 * The Iran Crisis and Afghanistan ... 1026

THE RISING TIDE OF CONSERVATISM ... 1028

The Religious Right ... 1028 * The Battle over the Equal Rights Amendment ... 1029 * The Abortion Controversy ... 1030 * The Tax Revolt ... 1031 * The Election of 1980 ... 1032

THE REAGAN REVOLUTION ... 1033

Reagan and American Freedom ... 1033

Voices of Freedom: *From* Redstockings Manifesto (1969), and *From* Jerry Falwell, *Listen, America!* (1980) ... 1034

Reaganomics ... 1036 * Reagan and Labor ... 1037 * The Problem of Inequality ... 1037 * The Second Gilded Age ... 1038 * Conservatives

and Reagan ... 1039 * Reagan and the Cold War ... 1040 * The Iran-Contra Affair ... 1042 * Reagan and Gorbachev ... 1042 * Reagan's Legacy ... 1042 * The Election of 1988 ... 1043

REVIEW ... 1045

27. GLOBALIZATION AND ITS DISCONTENTS, 1989-2000 ... 1046

THE POST-COLD WAR WORLD ... 1048

The Crisis of Communism ... 1048 * A New World Order? ... 1049 * The Gulf War ... 1050 * Visions of America's Role ... 1051 * The Election of Clinton ... 1051 * Clinton in Office ... 1052 * The "Freedom Revolution" ... 1053 * Clinton's Political Strategy ... 1053 * Clinton and World Affairs ... 1055 * The Balkan Crisis ... 1055 * Human Rights ... 1056

A NEW ECONOMY? ... 1056

The Computer Revolution ... 1057 * The Stock Market Boom and Bust ... 1058 * The Enron Syndrome ... 1059 * Fruits of Deregulation ... 1060 * Rising Inequality ... 1060

Voices of Freedom: From Bill Clinton, Speech on Signing of NAFTA (1993), and From Global Exchange, Seattle, Declaration for Global Democracy (December 1999) ... 1062

CULTURE WARS ... 1064

The Newest Immigrants ... 1065 * The New Diversity ... 1067 * African-Americans in the 1990s ... 1070 * The Role of the Courts ... 1071 * The Spread of Imprisonment ... 1071 * The Burden of Imprisonment ... 1072 * The Continuing Rights Revolution ... 1073 * Native Americans in 2000 ... 1073 * Multiculturalism ... 1074 * The Identity Debate ... 1074 * Cultural Conservatism ... 1075 * "Family Values" in Retreat ... 1076 * The Antigovernment Extreme ... 1077

IMPEACHMENT AND THE ELECTION OF 2000 ... 1078

The Impeachment of Clinton ... 1078 * The Disputed Election ... 1079 * The 2000 Result ... 1080 * A Challenged Democracy ... 1080

FREEDOM AND THE NEW CENTURY ... 1081

Exceptional America ... 1081 * Varieties of Freedom ... 1083

REVIEW ... 1085

28. A NEW CENTURY AND NEW CRISES ... 1086

THE WAR ON TERRORISM ... 1088

Bush before September 11 ... 1088 * "They Hate Freedom" ... 1089 * The Bush Doctrine ... 1090 * The "Axis of Evil" ... 1091 * The National Security Strategy ... 1091

AN AMERICAN EMPIRE? ... 1092

Confronting Iraq ... 1092 * The Iraq War ... 1093

Voices of Freedom: *From* The National Security Strategy of the United States (September 2002), and *From* President Barack Obama, Speech on the Middle East (2011) ... 1094

Another Vietnam? ... 1096 * The World and the War ... 1096

THE AFTERMATH OF SEPTEMBER 11 AT HOME ... 1097

Security and Liberty ... 1097 * The Power of the President ... 1099 * The Torture Controversy ... 1100 * The Economy under Bush ... 1101

THE WINDS OF CHANGE ... 1102

The 2004 Election ... 1102 * Bush's Second Term ... 1103 * Hurricane Katrina ... 1103 * The New Orleans Disaster ... 1104 * The Immigration Debate ... 1105 * Islam, America, and the "Clash of Civilizations" ... 1106 * The Constitution and Liberty ... 1107 * The Court and the President ... 1108 * The Midterm Elections of 2006 ... 1110 * The Housing Bubble ... 1111 * The Great Recession ... 1112 * "A Conspiracy against the Public" ... 1113 * The Collapse of Market Fundamentalism ... 1114 * Bush and the Crisis ... 1115

THE RISE OF OBAMA ... 1116

The 2008 Campaign ... 1117 * Obama's First Inauguration ... 1118 * Obama in Office ... 1118

OBAMA'S FIRST TERM ... 1120

The Continuing Economic Crisis ... 1120 * Obama and the World ... 1121 * The Republican Resurgence ... 1122 * The Occupy Movement ... 1123 * The 2012 Campaign ... 1124

LEARNING FROM HISTORY ... 1126

REVIEW ... 1129

APPENDIX

DOCUMENTS

The Declaration of Independence (1776)...A-2 * The Constitution of the United States (1787)...A-5 * *From* George Washington's Farewell Address (1796)...A-16 * The Seneca Falls Declaration of Sentiments and Resolutions (1848)...A-21 * *From* Frederick Douglass's "What, to the Slave, Is the Fourth of July?" Speech (1852)...A-24 * The Gettysburg Address (1863)...A-27 * Abraham Lincoln's Second Inaugural Address (1865)...A-28 * The Populist Platform of 1892...A-29 * Franklin D. Roosevelt's First Inaugural Address (1933)...A-32 * *From* The

Program for the March on Washington for Jobs and Freedom (1963)...A-35 ✶ Ronald Reagan's First Inaugural Address (1981)...A-36 ✶ Barack Obama's First Inaugural Address (2009)...A-39

TABLES AND FIGURES

Presidential Elections...A-42 ✶ Admission of States...A-50 ✶ Population of the United States...A-51 ✶ Historical Statistics of the United States: Labor Force—Selected Characteristics Expressed as a Percentage of the Labor Force, 1800–2010...A-52 ✶ Immigration, by Origin...A-52 ✶ Unemployment Rate, 1890–2013...A-53 ✶ Union Membership as a Percentage of Nonagricultural Employment, 1880–2012...A-53 ✶ Voter Participation in Presidential Elections 1824–2012...A-53 ✶ Birthrate, 1820–2011...A-53

GLOSSARY ★ ... A-55

CREDITS ★ ... A-79

INDEX ★ ... A-85

MAPS

CHAPTER 1
The First Americans...7
Native Ways of Life, ca. 1500...11
The Old World on the Eve of American Colonization,
    ca. 1500...19
Voyages of Discovery...22
Early Spanish Conquests and Explorations in the
    New World...32
The New World—New France and New Netherland,
    ca. 1650...39

CHAPTER 2
English Settlement in the Chesapeake, ca. 1650...58
English Settlement in New England, ca. 1640...72

CHAPTER 3
Eastern North America in the Seventeenth and Early
    Eighteenth Centuries...89
European Settlement and Ethnic Diversity on the
    Atlantic Coast of North America, 1760...108

CHAPTER 4
Atlantic Trading Routes...129
The Slave Trade in the Atlantic World,
    1460–1770...131
European Empires in North America, ca. 1750...153
Eastern North America after the Peace of Paris,
    1763...159

CHAPTER 5
The Revolutionary War in the North, 1775–1781...196
The Revolutionary War in the South, 1775–1781...198
North America, 1783...201

CHAPTER 6
Loyalism in the American Revolution...220

CHAPTER 7
Western Lands, 1782–1802...241
Western Ordinances, 1784–1787...244
Ratification of the Constitution...262
Indian Tribes, 1790...264

CHAPTER 8
The Presidential Election of 1800...287
The Louisiana Purchase...293
The War of 1812...301

CHAPTER 9
The Market Revolution: Roads and Canals, 1840...310
The Market Revolution: Western Settlement,
    1800–1820...313
Travel Times from New York City in 1800 and
    1830...314

The Market Revolution: The Spread of Cotton
    Cultivation, 1820–1840...316
Major Cities, 1840...320
Cotton Mills, 1820s...321

CHAPTER 10
The Missouri Compromise, 1820...357
The Americas, 1830...360
The Presidential Election of 1824...364
The Presidential Election of 1828...366
Indian Removals, 1830–1840...375
The Presidential Election of 1840...382

CHAPTER 11
Slave Population, 1860...392
Size of Slaveholdings, 1860...397
Distribution of Free Blacks, 1860...406
Major Crops of the South, 1860...409
Slave Resistance in the Nineteenth-Century Atlantic
    World...417

CHAPTER 12
Utopian Communities, Mid-Nineteenth
    Century...428

CHAPTER 13
The Trans-Mississippi West, 1830s–1840s...462
The Mexican War, 1846–1848...467
Gold-Rush California...470
Continental Expansion through 1853...472
The Compromise of 1850...476
The Kansas-Nebraska Act, 1854...478
The Railroad Network, 1850s...480
The Presidential Election of 1856...485
The Presidential Election of 1860...494

CHAPTER 14
The Secession of Southern States, 1860–1861...505
The Civil War in the East, 1861–1862...510
The Civil War in the West, 1861–1862...512
The Emancipation Proclamation...515
The Civil War, 1863...536
The Civil War, Late 1864–1865...542

CHAPTER 15
The Barrow Plantation...553
Sharecropping in the South, 1880...557
The Presidential Election of 1868...568
Reconstruction in the South, 1867–1877...581
The Presidential Election of 1876...582

CHAPTER 16
The Railroad Network, 1880...592
U.S. Steel: A Vertically Integrated Corporation...596
Indian Reservations, ca. 1890...611
Political Stalemate, 1876–1892...617

CHAPTER 17
Populist Strength, 1892...640
The Presidential Election of 1896...644
The Spanish-American War: The Pacific...663
The Spanish-American War: The Caribbean...663
American Empire, 1898...665

CHAPTER 18
The World on the Move, World Migration
    1815–1914...682
Socialist Towns and Cities, 1900–1920...690
The Presidential Election of 1912...710

CHAPTER 19
The Panama Canal Zone...717
The United States in the Caribbean,
    1898–1941...718
Colonial Possessions, 1900...720
World War I: The Western Front...725
Prohibition, 1915: Counties and States That Banned
    Liquor before the Eighteenth Amendment
    (Ratified 1919, Repealed 1933)...731
Europe in 1914...750
Europe in 1919...751

CHAPTER 20
The Presidential Election of 1928...790

CHAPTER 21
Columbia River Basin Project, 1949...801
The Presidential Election of 1932...802
The Tennessee Valley Authority...807
The Dust Bowl, 1935–1940...808

CHAPTER 22
World War II in the Pacific, 1941–1945...849
World War II in Europe, 1942–1945...851
Wartime Army and Navy Bases and
    Airfields...854
Japanese-American Internment, 1942–1945...868

CHAPTER 23
Cold War Europe, 1956...892
The Korean War, 1950–1953...894
The Presidential Election of 1948...905

CHAPTER 24
The Interstate Highway System...930
The Presidential Election of 1952...939
The Presidential Election of 1960...960

CHAPTER 25
The Presidential Election of 1964...974
The Vietnam War, 1964–1975...987
The Presidential Election of 1968...1004

CHAPTER 26
Center of Population, 1790–2010...1011
The Presidential Election of 1976...1023
The Presidential Election of 1980...1032
The United States in the Caribbean and Central
    America, 1954–2004...1041

CHAPTER 27
Eastern Europe after the Cold War...1050
The Presidential Election of 1992...1052
Maps of Diversity, 2000...1066
The Presidential Election of 2000...1080

CHAPTER 28
U.S. Presence in the Middle East, 1947–2012...1098
Israel, the West Bank, and Gaza Strip...1099
The Presidential Election of 2008...1117
The Presidential Election of 2012...1126

TABLES AND FIGURES

CHAPTER 1
Table 1.1 Estimated Regional Populations:
    The Americas, ca. 1500...31
Table 1.2 Estimated Regional Populations:
    The World, ca. 1500...31

CHAPTER 3
Table 3.1 Origins and Status of Migrants to British
    North American Colonies, 1700–1775...107

CHAPTER 4
Table 4.1 Slave Population as Percentage of Total
    Population of Original Thirteen Colonies,
    1770...135

CHAPTER 7
Table 7.1 Total Population and Black Population of
    the United States, 1790...267

CHAPTER 9
Table 9.1 Population Growth of Selected Western
    States, 1800–1850...315
Table 9.2 Total Number of Immigrants by Five-Year
    Period...324
Figure 9.1 Sources of Immigration, 1850...326

CHAPTER 11
Table 11.1 Growth of the Slave Population...393
Table 11.2 Slaveholding, 1850...394
Table 11.3 Free Black Population, 1860...407

CHAPTER 14
Figure 14.1 Resources for War: Union versus
    Confederacy...506

CHAPTER 16
Table 16.1 Indicators of Economic Change, 1870–1920...590
Figure 16.1 Railroad Mileage Built, 1830–1975...591

CHAPTER 17
Table 17.1 States with over 200 Lynchings, 1889–1918...652

CHAPTER 18
Table 18.1 Rise of the City, 1880–1920...681
Table 18.2 Immigrants and Their Children as Percentage of Population, Ten Major Cities, 1920...683
Table 18.3 Percentage of Women 14 Years and Older in the Labor Force, 1900–1930...684
Table 18.4 Percentage of Women Workers in Various Occupations, 1900–1920...685
Table 18.5 Sales of Passenger Cars, 1900–1925...686

CHAPTER 19
Table 19.1 The Great Migration...744

CHAPTER 20
Figure 20.1 Household Appliances, 1900–1930...762
Figure 20.2 The Stock Market, 1919–1939...765
Table 20.1 Selected Annual Immigration Quotas under the 1924 Immigration Act...782

CHAPTER 21
Figure 21.1 The Building Boom and Its Collapse, 1919–1939...809
Figure 21.2 Unemployment, 1925–1945...824

CHAPTER 22
Table 22.1 Labor Union Membership...855

CHAPTER 24
Figure 24.1 Real Gross Domestic Product per Capita, 1790–2000...925
Figure 24.2 Average Daily Television Viewing...929
Figure 24.3 The Baby Boom and Its Decline...931

CHAPTER 25
Figure 25.1 Percentage of Population below Poverty Level, by Race, 1959–1969...978

CHAPTER 26
Figure 26.1 Median Age at First Marriage, 1947–1981...1013
Table 26.1 Rate of Divorce: Divorces of Existing Marriages per 1,000 New Marriages, 1950–1980...1014
Table 26.2 The Misery Index, 1970–1980...1021
Figure 26.2 Real Average Weekly Wages, 1955–1990...1022
Figure 26.3 Changes in Families' Real Income, 1980–1990...1038

CHAPTER 27
Figure 27.1 U.S. Income Inequality, 1913–2003...1060
Table 27.1 Immigration to the United States, 1960–2010...1065
Figure 27.2 Birthplace of Immigrants, 1990–2000...1067
Figure 27.3 The Projected Non-White Majority: Racial and Ethnic Breakdown...1069
Figure 27.4 Unemployment Rate by Sex and Race, 1954–2000...1070
Table 27.2 Home Ownership Rates by Group, 1970–2000...1070
Figure 27.5 Institutional Inmates as a Percentage of the Population by Sex and Race, 1850–2010...1072
Figure 27.6 Change in Family Structure, 1970–2010...1076
Figure 27.7 Women in the Paid Workforce, 1940–2010...1077

CHAPTER 28
Figure 28.1 The Housing Bubble...1111
Figure 28.2 Portrait of a Recession...1112
Figure 28.3 Income Gains, 1947–2009...1121

★

For my mother,
Liza Foner (1909–2005),
an accomplished artist
who lived through
most of the twentieth century
and into the twenty-first

★

PREFACE

Give Me Liberty! An American History is a survey of American history from the earliest days of European exploration and conquest of the New World to the first decades of the twenty-first century. It offers students a clear, concise narrative whose central theme is the changing contours of American freedom.

I am extremely gratified by the response to the first three editions of *Give Me Liberty!*, which have been used in survey courses at many hundreds of two- and four-year colleges and universities throughout the country. The comments I have received from instructors and students encourage me to think that *Give Me Liberty!* has worked well in their classrooms. Their comments have also included many valuable suggestions for revisions, which I greatly appreciate. These have ranged from corrections of typographical and factual errors to thoughts about subjects that needed more extensive treatment. In making revisions for this Fourth Edition, I have tried to take these suggestions into account. I have also incorporated the findings and insights of new scholarship that has appeared since the original edition was written.

The most significant changes in this Fourth Edition reflect my desire to integrate the history of American religion more fully into the narrative. Today, this is

a thriving subfield of American historical writing, partly because of the increased prominence in our own time of debates over the relations between government and religion and over the definition of religious liberty—issues that are deeply rooted in the American experience. Changes relating to this theme may be found throughout the book, but some of the major additions seeking to illuminate the history of American religion are as follows:

Chapter 1 includes a new discussion of religious toleration and its limits in the seventeenth-century Dutch colony of New Netherland, which became New York after being seized by Great Britain in 1664. Chapter 2 expands the previous discussion of the complex relationship between church and state in Puritan New England. Chapter 4 examines the religious traditions brought to the American colonies by enslaved Africans. In Chapter 6, I have added a discussion of the Christian Republicanism of the era of the American Revolution, a set of ideas that linked public virtue in the new nation with religious conviction despite the separation of church and state. Chapter 9 now includes an extended discussion of the emergence of the Church of Latter-Day Saints (or the Mormon Church) and their experience of persecution, despite which they've become one of the largest and most rapidly growing denominations in the United States.

A further discussion of conflict between Mormons and other settlers in the West occurs in Chapter 16. That chapter also includes an expanded discussion of the Ghost Dance, an Indian religious movement of the late nineteenth century, and a new section on the role of Protestant leaders in the era's moral reform campaigns. In Chapter 17, a new section discusses the religious dimensions of the revised "memory" of the Civil War that rose to prominence in the 1890s. In Chapter 18, I have added a discussion of the spiritual elements in the early environmental movement, especially in relation to the career of the pioneer conservationist John Muir. The rise of religious fundamentalism, and its use of modern media like the radio to spread its message, is examined in Chapter 21. In Chapter 24, there is a new section on religion and the anticommunist crusade of the 1950s. Chapter 25 now contains a section on religious movements that arose in connection with the counterculture of the 1960s. Finally, I have added to Chapter 28, the book's final chapter, a new section on how the terrorist attacks of September 11, 2001, led to profound controversy over the role of Islam in American life, a debate that continues to this day.

As in the Second and Third Editions, the Voices of Freedom sections in each chapter include two documents illustrating the contested history of freedom in the United States. I have changed a number of them to reflect the new emphasis on the history of American religion. I have also revised the end-of-chapter bibliographies to reflect current scholarship.

The Fourth Edition sports a bright, award-winning design featuring enhanced pedagogy to give students more guidance as they move through chapters. New topic flags function as chapter outlines on the page. They provide easy visual cues that correspond to major points in the narrative and are handy tools for review. The chronology at the beginning of the chapter and the end-of-chapter review pages, including review questions and key terms with page references, have been revisited for the Fourth Edition. The aim of the pedagogy, as always, is to offer students guidance through the material without getting in the way of the presentation.

I have also added new images in each chapter to expand the visual representation of key ideas and personalities in the text. Taken together, I believe these changes enhance the purpose of *Give Me Liberty!*: to offer students a clear, concise, and thematically enriched introduction to American history.

Americans have always had a divided attitude toward history. On the one hand, they tend to be remarkably future-oriented, dismissing events of even the recent past as "ancient history" and sometimes seeing history as a burden to be overcome, a prison from which to escape. On the other hand, like many other peoples, Americans have always looked to history for a sense of personal or group identity and of national cohesiveness. This is why so many Americans devote time and energy to tracing their family trees and why they visit historical museums and National Park Service historical sites in ever-increasing numbers. My hope is that this book will convince readers with all degrees of interest that history does matter to them.

The novelist and essayist James Baldwin once observed that history "does not refer merely, or even principally, to the past. On the contrary, the great force of history comes from the fact that we carry it within us, ... [that] history is literally present in all that we do." As Baldwin recognized, the force of history is evident in our own world. Especially in a political democracy like the United States, whose government is designed to rest on the consent of informed citizens, knowledge of the past is essential—not only for those of us whose profession is the teaching and writing of history, but for everyone. History, to be sure, does not offer simple lessons or immediate answers to current questions. Knowing the history of immigration to the United States, and all of the tensions, turmoil, and aspirations associated with it, for example, does not tell us what current immigration policy ought to be. But without that knowledge, we have no way of understanding which approaches have worked and which have not—essential information for the formulation of future public policy.

History, it has been said, is what the present chooses to remember about the past. Rather than a fixed collection of facts, or a group of interpretations that cannot be challenged, our understanding of history is constantly changing. There is nothing unusual in the fact that each generation rewrites history to meet its own needs, or that scholars disagree among themselves on basic questions like the causes of the Civil War or the reasons for the Great Depression. Precisely because each generation asks different questions of the past, each generation formulates different answers. The past thirty years have witnessed a remarkable expansion of the scope of historical study. The experiences of groups neglected by earlier scholars, including women, African-Americans, working people, and others, have received unprecedented attention from historians. New subfields—social history, cultural history, and family history among them—have taken their place alongside traditional political and diplomatic history.

Give Me Liberty! draws on this voluminous historical literature to present an up-to-date and inclusive account of the American past, paying due attention to the

experience of diverse groups of Americans while in no way neglecting the events and processes Americans have experienced in common. It devotes serious attention to political, social, cultural, and economic history, and to their interconnections. The narrative brings together major events and prominent leaders with the many groups of ordinary people who make up American society. *Give Me Liberty!* has a rich cast of characters, from Thomas Jefferson to campaigners for woman suffrage, from Franklin D. Roosevelt to former slaves seeking to breathe meaning into emancipation during and after the Civil War.

Aimed at an audience of undergraduate students with little or no detailed knowledge of American history, *Give Me Liberty!* guides readers through the complexities of the subject without overwhelming them with excessive detail. The unifying theme of freedom that runs through the text gives shape to the narrative and integrates the numerous strands that make up the American experience. This approach builds on that of my earlier book, *The Story of American Freedom* (1998), although *Give Me Liberty!* places events and personalities in the foreground and is more geared to the structure of the introductory survey course.

Freedom, and the battles to define its meaning, has long been central to my own scholarship and undergraduate teaching, which focuses on the nineteenth century and especially the era of the Civil War and Reconstruction (1850-1877). This was a time when the future of slavery tore the nation apart and emancipation produced a national debate over what rights the former slaves, and all Americans, should enjoy as free citizens. I have found that attention to clashing definitions of freedom and the struggles of different groups to achieve freedom as they understood it offers a way of making sense of the bitter battles and vast transformations of that pivotal era. I believe that the same is true for American history as a whole.

No idea is more fundamental to Americans' sense of themselves as individuals and as a nation than freedom. The central term in our political language, freedom—or liberty, with which it is almost always used interchangeably—is deeply embedded in the record of our history and the language of everyday life. The Declaration of Independence lists liberty among mankind's inalienable rights; the Constitution announces its purpose as securing liberty's blessings. The United States fought the Civil War to bring about a new birth of freedom, World War II for the Four Freedoms, and the Cold War to defend the Free World. Americans' love of liberty has been represented by liberty poles, liberty caps, and statues of liberty, and acted out by burning stamps and burning draft cards, by running away from slavery, and by demonstrating for the right to vote. "Every man in the street, white, black, red, or yellow," wrote the educator and statesman Ralph Bunche in 1940, "knows that this is 'the land of the free' . . . 'the cradle of liberty.'"

The very universality of the idea of freedom, however, can be misleading. Freedom is not a fixed, timeless category with a single unchanging definition. Indeed, the history of the United States is, in part, a story of debates, disagreements, and struggles over freedom. Crises like the American Revolution, the Civil War, and the Cold War have permanently transformed the idea of freedom. So too have demands by various groups of Americans to enjoy greater freedom. The meaning of freedom has been constructed not only in congressional debates and political treatises, but on plantations and picket lines, in parlors and even bedrooms.

Over the course of our history, American freedom has been both a reality and a mythic ideal—a living truth for millions of Americans, a cruel mockery for others. For some, freedom has been what some scholars call a "habit of the heart," an ideal so taken for granted that it is lived out but rarely analyzed. For others, freedom is not a birthright but a distant goal that has inspired great sacrifice.

Give Me Liberty! draws attention to three dimensions of freedom that have been critical in American history: (1) the *meanings* of freedom; (2) the *social conditions* that make freedom possible; and (3) the *boundaries* of freedom that determine who is entitled to enjoy freedom and who is not. All have changed over time.

In the era of the American Revolution, for example, freedom was primarily a set of rights enjoyed in public activity—the right of a community to be governed by laws to which its representatives had consented and of individuals to engage in religious worship without governmental interference. In the nineteenth century, freedom came to be closely identified with each person's opportunity to develop to the fullest his or her innate talents. In the twentieth, the "ability to choose," in both public and private life, became perhaps the dominant understanding of freedom. This development was encouraged by the explosive growth of the consumer marketplace (a development that receives considerable attention in *Give Me Liberty!*), which offered Americans an unprecedented array of goods with which to satisfy their needs and desires. During the 1960s, a crucial chapter in the history of American freedom, the idea of personal freedom was extended into virtually every realm, from attire and "lifestyle" to relations between the sexes. Thus, over time, more and more areas of life have been drawn into Americans' debates about the meaning of freedom.

A second important dimension of freedom focuses on the social conditions necessary to allow freedom to flourish. What kinds of economic institutions and relationships best encourage individual freedom? In the colonial era and for more than a century after independence, the answer centered on economic autonomy, enshrined in the glorification of the independent small producer—the farmer, skilled craftsman, or shopkeeper—who did not have to depend on another person for his livelihood. As the industrial economy matured, new conceptions of economic freedom came to the fore: "liberty of contract" in the Gilded Age, "industrial freedom" (a say in corporate decision-making) in the Progressive era, economic security during the New Deal, and, more recently, the ability to enjoy mass consumption within a market economy.

The boundaries of freedom, the third dimension of this theme, have inspired some of the most intense struggles in American history. Although founded on the premise that liberty is an entitlement of all humanity, the United States for much of its history deprived many of its own people of freedom. Non-whites have rarely enjoyed the same access to freedom as white Americans. The belief in equal opportunity as the birthright of all Americans has coexisted with persistent efforts to limit freedom by race, gender, class, and in other ways.

Less obvious, perhaps, is the fact that one person's freedom has frequently been linked to another's servitude. In the colonial era and nineteenth century, expanding

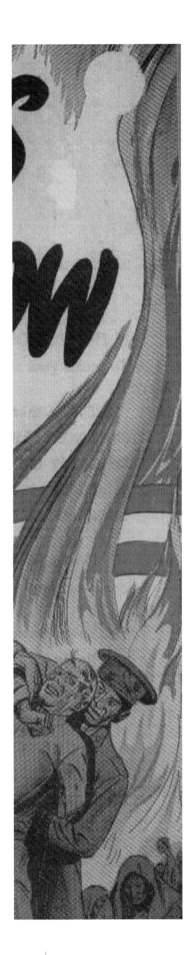

freedom for many Americans rested on the lack of freedom—slavery, indentured servitude, the subordinate position of women—for others. By the same token, it has been through battles at the boundaries—the efforts of racial minorities, women, and others to secure greater freedom—that the meaning and experience of freedom have been deepened and the concept extended into new realms.

Time and again in American history, freedom has been transformed by the demands of excluded groups for inclusion. The idea of freedom as a universal birthright owes much both to abolitionists who sought to extend the blessings of liberty to blacks and to immigrant groups who insisted on full recognition as American citizens. The principle of equal protection of the law without regard to race, which became a central element of American freedom, arose from the antislavery struggle and the Civil War and was reinvigorated by the civil rights revolution of the 1960s, which called itself the "freedom movement." The battle for the right of free speech by labor radicals and birth-control advocates in the first part of the twentieth century helped to make civil liberties an essential element of freedom for all Americans.

Although concentrating on events within the United States, *Give Me Liberty!* also, as indicated above, situates American history in the context of developments in other parts of the world. Many of the forces that shaped American history, including the international migration of peoples, the development of slavery, the spread of democracy, and the expansion of capitalism, were worldwide processes not confined to the United States. Today, American ideas, culture, and economic and military power exert unprecedented influence throughout the world. But beginning with the earliest days of settlement, when European empires competed to colonize North America and enrich themselves from its trade, American history cannot be understood in isolation from its global setting.

Freedom is the oldest of clichés and the most modern of aspirations. At various times in our history, it has served as the rallying cry of the powerless and as a justification of the status quo. Freedom helps to bind our culture together and exposes the contradictions between what America claims to be and what it sometimes has been. American history is not a narrative of continual progress toward greater and greater freedom. As the abolitionist Thomas Wentworth Higginson noted after the Civil War, "revolutions may go backward." Though freedom can be achieved, it may also be taken away. This happened, for example, when the equal rights granted to former slaves immediately after the Civil War were essentially nullified during the era of segregation. As was said in the eighteenth century, the price of freedom is eternal vigilance.

In the early twenty-first century, freedom continues to play a central role in American political and social life and thought. It is invoked by individuals and groups of all kinds, from critics of economic globalization to those who seek to secure American freedom at home and export it abroad. I hope that *Give Me Liberty!* will offer beginning students a clear account of the course of American history, and of its central theme, freedom, which today remains as varied, contentious, and ever-changing as America itself.

ACKNOWLEDGMENTS

All works of history are, to a considerable extent, collaborative books, in that every writer builds on the research and writing of previous scholars. This is especially true of a textbook that covers the entire American experience, over more than five centuries. My greatest debt is to the innumerable historians on whose work I have drawn in preparing this volume. The Suggested Reading list at the end of each chapter offers only a brief introduction to the vast body of historical scholarship that has influenced and informed this book. More specifically, however, I wish to thank the following scholars, who generously read portions of this work and offered valuable comments, criticisms, and suggestions:

Wayne Ackerson, Salisbury University
Mary E. Adams, City College of San Francisco
Jeff Adler, University of Florida
David Anderson, Louisiana Tech University
John Barr, Lone Star College, Kingwood
Lauren Braun-Strumfels, Raritan Valley Community College
James Broussard, Lebanon Valley College
Michael Bryan, Greenville Technical College
Stephanie Cole, The University of Texas at Arlington
Ashley Cruseturner, McLennan Community College
Jim Dudlo, Brookhaven College
Beverly Gage, Yale University
Monica Gisolfi, University of North Carolina, Wilmington
Adam Goudsouzian, University of Memphis
Mike Green, Community College of Southern Nevada
Vanessa Gunther, California State University, Fullerton
David E. Hamilton, University of Kentucky
Brian Harding, Mott Community College
Sandra Harvey, Lone Star College–Cy Fair
David Hsiung, Juniata College
James Karmel, Harford Community College
Kelly Knight, Penn State University
Marianne Leeper, Trinity Valley Community College
Jeffrey K. Lucas, University of North Carolina at Pembroke
Lillian E. Marrujo-Duck, City College of San Francisco
Kent McGaughy, HCC Northwest College
James Mills, University of Texas, Brownsville
Gil Montemayor, McLennan Community College
Jonathan Noyalas, Lord Fairfax Community College
Robert M. O'Brien, Lone Star College–Cy Fair

Joseph Palermo, California State University, Sacramento

Ann Plane, University of California, Santa Barbara

Nancy Marie Robertson, Indiana University-Purdue University Indianapolis

Esther Robinson, Lone Star College-Cy Fair

Richard Samuelson, California State University, San Bernadino

Diane Sager, Maple Woods Community College

John Shaw, Portland Community College

Mark Spencer, Brock University

David Stebenne, Ohio State University

Judith Stein, City College, City University of New York

George Stevens, Duchess Community College

Robert Tinkler, California State University, Chico

Elaine Thompson, Louisiana Tech University

David Weiman, Barnard College

William Young, Maple Woods Community College

I am particularly grateful to my colleagues in the Columbia University Department of History: Pablo Piccato, for his advice on Latin American history; Evan Haefeli and Ellen Baker, who read and made many suggestions for improvements in their areas of expertise (colonial America and the history of the West, respectively); and Sarah Phillips, who offered advice on treating the history of the environment.

I am also deeply indebted to the graduate students at Columbia University's Department of History who helped with this project. Theresa Ventura offered invaluable assistance in gathering material for the new sections placing American history in a global context. April Holm provided similar assistance for new coverage in this edition of the history of American religion and debates over religious freedom. James Delbourgo conducted research for the chapters on the colonial era. Beverly Gage did the same for the twentieth century. Daniel Freund provided all-round research assistance. Victoria Cain did a superb job of locating images. I also want to thank my colleagues Elizabeth Blackmar and Alan Brinkley for offering advice and encouragement throughout the writing of this book.

Many thanks to Joshua Brown, director of the American Social History Project, whose website, History Matters, lists innumerable online resources for the study of American history. Nancy Robertson at IUIPUI did a superb job revising and enhancing the in-book pedagogy. Monica Gisolfi (University of North Carolina, Wilmington) and Robert Tinkler (California State University, Chico) did excellent work on the Instructor's Manual and Test Bank. Kathleen Thomas (University of Wisconsin, Stout) helped greatly in the revisions of the companion media packages.

At W. W. Norton & Company, Steve Forman was an ideal editor—patient, encouraging, and always ready to offer sage advice. I would also like to thank Steve's assistant, Justin Cahill, for his indispensable and always cheerful help on all aspects of the project; Ellen Lohman and Debbie Nichols for their careful copyediting and proof reading work. Stephanie Romeo and Donna Ranieri for their resourceful attention to the illustrations program; Hope Miller Goodell and Chin-Yee Lai for their refinements of the book design; Mike Fodera and Debra Morton-Hoyt for splendid work on the covers for the Fourth Edition; Kim Yi for keeping the many threads of the project aligned and then tying them together; Sean Mintus for his efficiency and care in book production; Steve Hoge for orchestrating the rich media package that accompanies the textbook; Jessica Brannon-Wranowsky for the terrific new web quizzes and outlines; Nicole Netherton, Steve Dunn, and Mike Wright for their alert reads of the U.S. survey market and their hard work in helping establish *Give Me Liberty!* within it; and Drake McFeely, Roby Harrington, and Julia Reidhead for maintaining Norton as an independent, employee-owned publisher dedicated to excellence in its work.

Many students may have heard stories of how publishing companies alter the language and content of textbooks in an attempt to maximize sales and avoid alienating any potential reader. In this case, I can honestly say that W. W. Norton allowed me a free hand in writing the book and, apart from the usual editorial corrections, did not try to influence its content at all. For this I thank them, while I accept full responsibility for the interpretations presented and for any errors the book may contain. Since no book of this length can be entirely free of mistakes, I welcome readers to send me corrections at ef17@columbia.edu.

My greatest debt, as always, is to my family—my wife, Lynn Garafola, for her good-natured support while I was preoccupied by a project that consumed more than its fair share of my time and energy, and my daughter, Daria, who while a ninth and tenth grader read every chapter as it was written and offered invaluable suggestions about improving the book's clarity, logic, and grammar.

Eric Foner
New York City
July 2013

GIVE ME LIBERTY!

AN AMERICAN HISTORY

Fourth Edition

CHAPTER 19

SAFE FOR DEMOCRACY: THE UNITED STATES AND WORLD WAR I

★

1916–1920

In 1902, W. T. Stead published a short volume with the arresting title *The Americanization of the World; or, the Trend of the Twentieth Century*. Stead was an English editor whose sensational writings included an exposé of London prostitution, *Maiden Tribute of Modern Babylon*. He would meet his death in 1912 as a passenger on the *Titanic*, the ocean liner that foundered after striking an iceberg in the North Atlantic. Impressed by Americans' "exuberant energies," Stead predicted that the United States would soon emerge as "the greatest of world-powers." But what was most striking about his work was that Stead located the source of American power less in the realm of military might or territorial acquisition than in the country's single-minded commitment to the "pursuit of wealth" and the relentless international spread of American culture—art, music, journalism, even ideas about religion and gender relations. He foresaw a future in which the United States promoted its interests and values through an unending involvement in the affairs of other nations. Stead proved to be an accurate prophet.

The Spanish-American War had established the United States as an international empire. Despite the conquest of the Philippines and Puerto Rico, however, the country's overseas holdings remained tiny compared to those of Britain, France, and Germany. And no more were added, except for a strip of land surrounding the Panama Canal, acquired in 1903, and the Virgin Islands, purchased from Denmark in 1917. In 1900, Great Britain ruled over more than 300 million people in possessions scattered across the globe, and France had nearly 50 million subjects in Asia and Africa. Compared with these, the American presence in the world seemed very small. As Stead suggested, America's empire differed significantly from those of European countries—it was economic, cultural, and intellectual, rather than territorial.

The world economy at the dawn of the twentieth century was already highly globalized. An ever-increasing stream of goods, investments, and people flowed from country to country. Although Britain still dominated world banking and the British pound remained the major currency of international trade, the United States had become the leading industrial power. By 1914, it produced more than one-third of the world's manufactured goods. Already, Europeans complained of an "American invasion" of steel, oil, agricultural equipment, and consumer goods. Spearheads of American culture like movies and popular music were not far behind.

Europeans were fascinated by American ingenuity and mass production techniques. Many feared American products and culture would overwhelm their own. "What are the chief new features of London life?" one British writer asked in 1901. "They are the telephone, the portable camera, the phonograph, the electric street car, the automobile, the typewriter. . . . In every one of these the American maker is supreme." Meanwhile, hundreds of thousands of Americans traveled abroad each year in the early twentieth century. And American racial and ethnic groups became heavily engaged in overseas politics. Through fraternal, religious, and political organizations based in their ethnic and racial communities, Irish-Americans supported Irish independence, American Jews protested the treatment of their co-religionists in Russia, and black Americans hoped to uplift Africa. American influence was growing throughout the world.

FOCUS QUESTIONS

In what ways did the Progressive presidents promote the expansion of American power overseas? –*p. 717*

How did the United States get involved in World War I? –*p. 721*

How did the United States mobilize resources and public opinion for the war effort? –*p. 727*

How did the war affect race relations in the United States? –*p. 735*

Why was 1919 such a watershed year for the United States and the world? –*p. 747*

The Greatest Department Store on Earth, a cartoon from *Puck*, November 29, 1899, depicts Uncle Sam selling goods, mostly manufactured products, to the nations of the world. The search for markets overseas would be a recurring theme of twentieth-century American foreign policy.

1903	United States secures the Panama Canal Zone
1904	Roosevelt Corollary to the Monroe Doctrine
1905	The Niagara movement established
1907	Gentleman's Agreement with Japan
1909	National Association for the Advancement of Colored People organized
1910	Mexican Revolution begins
1914–1919	World War I
1915	*Lusitania* sinks
1916	Madison Grant's *The Passing of the Great Race*
	Randolph Bourne's "Trans-National America"
1917	Zimmerman Telegram intercepted
	United States enters the war
	Espionage Act passed
	Russian Revolution
1918	Woodrow Wilson's "Fourteen Points" speech
	Eugene V. Debs convicted under the Espionage Act
1918–1920	Worldwide flu epidemic
1919	Eighteenth Amendment
	Treaty of Versailles signed
1919–1920	Red Scare
1920	Senate rejects the Treaty of Versailles
	Nineteenth Amendment
1921	Tulsa Riot

America's growing connections with the outside world led to increasing military and political involvement. In the two decades after 1900, many of the basic principles that would guide American foreign policy for the rest of the century were formulated. The "open door"—the free flow of trade, investment, information, and culture—emerged as a key principle of American foreign relations. "Since the manufacturer insists on having the world as a market," wrote Woodrow Wilson, "the flag of his nation must follow him and the doors of nations which are closed against him must be battered down."

Americans in the twentieth century often discussed foreign policy in the language of freedom. At least in rhetoric, the United States ventured abroad—including intervening militarily in the affairs of other nations—not to pursue strategic goals or to make the world safe for American economic interests, but to promote liberty and democracy. A supreme faith in America's historic destiny and in the righteousness of its ideals enabled the country's leaders to think of the United States simultaneously as an emerging great power and as the worldwide embodiment of freedom.

More than any other individual, Woodrow Wilson articulated this vision of America's relationship to the rest of the world. His foreign policy, called by historians "liberal internationalism," rested on the conviction that economic and political progress went hand in hand. Thus, greater worldwide freedom would follow inevitably from increased American investment and trade abroad. Frequently during the twentieth century, this conviction would serve as a mask for American power and self-interest. It would also inspire sincere efforts to bring freedom to other peoples. In either case, liberal internationalism represented a shift from the nineteenth-century tradition of promoting freedom primarily by example, to active intervention to remake the world in the American image.

American involvement in World War I provided the first great test of Wilson's belief that American power could "make the world safe for democracy." Most Progressives embraced the country's participation in the war, believing that the United States could help to spread Progressive values throughout the world. But rather than bringing Progressivism to other peoples, the war destroyed it at home. The government quickly came to view critics of American involvement not simply as citizens with a different set of opinions, but as enemies of the very ideas of democracy and freedom. As a result, the war produced one of the most sweeping repressions of the right to dissent in all of American history.

AN ERA OF INTERVENTION

Just as they expanded the powers of the federal government in domestic affairs, the Progressive presidents were not reluctant to project American power outside the country's borders. At first, their interventions were confined to the Western Hemisphere, whose affairs the United States had claimed a special right to oversee ever since the Monroe Doctrine of 1823. Between 1901 and 1920, U.S. marines landed in Caribbean countries more than twenty times. Usually, they were dispatched to create a welcoming economic environment for American companies that wanted stable access to raw materials like bananas and sugar, and for bankers nervous that their loans to local governments might not be repaid.

"I Took the Canal Zone"

Just as he distinguished between good and bad trusts, Theodore Roosevelt divided the world into "civilized" and "uncivilized" nations. The former, he believed, had an obligation to establish order in an unruly world. Roosevelt became far more active in international diplomacy than most of his predecessors, helping, for example, to negotiate a settlement of the Russo-Japanese War of 1905, a feat for which he was awarded the Nobel Peace Prize. Closer to home, his policies were more aggressive. "I have always been fond of the West African proverb," he wrote, "'Speak softly and carry a big stick.'" And although he declared that the United States "has not the slightest desire for territorial aggrandizement at the expense of its southern neighbors," Roosevelt pursued a policy of intervention in Central America.

In his first major action in the region, Roosevelt engineered the separation of Panama from Colombia in order to facilitate the construction of a canal linking the Atlantic and Pacific Oceans. The idea of a canal across the fifty-one-mile-wide Isthmus of Panama had a long history. In 1879–1881, the French engineer Ferdinand de Lesseps attempted to construct such a waterway but failed because of inadequate funding and the toll exacted on his workers by yellow fever and malaria. Roosevelt had long been a proponent of American naval development. He was convinced that a canal would facilitate the movement of naval and commercial vessels between the two oceans. In 1903, when Colombia, of which Panama was a part, refused to cede land for the project, Roosevelt helped to set in motion an uprising by conspirators led by Philippe Bunau-Varilla, a representative of the Panama Canal Company. An American gunboat prevented the Colombian army from suppressing the rebellion.

Upon establishing Panama's independence, Bunau-Varilla signed a treaty giving the United States both the right to construct and operate a canal and sovereignty over the Canal Zone, a ten-mile-wide strip of land through which the route would run. A remarkable feat of engineering, the canal was the largest construction project in history to that date. Like the building of the transcontinental railroad in the 1860s and much construction work today, it involved the widespread use of immigrant labor. Most of the 60,000 workers came from the Caribbean islands of Barbados and Jamaica, but others hailed from Europe, Asia, and the United States. In keeping with American segregation policies, the best jobs were reserved for white Americans, who lived in their own communities complete with schools, churches, and libraries. It also required a massive effort to eradicate the mosquitoes that carried the tropical diseases responsible, in part, for the failure of earlier French efforts. When completed in 1914, the canal reduced the sea voyage between the East and West Coasts of the United States by 8,000 miles. "I took the Canal Zone," Roosevelt

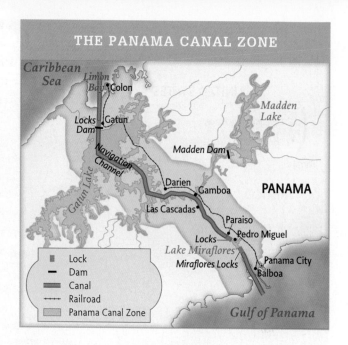

THE PANAMA CANAL ZONE

Constructed in the first years of the twentieth century, after Theodore Roosevelt helped engineer Panama's independence from Colombia, the Panama Canal drastically reduced the time it took for commercial and naval vessels to sail from the Atlantic to the Pacific Ocean.

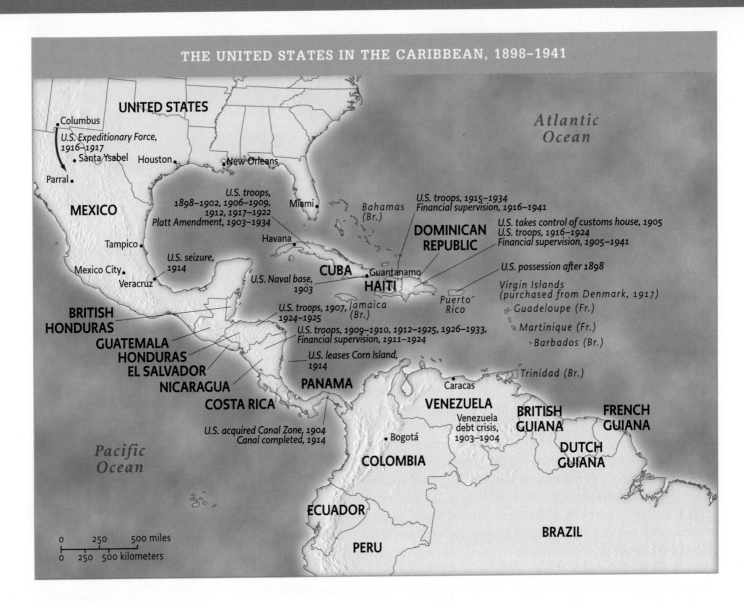

THE UNITED STATES IN THE CARIBBEAN, 1898–1941

UNITED STATES

Columbus
U.S. Expeditionary Force,
1916–1917
Santa Ysabel Houston
Parral
New Orleans

MEXICO

U.S. troops,
1898–1902, 1906–1909,
1912, 1917–1922
Platt Amendment, 1903–1934

Miami

Bahamas
(Br.)

U.S. troops, 1915–1934
Financial supervision, 1916–1941

DOMINICAN
REPUBLIC

U.S. takes control of customs house, 1905
U.S. troops, 1916–1924
Financial supervision, 1905–1941

Tampico

Havana

U.S. possession after 1898

Mexico City

U.S. seizure,
1914

CUBA

Virgin Islands
(purchased from Denmark, 1917)

Veracruz

U.S. Naval base,
1903

Guantanamo

HAITI

Puerto
Rico

Guadeloupe (Fr.)

BRITISH
HONDURAS

U.S. troops, 1907,
1924–1925

Jamaica
(Br.)

Martinique (Fr.)

GUATEMALA
HONDURAS
EL SALVADOR
NICARAGUA
COSTA RICA

U.S. troops, 1909–1910, 1912–1925, 1926–1933,
Financial supervision, 1911–1924

U.S. leases Corn Island,
1914

Barbados (Br.)

Trinidad (Br.)

PANAMA

Caracas

VENEZUELA

BRITISH
GUIANA

FRENCH
GUIANA

U.S. acquired Canal Zone, 1904
Canal completed, 1914

Venezuela
debt crisis,
1903–1904

DUTCH
GUIANA

Pacific
Ocean

Bogotá

COLOMBIA

Atlantic
Ocean

ECUADOR

BRAZIL

PERU

0   250   500 miles
0   250   500 kilometers

Between 1898 and 1941, the United States intervened militarily numerous times in Caribbean countries, generally to protect the economic interests of American banks and investors.

exulted. But the manner in which the canal had been initiated, and the continued American rule over the Canal Zone, would long remain a source of tension. In 1977, President Jimmy Carter negotiated treaties that led to turning over the canal's operation and control of the Canal Zone to Panama in the year 2000 (see Chapter 26).

The Roosevelt Corollary

Roosevelt's actions in Panama reflected a principle that came to be called the Roosevelt Corollary to the Monroe Doctrine. This held that the United States had the right to exercise "an international police power" in the Western Hemisphere—a significant expansion of Monroe's pledge to defend the hemisphere against European intervention. Early in Roosevelt's administration, British, Italian, and German naval forces blockaded Venezuela to ensure the payment of debts to European bankers. Roosevelt persuaded them to withdraw, but the incident convinced him that financial instability in the New World would invite intervention from the Old. In 1904, Roosevelt ordered

An international police power

American forces to seize the customs houses of the Dominican Republic to ensure payment of its debts to European and American investors. He soon arranged an "executive agreement" giving a group of American banks control over Dominican finances. In 1906, he dispatched troops to Cuba to oversee a disputed election; they remained in the country until 1909. Roosevelt also encouraged investment by American corporations like the United Fruit Company, whose huge banana plantations soon dominated the economies of Honduras and Costa Rica.

> *The U.S. in Latin America*

Roosevelt's successor, William Howard Taft, landed marines in Nicaragua to protect a government friendly to American economic interests. In general, however, Taft emphasized economic investment and loans from American banks, rather than direct military intervention, as the best way to spread American influence. As a result, his foreign policy became known as Dollar Diplomacy. In Honduras, Nicaragua, the Dominican Republic, and even Liberia—the West African nation established in 1816 as a home for freed American slaves—Taft pressed for more efficient revenue collection, stable government, and access to land and labor by American companies.

Moral Imperialism

The son of a Presbyterian minister, Woodrow Wilson brought to the presidency a missionary zeal and a sense of his own and the nation's moral righteousness. He appointed as secretary of state William Jennings Bryan, a strong anti-imperialist. Wilson repudiated Dollar Diplomacy and promised a new foreign policy that would respect Latin America's independence and free it from foreign economic domination. But Wilson could not abandon the conviction that the United States had a responsibility to teach other peoples the lessons of democracy. Moreover, he believed, the export of American manufactured goods and investments went hand in hand with the spread of democratic ideals. To Wilson, expanding American economic influence served a higher purpose than mere profit. Americans, he told a

The World's Constable, a cartoon commenting on Theodore Roosevelt's "new diplomacy," *in Judge*, January 14, 1905, portrays Roosevelt as an impartial policeman, holding in one hand the threat of force and in the other the promise of the peaceful settlement of disputes. Roosevelt stands between the undisciplined non-white peoples of the world and the imperialist powers of Europe and Japan.

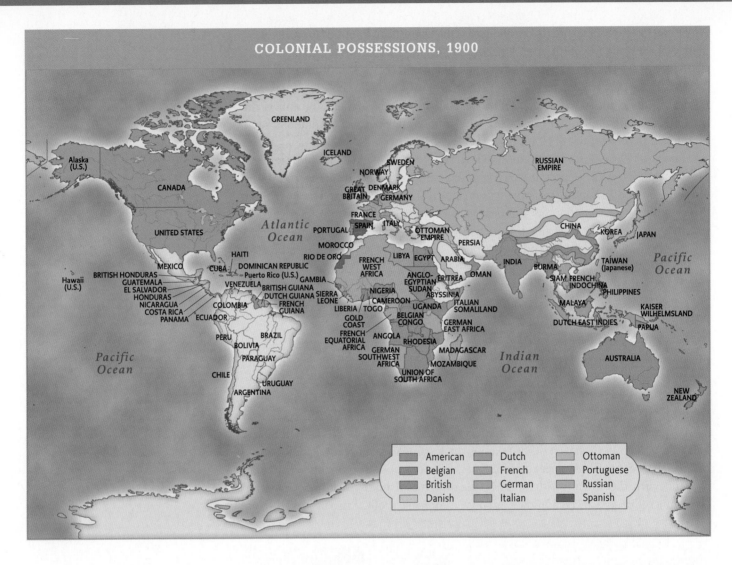

COLONIAL POSSESSIONS, 1900

American	Dutch	Ottoman
Belgian	French	Portuguese
British	German	Russian
Danish	Italian	Spanish

group of businessmen in 1916, were "meant to carry liberty and justice" throughout the world. "Go out and sell goods," he urged them, "that will make the world more comfortable and happy, and convert them to the principles of America."

Wilson's "moral imperialism" produced more military interventions in Latin America than the foreign policy of any president before or since. In 1915, he sent marines to occupy Haiti after the government refused to allow American banks to oversee its financial dealings. In 1916, he established a military government in the Dominican Republic, with the United States controlling the country's customs collections and paying its debts. American soldiers remained in the Dominican Republic until 1924 and in Haiti until 1934. They built roads and schools, but did little or nothing to promote democracy. Wilson's foreign policy underscored a paradox of modern American history: the presidents who spoke the most about freedom were likely to intervene most frequently in the affairs of other countries.

Wilson's interventions

Wilson and Mexico

Wilson's major preoccupation in Latin America was Mexico, where in 1911 a revolution led by Francisco Madero overthrew the government of dictator Porfirio Díaz.

Two years later, without Wilson's knowledge but with the backing of the U.S. ambassador and of American companies that controlled Mexico's oil and mining industries, military commander Victoriano Huerta assassinated Madero and seized power.

Wilson was appalled. The United States, he announced, would not extend recognition to a "government of butchers." He would "teach" Latin Americans, he added, "to elect good men." When civil war broke out in Mexico, Wilson ordered American troops to land at Vera Cruz to prevent the arrival of weapons meant for Huerta's forces. But to Wilson's surprise, Mexicans greeted the marines as invaders rather than liberators. Vera Cruz, after all, was where the forces of the conquistador Hernán Cortés had landed in the sixteenth century and those of Winfield Scott during the Mexican War. More than 100 Mexicans and 19 Americans died in the fighting that followed. Huerta left the presidency in 1914, but civil war continued, and neither side seemed grateful for Wilson's interference.

In 1916, the war spilled over into the United States when "Pancho" Villa, the leader of one faction, attacked Columbus, New Mexico, where he killed seventeen Americans. Wilson ordered 10,000 troops into northern Mexico on an expedition that unsuccessfully sought to arrest Villa. Mexico was a warning that it might be more difficult than Wilson assumed to use American might to reorder the internal affairs of other nations, or to apply moral certainty to foreign policy.

Pancho Villa

AMERICA AND THE GREAT WAR

In June 1914, a Serbian nationalist assassinated Archduke Franz Ferdinand, heir to the throne of the Austro-Hungarian empire, in Sarajevo, Bosnia. (Today, Sarajevo is the capital of Bosnia and Herzegovina.) This deed set in motion a chain of events that plunged Europe into the most devastating war the world had ever seen. In the years before 1914, European nations had engaged in a scramble to obtain colonial possessions overseas and had constructed a shifting series of alliances seeking military domination within Europe. In the aftermath of the assassination, Austria-Hungary, the major power in eastern Europe, declared war on Serbia. Within a little more than a month, because of the European powers' interlocking military alliances, Britain, France, Russia, and Japan (the Allies) found themselves at war with the Central Powers—Germany, Austria-Hungary, and the Ottoman empire, whose holdings included modern-day Turkey and much of the Middle East.

German forces quickly overran Belgium and part of northern France. The war then settled into a prolonged stalemate, with bloody, indecisive battles succeeding one another. New military technologies—submarines, airplanes, machine guns, tanks, and poison gas—produced unprecedented slaughter. In one five-month battle at Verdun, in 1916, 600,000 French and German soldiers perished—nearly as many combatants as in the entire American Civil War. By the time the war ended, an estimated 10 million soldiers, and uncounted millions of civilians, had perished. And the war was followed by widespread famine and a worldwide epidemic of influenza that killed an estimated 21 million people more.

The Great War, or World War I as it came to be called, dealt a severe blow to the optimism and self-confidence of Western civilization. For decades, philosophers,

A 1915 postcard portrays two soldiers—one American, one Mexican—at the border between the two countries shortly before Woodrow Wilson ordered American troops into Mexico. The photograph is intended to show a difference in discipline between the two.

reformers, and politicians had hailed the triumph of reason and human progress. Despite increasingly bitter rivalries between European powers, especially Germany and Britain, as they competed for political and military dominance at home and carved up Asia and Africa into rival empires, mankind seemed to have moved beyond the time when disputes were settled by war. The conflict was also a shock to European socialist and labor movements. Of the two great ideologies that had arisen in the nineteenth century, nationalism and socialism, the former proved more powerful. Karl Marx had called on the "workers of the world" to unite against their oppressors. Instead, they marched off to kill each other.

Neutrality and Preparedness

As war engulfed Europe, Americans found themselves sharply divided. British-Americans sided with their nation of origin, as did many other Americans who associated Great Britain with liberty and democracy and Germany with repressive government. On the other hand, German-Americans identified with Germany. Irish-Americans bitterly opposed any aid to the British, a sentiment reinforced in 1916 when authorities in London suppressed the Easter Rebellion, an uprising demanding Irish independence, and executed several of its leaders. Immigrants from the Russian empire, especially Jews, had no desire to see the United States aid the czar's regime. Indeed, the presence of Russia, the world's largest despotic state, as an ally of Britain and France made it difficult to see the war as a clear-cut battle between democracy and autocracy. Many feminists, pacifists, and social reformers, moreover, had become convinced that peace was essential to further efforts to enhance social justice at home. They lobbied vigorously against American involvement. So did large numbers of religious leaders, who viewed war as a barbaric throwback to a less Christian era.

Americans divided

Wilbur Wright, who with his brother Orville made the first powered flight in 1903, circling the Statue of Liberty six years later. World War I would reveal the military uses for this new technology.

When war broke out in 1914, President Wilson proclaimed American neutrality. But as in the years preceding the War of 1812, naval warfare in Europe reverberated in the United States. Britain declared a naval blockade of Germany and began to stop American merchant vessels. Germany launched submarine warfare against ships entering and leaving British ports. In May 1915, a German submarine sank the British liner *Lusitania* (which was carrying a large cache of arms) off the coast of Ireland, causing the death of 1,198 passengers, including 124 Americans. Wilson composed a note of protest so strong that Bryan resigned as secretary of state, fearing that the president was laying the foundation for military intervention. Bryan had advocated warning Americans not to travel on the ships of belligerents, but Wilson felt this would represent a retreat from the principle of freedom of the seas.

The sinking of the *Lusitania* outraged American public opinion and strengthened the hand of those who believed that the United States must prepare for possible entry into the war. These included longtime advocates of a stronger military establishment, like Theodore Roosevelt, and businessmen with close economic ties to Britain, the country's leading trading partner and the recipient

PEACE·HAS·HER·CONQUESTS·GREATER·FAR·THAN·WAR·

R.M.S. LUSITANIA
QUEEN OF THE SEAS.

The liner *Lusitania*, pictured on a "peace" postcard. Its sinking by a German submarine in 1915 strengthened the resolve of those who wished to see the United States enter the European war.

of more than $2 billion in wartime loans from American banks. Wilson himself had strong pro-British sympathies and viewed Germany as "the natural foe of liberty." By the end of 1915, he had embarked on a policy of "preparedness"— a crash program to expand the American army and navy.

Preparedness

The Road to War

In May 1916, Germany announced the suspension of submarine warfare against noncombatants. Wilson's preparedness program seemed to have succeeded in securing the right of Americans to travel freely on the high seas without committing American forces to the conflict. "He kept us out of war" became the slogan of his campaign for reelection. With the Republican Party reunited after its split in 1912, the election proved to be one of the closest in American history. Wilson defeated Republican candidate Charles Evans Hughes by only twenty-three electoral votes and about 600,000 popular votes out of more than 18 million cast. Partly because he seemed to promise not to send American soldiers to Europe, Wilson carried ten of the twelve states that had adopted woman suffrage. Without the votes of women, Wilson would not have been reelected.

Wilson's reelection

On January 22, 1917, Wilson called for a "peace without victory" in Europe and outlined his vision for a world order including freedom of the seas, restrictions on armaments, and self-determination for nations great and small. Almost immediately, however, Germany announced its intention to resume submarine warfare against ships sailing to or from the British Isles, and several American merchant vessels were sunk. The German government realized that its actions would probably lead Wilson to intervene, but German strategists gambled that the blockade would strangle Britain economically before the arrival of American troops.

In March 1917, British spies intercepted and made public the Zimmerman Telegram, a message by German foreign secretary Arthur Zimmerman calling on Mexico to join in a coming war against the United States and promising to help

Zimmerman Telegram

A 1916 Wilson campaign truck (a new development in political campaigning), promising peace, prosperity, and preparedness.

A new international order

it recover territory lost in the Mexican War of 1846–1848. A revolution in Russia that same month overthrew the czar and established a constitutional government, making it more plausible to believe that the United States would be fighting on the side of democracy. On April 2, Wilson went before Congress to ask for a declaration of war against Germany. "The world," he proclaimed, "must be made safe for democracy. Its peace must be planted upon the tested foundation of political liberty." The war resolution passed the Senate 82–6 and the House 373–50.

The Fourteen Points

Not until the spring of 1918 did American forces arrive in Europe in large numbers. By then, the world situation had taken a dramatic turn. In November 1917, a communist revolution headed by Vladimir Lenin overthrew the Russian government that had come to power the previous spring. Shortly thereafter, Lenin withdrew Russia from the war and published the secret treaties by which the Allies had agreed to divide up conquered territory after the war—an embarrassment for Wilson, who had promised a just peace.

Partly to assure the country that the war was being fought for a moral cause, Wilson in January 1918 issued the Fourteen Points, the clearest statement of American war aims and of his vision of a new international order. Among the key principles were self-determination for all nations, freedom of the seas, free trade, open diplomacy (an end to secret treaties), the readjustment of colonial claims with colonized people given "equal weight" in deciding their futures, and the creation of a "general association of nations" to preserve the peace. Wilson envisioned this last

In this painting from 1917, the Austrian painter Albin Egger-Leinz portrays World War I soldiers as faceless automatons marching in unison to the slaughter. By this time, the massive loss of life had produced widespread revulsion against the war.

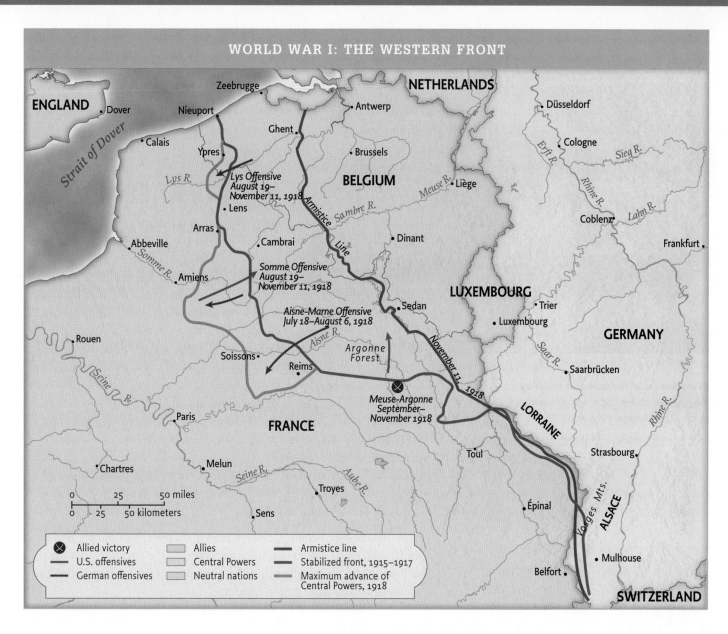

WORLD WAR I: THE WESTERN FRONT

After years of stalemate on the western front in World War I, the arrival of American troops in 1917 and 1918 shifted the balance of power and made possible the Allied victory.

provision, which led to the establishment after the war of the League of Nations, as a kind of global counterpart to the regulatory commissions Progressives had created at home to maintain social harmony and prevent the powerful from exploiting the weak. Although purely an American program, not endorsed by the other Allies, the Fourteen Points established the agenda for the peace conference that followed the war.

The United States threw its economic resources and manpower into the war. When American troops finally arrived in Europe, they turned the tide of battle. In the spring of 1918, they helped to repulse a German advance near Paris and by July were participating in a major Allied counteroffensive. In September, in the Meuse-Argonne campaign, more than 1 million American soldiers under General John J. Pershing helped to push back the outnumbered and exhausted German army.

Turning the tide of battle

World War I was the first war in which soldiers moved to the battlefront in motorized trucks. This photograph is from 1918.

With his forces in full retreat, the German kaiser abdicated on November 9. Two days later, Germany sued for peace. More than 100,000 Americans had died, a substantial number, but they were only 1 percent of the 10 million soldiers killed in the Great War.

THE WAR AT HOME

The Progressives' War

Looking back on American participation in the European conflict, Randolph Bourne summed up one of its lessons: "War is the health of the state." Bourne saw the expansion of government power as a danger, but it struck most Progressives as a golden opportunity. To them, the war offered the possibility of reforming American society along scientific lines, instilling a sense of national unity and self-sacrifice, and expanding social justice. That American power could now disseminate Progressive values around the globe heightened the war's appeal.

Almost without exception, Progressive intellectuals and reformers, joined by prominent labor leaders and native-born socialists, rallied to Wilson's support. The roster included intellectuals like John Dewey, journalists such as Walter Lippmann and Herbert Croly, AFL head Samuel Gompers, socialist writers like Upton Sinclair, and prominent reformers including Florence Kelley and Charlotte Perkins Gilman. In *The New Republic*, Dewey urged Progressives to recognize the "social possibilities of war." The crisis, he wrote, offered the prospect of attacking the "immense inequality of power" within the United States, thus laying the foundation for Americans to enjoy "effective freedom."

The Wartime State

An expanding state

Like the Civil War, World War I created, albeit temporarily, a national state with unprecedented powers and a sharply increased presence in Americans' everyday lives. Under the Selective Service Act of May 1917, 24 million men were required to register with the draft, and the army soon swelled from 120,000 to 5 million men. The war seemed to bring into being the New Nationalist state Theodore Roosevelt and so many Progressives had desired. New federal agencies moved to regulate industry, transportation, labor relations, and agriculture. Headed by Wall Street financier Bernard Baruch, the War Industries Board presided over all elements of war production from the distribution of raw materials to the prices of manufactured goods. To spur efficiency, it established standardized specifications for everything from automobile tires to shoe colors (three were permitted—black, brown, and white). The Railroad Administration took control of the nation's transportation system, and the Fuel Agency rationed coal and oil. The Food Administration instructed farmers on modern methods of cultivation and promoted the more efficient preparation of meals. Its director, Herbert Hoover, mobilized the shipment of American food to the war-devastated Allies, popularizing the slogan "Food will win the war."

These agencies generally saw themselves as partners of business as much as regulators. They guaranteed government suppliers a high rate of profit and encouraged cooperation among former business rivals by suspending antitrust laws. At the same time, however, the War Labor Board, which included representatives of government, industry, and the American Federation of Labor, pressed for the establishment of a minimum wage, eight-hour workday, and the right to form unions. During the war, wages rose substantially, working conditions in many industries improved, and union membership doubled. To finance the war, corporate and individual income taxes rose enormously. By 1918, the wealthiest Americans were paying 60 percent of their income in taxes. Tens of millions of Americans answered the call to demonstrate their patriotism by purchasing Liberty bonds. Once peace arrived, the wartime state quickly withered away. But for a time, the federal government seemed well on its way to fulfilling the Progressive task of promoting economic rationalization, industrial justice, and a sense of common national purpose.

The Propaganda War

During the Civil War, it had been left to private agencies—Union Leagues, the Loyal Publication Society, and others—to mobilize prowar public opinion. But the Wilson administration decided that patriotism was too important to leave to the private sector. Many Americans were skeptical about whether democratic America should enter a struggle between rival empires. Some vehemently opposed American participation, notably the Industrial Workers of the World (IWW) and the bulk of the Socialist Party, which in 1917 condemned the declaration of war as "a crime against the people of the United States" and called on "the workers of all countries" to refuse to fight. As the major national organization to oppose Wilson's policy, the Socialist Party became a rallying point for antiwar sentiment. In mayoral elections across the country in the fall of 1917, the Socialist vote averaged 20 percent, far above the party's previous total.

In April 1917, the Wilson administration created the Committee on Public Information (CPI) to explain to Americans and the world, as its director, George Creel, put it, "the cause that compelled America to take arms in defense of its liberties and free institutions." Enlisting academics, journalists, artists, and advertising men, the CPI flooded the country with prowar propaganda, using every available medium from pamphlets (of which it issued 75 million) to posters, newspaper advertisements, and motion pictures. It trained and dispatched across the country 75,000 Four-Minute Men, who delivered brief standardized talks (sometimes in Italian, Yiddish, and other immigrant languages) to audiences in movie theaters, schools, and other public venues.

Never before had an agency of the federal government attempted the "conscious and intelligent manipulation of the organized habits and opinions of the

HELLO!
THIS IS LIBERTY SPEAKING—
BILLIONS OF DOLLARS ARE NEEDED
AND NEEDED NOW

All combatants raised money by selling war bonds. In the German poster, the text reads: "The war loan is the way to peace. The enemies want it this way [referring to the mailed fist]. So subscribe." The fist conveys sheer power—it offers an image rather different from the representation of liberty on the American war poster.

masses," in the words of young Edward Bernays, a member of Creel's staff who would later create the modern profession of public relations. The CPI's activities proved, one adman wrote, that it was possible to "sway the ideas of whole populations, change their habits of life, create belief, practically universal in any policy or idea." In the 1920s, advertisers would use what they had learned to sell goods. But the CPI also set a precedent for active governmental efforts to shape public opinion in later international conflicts, from World War II to the Cold War and Iraq.

"The Great Cause of Freedom"

Mobilizing for democracy

The CPI couched its appeal in the Progressive language of social cooperation and expanded democracy. Abroad, this meant a peace based on the principle of national self-determination. At home, it meant improving "industrial democracy." A Progressive journalist, Creel believed the war would accelerate the movement toward solving the "age-old problems of poverty, inequality, oppression, and unhappiness." He took to heart a warning from historian Carl Becker that a simple contrast between German tyranny and American democracy would not seem plausible to the average worker: "You talk to him of our ideals of liberty and he thinks of the shameless exploitation of labor and of the ridiculous gulf between wealth and poverty." The CPI distributed pamphlets foreseeing a postwar society complete with a "universal eight-hour day" and a living wage for all.

Mobilizing for freedom

While "democracy" served as the key term of wartime mobilization, "freedom" also took on new significance. The war, a CPI advertisement proclaimed, was being fought in "the great cause of freedom." Thousands of persons, often draftees, were enlisted to pose in giant human tableaus representing symbols of liberty. One living representation of the Liberty Bell at Fort Dix, New Jersey, included 25,000 people. The most common visual image in wartime propaganda was the Statue of Liberty, employed especially to rally support among immigrants. "You came here seeking Freedom," stated a caption on one Statue of Liberty poster. "You must now help preserve it." Buying Liberty bonds became a demonstration of patriotism. Wilson's speeches cast the United States as a land of liberty fighting alongside a "concert of free people" to secure self-determination for the oppressed peoples of the world. The idea of freedom, it seems, requires an antithesis, and the CPI found one in the German kaiser and, more generally, the German nation and people. Government propaganda whipped up hatred of the wartime foe by portraying it as a nation of barbaric Huns.

Douglas Fairbanks, one of the era's most celebrated movie stars, addressing a 1918 rally urging people to buy Liberty Bonds.

The Coming of Woman Suffrage

The enlistment of "democracy" and "freedom" as ideological war weapons inevitably inspired demands for their expansion at home. In 1916, Wilson had cautiously endorsed votes for women. America's entry into the war threatened to tear the suffrage movement apart, since many advocates had been associated with opposition to American involvement. Indeed, among those who voted against the

Women during World War I: two women hauling ice—a job confined to men before the war—and woman suffrage demonstrators in front of the White House.

declaration of war was the first woman member of Congress, the staunch pacifist Jeannette Rankin of Montana. "I want to stand by my country, but I cannot vote for war," she said. Although defeated in her reelection bid in 1918, Rankin would return to Congress in 1940. She became the only member to oppose the declaration of war against Japan in 1941, which ended her political career. In 1968, at the age of eighty-five, Rankin took part in a giant march on Washington to protest the war in Vietnam.

As during the Civil War, however, most leaders of woman suffrage organizations enthusiastically enlisted in the effort. Women sold war bonds, organized patriotic rallies, and went to work in war production jobs. Some 22,000 served as clerical workers and nurses with American forces in Europe. Many believed wartime service would earn them equal rights at home.

At the same time, a new generation of college-educated activists, organized in the National Woman's Party, pressed for the right to vote with militant tactics many older suffrage advocates found scandalous. The party's leader, Alice Paul, had studied in England between 1907 and 1910 when the British suffrage movement adopted a strategy that included arrests, imprisonments, and vigorous denunciations of a male-dominated political system. How could the country fight for democracy abroad, Paul asked, while denying it to women at home? She compared Wilson to the Kaiser, and a group of her followers chained themselves to the White House fence, resulting in a seven-month prison sentence. When they began a hunger strike, the prisoners were force-fed.

Alice Paul

The combination of women's patriotic service and widespread outrage over the mistreatment of Paul and her fellow prisoners pushed the administration toward full-fledged support for woman suffrage. "We have made partners of the women in this war," Wilson proclaimed. "Shall we admit them only to a partnership of suffering and sacrifice and toil and not to a partnership of privilege and right?" In 1920, the long struggle ended with the ratification of the Nineteenth Amendment barring states from using sex as a qualification for the suffrage. The United States became the twenty-seventh country to allow women to vote.

A 1915 cartoon showing the western states where women had won the right to vote. Women in the East reach out to a western woman carrying a torch of liberty.

THE AWAKENING

Prohibition

The war gave a powerful impulse to other campaigns that had engaged the energies of many women in the Progressive era. Ironically, efforts to stamp out prostitution and protect soldiers from venereal disease led the government to distribute birth-control information and devices—the very action for which Margaret Sanger had recently been jailed, as noted in the previous chapter.

Prohibition, a movement inherited from the nineteenth century that had gained new strength and militancy in Progressive America, finally achieved national success during the war. Numerous impulses flowed into the renewed campaign to ban intoxicating liquor. Employers hoped it would create a more disciplined labor force. Urban reformers believed that it would promote a more orderly city environment and undermine urban political machines that used saloons as places to organize. Women reformers hoped Prohibition would protect wives and children from husbands who engaged in domestic violence when drunk or who squandered their wages at saloons. Many native-born Protestants saw Prohibition as a way of imposing "American" values on immigrants.

Like the suffrage movement, Prohibitionists first concentrated on state campaigns. By 1915, they had won victories in eighteen southern and midwestern states where the immigrant population was small and Protestant denominations like Baptists and Methodists strongly opposed drinking. But like the suffrage movement, Prohibitionists came to see national legislation as their best strategy. The war gave them added ammunition. Many prominent breweries were owned by German-Americans, making

A 1916 cartoon from the publication of the Women's Christian Temperance Union shows petitions for Prohibition flooding into Congress.

ON TO WASHINGTON!
STORM THE CAPITOL WITH PETITIONS FOR NATIONAL CONSTITUTIONAL

PROHIBITION, 1915: COUNTIES AND STATES THAT BANNED LIQUOR BEFORE THE EIGHTEENTH AMENDMENT (RATIFIED 1919, REPEALED 1933)

beer seem unpatriotic. The Food Administration insisted that grain must be used to produce food, not distilled into beer and liquor. In December 1917, Congress passed the Eighteenth Amendment, prohibiting the manufacture and sale of intoxicating liquor. It was ratified by the states in 1919 and went into effect at the beginning of 1920.

In the early years of the twentieth century, many states and localities in the South and West banned the manufacture and sale of alcoholic beverages. ("Wet" counties allowed alcoholic beverages, "dry" counties banned them.) Prohibition became national with the adoption of the Eighteenth Amendment in 1919.

Liberty in Wartime

World War I raised questions already glimpsed during the Civil War that would trouble the nation again during the McCarthy era and in the aftermath of the terrorist attacks of 2001: What is the balance between security and freedom? Does the Constitution protect citizens' rights during wartime? Should dissent be equated with lack of patriotism? The conflict demonstrated that during a war, traditional civil liberties are likely to come under severe pressure.

In 1917, Randolph Bourne ridiculed Progressives who believed they could mold the war according to their own "liberal purposes." The conflict, he predicted,

Security and freedom

ORGIE MANIACLE

ALL FOR HONOR

ALL FOR DEMOCRACY

ALL FOR WORLD PEACE

ALL FOR JESUS

EDITOR   CAPITALIST   POLITICIAN   MINISTER

Having Their Fling

A 1917 antiwar cartoon from the radical magazine *The Masses* depicts an editor, capitalist, politician, and minister celebrating American involvement in World War I and hoping to benefit from it. President Woodrow Wilson barred *The Masses* and other antiwar publications from the mails.

Debs in prison

would empower not reformers but the "least democratic forces in American life." The accuracy of Bourne's prediction soon become apparent. Despite the administration's idealistic language of democracy and freedom, the war inaugurated the most intense repression of civil liberties the nation has ever known. Perhaps the very nobility of wartime rhetoric contributed to the massive suppression of dissent. For in the eyes of Wilson and many of his supporters, America's goals were so virtuous that disagreement could only reflect treason to the country's values. "It is a fearful thing to lead this great peaceful people into war," Wilson remarked in his speech asking Congress to bring America into the conflict. Even he could not have predicted how significant an impact the war would have on American freedom.

The Espionage Act

For the first time since the Alien and Sedition Acts of 1798, the federal government enacted laws to restrict freedom of speech. The Espionage Act of 1917 prohibited not only spying and interfering with the draft but also "false statements" that might impede military success. The postmaster general barred from the mails numerous newspapers and magazines critical of the administration.

The victims ranged from virtually the entire socialist press and many foreign-language publications to *The Jeffersonian*, a newspaper owned by ex-Populist leader Tom Watson, which criticized the draft as a violation of states' rights. In 1918, the Sedition Act made it a crime to make spoken or printed statements that intended to cast "contempt, scorn, or disrepute" on the "form of government," or that advocated interference with the war effort. The government charged more than 2,000 persons with violating these laws. Over half were convicted. A court sentenced Ohio farmer John White to twenty-one months in prison for saying that the murder of innocent women and children by German soldiers was no worse than what the United States had done in the Philippines in the war of 1899–1903.

The most prominent victim was Eugene V. Debs, convicted in 1918 under the Espionage Act for delivering an antiwar speech. Before his sentencing, Debs gave the court a lesson in the history of American freedom, tracing the tradition of dissent from Thomas Paine to the abolitionists, and pointing out that the nation had never engaged in a war without internal opposition. Germany sent socialist leader Karl Liebknecht to prison for four years for opposing the war; in the United States, Debs's sentence was ten years. After the war's end, Wilson rejected the advice of his attorney general that he commute Debs's sentence. Debs ran for president while still in prison in 1920 and received 900,000 votes. It was left to Wilson's successor, Warren G. Harding, to release Debs from prison in 1921.

Coercive Patriotism

Even more extreme repression took place at the hands of state governments and private groups. Americans had long displayed the flag (and used it in advertisements for everything from tobacco products to variety shows). But during World War I, attitudes toward the American flag became a test of patriotism. Persons suspected of disloyalty were forced to kiss the flag in public; those who made statements critical of the flag could be imprisoned. During the war, thirty-three states outlawed the possession or display of red or black flags (symbols, respectively, of communism and anarchism), and twenty-three outlawed a newly created offense, "criminal syndicalism," the advocacy of unlawful acts to accomplish political change or "a change in industrial ownership."

"Who is the real patriot?" Emma Goldman asked while on trial for conspiring to violate the Selective Service Act. She answered, those who "love America with open eyes," who were not blind to "the wrongs committed in the name of patriotism." But from the federal government to local authorities and private groups, patriotism came to be equated with support for the government, the war, and the American economic system, while antiwar sentiment, labor radicalism, and sympathy for the Russian Revolution became "un-American." Minnesota established a Commission of Public Safety to root out disloyalty from the state. Local authorities formally investigated residents who failed to subscribe to Liberty Loans. Throughout the country, schools revised their course offerings to ensure their patriotism and required teachers to sign loyalty oaths.

The 250,000 members of the newly formed American Protective League (APL) helped the Justice Department identify radicals and critics of the war by spying on their neighbors and carrying out "slacker raids" in which thousands of men were stopped on the streets of major cities and required to produce draft registration cards. Many private groups seized upon the atmosphere of repression as a weapon against domestic opponents. Employers cooperated with the government in crushing the Industrial Workers of the World (IWW), a move long demanded by business interests. In July 1917, vigilantes in Bisbee, Arizona, rounded up some 1,200 striking copper miners and their sympathizers, herded them into railroad boxcars, and transported them into the desert, where they were abandoned. New Mexico's governor ordered them housed in tents and provided with food and water. Few ever returned to Bisbee. In August, a crowd in Butte, Montana, lynched IWW leader Frank Little. The following month, operating under one of the broadest warrants in American history, federal agents swooped down on IWW offices throughout the country, arresting hundreds of leaders and seizing files and publications.

Bisbee, Arizona

The war experience, commented Walter Lippmann, demonstrated "that the traditional liberties of speech and opinion rest on no solid foundation." Yet while some Progressives protested individual excesses, most failed to speak out against the broad suppression of freedom of expression. Civil liberties, by and large, had never been a major concern of Progressives, who had always viewed the national state as the embodiment of democratic purpose and insisted that freedom flowed from participating in the life of society, not standing in opposition. Strong believers in the use of national power to improve social conditions, Progressives found themselves ill prepared to develop a defense of minority rights against majority or governmental tyranny. From the AFL to *New Republic* intellectuals, moreover, supporters of

Progressives and civil liberties

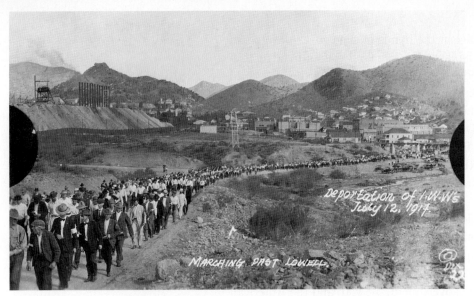

the war saw the elimination of socialists and alien radicals as a necessary prelude to the integration of labor and immigrants into an ordered society, an outcome they hoped would emerge from the war.

A long line of striking miners being led out of Bisbee, Arizona, in July 1917. Some 1,200 members of the Industrial Workers of the World were transported into the desert by armed vigilantes and abandoned there.

WHO IS AN AMERICAN?

In many respects, Progressivism was a precursor to major developments of the twentieth century—the New Deal, the Great Society, the socially active state. But in accepting the idea of "race" as a permanent, defining characteristic of individuals and social groups, Progressives bore more resemblance to nineteenth-century thinkers than to later twentieth-century liberals, with whom they are sometimes compared.

The "Race Problem"

Even before American participation in World War I, what contemporaries called the "race problem"—the tensions that arose from the country's increasing ethnic diversity—had become a major subject of public concern. "Race" referred to far more than black-white relations. The *Dictionary of Races of Peoples*, published in 1911 by the U.S. Immigration Commission, listed no fewer than forty-five immigrant "races," each supposedly with its own inborn characteristics. They ranged from Anglo-Saxons at the top down to Hebrews, Northern Italians, and, lowest of all, Southern Italians—supposedly violent, undisciplined, and incapable of assimilation.

In 1907, Congress had decreed that an American woman who married an alien automatically forfeited her American citizenship. Popular best-sellers like *The Passing of the Great Race*, published in 1916 by Madison Grant, president of the New York Zoological Society, warned that the influx of new immigrants and the low birthrate of native white women threatened the foundations of American civilization. The new science of eugenics, which studied the alleged mental characteristics of different races, gave anti-immigrant sentiment an air of professional expertise. If democracy could not flourish in the face of vast inequalities of economic power, neither, most Progressives believed, could it survive in a nation permanently divided along racial and ethnic lines.

Eugenics

Americanization and Pluralism

Somehow, the very nationalization of politics and economic life served to heighten awareness of ethnic and racial difference and spurred demands for "Americanization"—the creation of a more homogeneous national culture. A 1908

Demands for Americanization

play by the Jewish immigrant writer Israel Zangwill, *The Melting Pot*, gave a popular name to the process by which newcomers were supposed to merge their identity into existing American nationality. Public and private groups of all kinds—including educators, employers, labor leaders, social reformers, and public officials—took up the task of Americanizing new immigrants. The Ford Motor Company's famed sociological department entered the homes of immigrant workers to evaluate their clothing, furniture, and food preferences and enrolled them in English-language courses. Ford fired those who failed to adapt to American standards after a reasonable period of time. Americanization programs often targeted women as the bearers and transmitters of culture. In Los Angeles, teachers and religious missionaries worked to teach English to Mexican-American women so that they could then assimilate American values. Fearful that adult newcomers remained too stuck in their Old World ways, public schools paid great attention to Americanizing immigrants' children. The challenge facing schools, wrote one educator, was "to implant in their children, so far as can be done, the Anglo-Saxon conception of righteousness, law and order, and popular government."

A minority of Progressives questioned Americanization efforts and insisted on respect for immigrant subcultures. At Hull House, teachers offered English-language instruction but also encouraged immigrants to value their European heritage. Probably the most penetrating critique issued from the pen of Randolph Bourne, whose 1916 essay, "Trans-National America," exposed the fundamental flaw in the Americanization model. "There is no distinctive American culture," Bourne pointed out. Interaction between individuals and groups had produced the nation's music, poetry, and other cultural expressions. Bourne envisioned a democratic, cosmopolitan society in which immigrants and natives alike submerged their group identities in a new "trans-national" culture.

With President Wilson declaring that some Americans "born under foreign flags" were guilty of "disloyalty . . . and must be absolutely crushed," the federal and state governments demanded that immigrants demonstrate their unwavering devotion to the United States. The Committee on Public Information renamed

> *The melting pot*

> *Randolph Bourne*

An Americanization Celebration. A photograph of a Catholic assembly on National Slavic Day, September 3, 1914, illustrates how immigrants strove to demonstrate their patriotism. Children wear Old World dress, but most of the adults are in American clothing or nurses' uniforms.

WHO IS AN AMERICAN? | 735

VOICES OF FREEDOM

From EUGENE V. DEBS, SPEECH TO THE JURY BEFORE SENTENCING UNDER THE ESPIONAGE ACT (1918)

The most prominent spokesman for American socialism and a fervent opponent of American participation in World War I, Eugene V. Debs was arrested for delivering an antiwar speech and convicted of violating the Espionage Act. In his speech to the jury, he defended the right of dissent in wartime.

I wish to admit the truth of all that has been testified to in this proceeding. . . . Gentlemen, you have heard the report of my speech at Canton on June 16, and I submit that there is not a word in that speech to warrant the charges set out in the indictment. . . . In what I had to say there my purpose was to have the people understand something about the social system in which we live and to prepare them to change this system by perfectly peaceable and orderly means into what I, as a Socialist, conceive to be a real democracy. . . . I have never advocated violence in any form. I have always believed in education, in intelligence, in enlightenment; and I have always made my appeal to the reason and to the conscience of the people.

In every age there have been a few heroic souls who have been in advance of their time, who have been misunderstood, maligned, persecuted, sometimes put to death. . . . Washington, Jefferson,

Franklin, Paine, and their compeers were the rebels of their day. . . . But they had the moral courage to be true to their convictions. . . .

William Lloyd Garrison, Wendell Phillips, Elizabeth Cady Stanton . . . and other leaders of the abolition movement who were regarded as public enemies and treated accordingly, were true to their faith and stood their ground. . . . You are now teaching your children to revere their memories, while all of their detractors are in oblivion.

This country has been engaged in a number of wars and every one of them has been condemned by some of the people. The war of 1812 was opposed and condemned by some of the most influential citizens; the Mexican War was vehemently opposed and bitterly denounced, even after the war had been declared and was in progress, by Abraham Lincoln, Charles Sumner, Daniel Webster. . . . They were not indicted; they were not charged with treason. . . .

I believe in the Constitution. Isn't it strange that we Socialists stand almost alone today in upholding and defending the Constitution of the United States? The revolutionary fathers . . . understood that free speech, a free press and the right of free assemblage by the people were fundamental principles in democratic government. . . . I believe in the right of free speech, in war as well as in peace.

From W. E. B. DU BOIS, "RETURNING SOLDIERS," THE CRISIS (1919)

Scholar, poet, activist, founder of the National Association for the Advancement of Colored People and editor of its magazine, *The Crisis*, W. E. B. Du Bois was the most prominent black leader of the first half of the twentieth century. He supported black participation in World War I, but he insisted that black soldiers must now join in the struggle for freedom at home.

———————————

We are returning from war! *The Crisis* and tens of thousands of black men were drafted into a great struggle. For bleeding France and what she means and has meant and will mean to us and humanity and against the threat of German race arrogance, we fought gladly and to the last drop of blood; for America and her highest ideals, we fought in far-off hope; for the dominant southern oligarchy entrenched in Washington, we fought in bitter resignation. For the America that represents and gloats in lynching, disfranchisement, caste, brutality and devilish insult—for this, in the hateful upturning and mixing of things, we were forced by vindictive fate to fight, also.

But today we return! . . . We sing: This country of ours, despite all its better souls have done and dreamed, is yet a shameful land.

It *lynches*.

And lynching is barbarism of a degree of contemptible nastiness unparalleled in human history. Yet for fifty years we have lynched two Negroes a week, and we have kept this up right through the war.

It *disfranchises* its own citizens.

Disfranchisement is the deliberate theft and robbery of the only protection of poor against rich and black against white. The land that disfranchises its citizens and calls itself a democracy lies and knows it lies.

It encourages *ignorance*.

It has never really tried to educate the Negro. A dominate minority does not want Negroes educated. It wants servants. . . .

It *insults* us.

It has organized a nationwide and latterly a worldwide propaganda of deliberate and continuous insult and defamation of black blood wherever found. . . .

This is the country to which we Soldiers of Democracy return. This is the fatherland for which we fought! But it is *our* fatherland. It was right for us to fight. . . .

We *return fighting*.

Make way for Democracy!

QUESTIONS

1. *Why does Debs relate the history of war-time dissent in America?*

2. *What connections does Du Bois draw between blacks fighting abroad in the war and returning to fight at home?*

3. *In what ways does each author point up the contradiction between America's professed values and its actual conduct?*

A 1919 Americanization pageant in Milwaukee, in which immigrants encounter Abraham Lincoln and the Statue of Liberty.

the Fourth of July, 1918, Loyalty Day and asked ethnic groups to participate in patriotic pageants. New York City's celebration included a procession of 75,000 persons with dozens of floats and presentations linking immigrants with the war effort and highlighting their contributions to American society. Leaders of ethnic groups that had suffered discrimination saw the war as an opportunity to gain greater rights. Prominent Jewish leaders promoted enlistment and expressions of loyalty. The Chinese-American press insisted that even those born abroad and barred from citizenship should register for the draft, to "bring honor to the people of our race."

The Anti-German Crusade

German-Americans bore the brunt of forced Americanization. The first wave of German immigrants had arrived before the Civil War. By 1914, German-Americans numbered nearly 9 million, including immigrants and persons of German parentage. They had created thriving ethnic institutions including clubs, sports associations, schools, and theaters. On the eve of the war, many Americans admired German traditions in literature, music, and philosophy, and one-quarter of all the high school students in the country studied the German language. But after American entry into the war, the use of German and expressions of German culture became a target of prowar organizations. In Iowa, Governor William L. Harding issued a proclamation requiring that all oral communication in schools, public places, and over the telephone be conducted in English. Freedom of speech, he declared, did not include "the right to use a language other than the language of the country."

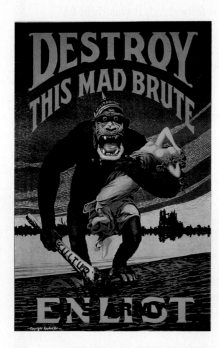

A vivid example of the anti-German propaganda produced by the federal government to encourage prowar sentiment during World War I.

By 1919, the vast majority of the states had enacted laws restricting the teaching of foreign languages. Popular words of German origin were changed: "hamburger" became "liberty sandwich," and "sauerkraut" was renamed "liberty cabbage." Many communities banned the playing of German music. The government jailed Karl Müch, the director of the Boston Symphony and a Swiss citizen, as an enemy alien after he insisted on including the works of German composers like Beethoven in his concerts. The war dealt a crushing blow to German-American culture. By 1920, the number of German-language newspapers had been reduced to 276 (one-third the number twenty years earlier), and only 1 percent of high school pupils still studied German. The Census of 1920 reported a 25 percent drop in the number of Americans admitting to having been born in Germany.

Toward Immigration Restriction

Even as Americanization programs sought to assimilate immigrants into American society, the war strengthened the conviction that certain kinds of undesirable persons ought to be excluded altogether. The new immigrants, one advocate of restriction declared, appreciated the values of democracy and freedom far less than "the Anglo-Saxon," as evidenced by their attraction to "extreme political doctrines" like anarchism and socialism. Stanford University psychologist Lewis Terman introduced the term "IQ" (intelligence quotient) in 1916, claiming that this single number could measure an individual's mental capacity. Intelligence tests administered to recruits by the army seemed to confirm scientifically that blacks and the new immigrants stood far below native white Protestants on the IQ scale, further spurring demands for immigration restriction.

In 1917, over Wilson's veto, Congress required that immigrants be literate in English or another language. The war accelerated other efforts to upgrade the American population. Some were inspired by the idea of improving the human race by discouraging reproduction among less "desirable" persons. Indiana in 1907 had passed a law authorizing doctors to sterilize insane and "feeble-minded" inmates in mental institutions so that they would not pass their "defective" genes on to children. Numerous other states now followed suit. In *Buck v. Bell* (1927), the Supreme Court upheld the constitutionality of these laws. Justice Oliver Wendell Holmes's opinion included the famous statement, "Three generations of imbeciles are enough." By the time the practice ended in the 1960s, some 63,000 persons had been involuntarily sterilized.

A 1919 cartoon, *Close the Gate,* warns that unrestricted immigration allows dangerous radicals to enter the United States.

Groups Apart: Mexicans, Puerto Ricans, and Asian-Americans

No matter how coercive, Americanization programs assumed that European immigrants and especially their children could eventually adjust to the conditions of American life, embrace American ideals, and become productive citizens enjoying the full blessings of American freedom. This assumption did not apply to non-white immigrants or to blacks. Although the melting-pot idea envisioned that newcomers from Europe would leave their ethnic enclaves and join the American mainstream, non-whites confronted ever-present boundaries of exclusion.

The war led to further growth of the Southwest's Mexican population. Wartime demand for labor from the area's mine owners and large farmers led the government to exempt Mexicans temporarily from the literacy test enacted in 1917. Mexicans were legally classified as white, and many Progressive reformers viewed the growing Mexican population as candidates for Americanization. Teachers and religious missionaries sought to instruct them in English, convert them to Protestantism, and in other ways promote their assimilation into the mainstream culture. Yet public officials in the Southwest treated them as a group apart. Segregation,

Mexicans in the Southwest

by law and custom, was common in schools, hospitals, theaters, and other institutions in states with significant Mexican populations. By 1920, nearly all Mexican children in California and the Southwest were educated in their own schools or classrooms. Phoenix, Arizona, established separate public schools for Indians, Mexicans, blacks, and whites.

Puerto Ricans also occupied an ambiguous position within American society. On the eve of American entry into World War I, Congress terminated the status "citizen of Puerto Rico" and conferred American citizenship on residents of the island. The aim was to dampen support for Puerto Rican independence and to strengthen the American hold on a strategic outpost in the Caribbean. The change did not grant islanders the right to vote for president, or representation in Congress. Puerto Rican men, nonetheless, were subject to the draft and fought overseas. José de Diego, the Speaker of the House of the island's legislature, wrote the president in 1917 asking that Puerto Rico be granted the democracy the United States was fighting for in Europe.

Even more restrictive were policies toward Asian-Americans. In 1906, the San Francisco school board ordered all Asian students confined to a single public school. When the Japanese government protested, president Theodore Roosevelt persuaded the city to rescind the order. He then negotiated the Gentlemen's Agreement of 1907 whereby Japan agreed to end migration to the United States except for the wives and children of men already in the country. In 1913, California barred all aliens incapable of becoming naturalized citizens (that is, Asians) from owning or leasing land.

The Gentlemen's Agreement

The Color Line

By far the largest non-white group, African-Americans, were excluded from nearly every Progressive definition of freedom described in Chapter 18. After their disenfranchisement in the South, few could participate in American democracy. Barred from joining most unions and from skilled employment, black workers had little access to "industrial freedom." A majority of adult black women worked outside the home, but for wages that offered no hope of independence. Predominantly domestic and agricultural workers, they remained unaffected by the era's laws regulating the hours and conditions of female labor. Nor could blacks, the majority desperately poor, participate fully in the emerging consumer economy, either as employees in the new department stores (except as janitors and cleaning women) or as purchasers of the consumer goods now flooding the marketplace.

Exclusion of blacks

Progressive intellectuals, social scientists, labor reformers, and suffrage advocates displayed a remarkable indifference to the black condition. Israel Zangwill did not include blacks in the melting-pot idea popularized by his Broadway play. Walter Weyl waited until the last fifteen pages of *The New Democracy* to introduce the "race problem." His comment, quoted in the previous chapter, that the chief obstacles to freedom were economic, not political, revealed little appreciation of how the denial of voting rights underpinned the comprehensive system of inequality to which southern blacks were subjected.

Progressives and race

Most settlement-house reformers accepted segregation as natural and equitable, assuming there should be white settlements for white neighborhoods and black settlements for black. White leaders of the woman suffrage movement said little about black disenfranchisement. In the South, members of upper-class white women's clubs sometimes raised funds for black schools and community centers. But suffrage leaders insisted that the vote was a racial entitlement, a "badge and synonym of freedom," in the words of Rebecca Felton of Georgia, that should not be denied to "free-born white women." During Reconstruction, women had been denied constitutional recognition because it was "the Negro's hour." Now, World War I's "woman's hour" excluded blacks. The amendment that achieved woman suffrage left the states free to limit voting by poll taxes and literacy tests. Living in the South, the vast majority of the country's black women did not enjoy its benefits.

> *Woman suffrage and race*

Roosevelt, Wilson, and Race

The Progressive presidents shared prevailing attitudes concerning blacks. Theodore Roosevelt shocked white opinion by inviting Booker T. Washington to dine with him in the White House and by appointing a number of blacks to federal offices. But in 1906, when a small group of black soldiers shot off their guns in Brownsville, Texas, killing one resident, and none of their fellows would name them, Roosevelt ordered the dishonorable discharge of three black companies—156 men in all, including six winners of the Congressional Medal of Honor. Roosevelt's ingrained belief in Anglo-Saxon racial destiny (he called Indians "savages" and blacks "wholly unfit for the suffrage") did nothing to lessen Progressive intellectuals' enthusiasm for his New Nationalism. Even Jane Addams, one of the few Progressives to take a strong interest in black rights and a founder of the National Association for the Advancement of Colored People (NAACP), went along when the Progressive Party convention of 1912 rejected a civil rights plank in its platform and barred black delegates from the South.

Woodrow Wilson, a native of Virginia, could speak without irony of the South's "genuine representative government" and its exalted "standards of liberty." His administration imposed racial segregation in federal departments in Washington, D.C., and dismissed numerous black federal employees. Wilson allowed D. W. Griffith's film *Birth of a Nation*, which glorified the Ku Klux Klan as the defender of white civilization during Reconstruction, to have its premiere at the White House in 1915. "Have you a 'new freedom' for white Americans and a new slavery for your African-American fellow citizens?" William Monroe Trotter, the militant black editor of the *Boston Guardian* and founder of the all-black National Equal Rights League, asked the president.

Blacks subject to disenfranchisement and segregation were understandably skeptical of the nation's claim to embody freedom and fully appreciated the ways the symbols of liberty could coexist with brutal racial violence. In one of hundreds of lynchings during the Progressive era, a white mob in Springfield, Missouri, in 1906 falsely accused three black men of rape, hanged them from an electric light pole, and burned their bodies in a public orgy of violence. Atop the pole stood a replica of the Statue of Liberty.

A cartoon from the *St. Louis Post-Dispatch,* April 17, 1906, commenting on the lynching of three black men in Springfield, Missouri. The shadow cast by the Statue of Liberty forms a gallows on the ground.

W. E. B. Du Bois, founder of the NAACP and editor of its magazine, *The Crisis*, in his New York office.

W. E. B. Du Bois and the Revival of Black Protest

Black leaders struggled to find a strategy to rekindle the national commitment to equality that had flickered brightly, if briefly, during Reconstruction. No one thought more deeply, or over so long a period, about the black condition and the challenge it posed to American democracy than the scholar and activist W. E. B. Du Bois. Born in Great Barrington, Massachusetts, in 1868, and educated at Fisk and Harvard universities, Du Bois lived to his ninety-fifth year. The unifying theme of his career was Du Bois's effort to reconcile the contradiction between what he called "American freedom for whites and the continuing subjection of Negroes." His book *The Souls of Black Folk* (1903) issued a clarion call for blacks dissatisfied with the accommodationist policies of Booker T. Washington to press for equal rights. Du Bois believed that educated African-Americans like himself—the "talented tenth" of the black community—must use their education and training to challenge inequality.

In some ways, Du Bois was a typical Progressive who believed that investigation, exposure, and education would lead to solutions for social problems. As a professor at Atlanta University, he projected a grandiose plan for decades of scholarly study of black life in order to make the country aware of racism and point the way toward its elimination. But he also understood the necessity of political action.

In 1905, Du Bois gathered a group of black leaders at Niagara Falls (meeting on the Canadian side since no American hotel would provide accommodations) and organized the Niagara movement, which sought to reinvigorate the abolitionist tradition. "We claim for ourselves," Du Bois wrote in the group's manifesto, "every single right that belongs to a freeborn American, political, civil, and social; and until we get these rights we will never cease to protest and assail the ears of America." The Declaration of Principles adopted at Niagara Falls called for restoring to blacks the right to vote, an end to racial segregation, and complete equality in economic and educational opportunity. These would remain the cornerstones of the black struggle for racial justice for decades to come. Four years later, Du Bois joined with a group of mostly white reformers shocked by a lynching in Springfield, Illinois (Lincoln's adult home), to create the National Association for the Advancement of Colored People. The NAACP, as it was known, launched a long struggle for the enforcement of the Fourteenth and Fifteenth Amendments.

The NAACP's legal strategy won a few victories. In *Bailey v. Alabama* (1911), the Supreme Court overturned southern "peonage" laws that made it a crime for sharecroppers to break their labor contracts. Six years later, it ruled unconstitutional a Louisville zoning regulation excluding blacks from living in certain parts of the city (primarily because it interfered with whites' right to sell their property as they saw fit). Overall, however, the Progressive era witnessed virtually no progress toward racial justice. At a time when Americans' rights were being reformulated, blacks, said Moorfield Story, the NAACP's president, enjoyed a "curious citizenship." They shared obligations like military service, but not

The Niagara movement

The NAACP

"the fundamental rights to which all men are entitled unless we repudiate . . . the Declaration of Independence."

Closing Ranks

Among black Americans, the wartime language of freedom inspired hopes for a radical change in the country's racial system. With the notable exception of William Monroe Trotter, most black leaders saw American participation in the war as an opportunity to make real the promise of freedom. To Trotter, much-publicized German atrocities were no worse than American lynchings; rather than making the world safe for democracy, the government should worry about "making the South safe for the Negroes." Yet the black press rallied to the war. Du Bois himself, in widely reprinted editorials, called on African-Americans to enlist in the army to help "make our own America a real land of the free."

Black participation in the Civil War had helped to secure the destruction of slavery and the achievement of citizenship. But during World War I, closing ranks did not bring significant gains. The navy barred blacks entirely, and the segregated army confined most of the 400,000 blacks who served in the war to supply units rather than combat. Wilson feared, as he noted in his diary, that the overseas experience would "go to their heads." And the U.S. Army campaigned strenuously to persuade the French not to treat black soldiers as equals—not to eat or socialize with them, or even shake their hands. Contact with African colonial soldiers fighting alongside the British and French did widen the horizons of black American soldiers. But while colonial troops marched in the victory parade in Paris, the Wilson administration did not allow black Americans to participate.

The Great Migration and the "Promised Land"

Nonetheless, the war unleashed social changes that altered the contours of American race relations. The combination of increased wartime production and a drastic falloff in immigration from Europe once war broke out opened thousands of industrial jobs to black laborers for the first time, inspiring a large-scale migration from South to North. On the eve of World War I, 90 percent of the African-American population still lived in the South. Most northern cities had tiny black populations, and domestic and service work still predominated among both black men and women in the North. But between 1910 and 1920, half a million blacks left the South. The black population of Chicago more than doubled, New York City's rose 66 percent, and smaller industrial cities like Akron, Buffalo, and Trenton showed similar gains.

Many motives sustained the Great Migration—higher wages in northern factories than were available in the South (even if blacks remained confined to menial and unskilled positions), opportunities for educating their children, escape from the threat of lynching, and the prospect of exercising the right to vote. Migrants spoke of a Second Emancipation, of "crossing over Jordan," and of leaving the realm of pharaoh for the Promised Land. One group from Mississippi stopped

> *Black soldiers*

A 1918 poster celebrates black soldiers in World War I as "True Sons of Freedom." At the upper right, Abraham Lincoln looks on, with a somewhat modified quotation from the Gettysburg Address.

TABLE 19.1 The Great Migration			
CITY	BLACK POPULATION, 1910	BLACK POPULATION, 1920	PERCENT INCREASE
New York	91,709	152,467	66.3%
Philadelphia	84,459	134,229	58.9
Chicago	44,103	109,458	148.2
St. Louis	43,960	69,854	58.9
Detroit	5,741	40,838	611.3
Pittsburgh	25,623	37,725	47.2
Cleveland	8,448	34,451	307.8

to sing, "I am bound for the land of Canaan," after their train crossed the Ohio River into the North.

The black migrants, mostly young men and women, carried with them "a new vision of opportunity, of social and economic freedom," as Alain Locke explained in the preface to his influential book, *The New Negro* (1925). Yet the migrants encountered vast disappointments—severely restricted employment opportunities, exclusion from unions, rigid housing segregation, and outbreaks of violence that made it clear that no region of the country was free from racial hostility. More white southerners than blacks moved north during the war, often with similar economic aspirations. But the new black presence, coupled with demands for change inspired by the war, created a racial tinderbox that needed only an incident to trigger an explosion.

Racial Violence, North and South

Violence in East St. Louis and Chicago

Dozens of blacks were killed during a 1917 riot in East St. Louis, Illinois, where employers had recruited black workers in an attempt to weaken unions (most of which excluded blacks from membership). In 1919, more than 250 persons died in riots in the urban North. Most notable was the violence in Chicago, touched off by the drowning by white bathers of a black teenager who accidentally crossed the unofficial dividing line between black and white beaches on Lake Michigan. The riot that followed raged for five days and involved pitched battles between the races throughout the city. By the time the National Guard restored order, 38 persons had been killed and more than 500 injured.

Violence was not confined to the North. In the year after the war ended, seventy-six persons were lynched in the South, including several returning black

Buildings in Tulsa, Oklahoma, burn during the city's riot of June 1921. An estimated 300 people died when white mobs destroyed the city's black neighborhood in the worst outbreak of racial violence in American history.

veterans wearing their uniforms. In Phillips County, Arkansas, attacks on striking black sharecroppers by armed white vigilantes left as many as 200 persons dead and required the intervention of the army to restore order. The worst race riot in American history occurred in Tulsa, Oklahoma, in 1921, when more than 300 blacks were killed and over 10,000 left homeless after a white mob, including police and National Guardsmen, burned an all-black section of the city to the ground. The violence erupted after a group of black veterans tried to prevent the lynching of a youth who had accidentally tripped and fallen on a white female elevator operator, causing rumors of rape to sweep the city.

Tulsa riot

The Rise of Garveyism

World War I kindled a new spirit of militancy. The East St. Louis riot of 1917 inspired a widely publicized Silent Protest Parade on New York's Fifth Avenue in which 10,000 blacks silently carried placards reading, "Mr. President, Why Not Make America Safe for Democracy?" In the new densely populated black ghettos of the North, widespread support emerged for the Universal Negro Improvement Association, a movement for African independence and black self-reliance launched by Marcus Garvey, a recent immigrant from Jamaica. Freedom for Garveyites meant national self-determination. Blacks, they insisted, should enjoy the same internationally recognized identity enjoyed by other peoples in the aftermath of the war. "Everywhere we hear the cry of freedom," Garvey proclaimed in 1921. "We desire a freedom that will lift us to the common standard of all men, . . . freedom that will give us a chance and opportunity to rise to the fullest of our ambition and that we cannot get in countries where other men rule and dominate." Du Bois and other established black leaders viewed Garvey as little more than a demagogue. They applauded when the government deported him after a conviction for mail fraud. But the massive following his movement achieved testified to the sense of betrayal that had been kindled in black communities during and after the war.

Marcus Garvey

The "silent parade" down Fifth Avenue, July 28, 1917, in which 10,000 black marchers protested the East St. Louis race riot.

1919

A Worldwide Upsurge

Global uprisings

The combination of militant hopes for social change and disappointment with the war's outcome was evident far beyond the black community. In the Union of Soviet Socialist Republics (or Soviet Union), as Russia had been renamed after the revolution, Lenin's government had nationalized landholdings, banks, and factories and proclaimed the socialist dream of a workers' government. The Russian Revolution and the democratic aspirations unleashed by World War I sent tremors of hope and fear throughout the world. Like 1848 and, in the future, 1968, 1919 was a year of worldwide social and political upheaval. Inspired by Lenin's call for revolution, communist-led governments came to power in Bavaria (a part of Germany) and Hungary. General strikes demanding the fulfillment of wartime promises of "industrial democracy" took place in Belfast, Glasgow, and Winnipeg. In Spain, anarchist peasants began seizing land. Crowds in India challenged British rule, and nationalist movements in other colonies demanded independence. "We are living and shall live all our lives in a revolutionary world," wrote Walter Lippmann.

The worldwide revolutionary upsurge produced a countervailing mobilization by opponents of radical change. Even as they fought the Germans, the Allies viewed the Soviet government as a dire threat and attempted to overturn it. In the summer of 1918, Allied expeditionary forces—British, French, Japanese, and Americans—landed in Russia to aid Lenin's opponents in the civil war that had engulfed the country. The last of them did not leave until 1920.

The Soviet Union

Wilson's policies toward the Soviet Union revealed the contradictions within the liberal internationalist vision. On the one hand, in keeping with the principles of the Fourteen Points and its goal of a worldwide economic open door, Wilson hoped to foster trade with the new government. On the other, fear of communism as a source of international instability and a threat to private property inspired military intervention in Russia. The Allies did not invite the Soviet Union to the Versailles peace conference, and Wilson refused to extend diplomatic recognition to Lenin's government. The Soviet regime survived, but in the rest of the world the tide of change receded. By the fall, the mass strikes had been suppressed and conservative governments had been installed in central Europe. Anticommunism would remain a pillar of twentieth-century American foreign policy.

Upheaval in America

The flu epidemic

In the United States, 1919 also brought unprecedented turmoil. It seemed all the more disorienting for occurring in the midst of a worldwide flu epidemic that killed between 20 and 40 million persons, including nearly 700,000 Americans. Racial violence, as noted above, was widespread. In June, bombs exploded at the homes of prominent Americans, including the attorney general, A. Mitchell Palmer, who escaped uninjured. Among aggrieved American workers, wartime language linking patriotism with democracy and freedom inspired hopes that an era of social justice and economic empowerment was at hand. In 1917, Wilson had told the AFL, "While we are fighting for freedom, we must see to it among other things that labor is free." Labor took him seriously—more seriously, it seems, than Wilson intended. The government, as one machinist put it, had "proclaimed to the World that the freedom and democracy we are fighting for shall be practiced in the industries of America."

By the war's end, many Americans believed that the country stood on the verge of what Herbert Hoover called "a new industrial order." Sidney Hillman, leader of the garment workers' union, was one of those caught up in the utopian dreams inspired by the war and reinforced by the Russian Revolution. "One can hear the footsteps of the Deliverer," he wrote. "Labor will rule and the World will be free." In 1919, more than 4 million workers engaged in strikes—the greatest wave of labor unrest in American history. There were walkouts, among many others, by textile workers, telephone operators, and Broadway actors. Throughout the country, workers appropriated the imagery and rhetoric of the war, parading in army uniforms with Liberty buttons, denouncing their employers as "kaisers," and demanding "freedom in the workplace." They were met by an unprecedented mobilization of employers, government, and private patriotic organizations.

Wave of strikes

The strike wave began in January 1919 in Seattle, where a walkout of shipyard workers mushroomed into a general strike that for once united AFL unions and the IWW. For five days, a committee of labor leaders oversaw city services, until federal troops arrived to end the strike. In September, Boston policemen struck for higher wages and shorter working hours. Declaring "there is no right to strike against the public safety," Massachusetts governor Calvin Coolidge called out the National Guard to patrol the city and fired the entire police force. In the nation's coalfields, a company manager observed, wartime propaganda had raised unrealistic expectations among workers, who took the promise of "an actual emancipation" too "literally." When the war ended, miners demanded an end to company absolutism. Their strike was ended by a court injunction obtained by Attorney General Palmer.

The Great Steel Strike

The wartime rhetoric of economic democracy and freedom helped to inspire the era's greatest labor uprising, the 1919 steel strike. Centered in Chicago, it united some 365,000 mostly immigrant workers in demands for union recognition, higher wages, and an eight-hour workday. Before 1917, the steel mills were little autocracies where managers arbitrarily established wages and working conditions and suppressed all efforts at union organizing. During the war, workers flooded into the Amalgamated Association, the union that had been nearly destroyed by its defeat at Homestead a generation earlier. By the end of 1918, they had won an eight-hour day. Employers' anti-union activities resumed following the armistice that ended the fighting. "For why this war?" asked one Polish immigrant steelworker at a union meeting. "For why we buy Liberty bonds? For the mills? No, for freedom and America—for everybody. No more [work like a] horse and wagon. For eight-hour day."

In response to the strike, steel magnates launched a concerted counterattack. Employers appealed to anti-immigrant sentiment among native-born workers, many of whom returned to work, and conducted a propaganda campaign that associated the strikers with the IWW, communism, and disloyalty. "Americanism vs. Alienism" was the issue of the strike, declared the *New York Tribune*. With middle-class opinion having turned against the labor movement and the police in Pittsburgh assaulting workers on the streets, the strike collapsed in early 1920.

An advertisement placed by a steel company in a Pittsburgh newspaper announces, in several languages, that the steel strike of 1919 "has failed." The use of the figure of Uncle Sam illustrates how the companies clothed their anti-union stance in the language of patriotism.

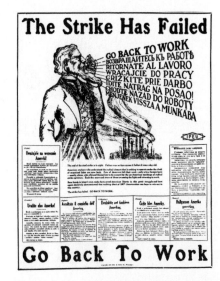

The Red Scare

Local police with literature seized from a Communist Party office in Cambridge, Massachusetts, November 1919.

Many Progressives hoped to see the wartime apparatus of economic planning continue after 1918. The Wilson administration, however, quickly dismantled the agencies that had established controls over industrial production and the labor market, although during the 1930s they would serve as models for some policies of Franklin D. Roosevelt's New Deal. Wartime repression of dissent, however, continued. It reached its peak with the Red Scare of 1919–1920, a short-lived but intense period of political intolerance inspired by the postwar strike wave and the social tensions and fears generated by the Russian Revolution.

Convinced that episodes like the steel strike were part of a worldwide communist conspiracy, Attorney General A. Mitchell Palmer in November 1919 and January 1920 dispatched federal agents to raid the offices of radical and labor organizations throughout the country. They carried search warrants so broad that they reminded those with a sense of history of the writs of assistance against which James Otis had eloquently protested as being destructive of liberty in 1761. The Palmer Raids were overseen by the twenty-four-year-old director of the Radical Division of the Justice Department, J. Edgar Hoover. More than 5,000 persons were arrested, most of them without warrants, and held for months without charge. The government deported hundreds of immigrant radicals, including Emma Goldman, the prominent radical speaker mentioned in the previous chapter. Hoover also began compiling files on thousands of Americans suspected of holding radical political ideas, a practice he would later continue as head of the Federal Bureau of Investigation.

The abuse of civil liberties in early 1920 was so severe that Palmer came under heavy criticism from Congress and much of the press. Secretary of Labor Louis Post began releasing imprisoned immigrants, and the Red Scare collapsed. Even the explosion of a bomb outside the New York Stock Exchange in September 1920, which killed forty persons, failed to rekindle it. (The perpetrators of this terrorist explosion, the worst on American soil until the Oklahoma City bombing of 1995, were never identified.) The reaction to the Palmer Raids planted the seeds for a new appreciation of the importance of civil liberties that would begin to flourish during the 1920s. But in their immediate impact, the events of 1919 and 1920 dealt a devastating setback to radical and labor organizations of all kinds and kindled an intense identification of patriotic Americanism with support for the political and economic status quo. The IWW had been effectively destroyed, and many moderate unions lay in disarray. The Socialist Party crumbled under the weight of governmental repression (the New York legislature expelled five Socialist members, and Congress denied Victor Berger the seat to which he had been elected from Wisconsin) and internal differences over the Russian Revolution.

Effects of Red Scare

Wilson at Versailles

The beating back of demands for fundamental social change was a severe rebuke to the hopes with which so many Progressives had enlisted in the war effort. Wilson's inability to achieve a just peace based on the Fourteen Points compounded the sense of failure. Late in 1918, the president traveled to France to attend the Versailles peace conference. Greeted by ecstatic Paris crowds, he declared that American soldiers had come to Europe "as crusaders, not merely to win a war, but to win a cause . . . to lead the world on the way of liberty." But he proved a less adept negotiator than his British and French counterparts, David Lloyd George and Georges Clemenceau.

While the Fourteen Points had called for "open covenants openly arrived at," the negotiations were conducted in secret. The Versailles Treaty did accomplish some of Wilson's goals. It established the League of Nations, the body central to his vision of a new international order. It applied the principle of self-determination to eastern Europe and redrew the map of that region. From the ruins of the Austro-Hungarian empire and parts of Germany and czarist Russia, new European nations emerged from the war—Finland, Poland, Czechoslovakia, Austria, Hungary, Latvia, Lithuania, Estonia, and Yugoslavia. Some enjoyed ethno-linguistic unity, while others comprised unstable combinations of diverse nationalities.

Part of the crowd that greeted President Woodrow Wilson in November 1918 when he traveled to Paris to take part in the peace conference. An electric sign proclaims "Long Live Wilson."

Despite Wilson's pledge of a peace without territorial acquisitions or vengeance, the Versailles Treaty was a harsh document that all but guaranteed future conflict in Europe. Clemenceau won for France the right to occupy the Saar Basin and Rhineland—iron- and coal-rich parts of Germany. The treaty placed strict limits on the size of Germany's future army and navy. Lloyd George persuaded Wilson to agree to a clause declaring Germany morally responsible for the war and setting astronomical reparations payments (they were variously estimated at between $33 billion and $56 billion), which crippled the German economy.

The Wilsonian Moment

To many people around the world, the Great War seemed like a civil war among the nations of Europe. The carnage destroyed European claims that theirs was a higher civilization, which gave them the right to rule over more barbaric peoples. In this sense, it helped to heighten the international prestige of the United States, a latecomer to the war. Like the ideals of the American Revolution, the Wilsonian rhetoric of self-determination reverberated across the globe, especially among oppressed minorities (including blacks in the United States) and colonial peoples seeking independence. In fact, these groups took Wilson's rhetoric more seriously than he did. Despite his belief in self-determination, he had supported the American annexation of the Philippines, believing that colonial peoples required a long period of tutelage before they were ready for independence.

Spread of Wilsonian ideals

Nonetheless, Wilsonian ideals quickly spread around the globe—not simply the idea that government must rest on the consent of the governed, but also Wilson's stress on the "equality of nations," large and small, and that international disputes should be settled by peaceful means rather than armed conflict. These stood

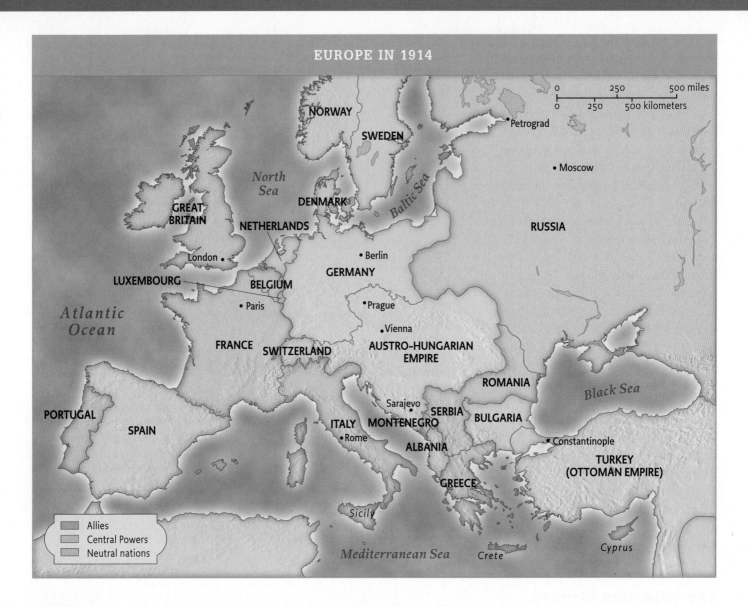

EUROPE IN 1914

World War I and the Versailles Treaty redrew the map of Europe and the Middle East. The Austro-Hungarian and Ottoman empires ceased to exist, and Germany and Russia were reduced in size.
A group of new states emerged in eastern Europe, embodying the principle of self-determination, one of Woodrow Wilson's Fourteen Points.

Self-determination

in sharp contrast to the imperial ideas and practices of Europe. In Eastern Europe, whose people sought to carve new, independent nations from the ruins of the Austro-Hungarian and Ottoman empires, many considered Wilson a "popular saint." The leading Arabic newspaper *Al-Ahram*, published in Egypt, then under British rule, gave extensive coverage to Wilson's speech asking Congress to declare war in the name of democracy, and to the Fourteen Points, and translated the Declaration of Independence into Arabic for its readers. In Beijing, students demanding that China free itself of foreign domination gathered at the American embassy shouting, "Long live Wilson." Japan proposed to include in the charter of the new League of Nations a clause recognizing the equality of all people, regardless of race. Hundreds of letters, petitions, and declarations addressed to President Wilson made their way to the Paris headquarters of the American delegation to the peace conference. Few reached the president, as his private secretary, Gilbert Close, carefully screened his mail.

Outside of Europe, however, the idea of "self-determination" was stillborn. When the peace conference opened, Secretary of State Robert Lansing warned that

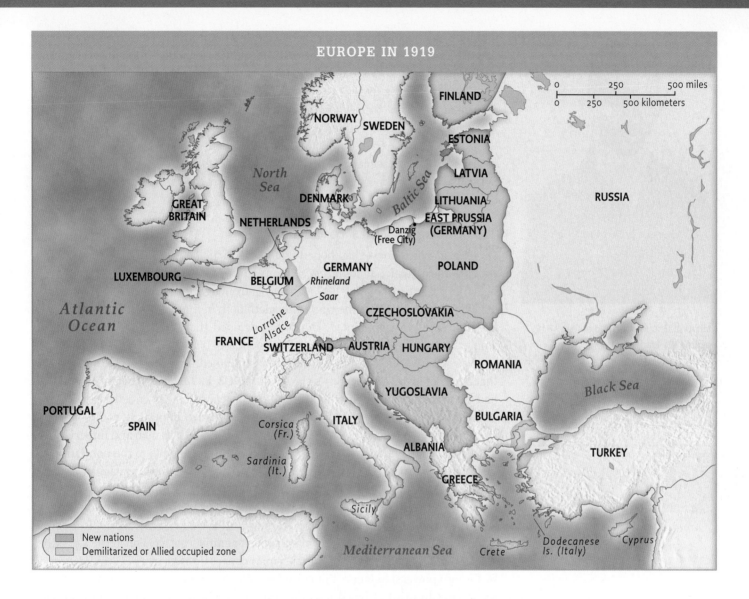

EUROPE IN 1919

0   250   500 miles
0   250   500 kilometers

FINLAND
NORWAY   SWEDEN
ESTONIA
LATVIA
North
Sea   DENMARK   Baltic Sea   LITHUANIA   RUSSIA
GREAT   Danzig   EAST PRUSSIA
BRITAIN   (Free City)   (GERMANY)
NETHERLANDS
GERMANY   POLAND
LUXEMBOURG   Rhineland
BELGIUM   Saar
Atlantic   CZECHOSLOVAKIA
Ocean   Lorraine
Alsace
FRANCE   AUSTRIA   HUNGARY
SWITZERLAND
ROMANIA
YUGOSLAVIA   Black Sea
PORTUGAL   ITALY
SPAIN   Corsica   BULGARIA
(Fr.)
ALBANIA   TURKEY
Sardinia
(It.)   GREECE
Sicily   Dodecanese   Cyprus
New nations   Mediterranean Sea   Crete   Is. (Italy)
Demilitarized or Allied occupied zone

the phrase was "loaded with dynamite" and would "raise hopes which can never be realized." Wilson's language, he feared, had put "dangerous" ideas "into the minds of certain races" and would inspire "impossible demands, and cause trouble in many lands." As Lansing anticipated, advocates of colonial independence descended on Paris to lobby the peace negotiators. Arabs demanded that a unified independent state be carved from the old Ottoman empire in the Middle East. Nguyen That Thanh, a young Vietnamese patriot working in Paris, pressed his people's claim for greater rights within the French empire. Citing the Declaration of Independence, he appealed unsuccessfully to Wilson to help bring an end to French rule in Vietnam. W. E. B. Du Bois organized a Pan-African Congress in Paris that put forward the idea of a self-governing nation to be carved out of Germany's African colonies. Koreans, Indians, Irish, and others also pressed claims for self-determination.

The British and French, however, had no intention of applying this principle to their own empires. They rebuffed the pleas of colonial peoples for self-rule. During the war, the British had encouraged Arab nationalism as a weapon against the

Imperial interests

Mahatma Ghandi, pictured here in 1919, became the leader of the nonviolent movement for independence for India. He was among those disappointed by the failure of the Versailles peace conference to apply the principle of self-determination to the colonial world.

Nationalism in the colonial world

Ottoman empire and had also pledged to create a homeland in Palestine for the persecuted Jews of Europe. In fact, the victors of World War I divided Ottoman territory into a series of new territories, including Syria, Lebanon, Iraq, and Palestine, controlled by the victorious Allies under League of Nations "mandates." South Africa, Australia, and Japan acquired former German colonies in Africa and Asia. Nor did Ireland achieve its independence at Versailles. Only at the end of 1921 did Britain finally agree to the creation of the Irish Free State, while continuing to rule the northeastern corner of the island. As for the Japanese proposal to establish the principle of racial equality, Wilson, with the support of Great Britain and Australia, engineered its defeat.

The Seeds of Wars to Come

Du Bois, as noted above, had hoped that black participation in the war effort would promote racial justice at home and self-government for colonies abroad. "We return," he wrote in *The Crisis* in May 1919, "we return from fighting, we return fighting. Make way for Democracy!" But the war's aftermath both in the United States and overseas left him bitterly disappointed. Du Bois concluded that Wilson had "never at any single moment meant to include in his democracy" black Americans or the colonial peoples of the world. "Most men today," he complained, "cannot conceive of a freedom that does not involve somebody's slavery." In 1903, in *The Souls of Black Folk*, Du Bois had made the memorable prediction that "the problem of the twentieth century is the problem of the color-line." He now forecast a "fight for freedom" that would pit "black and brown and yellow men" throughout the world against racism and imperialism.

Disappointment at the failure to apply the Fourteen Points to the non-European world created a pervasive cynicism about Western use of the language of freedom and democracy. Wilson's apparent willingness to accede to the demands of the imperial powers helped to spark a series of popular protest movements across the Middle East and Asia, and the rise of a new anti-Western nationalism. It inspired the May 4 movement in China, a mass protest against the decision at the Versailles peace conference to award certain German concessions (parts of China governed by foreign powers) to Japan. Some leaders, like Nguyen That Thanh, who took the name Ho Chi Minh, turned to communism, in whose name he would lead Vietnam's long and bloody struggle for independence. The Soviet leader Lenin, in fact, had spoken of "the right of nations to self-determination" before Wilson, and with the collapse of the Wilsonian moment, Lenin's reputation in the colonial world began to eclipse that of the American president. But whether communist or not, these movements announced the emergence of anticolonial nationalism as a major force in world affairs, which it would remain for the rest of the twentieth century.

"Your liberalness," one Egyptian leader remarked, speaking of Britain and America, "is only for yourselves." Yet ironically, when colonial peoples demanded to be recognized as independent members of the international community, they would invoke both the heritage of the American Revolution—the first colonial struggle that produced an independent nation—and the Wilsonian language whereby the self-governing nation-state is the most legitimate political institution, and all nations deserve equal respect.

As Du Bois recognized, World War I sowed the seeds not of a lasting peace but of wars to come. German resentment over the peace terms would help to fuel the rise of Adolf Hitler and the coming of World War II. In the breakup of Czechoslovakia and Yugoslavia, violence over the status of Northern Ireland, and the seemingly unending conflict in the Middle East between Arabs and Israelis, the world was still haunted by the ghost of Versailles.

The Treaty Debate

One final disappointment awaited Wilson on his return from Europe. He viewed the new League of Nations as the war's finest legacy. But many Americans feared that membership in the League would commit the United States to an open-ended involvement in the affairs of other countries. Wilson asserted that the United States could not save the world without being continually involved with it. His opponents, led by Senator Henry Cabot Lodge of Massachusetts, argued that the League threatened to deprive the country of its freedom of action.

A considerable majority of senators would have accepted the treaty with "reservations" ensuring that the obligation to assist League members against attack did not supersede the power of Congress to declare war. As governor of New Jersey and as president, Wilson had proved himself to be a skilled politician capable of compromising with opponents. In this case, however, convinced that the treaty reflected "the hand of God," Wilson refused to negotiate with congressional leaders. In October 1919, in the midst of the League debate, Wilson suffered a serious stroke. Although the extent of his illness was kept secret, he remained incapacitated for the rest of his term. In effect, his wife, Edith, headed the government for the next seventeen months. In November 1919 and again in March 1920, the Senate rejected the Versailles Treaty.

American involvement in World War I lasted barely nineteen months, but it cast a long shadow over the following decade—and, indeed, the rest of the century. In its immediate aftermath, the country retreated from international involvements. But in the long run, Wilson's combination of idealism and power politics had an enduring impact. His appeals to democracy, open markets, and a special American mission to instruct the world in freedom, coupled with a willingness to intervene abroad militarily to promote American interests and values, would create the model for twentieth-century American international relations.

On its own terms, the war to make the world safe for democracy failed. Even great powers cannot always bend the world to their purposes. The war brought neither stability nor democracy to most of the world, and it undermined freedom in the United States. It also led to the eclipse of Progressivism. Republican candidate Warren G. Harding, who had no connection with the party's Progressive wing, swept to victory in the presidential election of 1920. Harding's campaign centered on a "return to normalcy" and a repudiation of what he called "Wilsonism." He received 60 percent of the popular vote. Begun with idealistic goals and grand hopes for social change, American involvement in the Great War laid the foundation for one of the most conservative decades in the nation's history.

Interrupting the Ceremony, a 1918 cartoon from the *Chicago Tribune,* depicts Senate opponents of the Versailles Treaty arriving just in time to prevent the United States from becoming permanently ensnared in "foreign entanglements" through the League of Nations.

The enduring impact of Wilsonian policy

"Return to normalcy"

SUGGESTED READING

BOOKS

- Bederman, Gail. *Manliness and Civilization: A Cultural History of Race and Gender in the United States, 1880–1917* (1995). Explores how ideas concerning civilization and gender affected American foreign policy.

- Capozzola, Christopher. *Uncle Sam Wants You: World War I and the Making of the Modern American Citizen* (2008). A careful study of public and private efforts to enforce patriotic ideas and actions during World War I.

- Dawley, Alan. *Changing the World: American Progressives in War and Revolution* (2003). Presents the war as a fulfillment and betrayal of the Progressive impulse.

- Gilmore, Glenda E. *Gender and Jim Crow: Women and the Politics of White Supremacy in North Carolina, 1896–1920* (1996). A careful study of how black and white women negotiated the boundaries of segregation in a southern state.

- Green, Elna C. *Southern Strategies: Southern Women and the Woman Suffrage Question* (1997). Describes how southern women campaigned for the vote without challenging the subordinate status of African-Americans.

- Greene, Julie. *The Canal Builders: Making American Empire at the Panama Canal* (2009). Tells the story of the construction of the Panama Canal and the tens of thousands of workers who did the work.

- Grossman, James R. *Land of Hope: Chicago, Black Southerners, and the Great Migration* (1989). An in-depth study of the migration of blacks to one American city.

- Healy, David. *Drive to Hegemony: The United States in the Caribbean, 1898–1917* (1988). Examines American foreign policy in the Caribbean from McKinley to Wilson.

- Jensen, Kimberly. *Mobilizing Minerva: American Women in the First World War* (2008). Examines the participation of women in the war effort and its impact on gender relations.

- Kennedy, David M. *Over Here: The First World War and American Society* (1980). A comprehensive account of how the war affected domestic life in the United States.

- Manela, Erez. *The Wilsonian Moment* (2007). Details how the Wilsonian ideal of self-determination was received around the world, with results Wilson did not anticipate.

- Meier, August. *Negro Thought in America, 1880–1915* (1966). A pioneering study of the ideas of black leaders, including W. E. B. Du Bois.

- Mitchell, David J. *1919: Red Mirage* (1970). A global account of the upheavals of 1919.

- Preston, William, Jr. *Aliens and Dissenters: Federal Suppression of Radicals, 1903–1933* (1963). An influential study of the federal government's efforts to suppress dissenting ideas, especially during and immediately after World War I.

- Renda, Mary A. *Taking Haiti: Military Occupation and the Culture of U.S. Imperialism, 1915–1940* (2001). Examines the causes and consequences of the American occupation of Haiti.

- Stein, Judith. *The World of Marcus Garvey: Race and Class in Modern Society* (1986). Places the Garvey movement in an Atlantic perspective linking Africa, the United States, and the West Indies.

- Sullivan, Patricia. *Lift Every Voice: The NAACP and the Making of the Civil Rights Movement* (2009). A sweeping history of the country's preeminent civil rights organization, from its founding to the 1950s.

- Tuttle, William. *Race Riot: Chicago in the Red Summer of 1919* (1970). A vivid account of the most violent racial upheaval of the era.

WEBSITES

- Alcohol, Temperance, and Prohibition: http://dl.lib.brown.edu/temperance/

- First World War.com: www.firstworldwar.com/index.htm

- Red Scare: http://newman.baruch.cuny.edu/digital/redscare/

- The Bisbee Deportation of 1917: www.library.arizona.edu/exhibits/bisbee/

CHAPTER REVIEW AND ONLINE RESOURCES

REVIEW QUESTIONS

1. Explain the role of the United States in the global economy by 1920.

2. What were the assumptions underlying the Roosevelt Corollary? How did the doctrine affect U.S. relations with European nations and those in the Western hemisphere?

3. What did President Wilson mean by "moral imperialism," and what measures were taken to apply this to Latin America?

4. How did the ratification of both the Eighteenth and Nineteenth Amendments suggest both the restrictive and democratizing nature of Progressivism?

5. Why did Progressives see in the expansion of governmental powers in wartime an opportunity to reform American society?

6. What were the goals and methods of the Committee on Public Information during World War I?

7. What are governmental and private examples of coercive patriotism during the war? What were the effects of those efforts?

8. What were the major causes—both real and imaginary—of the Red Scare?

9. How did World War I and its aftermath provide African-Americans with opportunities?

10. Identify the goals of those pressing for global change in 1919, and of those who opposed them.

KEY TERMS

"liberal internationalism" (p. 716)

Panama Canal Zone (p. 717)

Roosevelt Corollary (p. 718)

Dollar Diplomacy (p. 719)

"moral imperialism" (p. 719)

sinking of the *Lusitania* (p. 722)

Zimmerman Telegram (p. 723)

Fourteen Points (p. 724)

Selective Service Act (p. 726)

War Industries Board (p. 726)

Espionage Act (p. 732)

Sedition Act (p. 732)

National Association for the Advancement of Colored People (p. 742)

Great Migration (p. 743)

Tulsa riot of 1921 (p. 745)

Garveyites (p. 745)

flu epidemic (p. 746)

Red Scare of 1919–1920 (p. 748)

Versailles Treaty (p. 749)

wwnorton.com/studyspace

Visit StudySpace for these resources and more:

- **Author Videos**
- **A chapter outline**
- **A practice quiz**
- **Interactive maps**
- **Multimedia documents**

PART 5

DEPRESSION AND WARS, 1920–1953

For the United States and the world at large, the decades between the end of World War I and the middle of the twentieth century marked one of the most painful eras in modern history. These years witnessed the Great Depression (1929–1939), World War II (1939–1945), and the advent of a Cold War that pitted the United States and the Soviet Union, former wartime allies, against each other in a global contest for power. These epochal events produced the deaths of tens of millions of people and wreaked economic havoc on hundreds of millions of others. By the end of this period, the United States and the world lived with the anxiety caused by the constant threat of nuclear war.

After World War I, the United States withdrew from active involvement in international affairs and enjoyed a decade of economic prosperity. During the 1920s, conservatism dominated the political arena. The labor movement suffered setback after setback, the government turned its back on many of the reforms of the Progressive era, and organized feminism faded from the public sphere. A nineteenth-century understanding of freedom based on liberty of contract in an unregulated marketplace gained a new lease on life during the administrations of Warren G. Harding and Calvin Coolidge.

If political dissent faded during the 1920s, cultural differences seemed stronger than ever. In the name of personal freedom, many Americans embraced a new culture, centered in the nation's cities, based on consumption and enjoyment of new mass forms of leisure and entertainment, including radio and motion pictures. Other Americans, living in rural areas of the South and West where traditional religion still held sway, saw the new urban culture as a threat to an understanding of freedom rooted in long-established moral values. During the 1920s, debates over immigration, Prohibition, the teaching of Darwin's theory of evolution in public schools, and the behavior of young, sexually liberated women in the nation's cities reflected the tension between older and newer cultures, each with its own definition of freedom.

The heady days of the 1920s came to an abrupt end with the stock market crash of 1929, which ushered in the Great Depression, the greatest economic crisis in American history. President Franklin D. Roosevelt presided over a profound political and social transformation in government, society, and the understandings of freedom. During his presidency, the federal government undertook unprecedented initiatives in an attempt to stimulate economic recovery and expand Americans' economic liberties. The government determined what farmers could plant, required employers to deal with unions, insured bank deposits, regulated the stock market, loaned money to home owners, and provided payments to a majority of the elderly and unemployed. It transformed the physical environment through hydroelectric dams, reforestation projects, and rural electrification. The New Deal helped to inspire, and was powerfully influenced by, a popular upsurge that redefined the idea of freedom to include a public guarantee of economic security for ordinary citizens.

Even as the United States struggled with the economic crisis, events abroad drew the country into the largest war in human history. The rise of powerful dictatorships bent on military expansion—Germany in Europe and Japan in Asia—led inexorably to World War II. Most Americans hoped to remain aloof from the crisis. When the Japanese attacked the American naval base at Pearl Harbor, Hawaii, on December 7, 1941, the United States entered the war. World War II expanded even further the size and power of the national government. War production finally ended the Depression and drew millions of Americans from rural areas into the army or to industrial centers in the North and West. The Four Freedoms—Roosevelt's statement of Allied war aims—became the wartime rallying cry. Unlike during World War I, the federal government promoted group equality as central to American freedom—although the internment of more than 100,000 Japanese-Americans revealed the limits of racial tolerance. The war also placed on the national agenda, for the first time since Reconstruction, the contradiction between the nation's rhetoric of freedom and the condition of its black population. It inspired an upsurge of black militancy, expressed in the slogan "double-V"—victory over enemies overseas, and over racial inequality at home.

No retreat into isolationism followed World War II. However, the wartime alliance among the United States, Britain, and the Soviet Union soon shattered, replaced by the worldwide contest known as the Cold War. By the 1950s, through a series of global anticommunist alliances, the United States had taken on a permanent military presence throughout the world. As in previous wars, freedom both helped to mobilize public support for the Cold War and was subtly changed in the process. The defense of freedom—increasingly equated with "free enterprise"—became the rationale for the doctrine of "containment," or global opposition to the spread of communism. The Cold War also inspired an anticommunist crusade within the United States. In the late 1940s and early 1950s, thousands of Americans accused of holding "subversive" beliefs lost their jobs, and an atmosphere of political conformity dominated public life. The battle to defend the "free world" abroad produced severe infringements on freedom at home.

CHAPTER 20

FROM BUSINESS CULTURE TO GREAT DEPRESSION

★

THE TWENTIES, 1920–1932

In May 1920, at the height of the postwar Red Scare, police arrested two Italian immigrants accused of participating in a robbery at a South Braintree, Massachusetts, factory in which a security guard was killed. Nicola Sacco, a shoemaker, and Bartolomeo Vanzetti, an itinerant unskilled laborer, were anarchists who dreamed of a society in which government, churches, and private property had been abolished. They saw violence as an appropriate weapon of class warfare. But very little evidence linked them to this particular crime. One man claimed to have seen Vanzetti at the wheel of the getaway car, but all the other eyewitnesses described the driver quite differently. Disputed tests on one of the six bullets in the dead man's body suggested that it might have been fired from a gun owned by Sacco. Neither fingerprints nor possession of stolen money linked either to the crime. In the atmosphere of anti-radical and anti-immigrant fervor, however, their conviction was a certainty. "I have suffered," Vanzetti wrote from prison, "for things that I am guilty of. I am suffering because I am a radical and indeed I am a radical; I have suffered because I was an Italian, and indeed I am an Italian."

Although their 1921 trial had aroused little public interest outside the Italian-American community, the case of Sacco and Vanzetti attracted international attention during the lengthy appeals that followed. There were mass protests in Europe against their impending execution. In the United States, the movement to save their lives attracted the support of an impressive array of intellectuals, including the novelist John Dos Passos, the poet Edna St. Vincent Millay, and Felix Frankfurter, a professor at Harvard Law School and a future justice of the Supreme Court. In response to the mounting clamor, the governor of Massachusetts appointed a three-member commission to review the case, headed by Abbott Lawrence Lowell, the president of Harvard University (and for many years an official of the Immigration Restriction League). The commission upheld the verdict and death sentences, and on August 23, 1927, Sacco and Vanzetti died in the electric chair. "It is not every prisoner," remarked the journalist Heywood Broun, "who has a president of Harvard throw the switch for him."

The Sacco-Vanzetti case laid bare some of the fault lines beneath the surface of American society during the 1920s. The case, the writer Edmund Wilson commented, "revealed the whole anatomy of American life, with all its classes, professions and points of view and . . . it raised almost every fundamental question of our political and social system." It demonstrated how long the Red Scare extended into the 1920s and how powerfully it undermined basic American freedoms. It reflected the fierce cultural battles that raged in many communities during the decade. To many native-born Americans, the two men symbolized an alien threat to their way of life. To Italian-Americans, including respectable middle-class organizations like the Sons of Italy that raised money for the defense, the outcome symbolized the nativist prejudices and stereotypes that haunted immigrant communities. To Dos Passos, the executions underscored the success of the anti-radical crusade: "They are stronger. They are rich. They hire and fire the politicians, the old judges, . . . the college presidents." Dos Passos's lament was a bitter comment on the triumph of pro-business conservatism during the 1920s.

FOCUS QUESTIONS

Who benefited and who suffered in the new consumer society of the 1920s? *–p. 761*

In what ways did the government promote business interests in the 1920s? *–p. 769*

Why did the protection of civil liberties gain importance in the 1920s? *–p. 775*

What were the major flash points between fundamentalism and pluralism in the 1920s? *–p. 777*

What were the causes of the Great Depression, and how effective were the government's responses by 1932? *–p. 789*

City Activities with Dance Hall. This mural, painted in 1930 by Thomas Hart Benton for the New School for Social Research in New York City, portrays aspects of 1920s urban life. On the left, hands reach for a bottle of liquor, a businessman reads a stock ticker, and patrons enjoy themselves at a dance hall and movie theater. Images on the right include a circus, a woman at a soda fountain, and scenes of family life.

1915   Reemergence of the Ku Klux Klan

1919   *Schenck v. United States*

1920   American Civil Liberties Union established

1921   Trial of Sacco and Vanzetti

1922   Washington Naval Arms Conference

          Cable Act

          Herbert Hoover's *American Individualism*

1923   *Adkins v. Children's Hospital*

          Meyer v. Nebraska

1924   Immigration Act of 1924

          Indian Citizenship Act of 1924

1925   Scopes trial

1927   Charles Lindbergh flies nonstop over the Atlantic

          Sacco and Vanzetti executed

1927–1928   President Coolidge vetoes McNary-Haugen farm bill

1929   Sheppard-Towner Act repealed

          Stock market crashes

1930   Hollywood adopts the Hays code

          Smoot-Hawley Tariff

1932   Reconstruction Finance Corporation established

          Bonus march on Washington

In popular memory, the decade that followed World War I is recalled as the Jazz Age or the Roaring Twenties. With its flappers (young, sexually liberated women), speakeasies (nightclubs that sold liquor in violation of Prohibition), and a soaring stock market fueled by easy credit and a get-rich-quick outlook, it was a time of revolt against moral rules inherited from the nineteenth century. Observers from Europe, where class divisions were starkly visible in work, politics, and social relations, marveled at the uniformity of American life. Factories poured out standardized consumer goods, their sale promoted by national advertising campaigns. Conservatism dominated a political system from which radical alternatives seemed to have been purged. Radio and the movies spread mass culture throughout the nation. Americans seemed to dress alike, think alike, go to the same movies, and admire the same larger-than-life national celebrities.

Many Americans, however, did not welcome the new secular, commercial culture. They resented and feared the ethnic and racial diversity of America's cities and what they considered the lax moral standards of urban life. The 1920s was a decade of profound social tensions—between rural and urban Americans, traditional and "modern" Christianity, participants in the burgeoning consumer culture and those who did not fully share in the new prosperity.

THE BUSINESS OF AMERICA

A Decade of Prosperity

"The chief business of the American people," said Calvin Coolidge, who became president after Warren G. Harding's sudden death from a heart attack in 1923, "is business." Rarely in American history had economic growth seemed more dramatic, cooperation between business and government so close, and business values so widely shared. After a sharp postwar recession that lasted into 1922, the 1920s was a decade of prosperity. Productivity and economic output rose dramatically as new industries—chemicals, aviation, electronics—flourished and older ones like food processing and the manufacture of household appliances adopted Henry Ford's moving assembly line.

The automobile was the backbone of economic growth. The most celebrated American factories now turned out cars, not textiles and steel as in the nineteenth century. Annual automobile production tripled during the 1920s, from 1.5 to 4.8 million. General Motors, which learned the secret of marketing numerous individual models and stylish designs, surpassed Ford with its cheap, standardized Model T (replaced in 1927 by the Model A). By 1929, half of all American families owned a car (a figure not reached in England until 1980). The automobile industry stimulated the expansion of steel, rubber, and oil production, road construction, and other sectors of the economy. It promoted tourism and the growth of suburbs (already, some commuters were driving to work) and helped to reduce rural isolation.

During the 1920s, American multinational corporations extended their sway throughout the world. With Europe still recovering from the Great War, American investment overseas far exceeded that of other countries. The dollar replaced the

A 1927 photograph shows Nicola Sacco and Bartolomeo Vanzetti outside the courthouse in Dedham, Massachusetts, surrounded by security agents and onlookers. They are about to enter the courthouse, where the judge will pronounce their death sentence.

British pound as the most important currency of international trade. American companies produced 85 percent of the world's cars and 40 percent of its manufactured goods. General Electric and International Telephone and Telegraph bought up companies in other countries. International Business Machines (IBM) was the world's leader in office supplies. American oil companies built new refineries overseas. American companies took control of raw materials abroad, from rubber in Liberia to oil in Venezuela.

One of the more unusual examples of the global spread of American corporations was Fordlandia, an effort by the auto manufacturer Henry Ford to create a town in the heart of Brazil's Amazon rain forest. Ford hoped to secure a steady supply of rubber for car tires. But as in the United States, where he had compelled immigrant workers to adopt American dress and diet, he wanted to bring local inhabitants up to what he considered the proper standard of life (this meant, for example, forbidding his workers from using alcohol and tobacco and trying to get them to eat brown rice and whole wheat bread instead of traditional Brazilian foods). Eventually, the climate and local insects destroyed the rubber trees that Ford's engineers, lacking experience in tropical agriculture, had planted much too close together, while the workers rebelled against the long hours of labor and regimentation of the community.

A New Society

During the 1920s, consumer goods of all kinds proliferated, marketed by salesmen and advertisers who promoted them as ways of satisfying Americans' psychological desires and everyday needs. Frequently purchased on credit

Advertisements, like this one for a refrigerator, promised that consumer goods would enable Americans to fulfill their hearts' desires.

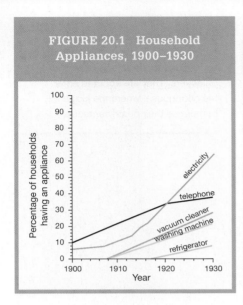

FIGURE 20.1 Household Appliances, 1900–1930

electricity

telephone

vacuum cleaner

washing machine

refrigerator

Percentage of households having an appliance

Year

The spread of the telephone network hastened the nation's integration and opened further job opportunities for women. Lewis Hine photographed this telephone operator in the 1920s.

through new installment buying plans, they rapidly altered daily life. Telephones made communication easier. Vacuum cleaners, washing machines, and refrigerators transformed work in the home and reduced the demand for domestic servants. Boosted by Prohibition and an aggressive advertising campaign that, according to the company's sales director, made it "impossible for the consumer to *escape*" the product, Coca-Cola became a symbol of American life.

Americans spent more and more of their income on leisure activities like vacations, movies, and sporting events. By 1929, weekly movie attendance had reached 80 million, double the figure of 1922. Hollywood films now dominated the world movie market. Movies had been produced early in the century in several American cities, but shortly before World War I filmmakers gravitated to Hollywood, a district of Los Angeles, attracted by the open space, year-round sunshine for outdoor filming, and varied scenery. In 1910, two French companies, Pathé and Gaumont, had been the world's leading film producers. By 1925, American releases outnumbered French by eight to one. In the 1920s, both companies abandoned film production for the more profitable business of distributing American films in Europe.

Radios and phonographs brought mass entertainment into Americans' living rooms. The number of radios in Americans' homes rose from 190,000 in 1923 to just under 5 million in 1929. These developments helped to create and spread a new celebrity culture, in which recording, film, and sports stars moved to the top of the list of American heroes. During the 1920s, more than 100 million records were sold each year. RCA Victor sold so many recordings of the great opera tenor Enrico Caruso that he is sometimes called the first modern celebrity. He was soon joined by the film actor Charlie Chaplin, baseball player Babe Ruth, and boxer Jack Dempsey. Ordinary Americans followed every detail of their lives. Perhaps the decade's greatest celebrity, in terms of intensive press coverage, was the aviator Charles Lindbergh, who in 1927 made the first solo nonstop flight across the Atlantic.

André Siegfried, a Frenchman who had visited the United States four times since the beginning of the century, commented in 1928 that a "new society" had come into being, in which Americans considered their "standard of living" a "sacred acquisition, which they will defend at any price." In this new "mass civilization," widespread acceptance of going into debt to purchase consumer goods had replaced the values of thrift and self-denial, central to nineteenth-century notions of upstanding character. Work, once seen as a source of pride in craft skill or collective empowerment via trade unions, now came to be valued as a path to individual fulfillment through consumption and entertainment.

The Limits of Prosperity

"Big business in America," remarked the journalist Lincoln Steffens, "is producing what the socialists held up as their goal—food, shelter, and clothing for all." But signs of future trouble could be seen beneath the prosperity of the 1920s. The fruits of increased production were very unequally distributed. Real wages for industrial workers (wages adjusted to take account of inflation) rose by one-quarter between 1922 and 1929, but corporate profits rose at more than twice that rate. The process of economic concentration continued unabated. A handful of firms dominated numerous sectors of the economy. In 1929, 1 percent of the nation's banks controlled half of its financial resources. Most of the small auto companies that had existed earlier in the century had fallen by the wayside. General Motors, Ford, and Chrysler now controlled four-fifths of the industry.

At the beginning of 1929, the share of national income of the wealthiest 5 percent of American families exceeded that of the bottom 60 percent. A majority of families had no savings, and an estimated 40 percent of the population remained in poverty, unable to participate in the flourishing consumer economy. Improved productivity meant that goods could be produced with fewer workers. During the 1920s, more Americans worked in the professions, retailing, finance, and education, but the number of manufacturing workers declined by 5 percent, the first such drop in the nation's history. Parts of New England were already experiencing the chronic unemployment caused by deindustrialization. Many of the region's textile companies failed in the face of low-wage competition from southern factories, or shifted production to take advantage of the South's cheap labor. Most advertisers directed their messages at businessmen and the middle class. At the end of the decade, 75 percent of American households still did not own a washing machine, and 60 percent had no radio.

During the 1920s, radio penetrated virtually the entire country. In this photograph, a farmer tunes in to a program while milking his cow.

The Farmers' Plight

Nor did farmers share in the decade's prosperity. The "golden age" of American farming had reached its peak during World War I, when the need to feed war-torn Europe and government efforts to maintain high farm prices had raised farmers' incomes and promoted the purchase of more land on credit. Thanks to mechanization and the increased use of fertilizer and insecticides, agricultural production continued to rise even when government subsidies ended and world demand stagnated. As a result, farm incomes declined steadily and banks foreclosed tens of thousands of farms whose owners were unable to meet mortgage payments.

For the first time in the nation's history, the number of farms and farmers declined during the 1920s. For example, half the farmers in Montana lost their land to foreclosure between 1921 and 1925. Extractive industries, like mining and lumber, also suffered as their products faced a glut on the world market. During the decade, some 3 million persons migrated out of rural areas. Many headed

Farmers, like this family of potato growers in rural Minnesota, did not share in the prosperity of the 1920s.

for southern California, whose rapidly growing economy needed new labor. The population of Los Angeles, the West's leading industrial center, a producer of oil, automobiles, aircraft, and, of course, Hollywood movies, rose from 575,000 to 2.2 million during the decade, largely because of an influx of displaced farmers from the Midwest. Well before the 1930s, rural America was in an economic depression.

The Image of Business

Even as unemployment remained high in Britain throughout the 1920s, and inflation and war reparations payments crippled the German economy, Hollywood films spread images of "the American way of life" across the globe. America, wrote the historian Charles Beard, was "boring its way" into the world's consciousness. In high wages, efficient factories, and the mass production of consumer goods, Americans seemed to have discovered the secret of permanent prosperity. Businessmen like Henry Ford and engineers like Herbert Hoover were cultural heroes. Photographers like Lewis Hine and Margaret Bourke-White and painters like Charles Sheeler celebrated the beauty of machines and factories. *The Man Nobody Knows*, a 1925 best-seller by advertising executive Bruce Barton, portrayed Jesus Christ as "the greatest advertiser of his day, . . . a virile go-getting he-man of business," who "picked twelve men from the bottom ranks and forged a great organization."

After the Ludlow Massacre of 1914, discussed in Chapter 18, John D. Rockefeller himself had hired a public relations firm to repair his tarnished image. Now, persuaded by the success of World War I's Committee on Public Information that it

America's image

River Rouge Plant, by the artist Charles Sheeler, exemplifies the "machine-age aesthetic" of the 1920s. Sheeler found artistic beauty in Henry Ford's giant automobile assembly factory.

was possible, as an advertising magazine put it, to "sway the minds of whole populations," numerous firms established public relations departments. They aimed to justify corporate practices to the public and counteract its long-standing distrust of big business.

They succeeded in changing popular attitudes toward Wall Street. Congressional hearings of 1912–1914 headed by Louisiana congressman Arsène Pujo had laid bare the manipulation of stock prices by a Wall Street "money trust." The Pujo investigation had reinforced the widespread view of the stock market as a place where insiders fleeced small investors—as, indeed, they frequently did. But in the 1920s, as the steadily rising price of stocks made front-page news, the market attracted more investors. Many assumed that stock values would rise forever. By 1928, an estimated 1.5 million Americans owned stock—still a small minority of the country's 28 million families, but far more than in the past.

The Decline of Labor

With the defeat of the labor upsurge of 1919 and the dismantling of the wartime regulatory state, business appropriated the rhetoric of Americanism and "industrial freedom" as weapons against labor unions. Some corporations during the 1920s implemented a new style of management. They

This graph illustrates the rapid rise and dramatic collapse of stock prices and the number of shares traded during the 1920s and early 1930s.

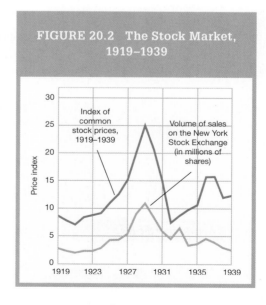

FIGURE 20.2 The Stock Market, 1919–1939

provided their employees with private pensions and medical insurance plans, job security, and greater workplace safety. They established sports programs to occupy their employees' leisure time. They spoke of "welfare capitalism," a more socially conscious kind of business leadership, and trumpeted the fact that they now paid more attention to the "human factor" in employment.

The American Plan

At the same time, however, employers in the 1920s embraced the American Plan, at whose core stood the open shop—a workplace free of both government regulation and unions, except, in some cases, "company unions" created and controlled by management. Collective bargaining, declared one group of employers, represented "an infringement of personal liberty and a menace to the institutions of a free people." Prosperity, they insisted, depended on giving business complete freedom of action. This message was reinforced in a propaganda campaign that linked unionism and socialism as examples of the sinister influence of foreigners on American life. Even the most forward-looking companies continued to employ strikebreakers, private detectives, and the blacklisting of union organizers to prevent or defeat strikes.

The decline of unions

During the 1920s, organized labor lost more than 2 million members, and unions agreed to demand after demand by employers in an effort to stave off complete elimination. In cities like Minneapolis, New Orleans, and Seattle, once centers of thriving labor movements, unions all but disappeared. Uprisings by the most downtrodden workers did occur sporadically throughout the decade. Southern textile mills witnessed desperate strikes by workers who charged employers with "making slaves out of the men and women" who labored there. Facing the combined opposition of business, local politicians, and the courts, as well as the threat of violence, such strikes were doomed to defeat.

The Equal Rights Amendment

The idealistic goals of World War I, wrote the young Protestant minister Reinhold Niebuhr, seemingly had been abandoned: "We are rapidly becoming the most conservative nation on earth." Like the labor movement, feminists struggled to adapt to the new political situation. The achievement of suffrage in 1920 eliminated the bond of unity between various activists, each "struggling for her own conception of freedom," in the words of labor reformer Juliet Stuart Poyntz. Black feminists insisted that the movement must now demand enforcement of the Fifteenth Amendment in the South, but they won little support from white counterparts. A few prominent feminists, including Elizabeth Cady Stanton's daughter Harriot Stanton Blatch, joined the rapidly diminishing Socialist Party, convinced that women should support an independent electoral force that promoted governmental protection of vulnerable workers.

Debate over the ERA

The long-standing division between two competing conceptions of woman's freedom—one based on motherhood, the other on individual autonomy and the right to work—now crystallized in the debate over an Equal Rights Amendment (ERA) to the Constitution promoted by Alice Paul and the National Women's Party. This amendment proposed to eliminate all legal distinctions "on account of sex." In Paul's opinion, the ERA followed logically from winning the right to vote.

Having gained political equality, she insisted, women no longer required special legal protection—they needed equal access to employment, education, and all the other opportunities of citizens. To supporters of mothers' pensions and laws limiting women's hours of labor, which the ERA would sweep away, the proposal represented a giant step backward. Apart from the National Women's Party, every major female organization, from the League of Women Voters to the Women's Trade Union League, opposed the ERA.

In the end, none of these groups achieved success in the 1920s. The ERA campaign failed, as did a proposed constitutional amendment giving Congress the power to prohibit child labor, which farm groups and business organizations opposed. In 1929, Congress repealed the Sheppard-Towner Act of 1921, a major achievement of the maternalist reformers that had provided federal assistance to programs for infant and child health.

Women's Freedom

If political feminism faded, the prewar feminist demand for personal freedom survived in the vast consumer marketplace and in the actual behavior of the decade's much-publicized liberated young women. Female liberation resurfaced as a lifestyle, the stuff of advertising and mass entertainment, stripped of any connection to political or economic radicalism. No longer one element in a broader program of social reform, sexual freedom now meant individual

Tipsy, a 1930 painting by the Japanese artist Kobayakawa Kiyoshi, illustrates the global appeal of the "new woman" of the 1920s. The subject, a *moga* ("modern girl" in Japanese), sits alone in a nightclub wearing Western clothing, makeup, and hairstyle, accompanied by a cigarette and a martini. The title of the work suggests that Kiyoshi does not entirely approve of her behavior, but he presents her as self-confident and alluring. Japanese police took a dim view of "modern" women, arresting those who applied makeup in public.

Many American authorities were no more welcoming to "new women." The superintendent of public buildings and grounds in Washington, D.C., decreed that women's bathing suits must fall no higher than six inches above the knee. Here, in 1922, he enforces his edict.

(*Left*) Advertisers marketed cigarettes to women as symbols of female independence. This 1929 ad for Lucky Strike promotes smoking cigarettes and bathing in risqué attire as breaking women's chains of servitude. (*Right*) An ad for Procter & Gamble laundry detergent urges modern women to modernize the methods of their employees. The text relates how a white woman in the Southwest persuaded Felipa, her Mexican-American domestic worker, to abandon her "primitive washing methods." Felipa, according to the ad, agrees that the laundry is now "whiter, cleaner, and fresher."

Marriage and the new freedom

autonomy or personal rebellion. With her bobbed hair, short skirts, public smoking and drinking, and unapologetic use of birth-control methods such as the diaphragm, the young, single "flapper" epitomized the change in standards of sexual behavior, at least in large cities. She frequented dance halls and music clubs where white people now performed "wild" dances like the Charleston that had long been popular in black communities. She attended sexually charged Hollywood films featuring stars like Clara Bow, the provocative "'It' Girl," and Rudolph Valentino, the original on-screen "Latin Lover." When Valentino died of a sudden illness in 1926, crowds of grieving women tried to storm the funeral home.

What had been scandalous a generation earlier—women's self-conscious pursuit of personal pleasure—became a device to market goods from automobiles to cigarettes. In 1904, a woman had been arrested for smoking in public in New York City. Two decades later, Edward Bernays, the "father" of modern public relations, masterminded a campaign to persuade women to smoke, dubbing cigarettes women's "torches of freedom." The new freedom, however, was available only during one phase of a woman's life. Once she married, what Jane Addams had called the "family claim" still ruled. And marriage, according to one advertisement, remained "the one pursuit that stands foremost in the mind of every girl and woman." Having found a husband, women were expected to seek freedom within the confines of the home, finding "liberation," according to the advertisements, in the use of new labor-saving appliances.

BUSINESS AND GOVERNMENT

The Retreat from Progressivism

In 1924, a social scientist remarked that the United States had just passed through "one of the most critical ten-year periods" in its history. Among the changes was the disintegration of Progressivism as a political movement and body of thought. The government's success in whipping up mass hysteria during the war seemed to undermine the very foundation of democratic thought—the idea of the rational, self-directed citizen. Followers of Sigmund Freud emphasized the unconscious, instinctual motivations of human behavior; scientists pointed to wartime IQ tests allegedly demonstrating that many Americans were mentally unfit for self-government. "The great bulk of people are stupid," declared one advertising executive, explaining why advertisements played on the emotions rather than providing actual information.

During the 1920s, Walter Lippmann published two of the most penetrating indictments of democracy ever written, *Public Opinion* and *The Phantom Public*, which repudiated the Progressive hope of applying "intelligence" to social problems in a mass democracy. Instead of acting out of careful consideration of the issues or even individual self-interest, Lippmann claimed, the American voter was ill-informed and prone to fits of enthusiasm. Not only were modern problems beyond the understanding of ordinary men and women (a sentiment that had earlier led Lippmann to favor administration by experts), but the independent citizen was nothing but a myth. Like advertising copywriters and journalists, he continued, the government had perfected the art of creating and manipulating public opinion—a process Lippmann called the "manufacture of consent."

> *Walter Lippmann*

In 1929, the sociologists Robert and Helen Lynd published *Middletown*, a classic study of life in Muncie, Indiana, a typical community in the American heartland. The Lynds found that new leisure activities and a new emphasis on consumption had replaced politics as the focus of public concern. Elections were no longer "lively centers" of public attention as in the nineteenth century, and voter participation had fallen dramatically. National statistics bore out their point; the turnout of eligible voters, over 80 percent in 1896, had dropped to less than 50 percent in 1924. Many factors helped to explain this decline, including the consolidation of one-party politics in the South, the long period of Republican dominance in national elections, and the enfranchisement of women, who for many years voted in lower numbers than men. But the shift from public to private concerns also played a part. "The American citizen's first importance to his country," declared a Muncie newspaper, "is no longer that of a citizen but that of a consumer."

The Republican Era

Government policies reflected the pro-business ethos of the 1920s. Recalling the era's prosperity, one stockbroker later remarked, "God, J. P. Morgan and the Republican Party were going to keep everything going forever." Business lobbyists dominated national conventions of the Republican Party. They called on the federal government to lower taxes on personal incomes and business profits, maintain high tariffs, and support employers' continuing campaign against

The policies of President Calvin Coolidge were music to the ears of big business, according to one 1920s cartoonist.

"This decision affirms your constitutional right to starve." A 1923 cartoon criticizes the Supreme Court decision declaring unconstitutional a Washington, D.C., law establishing a minimum wage for women. Justice George Sutherland, appointed to the Court the previous year by President Warren G. Harding, wrote the majority decision.

Teapot Dome

unions. The administrations of Warren G. Harding and Calvin Coolidge obliged. "Never before, here or anywhere else," declared the *Wall Street Journal*, "has a government been so completely fused with business." The two presidents appointed so many pro-business members of the Federal Reserve Board, the Federal Trade Commission, and other Progressive-era agencies that, complained Nebraska senator George W. Norris, they in effect repealed the regulatory system. The Harding administration did support Secretary of Commerce Herbert Hoover's successful effort to persuade the steel industry to reduce the workday from twelve to eight hours. But it resumed the practice of obtaining court injunctions to suppress strikes, as in a 1922 walkout of 250,000 railroad workers protesting a wage cut.

Under William Howard Taft, appointed chief justice in 1921, the Supreme Court remained strongly conservative. A resurgence of laissez-faire jurisprudence eclipsed the Progressive ideal of a socially active national state. The Court struck down a federal law that barred goods produced by child labor from interstate commerce. It even repudiated *Muller v. Oregon* (see Chapter 18) in a 1923 decision (*Adkins v. Children's Hospital*) overturning a minimum wage law for women in Washington, D.C. Now that women enjoyed the vote, the justices declared, they were entitled to the same workplace freedom as men. "This," lamented Florence Kelley, "is a new Dred Scott decision," which, in the name of liberty of contract, "fills those words with the bitterest and most cruel mockery."

Corruption in Government

Warren G. Harding took office as president in 1921 promising a return to "normalcy" after an era of Progressive reform and world war. Reflecting the prevailing get-rich-quick ethos, his administration quickly became one of the most corrupt in American history. A likeable, somewhat ineffectual individual—he called himself "a man of limited talents from a small town"—Harding seemed to have little regard for either governmental issues or the dignity of the presidency. Prohibition did not cause him to curb his appetite for liquor. He continued a previous illicit affair with a young Ohio woman, Nan Britton. The relationship did not become known until 1927, when Britton published *The President's Daughter*, about their child to whom Harding had left nothing in his will.

Although his cabinet included men of integrity and talent, like Secretary of State Charles Evans Hughes and Secretary of Commerce Herbert Hoover, Harding also surrounded himself with cronies who used their offices for private gain. Attorney General Harry Daugherty accepted payments not to prosecute accused criminals. The head of the Veterans' Bureau, Charles Forbes, received kickbacks from the sale of government supplies. The most notorious scandal involved Secretary of the Interior Albert Fall, who accepted nearly $500,000 from private businessmen to whom he leased government oil reserves at Teapot Dome, Wyoming. Fall became the first cabinet member in history to be convicted of a felony.

The Election of 1924

Harding's successor, Calvin Coolidge, who as governor of Massachusetts had won national fame for using state troops against striking Boston policemen in 1919, was a dour man of few words. But in contrast to his predecessor he seemed to exemplify

A 1924 cartoon commenting on the scandals of the Harding administration. The White House, Capitol, and Washington Monument have been sold to the highest bidder.

Yankee honesty. The scandals subsided, but otherwise Coolidge continued his predecessor's policies. He twice vetoed the McNary-Haugen bill, the top legislative priority of congressmen from farm states. This bill sought to have the government purchase agricultural products for sale overseas in order to raise farm prices. Coolidge denounced it as an unwarranted interference with the free market. In 1924, Coolidge was reelected in a landslide, defeating John W. Davis, a Wall Street lawyer nominated on the 103rd ballot by a badly divided Democratic convention. (This was when the comedian Will Rogers made the quip, often repeated in future years, "I am a member of no organized political party; I am a Democrat.")

> *The election of Coolidge*

One-sixth of the electorate in 1924 voted for Robert La Follette, running as the candidate of a new Progressive Party, which called for greater taxation of wealth, the conservation of natural resources, public ownership of the railroads, farm relief, and the end of child labor. Although such ideas had been proposed many times before World War I, Coolidge described the platform as a blueprint for a "communistic and socialistic" America. Despite endorsements from veteran Progressives like Jane Addams and John Dewey and the American Federation of Labor, La Follette could raise no more than $250,000 for his campaign. He carried only his native Wisconsin. But his candidacy demonstrated the survival of some currents of dissent in a highly conservative decade.

> *Robert La Follette*

Economic Diplomacy

Foreign affairs also reflected the close working relationship between business and government. "Any student of modern diplomacy," declared Huntington Wilson, a State Department official, "knows that in these days of competition, capital, trade,

VOICES OF FREEDOM

From ANDRÉ SIEGFRIED, "THE GULF BETWEEN," *ATLANTIC MONTHLY* (MARCH 1928)

The French writer André Siegfried in 1928 commented on the rise of an industrial economy and consumer culture and the changes they produced in American society.

Never has Europe more eagerly observed, studied, discussed America; and never . . . have the two continents been wider apart in their aspirations and ideals. . . . Europe, after all, is not very different from what it was a generation ago; but there has been born since then a new America. . . .

The conquest of the continent has been completed, and—all recent American historians have noted the significance of the event—the western frontier has disappeared; the pioneer is no longer needed, and, with him, the mystic dream of the West . . . has faded away. Thus came the beginning of the era of organization: the new problem was not to conquer adventurously but to produce methodically. The great man of the new generation was no longer a pioneer like Lincoln . . . but . . . Henry Ford. From this time on, America has been no more an unlimited prairie with pure and

infinite horizons, in which free men may sport like wild horses, but a huge factory of prodigious efficiency. . . .

In the last twenty-five or thirty years America has produced a new civilization. . . . From a *moral point of view*, it is obvious that Americans have come to consider their standard of living as a somewhat sacred acquisition, which they will defend at any price. This means that they would be ready to make many an intellectual or even moral concession in order to maintain that standard.

From a *political point of view*, it seems that the notion of efficiency of production is on the way to taking [precedence over] the very notion of liberty. In the name of efficiency, one can obtain, from the American, all sorts of sacrifices in relation to his personal and even to certain of his political liberties. . . .

Mass production and mass civilization, its natural consequence, are the true characteristics of the new American society. . . . Lincoln, with his Bible and classical tradition, was easier for Europe to understand than Ford, with his total absence of tradition and his proud creation of new methods and new standards, especially conceived for a world entirely different from our own.

From MAJORITY OPINION, JUSTICE JAMES C. MCREYNOLDS, IN *MEYER V. NEBRASKA* (1923)

A landmark in the development of civil liberties, the Supreme Court's decision in *Meyer v. Nebraska* rebuked the coercive Americanization impulse of World War I, overturning a Nebraska law that required all school instruction to take place in English.

The problem for our determination is whether the statute [prohibiting instruction in a language other than English] as construed and applied unreasonably infringes the liberty guaranteed . . . by the Fourteenth Amendment. . . .

The American people have always regarded education and acquisition of knowledge as matters of supreme importance which should be diligently promoted. . . . The calling always has been regarded as useful and honorable, essential, indeed, to the public welfare. Mere knowledge of the German language cannot reasonably be regarded as harmful. Heretofore it has been commonly looked upon as helpful and desirable. [Meyer] taught this language in school as part of his occupation. His right to teach and the right of parents to engage him so to instruct their children, we think, are within the liberty of the Amendment.

It is said the purpose of the legislation was to promote civil development by inhibiting training and education of the immature in foreign tongues and ideals before they could learn English and acquire American ideals. . . . It is also affirmed that the foreign born population is very large, that certain communities commonly use foreign words, follow foreign leaders, move in a foreign atmosphere, and that the children are therefore hindered from becoming citizens of the most useful type and the public safety is impaired.

That the State may do much, go very far, indeed, in order to improve the quality of its citizens, physically, mentally, and morally, is clear; but the individual has certain fundamental rights which must be respected. The protection of the Constitution extends to all, to those who speak other languages as well as to those born with English on the tongue. Perhaps it would be highly advantageous if all had ready understanding of our ordinary speech, but this cannot be coerced by methods which conflict with the Constitution. . . . No emergency has arisen which rendered knowledge by a child of some language other than English so clearly harmful as to justify its inhibition with the consequent infringement of rights long freely enjoyed.

QUESTIONS

1. *Why does Siegfried feel Europeans no longer find America understandable?*

2. *How does the decision in* Meyer v. Nebraska *expand the definition of liberty protected by the Fourteenth Amendment?*

3. *How do the two excerpts reflect the changes American society experienced in the 1910s and 1920s?*

A German cartoon inspired by President Calvin Coolidge's dispatch of American troops to Nicaragua. While Coolidge insisted that the United States acted in the interest of preserving international order, residents of other countries often saw the United States as a grasping imperial power.

Intervention in Nicaragua and its consequences

agriculture, labor and statecraft all go hand in hand if a country is to profit." The 1920s marked a retreat from Wilson's goal of internationalism in favor of unilateral American actions mainly designed to increase exports and investment opportunities overseas. Indeed, what is sometimes called the "isolationism" of the 1920s represented a reaction against the disappointing results of Wilson's military and diplomatic pursuit of freedom and democracy abroad. The United States did play host to the Washington Naval Arms Conference of 1922 that negotiated reductions in the navies of Britain, France, Japan, Italy, and the United States. But the country remained outside the League of Nations. Even as American diplomats continued to press for access to markets overseas, the Fordney-McCumber Tariff of 1922 raised taxes on imported goods to their highest levels in history, a repudiation of Wilson's principle of promoting free trade.

Much foreign policy was conducted through private economic relationships rather than governmental action. The United States emerged from World War I as both the world's foremost center of manufacturing and the major financial power, thanks to British and French debts for American loans that had funded their war efforts. During the 1920s, New York bankers, sometimes acting on their own and sometimes with the cooperation of the Harding and Coolidge administrations, solidified their international position by extending loans to European and Latin American governments. They advanced billions of dollars to Germany to enable the country to meet its World War I reparations payments. American industrial firms, especially in auto, agricultural machinery, and electrical equipment manufacturing, established plants overseas to supply the world market and take advantage of inexpensive labor. American investors gained control over raw materials such as copper in Chile and oil in Venezuela. In 1928, in the so-called Red Line Agreement, British, French, and American oil companies divided oil-producing regions in the Middle East and Latin America among themselves.

As before World War I, the government dispatched soldiers when a change in government in the Caribbean threatened American economic interests. Having been stationed in Nicaragua since 1912, American marines withdrew in 1925. But the troops soon returned in an effort to suppress a nationalist revolt headed by General Augusto César Sandino. Having created a National Guard headed by General Anastasio Somoza, the marines finally departed in 1933. A year later, Somoza assassinated Sandino and seized power. For the next forty-five years, he and his family ruled and plundered Nicaragua. Somoza was overthrown in 1978 by a popular movement calling itself the Sandinistas (see Chapter 26).

THE BIRTH OF CIVIL LIBERTIES

Among the casualties of World War I and the 1920s was Progressivism's faith that an active federal government embodied the national purpose and enhanced the enjoyment of freedom. Wartime and postwar repression, Prohibition, and the pro-business policies of the 1920s all illustrated, in the eyes of many Progressives, how public power could go grievously wrong.

This lesson opened the door to a new appreciation of civil liberties—rights an individual may assert even against democratic majorities—as essential elements of American freedom. Building on prewar struggles for freedom of expression by labor unions, socialists, and birth-control advocates, some reformers now developed a greater appreciation of the necessity of vibrant, unrestricted political debate. In the name of a "new freedom for the individual," the 1920s saw the birth of a coherent concept of civil liberties and the beginnings of significant legal protection for freedom of speech against the government.

Rights of the individual

The "Free Mob"

Wartime repression continued into the 1920s. Under the heading "Sweet Land of Liberty," *The Nation* magazine in 1923 detailed recent examples of the degradation of American freedom—lynchings in Alabama, Arkansas, and Florida; the beating by Columbia University students of an undergraduate who had written a letter defending freedom of speech and the press; the arrest of a union leader in New Jersey and 400 members of the IWW in California; refusal to allow a socialist to speak in Pennsylvania. Throughout the 1920s, artistic works with sexual themes were subjected to rigorous censorship. The Postal Service removed from the mails books it deemed obscene. The Customs Service barred works by the sixteenth-century French satirist Rabelais, the modern novelist James Joyce, and many others from entering the country. A local crusade against indecency made the phrase "Banned in Boston" a term of ridicule among upholders of artistic freedom. Boston's Watch and Ward Committee excluded sixty-five books from the city's bookstores, including works by the novelists Upton Sinclair, Theodore Dreiser, and Ernest Hemingway.

Curbing free speech

Hollywood producers feared that publicity over actress Mary Pickford's divorce, actor Wallace Reid's death from a drug overdose, and a murder trial involving actor Fatty Arbuckle would reinforce the belief that movies promoted immorality. In 1930, the film industry adopted the Hays code, a sporadically enforced set of guidelines that prohibited movies from depicting nudity, long kisses, and adultery, and barred scripts that portrayed clergymen in a negative light or criminals sympathetically. (The code in some ways anticipated recent efforts by television networks, music companies, and video game producers to adopt self-imposed guidelines to fend off governmental regulation.) Filmmakers hoped that self-censorship would prevent censorship by local governments, a not uncommon occurrence since the courts deemed movies a business subject to regulation, not a form of expression. Not until 1951, in a case involving *The Miracle*, a film many Catholics found offensive, would the Supreme Court declare movies an artistic form protected by the First Amendment.

The Hays code for movies

Even as Europeans turned in increasing numbers to American popular culture and consumer goods, some came to view the country as a repressive cultural wasteland. Americans, commented the British novelist D. H. Lawrence, who lived for a time in the United States, prided themselves on being the "land of the free," but "the free mob" had destroyed the right to dissent. "I have never been in any country," he wrote, "where the individual has such an abject fear of his fellow countrymen." Disillusionment with the conservatism of American politics and the

The Lost Generation

materialism of the culture inspired some American artists and writers to emigrate to Paris. The Lost Generation of cultural exiles included novelists and poets like Ernest Hemingway, Gertrude Stein, and F. Scott Fitzgerald. Europe, they felt, valued art and culture, and appreciated unrestrained freedom of expression (and, of course, allowed individuals to drink legally).

A "Clear and Present Danger"

During World War I, the Unitarian minister John Haynes Holmes later recalled, "there suddenly came to the fore in our nation's life the new issue of civil liberties." The arrest of antiwar dissenters under the Espionage and Sedition Acts inspired the formation in 1917 of the Civil Liberties Bureau, which in 1920 became the American Civil Liberties Union (ACLU). For the rest of the century, the ACLU would take part in most of the landmark cases that helped to bring about a "rights revolution." Its efforts helped to give meaning to traditional civil liberties like freedom of speech and invented new ones, like the right to privacy. When it began, however, the ACLU was a small, beleaguered organization. A coalition of pacifists, Progressives shocked by wartime repression, and lawyers outraged at what they considered violations of Americans' legal rights, it saw its own pamphlets defending free speech barred from the mails by postal inspectors.

The American Civil Liberties Union

Prior to World War I, the Supreme Court had done almost nothing to protect the rights of unpopular minorities. Now, it was forced to address the question of the permissible limits on political and economic dissent. In its initial decisions, it dealt the concept of civil liberties a series of devastating blows. In 1919, the Court upheld the constitutionality of the Espionage Act and the conviction of Charles T. Schenck, a socialist who had distributed antidraft leaflets through the mails. Speaking for the Court, Justice Oliver Wendell Holmes declared that the First Amendment did not prevent Congress from prohibiting speech that presented a "clear and present danger" of inspiring illegal actions. Free speech, he observed, "would not protect a man in falsely shouting fire in a theater and causing a panic."

Schenck v. United States

For the next half-century, Holmes's doctrine would remain the basic test in First Amendment cases. Since the Court usually allowed public officials to decide what speech was in fact "dangerous," it hardly provided a stable basis for the defense of free expression in times of crisis. A week after *Schenck v. United States*, the Court unanimously upheld the conviction of Eugene V. Debs for a speech condemning the war. It also affirmed the wartime jailing of the editor of a German-language newspaper whose editorials had questioned the draft's constitutionality.

The Court and Civil Liberties

Also in 1919, the Court upheld the conviction of Jacob Abrams and five other men for distributing pamphlets critical of American intervention in Russia after the Bolshevik revolution. This time, however, Holmes and Louis Brandeis dissented, marking the emergence of a court minority committed to a broader defense of free speech. Six years after *Abrams*, the two again dissented when the majority upheld the conviction of Benjamin Gitlow, a communist whose *Left-wing Manifesto* calling for revolution led to his conviction under a New York law prohibiting "criminal anarchy." "The only meaning of free speech," Holmes now declared, was that advocates of every set of beliefs, even "proletarian dictatorship," should have the right to convert the public to their views in the great "marketplace of ideas" (an apt metaphor for a consumer society). In approving Gitlow's conviction, the Court majority observed that the Fourteenth Amendment obligated the states to refrain from unreasonable restraints on freedom of speech and the press. The comment marked a major step in the long process by which the Bill of Rights was transformed from an ineffective statement of principle into a significant protection of Americans' freedoms.

> The "marketplace of ideas"

The tide of civil-liberties decision making slowly began to turn. By the end of the 1920s, the Supreme Court had voided a Kansas law that made it a crime to advocate unlawful acts to change the political or economic system, and one from Minnesota authorizing censorship of the press. The new regard for free speech went beyond political expression. In 1930, the Court threw out the conviction of Mary Ware Dennett for sending a sex-education pamphlet, *The Sex Side of Life*, through the mails. Three years later, a federal court overturned the Customs Service's ban on James Joyce's novel *Ulysses*, a turning point in the battle against the censorship of works of literature.

Meanwhile, Brandeis was crafting an intellectual defense of civil liberties on grounds somewhat different from Holmes's model of a competitive market in ideas. In 1927, the Court upheld the conviction of the prominent California socialist and women's rights activist Anita Whitney for attending a convention of the Communist Labor Party where speakers advocated violent revolution. Brandeis voted with the majority on technical grounds. But he issued a powerful defense of freedom of speech as essential to active citizenship in a democracy: "Those who won our independence believed . . . that freedom to think as you will and to speak as you think are indispensable to the discovery and spread of political truth. . . . The greatest menace to freedom is an inert people." A month after the decision, the governor of California pardoned Whitney, terming freedom of speech the "indispensable birthright of every free American." The intrepid Mrs. Whitney was soon back in court for violating a California law making it a crime to display a red flag. In 1931, the Supreme Court overturned the law as "repugnant to the guaranty of liberty contained in the Fourteenth Amendment." A judicial defense of civil liberties was slowly being born.

> *A broader defense of free speech*

THE CULTURE WARS

The Fundamentalist Revolt

Although many Americans embraced modern urban culture with its religious and ethnic pluralism, mass entertainment, and liberated sexual rules, others found it alarming. Many evangelical Protestants felt threatened by the decline of traditional values and the increased visibility of Catholicism and Judaism because of immigration. They also resented the growing presence within mainstream Protestant denominations of "modernists" who sought to integrate science and religion and adapt Christianity to the new secular culture. "The day is past," declared Harry Emerson Fosdick, pastor of New York's First Presbyterian Church and a prominent

A 1923 lithograph by George Bellows captures the dynamic style of the most prominent evangelical preacher of the 1920s, Billy Sunday.

Billy Sunday

Federal agents with confiscated liquor in Colorado in 1920, shortly after the advent of Prohibition.

modernist, "when you can ask thoughtful men to hold religion in one compartment of their minds and their modern world view in another."

Convinced that the literal truth of the Bible formed the basis of Christian belief, fundamentalists launched a campaign to rid Protestant denominations of modernism and to combat the new individual freedoms that seemed to contradict traditional morality. Their most flamboyant apostle was Billy Sunday, a talented professional baseball player who became a revivalist preacher. Between 1900 and 1930, Sunday drew huge crowds with a highly theatrical preaching style and a message denouncing sins ranging from Darwinism to alcohol. He was said to have preached to 100 million people during his lifetime—more than any other individual in history.

Much of the press portrayed fundamentalism as a movement of backwoods bigots. In fact, it was a national phenomenon. Even in New York City, the center of the new modern culture, Fosdick was removed from his ministry in 1924 (whereupon John D. Rockefeller Jr. built the interdenominational Riverside Church for him). Fundamentalism remained an important strain of 1920s culture and politics. Prohibition, which fundamentalists strongly supported, succeeded in reducing the consumption of alcohol as well as public drunkenness and drink-related diseases. Not until 1975 would per capita consumption of alcohol reach its pre-Prohibition level of 2.6 gallons per year.

Prohibition, however, remained a deeply divisive issue. The greatest expansion of national authority since Reconstruction, it raised major questions of local rights, individual freedom, and the wisdom of attempting to impose religious and moral values on the entire society through legislation. It divided the Democratic Party into "wet" and "dry" wings, leading to bitter battles at the party's 1924 and 1928 national conventions. Too many Americans deemed Prohibition a violation of individual freedom for the flow of illegal liquor to stop. In urban areas, Prohibition led to large profits for the owners of illegal speakeasies and the "bootleggers" who supplied them. It produced widespread corruption as police and public officials accepted bribes to turn a blind eye to violations of the law. These developments reinforced fundamentalists' identification of urban life and modern notions of freedom with immorality and a decline of Christian liberty.

◀ *Defiance of Prohibition*

The Scopes Trial

In 1925, a trial in Tennessee threw into sharp relief the division between traditional values and modern, secular culture. John Scopes, a teacher in a Tennessee public school, was arrested for violating a state law that prohibited the teaching of Charles Darwin's theory of evolution. His trial became a national sensation. The proceedings were even carried live on national radio.

The Scopes trial reflected the enduring tension between two American definitions of freedom. Fundamentalist Christians, strongest in rural areas of the South and West, clung to the traditional idea of "moral" liberty—voluntary adherence to time-honored religious beliefs. The theory that man had evolved over millions of years from ancestors like apes contradicted the biblical account of creation. Those who upheld the Tennessee law identified evolutionists with feminists, socialists, and religious modernists, all of whom, they claimed, substituted human judgment for the word of God. To Scopes's defenders, including the American Civil Liberties Union, which had persuaded him to violate the law in order to test its constitutionality, freedom meant above all the right to independent thought and individual self-expression. To them, the Tennessee law offered a lesson in the dangers of religious intolerance and the merger of church and state.

The renowned labor lawyer Clarence Darrow defended Scopes. The trial's highlight came when Darrow called William Jennings Bryan to the stand as an "expert witness" on the Bible. Viewing the trial as a "duel to the death" between science and Christianity, he accepted Darrow's challenge. But Bryan revealed an almost complete ignorance of modern science and proved unable to respond effectively to Darrow's sarcastic questioning. Does the serpent really crawl on its belly as punishment for having tempted Eve in the Garden of Evil? When Bryan answered "yes," Darrow inquired how it got around before being cursed—on its tail? Asked whether God had actually created the world in six days, Bryan

The Anti-Evolution League selling its publications outside the Tennessee courthouse where the Scopes trial was taking place.

Because of extreme heat, some sessions of the Scopes trial were held outdoors, in front of the courthouse in Dayton, Tennessee. A photographer snapped this picture of the trial's climactic moment, when Clarence Darrow (standing at the center) questioned William Jennings Bryan (seated) about interpretation of the Bible.

replied that these should be understood as ages, "not six days of twenty-four hours"—thus opening the door to the very nonliteral interpretation of the Bible fundamentalists rejected.

The jury found Scopes guilty, although the Tennessee supreme court later overturned the decision on a technicality. Shortly after the trial ended, Bryan died and the movement for anti-evolution laws disintegrated. Fundamentalists retreated for many years from battles over public education, preferring to build their own schools and colleges where teaching could be done as they saw fit and preachers were trained to spread their interpretation of Christianity. The battle would be rejoined, however, toward the end of the twentieth century, when fundamentalism reemerged as an important force in politics. To this day, the teaching of the theory of evolution in public schools arouses intense debate in parts of the United States.

Fundamentalism

The Second Klan

Few features of urban life seemed more alien to rural and small-town native-born Protestants than their immigrant populations and cultures. The wartime obsession with "100 percent Americanism" continued into the 1920s, a decade of citizenship education programs in public schools, legally sanctioned visits to immigrants' homes to investigate their household arrangements, and vigorous efforts by employers to instill appreciation for "American values." Only "an agile and determined immigrant," commented the *Chicago Tribune*, could "hope to escape Americanization by at least one of the many processes now being prepared for his special benefit." In 1922, Oregon became the only state ever to require all students to attend public schools—a measure aimed, said the state's attorney general, at abolishing parochial education and preventing "bolshevists, syndicalists and communists" from organizing their own schools.

"100 percent Americanism"

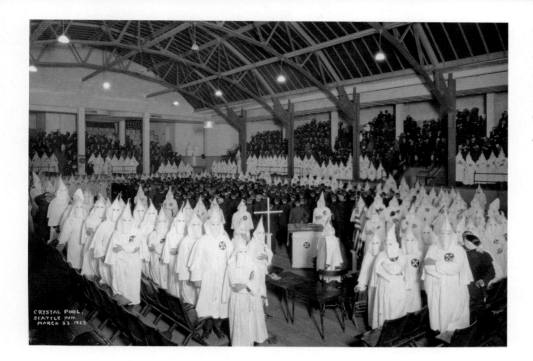

A Ku Klux Klan gathering in Seattle, Washington, in 1923. The unrobed members of the audience are covering their faces to avoid identification. Unlike the Klan of the Reconstruction era, the second Ku Klux Klan was more powerful in the North and West than in the South.

Perhaps the most menacing expression of the idea that enjoyment of American freedom should be limited on religious and ethnic grounds was the resurgence of the Ku Klux Klan in the early 1920s. The Klan had been reborn in Atlanta in 1915 after the lynching of Leo Frank, a Jewish factory manager accused of killing a teenage girl. By the mid-1920s, it claimed more than 3 million members, nearly all white, native-born Protestants, many of whom held respected positions in their communities. Unlike the Klan of Reconstruction, the organization now sank deep roots in parts of the North and West. It became the largest private organization in Indiana, and for a time controlled the state Republican Party. It was partly responsible for the Oregon law banning private schools. In southern California, its large marches and auto parades made the Klan a visible presence. The new Klan attacked a far broader array of targets than during Reconstruction. American civilization, it insisted, was endangered not only by blacks but by immigrants (especially Jews and Catholics) and all the forces (feminism, unions, immorality, even, on occasion, the giant corporations) that endangered "individual liberty."

> *Klan in the North and West*

Closing the Golden Door

The Klan's influence faded after 1925, when its leader in Indiana was convicted of assaulting a young woman. But the Klan's attacks on modern secular culture and political radicalism and its demand that control of the nation be returned to "citizens of the old stock" reflected sentiments widely shared in the 1920s. The decade witnessed a flurry of legislation that offered a new answer to the venerable question "Who is an American?" Some new laws redrew the boundary of citizenship to include groups previously outside it. With women now recognized as part of the political nation, Congress in the Cable Act of 1922 overturned the 1907 law requiring American women who married foreigners to assume the citizenship of the husband—except in the case of those who married Asians, who still forfeited their nationality. Two years later, it declared all Indians born in the United States to be American citizens, although many western states continued to deny the vote to those living on reservations.

Far more sweeping was a fundamental change in immigration policy. Immigration restriction had a long history. The Naturalization Act of 1790 had barred blacks and Asians from naturalization, with the ban lifted for the former in 1870. Beginning in 1875, various classes of immigrants had been excluded, among them prostitutes, the mentally retarded, and those with contagious diseases. Nonetheless, prior to World War I virtually all the white persons who wished to pass through the "golden door" into the United States and become citizens were able to do so. During the 1920s, however, the pressure for wholesale immigration restriction became irresistible. One index of the changing political climate was that large employers dropped their traditional opposition. Fears of immigrant radicalism now outweighed the desire for cheap unskilled labor, especially since mechanization had halted the growth of the industrial labor force and the

Immigration restriction

TABLE 20.1 Selected Annual Immigration Quotas under the 1924 Immigration Act

COUNTRY	QUOTA	IMMIGRANTS IN 1914
Northern and Western Europe:		
Great Britain and Northern Ireland	65,721	48,729 (Great Britain only)
Germany	25,957	35,734
Ireland	17,853	24,688 (includes Northern Ireland)
Scandinavia (Sweden, Norway, Denmark, Finland)	7,241	29,391
Southern and Eastern Europe:		
Poland	6,524	(Not an independent state; included in Germany, Russia, and Austria-Hungary)
Italy	5,802	283,738
Russia	2,784	255,660
Other:		
Africa (total of various colonies and countries)	1,000	1,539
Western Hemisphere	No quota limit	122,695
Asia (China, India, Japan, Korea)	0	11,652

Great Migration of World War I had accustomed industrialists to employing African-Americans.

In 1921, a temporary measure restricted immigration from Europe to 357,000 per year (one-third of the annual average before the war). Three years later, Congress permanently limited European immigration to 150,000 per year, distributed according to a series of national quotas that severely restricted the numbers from southern and eastern Europe. The law aimed to ensure that descendants of the old immigrants forever outnumbered the children of the new. However, to satisfy the demands of large farmers in California who relied heavily on seasonal Mexican labor, the 1924 law established no limits on immigration from the Western Hemisphere.

The 1924 law did bar the entry of all those ineligible for naturalized citizenship—that is, the entire population of Asia, even though Japan had fought on the American side in World War I. The only Asians still able to enter the United States were residents of the Philippines, who were deemed to be "American nationals" (although not citizens) because the islands had been U.S. territory since the Spanish-American War. Largely to bar further Philippine immigration, Congress in 1934 established a timetable for the islands' independence, which was finally achieved in 1946. The 1934 law established an immigration quota of fifty Filipinos a year to the mainland United States, but allowed their continued entry into the Hawaiian Islands to work as plantation laborers.

Although a few Chinese had tried to enter the country in the past in spite of exclusion legislation, the law of 1924 established, in effect, for the first time a new category—the "illegal alien." With it came a new enforcement mechanism, the Border Patrol, charged with policing the land boundaries of the United States and empowered to arrest and deport persons who entered the country in violation of the new nationality quotas or other restrictions. Later associated almost exclusively with Latinos, "illegal aliens" at first referred mainly to southern and eastern Europeans who tried to sneak across the border from Mexico or Canada.

> *The "illegal alien"*

The Only Way to Handle It, a cartoon endorsing immigration restriction.

Race and the Law

The new immigration law reflected the heightened emphasis on "race" as a determinant of public policy. By the early 1920s, political leaders of both North and South agreed upon the relegation of blacks to second-class citizenship. In a speech in Alabama in 1921, President Harding unconsciously echoed W. E. B. Du Bois by affirming that the "problem" of race was a global one, not confined to the South. Unlike Du Bois, he believed the South showed the way to the problem's solution. "It would be helpful," he added, "to have that word 'equality' eliminated from this consideration." Clearly, the Republican Party of the Civil War era was dead.

But "race policy" meant far more than black-white relations. "America must be kept American," declared President Coolidge in signing the 1924 immigration law. His secretary of labor, James J. Davis, commented that immigration policy, once based on the need for labor and the notion of the United States as an asylum of liberty, must now rest on a biological definition of the ideal population. Although enacted by a highly conservative Congress strongly influenced by nativism, the 1924 immigration law also reflected the Progressive desire to

> *A "biologically ideal" population*

The immigration law of 1924 established the Border Patrol to stop those barred from entry from sneaking into the United States from Mexico. At first, the patrol was a modest operation. Here, two officers police the California-Mexico border.

improve the "quality" of democratic citizenship and to employ scientific methods to set public policy. It revealed how these aims were overlaid with pseudo-scientific assumptions about the superiority and inferiority of particular "races."

The seemingly "scientific" calculation of the new quotas—based on the "national origins" of the American population dating back to 1790—involved a highly speculative analysis of past census returns, with the results altered to increase allowable immigration by politically influential groups like Irish-Americans. Non-whites (one-fifth of the population in 1790) were excluded altogether when calculating quotas—otherwise, Africa would have received a far higher quota than the tiny number allotted to it. But then, the entire concept of race as a basis for public policy lacked any rational foundation. The Supreme Court admitted as much in 1923 when it rejected the claim of Bhagat Singh Thind, an Indian-born World War I veteran, who asserted that as a "pure Aryan," he was actually white and could therefore become an American citizen. "White," the Court declared, was not a scientific concept at all, but part of "common speech, to be interpreted with the understanding of the common man" (a forthright statement of what later scholars would call the "social construction" of race).

Pluralism and Liberty

During the 1920s, some Americans challenged the idea that southern and eastern Europeans were unfit to become citizens, or could only do so by abandoning their traditions in favor of Anglo-Saxon ways. Horace Kallen, himself of German-Jewish origin, in 1924 coined the phrase "cultural pluralism" to describe a society that gloried in ethnic diversity rather than attempting to suppress it. Toleration of difference was part of the "American Idea," Kallen wrote. Anthropologists like Franz Boas, Alfred Kroeber, and Ruth Benedict insisted that no scientific basis existed for theories of racial superiority or for the notion that societies and races could be ranked on a fixed scale running from "primitive" to "civilized."

"Cultural pluralism"

These writings, however, had little immediate impact on public policy. In the 1920s, the most potent defense of a pluralist vision of American society came from the new immigrants themselves. Every major city still contained ethnic enclaves with their own civic institutions, theaters, churches, and foreign-language newspapers. Their sense of separate identity had been heightened by the emergence of independent nation-states in eastern Europe after the war. It would be wrong, to be sure, to view ethnic communities as united in opposition to Americanization. In a society increasingly knit together by mass culture and a consumer economy, few could escape the pull of assimilation. The department store, dance hall, and motion picture theater were as much agents of Americanization as the school and workplace. From the perspective of many immigrant women, moreover, assimilation often seemed not so much the loss of an inherited culture as a loosening of

Assimilation

patriarchal bonds and an expansion of freedom. But most immigrants resented the coercive aspects of Americanization programs, so often based on the idea of the superiority of Protestant mainstream culture.

Promoting Tolerance

In the face of immigration restriction, Prohibition, a revived Ku Klux Klan, and widespread anti-Semitism and anti-Catholicism, immigrant groups asserted the validity of cultural diversity and identified toleration of difference—religious, cultural, and individual—as the essence of American freedom. In effect, they reinvented themselves as "ethnic" Americans, claiming an equal share in the nation's life but, in addition, the right to remain in many respects culturally distinct. The Roman Catholic Church urged immigrants to learn English and embrace "American principles," but it continued to maintain separate schools and other institutions. In 1924, the Catholic Holy Name Society brought 10,000 marchers to Washington to challenge the Klan and to affirm Catholics' loyalty to the nation. Throughout the country, organizations like the Anti-Defamation League of B'nai B'rith (founded in 1916 to combat anti-Semitism) and the National Catholic Welfare Council lobbied, in the name of "personal liberty," for laws prohibiting discrimination against immigrants by employers, colleges, and government agencies. The Americanization movement, declared a Polish newspaper in Chicago, had "not the smallest particle of the true American spirit, the spirit of freedom, the brightest virtue of which is the broadest possible tolerance."

Ethnic Americans

The efforts of immigrant communities to resist coerced Americanization and of the Catholic Church to defend its school system broadened the definition of liberty for all Americans. In landmark decisions, the Supreme Court struck down Oregon's law, mentioned earlier, requiring all students to attend public schools and Nebraska's prohibiting teaching in a language other than English—one of the anti-German measures of World War I. "The protection of the Constitution," the

Freedom broadened

The Zion Lutheran Church in Nebraska where Robert Meyer was arrested for teaching a Bible lesson in German, in violation of state law. The case led to the landmark Supreme Court decision of *Meyer v. Nebraska*, an important rebuke to World War I xenophobia.

decision in *Meyer v. Nebraska* (1923) declared, "extends to all, to those who speak other languages as well as to those born with English on the tongue," a startling rebuke to enforced Americanization. The decision expanded the freedom of all immigrant groups. In its aftermath, federal courts overturned various Hawaii laws imposing special taxes and regulations on private Japanese-language schools. In these cases, the Court also interpreted the Fourteenth Amendment's guarantee of equal liberty to include the right to "marry, establish a home and bring up children" and to practice religion as one chose, "without interference from the state." The decisions gave pluralism a constitutional foundation and paved the way for the Court's elaboration, two generations later, of a constitutional right to privacy.

A foundation for pluralism

The Emergence of Harlem

The 1920s also witnessed an upsurge of self-consciousness among black Americans, especially in the North's urban ghettos. With European immigration all but halted, the Great Migration of World War I continued apace. Nearly 1 million blacks left the South during the 1920s, and the black population of New York, Chicago, and other urban centers more than doubled. New York's Harlem gained an international reputation as the "capital" of black America, a mecca for migrants from the South and immigrants from the West Indies, 150,000 of whom entered the United States between 1900 and 1930. Unlike the southern newcomers, most of whom had been agricultural workers, the West Indians included a large number of well-educated professional and white-collar workers.

The capital of black America

A black family arriving in Chicago in 1922, as part of the Great Migration from the rural South.

Their encounter with American racism appalled them. "I had heard of prejudice in America," wrote the poet and novelist Claude McKay, who emigrated from Jamaica in 1912, "but never dreamed of it being so intensely bitter."

The 1920s became famous for "slumming," as groups of whites visited Harlem's dance halls, jazz clubs, and speakeasies in search of exotic adventure. The Harlem of the white imagination was a place of primitive passions, free from the puritanical restraints of mainstream American culture. The real Harlem was a community of widespread poverty, its residents confined to low-wage jobs and, because housing discrimination barred them from other neighborhoods, forced to pay exorbitant rents. Most Harlem businesses were owned by whites; even the famed Cotton Club excluded black customers and employed only light-skinned dancers in its renowned chorus line. Few blacks, North or South, shared in the prosperity of the 1920s.

The Harlem Renaissance

But Harlem also contained a vibrant black cultural community that established links with New York's artistic mainstream. Poets and novelists like Countee Cullen, Langston Hughes, and Claude McKay were befriended and sponsored by white intellectuals and published by white presses. Broadway for the first time presented black actors in serious dramatic roles, as well as shows like *Dixie to Broadway* and *Blackbirds* that featured great entertainers like the singers Florence Mills and Ethel Waters and the tap dancer Bill Robinson. At the same time, the theater flourished in Harlem, freeing black writers and actors from the constraints imposed by white producers.

The term "New Negro," associated in politics with pan-Africanism and the militancy of the Garvey movement, in art meant the rejection of established stereotypes and a search for black values to put in their place. This quest led the writers of what came to be called the Harlem Renaissance to the roots of the black experience—Africa, the rural South's folk traditions, and the life of the urban ghetto. Claude McKay made the major character of his novel *Home to Harlem* (1928) a free spirit who wandered from one scene of exotic life to another in search of a beautiful girl he had known. W. E. B. Du Bois feared that a novel like McKay's, with its graphic sex and violence, actually reinforced white prejudices about black life. Harlem Renaissance writings, however, also contained a strong element of protest. This mood was exemplified by McKay's poem "If We Must Die," a response to the race riots of 1919. The poem affirmed that blacks would no longer allow themselves to be murdered defenselessly by whites:

> If we must die, let it not be like hogs
> Hunted and penned in an inglorious spot,
> While round us bark the mad and hungry dogs,
> Making their mock at our accursed lot. . . .
> Like men we'll face the murderous, cowardly pack,
> Pressed to the wall, dying, but fighting back!

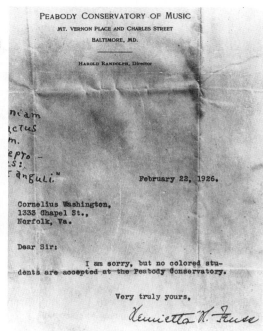

Racism severely limited the opportunities open to black Americans. Here, the internationally renowned Peabody Conservatory of Music informs a black applicant that he cannot pursue his musical education there.

The "New Negro"

Segregated institutions sprang up to serve the expanding black communities created by the Great Migration. Here, black residents of the nation's capital enjoy an outing at Suburban Gardens, a black-owned amusement park.

Winston Churchill would invoke McKay's words to inspire the British public during World War II. The celebrated case of Ossian Sweet, a black physician who moved into a previously all-white Detroit neighborhood in 1925, reflected the new spirit of assertiveness among many African-Americans. When a white mob attacked his home, someone (probably Sweet's brother) fired into the crowd, killing a man. Indicted for murder along with his two brothers, Sweet was defended by Clarence Darrow, fresh from his participation in the Scopes trial. The jury proved unable to agree on a verdict. A second prosecution, of Sweet's brother, ended in acquittal.

THE GREAT DEPRESSION

The Election of 1928

Few men elected as president have seemed destined for a more successful term in office than Herbert Hoover. Born in Iowa in 1874, the son of a blacksmith and his schoolteacher wife, Hoover accumulated a fortune as a mining engineer working for firms in Asia, Africa, and Europe. During and immediately after World War I, he gained international fame by coordinating overseas food relief. The British economist John Maynard Keynes, a severe critic of the 1919 Versailles Treaty, called Hoover "the only man" to emerge from the peace conference "with an enhanced reputation." He "had never known failure," wrote the novelist Sherwood Anderson. Hoover seemed to exemplify what was widely called the "new era" of American capitalism. In 1922, while serving as secretary of commerce, he published *American Individualism*, which condemned government regulation as an interference with the economic opportunities of ordinary Americans, but also insisted that self-interest should be subordinated to public service. Hoover considered himself a Progressive, although he preferred what he called "associational action," in which private agencies directed regulatory and welfare policies, to government intervention in the economy.

Hoover and the "new era"

After "silent Cal" Coolidge in 1927 handed a piece of paper to a group of reporters that stated, "I do not choose to run for president in 1928," Hoover quickly emerged as his successor. Accepting the Republican nomination, Hoover celebrated the decade's prosperity and promised that poverty would "soon be banished from this earth." His Democratic opponent was Alfred E. Smith, the first Catholic to be nominated by a major party. Born into poverty on New York's Lower East Side, Smith had become a fixture in Tammany Hall politics. Although he had no family connection with the new immigrants from southern and eastern Europe (his grandparents had emigrated from Ireland), Smith emerged as their symbolic spokesman. The Triangle fire of 1911 made him an advocate of Progressive social legislation. He served three terms as governor of New York, securing passage of laws limiting the hours of working women and children and establishing widows' pensions. Smith denounced the Red Scare and called for the repeal of Prohibition. His bid for the Democratic nomination in 1924 had been blocked by delegates beholden to nativists and Klansmen, but he secured the nod four years later.

A 1928 campaign poster for the Republican ticket of Herbert Hoover and Charles Curtis.

Given the prevailing prosperity and his own sterling reputation, Hoover's victory was inevitable. Other than on Prohibition, moreover, the Democratic platform did not differ much from the Republican one, leaving little to discuss except the candidates' personalities and religions. Smith's Catholicism became the focus of the race. Many Protestant ministers and religious publications denounced him for his faith. For the first time since Reconstruction, Republicans carried several southern states, reflecting the strength of anti-Catholicism and nativism among religious fundamentalists. "Hoover," wrote one previously Democratic southern newspaper editor, "is sprung from American soil and stock," while Smith represented "the aliens." On the other hand, Smith carried the nation's twelve largest cities and won significant support in economically struggling farm areas. With more than 58 percent of the vote, Hoover was elected by a landslide. But Smith's campaign helped to lay the foundation for the triumphant Democratic coalition of the 1930s, based on urban ethnic voters, farmers, and the South.

President Herbert Hoover (to the right, next to the woman), at the opening day baseball game in Washington, April 17, 1929.

The Coming of the Depression

On October 21, 1929, President Hoover traveled to Michigan to take part in the Golden Anniversary of the Festival of Light, organized by Henry Ford to commemorate the invention of the lightbulb by Thomas Edison fifty years earlier. Hoover's speech was a tribute to progress, and especially to the businessmen and scientists

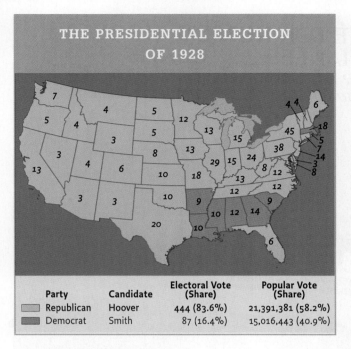

THE PRESIDENTIAL ELECTION OF 1928

Party	Candidate	Electoral Vote (Share)	Popular Vote (Share)
Republican	Hoover	444 (83.6%)	21,391,381 (58.2%)
Democrat	Smith	87 (16.4%)	15,016,443 (40.9%)

Roots of the Depression

Three months before the stock market crash, *The Magazine of Wall Street* was avidly encouraging readers to purchase stocks.

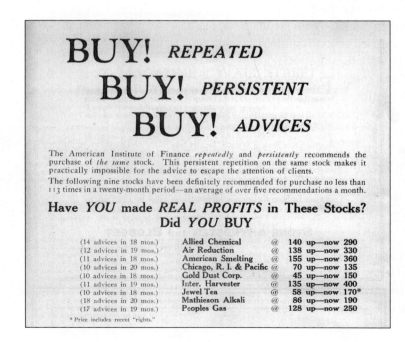

BUY! *REPEATED*
BUY! *PERSISTENT*
BUY! *ADVICES*

The American Institute of Finance *repeatedly* and *persistently* recommends the purchase of *the same* stock. This persistent repetition on the same stock makes it practically impossible for the advice to escape the attention of clients.

The following nine stocks have been definitely recommended for purchase no less than 113 times in a twenty-month period—an average of over five recommendations a month.

Have *YOU* made *REAL PROFITS* in These Stocks? Did *YOU* BUY

(14 advices in 18 mos.)	Allied Chemical	@	140 up—now 290
(12 advices in 19 mos.)	Air Reduction	@	138 up—now 330
(11 advices in 18 mos.)	American Smelting	@	155 up—now 360
(10 advices in 20 mos.)	Chicago, R. I. & Pacific	@	70 up—now 135
(10 advices in 18 mos.)	Gold Dust Corp.	@	45 up—now 150
(11 advices in 19 mos.)	Inter. Harvester	@	135 up—now 400
(10 advices in 18 mos.)	Jewel Tea	@	58 up—now 170*
(18 advices in 20 mos.)	Mathieson Alkali	@	86 up—now 190
(17 advices in 19 mos.)	Peoples Gas	@	128 up—now 250

* Price includes recent "rights."

from whose efforts "we gain constantly in better standards of living, more stability of employment . . . and decreased suffering." Eight days later, on Black Tuesday, the stock market crashed. As panic selling set in, more than $10 billion in market value (equivalent to more than ten times that amount in today's money) vanished in five hours. Soon, the United States and, indeed, the entire world found itself in the grip of the Great Depression, the greatest economic disaster in modern history.

The stock market crash did not, by itself, cause the Depression. Even before 1929, signs of economic trouble had become evident. Southern California and Florida experienced frenzied real-estate speculation and then spectacular busts, with banks failing, land remaining undeveloped, and mortgages foreclosed. The highly unequal distribution of income and the prolonged depression in farm regions reduced American purchasing power. Sales of new autos and household consumer goods stagnated after 1926. European demand for American goods also declined, partly because industry there had recovered from wartime destruction.

A fall in the bloated stock market, driven ever higher during the 1920s by speculators, was inevitable. But it came with such severity that it destroyed many of the investment companies that had been created to buy and sell stock, wiping out thousands of investors, and it greatly reduced business and consumer confidence. Around 26,000 businesses failed in 1930. Those that survived cut back on further investment and began laying off workers. The global financial system, which was based on the gold standard, was ill-equipped to deal with the downturn. Germany defaulted on reparations payments to France and Britain, leading these governments to stop repaying debts to American banks. Throughout the industrial world, banks failed as depositors withdrew money, fearful that they could no longer count on the promise to redeem paper money in gold. Millions of families lost their life savings.

Although stocks recovered somewhat in 1930, they soon resumed their relentless downward slide. Between 1929 and 1932, the price of a share of U.S. Steel fell from $262 to $22, and General Motors from $73 to $8. Four-fifths of the Rockefeller family fortune disappeared. William C. Durant, one of the founders of General Motors, lost all his money and ended up running a bowling alley in Flint, Michigan. In 1932, the economy hit rock bottom. Since 1929, the gross national product (the value of all the goods and services in the country) had fallen by one-third, prices by nearly 40 percent, and more than 11 million Americans—25 percent of the labor force—could not find work. U.S. Steel, which had employed 225,000 full-time workers in 1929, had none at the end of 1932, when it was operating at only

12 percent of capacity. Those who retained their jobs confronted reduced hours and dramatically reduced wages. Every industrial economy suffered, but the United States, which had led the way in prosperity in the 1920s, was hit hardest of all.

Americans and the Depression

The Depression transformed American life. Hundreds of thousands of people took to the road in search of work. Hungry men and women lined the streets of major cities. In Detroit, 4,000 children stood in bread lines each day seeking food. Thousands of families, evicted from their homes, moved into ramshackle shantytowns, dubbed Hoovervilles, that sprang up in parks and on abandoned land. Cities quickly spent the little money they had available for poor relief. In Chicago, where half the working population was unemployed at the beginning of 1932, Mayor Anton Cermak telephoned people individually, begging them to pay their taxes. "We saw want and despair walking the streets," wrote a Chicago social worker, "and our friends, sensible, thrifty families, reduced to poverty." When the Soviet Union advertised its need for skilled workers, it received more than 100,000 applications from the United States.

The Depression actually reversed the long-standing movement of population from farms to cities. Many Americans left cities to try to grow food for their families. In 1935, 33 million people lived on farms—more than at any previous point in American history. But rural areas, already poor, saw families reduce the number of meals per day and children go barefoot. With the future shrouded in uncertainty, the American suicide rate rose to the highest level in the nation's history, and the birthrate fell to the lowest.

"The American way of life," the confident slogan of the consumer culture, and common sayings like "safe as a bank" took on a hollow ring. The image of big business, carefully cultivated during the 1920s, collapsed as congressional investigations revealed massive irregularities committed by bankers and stockbrokers. Banks had knowingly sold worthless bonds. Prominent Wall Streeters had unloaded their own portfolios while advising small investors to maintain their

Oct. 29—Dies Irae, a 1929 lithograph by James N. Rosenberg, depicts skyscrapers tottering, stockbrokers jumping from windows, and crowds panicking as the stock market crashes. The title means "Day of Wrath."

Unemployed men lined up outside a Chicago soup kitchen in 1931. Charitable institutions like this one were overwhelmed by the advent of the Great Depression.

Police battling "bonus marchers" in Washington, D.C., July 1932. Soon afterward, President Hoover sent federal troops to evict the marchers.

holdings. Richard Whitney, the president of the New York Stock Exchange, was convicted of stealing funds from customers, including from a fund to aid widows and orphans. He ended up in jail.

Resignation and Protest

Many Americans reacted to the Depression with resignation or blamed themselves for economic misfortune. Others responded with protests that were at first spontaneous and uncoordinated, since unions, socialist organizations, and other groups that might have provided disciplined leadership had been decimated during the 1920s. In the spring of 1932, 20,000 unemployed World War I veterans descended on Washington to demand early payment of a bonus due in 1945, only to be driven away by federal soldiers led by the army's chief of staff, Douglas MacArthur. Throughout the country, the unemployed demonstrated for jobs and public relief. That summer, led by the charismatic Milo Reno, a former Iowa Populist, the National Farmers' Holiday Association protested low prices by temporarily blocking roads in the Midwest to prevent farm goods from getting to market.

Only the minuscule Communist Party seemed able to give a political focus to the anger and despair. "The most fully employed persons I met during the Depression," one labor leader later recalled, "were the Communists." They "brought misery out of hiding," forming unemployed councils, sponsoring marches and demonstrations for public assistance, and protesting the eviction of unemployed families from their homes. The press discussed the idea that the United States was on the verge of a revolution. The insurance firm Lloyd's of London reported an upsurge in American requests for riot insurance. The Hoover administration in 1931 opposed efforts to save money by reducing the size of the army, warning that this would "lessen our means of maintaining domestic peace and order."

Hoover's Response

In the eyes of many Americans, President Hoover's response to the Depression seemed inadequate and uncaring. Leading advisers, including Andrew Mellon,

The celebrated photographer Dorothea Lange took this photograph of an unemployed man on a San Francisco breadline in 1933.

Communist Party headquarters in New York City, 1932. The banners illustrate the variety of activities the party organized in the early 1930s.

the wealthy secretary of the treasury, told Hoover that economic downturns were a normal part of capitalism, which weeded out unproductive firms and encouraged moral virtue among the less fortunate. Businessmen strongly opposed federal aid to the unemployed, and many publications called for individual "belt-tightening" as the road to recovery. Some initially saw a silver lining in the Depression. Wages had fallen so sharply, reported *Fortune* magazine, that "you can have your garden taken care of in Los Angeles for $1 a week" or hire an "affable Negro to fry your chicken and do your washing for $8 a month in Virginia."

The federal government had never faced an economic crisis as severe as the Great Depression. Few political leaders understood how important consumer spending had become in the American economy. Most held to the conventional view that government intervention to aid those who had lost their jobs would do little to spur economic recovery and would encourage Americans to rely on government charity to address misfortune. In 1931, Hoover quoted former president Grover Cleveland from four decades earlier: "The Government should not support the people. . . . Federal aid . . . weakens the sturdiness of our national character."

Strongly opposed on principle to direct federal intervention in the economy, Hoover remained committed to "associational action." He put his faith in voluntary steps by business to maintain investment and employment—something few found it possible to do—and efforts by local charity organizations to assist needy neighbors. He called numerous conferences of business and labor leaders

> Hoover's approach

A Hooverville—a shantytown created by homeless squatters—outside Seattle, Washington, in 1933.

and established commissions to encourage firms to cooperate in maintaining prices and wages without governmental dictation. Hoover attempted to restore public confidence, making frequent public statements that "the tide had turned." But these made him increasingly seem out of touch with reality. About the unemployed men who appeared on city streets offering apples at five cents apiece, Hoover would later write, "Many persons left their jobs for the more profitable one of selling apples."

The Worsening Economic Outlook

Some administration remedies, like the Smoot-Hawley Tariff, which Hoover signed with some reluctance in 1930, made the economic situation worse. Raising the already high taxes on imported goods, it inspired similar increases abroad, further reducing international trade. A tax increase Hoover pushed through Congress in 1932 in an attempt to balance the federal budget further reduced Americans' purchasing power. Other initiatives inspired ridicule. When he approved funds to provide food for livestock, one observer remarked that the president would feed "jackasses but . . . not starving babies."

Government action

By 1932, Hoover had to admit that voluntary action had failed to stem the Depression. He signed laws creating the Reconstruction Finance Corporation, which loaned money to failing banks, railroads, and other businesses, and the Federal Home Loan Bank System, which offered aid to home owners threatened with foreclosure. Having vetoed previous bills to create employment through public-works projects like road and bridge construction, he now approved a measure appropriating nearly $2 billion for such initiatives and helping to fund local relief efforts. These were dramatic departures from previous federal economic policy. But further than this, Hoover would not go. He adamantly opposed offering direct relief to the unemployed—it would do them a "disservice," he told Congress.

An unemployed man and woman selling apples on a city street during the Great Depression.

Freedom in the Modern World

In 1927, the New School for Social Research in New York City organized a series of lectures on the theme of Freedom in the Modern World. Founded eight years earlier as a place where "free thought and intellectual integrity" could flourish in the wake of wartime repression, the school's distinguished faculty included the philosopher John Dewey and historian Charles Beard (who had resigned from Columbia University in 1917 to protest the dismissal of antiwar professors). The lectures painted a depressing portrait of American freedom on the eve of the Great Depression. "The idea of freedom," declared economist Walton H. Hamilton, had become "an intellectual instrument for looking backward. . . . Liberty of contract has been made the be-all and end-all of personal freedom; . . . the domain of business has been defended against control from without in the name of freedom." The free exchange of ideas, moreover, had not recovered from the crisis of World War I. The "sacred dogmas of patriotism and Big Business," said the educator Horace Kallen, dominated teaching, the press, and public debate. A definition of freedom reigned supreme that celebrated the unimpeded reign of economic enterprise yet tolerated the surveillance of private life and individual conscience.

> *Assessing freedom in the 1920s*

The prosperity of the 1920s had reinforced this definition of freedom. With the economic crash, compounded by the ineffectiveness of the Hoover administration's response, it would be discredited. By 1932, the seeds had already been planted for a new conception of freedom that combined two different elements in a sometimes uneasy synthesis. One was the Progressive belief in a socially conscious state making what Dewey called "positive and constructive changes" in economic arrangements. The other, which arose in the 1920s, centered on respect for civil liberties and cultural pluralism and declared that realms of life like group identity, personal behavior, and the free expression of ideas lay outside legitimate state concern. These two principles would become the hallmarks of modern liberalism, which during the 1930s would redefine American freedom.

> *A new conception of freedom*

SUGGESTED READING

BOOKS

- Boyle, Kevin. *Arc of Justice: A Saga of Race, Civil Rights, and Murder in the Jazz Age* (2004). A history of the Sweet case, placing it in the context of postwar Detroit and the nation.

- Cohen, Warren I. *Empire without Tears: America's Foreign Relations, 1921–1933* (1987). A careful examination of American foreign policy between the presidencies of Wilson and Roosevelt.

- Dumenil, Lynn. *The Modern Temper: America in the Twenties* (1995). A brief survey of the main political and cultural trends of the decade.

- Garraty, John A. *The Great Depression* (1986). Places the Depression in a global context and compares various governments' responses to it.

- Gerstle, Gary. *American Crucible: Race and Nation in the Twentieth Century* (2002). A sweeping survey of how changing ideas of race have affected the concept of American nationality, with a strong account of the debates of the 1920s.

- Grandin, Greg. *Fordlandia: The Rise and Fall of Henry Ford's Forgotten Jungle City* (2009). Tells the fascinating story of Ford's effort to create a planned community in Brazil's Amazon rain forest.

- Higham, John. *Strangers in the Land: Patterns of American Nativism, 1860–1925* (1955). A classic account of American hostility to immigrants, concluding with the immigration restriction of 1924.

- Larson, Edward. *Summer for the Gods: The Scopes Trial and America's Continuing Debate over Science and Religion* (1998). A history of the famous trial and the enduring debate over evolution.

- Lerner, Michael A. *Dry Manhattan: Prohibition in New York City* (2007). An account of the success and failure of Prohibition in the nation's largest city.

- Lewis, David L. *When Harlem Was in Vogue* (1981). A lively account of the Harlem Renaissance of the 1920s.

- Maclean, Nancy. *Behind the Mask of Chivalry: The Making of the Second Ku Klux Klan* (1994). A careful analysis of the membership and motivations of the Ku Klux Klan of the 1920s.

- Marchand, Roland. *Advertising the American Dream: Making Way for Modernity, 1920–1940* (1985). Examines how advertisers responded to and helped to shape changes in American life between the two world wars.

- Marsden, George M. *Fundamentalism and American Culture: The Shaping of Twentieth-Century Evangelicism, 1870–1925* (1980). Traces the ups and downs of American fundamentalism, culminating in the Scopes trial.

- Murphy, Paul L. *World War I and the Origin of Civil Liberties in the United States* (1979). An analysis of how the repression of free speech during World War I paved the way for a heightened awareness of the importance of civil liberties.

- Ngai, Mae. *Impossible Subjects: Illegal Aliens and the Making of Modern America* (2004). An influential examination of immigration policy toward Mexicans and Asians, and the development of the legal category of "illegal alien."

- Ross, William G. *Forging New Freedoms: Nativism, Education, and the Constitution, 1917–1927* (1994). Discusses battles over cultural pluralism in the 1920s and how they laid the groundwork for an expanded definition of personal liberty.

WEBSITES

- Emergence of Advertising in America: http://library.duke.edu/digitalcollections/eaa/

- Harlem History: www.columbia.edu/cu/iraas/harlem/index.html

- Pluralism and Unity: www.expo98.msu.edu

- Prosperity and Thrift: Coolidge Era and the Consumer Economy: http://memory.loc.gov/ammem/coolhtml/coolhome.html

CHAPTER REVIEW AND ONLINE RESOURCES

REVIEW QUESTIONS

1. How did consumerism and the idea of the "American way of life" affect people's understanding of American values, including the meaning of freedom, in the 1920s?

2. Which groups did not share in the prosperity of the 1920s and why?

3. How did business practices and policies lead to a decline in union membership in the 1920s?

4. President Calvin Coolidge said that "the chief business of the American people is business." How did the federal government's policies and practices in the 1920s reflect this understanding of the importance of business interests?

5. Who supported restricting immigration in the 1920s and why? Why were they more successful in gaining federal legislation to limit immigration in these years?

6. Did U.S. society in the 1920s reflect the concept of cultural pluralism as explained by Horace Kallen? Why or why not?

7. Identify the causes of the Great Depression.

8. What principles guided President Hoover's response to the Great Depression, and how did this restrict his ability to help the American people?

9. What issues were of particular concern to religious fundamentalists in these years and why?

10. In what ways did the ideas about (and the reality of) proper roles for women change in these years?

KEY TERMS

Sacco-Vanzetti case (p. 759)

rise of the stock market (p. 765)

"welfare capitalism" (p. 766)

Equal Rights Amendment (p. 766)

the "flapper" (p. 768)

Teapot Dome scandal (p. 770)

Adkins v. Children's Hospital (p. 770)

McNary-Haugen farm bill (p. 771)

Hays code (p. 775)

American Civil Liberties Union (p. 776)

"clear and present danger" (p. 776)

fundamentalism (p.778)

Scopes trial (p. 779)

second Ku Klux Klan (p. 780)

immigration restriction (p. 782)

"illegal alien" (p. 783)

the "New Negro" (p. 787)

stock market crash (p. 790)

bonus marchers (p. 792)

Reconstruction Finance Corporation (p. 794)

wwnorton.com/studyspace

Visit StudySpace for these resources and more:

-   **Author Videos**
-   **A chapter outline**
-   **A practice quiz**
-   **Interactive maps**
-   **Multimedia documents**

CHAPTER 21

THE NEW DEAL

★

1932–1940

Early in 1941, the unemployed Woody Guthrie, soon to become one of the country's most popular songwriters and folk singers, brought his family to Portland, Oregon. He hoped to star in a film about the great public-works projects under way on the Columbia River. Given a temporary job by the Bonneville Power Authority, the public agency that controlled the Columbia dams, Guthrie produced a song every day for the next month. One, "Roll on, Columbia," became a popular statement of the benefits that resulted when government took the lead in improving the lot of ordinary citizens:

> And on up the river is the Grand Coulee Dam,
> The biggest thing built by the hand of a man,
> To run the great factories and water the land,
> So, roll on, Columbia, roll on. . . .
> Your power is turning our darkness to dawn.
> So, roll on, Columbia, roll on.©

The Columbia River winds its way on a 1,200-mile course from Canada through Washington and Oregon to the Pacific Ocean. Because of its steep descent from uplands to sea level, it produces an immense amount of energy. Residents of the economically underdeveloped Pacific Northwest had long dreamed of tapping this unused energy for electricity and irrigation. But not until the 1930s did the federal government launch the program of dam construction that transformed the region. The project created thousands of jobs for the unemployed, and the network of dams produced abundant cheap power.

When the Grand Coulee Dam went into operation in 1941, it was the largest man-made structure in world history. It eventually produced more than 40 percent of the nation's hydroelectric power. The dam provided the cheapest electricity in the country for towns that sprang up out of nowhere, farms on what had once been deserts in eastern Washington and Oregon, and factories that would soon be producing aluminum for World War II airplanes. The project also had less appealing consequences. From time immemorial, the Columbia River had been filled with salmon. But the Grand Coulee Dam made no provision for the passage of fish, and the salmon all but vanished. This caused little concern during the Depression but became a source of controversy later in the century as Americans became more concerned about preserving the natural environment.

The Grand Coulee Dam was part of what one scholar has called a "public works revolution" that transformed the American economy and landscape during the 1930s. The Roosevelt administration spent far more money on building roads, dams, airports, bridges, and housing than on any other activity.

Franklin D. Roosevelt believed regional economic development like that in the Northwest would promote economic growth, ease the domestic and working lives of ordinary Americans, and keep control of key natural resources in public rather than private hands. "It promises," one supporter wrote, "a world replete with more freedom and happiness than mankind has ever known."

The Columbia River project reflected broader changes in American life and thought during the New Deal of the 1930s. Roosevelt oversaw the transformation

FOCUS QUESTIONS

What were the major policy initiatives of the New Deal in the Hundred Days? –p. 801

Who were the main proponents of economic justice in the 1930s, and what measures did they advocate? –p. 811

What were the major initiatives of the Second New Deal, and how did they differ from the First New Deal? –p. 815

How did the New Deal recast the meaning of American freedom? –p. 819

How did New Deal benefits apply to women and minorities? –p. 825

How did the Popular Front influence American culture in the 1930s? –p. 831

This panel depicting the construction of a dam was painted in 1939 by William Gropper as part of a mural for the new Department of Interior building in Washington, D.C. Like other artists who found it difficult to obtain work, he was hired by the Works Progress Administration to paint murals for government buildings. This one was inspired by the construction of the Grand Coulee Dam on the Columbia River, one of the many New Deal projects that expanded the nation's infrastructure and provided employment to victims of the Depression.

1931   Scottsboro case

1933   Franklin Roosevelt inaugurated president

       Bank holiday

       The Hundred Days and the First New Deal

       21st Amendment ratified

1934   Huey Long launches the Share Our Wealth movement

       American Liberty League established

       Herbert Hoover's *The Challenge to Liberty*

1934–1940   Height of the Dust Bowl

1935   Second New Deal launched

       Supreme Court rules the National Recovery Association unconstitutional

       John L. Lewis organizes the Congress of Industrial Organizations

1936   Supreme Court rules the Agricultural Adjustment Act unconstitutional

       New Deal coalition leads to Democratic landslide

       John Maynard Keynes's *The General Theory of Employment, Interest, and Money*

1936–1937   United Auto Workers sit-down strike

1938   House Un-American Activities Committee established

       Fair Labor Standards Act passed

1939   John Steinbeck's *The Grapes of Wrath*

of the Democratic Party into a coalition of farmers, industrial workers, the reform-minded urban middle class, liberal intellectuals, northern African-Americans, and, somewhat incongruously, the white supremacist South, united by the belief that the federal government must provide Americans with protection against the dislocations caused by modern capitalism. "Liberalism," traditionally understood as limited government and free market economics, took on its modern meaning. Thanks to the New Deal, it now referred to active efforts by the national government to modernize and regulate the market economy and to uplift less fortunate members of society.

Freedom, too, underwent a transformation during the 1930s. The Depression had discredited the ideas that social progress rests on the unrestrained pursuit of wealth and that, apart from unfortunates like widows and orphans, most poverty is self-inflicted. The New Deal elevated a public guarantee of economic security to the forefront of American discussions of freedom. The 1930s were a decade of dramatic social upheaval. Social and political activists, most notably a revitalized labor movement, placed new issues on the political agenda. When one writer in 1941 published a survey of democratic thought beginning in the ancient world, he concluded that what distinguished his own time was its awareness of "the social conditions of freedom." Thanks to the New Deal, he wrote, "economic security" had "at last been recognized as a political condition of personal freedom." Regional economic development like that in the Northwest reflected this understanding of freedom. So did other New Deal measures, including the Social Security Act, which offered aid to the unemployed and aged, and the Fair Labor Standards Act, which established a national minimum wage.

Yet while the New Deal significantly expanded the meaning of freedom, it did not erase freedom's boundaries. Its benefits flowed to industrial workers but not tenant farmers, to men far more fully than to women, and to white Americans more than blacks, who, in the South, still were deprived of the basic rights of citizenship.

THE FIRST NEW DEAL

FDR and The Election of 1932

It is indeed paradoxical that Franklin D. Roosevelt, who had been raised in privilege on a New York country estate, came to be beloved as the symbolic representative of ordinary citizens. But like Lincoln, with whom he is often compared, Roosevelt's greatness lay in his willingness to throw off the "dogmas of the quiet past" (Lincoln's words) to confront an unprecedented national crisis. FDR, as he liked to be called, was born in 1882, a fifth cousin of Theodore Roosevelt. He graduated from Harvard in 1904 and six years later won election to the New York legislature from Duchess County, site of his family's home at Hyde Park. After serving as undersecretary of the navy during World War I, he ran for vice president on the ill-fated Democratic ticket of 1920 headed by James M. Cox. In 1921, he contracted polio and lost the use of his legs, a fact carefully concealed from the

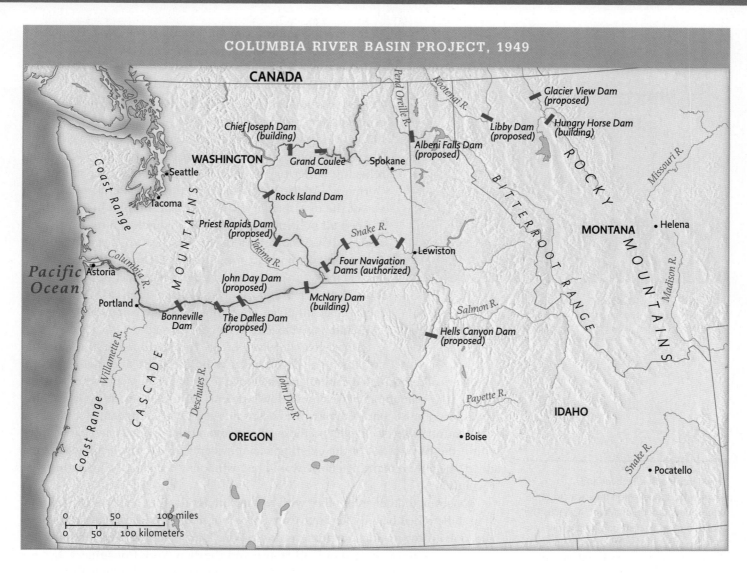

COLUMBIA RIVER BASIN PROJECT, 1949

A 1949 map of the Columbia River project, showing its numerous dams, including the Grand Coulee, the largest man-made structure in the world at the time of its opening in 1941.

public in that pre-television era. Very few Americans realized that the president who projected an image of vigorous leadership during the 1930s and World War II was confined to a wheelchair.

In his speech accepting the Democratic nomination for president in 1932, Roosevelt promised a "new deal" for the American people. But his campaign offered only vague hints of what this might entail. Roosevelt spoke of the government's responsibility to guarantee "every man . . . a right to make a comfortable living." But he also advocated a balanced federal budget and criticized his opponent, President Hoover, for excessive government spending. The biggest difference between the parties during the campaign was the Democrats' call for the repeal of Prohibition, although Roosevelt certainly suggested a greater awareness of the plight of ordinary Americans and a willingness to embark on new ways to address the Great Depression. Battered by the economic crisis, Americans in 1932 were desperate for new leadership, and Roosevelt won a resounding victory.

A "new deal"

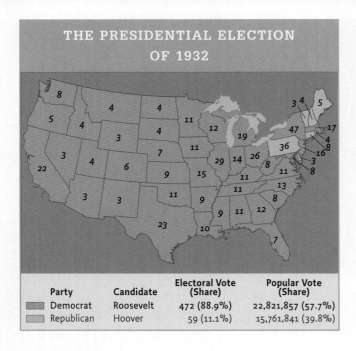

THE PRESIDENTIAL ELECTION OF 1932

Party	Candidate	Electoral Vote (Share)	Popular Vote (Share)
Democrat	Roosevelt	472 (88.9%)	22,821,857 (57.7%)
Republican	Hoover	59 (11.1%)	15,761,841 (39.8%)

He received 57 percent of the popular vote, and Democrats swept to a commanding majority in Congress.

The Coming of the New Deal

The Depression did not produce a single pattern of international public response. For nearly the entire decade of the 1930s, conservative governments ruled Britain and France. They were more interested in preserving public order than relieving suffering or embarking on policy innovations. In Germany, Adolf Hitler, leader of the Nazi Party, established one of the most brutal dictatorships in human history. Hitler banned all political opposition and launched a reign of terror against Jews and others deemed to be "un-German." In the Soviet Union, another tyrant, Joseph Stalin, embarked on successive five-year plans that at great social cost produced rapid industrialization and claimed to have eliminated unemployment. The militarist government of Japan invaded China in 1937, and hoped to extend its rule throughout Asia.

Roosevelt conceived of the New Deal as an alternative to socialism on the left, Nazism on the right, and the inaction of upholders of unregulated capitalism. He hoped to reconcile democracy, individual liberty, and economic recovery and development. "You have made yourself," the British economist John Maynard Keynes wrote to FDR, "the trustee for those in every country who seek to mend the evils of our condition by reasoned experiment within the framework of the existing social system." If Roosevelt failed, Keynes added, the only remaining choice would be "orthodoxy" (that is, doing nothing) or "revolution."

Roosevelt did not enter office with a blueprint for dealing with the Depression. At first, he relied heavily for advice on a group of intellectuals and social workers who took up key positions in his administration. They included Secretary of Labor Frances Perkins, a veteran of Hull House and the New York Consumers' League who had been among the eyewitnesses to the Triangle fire of 1911; Harry Hopkins, who had headed emergency relief efforts during Roosevelt's term as governor of New York; Secretary of the Interior Harold Ickes, a veteran of Theodore Roosevelt's Progressive campaign of 1912; and Louis Brandeis, who had advised Woodrow Wilson during the 1912 campaign and now offered political advice to FDR while serving on the Supreme Court.

The presence of these individuals reflected how Roosevelt drew on the reform traditions of the Progressive era. But Progressivism, as noted in Chapter 18, was hardly a unified movement, and Roosevelt's advisers did not speak with one voice. Brandeis believed that large corporations not only wielded excessive power but had contributed to the Depression by keeping prices artificially high and failing to increase workers' purchasing power. They should be broken up, he insisted, not regulated. But the "brains trust"—a group of academics that included a number of Columbia University

Presidents Herbert Hoover and Franklin D. Roosevelt on their way to the latter's inauguration on March 4, 1933. The two men strongly disliked one another. They barely spoke during the ride and never saw each other again after that day.

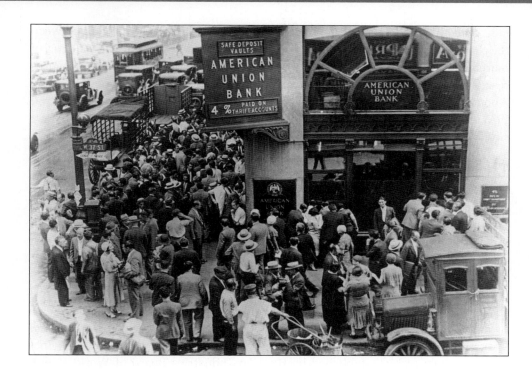

A "run" on a bank: crowds of people wait outside a New York City bank, hoping to withdraw their money.

professors—saw bigness as inevitable in a modern economy. The competitive marketplace, they argued, was a thing of the past, and large firms needed to be managed and directed by the government, not dismantled. Their view prevailed during what came to be called the First New Deal.

The Banking Crisis

"This nation asks for action and action now," Roosevelt announced on taking office on March 4, 1933. The country, wrote the journalist and political commentator Walter Lippmann, "was in such a state of confused desperation that it would have followed almost any leader anywhere he chose to go." FDR spent much of 1933 trying to reassure the public. In his inaugural address, he declared that "the only thing we have to fear is fear itself." (See the Appendix for the full text.)

> *"fear itself"*

Roosevelt confronted a banking system on the verge of collapse. As bank funds invested in the stock market and corporate bonds lost their value and panicked depositors withdrew their savings, bank after bank had closed its doors. By March 1933, banking had been suspended in a majority of the states—that is, people could not gain access to money in their bank accounts. Roosevelt declared a "bank holiday," temporarily halting all bank operations, and called Congress into special session. On March 9, it rushed to pass the Emergency Banking Act, which provided funds to shore up threatened institutions.

Further measures soon followed that transformed the American financial system. The Glass-Steagall Act barred commercial banks from becoming involved in the buying and selling of stocks. Until its repeal in the 1990s, the law prevented many of the irresponsible practices that had contributed to the stock market crash. The same law established the Federal Deposit Insurance Corporation (FDIC), a government system that insured the accounts of individual depositors. And Roosevelt

> *The Glass-Steagall Act*

took the United States off the gold standard—that is, he severed the link between the country's currency and its gold reserves, thus making possible the issuance of more money in the hope of stimulating business activity. Together, these measures rescued the financial system and greatly increased the government's power over it. About 5,000 banks—one-third of the nation's total—had failed between 1929 and 1933, representing a loss of tens of millions of dollars to depositors. In 1936, not a single bank failed in the United States.

The NRA

The Emergency Banking Act was the first of an unprecedented flurry of legislation during the first three months of Roosevelt's administration, a period known as the "Hundred Days." Seizing on the sense of crisis and the momentum of his electoral victory, Roosevelt won rapid passage of laws he hoped would promote economic recovery. He persuaded Congress to create a host of new agencies, whose initials soon became part of the language of politics—NRA, AAA, CCC. Never in American history had a president exercised such power or so rapidly expanded the role of the federal government in people's lives.

The centerpiece of Roosevelt's plan for combating the Depression, the National Industrial Recovery Act, was to a large extent modeled on the government–business partnership established by the War Industries Board of World War I, although in keeping with FDR's nondogmatic approach, it also owed something to Herbert Hoover's efforts to build stronger government–business cooperation. Roosevelt called it "the most important and far-reaching legislation ever enacted by the American Congress." The act established the National Recovery Administration (NRA), which would work with groups of business leaders to establish industry codes that set standards for output, prices, and working conditions. Thus, "cutthroat" competition (in which companies took losses to drive competitors out of business) would be ended. These industry-wide arrangements would be exempt from antitrust laws.

The Spirit of the New Deal, a 1933 cartoon in the *Washington Star*, depicts the federal government, through the National Recovery Administration, promoting peace between workers and employers.

The Hundred Days

The NRA reflected how even in its early days, the New Deal reshaped understandings of freedom. In effect, FDR had repudiated the older idea of liberty based on the idea that the best way to encourage economic activity and ensure a fair distribution of wealth was to allow market competition to operate, unrestrained by the government. And to win support from labor, section 7a of the new law recognized the workers' right to organize unions—a departure from the "open shop" policies of the 1920s and a step toward government support for what workers called "industrial freedom."

Headed by Hugh S. Johnson, a retired general and businessman, the NRA quickly established codes that set standards for production, prices, and wages in the textile, steel, mining, and auto industries. Johnson launched a publicity campaign to promote the NRA and its symbol, the Blue Eagle, which stores and factories that abided by the codes displayed. But after initial public enthusiasm, the NRA became mired in controversy. Large companies dominated the code-writing process. An inquiry conducted by the labor lawyer Clarence Darrow in 1934 concluded that they used the NRA to drive up prices, limit production, lay off workers, and divide markets among themselves at the expense of smaller competitors. Many anti-union employers ignored section 7a. The government lacked the manpower to police the 750 codes in effect by 1935. The NRA produced neither economic recovery nor peace between employers and workers. It did, however, help to undercut the pervasive sense that the federal government was doing nothing to deal with the economic crisis.

Government Jobs

The Hundred Days also brought the government into providing relief to those in need. Roosevelt and most of his advisers shared the widespread fear that direct government payments to the unemployed would undermine individual self-reliance. Indeed, one of the first measures of the Hundred Days had been the Economy Act, which reduced federal spending in an attempt to win the confidence of the business community. But with nearly a quarter of the workforce unemployed, spending on relief was unavoidable. In May 1933, Congress created the Federal Emergency Relief Administration, to make grants to local agencies that aided those impoverished by the Depression. FDR, however, much preferred to create temporary jobs, thereby combating unemployment while improving the nation's infrastructure of roads, bridges, public buildings, and parks.

In March 1933, Congress established the Civilian Conservation Corps (CCC), which set unemployed young men to work on projects like forest preservation, flood control, and the improvement of national parks and wildlife preserves. By the time the program ended in 1942, more than 3 million persons had passed through CCC camps, where they received government wages of $30 per month.

Relief

Civilian Conservation Corps

A Civilian Conservation Corps workforce in Yosemite National Park, 1935.

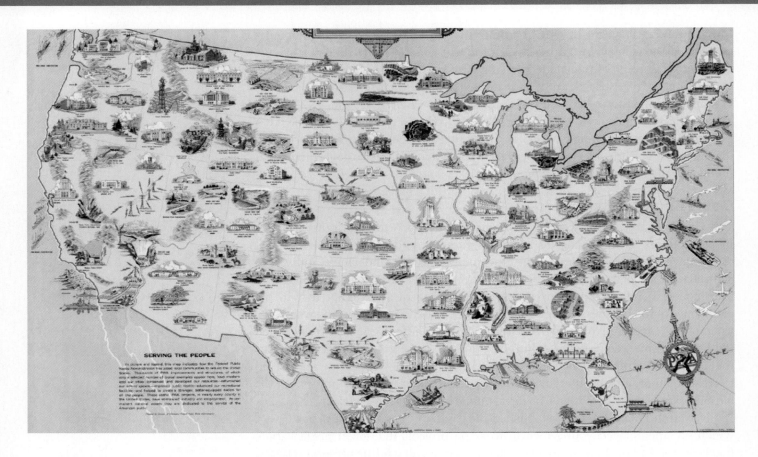

SERVING THE PEOPLE

A map published by the Public Works Administration in 1935 depicts some of the numerous infrastructure projects funded by the New Deal. Among the most famous public-works projects are the Triborough Bridge in New York City, the Key West Highway in Florida, and the Grand Coulee Dam in Washington. Overall, the New Deal spent $250 billion (in today's money) to construct, among other things, 40,000 public buildings, 72,000 schools, 80,000 bridges, and 8,000 parks.

The TVA

Public-Works Projects

One section of the National Industrial Recovery Act created the Public Works Administration (PWA), with an appropriation of $3.3 billion. Directed by Secretary of the Interior Harold Ickes, it contracted with private construction companies to build roads, schools, hospitals, and other public facilities, including New York City's Triborough Bridge and the Overseas Highway between Miami and Key West, Florida. In November, yet another agency, the Civil Works Administration (CWA), was launched. Unlike the PWA, it directly hired workers for construction projects. By January 1934, it employed more than 4 million persons in the construction of highways, tunnels, courthouses, and airports. But as the cost spiraled upward and complaints multiplied that the New Deal was creating a class of Americans permanently dependent on government jobs, Roosevelt ordered the CWA dissolved.

Some New Deal public-works initiatives looked to government-planned economic transformation as much as economic relief. The Tennessee Valley Authority (TVA), another product of the Hundred Days, built a series of dams to prevent floods and deforestation along the Tennessee River and to provide cheap electric power for homes and factories in a seven-state region where many families still lived in isolated log cabins. The TVA put the federal government, for the first time, in the business of selling electricity in competition with private companies. It was a preview of the program of regional planning that spurred the economic development of the West.

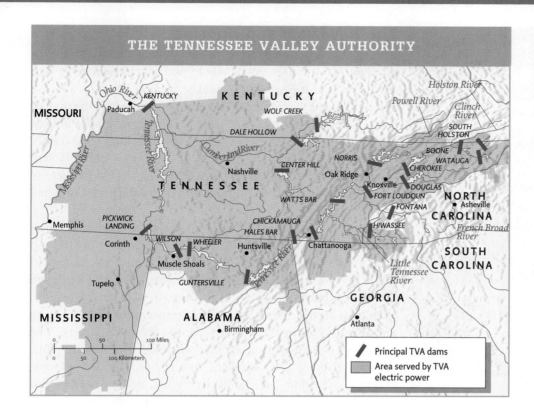

THE TENNESSEE VALLEY AUTHORITY

Principal TVA dams

Area served by TVA electric power

A map showing the reach of the Tennessee Valley Authority, covering all or parts of seven southeastern states. Numerous reservoirs and power plants dot the landscape.

The New Deal and Agriculture

Another policy initiative of the Hundred Days addressed the disastrous plight of American farmers. The Agricultural Adjustment Act (AAA) authorized the federal government to try to raise farm prices by setting production quotas for major crops and paying farmers to plant less. Many crops already in the field were destroyed. In 1933, the government ordered more than 6 million pigs slaughtered as part of the policy, a step critics found strange at a time of widespread hunger.

The AAA succeeded in significantly raising farm prices and incomes. But not all farmers benefited. Benefits flowed to property-owning farmers, ignoring the large number who worked on land owned by others. The AAA policy of paying landowning farmers not to grow crops encouraged the eviction of thousands of poor tenants and sharecroppers. Many joined the rural exodus to cities or to the farms of the West Coast.

The AAA

The onset in 1930 of a period of unusually dry weather in the nation's heartland worsened the Depression's impact on rural America. By mid-decade, the region suffered from the century's most severe drought. Mechanized agriculture in this semiarid region had pulverized the topsoil and killed native grasses that prevented erosion. Winds now blew much of the soil away, creating the Dust Bowl, as the affected areas of Oklahoma, Texas, Kansas, and Colorado were called. A local newspaper described the situation in Cimarron County, Oklahoma: "Not a blade of wheat; cattle dying on the range, ninety percent of the poultry dead because of the sand storms, milk cows gone dry." One storm in 1934 carried dust as far as Washington, D.C. The drought and dust storms displaced more than 1 million farmers. John Steinbeck's novel *The Grapes of Wrath* (1939) and a popular film based on the book captured their plight, tracing a dispossessed family's trek from Oklahoma to California.

The Dust Bowl

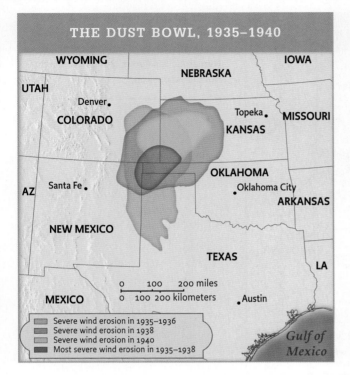

THE DUST BOWL, 1935–1940

WYOMING

UTAH

Denver

COLORADO

AZ   Santa Fe

NEW MEXICO

NEBRASKA

IOWA

Topeka   MISSOURI

KANSAS

OKLAHOMA
Oklahoma City

ARKANSAS

TEXAS   LA

0   100   200 miles
0   100 200 kilometers

MEXICO   Austin

Gulf of
Mexico

Severe wind erosion in 1935–1936
Severe wind erosion in 1938
Severe wind erosion in 1940
Most severe wind erosion in 1935–1938

The New Deal and Housing

Owning one's home had long been a widely shared American ambition. "A man is not a whole and complete man," Walt Whitman had written in the 1850s, "unless he owns a house and the ground it stands on." For many members of the middle class, home ownership had become a mark of respectability. For workers, it offered economic security at a time of low wages, erratic employment, and limited occupational mobility. On the eve of World War I, a considerably higher percentage of immigrant workers than the native-born middle class owned their homes.

The Depression devastated the American housing industry. The construction of new residences all but ceased, and banks and savings and loan associations that had financed home ownership collapsed or, to remain afloat, foreclosed on many homes (a quarter of a million in 1932 alone). In 1931, President Hoover convened a Conference on Home Building and Home Ownership to review the housing crisis. The president called owning a home an American "birthright," the embodiment of the spirit of "enterprise, of independence, and of . . . freedom." Rented apartments, he pointed out, did not inspire "immortal ballads" like *Home, Sweet Home* or *The Little Gray Home in the West*. Papers presented at the conference revealed that millions of Americans lived in overcrowded, unhealthy urban slums or in ramshackle rural dwellings. Private enterprise alone, it seemed clear, was unlikely to solve the nation's housing crisis.

Hoover's administration established a federally sponsored bank to issue home loans. Not until the New Deal, however, did the government systematically enter

A giant dust storm engulfs a town in western Kansas on April 14, 1935, known as Black Sunday in the American West.

Sunday April 14, 1935
Dust Clouds Rolling Over The Prairies
Stovall Studio Dodge City, Kansas #5

Sharecroppers evicted from the farms on which they had been working in New Madrid County, Missouri, as a result of government subsidies to farm owners to reduce crop production.

the housing market. Roosevelt spoke of "the security of the home" as a fundamental right akin to "the security of livelihood, and the security of social insurance." In 1933 and 1934, his administration moved energetically to protect home owners from foreclosure and to stimulate new construction. The Home Owners Loan Corporation and Federal Housing Administration (FHA) insured millions of long-term mortgages issued by private banks. At the same time, the federal government itself built thousands of units of low-rent housing. New Deal housing policy represented a remarkable departure from previous government practice. Thanks to the FHA and, later, the Veterans' Administration, home ownership came within the reach of tens of millions of families. It became cheaper for most Americans to buy single-family homes than to rent apartments.

Other important measures of Roosevelt's first two years in office included the ratification of the Twenty-first Amendment to the Constitution, which repealed Prohibition; the establishment of the Federal Communications Commission to oversee the nation's broadcast airwaves and telephone communications; and the creation of the Securities and Exchange Commission to regulate the stock and bond markets. Taken together, the First New Deal was a series of experiments, some of which succeeded and some of which did not. They transformed the role of the federal government, constructed numerous public facilities, and provided relief to millions of needy persons. But they did not end the Depression. Some 10 million Americans—more than 20 percent of the workforce—remained unemployed when 1934 came to an end.

As it did in other sectors of the economy, the Great Depression led to a collapse in the construction industry.

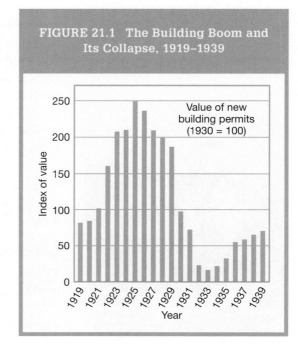

FIGURE 21.1 The Building Boom and Its Collapse, 1919–1939

Value of new building permits (1930 = 100)

Index of value

Year

Russell Lee's 1939 photograph of a migrant family saying grace before eating by the side of the road near Fort Gibson, Oklahoma, shows how, even in the most difficult circumstances, families struggled to maintain elements of their normal lives.

The Illegal Act, a cartoon critical of the Supreme Court's decision declaring the NRA unconstitutional. FDR tells a drowning Uncle Sam, "I'm sorry, but the Supreme Court says I must chuck you back in."

The Court and the New Deal

In 1935, the Supreme Court, still controlled by conservative Republican judges who held to the nineteenth-century understanding of freedom as liberty of contract, began to invalidate key New Deal laws. First came the NRA, declared unconstitutional in May in a case brought by the Schechter Poultry Company of Brooklyn, which had been charged with violating the code adopted by the chicken industry. In a unanimous decision, the Court declared the NRA unlawful because in its codes and other regulations it delegated legislative powers to the president and attempted to regulate local businesses that did not engage in interstate commerce. In January 1936, the AAA fell in *United States v. Butler*, which declared it an unconstitutional exercise of congressional power over local economic activities. In June, by a 5-4 vote, the justices ruled that New York could not establish a minimum wage for women and children.

Having failed to end the Depression or win judicial approval, the First New Deal ground to a halt. Meanwhile, pressures were mounting outside Washington that propelled the administration toward more radical departures in policy.

THE GRASSROOTS REVOLT

Labor's Great Upheaval

The most striking development of the mid-1930s was the mobilization of millions of workers in mass-production industries that had successfully resisted unionization. "Labor's great upheaval," as this era of unprecedented militancy was called, came as a great surprise. Unlike in the past, however, the federal government now seemed to be on the side of labor, a commitment embodied in the National Industrial Recovery Act and in the Wagner Act (discussed later) of 1935, which granted workers the legal right to form unions. With the severe reduction of European immigration, ethnic differences among workers had diminished in importance. American-born children of the new immigrants now dominated the industrial labor force, and organizers no longer had to distribute materials in numerous languages as the IWW had done. And a cadre of militant labor leaders, many of them socialists and communists with long experience in organization, had survived the repression of the 1920s. They provided leadership to the labor upsurge.

American factories at the outset of the New Deal were miniature dictatorships in which unions were rare, workers could be beaten by supervisors and fired at will, and management determined the length of the workday and speed of the assembly line. In industrial communities scattered across the country, local government firmly supported the companies. "Jesus Christ couldn't speak in Duquesne for the union," declared the mayor of that Pennsylvania steel town. Workers' demands during the 1930s went beyond better wages. They included an end to employers' arbitrary power in the workplace, and basic civil liberties for workers, including the right to picket, distribute literature, and meet to discuss their grievances. All these goals required union recognition.

Roosevelt's election as president did much to rekindle hope among those who called themselves, in the words of a worker writing to Secretary of Labor Frances Perkins, "slaves of the depression." His inauguration unleashed a flood of poignant letters to the federal government describing what a Louisiana sugar laborer called the "terrible and inhuman condition" of many workers. Labor organizers spread the message that the "political liberty for which our forefathers fought" had been "made meaningless by economic inequality" and "industrial despotism." "We are free Americans," declared the Steel Workers Organizing Committee. "We shall exercise our inalienable rights to organize into a great industrial union."

Labor's great upheaval exploded in 1934, a year that witnessed no fewer than 2,000 strikes. Many produced violent confrontations between workers and the local police. In Toledo, Ohio, 10,000 striking auto workers surrounded the Electric Auto-Lite factory, where managers had brought strikebreakers to take their jobs, leading to a seven-hour fight with police and the National Guard. In Minneapolis, where an organization of businessmen known as the Citizens Alliance controlled the city government, a four-month strike by truck drivers led to pitched battles in the streets and the governor declaring martial law. San Francisco experienced the country's first general strike since 1919. It began with a walkout of dockworkers led by the fiery communist Harry Bridges. Workers demanded recognition of the International Longshoremen's Association and an end to the hated "shape up" system in which they had to gather en masse each day to wait for work assignments. The year 1934 also witnessed a strike of 400,000 textile workers in states from New England to the Deep South, demanding recognition of the United Textile Workers. Many of these walkouts, including those in Toledo, Minneapolis, and San Francisco, won at least some of the workers' demands. But the textile strike failed.

> *Conditions in American factories*

Pennsylvania Steelworkers outside the Local Headquarters of the Steel Workers Organizing Committee, a 1938 photograph by Arnold Rothstein.

Signs carried by striking cotton mill workers in Lumberton, North Carolina, in 1937 illustrate how the labor movement revived the nineteenth-century language of "wage slavery" to demand union recognition.

The Rise of the CIO

The labor upheaval posed a challenge to the American Federation of Labor's traditional policy of organizing workers by craft—welders or machine repairers, for example—rather than seeking to mobilize all the workers in a given industry, such as steel manufacturing. In 1934, thirty AFL leaders called for the creation of unions of industrial workers. When the AFL convention of 1935 refused, the head of the United Mine Workers, John L. Lewis, led a walkout that produced a new labor organization, the Congress of Industrial Organizations (CIO). It set out to create unions in the main bastions of the American economy. It aimed, said Lewis, at nothing less than to secure "economic freedom and industrial democracy" for American workers—a fair share in the wealth produced by their labor, and a voice in determining the conditions under which they worked.

> *John L. Lewis*

In December 1936, unions, most notably the United Auto Workers (UAW), a fledgling CIO union, unveiled the sit-down, a strikingly effective tactic that the IWW had pioneered three decades earlier. Rather than walking out of a plant, thus enabling management to bring in strikebreakers, workers halted production but remained inside. In the UAW's first sit-down strike, 7,000 General Motors workers seized control of the Fisher Body Plant in Cleveland. Sit-downs soon spread to GM plants in Flint, Michigan, the nerve center of automobile production. When local police tried to storm the Flint plants, workers fought them off. Democratic governor Frank Murphy, who had been elected with strong support from the CIO, declared his unwillingness to use force to dislodge the strikers. The strikers demonstrated a remarkable spirit of unity. They cleaned the plant, oiled the idle machinery, settled disputes among themselves, prepared meals, and held concerts of labor songs.

> *The UAW's sit-down strike*

Workers' wives shuttled food into the plant. "They made a palace out of what had been their prison," wrote one reporter. On February 11, General Motors agreed to negotiate with the UAW. Not until 1941 would the bitterly anti-union Henry Ford sign a labor contract. But by the end of 1937, the UAW claimed 400,000 members.

The victory in the auto industry reverberated throughout industrial America. Steelworkers had suffered memorable defeats in the struggle for unionization, notably at Homestead in 1892 and in the Great Steel Strike of 1919. U.S. Steel, the country's single most important business firm, owner of an industrial empire that stretched across several states and employed more than 200,000 workers, had been among the strongest opponents

Sit-down strike at a General Motors factory in Flint, Michigan, 1937.

of unionization. But in March 1937, fearing a sit-down campaign and aware that it could no longer count on the aid of state and federal authorities, the company agreed to recognize the Steel Workers Organizing Committee (forerunner of the United Steelworkers of America). Smaller steel firms, however, refused to follow suit. On Memorial Day, 1937, company guards and Chicago police fired on a picnic of striking Republic Steel workers, killing ten persons. Not until 1942 would Republic sign a labor contract.

Union membership nonetheless reached 9 million by 1940, more than double the number in 1930. The coming of the union, said a member of New York City's transit workers' organization, enabled workers "to go to our bosses and talk to them like men, instead of . . . like slaves." Unions frequently demanded and won a say in workplace management, including the right to contest the amount and pace of work and the introduction of new technology. They gained new grievance procedures and seniority systems governing hiring, firing, and promotions. The CIO unions helped to stabilize a chaotic employment situation and offered members a sense of dignity and freedom.

Labor and Politics

Throughout the industrial heartland, the labor upsurge altered the balance of economic power and propelled to the forefront of politics labor's goal of a fairer, freer, more equal America. Unlike the AFL, traditionally hostile to government intervention in labor-management relations, the CIO put forward an ambitious program for federal action to shield Americans from economic and social insecurity, including public housing, universal health care, and unemployment and old age insurance.

Building on the idea, so prominent in the 1920s, that the key to prosperity lay in an American standard of living based on mass consumption, CIO leaders explained the Depression as the result of an imbalance of wealth and income. The role of unions, in cooperation with the government, they argued, was to "create a consumer's demand" by raising wages and redistributing wealth. Only in this way could society absorb the products that rolled off modern assembly lines. The pathbreaking 1937 agreement between the UAW and General Motors spoke of a "rate of pay commensurate with an American standard of living." By mid-decade, many New Dealers accepted the "underconsumptionist" explanation of the Depression, which saw lack of sufficient consumer demand as its underlying cause. They concluded that the government must act to raise dramatically wage earners' share of the national income.

"An American standard of living"

Voices of Protest

Other popular movements of the mid-1930s also placed the question of economic justice on the political agenda. In California, the novelist Upton Sinclair won the Democratic nomination for governor in 1934 as the head of the End Poverty in California movement. Sinclair called for the state to use idle factories and land in cooperative ventures that would provide jobs for the unemployed. He lost the election after being subjected to one of the first modern "negative" media campaigns. Sinclair's opponents circulated false newsreels showing armies of unemployed men marching to California to support his candidacy and a fake endorsement from the Communist Party.

Huey Long

The rise to national prominence of Huey Long offered another sign of popular dissatisfaction with the slow pace of economic recovery. Long's career embodied both Louisiana's Populist and Socialist traditions (Winn Parish, his home, had voted for both of these third parties) and the state's heritage of undemocratic politics. Driven by intense ambition and the desire to help uplift the state's "common people," Long won election as governor in 1928 and in 1930 took a seat in the U.S. Senate. From Washington, he dominated every branch of state government. He used his dictatorial power to build roads, schools, and hospitals and to increase the tax burden on Louisiana's oil companies.

One of the most colorful characters in twentieth-century American politics, Long was referred to by both admirers and critics as the "Kingfish." In 1934, he launched the Share Our Wealth movement, with the slogan "Every Man a King." He called for the confiscation of most of the wealth of the richest Americans in order to finance an immediate grant of $5,000 and a guaranteed job and annual income for all citizens. In his inimitable style, Long explained his goal: "Let's pull down these huge piles of gold until there shall be a real job, not a little old sow-belly, black-eyed pea job but a real spending money, beefsteak and gravy . . . Ford in the garage . . . red, white, and blue job for every man." Long claimed a following of 5 million. He was on the verge of announcing a run for president when the son of a defeated political rival assassinated him in 1935.

Dr. Francis Townsend, a California physician, meanwhile won wide support for a plan by which the government would make a monthly payment of $200 to older Americans, with the requirement that they spend it immediately. This, he argued, would boost the economy. By the end of 1934, Townsend Clubs claimed more than 2 million members. Along with the rise of the CIO, these signs of popular discontent helped to spark the Second New Deal.

Huey Long, the "Kingfish" of Louisiana politics, in full rhetorical flight. The photo was probably taken in 1934, when Long was in the Senate but still running the state government.

Religion on the Radio

Religious leaders of various denominations took advantage of the mass media to spread their beliefs. Ironically, many fundamentalists used the most modern techniques of communication, including the radio and popular entertainment, to promote their anti-modernist message. They found in the radio a way of bringing their views directly to ordinary Americans, bypassing established churches and their leaders. During the 1920s, Aimee Semple McPherson, a Los Angeles revivalist, had her own radio station, which broadcast sermons from the International Church of the Foursquare Gospel she had founded. McPherson also traveled the country as a revivalist preacher. Her sermons used elaborate sets, costumes, and special effects borrowed from the movie industry. By the 1940s, national religious broadcast networks emerged, with a reliable and dedicated listening audience. In later decades, fundamentalist Christians would take advantage of television and the Internet to disseminate their religious and political views.

Also in the mid-1930s, the "radio priest," Father Charles E. Coughlin, attracted millions of listeners with weekly broadcasts attacking Wall Street bankers and greedy capitalists, and calling for government ownership of key industries as a way of combating the Depression. Initially a strong supporter of FDR, Coughlin became increasingly critical of the president for what he considered the failure of the New Deal to promote social justice. His crusade would later shift to anti-Semitism and support for European fascism.

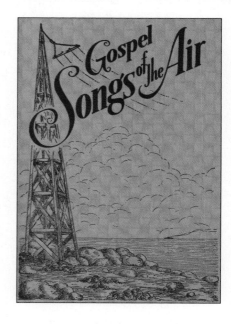

The cover of a songbook to accompany a radio broadcast from the Chicago Gospel Tabernacle. A radio tower dominates the image.

THE SECOND NEW DEAL

In 1935, President Roosevelt sent a message to 100,000 American clergymen asking about economic and social conditions in their communities. The responses indicated that their financially hard-pressed churches could not respond effectively via traditional charity to the massive needs of their congregations. This was one among many illustrations of the critical importance of government intervention in relieving the widespread hardship caused by the Depression.

Spurred by the failure of his initial policies to pull the country out of the Depression and the growing popular clamor for greater economic equality, and buoyed by Democratic gains in the midterm elections of 1934, Roosevelt in 1935 launched the Second New Deal. The first had focused on economic recovery. The emphasis of the second was economic security—a guarantee that Americans would be protected against unemployment and poverty. "Boys," Roosevelt's relief administrator, Harry Hopkins, told his staff, "this is our hour. We've got to get everything we want—a [public] works program, social security, wages and hours, everything—now or never."

Economic security

The idea that lack of consumer demand caused the Depression had been popularized by Huey Long, Francis Townsend, and the CIO. By 1935, more and more New Dealers had concluded that the government should no longer try to plan business recovery but should try to redistribute the national income so as to sustain mass purchasing power in the consumer economy. A series of measures in 1935 attacked head-on the problem of weak demand and economic inequality. Congress

The Rural Electrification Agency

Farm assistance

levied a highly publicized tax on large fortunes and corporate profits—a direct response to the popularity of Huey Long's Share Our Wealth campaign. It created the Rural Electrification Agency (REA) to bring electric power to homes that lacked it—80 percent of farms were still without electricity in 1934—in part to enable more Americans to purchase household appliances.

The REA proved to be one of the Second New Deal's most successful programs. By 1950, 90 percent of the nation's farms had been wired for electricity, and almost all now possessed radios, electric stoves, refrigerators, and mechanical equipment to milk cows. In addition, the federal government under the Second New Deal tried to promote soil conservation and family farming. This effort resulted from the belief that the country would never achieve prosperity so long as farmers' standard of living lagged well behind that of city dwellers, and that rural poverty resulted mainly from the poor use of natural resources. Thus, farmers received federal assistance in reducing soil loss in their fields. The federal government also purchased significant amounts of marginal and eroded land and converted these areas from farms into national grasslands and parks. It encouraged more environmentally conscious agricultural techniques. These measures (like those of the AAA) mainly benefited landowners, not sharecroppers, tenants, or migrant workers. In the long run, the Second New Deal failed to arrest the trend toward larger farms and fewer farmers.

The WPA and the Wagner Act

In 1934, Roosevelt had severely curtailed federal employment for those in need. Now, he approved the establishment of the Works Progress Administration (WPA), which hired some 3 million Americans, in virtually every walk of life, each year until it ended in 1943. Under Harry Hopkins's direction, the WPA changed the physical face of the United States. It constructed thousands of public buildings and bridges, more than 500,000 miles of roads, and 600 airports. It built stadiums, swimming pools, and sewage treatment plants. Unlike previous work relief programs, the WPA employed many out-of-work white-collar workers and professionals, even doctors and dentists.

Perhaps the most famous WPA projects were in the arts. The WPA set hundreds of artists to work decorating public buildings with murals. It hired writers to produce local histories and guidebooks to the forty-eight states and to record the recollections of ordinary Americans, including hundreds of former slaves. Its Federal Theater Project put on plays, including an all-black production of *Macbeth* and Sinclair Lewis's drama *It Can't Happen Here*, about fascism coming to the United States. The Federal Music Project established orchestras and choral groups, and the Federal Dance Project sponsored ballet and modern dance programs. Thanks to the WPA, audiences across the country enjoyed their first glimpse of live musical and theatrical performances and their first opportunity to view exhibitions of American art. Also in 1935, Congress created the National Youth Administration to provide relief to American teenagers and young adults.

Another major initiative of the Second New Deal, the Wagner Act, was known at the time as "Labor's Magna Carta" (a reference to an early landmark in the history of freedom). This brought democracy into the American workplace by empowering the National Labor Relations Board to supervise elections in which employees voted on union representation. It also outlawed "unfair labor practices,"

A poster by the artist Vera Bock for the Federal Art Project of the Works Progress Administration depicts farmers and laborers joining hands to produce prosperity.

An art exhibit in a New York City alley in 1938. The Works Progress Administration tried to broaden the audience for art by displaying it in unusual venues.

including the firing and blacklisting of union organizers. The bill's main sponsor, Robert Wagner of New York, told the Senate that the ability of workers to pool their strength through collective bargaining represented the "next step" in "the evolution of American freedom." He also promised that unionization and higher wages would aid economic recovery by boosting the purchasing power of ordinary Americans.

The American Welfare State

The centerpiece of the Second New Deal was the Social Security Act of 1935. It embodied Roosevelt's conviction that the national government had a responsibility to ensure the material well-being of ordinary Americans. It created a system of unemployment insurance, old age pensions, and aid to the disabled, the elderly poor, and families with dependent children.

The Social Security Act

None of these were original ideas. The Progressive platform of 1912 had called for old age pensions. Assistance to poor families with dependent children descended from the mothers' pensions promoted by maternalist reformers. Many European countries had already adopted national unemployment insurance plans. What was new, however, was that in the name of economic security, the American government would now supervise not simply temporary relief but a permanent system of social insurance.

The Social Security Act launched the American version of the welfare state—a term that originated in Britain during World War II to refer to a system of income assistance, health coverage, and social services for all citizens. The act illustrated both the extent and the limits of the changes ushered in by the Second New Deal. The American welfare state marked a radical departure from previous government policies, but compared with similar programs in Europe, it has always been far more decentralized, involved lower levels of public spending, and covered fewer

A 1935 poster promoting the new Social Security system.

Role of government

citizens. The original Social Security bill, for example, envisioned a national system of health insurance. But Congress dropped this after ferocious opposition from the American Medical Association, which feared government regulation of doctors' activities and incomes.

The Social Security System

Some New Dealers desired a program funded by the federal government's general tax revenues, and with a single set of eligibility standards administered by national officials. But Secretary of Labor Frances Perkins, along with powerful members of Congress, wished to keep relief in the hands of state and local authorities and believed that workers should contribute directly to the cost of their own benefits. Roosevelt himself preferred to fund Social Security by taxes on employers and workers, rather than out of general government revenues. He wanted to ensure that Social Security did not add to the federal deficit and believed that paying such taxes gave contributors "a legal, moral, and political right" to collect their old age pensions and unemployment benefits, which no future Congress could rescind.

As a result, Social Security emerged as a hybrid of national and local funding, control, and eligibility standards. Old age pensions were administered nationally but paid for by taxes on employers and employees. Such taxes also paid for payments to the unemployed, but this program was highly decentralized, with the states retaining considerable control over the level of benefits. The states paid most of the cost of direct poor relief, under the program called Aid to Dependent Children, and eligibility and the level of payments varied enormously from place to place. As will be discussed later, the combination of local administration and the fact that domestic and agricultural workers were not covered by unemployment and old age benefits meant that Social Security at first excluded large numbers of Americans, especially unmarried women and non-whites.

Nonetheless, Social Security represented a dramatic departure from the traditional functions of government. The Second New Deal transformed the relationship between the federal government and American citizens. Before the 1930s, national political debate often revolved around the question of *whether* the federal government should intervene in the economy. After the New Deal, debate rested on *how* it should intervene. In addition, the government assumed a responsibility, which it has never wholly relinquished, for guaranteeing Americans a living wage and protecting them against economic and personal misfortune. "Laissez-faire is dead," wrote Walter Lippmann, "and the modern state has become responsible for the modern economy [and] the task of insuring . . . the standard of life for its people."

A RECKONING WITH LIBERTY

The Depression made inevitable, in the words of one writer, a "reckoning with liberty." For too many Americans, Roosevelt proclaimed, "life was no longer free; liberty no longer real; men could no longer follow the pursuit of happiness." The 1930s produced an outpouring of books and essays on freedom. The large majority took for granted the need for a new definition. In a volume entitled *Land of the Free* (1938), the poet Archibald MacLeish used photographs of impoverished migrants and sharecroppers to question the reality of freedom in desperate times. "We told ourselves we were free," he wrote. Now, "we wonder if the liberty is done . . . or if there's something different men can mean by Liberty."

Like the Civil War, the New Deal recast the idea of freedom by linking it to the expanding power of the national state. "Our democracy," wrote Father John A. Ryan, a prominent Catholic social critic, "finds itself . . . in a new age where not political freedom but social and industrial freedom is the most insistent cry." Influenced by Ryan, the National Catholic Welfare Conference in 1935 declared that "social justice" required a government guarantee of continuous employment and a "decent livelihood and adequate security" for all Americans. A 1935 survey by *Fortune* magazine found that among poor respondents, 90 percent believed that the government should guarantee that "every man who wants work has a job."

FDR delivering one of his "fireside chats" in 1938. Roosevelt was the first president to make effective use of the radio to promote his policies.

FDR and the Idea of Freedom

Along with being a superb politician, Roosevelt was a master of political communication. At a time when his political opponents controlled most newspapers, he harnessed radio's power to bring his message directly into American homes. By the mid-1930s, more than two-thirds of American families owned radios. They listened avidly to Roosevelt's radio addresses, known as "fireside chats."

Roosevelt adeptly appealed to traditional values in support of new policies. He gave the term "liberalism" its modern meaning. In the nineteenth century, liberalism had been a shorthand for limited government and free-market economics. Roosevelt consciously chose to employ it to describe a large, active, socially conscious state. He reclaimed the word "freedom" from conservatives and made it a rallying cry for the New Deal. In his second fireside chat, Roosevelt juxtaposed his own definition of liberty as "greater security for the average man" to the older notion of liberty of contract, which served the interests of "the privileged few." Henceforth, he would consistently link freedom with economic security and identify entrenched economic inequality as its greatest enemy. "The liberty of a democracy," he declared in 1938, was not safe if citizens could not "sustain an acceptable standard of living."

Freedom and economic security

Even as Roosevelt invoked the word to uphold the New Deal, "liberty"—in the sense of freedom from powerful government—became the fighting slogan of his opponents. Their principal critique of the New Deal was that its "reckless spending" undermined fiscal responsibility and its new government regulations restricted American freedom. When conservative businessmen and politicians in 1934 formed an organization to mobilize opposition to Roosevelt's policies, they called it the American Liberty League. Robert Taft of Ohio, leader of the Republicans in Congress, accused Roosevelt of sacrificing "individual freedom" in a misguided effort to "improve the conditions of the poor."

Opposition to the New Deal

As the 1930s progressed, opponents of the New Deal invoked the language of liberty with greater and greater passion. The U.S. Chamber of Commerce charged FDR with attempting to "Sovietize" America. Even though his own administration had abandoned laissez-faire in the face of economic disaster,

VOICES OF FREEDOM

From FRANKLIN D. ROOSEVELT, "FIRESIDE CHAT" (1934)

President Roosevelt pioneered the use of the new mass medium of radio to speak directly to Americans in their homes. He used his "fireside chats" to mobilize support for New Deal programs, link them with American traditions, and outline his definition of freedom.

To those who say that our expenditures for public works and other means for recovery are a waste that we cannot afford, I answer that no country, however rich, can afford the waste of its human resources. Demoralization caused by vast unemployment is our greatest extravagance. Morally, it is the greatest menace to our social order. Some people try to tell me that we must make up our minds that in the future we shall permanently have millions of unemployed just as other countries have had them for over a decade. What may be necessary for those countries is not my responsibility to determine. But as for this country, I stand or fall by my refusal to accept as a necessary condition of our future a permanent army of unemployed. . . .

In our efforts for recovery we have avoided, on the one hand, the theory that business should and must be taken over into an all-embracing Government. We have avoided, on the other hand, the equally untenable theory that it is an interference with liberty to offer reasonable help when private enterprise is in need of help. The course we have followed fits the American practice of Government, a practice of taking action step by step, of regulating only to meet concrete needs, a practice of courageous recognition of change. I believe with Abraham Lincoln, that "the legitimate object of Government is to do for a community of people whatever they need to have done but cannot do at all or cannot do so well for themselves in their separate and individual capacities."

I am not for a return to that definition of liberty under which for many years a free people were being gradually regimented into the service of the privileged few. I prefer and I am sure you prefer that broader definition of liberty under which we are moving forward to greater freedom, to greater security for the average man than he has ever known before in the history of America.

From JOHN STEINBECK, *THE HARVEST GYPSIES: ON THE ROAD TO THE GRAPES OF WRATH* (1938)

John Steinbeck's popular novel *The Grapes of Wrath* (1939), and the film version that followed shortly thereafter, focused national attention on the plight of homeless migrants displaced from their farms as a result of the Great Depression. Before that book appeared, Steinbeck had published a series of newspaper articles based on eyewitness accounts of the migrants, which became the basis for his novel.

In California, we find a curious attitude toward a group that makes our agriculture successful. The migrants are needed, and they are hated. . . . The migrants are hated for the following reasons, that they are ignorant and dirty people, that they are carriers of disease, that they increase the necessity for police and the tax bill for schooling in a community, and that if they are allowed to organize they can, simply by refusing to work, wipe out the season's crops. . . .

Let us see what kind of people they are, where they come from, and the routes of their wanderings. In the past they have been of several races, encouraged to come and often imported as cheap labor. Chinese in the early period, then Filipinos, Japanese and Mexicans. These were foreigners, and as such they were ostracized and segregated and herded about. . . . But in recent years the foreign migrants have begun to organize, and at this danger they have been deported in great numbers, for there was a new reservoir from which a great quantity of cheap labor could be obtained.

The drought in the middle west has driven the agricultural populations of Oklahoma, Nebraska and parts of Kansas and Texas westward. . . . Thousands of them are crossing the borders in ancient rattling automobiles, destitute and hungry and homeless, ready to accept any pay so that they may eat and feed their children. . . .

The earlier foreign migrants have invariably been drawn from a peon class. This is not the case with the new migrants. They are small farmers who have lost their farms, or farm hands who have lived with the family in the old American way. . . . They have come from the little farm districts where democracy was not only possible but inevitable, where popular government, whether practiced in the Grange, in church organization or in local government, was the responsibility of every man. And they have come into the country where, because of the movement necessary to make a living, they are not allowed any vote whatever, but are rather considered a properly unprivileged class. . . .

As one little boy in a squatter's camp said, "When they need us they call us migrants, and when we've picked their crop, we're bums and we got to get out."

QUESTIONS

1. *What does Roosevelt mean by the difference between the definition of liberty that has existed in the past and his own "broader definition of liberty"?*

2. *According to Steinbeck, how do Depression-era migrant workers differ from those in earlier periods?*

3. *Do the migrant workers described by Steinbeck enjoy liberty as Roosevelt understands it?*

This 1935 cartoon by William Gropper portrays Uncle Sam as Gulliver tied down by Lilliputians in the famous eighteenth-century novel *Gulliver's Travels* by Jonathan Swift. In this case, the bonds are the numerous agencies and laws created by the New Deal, which, Gropper suggests, are inhibiting the country from getting back on its feet during the Great Depression.

former president Hoover launched strident attacks on his successor for endangering "fundamental American liberties." In *The Challenge to Liberty* (1934), Hoover called the New Deal "the most stupendous invasion of the whole spirit of liberty" the nation had ever seen.

The Election of 1936

Politics and class divisions

By 1936, with working-class voters providing massive majorities for the Democratic Party and businesses large and small bitterly estranged from the New Deal, politics reflected class divisions more completely than at any other time in American history. Conceptions of freedom divided sharply as well. Americans, wrote George Soule, editor of *The New Republic*, confronted "two opposing systems of concepts about liberty," reflecting "the needs and purposes of two opposing [parts] of the population." One was the idea of "freedom for private enterprise," the other "socialized liberty" based on "an equitably shared abundance."

A fight for the possession of "the ideal of freedom," reported the *New York Times*, emerged as the central issue of the presidential campaign of 1936. The Democratic platform insisted that in a modern economy the government has an obligation to establish a "democracy of opportunity for all the people." In his speech accepting renomination, Roosevelt launched a blistering attack against "economic royalists" who, he charged, sought to establish a new tyranny over the "average man." Economic rights, he went on, were the precondition of liberty—poor men "are not free men." Throughout the campaign, FDR would insist that the threat posed to economic freedom by the "new despotism" of large corporations was the main issue of the election.

As Roosevelt's opponent, Republicans chose Kansas governor Alfred Landon, a former Theodore Roosevelt Progressive. Landon denounced Social Security and other measures as threats to individual liberty. Opposition to the New Deal planted the seeds for the later flowering of an antigovernment conservatism bent on upholding the free market and dismantling the welfare state. But in 1936 Roosevelt won a landslide reelection, with more than 60 percent of the popular vote. He carried every state except Maine and Vermont. Roosevelt's victory was all the more remarkable in view of the heavy support most of the nation's newspapers and nearly the entire business community gave to the Republicans. His success stemmed from strong backing from organized labor and his ability to unite southern white and northern black voters, Protestant farmers and urban Catholic and Jewish ethnics, industrial workers and middle-class home owners. These groups made up the so-called New Deal coalition, which would dominate American politics for nearly half a century.

Fall In!, a cartoon commenting on Roosevelt's proposal to "pack" the Supreme Court, from the *Richmond Times-Dispatch*, January 8, 1937.

The Court Fight

Roosevelt's second inaugural address was the first to be delivered on January 20. In order to lessen a newly elected president's wait before taking office, the recently ratified Twentieth Amendment had moved inauguration day from March 4. FDR called on the nation to redouble its efforts to aid those "who have too little." The Depression, he admitted, had not been conquered: "I see one-third of a nation ill-housed, ill-clad, and ill-nourished." Emboldened by his electoral triumph, Roosevelt now made what many considered a serious political miscalculation. On the pretense that several members of the Supreme Court were too old to perform their functions, he proposed that the president be allowed to appoint a new justice for each one who remained on the Court past age seventy (an age that six of the nine had already surpassed). FDR's aim, of course, was to change the balance of power on a Court that, he feared, might well invalidate Social Security, the Wagner Act, and other measures of the Second New Deal.

"Court packing" plan

The plan aroused cries that the president was an aspiring dictator. Congress rejected it. But Roosevelt accomplished his underlying purpose. The Supreme Court, it is sometimes said, follows the election returns. Coming soon after Roosevelt's landslide victory of 1936, the threat of "Court packing" inspired an astonishing about-face on the part of key justices. Beginning in March 1937, the Court suddenly revealed a new willingness to support economic regulation by both the federal government and the states. It upheld a minimum wage law of the state of Washington similar to the New York measure it had declared unconstitutional a year earlier. It turned aside challenges to Social Security and the Wagner Act. In subsequent cases, the Court affirmed federal power to regulate wages, hours, child labor, agricultural production, and numerous other aspects of economic life.

The about-face for the Court

Announcing a new judicial definition of freedom, Chief Justice Charles Evans Hughes pointed out that the words "freedom of contract" did not appear in the Constitution. "Liberty," however, did, and this, Hughes continued, required "the protection of law against the evils which menace the health, safety, morals, and

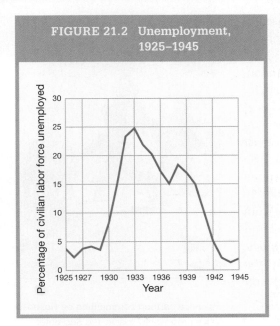

FIGURE 21.2 Unemployment, 1925–1945

The New Deal did not really solve the problem of unemployment, which fell below 10 percent only in 1941, as the United States prepared to enter World War II.

Keynesian economics

welfare of the people." The Court's new willingness to accept the New Deal marked a permanent change in judicial policy. Having declared dozens of economic laws unconstitutional in the decades leading up to 1937, the justices have rarely done so since.

The End of the Second New Deal

Even as the Court made its peace with Roosevelt's policies, the momentum of the Second New Deal slowed. The landmark United States Housing Act did pass in 1937, initiating the first major national effort to build homes for the poorest Americans. But the Fair Labor Standards bill failed to reach the floor for over a year. When it finally passed in 1938, it banned goods produced by child labor from interstate commerce, set forty cents as the minimum hourly wage, and required overtime pay for hours of work exceeding forty per week. This last major piece of New Deal legislation established the practice of federal regulation of wages and working conditions, another radical departure from pre-Depression policies.

The year 1937 also witnessed a sharp downturn of the economy. With economic conditions improving in 1936, Roosevelt had reduced federal funding for farm subsidies and WPA work relief. The result was disastrous. As government spending fell, so did business investment, industrial production, and the stock market. Unemployment, still 14 percent at the beginning of 1937, rose to nearly 20 percent by year's end.

In 1936, in *The General Theory of Employment, Interest, and Money*, John Maynard Keynes had challenged economists' traditional belief in the sanctity of balanced budgets. Large-scale government spending, he insisted, was necessary to sustain purchasing power and stimulate economic activity during downturns. Such spending should be enacted even at the cost of a budget deficit (a situation in which the government spends more money than it takes in). By 1938, Roosevelt was ready to follow this prescription, which would later be known as Keynesian economics. In April, he asked Congress for billions more for work relief and farm aid. By the end of the year, the immediate crisis had passed. But the events of 1937–1938 marked a major shift in New Deal philosophy. Rather than economic planning, as in 1933–1934, or economic redistribution, as in 1935–1936, public spending would now be the government's major tool for combating unemployment and stimulating economic growth. The Second New Deal had come to an end.

THE LIMITS OF CHANGE

Roosevelt conceived of the Second New Deal, and especially Social Security, as expanding the meaning of freedom by extending assistance to broad groups of needy Americans—the unemployed, elderly, and dependent—as a right of citizenship, not charity or special privilege. But political realities, especially the power of inherited ideas about gender and black disenfranchisement in the South, powerfully affected the drafting of legislation. New Deal programs were justified

Eleanor Roosevelt transformed the role of First Lady by taking an active and visible part in public life. Here she visits a West Virginia coal mine in 1933.

as ways of bringing economic security to "the people" rather than to specific disadvantaged groups. But different Americans experienced the New Deal in radically different ways.

The New Deal and American Women

The New Deal brought more women into government than ever before in American history. A number of talented women, including Secretary of Labor Frances Perkins, advised the president and shaped public policy. Most prominent of all was Eleanor Roosevelt, FDR's distant cousin whom he had married in 1905. She transformed the role of First Lady, turning a position with no formal responsibilities into a base for political action. She traveled widely, spoke out on public issues, wrote a regular newspaper column that sometimes disagreed openly with her husband's policies, and worked to enlarge the scope of the New Deal in areas like civil rights, labor legislation, and work relief.

Eleanor Roosevelt

But even as the New Deal increased women's visibility in national politics, organized feminism, already in disarray during the 1920s, disappeared as a political force. Indeed, the Depression inspired widespread demands for women to remove themselves from the labor market to make room for unemployed men. Because the Depression hit industrial employment harder than low-wage clerical and service jobs where women predominated, the proportion of the workforce made up of women rose. The government tried to reverse this trend. The Economy Act of 1933 prohibited both members of a married couple from holding federal jobs. Until its repeal in 1937, it led to the dismissal of numerous female civil

The disappearance of organized feminism

service employees whose husbands worked for the government. Many states and localities prohibited the hiring of women whose husbands earned a "living wage," and employers from banks to public school systems barred married women from jobs. Although the CIO organized female workers, it, too, adhered to the idea that women should be supported by men. "The working wife whose husband is employed," said a vice president of the United Auto Workers, "should be barred from industry."

Most New Deal programs did not exclude women from benefits (although the CCC restricted its camps to men). But the ideal of the male-headed household powerfully shaped social policy. Since paying taxes on one's wages made one eligible for the most generous Social Security programs—old age pensions and unemployment insurance—they left most women uncovered, since they did not work outside the home. The program excluded the 3 million mostly female domestic workers altogether. "Those who need protection most are completely overlooked," the sister of a household worker complained to Secretary of Labor Perkins. "What about the poor domestics, both in private homes and private institutions. What have you done for them? Nothing."

Women and Social Security

The Southern Veto

Roosevelt made the federal government the symbolic representative of all the people, including racial and ethnic groups generally ignored by previous administrations. Yet the power of the Solid South helped to mold the New Deal welfare state into an entitlement of white Americans. After the South's blacks lost the right to vote around the turn of the century, Democrats enjoyed a political monopoly in the region. Democratic members of Congress were elected again and again. With results predetermined, many whites did not bother to vote (only about 20 percent of eligible southern voters cast ballots in the election of 1920). But this tiny electorate had an enormous impact on national policy. Committee chairmanships in Congress rest on seniority—how many years a member has served in office. Beginning in 1933, when Democrats took control of Congress, southerners took the key leadership positions. Despite his personal popularity, Roosevelt felt he could not challenge the power of southern Democrats if he wished legislation to pass. At their insistence, the Social Security law excluded agricultural and domestic workers, the largest categories of black employment.

The Solid South and the New Deal

Roosevelt spoke of Social Security's universality, but the demand for truly comprehensive coverage came from the political left and black organizations. Congressman Ernest Lundeen of Minnesota in 1935 introduced a bill establishing a federally controlled system of old age, unemployment, and health benefits for all wage workers, plus support for female heads of households with dependents. Black organizations like the Urban League and the NAACP supported the Lundeen bill and lobbied strenuously for a system that enabled agricultural and domestic workers to receive unemployment and old age benefits and that established national relief standards. The Social Security Act, however, not Lundeen's proposal, became law. Its limitations, complained the *Pittsburgh Courier*, a black newspaper, reflected the power of "reactionary elements in the South who cannot bear the thought of

Blacks and Social Security

Negroes getting pensions and compensations" and who feared that the inclusion of black workers would disrupt the region's low-wage, racially divided labor system.

The Stigma of Welfare

Because of the "southern veto," the majority of black workers found themselves confined to the least generous and most vulnerable wing of the new welfare state. The public assistance programs established by Social Security, notably aid to dependent children and to the poor elderly, were open to all Americans who could demonstrate financial need. But they set benefits at extremely low levels and authorized the states to determine eligibility standards, including "moral" behavior as defined by local authorities. As a result, public assistance programs allowed for widespread discrimination in the distribution of benefits. Because recipients did not pay Social Security taxes, they soon came to bear the humiliating stigma of dependency on government handouts, which would soon come to be known as "welfare."

Public assistance

In 1942, the National Resources Planning Board noted that because of their exclusion from programs "which give aid under relatively favorable conditions," blacks were becoming disproportionately dependent on welfare, a program widely viewed with popular disfavor. The situation, the report concluded, seemed certain to stigmatize blacks as recipients of unearned government assistance, and welfare as a program for minorities, thus dooming it forever to inadequate "standards of aid." Over time, this is precisely what happened, until the federal government abolished its responsibility for welfare in 1996, during the presidency of Bill Clinton.

The Indian New Deal

Overall, the Depression and New Deal had a contradictory impact on America's racial minorities. Under Commissioner of Indian Affairs John Collier, the administration launched an "Indian New Deal." Collier ended the policy of forced assimilation and allowed Indians unprecedented cultural autonomy. He replaced boarding schools meant to eradicate the tribal heritage of Indian children with schools on reservations, and dramatically increased spending on Indian health. He secured passage of the Indian Reorganization Act of 1934, ending the policy, dating back to the Dawes Act of 1887, of dividing Indian lands into small plots for individual families and selling off the rest. Federal authorities once again recognized Indians' right to govern their own affairs, except where specifically limited by national laws. Such limitations, however, could weigh heavily on Indian tribes. The Navajos, the nation's largest tribe, refused to cooperate with the Reorganization Act as a protest against a federal soil conservation program that required them to reduce their herds of livestock.

Changes in Indian policy

The New Deal marked the most radical shift in Indian policy in the nation's history. But living conditions on the desperately poor reservations did not significantly improve, and New Deal programs often ignored Indians' interests. The building of the Grand Coulee Dam on the Columbia River flooded

A large crowd of Mexican-Americans waiting to leave Los Angeles in 1932 as part of the repatriation campaign.

thousands of acres where Indians had hunted and fished for centuries. But the government did not make any of the irrigation water available to the region's reservations.

The New Deal and Mexican-Americans

For Mexican-Americans, the Depression was a wrenching experience. With demand for their labor plummeting, more than 400,000 (one-fifth of the population of Mexican origin) returned to Mexico, some voluntarily, others at the strong urging of local authorities in the Southwest. A majority of those "encouraged" to leave the country were recent immigrants, but they included perhaps 200,000 Mexican-American children who had been born in the United States and were therefore citizens. Those who remained mostly worked in grim conditions in California's vegetable and fruit fields, whose corporate farms benefited enormously from New Deal dam construction that provided them with cheap electricity and water for irrigation. The Wagner and Social Security Acts did not apply to agricultural laborers. When the workers tried to organize a union as part of the decade's labor upsurge, they were brutally suppressed. In his 1939 book *Factories in the Field*, the writer Carey McWilliams exposed the low wages, inadequate housing, and political repression under which the migrant laborers suffered, which the New Deal did nothing to alleviate.

Mexican-American leaders struggled to develop a consistent strategy for their people. They sought greater rights by claiming to be white Americans—in order to not suffer the same discrimination as African-Americans—but also sought the

Repatriation of Mexican-Americans

backing of the Mexican government and promoted a mystical sense of pride and identification with Mexican heritage later given the name *la raza*.

Last Hired, First Fired

As the "last hired and first fired," African-Americans were hit hardest by the Depression. Even those who retained their jobs now faced competition from unemployed whites who had previously considered positions like waiter and porter beneath them. With an unemployment rate double that of whites, blacks benefited disproportionately from direct government relief and, especially in northern cities, jobs on New Deal public-works projects. Half of the families in Harlem received public assistance during the 1930s.

> *Unemployment for blacks*

The Depression propelled economic survival to the top of the black agenda. Demonstrations in Harlem demanded jobs in the neighborhood's white-owned stores, with the slogan "Don't Buy Where You Can't Work." W. E. B. Du Bois abandoned his earlier goal of racial integration as unrealistic for the foreseeable future. Blacks, he wrote, must recognize themselves as "a nation within a nation." He called on blacks to organize for economic survival by building an independent, cooperative economy within their segregated communities, and to gain control of their own separate schools (a position reminiscent of that of Booker T. Washington, whom he had earlier condemned).

A New Deal for Blacks

Although Roosevelt seems to have had little personal interest in race relations or civil rights, he appointed Mary McLeod Bethune, a prominent black educator, as a special adviser on minority affairs and a number of other blacks to important federal positions. Key members of his administration, including his wife, Eleanor, and Secretary of the Interior Harold Ickes, a former president of the Chicago chapter of the NAACP, directed national attention to the injustices of segregation, disenfranchisement, and lynching. In 1939, Eleanor Roosevelt resigned from the Daughters of the American Revolution when the organization refused to allow the black singer Marian Anderson to present a concert at Constitution Hall in Washington. The president's wife arranged for Anderson to sing on the steps of the Lincoln Memorial and for the concert to be broadcast nationally on the radio.

Thanks to the New Deal, Bethune proclaimed, a "new day" had dawned when blacks would finally reach "the promised land of liberty." The decade witnessed a historic shift in black voting patterns. In

Future congressman Adam Clayton Powell, Jr., (at center with billboard) taking part in a "Don't Buy Where You Can't Work" demonstration in Harlem during the Depression. The campaign targeted stores that served black customers but refused to hire black employees. Photograph © Morgan and Marvin Smith.

A map of Philadelphia prepared by the Home Owners' Loan Corporation illustrates how federal agencies engaged in "red-lining" of neighborhoods containing blue collar and black residents. The colors correspond to the agency's perception of an area's real-estate prospects. Wealthy neighborhoods, colored green and given the best credit ratings, were expected to be racially and ethnically homogenous. White-collar districts, in blue, were second best. Red districts, the worst, had an "undesirable population." The corporation prepared maps like this for many cities and shared them with private lenders and the Federal Housing Administration, resulting in massive disinvestment in "red" districts.

the North and West, where they enjoyed the right to vote, blacks in 1934 and 1936 abandoned their allegiance to the party of Lincoln and emancipation in favor of Democrats and the New Deal. But their hopes for broad changes in the nation's race system were disappointed. Despite a massive lobbying campaign, southern congressmen prevented passage of a federal antilynching law. FDR offered little support. "I did not choose the tools with which I must work," he told Walter White of the NAACP; he could not jeopardize his economic programs by alienating powerful members of Congress. The CCC established segregated work camps. Because of the exclusion of agricultural and domestic workers, Social Security's old age pensions and unemployment benefits and the minimum wages established by the Fair Labor Standards Act left uncovered 60 percent of all employed blacks and 85 percent of black women.

Federal Discrimination

Federal housing policy, which powerfully reinforced residential segregation, revealed the limits of New Deal freedom. As in the case of Social Security, local officials put national housing policy into practice in a way that reinforced existing racial boundaries. Nearly all municipalities, North as well as South, insisted that housing built or financially aided by the federal government be racially segregated. (In Texas, some communities financed three sets of housing projects—for whites, blacks, and Mexicans.) The Federal Housing Administration, moreover, had no hesitation about insuring mortgages that contained clauses barring future sales to non-white buyers, and it refused to channel money into integrated neighborhoods. In some cases, the presence of a single black family led the agency to declare an entire block off-limits for federal mortgage insurance. Along with discriminatory practices by private banks and real-estate companies, federal policy became a major factor in further entrenching housing segregation in the United States.

Federal employment practices also discriminated on the basis of race. As late as 1940, of the 150,000 blacks holding federal jobs, only 2 percent occupied positions other than clerk or custodian. In the South, many New Deal construction projects refused to hire blacks at all. "They give all the work to white people and give us nothing," a black resident of Mississippi wrote to FDR in 1935. The New Deal began the process of modernizing southern agriculture, but tenants, black and white, footed much of the bill. Tens of thousands of sharecroppers, as noted earlier, were driven off the land as a result of the AAA policy of raising crop prices by paying landowners to reduce cotton acreage.

Support for civil rights would eventually become a test of liberal credentials. But in the 1930s, one could advocate Roosevelt's economic program and oppose antilynching legislation and moves to incorporate black workers within Social Security. Theodore Bilbo, the notoriously racist senator from Mississippi, was one of the New Deal's most loyal backers. Not until the Great Society of the 1960s would those left out of Social Security and other New Deal programs—racial minorities, many women, migrants and other less privileged workers—win inclusion in the American welfare state.

Nonetheless, in a society in which virtually all institutions, public and private, created and reinforced patterns of discrimination, the New Deal helped to create an atmosphere that made possible challenges to the racial and ethnic status quo and the rise of a new, more inclusive vision of American freedom.

A NEW CONCEPTION OF AMERICA

If the New Deal failed to dismantle the barriers that barred non-whites from full participation in American life, the 1930s witnessed the absorption of other groups into the social mainstream. With Catholics and Jews occupying prominent posts in the Roosevelt administration and new immigrant voters forming an important part of its electoral support, the New Deal made ethnic pluralism a living reality in American politics. One of Roosevelt's first acts on taking office had been to sign the Beer and Wine Revenue Act, an anticipation of the constitutional amendment repealing prohibition. While promoted as a way to revive employment in the liquor industry and boost tax revenues, it also represented a repudiation of the linkage of politics and Protestant morality. The election of the Italian-American Fiorello La Guardia as mayor of New York City in 1933 symbolized the coming to power of the new immigrants. Although elected as a Republican, La Guardia worked closely with FDR and launched his own program of spending on housing, parks, and public works. La Guardia's was one of numerous "little New Deals" that brought ethnic working-class voters to power in communities throughout the industrial heartland.

New immigrants and the mainstream

Thanks to the virtual cutoff of southern and eastern European immigration in 1924, the increasing penetration of movies, chain stores, and mass advertising into ethnic communities, and the common experience of economic crisis, the 1930s witnessed an acceleration of cultural assimilation. But the process had a different content from the corporate-sponsored Americanization plans of the preceding years. For the children of the new immigrants, labor and political activism became agents of a new kind of Americanization. One could participate fully in the broader society without surrendering one's ideals and ethnic identity. "Unionism is Americanism" became a CIO rallying cry. "The Mesabi Range," a Minnesota miner wrote to Secretary of Labor Perkins, complaining of low wages and management hostility to unions in the iron-rich region, "isn't Americanized yet."

The Heyday of American Communism

In the mid-1930s, for the first time in American history, the left—an umbrella term for socialists, communists, labor radicals, and many New Deal liberals—enjoyed

The left

A card issued by the Communist Party during the 1936 campaign illustrates the party's attempt at "Americanization" (note the images of the American Revolution and Abraham Lincoln), as well as its emphasis on interracialism. James Ford, an African-American, was the party's vice-presidential candidate.

a shaping influence on the nation's politics and culture. The CIO and Communist Party became focal points for a broad social and intellectual impulse that helped to redraw the boundaries of American freedom. An obscure, faction-ridden organization when the Depression began, the Communist Party experienced remarkable growth during the 1930s. The party's membership never exceeded 100,000, but several times that number passed through its ranks.

The party's commitment to socialism resonated with a widespread belief that the Depression had demonstrated the bankruptcy of capitalism. But it was not so much the party's ideology as its vitality—its involvement in a mind-boggling array of activities, including demonstrations of the unemployed, struggles for industrial unionism, and a renewed movement for black civil rights—that for a time made it the center of gravity for a broad democratic upsurge. At the height of the Popular Front—a period during the mid-1930s when the Communist Party sought to ally itself with socialists and New Dealers in movements for social change, urging reform of the capitalist system rather than revolution—Communists gained an unprecedented respectability. Earl Browder, the party's leader, even appeared on the cover of *Time* magazine. It is one of the era's ironies that an organization with an undemocratic structure and closely tied to Stalin's dictatorial regime in Russia should have contributed to the expansion of freedom in the United States. But the Communist Party helped to imbue New Deal liberalism with a militant spirit and a more pluralistic understanding of Americanism.

Redefining the People

In theater, film, and dance, the Popular Front vision of American society sank deep roots and survived much longer than the political moment from which it sprang. In this broad left-wing culture, social and economic radicalism, not support for the status quo, defined true Americanism, ethnic and racial diversity was the glory of American society, and the "American way of life" meant unionism and social

History of Southern Illinois, a mural sponsored by the Illinois Federal Art Project, illustrates the widespread fascination during the 1930s with American traditions and the lives of ordinary Americans. On the left, a man strums a guitar, while workers labor on the waterfront.

A Dorothea Lange photograph of a sharecropper and his family outside their modest home.

citizenship, not the unbridled pursuit of wealth. The American "people," viewed by many intellectuals in the 1920s as representing mean-spirited fundamentalism and crass commercialism, were suddenly rediscovered as embodiments of democratic virtue.

The "common man," Roosevelt proclaimed, embodied "the heart and soul of our country." During the 1930s, artists and writers who strove to create socially meaningful works eagerly took up the task of depicting the daily lives of ordinary farmers and city dwellers. Art about the people—such as Dorothea Lange's photographs of migrant workers and sharecroppers—and art created by the people—such as black spirituals—came to be seen as expressions of genuine Americanism. The Federal Music Project dispatched collectors with tape recorders to help preserve American folk music. Films celebrated populist figures who challenged and defeated corrupt businessmen and politicians, as in *Mr. Deeds Goes to Town* (1936) and *Mr. Smith Goes to Washington* (1939). New immigrants, especially Jews and Italians, played a prominent role in producing and directing Hollywood films of the 1930s. Their movies, however, glorified not urban ethnic communities but ordinary small-town middle-class Americans.

Promoting Diversity

"A new conception of America is necessary," wrote the immigrant labor radical Louis Adamic in 1938. Despite bringing ethnic and northern black voters into its political coalition, the Democratic Party said little about ethno-cultural issues, fearful of rekindling the divisive battles of the 1920s. But the Popular Front forthrightly sought to promote the idea that the country's strength lay in diversity, tolerance, and the rejection of ethnic prejudice and

A scene from the Emancipation episode of Martha Graham's *American Document*, photographed by Barbara Morgan. The dancers are Martha Graham and Erick Hawkins. Photograph © Barbara Morgan, Barbara Morgan Archive.

class privilege. The CIO avidly promoted the idea of ethnic and racial inclusiveness. It broke decisively with the AFL's tradition of exclusionary unionism. The CIO embraced cultural pluralism—an idea, as noted in Chapter 20, previously associated with intellectuals like Horace Kallen and the self-defense of ethnic and Catholic communities against enforced Americanization. "We are the only Americans who take them into our organization as equals," wrote labor organizer Rose Pesotta, referring to the Mexican-Americans who flocked to the Cannery and Agricultural Workers union.

Popular Front culture presented a heroic but not uncritical picture of the country's past. Martha Graham's modern dance masterpiece *American Document* (1938), an embodiment of Popular Front aesthetics with its emphasis on America's folk traditions and multi-ethnic heritage, centered its account of history on the Declaration of Independence and the Gettysburg Address. Yet Graham did not neglect what her narrator called "things we are ashamed of," including the dispossession of the Indians and the plight of the unemployed. Graham's answer to Hector St. John de Crèvecoeur's old question, "What, then, is the American, this new man?" was that Americans were not only middle-class Anglo-Saxons but also blacks, immigrants, and the working class. Earl Robinson's song "Ballad for Americans," a typical expression of Popular Front culture that celebrated the religious, racial, and ethnic diversity of American society, became a national hit and was performed in 1940 at the Republican national convention.

Challenging the Color Line

It was fitting that "Ballad for Americans" reached the top of the charts in a version performed by the magnificent black singer Paul Robeson. Popular Front culture moved well beyond New Deal liberalism in condemning racism as incompatible with true Americanism. In the 1930s, groups like the American Jewish Committee and the National Conference of Christians and Jews actively promoted ethnic and religious tolerance, defining pluralism as "the American way." But whether in Harlem or East Los Angeles, the Communist Party was the era's only predominantly white organization to make fighting racism a top priority. "The communists," declared Charles H. Houston, the NAACP's chief lawyer, "made it impossible for any aspirant to Negro leadership to advocate less than full economic, political and social equality."

Communist influence spread even to the South. The Communist-dominated International Labor Defense mobilized popular support for black defendants victimized by a racist criminal justice system. It helped to make the Scottsboro case an international cause célèbre. The case revolved around nine young black men arrested for the rape of two white women in Alabama in 1931. Despite the

The "Scottsboro boys"

weakness of the evidence against the "Scottsboro boys" and the fact that one of the two accusers recanted, Alabama authorities three times put them on trial and three times won convictions. Landmark Supreme Court decisions overturned the first two verdicts and established legal principles that greatly expanded the definition of civil liberties—that defendants have a constitutional right to effective legal representation, and that states cannot systematically exclude blacks from juries. But the Court allowed the third set of convictions to stand, which led to prison sentences for five of the defendants. In 1937, a defense lawyer worked out a deal whereby Alabama authorities released nearly all the defendants on parole, although the last of the Scottsboro boys did not leave prison until thirteen years had passed.

Despite considerable resistance from white workers determined to preserve their monopoly of skilled positions and access to promotions, the CIO welcomed black members and advocated the passage of antilynching laws and the return of voting rights to southern blacks. The CIO brought large numbers of black industrial workers into the labor movement for the first time and ran extensive educational campaigns to persuade white workers to recognize the interests they shared with their black counterparts. Black workers, many of them traditionally hostile to unions because of their long experience of exclusion, responded with enthusiasm to CIO organizing efforts. The union offered the promise of higher wages, dignity in the workplace, and an end to the arbitrary power of often racist foremen. Ed McRea, a white CIO organizer in Memphis, Tennessee, reported that he had little difficulty persuading black workers of the value of unionization: "You didn't have any trouble explaining this to blacks, with the kinds of oppression and conditions they had. It was a question of freedom."

The "Scottsboro boys," flanked by two prison guards, with their lawyer, Samuel Liebowitz.

Labor and Civil Liberties

Another central element of Popular Front public culture was its mobilization for civil liberties, especially the right of labor to organize. The struggle to launch industrial unions encountered sweeping local restrictions on freedom of speech as well as repression by private and public police forces. Nationwide publicity about the wave of violence directed against the Southern Tenant Farmers Union in the South and the CIO in industrial communities in the North elevated the rights of labor to a central place in discussions of civil liberties. The American Civil Liberties Union, primarily concerned in the 1920s with governmental repression, by 1934 concluded that "the masters of property" posed as great a danger to freedom of speech and assembly as political authorities.

Efforts to organize labor

Beginning in 1936, a Senate subcommittee headed by Robert M. La Follette Jr. exposed the methods employers used to combat unionization, including spies and private police forces. Workers had "no liberties at all," an employee of General Motors wrote to the committee from Saginaw, Michigan. The extensive violence unleashed against strikers in California's cotton and lettuce fields made that state, the committee report concluded, seem more like a "European dictatorship" than part of the United States.

Labor militancy helped to produce an important shift in the understanding of civil liberties. Previously conceived of as individual rights that must be protected against infringement by the government, the concept now expanded to include violations of free speech and assembly by powerful private groups. As a result, just as the federal government emerged as a guarantor of economic security, it also became a protector of freedom of expression.

By the eve of World War II, civil liberties had assumed a central place in the New Deal understanding of freedom. In 1939, Attorney General Frank Murphy established a Civil Liberties Unit in the Department of Justice. "For the first time in our history," Murphy wrote the president, "the full weight of the Department will be thrown behind the effort to preserve in this country the blessings of liberty." Meanwhile, the same Supreme Court that in 1937 relinquished its role as a judge of economic legislation moved to expand its authority over civil liberties. The justices insisted that constitutional guarantees of free thought and expression were essential to "nearly every other form of freedom" and therefore deserved special protection by the courts. Thus, civil liberties replaced liberty of contract as the judicial foundation of freedom. In 1937, the Court overturned on free speech grounds the conviction of Angelo Herndon, a Communist organizer jailed in Georgia for "inciting insurrection." Three years later, it invalidated an Alabama law that prohibited picketing in labor disputes. Since 1937, the large majority of state and national laws overturned by the courts have been those that infringe on civil liberties, not on the property rights of business.

The new appreciation of free expression was hardly universal. In 1938, the House of Representatives established an Un-American Activities Committee to investigate disloyalty. Its expansive definition of "un-American" included communists, labor radicals, and the left of the Democratic Party, and its hearings led to the dismissal of dozens of federal employees on charges of subversion. Two years later, Congress enacted the Smith Act, which made it a federal crime to "teach, advocate, or encourage" the overthrow of the government. A similar pursuit of radical views took place at the state level. The New York legislature's Rapp-Coudert Committee held sweeping hearings investigating "subversive" influences in New York City's public colleges, resulting in the firing in 1941 of some sixty faculty members charged with communist sympathies.

The End of the New Deal

By then the New Deal, as an era of far-reaching social reform, had already begun to recede. One reason was that more and more southern Democrats were finding themselves at odds with Roosevelt's policies. In 1938, the administration released a "Report on Economic Conditions in the South," along with a letter by the president referring to the region as "the nation's No. 1 economic problem." The document revealed that the South lagged far behind other parts of the country in industrialization and investment in education and public health. Its per capita income stood at half that of the rest of the nation. Also in 1938, a new generation of homegrown radicals—southern New Dealers, black activists, labor leaders, communists, even a few elected officials—founded the Southern Conference for Human Welfare to work for unionization, unemployment relief, and racial justice.

Until the late 1930s, prominent southern Democrats had been strong supporters of the New Deal, while at the same time working to shape legislation to allow for the local administration of relief and the exclusion of most black workers. Now,

Free expression

The House Un-American Activities Committee

southern business and political leaders feared that continuing federal intervention in their region would encourage unionization and upset race relations. Roosevelt concluded that the enactment of future New Deal measures required a liberalization of the southern Democratic Party. In 1938, he tried to persuade the region's voters to replace conservative congressmen with ones who would support his policies. The South's small electorate dealt him a stinging rebuke. In the North, where the economic downturn, the "Court-packing" plan, and the upsurge of CIO militancy alarmed many middle-class voters, Republicans increased their congressional representation.

Southern leaders and the New Deal

A period of political stalemate followed the congressional election of 1938. For many years, a conservative coalition of southern Democrats and northern Republicans dominated Congress. Further reform initiatives became almost impossible, and Congress moved to abolish existing ones, beginning with the Federal Theater Project, which had alarmed conservatives because of the presence of radicals and homosexuals on its payroll. Congress repealed an earlier tax on corporate profits and rejected a proposed program of national medical insurance. The administration, moreover, increasingly focused its attention on the storm gathering in Europe. Even before December 1941, when the United States entered World War II, "Dr. Win the War," as Roosevelt put it, had replaced "Dr. New Deal."

The New Deal in American History

Given the scope of the economic calamity it tried to counter, the New Deal seems in many ways quite limited. Compared to later European welfare states, Social Security remained restricted in scope and modest in cost. The New Deal failed to address the problem of racial inequality, which in some ways it actually worsened.

Failures and accomplishments of the New Deal

Yet even as the New Deal receded, its substantial accomplishments remained. It greatly expanded the federal government's role in the American economy and made it an independent force in relations between industry and labor. The government influenced what farmers could and could not plant, required employers to deal with unions, insured bank deposits, regulated the stock market, loaned money to home owners, and provided payments to a majority of the elderly and unemployed. It transformed the physical environment through hydroelectric dams, reforestation projects, rural electrification, and the construction of innumerable public facilities. It restored faith in democracy and made the government an institution directly experienced in Americans' daily lives and directly concerned with their welfare. It redrew the map of American politics. It helped to inspire, and was powerfully influenced by, a popular upsurge that recast the idea of freedom to include a public guarantee of economic security for ordinary citizens and that identified economic inequality as the greatest threat to American freedom.

The New Deal certainly improved economic conditions in the United States. But it did not generate sustained prosperity. More than 15 percent of the workforce remained unemployed in 1940. Only the mobilization of the nation's resources to fight World War II would finally end the Great Depression.

SUGGESTED READING

BOOKS

- Brinkley, Alan. *Voices of Protest: Huey Long, Father Coughlin, and the Great Depression* (1982). An account of the political careers of two key figures of the New Deal era and their influence on national events.

- Carpenter, Joel A. *Revive Us Again: The Reawakening of American Fundamentalism* (1999). Shows how evangelicals adapted to the Depression and used mass communications to spread their message.

- Cohen, Lizabeth. *Making a New Deal: Industrial Workers in Chicago, 1919–1939* (1990). Describes how the assimilation of immigrants and their children paved the way for the creation of the New Deal political coalition.

- Denning, Michael. *The Cultural Front: The Laboring of American Culture in the Twentieth Century* (1996). A comprehensive account of the rise of cultural activity associated with the political left and the New Deal.

- Dickstein, Morris. *Dancing in the Dark: A Cultural History of the Great Depression* (2009). A comprehensive survey of how the Depression and New Deal affected the arts in the United States.

- Katznelson, Ira. *When Affirmative Action Was White* (2005). An examination of the racial exclusion built into many New Deal policies, and their long-term consequences.

- Kessler-Harris, Alice. *In Pursuit of Equity: Men, Women, and the Quest for Economic Citizenship in 20th-Century America* (2001). Explores how assumptions regarding the proper roles of men and women helped to shape New Deal measures such as Social Security.

- Kirby, Jack T. *Rural Worlds Lost: The American South, 1920–1960* (1987). Traces the transformation of the South in these four decades, with emphasis on how the New Deal affected the southern states.

- Leuchtenberg, William E. *Franklin D. Roosevelt and the New Deal, 1932–1940* (1963). Still the standard one-volume account of Roosevelt's first two terms as president.

- Maher, Neil. *Nature's New Deal: The Civilian Conservation Corps and the Roots of the American Environmental Movement* (2007). A history of one of the most significant New Deal agencies and how it affected attitudes toward the natural environment.

- Naison, Mark. *Communists in Harlem during the Depression* (1983). Examines the rise and decline of the Communist Party in a center of black life, and its impact on the movement for racial justice.

- Phillips, Sarah T. *The Land, This Nation: Conservation, Rural America, and the New Deal* (2007). Examines New Deal policies regarding agricultural development, rural conservation, and land use, and its attempt to modernize and uplift rural life.

- Sanchez, George. *Becoming Mexican American: Ethnicity, Culture, and Identity in Chicano Los Angeles, 1900–1945* (1995). A careful study of Mexican-Americans in Los Angeles, including their participation in the social unrest of the 1930s and the movement for deporting them during that decade.

- Sitkoff, Harvard. *A New Deal for Blacks: The Emergence of Civil Rights as a National Issue* (1978). Discusses the changing approach of the Roosevelt administration toward black Americans.

- Smith, Jason B. *Building New Deal Liberalism: The Political Economy of Public Works* (2006). Places the great construction projects of the 1930s at the center of New Deal economic policy.

- Sullivan, Patricia. *Days of Hope: Race and Democracy in the New Deal Era* (1996). Analyzes how the New Deal inspired the emergence of a biracial movement for civil rights in the South.

- Worster, Donald. *Dust Bowl: The Southern Plains in the 1930s* (1979). A social and environmental history of one of the key episodes in rural America during the 1930s.

- Zieger, Robert H. *The CIO, 1935–1955* (1995). A comprehensive history of the Congress of Industrial Organizations, the major labor group to emerge during the New Deal.

WEBSITES

- America from the Great Depression to World War II: http://memory.loc.gov/ammem/fsowhome.html

- FDR Cartoon Archive: www.nisk.k12.ny.us/fdr/FDRcartoons.html

- Flint Sit-Down Strike: www.historicalvoices.org/flint/

- New Deal Network: http://newdeal.feri.org

CHAPTER REVIEW AND ONLINE RESOURCES

REVIEW QUESTIONS

1. Discuss how regional planning such as the Tennessee Valley Authority and the Columbia River project reflected broader changes in American life during the New Deal.

2. What actions did President Roosevelt and Congress take to help the banking system recover as well as to reform how it operated in the long run?

3. How did the actions of the AAA benefit many farmers, injure others, and provoke attacks by conservatives?

4. Explain what labor did in the 1930s to rise from being "slaves of the depression" to secure "economic freedom and industrial democracy" for American workers.

5. How did the emphasis of the Second New Deal differ from the First New Deal?

6. How did the entrenched power of southern white conservatives limit African-Americans' ability to enjoy the full benefits of the New Deal and eliminate racial violence and discrimination? Why did African-Americans still support the Democratic Party?

7. Analyze the effects of the Indian Reorganization Act of 1934 on Native Americans.

8. Explain how New Deal programs contributed to the stigma of blacks as welfare-dependent.

9. How did the New Deal build on traditional ideas about the importance of homeownership to Americans and how did it change Americans' ability to own their own homes?

10. What were the major characteristics of liberalism by 1939?

KEY TERMS

bank holiday (p. 803)

Emergency Banking Act (p. 803)

the Hundred Days (p. 804)

National Recovery Administration (p. 804)

Civilian Conservation Corps (p. 805)

Public Works Administration (p. 806)

Dust Bowl (p. 807)

Federal Housing Administration (p. 809)

sit-down strike (p. 812)

Congress of Industrial Organizations (p. 812)

Share Our Wealth movement (p. 814)

Works Progress Administration (p. 816)

welfare state (p. 817)

Social Security Act (p. 817)

court-packing plan (p. 823)

minimum wage laws (p. 823)

Indian New Deal (p. 827)

the Popular Front (p. 832)

"Scottsboro boys" (p. 834)

House Un-American Activities Committee (p. 836)

wwnorton.com/studyspace

Visit StudySpace for these resources and more:

- **Author Videos**
- **A chapter outline**
- **A practice quiz**
- **Interactive maps**
- **Multimedia documents**

CHAPTER 22

FIGHTING FOR THE FOUR FREEDOMS: WORLD WAR II

★

1941–1945

Dusty Road to Formia. June 44

By far the most popular works of art produced during World War II were paintings of the Four Freedoms by the magazine illustrator Norman Rockwell. In his State of the Union Address, delivered before Congress on January 6, 1941, President Roosevelt spoke eloquently of a future world order founded on the "essential human freedoms": freedom of speech, freedom of worship, freedom from want, and freedom from fear. The Four Freedoms became Roosevelt's favorite statement of Allied aims. At various times, he compared them with the Ten Commandments, the Magna Carta, and the Emancipation Proclamation. They embodied, Roosevelt declared in a 1942 radio address, the "rights of men of every creed and every race, wherever they live," and made clear "the crucial difference between ourselves and the enemies we face today."

Rockwell's paintings succeeded in linking the Four Freedoms with the defense of traditional American values. "Words like freedom or liberty," declared one wartime advertisement, "draw close to us only when we break them down into the homely fragments of daily life." This insight helps to explain Rockwell's astonishing popularity. Born in New York City in 1894, Rockwell had lived in the New York area until 1939, when he and his family moved to Arlington, Vermont, where they could enjoy, as he put it, "the clean, simple country life, as opposed to the complicated world of the city." Drawing on the lives of his Vermont neighbors, Rockwell translated the Four Freedoms into images of real people situated in small-town America. Each of the paintings focuses on an instantly recognizable situation. An ordinary citizen rises to speak at a town meeting; members of different religious groups are seen at prayer; a family enjoys a Thanksgiving dinner; a mother and father stand over a sleeping child.

The Four Freedoms paintings first appeared in the Saturday Evening Post early in 1943. Letters of praise poured in to the magazine's editors. The government produced and sold millions of reprints. The paintings toured the country as the centerpiece of the Four Freedoms Show, which included theatrical presentations, parades, and other events aimed at persuading Americans to purchase war bonds. By the end of its tour, the Four Freedoms Show had raised $133 million.

Even as Rockwell invoked images of small-town life to rally Americans to the war effort, however, the country experienced changes as deep as at any time in its history. Many of the economic trends and social movements that we associate with the last half of the twentieth century had their roots in the war years. As during World War I, but on a far larger scale, wartime mobilization expanded the size and scope of government and energized the economy. The gross national product more than doubled and unemployment disappeared as war production finally conquered the Depression. The demand for labor drew millions of women into the workforce and sent a tide of migrants from rural America to the industrial cities of the North and West, permanently altering the nation's social geography. Some 30 million Americans moved during the war, half going into military service and half taking up new jobs.

World War II gave the country a new and lasting international role and greatly strengthened the idea that American security was global in scope and could only be protected by the worldwide triumph of core American values.

FOCUS QUESTIONS

What steps led to American participation in World War II? –p. 843

How did the United States mobilize economic resources and promote popular support for the war effort? –p. 853

What visions of America's postwar role began to emerge during the war? –p. 861

How did American minorities face threats to their freedom at home and abroad during World War II? –p. 863

How did the end of the war begin to shape the postwar world? –p. 877

Ben Hurwitz, a soldier from New York City who fought in North Africa and Italy during World War II, made numerous sketches of his experiences. Here American troops pass a wrecked German tank in southern Italy in June 1944.

1931	Japan invades Manchuria
1933	U.S. recognizes Soviet Union
1935–1939	Congress passes Neutrality Acts
1937	Sino-Japanese War begins
1938	Munich agreement
1939	Germany invades Poland
1940	Draft established
1941	Four Freedoms speech
	Henry Luce's *The American Century*
	Lend-Lease Act
	Executive Order 8802
	Atlantic Charter
	Pearl Harbor attacked
1942	Executive Order 9066
	Battle of Midway Island
	Congress of Racial Equality (CORE) formed
1943	"Zoot" suit riots
	Detroit race riot
	Congress lifts Chinese Exclusion Act
1944	*Smith v. Allwright*
	D-Day
	GI Bill of Rights
	Bretton Woods conference
	Korematsu v. United States
	Battle of the Bulge
1945	Yalta conference
	Roosevelt dies; Harry Truman becomes president
	V-E Day (May)
	Atomic bombs dropped on Japan
	V-J Day (September)

Government military spending sparked the economic development of the South and West, laying the foundation for the rise of the modern Sunbelt. The war created a close link between big business and a militarized federal government—a "military-industrial complex," as President Dwight D. Eisenhower would later call it—that long survived the end of fighting.

World War II also redrew the boundaries of American nationality. In contrast to World War I, the government recognized the "new immigrants" of the early twentieth century and their children as loyal Americans. Black Americans' second-class status assumed, for the first time since Reconstruction, a prominent place on the nation's political agenda. But toleration had its limits. With the United States at war with Japan, the federal government removed more than 100,000 Japanese-Americans, the majority of them American citizens, from their homes and placed them in internment camps.

As a means of generating support for the struggle, the Four Freedoms provided a crucial language of national unity. But this unity obscured divisions within American society that the war in some ways intensified, divisions reflected in debates over freedom. While some Americans looked forward to a worldwide New Deal, others envisioned "free enterprise" replacing government intervention in the economy. The war gave birth to the modern civil rights movement but strengthened the commitment of many white Americans to maintain the existing racial order. The movement of women into the labor force challenged traditional gender relations, but most men and not a few women longed for the restoration of family life with a male breadwinner and a wife responsible for the home.

Even Rockwell's popular paintings suggested some of the ambiguities within the idea of freedom. With the exception of Freedom of Speech, which depicts civic democracy in action, the paintings emphasized private situations. The message seemed to be that Americans were fighting to preserve freedoms enjoyed individually or within the family rather than in the larger public world. This emphasis on freedom as an element of private life would become more and more prominent in postwar America.

FIGHTING WORLD WAR II

Good Neighbors

During the 1930s, with Americans preoccupied by the economic crisis, international relations played only a minor role in public affairs. From the outset of his administration, nonetheless, FDR embarked on a number of departures in foreign policy. In 1933, hoping to stimulate American trade, he exchanged ambassadors with the Soviet Union, whose government his Republican predecessors had stubbornly refused to recognize.

Roosevelt also formalized a policy initiated by Herbert Hoover by which the United States repudiated the right to intervene militarily in the internal affairs of Latin American countries. This Good Neighbor Policy, as it was called, had mixed

The immensely popular Office of War Information poster reproducing Norman Rockwell's paintings of the Four Freedoms, President Franklin D. Roosevelt's shorthand for American purposes in World War II.

results. During the 1930s, the United States withdrew its troops from Haiti and Nicaragua. FDR accepted Cuba's repeal of the Platt Amendment (discussed in Chapter 17), which had authorized American military interventions on that island. These steps offered a belated recognition of the sovereignty of America's neighbors. But while Roosevelt condemned "economic royalists" (wealthy businessmen) at home, like previous presidents he felt comfortable dealing with undemocratic governments friendly to American business interests abroad. The United States lent its support to dictators like Anastasio Somoza in Nicaragua, Rafael Trujillo

Molina in the Dominican Republic, and Fulgencio Batista in Cuba. "He may be a son of a bitch, but he's *our* son of a bitch," FDR said of Somoza.

However, as the international crisis deepened in the 1930s, the Roosevelt administration took steps to counter German influence in Latin America by expanding hemispheric trade and promoting respect for American culture. Nelson Rockefeller, the head of an office that hoped to expand cultural relations in the hemisphere, sent the artists of the American Ballet Caravan and the NBC Symphony Orchestra on Latin American tours. This was a far different approach to relations with Central and South America than the military interventions of the first decades of the century.

The Road to War

Aggression in Asia and Europe

Ominous developments in Asia and Europe quickly overshadowed events in Latin America. By the mid-1930s, it seemed clear that the rule of law was disintegrating in international relations and that war was on the horizon. In 1931, seeking to expand its military and economic power in Asia, Japan invaded Manchuria, a province of northern China. Six years later, its troops moved farther into China. When the Japanese overran the city of Nanjing, they massacred an estimated 300,000 Chinese prisoners of war and civilians.

An aggressive power threatened Europe as well. After brutally consolidating his rule in Germany, Adolf Hitler embarked on a campaign to control the entire continent. In violation of the Versailles Treaty, he feverishly pursued German rearmament. In 1936, he sent troops to occupy the Rhineland, a demilitarized zone between France and Germany established after World War I. The failure of Britain, France, and the United States to oppose this action convinced Hitler that the democracies could not muster the will to halt his aggressive plans. Italian leader Benito Mussolini, the founder of fascism, a movement similar to Hitler's Nazism, invaded and conquered Ethiopia. When General Francisco Franco in 1936 led an uprising against the democratically elected government of Spain, Hitler poured in arms, seeing the conflict as a testing ground for new weaponry. In 1939, Franco emerged victorious from a bitter civil war, establishing yet another fascist government in Europe. As part of a campaign to unite all Europeans of German origin in a single empire, Hitler in 1938 annexed Austria and the Sudetenland, an ethnically German part of Czechoslovakia. Shortly thereafter, he gobbled up all of that country.

As the 1930s progressed, Roosevelt became more and more alarmed at Hitler's aggression as well as his accelerating campaign against Germany's Jews, whom the Nazis stripped of citizenship and property and began to deport to concentration camps. In a 1937 speech in Chicago, FDR called for international action to "quarantine" aggressors. But no further steps followed. Roosevelt had little choice but to follow the policy of "appeasement" adopted by Britain and France, who hoped that agreeing to Hitler's demands would prevent war. British prime minister Neville Chamberlain returned from the Munich conference of 1938, which awarded Hitler the Sudetenland, proclaiming that he had guaranteed "peace in our time."

Isolationism

To most Americans, the threat arising from Japanese and German aggression seemed very distant. Moreover, Hitler had more than a few admirers in the United States. Obsessed with the threat of communism, some Americans approved his

This Hand Guides the Reich, a Nazi propaganda poster from 1930s Germany. The bottom text reads: "German youth follow it in the ranks of Hitler Youth."

expansion of German power as a counterweight to the Soviet Union. Businessmen did not wish to give up profitable overseas markets. Henry Ford did business with Nazi Germany throughout the 1930s. Indeed, Ford plants there employed slave labor provided by the German government. Trade with Japan also continued, including shipments of American trucks and aircraft and considerable amounts of oil. Until 1941, 80 percent of Japan's oil supply came from the United States.

Many Americans remained convinced that involvement in World War I had been a mistake. Senate hearings in 1934–1935 headed by Gerald P. Nye of North Dakota revealed that international bankers and arms exporters had pressed the Wilson administration to enter that war and had profited handsomely from it. Pacifism spread on college campuses, where tens of thousands of students took part in a "strike for peace" in 1935. Ethnic allegiances reinforced Americans' traditional reluctance to enter foreign conflicts. Many Americans of German and Italian descent celebrated the expansion of national power in their countries of origin, even when they disdained their dictatorial governments. Irish-Americans remained strongly anti-British.

Isolationism—the 1930s version of Americans' long-standing desire to avoid foreign entanglements—dominated Congress. Beginning in 1935, lawmakers passed a series of Neutrality Acts that banned travel on belligerents' ships and the sale of arms to countries at war. These policies, Congress hoped, would allow the United States to avoid the conflicts over freedom of the seas that had contributed to involvement in World War I. Despite the fact that the Spanish Civil War pitted a democratic government against an aspiring fascist dictator, the Western democracies, including the United States, imposed an embargo on arms shipments to both sides. Some 3,000 Americans volunteered to fight in the Abraham Lincoln Brigade on the side of the Spanish republic. But with Germany supplying the forces of Franco, the decision by democratic countries to abide by the arms embargo contributed substantially to his victory.

> *The Neutrality Acts*

War in Europe

In the Munich agreement of 1938, Britain and France had caved in to Hitler's aggression. In 1939, the Soviet Union proposed an international agreement to oppose further German demands for territory. Britain and France, who distrusted Stalin and saw Germany as a bulwark against the spread of communist influence in Europe, refused. Stalin then astonished the world by signing a nonaggression pact with Hitler, his former sworn enemy. On September 1, immediately after the signing of the Nazi–Soviet pact, Germany invaded Poland. This time, Britain and France, who had pledged to protect Poland against aggression, declared war. But Germany appeared unstoppable. Within a year, the Nazi *blitzkrieg* (lightning war) had overrun Poland and much of Scandinavia, Belgium, and the Netherlands. On June 14, 1940, German troops occupied Paris. Hitler now dominated nearly all of Europe, as well as North Africa. In September 1940, Germany, Italy, and Japan created a military alliance known as the Axis.

In a 1940 cartoon, war clouds engulf Europe, while Uncle Sam observes that the Atlantic Ocean no longer seems to shield the United States from involvement.

A newsreel theater in New York's Times Square announces Hitler's *blitzkrieg* in Europe in the spring of 1940.

For one critical year, Britain stood virtually alone in fighting Germany. Winston Churchill, who became prime minister in 1940, vowed to resist a threatened Nazi invasion. In the Battle of Britain of 1940–1941, the German air force launched devastating attacks on London and other cities. The Royal Air Force eventually turned back the air assault. But Churchill pointedly called on the "new world, with all its power and might," to step forward to rescue the old.

Toward Intervention

Roosevelt viewed Hitler as a mad gangster whose victories posed a direct threat to the United States. But most Americans remained desperate to remain out of the conflict. "What worries me, especially," FDR wrote to Kansas editor William Allen White, "is that public opinion over here is patting itself on the back every morning and thanking God for the Atlantic Ocean and the Pacific Ocean." After a tumultuous debate, Congress in 1940 agreed to allow the sale of arms to Britain on a "cash and carry" basis—that is, they had to be paid for in cash and transported in British ships. It also approved plans for military rearmament. But with a presidential election looming, Roosevelt was reluctant to go further. Opponents of involvement in Europe organized the America First Committee, with hundreds of thousands of members and a leadership that included well-known figures like Henry Ford, Father Coughlin, and Charles A. Lindbergh.

In 1940, breaking with a tradition that dated back to George Washington, Roosevelt announced his candidacy for a third term as president. The international situation was too dangerous and domestic recovery too fragile, he insisted, for him to leave office. Republicans chose as his opponent a political amateur, Wall Street businessman and lawyer Wendell Willkie. Differences between the candidates were far more muted than in 1936. Both supported the law, enacted in September 1940, that established the nation's first peacetime draft. Willkie endorsed New Deal social legislation. He captured more votes than Roosevelt's previous opponents, but FDR still emerged with a decisive victory. Soon after his victory, in a fireside chat in December 1940, Roosevelt announced that the United States would become the "great arsenal of democracy," providing Britain and China with military supplies in their fight against Germany and Japan.

During 1941, the United States became more and more closely allied with those fighting Germany and Japan. But with Britain virtually bankrupt, it could no longer pay for supplies. At Roosevelt's urging, Congress passed the Lend-Lease Act, which authorized military aid so long as countries promised somehow to return it all after the war. Under the law's provisions, the United States funneled billions of dollars' worth of arms to Britain and China, as well as the Soviet Union, after Hitler renounced his nonaggression pact and invaded that country in June 1941. FDR also froze Japanese assets in the United States, halting virtually all trade between the countries, including the sale of oil vital to Japan.

Those who believed that the United States must intervene to stem the rising tide of fascism tried to awaken a reluctant country to prepare for war. Interventionists popularized slogans that would become central to wartime mobilization. In June 1941, refugees from Germany and the occupied countries of Europe joined with Americans to form the Free World Association, which sought to bring the United States into the war against Hitler. The same year saw the formation of Freedom

House. With a prestigious membership that included university presidents, ministers, businessmen, and labor leaders, Freedom House described the war raging in Europe as an ideological struggle between dictatorship and the "free world." In October 1941, it sponsored a "Fight for Freedom" rally at New York's Madison Square Garden, complete with a patriotic variety show entitled "It's Fun to Be Free." The rally ended by demanding an immediate declaration of war against Germany.

Pearl Harbor

Until November 1941, the administration's attention focused on Europe. But at the end of that month, intercepted Japanese messages revealed that an assault in the Pacific was imminent. No one, however, knew where it would come. On December 7, 1941, Japanese planes, launched from aircraft carriers, bombed the naval base at Pearl Harbor in Hawaii, the first attack by a foreign power on American soil since the War of 1812. Pearl Harbor was a complete and devastating surprise. In a few hours, more than 2,000 American servicemen were killed, and 187 aircraft and 18 naval vessels, including 8 battleships, had been destroyed or damaged. By a stroke of fortune, no aircraft carriers—which would prove decisive in the Pacific war—happened to be docked at Pearl Harbor on December 7.

> *December 7, 1941*

To this day, conspiracy theories abound suggesting that FDR knew of the attack and did nothing to prevent it so as to bring the United States into the war. No credible evidence supports this charge. Indeed, with the country drawing ever closer to intervention in Europe, Roosevelt hoped to keep the peace in the Pacific. But Secretary of Labor Frances Perkins, who saw the president after the attack, remarked that he seemed calm—"his terrible moral problem had been resolved." Terming December 7 "a date which will live in infamy," Roosevelt asked Congress for a declaration of war against Japan. The combined vote in Congress was 388 in favor and 1 against—pacifist Jeanette Rankin of Montana, who had also voted

The battleships *West Virginia* and *Tennessee* in flames during the Japanese attack on Pearl Harbor. Both were repaired and later took part in the Pacific war.

Some of the 13,000 American troops forced to surrender to the Japanese on Corregidor Island in the Philippines in May 1942.

Members of the U.S. Marine Corps, Navy, and Coast Guard taking part in an amphibious assault during the "island hopping" campaign in the Pacific theater of World War II.

against American entry into World War I. The next day, Germany declared war on the United States. America had finally joined the largest war in human history.

The War in the Pacific

World War II has been called a "gross national product war," meaning that its outcome turned on which coalition of combatants could outproduce the other. In retrospect, it appears inevitable that the entry of the United States, with its superior industrial might, would ensure the defeat of the Axis powers. But the first few months of American involvement witnessed an unbroken string of military disasters. Having earlier occupied substantial portions of French Indochina (now Vietnam, Laos, and Cambodia), Japan in early 1942 conquered Burma (Myanmar) and Siam (Thailand). Japan also took control of the Dutch East Indies (Indonesia), whose extensive oil fields could replace supplies from the United States. And it occupied Guam, the Philippines, and other Pacific islands. At Bataan, in the Philippines, the Japanese forced 78,000 American and Filipino troops to lay down their arms—the largest surrender in American military history. Thousands perished on the ensuing "death march" to a prisoner-of-war camp, and thousands more

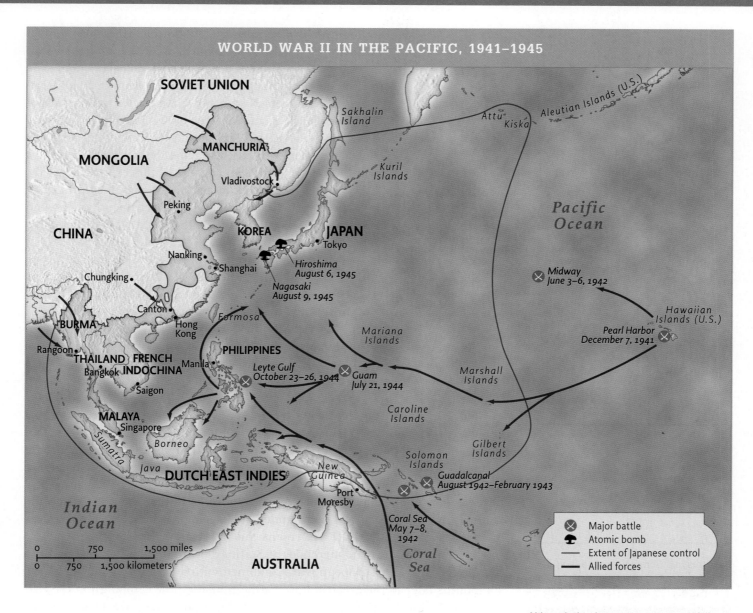

WORLD WAR II IN THE PACIFIC, 1941–1945

died of disease and starvation after they arrived. At the same time, German submarines sank hundreds of Allied merchant and naval vessels during the Battle of the Atlantic.

Soon, however, the tide of battle began to turn. In May 1942, in the Battle of the Coral Sea, the American navy turned back a Japanese fleet intent on attacking Australia. The following month, it inflicted devastating losses on the Japanese navy in the Battle of Midway Island. These victories allowed American forces to launch the bloody campaigns that one by one drove the Japanese from fortified islands like Guadalcanal and the Solomons in the western Pacific and brought American troops ever closer to Japan.

The War in Europe

In November 1942, British and American forces invaded North Africa and by May 1943 forced the surrender of the German army commanded by General Erwin

Although the Japanese navy never fully recovered from its defeats at the Coral Sea and Midway in 1942, it took three more years for American forces to near the Japanese homeland.

German prisoners of war guarded by an American soldier shortly after D-Day in June 1944. By this time, the Germans were drafting very young men into their armies.

Prisoners at a German concentration camp liberated by Allied troops in 1945.

Rommel. By the spring of 1943, the Allies also gained the upper hand in the Atlantic, as British and American destroyers and planes devastated the German submarine fleet. But even though Roosevelt was committed to liberating Europe from Nazi control, American troops did not immediately become involved on the European continent. As late as the end of 1944, more American military personnel were deployed in the Pacific than against Germany. In July 1943, American and British forces invaded Sicily, beginning the liberation of Italy. A popular uprising in Rome overthrew the Mussolini government, whereupon Germany occupied most of the country. Fighting there raged throughout 1944.

The major involvement of American troops in Europe did not begin until June 6, 1944. On that date, known as D-Day, nearly 200,000 American, British, and Canadian soldiers under the command of General Dwight D. Eisenhower landed in Normandy in northwestern France. More than a million troops followed them ashore in the next few weeks, in the most massive sea-land operation in history. After fierce fighting, German armies retreated eastward. By August, Paris had been liberated.

The crucial fighting in Europe, however, took place on the eastern front, the scene of an epic struggle between Germany and the Soviet Union. More than 3 million German soldiers took part in the 1941 invasion. After sweeping through western Russia, German armies in August 1942 launched a siege of Stalingrad, a city located deep inside Russia on the Volga River. This proved to be a catastrophic mistake. Bolstered by an influx of military supplies from the United States, the Russians surrounded the German troops and forced them to surrender. Some 800,000 Germans and 1.2 million Russians perished in the fighting. The German surrender at Stalingrad in January 1943 marked the turning point of the European war. Combined with a Russian victory at Kursk six months later in the greatest tank battle in history, the campaign in the east devastated Hitler's forces and sent surviving units on a long retreat back toward Germany.

Of 13.6 million German casualties in World War II, 10 million came on the Russian front. They represented only part of the war's vast toll in human lives. Millions of Poles and at least 20 million Russians, probably many more, perished—not only soldiers but civilian victims of starvation, disease, and massacres by German soldiers. After his armies had penetrated eastern Europe in 1941, moreover, Hitler embarked on the "final solution"—the mass extermination of "undesirable" peoples—Slavs, gypsies, homosexuals, and, above all, Jews. By 1945, 6 million Jewish men, women, and children had died in Nazi death camps. What came to be called the Holocaust was the horrifying culmination of the Nazi belief that Germans constituted a "master race" destined to rule the world.

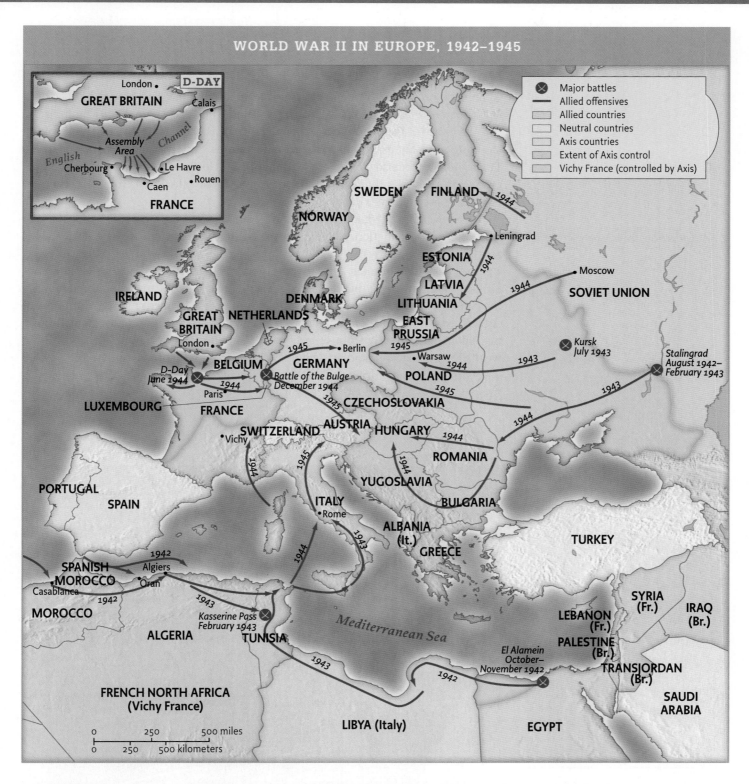

WORLD WAR II IN EUROPE, 1942–1945

D-DAY

GREAT BRITAIN
London
Calais
Assembly Area
English Channel
Cherbourg
Le Havre
Caen
Rouen
FRANCE

⊗ Major battles
— Allied offensives
☐ Allied countries
☐ Neutral countries
☐ Axis countries
☐ Extent of Axis control
☐ Vichy France (controlled by Axis)

SWEDEN
FINLAND
1944
NORWAY

Leningrad
ESTONIA
1944
LATVIA
1944
Moscow
SOVIET UNION

IRELAND
DENMARK
LITHUANIA
EAST PRUSSIA

GREAT BRITAIN
NETHERLANDS
London
1945 → Berlin
GERMANY
1945
Warsaw
1944
1943
⊗ Kursk July 1943
⊗ Stalingrad August 1942–February 1943

D-Day June 1944
BELGIUM
Battle of the Bulge December 1944
POLAND
1943
1944
Paris
1944
LUXEMBOURG
FRANCE
1945
CZECHOSLOVAKIA
1945
1944

SWITZERLAND
AUSTRIA
HUNGARY
1944
Vichy
1944
1945
ROMANIA

PORTUGAL
SPAIN
YUGOSLAVIA
BULGARIA
1944

ITALY
Rome
ALBANIA (It.)
GREECE
TURKEY

1944
1943

SPANISH MOROCCO
Algiers
Oran
1942
SYRIA (Fr.)
IRAQ (Br.)
Casablanca
1942
LEBANON (Fr.)
MOROCCO
1943
Kasserine Pass February 1943 ⊗
Mediterranean Sea
PALESTINE (Br.)
ALGERIA
TUNISIA
El Alamein October–November 1942
TRANSJORDAN (Br.)

FRENCH NORTH AFRICA (Vichy France)
1943
1942
⊗
SAUDI ARABIA

LIBYA (Italy)
EGYPT

0   250   500 miles
0   250   500 kilometers

Most of the land fighting in Europe during World War II took place on the eastern front between the German and Soviet armies.

THE HOME FRONT

Mobilizing for War

At home, World War II transformed the role of the national government. FDR created federal agencies like the War Production Board, the War Man power Commission, and the Office of Price Administration to regulate the allocation of labor, control the shipping industry, establish manufacturing quotas, and fix wages, prices, and rents. The number of federal workers rose from 1 million to 4 million, part of a tremendous growth in new jobs that pushed the unemployment rate down from 14 percent in 1940 to 2 percent three years later.

The government built housing for war workers and forced civilian industries to retool for war production. Michigan's auto factories now turned out trucks, tanks, and jeeps for the army. By 1944, American factories produced a ship every day and a plane every five minutes. The gross national product rose from $91 billion to $214 billion during the war, and the federal government's expenditures amounted to twice the combined total of the previous 150 years. The government marketed billions of dollars' worth of war bonds, increased taxes, and began the practice of withholding income tax directly from weekly paychecks. Before the war, only the 4 million wealthiest Americans paid income taxes; by 1945, more than 40 million did so. The government, one historian writes, moved during the war from "class taxation" to "mass taxation."

Redirecting the economy

A list of jobs available in Detroit in July 1941 illustrates how war-related production ended the Great Depression even before the United States entered the conflict.

Business and the War

The relationship between the federal government and big business changed dramatically from the days of the Second New Deal. "If you are going to go to war in a capitalist country," observed Secretary of War Henry Stimson, "you had better let business make money out of the process." As corporate executives flooded into federal agencies concerned with war production, Roosevelt offered incentives to spur production—low-interest loans, tax concessions, and contracts with guaranteed profits. The great bulk of federal spending went to the largest corporations, furthering the long-term trend toward economic concentration. By the end of the war, the 200 biggest industrial companies accounted for almost half of all corporate assets in the United States.

Americans marveled at the achievements of wartime manufacturing. Thousands of aircraft, 100,000 armored vehicles, and 2.5 million trucks rolled off American assembly lines, and entirely new products like synthetic rubber replaced natural resources now controlled by Japan. Government-sponsored scientific research perfected inventions like radar, jet engines, and early computers that helped to win the war and would have a large impact on postwar life. These accomplishments not only made it possible to win a two-front war but also helped to restore the reputation of business and businessmen, which had reached a low point during the Depression.

> *Wartime manufacturing*

Federal funds reinvigorated established manufacturing areas and created entirely new industrial centers. World War II saw the West Coast emerge as a focus of military-industrial production. The government invested billions of dollars in

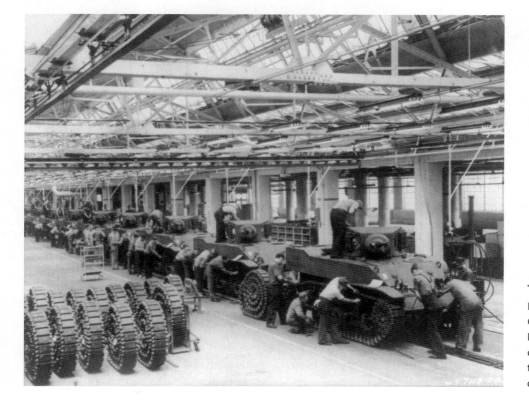

M-5 tanks on the assembly line at a Detroit Cadillac plant, in a 1942 photograph. During the war, General Motors and other automakers produced vehicles for the armed forces rather than cars for consumers.

WARTIME ARMY AND NAVY BASES AND AIRFIELDS

Legend:
- Airfields, bases, and stations
- Army camps, forts, and posts
- Naval bases

Scale: 0—250—500 miles; 0—250—500 kilometers

As this map indicates, the military and naval facilities built by the federal government during World War II were concentrated in the South and West, sparking the economic development of these regions.

Economic shift in the South

the shipyards of Seattle, Portland, and San Francisco and in the steel plants and aircraft factories of southern California. By the war's end, California had received one-tenth of all federal spending, and Los Angeles had become the nation's second largest manufacturing center. Nearly 2 million Americans moved to California for jobs in defense-related industries, and millions more passed through for military training and embarkation to the Pacific war.

In the South, the combination of rural out-migration and government investment in military-related factories and shipyards hastened a shift from agricultural to industrial employment. During the war, southern per capita income rose from 60 percent to 70 percent of the national average. But the South remained very poor when the war ended. Much of its rural population still lived in small wooden shacks with no indoor plumbing. The region had only two cities—Houston and New Orleans—with populations exceeding 500,000. Despite the expansion of war production, the South's economy still relied on agriculture and extractive industries—mining, lumber, oil—or manufacturing linked to farming, like the production of cotton textiles.

Labor in Wartime

Organized labor repeatedly described World War II as a crusade for freedom that would expand economic and political democracy at home and abroad and win for unions a major voice in politics and industrial management. During the war, labor entered a three-sided arrangement with government and business that allowed union membership to soar to unprecedented levels. In order to secure industrial peace and stabilize war production, the federal government forced reluctant employers to recognize unions. In 1944, when Montgomery Ward, the large mail-order company, defied a pro-union order, the army seized its headquarters and physically evicted its president. For their part, union leaders agreed not to strike and conceded employers' right to "managerial prerogatives" and a "fair profit."

Despite the gains produced by labor militancy during the 1930s, unions only became firmly established in many sectors of the economy during World War II. By 1945, union membership stood at nearly 15 million, one-third of the non-farm labor force and the highest proportion in American history. But if labor became a partner in government, it was very much a junior partner. The decline of the New Deal, already evident in the late 1930s, proceeded during the war. Congress continued to be dominated by a conservative alliance of Republicans and southern Democrats. They left intact core New Deal programs like Social Security but eliminated agencies thought to be controlled by leftists, including the Civilian Conservation Corps, National Youth Administration, and Works Progress Administration. Congress rejected Roosevelt's call for a cap on personal incomes and set taxes on corporate profits at a level far lower than FDR requested. Despite the "no-strike" pledge, 1943 and 1944 witnessed numerous brief walkouts in which workers protested the increasing speed of assembly-line production and the disparity between wages frozen by government order and expanding corporate profits.

Fighting for the Four Freedoms

Previous conflicts, including the Mexican War and World War I, had deeply divided American society. In contrast, World War II came to be remembered as the Good War, a time of national unity in pursuit of indisputably noble goals. But all wars require the mobilization of patriotic public opinion. By 1940, "To sell *goods*, we must sell *words*" had become a motto of advertisers. Foremost among the words that helped to "sell" World War II was "freedom."

Talk of freedom pervaded wartime America. To Roosevelt, the Four Freedoms expressed deeply held American values worthy of being spread worldwide. Freedom from fear meant not only a longing for peace but a more general desire for security in a world that appeared to be out of control. Freedom of speech and religion scarcely required detailed explanation. But their prominent place among the Four Freedoms accelerated the process by which First Amendment protections of free expression moved to the center of Americans' definition of liberty. In 1941, the administration celebrated with considerable fanfare the 150th anniversary of the Bill of Rights (the first ten amendments to the Constitution). FDR described their protections against tyrannical government as defining characteristics of American

TABLE 22.1 Labor Union Membership	
YEAR	NUMBER OF MEMBERS
1933	2,857,000
1934	3,728,000
1935	3,753,000
1936	4,107,000
1937	5,780,000
1938	8,265,000
1939	8,980,000
1940	8,944,000
1941	10,489,000
1942	10,762,000
1943	13,642,000
1944	14,621,000
1945	14,796,000

One of the patriotic war posters issued by the Office of War Information during World War II, linking modern-day soldiers with patriots of the American Revolution as fighters for freedom, a major theme of government efforts to mobilize support for the war.

1778 1943

AMERICANS
will <u>always</u> fight for liberty

In this recruitment poster for the Boy Scouts, a svelte Miss Liberty prominently displays the Bill of Rights, widely celebrated during World War II as the centerpiece of American freedom.

life, central to the rights of "free men and free women." In 1943, the Supreme Court reversed a 1940 ruling and, on First Amendment grounds, upheld the right of Jehovah's Witnesses to refuse to salute the American flag in public schools. The decision stood in sharp contrast to the coercive patriotism of World War I, and it affirmed the sanctity of individual conscience as a bedrock of freedom, even in times of crisis. The justices contrasted the American system of constitutional protection for unpopular minorities with Nazi tyranny.

Freedom from Want

The "most ambiguous" of the Four Freedoms, *Fortune* magazine remarked, was freedom from want. Yet this "great inspiring phrase," as a Pennsylvania steelworker put it in a letter to the president, seemed to strike the deepest chord in a nation just emerging from the Depression. Roosevelt initially meant it to refer to the elimination of barriers to international trade. But he quickly came to link freedom from want to an economic goal more relevant to the average citizen—protecting the future "standard of living of the American worker and farmer" by guaranteeing that the Depression would not resume after the war. This, he declared, would bring "real freedom for the common man."

When Norman Rockwell's paintings of the Four Freedoms first appeared in the *Saturday Evening Post*, each was accompanied by a brief essay. Three of these essays, by the celebrated authors Stephen Vincent Benét, Booth Tarkington, and Will Durant, emphasized that the values Rockwell depicted were essentially American and the opposite of those of the Axis powers. For *Freedom from Want*, the editors chose an unknown Filipino poet, Carlos Bulosan, who had emigrated to the United States at the age of sixteen. Bulosan's essay showed how the Four

Patriotic Fan. This fan, marketed to women during World War II, illustrates how freedom and patriotism were closely linked. At the far left and right, owners are instructed in ways to help win the war and preserve American freedom. The five middle panels suggest some of the era's definitions of freedom: freedom "to listen" (presumably without government censorship); self-government; freedom of assembly; the right to choose one's work; and freedom "to play."

Freedoms could inspire hopes for a better future as well as nostalgia for Rockwell's imagined small-town past. Bulosan wrote of those Americans still outside the social mainstream—migrant workers, cannery laborers, black victims of segregation—for whom freedom meant having enough to eat, sending their children to school, and being able to "share the promise and fruits of American life."

The Office of War Information

The history of the Office of War Information (OWI), created in 1942 to mobilize public opinion, illustrates how the political divisions generated by the New Deal affected efforts to promote the Four Freedoms. The liberal Democrats who dominated the OWI's writing staff sought to make the conflict "a 'people's war' for freedom." The OWI feared that Americans had only a vague understanding of the war's purposes and that the populace seemed more fervently committed to paying back the Japanese for their attack on Pearl Harbor than ridding the world of fascism. They utilized radio, film, the press, and other media to give the conflict an ideological meaning, while seeking to avoid the nationalist hysteria of World War I.

> *Mobilizing public opinion*

Wartime mobilization drew on deep-seated American traditions. The portrait of the United States holding aloft the torch of liberty in a world overrun by oppression reached back at least as far as the American Revolution. The description of a world half slave and half free recalled the Great Emancipator. But critics charged that the OWI seemed most interested in promoting the definition of freedom Roosevelt had emphasized during the 1930s. One of its first pamphlets listed as elements of freedom the right to a job at fair pay and to adequate food, clothing, shelter, and medical care. Concerned that the OWI was devoting as much time to

Each side in World War II invoked history to rally support for its cause. "Rise of Asia" depicts Japan liberating Asia from ABCD imperial oppressors (America, Britain, Chinese, Dutch), while the poster issued by the Office of War Information in the United States links the words of Abraham Lincoln to the struggle against Nazi tyranny.

promoting New Deal social programs as to the war effort, Congress eliminated most of its funding.

The Fifth Freedom

After Congress curtailed the OWI, the "selling of America" became overwhelmingly a private affair. Under the watchful eye of the War Advertising Council, private companies joined in the campaign to promote wartime patriotism, while positioning themselves and their brand names for the postwar world. Alongside advertisements urging Americans to purchase war bonds, guard against revealing military secrets, and grow "victory gardens" to allow food to be sent to the army, the war witnessed a burst of messages marketing advertisers' definition of freedom. Without directly criticizing Roosevelt, they repeatedly suggested that he had overlooked a fifth freedom. The National Association of Manufacturers and individual companies bombarded Americans with press releases, radio programs, and advertisements attributing the amazing feats of wartime production to "free enterprise."

Prosperity at home

Americans on the home front enjoyed a prosperity many could scarcely remember. Despite the rationing of scarce consumer items like coffee, meat, and gasoline, consumers found more goods available in 1944 than when the war began. With the memory of the Depression still very much alive, businessmen predicted a postwar world filled with consumer goods, with "freedom of choice" among abundant possibilities assured if only private enterprise were liberated from government controls. One advertisement for Royal typewriters, entitled "What This War Is All About," explained that victory would "hasten the day when you . . . can once more walk into any store in the land and buy anything you want." Certainly,

In this advertisement by the Liberty Motors and Engineering Corporation, published in the February 1944 issue of *Fortune*, Uncle Sam offers the Fifth Freedom—"free enterprise"—to war-devastated Europe. To spread its message, the company offered free enlargements of its ad.

ads suggested, the war did not imply any alteration in American institutions. "I'm
fighting for freedom," said a soldier in an ad by the Nash-Kelvinator Corporation.
"So don't anybody tell me I'll find America changed."

Women at Work

During the war, the nation engaged in an unprecedented mobilization of "woman-
power" to fill industrial jobs vacated by men. OWI publications encouraged
women to go to work, Hollywood films glorified the independent woman, and
private advertising celebrated the achievements of Rosie the Riveter, the female
industrial laborer depicted as muscular and self-reliant in Norman Rockwell's
famous magazine cover. With 15 million men in the armed forces, women in 1944
made up more than one-third of the civilian labor force, and 350,000 served in
auxiliary military units.

Even though most women workers still labored in clerical and service jobs,
new opportunities suddenly opened in industrial, professional, and government positions previously restricted to men. On the West Coast, one-third of
the workers in aircraft manufacturing and shipbuilding were women. For the
first time in history, married women in their thirties outnumbered the young
and single among female workers. Women forced unions like the United Auto
Workers to confront issues like equal pay for equal work, maternity leave, and
childcare facilities for working mothers. Defense companies sponsored swing
bands and dances to boost worker morale and arranged dates between male

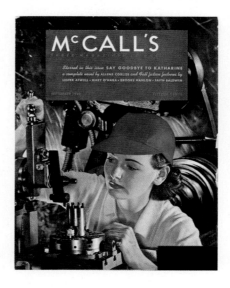

Unlike the lathe operator below, the
woman operating industrial machinery on
the cover of the September 1942 issue of
McCall's magazine remains glamorous,
with makeup in place and hair unruffled.

A female lathe operator in a Texas plant
that produced transport planes.

This print, part of the *America in the War* exhibition shown simultaneously in twenty-six American museums in 1943, offers a stylized image of women workers assembling shells in a factory while men march off to war.

and female workers. Having enjoyed what one wartime worker called "a taste of freedom"—doing "men's" jobs for men's wages and, sometimes, engaging in sexual activity while unmarried—many women hoped to remain in the labor force once peace returned.

The Pull of Tradition

"We as a nation," proclaimed one magazine article, "must change our basic attitude toward the work of women." But change proved difficult. The government, employers, and unions depicted work as a temporary necessity, not an expansion of women's freedom. Advertisements assured women laboring in factories that they, too, were "fighting for freedom." But their language spoke of sacrifice and military victory, not rights, independence, or self-determination. One union publication even declared, "There should be a law requiring the women who have taken over men's jobs to be laid off after the war." When the war ended, most female war workers, especially those in better-paying industrial employment, did indeed lose their jobs.

Despite the upsurge in the number of working women, the advertisers' "world of tomorrow" rested on a vision of family-centered prosperity. Like Norman Rockwell's Four Freedoms paintings, these wartime discussions of freedom simultaneously looked forward to a day of material abundance and back to a time when the family stood as the bedrock of society. The "American way of life" celebrated during the war centered on the woman with "a husband to meet every night at the door," and a home stocked with household appliances and consumer goods. Advertisements portrayed working women dreaming of their boyfriends in the army and emphasized that with the proper makeup, women could labor in a factory and remain attractive to men. Men in the army seem to have assumed that they would return home to resume traditional family life. In one wartime radio program, a young man described his goal for peacetime: "Havin' a home and some kids, and breathin' fresh air out in the suburbs . . . livin' and workin' decent, like free people."

VISIONS OF POSTWAR FREEDOM

Toward an American Century

The prospect of an affluent future provided a point of unity between New Dealers and conservatives, business and labor. And the promise of prosperity to some extent united two of the most celebrated blueprints for the postwar world. One was *The American Century*, publisher Henry Luce's 1941 effort to mobilize the American people both for the coming war and for an era of postwar world leadership. Americans, Luce's book insisted, must embrace the role history had thrust upon them as the "dominant power in the world." They must seize the opportunity to share with "all peoples" their "magnificent industrial products" and the "great American ideals," foremost among which stood "love of freedom." After the war, American power and American values would underpin a previously unimaginable prosperity— "the abundant life," Luce called it—produced by "free economic enterprise."

Luce's The American Century

The idea of an American mission to spread democracy and freedom goes back to the Revolution. But traditionally, it had envisioned the country as an example, not an active agent imposing the American model throughout the globe. Luce's essay anticipated important aspects of the postwar world. But its bombastic rhetoric and a title easily interpreted as a call for an American imperialism aroused immediate opposition among liberals and the left. Henry Wallace offered their response in "The Price of Free World Victory," an address delivered in May 1942 to the Free World Association.

Wallace, secretary of agriculture during the 1930s and one of the more liberal New Dealers, had replaced Vice President John Nance Garner as Roosevelt's running mate in 1940. In contrast to Luce's American Century, a world of business dominance no less than of American power, Wallace predicted that the war would usher in a "century of the common man." The "march of freedom," said Wallace, would continue in the postwar world. That world, however, would be marked by international cooperation, not any single power's rule. Governments acting to "humanize" capitalism and redistribute economic resources would eliminate hunger, illiteracy, and poverty.

Henry Wallace

Luce and Wallace both spoke the language of freedom. Luce offered a confident vision of worldwide free enterprise, while Wallace anticipated a global New Deal. But they had one thing in common—a new conception of America's role in the world, tied to continued international involvement, the promise of economic abundance, and the idea that the American experience should serve as a model for all other nations. Neither took into account the ideas that other countries might have developed as to how to proceed once the war had ended.

"The Way of Life of Free Men"

Even as Congress moved to dismantle parts of the New Deal, liberal Democrats and their left-wing allies unveiled plans for a postwar economic policy that would allow all Americans to enjoy freedom from want. In 1942 and 1943, the reports of the National Resources Planning Board (NRPB) offered a blueprint for a peacetime economy based on full employment, an expanded welfare state, and a widely shared American standard of living. Economic security and full employment were the board's watchwords. It called for a "new bill of rights" that would include all Americans in an expanded Social Security system and guarantee access to education, health care, adequate housing, and jobs for able-bodied adults. Labor and farm organizations, church and civil rights groups, and liberal New Dealers hailed the reports as offering a "vision of freedom" for the postwar world. The NRPB's plan for a "full-employment economy" with a "fair distribution of income," said *The Nation*, embodied "the way of life of free men."

The reports continued a shift in liberals' outlook that dated from the late 1930s. Rather than seeking to reform the institutions of capitalism, liberals would henceforth rely on government spending to secure full employment, social welfare, and mass consumption, while leaving the operation of the economy in private hands. The reports appeared to reflect the views of British economist John Maynard Keynes, who, as noted in the previous chapter, had identified government spending as the best way to promote economic growth, even if it caused budget deficits. The war had, in effect, ended the Depression by implementing a military version of

Despite the new independence enjoyed by millions of women, propaganda posters during World War II emphasized the male-dominated family as an essential element of American freedom.

...where the family is a sacred institution. Where children love, honor and respect their parents ...where a man's home is his castle ★ This is *your* America

Keynesianism. In calling for massive spending on job creation and public works—urban redevelopment, rural electrification, an overhaul of the transportation system, and the like—the NRPB proposed the continuation of Keynesian spending in peacetime. But this went so far beyond what Congress was willing to support that it eliminated the NRPB's funding.

An Economic Bill of Rights

Roosevelt had not publicized or promoted the NRPB reports of 1942 and 1943. Yet mindful that public-opinion polls showed a large majority of Americans favoring a guarantee of employment for those who could not find work, the president in 1944 called for an "Economic Bill of Rights." The original Bill of Rights restricted the power of government in the name of liberty. FDR proposed to expand its power in order to secure full employment, an adequate income, medical care, education, and a decent home for all Americans. "True individual freedom," he declared, "cannot exist without economic security and independence."

Already ill and preoccupied with the war, Roosevelt spoke only occasionally of the Economic Bill of Rights during the 1944 presidential campaign. The replacement of Vice President Henry Wallace by Harry S. Truman, then a little-known senator from Missouri, suggested that the president did not intend to do battle with Congress over social policy. Congress did not enact the Economic Bill of Rights. But in 1944, it extended to the millions of returning veterans an array of benefits, including unemployment pay, scholarships for further education, low-cost mortgage loans, pensions, and job training. The Servicemen's Readjustment Act, or GI Bill of Rights, was one of the most far-reaching pieces of social legislation in American history. Aimed at rewarding members of the armed forces for their service and preventing the widespread unemployment and economic disruption that had followed World War I, it profoundly shaped postwar society. By 1946, more than 1 million veterans were attending college under its provisions, making up half of total college enrollment. Almost 4 million would receive home mortgages, spurring the postwar suburban housing boom.

During 1945, unions, civil rights organizations, and religious groups urged Congress to enact the Full Employment Bill, which tried to do for the entire economy what the GI Bill promised veterans. The measure established a "right to employment" for all Americans and required the federal government to increase its level of spending to create enough jobs in case the economy failed to do so. The target of an intense business lobbying campaign, the bill only passed in 1946 with the word "Full" removed from its title and after its commitment to governmental job creation had been eliminated. But as the war drew to

Economic security

Ben Shahn's poster, *Our Friend*, for the Congress of Industrial Organizations' political action committee, urges workers to vote for FDR during his campaign for a fourth term. Art © Estate of Ben Shahn/Licensed by VAGA, New York, NY.

a close, most Americans embraced the idea that the government must continue to play a major role in maintaining employment and a high standard of living.

The Road to Serfdom

The failure of the Full Employment Bill confirmed the political stalemate that had begun with the elections of 1938. It also revealed the renewed intellectual respectability of fears that economic planning represented a threat to liberty. When the *New Republic* spoke of full employment as the "road to freedom," it subtly acknowledged the impact of *The Road to Serfdom* (1944), a surprise best-seller by Friedrich A. Hayek, a previously obscure Austrian-born economist. Hayek claimed that even the best-intentioned government efforts to direct the economy posed a threat to individual liberty. He offered a simple message—"planning leads to dictatorship."

Coming at a time when the miracles of war production had reinvigorated belief in the virtues of capitalism, and with the confrontation with Nazism highlighting the danger of merging economic and political power, Hayek offered a new intellectual justification for opponents of active government. In a complex economy, he insisted, no single person or group of experts could possibly possess enough knowledge to direct economic activity intelligently. A free market, he wrote, mobilizes the fragmented and partial knowledge scattered throughout society far more effectively than a planned economy.

Friedrich A. Hayek and laissez-faire economics

Unlike many of his disciples, Hayek was not a doctrinaire advocate of laissez-faire. His book endorsed measures that later conservatives would denounce as forms of socialism—minimum wage and maximum hours laws, antitrust enforcement, and a social safety net guaranteeing all citizens a basic minimum of food, shelter, and clothing. Hayek, moreover, criticized traditional conservatives for fondness for social hierarchy and authoritarian government. "I am not a conservative," he would later write. But by equating fascism, socialism, and the New Deal and by identifying economic planning with a loss of freedom, he helped lay the foundation for the rise of modern conservatism and a revival of laissez-faire economic thought. As the war drew to a close, the stage was set for a renewed battle over the government's proper role in society and the economy, and the social conditions of American freedom.

THE AMERICAN DILEMMA

The unprecedented attention to freedom as the defining characteristic of American life had implications that went far beyond wartime mobilization. World War II reshaped Americans' understanding of themselves as a people. The struggle against Nazi tyranny and its theory of a master race discredited ethnic and racial inequality. Originally promoted by religious and ethnic minorities in the 1920s and the Popular Front in the 1930s, a pluralist vision of American society now became part of official rhetoric. What set the United States apart from its wartime foes, the government insisted, was not only dedication to the ideals of the Four Freedoms but also the principle that Americans of all races, religions, and national origins could enjoy those freedoms equally. Racism was the enemy's philosophy; Americanism rested on toleration of diversity and equality for all. By

Embracing pluralism

Arthur Poinier's cartoon for the *Detroit Free Press*, June 19, 1941, illustrates how, during World War II, white ethnics (of British, German, Irish, French, Polish, Italian, and Scandinanvian descent) were incorporated within the boundaries of American freedom.

the end of the war, the new immigrant groups had been fully accepted as loyal ethnic Americans, rather than members of distinct and inferior "races." And the contradiction between the principle of equal freedom and the actual status of blacks had come to the forefront of national life.

Patriotic Assimilation

Among other things, World War II created a vast melting pot, especially for European immigrants and their children. Millions of Americans moved out of urban ethnic neighborhoods and isolated rural enclaves into the army and industrial plants where they came into contact with people of very different backgrounds. What one historian has called their "patriotic assimilation" differed sharply from the forced Americanization of World War I. While the Wilson administration had established Anglo-Saxon culture as a national norm, Roosevelt promoted pluralism as the only source of harmony in a diverse society. The American way of life, wrote the novelist Pearl Buck in an OWI pamphlet, rested on brotherhood—the principle that "persons of many lands can live together . . . and if they believe in freedom they can become a united people."

Government and private agencies eagerly promoted equality as the definition of Americanism and a counterpoint to Nazism. Officials rewrote history to establish racial and ethnic tolerance as the American way. To be an American, FDR declared, had always been a "matter of mind and heart," and "never . . . a matter of race or ancestry"—a statement more effective in mobilizing support for the war than in accurately describing the nation's past. Mindful of the intolerance spawned by World War I, the OWI highlighted nearly every group's contributions to American life and celebrated the strength of a people united in respect for diversity. One OWI pamphlet described prejudice as a foreign import rather than a homegrown product and declared bigots more dangerous than spies—they were "fighting for the enemy."

Racism and nativism discredited

Horrified by the uses to which the Nazis put the idea of inborn racial difference, biological and social scientists abandoned belief in a link among race, culture, and intelligence, an idea only recently central to their disciplines. Ruth Benedict's *Races and Racism* (1942) described racism as "a travesty of scientific knowledge." In the same year, Ashley Montagu's *Man's Most Dangerous Myth: The Fallacy of Race* became a best-seller. By the war's end, racism and nativism had been stripped of intellectual respectability, at least outside the South, and were viewed as psychological disorders.

Hollywood, too, did its part, portraying fighting units whose members, representing various regional, ethnic, and religious backgrounds, put aside group loyalties and prejudices for the common cause. *Air Force* featured a bomber crew that included an Anglo-Saxon officer, a Jewish sergeant, and a Polish-American gunner. In the film *Bataan*, the ethnically balanced platoon included a black soldier, even though the real army was racially segregated. The war's most popular motion picture, *This Is the Army*, starring, among others, future president Ronald Reagan, offered a vision of postwar society that celebrated the ethnic diversity of the American people.

Intolerance, of course, hardly disappeared from American life. One correspondent complained to Norman Rockwell that he included too many "foreign-looking" faces in his *Freedom of Worship* painting. Many business and government circles still

The persistence of prejudice

excluded Jews. Along with the fact that early reports of the Holocaust were too terrible to be believed, anti-Semitism contributed to the government's unwillingness to allow more than a handful of European Jews (21,000 during the course of the war) to find refuge in the United States. Roosevelt himself learned during the war of the extent of Hitler's "final solution" to the Jewish presence in Europe. But he failed to authorize air strikes that might have destroyed German death camps.

Nonetheless, the war made millions of ethnic Americans, especially the children of the new immigrants, feel fully American for the first time. During the war, one New York "ethnic" recalled, "the Italo-Americans stopped being Italo and started becoming Americans." But the event that inspired this comment, the Harlem race riot of 1943, suggested that patriotic assimilation stopped at the color line.

The *Bracero* Program

The war had a far more ambiguous meaning for non-white groups than for whites. On the eve of Pearl Harbor, racial barriers remained deeply entrenched in American life. Southern blacks were still trapped in a rigid system of segregation. Asians could not emigrate to the United States or become naturalized citizens. As noted in the previous chapter, more than 400,000 Mexican-Americans had been "voluntarily" repatriated by local authorities in the Southwest during the Depression. Most American Indians still lived on reservations, in dismal poverty.

The war set in motion changes that would reverberate in the postwar years. Under the *bracero* program agreed to by the Mexican and American governments in 1942 (the name derives from *brazo*, the Spanish word for arm), tens of thousands of contract laborers crossed into the United States to take up jobs as domestic and agricultural workers. Initially designed as a temporary response to the wartime labor shortage, the program lasted until 1964. During the period of the *bracero* program, more than 4.5 million Mexicans entered the United States under government labor contracts (while a slightly larger number were arrested for illegal entry by the Border Patrol). *Braceros* were supposed to receive decent housing and wages. But since they could not become citizens and could be deported at any time, they found it almost impossible to form unions or secure better working conditions.

Mexican contract workers

Although the *bracero* program reinforced the status of immigrants from Mexico as an unskilled labor force, wartime employment opened new opportunities for second-generation Mexican-Americans. Hundreds of thousands of men and women emerged from ethnic neighborhoods, or *barrios*, to work in defense industries and serve in the army (where, unlike blacks, they fought alongside whites). A new "Chicano" culture—a fusion of Mexican heritage and American experience—was being born. Contact with other groups led many to learn English and sparked a rise in interethnic marriages.

New opportunities for Mexican-Americans

Mexican-American Rights

The "zoot suit" riots of 1943, in which club-wielding sailors and policemen attacked Mexican-American youths wearing flamboyant clothing on the streets of Los Angeles, illustrated the limits of wartime tolerance. "Our Latin American boys," complained one activist, "are not segregated at the front line. . . . They are dying that democracy may live." Yet when they return home, the activist continued, "they are not considered good enough to go into a café." But the contrast between the war's rhetoric of freedom and pluralism and the reality of continued discrimination

The "zoot suit" riots

inspired a heightened consciousness of civil rights. For example, Mexican-Americans brought complaints of discrimination before the Fair Employment Practices Commission (FEPC) to fight the practice in the Southwest of confining them to the lowest-paid work or paying them lower wages than white workers doing the same jobs.

Perhaps half a million Mexican-American men and women served in the armed forces. And with discrimination against Mexicans an increasing embarrassment in view of Roosevelt's Good Neighbor policy, Texas (the state with the largest population of Mexican descent) in 1943 unanimously passed the oddly named Caucasian Race—Equal Privileges resolution. It stated that since "all the nations of the North and South American continents" were united in the struggle against Nazism, "all persons of the Caucasian race" were entitled to equal treatment in places of public accommodation. Since Texas law had long defined Mexicans as white, the measure applied to them while not challenging the segregation of blacks. The resolution lacked an enforcement mechanism. Indeed, because of continued discrimination in Texas, the Mexican government for a time prohibited the state from receiving laborers under the *bracero* program.

> *Texas and Mexican-Americans*

Indians During the War

The war also brought many American Indians closer to the mainstream of American life. Some 25,000 served in the army (including the famous Navajo "code-talkers," who transmitted messages in their complex native language, which the Japanese could not decipher). Insisting that the United States lacked the authority to draft Indian men into the army, the Iroquois issued their own declaration of war against the Axis powers. Tens of thousands of Indians left reservations for jobs in war industries. Exposed for the first time to urban life and industrial society, many chose not to return to the reservations after the war ended (indeed, the reservations did not share in wartime prosperity). Some Indian veterans took advantage of the GI Bill to attend college after the war, an opportunity that had been available to very few Indians previously.

> *The Navajo "code-talkers"*

Asian-Americans in Wartime

Asian-Americans' war experience was paradoxical. More than 50,000—the children of immigrants from China, Japan, Korea, and the Philippines—fought in the army, mostly in all-Asian units. With China an ally in the Pacific war, Congress in 1943 ended decades of complete exclusion by establishing a nationality quota for Chinese immigrants. The annual limit of 105 hardly suggested a desire for a large-scale influx. But the image of the Chinese as gallant fighters defending their country against Japanese aggression called into question long-standing racial stereotypes. As in the case of Mexican-Americans, large numbers of Chinese-Americans moved out of ethnic ghettos to work alongside whites in jobs on the home front.

The experience of Japanese-Americans was far different. Many Americans viewed the war against Germany as an ideological struggle. But both sides saw the Pacific war as a race war. Japanese propaganda depicted Americans as a self-indulgent people contaminated by ethnic and racial diversity as opposed to the racially "pure" Japanese. In the United States, long-standing prejudices and the

Wartime propaganda in the United States sought to inspire hatred against the Pacific foe. This poster, issued by the U.S. Army, recalls the Bataan death march in the Philippines.

What are YOU going to do about it?

5200 Yank Prisoners Killed by Jap Torture In Philippines; Cruel 'March of Death' Described

STAY ON THE JOB UNTIL EVERY MURDERING JAP IS WIPED OUT!

shocking attack on Pearl Harbor combined to produce an unprecedented hatred of Japan. "In all our history," according to one historian, "no foe has been detested as were the Japanese." Government propaganda and war films portrayed the Japanese foe as rats, dogs, gorillas, and snakes—bestial and subhuman. They blamed Japanese aggression on a violent racial or national character, not, as in the case of Germany and Italy, on tyrannical rulers.

About 70 percent of Japanese-Americans in the continental United States lived in California, where they dominated vegetable farming in the Los Angeles area. One-third were first-generation immigrants, or *issei*, but a substantial majority were *nisei*—American-born, and therefore citizens. Many of the latter spoke only English, had never been to Japan, and had tried to assimilate despite prevailing prejudice. But the Japanese-American community could not remain unaffected by the rising tide of hatred. The government bent over backward to include German-Americans and Italian-Americans in the war effort. It ordered the arrest of only a handful of the more than 800,000 German and Italian nationals in the United States when the war began. But it viewed every person of Japanese ethnicity as a potential spy.

Nisei

Japanese-American Internment

California, as discussed in Chapter 19, had a long history of hostility toward the Japanese. Now, inspired by exaggerated fears of a Japanese invasion of the West Coast and pressured by whites who saw an opportunity to gain possession of Japanese-American property, the military persuaded FDR to issue Executive Order 9066. Promulgated in February 1942, this ordered the relocation of all persons of Japanese descent from the West Coast. That spring and summer, authorities removed more than 110,000 men, women, and children—nearly two-thirds of them American citizens—to camps far from their homes. The order did not apply to persons of Japanese descent living in Hawaii, where they represented nearly 40 percent of the population. Despite Hawaii's vulnerability, its economy could not function without Japanese-American labor. But the treatment of mainland Japanese-Americans provided ammunition for Japan's claim that its aggressions in Asia were intended to defend the rights of non-white peoples against colonial rule and a racist United States.

The internees were subjected to a quasi-military discipline in the camps. Living in former horse stables, makeshift shacks, or barracks behind barbed wire fences, they were awakened for roll call at 6:45 each morning and ate their meals (which rarely included the Japanese cooking to which they were accustomed) in giant mess halls. Armed guards patrolled the camps, and searchlights shone all night. Privacy was difficult to come by, and medical facilities were often nonexistent. Nonetheless, the internees did their best to create an atmosphere of home, decorating their accommodations with pictures, flowers, and curtains, planting vegetable gardens, and setting up activities like sports clubs and art classes for themselves.

Internment revealed how easily war can undermine basic freedoms. There were no court hearings, no due process, and no writs of habeas corpus. One searches the wartime record in vain for public protests among non-Japanese

Fumiko Hayashida holds her thirteen-month-old daughter, while waiting for relocation to an internment camp. Both wear baggage tags, as if they were pieces of luggage. This photo, taken by a journalist for the *Seattle Post-Intelligencer*, came to symbolize the entire internment experience. Ms. Hayashida celebrated her 100th birthday in 2011.

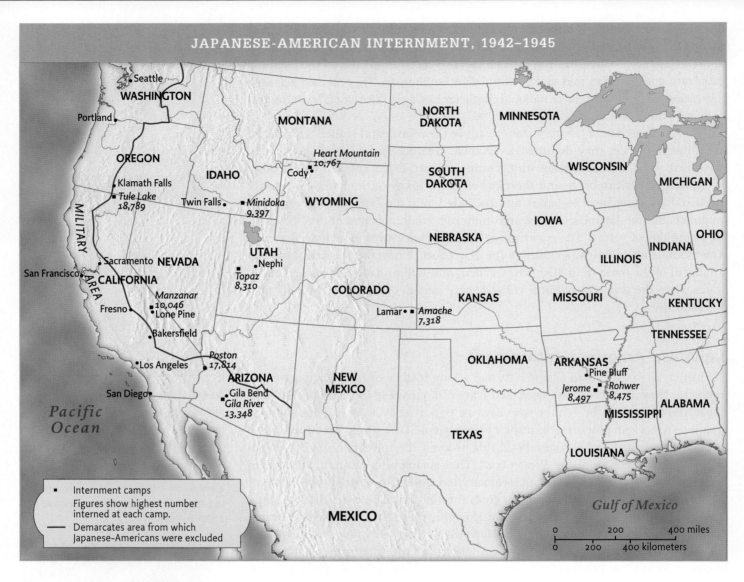

JAPANESE-AMERICAN INTERNMENT, 1942–1945

Legend:
- Internment camps. Figures show highest number interned at each camp.
- Demarcates area from which Japanese-Americans were excluded

Camps and figures shown on map:
- Tule Lake 18,789
- Minidoka 9,397
- Heart Mountain 10,767
- Topaz 8,310
- Manzanar 10,046
- Poston 17,814
- Gila River 13,348
- Amache 7,318
- Jerome 8,497
- Rohwer 8,475

More than 100,000 Japanese-Americans—the majority American citizens—were forcibly moved from their homes to internment camps during World War II.

The Korematsu *decision*

against the gravest violation of civil liberties since the end of slavery. The press supported the policy almost unanimously. In Congress, only Senator Robert Taft of Ohio spoke out against it. Groups publicly committed to fighting discrimination, from the Communist Party to the NAACP and the American Jewish Committee, either defended the policy or remained silent.

The courts refused to intervene. In 1944, in *Korematsu v. United States*, the Supreme Court denied the appeal of Fred Korematsu, a Japanese-American citizen who had been arrested for refusing to present himself for internment. Speaking for a 6-3 majority, Justice Hugo Black, usually an avid defender of civil liberties, upheld the legality of the internment policy, insisting that an order applying only to persons of Japanese descent was not based on race. The Court has never overturned the *Korematsu* decision. As Justice Robert H. Jackson warned in his dissent, it "lies about like a loaded weapon ready for the hand of any authority that can bring forward a plausible claim" of national security.

The government marketed war bonds to the internees. It established a loyalty oath program, expecting Japanese-Americans to swear allegiance to the government that had imprisoned them and to enlist in the army. Some young men refused, and about 200 were sent to prison for resisting the draft. "Let us out and then maybe I'll think about risking my skin for 'the land of the free,'" one of the resisters remarked. But 20,000 Japanese-Americans joined the armed forces from the camps, along with another 13,000 from Hawaii. A long campaign for acknowledgment of the injustice done to Japanese-Americans followed the end of the war. In 1988, Congress apologized for internment and provided $20,000 in compensation to each surviving victim. President Bill Clinton subsequently awarded Fred Korematsu the Presidential Medal of Freedom.

Blacks and the War

Although the treatment of Japanese-Americans revealed the stubborn hold of racism in American life, the wartime message of freedom portended a major transformation in the status of blacks. "There never has been, there isn't now, and there never will be," Roosevelt declared, "any race of people on the earth fit to serve as masters over their fellow men." Yet Nazi Germany cited American practices as proof of its own race policies. Washington remained a rigidly segregated city, and the Red Cross refused to mix blood from blacks and whites in its blood banks (thereby, critics charged, in effect accepting Nazi race theories). Charles Drew, the black scientist who pioneered the techniques of storing and shipping blood plasma—a development of immense importance to the treatment of wounded soldiers—protested bitterly against this policy, pointing out that it had no scientific basis. In 1940 and 1941, even as Roosevelt called for aid to the free peoples of Europe, thirteen lynchings took place in the United States.

The war spurred a movement of black population from the rural South to the cities of the North and West that dwarfed the Great Migration of World War I and the 1920s. About 700,000 black migrants poured out of the South on what they called "liberty trains," seeking jobs in the industrial heartland. They encountered sometimes violent hostility, nowhere more so than in Detroit, where angry white residents forced authorities to evict black tenants from a new housing project. In 1943, a fight at a Detroit city park spiraled into a race riot that left thirty-four persons dead, and a "hate strike" of 20,000 workers protested the upgrading of black employees in a plant manufacturing aircraft engines. The war failed to end lynching. Isaac Simmons, a black minister, was murdered in 1944 for refusing to sell his land to a white man who believed it might contain oil. The criminals went unpunished. This took place in Liberty, Mississippi.

Blacks and Military Service

When World War II began, the air force and marines had no black members. The army restricted the number of black enlistees and contained only five black officers, three of them chaplains. The navy accepted blacks only as waiters and cooks.

During the war, more than 1 million blacks served in the armed forces. They did so in segregated units, largely confined to construction, transport, and

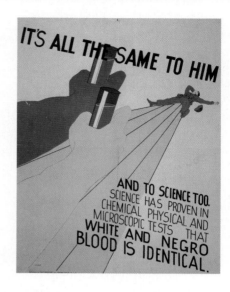

During World War II, Red Cross blood banks separated blood from black and white Americans—one illustration of the persistence of racial segregation. This 1943 poster by the NAACP points out that the concept of "Negro" and "white" blood has no scientific basis.

Race riot in Detroit

other noncombat tasks. Many northern black draftees were sent to the South for military training, where they found themselves excluded from movie theaters and servicemen's clubs on military bases and abused when they ventured into local towns. Black soldiers sometimes had to give up their seats on railroad cars to accommodate Nazi prisoners of war. "Nothing so lowers Negro morale," wrote the NAACP's magazine, *The Crisis*, "as the frequent preferential treatment of Axis prisoners of war in contrast with Army policy toward American troops who happen to be Negro."

Segregation in the armed forces

When southern black veterans returned home and sought benefits through the GI Bill, they encountered even more evidence of racial discrimination. On the surface, the GI Bill contained no racial differentiation in offering benefits like health care, college tuition assistance, job training, and loans to start a business or purchase a farm. But local authorities who administered its provisions allowed southern black veterans to use its education benefits only at segregated colleges, limited their job training to unskilled work and low-wage service jobs, and limited loans for farm purchase to white veterans.

Birth of the Civil Rights Movement

In 1942, a public-opinion survey sponsored by the army's Bureau of Intelligence found that the vast majority of white Americans were "unaware that there is any such thing as a 'Negro problem' " and were convinced that blacks were satisfied with their social and economic conditions. They would soon discover their mistake.

The war years witnessed the birth of the modern civil rights movement. Angered by the almost complete exclusion of African-Americans from jobs in the rapidly expanding war industries (of 100,000 aircraft workers in 1940, fewer than 300 were blacks), the black labor leader A. Philip Randolph in July 1941 called for a March on Washington. His demands included access to defense employment, an end to segregation, and a national antilynching law. Randolph, who as founder of the Brotherhood of Sleeping Car Porters had long battled racism among both employers and unions, hurled Roosevelt's rhetoric back at the president. Randolph declared racial discrimination "undemocratic, un-American, and pro-Hitler."

The prospect of thousands of angry blacks descending on Washington, remarked one official, "scared the government half to death." To persuade Randolph to call off the march, Roosevelt issued Executive Order 8802, which banned discrimination in defense jobs and established a Fair Employment Practices Commission (FEPC) to monitor compliance. The black press hailed the order as a new Emancipation Proclamation.

Essentially an investigative agency, the FEPC lacked enforcement powers. But its very existence marked a significant shift in public policy. Its hearings exposed patterns of racial exclusion so ingrained that firms at first freely admitted that their want ads asked for "colored" applicants for positions as porters and janitors and "white" ones for skilled jobs, and that they allowed black women to work only as laundresses and cooks. The first federal agency since Reconstruction to campaign for equal opportunity for black Americans, the FEPC played an important role in obtaining jobs for black workers in industrial plants and shipyards. In southern

This Is the Enemy, a 1942 poster by Victor Ancona and Karl Koehler, suggests a connection between Nazism abroad and lynching at home.

California, the aircraft manufacturer Lockheed ran special buses into black neighborhoods to bring workers to its plants. By 1944, more than 1 million blacks, 300,000 of them women, held manufacturing jobs. ("My sister always said that Hitler was the one that got us out of the white folks' kitchen," recalled one black woman.)

The Double-V

When the president "said that we should have the Four Freedoms," a black steel-worker declared, he meant to include "all races." During the war, NAACP membership grew from 50,000 to nearly 500,000. The Congress of Racial Equality (CORE), founded by an interracial group of pacifists in 1942, held sit-ins in northern cities to integrate restaurants and theaters. After a Firestone tire factory in Memphis fired a black woman for trying to enter a city bus before white passengers had been seated, black workers at the plant went on strike until she was reinstated.

In February 1942, the *Pittsburgh Courier* coined the phrase that came to symbolize black attitudes during the war—the "double-V." Victory over Germany and Japan, it insisted, must be accompanied by victory over segregation at home. While the Roosevelt administration and the white press saw the war as an expression of American ideals, black newspapers pointed to the gap between those ideals and reality. Side by side with ads for war bonds, *The Crisis* insisted that a segregated army "cannot fight for a free world."

Surveying wartime public opinion, a political scientist concluded that "symbols of national solidarity" had very different meanings to white and black Americans. To blacks, freedom from fear meant, among other things, an end to lynching, and freedom from want included doing away with "discrimination in getting jobs." If, in whites' eyes, freedom was a "possession to be defended," he observed, to blacks and other racial minorities it remained a "goal to be achieved." "*Our* fight for freedom," said a returning black veteran of the Pacific war, "begins when we get to San Francisco."

What the Negro Wants

During the war, a broad political coalition centered on the left but reaching well beyond it called for an end to racial inequality in America. The NAACP and American Jewish Congress cooperated closely in advocating laws to ban discrimination in employment and housing. Despite considerable resistance from rank-and-file white workers, CIO unions, especially those with strong left-liberal and communist influence, made significant efforts to organize black workers and win them access to skilled positions. AFL craft unions by and large continued their long tradition of excluding black workers. But during World War II, the CIO was probably more racially integrated than any labor organization since the Knights of Labor in the 1880s.

The new black militancy created a crisis for moderate white southerners. They now saw their middle ground evaporating as blacks demanded an end to segregation while southern politicians took up the cry of protecting white supremacy. The latter also spoke the language of freedom. Defenders of the racial status quo interpreted freedom to mean the right to shape their region's institutions without outside interference. The "war emergency," insisted Governor Frank Dixon of Alabama, "should not be used as a pretext to bring about the abolition of the color line."

Another This Is America *propaganda poster emphasizes the American dream of equal opportunity for all. All the children in the classroom, however, are white.*

Labor and race

VOICES OF FREEDOM

From HENRY R. LUCE, *THE AMERICAN CENTURY* (1941)

Even before the United States entered World War II, some Americans were thinking of a postwar world in which the United States would exert its influence throughout the globe. One influential call for Americans to accept the burden of world leadership was a short book by Henry R. Luce, the publisher of *Life* and *Time* magazines.

In the field of national policy, the fundamental trouble with America has been, and is, that whereas their nation became in the 20th Century the most powerful and the most vital nation in the world, nevertheless Americans were unable to accommodate themselves spiritually and practically to that fact. Hence they have failed to play their part as a world power—a failure which has had disastrous consequences for themselves and for all mankind. And the cure is this: to accept wholeheartedly our duty and our opportunity as the most powerful and vital nation in the world and in consequence to exert upon the world the full impact of our influence, for such purposes as we see fit and by such means as we see fit. . . .

Our world of 2,000,000,000 human beings is for the first time in history one world, fundamentally indivisible. . . . Our world, again for the first time in human history, is capable of producing all the material needs of the entire human family. . . . The world of the 20th Century, if it is to

come to life in any nobility of health and vigor, must be to a significant degree an American Century. . . .

In postulating the indivisibility of the contemporary world, one does not necessarily imagine that anything like a world state—a parliament of men—must be brought about in this century. Nor need we assume that war can be abolished. . . . Large sections of the human family may be effectively organized into opposition to one another. Tyrannies may require a large amount of living space. But Freedom requires and will require far greater living space than Tyranny. . . . Justice will come near to losing all meaning in the minds of men unless Justice can have approximately the same fundamental meanings in many lands and among many peoples. . . .

As to the . . . promise of adequate production for all mankind, the "more abundant life," be it noted that this is characteristically an American promise. . . . What we must insist on is that the abundant life is predicated on Freedom. . . . Without Freedom, there will be no abundant life. With Freedom, there can be.

And finally there is the belief—shared let us remember by most men living—that the 20th Century must be to a significant degree an American Century. . . . As America enters dynamically upon the world scene, we need most of all to seek and to bring forth a vision of America as a world power and to bring forth a vision . . . which will guide us to the authentic creation of the 20th Century—our Century.

From CHARLES H. WESLEY, "THE NEGRO HAS ALWAYS WANTED THE FOUR FREEDOMS," IN *WHAT THE NEGRO WANTS* (1944)

In 1944, the University of North Carolina Press published *What the Negro Wants*, a book of essays by fourteen prominent black leaders. Virtually every contributor called for the right to vote in the South, the dismantling of segregation, and access to the "American standard of living." Several essays also linked the black struggle for racial justice with movements against European imperialism in Africa and Asia. When he read the manuscript, W. T. Couch, the director of the press, was stunned. "If this is what the Negro wants," he told the book's editor, "nothing could be clearer than what he needs, and needs most urgently, is to revise his wants." In this excerpt, the historian Charles H. Wesley explains that blacks are denied each of the Four Freedoms, and also illustrates how the war strengthened black internationalism.

[Negroes] have wanted what other citizens of the United States have wanted. They have wanted freedom and opportunity. They have wanted the pursuit of the life vouchsafed to all citizens of the United States by our own liberty documents. They have wanted freedom of speech, [but] they were supposed to be silently acquiescent in all aspects of their life. . . . They have wanted freedom of religion, for they had been compelled to "steal away to Jesus" . . . in order to worship God as they desired. . . . They have wanted freedom from want. . . . However, the Negro has remained a marginal worker and the competition with white workers has left him in want in many localities of an economically sufficient nation. They have wanted freedom from fear. They have been cowed, browbeaten or beaten, as they have marched through the years of American life. . . .

The Negro wants democracy to begin at home. . . . The future of our democratic life is insecure so long as the hatred, disdain and disparagement of Americans of African ancestry exist. . . .

The Negro wants not only to win the war but also to win the peace. . . . He wants the peace to be free of race and color restrictions, of imperialism and exploitation, and inclusive of the participation of minorities all over the world in their own governments. When it is said that we are fighting for freedom, the Negro asks, "Whose freedom?" Is it the freedom of a peace to exploit, suppress, exclude, debase and restrict colored peoples in India, China, Africa, Malaya in the usual ways? . . . Will Great Britain and the United States specifically omit from the Four Freedoms their minorities and subject peoples? The Negro does not want such a peace.

QUESTIONS

1. *What values does Luce wish America to spread to the rest of the world?*

2. *Why does Wesley believe that black Americans are denied the Four Freedoms?*

3. *Do Luce and Wesley envision different roles for the United States in the postwar world?*

Even as the war gave birth to the modern civil rights movement, it also planted the seeds for the South's "massive resistance" to desegregation during the 1950s.

Progress on race

In the rest of the country, however, the status of black Americans assumed a place at the forefront of enlightened liberalism. Far more than in the 1930s, federal officials spoke openly of the need for a dramatic change in race relations. American democracy, noted Secretary of War Stimson, had not yet addressed "the persistent legacy of the original crime of slavery." Progress came slowly. But the National War Labor Board banned racial wage differentials. In *Smith v. Allwright* (1944), the Supreme Court outlawed all-white primaries, one of the mechanisms by which southern states deprived blacks of political rights. In the same year, the navy began assigning small numbers of black sailors to previously all-white ships. In the final months of the war, it ended segregation altogether, and the army established a few combat units that included black and white soldiers.

Willkie's One World

After a world tour in 1942 to rally support for the Allies, Wendell Willkie, Roosevelt's opponent of 1940, published *One World*. It sold 1 million copies, faster than any nonfiction work in American history. Willkie's travels persuaded him that Asia, Africa, and Latin America would play a pivotal role in the postwar era. But the book's great surprise came in Willkie's attack on "our imperialisms at home." Unless the United States addressed the "mocking paradox" of racism, he insisted, its claim to world leadership would lack moral authority. "If we want to talk about freedom," Willkie wrote, "we must mean freedom for everyone inside our frontiers."

An American Dilemma

No event reflected the new concern with the status of black Americans more than the publication in 1944 of *An American Dilemma*, a sprawling account of the country's racial past, present, and future written by the Swedish social scientist Gunnar Myrdal. The book offered an uncompromising portrait of how deeply racism was entrenched in law, politics, economics, and social behavior. But Myrdal combined this sobering analysis with admiration for what he called the American Creed—belief in equality, justice, equal opportunity, and freedom. The war, he argued, had made Americans more aware than ever of the contradiction between this creed and the reality of racial inequality. He concluded that "there is bound to be a redefinition of the Negro's status as a result of this War."

Myrdal's notion of a conflict between American values and American racial policies was hardly new—Frederick Douglass and W. E. B. Du Bois had said much the same thing. But in the context of a worldwide struggle against Nazism and rising black demands for equality at home, his book struck a chord. It identified a serious national problem and seemed to offer an almost painless path to peaceful change, in which the federal government would take

World War II reinvigorated the movement for civil rights. Here African-Americans attempt to register to vote in Atlanta, Georgia.

the lead in outlawing discrimination. This coupling of an appeal to American principles with federal social engineering established a liberal position on race relations that would survive for many years.

By 1945, support for racial justice had finally taken its place on the liberal-left agenda alongside full employment, civil liberties, and the expansion of the New Deal welfare state. Roosevelt himself rarely spoke out on racial issues. But many liberals insisted that racial discrimination must be confronted head-on through federal antilynching legislation, equal opportunity in the workplace, an end to segregated housing and schools, and the expansion of Social Security programs to cover agricultural and domestic workers. This wartime vision of a racially integrated full employment economy formed a bridge between the New Deal and the Great Society of the 1960s (see Chapter 25).

> *Wartime vision of racial justice*

Black Internationalism

In the nineteenth century, black radicals like David Walker and Martin Delany had sought to link the fate of African-Americans with that of peoples of African descent in other parts of the world, especially the Caribbean and Africa. In the first decades of the twentieth century, this kind of international consciousness was reinvigorated. In a sense, the global imposition of white supremacy brought forth a feeling of racial solidarity across national and geographic lines. Garveyism (discussed in Chapter 19) was one example; another was reflected in the five Pan-African Congresses that met between 1919 and 1945. Attended by black intellectuals from the United States, the Caribbean, Europe, and Africa, these gatherings denounced the colonial rule of Africa and sought to establish a sense of unity among all people in the African diaspora (a term used to describe the scattering of a people with a single national, religious, or racial identity). At the home of George Padmore, a West Indian labor

> *Pan-African Congresses*

Paul Robeson, the black actor, singer, and battler for civil rights, leading Oakland dockworkers in singing the national anthem in 1942. World War II gave a significant boost to the vision, shared by Robeson and others on the left, of an America based on genuine equality.

organizer and editor living in London, black American leaders like W. E. B. Du Bois and Paul Robeson came into contact with future leaders of African independence movements such as Jomo Kenyatta (Kenya), Kwame Nkrumah (Ghana), and Nnamdi Azikiwe (Nigeria). "I discovered Africa in London," Robeson remarked.

A global cause

Through these gatherings, Du Bois, Robeson, and others developed an outlook that linked the plight of black Americans with that of people of color worldwide. Racism, they came to believe, originated not in irrational hatred but in the slave trade and slavery. In the modern age, it was perpetuated by colonialism. Thus, freeing Africa from colonial rule would encourage greater equality at home.

World War II stimulated among African-Americans an even greater awareness of the links between racism in the United States and colonialism abroad. In 1942, the *Pittsburgh Courier*, a major black newspaper, began publishing regular columns on events in India (where the British had imprisoned leaders of the movement for national independence) and China. In the same year, Robeson founded the Council on African Affairs, which tried to place colonial liberation at the top of the black American agenda.

THE END OF THE WAR

As 1945 opened, Allied victory was assured. In December 1944, in a desperate gamble, Hitler launched a surprise counterattack in France that pushed Allied forces back fifty miles, creating a large bulge in their lines. The largest single battle ever fought by the U.S. Army, the Battle of the Bulge produced more than 70,000 American casualties. But by early 1945 the assault had failed.

In March, American troops crossed the Rhine River and entered the industrial heartland of Germany. Hitler took his own life, and shortly afterward Soviet forces occupied Berlin. On May 8, known as V-E Day (for victory in Europe), came the formal end to the war against Germany. In the Pacific, American forces moved ever closer to Japan. They had reconquered Guam in August 1944 and landed in the Philippines two months later, where they destroyed most of the remainder of the enemy fleet in the naval battle of Leyte Gulf.

V-E Day

"The Most Terrible Weapon"

Franklin D. Roosevelt defeated Republican nominee Thomas E. Dewey, the governor of New York, to win an unprecedented fourth term in 1944. But FDR did not live to see the Allied victory. He succumbed to a stroke on April 12, 1945. To his successor, Harry S. Truman, fell one of the most momentous decisions ever confronted by an American president—whether to use the atomic bomb against Japan. Truman did not know about the bomb until after he became president. Then, Secretary of War Stimson informed him that the United States had secretly developed "the most terrible weapon ever known in human history."

Truman and the atomic bomb

The bomb was a practical realization of the theory of relativity, a rethinking of the laws of physics developed early in the twentieth century by the German scientist Albert Einstein. Energy and matter, Einstein showed, represented two forms of the same phenomenon. According to his famous equation $E = mc^2$, the energy contained in matter equals its mass times the speed of light squared—an enormous amount. By using certain forms of uranium, or the man-made element plutonium, an atomic reaction could be created that transformed part of the mass into energy. This energy could be harnessed to provide a form of controlled power, or it could be unleashed in a tremendous explosion.

Having fled to the United States from Hitler's Germany, Einstein in 1939 warned Roosevelt that Nazi scientists were trying to develop an atomic weapon and urged the president to do likewise. In the following year, FDR authorized what came to be known as the Manhattan Project, a top-secret program in which American scientists developed an atomic bomb during World War II. The weapon was tested successfully in New Mexico in July 1945.

> *Manhattan Project*

The Dawn of the Atomic Age

On August 6, 1945, an American plane dropped an atomic bomb that detonated over Hiroshima, Japan—a target chosen because almost alone among major Japanese cities, it had not yet suffered damage. In an instant, nearly every building in the city was destroyed. Of the city's population of 280,000 civilians and 40,000 soldiers, approximately 70,000 died immediately. Because atomic bombs release deadly radiation, the death toll kept rising in the months that followed. By the end of the year, it reached at least 140,000. Thousands more perished over the next five years. On August 9, the United States exploded a second bomb over Nagasaki, killing 70,000 persons. On the same day, the Soviet Union declared war on Japan and invaded Manchuria. Within a week, Japan surrendered.

> *Hiroshima and Nagasaki*

After the dropping of the atomic bomb on Hiroshima, Japan, the federal government restricted the circulation of images of destruction. But soon after the end of the war it dispatched photographers to compile a Strategic Bombing Survey, to assess the bomb's impact. This photograph, which long remained classified, shows the remains of an elementary school.

Because of the enormous cost in civilian lives—more than twice America's military fatalities in the entire Pacific war—the use of the bomb remains controversial. The Japanese had fought ferociously while being driven from one Pacific island after another. An American invasion of Japan, some advisers warned Truman, might cost as many as 250,000 American lives. No such invasion was planned, however, until 1946, and considerable evidence had accumulated that Japan was nearing surrender. Already some of its officials had communicated a willingness to end the war if Emperor Hirohito could remain on his throne. This fell short of the Allies' demand for "unconditional surrender," but the victors would, in the end, agree to Hirohito's survival. Japan's economy had been crippled and its fleet destroyed, and it would now have to fight the Soviet Union as well as the United States. Some of the scientists who had worked on the bomb urged Truman to demonstrate its power to international observers. But Truman did not hesitate. The bomb was a weapon, and weapons are created to be used.

Assessing the use of the bomb

The Nature of the War

The dropping of the atomic bombs was the logical culmination of the way World War II had been fought. All wars inflict suffering on noncombatants. But never before had civilian populations been so ruthlessly targeted. Military personnel represented 90 percent of those who died in World War I. But of the estimated 50 million persons who perished during World War II (including 400,000 American soldiers), perhaps 20 million were civilians. Germany had killed millions of members of "inferior races." It had repeatedly bombed London and other cities. The Allies carried out even more deadly air assaults on civilian populations. Early in 1945, the firebombing of Dresden killed some 100,000 people, mostly women, children, and elderly men. On March 9, nearly the same number died in an inferno caused by the bombing of Tokyo.

The war and civilian populations

Four years of war propaganda had dehumanized the Japanese in American eyes, and few persons criticized Truman's decision in 1945. But public doubts began to surface, especially after John Hersey published *Hiroshima* (1946), a graphic account of the horrors suffered by the civilian population. General Dwight D. Eisenhower, who thought the use of the bomb unnecessary, later wrote, "I hated to see our country be the first to use such a weapon."

Planning the Postwar World

Even as the war raged, a series of meetings between Allied leaders formulated plans for the postwar world. Churchill, Roosevelt, and Stalin met at Tehran, Iran, in 1943, and at Yalta, in the southern Soviet Union, early in 1945, to hammer out agreements. The final "Big Three" conference took place at Potsdam, near Berlin, in July 1945. It involved Stalin, Truman, and Churchill (replaced midway in the talks by Clement Attlee, who became prime minister when his Labour Party swept the British elections). At Potsdam, the Allied leaders established a military administration for Germany and agreed to place top Nazi leaders on trial for war crimes.

The "Big Three" conferences

Relations among the three Allies were often uneasy, as each maneuvered to maximize its postwar power. Neither Britain nor the United States trusted

Stalin. The delay in the Allied invasion of France until 1944, which left the Soviets to do the bulk of the fighting against Germany, angered the Russians. But since Stalin's troops had won the war on the eastern front, it was difficult to resist his demand that eastern Europe become a Soviet sphere of influence (a region whose governments can be counted on to do a great power's bidding).

Yalta and Bretton Woods

At Yalta, Roosevelt and Churchill entered only a mild protest against Soviet plans to retain control of the Baltic states (Estonia, Latvia, and Lithuania) and a large part of eastern Poland, in effect restoring Russia's pre–World War I western borders. Stalin agreed to enter the war against Japan later in 1945, to include noncommunists in the pro-Soviet government of Poland, and to allow "free and unfettered elections" there. But he was intent on establishing communism in eastern Europe. He believed, as he put it to Yugoslav communist leader Josip Broz ("Tito"), that in modern war, "whoever occupies a territory also imposes his own social system." Yalta saw the high-water mark of wartime American–Soviet cooperation. But it planted seeds of conflict, since the participants soon disagreed over the fate of eastern Europe.

Tension also existed between Britain and the United States. Churchill rejected American pressure to place India and other British colonies on the road to independence. He concluded private deals with Stalin to divide southern and eastern Europe into British and Soviet spheres of influence.

Britain also resisted, unsuccessfully, American efforts to reshape and dominate the postwar economic order. A meeting of representatives of forty-five nations at Bretton Woods, New Hampshire, in July 1944 replaced the British pound with the dollar as the main currency for international transactions. During the 1930s, as noted in the previous chapter, FDR had taken the United States off the gold standard, allowing the government to issue more money in the hope of stimulating business activity. The Bretton Woods conference reestablished the link between the dollar and gold. It set the dollar's value at $35 per ounce of gold and gave other currencies a fixed relationship to the dollar. The conference also created two American-dominated financial institutions. The World Bank would provide money to developing countries and to help rebuild Europe. The International Monetary Fund would work to prevent governments from devaluing their currencies to gain an advantage in international trade, as many had done during the Depression.

Although the details took many years to emerge, Bretton Woods created the framework for the postwar capitalist economic system, based on a freer international flow of goods and investment and a recognition of the United States as the

The Big Three—Stalin, Roosevelt, and Churchill—at their first meeting, in Tehran, Iran, in 1943, where they discussed the opening of a second front against Germany in western Europe.

Shaping the postwar economic order

world's financial leader. Determined to avoid a recurrence of the Great Depression, American leaders believed that the removal of barriers to free trade would encourage the growth of the world economy, an emphasis that remains central to American foreign policy to this day.

The United Nations

Early in the war, the Allies also agreed to establish a successor to the League of Nations. In a 1944 conference at Dumbarton Oaks, near Washington, D.C., they developed the structure of the United Nations (UN). There would be a General Assembly—essentially a forum for discussion where each member enjoyed an equal voice—and a Security Council responsible for maintaining world peace. Along with ten rotating members, the council would have five permanent ones—Britain, China, France, the Soviet Union, and the United States—each with the power to veto resolutions. In June 1945, representatives of fifty-one countries met in San Francisco to adopt the UN Charter, which outlawed force or the threat of force as a means of settling international disputes. In July, the U.S. Senate endorsed the charter. In contrast to the bitter dispute over membership in the League of Nations after World War I, only two members of the U.S. Senate voted against joining the UN. At the conclusion of the San Francisco conference that established the United Nations, President Truman urged Americans to recognize that "no matter how great our strength, we must deny ourselves the license to do always as we please. This is the price which each nation will have to pay for world peace. . . . And what a reasonable price that is."

The UN Charter

Peace, but Not Harmony

World War II produced a radical redistribution of world power. Japan and Germany, the two dominant military powers in their regions before the war, were utterly defeated. Britain and France, though victorious, were substantially weakened. Only the United States and the Soviet Union were able to project significant influence beyond their national borders.

Overall, however, the United States was clearly the dominant world power. "What Rome was to the ancient world," wrote the journalist Walter Lippmann, "America is to be to the world of tomorrow." But peace did not usher in an era of international harmony. The Soviet occupation of eastern Europe created a division soon to be solidified in the Cold War. The dropping of the atomic bombs left a worldwide legacy of fear.

The dominant world power

It remained to be seen how seriously the victorious Allies took their wartime rhetoric of freedom. In August 1941, four months before the United States entered the war, FDR and British prime minister Winston Churchill had met for a conference, on warships anchored off the coast of Newfoundland, and issued the Atlantic Charter. The charter promised that "the final destruction of Nazi tyranny" would be followed by open access to markets, the right of "all peoples" to choose their form of government, and a global extension of the New Deal so that people everywhere would enjoy "improved labor standards, economic advancement and social security." It referred specifically to two of Roosevelt's Four Freedoms—freedom from want and freedom

Atlantic Charter For Whom?

QUIET! THE TIME IS NOT YET RIPE!

CHURCHILL

WHITE RACES

COLORED RACES

This 1943 cartoon from the *Chicago Defender*, a black newspaper, questions whether non-white peoples will be accorded the right to choose their own government, as promised in the Atlantic Charter agreed to two years earlier by Franklin D. Roosevelt and Winston Churchill. Churchill insisted the principle only applied to Europeans.

from fear. But freedom of speech and of worship had been left out because of British reluctance to apply them to its colonial possessions, especially India.

The Four Freedoms speech and the Atlantic Charter had been primarily intended to highlight the differences between Anglo-American ideals and Nazism. Nonetheless, they had unanticipated consequences. As one of Roosevelt's speech-writers remarked, "when you state a moral principle, you are stuck with it, no matter how many fingers you have kept crossed at the moment." The language with which World War II was fought helped to lay the foundation for postwar ideals of human rights that extend to all mankind.

During the war, Mahatma Gandhi, the Indian nationalist leader, wrote to Roosevelt that the idea "that the Allies are fighting to make the world safe for freedom of the individual and for democracy seems hollow, so long as India, and for that matter, Africa, are exploited by Great Britain, and America has the Negro problem in her own home." Allied victory saved mankind from a living nightmare—a worldwide system of dictatorial rule and slave labor in which peoples deemed inferior suffered the fate of European Jews and of the victims of Japanese outrages in Asia. But disputes over the freedom of colonial peoples overseas and non-whites in the United States foretold more wars and social upheavals to come.

Human rights

SUGGESTED READING

BOOKS

- Ambrose, Stephen E. *Citizen Soldiers* (1997). Discusses the experience of American soldiers fighting in Europe from D-Day to the end of the war.

- Anderson, Karen. *Wartime Women: Sex Roles, Family Relations, and the Status of Women during World War II* (1981). Explores how the experience of World War II opened new opportunities for women and challenged existing gender conventions.

- Blum, John M. *V Was for Victory: Politics and American Culture during World War II* (1976). A comprehensive account of the home front during World War II.

- Borgwardt, Elizabeth. *A New Deal for the World: America's Vision for Human Rights* (2005). The emergence during the war of the idea of human rights as an international entitlement.

- Brinkley, Alan. *The End of Reform: New Deal Liberalism in Recession and War* (1995). Describes how liberals' ideas and policies moved away, during the late New Deal and the war, from combating inequalities of economic power.

- Daniels, Rogers. *Prisoners without Trial: Japanese Americans in World War II* (1993). A brief history of the internment of Japanese-Americans during the war.

- Dower, John W. *War without Mercy: Race and Power in the Pacific War* (1986). Explores how racial fears and antagonisms motivated both sides in the Pacific theater.

- Frydl, Kathleen. *The G.I. Bill* (2009). How this important piece of legislation changed American society.

- Isserman, Maurice. *Which Side Were You On? The American Communist Party during World War II* (1982). Traces the Communist Party's changing political positions during World War II.

- Kennedy, David M. *Freedom from Fear: The American People in Depression and War, 1929–1945* (1999). A detailed and lively account of American history from the Great Depression through the end of World War II.

- Lichtenstein, Nelson. *Labor's War at Home: The CIO in World War II* (1982). Examines the war's impact on workers and the labor movement.

- Rhodes, Richard. *The Making of the Atomic Bomb* (1986). A dramatic account of how the atomic bomb was created.

- Von Eschen, Penny. *Race against Empire: Black Americans and Anticolonialism, 1937–1957* (1997). Examines how black Americans responded to the rise of movements for colonial independence overseas during and after World War II.

- Wyman, David S. *The Abandonment of the Jews: America and the Holocaust, 1941–1945* (1984). A sharply critical account of the Roosevelt administration's response to Hitler's effort to exterminate European Jews.

- Zelizer, Julian E. *Arsenal of Democracy: The Politics of National Security—From World War II to the War on Terrorism* (2009). Traces the origins of the national security state from Roosevelt's "arsenal of democracy" speech of 1940 to the present, stressing the tension between the two elements, arsenal and democracy.

WEBSITES

- A More Perfect Union: Japanese Americans and the U.S. Constitution: http://americanhistory.si.edu/perfectunion/experience/index.html

- A People at War: www.archives.gov/exhibits/a_people_at_war/a_people_at_war.html

- "A Summons to Comradeship": World War I and World War II Posters and Postcards: http://digital.lib.umn.edu/warposters/warpost.html

- Remembering Nagasaki: www.exploratorium.edu/nagasaki/

CHAPTER REVIEW AND ONLINE RESOURCES

REVIEW QUESTIONS

1. Why did most Americans support isolationism in the 1930s?

2. What factors after 1939 led to U.S. involvement in World War II?

3. How did government, business, and labor work together to promote wartime production, and how did the war affect each group?

4. How did different groups understand or experience the Four Freedoms differently?

5. Explain how conservatives in Congress and business used the war effort to attack the goals and legacy of the New Deal.

6. How did the war alter the lives of women on the home front, and what did different groups think would happen to the status of women after the war?

7. How did a war fought to bring "essential human freedoms" to the world fail to protect the home-front liberties of blacks, Indians, Japanese-Americans, and Mexican-Americans?

8. Explain how World War II promoted an awareness of the links between racism in the United States and colonialism around the world.

9. What was the impact of the GI Bill of Rights on American society, including minorities?

10. Describe how the decisions made at the Bretton Woods conference in 1944 created the framework for postwar U.S. economic and foreign policy.

KEY TERMS

Four Freedoms (p. 841)

Good Neighbor Policy (p. 842)

isolationism (p. 844)

Neutrality Acts (p. 845)

"Arsenal of Democracy" (p. 846)

Lend-Lease Act (p. 846)

D-Day (p. 850)

Holocaust (p. 850)

Rosie the Riveter (p. 859)

GI Bill of Rights (p. 862)

"patriotic assimilation" (p. 864)

bracero program (p. 865)

zoot suit riots (p. 865)

Executive Order 9066 (p. 867)

Korematsu v. United States (p. 868)

second Great Migration (p. 869)

Executive Order 8802 (p. 870)

"double-V" (p. 871)

Manhattan Project (p. 877)

Yalta conference (p. 878)

Bretton Woods conference (p. 879)

United Nations (p. 880)

Atlantic Charter (p. 880)

wwnorton.com/studyspace

Visit StudySpace for these resources and more:

- **Author Videos**
- **A chapter outline**
- **A practice quiz**
- **Interactive maps**
- **Multimedia documents**

CHAPTER 23

THE UNITED STATES AND THE COLD WAR

★

1945-1953

On September 16, 1947, the 160th anniversary of the signing of the Constitution, the Freedom Train opened to the public in Philadelphia. A traveling exhibition of 133 historical documents, the train, bedecked in red, white, and blue, soon embarked on a sixteen-month tour that took it to more than 300 American cities. Never before or since have so many cherished pieces of Americana—among them the Mayflower Compact, the Declaration of Independence, and the Gettysburg Address—been assembled in one place. After leaving the train, visitors were encouraged to rededicate themselves to American values by taking the Freedom Pledge and adding their names to a Freedom Scroll.

The idea for the Freedom Train, perhaps the most elaborate peacetime patriotic campaign in American history, originated in 1946 with the Department of Justice. President Harry S. Truman endorsed it as a way of contrasting American freedom with "the destruction of liberty by the Hitler tyranny." Since direct government funding raised fears of propaganda, however, the administration turned the project over to a nonprofit group, the American Heritage Foundation, headed by Winthrop W. Aldrich, chairman of Chase Manhattan Bank.

By any measure, the Freedom Train was an enormous success. It attracted more than 3.5 million visitors, and millions more took part in the civic activities that accompanied its journey, including labor-management forums, educational programs, and patriotic parades. The powerful grassroots response to the train, wrote *The New Republic*, revealed a popular hunger for "tangible evidence of American freedom." Behind the scenes, however, the Freedom Train demonstrated that the meaning of freedom remained as controversial as ever.

The liberal staff members at the National Archives who proposed the initial list of documents had included the Wagner Act of 1935, which guaranteed workers the right to form unions, as well as President Roosevelt's Four Freedoms speech of 1941, with its promise to fight "freedom from want." The more conservative American Heritage Foundation removed these documents. They also deleted from the original list the Fourteenth and Fifteenth Amendments, which had established the principle of equal civil and political rights regardless of race after the Civil War, and FDR's 1941 order establishing the Fair Employment Practices Commission, which Congress had recently allowed to expire. In the end, nothing on the train referred to organized labor or any twentieth-century social legislation. The only documents relating to blacks were the Emancipation Proclamation, the Thirteenth Amendment, and a 1776 letter by South Carolina patriot Henry Laurens criticizing slavery.

Many black Americans initially voiced doubts regarding the exhibit. On the eve of the train's unveiling, the poet Langston Hughes wondered whether there would be "Jim Crow on the Freedom Train." "When it stops in Mississippi," Hughes asked, "will it be made plain / Everybody's got a right to board the Freedom Train?" In fact, with the Truman administration about to make civil rights a major priority, the train's organizers announced that they would not permit segregated viewing. In an unprecedented move, the American Heritage Foundation canceled visits to Memphis, Tennessee, and

FOCUS QUESTIONS

What series of events and ideological conflicts prompted the Cold War? –p. 887

How did the Cold War reshape ideas of American freedom? –p. 897

What were the major initiatives of Truman's domestic policies? –p. 901

What effects did the anticommunism of the Cold War have on American politics and culture? –p. 907

The Cold War led to widespread fears of a communist takeover in the United States (a task far beyond the capacity of the minuscule American Communist Party). This image is part of the cover of a comic book warning of the danger that communists might overthrow the government, and detailing the horrors of life in a communist America. It was published in 1947 by the Catechetical Guild Educational Society of St. Paul, Minnesota, a religious organization. Church groups distributed some 4 million copies. The text on the bottom of the full cover read "America Under Communism!"

1945   Yalta conference

1946   Philippines granted independence

1947   Truman Doctrine

       Federal Employee Loyalty program

       Jackie Robinson integrates major league baseball

       Marshall Plan

       Taft-Hartley Act

       Freedom Train exhibition

       House Un-American Activities Committee investigates Hollywood

1948   UN adopts Universal Declaration of Human Rights

       Truman desegregates military

1948–   Berlin blockade and airlift
1949

1949   North Atlantic Treaty Organization established

       Soviet Union tests atomic bomb

       People's Republic of China established

1950   McCarthy's Wheeling, WV, speech

       NSC-68 issued

       McCarran Internal Security Act

1950–   Korean War
1953

1951   *Dennis v. United States*

1953   Julius and Ethel Rosenberg executed for spying

1954   Army-McCarthy hearings

1955   Warsaw Pact organized

Birmingham, Alabama, when local authorities insisted on separating visitors by race. The Freedom Train visited forty-seven other southern cities without incident and was hailed in the black press for breaching, if only temporarily, the walls of segregation.

Even as the Freedom Train reflected a new sense of national unease about expressions of racial inequality, its journey also revealed the growing impact of the Cold War. Originally intended to contrast American freedom with Nazi tyranny, the train quickly became caught up in the emerging struggle with communism. In the spring of 1947, a few months before the train was dedicated, President Truman committed the United States to the worldwide containment of Soviet power and inaugurated a program to root out "disloyal" persons from government employment. Soon, Attorney General Tom C. Clark was praising the Freedom Train as a means of preventing "foreign ideologies" from infiltrating the United States and of "aiding the country in its internal war against subversive elements." The Federal Bureau of Investigation began compiling reports on those who found the train objectionable. The Freedom Train revealed how the Cold War helped to reshape freedom's meaning, identifying it ever more closely with anticommunism, "free enterprise," and the defense of the social and economic status quo.

ORIGINS OF THE COLD WAR

The Two Powers

The United States emerged from World War II as by far the world's greatest power. Although most of the army was quickly demobilized, the country boasted the world's most powerful navy and air force. The United States accounted for half the world's manufacturing capacity. It alone possessed the atomic bomb. As discussed in the previous chapter, the Roosevelt administration was determined to avoid a retreat to isolationism like the one that followed World War I. It believed that the United States could lead the rest of the world to a future of international cooperation, expanding democracy, and ever-increasing living standards. New institutions like the United Nations and World Bank had been created to promote these goals. American leaders also believed that the nation's security depended on the security of Europe and Asia, and that American prosperity required global economic reconstruction.

The only power that in any way could rival the United States was the Soviet Union, whose armies now occupied most of eastern Europe, including the eastern part of Germany. Its crucial role in defeating Hitler and its claim that communism had wrested a vast backward nation into modernity gave the Soviet Union considerable prestige in Europe and among colonial peoples struggling for independence. Like the United States, the Soviets looked forward to a world order modeled on their own society and values. Having lost more than 20 million dead and suffered vast devastation during the war, however, Stalin's government was in no position to embark on new military adventures. "Unless they were completely out of their minds," said American undersecretary of state Dean Acheson, the Russians were hardly likely to go to war with the far more powerful United States. But having done by far the largest amount of ground fighting in the defeat of Hitler, the Soviet government remained determined to establish a sphere of influence in eastern Europe, through which Germany had twice invaded Russia in the past thirty years.

The Roots of Containment

FDR seems to have believed that the United States could maintain friendly relations with the Soviet Union once World War II ended. In retrospect, however, it seems all but inevitable that the two major powers to emerge from the war would come into conflict. Born of a common foe rather than common long-term interests, values, or history, their wartime alliance began to unravel almost from the day that peace was declared.

The first confrontation of the Cold War took place in the Middle East. At the end of World War II, Soviet troops had occupied parts of northern Iran, hoping to pressure that country to grant it access to its rich oil fields. Under British and American pressure, however, Stalin quickly withdrew Soviet forces. At the same time, the Soviets installed procommunist governments in Poland, Romania, and Bulgaria, a step they claimed was no different from American domination of Latin America or Britain's determination to maintain its own empire. But many Americans became convinced that Stalin was violating the promise of free elections in Poland that had been agreed to at the Yalta conference of 1945.

Early in 1946, in his famous Long Telegram from Moscow, American diplomat George Kennan advised the Truman administration that the Soviets could not be dealt with as a normal government. Communist ideology drove them to try to expand their power throughout the world, he claimed, and only the United States had the ability to stop them. While Kennan believed that the Russians could not be dislodged from control of eastern Europe, his telegram laid the foundation for what became known as the policy of "containment," according to which the United States committed itself to preventing any further expansion of Soviet power.

The Iron Curtain

Shortly afterward, in a speech at Fulton, Missouri, Britain's former wartime prime minister Winston Churchill declared that an "iron curtain" had descended across Europe, partitioning the free West from the communist East. Churchill's speech helped to popularize the idea of an impending long-term struggle between the United States and the Soviets. But not until March 1947, in a speech announcing what came to be known as the Truman Doctrine, did the president officially embrace the Cold War as the foundation of American foreign policy and describe it as a worldwide struggle over the future of freedom.

The Truman Doctrine

Harry S. Truman never expected to become president. Until Democratic party leaders chose him to replace Henry Wallace as Roosevelt's running mate in 1944, he was an undistinguished senator from Missouri who had risen in politics

The cover of a comic book promoting the Freedom Train in 1948. The image links the train to Paul Revere's ride and, more broadly, the revolutionary era.

Kennan's Long Telegram

Churchill's speech

President Harry S. Truman delivering his Truman Doctrine speech before Congress on March 12, 1947.

A page from a Dutch pamphlet promoting the Marshall Plan.

WITHOUT THE MARSHALL PLAN

YOUR BREAD WOULD BE BARE......

AND SO WOULD YOUR CHILDREN!

through his connection with the boss of the Kansas City political machine, Tom Pendergast. When he assumed the presidency after Roosevelt's death in April 1945, Truman found himself forced to decide foreign policy debates in which he had previously played virtually no role.

Convinced that Stalin could not be trusted and that the United States had a responsibility to provide leadership to a world that he tended to view in stark, black-and-white terms, Truman soon determined to put the policy of containment into effect. The immediate occasion for this epochal decision came early in 1947 when Britain informed the United States that because its economy had been shattered by the war, it could no longer afford its traditional international role. Britain had no choice but to end military and financial aid to two crucial governments—Greece, a monarchy threatened by a communist-led rebellion, and Turkey, from which the Soviets were demanding joint control of the straits linking the Black Sea and the Mediterranean. Britain asked the United States to fill the vacuum.

The Soviet Union had little to do with the internal problems of Greece and Turkey, where opposition to corrupt, undemocratic regimes was largely homegrown. Neither had held truly free elections. But they occupied strategically important sites at the gateway to southeastern Europe and the oil-rich Middle East. Truman had been told by Senate leader Arthur Vandenberg that the only way a reluctant public and Congress would support aid to these governments was for the president to "scare hell" out of the American people. To rally popular backing, Truman rolled out the heaviest weapon in his rhetorical arsenal—the defense of freedom. As the leader of the "free world," the United States must now shoulder the responsibility of supporting "freedom-loving peoples" wherever communism threatened them. Twenty-four times in the eighteen-minute speech, Truman used the words "free" or "freedom."

Building on the wartime division of the globe into free and enslaved worlds, and invoking a far older vision of an American mission to defend liberty against the forces of darkness, the Truman Doctrine created the language through which most Americans came to understand the postwar world. More than any other statement a prominent senator would write, this speech established "the guiding spirit of American foreign policy." Truman succeeded in persuading both Republicans and Democrats in Congress to support his policy, beginning a long period of bipartisan support for the containment of communism. As Truman's speech to Congress suggested, the Cold War was, in part, an ideological conflict. Both sides claimed to be promoting freedom and social justice while defending their own security, and each offered its social system as a model the rest of the world should follow.

While his request to Congress was limited to $400 million in military aid to two governments (aid that enabled both Greece and Turkey to defeat their domestic foes), Truman's rhetoric suggested that the United States had assumed a permanent global responsibility. The speech set a precedent for American assistance to anti-communist regimes throughout the world, no matter how undemocratic, and for the creation of a set of global military alliances directed against the Soviet Union.

There soon followed the creation of new national security bodies immune from democratic oversight, such as the Atomic Energy Commission, National Security Council, and Central Intelligence Agency (CIA), the last established in 1947 to gather intelligence and conduct secret military operations abroad.

The Marshall Plan

The language of the Truman Doctrine and the future it sketched of open-ended worldwide responsibilities for the United States alarmed many Americans. "Are we to shoulder the mantle of nineteenth-century British imperialism?" asked the *San Francisco Chronicle*. "Are we asking for a third world war?" But the threat of American military action overseas formed only one pillar of containment. Secretary of State George C. Marshall spelled out the other in a speech at Harvard University in June 1947. Marshall pledged the United States to contribute billions of dollars to finance the economic recovery of Europe. Two years after the end of the war, much of the continent still lay in ruins. Food shortages were widespread, and inflation was rampant. The economic chaos, exacerbated by the unusually severe winter of 1946–1947, had strengthened the communist parties of France and Italy. American policymakers feared that these countries might fall into the Soviet orbit.

> *Marshall's speech*

The Marshall Plan offered a positive vision to go along with containment. It aimed to combat the idea, widespread since the Great Depression, that capitalism was in decline and communism the wave of the future. It defined the threat to American security not so much as Soviet military power but as economic and political instability, which could be breeding grounds for communism. Avoiding Truman's language of a world divided between free and unfree blocs, Marshall insisted, "Our policy is directed not against any country or doctrine, but against hunger, poverty, desperation, and chaos." Freedom meant more than simply anticommunism—it required the emergence of the "political and social conditions in which free institutions can exist." In effect, the Marshall Plan envisioned a New Deal for Europe, an extension to that continent of Roosevelt's wartime Four Freedoms. As a booklet explaining the idea to Europeans put it, the aim was "a higher standard of living for the entire nation; maximum employment for workers and farmers; greater production." Or, in the words of a slogan used to popularize the Marshall Plan, "Prosperity Makes You Free."

Bales of American cotton in a warehouse at the French port of Le Havre, 1949. Part of the Marshall Plan aid program, the shipment helped to revive the French cotton industry.

The Marshall Plan proved to be one of the most successful foreign aid programs in history. By 1950, western European production exceeded prewar levels and the region was poised to follow the United States down the road to a mass-consumption society. Since the Soviet Union refused to participate, fearing American control over the economies of eastern Europe, the Marshall Plan further solidified the division of the continent. At the same time, the United

States worked out with twenty-three other Western nations the General Agreement on Tariffs and Trade (GATT), which proposed to stimulate freer trade among the participants, creating an enormous market for American goods and investment.

The Reconstruction of Japan

Under the guidance of General Douglas MacArthur, the "supreme commander" in Japan until 1948, the country adopted a new, democratic constitution and eliminated absentee landlordism so that most tenant farmers became owners of land. Thanks to American insistence, and against the wishes of most Japanese leaders, the new constitution gave women the right to vote for the first time in Japan's history. (A century after the Seneca Falls convention, women's suffrage had become an intrinsic part of American understandings of freedom.) Furthermore, Article 9 of the new constitution stated that Japan would renounce forever the policy of war and armed aggression, and would maintain only a modest self-defense force.

The United States also oversaw the economic reconstruction of Japan. Initially, the United States proposed to dissolve Japan's giant industrial corporations, which had contributed so much to the nation's war effort. But this plan was abandoned in 1948 in favor of an effort to rebuild Japan's industrial base as a bastion of anticommunist strength in Asia. By the 1950s, thanks to American economic assistance, the adoption of new technologies, and low spending on the military, Japan's economic recovery was in full swing.

The Berlin Blockade and NATO

Meanwhile, the Cold War intensified and, despite the Marshall Plan, increasingly took a militaristic turn. At the end of World War II, each of the four victorious powers assumed control of a section of occupied Germany, and of Berlin, located deep in the Soviet zone. In June 1948, the United States, Britain, and France introduced a separate currency in their zones, a prelude to the creation of a new West German

A new constitution

Economic recovery

Occupation of Germany

Children in Berlin celebrate the arrival of a plane bringing supplies to counter the Soviet blockade of the city in 1948.

government that would be aligned with them in the Cold War. In response, the Soviets cut off road and rail traffic from the American, British, and French zones of occupied Germany to Berlin (although Stalin kept supply routes open from the east, since Soviet forces occupied part of the divided city).

An eleven-month airlift followed, with Western planes supplying fuel and food to their zones of the city. When Stalin lifted the blockade in May 1949, the Truman administration had won a major victory. Soon, two new nations emerged, East and West Germany, each allied with a side in the Cold War. Berlin itself remained divided. The city's western part survived as an isolated enclave within East Germany. Not until 1991 would Germany be reunified.

The Berlin airlift

Also in 1949, the Soviet Union tested its first atomic bomb, ending the American monopoly of the weapon. In the same year, the United States, Canada, and ten western European nations established the North Atlantic Treaty Organization (NATO), pledging mutual defense against any future Soviet attack. Soon, West Germany became a crucial part of NATO. Many Europeans feared German rearmament. But France and other victims of Nazi aggression saw NATO as a kind of "double containment," in which West Germany would serve as a bulwark against the Soviets while integration into the Western alliance tamed and "civilized" German power. The North Atlantic Treaty was the first long-term military alliance between the United States and Europe since the Treaty of Amity and Commerce with France during the American Revolution. The Soviets formalized their own eastern European alliance, the Warsaw Pact, in 1955.

NATO

The Growing Communist Challenge

In 1949, communists led by Mao Zedong emerged victorious in the long Chinese civil war—a serious setback for the policy of containment. Assailed by Republicans for having "lost" China (which, of course, the United States never "had" in the first place), the Truman administration refused to recognize the new government—the People's Republic of China—and blocked it from occupying China's seat at the United Nations. Until the 1970s, the United States insisted that the ousted regime, which had been forced into exile on the island of Taiwan, remained the legitimate government of China.

"Losing" China

In the wake of Soviet-American confrontations over southern and eastern Europe and Berlin, the communist victory in China, and Soviet success in developing an atomic bomb, the National Security Council approved a call for a permanent military build-up to enable the United States to pursue a global crusade against communism. Known as NSC-68, this 1950 manifesto described the Cold War as an epic struggle between "the idea of freedom" and the "idea of slavery under the grim oligarchy of the Kremlin." At stake in the world conflict, it insisted, was nothing less than "the survival of the free world." One of the most important policy statements of the early Cold War, NSC-68 helped to spur a dramatic increase in American military spending.

NSC-68

The Korean War

Initially, American postwar policy focused on Europe. But it was in Asia that the Cold War suddenly turned hot. Occupied by Japan during World War II, Korea had been divided in 1945 into Soviet and American zones. These soon evolved into two governments: communist North Korea, and anticommunist South Korea,

COLD WAR EUROPE, 1956

ICELAND

NORWAY
SWEDEN
FINLAND

North Sea

IRELAND
DENMARK
GREAT BRITAIN
London
NETHERLANDS
Berlin
POLAND
SOVIET UNION
Atlantic Ocean
BELGIUM
Bonn
EAST GERMANY
Warsaw
WEST GERMANY
Paris
LUXEMBOURG
Prague
CZECHOSLOVAKIA
FRANCE
AUSTRIA
SWITZERLAND
HUNGARY
Budapest
ROMANIA
Bucharest
Baltic Sea

PORTUGAL
Lisbon
SPAIN
Corsica
ITALY
YUGOSLAVIA
Sofia
BULGARIA
Black Sea
Tirane
ALBANIA
Sardinia
GREECE
Ankara
TURKEY
Athens
Sicily

MOROCCO
TUNISIA
Mediterranean Sea
Crete
CYPRUS (Great Britain)
LEBANON
SYRIA
IRAQ

ALGERIA (France)
ISRAEL
JORDAN

LIBYA
EGYPT
SAUDI ARABIA
Red Sea

Occupation Zones
- American
- British
- French
- Soviet

Berlin Wall, 1961
West Berlin
East Berlin

NATO countries
Warsaw Pact countries

0   250   500 miles
0   250   500 kilometers

The division of Europe between communist and noncommunist nations, solidified by the early 1950s, would last for nearly forty years.

Chinese communists carrying portraits of Mao Zedong, who took control of the country's government in 1949 after a long civil war.

undemocratic but aligned with the United States. In June 1950, the North Korean army invaded the south, hoping to reunify the country under communist control. North Korean soldiers soon occupied most of the peninsula. Viewing Korea as a clear test of the policy of containment, the Truman administration persuaded the United Nations Security Council to authorize the use of force to repel the invasion. (The Soviets, who could have vetoed the resolution, were boycotting Security Council meetings to protest the refusal to seat communist China.)

North Korean invasion

American troops did the bulk of the fighting on this first battlefield of the Cold War. In September 1950, General Douglas MacArthur launched a daring counterattack at Inchon, behind North Korean lines. The invading forces retreated northward, and MacArthur's army soon occupied most of North Korea. Truman now hoped to unite Korea under a pro-American government. But in October 1950, when UN forces neared the Chinese border, hundreds of thousands of Chinese troops intervened, driving them back in bloody fighting. MacArthur demanded the right to push north again and possibly even invade China and use nuclear weapons against it. But Truman, fearing an all-out war on the Asian mainland, refused. MacArthur did not fully accept the principle of civilian control of the military. When he went public with criticism of the president, Truman removed him from command. The war then settled into a stalemate around the thirty-eighth parallel, the original boundary between the two Koreas. Not until 1953 was an armistice agreed to, essentially restoring the prewar status quo. There has never been a formal peace treaty ending the Korean War.

Inchon

Chinese intervention

More than 33,000 Americans died in Korea. The Asian death toll reached an estimated 1 million Korean soldiers and 2 million civilians (many of them victims of starvation after American bombing destroyed irrigation systems essential to rice cultivation), along with hundreds of thousands of Chinese troops. Korea made it clear that the Cold War, which began in Europe, had become a global conflict.

A global conflict

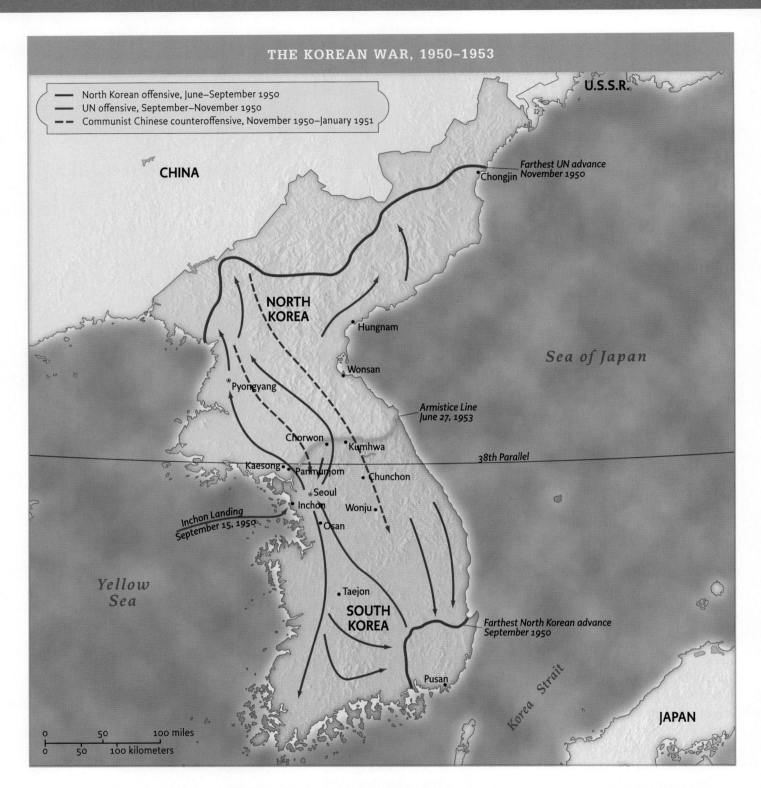

THE KOREAN WAR, 1950–1953

——— North Korean offensive, June–September 1950
——— UN offensive, September–November 1950
– – – Communist Chinese counteroffensive, November 1950–January 1951

U.S.S.R.

CHINA

NORTH KOREA

Farthest UN advance
November 1950

Chongjin

Hungnam

Sea of Japan

Wonsan

Pyongyang

Armistice Line
June 27, 1953

Chorwon

Kumhwa

38th Parallel

Kaesong

Panmunjom

Chunchon

Seoul

Inchon

Wonju

Inchon Landing
September 15, 1950

Osan

Yellow
Sea

Taejon

SOUTH KOREA

Farthest North Korean advance
September 1950

Pusan

Korea Strait

JAPAN

0   50   100 miles
0   50   100 kilometers

As this map indicates, when General Douglas MacArthur launched his surprise landing at Inchon, North Korean forces controlled nearly the entire Korean peninsula.

A photograph of a street battle in Seoul, South Korea, during the Korean War illustrates the ferocity of the fighting.

Taken together, the events of 1947–1953 showed that the world had moved very far from the hopes for global harmony symbolized by the founding of the United Nations in 1945. No longer did the United States speak of One World (the title of Wendell Willkie's influential wartime book). Instead, the world had been divided in two. The United States now stood as the undisputed leader of what was increasingly known as the West (although it included Japan, where permanent American military bases were established), or the Free World. NATO was soon followed by SEATO in Southeast Asia and CENTO in the Middle East, forming a web of military alliances that ringed the Soviet Union and China.

Cold War Critics

In the Soviet Union, Stalin had consolidated a brutal dictatorship that jailed or murdered millions of Soviet citizens. With its one-party rule, stringent state control of the arts and intellectual life, and government-controlled economy, the Soviet Union presented a stark opposite of democracy and "free enterprise." As a number of contemporary critics, few of them sympathetic to Soviet communism, pointed out, however, casting the Cold War in terms of a worldwide battle between freedom and slavery had unfortunate consequences. George Kennan, whose Long Telegram had inspired the policy of containment, observed that such language made it impossible to view international crises on a case-by-case basis, or to determine which genuinely involved either freedom or American interests.

In a penetrating critique of Truman's policies, Walter Lippmann, one of the nation's most prominent journalists, objected to turning foreign policy into an "ideological crusade." To view every challenge to the status quo as part of a contest with the Soviet Union, Lippmann correctly predicted, would require the United States to recruit and subsidize an "array of satellites, clients, dependents and

Stalin's brutal dictatorship

Walter Lippmann

puppets." It would have to intervene continuously in the affairs of nations whose political problems did not arise from Moscow and could not be easily understood in terms of the battle between freedom and slavery. World War II, he went on, had shaken the foundations of European empires. In the tide of revolutionary nationalism now sweeping the world, communists were certain to play an important role. It would be a serious mistake, Lippmann warned, for the United States to align itself against the movement for colonial independence in the name of anticommunism.

Imperialism and Decolonization

The Free World

World War II had increased awareness in the United States of the problem of imperialism and had led many African-Americans to identify their own struggle for equality with the strivings of non-white colonial peoples overseas. Many movements for colonial independence borrowed the language of the American Declaration of Independence in demanding the right to self-government. Liberal Democrats and black leaders urged the Truman administration to take the lead in promoting worldwide decolonization, insisting that a Free World worthy of the name should not include colonies and empires. In 1946, the United States granted independence to the Philippines, a move hailed by nationalist movements in other colonies. But as the Cold War developed, the United States backed away from pressuring its European allies to move toward granting self-government to colonies like French Indochina, the Dutch East Indies, and British possessions like the Gold Coast and Nigeria in Africa and Malaya in Asia. Even after granting independence to India and Pakistan in 1947, Britain was determined to retain much of its empire.

In practice, geopolitical and economic interests shaped American foreign policy as powerfully as the idea of freedom. But American policymakers used the language of a crusade for freedom to justify actions around the world that had little to do with freedom by almost any definition. No matter how repressive to its own people, if a nation joined the worldwide anticommunist alliance led by the United States, it was counted as a member of the Free World. The Republic of South Africa, for example, was considered a part of the Free World even though its white minority had deprived the black population of nearly all their rights. Was there not some way, one critic asked, that the United States could accept "the aid of tyrants" on practical grounds "without corrupting our speeches by identifying tyranny with freedom"?

THE COLD WAR AND THE IDEA OF FREEDOM

Among other things, the Cold War was an ideological struggle, a battle, in a popular phrase of the 1950s, for the "hearts and minds" of people throughout the world. Like other wars, it required popular mobilization, in which the idea of freedom played a central role. During the 1950s, freedom became an inescapable theme of academic research, popular journalism, mass culture, and official pronouncements. Henry Luce, who had popularized the idea of an American Century, explained that "freedom" was the "one word out of the whole human vocabulary" through which *Time* magazine could best explain America to the rest of the world. In many ways, the Cold War established the framework for the discussion of freedom.

The Cultural Cold War

One of the more unusual Cold War battlefields involved American history and culture. Many scholars read the American Creed of pluralism, tolerance, and equality back into the past as a timeless definition of Americanism, ignoring the powerful ethnic and racial strains with which it had always coexisted. Under the code name "Militant Liberty," national security agencies encouraged Hollywood to produce anticommunist movies, such as *The Red Menace* (1949) and *I Married a Communist* (1950), and urged that film scripts be changed to remove references to less-than-praiseworthy aspects of American history, such as Indian removal and racial discrimination.

The Central Intelligence Agency and Defense Department emerged as unlikely patrons of the arts. As noted in Chapter 21, the federal government had openly financed all sorts of artistic works during the 1930s. But Cold War funding for the arts remained top-secret—in part because Congress proved reluctant to spend money for this purpose, in part because Americans charged communist governments with imposing artistic conformity. In an effort to influence public opinion abroad, the Soviet Union sponsored tours of its world-famous ballet companies, folk dance troupes, and symphony orchestras. To counteract the widespread European view of the United States as a cultural backwater, the CIA secretly funded an array of overseas publications, conferences, publishing houses, concerts, and art exhibits. And to try to improve the international image of American race relations, the government sent jazz musicians and other black performers abroad, especially to Africa and Asia.

Works produced by artists who considered themselves thoroughly nonpolitical became weapons in the cultural Cold War. The CIA promoted the so-called New York school of painters, led by Jackson Pollock. For Pollock, the essence of art lay in the process of creation, not the final product. His "action" paintings, made by spontaneously dripping and pouring paint over large canvases, produced works of vivid color and energy but without any recognizable subject matter. Many members of Congress much preferred Norman Rockwell's readily understandable illustrations of small-town life to Pollock's "abstract expressionism." Some called Pollock's works un-American and wondered aloud if they were part of a communist plot. But the CIA funded the Museum of Modern Art in New York, which championed the New York school, and helped arrange for exhibitions overseas. It hoped to persuade Europeans not only that these paintings demonstrated that the United States represented artistic leadership as well as military power, but that such art embodied the free, individual expression denied to artists in communist countries. Pollock's paintings, John Cage's musical compositions, which incorporated chance sounds rather than a fixed score, and the "graceful freedom" of George Balanchine's choreography were all described as artistic reflections of the essence of American life.

A poster for *The Red Menace*, one of numerous anticommunist films produced by Hollywood during the 1950s.

Freedom and Totalitarianism

Along with freedom, the Cold War's other great mobilizing concept was "totalitarianism." The term originated in Europe between the world wars to describe fascist Italy and Nazi Germany—aggressive, ideologically driven states that sought to

Visitors to the Museum of Modern Art in New York City contemplate a work by Jackson Pollock, whose paintings exemplified the artistic school of abstract expressionism, promoted during the Cold War as a reflection of American freedom. The paintings had no recognizable subject other than reminding the viewer of how Pollock had created them, by flinging paint at the canvas. "I want to express my feelings, rather than illustrate them," Pollock declared.

The idea of "totalitarianism"

subdue all of civil society, including churches, unions, and other voluntary associations, to their control. Such states, according to the theory of totalitarianism, left no room for individual rights or alternative values and therefore could never change from within. By 1950, the year the McCarran Internal Security Act barred "totalitarians" from entering the United States, the term had become a shorthand way of describing those on the other side in the Cold War. As the eventual collapse of communist governments in eastern Europe and the Soviet Union would demonstrate, the idea of totalitarianism greatly exaggerated the totality of government control of private life and thought in these countries. But its widespread use reinforced the view that the greatest danger to freedom lay in an overly powerful government.

Just as the conflict over slavery redefined American freedom in the nineteenth century and the confrontation with the Nazis shaped understandings of freedom during World War II, the Cold War reshaped them once again. Russia had already conquered America, the poet Archibald MacLeish complained in 1949, since politics was conducted "under a kind of upside-down Russian veto." Whatever Moscow stood for was by definition the opposite of freedom, including anything to which the word "socialized" could be attached. In the largest public relations campaign in American history, the American Medical Association raised the specter of "socialized medicine" to discredit and defeat Truman's proposal for national health insurance. The real-estate industry likewise mobilized against public housing, terming it "socialized housing," similar to policies undertaken by Moscow.

The Rise of Human Rights

The Cold War also affected the emerging concept of human rights. The idea that there are rights that are applicable to all of humanity originated during the eighteenth century in the Enlightenment and the American and French Revolutions.

The atrocities committed during World War II, as well as the global language of the Four Freedoms and the Atlantic Charter, forcefully raised the issue of human rights in the postwar world. After the war, the victorious Allies put numerous German officials on trial before special courts at Nuremberg for crimes against humanity. For the first time, individuals were held directly accountable to the international community for violations of human rights. The trials resulted in prison terms for many Nazi officials and the execution of ten leaders.

The United Nations Charter includes strong language prohibiting discrimination on the basis of race, sex, or religion. In 1948, the UN General Assembly approved a far more sweeping document, the Universal Declaration of Human Rights, drafted by a committee chaired by Eleanor Roosevelt. It identified a broad range of rights to be enjoyed by people everywhere, including freedom of speech, religious toleration, and protection against arbitrary government, as well as social and economic entitlements like the right to an adequate standard of living and access to housing, education, and medical care. The document had no enforcement mechanism. Some considered it an exercise in empty rhetoric. But the core principle—that a nation's treatment of its own citizens should be subject to outside evaluation—slowly became part of the language in which freedom was discussed.

Ambiguities of Human Rights

The American and French Revolutions of the late eighteenth century had introduced into international relations the idea of basic rights belonging to all persons simply because they are human. In a sense, this was the origin of the idea of "human

Human Rights. This cartoon from 1947 depicts delegates to a meeting of the UN Human Rights Commission as unruly schoolchildren. Eleanor Roosevelt lectures delegates from various countries about human rights. "Now children," she says, "all together: 'The rights of the individual are above the rights of the state.'" At the lower left, John Foster Dulles, an American delegate, aims a slingshot at the Soviet ambassador to the UN, Andrei Y. Vishinsky, who stands in the lower right corner wearing a dunce cap. Charles Malik of Lebanon offers the teacher an apple. Several delegates seem bored; others are attentive.

rights"—principles so fundamental that no government has a right to violate them. The antislavery movement had turned this idea into a powerful weapon against the legitimacy of slavery. Yet the debates over the Universal Declaration of Human Rights revealed the tensions inherent in the idea, tensions that persist to the present day. To what extent do human rights supersede national sovereignty? Who has the authority to enforce human rights that a government is violating? The United Nations? Regional bodies like the Organization of American States and the European Union? A single country (as the United States would claim to be doing in the Iraq War that began in 2003)? The Covenant of the League of Nations—the predecessor of the United Nations created after World War I—had contained a clause allowing the league to intervene when a government violated the rights of its own citizens.

Debates over human rights

One reason for the lack of an enforcement mechanism in the Universal Declaration of Human Rights was that both the United States and the Soviet Union refused to accept outside interference in their internal affairs or restraints on their ability to conduct foreign policy as they desired. John Foster Dulles, an American delegate to the conference that created the UN, opposed any statement affirming human rights out of fear that it would lead to an international investigation of "the Negro question in this country." In 1947, the NAACP did file a petition with the United Nations asking it to investigate racism in the United States as a violation of human rights. Conditions in states like Mississippi should be of concern to all mankind, it argued, because if democracy failed to function in "the leading democracy in the world," the prospects for democracy were weakened everywhere. But the UN decided that it lacked jurisdiction. Nonetheless, since the end of World War II, the enjoyment of human rights has increasingly taken its place in definitions of freedom across the globe, especially, perhaps, where such rights are flagrantly violated.

After the Cold War ended, the idea of human rights would play an increasingly prominent role in world affairs. But during the 1950s, Cold War imperatives shaped the concept. Neither the United States nor the Soviet Union could resist emphasizing certain provisions of the Universal Declaration while ignoring others. The Soviets claimed to provide all citizens with social and economic rights, but violated democratic rights and civil liberties. Many Americans condemned the nonpolitical rights as a step toward socialism. In 1950, Freedom House began yearly assessments of the status of freedom in the world's nations. It adopted purely political criteria, emphasizing citizens' rights to participate in open elections and to speak out on public issues. Considering access to employment, housing, education, medical care, and the like as part of the definition of freedom, the reports argued, would be a serious mistake.

Human rights in world affairs

Eleanor Roosevelt saw the Universal Declaration of Human Rights as an integrated body of principles, a combination of traditional civil and political liberties with the social conditions of freedom outlined in her husband's Economic Bill of Rights of 1944. But to make it easier for member states to ratify the document, the UN divided it into two "covenants"—Civil and Political Rights, and Economic, Social, and Cultural Rights. It took until 1992 for the U.S. Congress to ratify the first. It has never approved the second.

THE TRUMAN PRESIDENCY

The Fair Deal

With the end of World War II, President Truman's first domestic task was to preside over the transition from a wartime to a peacetime economy. More than 12 million men remained in uniform in August 1945. They wanted nothing more than to return home to their families. Demobilization proceeded at a rapid pace. Within a year, the armed forces had been reduced to 3 million. Some returning soldiers found the adjustment to civilian life difficult. The divorce rate in 1945 rose to double its pre-war level. Others took advantage of the GI Bill of Rights (discussed in the previous chapter) to obtain home mortgages, set up small businesses, and embark on college educations. The majority of returning soldiers entered the labor force—one reason why more than 2 million women workers lost their jobs. The government abolished wartime agencies that regulated industrial production and labor relations, and it dismantled wartime price controls, leading to a sharp rise in prices.

> *Economic transition*

In the immediate aftermath of World War II, President Truman, backed by party liberals and organized labor, moved to revive the stalled momentum of the New Deal. Truman's program, which he announced in September 1945 and would later call the Fair Deal, focused on improving the social safety net and raising the standard of living of ordinary Americans. He called on Congress to increase the minimum wage, enact a program of national health insurance, and expand public housing, Social Security, and aid to education. Truman, complained one Republican leader, was "out–New Dealing the New Deal."

> *Raising the standard of living*

The Postwar Strike Wave

In 1946, a new wave of labor militancy swept the country. The AFL and CIO launched Operation Dixie, a campaign to bring unionization to the South and, by so doing, shatter the hold of anti-labor conservatives on the region's politics. More than 200 labor organizers entered the region, seeking support especially in the southern textile industry, the steel industry in the Birmingham region, and agriculture. With war production at an end, overtime work diminished even as inflation soared following the removal of price controls. The resulting drop in workers' real income sparked the largest strike wave in American history. Nearly 5 million workers—including those in the steel, auto, coal, and other key industries—walked off their jobs, demanding wage increases. The strike of 750,000 steelworkers represented the largest single walkout in American history to that date. Even Hollywood studios shut down because of a strike of actors and other employees of the movie industry that lasted for the better part of a year. One historian calls this period "the closest thing to a national general strike in industry in the twentieth century."

A few of the numerous World War II veterans who attended college after the war, thanks to the GI Bill.

President Truman feared the strikes would seriously disrupt the economy. When railroad workers stopped work and set up picket lines, the infuriated president prepared a speech in which he threatened to draft them all into the army and "hang a few traitors"—language toned down by his advisers. The walkout soon ended, as did a coal strike after the Truman administration secured a court order requiring the miners to return to work. To resolve other strikes, Truman appointed federal "fact-finding boards," which generally recommended wage increases, although not enough to restore workers' purchasing power to wartime levels.

The Republican Resurgence

In the congressional elections of 1946, large numbers of middle-class voters, alarmed by the labor turmoil, voted Republican. Many workers, disappointed by Truman's policies, stayed at home. This was a lethal combination for the Democratic Party. For the first time since the 1920s, Republicans swept to control of both houses of Congress. Meanwhile, in the face of vigorous opposition from southern employers and public officials and the reluctance of many white workers to join interracial labor unions, Operation Dixie had failed to unionize the South or dent the political control of conservative Democrats in the region. The election of 1946 ensured that a conservative coalition of Republicans and southern Democrats would continue to dominate Congress.

Congress turned aside Truman's Fair Deal program. It enacted tax cuts for wealthy Americans and, over the president's veto, in 1947 passed the Taft-Hartley Act, which sought to reverse some of the gains made by organized labor in the past decade. The measure authorized the president to suspend strikes by ordering an eighty-day "cooling-off period," and it banned sympathy strikes and secondary boycotts (labor actions directed not at an employer but at those who did business with him). It outlawed the closed shop, which required a worker to be a union member when taking up a job, and authorized states to pass "right-to-work" laws, prohibiting other forms of compulsory union membership. It also forced union officials to swear that they were not communists. While hardly a "slave-labor bill," as the AFL and CIO called it, the Taft-Hartley Act made it considerably more difficult to bring unorganized workers into unions. Over time, as population and capital investment shifted to states with "right-to-work" laws like Texas, Florida, and North Carolina, Taft-Hartley contributed to the decline of organized labor's share of the nation's workforce.

The Taft-Hartley Act of 1947

Postwar Civil Rights

During his first term, Truman reached out in unprecedented ways to the nation's black community. The war, as noted in the previous chapter, had inspired a new black militancy and led many whites to reject American racial practices as reminiscent of Hitler's theory of a master race. In the years immediately following World War II, the status of black Americans enjoyed a prominence in national affairs unmatched since Reconstruction.

Between 1945 and 1951, eleven states from New York to New Mexico established fair employment practices commissions, and numerous cities passed laws against

The postwar status of black Americans

An NAACP youth march against racial segregation in Houston, Texas, in 1947 illustrates the civil rights upsurge of the years immediately following the end of World War II.

discrimination in access to jobs and public accommodations. (Some of these measures addressed other racial groups besides blacks: for example, California in 1947 repealed its laws permitting local school districts to provide segregated education for children of Chinese descent and those barring aliens from owning land.) A broad civil rights coalition involving labor, religious groups, and black organizations supported these measures. The NAACP, its ranks swollen during the war, launched a voter registration campaign in the South. By 1952, 20 percent of black southerners were registered to vote, nearly a seven-fold increase since 1940. (Most of the gains took place in the Upper South—in Alabama and Mississippi, the heartland of white supremacy, the numbers barely budged.) Law enforcement agencies finally took the crime of lynching seriously. In 1952, for the first time since record keeping began seventy years earlier, no lynchings took place in the United States.

In another indication that race relations were in flux, the Brooklyn Dodgers in 1947 challenged the long-standing exclusion of black players from major league baseball by adding Jackie Robinson to their team. Robinson, who possessed both remarkable athletic ability and a passion for equality, had been tried and acquitted for insubordination in 1944 when he refused to move to the back of a bus at Fort Hood, Texas, while serving in the army. But he promised Dodger owner Branch

Jackie Robinson sliding into third base, 1949.

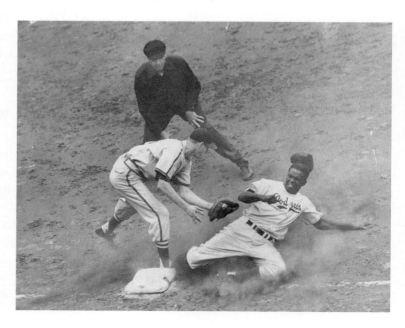

Rickey that he would not retaliate when subjected to racist taunts by opposing fans and players. His dignity in the face of constant verbal abuse won Robinson nationwide respect, and his baseball prowess earned him the Rookie of the Year award. His success opened the door to the integration of baseball and led to the demise of the Negro Leagues, to which black players had previously been confined.

To Secure These Rights

In October 1947, a Commission on Civil Rights appointed by the president issued *To Secure These Rights*, one of the most devastating indictments ever published of racial inequality in America. It called on the federal government to assume the responsibility for abolishing segregation and ensuring equal treatment in housing, employment, education, and the criminal justice system. Truman hailed the report as "an American charter of human freedom." The impact of America's race system on the nation's ability to conduct the Cold War was not far from his mind. Truman noted that if the United States were to offer the "peoples of the world" a "choice of freedom or enslavement," it must "correct the remaining imperfections in our practice of democracy."

In February 1948, Truman presented an ambitious civil rights program to Congress, calling for a permanent federal civil rights commission, national laws against lynching and the poll tax, and action to ensure equal access to jobs and education. Congress, as Truman anticipated, approved none of his proposals. But in July 1948, just as the presidential campaign was getting under way, Truman issued an executive order desegregating the armed forces. The armed services became the first large institution in American life to promote racial integration actively and to attempt to root out long-standing racist practices. The Korean War would be the first American conflict fought by an integrated army since the War of Independence.

Desegregating the armed forces

Truman genuinely despised racial discrimination. But his focus on civil rights also formed part of a strategy to win reelection by reinvigorating and expanding the political coalition Roosevelt had created. With calls for federal health insurance, the repeal of the Taft-Hartley Act, and aid to public education, the Democratic platform of 1948 was the most progressive in the party's history. Led by Hubert Humphrey, the young mayor of Minneapolis, party liberals overcame southern resistance and added a strong civil rights plank to the platform.

The Dixiecrat and Wallace Revolts

"I say the time has come," Humphrey told the Democratic national convention, "to walk out of the shadow of states' rights and into the sunlight of human rights." Whereupon numerous southern delegates—dubbed Dixiecrats by the press—walked out of the gathering. They soon formed the States' Rights Democratic Party and nominated for president Governor Strom Thurmond of South Carolina. Although his platform called for the "complete segregation of the races" and his campaign drew most of its support from those alarmed by Truman's civil rights initiatives, Thurmond denied charges of racism. The real issue of the election, Thurmond insisted, was freedom—the States' Rights Democratic Party, he declared, stood for "individual liberty and freedom, the right of people to govern

The 1948 Democratic national convention

themselves." Truman's plans for extending federal power into the South to enforce civil rights, Thurmond charged, would "convert America into a Hitler state."

Also in 1948, a group of left-wing critics of Truman's foreign policy formed the Progressive Party and nominated former vice president Henry A. Wallace for president. Wallace advocated an expansion of social welfare programs at home and denounced racial segregation even more vigorously than Truman. When he campaigned in the South, angry white crowds attacked him. But his real difference with the president concerned the Cold War. Wallace called for international control of nuclear weapons and a renewed effort to develop a relationship with the Soviet Union based on economic cooperation rather than military confrontation. He announced his willingness to accept support from all Americans who agreed with him, including socialists and communists. The influence of the now much-reduced Communist Party in Wallace's campaign led to an exodus of New Deal liberals and severe attacks on his candidacy. A vote for Wallace, Truman declared, was in effect a vote for Stalin.

> *Henry A. Wallace*

The 1948 Campaign

Wallace threatened to draw votes from Truman on the left, and Thurmond to undermine the president's support in the South, where whites had voted solidly for the Democrats throughout the twentieth century. But Truman's main opponent, fortunately for the president, was the colorless Republican Thomas A. Dewey. Certain of victory and an ineffective speaker and campaigner, Dewey seemed unwilling to commit himself on controversial issues. His speeches, wrote one hostile newspaper, amounted to nothing more than clichés: "Agriculture is important. Our rivers are full of fish. You cannot have freedom without liberty. Our future lies ahead." Truman, by contrast, ran an aggressive campaign. He crisscrossed the country by train, delivering fiery attacks on the Republican-controlled "do-nothing Congress." Truman revived New Deal rhetoric denouncing Wall Street and charged his opponent with threatening to undermine Social Security and other New Deal benefits. "Don't let them take it away," he repeated over and over.

The four-way 1948 campaign was the last before television put a premium on brief political advertisements and entertaining slogans rather than substantive debate, and the last in which a full spectrum of ideologies was presented to the American public. Virtually every public-opinion poll and newspaper report predicted a Dewey victory. Truman's success—by 303 to 189 electoral votes—represented one of the greatest upsets in American political history. For the first time since 1868, blacks (in the North, where they enjoyed the right to vote) played a decisive role in the outcome. Thurmond carried four Deep South states, demonstrating that the race issue, couched in terms of individual freedom, had the potential of leading traditionally Democratic white voters to desert their party. In retrospect, the States' Rights campaign offered a preview of the political transformation that by the end of the twentieth century would leave every southern state in the Republican column. As for

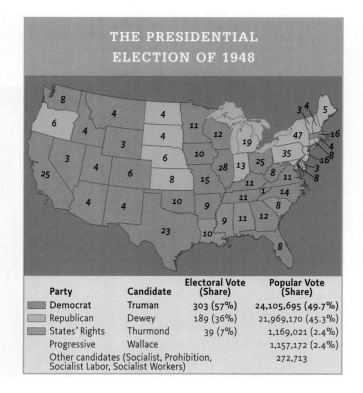

THE PRESIDENTIAL ELECTION OF 1948

Party	Candidate	Electoral Vote (Share)	Popular Vote (Share)
Democrat	Truman	303 (57%)	24,105,695 (49.7%)
Republican	Dewey	189 (36%)	21,969,170 (45.3%)
States' Rights	Thurmond	39 (7%)	1,169,021 (2.4%)
Progressive	Wallace		1,157,172 (2.4%)
Other candidates (Socialist, Prohibition, Socialist Labor, Socialist Workers)			272,713

Wallace, he suffered the humiliation of polling fewer popular votes (1.16 million) than Thurmond (1.17 million). His crushing defeat inaugurated an era in which public criticism of the foundations of American foreign policy became all but impossible.

THE ANTICOMMUNIST CRUSADE

For nearly half a century, the Cold War profoundly affected American life. There would be no return to "normalcy" as after World War I. The military-industrial establishment created during World War II would be permanent, not temporary. The United States retained a large and active federal government and poured money into weapons development and overseas bases. National security became the stated reason for a host of government projects, including aid to higher education and the building of a new national highway system (justified by the need to speed the evacuation of major cities in the event of nuclear war). The Cold War encouraged a culture of secrecy and dishonesty. Not until decades later was it revealed that during the 1950s and 1960s both the Soviet and American governments conducted experiments in which unwitting soldiers were exposed to chemical, biological, and nuclear weapons. American nuclear tests, conducted on Pacific islands and in Nevada, exposed thousands of civilians to radiation that caused cancer and birth defects.

Cold War military spending helped to fuel economic growth and support scientific research that not only perfected weaponry but also led to improved aircraft, computers, medicines, and other products with a large impact on civilian life. Since much of this research took place at universities, the Cold War promoted the rapid expansion of American higher education. The Cold War reshaped immigration policy, with refugees from communism being allowed to enter the United States regardless of national-origin quotas. The international embarrassment caused

National security and government policy

A postcard promoting tourism to Las Vegas highlights as one attraction the city's proximity to a nuclear test site. Witnessing nearby atomic explosions became a popular pastime in the city. The government failed to issue warnings of the dangers of nuclear fallout, and only years later did it admit that many onlookers had contracted diseases from radiation.

by American racial policies contributed to the dismantling of segregation. And like other wars, the Cold War encouraged the drawing of a sharp line between patriotic Americans and those accused of being disloyal. Containment—not only of communism but of unorthodox opinions of all kinds—took place at home as well as abroad. At precisely the moment when the United States celebrated freedom as the foundation of American life, the right to dissent came under attack.

Loyalty and Disloyalty

Dividing the world between liberty and slavery automatically made those who could be linked to communism enemies of freedom. Although the assault on civil liberties came to be known as McCarthyism, it began before Senator Joseph R. McCarthy of Wisconsin burst onto the national scene in 1950. In 1947, less than two weeks after announcing the Truman Doctrine, the president established a loyalty review system in which government employees were required to demonstrate their patriotism without being allowed to confront accusers or, in some cases, knowing the charges against them. Along with persons suspected of disloyalty, the new national security system also targeted homosexuals who worked for the government. They were deemed particularly susceptible to blackmail by Soviet agents as well as supposedly lacking in the manly qualities needed to maintain the country's resolve in the fight against communism. Ironically, the government conducted an anti-gay campaign at the very time that gay men enjoyed a powerful presence in realms of culture and commercial life being promoted as expressions of American freedom—modern art and ballet, fashion, and advertising. The loyalty program failed to uncover any cases

Loyalty review system

Movie stars, led by actors Humphrey Bogart and Lauren Bacall, on their way to attend the 1947 hearings of the House Un-American Activities Committee, in a demonstration of support for those called to testify about alleged communist influence in Hollywood.

of espionage. But the federal government dismissed several hundred persons from their jobs, and thousands resigned rather than submit to investigation.

Also in 1947, the House Un-American Activities Committee (HUAC) launched a series of hearings about communist influence in Hollywood. Calling well-known screenwriters, directors, and actors to appear before the committee ensured it a wave of national publicity, which its members relished. Celebrities like producer Walt Disney and actors Gary Cooper and Ronald Reagan testified that the movie industry harbored numerous communists. But ten "unfriendly witnesses" refused to answer the committee's questions about their political beliefs or to "name names" (identify individual communists) on the grounds that the hearings violated the First Amendment's guarantees of freedom of speech and political association. The committee charged the Hollywood Ten, who included the prominent screenwriters Ring Lardner Jr. and Dalton Trumbo, with contempt of Congress, and they served jail terms of six months to a year. Hollywood studios blacklisted them (denied them employment), along with more than 200 others who were accused of communist sympathies or who refused to name names.

The HUAC hearings in Hollywood

The Spy Trials

A series of highly publicized legal cases followed, which fueled the growing anti-communist hysteria. Whittaker Chambers, an editor at *Time* magazine, testified before HUAC that during the 1930s, Alger Hiss, a high-ranking State Department official, had given him secret government documents to pass to agents of the Soviet Union. Hiss vehemently denied the charge, but a jury convicted him of perjury and he served five years in prison. A young congressman from California and a member of HUAC, Richard Nixon achieved national prominence because of his dogged pursuit of Hiss. In another celebrated case, the Truman administration put the leaders of the Communist Party on trial for advocating the overthrow of the government. In 1951, eleven of them were sentenced to five years in prison.

The most sensational trial involved Julius and Ethel Rosenberg, a working-class Jewish communist couple from New York City (quite different from Hiss, a member of the eastern Protestant "establishment"). In 1951, a jury convicted the Rosenbergs of conspiracy to pass secrets concerning the atomic bomb to Soviet agents during World War II (when the Soviets were American allies). Their chief accuser was David Greenglass, Ethel Rosenberg's brother, who had worked at the Los Alamos nuclear research center.

The case against Julius Rosenberg rested on highly secret documents that could not be revealed in court. (When they were released many years later, the scientific information they contained seemed too crude to justify the government's charge that Julius had passed along the "secret of the atomic bomb," although he may have helped the Soviets speed up their atomic program.) The government had almost no evidence against Ethel Rosenberg, and Greenglass later admitted that he had lied in some of his testimony about her. Indeed, prosecutors seem to have indicted her in the hope of pressuring Julius to confess and implicate others. But in the atmosphere of hysteria, their conviction was certain. Even though they had been convicted of conspiracy, a far weaker charge than spying or treason, Judge Irving Kaufman called

Demonstrators at a 1953 rally in Washington, D.C., demanding the execution of Julius and Ethel Rosenberg.

their crime "worse than murder." They had helped, he declared, to "cause" the Korean War. Despite an international outcry, the death sentence was carried out in 1953. Controversy still surrounds the degree of guilt of both Hiss and the Rosenbergs, although almost no one today defends the Rosenbergs' execution. But these trials powerfully reinforced the idea that an army of Soviet spies was at work in the United States.

McCarthy and McCarthyism

In this atmosphere, a little-known senator from Wisconsin suddenly emerged as the chief national pursuer of subversives and gave a new name to the anticommunist crusade. Joseph R. McCarthy had won election to the Senate in 1946, partly on the basis of a fictional war record (he falsely claimed to have flown combat missions in the Pacific). In a speech at Wheeling, West Virginia, in February 1950, McCarthy announced that he had a list of 205 communists working for the State Department. The charge was preposterous, the numbers constantly changed, and McCarthy never identified a single person guilty of genuine disloyalty. But with a genius for self-promotion, McCarthy used the Senate subcommittee he chaired to hold hearings and level wild charges against numerous individuals as well as the Defense Department, the Voice of America, and other government agencies. Although many Republicans initially supported his rampage as a weapon against the Truman administration, McCarthy became an embarrassment to the party after the election of Republican Dwight D. Eisenhower as president in 1952. But McCarthy did not halt his campaign. He even questioned Eisenhower's anticommunism.

Senator Joseph R. McCarthy at the Army-McCarthy hearings of 1954. McCarthy points to a map detailing charges about the alleged extent of the communist menace, while the army's lawyer, Joseph Welch, listens in disgust.

McCarthy's downfall came in 1954, when a Senate committee investigated his charges that the army had harbored and "coddled" communists. The nationally televised Army-McCarthy hearings revealed McCarthy as a bully who browbeat witnesses and made sweeping accusations with no basis in fact. The dramatic high point came when McCarthy attacked the loyalty of a young lawyer in the firm of Joseph Welch, the army's chief lawyer. "Let us not assassinate this lad further," Welch pleaded. "You have done enough. Have you no sense of decency, sir?" After the hearings ended, the Republican-controlled Senate voted to "condemn" McCarthy for his behavior. He died three years later. But the word "McCarthyism" had entered the political vocabulary, a shorthand for character assassination, guilt by association, and abuse of power in the name of anticommunism.

"Fire!" Cartoonist Herbert Block, known as "Herblock," offered this comment in 1949 on the danger to American freedom posed by the anticommunist crusade.

An Atmosphere of Fear

By the early 1950s, the anticommunist crusade had created a pervasive atmosphere of fear. One commentator described Washington, D.C., as a city rife with "spying, suspicion, [and] defamation by rumor," with "democratic freedoms" at risk as power slipped into the hands of those "whose values are the values of dictatorship and whose methods are the methods of the police state." But anticommunism was as much a local as a national phenomenon. States created their own committees, modeled on HUAC, that investigated suspected communists and other dissenters. States and localities required loyalty oaths of teachers, pharmacists, and members of other professions, and they banned communists from fishing, holding a driver's license, and, in Indiana, working as a professional wrestler.

State and local actions

Private organizations like the American Legion, National Association of Manufacturers, and Daughters of the American Revolution also persecuted individuals for their beliefs. The Better America League of southern California gathered the names of nearly 2 million alleged subversives in the region. Previous membership in organizations with communist influence or even participation in campaigns in which communists had taken part, such as the defense of the government of Spain during the Spanish Civil War of the 1930s, suddenly took on sinister implications. Throughout the country in the late 1940s and 1950s, those who failed to testify about their past and present political beliefs and to inform on possible communists frequently lost their jobs.

Local anticommunist groups forced public libraries to remove from their shelves "un-American" books like the tales of Robin Hood, who took from the rich to give to the poor. Universities refused to allow left-wing speakers to appear on campus and fired teachers who refused to sign loyalty oaths or to testify against others.

As during World War I, the courts did nothing to halt the political repression, demonstrating once again James Madison's warning that popular hysteria could override "parchment barriers" like the Bill of Rights that sought to prevent infringements on freedom. In 1951, in *Dennis v. United States*, the Supreme Court upheld the jailing of Communist Party leaders even though the charges concerned their beliefs, not any actions they had taken. Even many liberals retreated from the idea that freedom of expression was a birthright of all Americans. The American Civil Liberties Union condemned McCarthy's tactics but refused to defend the indicted Communist Party leaders.

The Uses of Anticommunism

There undoubtedly were Soviet spies in the United States. Yet the tiny Communist Party hardly posed a threat to American security. And the vast majority of those jailed or deprived of their livelihoods during the McCarthy era were guilty of nothing more than holding unpopular beliefs and engaging in lawful political activities.

Anticommunist groups and goals

Anticommunism had many faces and purposes. A popular mass movement, it grew especially strong among ethnic groups like Polish-Americans, with roots in eastern European countries now dominated by the Soviet Union, and among American Catholics in general, who resented and feared communists' hostility to religion. Government agencies like the Federal Bureau of Investigation (FBI) used anticommunism to expand their power. Under director J. Edgar Hoover, the FBI developed files on thousands of American citizens, including political dissenters, homosexuals, and others, most of whom had no connection to communism.

Anticommunism also served as a weapon wielded by individuals and groups in battles unrelated to defending the United States against subversion. McCarthy and his Republican followers often seemed to target not so much Stalin as the legacy of Roosevelt and the New Deal. For many Democrats, aggressive anticommunism became a form of self-defense against Republican charges of disloyalty and a weapon in a struggle for the party's future. The campaign against subversion redrew the boundaries of acceptable Democratic liberalism to exclude both communists and those willing to cooperate with them as in the days of the Popular Front. Indeed, "sympathetic association" with communists—past or present—became grounds for dismissal from one's job under the government's loyalty program.

As the historian Henry Steele Commager argued in a 1947 magazine article, the anticommunist crusade promoted a new definition of loyalty—conformity. Anything other than "uncritical and unquestioning acceptance of America as it is," wrote Commager, could now be labeled unpatriotic. For business, anticommunism became part of a campaign to identify government intervention in the economy with socialism. White supremacists employed anticommunism against black civil rights, business used it against unions, and upholders of sexual morality and traditional gender roles raised the cry of subversion against feminism and homosexuality, both supposedly responsible for eroding the country's fighting spirit. (Those barred from government service now included homosexuals and members of nudist colonies.)

Loyalty and conformity

Anticommunist Politics

At its height, from the late 1940s to around 1960, the anticommunist crusade powerfully structured American politics and culture. Especially after their unexpected defeat in 1948, Republicans in Congress used a drumbeat of charges of subversion to block Truman's political program. The most important actions of Congress were ones the president opposed. After launching the government's loyalty program in 1947, Truman had become increasingly alarmed at the excesses of the anticommunist crusade. He vetoed the McCarran Internal Security Bill of 1950, which required "subversive" groups to register with the government, allowed the denial of passports to their members, and authorized their deportation or detention on presidential order. But Congress quickly gave the measure the two-thirds majority necessary for it to become law.

The McCarran-Walter Act of 1952, the first major piece of immigration legislation since 1924, also passed over the president's veto. Truman had appointed a Commission on Immigration, whose report, *Whom Shall We Welcome?*, called for replacing the quotas based on national origins with a more flexible system taking into account family reunion, labor needs, and political asylum. But the McCarran-Walter Act kept the quotas in place. It also authorized the deportation of immigrants identified as communists, even if they had become citizens. But the renewed fear of aliens sparked by the anticommunist crusade went far beyond communists. In 1954, the federal government launched Operation Wetback, which employed the military to invade Mexican-American neighborhoods and round up and deport illegal aliens. Within a year, some 1 million Mexicans had been deported.

The McCarran-Walter Act of 1952

Truman did secure passage of a 1950 law that added previously excluded self-employed and domestic workers to Social Security. Otherwise, however, the idea of expanding the New Deal welfare state faded. In its place, private welfare

VOICES OF FREEDOM

From WILL HERBERG, *PROTESTANT, CATHOLIC, JEW* (1955)

The Jewish philosopher Will Herberg was one of the more influential writers of the 1950s. In this excerpt, he analyzes the concept of the American Way of Life, a key slogan of the Cold War.

What is this American Way of Life that we have said constitutes the "common religion" of American society? . . . The American Way of Life is the symbol by which Americans define themselves and establish their unity. . . . On its political side it means the Constitution; on its economic side, "free enterprise"; on its social side, an equalitarianism which is not only compatible with but indeed actually implies vigorous economic competition and high mobility. . . .

The American Way of Life is humanitarian, "forward looking," optimistic. Americans are easily the most generous and philanthropic people in the world, in terms of their ready and unstinting response to suffering anywhere on the globe. The American believes in progress, in self-improvement, and quite fanatically in education. But above all, the American is idealistic. . . . And because they are so idealistic, Americans tend to be moralistic: they are inclined to see all issues as plain and simple, black and white, issues of morality. Every struggle in which they are seriously engaged becomes a "crusade." To Mr. Eisenhower, who in many ways exemplifies American religion in a particularly representative way, the second world war was a "crusade" (as was the first to Woodrow Wilson) . . . and so is his administration—a "battle for the republic" against "godless Communism" abroad and against "corruption and materialism" at home. . . . It is the secret of what outsiders must take to be the incredible self-righteousness of the American people, who tend to see the world divided into an innocent, virtuous America confronted with a corrupt, devious, and guileful Europe and Asia.

From HENRY STEELE COMMAGER, "WHO IS LOYAL TO AMERICA?" *HARPER'S* (SEPTEMBER 1947)

In a sharply worded essay written in 1947, the prominent historian Henry Steele Commager commented on how the anticommunist crusade was stifling the expression of dissent and promoting an idea of patriotism that equated loyalty to the nation with the uncritical acceptance of American society and institutions.

Increasingly, Congress is concerned with the eradication of disloyalty and the defense of Americanism, and scarcely a day passes . . . that the outlines of the new loyalty and the new Americanism are not etched more sharply in public policy. . . . In the making is a revival of the red hysteria of the early 1920s, one of the shabbiest chapters in the history of American democracy, and more than a revival, for the new crusade is designed not merely to frustrate Communism but to formulate a positive definition of Americanism, and a positive concept of loyalty.

What is this new loyalty? It is, above all, conformity. It is the uncritical and unquestioning acceptance of America as it is—the political institutions, the social relationships, the economic practices. It rejects inquiry into the race question or socialized medicine, or public housing, or into the wisdom or validity of our foreign policy. It regards as particularly heinous any challenge to what is called "the system of private enterprise," identifying that system with Americanism. It abandons . . . the once popular concept of progress, and regards America as a finished product, perfect and complete.

It is, it must be added, easily satisfied. For it wants not intellectual conviction nor spiritual conquest, but mere outward conformity. In matters of loyalty, it takes the word for the deed, the gesture for the principle. It is content with the flag salute. . . . It is satisfied with membership in respectable organizations and, as it assumes that every member of a liberal organization is a Communist, concludes that every member of a conservative one is a true American. It has not yet learned that not everyone who saith Lord, Lord, shall enter into the kingdom of Heaven. It is designed neither to discover real disloyalty nor to foster true loyalty.

The concept of loyalty as conformity is a false one. It is narrow and restrictive, denies freedom of thought and of conscience. . . . What do men know of loyalty who make a mockery of the Declaration of Independence and the Bill of Rights?

QUESTIONS

1. *What does Herberg think are the strengths and weaknesses of the American outlook?*

2. *Why does Commager feel that the new patriotism makes "a mockery" of the Bill of Rights?*

3. *How does Herberg's analysis help to explain the violations of civil liberties deplored by Commager?*

arrangements proliferated. The labor contracts of unionized workers established health insurance plans, automatic cost of living wage increases, paid vacations, and pension plans that supplemented Social Security. Western European governments provided these benefits to all citizens. In the United States, union members in major industries enjoyed them, but not the nonunionized majority of the population, a situation that created increasing inequality among laboring Americans.

The Cold War and Organized Labor

Every political and social organization had to cooperate with the anticommunist crusade or face destruction, a wrenching experience for movements like labor and civil rights, in which communists had been some of the most militant organizers. After the passage of the Taft-Hartley Act of 1947, which withdrew bargaining rights and legal protection from unions whose leaders failed to swear that they were not communists, the CIO expelled numerous left-wing officials and eleven communist-led unions, representing nearly 1 million workers. Organized labor emerged as a major supporter of the foreign policy of the Cold War. Internal battles over the role of communists and their allies led to the purging of some of the most militant union leaders, often the ones most committed to advancing equal rights to women and racial minorities in the workplace. This left organized labor less able to respond to the economy's shift to an emphasis on service rather than manufacturing, and to the rise of the civil rights movement.

Cold War Civil Rights

The civil rights movement also underwent a transformation. At first, mainstream black organizations like the NAACP and Urban League protested the Truman administration's loyalty program. They wondered aloud why the program and congressional committees defined communism as "un-American," but not racism. Anticommunist investigators often cited attendance at interracial gatherings as evidence of disloyalty. But while a few prominent black leaders, notably the singer and actor Paul Robeson and the veteran crusader for equality W. E. B. Du Bois, became outspoken critics of the Cold War, most felt they had no choice but to go along. The NAACP purged communists from local branches. When the government deprived Robeson of his passport and indicted Du Bois for failing to register as an agent of the Soviet Union, few prominent Americans, white or black, protested. (The charge against Du Bois was so absurd that even at the height of McCarthyism, the judge dismissed it.)

> *Black organizations and the Cold War*

The Cold War caused a shift in thinking and tactics among civil rights groups. Organizations like the Southern Conference for Human Welfare, in which communists and noncommunists had cooperated in linking racial equality with labor organizing and economic reform, had been crucial to the struggles of the 1930s and war years. Their demise left a gaping hole that the NAACP, with its narrowly legalistic strategy, could not fill. Black organizations embraced the language of the Cold War and used it for their own purposes. They insisted that by damaging the

American image abroad, racial inequality played into the Russians' hands. Thus, they helped to cement Cold War ideology as the foundation of the political culture, while complicating the idea of American freedom.

President Truman, as noted above, had called for greater attention to civil rights in part to improve the American image abroad. All in all, however, the height of the Cold War was an unfavorable time to raise questions about the imperfections of American society. In 1947, two months after the Truman Doctrine speech, Undersecretary of State Dean Acheson delivered a major address defending the president's pledge to aid "free peoples" seeking to preserve their "democratic institutions." Acheson chose as his audience the Delta Council, an organization of Mississippi planters, bankers, and merchants. He seemed unaware that to make the case for the Cold War, he had ventured into what one historian has called the "American Siberia," a place of grinding poverty whose black population (70 percent of the total) enjoyed neither genuine freedom nor democracy. Most of the Delta's citizens were denied the very liberties supposedly endangered by communism.

After 1948, little came of the Truman administration's civil rights flurry. State and local laws banning discrimination in employment and housing remained largely unenforced. In 1952, the Democrats showed how quickly the issue had faded by nominating for president Adlai Stevenson of Illinois, a candidate with little interest in civil rights, with southern segregationist John Sparkman as his running mate. The following year, Hortense Gabel, director of the eminently respectable New York State Committee Against Discrimination in Housing, reported that the shadow of fear hung over the civil rights movement. Given the persecution of dissent and the widespread sentiment that equated any criticism of American society with disloyalty, "a great many people are shying away from all activity in the civil liberties and civil rights fronts."

Time would reveal that the waning of the civil rights impulse was only temporary. But it came at a crucial moment, the late 1940s and early 1950s, when the United States experienced the greatest economic boom in its history. The rise of an "affluent society" transformed American life, opening new opportunities for tens of millions of white Americans in rapidly expanding suburbs. But it left blacks trapped in the declining rural areas of the South and urban ghettos of the North. The contrast between new opportunities and widespread prosperity for whites and continued discrimination for blacks would soon inspire a civil rights revolution and, with it, yet another redefinition of American freedom.

Blacks, led by A. Philip Randolph (*left*), picketing at the 1948 Democratic national convention. The delegates' adoption of a strong civil rights plank led representatives of several southern states to withdraw and nominate their own candidate for president, Strom Thurmond.

The waning civil rights impulse

SUGGESTED READING

BOOKS

- Biondi, Martha. *To Stand and Fight: The Struggle for Civil Rights in Postwar New York City* (2003). A comprehensive account of the broad coalition that battled for racial justice in New York City, in areas such as jobs, education, and housing.

- Canaday, Margot. *The Straight State: Sexuality and Citizenship in Twentieth-Century America* (2009). Details the federal government's efforts to stigmatize and punish homosexuality.

- Donovan, Robert. *Conflict and Crisis: The Presidency of Harry S. Truman, 1945–1948* (1977). A careful account of Truman's first administration and his surprising election victory in 1948.

- Dudziak, Mary L. *Cold War Civil Rights: Race and the Image of American Democracy* (2000). Analyzes how the Cold War influenced and in some ways encouraged the civil rights movement at home.

- Gaddis, John. *Strategies of Containment: A Critical Analysis of Postwar American National Security* (1982). An influential analysis of the development of the containment policy central to American foreign policy during the Cold War.

- Glendon, Mary Ann. *A World Made New: Eleanor Roosevelt and the Universal Declaration of Human Rights* (2001). Relates the drafting of the Universal Declaration of Human Rights and the response of governments around the world, including the United States.

- Hogan, Michael. *The Marhsall Plan* (1987). A detailed look at a pillar of early Cold War policy.

- Hunt, Michael. *Ideology and U.S. Foreign Policy* (1987). Discusses how ideas, including the idea of freedom, have shaped America's interactions with the rest of the world.

- Leffler, Melvyn P. *A Preponderance of Power: National Security, the Truman Administration, and the Cold War* (1992). An influential account of the origins of the Cold War.

- Lipsitz, George. *Rainbow at Midnight: Labor and Culture in the 1940s* (1994). Examines the labor movement and its role in American life in the decade of perhaps its greatest influence.

- Saunders, Frances S. *The Cultural Cold War: The CIA and the World of Arts and Letters* (2000). Describes how the CIA and other government agencies secretly funded artists and writers as part of the larger Cold War.

- Schrecker, Ellen. *Many Are the Crimes: McCarthyism in America* (1998). A full account of the anticommunist crusade at home and its impact on American intellectual and social life.

- Stueck, William. *The Korean War: An International History* (1995). Studies the Korean War in its full global context.

- Sugrue, Thomas. *Origins of the Urban Crisis: Race and Inequality in Postwar Detroit* (1996). Explores race relations in a key industrial city after World War II and how they set the stage for the upheavals of the 1960s.

- Williams, William A. *The Tragedy of American Diplomacy* (1959). An influential critique of America's Cold War foreign policy.

WEBSITES

- Cold War International History Project: www.wilsoncenter .org/program/cold-war-international-history-project

- Korea + 50: No Longer Forgotten: www.trumanlibrary .org/korea/

CHAPTER REVIEW AND ONLINE RESOURCES

REVIEW QUESTIONS

1. What major ideological conflicts, security interests, and events brought about the Cold War?

2. President Truman referred to the Truman Doctrine and the Marshall Plan as "two halves of the same walnut." Explain the similarities and differences between these two aspects of containment.

3. How did the tendency of both the United States and the Soviet Union to see all international events through the lens of the Cold War lessen each country's ability to understand what was happening in other countries around the world?

4. Why did the United States not support movements for colonial independence around the world?

5. How did the government attempt to shape public opinion during the Cold War?

6. Explain the differences between the United States's and the Soviet Union's application of the UN Universal Declaration of Human Rights.

7. How did the anticommunist crusade affect organized labor in the postwar period?

8. What accounts for the Republican resurgence in these years?

9. What were the major components of Truman's Fair Deal? Which ones were implemented and which ones not?

10. How did the Cold War affect civil liberties in the United States?

KEY TERMS

containment (p. 886)

Long Telegram (p. 887)

"iron curtain" speech (p. 887)

Truman Doctrine (p. 887)

Marshall Plan (p. 889)

National Security Council (p. 889)

General Agreement on Tariffs and Trade (p. 890)

North Atlantic Treaty Organization (p. 891)

NSC-68 (p. 891)

decolonization (p. 896)

"Militant Liberty" (p. 897)

totalitarianism (p. 897)

the Fair Deal (p. 901)

Taft-Hartley Act (p. 902)

Dixiecrats (p. 904)

loyalty review system (p. 907)

Hollywood Ten (p. 908)

Army-McCarthy hearings (p. 909)

conformity (p. 911)

McCarran-Walter Act (p. 911)

wwnorton.com/studyspace

Visit StudySpace for these resources and more:

- **Author Videos**
- **A chapter outline**
- **A practice quiz**
- **Interactive maps**
- **Multimedia documents**

PART 6

WHAT KIND OF NATION?

1953–2012

I n the last half of the twentieth century, the United States experienced profound changes both at home and in its role in the larger world. The Cold War produced increasing American involvement in the affairs of other nations across the globe. Sometimes indirectly, sometimes through direct military intervention, the United States sought to prevent the further spread of communism and to ensure the existence of governments friendly to American strategic and economic interests. The sudden and unexpected collapse of communism in the Soviet Union and eastern Europe between 1989 and 1991 left the United States by far the world's foremost military power. At home, these years witnessed far-reaching changes in the nature of American society and a dramatic expansion in the rights of American citizens and their understandings of freedom.

On the surface, the decade of the 1950s seemed uneventful. It was a time of widespread affluence in the United States, the beginning of an unprecedented economic expansion that lasted until the early 1970s. Millions of Americans moved to the suburbs, where they enjoyed access to an astonishing array of

consumer goods that poured out of American factories, including cars, television sets, and household appliances. The postwar "baby boom" dramatically increased the population. American understandings of freedom centered on the enjoyment of economic affluence and consumer choice within the context of traditional family life, with women finding fulfillment within their suburban homes.

Even during this time of "consensus," when sharp political divisions and economic strife seemed to have vanished from American life, seeds of discontent sprouted. A few artists and social commentators began to criticize the stifling atmosphere of conformity. The Supreme Court's decision in 1954 outlawing racial segregation in public schools, justified, in part, by the damage Jim Crow inflicted on the world standing of the United States in the Cold War, helped to inspire the revival of the struggle for racial justice. The Montgomery bus boycott of 1955 launched the southern phase of the civil rights movement, which forced the entire country to rethink whether the United States could genuinely call itself "the land of the free" if it confined millions of Americans to second-class citizenship.

These seeds of protest flowered in the 1960s, a decade of social conflict and of dramatic expansion of the boundaries of American freedom. The civil rights revolution reached its climax with demonstrations throughout the South and the passage in 1964 and 1965 of national laws protecting blacks' civil rights and restoring to them the right to vote in the South. Although the movement splintered thereafter and the nation failed to address adequately the economic plight of non-whites trapped in decaying urban ghettos, the 1960s ended with the structure of legal segregation having been dismantled. The black movement inspired other aggrieved groups—Latinos, Indians, homosexuals, and women—to press their own grievances and claim their own "liberation." Their efforts further enlarged freedom's boundaries and helped to propel the idea of freedom into the most intimate areas of life. Under the leadership of Chief Justice Earl Warren, the Supreme Court gave constitutional recognition to the "rights revolution." By the end of the decade, both the meaning and the boundaries of freedom had expanded enormously.

At the same time, the country became more and more deeply involved in the Vietnam War. In this Cold War conflict, American policymakers viewed the nationalist movement in Vietnam, led by homegrown communists, as part of a worldwide conspiracy directed from Moscow. As the United States committed hundreds of thousands of soldiers to Vietnam in the mid-1960s, the foreign policy consensus disintegrated. For the first time in American history, college students took the lead in radical protest, organizing massive protests against the war. Political disaffection helped to spawn the counterculture, a youth rebellion against prevailing middle-class mores. Having brought twentieth-century liberalism to its high point with his Great Society programs that sought to uplift the poor, encourage the arts, and provide medical care to the aged and needy, President Lyndon B. Johnson saw his party split over the war and his public support disintegrate.

Known as a time of radical protest, the 1960s also spawned a conservative backlash against the civil rights movement, the sexual revolution, public disorder, and the expansion of federal power. During the 1970s and 1980s, businessmen, antigovernment activists, a Christian Right that sought to restore what it considered to be traditional moral values, and Cold Warriors who desired a reinvigorated anticommunist crusade came together in an increasingly powerful conservative coalition. Their rise to power was hastened by the end of the postwar economic boom in 1973 and the inability of President Jimmy Carter to address the slump effectively. In 1980, conservative Ronald Reagan was elected president, ushering in the Reagan Revolution.

Reagan drastically increased military spending, cut funding for some social programs, reduced taxes, and attacked labor unions. Like Franklin D. Roosevelt, he consciously sought to redefine the meaning of freedom, associating it with anticommunism, free enterprise, and reduced government intervention in the economy. Although he put into effect conservative economic policies, Reagan failed to halt the rights revolution that had begun in the 1960s. Throughout the 1980s and 1990s, many conservatives lamented the fact that fewer and fewer women were embracing the traditional role of

homemaker and that gays were gaining more and more recognition of their rights. Although conservatives launched a furious campaign to overturn the Supreme Court's 1973 decision legalizing abortion, they failed to achieve success. Moreover, thanks to a 1965 law that ended the national-origins quotas for immigrants, newcomers from Asia and Latin America poured into the United States, setting off political battles over the country's increasingly visible racial and ethnic diversity.

The abrupt end of the Cold War between 1989 and 1991 left the United States as the world's lone superpower. This reinforced prevailing American understandings of freedom, emphasizing political democracy, free markets, and unrestrained individual choice in personal matters. During the 1990s, Americans became increasingly aware of the process of "globalization"—the international flow of people, investment, goods, and information across national boundaries. Some welcomed it as an expansion of economic freedom. Others worried that manufacturing jobs were leaving the United States for low-wage areas abroad and that crucial decisions affecting people's day-to-day lives were being made by institutions like the World Bank and World Trade Organization, over which no democratic control existed.

Events at the dawn of the twenty-first century revealed the extent and limitations of American power. The attacks of September 11, 2001, which killed some 3,000 persons, highlighted the nation's vulnerability at a time when terrorists, like goods and money, seemed able to cross national boundaries with ease. In response, President George W. Bush committed the United States to a "war on terrorism," a war without easily definable enemies, a predictable timetable, or a clear definition of victory. The federal government claimed the power to arrest persons suspected of involvement with terrorism, primarily individuals of Middle Eastern origin, without charge and to hold them indefinitely. The 2003 Iraq War, launched by the United States and Great Britain over the opposition of most members of the United Nations, suggested that in the post–Cold War world, America no longer needed to build alliances or concern itself with world opinion. Although the invasion successfully overthrew the Iraqi dictator Saddam Hussein, an anti-American insurgency soon developed, along with strife between Iraq's Shiite and Sunni Muslims. By the end of 2006, the United States was bogged down in a seemingly interminable war, which was soon becoming increasingly unpopular at home.

These events raised anew vital questions already debated many times in the country's history. What is the balance between civil liberties and security in times of crisis? What are the economic conditions of freedom? Should the country consider itself a democracy or an empire? Should certain groups have their rights diminished because of their racial or ethnic origins? The answers to these questions would go a long way toward defining the meaning and boundaries of American freedom in the twenty-first century.

CHAPTER 24

AN AFFLUENT SOCIETY

★

1953–1960

In 1958, during a "thaw" in the Cold War, the United States and the Soviet Union agreed to exchange national exhibitions in order to allow citizens of each "superpower" to become acquainted with life in the other. The Soviet Exhibition, unveiled in New York City in June 1959, featured factory machinery, scientific advances, and other illustrations of how communism had modernized a backward country. The following month, the American National Exhibition opened in Moscow. A showcase of consumer goods and leisure equipment, complete with stereo sets, a movie theater, home appliances, and twenty-two different cars, the exhibit, Newsweek observed, hoped to demonstrate the superiority of "modern capitalism with its ideology of political and economic freedom." Yet the exhibit's real message was not freedom but consumption—or, to be more precise, the equating of the two.

When Vice President Richard Nixon prepared for his trip to Moscow to launch the exhibition, a former ambassador to Russia urged him to emphasize American values: "We are idealists; they are materialists." But the events of the opening day seemed to reverse these roles. Nixon devoted his address, entitled "What Freedom Means to Us," not to freedom of expression or differing forms of government, but to the "extraordinarily high standard of living" in the United States, with its 56 million cars and 50 million television sets. The United States, he declared, had achieved what Soviets could only dream of—"prosperity for all in a classless society."

The Moscow exhibition became the site of a classic Cold War confrontation over the meaning of freedom—the "kitchen debate" between Nixon and Soviet premier Nikita Khrushchev. Twice during the first day Nixon and Khrushchev engaged in unscripted debate about the merits of capitalism and communism. The first took place in the kitchen of a model suburban ranch house, the second in a futuristic "miracle kitchen" complete with a mobile robot that swept the floors. Supposedly the home of an average steelworker, the ranch house was the exhibition's centerpiece. It represented, Nixon declared, the mass enjoyment of American freedom within a suburban setting—freedom of choice among products, colors, styles, and prices. It also implied a particular role for women. Throughout his exchanges with Khrushchev, Nixon used the words "women" and "housewives" interchangeably. Pointing to the automatic floor sweeper, the vice president remarked that in the United States "you don't need a wife."

Nixon's decision to make a stand for American values in the setting of a suburban kitchen was a brilliant stroke. Nixon recognized that "soft power"—the penetration across the globe of American goods and popular culture—was an even more potent form of influence than military might. Indeed, his stance reflected the triumph during the 1950s of a conception of freedom centered on economic abundance and consumer choice within the context of traditional family life—a vision that seemed to offer far more opportunities for the "pursuit of happiness" to men than women. In reply, Khrushchev ridiculed consumer culture and the American obsession with household gadgets. "Don't you have a machine," he quipped, "that puts food in the mouth and pushes it down?" Many of the items on display, he continued, served "no useful purpose." Yet, in a sense,

FOCUS QUESTIONS

What were the main characteristics of the affluent society of the 1950s? –p. 925

How were the 1950s a period of consensus in both domestic policies and foreign affairs? –p. 939

What were the major thrusts of the civil rights movement in this period? –p. 949

What was the significance of the presidential election of 1960? –p. 959

A portrait of affluence: In this photograph by Alex Henderson, Steve Czekalinski, an employee of the DuPont Corporation, poses with his family and the food they consumed in a single year, 1951. The family spent $1,300 (around $11,000 in today's money) on food, including 699 bottles of milk, 578 pounds of meat, and 131 dozen eggs. Nowhere else in the world in 1951 was food so available and inexpensive.

1946	*Mendez v. Westminster*
1947	Levittown development starts
1950	David Riesman's *The Lonely Crowd*
1952	United States detonates first hydrogen bomb
1953	Soviet Union detonates hydrogen bomb
	CIA-led Iranian coup
1954	*Brown v. Board of Education*
	CIA-led Guatemalan coup
	Geneva Accords for Vietnam
1955	AFL and CIO merge
	Allen Ginsberg's *Howl*
1955–1956	Montgomery bus boycott
1956	"Southern Manifesto"
	Federal-Aid Highway Act
	Suez crisis
1957	Eisenhower Doctrine
	Southern Christian Leadership Conference organized
	Integration of Little Rock's Central High School
	Sputnik launched
	Jack Kerouac's *On the Road*
1958	National Defense Education Act
1959	Nixon-Khrushchev "kitchen debate"
1960	John F. Kennedy elected president
1962	Milton Friedman's *Capitalism and Freedom*

the Soviet leader conceded the debate when he predicted—quite incorrectly—that within seven years his country would surpass the United States in the production of consumer goods. For if material abundance was a battleground in the Cold War, American victory was certain.

THE GOLDEN AGE

The end of World War II was followed by what one scholar has called the "golden age" of capitalism, a period of economic expansion, stable prices, low unemployment, and rising standards of living that continued until 1973. Between 1946 and 1960, the American gross national product more than doubled and much of the benefit flowed to ordinary citizens in rising wages. In every measurable way—diet, housing, income, education, recreation—most Americans lived better than their parents and grandparents had. By 1960, an estimated 60 percent of Americans enjoyed what the government defined as a middle-class standard of living. The official poverty rate, 30 percent of all families in 1950, had declined to 22 percent a decade later (still, to be sure, representing more than one in five Americans).

Numerous innovations came into widespread use in these years, transforming Americans' daily lives. They included television, home air-conditioning, automatic dishwashers, inexpensive long-distance telephone calls, and jet air travel. Services like electricity, central heating, and indoor plumbing that within living memory had been enjoyed only by the rich and solidly middle class now became features of common life.

A Changing Economy

Despite the economic recovery of western Europe and Japan after World War II, the United States remained the world's predominant industrial power. Major industries like steel, automobiles, and aircraft dominated the domestic and world markets for their products. Like other wars, the Cold War fueled industrial production and promoted a redistribution of the nation's population and economic resources. The West, especially the Seattle area, southern California, and the Rocky Mountain states, benefited enormously from government contracts for aircraft, guided missiles, and radar systems. The South became the home of numerous military bases and government-funded shipyards. Growth in the construction of aircraft engines and submarines counterbalanced the decline of New England's old textile and machinery industries, many of which relocated in the South to take advantage of low-cost nonunion labor.

In retrospect, the 1950s appear as the last decade of the industrial age in the United States. Since then, the American economy has shifted rapidly toward services, education, information, finance, and entertainment, while employment in manufacturing has declined. Even during the 1950s, the number of factory laborers fell slightly while clerical workers grew by nearly 25 percent and salaried employees in large corporate enterprises rose by 60 percent. Unions' very success in raising wages inspired employers to mechanize more and more elements of manufacturing in order to reduce labor costs. In 1956, for the first

Vice President Richard Nixon and Soviet premier Nikita Khrushchev during the "kitchen debate," a discussion, among other things, of the meaning of freedom, which took place in 1959 at the American National Exposition in Moscow. Khrushchev makes a point while a woman demonstrates a washing machine.

time in American history, white-collar workers outnumbered blue-collar factory and manual laborers.

The long-term trend toward fewer and larger farms continued. During the 1950s, the farm population fell from 23 million to 15 million, yet agricultural production rose by 50 percent, thanks to more efficient machinery, the application of chemical fertilizers and insecticides, increased use of irrigation to open land to cultivation in the West, and the development of new crop strains. The decade witnessed an acceleration of the transformation of southern life that had begun during World War II. New tractors and harvesting machinery and a continuing shift from cotton production to less labor-intensive soybean and poultry raising reduced the need for farm workers. More than 3 million black and white hired hands and sharecroppers migrated out of the region. The center of gravity of American farming shifted decisively to Texas, Arizona, and especially California. The large corporate farms of California, worked by Latino and Filipino migrant laborers, poured forth an endless supply of fruits and vegetables for the domestic and world markets. Items like oranges and orange juice, once luxuries, became an essential part of the American diet.

A Suburban Nation

The main engines of economic growth during the 1950s, however, were residential construction and spending on consumer goods. The postwar baby boom (discussed later) and the shift of population from cities to suburbs created an enormous demand for housing, television sets, home appliances,

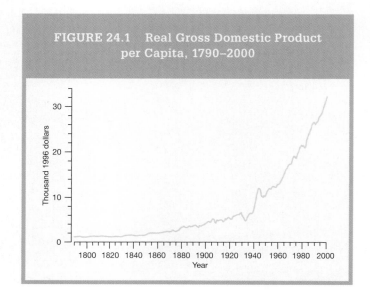

FIGURE 24.1   Real Gross Domestic Product per Capita, 1790–2000

Levittown, New York, perhaps the nation's most famous suburban community, photographed in 1954. Eventually, home owners would make individualized changes to their houses, so today Levittown looks far less uniform than when it was built.

This aerial view of Westchester, a community in Los Angeles, California, in 1949, illustrates how suburban "sprawl" spread over the landscape in the postwar era.

and cars. By 1960, suburban residents of single-family homes outnumbered urban dwellers and those living in rural areas. (Today, they outnumber both combined.)

During the 1950s, the number of houses in the United States doubled, nearly all of them built in the suburbs that sprang up across the landscape. The dream of home ownership, the physical embodiment of hopes for a better life, came within reach of the majority of Americans. Developers pioneered inexpensive mass-building techniques, and government-backed low-interest loans to returning veterans allowed working-class men and women in large numbers to purchase homes. William and Alfred Levitt, who shortly after the war built the first Levittown on 1,200 acres of potato fields on Long Island near New York City, became the most famous suburban developers. Levittown's more than 10,000 houses were assembled quickly from prefabricated parts and priced well within the reach of most Americans. Levittown was soon home to 40,000 people. At the same time, suburbs required a new form of shopping center—the mall—to which people drove in their cars. In contrast to traditional mixed-use city centers crowded with pedestrians, malls existed solely for shopping and had virtually no public space.

The Growth of the West

But it was California that became the most prominent symbol of the postwar suburban boom. Between World War II and 1975, more than 30 million Americans moved west of the Mississippi River. One-fifth of the population growth of the 1950s occurred in California alone. In 1963, it surpassed New York to become the nation's most populous state.

Ernst Haas's 1969 photograph of Albuquerque, New Mexico, could have been taken in any one of scores of American communities. As cities spread out, "strips," consisting of motels, gas stations, and nationally franchised businesses, became common. Meanwhile, older downtown business sections stagnated.

Most western growth took place in metropolitan areas, not on farms. But "centerless" western cities like Houston, Phoenix, and Los Angeles differed greatly from traditional urban centers in the East. Rather than consisting of downtown business districts linked to residential neighborhoods by public transportation, western cities were decentralized clusters of single-family homes and businesses united by a web of highways. The Los Angeles basin, the largest western suburban region, had once had an extensive system of trains, trolleys, and buses. But local governments dismantled these lines after World War II, and the state and federal governments replaced them with freeways for cars and trucks. Suburban growth spilled into farm regions like the San Fernando and San Bernardino valleys. By one estimate, one-third of southern California's land area (presumably not including mountains and deserts) was paved over with roads and parking lots. Life centered around the car; people drove to and from work and did their shopping at malls reachable only by driving. In other sections of the country as well, shopping shifted to suburban centers, and old downtown business districts stagnated. The spread of suburban homes created millions of new lawns. Today, more land is cultivated in grass than any agricultural crop in the United States.

The Los Angeles basin

A Consumer Culture

"The consumer is the key to our economy," declared Jack Straus, chairman of the board of Macy's, New York City's leading department store. "Our ability to consume is endless. The luxuries of today are the necessities of tomorrow." The roots of the consumer culture of the 1950s date back to the 1920s and even earlier. But never before had affluence, or consumerism, been so widespread. In a consumer culture, the measure of freedom became the ability to gratify market desires. Modern

In this 1950 photograph, television sets move through an assembly line.

Introduced in 1954, the frozen TV dinner was marketed in a package designed to look like a TV set. Within a year, Swanson had sold 25 million dinners.

society, wrote Clark Kerr, president of the University of California, may well have reduced freedom "in the workplace" by subjecting workers to stringent discipline on the job, but it offered a far greater range of "goods and services," and therefore "a greater scope of freedom" in Americans' "personal lives."

In a sense, the 1950s represented the culmination of the long-term trend in which consumerism replaced economic independence and democratic participation as central definitions of American freedom. Attitudes toward debt changed as well. Low interest rates and the spread of credit cards encouraged Americans to borrow money to purchase consumer goods. Americans became comfortable living in never-ending debt, once seen as a loss of economic freedom.

Consumer culture demonstrated the superiority of the American way of life to communism and virtually redefined the nation's historic mission to extend freedom to other countries. From Coca-Cola to Levi's jeans, American consumer goods, once a status symbol for the rich in other countries, were now marketed to customers around the globe. The country's most powerful weapon in the Cold War, insisted a reporter for *House Beautiful* magazine, was "the freedom offered by washing machines and dishwashers, vacuum cleaners, automobiles, and refrigerators."

The TV World

Thanks to television, images of middle-class life and advertisements for consumer goods blanketed the country. By the end of the 1950s, nearly nine of ten American families owned a TV set. Television replaced newspapers as the most common source of information about public events, and TV watching became the nation's leading leisure activity. Television changed Americans' eating habits (the frozen

TV dinner, heated and eaten while watching a program, went on sale in 1954), and it provided Americans of all regions and backgrounds with a common cultural experience.

With a few exceptions, like the Army-McCarthy hearings mentioned in the previous chapter, TV avoided controversy and projected a bland image of middle-class life. Popular shows of the early 1950s, such as *The Goldbergs* (with Jewish immigrants as the central characters) and *The Honeymooners* (in which Jackie Gleason played a bus driver), featured working-class families living in urban apartments. By the end of the decade, they had been replaced as the dominant programs by quiz shows, westerns, and comedies set in suburban homes like *Leave It to Beaver* and *The Adventures of Ozzie and Harriet*. Television also became the most effective advertising medium ever invented. To polish their image, large corporations sponsored popular programs—*The General Electric Theater* (hosted for several years by Ronald Reagan), *Alcoa Presents*, and others. TV ads, aimed primarily at middle-class suburban viewers, conveyed images of the good life based on endless consumption.

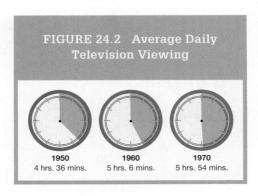

FIGURE 24.2   Average Daily Television Viewing

1950	1960	1970
4 hrs. 36 mins.	5 hrs. 6 mins.	5 hrs. 54 mins.

A New Ford

"The concept of freedom," wrote one commentator in 1959, "has become as familiar to us as an old hat or a new Ford." And a new Ford—or Chrysler or Chevrolet—now seemed essential to the enjoyment of freedom's benefits. Along with a home and television set, the car became part of what sociologists called "the standard consumer package" of the 1950s. By 1960, 80 percent of American families owned at least one car, and 14 percent had two or more, nearly all manufactured in the United States. Most were designed to go out of style within a year or two, promoting further purchases.

Auto manufacturers and oil companies vaulted to the top ranks of corporate America. Detroit and its environs were home to immense auto factories. The River Rouge complex had 62,000 employees, Willow Run 42,000. Since the military

A 1959 Cadillac Eldorado Biarritz, an example of the design excesses of 1950s car makers. Behemoths like this, which got less than fifteen miles to a gallon of gasoline, depended on the availability of cheap fuel. When gas prices rose in later decades, consumers turned to smaller, more fuel-efficient foreign cars.

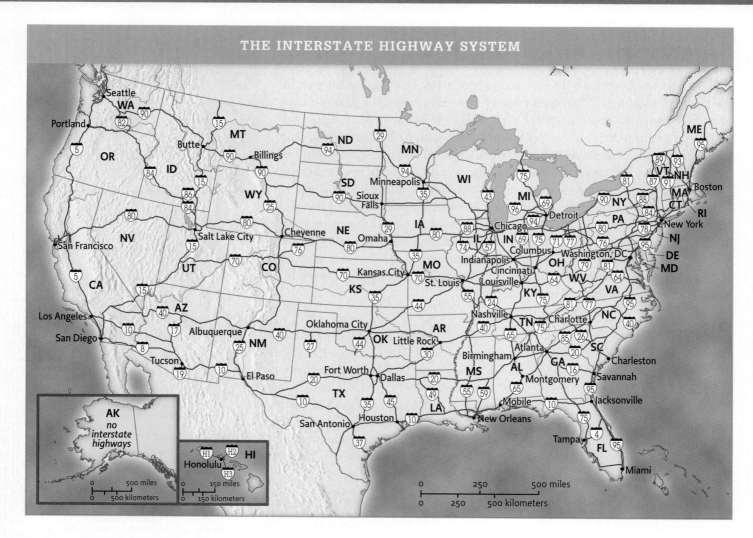

THE INTERSTATE HIGHWAY SYSTEM

Begun in 1956 and completed in 1993, the interstate highway system dramatically altered the American landscape and Americans' daily lives. It made possible more rapid travel by car and stimulated the growth of suburbs along its many routes.

The car and daily life

increasingly needed high-technology goods rather than the trucks and tanks that had rolled off assembly lines in World War II, the region around the Great Lakes lagged in defense contracts. In the long term, the continued funneling of federal dollars from the North and Midwest to the Sunbelt would prove devastating to the old industrial heartland. But during the 1950s, the booming automobile industry, with its demand for steel, rubber, and other products, assured the region's continued prosperity.

The automobile, the pivot on which suburban life turned, transformed the nation's daily life, just as the interstate highway system (discussed later) transformed Americans' travel habits, making possible long-distance vacationing by car and commuting to work from ever-increasing distances. The result was an altered American landscape, leading to the construction of motels, drive-in movie theaters, and roadside eating establishments. The first McDonald's fast food restaurant opened in Illinois in 1954. Within ten years, having been franchised by California businessman Ray Kroc, approximately 700 McDonald's stands had been built, which had sold over 400 million hamburgers. The car symbolized the identification of freedom with individual mobility and private choice. On the road, Americans were constantly reminded in advertising, television shows, and popular songs, they truly enjoyed freedom. They could imagine themselves as modern versions of western pioneers, able to leave behind urban crowds and workplace pressures for the "open road."

Women at Work and at Home

The emergence of suburbia as a chief site of what was increasingly called the "American way of life" placed pressure on the family—and especially women—to live up to freedom's promise. After 1945, women lost most of the industrial jobs they had performed during the war. As during most of American history, women who worked outside the home remained concentrated in low-salary, nonunion jobs, such as clerical, sales, and service labor, rather than better-paying manufacturing positions. After a sharp postwar drop in female employment, the number of women at work soon began to rise. By 1955, it exceeded the level of World War II. But the nature and aims of women's work had changed. The modern woman, said *Look* magazine, worked part-time, to help support the family's middle-class lifestyle, not to help pull it out of poverty or to pursue personal fulfillment or an independent career. Working women in 1960 earned, on average, only 60 percent of the income of men.

Despite the increasing numbers of wage-earning women, the suburban family's breadwinner was assumed to be male, while the wife remained at home. Films, TV shows, and advertisements portrayed marriage as the most important goal of American women. And during the 1950s, men and women reaffirmed the virtues of family life. They married younger (at an average age of twenty-two for men and twenty for women), divorced less frequently than in the past, and had more children (3.2 per family). A "baby boom" that lasted into the mid-1960s followed the end of the war. At a time of low immigration, the American population rose by nearly 30 million (almost 20 percent) during the 1950s. The increase arose mostly from the large number of births, but it also reflected the fact that Americans now lived longer than in the past, thanks to the wide availability of "miracle drugs" like penicillin that had been developed during World War II to combat bacterial infections.

The family also became a weapon in the Cold War. The ability of women to remain at home, declared a government official, "separates us from the Communist world," where a high percentage of women worked. To be sure, the family life exalted during the 1950s differed from the patriarchal household of old. It was a modernized relationship, in

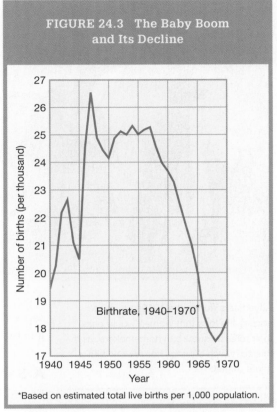

FIGURE 24.3 The Baby Boom and Its Decline

Number of births (per thousand)

Birthrate, 1940–1970*

Year

*Based on estimated total live births per 1,000 population.

Jack Gould's 1946 photograph of a hospital maternity ward captures the first year of the postwar baby boom.

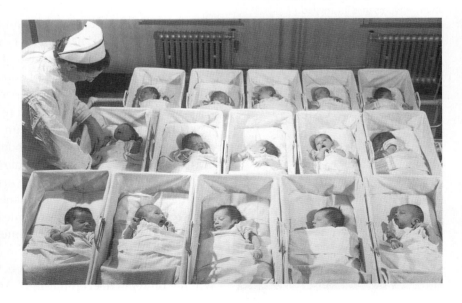

Advertisers during the 1950s sought to convey the idea that women would enjoy their roles as suburban homemakers, as in this ad, which equates housework with a game of golf.

Elliott Erwitt's photograph of a young mother in New Rochelle, a suburb of New York City, suggests that life for the suburban woman could be less idyllic than many advertisements implied.

which both partners reconciled family obligations with personal fulfillment through shared consumption, leisure activities, and sexual pleasure. Thanks to modern conveniences, the personal freedom once associated with work could now be found at home. Frozen and prepared meals, exulted one writer in 1953, offered housewives "freedom from tedium, space, work, and their own inexperience"—quite a change from the Four Freedoms of World War II.

Like other forms of dissent, feminism seemed to have disappeared from American life or was widely dismissed as evidence of mental disorder. Prominent psychologists insisted that the unhappiness of individual women or even the desire to work for wages stemmed from a failure to accept the "maternal instinct." "The independent woman," declared the book *Modern Woman: The Lost Sex* (1947) "is a contradiction in terms." The idea of domestic life as a refuge and of full-time motherhood as a woman's "sphere" had a long history in the United States. But in the postwar suburbs, where family life was physically separated from work, relatives, and the web of social organizations typical of cities, it came close to realization.

A Segregated Landscape

For millions of city dwellers, the suburban utopia fulfilled the dream, postponed by depression and war, of home ownership and middle-class incomes. For beneficiaries of postwar prosperity, in the words of a Boston worker who made heroic sacrifices to move his family to the suburbs, the home became "the center of freedom." The move to the suburbs also promoted Americanization, cutting residents off from urban ethnic communities and bringing them fully into the world of mass consumption. But if the suburbs offered a new site for the enjoyment of American freedom, they retained at least one familiar characteristic—rigid racial boundaries.

Suburbia has never been as uniform as either its celebrants or its critics claimed. There are upper-class suburbs, working-class suburbs, industrial suburbs, and "suburban" neighborhoods within city limits. But if the class uniformity of suburbia has been exaggerated, its racial uniformity was all too real. As late as the 1990s, nearly 90 percent of suburban whites lived in communities with non-white populations of less than 1 percent—the legacy of decisions by government, real-estate developers, banks, and residents.

During the postwar suburban boom, federal agencies continued to insure mortgages that barred resale of houses to non-whites, thereby financing housing segregation. Even after the Supreme Court in 1948 declared such provisions legally unenforceable, banks and private developers barred non-whites from the suburbs and the government refused to subsidize their mortgages except in segregated enclaves. In 1960, blacks represented less than 3 percent of the population of Chicago's suburbs. The vast new communities built by William Levitt refused to allow blacks, including army veterans, to rent or purchase homes. "If we sell one house to a Negro family," Levitt explained, "then 90 or 95 percent of our white customers will not buy into the community." After a lawsuit, Levitt finally agreed during the

1960s to sell homes to non-whites, but at a pace that can only be described as glacial. In 1990, his Long Island community, with a population of 53,000, included 127 black residents.

Public Housing and Urban Renewal

A Housing Act passed by Congress in 1949 authorized the construction of more than 800,000 units of public housing in order to provide a "decent home for every American family." But the law set an extremely low ceiling on the income of residents—a rule demanded by private contractors seeking to avoid competition from the government in building homes for the middle class. This regulation limited housing projects to the very poor. Since white urban and suburban neighborhoods successfully opposed the construction of public housing, it was increasingly confined to segregated neighborhoods in inner cities, reinforcing the concentration of poverty in urban non-white neighborhoods. At the same time, under programs of "urban renewal," cities demolished poor neighborhoods in city centers that occupied potentially valuable real estate. In their place, developers constructed retail centers and all-white middle-income housing complexes, and states built urban public universities like Wayne State in Detroit and the University of Illinois at Chicago. Los Angeles displaced a neighborhood of mixed ethnic groups in Chavez Ravine in order to build a stadium for the Dodgers, whose move in 1958 after sixty-eight years in Brooklyn seemed to symbolize the growing importance of California on the national scene. White residents displaced by urban renewal often moved to the suburbs. Non-whites, unable to do so, found housing in run-down city neighborhoods.

Suburban builders sometimes openly advertised the fact that their communities excluded minorities. This photograph was taken in southern California in 1948.

An aerial photograph of Boulevard Houses, a low-income housing project in Brooklyn, illustrates how public housing concentrated poor Americans in structures separated from surrounding neighborhoods.

The Divided Society

Suburbanization hardened the racial lines of division in American life. Between 1950 and 1970, about 7 million white Americans left cities for the suburbs. Meanwhile, nearly 3 million blacks moved from the South to the North, greatly increasing the size of existing urban ghettos and creating entirely new ones. And half a million Puerto Ricans, mostly small coffee and tobacco farmers and agricultural laborers forced off the land when American sugar companies expanded their landholdings on the island, moved to the mainland. Most ended up in New York City's East Harlem, until then an Italian-American community. Although set in a different part of New York, the popular Broadway musical *West Side Story* dramatized the tensions between Puerto Rican newcomers and longtime urban residents. By the late

Students at an East Harlem elementary school in 1947. Most have recently migrated from Puerto Rico to the mainland with their families, although some are probably children of the area's older Italian-American community.

1960s, more Puerto Ricans lived in New York City than San Juan, the island's capital.

The process of racial exclusion became self-reinforcing. Non-whites remained concentrated in manual and unskilled jobs, the result of employment discrimination and their virtual exclusion from educational opportunities at public and private universities, including those outside the South. In 1950, only 12 percent of employed blacks held white-collar positions, compared with 45 percent of whites. As the white population and industrial jobs fled the old city centers for the suburbs, poorer blacks and Latinos remained trapped in urban ghettos, seen by many whites as places of crime, poverty, and welfare.

Suburbanites, for whom the home represented not only an emblem of freedom but the family's major investment, became increasingly fearful that any non-white presence would lower the quality of life and destroy property values. *Life* magazine quoted a white suburbanite discussing a prospective black neighbor: "He's probably a nice guy, but every time I see him, I see $2,000 drop off the value of my house." Residential segregation was reinforced by "blockbusting"—a tactic of real-estate brokers who circulated exaggerated warnings of an impending influx of non-whites, to persuade alarmed white residents to sell their homes hastily. Because of this practice, some all-white neighborhoods quickly became all-minority enclaves rather than places where members of different races lived side by side.

"Freedom is equal housing too" became a slogan in the campaign for residential integration. But suburban home ownership long remained a white entitlement, with the freedom of non-whites to rent or purchase a home where they desired overridden by the claims of private property and "freedom of association." Even as the old divisions between white ethnic Americans faded in the suburban melting pot, racial barriers in housing, and therefore in public education and jobs, were reinforced.

Cold War affluence coexisted with urban decay and racism, the seeds from which protest would soon flower. Yet to many observers in the 1950s it seemed that the ills of American society had been solved. Scholars celebrated the "end of ideology" and the triumph of a democratic, capitalist "consensus" in which all Americans except the maladjusted and fanatics shared the same liberal values of individualism, respect for private property, and belief in equal opportunity. If problems remained, their solutions required technical adjustments, not structural change or aggressive political intervention.

Religion and Anticommunism

Both Protestant and Roman Catholic religious leaders played crucial roles in the spread of anticommunism and Cold War culture. Official American values celebrated the nation's religiosity as opposed to "godless" communism. During the 1950s, a majority of Americans—the highest percentage in the nation's history—were affiliated with a church or synagogue. In 1954, to "strengthen our national resistance to communism," Congress added the words "under God" to the Pledge of Allegiance. In 1957, "In God We Trust" was included on paper money. Big-budget Hollywood films like *The Ten Commandments* and *Ben Hur* celebrated early Judaism and Christianity. As noted in the previous chapter, Soviet domination of strongly

Church affiliations

Catholic eastern Europe inspired powerful currents of anticommunism among Catholic ethnic groups in the United States. Leading clerics like Bishop Fulton J. Sheen of the Catholic church and Protestant evangelist Billy Graham used radio and television to spread to millions a religious message heavily imbued with anticommunism. Communism, Graham declared, was not only an economic and political outlook but a religion—one "inspired, directed and motivated by the Devil himself."

As for religious differences, the source of persistent tension in American history, these were absorbed within a common "Judeo-Christian" heritage, a notion that became central to the cultural and political dialogue of the 1950s. This newly invented tradition sought to demonstrate that Catholics, Protestants, and Jews shared the same history and values and had all contributed to the evolution of American society. In the era of McCarthyism, ideological differences may have been un-American, but group pluralism reigned supreme, with the free exercise of religion yet another way of differentiating the American way of life from life under communism.

The idea of a unified Judeo-Christian tradition overlooked the long history of hostility among religious denominations. But it reflected the decline of anti-Semitism and anti-Catholicism in the wake of World War II, as well as the ongoing secularization of American life. As Will Herberg argued in his influential book *Protestant-Catholic-Jew* (1955), religion now had less to do with spiritual activities or sacred values than with personal identity, group assimilation, and the promotion of traditional morality. In an affluent suburban society, Herberg argued, the "common religion" was the American way of life, a marriage of democratic values and economic prosperity—in a phrase, "free enterprise."

Selling Free Enterprise

The economic content of Cold War freedom increasingly came to focus on consumer capitalism, or, as it was now universally known, "free enterprise." More than

An image from a booklet issued by the American Economic Foundation illustrates the linkage of anticommunism and religious faith during the Cold War. The hairy hand in the bottom half of the drawing represents the communist threat, which endangers religious freedom in the United States. Most of the booklet, however, dealt with the superiority of free enterprise to communism.

This postage stamp depicts four chaplains who perished during the sinking of an American ship during World War II. Its original design listed their denominations: Catholic, Protestant, and Jewish. When the stamp was issued in 1948, these words were omitted, in keeping with the emphasis on the newly invented idea of a Judeo-Christian tradition shared by all Americans.

political democracy or freedom of speech, which many allies of the United States outside western Europe lacked, an economic system resting on private ownership united the nations of the Free World. A week before his Truman Doctrine speech, in a major address on economic policy, the president reduced Roosevelt's Four Freedoms to three. Freedom of speech and worship remained, but freedom from want and fear had been replaced by freedom of enterprise, "part and parcel," said Truman, of the American way of life.

Even more than during World War II, what one historian calls the "selling of free enterprise" became a major industry, involving corporate advertising, school programs, newspaper editorials, and civic activities. Convinced that ads represented "a new weapon in the world-wide fight for freedom," the Advertising Council invoked cherished symbols like the Statue of Liberty and the Liberty Bell in the service of "competitive free enterprise." To be sure, the free enterprise campaigners did not agree on every issue. Some businessmen believed that defending free enterprise required rolling back much of the power that labor unions had gained in the past decade, dismantling New Deal regulations, and restricting the economic role of government. Representing what might be called business's more liberal wing, the Advertising Council, in its "American Economic System" ad campaign of 1949, reaffirmed labor's right to collective bargaining and the importance of government–business cooperation. Indeed, despite talk of the glories of the free market, government policies played a crucial role in the postwar boom. The rapid expansion of the suburban middle class owed much to federal tax subsidies, mortgage guarantees for home purchases, dam and highway construction, military contracts, and benefits under the GI Bill.

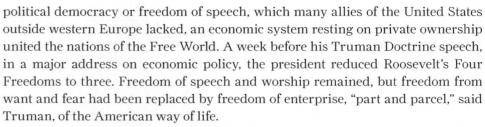

Selling free enterprise

People's Capitalism

Free enterprise seemed an odd way of describing an economy in which a few large corporations dominated key sectors. Until well into the twentieth century, most ordinary Americans had been deeply suspicious of big business, associating it with images of robber barons who manipulated politics, suppressed economic competition, and treated their workers unfairly. Americans, wrote David Lilienthal, chairman of the Atomic Energy Commission, must abandon their traditional fear that concentrated economic power endangered "our very liberties." Large-scale production was not only necessary to fighting the Cold War, but it enhanced freedom by multiplying consumer goods. "By freedom," wrote Lilienthal, "I mean essentially *freedom to choose*. . . . It means a maximum range of choice for the consumer when he spends his dollar." By the end of the 1950s, public-opinion surveys revealed that more than 80 percent of Americans believed that "our freedom depends on the free enterprise system."

TV became the most effective advertising medium in history. Here, an advertisement for Ford, one of the largest American corporations, is being filmed. The background evokes the idea of driving on the open road as a form of individual freedom.

The United States, declared *Fortune* magazine, anticipating Vice President Nixon's remark in the 1959 kitchen debate, had achieved the Marxist goal of a classless society. A sharp jump in the number of individuals investing in Wall Street inspired talk of a new "people's capitalism." In 1953, 4.5 million Americans—only slightly more than in 1928—owned shares of stock. By the mid-1960s, the number had grown to 25 million. In the face of widespread abundance, who could deny that the capitalist marketplace embodied individual freedom or that poverty would soon be a thing of the past? "It was American Freedom," proclaimed *Life* magazine, "by which and through which this amazing achievement of wealth and power was fashioned."

The Libertarian Conservatives

During the 1950s, a group of thinkers began the task of reviving conservatism and reclaiming the idea of freedom from liberals. Although largely ignored outside their own immediate circle, they developed ideas that would define conservative thought for the next half-century. One was opposition to a strong national government, an outlook that had been given new political life in conservatives' bitter reaction against the New Deal. To these "libertarian" conservatives, freedom meant individual autonomy, limited government, and unregulated capitalism.

New directions for conservative thought

These ideas had great appeal to conservative entrepreneurs, especially in the rapidly growing South and West. Many businessmen who desired to pursue their economic fortunes free of government regulation, high taxes, and labor unions found intellectual reinforcement in the writings of the young economist Milton Friedman. In 1962, Friedman published *Capitalism and Freedom*, which identified the free market as the necessary foundation for individual liberty. This was not an uncommon idea during the Cold War, but Friedman pushed it to extreme conclusions. He called for turning over to the private sector virtually all government functions and the repeal of minimum wage laws, the graduated income tax, and the Social Security system. Friedman extended the idea of unrestricted free choice into virtually every realm of life. Government, he insisted, should seek to regulate neither the economy nor individual conduct.

The New Conservatism

Friedman was indirectly criticizing not only liberalism but also the "new conservatism," a second strand of thought that became increasingly prominent in the 1950s. Convinced that the Free World needed to arm itself morally and intellectually, not just militarily, for the battle against communism, "new conservatives" like writers Russell Kirk and Richard Weaver insisted that toleration of difference—a central belief of modern liberalism—offered no substitute for the search for absolute truth. Weaver's book, *Ideas Have Consequences* (1948), a rambling philosophical treatise that surprisingly became the most influential statement of this new traditionalism, warned that the West was suffering from moral decay and called for a return to a civilization based on values grounded in the Christian tradition and in timeless notions of good and evil.

Conservatives and the search for values

The "new conservatives" understood freedom as first and foremost a moral condition. It required a decision by independent men and women to lead virtuous lives, or governmental action to force them to do so. Although they wanted government expelled from the economy, new conservatives trusted it to regulate personal behavior, to restore a Christian morality they saw as growing weaker and weaker in American society.

Here lay the origins of a division in conservative ranks that would persist into the twenty-first century. Unrestrained individual choice and moral virtue are radically different starting points from which to discuss freedom. Was the purpose of conservatism, one writer wondered, to create the "free man" or the "good man"? Libertarian conservatives spoke the language of progress and personal autonomy; the "new conservatives" emphasized tradition, community, and moral commitment. The former believed that too many barriers existed to the pursuit of individual liberty. The latter condemned an excess of individualism and a breakdown of common values.

Fortunately for conservatives, political unity often depends less on intellectual coherence than on the existence of a common foe. And two powerful enemies became focal points for the conservative revival—the Soviet Union abroad and the federal government at home. Anticommunism, however, did not clearly distinguish conservatives from liberals, who also supported the Cold War. What made conservatism distinct was its antagonism to "big government" in America, at least so long as it was controlled by liberals who, conservatives believed, tolerated or encouraged immorality. Republican control of the presidency did not lessen conservatives' hostility to the federal government, partly because they did not consider President Eisenhower one of their own.

Division in conservatism

Dwight D. Eisenhower's popularity was evident at this appearance in Baltimore during the 1952 presidential campaign.

THE EISENHOWER ERA

Ike and Nixon

Dwight D. Eisenhower, or "Ike," as he was affectionately called, emerged from World War II as the military leader with the greatest political appeal, partly because his public image of fatherly warmth set him apart from other successful generals like the arrogant Douglas MacArthur. Eisenhower's party affiliation was unknown. In 1948, he voted for Truman, and he accepted Truman's invitation to return to Europe as Supreme Commander of NATO forces. Both parties wanted him as their candidate in 1952. But Eisenhower became convinced that Senator Robert A. Taft of Ohio, a leading contender for the Republican nomination, would lead the United States back toward isolationism. Eisenhower entered the contest and won the Republican nomination.

As his running mate, Eisenhower chose Richard Nixon of California, a World War II veteran who had made a name for himself by vigorous anticommunism. In his first campaign for Congress, in 1946, Nixon attacked his opponent as an advocate of "state socialism." He gained greater fame by his pursuit of Alger Hiss while a member of the House Un-American Activities Committee. Nixon won election to the U.S. Senate in 1950 in a campaign in which he suggested that the Democratic candidate, Congresswoman Helen Gahagan Douglas, had communist sympathies.

These tactics gave Nixon a lifelong reputation for opportunism and dishonesty. But Nixon was also a shrewd politician, who pioneered efforts to transform the Republican Party's image from defender of business to champion of the "forgotten man"—the hardworking citizen burdened by heavy taxation and unresponsive government bureaucracies. "Freedom for the individual, for private enterprise," he insisted, had made America great. In using populist language to promote free market economics, Nixon helped to lay the foundation for the triumph of conservatism a generation later.

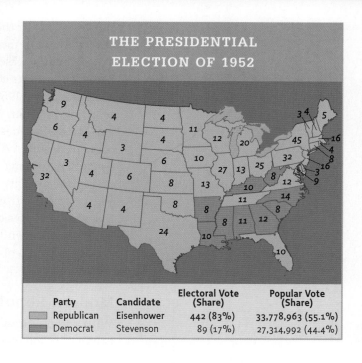

THE PRESIDENTIAL ELECTION OF 1952

Party	Candidate	Electoral Vote (Share)	Popular Vote (Share)
Republican	Eisenhower	442 (83%)	33,778,963 (55.1%)
Democrat	Stevenson	89 (17%)	27,314,992 (44.4%)

The 1952 Campaign

Almost as soon as he won the vice-presidential nomination, Nixon ran into trouble over press reports that wealthy Californians had created a private fund for his family. Eisenhower considered dropping him from the ticket. But in an emotional nationally televised thirty-minute address in which he drew attention to his ordinary upbringing, war service, and close-knit family, Nixon denied the accusations. The "Checkers speech," named after the family dog—the one gift Nixon acknowledged receiving, but insisted he would not return—rescued his political career. It illustrated how television was beginning to transform politics by allowing candidates to bring a carefully crafted image directly into Americans' living rooms. The 1952 campaign became the first to make extensive use of TV ads. Parties, one observer complained, were "selling the president like toothpaste."

More important to the election's outcome, however, was Eisenhower's popularity (invoked in the Republican campaign slogan "I Like Ike") and the public's weariness with the Korean War. Ike's pledge to "go to Korea" in search of peace signaled his intention to bring the conflict to an end. He won a resounding victory over the Democratic candidate, Adlai Stevenson. Four years later, Eisenhower again defeated Stevenson, by an even wider margin. His popularity, however, did not extend to his party. Republicans won a razor-thin majority in Congress in 1952, but Democrats regained control in 1954 and retained it for the rest of the decade. In 1956, Eisenhower became the first president to be elected without his party controlling either house of Congress.

Ike's appeal

In his two campaigns for president, the Texas-born Eisenhower made remarkable inroads in the Democratic South, a harbinger of the region's later political realignment. In 1952, he carried eight former slave states and won 48 percent of the votes cast in the states of the Confederacy. He ran strongly among moderate whites living in metropolitan and suburban areas of the upper South and border states. But his personal appeal did not translate into a "coattail" effect. For the time being, Democrats continued to control almost all southern state and local offices.

During the 1950s, voters at home and abroad seemed to find reassurance in selecting familiar, elderly leaders to govern them. At age sixty-two, Eisenhower was one of the oldest men ever elected president. But he seemed positively youthful compared with Winston Churchill, who returned to office as prime minister of Great Britain at age seventy-seven, Charles DeGaulle, who assumed the presidency of France at sixty-eight, and Konrad Adenauer, who served as chancellor of West Germany from age seventy-three until well into his eighties. In retrospect, Eisenhower's presidency seems almost uneventful, at least in domestic affairs—an interlude between the bitter party battles of the Truman administration and the social upheavals of the 1960s.

Modern Republicanism

With a Republican serving as president for the first time in twenty years, the tone in Washington changed. Wealthy businessmen dominated Eisenhower's cabinet. Defense Secretary Charles Wilson, the former president of General Motors, made the widely publicized statement: "What is good for the country is good for General Motors, and vice versa." A champion of the business community and a fiscal conservative, Ike worked to scale back government spending, including the military budget. But while right-wing Republicans saw his victory as an invitation to roll back the New Deal, Eisenhower realized that such a course would be disastrous. "Should any political party attempt to abolish Social Security, unemployment insurance, and eliminate labor laws and farm programs," he declared, "you would not hear of that party again in our political history."

Eisenhower called his domestic agenda Modern Republicanism. It aimed to sever his party's identification in the minds of many Americans with Herbert Hoover, the Great Depression, and indifference to the economic conditions of ordinary citizens. The core New Deal programs not only remained in place, but expanded. In 1955, millions of agricultural workers became eligible for the first time for Social Security. Nor did Ike reduce the size and scope of government. Despite the use of "free enterprise" as a weapon in the Cold War, the idea of a "mixed economy" in which the government played a major role in planning economic activity was widely accepted throughout the Western world. America's European allies like Britain and France expanded their welfare states and nationalized key industries like steel, shipbuilding, and transportation (that is, the government bought them from private owners and operated and subsidized them).

The United States had a more limited welfare state than western Europe and left the main pillars of the economy in private hands. But it too used government spending to promote productivity and boost employment. Eisenhower presided over the largest public-works enterprise in American history, the building of the 41,000-mile interstate highway system. As noted in the previous chapter, Cold War arguments—especially the need to provide rapid exit routes from cities in

> Accepting the New Deal

"Do you call C-minus catching up with Russia?" Alan Dunn's cartoon for the *New Yorker* magazine comments on how Soviet success in launching an artificial earth satellite spurred a focus on improving scientific education in the United States.

the event of nuclear war—justified this multibillion-dollar project. But automobile manufacturers, oil companies, suburban builders, and construction unions had very practical reasons for supporting highway construction regardless of any Soviet threat. When the Soviets launched *Sputnik*, the first artificial earth satellite, in 1957, the administration responded with the National Defense Education Act, which for the first time offered direct federal funding to higher education.

Sputnik

All in all, rather than dismantling the New Deal, Eisenhower's modern Republicanism consolidated and legitimized it. By accepting its basic premises, he ensured that its continuation no longer depended on Democratic control of the presidency.

The Social Contract

The 1950s also witnessed an easing of the labor conflict of the two previous decades. The passage of the Taft-Hartley Act in 1947 (discussed in the previous chapter) had reduced labor militancy. In 1955, the AFL and CIO merged to form a single organization representing 35 percent of all nonagricultural workers. In leading industries, labor and management hammered out what has been called a new "social contract." Unions signed long-term agreements that left decisions regarding capital investment, plant location, and output in management's hands, and they agreed to try to prevent unauthorized "wildcat" strikes. Employers stopped trying to eliminate existing unions and granted wage increases and fringe benefits such as private pension plans, health insurance, and automatic adjustments to pay to reflect rises in the cost of living.

Labor and management cooperation

Unionized workers shared fully in 1950s prosperity. Although the social contract did not apply to the majority of workers, who did not belong to unions, it did bring benefits to those who labored in nonunion jobs. For example, trade unions in the 1950s and 1960s were able to use their political power to win a steady increase in the minimum wage, which was earned mostly by nonunion workers at the bottom of the employment pyramid. But these "spillover effects" were limited. The majority of workers did not enjoy anything close to the wages, benefits, and job security of unionized workers in such industries as automobiles and steel.

Benefits for nonunion workers

Indeed, nonunion employers continued to fight vehemently against labor organization, and groups like the National Association of Manufacturers still viewed unions as an unacceptable infringement on the power of employers. Some firms continued to shift jobs to the less-unionized suburbs and South. By the end of the 1950s, the social contract was weakening. In 1959, the steel industry sought to tighten work rules and limit wage increases in an attempt to boost profits battered by a recession that hit two years earlier. The plan sparked a strike of 500,000 steelworkers, which successfully beat back the proposed changes.

Massive Retaliation

Soon after he entered office, Eisenhower approved an armistice that ended fighting in Korea. But this failed to ease international tensions. Ike took office at a time when the Cold War had entered an extremely dangerous phase. In 1952, the United States exploded the first hydrogen bomb—a weapon far more powerful than those that

The hydrogen bomb

had devastated Hiroshima and Nagasaki. The following year, the Soviets matched this achievement. Both sides feverishly developed long-range bombers capable of delivering weapons of mass destruction around the world.

A professional soldier, Ike hated war, which he viewed as a tragic waste. "Every gun that is made," he said in 1953, "every warship launched . . . signifies a theft from those who hunger and are not fed." But his secretary of state, John Foster Dulles, was a grim Cold Warrior. In 1954, Dulles announced an updated version of the doctrine of containment. "Massive retaliation," as it was called, declared that any Soviet attack on an American ally would be countered by a nuclear assault on the Soviet Union itself. In some ways, this reliance on the nuclear threat was a way to enable the budget-conscious Eisenhower to reduce spending on conventional military forces. During his presidency, the size of the armed services fell by nearly half. But the number of American nuclear warheads rose from 1,000 in 1953 to 18,000 in 1960.

Massive retaliation ran the risk that any small conflict, or even a miscalculation, could escalate into a war that would destroy both the United States and the Soviet Union. Critics called the doctrine "brinksmanship," warning of the danger of Dulles's apparent willingness to bring the world to the brink of nuclear war. The reality that all-out war would result in "mutual assured destruction" (or MAD, in military shorthand) did succeed in making both great powers cautious in their direct dealings with one another. But it also inspired widespread fear of impending nuclear war. Government programs encouraging Americans to build bomb shelters in their backyards, and school drills that trained children to hide under their desks in the event of an atomic attack, aimed to convince Americans that nuclear war was survivable. But these measures only increased the atmosphere of fear.

Massive retaliation

An advertisement for a government film explaining to children how to survive a nuclear attack by hiding under their desks. Thousands of schools instituted these "duck and cover" drills. They were meant to reduce Americans' fear of nuclear war.

Ike and the Russians

In his inaugural address, Eisenhower repeated the familiar Cold War formula: "Freedom is pitted against slavery; lightness against dark." But the end of the Korean War and the death of Stalin, both of which occurred in 1953, convinced him that rather than being blind zealots, the Soviets were reasonable and could be dealt with in conventional diplomatic terms. In 1955, Ike met in Geneva, Switzerland, with Nikita Khrushchev, the new Soviet leader, at the first "summit" conference since Potsdam a decade earlier. The following year, Khrushchev delivered a speech to the Communist Party Congress in Moscow that detailed Stalin's crimes, including purges of political opponents numbering in the millions. The revelations created a crisis of belief among communists throughout the world. In the United States, three-quarters of the remaining Communist Party members abandoned the organization, realizing that they had been blind to the nature of Stalin's rule.

Khrushchev's call in the same 1956 speech for "peaceful coexistence" with the United States raised the possibility of an easing of the Cold War. The "thaw" was abruptly shaken that fall, however, when Soviet troops put down an anticommunist uprising in Hungary. Many conservative Republicans had urged eastern Europeans to resist communist rule, and Secretary of State Dulles himself had declared "liberation," rather than containment, to be the goal of American policy. But Eisenhower refused to extend aid to the Hungarian rebels, an indication that he believed it impossible to "roll back" Soviet domination of eastern Europe.

In 1958, the two superpowers agreed to a voluntary halt to the testing of nuclear weapons. The pause lasted until 1961. It had been demanded by the National Committee for a Sane Nuclear Policy, which publicized the danger to public health posed by radioactive fallout from nuclear tests. In 1959, Khrushchev toured the United States and had a friendly meeting with Eisenhower at Camp David. But the spirit of cooperation ended abruptly in 1960, when the Soviets shot down an American U-2 spy plane over their territory. Eisenhower first denied that the plane had been involved in espionage and refused to apologize even after the Russians produced the captured pilot. The incident torpedoed another planned summit meeting.

The Emergence of the Third World

Even as Europe, where the Cold War began, settled into what appeared to be a permanent division between a communist East and a capitalist West, an intense rivalry, which sometimes took a military form, persisted in what came to be called the Third World. The term was invented to describe developing countries aligned with neither of the two Cold War powers and desirous of finding their own model of development between Soviet centralized economic planning and free market capitalism. The Bandung Conference, which brought leaders of twenty-nine Asian and African nations together in Indonesia in 1955, seemed to announce the emergence of a new force in global affairs, representing a majority of the world's population. But none of these countries could avoid being strongly affected by the political, military, and economic contest of the Cold War.

The post–World War II era witnessed the crumbling of European empires. The "winds of change," said British prime minister Harold Macmillan, were sweeping Africa and Asia. Decolonization began when India and Pakistan (the latter carved out of India to give Muslims their own nation) achieved independence in 1947. Ten years later, Britain's Gold Coast colony in West Africa emerged as the independent nation of Ghana. Other new nations—including Indonesia, Malaysia, Nigeria, Kenya, and Tanzania—soon followed. In 1975, Portugal, which five centuries earlier had created the first modern overseas empire, granted independence to its African colonies of Mozambique and Angola.

Decolonization presented the United States with a complex set of choices. It created power vacuums in the former colonies into which, Americans feared, communists would move. The Soviet Union strongly supported the dissolution of Europe's overseas empires, and communists participated in movements for colonial independence. Many noncommunist leaders, like Jawaharlal Nehru of India and Kwame Nkrumah of Ghana, saw socialism of one sort or another as the best route to achieving economic independence and narrowing the social inequalities fostered by imperialism. Most of the new Third World nations resisted alignment

A man helps his daughter into a backyard bomb shelter in Garden City, Long Island, New York, in a photograph from 1955. Manufacturers of such shelters assured purchasers that occupants could survive for five days after a nuclear attack.

Decolonization begins

with either major power bloc, hoping to remain neutral in the Cold War. On the other hand, many nationalists sincerely admired the United States and, indeed, saw the American struggle for independence as a model for their own struggles. Ho Chi Minh, the communist leader of the Vietnamese movement against rule by France, modeled his 1945 proclamation of nationhood on the American Declaration of Independence. He even requested that President Truman establish a protectorate over Vietnam to guarantee its independence.

The Cold War in the Third World

<table>
<tr><td>Containment and the
Third World</td></tr>
</table>

By the end of the 1950s, the division of Europe appeared to be set in stone. Much of the focus of the Cold War shifted to the Third World. The policy of containment easily slid over into opposition to any government, whether communist or not, that seemed to threaten American strategic or economic interests. Jacobo Arbenz Guzmán in Guatemala and Mohammed Mossadegh in Iran were elected, homegrown nationalists, not agents of Moscow. But they were determined to reduce foreign corporations' control over their countries' economies. Arbenz embarked on a sweeping land-reform policy that threatened the domination of Guatemala's economy by the American-owned United Fruit Company. Mossadegh nationalized the Anglo-Iranian Oil Company, whose refinery in Iran was Britain's largest remaining overseas asset. Their foes quickly branded both as communists. In 1953 and 1954, the Central Intelligence Agency organized the ouster of both governments—a clear violation of the UN Charter, which barred a member state from taking military action against another except in self-defense.

Mohammed Mossadegh, prime minister of Iran, views the Liberty Bell during his visit to the United States in 1951. The U.S.-sponsored coup that overthrew Mossadegh in 1953 created resentments that helped lead to Iran's Islamic Revolution twenty-five years later.

In 1956, Israel, France, and Britain—without prior consultation with the United States—invaded Egypt after the country's nationalist leader, Gamal Abdel Nasser, nationalized the Suez Canal, jointly owned by Britain and France. A furious Eisenhower forced them to abandon the invasion. After the Suez fiasco, the United States moved to replace Britain as the dominant Western power in the Middle East, and American companies increasingly dominated the region's oil fields. In 1957, Eisenhower extended the principle of containment to the region, issuing the Eisenhower Doctrine, which pledged the United States to defend Middle Eastern governments threatened by communism or Arab nationalism. A year later, Ike dispatched 5,000 American troops to Lebanon to protect a government dominated by

The military junta installed in Guatemala by the CIA in 1954 enters Guatemala City in a Jeep driven by CIA agent Carlos Castillo Armas. Although hailed by the Eisenhower administration as a triumph for freedom, the new government suppressed democracy in Guatemala and embarked on a murderous campaign to stamp out opposition.

pro-Western Christians against Nasser's effort to bring all Arab states into a single regime under his rule.

Origins of the Vietnam War

In Vietnam, the expulsion of the Japanese in 1945 led not to independence but to a French military effort to preserve their Asian empire, which dated to the late nineteenth century, against Ho Chi Minh's nationalist forces. Anticommunism led the United States into deeper and deeper involvement. Following a policy initiated by Truman, the Eisenhower administration funneled billions of dollars in aid to bolster French efforts. By the early 1950s, the United States was paying four-fifths of the cost of the war. Wary of becoming bogged down in another land war in Asia immediately after Korea, however, Ike declined to send in American troops when France requested them to avert defeat in 1954. He also rejected the National Security Council's advice to use nuclear weapons, leaving France no alternative but to agree to Vietnamese independence.

Save the Holy Places, a 1948 cartoon by Herbert Block, suggests that American diplomacy in the Middle East was primarily concerned with access to oil.

A peace conference in Geneva divided Vietnam temporarily into northern and southern districts, with elections scheduled for 1956 to unify the country. But the staunchly anticommunist southern leader Ngo Dinh Diem, urged on by the United States, refused to hold elections, which would almost certainly have resulted in a victory for Ho Chi Minh's communists. Diem's close ties to wealthy Catholic families—in predominantly Buddhist South Vietnam—and to landlords in a society dominated by small farmers who had been promised land by Ho alienated an increasing number of his subjects. American aid poured into South Vietnam in order to bolster the Diem regime. By the time Eisenhower left office, Diem nevertheless faced a full-scale guerrilla revolt by the communist-led National Liberation Front.

The Diem regime

Events in Guatemala, Iran, and Vietnam, considered great successes at the time by American policymakers, cast a long shadow over American foreign relations. Little by little, the United States was becoming accustomed to intervention, both open and secret, in far-flung corners of the world. Despite the Cold War rhetoric of freedom, American leaders seemed more comfortable dealing with reliable military regimes than democratic governments. A series of military governments succeeded Arbenz. The shah of Iran replaced Mossadegh and agreed to give British and American oil companies 40 percent of his nation's oil revenues. He remained in office until 1979 as one of the world's most tyrannical rulers, until his overthrow in a revolution led by the fiercely anti-American radical Islamist Ayatollah Khomeini. In Vietnam, the American decision to prop up Diem's regime laid the groundwork for what would soon become the most disastrous military involvement in American history.

Mass Society and Its Critics

The fatherly Eisenhower seemed the perfect leader for the placid society of the 1950s. Consensus was the dominant ideal in an era in which McCarthyism had defined criticism of the social and economic order as disloyalty and most Americans located the enjoyment of freedom in private pleasures rather than the public sphere. With the mainstreams of both parties embracing the Cold War, political debate took place within extremely narrow limits. Even *Life* magazine commented that American freedom might be in greater danger from "disuse" than from communist subversion.

Dissenting voices could be heard. Some intellectuals wondered whether the celebration of affluence and the either-or mentality of the Cold War obscured the extent to which the United States itself fell short of the ideal of freedom. The sociologist C. Wright Mills challenged the self-satisfied vision of democratic pluralism that dominated mainstream social science in the 1950s. Mills wrote of a "power elite"—an interlocking directorate of corporate leaders, politicians, and military men whose domination of government and society had made political democracy obsolete. Freedom, Mills insisted, meant more than "the chance to do as one pleases." It rested on the ability "to formulate the available choices," and this most Americans were effectively denied.

C. Wright Mills and the "power elite"

Even as the government and media portrayed the United States as a beacon of liberty locked in a titanic struggle with its opposite, one strand of social analysis in the 1950s contended that Americans did not enjoy genuine freedom. These critics identified as the culprit not the unequal structure of power criticized by Mills, but the modern age itself, with its psychological and cultural discontents. Modern mass society, some writers worried, inevitably produced loneliness and anxiety, causing mankind to yearn for stability and authority, not freedom. In *The Lonely Crowd* (1950), the decade's most influential work of social analysis, the sociologist David Riesman described Americans as "other-directed" conformists who lacked the inner resources to lead truly independent lives. Other social critics charged that corporate bureaucracies had transformed employees into "organization men" incapable of independent thought.

Some commentators feared that the Russians had demonstrated a greater ability to sacrifice for common public goals than Americans. What kind of nation, the economist John Kenneth Galbraith asked in *The Affluent Society* (1958), neglected investment in schools, parks, and public services, while producing ever more goods to fulfill desires created by advertising? Was the spectacle of millions of educated middle-class women seeking happiness in suburban dream houses a reason for celebration or a waste of precious "woman power" at a time when the Soviets trumpeted the accomplishments of their female scientists, physicians, and engineers? Books like Galbraith's, along with William Whyte's *The Organization Man* (1956) and Vance Packard's *The Hidden Persuaders* (1957), which criticized the monotony of modern work, the emptiness of suburban life, and the pervasive influence of advertising, created the vocabulary for an assault on the nation's social values that lay just over the horizon. In the 1950s, however, while criticism of mass society became a minor industry among intellectuals, it failed to dent widespread complacency about the American way.

Rebels without a Cause

The social critics did not offer a political alternative or have any real impact on the parties or government. Nor did other stirrings of dissent. With teenagers a growing part of the population thanks to the baby boom, the emergence of a popular culture geared to the emerging youth market suggested that signifi-

cant generational tensions lay beneath the bland surface of 1950s life. J. D. Salinger's 1951 novel *Catcher in the Rye* and the 1955 films *Blackboard Jungle* and *Rebel without a Cause* (the latter starring James Dean as an aimlessly rebellious youth) highlighted the alienation of at least some young people from the world of adult respectability. These works helped to spur a mid-1950s panic about "juvenile delinquency." *Time* magazine devoted a cover story to "Teenagers on the Rampage," and a Senate committee held hearings in 1954 on whether violent comic books caused criminal behavior among young people. (One witness even criticized Superman comics for arousing violent emotions

Commuters returning from work in downtown Chicago, leaving the railroad station at suburban Park Forest, Illinois, in 1953. Social critics of the 1950s claimed that Americans had become "organization men," too conformist to lead independent lives.

Rebels without a cause. Teenagers, photographed at Coney Island, Brooklyn, in the late 1950s.

Elvis Presley's gyrating hips appealed to teenagers but alarmed many adults during the 1950s.

among its readers.) To head off federal regulation, publishers—like movie producers in the 1920s—adopted a code of conduct for their industry that strictly limited the portrayal of crime and violence in comic books.

Cultural life during the 1950s seemed far more daring than politics. Indeed, many adults found the emergence of a mass-marketed teenage culture that rejected middle-class norms more alarming than the actual increase in juvenile arrests. Teenagers wore leather jackets and danced to rock-and-roll music that brought the hard-driving rhythms and sexually provocative movements of black musicians and dancers to enthusiastic young white audiences. They made Elvis Presley, a rock-and-roll singer with an openly sexual performance style, an immensely popular entertainment celebrity.

Challenges of various kinds also arose to the family-centered image of personal fulfillment. *Playboy* magazine, which began publication in 1953, reached a circulation of more than 1 million copies per month by 1960. It extended the consumer culture into the most intimate realms of life, offering men a fantasy world of sexual gratification outside the family's confines. Although considered sick or deviant by the larger society and subject to constant police harassment, gay men and lesbians created their own subcultures in major cities.

The Beats

In New York City and San Francisco, as well as college towns like Madison, Wisconsin, and Ann Arbor, Michigan, the Beats, a small group of poets and writers, railed against mainstream culture. The novelist Jack Kerouac coined the term "beat"—a

A Beat coffeehouse in San Francisco, photographed in 1958, where poets, artists, and others who rejected 1950s mainstream culture gathered.

play on "beaten down" and "beatified" (or saintlike). His *On the Road*, written in the early 1950s but not published until 1957, recounted in a seemingly spontaneous rush of sights, sounds, and images its main character's aimless wanderings across the American landscape. The book became a bible for a generation of young people who rejected the era's middle-class culture but had little to put in its place.

"I saw the best minds of my generation destroyed by madness, starving hysterical naked," wrote the Beat poet Allen Ginsberg in *Howl* (1955), a brilliant protest against materialism and conformism written while the author was under the influence of hallucinogenic drugs. Ginsberg became nationally known when San Francisco police in 1956 confiscated his book and arrested bookstore owners for selling an obscene work. (A judge later overturned the ban on the grounds that *Howl* possessed redeeming social value.) Rejecting the work ethic, the "desperate materialism" of the suburban middle class, and the militarization of American life by the Cold War, the Beats celebrated impulsive action, immediate pleasure (often enhanced by drugs), and sexual experimentation. Despite Cold War slogans, they insisted, personal and political repression, not freedom, were the hallmarks of American society.

Allen Ginsberg

THE FREEDOM MOVEMENT

Not until the 1960s would young white rebels find their cause, as the seeds of dissent planted by the social critics and Beats flowered in an outpouring of political activism, new attitudes toward sexuality, and a full-fledged generational rebellion. A more immediate challenge to the complacency of the 1950s arose from the twentieth century's greatest citizens' movement—the black struggle for equality.

Origins of the Movement

Today, with the birthday of Martin Luther King Jr. a national holiday and the struggles of Montgomery, Little Rock, Birmingham, and Selma celebrated as heroic episodes in the history of freedom, it is easy to forget that at the time, the civil rights revolution came as a great surprise. Looking back, its causes seem clear: the destabilization of the racial system during World War II; the mass migration out of the segregated South that made black voters an increasingly important part of the Democratic Party coalition; and the Cold War and rise of independent states in the Third World, both of which made the gap between America's rhetoric and its racial reality an international embarrassment. Yet few predicted the emergence of the southern mass movement for civil rights.

Immediate causes

In *An American Dilemma* (1944), Gunnar Myrdal had suggested that the challenge to racial inequality would arise in the North, where blacks had far greater opportunities for political organization than in the South. With blacks' traditional allies on the left decimated by McCarthyism, most union leaders unwilling to challenge racial inequalities within their own ranks, and the NAACP concentrating on court battles, new constituencies and new tactics were sorely needed. The movement found in the southern black church the organizing power for a militant, nonviolent assault on segregation.

The southern black church

VOICES OF FREEDOM

From MARTIN LUTHER KING JR., SPEECH AT MONTGOMERY, ALABAMA (DECEMBER 5, 1955)

On the evening of Rosa Parks's arrest for refusing to give up her seat on a Montgomery bus to a white passenger, a mass rally of local African-Americans decided to boycott city buses in protest. In his speech to the gathering, the young Baptist minister Martin Luther King Jr. invoked Christian and American ideals of justice and democracy—themes he would strike again and again during his career as the leading national symbol of the civil rights struggle.

We are here this evening . . . because first and foremost we are American citizens, and we are determined to apply our citizenship to the fullness of its means. We are here also because of our love for democracy. . . . Just the other day . . . one of the finest citizens in Montgomery—not one of the finest Negro citizens but one of the finest citizens in Montgomery—was taken from a bus and carried to jail and arrested because she refused to give her seat to a white person. . . .

Mrs. Rosa Parks is a fine person. And since it had to happen I'm happy that it happened to a person like Mrs. Parks, for nobody can doubt the boundless outreach of her integrity! Nobody can doubt the height of her character, nobody can doubt that depth of her Christian commitment and devotion to the teachings of Jesus. And I'm happy since it

had to happen, it happened to a person that nobody can call a disturbing factor in the community. Mrs. Parks is a fine Christian person, unassuming, and yet there is integrity and character there. And just because she refused to get up, she was arrested.

I want to say, that we are not here advocating violence. We have never done that. . . . We believe in the teachings of Jesus. The only weapon that we have in our hands this evening is the weapon of protest. . . . There will be no white persons pulled out of their homes and taken out to some distant road and lynched. . . .

We are not wrong in what we are doing. If we are wrong, then the Supreme Court of this nation is wrong. If we are wrong, the Constitution of the United States is wrong. If we are wrong, God Almighty is wrong. . . . If we are wrong, justice is a lie. . . .

We, the disinherited of this land, we who have been oppressed so long, are tired of going through the long night of captivity. And now we are reaching out for the daybreak of freedom and justice and equality. . . . Right here in Montgomery when the history books are written in the future, somebody will have to say, "There lived a race of people, a *black* people, . . . a people who had the moral courage to stand up for their rights. And thereby they injected a new meaning into the veins of history and of civilization."

From THE SOUTHERN MANIFESTO (1956)

Drawn up early in 1956 and signed by 101 southern members of the Senate and House of Representatives, the Southern Manifesto repudiated the Supreme Court decision in *Brown v. Board of Education* and offered support to the campaign of resistance in the South.

The unwarranted decision of the Supreme Court in the public school cases is now bearing the fruit always produced when men substitute naked power for established law. . . .

We regard the decisions of the Supreme Court in the school cases as a clear abuse of judicial power. It climaxes a trend in the Federal Judiciary undertaking to legislate, in derogation [violation] of the authority of Congress, and to encroach upon the reserved rights of the States and the people.

The original Constitution does not mention education. Neither does the 14th Amendment nor any other amendment. The debates preceding the submission of the 14th Amendment clearly show that there was no intent that it should affect the system of education maintained by the States.

In the case of *Plessy v. Ferguson* in 1896 the Supreme Court expressly declared that under the 14th Amendment no person was denied any of his rights if the States provided separate but equal facilities. This decision . . . restated time and again, became a part of the life of the people of many of the States and confirmed their habits, traditions, and way of life. It is founded on elemental humanity and commonsense, for parents should not be deprived by Government of the right to direct the lives and education of their own children.

Though there has been no constitutional amendment or act of Congress changing this established legal principle almost a century old, the Supreme Court of the United States, with no legal basis for such action, undertook to exercise their naked judicial power and substituted their personal political and social ideas for the established law of the land.

This unwarranted exercise of power by the Court, contrary to the Constitution, is creating chaos and confusion in the States principally affected. It is destroying the amicable relations between the white and Negro races that have been created through 90 years of patient effort by the good people of both races. It has planted hatred and suspicion where there has been heretofore friendship and understanding.

With the gravest concern for the explosive and dangerous condition created by this decision and inflamed by outside meddlers: . . . we commend the motives of those States which have declared the intention to resist forced integration by any lawful means. . . .

QUESTIONS

1. *How do religious convictions shape King's definition of freedom?*

2. *Why does the Southern Manifesto claim that the Supreme Court decision is a threat to constitutional government?*

3. *How do these documents illustrate contrasting understandings of freedom in the wake of the civil rights movement?*

A segregated school in West Memphis, Arkansas, photographed for *Life* magazine in 1949. Education in the South was separate but hardly equal.

The persistence of Jim Crow

The United States in the 1950s was still a segregated, unequal society. Half of the nation's black families lived in poverty. Because of labor contracts that linked promotions and firings to seniority, non-white workers, who had joined the industrial labor force later than whites, lost their jobs first in times of economic downturn. In the South, evidence of Jim Crow abounded—in separate public institutions and the signs "white" and "colored" at entrances to buildings, train carriages, drinking fountains, restrooms, and the like. In the North and West, the law did not require segregation, but custom barred blacks from many colleges, hotels, and restaurants, and from most suburban housing. Las Vegas, Nevada, for example, was as strictly segregated as any southern city. Hotels and casinos did not admit blacks except in the most menial jobs. Lena Horne, Sammy Davis Jr., Louis Armstrong, and other black entertainers played the hotel-casinos on the "strip" but could not stay as guests where they performed.

In 1950, seventeen southern and border states and Washington, D.C., had laws requiring the racial segregation of public schools, and several others permitted local districts to impose it. Around 40 percent of the nation's 28 million schoolchildren studied in legally segregated schools, and millions more attended classes in northern communities where housing patterns and school district lines created de facto segregation—separation in fact if not in law. Few white Americans felt any urgency about confronting racial inequality. "Segregation," the white writer John Egerton later recalled, "didn't restrict me in any way, so it was easy to accept things the way they were, to take my freedom for granted and not worry about anyone else's."

The Legal Assault on Segregation

With Truman's civil rights initiative having faded and the Eisenhower administration being reluctant to address the issue, it fell to the courts to confront the problem of racial segregation. In the Southwest, the League of United Latin American Citizens (LULAC), the equivalent of the NAACP, challenged restrictive housing, employment discrimination, and the segregation of Latino students. They won an important victory in 1946 in the case of *Mendez v. Westminster*, when the California Supreme Court ordered the schools of Orange County desegregated. In response, the state legislature repealed all school laws requiring racial segregation. The governor who signed the measure, Earl Warren, had presided over the internment of Japanese-Americans during World War II as the state's attorney general. After the war, he became convinced that racial inequality had no place in American life. When Chief Justice Fred Vinson died in 1953, Eisenhower appointed Earl Warren to replace him. Warren would play the key role in deciding *Brown v. Board of Education*, the momentous case that outlawed school segregation.

> *LULAC and* Mendez v. Westminster

For years, the NAACP, under the leadership of attorneys Charles Hamilton Houston and Thurgood Marshall, had pressed legal challenges to the "separate but equal" doctrine laid down by the Court in 1896 in *Plessy v. Ferguson* (see Chapter 17). At first, the NAACP sought to gain admission to white institutions of higher learning for which no black equivalent existed. In 1938, the Supreme Court ordered the University of Missouri Law School to admit Lloyd Gaines, a black student, because the state had no such school for blacks. Missouri responded by setting up a segregated law school, satisfying the courts. But in 1950, the Supreme Court unanimously ordered Heman Sweatt admitted to the University of Texas Law School even though the state had established a "school" for him in a basement containing three classrooms and no library. There was no way, the Court declared, that this hastily constructed law school could be "equal" to the prestigious all-white institution.

> *Thurgood Marshall and the NAACP*

The *Brown* Case

Marshall now launched a frontal assault on segregation itself. He brought the NAACP's support to local cases that had arisen when black parents challenged unfair school policies. To do so required remarkable courage. In Clarendon County, South Carolina, Levi Pearson, a black farmer who brought a lawsuit on behalf of his children, saw his house burned to the ground. The Clarendon case attacked not segregation itself but the unequal funding of schools. The local school board spent $179 per white child and $43 per black, and unlike white pupils, black children attended class in buildings with no running water or indoor toilets and were not provided with buses to transport them to classes. Five such cases from four states and the District of Columbia were combined in a single appeal that reached the Supreme Court late in 1952.

When cases are united, they are listed alphabetically and the first case gives the entire decision its name. In this instance, the first case arose from a state outside the old Confederacy. Oliver Brown went to court because his daughter, a third grader, was forced to walk across dangerous railroad tracks each morning rather than being allowed to attend a nearby school restricted to whites. His lawsuit became *Brown v. Board of Education of Topeka, Kansas.*

Thurgood Marshall decided that the time had come to attack not the unfair applications of the "separate but equal" principle but the doctrine itself. Even with

Linda Brown's parents sued the school board of Topeka, Kansas, demanding that it admit their daughter to a school near her home restricted to whites, rather than requiring her to walk across dangerous railroad tracks, each day, as in this photograph, to attend a black school. The result was the Supreme Court's landmark *Brown* decision outlawing school segregation.

the same funding and facilities, he insisted, segregation was inherently unequal since it stigmatized one group of citizens as unfit to associate with others. Drawing on studies by New York psychologists Kenneth and Mamie Clark, Marshall argued that segregation did lifelong damage to black children, undermining their self-esteem. In its legal brief, the Eisenhower administration did not directly support Marshall's position, but it urged the justices to consider "the problem of racial discrimination . . . in the context of the present world struggle between freedom and tyranny." Other peoples, it noted, "cannot understand how such a practice can exist in a country which professes to be a staunch supporter of freedom, justice, and democracy."

The new chief justice, Earl Warren, managed to create unanimity on a divided Court, some of whose members disliked segregation but feared that a decision to outlaw it would spark widespread violence. On May 17, 1954, Warren himself read aloud the decision, only eleven pages long. Segregation in public education, he concluded, violated the equal protection of the laws guaranteed by the Fourteenth Amendment. "In the field of education, the doctrine of 'separate but equal' has no place. Separate educational facilities are inherently unequal."

The black press hailed the *Brown* decision as a "second Emancipation Proclamation." And like its predecessor it was in many ways a limited document. The decision did not address segregation in institutions other than public schools or ban all racial classifications in the law, such as statutes prohibiting interracial marriage. It did not address the de facto school segregation of the North, which rested on housing patterns rather than state law. It did not order immediate implementation but instead called for hearings as to how segregated schooling should be dismantled. But *Brown* marked the emergence of the "Warren Court" as an active agent of social change. And it inspired a wave of optimism that discrimination would soon disappear. "What a wonderful world of possibilities are unfolded for the children," wrote the black novelist Ralph Ellison.

The Montgomery Bus Boycott

Brown did not cause the modern civil rights movement, which, as noted in the previous two chapters, began during World War II and continued in cities like New York after the war. But the decision did ensure that when the movement resumed after waning in the early 1950s, it would have the backing of the federal courts. Mass action against Jim Crow soon reappeared. On December 1, 1955, Rosa Parks, a black tailor's assistant who had just completed her day's work in a Montgomery, Alabama, department store, refused to surrender her seat on a city bus to a white rider, as required by local law. Parks's arrest sparked a yearlong bus boycott, the beginning of the mass phase of the civil rights movement in the South. Within a decade, the civil rights revolution had overturned the structure of legal segregation and regained the right to vote for black southerners. In 2000, *Time* magazine named Rosa Parks one of the 100 most significant persons of the twentieth century.

Parks is widely remembered today as a "seamstress with tired feet," a symbol of ordinary blacks' determination to resist the daily injustices and indignities of the Jim Crow South. In fact, her life makes clear that the civil rights revolution built on

The mug shot of Rosa Parks, taken in December 1955 at a Montgomery, Alabama, police station after she was arrested for refusing to give up her seat on a city bus to a white passenger.

earlier struggles. Parks was a veteran of black politics. During the 1930s, she took part in meetings protesting the conviction of the Scottsboro Boys. She served for many years as secretary to E. D. Nixon, the local leader of the NAACP. In 1943, she tried to register to vote, only to be turned away because she supposedly failed a literacy test. After two more attempts, Parks succeeded in becoming one of the few blacks in Montgomery able to cast a ballot. In 1954, she attended a training session for political activists at the Highlander School in Tennessee, a meeting ground for labor and civil rights radicals.

No one knows exactly why Parks decided not to give up her seat that day. Perhaps it was because an all-white jury in Mississippi had just acquitted the murderers of Emmett Till, a black teenager who had allegedly whistled at a white woman. Jo Ann Robinson, a professor at the all-black Alabama State University, had been calling for a boycott of public transportation since 1954. When news of Parks's arrest spread, hundreds of blacks gathered in a local church and vowed to refuse to ride the buses until accorded equal treatment. For 381 days, despite legal harassment and occasional violence, black maids, janitors, teachers, and students walked to their destinations or rode an informal network of taxis. Finally, in November 1956, the Supreme Court ruled segregation in public transportation unconstitutional. The boycott ended in triumph.

Black residents of Montgomery, Alabama, walking to work during the bus boycott of 1955–1956.

The Daybreak of Freedom

The Montgomery bus boycott marked a turning point in postwar American history. It launched the movement for racial justice as a nonviolent crusade based in the black churches of the South. It gained the support of northern liberals and focused unprecedented and unwelcome international attention on the country's racial policies. And it marked the emergence of twenty-six-year-old Martin Luther King Jr., who had recently arrived in Montgomery to become pastor of a Baptist church, as the movement's national symbol. On the night of the first protest meeting, King's call to action electrified the audience: "We, the disinherited of this land, we who have been oppressed so long, are tired of going through the long night of captivity. And now we are reaching out for the daybreak of freedom and justice and equality."

The rise of Martin Luther King Jr.

From the beginning, the language of freedom pervaded the black movement. It resonated in the speeches of civil rights leaders and in the hand-lettered placards of the struggle's foot soldiers. On the day of Rosa Parks's court appearance in December 1955, even before the bus boycott had officially been announced, a torn piece of cardboard appeared on a bus shelter in Montgomery's Court Square, advising passengers: "Don't ride the buses today. Don't ride it for freedom." During the summer of 1964, when civil rights activists established "freedom schools" for black children across Mississippi, lessons began with students being asked to define the word. Some gave specific answers ("going to public libraries"), some more abstract ("standing up for your rights"). Some insisted that freedom meant legal equality, others saw it as liberation from years of deference to and fear of whites. "Freedom of the mind," wrote one, was the greatest freedom of all.

The movement and freedom

For adults as well, freedom had many meanings. It meant enjoying the political rights and economic opportunities taken for granted by whites. It required eradicating historic wrongs such as segregation, disenfranchisement, confinement to low-wage jobs, and the ever-present threat of violence. It meant the right to be served at lunch counters and downtown department stores, central locations in the consumer culture, and to be addressed as "Mr.," "Miss," and "Mrs.," rather than "boy" and "auntie."

The Leadership of King

In King's soaring oratory, the protesters' understandings of freedom fused into a coherent whole. For the title of his first book, relating the boycott's history, King chose the title *Stride Toward Freedom*. His most celebrated oration, the "I Have a Dream" speech of 1963, began by invoking the unfulfilled promise of emancipation ("one hundred years later, the Negro still is not free") and closed with a cry borrowed from a black spiritual: "Free at last! Free at last! Thank God Almighty, we are free at last!"

A master at appealing to the deep sense of injustice among blacks and to the conscience of white America, King presented the case for black rights in a vocabulary that merged the black experience with that of the nation. Having studied the writings on peaceful civil disobedience of Henry David Thoreau and Mohandas (Mahatma) Gandhi, as well as the nonviolent protests the Congress of Racial Equality had organized in the 1940s, King outlined a philosophy of struggle in which evil must be met with good, hate with Christian love, and violence with peaceful demands for change. "There will be no white persons pulled out of their homes and taken out to some distant road and lynched," he declared in his speech at the launching of the Montgomery bus boycott.

Peaceful civil disobedience

Echoing Christian themes derived from his training in the black church, King's speeches resonated deeply in both black communities and the broader culture. He repeatedly invoked the Bible to preach justice and forgiveness, even toward those "who desire to deprive you of freedom." Like Frederick Douglass before him, King appealed to white America by stressing the protesters' love of country and devotion to national values. The "daybreak of freedom," King made clear, meant a new dawn for the whole of American society. And like W. E. B. Du Bois, he linked the American "color line" with the degradation of non-white peoples overseas. "The great struggle of the Twentieth Century," he declared in a 1956 sermon, "has been between the exploited masses questing for freedom and the colonial powers seeking to maintain their domination." If Africa was gaining its freedom, he asked, why must black America lag behind?

King and the history of black leadership

Massive Resistance

Buoyed by success in Montgomery, King in 1956 took the lead in forming the Southern Christian Leadership Conference, a coalition of black ministers and civil rights activists, to press for desegregation. But despite the movement's success in popular mobilization, the fact that Montgomery's city fathers agreed to the boycott's demands only after a Supreme Court ruling indicated that without national backing, local action might not be enough to overturn Jim Crow. The white South's refusal to accept the *Brown* decision reinforced the conviction that black citizens could not gain their constitutional rights without Washington's intervention. This

The SCLC

was not immediately forthcoming. When the Supreme Court finally issued its implementation ruling in 1955, the justices declared that desegregation should proceed "with all deliberate speed." This vague formulation unintentionally encouraged a campaign of "massive resistance" that paralyzed civil rights progress in much of the South.

In 1956, 82 of 106 southern congressmen—and every southern senator except Lyndon B. Johnson of Texas and Albert Gore and Estes Kefauver of Tennessee—signed a Southern Manifesto, denouncing the *Brown* decision as a "clear abuse of judicial power," and calling for resistance to "forced integration" by "any lawful means." State after state passed laws to block desegregation. Some made it illegal for the NAACP to operate within their borders. Virginia pioneered the strategy of closing any public schools ordered to desegregate and offering funds to enable white pupils, but not black, to attend private institutions. Prince Edward County, Virginia, shut its schools entirely in 1959; not until 1964 did the Supreme Court order them reopened. Many states adopted "freedom of choice" plans that allowed white students to opt out of integrated schools. As a symbol of defiance, Georgia's legislature incorporated the Confederate battle flag into its state flag in 1956, and Alabama and South Carolina soon began flying the battle flag over their state capitol buildings.

Eisenhower and Civil Rights

The federal government tried to remain aloof from the black struggle. Thanks to the efforts of Senate majority leader Lyndon B. Johnson, who hoped to win liberal support for a run for president in 1960, Congress in 1957 passed the first national civil rights law since Reconstruction. It targeted the denial of black voting rights

Opponents of racial integration raised all sorts of lurid fears about the consequences if blacks and whites attended school together.

Federal troops escort black children to Little Rock Central High School, enforcing a court order for integration in 1957.

The Problem We All Live With. This 1964 painting by Norman Rockwell, which accompanied an article in *Look* magazine, depicts federal marshals escorting six-year-old Ruby Bridges to kindergarten in New Orleans in 1960 in accordance with a court order to integrate the city's schools. "There was a large crowd of people outside the school," she later recalled. "They were throwing things and shouting." But Rockwell, intent on focusing on the child, presents the mob only through their graffiti and tomatoes thrown against the wall, and does not show the faces of the marshals. Because of the decision to send her to the formerly white school, Bridges's father lost his job, and her grandparents, who worked as sharecroppers in Mississippi, were evicted from their land. In 2001, President Bill Clinton presented her with the Presidential Citizens Medal.

> **Little Rock**

> **Segregation and America's reputation abroad**

in the South, but with weak enforcement provisions it added few voters to the rolls. President Eisenhower failed to provide moral leadership. He called for Americans to abide by the law, but he made it clear that he found the whole civil rights issue distasteful. He privately told aides that he disagreed with the Supreme Court's reasoning. Ike failed to act in 1956 when a federal court ordered that Autherine Lucy be admitted to the University of Alabama; a mob prevented her from registering and the board of trustees expelled her. The university remained all white into the 1960s.

In 1957, however, after Governor Orval Faubus of Arkansas used the National Guard to prevent the court-ordered integration of Little Rock's Central High School, Eisenhower dispatched federal troops to the city. In the face of a howling mob, soldiers of the 101st Airborne Division escorted nine black children into the school. Events in Little Rock showed that in the last instance, the federal government would not allow the flagrant violation of court orders. But because of massive resistance, the pace of the movement slowed in the final years of the 1950s. When Eisenhower left office, fewer than 2 percent of black students attended desegregated schools in the states of the old Confederacy.

The World Views the United States

Ever since the beginning of the Cold War, American leaders had worried about the impact of segregation on the country's international reputation. President Truman had promoted his civil rights initiative, in part, by reminding Americans that they could not afford to "ignore what the world thinks of our record." The State Department filed a brief in the *Brown* case noting the damage segregation was doing to the country's image overseas.

Foreign nations and colonies paid close attention to the unfolding of the American civil rights movement. The global reaction to the *Brown* decision was overwhelmingly positive. "At Last! Whites and Blacks in the United States on the same school benches!" proclaimed a newspaper in Senegal, West Africa. But the slow pace of change led to criticism that embarrassed American diplomats seeking to win the loyalty of people in the non-white world. In a public forum in India, the American ambassador was peppered with questions about American race relations. Was it true that the Haitian ambassador to the United States had to live in a black ghetto in Washington? Why did no black person hold a high public office? Of course, the Soviet Union played up American race relations as part of the global "battle for hearts and minds of men" that was a key part of the Cold War.

THE ELECTION OF 1960

Kennedy and Nixon

The presidential campaign of 1960 turned out to be one of the closest in American history. Republicans chose Vice President Richard Nixon as their candidate to succeed Eisenhower. Democrats nominated John F. Kennedy, a senator from Massachusetts and a Roman Catholic, whose father, a millionaire Irish-American businessman, had served as ambassador to Great Britain during the 1930s. Kennedy's chief rivals for the nomination were Hubert Humphrey, leader of the party's liberal wing, and Lyndon B. Johnson of Texas, the Senate majority leader, who accepted Kennedy's offer to run for vice president.

The atmosphere of tolerance promoted by World War II had weakened traditional anti-Catholicism. But as recently as 1949, Paul Blanshard's *American Freedom and Catholic Power,* which accused the church of being antidemocratic, morally repressive, and essentially un-American, had become a national best-seller. Many Protestants remained reluctant to vote for a Catholic, fearing that Kennedy would

JFK

The 1960 presidential campaign produced a flood of anti-Catholic propaganda. Kennedy's victory, the first for an American Catholic, was a major step in the decline of this long-standing prejudice.

A photograph of John F. Kennedy and his wife, Jacqueline, strolling along the pier at Hyannisport, Massachusetts, illustrates their youthful appeal.

be required to support church doctrine on controversial public issues or, in a more extreme version, take orders from the pope. Kennedy addressed the question directly. "I do not speak for my church on public matters," he insisted, and "the church does not speak for me." His defeat of Humphrey in the Democratic primary in overwhelmingly Protestant West Virginia put the issue of his religion to rest. At age forty-three, Kennedy became the youngest major-party nominee for president in the nation's history.

Both Kennedy and Nixon were ardent Cold Warriors. But Kennedy pointed to Soviet success in putting *Sputnik*, the first earth satellite, into orbit and subsequently testing the first intercontinental ballistic missile (ICBM) as evidence that the United States had lost the sense of national purpose necessary to fight the Cold War. He warned that Republicans had allowed a "missile gap" to develop in which the Soviets had achieved technological and military superiority over the United States. In fact, as both Kennedy and Nixon well knew, American economic and military capacity far exceeded that of the Soviets. But the charge persuaded many Americans that the time had come for new leadership. The stylishness of Kennedy's wife, Jacqueline, which stood in sharp contrast to the more dowdy public appearance of Mamie Eisenhower and Pat Nixon, reinforced the impression that Kennedy would conduct a more youthful, vigorous presidency.

In the first televised debate between presidential candidates, judging by viewer response, the handsome Kennedy bested Nixon, who was suffering from a cold and appeared tired and nervous. Those who heard the encounter on the radio thought Nixon had won, but, on TV, image counted for more than substance. In November, Kennedy eked out a narrow victory, winning the popular vote by only 120,000 out of 69 million votes cast (and, Republicans charged, benefiting from a fraudulent vote count by the notoriously corrupt Chicago Democratic machine).

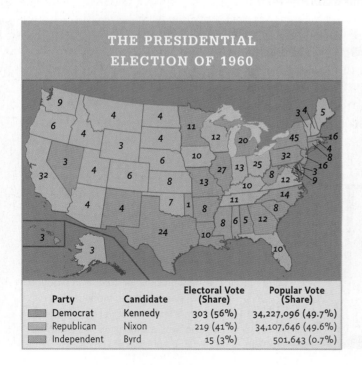

THE PRESIDENTIAL ELECTION OF 1960

Party	Candidate	Electoral Vote (Share)	Popular Vote (Share)
Democrat	Kennedy	303 (56%)	34,227,096 (49.7%)
Republican	Nixon	219 (41%)	34,107,646 (49.6%)
Independent	Byrd	15 (3%)	501,643 (0.7%)

The End of the 1950s

In January 1961, shortly before leaving office, Eisenhower delivered a televised Farewell Address, modeled to some extent on George Washington's address of 1796. Knowing that the missile gap was a myth, Ike warned against the drumbeat of calls for a new military buildup. He urged Americans to think about the dangerous power of what he called the "military-industrial complex"—the conjunction of "an immense military establishment" with a "permanent arms industry"—with an influence felt in "every office" in the land. "We must never let the weight of this combination," he advised his countrymen, "endanger our liberties or democratic processes." Few Americans shared Ike's concern—far more saw the alliance of the Defense Department and private industry as a source of jobs and national security rather than a threat to democracy. A few years later, however, with the United States locked in an increasingly unpopular war, Eisenhower's warning would come to seem prophetic.

WHY WAIT TILL 1955
We Might Not Even Be Alive

Residents of Los Angeles don gas masks at a 1954 luncheon to protest the government's failure to combat the air pollution, or "smog," that hung over the city.

By then, other underpinnings of 1950s life were also in disarray. The tens of millions of cars that made suburban life possible were spewing toxic lead, an additive to make gasoline more efficient, into the atmosphere. Penned in to the east by mountains that kept automobile emissions from being dispersed by the wind, Los Angeles had become synonymous with smog, a type of air pollution produced by cars. Chlorofluorocarbons, used in air conditioners, deodorants, and aerosol hair sprays, were releasing chemicals into the atmosphere that damaged the ozone layer, producing global warming and an increase in skin cancer. (Both leaded gasoline and chlorofluorocarbons had been invented by General Motors research scientist Thomas Midgley. He "had more impact on the atmosphere," writes one historian, "than any other single organism" in the history of the world.) The chemical insecticides that enabled agricultural conglomerates to produce the country's remarkable abundance of food were poisoning farm workers, consumers, and the water supply. Housewives were rebelling against a life centered in suburban dream houses. Blacks were increasingly impatient with the slow progress of racial change. The United States, in other words, had entered that most turbulent of decades, the 1960s.

SUGGESTED READING

BOOKS

- Branch, Taylor. *Parting the Waters: America in the King Years, 1954–1963* (1988). A comprehensive account of the civil rights movement from the *Brown* decision to the early 1960s.

- Cohen, Lizabeth. *A Consumer's Republic: The Politics of Mass Consumption in Postwar America* (2003). Considers how the glorification of consumer freedom shaped American public policy and the physical landscape.

- De Grazia, Victoria. *Irresistible Empire: America's Advance through Twentieth-Century Europe* (2005). An examination of American "soft power" and its triumphant penetration of twentieth-century Europe.

- Fones-Wolf, Elizabeth A. *Selling Free Enterprise: The Business Assault on Labor and Liberalism, 1945–1960* (1994). Examines the carefully developed campaign whereby business leaders associated capitalism and a union-free workplace with freedom.

- Freeman, Joshua B. *Working-Class New York: Life and Labor since World War II* (2000). An account of the lives of laborers in the nation's largest city, tracing the rise and decline of the labor movement.

- Inboden, William. *Religion and American Foreign Policy, 1945–1960: The Soul of Containment* (2008). How religious groups influenced American diplomacy at the height of the Cold War.

- Jackson, Kenneth T. *Crabgrass Frontier: The Suburbanization of America* (1985). The standard account of the development of American suburbia.

- Jacobs, Meg. *Pocketbook Politics: Economic Citizenship in Twentieth-Century America* (2005). Discusses how consumer freedom became central to Americans' national identity after World War II.

- Klarman, Michael J. *From Jim Crow to Civil Rights: The Supreme Court and the Struggle for Racial Equality* (2004). A full study of Supreme Court cases dealing with civil rights, and how they both reflected and helped to stimulate social change.

- Klein, Jennifer. *For All These Rights: Business, Labor, and the Shaping of America's Public-Private Welfare State* (2003). Examines the development of the "social contract" of the 1950s whereby many workers received social benefits from their employers rather than the government.

- May, Elaine T. *Homeward Bound: American Families in the Cold War Era* (1988). Studies the nuclear family as a bastion of American freedom during the Cold War, at least according to official propaganda.

- Nicolaides, Becky M. *My Blue Heaven: Life and Politics in the Working-Class Suburbs of Los Angeles, 1920–1965* (2002). Traces the transformation of Southgate, an industrial neighborhood of Los Angeles, into an all-white suburb, and the political results.

- Patterson, James T. *Grand Expectations: The United States, 1945–1974* (1996). A comprehensive account of American history over the three decades following World War II.

- Pells, Richard. *The Liberal Mind in a Conservative Age: American Intellectuals in the 1940s and 1950s* (1984). Examines how American writers and artists responded to the Cold War.

- Phillips-Fein, Kim. *Invisible Hands: The Making of the Conservative Movement from the New Deal to Reagan* (2009). Relates how a group of economic thinkers and businessmen worked to fashion a conservative movement in an attempt to reverse many of the policies of the New Deal.

- Wall, Wendy L. *Inventing the "American Way": The Politics of Consensus from the New Deal to the Civil Rights Movement* (2008). A careful examination of the political and ideological world of the Cold War era.

- Westad, Odd Arne. *The Global Cold War* (2005). A wide-ranging analysis of how the Cold War played out in the Third World.

WEBSITES

- Brown v. Board of Education: www.lib.umich.edu/exhibits/brownarchive/

- Herblock's History: Political Cartoons from the Crash to the Millennium: www.loc.gov/rr/print/swann/herblock/

- Levittown: Documents of an Ideal American Suburb: http://tigger.uic.edu/~pbhales/Levittown.html

CHAPTER REVIEW AND ONLINE RESOURCES

REVIEW QUESTIONS

1. Explain the meaning of the "American standard of living" during the 1950s.

2. Describe how the automobile transformed American communities and culture in the 1950s.

3. Identify the prescribed roles and aspirations for women during the social conformity of the 1950s.

4. How did governmental policies, business practices, and individual choices contribute to racially segregated suburbs?

5. Explain the ideological rifts between conservatives in the 1950s. Why did many view President Eisenhower as "not one of them"?

6. What was the new "social contract" between labor and management, and how did it benefit both sides as well as the nation as a whole?

7. How did the United States and Soviet Union shift the focus of the Cold War to the Third World?

8. What were the most significant factors that contributed to the growing momentum of the civil rights movement in the 1950s?

9. How did many southern whites, led by their elected officials, resist desegregation and civil rights in the name of "freedom"?

10. How and why did the federal government's concern with U.S. relations overseas shape its involvement with the *Brown v. Board of Education* case?

KEY TERMS

Levittown (p. 926)

"baby boom" (p. 931)

housing segregation (p. 932)

urban renewal (p. 933)

"In God We Trust" (p. 934)

Interstate highway system (p. 940)

Sputnik (p. 941)

National Defense Education Act (p. 941)

massive retaliation (p. 942)

Iranian coup (p. 944)

Geneva Accords (p. 946)

juvenile delinquency (p. 947)

rock-and-roll music (p. 948)

the Beats (p. 948)

League of United Latin American Citizens (p. 953)

Brown v. Board of Education (p. 953)

Montgomery bus boycott (p. 954)

"Southern Manifesto" (p. 957)

"missile gap" (p. 960)

military-industrial complex (p. 960)

wwnorton.com/studyspace

Visit StudySpace for these resources and more:

- **Author Videos**
- **A chapter outline**
- **A practice quiz**
- **Interactive maps**
- **Multimedia documents**

CHAPTER 25

THE SIXTIES

★

1960–1968

On the afternoon of February 1, 1960, four students from North Carolina Agricultural and Technical State University, a black college in Greensboro, North Carolina, entered the local Woolworth's department store. After making a few purchases, they sat down at the lunch counter, an area reserved for whites. Told that they could not be served, they remained in their seats until the store closed. They returned the next morning and the next. As the protest continued, other students, including a few local whites, joined in. Demonstrations spread across the country. After resisting for five months, Woolworth's in July agreed to serve black customers at its lunch counters.

The sit-in reflected mounting frustration at the slow pace of racial change. White Greensboro prided itself on being free of prejudice. In 1954, the city had been the first in the South to declare its intention of complying with the Brown decision. But by 1960 only a handful of black students had been admitted to all-white schools, the economic gap between blacks and whites had not narrowed, and Greensboro was still segregated.

More than any other event, the Greensboro sit-in launched the 1960s: a decade of political activism and social change. Sit-ins had occurred before, but never had they sparked so massive a response. Similar demonstrations soon took place throughout the South, demanding the integration not only of lunch counters but of parks, pools, restaurants, bowling alleys, libraries, and other facilities as well. By the end of 1960, some 70,000 demonstrators had taken part in sit-ins. Angry whites often assaulted them. But having been trained in nonviolent resistance, the protesters did not strike back.

Even more than elevating blacks to full citizenship, declared the writer James Baldwin, the civil rights movement challenged the United States to rethink "what it really means by freedom"—including whether freedom applied to all Americans or only to part of the population. With their freedom rides, freedom schools, freedom marches, and the insistent cry "freedom now," black Americans and their white allies made freedom once again the rallying cry of the dispossessed. Thousands of ordinary men and women—maids and laborers alongside students, teachers, businessmen, and ministers—risked physical and economic retribution to lay claim to freedom. Their courage inspired a host of other challenges to the status quo, including a student movement known as the New Left, the "second wave" of feminism, and activism among other minorities.

By the time the decade ended, these movements had challenged the 1950s' understanding of freedom linked to the Cold War abroad and consumer choice at home. They exposed the limitations of traditional New Deal liberalism. They forced a reconsideration of the nation's foreign policy and extended claims to freedom into the most intimate areas of life. They made American society confront the fact that certain groups, including students, women, members of racial minorities, and homosexuals, felt themselves excluded from full enjoyment of American freedom.

Reflecting back years later on the struggles of the 1960s, one black organizer in Memphis remarked, "All I wanted to do was to live in a free country." Of the movement's accomplishments, he added, "You had to fight for every inch of it. Nobody gave you anything. Nothing."

FOCUS QUESTIONS

What were the major events in the civil rights movement of the early 1960s? –p. 967

What were the major crises and policy initiatives of the Kennedy presidency? –p. 969

What were the purposes and strategies of Johnson's Great Society programs? –p. 973

How did the civil rights movement change in the mid-1960s? –p. 979

How did the Vietnam War transform American politics and culture? –p. 983

What were the sources and significance of the rights revolution of the late 1960s? –p. 995

In what ways was 1968 a climactic year for the Sixties? –p. 1003

An antiwar demonstrator offers a flower to Military Police stationed outside the Pentagon at a 1967 rally against the Vietnam War. Some 100,000 protesters took part in this demonstration.

THE CIVIL RIGHTS REVOLUTION

1960   Greensboro, N.C., sit-in

        Young Americans for
        Freedom founded

1961   Bay of Pigs

        Freedom Rides

        Berlin Wall constructed

1962   Port Huron Statement

        University of Mississippi
        desegregated

        Rachel Carson's *Silent Spring*

        Cuban missile crisis

1963   Betty Friedan's *The
        Feminine Mystique*

        King's "Letter from
        Birmingham Jail"

        March on Washington

        Kennedy assassinated

1964   Freedom Summer

        Civil Rights Act passed

        Gulf of Tonkin resolution

1965–   Great Society
1967

1965   Voting Rights Act

        Watts uprising

        Hart-Celler Act

1966   National Organization for
        Women organized

1968   Tet offensive

        Martin Luther King Jr.
        assassinated

        American Indian movement
        founded

        Richard Nixon elected

1969   Police raid on Stonewall Inn

        Woodstock festival

1973   *Roe v. Wade*

The Rising Tide of Protest

With the sit-ins, college students for the first time stepped onto the stage of American history as the leading force for social change. In April 1960, Ella Baker, a longtime civil rights organizer, called a meeting of young activists in Raleigh, North Carolina. About 200 black students and a few whites attended. Out of the gathering came the Student Non-Violent Coordinating Committee (SNCC), dedicated to replacing the culture of segregation with a "beloved community" of racial justice and to empowering ordinary blacks to take control of the decisions that affected their lives. "We can't count on adults," declared SNCC organizer Robert Moses. "Very few . . . are not afraid of the tremendous pressure they will face. This leaves the young people to be the organizers, the agents of social and political change."

Other forms of direct action soon followed the sit-ins. Blacks in Biloxi and Gulfport, Mississippi, engaged in "wade-ins," demanding access to segregated public beaches. Scores were arrested and two black teenagers were killed. In 1961, the Congress of Racial Equality (CORE) launched the Freedom Rides. Integrated groups traveled by bus into the Deep South to test compliance with court orders banning segregation on interstate buses and trains and in terminal facilities. Violent mobs assaulted them. Near Anniston, Alabama, a firebomb was thrown into the vehicle and the passengers beaten as they escaped. In Birmingham, Klansmen attacked riders with bats and chains, while police refused to intervene. Many of the Freedom Riders were arrested. But their actions led the Interstate Commerce Commission to order buses and terminals desegregated.

As protests escalated, so did the resistance of local authorities. Late in 1961, SNCC and other groups launched a campaign of nonviolent protests against racial discrimination in Albany, Georgia. The protests lasted a year, but despite filling the jails with demonstrators—a tactic adopted by the movement to gain national sympathy—they failed to achieve their goals. In September 1962, a court ordered the University of Mississippi to admit James Meredith, a black student. The state police stood aside as a mob, encouraged by Governor Ross Barnett, rampaged through the streets of Oxford, where the university is located. Two bystanders lost their lives in the riot. President Kennedy was forced to dispatch the army to restore order.

Birmingham

The high point of protest came in the spring of 1963, when demonstrations took place in towns and cities across the South, dramatizing black discontent over inequality in education, employment, and housing. In one week in June, there were more than 15,000 arrests in 186 cities. The dramatic culmination came in Birmingham, Alabama, a citadel of segregation. Even for the Deep South, Birmingham was a violent city—there had been over fifty bombings of black homes and institutions since World War II. Local blacks had been demonstrating, with no result, for greater economic opportunities and an end to segregation by local businesses.

Participants in a sit-in in Raleigh, North Carolina, in 1960. The protesters, probably students from a local college, brought books and newspapers to emphasize the seriousness of their intentions and their commitment to nonviolence.

With the movement flagging, some of its leaders invited Martin Luther King Jr. to come to Birmingham. While serving a nine-day prison term in April 1963 for violating a ban on demonstrations, King composed one of his most eloquent pleas for racial justice, the "Letter from Birmingham Jail." Responding to local clergymen who counseled patience, King related the litany of abuses faced by black southerners, from police brutality to the daily humiliation of having to explain to their children why they could not enter amusement parks or public swimming pools. The "white moderate," King declared, must put aside fear of disorder and commit himself to racial justice.

In May, King made the bold decision to send black schoolchildren into the streets of Birmingham. Police chief Eugene "Bull" Connor unleashed his forces against the thousands of young marchers. The images, broadcast on television, of children being assaulted with nightsticks, high-pressure fire hoses, and attack dogs produced a wave of revulsion throughout the world and turned the Birmingham campaign into a triumph for the civil rights movement. It led President Kennedy, as will be related later, to endorse the movement's goals. Leading businessmen, fearing that the city was becoming an international symbol of brutality, brokered an end to the demonstrations that desegregated downtown stores and restaurants and promised that black salespeople would be hired.

But more than these modest gains, the events in Birmingham forced white Americans to decide whether they had more in common with fellow citizens demanding their basic rights or with violent segregationists. The question became more insistent in the following weeks. In June 1963, a sniper killed Medgar Evers, field secretary of the NAACP in Mississippi. In September, a bomb exploded at a black Baptist church in Birmingham, killing four young girls. (Not until the year 2002 was the last of those who committed this act of domestic terrorism tried and convicted.)

Civil rights demonstrators in Orangeburg, South Carolina, in 1960.

A police officer takes picket signs from young demonstrators in downtown Birmingham, Alabama, during the civil rights campaign of 1963. One sign illustrates how religious beliefs helped to inspire the protesters.

A fireman assaulting young African-American demonstrators with a high-pressure hose during the climactic demonstrations in Birmingham. Broadcast on television, such pictures proved a serious problem for the United States in its battle for the "hearts and minds" of people around the world and forced the Kennedy administration to confront the contradiction between the rhetoric of freedom and the reality of racism.

The March on Washington

On August 28, 1963, two weeks before the Birmingham church bombing, 250,000 black and white Americans converged on the nation's capital for the March on Washington, often considered the high point of the nonviolent civil rights movement. Organized by a coalition of civil rights, labor, and church organizations led by A. Philip Randolph, the black unionist who had threatened a similar march in 1941, it was the largest public demonstration in the nation's history to that time. Calls for the passage of a civil rights bill pending before Congress took center stage. But the march's goals also included a public-works program to reduce unemployment, an increase in the minimum wage, and a law barring discrimination in employment. These demands, and the marchers' slogan, "Jobs and Freedom," revealed how the black movement had, for the moment, forged an alliance with white liberal groups. On the steps of the Lincoln Memorial, King delivered his most famous speech, including the words, "I have a dream that one day this nation will rise up and live out the true meaning of its creed: 'We hold these truths to be self-evident, that all men are created equal.'"

The March on Washington reflected an unprecedented degree of black-white cooperation in support of racial and economic justice. But it also revealed some of the movement's limitations, and the tensions within it. Even though female activists like Jo Ann Robinson and Ella Baker had played crucial roles in civil rights organizing, every speaker at the Lincoln Memorial was male. The organizers ordered SNCC leader John Lewis (later a congressman from Georgia) to tone down his speech, the original text of which called on blacks to "free ourselves of the chains of political and economic slavery" and march "through the heart of Dixie the way Sherman did . . . and burn Jim Crow to the ground." Lewis's rhetoric forecast the more militant turn many in the movement would soon be taking.

"Seek the freedom in 1963 promised in 1863," read one banner at the March on Washington. And civil rights activists resurrected the Civil War–era vision of national authority as the custodian of American freedom. Despite the fact that the federal government had for many decades promoted segregation, blacks' historical experience suggested that they had more hope for justice from national power than from local governments or civic institutions—home owners' associations, businesses, private clubs—still riddled with racism. It remained unclear whether the federal government would take up this responsibility.

Three participants in the 1963 March on Washington stand in front of the White House with signs invoking freedom and the memory of slavery.

THE KENNEDY YEARS

John F. Kennedy served as president for less than three years and, in domestic affairs, had few tangible accomplishments. But his administration is widely viewed today as a moment of youthful glamour, soaring hopes, and dynamic leadership at home and abroad. Later revelations of the sexual liaisons Kennedy obsessively pursued while in the White House have not significantly damaged his reputation among the general public.

Kennedy's inaugural address of January 1961 announced a watershed in American politics: "The torch has been passed," he declared, "to a new generation of Americans" who would "pay any price, bear any burden," to "assure the survival and success of liberty." The speech seemed to urge Americans to move beyond the self-centered consumer culture of the 1950s: "Ask not what your country can do for you; ask what you can do for your country." But while the sit-ins were by now a year old, the speech said nothing about segregation or race. At the outset of his presidency, Kennedy regarded civil rights as a distraction from his main concern— vigorous conduct of the Cold War.

"The torch has been passed"

Kennedy and the World

Kennedy's agenda envisioned new initiatives aimed at countering communist influence in the world. One of his administration's first acts was to establish the Peace Corps, which sent young Americans abroad to aid in the economic and educational progress of developing countries and to improve the image of the

The Peace Corps

United States there. By 1966, more than 15,000 young men and women were serving as Peace Corps volunteers. When the Soviets in April 1961 launched a satellite carrying the first man into orbit around the earth, Kennedy announced that the United States would mobilize its resources to land a man on the moon by the end of the decade. The goal seemed almost impossible when announced, but it was stunningly accomplished in 1969.

Kennedy also formulated a new policy toward Latin America, the Alliance for Progress. A kind of Marshall Plan for the Western Hemisphere, although involving far smaller sums of money, it aimed, Kennedy said, to promote both "political" and "material freedom." Begun in 1961 with much fanfare about alleviating poverty and counteracting the appeal of communism, the Alliance for Progress failed. Unlike the Marshall Plan, military regimes and local elites controlled Alliance for Progress aid. They enriched themselves while the poor saw little benefit.

Kennedy as Cold Warrior

Like his predecessors, Kennedy viewed the entire world through the lens of the Cold War. This outlook shaped his dealings with Fidel Castro, who had led a revolution that in 1959 ousted Cuban dictator Fulgencio Batista. Until Castro took power, Cuba was an economic dependency of the United States. When his government began nationalizing American landholdings and other investments and signed an agreement to sell sugar to the Soviet Union, the Eisenhower administration suspended trade with the island. The CIA began training anti-Castro exiles for an invasion of Cuba.

The Bay of Pigs disaster

In April 1961, Kennedy allowed the CIA to launch its invasion, at a site known as the Bay of Pigs. Military advisers predicted a popular uprising that would quickly topple the Castro government. But the assault proved to be a total failure. Of 1,400 invaders, more than 100 were killed and 1,100 captured. Cuba became ever more closely tied to the Soviet Union. The Kennedy administration tried other methods, including assassination attempts, to get rid of Castro's government.

The Missile Crisis

Meanwhile, relations between the two "superpowers" deteriorated. In August 1961, in order to stem a growing tide of emigrants fleeing from East to West Berlin, the Soviets constructed a wall separating the two parts of the city. Until its demolition in 1989, the Berlin Wall would stand as a tangible symbol of the Cold War and the division of Europe.

The most dangerous crisis of the Kennedy administration, and in many ways of the entire Cold War, came in October 1962, when American spy planes discovered that the Soviet Union was installing missiles in Cuba capable of reaching the United States with nuclear weapons. Rejecting advice from military leaders that he authorize an attack on Cuba, which would almost certainly have triggered a Soviet response in Berlin and perhaps a nuclear war, Kennedy imposed a block-

The Cuba blockade

ade, or "quarantine," of the island and demanded the missiles' removal. After tense behind-the-scenes negotiations, Soviet premier Nikita Khrushchev agreed to withdraw the missiles; Kennedy pledged that the United States would not invade Cuba and secretly agreed to remove American Jupiter missiles from Turkey, from which they could reach the Soviet Union.

For thirteen days, the world teetered on the brink of all-out nuclear war. The crisis seems to have lessened Kennedy's passion for the Cold War. Indeed, he appears to have been shocked by the casual way military leaders spoke of "winning" a nuclear exchange in which tens of millions of Americans and Russians were certain to die. In 1963, Kennedy moved to reduce Cold War tensions. In a speech at American University, he called for greater cooperation with the Soviets. That summer, the two countries agreed to a treaty banning the testing of nuclear weapons in the atmosphere and in space. In announcing the agreement, Kennedy paid tribute to the small movement against nuclear weapons that had been urging such a ban for several years. He even sent word to Castro through a journalist that he desired a more constructive relationship with Cuba.

The test-ban treaty

Kennedy and Civil Rights

In his first two years in office, Kennedy was preoccupied with foreign policy. But in 1963, the crisis over civil rights eclipsed other concerns. Until then, Kennedy had been reluctant to take a forceful stand on black demands. He seemed to share FBI director J. Edgar Hoover's fear that the movement was inspired by communism. Attorney General Robert F. Kennedy, the president's brother, approved FBI wiretaps on King. Despite promising during the 1960 campaign to ban discrimination in federally assisted housing, Kennedy waited until the end of 1962 to issue the order. He used federal force when obstruction of the law became acute, as at the University of Mississippi. But he failed to protect civil rights workers from violence, insisting that law enforcement was a local matter.

Events in Birmingham in May 1963 forced Kennedy's hand. Kennedy realized that the United States simply could not declare itself the champion of freedom throughout the world while maintaining a system of racial inequality at home. In June, he went on national television to call for the passage of a law banning discrimination in all places of public accommodation, a major goal of the civil rights movement. The nation, he asserted, faced a moral crisis: "We preach freedom

The impact of Birmingham

James Meredith, the first black student to attend the University of Mississippi, in a classroom where white classmates refused to sit near him.

New York City train passengers reading the news of President Kennedy's assassination, November 22, 1963.

around the world, . . . but are we to say to the world, and much more importantly, to each other, that this is a land of the free except for Negroes?"

Kennedy did not live to see his civil rights bill enacted. On November 22, 1963, while riding in a motorcade through Dallas, Texas, he was shot and killed. Most likely, the assassin was Lee Harvey Oswald, a troubled former marine. Partly because Oswald was murdered two days later by a local nightclub owner while in police custody, speculation about a possible conspiracy continues to this day. In any event, Kennedy's death brought an abrupt and utterly unexpected end to his presidency. As with Pearl Harbor or September 11, 2001, an entire generation would always recall the moment when they first heard the news of Kennedy's death. It fell to his successor, Lyndon B. Johnson, to secure passage of the civil rights bill and to launch a program of domestic liberalism far more ambitious than anything Kennedy had envisioned.

LYNDON JOHNSON'S PRESIDENCY

Unlike John F. Kennedy, raised in a wealthy and powerful family, Lyndon Johnson grew up in one of the poorest parts of the United States, the central Texas hill country. Kennedy seemed to view success as his birthright; Johnson had to struggle ferociously to achieve wealth and power. By the 1950s, he had risen to become majority leader of the U.S. Senate. But Johnson never forgot the poor Mexican and white children he had taught in a Texas school in the early 1930s. Far more interested than Kennedy in domestic reform, he continued to hold the New Deal view that government had an obligation to assist less-fortunate members of society.

Lyndon B. Johnson being sworn in as president on the plane taking him to Washington from Dallas. On the left is Lady Bird Johnson, and on the right, Jacqueline Kennedy.

The Civil Rights Act of 1964

When he became president, nobody expected that Johnson would make the passage of civil rights legislation his first order of business or that he would come to identify himself with the black movement more passionately than any previous president. Just five days after Kennedy's assassination, however, Johnson called on Congress to enact the civil rights bill as the most fitting memorial to his slain predecessor. "We have talked long enough about equal rights in this country," he declared. "It is now time to write the next chapter and write it in the books of law."

In 1964, Congress passed the Civil Rights Act, which prohibited racial discrimination in employment, institutions like hospitals and schools, and privately owned public accommodations such as restaurants, hotels, and theaters. It also banned discrimination on the grounds of sex—a provision added by opponents of civil rights in an effort to derail the entire bill and embraced by liberal and female members of Congress as a way to broaden its scope. Johnson knew that many whites opposed the new law. After signing it, he turned to an aide and remarked, "I think we delivered the South to the Republican Party."

Freedom Summer

The 1964 law did not address a major concern of the civil rights movement—the right to vote in the South. That summer, a coalition of civil rights groups, including SNCC, CORE, and the NAACP, launched a voter registration drive in Mississippi. Hundreds of white college students from the North traveled to the state to take part in Freedom Summer. An outpouring of violence greeted the campaign, including thirty-five bombings and numerous beatings of civil rights workers. In June, three young activists—Michael Schwerner and Andrew Goodman, white students from the North, and James Chaney, a local black youth, were kidnapped by a group headed by a deputy sheriff and murdered near Philadelphia, Mississippi. Between 1961 and 1965, an estimated twenty-five black civil rights workers paid with their lives. But the deaths of the two white students focused unprecedented attention on Mississippi and on the apparent inabil ity of the federal government to protect citizens seeking to enjoy their constitutional rights. (In June 2005, forty-one years after Freedom Summer, a Mississippi jury convicted a member of the Ku Klux Klan of manslaughter in the deaths of the three civil rights workers.)

> *The 1964 voter registration drive*

Freedom Summer led directly to one of the most dramatic confrontations of the civil rights era—the campaign by the Mississippi Freedom Democratic Party (MFDP) to take the seats of the state's all-white official party at the 1964 Democratic national convention in Atlantic City, New Jersey. With blacks unable to participate in the activities of the Democratic Party or register to vote, the civil rights movement in Mississippi had created the MFDP, open to all residents of the state. At televised hearings before the credentials committee, Fannie Lou Hamer of the MFDP held

> *The MFDP*

Fannie Lou Hamer testifying at the Democratic national convention of 1964 on behalf of the Mississippi Freedom Democratic Party.

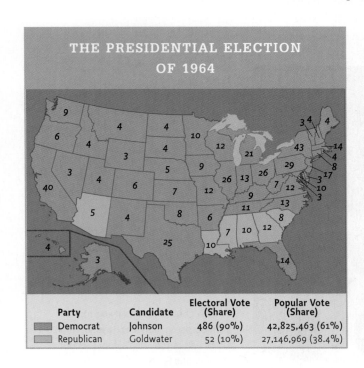

Fannie Lou Hamer

a national audience spellbound with her account of growing up in poverty in the Yazoo-Mississippi Delta and of the savage beatings she had endured at the hands of police. Like many other black activists, Hamer was a deeply religious person who believed that Christianity rested on the idea of freedom and that the movement had been divinely inspired. "Is this America," she asked, "the land of the free and home of the brave, where . . . we [are] threatened daily because we want to live as decent human beings?" Johnson feared a southern walkout, as had happened at the 1948 party convention, if the MFDP were seated. Party liberals, including Johnson's running mate, Hubert Humphrey, pressed for a compromise in which two black delegates would be granted seats. But the MFDP rejected the proposal.

The 1964 Election

The events at Atlantic City severely weakened black activists' faith in the responsiveness of the political system and forecast the impending breakup of the coalition between the civil rights movement and the liberal wing of the Democratic Party. For the moment, however, the movement rallied behind Johnson's campaign for reelection. Johnson's opponent, Senator Barry Goldwater of Arizona, had published *The Conscience of a Conservative* (1960), which sold more than 3 million copies. The book demanded a more aggressive conduct of the Cold War (he even suggested that nuclear war might be "the price of freedom"). But Goldwater directed most of his critique against "internal" dangers to freedom, especially the New Deal welfare state, which he believed stifled individual initiative and independence. He called for the substitution of private charity for public welfare programs and Social Security, and the abolition of the graduated income tax. Goldwater had voted against the Civil Rights Act of 1964. His acceptance speech at the Republican national convention contained the explosive statement, "Extremism in the defense of liberty is no vice."

Stigmatized by the Democrats as an extremist who would repeal Social Security and risk nuclear war, Goldwater went down to a disastrous defeat. Johnson received almost 43 million votes to Goldwater's 27 million. Democrats swept to two-to-one majorities in both houses of Congress. Although few realized it, the 1964 campaign marked a milestone in the resurgence of American conservatism. Goldwater's success in the Deep South, where he carried five states, coupled with the surprisingly strong showing of segregationist governor George Wallace of Alabama in Democratic primaries in Wisconsin, Indiana, and Maryland, suggested that politicians could strike electoral gold by appealing to white opposition to the civil rights movement.

One indication of problems for the Democrats came in California, with the passage by popular referendum of Proposition 14, which repealed a 1963 law banning racial discrimination in the sale of real estate. Backed by the state's realtors and developers, California conservatives made the "freedom" of home owners to control their property the rallying cry of the campaign against the fair housing law. Although Johnson

THE PRESIDENTIAL ELECTION OF 1964

Party	Candidate	Electoral Vote (Share)	Popular Vote (Share)
Democrat	Johnson	486 (90%)	42,825,463 (61%)
Republican	Goldwater	52 (10%)	27,146,969 (38.4%)

carried California by more than 1 million votes, Proposition 14 received a considerable majority, winning three-fourths of the votes cast by whites.

The Conservative Sixties

The 1960s, today recalled as a decade of radicalism, clearly had a conservative side as well. With the founding in 1960 of Young Americans for Freedom (YAF), conservative students emerged as a force in politics. There were striking parallels between the Sharon Statement, issued by ninety young people who gathered at the estate of conservative intellectual William F. Buckley in Sharon, Connecticut, to establish YAF, and the Port Huron Statement of SDS of 1962 (discussed later in this chapter). Both manifestos portrayed youth as the cutting edge of a new radicalism, and both claimed to offer a route to greater freedom. The Sharon Statement summarized beliefs that had circulated among conservatives during the past decade—the free market underpinned "personal freedom," government must be strictly limited, and "international communism," the gravest threat to liberty, must be destroyed.

Young Americans for Freedom

YAF aimed initially to take control of the Republican Party from leaders who had made their peace with the New Deal and seemed willing to coexist with communism. YAF members became Barry Goldwater's shock troops in 1964. Despite his landslide defeat in the general election, Goldwater's nomination was a remarkable triumph for a movement widely viewed as composed of fanatics out to "repeal the twentieth century."

Goldwater also brought new constituencies to the conservative cause. His campaign aroused enthusiasm in the rapidly expanding suburbs of southern California and the Southwest. Orange County, California, many of whose residents had recently arrived from the East and Midwest and worked in defense-related industries, became a nationally known center of grassroots conservative activism.

Conservative strength

A 1967 rally by members of Young Americans for Freedom, a conservative group that flourished in the 1960s.

A white resident of Selma offers her support to civil rights demonstrators.

The funds that poured into the Goldwater campaign from the Sunbelt's oilmen and aerospace entrepreneurs established a new financial base for conservatism. And by carrying five states of the Deep South, Goldwater showed that the civil rights revolution had redrawn the nation's political map, opening the door to a "southern strategy" that would eventually lead the entire region into the Republican Party.

Well before the rise of Black Power, a reaction against civil rights gains offered conservatives new opportunities and threatened the stability of the Democratic coalition. During the 1950s, many conservatives had responded favorably to southern whites' condemnation of the *Brown v. Board of Education* desegregation decision as an invasion of states' rights. The *National Review*, an influential conservative magazine, referred to whites as "the advanced race" and defended black disenfranchisement on the grounds that "the claims of civilization supersede those of universal suffrage." In 1962, YAF bestowed its Freedom Award on Senator Strom Thurmond of South Carolina, one of the country's most prominent segregationists. During the 1960s, most conservatives abandoned talk of racial superiority and inferiority. But conservative appeals to law and order, "freedom of association," and the evils of welfare often had strong racial overtones. Racial divisions would prove to be a political gold mine for conservatives.

The Voting Rights Act

Selma, Alabama

One last legislative triumph, however, lay ahead for the civil rights movement. In January 1965, King launched a voting rights campaign in Selma, Alabama, a city where only 355 of 15,000 black residents had been allowed to register to vote. In March, defying a ban by Governor Wallace, King attempted to lead a march from Selma to the state capital, Montgomery. When the marchers reached the bridge leading out of the city, state police assaulted them with cattle prods, whips, and tear gas.

LBJ's support

Once again, violence against nonviolent demonstrators flashed across television screens throughout the world, compelling the federal government to take action. Calling Selma a milestone in "man's unending search for freedom," Johnson asked Congress to enact a law securing the right to vote. He closed his speech by quoting the demonstrators' song, "We Shall Overcome." Never before had the movement received so powerful an endorsement from the federal government. Congress quickly passed the Voting Rights Act of 1965, which allowed federal officials to register voters. Black southerners finally regained the suffrage that had been stripped from them at the turn of the twentieth century. In addition, the Twenty-fourth Amendment to the Constitution outlawed the poll tax, which had long prevented poor blacks (and some whites) from voting in the South.

Immigration Reform

The Hart-Celler Act and its consequences

By 1965, the civil rights movement had succeeded in eradicating the legal bases of second-class citizenship. The belief that racism should no longer serve as a basis of public policy spilled over into other realms. In 1965, the Hart-Celler Act abandoned the national-origins quota system of immigration, which had excluded Asians and severely restricted southern and eastern Europeans. The law established new, racially neutral criteria for immigration, notably family reunification and possession of skills in demand in the United States. On the other hand, because of growing hostility in the Southwest to Mexican immigration, the law established the first limit, 120,000, on newcomers from the Western Hemisphere. This created, for the first time, the category of "illegal aliens" from the Americas. The act set the quota for the rest of the world at 170,000. The total annual number of immigrants, 290,000, represented a lower percentage of the American population than had been admitted when the nationality quotas were established in 1924. However, because of special provisions for refugees from communist countries, immigration soon exceeded these caps.

The new law had many unexpected results. At the time, immigrants represented only 5 percent of the American population—the lowest proportion since the 1830s. No one anticipated that the new quotas not only would lead to an explosive rise in immigration but also would spark a dramatic shift in which newcomers from Latin America, the Caribbean, and Asia came to outnumber those from Europe. Taken together, the civil rights revolution and immigration reform marked the triumph of a pluralist conception of Americanism. By 1976, 85 percent of respondents to a public-opinion survey agreed with the statement, "The United States was meant to be . . . a country made up of many races, religions, and nationalities."

> *New wave of immigration*

The Great Society

After his landslide victory of 1964, Johnson outlined the most sweeping proposal for governmental action to promote the general welfare since the New Deal. Johnson's initiatives of 1965–1967, known collectively as the Great Society, provided health services to the poor and elderly in the new Medicaid and Medicare programs and poured federal funds into education and urban development. New cabinet offices—the Departments of Transportation and of Housing and Urban Development—and new agencies, such as the Equal Employment Opportunity Commission, the National Endowments for the Humanities and for the Arts, and a national public broadcasting network, were created. These measures greatly expanded the powers of the federal government, and they completed and extended the social agenda (with the exception of national health insurance) that had been stalled in Congress since 1938.

> *Medicaid and Medicare*

Unlike the New Deal, however, the Great Society was a response to prosperity, not depression. The mid-1960s were a time of rapid economic expansion, fueled by increased government spending and a tax cut on individuals and businesses initially proposed by Kennedy and enacted in 1964. Johnson and Democratic liberals believed that economic growth made it possible to fund ambitious new government programs and to improve the quality of life.

As part of his War on Poverty, President Lyndon Johnson visited Appalachia, one of the poorest places in the United States.

The War on Poverty

The centerpiece of the Great Society, however, was the crusade to eradicate poverty, launched by Johnson early in 1964. After the talk of universal affluence during the 1950s, economic deprivation had been rediscovered by political leaders, thanks in part to Michael Harrington's 1962 book *The Other America*. Harrington revealed that 40 to 50 million Americans lived in poverty, often in isolated rural areas or urban slums "invisible" to the middle class. The civil rights movement heightened the

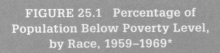

FIGURE 25.1 Percentage of Population Below Poverty Level, by Race, 1959–1969*

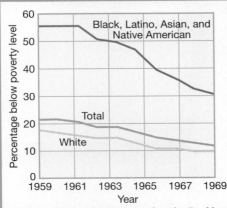

*The poverty threshold for a non-farm family of four was $3,743 in 1969 and $2,973 in 1959.

During the 1960s, an expanding economy and government programs assisting the poor produced a steady decrease in the percentage of Americans living in poverty.

urgency of the issue, even though, as Harrington made clear, whites made up a majority of the nation's poor.

During the 1930s, Democrats had attributed poverty to an imbalance of economic power and flawed economic institutions. In the 1960s, the administration attributed it to an absence of skills and a lack of proper attitudes and work habits. Thus, the War on Poverty did not consider the most direct ways of eliminating poverty—guaranteeing an annual income for all Americans, creating jobs for the unemployed, promoting the spread of unionization, or making it more difficult for businesses to shift production to the low-wage South or overseas. Nor did it address the economic changes that were reducing the number of well-paid manufacturing jobs and leaving poor families in rural areas like Appalachia and decaying urban ghettos with little hope of economic advancement.

One of the Great Society's most popular and successful components, food stamps, offered direct aid to the poor. But, in general, the War on Poverty concentrated not on direct economic aid but on equipping the poor with skills and rebuilding their spirit and motivation. The new Office of Economic Opportunity oversaw a series of initiatives designed to lift the poor into the social and economic mainstream. It provided Head Start (an early childhood education program), job training, legal services, and scholarships for poor college students. It also created VISTA, a domestic version of the Peace Corps for the inner cities. In an echo of SNCC's philosophy of empowering ordinary individuals to take control of their lives, the War on Poverty required that poor people play a leading part in the design and implementation of local policies, a recipe for continuing conflict with local political leaders accustomed to controlling the flow of federal dollars.

Freedom and Equality

Johnson defended the Great Society in a vocabulary of freedom derived from the New Deal, when his own political career began, and reinforced by the civil rights movement. Soon after assuming office in 1963, he resurrected the phrase "freedom from want," all but forgotten during the 1950s. Echoing FDR, Johnson told the 1964 Democratic convention, "The man who is hungry, who cannot find work or educate his children, who is bowed by want, that man is not fully free." Recognizing that black poverty was fundamentally different from white, since its roots lay in "past injustice and present prejudice," Johnson sought to redefine the relationship between freedom and equality. Economic liberty, he insisted, meant more than equal opportunity: "You do not wipe away the scars of centuries by saying: Now you are free to go where you want, do as you desire, and choose the leaders you please. . . . We seek . . . not just equality as a right and a theory, but equality as a fact and as a result."

Johnson's vision

Johnson's Great Society may not have achieved equality "as a fact," but it represented a remarkable reaffirmation of the idea of social citizenship. It was the most expansive effort in the nation's history to mobilize the powers of the national government to address the needs of the least-advantaged Americans, especially those, like blacks, largely excluded from the original New Deal entitlements such as Social Security.

Coupled with the decade's high rate of economic growth, the War on Poverty succeeded in reducing the incidence of poverty from 22 percent to 13 percent of American families during the 1960s. It has fluctuated around the latter figure ever since. The sum spent, however, was too low to end poverty altogether or to transform conditions of life in poor urban neighborhoods. By the 1990s, thanks to the civil rights movement and the Great Society, the historic gap between whites and blacks in education, income, and access to skilled employment narrowed considerably. But with deindustrialization and urban decay affecting numerous families and most suburbs still being off-limits to non-whites, the median wealth of white households remained ten times greater than that of blacks, and nearly a quarter of all black children still lived in poverty.

> *The War on Poverty*

THE CHANGING BLACK MOVEMENT

Even at its moment of triumph, the civil rights movement confronted a crisis as it sought to move from access to schools, public accommodations, and the voting booth to the economic divide separating blacks from other Americans. In the mid-1960s, economic issues rose to the forefront of the civil rights agenda. Violent outbreaks in black ghettos outside the South drew attention to the national scope of racial injustice and to inequalities in jobs, education, and housing that the dismantling of legal segregation left intact. Much of the animosity that came to characterize race relations arose from the belief of many whites that the legislation of 1964 and 1965 had fulfilled the nation's obligation to assure blacks equality before the law, while blacks pushed for more government action, sparking fears of "reverse discrimination."

In 1965, Martin Luther King Jr. and the black labor leader A. Philip Randolph called for a Freedom Budget, which they claimed would eliminate poverty by 1975. The proposal illustrated how the focus of the civil rights movement was shifting from desegregation to economic inequality.

The Ghetto Uprisings

The first riots—really, battles between angry blacks and the predominantly white police (widely seen by many ghetto residents as an occupying army)—erupted in Harlem in 1964. Far larger was the Watts uprising of 1965, which took place in the black ghetto of Los Angeles only days after Johnson signed the Voting Rights Act. An estimated 50,000 persons took part in this "rebellion," attacking police and firemen, looting white-owned businesses, and burning buildings. It required 15,000 police and National Guardsmen to restore order, by which time thirty-five people lay dead, 900 were injured, and $30 million worth of property had been destroyed.

By the summer of 1967, violence had become so widespread that some feared racial civil war. Urban uprisings in that year left twenty-three dead in Newark and forty-three in Detroit, where entire blocks went up in flames and property damage ran into the hundreds of millions of dollars. The violence led Johnson to appoint a commission headed by Illinois governor Otto Kerner to study the causes of urban rioting. Released in 1968, the Kerner Report blamed the violence on "segregation and poverty" and offered a powerful indictment of "white racism." It depicted a country in danger of being torn apart by racial antagonism: "Our nation is moving

A "Freedom Budget" for All Americans

$1.00

BUDGETING OUR RESOURCES, 1966-1975
TO ACHIEVE "FREEDOM FROM WANT"

✓ Abolition of poverty
✓ Guaranteed full employment
✓ Full production and high economic growth
✓ Adequate minimum wages
✓ Farm income parity
✓ Guaranteed incomes for all unable to work

✓ A decent home for every American family
✓ Modern health services for all
✓ Full educational opportunity for all
✓ Updated social security and welfare programs
✓ Equitable tax and money policies

A. PHILIP RANDOLPH INSTITUTE

A semblance of normal life resumes amid the rubble of the Watts uprising of August 1965.

toward two societies, one black, one white—separate and unequal." But the report failed to offer any clear proposals for change.

With black unemployment twice that of whites and the average black family income little more than half the white norm, the movement looked for ways to "make freedom real" for black Americans. In 1964, King called for a "Bill of Rights for the Disadvantaged" to mobilize the nation's resources to abolish economic deprivation. His proposal was directed against poverty in general, but King also insisted that after "doing something special *against* the Negro for hundreds of years," the United States had an obligation to "do something special *for* him now"—an early call for what would come to be known as "affirmative action." A. Philip Randolph and civil rights veteran Bayard Rustin proposed a Freedom Budget, which envisioned spending $100 billion over ten years on a federal program of job creation and urban redevelopment.

A new bill of rights

Chicago Freedom movement

In 1966, King launched the Chicago Freedom movement, with demands quite different from its predecessors in the South—an end to discrimination by employers and unions, equal access to mortgages, the integration of public housing, and the construction of low-income housing scattered throughout the region. Confronting the entrenched power of Mayor Richard J. Daley's political machine and the ferocious opposition of white home owners, the movement failed. King's tactics—marches, sit-ins, mass arrests—proved ineffective in the face of the North's less pervasive but still powerful system of racial inequality. As he came to realize the difficulty of combating the economic plight of black America, King's language became more and more radical. He called for nothing less than a "revolution in values" that would create a "better distribution of wealth" for "all God's children."

Malcolm X

The civil rights movement's first phase had produced a clear set of objectives, far-reaching accomplishments, and a series of coherent if sometimes competitive organizations. The second witnessed political fragmentation and few significant victories. Even during the heyday of the integration struggle, the fiery orator Malcolm X had insisted that blacks must control the political and economic resources of their communities and rely on their own efforts rather than working with whites. Having committed a string of crimes as a youth, Malcolm Little was converted in jail to the teachings of the Nation of Islam, or Black Muslims, who preached a message of white evil and black self-discipline. Malcolm dropped his "slave surname" in favor of "X," symbolizing blacks' separation from their African ancestry. On his release from prison he became a spokesman for the Muslims and a sharp critic of the ideas of integration and nonviolence, and of King's practice of appealing to American values. "I don't see any American dream," he proclaimed. "I see an American nightmare."

On a 1964 trip to Mecca, Saudi Arabia, Islam's spiritual home, Malcolm X witnessed harmony among Muslims of all races. He now began to speak of the possibility of interracial cooperation for radical change in the United States. But when members of the Nation of Islam assassinated him in February 1965 after he had formed his own Organization of Afro-American Unity, Malcolm X left neither a consistent ideology nor a coherent movement. Most whites considered him an apostle of racial violence. However, his call for blacks to rely on their own resources struck a chord among the urban poor and younger civil rights activists. His *Autobiography*, published in 1966, became a great best-seller. Today, streets, parks, and schools are named after him.

> *Black control*

Female students on the campus of Howard University in Washington, D.C., sport the Afro, a hairstyle representative of the "black is beautiful" campaign of the 1960s.

The Rise of Black Power

Malcolm X was the intellectual father of "Black Power," a slogan that came to national attention in 1966 when SNCC leader Stokely Carmichael used it during a civil rights march in Mississippi. Black Power immediately became a rallying cry for those bitter over the federal government's failure to stop violence against civil rights workers, white attempts to determine movement strategy (as at the Democratic convention of 1964), and the civil rights movement's failure to have any impact on the economic problems of black ghettos.

One who embraced the idea proclaimed, "Black Power means Black Freedom"—freedom, especially, from whites who tried to dictate the movement's goals. A highly imprecise idea, Black Power suggested everything from the election of more black officials (hardly a radical notion) to the belief that black Americans were a colonized people whose freedom could be won only through a revolutionary struggle for self-determination. But however employed, the idea reflected the radicalization of young civil rights activists and sparked an explosion of racial self-assertion, reflected in the slogan "Black is beautiful." The abandonment of the word "Negro" in favor

Betye Saar's 1972 installation, *The Liberation of Aunt Jemima*, illustrates modes of thought associated with Black Power. Quaker Oats Company has long used an image of a black woman reminiscent of the stereotypical slave "mammy" as a symbol for its brand of pancake mix. Saar gives Aunt Jemima a rifle to go along with her broom. In front of her is another Aunt Jemima, holding a light-skinned baby, a symbol, according to the artist, of the sexual exploitation of black women by white men. Images in the background reveal how Quaker Oats had already modified its advertising image, giving her a smaller kerchief and an Afro hairdo. By the end of the twentieth century, the kerchief had disappeared entirely, and Aunt Jemima had become slimmer and younger and was not smiling quite so broadly.

of "Afro-American" and the popularity of black beauty pageants, African styles of dress, and the "natural," or "Afro," hairdo among both men and women signified much more than a change in language and fashion. They reflected a new sense of racial pride and a rejection of white norms.

Inspired by the idea of black self-determination, SNCC and CORE repudiated their previous interracialism, and new militant groups sprang into existence. Most prominent of the new groups, in terms of publicity, if not numbers, was the Black Panther Party. Founded in Oakland, California, in 1966, it became notorious for advocating armed self-defense in response to police brutality. It demanded the release of black prisoners because of racism in the criminal justice system. The party's youthful members alarmed whites by wearing military garb, although they also ran health clinics, schools, and children's breakfast programs. But internal disputes and a campaign against the Black Panthers by police and the FBI, which left several leaders dead in shootouts, destroyed the organization.

By 1967, with the escalation of U.S. military involvement in Vietnam, the War on Poverty had ground to a halt. By then, with ghetto uprisings punctuating the urban landscape, the antiwar movement assuming massive proportions, and millions of young people ostentatiously rejecting mainstream values, American society faced its greatest crisis since the Depression.

VIETNAM AND THE NEW LEFT

Old and New Lefts

To most Americans, the rise of a protest movement among white youth came as a complete surprise. For most of the century, colleges had been conservative institutions that drew their students from a privileged segment of the population. During the 1950s, young people had been called a "silent generation." If blacks' grievances appeared self-evident, those of white college students were difficult to understand. What persuaded large numbers of children of affluence to reject the values and institutions of their society? In part, the answer lay in a redefinition of the meaning of freedom by what came to be called the New Left.

What made the New Left new was its rejection of the intellectual and political categories that had shaped radicalism and liberalism for most of the twentieth century. It challenged not only mainstream America but also what it dismissively called the Old Left. Unlike the Communist Party, it did not take the Soviet Union as a model or see the working class as the main agent of social change. Instead of economic equality and social citizenship, the language of New Deal liberals, the New Left spoke of loneliness, isolation, and alienation, of powerlessness in the face of bureaucratic institutions and a hunger for authenticity that affluence could not provide. These discontents galvanized a mass movement among what was rapidly becoming a major sector of the American population. By 1968, thanks to the coming of age of the baby-boom generation and the growing number of jobs that required post–high school skills, more than 7 million students attended college, more than the number of farmers or steelworkers.

Members of Students for a Democratic Society (SDS) at a 1963 National Council meeting in Indiana. Despite their raised fists, they appear eminently respectable compared to radicals who emerged later in the decade. The group is entirely white.

The New Left was not as new as it claimed. Its call for a democracy of citizen participation harked back to the American Revolution, and its critique of the contrast between American values and American reality, to the abolitionists. Its emphasis on authenticity in the face of conformity recalled the bohemians of the years before World War I, and its critique of consumer culture drew inspiration from 1950s writers on mass society. But the New Left's greatest inspiration was the black freedom movement. More than any other event, the sit-ins catalyzed white student activism.

Here was the unlikely combination that created the upheaval known as The Sixties—the convergence of society's most excluded members demanding full access to all its benefits, with the children of the middle class rejecting the social mainstream. The black movement and white New Left shared basic assumptions—that the evils to be corrected were deeply embedded in social institutions and that only direct confrontation could persuade Americans of the urgency of far-reaching change.

An unlikely coalition

The Fading Consensus

The years 1962 and 1963 witnessed the appearance of several pathbreaking books that challenged one or another aspect of the 1950s consensus. James Baldwin's *The Fire Next Time* gave angry voice to the black revolution. Rachel Carson's *Silent Spring* exposed the environmental costs of economic growth. Michael Harrington's *The Other America* revealed the persistence of poverty amid plenty. *The Death and Life of Great American Cities*, by Jane Jacobs, criticized urban renewal, the removal of the poor from city centers, and the destruction of neighborhoods to build highways, accommodating cities to the needs of drivers rather than pedestrians. What made

Pivotal books

cities alive, she insisted, was density and diversity, the social interaction of people of different backgrounds encountering each other on urban streets.

Yet in some ways the most influential critique of all arose in 1962 from Students for a Democratic Society (SDS), an offshoot of the socialist League for Industrial Democracy. Meeting at Port Huron, Michigan, some sixty college students adopted a document that captured the mood and summarized the beliefs of this generation of student protesters.

The Port Huron Statement

The Port Huron Statement devoted four-fifths of its text to criticism of institutions ranging from political parties to corporations, unions, and the military-industrial complex. But what made the document the guiding spirit of a new radicalism was the remainder, which offered a new vision of social change. "We seek the establishment," it proclaimed, of "a democracy of individual participation, [in which] the individual shares in those social decisions determining the quality and direction of his life." Freedom, for the New Left, meant "participatory democracy." Although rarely defined with precision, this became a standard by which students judged existing social arrangements—workplaces, schools, government—and found them wanting.

The Rise of SDS

By the end of 1962, SDS had grown to 8,000 members. Then, in 1964, events at the University of California at Berkeley revealed the possibility for a far broader mobilization of students in the name of participatory democracy. A Cold War "multiversity," Berkeley was an immense, impersonal institution where enrollments in many classes approached 1,000 students. The spark that set student protests

Mario Savio, a leader of the 1964 Free Speech movement at the University of California, Berkeley, addressing a crowd on campus from the roof of a police car.

alight was a new rule prohibiting political groups from using a central area of the campus to spread their ideas. Students—including conservatives outraged at being barred from distributing their own literature—responded by creating the Free Speech movement. Freedom of expression, declared Mario Savio, a student leader, "represents the very dignity of what a human being is. . . . That's what marks us off from the stones and the stars. You can speak freely." Likening the university to a factory, Savio called on students to "throw our body against the machines."

Thousands of Berkeley students became involved in the protests in the months that followed. Their program moved from demanding a repeal of the new rule to a critique of the entire structure of the university and of an education geared toward preparing graduates for corporate jobs. When the university gave in on the speech ban early in 1965, one activist exulted that the students had succeeded in reversing "the world-wide drift from freedom."

America and Vietnam

By 1965 the black movement and the emergence of the New Left had shattered the climate of consensus of the 1950s. But what transformed protest into a full-fledged generational rebellion was the war in Vietnam. What one historian has called "the greatest miscalculation in the history of American foreign relations" was a logical extension of Cold War policies and assumptions. The war tragically revealed the danger that Walter Lippmann had warned of at the outset of the Cold War—viewing the entire world and every local situation within it through the either-or lens of an anticommunist crusade. A Vietnam specialist in the State Department who attended a policy meeting in August 1963 later recalled "the abysmal ignorance around the table of the particular facts of Vietnam. . . . They made absolutely no distinctions between countries with completely different historical experiences. . . . They [believed] that we could manipulate other states and build nations; that we knew all the answers."

Few Americans had any knowledge of Vietnam's history and culture. Successive administrations reduced a complex struggle for national independence, led by homegrown communists who enjoyed widespread support throughout their country in addition to Soviet backing, to a test of "containment." As noted in the previous chapter, the Truman and Eisenhower administrations had cast their lot with French colonialism in the region. After the French defeat, they financed the creation of a pro-American South Vietnamese government, in violation of the Geneva Accords of 1954 that had promised elections to unify Vietnam. By the 1960s, the United States was committed to the survival of this corrupt regime.

Fear that the public would not forgive them for "losing" Vietnam made it impossible for Presidents Kennedy and Johnson to remove the United States from an increasingly untenable situation. Kennedy's foreign policy advisers saw Vietnam as a test of whether the United States could, through "counterinsurgency"—intervention to counter internal uprisings in noncommunist countries—halt the spread of Third World revolutions. Despite the dispatch of increased American aid and numerous military advisers, South Vietnamese leader Ngo Dinh Diem lost control of the countryside to the communist-led Viet Cong. Diem resisted American advice to broaden his government's base of support. In October 1963, after large Buddhist

Secretary of Defense Robert McNamara, on the left, and his deputy, Cyrus Vance, at a May 1965 meeting at the White House where the war in Vietnam was discussed. A bust of President Kennedy stands in the background. McNamara later wrote in his memoirs that his misgivings only grew as the war progressed.

Gulf of Tonkin resolution

Intervention in the Dominican Republic

demonstrations against his regime, the United States approved a military coup that led to Diem's death. When Kennedy was assassinated the following month, there were 17,000 American military advisers in South Vietnam. Shortly before his death, according to the notes of a White House meeting, Kennedy questioned "the wisdom of involvement in Vietnam." But he took no action to end the American presence.

Lyndon Johnson's War

Lyndon B. Johnson came to the presidency with little experience in foreign relations. Johnson had misgivings about sending American troops to Vietnam. But he knew that Republicans had used the "loss" of China as a weapon against Truman. "I am not going to be the president," he vowed, "who saw Southeast Asia go the way China went."

In August 1964, North Vietnamese vessels encountered an American ship on a spy mission off its coast. When North Vietnamese patrol boats fired on the American vessel, Johnson proclaimed that the United States was a victim of "aggression." In response, Congress passed the Gulf of Tonkin resolution, authorizing the president to take "all necessary measures to repel armed attack" in Vietnam. Only two members—Senators Ernest Gruening of Alaska and Wayne Morse of Oregon—voted against giving Johnson this blank check. The nearest the United States ever came to a formal declaration of war, the resolution passed without any discussion of American goals and strategy in Vietnam. (Over forty years later, in December 2005, the National Security Agency finally released hundreds of pages of secret documents that made it clear that no North Vietnamese attack had actually taken place.)

During the 1964 campaign, Johnson insisted that he had no intention of sending American troops to Vietnam. But immediately after Johnson's reelection, the National Security Council recommended that the United States begin air strikes against North Vietnam and introduce American ground troops in the south. When the Viet Cong in February 1965 attacked an American air base in South Vietnam, Johnson put the plan into effect. At almost the same time, he intervened in the Dominican Republic. Here, military leaders in 1963 had overthrown the left-wing but noncommunist Juan Bosch, the country's first elected president since 1924. In April 1965, another group of military men attempted to restore Bosch to power but were defeated by the ruling junta. Fearing the unrest would lead to "another Cuba," Johnson dispatched 22,000 American troops. The intervention outraged many Latin Americans. But the operation's success seemed to bolster Johnson's determination in Vietnam.

By 1968, the number of American troops in Vietnam exceeded half a million, and the conduct of the war had become more and more brutal. The North Vietnamese mistreated American prisoners of war held in a camp known sardonically

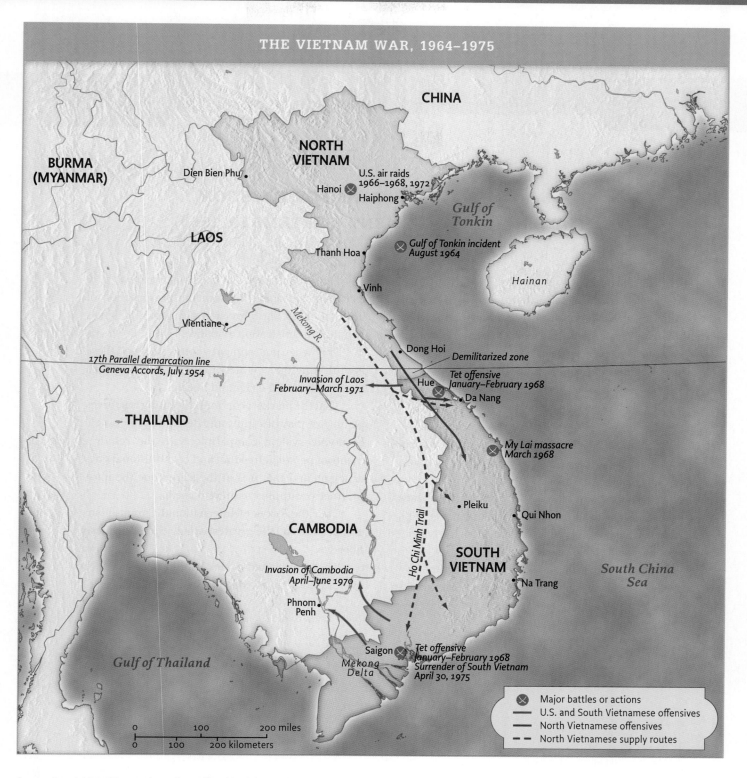

THE VIETNAM WAR, 1964–1975

A war of aerial bombing and small guerilla skirmishes rather than fixed land battles, at the time it was fought, Vietnam was the longest war in American history and the only one the United States has lost.

VOICES OF FREEDOM

From YOUNG AMERICANS FOR FREEDOM, THE SHARON STATEMENT (SEPTEMBER 1960)

Although the 1960s is usually thought of as a decade of youthful radicalism, it also witnessed the growth of conservative movements. The Sharon Statement marked the emergence of Young Americans for Freedom as a force for conservatism in American politics.

In this time of moral and political crisis, it is the responsibility of the youth of America to affirm certain eternal truths. We, as young conservatives, believe:

That foremost among the transcendent values is the individual's use of his God-given free will, whence derives his right to be free from the restrictions of arbitrary force;

That liberty is indivisible, and that political freedom cannot long exist without economic freedom;

That the purposes of government are to protect those freedoms through the preservation of internal order, the provision of national defense, and the administration of justice;

That when government ventures beyond these lawful functions, it accumulates power which tends to diminish order and liberty; . . .

That the market economy, allocating resources by the free play of supply and demand, is the single economic system compatible with the requirements of personal freedom and constitutional government, and that it is at the same time the most productive supplier of human needs; . . .

That the forces of international Communism are, at present, the greatest single threat to these liberties;

That the United States should stress victory over, rather than coexistence with, this menace.

From TOM HAYDEN AND OTHERS, THE PORT HURON STATEMENT (JUNE 1962)

One of the most influential documents of the 1960s emerged in 1962 from a meeting sponsored by the Students for a Democratic Society in Port Huron, Michigan. Its call for a "democracy of individual participation" inspired many of the social movements of the decade and offered a critique of institutions ranging from the government to universities that failed to live up to this standard.

———————————

We are the people of this generation, bred in at least modest comfort, housed now in universities, looking uncomfortably to the world we inherit. . . . Freedom and equality for each individual, government of, by, and for the people—these American values we found good principles by which we could live as men.

As we grew, however, our comfort was penetrated by events too troubling to dismiss. First, the . . . Southern struggle against racial bigotry compelled most of us from silence to activism. Second, . . . the proclaimed peaceful intentions of the United States contradicted its economic and military investments in the Cold War. . . . The conventional moral terms of the age, the politician moralities—"free world," "people's democracies"—reflect realities poorly if at all, and seem to function more as ruling myths than as descriptive principles. But neither has our experience in the universities brought us moral enlightenment. Our professors and administrators sacrifice controversy to public relations; . . . their skills and silence are purchased by investors in the arms race. . . .

We regard *men* as infinitely precious and possessed of unfulfilled capacities for reason, freedom, and love. In affirming these principles we are aware of countering perhaps the dominant conceptions of man in the twentieth century: that he is a thing to be manipulated, and that he is inherently incapable of directing his own affairs. We oppose the depersonalization that reduces human beings to the status of things—if anything, the brutalities of the twentieth century teach that means and ends are intimately related, that vague appeals to "posterity" cannot justify the mutilations of the present. . . . We see little reason why men cannot meet with increasing skill the complexities and responsibilities of their situation, if society is organized not for minority, but for majority, participation in decision-making.

We would replace power rooted in possession, privilege, or circumstance by power and uniqueness rooted in love, reflectiveness, reason, and creativity. As a social system we seek the establishment of a democracy of individual participation [so] that the individual [can] share in those social decisions determining the quality and direction of his life. . . . A new left must consist of younger people. . . . [It] must start controversy throughout the land, if national policies and national apathy are to be reversed.

QUESTIONS

1. *How do the young conservatives who wrote the Sharon Statement understand freedom?*

2. *What do the authors of the Port Huron Statement appear to mean by participatory democracy?*

3. *What are the main differences, and are there any similarities, between the outlooks of the young conservatives and the young radicals?*

American soldiers in South Vietnam carrying wounded men to safety after a 1966 battle.

by the inmates as the Hanoi Hilton. (One prisoner of war, John McCain, who spent six years there, courageously refused to be exchanged unless his companions were freed with him. McCain later became a senator from Arizona and the Republican candidate for president in 2008.) American planes dropped more tons of bombs on the small countries of North and South Vietnam than both sides used in all of World War II. They spread chemicals that destroyed forests to deprive the Viet Cong of hiding places and dropped bombs filled with napalm, a gelatinous form of gasoline that burns the skin of anyone exposed to it. The army pursued Viet Cong and North Vietnamese forces in "search and destroy" missions that often did not distinguish between combatants and civilians. Weekly reports of enemy losses or "body counts" became a fixation of the administration. But the United States could not break its opponents' ability to fight or make the South Vietnamese government any more able to survive on its own.

The Antiwar Movement

As casualties mounted and American bombs poured down on North and South Vietnam, the Cold War foreign policy consensus began to unravel. By 1968, the war had sidetracked much of the Great Society and had torn families, universities, and the Democratic Party apart. With the entire political leadership, liberal no less than conservative, committed to the war for most of the 1960s, young activists lost all confidence in "the system."

Opposition to the war became the organizing theme that united people with all kinds of doubts and discontents. "We recoil with horror," said a SNCC position paper, "at the inconsistency of a supposedly 'free' society where responsibility to freedom is equated with the responsibility to lend oneself to military aggression." With college students exempted from the draft, the burden of fighting fell on the working class and the poor. In 1967, Martin Luther King Jr. condemned the administration's Vietnam policy as an unconscionable use of violence and for draining resources from needs at home. At this point, King was the most prominent American to speak out against the war.

As for SDS, the war seemed the opposite of participatory democracy, since American involvement had come through secret commitments and decisions made by political elites, with no real public debate. In April 1965, SDS invited opponents of American policy in Vietnam to assemble in Washington, D.C. The turnout of 25,000 amazed the organizers, offering the first hint that the antiwar movement would soon enjoy a mass constituency. At the next antiwar rally, in November 1965, SDS leader Carl Ogelsby openly challenged the foundations of

An antiwar placard parodies a famous army recruiting poster from World War I. The original read, "I Want You."

I WANT OUT

Cold War thinking. He linked Vietnam to a critique of American interventions in Guatemala and Iran, support for South African apartheid, and Johnson's dispatch of troops to the Dominican Republic, all rooted in obsessive anticommunism. Some might feel, Ogelsby concluded, "that I sound mighty anti-American. To these, I say: 'Don't blame *me* for *that*! Blame those who mouthed my liberal values and broke my American heart.'" The speech, observed one reporter, marked a "declaration of independence" for the New Left.

By 1967, young men were burning their draft cards or fleeing to Canada to avoid fighting in what they considered an unjust war. In October of that year, 100,000 antiwar protesters assembled at the Lincoln Memorial in Washington, D.C. Many marched across the Potomac River to the Pentagon, where photographers captured them placing flowers in the rifle barrels of soldiers guarding the nerve center of the American military.

Two young members of the counterculture at their wedding in New Mexico.

The Counterculture

The New Left's definition of freedom initially centered on participatory democracy, a political concept. But as the 1960s progressed, young Americans' understanding of freedom increasingly expanded to include cultural freedom as well. Although many streams flowed into the generational rebellion known as the "counterculture," the youth revolt was inconceivable without the war's destruction of young Americans' belief in authority. By the late 1960s, millions of young people openly rejected the values and behavior of their elders. Their ranks included not only college students but also numerous young workers, even though most unions strongly opposed antiwar demonstrations and countercultural displays (a reaction that further separated young radicals from former allies on the traditional left). For the first time in American history, the flamboyant rejection of respectable norms in clothing, language, sexual behavior, and drug use, previously confined

Timothy Leary, promoter of the hallucinogenic drug LSD, listening to the band Quicksilver Messenger Service at the Human Be-In in San Francisco in 1967.

A poster listing some of the performers who took part in the Woodstock festival in 1969. A dove of peace sits on the guitar, symbolizing the overlap between the antiwar movement and counterculture.

to artists and bohemians, became the basis of a mass movement. Its rallying cry was "liberation."

Here was John Winthrop's nightmare of three centuries earlier come to pass—a massive redefinition of freedom as a rejection of all authority. "Your sons and your daughters are beyond your command," Bob Dylan's song "The Times They Are A-Changin'" bluntly informed mainstream America. To be sure, the counterculture in some ways represented not rebellion but the fulfillment of the consumer marketplace. It extended into every realm of life the definition of freedom as the right to individual choice. Given the purchasing power of students and young adults, countercultural emblems—colorful clothing, rock music, images of sexual freedom, even symbols of black revolution and Native American resistance—were soon being mass-marketed as fashions of the day. Self-indulgence and self-destructive behavior were built into the counterculture. To followers of Timothy Leary, the Harvard scientist turned prophet of mind-expansion, the psychedelic drug LSD embodied a new freedom—"the freedom to expand your own consciousness." In 1967, Leary organized a Human Be-In in San Francisco, where he urged a crowd of 20,000 to "turn on, tune in, drop out."

Personal Liberation and the Free Individual

But there was far more to the counterculture than new consumer styles or the famed trio of sex, drugs, and rock and roll. To young dissenters, personal liberation represented a spirit of creative experimentation, a search for a way of life in which friendship and pleasure eclipsed the single-minded pursuit of wealth. It meant a release from bureaucratized education and work, repressive rules of personal behavior, and, above all, a militarized state that, in the name of freedom, rained destruction on a faraway people. It also encouraged new forms of radical action. "Underground" newspapers pioneered a personal and politically committed style of journalism. The Youth International Party, or "yippies," introduced humor and theatricality as elements of protest. From the visitor's gallery of the New York Stock Exchange, yippie founder Abbie Hoffman showered dollar bills onto the floor, bringing trading to a halt as brokers scrambled to retrieve the money.

The counterculture emphasized the ideal of community, establishing quasi-independent neighborhoods in New York City's East Village and San Francisco's Haight-Ashbury district and, in an echo of nineteenth-century utopian communities like New Harmony, some 2,000 communes nationwide. Rock festivals, like Woodstock in upstate New York in 1969, brought together hundreds of thousands of young people to celebrate their alternative lifestyle and independence from adult authority. The opening song at Woodstock, performed by Richie Havens, began with eight repetitions of the single word "freedom."

Faith and the Counterculture

Religious conviction, as has been noted, helped to inspire the civil rights movement. A different religious development, the sweeping reforms initiated in Roman

A gathering of "Jesus People," one of the religious groups that sprang up in the 1960s.

Catholic practice (such as the delivery of the Mass in local languages, not Latin) by the Second Vatican Council of 1962–65, led many priests, nuns, and lay Catholics to become involved in social justice movements. This produced a growing split in the church between liberals and conservatives. "Liberation theology," a movement that swept across parts of Latin America in which priests helped to mobilize rural peasants to combat economic inequality, also reverberated among some Catholics in the United States. Many members of the New Left were motivated by a quest for a new sense of brotherhood and social responsibility, which often sprang from Christian roots. Like adherents of the Social Gospel of the late nineteenth century, many young people came to see a commitment to social change as a fulfillment of Christian values.

The quest for personal authenticity, a feature of the counterculture, led to a flowering of religious and spiritual creativity and experimentation. The Jesus People (called by their detractors Jesus Freaks) saw the hippy lifestyle, with its long hair, unconventional attire, and quest for universal love, as an authentic expression of the outlook of the early church. Like nineteenth-century forebears, Jesus People created Christian communes; they also held religiously oriented rock concerts. The Sixties also witnessed a burgeoning interest in eastern religions. The Beats of the 1950s had been attracted to Buddhism as a religion that rejected violence and materialism—the antithesis of what they saw as key features of American society. Now, practices derived from Hinduism like yoga and meditation became popular with members of the counterculture and even in the suburban mainstream as a way of promoting spiritual and physical well-being. Some Americans traveled to Tibet and India to seek spiritual guidance from "gurus" (religious teachers) there.

More sinister was the emergence of religious cults based on single-minded devotion to a charismatic leader. The one with the most tragic outcome was the People's Temple, founded by Jim Jones, whose religious outlook combined intense spiritual commitment with strong criticism of racism. He attracted a racially mixed

Among the religious developments of the 1960s was the spread of interest in eastern religions and religious practices. The cover of *Yoga Journal* illustrates how one practice entered the mainstream of American life.

community of devout followers, whom he led from Indianapolis to San Francisco and finally to Guyana. There, in 1978 over 900 men, women, and children perished in a mass suicide/murder ordered by Jones.

THE NEW MOVEMENTS AND THE RIGHTS REVOLUTION

The civil rights revolution, soon followed by the rise of the New Left, inspired other Americans to voice their grievances and claim their rights. Many borrowed the confrontational tactics of the black movement and activist students, adopting their language of "power" and "liberation" and their rejection of traditional organizations and approaches. By the late 1960s, new social movements dotted the political landscape.

The counterculture's notion of liberation centered on the free individual. Nowhere was this more evident than in the place occupied by sexual freedom in the generational rebellion. Starting in 1960, the mass marketing of birth-control pills made possible what "free lovers" had long demanded—the separation of sex from procreation. By the late 1960s, sexual freedom had become as much an element of the youth rebellion as long hair and drugs. Rock music celebrated the free expression of sexuality. The musical *Hair*, which gave voice to the youth rebellion, flaunted nudity on Broadway. The sexual revolution was central to another mass movement that emerged in the 1960s—the "second wave" of feminism.

> *The sexual revolution*

The Feminine Mystique

The achievement of the vote had not seemed to affect women's lack of power and opportunity. When the 1960s began, only a handful of women held political office, newspapers divided job ads into "male" and "female" sections, with the latter limited to low-wage clerical positions, and major universities limited the number of female students they accepted. In many states, husbands still controlled their wives' earnings. As late as 1970, the Ohio Supreme Court held that a wife was "at most a superior servant to her husband," without "legally recognized feelings or rights."

During the 1950s, some commentators had worried that the country was wasting its "woman power," a potential weapon in the Cold War. But the public reawakening of feminist consciousness did not get its start until the publication in 1963 of Betty Friedan's *The Feminine Mystique*. Friedan had written pioneering articles during the 1940s on pay discrimination against women workers and racism in the workplace for the newspaper of the United Electrical Workers' union. But, like other social critics of the 1950s, she now took as her themes the emptiness of consumer culture and the discontents of the middle class. Her opening chapter, "The Problem That Has No Name," painted a devastating picture of talented, educated women trapped in a world that viewed marriage and motherhood as their primary goals. Somehow, after more than a century of agitation for access

> *Betty Friedan*

to the public sphere, women's lives still centered on the home. In Moscow in 1959, Richard Nixon had made the suburban home an emblem of American freedom. For Friedan, invoking the era's most powerful symbol of evil, it was a "comfortable concentration camp."

Few books have had the impact of *The Feminine Mystique*. Friedan was deluged by desperate letters from female readers relating how the suburban dream had become a nightmare. "Freedom," wrote an Atlanta woman, "was a word I had always taken for granted. [I now realized that] I had voluntarily enslaved myself." To be sure, a few of Friedan's correspondents insisted that for a woman to create "a comfortable, happy home for her family" was "what God intended." But the immediate result of *The Feminine Mystique* was to focus attention on yet another gap between American rhetoric and American reality.

The law slowly began to address feminist concerns. In 1963, Congress passed the Equal Pay Act, barring sex discrimination among holders of the same jobs. The Civil Rights Act of 1964, as noted earlier, prohibited inequalities based on sex as well as race. Deluged with complaints of discrimination by working women, the Equal Employment Opportunity Commission established by the law became a major force in breaking down barriers to female employment. The year 1966 saw the formation of the National Organization for Women (NOW), with Friedan as president. Modeled on civil rights organizations, it demanded equal opportunity in jobs, education, and political participation and attacked the "false image of women" spread by the mass media.

Women's Liberation

If NOW grew out of a resurgence of middle-class feminism, a different female revolt was brewing within the civil rights and student movements. As in the days of abolitionism, young women who had embraced an ideology of social equality and personal freedom and learned methods of political organizing encountered inequality and sexual exploitation. Women like Ella Baker and Fannie Lou Hamer had played major roles in grassroots civil rights organizing. But many women in the movement found themselves relegated to typing, cooking, and cleaning for male coworkers. Some were pressured to engage in sexual liaisons. Echoing the words of Abby Kelley a century earlier, a group of female SNCC activists concluded in a 1965 memorandum that "there seem to be many parallels that can be drawn between the treatment of Negroes and the treatment of women in our society

In 1967, in a celebrated incident arising from the new feminism, a race official tried to eject Kathrine Switzer from the Boston Marathon, only to be pushed aside by other runners. Considered too fragile for the marathon (whose course covers more than twenty-six miles), women were prohibited from running. Switzer completed the race and today hundreds of thousands of women around the world compete in marathons each year.

A 1970 women's liberation demonstration at the Statue of Liberty.

as a whole." What bothered them most was the status of women within the movement, where assumptions of male supremacy seemed as deeply rooted as in society at large.

The same complaints arose in SDS. "The Movement is supposed to be for human liberation," wrote one student leader. "How come the condition of women inside it is no better than outside?" The rapidly growing number of women in college provided a ready-made constituency for the new feminism. By 1967, women throughout the country were establishing "consciousness-raising" groups to discuss the sources of their discontent. The time, many concluded, had come to establish a movement of their own, more radical than NOW. The new feminism burst onto the national scene at the Miss America beauty pageant of 1968, when protesters filled a "freedom trash can" with objects of "oppression"—girdles, brassieres, high-heeled shoes, and copies of *Playboy* and *Cosmopolitan*. (Contrary to legend, they did not set the contents on fire, which would have been highly dangerous on the wooden boardwalk. But the media quickly invented a new label for radical women—"bra burners.") Inside the hall, demonstrators unfurled banners carrying the slogans "Freedom for Women" and "Women's Liberation."

Personal Freedom

The women's liberation movement inspired a major expansion of the idea of freedom by insisting that it should be applied to the most intimate realms of life. Introducing the terms "sexism" and "sexual politics" and the phrase "the personal is political" into public debate, they insisted that sexual relations, conditions of marriage, and standards of beauty were as much "political" questions as the war, civil rights, and the class tensions that had traditionally inspired the left to action. The idea that family life is not off-limits to considerations of power and justice repudiated the family-oriented public culture of the 1950s, and it permanently changed Americans' definition of freedom.

The abortion issue

Radical feminists' first public campaign demanded the repeal of state laws that underscored women's lack of self-determination by banning abortions or leaving it up to physicians to decide whether a pregnancy could be terminated. Without the right to control her own reproduction, wrote one activist, "woman's other 'freedoms' are tantalizing mockeries that cannot be exercised." In 1969, a group of feminists disrupted legislative hearings on New York's law banning abortions, where the experts scheduled to testify consisted of fourteen men and a Roman Catholic nun.

The call for legalized abortions merged the nineteenth-century demand that a woman control her own body with the Sixties emphasis on sexual freedom. But the concerns of women's liberation went far beyond sexuality. *Sisterhood Is Powerful*, an influential collection of essays, manifestos, and personal accounts published in 1970, touched on a remarkable array of issues, from violence against women to inequalities in the law, churches, workplaces, and family life. By this time, feminist ideas had entered the mainstream. In 1962, a poll showed that two-thirds of American women did not feel themselves to be victims of discrimination. By 1974, two-thirds did.

Gay Liberation

In a decade full of surprises, perhaps the greatest of all was the emergence of the movement for gay liberation. Efforts of one kind or another for greater rights for racial minorities and women had a long history. Homosexuals, wrote Harry Hay, who in 1951 founded the Mattachine Society, the first gay rights organization, were "the one group of disadvantaged people who didn't even think of themselves as a group." Gay men and lesbians had long been stigmatized as sinful or mentally disordered. Most states made homosexual acts illegal, and police regularly harassed the gay subcultures that existed in major cities like San Francisco and New York. McCarthyism, which viewed homosexuality as a source of national weakness, made the discrimination to which gays were subjected even worse. Although homosexuals had achieved considerable success in the arts and fashion, most kept their sexual orientation secret, or "in the closet."

Part of the Gay Liberation Day demonstration in New York City in June 1970.

The Mattachine Society had worked to persuade the public that apart from their sexual orientation, gays were average Americans who ought not to be persecuted. But as with other groups, the Sixties transformed the gay movement. If one moment marked the advent of "gay liberation," it was a 1969 police raid on the Stonewall Inn in New York's Greenwich Village, a gathering place for homosexuals. Rather than bowing to police harassment, as in the past, gays fought back. Five days of rioting followed, and a militant movement was born. Gay men and lesbians stepped out of the "closet" to insist that sexual orientation is a matter of rights, power, and identity. Prejudice against homosexuals persisted. But within a few years, "gay pride" marches were being held in numerous cities.

César Chavez speaking at a 1965 rally to support the national grape boycott. *Huelga*, on the banner behind him, means *"strike"* in Spanish. On the front of the platform is an image of Our Lady of Guadalupe, the patron saint of Mexico. Like the civil rights movement, the United Farm Workers merged religious and political language and imagery.

Latino Activism

As in the case of blacks, a movement for legal rights had long flourished among Mexican-Americans. But the mid-1960s saw the flowering of a new militancy challenging the group's second-class economic status. Like Black Power advocates, the movement emphasized pride in both the Mexican past and the new Chicano culture that had arisen in the United States. Unlike the Black Power movement and SDS, it was closely linked to labor struggles. Beginning in 1965, César Chavez, the son of migrant farm workers and a disciple of King, led a series of nonviolent protests, including marches, fasts, and a national boycott of California grapes, to pressure growers to agree to labor contracts with the United Farm Workers union (UFW). The UFW was as much a mass movement for civil rights as a campaign for economic betterment. The boycott mobilized Latino communities throughout

the Southwest and drew national attention to the pitifully low wages and oppressive working conditions of migrant laborers. In 1970, the major growers agreed to contracts with the UFW.

In New York City, the Young Lords Organization, modeled on the Black Panthers, staged street demonstrations to protest the high unemployment rate among the city's Puerto Ricans and the lack of city services in Latino neighborhoods. (In one protest, they dumped garbage on city streets to draw attention to the city's failure to collect refuse in poor areas.) Like SNCC and SDS, the Latino movement gave rise to feminist dissent. Many Chicano and Puerto Rican men regarded feminist demands as incompatible with the Latino heritage of *machismo* (an exaggerated sense of manliness, including the right to dominate women). Young female activists, however, viewed the sexual double standard and the inequality of women as incompatible with freedom for all members of *la raza* (the race, or people).

Women and Latino activism

Red Power

The 1960s also witnessed an upsurge of Indian militancy. The Truman and Eisenhower administrations had sought to dismantle the reservation system and integrate Indians into the American mainstream—a policy known as "termination," since it meant ending recognition of the remaining elements of Indian sovereignty. Many Indian leaders protested vigorously against this policy, and it was abandoned by President Kennedy. Johnson's War on Poverty channeled increased federal funds to reservations. But like other minority groups, Indian activists compared their own status to that of underdeveloped countries overseas. They demanded not simply economic aid but self-determination, like the emerging nations of the Third World. Using language typical of the late 1960s, Clyde Warrior, president of the National Indian Youth Council, declared, "We are not free in the most basic sense of the word. We are not allowed to make those basic human choices about our personal life and the destiny of our communities."

Founded in 1968, the American Indian movement staged protests demanding greater tribal self-government and the restoration of economic resources guaranteed in treaties. In 1969, a group calling itself "Indians of All Nations" occupied (or from their point of view, reoccupied) Alcatraz Island in San Francisco Bay, claiming that it had been illegally seized from its original inhabitants. The protest, which lasted into 1971, launched the Red Power movement. In the years that followed, many Indian tribes would win greater control over education and economic development on the reservations. Indian activists would bring land claims suits, demanding and receiving monetary settlements for past dispossession. As a result of a rising sense of self-respect, the number of Americans identifying themselves as Indians doubled between 1970 and 1990.

The occupation of Alcatraz Island in San Francisco Bay in 1969 by "Indians of All Tribes" symbolized the emergence of a new militancy among Native Americans.

Silent Spring

Liberation movements among racial minorities, women, and gays challenged long-standing social inequalities. Another movement, environmentalism, called into question different pillars of American life—the equation of progress with endless increases in consumption and the faith that science, technology, and economic growth would advance the social welfare. Concern for preserving the natural environment dated back to the creation of national parks and other conservation efforts during the Progressive era. But in keeping with the spirit of the Sixties, the new environmentalism was more activist and youth-oriented, and it spoke the language of empowering citizens to participate in decisions that affected their lives. Its emergence reflected the very affluence celebrated by proponents of the American Way. As the "quality of life"—including physical fitness, health, and opportunities to enjoy leisure activities—occupied a greater role in the lives of middle-class Americans, the environmental consequences of economic growth received increased attention. When the 1960s began, complaints were already being heard about the bulldozing of forests for suburban development and the contamination produced by laundry detergents and chemical lawn fertilizers seeping into drinking supplies.

Environmental activism

The publication in 1962 of *Silent Spring* by the marine biologist Rachel Carson brought home to millions of readers the effects of DDT, an insecticide widely used by home owners and farmers against mosquitoes, gypsy moths, and other insects. In chilling detail, Carson related how DDT killed birds and animals and caused sickness among humans. Chemical and pesticide companies launched a campaign to discredit her—some critics called the book part of a communist plot. *Time* magazine even condemned Carson as "hysterical" and "emotional"—words typically used by men to discredit women.

Rachel Carson

The New Environmentalism

Carson's work launched the modern environmental movement. The Sierra Club, founded in the 1890s to preserve forests, saw its membership more than triple, and other groups sprang into existence to alert the country to the dangers of water contamination, air pollution, lead in paint, and the extinction of animal species. Nearly every state quickly banned the use of DDT. In 1969, television brought home to a national audience the death of birds and fish and the despoiling of beaches caused by a major oil spill off the coast of California, exposing the environmental dangers of oil transportation and ocean drilling for oil.

The postwar economic boom, with its seemingly limitless demand for resources like land, energy, and building materials, placed enormous stress on the natural environment. As highways and suburbs paved over the landscape, more and more Americans became committed to the survival of places of natural beauty.

Despite vigorous opposition from business groups that considered its proposals a violation of property rights, environmentalism attracted the broadest bipartisan support of any of the new social movements. Under Republican president Richard Nixon, Congress during the late 1960s and early 1970s passed a series of measures to protect the environment, including the Clean Air and Clean Water Acts and the Endangered Species Act. On April 22, 1970, the first Earth Day, some 20 million people, most of them under the age of thirty, participated in rallies, concerts, and teach-ins.

Environmental legislation

Consumer activism

Closely related to environmentalism was the consumer movement, spearheaded by the lawyer Ralph Nader. His book *Unsafe at Any Speed* (1965) exposed how auto manufacturers produced highly dangerous vehicles. General Motors, whose Chevrolet Corvair Nader singled out for its tendency to roll over in certain driving situations, hired private investigators to discredit him. When their campaign was exposed, General Motors paid Nader a handsome settlement, which he used to fund investigations of other dangerous products and of misleading advertising.

Nader's campaigns laid the groundwork for the numerous new consumer protection laws and regulations of the 1970s. Unlike 1960s movements that emphasized personal liberation, environmentalism and the consumer movement called for limiting some kinds of freedom—especially the right to use private property in any way the owner desired—in the name of a greater common good.

The Rights Revolution

It is one of the more striking ironies of the 1960s that although the "rights revolution" began in the streets, it achieved constitutional legitimacy through the Supreme Court, historically the most conservative branch of government. Under the guidance of Chief Justice Earl Warren, the Court vastly expanded the rights enjoyed by all Americans and placed them beyond the reach of legislative and local majorities.

As noted in Chapter 21, the Court's emergence as a vigorous guardian of civil liberties had been foreshadowed in 1937, when it abandoned its commitment to freedom of contract while declaring that the right of free expression deserved added protection. The McCarthy era halted progress toward a broader conception of civil liberties. It resumed on June 17, 1957, known as "Red Monday" by conservatives, when the Court moved to rein in the anticommunist crusade. The justices overturned convictions of individuals for advocating the overthrow of the government, failing to answer questions before the House Un-American Activities Committee, and refusing to disclose their political beliefs to state officials. The government, Warren declared, could prosecute illegal actions, but not "unorthodoxy or dissent." By the time Warren retired in 1969, the Court had reaffirmed the right of even the most unpopular viewpoints to First Amendment protection and had dismantled the Cold War loyalty security system.

Civil liberties had gained strength in the 1930s because of association with the rights of labor; in the 1950s and 1960s, they became intertwined with civil rights. Beginning with *NAACP v. Alabama* in 1958, the Court struck down southern laws that sought to destroy civil rights organizations by forcing them to make public their membership lists. In addition, in the landmark ruling in *New York Times v. Sullivan* (1964), it overturned a libel judgment by an Alabama jury against the nation's leading newspaper for carrying an advertisement critical of how local officials treated civil rights demonstrators. The "central meaning of the First Amendment," the justices declared, lay in the right of citizens to criticize their government. For good measure, they declared the Sedition Act of 1798 unconstitutional over a century and a half after it had expired. Before the 1960s, few Supreme Court cases had dealt with newspaper publishing. *Sullivan* created the modern constitutional law of freedom of the press.

Karl Hubenthal's December 8, 1976, cartoon for the *Los Angeles Herald-Examiner* celebrates the rights revolution as an expansion of American liberty.

The Court in the 1960s continued the push toward racial equality, overturning numerous local Jim Crow laws. In *Loving v. Virginia* (1967), it declared unconstitutional the laws still on the books in sixteen states that prohibited interracial marriage. This aptly named case arose from the interracial marriage of Richard and Mildred Loving. Barred by Virginia law from marrying, they did so in Washington, D.C., and later returned to their home state. Two weeks after their arrival, the local sheriff entered their home in the middle of the night, roused the couple from bed, and arrested them. The Lovings were sentenced to five years in prison, although the judge gave them the option of leaving Virginia instead. They departed for Washington, but five years later, wishing to return, they sued in federal court, claiming that their rights had been violated. In 1968, in *Jones v. Alfred H. Mayer Co.*, the Court forbade discrimination in the rental or sale of housing. Eliminating "badges of slavery," such as unequal access to housing, the ruling suggested, was essential to fulfilling at long last the promise of emancipation.

Richard and Mildred Loving with their children in a 1965 photograph by Grey Villet. Their desire to live in Virginia as man and wife led to a Supreme Court decision declaring unconstitutional state laws that barred interracial marriages.

Policing the States

The Court simultaneously pushed forward the process of imposing upon the states the obligation to respect the liberties outlined in the Bill of Rights. It required states to abide by protections against illegal search and seizure, the right of a defendant to a speedy trial, the prohibition against cruel and unusual punishment, and the right of poor persons accused of a crime to receive counsel from publicly supplied attorneys. Among the most important of these decisions was the 5-4 ruling in *Miranda v. Arizona* (1966). This held that an individual in police custody must be informed of the rights to remain silent and to confer with a lawyer before answering questions and must be told that any statements might be used in court. The decision made "Miranda warnings" standard police practice.

The cartoonist Herblock's comment on critics of the Supreme Court's decision barring prayer in public schools.

The Court also assumed the power to oversee the fairness of democratic procedures at the state and local levels. *Baker v. Carr* (1962) established the principle that districts electing members of state legislatures must be equal in population. This "one-man, one-vote" principle overturned apportionment systems in numerous states that had allowed individuals in sparsely inhabited rural areas to enjoy the same representation as residents of populous city districts.

The justices also moved to reinforce the "wall of separation" between church and state. In 1961, they unanimously declared unconstitutional a clause in Maryland's constitution requiring that public officials declare their belief "in the existence of God." In the following year, in *Engel v. Vitale*, they decreed that prayers and Bible readings in public schools also violated the First Amendment. President Kennedy pointed out that Americans remained perfectly free to pray at home or in church, but these rulings proved to be the most unpopular of all the Warren Court's decisions. Polls showed that 80 percent of Americans favored allowing prayer in public schools.

THE NEW MOVEMENTS AND THE RIGHTS REVOLUTION |

A 1968 poster produced by the Student Nonviolent Coordinating Committee starkly captures the impatient spirit of the social movements of the Sixties.

Griswold *and* Roe

The Right to Privacy

The Warren Court not only expanded existing liberties but also outlined entirely new rights in response to the rapidly changing contours of American society. Most dramatic was its assertion of a constitutional right to privacy in *Griswold v. Connecticut* (1965), which overturned a state law prohibiting the use of contraceptives. Justice William O. Douglas, who wrote the decision, had once declared, "The right to be let alone is the beginning of all freedom." Apart from decisions of the 1920s that affirmed the right to marry and raise children without government interference, however, few legal precedents existed regarding privacy. The Constitution does not mention the word. Nonetheless, Douglas argued that a constitutionally protected "zone of privacy" within marriage could be inferred from the "penumbras" (shadows) of the Bill of Rights.

Griswold linked privacy to the sanctity of marriage. But the Court soon transformed it into a right of individuals. It extended access to birth control to unmarried adults and ultimately to minors—an admission by the Court that law could not reverse the sexual revolution. These decisions led directly to the most controversial decision that built on the rulings of the Warren Court (even though it occurred in 1973, four years after Warren's retirement). This was *Roe v. Wade*, which created a constitutional right to terminate a pregnancy. The Court declared access to abortion a fundamental freedom protected by the Constitution, a fulfillment of radical feminists' earliest demand. *Roe* provoked vigorous opposition, which has continued to this day. Only two states banned contraception when *Griswold* was decided; *Roe* invalidated the laws of no fewer than forty-six.

Griswold and *Roe* unleashed a flood of rulings and laws that seemed to accept the feminist view of the family as a collection of sovereign individuals rather than a unit with a single head. The legal rights of women within the domestic sphere expanded dramatically. Law enforcement authorities for the first time began to prosecute crimes like rape and assault by husbands against their wives. Today, some notion of privacy is central to most Americans' conception of freedom.

The rights revolution completed the transformation of American freedom from a set of entitlements enjoyed mainly by white men into an open-ended claim to equality, recognition, and self-determination. For the rest of the century, the government and legal system would be inundated by demands by aggrieved groups of all kinds, and the Supreme Court would devote much of its time to defining the rights of Americans.

1968

A Year of Turmoil

The Sixties reached their climax in 1968, a year when momentous events succeeded each other so rapidly that the foundations of society seemed to be dissolving. Late January 1968 saw the Tet offensive, in which Viet Cong and North Vietnamese troops launched well-organized uprisings in cities throughout South Vietnam, completely surprising American military leaders. The United States drove back the offensive and inflicted heavy losses. But the intensity of the fighting, brought into America's homes on television, shattered public confidence in the Johnson administration, which had repeatedly proclaimed victory to be "just around the corner." Leading members of the press and political establishment joined the chorus criticizing American involvement. Eugene McCarthy, an antiwar senator from Minnesota, announced that he would seek the Democratic nomination. In March, aided by a small army of student volunteers, McCarthy received more than 40 percent of the vote in the New Hampshire primary. With public support dissolving, Johnson rejected the military's request to send 200,000 more troops to Vietnam. In March, he stunned the nation by announcing that he had decided not to seek reelection. Peace talks soon opened in Paris.

Striking sanitation workers in Memphis, Tennessee. As their signs suggest, they demanded respect as well as higher wages. Having traveled to Memphis to support the strikers, Martin Luther King Jr. was assassinated on April 4, 1968.

Meanwhile, Martin Luther King Jr. was organizing a Poor People's March, hoping to bring thousands of demonstrators to Washington to demand increased anti-poverty efforts. On April 4, having traveled to Memphis to support a strike of the city's grossly underpaid black garbage collectors, King was killed by a white assassin. The greatest outbreak of urban violence in the nation's history followed in ghettos across the country. Washington, D.C., had to be occupied by soldiers before order was restored. As a gesture to King's memory, Congress passed its last major civil rights law, the Open Housing Act, which prohibited discrimination in the sale and rental of homes and apartments, although with weak enforcement mechanisms.

At the end of April, students protesting Columbia University's involvement in defense research and its plan to build a gymnasium in a public park occupied seven campus buildings. New York police removed them in an assault that left hundreds of protesters and bystanders injured and led to a strike that closed the campus. In June, a young Palestinian nationalist assassinated Robert F. Kennedy, who was seeking the Democratic nomination as an opponent of the war. In August, tens of thousands of antiwar activists descended on Chicago for protests at the Democratic national convention, where the delegates nominated Vice President Hubert Humphrey as their presidential candidate. The city's police, never known for restraint, assaulted the marchers with nightsticks, producing hundreds of injuries outside the convention hall and pandemonium inside it.

The 1968 Democratic national convention

A later investigation called the event a "police riot." Nonetheless, the government indicted eight political radicals for conspiring to incite the violence. They included Tom Hayden of SDS, yippie leader Abbie Hoffman, and Bobby Seale of the Black Panthers. Five were found guilty after a tumultuous trial. But an appeals court overturned the convictions because Judge Julius Hoffman (no relation to Abbie Hoffman) had been flagrantly biased against the defendants.

A mural in Belfast, Northern Ireland, depicts the black American abolitionist Frederick Douglass, illustrating how the movement for Catholic civil rights associated itself with the struggle for racial justice in the United States. The text points out that Douglass lectured in Ireland in the 1840s on abolitionism, women's rights, and Irish independence.

The Global 1968

Like 1848 and 1919, 1968 was a year of worldwide upheaval. In many countries, young radicals challenged existing power structures, often borrowing language and strategies from the decade's social movements in the United States and adapting them to their own circumstances. Television carried events in one country instantaneously across the globe.

Massive antiwar demonstrations took place in London, Rome, Paris, Munich, and Tokyo, leading to clashes with police and scores of injuries. In Italy, students occupied university buildings, bringing education to a halt. In Paris, a nationwide student uprising began in May 1968 that echoed American demands for educational reform and personal liberation. Unlike in the United States, millions of French workers soon joined the protest, adding their own demands for higher wages and greater democracy in the workplace. The result was a general strike that paralyzed the country and nearly led to the collapse of the government before it ended. In communist Czechoslovakia, leaders bent on reform came to power by promising to institute "socialism with a human face," only to be ousted by a Soviet invasion. Soldiers fired on students demonstrating for greater democracy on the eve of the opening of the Olympic Games in Mexico City, leading to more than 500 deaths. In Northern Ireland, which remained part of Great Britain after the rest of Ireland achieved independence, the police attacked a peaceful march of Catholics demanding an end to religious discrimination who were inspired by the American civil rights movement. This event marked the beginning of The Troubles, a period of both peaceful protest and violent conflict in the region that did not end until the turn of the twenty-first century.

And throughout the world, the second wave of American feminism found echoes among women who resented being relegated to unequal citizenship. American women influenced, and were influenced by, movements in other countries, particularly in Europe, which demanded equal rights and challenged demeaning representations of women in advertising and the mass media. As in the United States, personal liberation, including a woman's right to control her own body, became a rallying cry. In Catholic European countries like France and Italy, women's movements won significant legal changes, making it easier to obtain divorces and decriminalizing abortion. *Our Bodies, Ourselves*, a book originally published in 1973 by a group of Boston women, dealt frankly with widely misunderstood aspects of women's health, including pregnancy and childbirth, menopause, birth control, and sexually transmitted diseases. It was quickly translated into twenty languages.

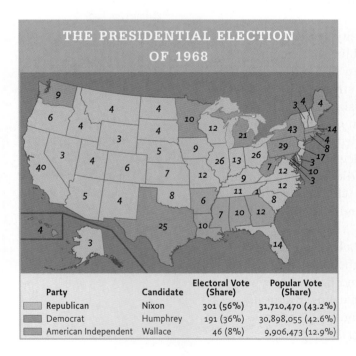

THE PRESIDENTIAL ELECTION OF 1968

Party	Candidate	Electoral Vote (Share)	Popular Vote (Share)
Republican	Nixon	301 (56%)	31,710,470 (43.2%)
Democrat	Humphrey	191 (36%)	30,898,055 (42.6%)
American Independent	Wallace	46 (8%)	9,906,473 (12.9%)

Nixon's Comeback

In the United States, instead of radical change, the year's events opened the door for a conservative reaction. Turmoil in the streets produced a demand for public order. Black militancy produced white "backlash," which played an increasing role in politics. The fact that the unelected Supreme Court was inventing and protecting "rights" fed the argument that faraway bureaucrats rode roughshod over local traditions.

In August, Richard Nixon capped a remarkable political comeback by winning the Republican nomination. He campaigned as the champion of the "silent majority"—ordinary Americans who believed that change had gone too far—and called for a renewed commitment to "law and order." Humphrey could not overcome the deep divide in his party. With 43 percent of the vote, Nixon had only a razor-thin margin over his Democratic rival. But George Wallace, running as an independent and appealing to resentments against blacks' gains, Great Society programs, and the Warren Court, received an additional 13 percent. Taken together, the Nixon and Wallace totals, which included a considerable number of former Democratic voters, indicated that four years after Johnson's landslide election ushered in the Great Society, liberalism was on the defensive.

The year 1968 did not mark the end of the 1960s. The Great Society would achieve an unlikely culmination during the Nixon administration. The second wave of feminism achieved its largest following during the 1970s. Nixon's election did, however, inaugurate a period of growing conservatism in American politics. The conservative ascendancy would usher in yet another chapter in the story of American freedom.

Signs, a 1970 painting by Robert Rauschenberg, presents a collage of images from the turbulent 1960s, including (clockwise from the upper-left corner) troops putting down urban rioting, Robert F. Kennedy, singer Janis Joplin, peace demonstrators, John F. Kennedy, Martin Luther King Jr. after his assassination, and an astronaut on the moon. Art © Robert Rauschenberg Foundation/Licensed by VAGA, New York, NY.

The Legacy of the Sixties

The 1960s transformed American life in ways unimaginable when the decade began. It produced new rights and new understandings of freedom. It made possible the entrance of numerous members of racial minorities into the mainstream of American life, while leaving unsolved the problem of urban poverty. It set in motion a transformation of the status of women. It changed what Americans expected from government—from clean air and water to medical coverage in old age. At the same time, it undermined public confidence in national leaders. Relations between young and old, men and women, and white and non-white, along with every institution in society, changed as a result.

Just as the Civil War and New Deal established the framework for future political debates, so, it seemed, Americans were condemned to refight the battles of the 1960s long after the decade had ended. Race relations, feminism, social policy, the nation's proper role in world affairs—these issues hardly originated in the 1960s. But the events of those years made them more pressing and more divisive. As the country became more conservative, the Sixties would be blamed for every imaginable social ill, from crime and drug abuse to a decline of respect for authority. Yet during the 1960s, the United States had become a more open, more tolerant—in a word, a freer—country.

SUGGESTED READING

BOOKS

- Anderson, John A., III. *The Other Side of the Sixties: Young Americans for Freedom and the Rise of Conservative Politics* (1997). Considers conservative students of the 1960s and how they laid the groundwork for the later growth of their movement.

- Brick, Howard. *Age of Contradiction: American Thought and Culture in the 1960s* (1998). A careful examination of the complex currents of thought that circulated during the decade.

- Carson, Clayborne. *In Struggle: SNCC and the Black Awakening of the 1960s* (1981). A study of the Student Non-Violent Coordinating Committee and its impact on the 1960s.

- D'Emilio, John. *Sexual Politics, Sexual Communities: The Making of a Homosexual Minority in the United States, 1940-1970* (1983). Explores the status of gay men and lesbians in mid-twentieth-century America and the rise of the gay movement.

- Dierenfield, Bruce. *The Battle over School Prayer: How* Engel v. Vitale *Changed America* (2007). One controversial Supreme Court decision of the 1960s and its long-term consequences.

- Dittmer, John. *Local People: The Struggle for Civil Rights in Mississippi* (1994). Traces the civil rights movement in one state, looked at from the experience of grassroots activists.

- Herring, George C. *America's Longest War: The United States and Vietnam, 1950-1975* (2002 ed.). The fullest study of how the United States became involved in the war in Vietnam, and the course of the conflict.

- Horwitz, Morton J. *The Warren Court and the Pursuit of Justice* (1998). Analyzes how the Supreme Court redefined the rights of Americans under Chief Justice Earl Warren.

- Isserman, Maurice, and Michael Kazin. *America Divided: The Civil War of the 1960s* (2000). A comprehensive account of the social movements and political debates of the 1960s.

- McCartin, James P. *Prayers of the Faithful: The Shifting Spiritual Life of American Catholics* (2010). Examines the impact of the 1960s on the Catholic Church.

- Porter, Gareth. *Perils of Dominance: Imbalance of Power and the Road to Vietnam* (2005). Discusses the assumptions of policymakers and their effect on foreign policy, especially the idea that American power could not be resisted.

- Rosen, Ruth. *The World Split Open: How the Modern Women's Movement Changed America* (2000). Considers how the "second wave" of feminism transformed the lives of American women and men.

- Rossinow, Douglas C. *The Politics of Authenticity: Liberalism, Christianity, and the New Left in America* (1998). A careful look at some of the intellectual and religious roots of New Left radicalism.

- Sale, Kirkpatrick. *The Green Revolution: The American Environmental Movement, 1962-1992* (1993). A brief history of one of the most significant movements to emerge from the 1960s.

- Skretny, John. *The Minority Rights Revolution* (2002). An account of the rights revolution and how it affected American society and its understanding of the rights of citizens.

WEBSITES

- A Visual Journey: Photographs by Lisa Law, 1965–1971: http://americanhistory.si.edu/lisalaw/1.htm

- Free Speech Movement Digital Archive: http://bancroft.berkeley.edu/FSM/

- Freedom Now!: www.stg.brown.edu/projects/FreedomNow/

- The Wars for Vietnam, 1945–1975: http://vietnam.vassar.edu/index.html

CHAPTER REVIEW AND ONLINE RESOURCES

REVIEW QUESTIONS

1. How did the idea of a "zone of privacy" build on or change earlier notions of rights and freedom?

2. In what ways were President Kennedy's foreign policy decisions shaped by Cold War ideology?

3. How did immigration policies change in these years, and what were the consequences for the composition of the population in the United States?

4. Explain why many blacks, especially in the North, did not believe that the civil rights legislation went far enough in promoting black freedom.

5. What were the effects of President Johnson's Great Society and War on Poverty programs?

6. In what ways was the New Left not as new as it claimed?

7. How did the goals and actions of the United States in Vietnam cause controversy at home and abroad?

8. Discuss the impact of the Civil Right movement on other movements for social change in the 1960s.

9. Identify the origins, goals, and composition of the feminist, or women's liberation, movement.

10. Describe how the social movement of the 1960s in the United States become part of global movements for change by 1968. How did those connections affect the United States's position in the world?

11. How did the counterculture expand the meaning of freedom in these years?

KEY TERMS

Student Non-Violent Coordinating
    Committee (p. 966)

Freedom Rides (p. 966)

March on Washington (p. 968)

Bay of Pigs (p. 970)

Berlin Wall (p. 970)

Cuban missile crisis (p. 970)

Civil Rights Act (p. 972)

Voting Rights Act (p. 976)

Hart-Celler Act (p. 976)

Great Society (p. 977)

War on Poverty (p. 977)

Black Power (p. 981)

Port Huron Statement (p. 984)

Gulf of Tonkin resolution (p. 986)

counterculture (p. 991)

The Feminine Mystique (p. 994)

National Organization for Women
    (p. 995)

Stonewall Inn (p. 997)

American Indian movement (p. 998)

Silent Spring (p. 999)

"zone of privacy" (p. 1002)

wwnorton.com/studyspace

Visit StudySpace for these resources and more:

- **Author Videos**
- **A chapter outline**
- **A practice quiz**
- **Interactive maps**
- **Multimedia documents**

CHAPTER 26

THE TRIUMPH OF CONSERVATISM

★

1969-1988

Beginning with the dramatic 1960 contest between John F. Kennedy and Richard M. Nixon, the journalist Theodore White published bestselling accounts of four successive races for the presidency. Covering the 1964 election, White attended civil rights demonstrations and rallies for Barry Goldwater, the Republican nominee. White noticed something that struck him as odd: "The dominant word of these two groups, which loathe each other, is 'freedom.' Both demand either Freedom Now or Freedom for All. The word has such emotive power behind it that . . . a reporter is instantly denounced for questioning what they mean by the word 'freedom.'" The United States, White concluded, sorely needed "a commonly agreed-on concept of freedom."

White had observed firsthand the struggle over the meaning of freedom set in motion by the 1960s, as well as the revival of conservatism in the midst of an era known for radicalism. Goldwater's campaign helped to crystallize and popularize ideas that would remain the bedrock of conservatism for years to come. To intense anticommunism, Goldwater added a critique of the welfare state for destroying "the dignity of the individual." He demanded a reduction in taxes and governmental regulations. Goldwater showed that with liberals in control in Washington, conservatives could claim for themselves the tradition of antigovernment populism, thus broadening their electoral base and countering their image as upper-crust elitists.

The second half of the 1960s and the 1970s would witness pivotal developments that reshaped American politics—the breakup of the political coalition forged by Franklin D. Roosevelt; an economic crisis that traditional liberal remedies seemed unable to solve; a shift of population and economic resources to conservative strongholds in the Sunbelt of the South and West; the growth of an activist, conservative Christianity increasingly aligned with the Republican Party; and a series of setbacks for the United States overseas. Together, they led to growing popularity for conservatives' ideas, including their understanding of freedom.

PRESIDENT NIXON

From the vantage point of the early twenty-first century, it is difficult to recall how marginal conservatism seemed at the end of World War II. Associated in many minds with conspiracy theories, anti-Semitism, and preference for social hierarchy over democracy and equality, conservatism seemed a relic of a discredited past. When conservative ideas did begin to spread, liberals explained them as a rejection of the modern world by the alienated or psychologically disturbed.

Nonetheless, as noted in the previous two chapters, the 1950s and 1960s witnessed a conservative rebirth. And in 1968, a "backlash" among formerly Democratic voters against both black assertiveness and antiwar demonstrations helped to propel Richard Nixon into the White House. But conservatives found Nixon no more to their liking than his predecessors. Nixon echoed conservative language, especially in his condemnation of student protesters and his calls for

What were the major policies of the Nixon administration on social and economic issues? –p. 1011

How did Vietnam and the Watergate scandal affect popular trust in the government? –p. 1017

In what ways did the opportunities of most Americans diminish in the 1970s? –p. 1021

What were the roots of the rise of conservatism in the 1970s? –p. 1029

How did the Reagan presidency affect Americans both at home and abroad? –p. 1033

Ronald Reagan addressing the Republican national convention of 1980, which nominated him for president. His election that fall brought modern conservatism to the White House and launched the Reagan Revolution.

1968	Oil discovered in Alaska
	My Lai massacre
1970	U.S. invades Cambodia
1971	Pentagon Papers published
	U.S. goes off gold standard
1972	Nixon travels to the People's Republic of China
	Congress passes the Equal Rights Amendment for ratification
	SALT is signed
	Congress approves Title IX
1973	Pairs Peace Accords end U.S. involvement in Vietnam War
	CIA-aided Chilean coup
	War Powers Act
1974	Nixon resigns in Watergate scandal
1975	Collapse of South Vietnamese government
1976	Jimmy Carter elected
1978	*Regents of the University of California v. Bakke*
	Camp David Accords signed between Israel and Egypt
1979	Three Mile Island accident
	Sagebrush Rebellion
	Sixty-six Americans taken hostage in Iran
1980	Ronald Reagan elected
1981	Air traffic controllers' strike
1983	Strategic Defense Initiative
1985–1987	Iran-Contra affair
1986	*Bowers v. Hardwick*

law and order, but in office he expanded the welfare state and moved to improve American relations with the Soviet Union and China. During his presidency, the social changes set in motion by the 1960s—seen by conservatives as forces of moral decay—continued apace.

Nixon's Domestic Policies

Having won the presidency by a very narrow margin, Nixon moved toward the political center on many issues. A shrewd politician, he worked to solidify his support among Republicans while reaching out to disaffected elements of the Democratic coalition. It is difficult to characterize Nixon's domestic agenda according to the traditional categories of liberal and conservative. Mostly interested in foreign policy, he had no desire to battle Congress, still under Democratic control, on domestic issues. Just as Eisenhower had helped to institutionalize the New Deal, Nixon accepted and even expanded many elements of the Great Society.

Conservatives applauded Nixon's New Federalism, which offered federal "block grants" to the states to spend as they saw fit, rather than for specific purposes dictated by Washington. On the other hand, the Nixon administration created a host of new federal agencies. The Environmental Protection Agency oversaw programs to combat water and air pollution, cleaned up hazardous wastes, and required "environmental impact" statements from any project that received federal funding. The Occupational Safety and Health Administration sent inspectors into the nation's workplaces. The National Transportation Safety Board instructed automobile makers on how to make their cars safer.

Nixon spent lavishly on social services and environmental initiatives. He abolished the Office of Economic Opportunity, which had coordinated Johnson's War on Poverty. But he signed congressional measures that expanded the food stamp program and indexed Social Security benefits to inflation—meaning that they would rise automatically as the cost of living increased. The Endangered Species Act prohibited spending federal funds on any project that might extinguish an animal species. The Clean Air Act set air quality standards for carbon monoxide and other chemicals released by cars and factories and led to a dramatic decline in air pollution.

Nixon and Welfare

Perhaps Nixon's most startling initiative was his proposal for a Family Assistance Plan, or "negative income tax," that would replace Aid to Families with Dependent Children (AFDC) by having the federal government guarantee a minimum income for all Americans. Universally known as "welfare," AFDC provided assistance, often quite limited, to poor families who met local eligibility requirements. Originally a New Deal program that mainly served the white poor, welfare had come to be associated with blacks, who by 1970 accounted for nearly half the recipients. The AFDC rolls expanded rapidly during the 1960s, partly because the federal government relaxed eligibility standards. This arose from an increase in births to unmarried women, which produced a sharp rise in the number of poor female-headed households, and from an aggressive campaign by welfare rights groups to encourage people to apply for benefits. Conservative politicians now attacked

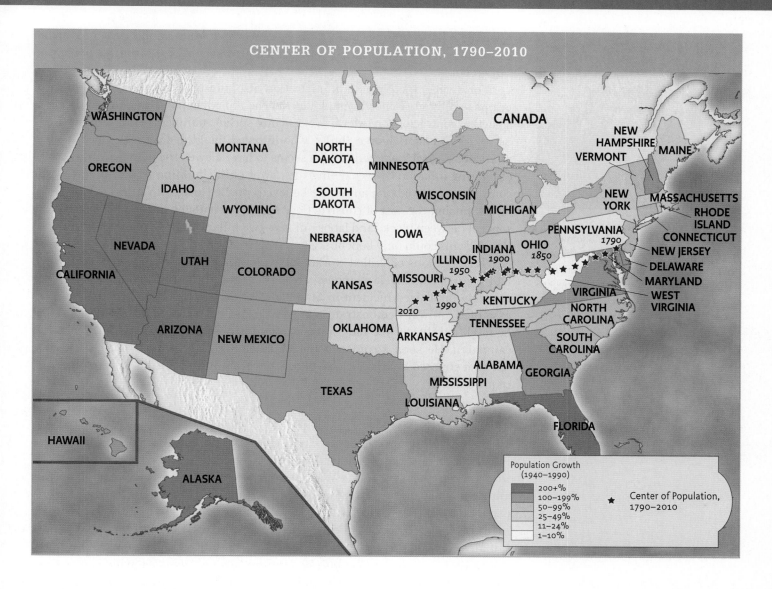

CENTER OF POPULATION, 1790–2010

recipients of welfare as people who preferred to live at the expense of honest taxpayers rather than by working.

A striking example of Nixon's willingness to break the political mold, his plan to replace welfare with a guaranteed annual income failed to win approval by Congress. It proved too radical for conservatives, who saw it as a reward for laziness, while liberals denounced the proposed level of $1,600 per year for a needy family of four as inadequate.

Nixon and Race

Nixon's racial policies offer a similarly mixed picture. To consolidate support in the white South, he nominated to the Supreme Court Clement Haynsworth and G. Harold Carswell, conservative southern jurists with records of support for segregation. Both were rejected by the Senate. On the other hand, because the courts finally lost patience with southern delaying tactics, extensive racial integration at last came

Richard Nixon (on the right) and former Alabama governor George Wallace at an "Honor America" celebration in February 1974. Nixon's "southern strategy" sought to woo Wallace's supporters into the Republican Party.

to public schools in the South. In Nixon's first three years in office, the proportion of southern black students attending integrated schools rose from 32 percent to 77 percent.

For a time, the Nixon administration also pursued "affirmative action" programs to upgrade minority employment. The Philadelphia Plan required that construction contractors on federal projects hire specific numbers of minority workers. Secretary of Labor George Shultz, who initiated the idea, sincerely hoped to open more jobs for black workers. Nixon seems to have viewed the plan mainly as a way of fighting inflation by weakening the power of the building trades unions. Their control over the labor market, he believed, pushed wages to unreasonably high levels, raising the cost of construction. And, he calculated, if the plan caused dissension between blacks and labor unions—two pillars of the Democratic coalition—Republicans could only benefit.

Trade unions of skilled workers like plumbers and electrical workers, which had virtually no black members, strongly opposed the Philadelphia Plan. After a widely publicized incident in May 1970, when a group of construction workers assaulted antiwar demonstrators in New York City, Nixon suddenly decided that he might be able to woo blue-collar workers in preparation for his 1972 reelection campaign. He soon abandoned the Philadelphia Plan in favor of an ineffective one that stressed voluntary local efforts toward minority hiring instead of federal requirements.

The Burger Court

When Earl Warren retired as chief justice in 1969, Nixon appointed Warren Burger, a federal court-of-appeals judge, to succeed him. An outspoken critic of the "judicial activism" of the Warren Court—its willingness to expand old rights and create new ones by overturning acts of Congress and the states—Burger was expected to lead the justices in a conservative direction. But like Nixon, he surprised many of his supporters. While the pace of change slowed, the Burger Court, at least initially, consolidated and expanded many of the judicial innovations of the 1960s.

In 1971, in *Swann v. Charlotte-Mecklenburg Board of Education*, which arose from North Carolina, the justices unanimously approved a lower court's plan that required the extensive transportation of students to achieve school integration. The decision led to hundreds of cases in which judges throughout the country ordered the use of busing as a tool to achieve integration. With many white parents determined to keep their children in neighborhood schools and others willing to move to the suburbs or enroll them in private academies to avoid integration, busing became a lightning rod for protests. One of the most bitter fights took place in Boston in the mid-1970s. Residents of the tightly knit Irish-American community of South Boston demonstrated vociferously and sometimes violently against a busing plan decreed by a local judge.

The Supreme Court soon abandoned the idea of overturning local control of schools, or moving students great distances to achieve integration. In 1973, it rebuffed a group of Texas Latinos who sued to overturn the use of property taxes to finance public education. Because of the great disparity in wealth between districts, spending on predominantly Mexican-American schools stood far below that for white ones. But in *San Antonio Independent School District v. Rodriguez*, a 5-4 Court

The school busing issue

San Antonio v. Rodriguez

majority ruled that the Constitution did not require equality of school funding. In the following year, in *Milliken v. Bradley* (1974), the justices overturned a lower court order that required Detroit's predominantly white suburbs to enter into a regional desegregation plan with the city's heavily minority school system. By absolving suburban districts of responsibility for assisting in integrating urban schools, the decision guaranteed that housing segregation would be mirrored in public education. Indeed, by the 1990s, public schools in the North were considerably more segregated than those in the South.

> Milliken v. Bradley

The Court and Affirmative Action

Efforts to promote greater employment opportunities for minorities also spawned politically divisive legal issues. Many whites came to view affirmative action programs as a form of "reverse discrimination." Even as affirmative action programs quickly spread from blacks to encompass women, Latinos, Asian-Americans, and Native Americans, conservatives demanded that the Supreme Court invalidate all such policies. The justices refused, but they found it difficult to devise a consistent approach to this politically charged issue.

In *Griggs v. Duke Power Company* (1971), the Court ruled that even racially neutral job requirements such as a written examination were illegal if they operated to exclude a disproportionate number of non-white applicants and were not directly related to job performance. Later in the decade, in *United Steelworkers of America v. Weber* (1979), it upheld a program devised by the Kaiser Aluminum & Chemical Corporation and its union that set quotas for training and hiring non-white workers in skilled jobs. Since this private, voluntary agreement did not involve government action, the Court ruled, it did not violate the Fourteenth Amendment's ban on state policies that discriminated among citizens.

The justices, however, proved increasingly hostile to governmental affirmative action policies. In *Regents of the University of California v. Bakke* (1978), the Court overturned an admissions program of the University of California at Davis, a public university, which set aside 16 of 100 places in the entering medical school class for minority students. Justice Lewis F. Powell, a Nixon appointee who cast the deciding vote in the 5-4 decision, rejected the idea of fixed affirmative action quotas. He added, however, that race could be used as one factor among many in admissions decisions, so affirmative action continued at most colleges and universities.

The Continuing Sexual Revolution

To the alarm of conservatives, during the 1970s the sexual revolution passed from the counterculture into the social mainstream. The number of Americans who told public-opinion polls that premarital sex was wrong plummeted. The number of divorces soared, reaching more than 1 million in 1975, double the number ten years earlier. The age at which both men and women married rose dramatically. The figure for divorces in 1975 exceeded the number of first-time marriages. A popular 1978 film, *An Unmarried Woman*, portrayed the dissolution of a marriage as a triumph for the wife, who discovered her potential for individual growth only after being abandoned

One result of the sexual revolution was a sharp rise in the age at which Americans chose to marry, and an increase in the number of divorces.

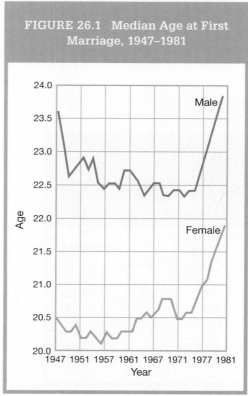

FIGURE 26.1 Median Age at First Marriage, 1947–1981

Daryl Koehn, of Kansas, celebrates in 1977 on learning that she has been chosen as one of the first group of women allowed to study at Oxford University as a Rhodes Scholar. Since their establishment in 1903, the scholarships had been limited to men.

The gay and lesbian movement

TABLE 26.1 Rate of Divorce: Divorces of Existing Marriages per 1,000 New Marriages, 1950–1980

YEAR	DIVORCES
1950	385
1955	377
1960	393
1965	479
1970	708
1975	1,036
1980	1,189

by her husband. As a result of women's changing aspirations and the availability of birth control and legal abortions, the American birthrate declined dramatically. By 1976, the average woman was bearing 1.7 children during her lifetime, less than half the figure of 1957 and below the level at which a population reproduces itself. A 1971 survey of the last five graduating classes at Bryn Mawr, an elite women's college, reported the birth of more than seventy children. A similar survey covering the classes of 1971 through 1975 found that only three had been born.

During the Nixon years, women made inroads into areas from which they had long been excluded. In 1972, Congress approved Title IX, which banned gender discrimination in higher education, and the Equal Credit Opportunity Act, which required that married women be given access to credit in their own name. The giant corporation American Telephone and Telegraph (AT&T) entered into a landmark agreement in which it agreed to pay millions of dollars to workers who had suffered gender discrimination and to upgrade employment opportunities for women. The number of women at work continued its upward climb. In 1960, only 20 percent of women with young children had been in the workforce. The figure reached 40 percent in 1980, and 55 percent in 1990. Working women were motivated by varied aims. Some sought careers in professions and skilled jobs previously open only to men. Others, spurred by the need to bolster family income as the economy faltered, flooded into the traditional, low-wage, "pink-collar" sector, working as cashiers, secretaries, and telephone operators.

In addition, the gay and lesbian movement, born at the end of the 1960s, expanded greatly during the 1970s and became a major concern of the right. In 1969, there had been about fifty local gay rights groups in the United States; ten years later, their numbers reached into the thousands. They began to elect local officials, persuaded many states to decriminalize homosexual relations, and succeeded in convincing cities with large gay populations to pass antidiscrimination laws. They actively encouraged gay men and lesbians to "come out of the closet"—that is, to reveal their sexual orientation. During the 1970s, the American Psychiatric Association removed homosexuality from its list of mental diseases.

As pre–World War I bohemians saw many of their ideas absorbed into the mass culture of the 1920s, values and styles of the 1960s became part of 1970s America, dubbed by the writer Tom Wolfe the "Me Decade." When asked in a Gallup poll to rate a series of ideas, respondents gave the highest ranking not to "following God's will," "high income," or "a sense of accomplishment," but to "freedom to choose." The demand of student protesters that individuals be empowered to determine their own "lifestyle" emerged in depoliticized form in Americans' obsession with self-improvement through fitness programs, health food diets, and new forms of psychological therapy.

Nixon and Détente

Just as domestic policies and social trends under Nixon disappointed conservatives, they viewed his foreign policy as dangerously "soft" on communism. To be sure, in the Third World, Nixon and Henry Kissinger, his national security adviser and secretary of state, continued their predecessors' policy of attempting to undermine governments deemed dangerous to American strategic or economic interests. Nixon funneled arms to dictatorial pro-American regimes in Iran, the Philippines, and South Africa. After Chile in 1970 elected socialist Salvador Allende as president, the CIA worked with his domestic opponents to destabilize the regime. On September 11, 1973, Allende was overthrown and killed in a military coup, which installed a bloody dictatorship under General Augusto Pinochet. Thousands of Allende backers, including a few Americans then in Chile, were tortured and murdered, and many others fled the country. The Nixon administration knew of the coup plans in advance but failed to warn Allende, and it continued to back Pinochet despite his brutal policies. Democracy did not return to Chile until the end of the 1980s.

The Allende affair

In his relations with the major communist powers, however, Nixon fundamentally altered Cold War policies. Nixon had launched his political career as a fierce and, critics charged, unscrupulous anticommunist. But in the language of foreign relations, he and Kissinger were "realists." They had more interest in power than ideology and preferred international stability to relentless conflict. Nixon also hoped that if relations with the Soviet Union improved, the Russians would influence North Vietnam to agree to an end to the Vietnam War on terms acceptable to the United States.

Nixon and Kissinger's "realist" foreign policy

Nixon realized that far from being part of a unified communist bloc, China had its own interests, different from those of the Soviet Union, and was destined to play a major role on the world stage. The policy of refusing to recognize China's communist government had reached a dead end. In 1971, Kissinger flew secretly to China, paving the way for Nixon's own astonishing public visit of February 1972. The trip led to the Beijing government's taking up China's seat at the United Nations, previously occupied by the exiled regime on Taiwan. Full diplomatic relations between the United States and the People's Republic of China were not established until 1979. But Nixon's visit sparked a dramatic increase in trade between the two countries.

Nixon in China

Richard Nixon at a banquet celebrating his visit to China in February 1972. To his right is Premier Chou En-lai.

Three months after his trip to Beijing, Nixon became the first American president to visit the Soviet Union, where he engaged in intense negotiations with his Soviet counterpart, Leonid Brezhnev. Out of this "summit" meeting came agreements for increased trade and two landmark arms-control treaties. SALT (named for the Strategic Arms Limitation Talks under way since 1969) froze each country's arsenal of intercontinental missiles capable of carrying nuclear warheads. The Anti–Ballistic Missile Treaty banned the development of systems designed to intercept incoming missiles, so that neither side would be tempted to attack the other without fearing devastating retaliation. Nixon and Brezhnev proclaimed a new era of "peaceful coexistence," in which "détente" (cooperation) would replace the hostility of the Cold War.

VIETNAM AND WATERGATE

Nixon and Vietnam

Despite Nixon's foreign policy triumphs, one issue would not go away—Vietnam. Nixon ran for president in 1968 declaring that he had a "secret plan" to end the war. On taking office, he announced a new policy, Vietnamization. Under this plan, American troops would gradually be withdrawn while South Vietnamese soldiers, backed by continued American bombing, did more and more of the fighting. But Vietnamization neither limited the war nor ended the antiwar movement. Hoping to cut North Vietnamese supply lines, Nixon in 1970 ordered American troops into neutral Cambodia. The invasion did not achieve its military goals, but it destabilized the Cambodian government and set in motion a chain of events that eventually brought to power the Khmer Rouge. Before being ousted by a Vietnamese invasion in 1979, this local communist movement attempted to force virtually all Cambodians into rural communes and committed widespread massacres in that unfortunate country.

The invasion of Cambodia and its consequences

As the war escalated, protests again spread on college campuses. In the wake of the killing of four antiwar protesters at Kent State University by the Ohio National Guard and two by police at Jackson State University in Mississippi, the student movement reached its high-water mark. In the spring of 1970, more than 350 colleges and universities experienced strikes, and troops occupied 21 campuses.

The protests at Kent State, a public university with a largely working-class student body, and Jackson State, a black institution, demonstrated how antiwar sentiment had spread far beyond elite campuses like Berkeley and Columbia.

At the same time, troop morale in Vietnam plummeted. Although all young men were subject to the draft, for most of the war college students received exemptions. As a result, the army was predominantly composed of working-class whites and members of racial minorities. Unlike in previous wars, blacks complained not about exclusion from the army but about the high number of black soldiers among the casualties.

The same social changes sweeping the home front were evident among troops in Vietnam. Soldiers experimented with drugs, openly wore peace and black-power symbols, refused orders, and even assaulted unpopular officers. In 1971, thousands deserted the army, while at home Vietnam veterans held antiwar demonstrations. The decline of discipline within the army convinced increasing numbers of high-ranking officers that the United States must extricate itself from Vietnam.

Public support for the war was rapidly waning. In 1969, the *New York Times* published details of the My Lai massacre of 1968, in which a company of American troops had killed some 350 South Vietnamese civilians. After a military investigation, one soldier, Lieutenant William Calley, was found guilty of directing the atrocity. (The courts released him from prison in

Tear gas envelops the campus as members of the Ohio National Guard prepare to fire on student demonstrators at Kent State University. Shortly after this photo was taken, four students lay dead.

1974.) In 1971, the *Times* began publishing the Pentagon Papers, a classified report prepared by the Defense Department that traced American involvement in Vietnam back to World War II and revealed how successive presidents had misled the American people about it. In a landmark freedom-of-the-press decision, the Supreme Court rejected Nixon's request for an injunction to halt publication. In 1973, Congress passed the War Powers Act. The most vigorous assertion of congressional control over foreign policy in the nation's history, it required the president to seek congressional approval for the commitment of American troops overseas.

In 1971, in one of the most dramatic demonstrations of the entire era, hundreds of veterans deposited on the steps of the Capitol medals they had received while fighting in Vietnam.

The End of the Vietnam War

Early in 1973, Nixon achieved what had eluded his predecessors—a negotiated settlement in Vietnam. The Paris peace agreement, the result of five years of talks, made possible the final withdrawal of American troops. The compromise left in place the government of South Vietnam, but it also left North Vietnamese and Viet Cong soldiers in control of parts of the South. American bombing ceased, and the military draft came to an end. Henceforth, volunteers would make up the armed forces. But the agreement did not solve the basic issue of the war—whether Vietnam would be one country or two. That question was answered in the spring of 1975, when the North Vietnamese launched a final military offensive. The government of South Vietnam collapsed; the United States did not intervene except to evacuate the American embassy, and Vietnam was reunified under communist rule.

The only war the United States has ever lost, Vietnam was a military, political, and social disaster. By the time it ended, 58,000 Americans had been killed, along with 3 million to 4 million Vietnamese. The war cost the United States many hundreds of millions of dollars and diverted funds from needs at home. But the nonmonetary price was far higher. Vietnam undermined Americans' confidence in their own institutions and challenged long-standing beliefs about the country and its purposes. The divisions caused by the war continued in debates over its legacy that persisted for many years. The war's supporters blamed critics at home for undermining a successful and winnable military effort. Others took the lesson that the United States should be extremely reluctant to commit its armed forces overseas—an outlook sometimes called the Vietnam Syndrome.

Two decades after the war ended, former secretary of defense Robert McNamara published a memoir in which he admitted that the policy he had helped to shape had been "terribly wrong." Ignorance of the history and culture of Vietnam and a misguided belief that every communist movement in the world was a puppet of Moscow, he wrote, had led the country into a war that he now profoundly

The consequences of the war

Buttons and flags for sale at a rally in the early 1970s illustrate the linkage of support for the Vietnam War and strong feelings of patriotism, building blocks of the new conservatism.

regretted. The *New York Times* rejected McNamara's apology. The "ghosts of those unlived lives," the young men sent to their death "for no purpose," it declared, could not so easily be wished away. But the *Times* itself, like the rest of the political establishment, had supported the war for most of its duration. For far too long, they had accepted its basic premise—that the United States had the right to decide the fate of a faraway people about whom it knew almost nothing.

Watergate

By the time the war ended, Richard Nixon was no longer president. His domestic policies and foreign policy successes had contributed greatly to his reelection in 1972. He won a landslide victory over liberal Democrat George McGovern, receiving 60 percent of the popular vote. Nixon made deep inroads into former Democratic strongholds in the South and among working-class white northerners. He carried every state but Massachusetts. But his triumph soon turned into disaster.

Nixon was obsessed with secrecy and could not accept honest difference of opinion. He viewed every critic as a threat to national security and developed an "enemies list" that included reporters, politicians, and celebrities unfriendly to the administration. When the Pentagon Papers were published, Nixon created a special investigative unit known as the "plumbers" to gather information about Daniel Ellsberg, the former government official who had leaked them to the press. The plumbers raided the office of Ellsberg's psychiatrist in search of incriminating records. In June 1972, five former employees of Nixon's reelection committee took part in a break-in at Democratic Party headquarters in the Watergate apartment complex in Washington, D.C. A security guard called police, who arrested the intruders.

No one knows precisely what the Watergate burglars were looking for (perhaps they intended to install listening devices), and the botched robbery played little role in the 1972 presidential campaign. But in 1973, Judge John J. Sirica, before whom the burglars were tried, determined to find out who had sponsored the break-in. A pair of *Washington Post* journalists began publishing investigative stories that made it clear that persons close to the president had ordered the burglary and then tried to "cover up" White House involvement. Congressional hearings followed that revealed a wider pattern of wiretapping, break-ins, and attempts to sabotage political opposition. When it became known that Nixon had made tape recordings of conversations in his office, Archibald Cox, a special prosecutor the president had reluctantly appointed to investigate the Watergate affair, demanded copies. In October 1973, Nixon proposed to allow Senator John C. Stennis of Mississippi

The Watergate hearings

to review the tapes, rather than releasing them. When Cox refused to agree, Nixon fired him, whereupon Attorney General Elliot Richardson resigned in protest. These events, known as the Saturday Night Massacre, further undermined Nixon's standing. The Supreme Court unanimously ordered Nixon to provide them—a decision that reaffirmed the principle that the president is not above the law.

Nixon's Fall

Week after week, revelations about the scandal unfolded. By mid-1974, it had become clear that whether or not Nixon knew in advance of the Watergate break-in, he had become involved immediately afterward in authorizing payments to the burglars to remain silent or commit perjury, and he had ordered the FBI to halt its investigation of the crime. In August 1974, the House Judiciary Committee voted to recommend that Nixon be impeached for conspiracy to obstruct justice. His political support having evaporated, Nixon became the only president in history to resign.

> *Nixon's resignation*

Nixon's presidency remains a classic example of the abuse of political power. In 1973, his vice president, Spiro T. Agnew, resigned after revelations that he had accepted bribes from construction firms while serving as governor of Maryland. Nixon's attorney general, John Mitchell, and White House aides H. R. Haldeman and John Ehrlichman were convicted of obstruction of justice in the Watergate affair and went to jail. As for the president, he insisted that he had done nothing wrong—or at any rate, that previous presidents had also been guilty of lying and illegality.

Although it hardly excused his behavior, Nixon had a point. His departure from office was followed by Senate hearings headed by Frank Church of Idaho that laid bare a history of abusive actions that involved every administration since the beginning of the Cold War. In violation of the law, the FBI had spied on millions of Americans and had tried to disrupt the civil rights movement. The CIA had conducted secret operations to overthrow foreign governments and had tried to assassinate foreign leaders. It had even recruited a secret army to fight in Laos, a neighbor of Vietnam. Abuses of power, in other words, went far beyond the misdeeds of a single president.

Herbert Block's 1973 cartoon depicts Americans' disbelief as revelations related to the Watergate scandal unfolded in Washington.

Along with Watergate, the Pentagon Papers, and the Vietnam War itself, the Church Committee revelations seriously undermined Americans' confidence in their own government. They led Congress to enact new restrictions on the power of the FBI and CIA to spy on American citizens or conduct operations abroad without the knowledge of lawmakers. Congress also strengthened the Freedom of Information Act (FOIA), initially enacted in 1966. Since 1974, the FOIA has allowed scholars, journalists, and ordinary citizens to gain access to millions of pages of records of federal agencies.

Liberals, who had despised Nixon throughout his career, celebrated his downfall. They did not realize that the revulsion against Watergate undermined the foundations of liberalism itself, already weakened by the divisions of the 1960s. For liberalism rests, in part, on belief in the ability of government, especially the federal government, to solve social problems and promote both the public good and individual freedom. Nixon's fall and the revelations of years of governmental misconduct helped to convince many Americans that conservatives were correct

when they argued that to protect liberty it was necessary to limit Washington's power over Americans' lives. The Watergate crisis also distracted attention from the economic crisis that began in the fall of 1973. Its inability to fashion a response to this crisis, which gripped the United States for much of the 1970s, dealt liberalism yet another blow.

THE END OF THE GOLDEN AGE

The Decline of Manufacturing

During the 1970s, the long period of postwar economic expansion and consumer prosperity came to an end, succeeded by slow growth and high inflation. For the only time in the twentieth century, other than the 1930s, the average American ended the 1970s poorer than when the decade began. There were many reasons for the end of capitalism's "golden age." With American prosperity seemingly unassailable and the military-industrial complex thriving, successive administrations had devoted little attention to the less positive economic consequences of the Cold War. To strengthen its anticommunist allies, the United States promoted the industrial reconstruction of Japan and Germany and the emergence of new centers of manufacturing in places like South Korea and Taiwan. It encouraged American companies to invest in overseas plants and did not complain when allies protected their own industries while seeking unrestricted access to the American market. Imports of foreign steel, for example, led to growing problems for this key industry at home. The strong dollar, linked to gold by the Bretton Woods agreement of 1944, made it harder to sell American goods overseas (discussed in Chapter 22).

Economic weakness

In 1971, for the first time in the twentieth century, the United States experienced a merchandise trade deficit—that is, it imported more goods than it exported. By 1980, nearly three-quarters of goods produced in the United States were competing with foreign-made products and the number of manufacturing workers, 38 percent of the American workforce in 1960, had fallen to 28 percent.

In 1971, Nixon announced the most radical change in economic policy since the Great Depression. He took the United States off the gold standard, ending the Bretton Woods agreement that fixed the value of the dollar and other currencies in terms of gold. Henceforth, the world's currencies would "float" in relation to one another, their worth determined not by treaty but by international currency markets. Nixon hoped that lowering the dollar's value in terms of the German mark and Japanese yen would promote exports by making American goods cheaper overseas and reduce imports since foreign products would be more expensive in the United States. But the end of fixed currency rates injected a new element of instability into the world economy. Nixon also ordered wages and prices frozen for ninety days.

Currency values and trade

Stagflation

These policies temporarily curtailed inflation and reduced imports. But in 1973, a brief war broke out between Israel and its neighbors Egypt and Syria. Middle Eastern Arab states retaliated for Western support of Israel by quadrupling the price of oil and suspending the export of oil to the United States for several months. Long lines of cars appeared at American gas stations, which either ran out of fuel or limited how much a customer could buy. A second "oil shock" occurred in 1979 as a result of the revolution that overthrew the shah of Iran, discussed later.

Because the rapidly growing demand for fuel by cars and factories outstripped domestic supplies, by 1973 the United States imported one-third of its oil. Europe and Japan depended even more heavily on oil imports. To promote energy conservation, Congress lowered the speed limit on interstate highways to fifty-five miles per hour, and many public buildings reduced heat and lighting.

The energy crisis of the 1970s drew increased attention to domestic energy resources like oil, coal, and natural gas. While the rest of the economy stagnated, western energy production grew apace. Oil was discovered in Alaska in 1968, and in 1977 a pipeline opened to facilitate its shipment to the rest of the country. Coal production in Wyoming boomed. Western energy companies benefited from the high oil prices set by OPEC—the Organization of Petroleum Exporting Countries.

But rising oil prices rippled through the world economy, contributing to the combination of stagnant economic growth and high inflation known as "stagflation." Between 1973 and 1981, the rate of inflation in developed countries was 10 percent per year, and the rate of economic growth only 2.4 percent, a sharp deterioration from the economic conditions of the 1960s. The so-called misery index—the sum of the unemployment and inflation rates—stood at 10.8 when the decade began. By 1980, it had almost doubled. As oil prices rose, many Americans shifted from large domestically produced cars, known for high gasoline consumption, to smaller, more fuel-efficient imports. By the end of the decade, Japan had become the world's leading automobile producer, and imports accounted for nearly 25 percent of car sales in the United States.

Drivers lining up to purchase gas during the oil crisis of 1973–1974.

The Beleaguered Social Compact

The economic crisis contributed to a breakdown of the postwar social compact. Faced with declining profits and rising overseas competition, corporations stepped up the trend,

	TABLE 26.2 The Misery Index, 1970–1980		
YEAR	RATE OF INFLATION (%)	RATE OF UNEMPLOYMENT (%)	MISERY INDEX (%)
1970	5.9	4.9	10.8
1971	4.3	5.9	10.2
1972	3.3	5.6	8.9
1973	6.2	4.9	11.1
1974	11.0	5.6	16.6
1975	9.1	8.5	17.6
1976	5.8	7.7	13.5
1977	6.5	7.1	13.6
1978	7.7	6.1	13.8
1979	11.3	5.8	17.1
1980	13.5	7.1	20.6

The World Trade Center under construction in New York City in the 1970s.

Because of economic dislocations and deindustrialization, Americans' real wages (wages adjusted to take account of inflation) peaked in the early 1970s and then began a sharp, prolonged decline.

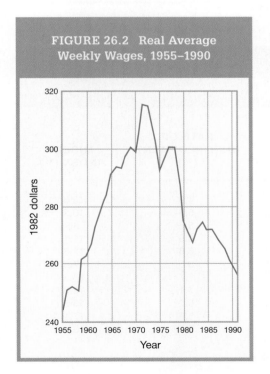

FIGURE 26.2 Real Average Weekly Wages, 1955–1990

already under way before 1970, toward eliminating well-paid manufacturing jobs through automation and shifting production to low-wage areas of the United States and overseas. The effects on older industrial cities were devastating. By 1980, Detroit and Chicago had lost more than half the manufacturing jobs that had existed three decades earlier.

Smaller industrial cities suffered even sharper declines. As their tax bases shriveled, many found themselves unable to maintain public services. In Paterson, New Jersey, where great silk factories had arisen in the early twentieth century, deindustrialization left a landscape of abandoned manufacturing plants. The poverty rate reached 20 percent, the city sold off public library buildings to raise cash, and the schools became so run down and overcrowded that the state government took control. The accelerating flow of jobs, investment, and population to the nonunion, low-wage states of the Sunbelt increased the political influence of this conservative region. Of population growth in metropolitan areas, during the 1970s, 96 percent occurred in the South and West. San Jose and Phoenix, with populations around 100,000 in 1950, neared 1 million by 1990.

In some manufacturing centers, political and economic leaders welcomed the opportunity to remake their cities as finance, information, and entertainment hubs. In New York, the construction of the World Trade Center, completed in 1977, symbolized this shift in the economy. Until destroyed by terrorists twenty-four years later, the 110-story "twin towers" stood as a symbol of New York's grandeur. But to make way for the World Trade Center, the city displaced hundreds of small electronics, printing, and other firms, causing the loss of thousands of manufacturing jobs.

Labor on the Defensive

Always a junior partner in the Democratic coalition, the labor movement found itself forced onto the defensive. It has remained there ever since. One example of the weakening of unions' power came in 1975 with the New York City fiscal crisis. Deeply in debt and unable to market its bonds, the city faced the prospect of bankruptcy. The solution to the crisis required a reduction of the city's workforce, severe cuts in the budgets of schools, parks, and the subway system, and an end to the century-old policy of free tuition at the City University. Even in this center of unionism, working-class New Yorkers had no choice but to absorb job losses and a drastic decline in public services.

The weakening of unions and the continuation of the economy's long-term shift from manufacturing to service employment had an adverse impact on ordinary Americans. Between 1953 and 1973, median family income had doubled. But beginning in 1973, real wages essentially did not rise for twenty years. The 1970s was one of only two decades in the twentieth century (the other being the 1930s) that ended with Americans on average poorer than when it began. The popular song "The River," by Bruce Springsteen, captured the woes of blue-collar workers: "Is a dream a lie if it don't come true / Or is it something worse?"

Ford as President

Economic problems dogged the presidencies of Nixon's successors. Gerald Ford, who had been appointed to replace Vice President Agnew, succeeded to the White House when Nixon resigned. Ford named Nelson Rockefeller of New York as his own vice president. Thus, for the only time in American history, both offices were occupied by persons for whom no one had actually voted. Among his first acts as president, Ford pardoned Nixon, shielding him from prosecution for obstruction of justice. Ford claimed that he wanted the country to put the Watergate scandal behind it. But the pardon proved to be widely unpopular.

In domestic policy, Ford's presidency lacked significant accomplishment. Ford and his chief economic adviser, Alan Greenspan, believed that Americans spent too much on consumption and saved too little, leaving business with insufficient money for investment. They called for cutting taxes on business and lessening government regulation of the economy. But the Democratic majority in Congress was in no mood to accept these traditional Republican policies. To combat inflation, Ford urged Americans to shop wisely, reduce expenditures, and wear WIN buttons (for "Whip Inflation Now"). Although inflation fell, joblessness continued to rise. During the steep recession of 1974–1975 unemployment exceeded 9 percent, the highest level since the Depression.

In the international arena, 1975 witnessed the major achievement of Ford's presidency. In a continuation of Nixon's policy of détente, the United States and Soviet Union signed an agreement at Helsinki, Finland, that recognized the permanence of Europe's post–World War II boundaries (including the division of Germany). In addition, both superpowers agreed to respect the basic liberties of their citizens. Secretary of State Kissinger and his Soviet counterpart, Andrey Gromyko, assumed that this latter pledge would have little practical effect. But over time, the Helsinki Accords inspired movements for greater freedom within the communist countries of eastern Europe.

President Gerald Ford tried to enlist Americans in his "Whip Inflation Now" program. It did not succeed.

The Carter Administration

In the presidential election of 1976, Jimmy Carter, a former governor of Georgia, narrowly defeated Ford. A graduate of the U.S. Naval Academy who later became a peanut farmer, Carter was virtually unknown outside his state when he launched his campaign for the Democratic nomination. But realizing that Watergate and Vietnam had produced a crisis in confidence in the federal government, he turned his obscurity into an advantage. Carter ran for president as an "outsider," making a virtue of the fact that he had never held federal office. A devout "born-again" Baptist, he spoke openly of his religious convictions. His promise, "I'll never lie to you," resonated with an electorate tired of official dishonesty.

Carter had much in common with Progressives of the early twentieth century. His passions were making government more efficient, protecting the environment, and raising the moral tone of politics. Unlike the Progressives, however,

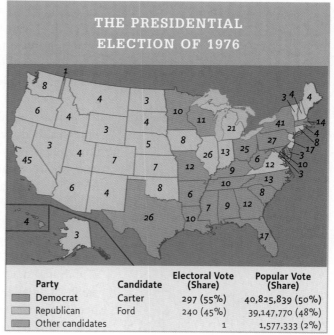

THE PRESIDENTIAL ELECTION OF 1976

Party	Candidate	Electoral Vote (Share)	Popular Vote (Share)
Democrat	Carter	297 (55%)	40,825,839 (50%)
Republican	Ford	240 (45%)	39,147,770 (48%)
Other candidates		1	1,577,333 (2%)

The deregulation of the airline industry produced lower fares but also a drastic decline in service. Before deregulation, with prices fixed, airlines sought to attract customers by providing good service in all classes. Today, fares are low, but passengers are jammed in like sardines and have to pay for checked baggage, onboard meals, and other amenities.

Three Mile Island

he embraced the aspirations of black Americans. As president, Carter appointed an unprecedented number of blacks to important positions, including Andrew Young, a former lieutenant of Martin Luther King Jr., as ambassador to the United Nations.

Carter and the Economic Crisis

The Democratic party found itself ill-equipped to deal with the economic crisis. The social upheavals of the 1960s had led to the emergence of politicians known as the New Democrats. Representing affluent urban and suburban districts, they viewed issues like race relations, gender equality, the environment, and improving the political process as more central than traditional economic matters. Although his party controlled both houses, Carter often found himself at odds with Congress. He viewed inflation, not unemployment, as the country's main economic problem, and to combat it he promoted cuts in spending on domestic programs. In the hope that increased competition would reduce prices, his administration deregulated the trucking and airline industries. Anticipating what would come to be called the supply-side economics of the Reagan administration, Carter in 1978 inaugurated tax cuts for wealthier Americans in the hope that this would stimulate investment and encourage economic growth. In 1980, with Carter's approval, Congress repealed usury laws—laws that limit how much interest lenders can charge—allowing credit card companies to push their interest rates up to 20 percent or even higher. Carter supported the Federal Reserve Bank's decision to raise interest rates to curtail economic activity until both wages and prices fell, traditionally a Republican policy. But oil prices kept rising, thanks to the overthrow of the shah of Iran, discussed later, and inflation did not decline.

Carter also believed that expanded use of nuclear energy could help reduce dependence on imported oil. For years, proponents of nuclear power had hailed it as an inexpensive way of meeting the country's energy needs. By the time Carter took office, more than 200 nuclear plants were operating or on order. But in 1979 the industry suffered a near-fatal blow when an accident at the Three Mile Island plant in Pennsylvania released a large amount of radioactive steam into the atmosphere. The rise of the environmental movement had promoted public skepticism about scientific experts who touted the miraculous promise of technological innovations without concern for their social consequences. The Three Mile Island mishap reinforced fears about the environmental hazards associated with nuclear energy and put a halt to the industry's expansion.

Since the New Deal, Democrats had presented themselves as the party of affluence and economic growth. But Carter seemed to be presiding over a period of national decline. It did not help his popularity when, in a speech in 1979, he spoke of a national "crisis of confidence" and seemed to blame it on the American people themselves and their "mistaken idea of freedom" as "self-indulgence and consumption."

The 1979 accident at the Three Mile Island nuclear plant in Pennsylvania brought a halt to the industry's expansion.

The Emergence of Human Rights Politics

Under Carter, a commitment to promoting human rights became a centerpiece of American foreign policy for the first time. He was influenced by the proliferation of information about global denials of human rights spread by nongovernmental agencies like Amnesty International and the International League for Human Rights. The American membership of Amnesty International, a London-based organization, grew from 6,000 to 35,000 between 1970 and 1976. Its reports marked a significant break with dominant ideas about international affairs since World War II, which had viewed the basic division in the world as between communist and noncommunist countries. Such reports, along with congressional hearings, fact-finding missions, and academic studies of human rights, exposed misdeeds not only by communist countries but also by American allies, especially the death squads of Latin American dictatorships. Amnesty International pressured the United States to try to do something to promote human rights abroad. In 1977, Amnesty International received the Nobel Peace Prize, an indication of the rapid emergence of human rights as an international issue.

Amnesty International

In 1978, Carter cut off aid to the brutal military dictatorship governing Argentina, which in the name of anticommunism had launched a "dirty war" against its own citizens, kidnapping off the streets and secretly murdering an estimated 10,000 to 30,000 persons. Carter's action was a dramatic gesture, as Argentina was one of the most important powers in Latin America and previous American administrations had turned a blind eye to human rights abuses by Cold War allies. By the end of his presidency, the phrase "human rights" had acquired political potency. Its very vagueness was both a weakness and a strength. It was difficult to define exactly what rights should and should not be considered universally applicable, but various groups could and did unite under the umbrella of global human rights.

Carter's human rights foreign policy

President Jimmy Carter *(center)*, Egyptian president Anwar Sadat *(left)*, and Israeli prime minister Menachem Begin *(right)* celebrating the signing of the 1979 peace treaty between Israel and Egypt.

Carter's effectiveness

Carter believed that in the post-Vietnam era, American foreign policy should de-emphasize Cold War thinking. Combating poverty in the Third World, preventing the spread of nuclear weapons, and promoting human rights should take priority over what he called "the inordinate fear of communism that once led us to embrace any dictator who joined us in that fear." In one of his first acts as president, he offered an unconditional pardon to Vietnam-era draft resisters. In a 1977 address, he insisted that foreign policy could not be separated from "questions of justice, equity, and human rights."

Carter's emphasis on pursuing peaceful solutions to international problems and his willingness to think outside the Cold War framework yielded important results. In 1979, he brought the leaders of Egypt and Israel to the presidential retreat at Camp David and brokered a historic peace agreement between the two countries. He improved American relations with Latin America by agreeing to a treaty, ratified by the Senate in 1978, that provided for the transfer of the Panama Canal to local control by the year 2000. In 1979, he resisted calls for intervention when a popular revolution led by the left-wing Sandinista movement overthrew Nicaraguan dictator Anastasio Somoza, a longtime ally of the United States. Carter attempted to curb the murderous violence of death squads allied to the right-wing government of El Salvador, and in 1980 he suspended military aid after the murder of four American nuns by members of the country's army. He signed the SALT II agreement with the Soviets, which reduced the number of missiles, bombers, and nuclear warheads.

Both conservative Cold Warriors and foreign policy "realists" severely criticized Carter's emphasis on human rights. He himself found it impossible to translate rhetoric into action. He criticized American arms sales to the rest of the world. But with thousands of jobs and billions of dollars in corporate profits at stake, he did nothing to curtail them. The United States continued its support of allies with records of serious human rights violations such as the governments of Guatemala, the Philippines, South Korea, and Iran. Indeed, the American connection with the shah of Iran, whose secret police regularly jailed and tortured political opponents, proved to be Carter's undoing.

The Iran Crisis and Afghanistan

Occupying a strategic location on the southern border of the Soviet Union, Iran was a major supplier of oil and an importer of American military equipment. At the end of 1977, Carter traveled there to help celebrate the shah's rule, causing the internal opposition to become more and more anti-American. Early in 1979, a popular revolution inspired by the exiled Muslim cleric Ayatollah Khomeini overthrew the shah and declared Iran an Islamic republic.

The Iranian revolution marked an ideological shift in opposition movements in the Middle East from socialism and Arab nationalism to religious fundamentalism. This would have important long-term consequences for the United States. More immediately, when Carter in November 1979 allowed the deposed shah to seek medical treatment in the United States, Khomeini's followers invaded the American embassy in Tehran and seized sixty-six hostages. Fourteen people (which included women, African-American men, and a white man in ill health) were soon released, leaving fifty-two captives. They did not regain their freedom until January 1981, on the day Carter's term as president ended. Events in Iran made Carter seem helpless and inept and led to a rapid fall in his popularity.

American hostages being paraded by their Iranian captors on the first day of the occupation of the American embassy in Tehran in 1979. Television gave extensive coverage to the plight of the hostages, leading many Americans to view the Carter administration as weak and inept.

Another crisis that began in 1979 undermined American relations with Moscow. At the end of that year, the Soviet Union sent thousands of troops into Afghanistan to support a friendly government threatened by an Islamic rebellion. In the long run, Afghanistan became the Soviet Vietnam, an unwinnable conflict whose mounting casualties seriously weakened the government at home. Initially, however, it seemed another example of declining American power.

Declaring the invasion the greatest crisis since World War II (a considerable exaggeration), the president announced the Carter Doctrine, declaring that the United States would use military force, if necessary, to protect its interests in the Persian Gulf. He placed an embargo on grain exports to the Soviet Union and organized a Western boycott of the 1980 Olympics, which took place in Moscow. He withdrew the SALT II treaty from consideration by the Senate and dramatically increased American military spending. In a reversion to the Cold War principle that any opponent of the Soviet Union deserved American support, the United States funneled aid to fundamentalist Muslims in Afghanistan who fought a decade-long guerrilla war against the Soviets. The alliance had unforeseen consequences. A faction of Islamic fundamentalists known as the Taliban eventually came to power in Afghanistan. Tragically, they would prove as hostile to the United States as to Moscow.

Actions in Afghanistan

In an unsuccessful attempt to bring down inflation, Carter had abandoned the Keynesian economic policy of increased government spending to combat recession in favor of high interest rates. He had cut back on social spending and the federal government's economic regulations, while projecting a major increase in the military budget. By 1980, détente had been eclipsed and the Cold War reinvigorated. Thus, many of the conservative policies associated with his successor, Ronald Reagan, were already in place when Carter's presidency ended.

THE RISING TIDE OF CONSERVATISM

The combination of domestic and international dislocations during the 1970s created a widespread sense of anxiety among Americans and offered conservatives new political opportunities. Economic problems heightened the appeal of lower taxes, reduced government regulation, and cuts in social spending to spur business investment. Fears about a decline of American power in the world led to calls for a renewal of the Cold War. The civil rights and sexual revolutions produced resentments that undermined the Democratic coalition. Rising urban crime rates reinforced demands for law and order and attacks on courts considered too lenient toward criminals. These issues brought new converts to the conservative cause.

As the 1970s went on, conservatives abandoned overt opposition to the black struggle for racial justice. The fiery rhetoric and direct confrontation tactics of Bull Connor, George Wallace, and other proponents of massive resistance were succeeded by appeals to freedom of association, local control, and resistance to the power of the federal government. This language of individual freedom resonated throughout the country, appealing especially to the growing, predominantly white, suburban population that was fleeing the cities and their urban problems. The suburbs would become one of the bastions of modern conservatism.

But it was not just a reaction to the 1960s and the spread of conservative ideas that nourished the movement. Like predecessors as diverse as the civil rights and labor movements, conservatives organized at the grass roots. In order to spread conservative doctrines, they ran candidates for office even when they had little chance of winning, and worked to change the policies of local institutions like school boards, town councils, and planning commissions.

One set of recruits was the "neoconservatives," a group of intellectuals who charged that the 1960s had produced a decline in moral standards and respect for authority. Once supporters of liberalism, they had come to believe that even well-intentioned government social programs did more harm than good. Welfare, for example, not only failed to alleviate poverty but also encouraged single motherhood and undermined the work ethic. High taxes and expensive government regulations drained resources from productive enterprises, stifling economic growth. Neoconservatives repudiated the attempts by Nixon, Ford, and Carter to reorient foreign policy away from the Cold War. Carter's focus on human rights and alleged blindness to the Soviet threat, they argued, endangered the "survival of freedom." Conservative "think tanks" created during the 1970s, like the Heritage Foundation and the American Enterprise Institute, refined and spread these ideas.

The Religious Right

The rise of religious fundamentalism during the 1970s expanded conservatism's popular base. Challenged by the secular and material concerns of American society, some denominations tried to bring religion into harmony with these interests; others reasserted more traditional religious values. The latter approach seemed to appeal to growing numbers of Americans. Even as membership in mainstream denominations like Episcopalianism and Presbyterianism declined, evangelical Protestantism flourished. Some observers spoke of a Third Great Awakening (like

Issues for conservatives

Conservatives and freedom

Neoconservatives

those of the 1740s and early nineteenth century). The election of Carter, the first "born-again" Christian to become president, highlighted the growing influence of evangelical religion. But unlike Carter, most fundamentalists who entered politics did so as conservatives.

Of course, there was nothing new about the involvement of churches in political life. There is a long tradition in American history of moral stewardship—devout Christians taking on responsibility for social reform and using political means to combat what they perceive as individual or collective sins. During the 1960s, many members of the burgeoning evangelical churches of the suburbs, South, and West had become more and more alienated from a culture that seemed to them to trivialize religion and promote immorality. Evangelicals of different denominations increasingly came to feel that they had more in common with each other than with more liberal coreligionists. They demanded the reversal of Supreme Court decisions banning prayer in public schools, protecting pornography as free speech, and legalizing abortion. Although it spoke of restoring traditional values, the Religious Right proved remarkably adept at using modern technology, including mass mailings and televised religious programming, to raise funds for their crusade and spread their message. In 1979, Jerry Falwell, a Virginia minister, created the self-styled Moral Majority, devoted to waging a "war against sin" and electing "pro-life, pro-family, pro-America" candidates to office. Falwell identified supporters of abortion rights, easy divorce, and "military unpreparedness" as the forces of Satan, who sought to undermine God's "special plans for this great, free country of ours."

Christian conservatives seemed most agitated by the ongoing sexual revolution, which they saw as undermining the traditional family and promoting immorality. As a result of the 1960s, they believed, American freedom was out of control. The growing assertiveness of the new gay movement spurred an especially fierce reaction. In 1977, after a campaign led by the popular singer Anita Bryant, a familiar fixture in televised orange juice commercials, Dade County, Florida, passed an anti-gay ordinance under the banner "Save Our Children."

The Battle over the Equal Rights Amendment

During the 1970s, "family values" moved to the center of conservative politics, nowhere more so than in the battle over the Equal Rights Amendment (ERA). Originally proposed during the 1920s by Alice Paul and the Women's Party, the ERA

Phyllis Schlafly Campaigning against the Equal Rights Amendment. The activist Phyllis Schlafly, pictured here leading a rally at the Illinois State Capitol in 1978, was instrumental in grassroots organization of conservative men and women in opposition to the proposed Equal Rights Amendment to the Constitution, which would have barred all legal inequalities based on sex. She claimed that the amendment would take away "the right to be a housewife." The amendment's defeat was a major victory for the conservative movement.

Doug Marlette's cartoon comments on the continuing gap in pay between men and women, the kind of inequality that inspired support for the proposed Equal Rights Amendment.

had been revived by second-wave feminists. In the wake of the rights revolution, the amendment's affirmation that "equality of rights under the law" could not be abridged "on account of sex" hardly seemed controversial. In 1972, with broad bipartisan support, Congress approved the ERA and sent it to the states for ratification. Designed to eliminate obstacles to the full participation of women in public life, it aroused unexpected protest from those who claimed it would discredit the role of wife and homemaker.

The ERA debate reflected a division among women as much as a battle of the sexes. To its supporters, the amendment offered a guarantee of women's freedom in the public sphere. To its foes, freedom for women still resided in the divinely appointed roles of wife and mother. Phyllis Schlafly, who helped to organize opposition to the ERA, insisted that the "free enterprise system" was the "real liberator of women," since labor-saving home appliances offered more genuine freedom than "whining about past injustices" or seeking fulfillment outside the home. Opponents claimed that the ERA would let men "off the hook" by denying their responsibility to provide for their wives and children. Polls consistently showed that a majority of Americans, male and female, favored the ERA. But thanks to the mobilization of conservative women, the amendment failed to achieve ratification by the required thirty-eight states.

Women divided

The Abortion Controversy

An even more bitter battle emerged in the 1970s over abortion rights, another example, to conservatives, of how liberals in office promoted sexual immorality at the expense of moral values. The movement to reverse the 1973 *Roe v. Wade* decision began among Roman Catholics, whose church condemned abortion under any circumstances. But it soon enlisted evangelical Protestants and social conservatives more generally. Life, the movement insisted, begins at conception, and abortion is

A 1979 anti-abortion rally in Washington, D.C., on the sixth anniversary of the Supreme Court's decision in *Roe v. Wade*, which barred states from limiting a woman's right to terminate a pregnancy.

nothing less than murder. Between this position and the feminist insistence that a woman's right to control her body includes the right to a safe, legal abortion, compromise was impossible. Ironically, both sides showed how the rights revolution had reshaped the language of politics. Defenders of abortion exalted "the right to choose" as the essence of freedom. Opponents called themselves the "right to life" movement and claimed to represent the rights of the "unborn child."

The abortion issue drew a bitter, sometimes violent line through American politics. It affected battles over nominees to judicial positions and led to demonstrations at family-planning and abortion clinics. The anti-abortion movement won its first victory in 1976 when Congress, over President Ford's veto, ended federal funding for abortions for poor women through the Medicaid program. By the 1990s, a few fringe anti-abortion activists were placing bombs at medical clinics and murdering doctors who terminated pregnancies. To the end of the century, most women would continue to have the legal right of access to abortion. But in many areas the procedure became more and more difficult to obtain as hospitals and doctors stopped providing it.

Women demonstrating in support for abortion rights.

The Tax Revolt

With liberals unable to devise an effective policy to counteract deindustrialization and declining real wages, economic anxieties also created a growing constituency for conservative economics. Unlike during the Great Depression, economic distress inspired a critique of government rather than of business. New environmental regulations led to calls for less government intervention in the economy. These were most strident in the West, where measures to protect the environment threatened irrigation projects and private access to public lands. But everywhere, the economy's descent from affluence to "stagflation" increased the appeal of the

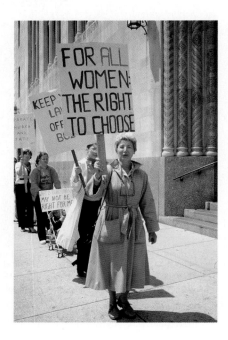

conservative argument that government regulation raised business costs and eliminated jobs.

Economic decline also broadened the constituency receptive to demands for lower taxes. To conservatives, tax reductions served the dual purpose of enhancing business profits and reducing the resources available to government, thus making new social programs financially impossible.

California's Proposition 13

In 1978, conservatives sponsored and California voters approved Proposition 13, a ban on further increases in property taxes. The vote demonstrated that the level of taxation could be a powerful political issue. Proposition 13 proved to be a windfall for businesses and home owners, while reducing funds available for schools, libraries, and other public services. Many voters, however, proved willing to accept this result of lower taxes. As anti-tax sentiment flourished throughout the country, many states followed California's lead.

Sagebrush Rebellion

A parallel upsurge of grassroots conservatism was reflected in the Sagebrush Rebellion (the name given to a bill passed by the Nevada legislature in 1979). Using the language of freedom from government tyranny, leaders in western states denounced control of large areas of land by the Bureau of Land Management in Washington, D.C., and insisted that the states themselves be given decision-making power over issues like grazing rights, mining development, and whether public lands should be closed to fishing and hunting. With the federal government reluctant to give up control over public lands in the West, the Sagebrush Rebellion had few concrete accomplishments, but it underscored the rising tide of antigovernment sentiment.

The Election of 1980

By 1980, Carter's approval rating had fallen to 21 percent—lower than Nixon's at the time of his resignation. A conservative tide seemed to be rising throughout the Western world. In 1979, Margaret Thatcher became prime minister of Great Britain. She promised to restore economic competitiveness by curtailing the power of unions, reducing taxes, selling state-owned industries to private owners, and cutting back the welfare state. In the United States, Ronald Reagan's 1980 campaign for the presidency brought together the many strands of 1970s conservatism. He pledged to end stagflation and restore the country's dominant role in the world and its confidence in itself. "Let's make America great again," he proclaimed. "The era of self-doubt is over."

Reagan also appealed skillfully to "white backlash." He kicked off his campaign in Philadelphia, Mississippi, where three civil rights workers had been murdered in 1964, with a speech emphasizing his belief in states' rights. Many white southerners understood this doctrine as including opposition to federal intervention on behalf of civil rights. During the campaign, Reagan repeatedly condemned welfare "cheats," school busing, and affirmative action. The Republican platform reversed the party's long-standing support for the Equal Rights Amendment and condemned moral permissiveness. Although not personally religious and the first divorced man

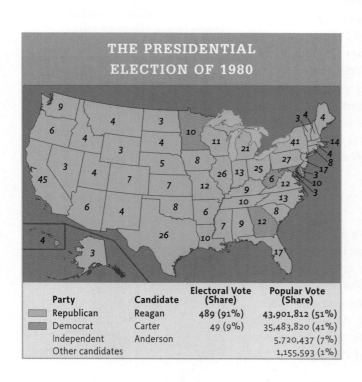

THE PRESIDENTIAL ELECTION OF 1980

	Party	Candidate	Electoral Vote (Share)	Popular Vote (Share)
	Republican	Reagan	489 (91%)	43,901,812 (51%)
	Democrat	Carter	49 (9%)	35,483,820 (41%)
	Independent	Anderson		5,720,437 (7%)
	Other candidates			1,155,593 (1%)

to run for president, Reagan won the support of the Religious Right and conservative upholders of "family values."

Riding a wave of dissatisfaction with the country's condition, Reagan swept into the White House. He carried such Democratic strongholds as Illinois, Texas, and New York. Because moderate Republican John Anderson, running for president as an independent, received about 7 percent of the popular vote, Reagan won only a bare majority, although he commanded a substantial margin in the electoral college. Carter received 41 percent, a humiliating defeat for a sitting president.

Jimmy Carter's reputation improved after he left the White House. He went to work for Habitat for Humanity, an organization that constructs homes for poor families. In the 1990s, he negotiated a cease-fire between warring Muslim and Serb forces in Bosnia and arranged a peaceful transfer of power from the military to an elected government in Haiti. In 2002, Carter was awarded the Nobel Peace Prize. His presidency, however, is almost universally considered a failure. And his defeat in 1980 launched the Reagan Revolution, which completed the transformation of freedom from the rallying cry of the left to a possession of the right.

A delegate to the Republican national convention of 1980 wears a hat festooned with the flags of the United States and Texas, and a button with a picture of her hero, Ronald Reagan.

THE REAGAN REVOLUTION

Ronald Reagan followed a most unusual path to the presidency. Originally a New Deal Democrat and head of the Screen Actors Guild (the only union leader ever to reach the White House), he emerged in the 1950s as a spokesman for the General Electric Corporation, preaching the virtues of unregulated capitalism. His nominating speech for Barry Goldwater at the 1964 Republican convention brought Reagan to national attention. Two years later, California voters elected Reagan as governor, establishing him as conservatives' best hope of capturing the presidency. In 1976, he challenged President Ford for the Republican nomination and came close to winning it. His victory in 1980 brought to power a diverse coalition of old and new conservatives: Sunbelt suburbanites and urban working-class ethnics; antigovernment crusaders and advocates of a more aggressive foreign policy; libertarians who believed in freeing the individual from restraint and the Christian Right, which sought to restore what they considered traditional moral values to American life.

Before entering politics, Ronald Reagan was a prominent actor and a spokesperson for General Electric. In this 1958 photograph he demonstrates the use of a GE oven.

Reagan and American Freedom

Reagan's opponents often underestimated him. By the time he left office at the age of seventy-seven, he had become the oldest man ever to serve as president. He "rose at the crack of noon," as one reporter put it, and relied on his wife to arrange his official schedule. Unlike most modern presidents, he was content to outline broad policy themes and leave their implementation to others.

Reagan, however, was hardly a political novice, having governed California during the turbulent 1960s. An excellent public speaker, his optimism and affability appealed to large numbers of Americans. Reagan made conservatism seem progressive, rather than an attempt to turn back the tide of progress. He frequently quoted Thomas Paine: "We have it in our power to begin the world over again."

VOICES OF FREEDOM

From REDSTOCKINGS MANIFESTO (1969)

Redstockings was one of the radical feminist movements that arose in the late 1960s. Based in New York, it issued this manifesto, which, in language typical of the era, illustrates how at its most radical edge, feminism had evolved from demands for equal treatment for women to a total critique of male power and a call for women's "liberation."

After centuries of individual and preliminary political struggle, women are uniting to achieve their final liberation from male supremacy. Redstockings is dedicated to building this unity and winning our freedom.

Women are an oppressed class. Our oppression is total, affecting every facet of our lives. We are exploited as sex objects, breeders, domestic servants, and cheap labor. We are considered inferior beings, whose only purpose is to enhance men's lives. Our humanity is denied. Our prescribed behavior is enforced by the threat of physical violence.

Because we have lived so intimately with our oppressors, in isolation from each other, we have been kept from seeing our personal suffering as a political condition. . . .

We identify the agents of our oppression as men. Male supremacy is the oldest, most basic form of domination. . . . Men have controlled all political, economic, and cultural institutions and backed up this control with physical force. . . .

Our chief task at present is to develop female class consciousness through sharing experience and publicly exposing the sexist foundation of all our institutions. Consciousness-raising is not "therapy," which implies the existence of individual solutions and falsely assumes that the male-female relationship is purely personal, but the only method by which we can ensure that our program for liberation is based on the concrete realities of our lives. . . . The first requirement for raising class consciousness is honesty, in private and in public, with ourselves and other women.

We identify with all women. We define our best interest as that of the poorest, most brutally exploited women. . . .

We call on all our sisters to unite with us in struggle.

We call on all men to give up their male privileges and support women's liberation in the interest of our humanity and their own.

July 7, 1969, New York City

From JERRY FALWELL, *LISTEN, AMERICA!* (1980)

The Reverend Jerry Falwell, a Virginia minister who in 1979 founded the self-proclaimed Moral Majority, was one of the leading conservative activists of the 1970s and 1980s. In language reminiscent of Puritan jeremiads about the decline of moral values, Falwell helped to mobilize evangelical Christians to ally with the Republican Party.

We must reverse the trend America finds herself in today. Young people between the ages of twenty-five and forty have been born and reared in a different world than Americans of years past. The television set has been their primary baby-sitter. From the television set they have learned situation ethics and immorality—they have learned a loss of respect for human life. They have learned to disrespect the family as God has established it. They have been educated in a public-school system that is permeated with secular humanism. They have been taught that the Bible is just another book of literature. They have been taught that there are no absolutes in our world today. They have been introduced to the drug culture. They have been reared by the family and the public school in a society that is greatly void of discipline and character-building. . . .

Every American who looks at the facts must share a deep concern and burden for our country. . . . If Americans will face the truth, our nation can be turned around and can be saved from the evils and the destruction that have fallen upon every other nation that has turned its back on God. . . .

I personally feel that the home and the family are still held in reverence by the vast majority of the American public. I believe there is still a vast number of Americans who love their country, are patriotic, and are willing to sacrifice for her. . . . I believe that Americans want to see this country come back to basics, back to values, back to biblical morality, back to sensibility, and back to patriotism. . . .

It is now time to take a stand on certain moral issues, and we can only stand if we have leaders. We must stand against the Equal Rights Amendment, the feminist revolution, and the homosexual revolution. . . . The hope of reversing the trends of decay in our republic now lies with the Christian public in America. We cannot expect help from the liberals. They certainly are not going to call our nation back to righteousness and neither are the pornographers, the smut peddlers, and those who are corrupting our youth. Moral Americans must be willing to put their reputations, their fortunes, and their very lives on the line for this great nation of ours. Would that we had the courage of our forefathers who knew the great responsibility that freedom carries with it.

QUESTIONS

1. *How do the authors of the Redstockings Manifesto seem to define women's freedom?*

2. *What does Falwell see as the main threats to moral values?*

3. *How do the two documents differ in their views about the role of women in American society?*

Reagan repeatedly invoked the idea that America has a divinely appointed mission as a "beacon of liberty and freedom." Freedom, indeed, became the watchword of the Reagan Revolution. In his public appearances and state papers, Reagan used the word more often than any president before him.

Reagan as leader

Reagan reshaped the nation's agenda and political language more effectively than any president since Franklin D. Roosevelt. Like FDR, he seized on the vocabulary of his opponents and gave it new meaning. Reagan promised to free government from control by "special interests," but these were racial minorities, unionists, and others hoping to use Washington's power to attack social inequalities, not businessmen seeking political favors, the traditional target of liberals. His Justice Department made the principle that the Constitution must be "color-blind"—a remark hurled at the Supreme Court majority by Justice John Marshall Harlan in 1896 to challenge a system of legal segregation—a justification for gutting civil rights enforcement.

Overall, Reagan proved remarkably successful at seizing control of the terms of public debate. On issues ranging from taxes to government spending, national security, crime, welfare, and "traditional values," he put Democrats on the defensive. But he also proved to be a pragmatist, recognizing when to compromise so as not to fragment his diverse coalition of supporters.

Reaganomics

Like Roosevelt and Johnson before him, Reagan spoke of "economic freedom" and proposed an "economic Bill of Rights." But in contrast to his predecessors, who used these phrases to support combating poverty and strengthening economic security, economic freedom for Reagan meant curtailing the power of unions, dismantling regulations, and radically reducing taxes. Taxation, he declared, violated the principle that "the right to earn your own keep and keep what you earn" was "what it means to be free."

Tax reform

In 1981, Reagan persuaded Congress to reduce the top tax rate from 70 percent to 50 percent and to index tax brackets to take inflation into account. Five years later, the Tax Reform Act reduced the rate on the wealthiest Americans to 28 percent. These measures marked a sharp retreat from the principle of progressivity (the idea that the wealthy should pay a higher percentage of their income in taxes than other citizens), one of the ways twentieth-century societies tried to address the unequal distribution of wealth. Reagan also appointed conservative heads of regulatory agencies, who cut back on environmental protection and workplace safety rules about which business had complained for years.

Supply-side economics

Since the New Deal, liberals had tried to promote economic growth by using the power of the government to bolster ordinary Americans' purchasing power. Reagan's economic program, known as "supply-side economics" by proponents and "trickle-down economics" by critics, relied on high interest rates to curb inflation and lower tax rates, especially for businesses and high-income Americans, to stimulate private investment. The policy assumed that cutting taxes would inspire Americans at all income levels to work harder, since they would keep more of the money they earned. Everyone would benefit from increased business profits, and because of a growing economy, government receipts would rise despite lower tax rates.

This photograph of the remains of the Bethlehem Steel plant in Lackawanna, New York, which closed in 1982, depicts the aftermath of deindustrialization. Today, the site is a wind farm, with eight windmills helping to provide electricity for the city.

Reagan and Labor

Reagan inaugurated an era of hostility between the federal government and organized labor. In August 1981, when 13,000 members of PATCO, the union of air traffic controllers, began a strike in violation of federal law, Reagan fired them all. He used the military to oversee the nation's air traffic system until new controllers could be trained. Reagan's action inspired many private employers to launch anti-union offensives. The hiring of workers to replace permanently those who had gone on strike, a rare occurrence before 1980, became widespread. Manufacturing employment, where union membership was concentrated, meanwhile continued its long-term decline. By the mid-1990s, the steel industry employed only 170,000 persons—down from 600,000 in 1973. When Reagan left office, both the service and retail sectors employed more Americans than manufacturing, and only 11 percent of workers with non-government jobs were union members.

The air traffic controllers' strike

"Reaganomics," as critics dubbed the administration's policies, initially produced the most severe recession since the 1930s. A long period of economic expansion, however, followed the downturn of 1981–1982. As companies "downsized" their workforces, shifted production overseas, and took advantage of new technologies such as satellite communications, they became more profitable. At the same time, the rate of inflation, 13.5 percent at the beginning of 1981, declined to 3.5 percent in 1988, partly because a period of expanded oil production that drove down prices succeeded the shortages of the 1970s.

The Problem of Inequality

Together, Reagan's policies, rising stock prices, and deindustrialization resulted in a considerable rise in economic inequality. By the mid-1990s, the richest 1 percent of Americans owned 40 percent of the nation's wealth, twice their share twenty

A homeless Los Angeles family, forced to live in their car, photographed in 1983.

The wealthiest American families benefited the most from economic expansion during the 1980s, while the poorest 40 percent of the population saw their real incomes decline. (Real income indicates income adjusted to take account of inflation.)

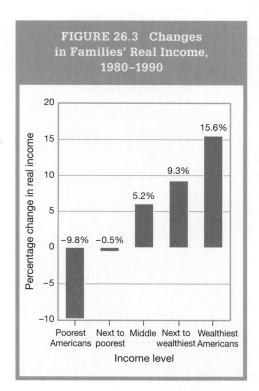

FIGURE 26.3   Changes in Families' Real Income, 1980–1990

years earlier. Most spent their income not on productive investments and charity as supply-side economists had promised, but on luxury goods, real-estate speculation, and corporate buyouts that often led to plant closings as operations were consolidated. The income of middle-class families, especially those with a wife who did not work outside the home, stagnated while that of the poorest one-fifth of the population declined. Because of falling investment in public housing, the release of mental patients from state hospitals, and cuts in welfare, homeless persons became a visible fixture on the streets of cities from New York to Los Angeles.

Deindustrialization and the decline of the labor movement had a particularly devastating impact on minority workers, who had only recently gained a foothold in better-paying manufacturing jobs. Thanks to the opening of colleges and professional schools to minority students as a result of the civil rights movement and affirmative action programs, the black middle class expanded considerably. But black workers, traditionally the last hired and first fired, were hard hit by economic changes.

During the 1970s, Jim Crow had finally ended in many workplaces and unions. But just as decades of painful efforts to obtain better jobs bore fruit, hundreds of thousands of black workers lost their jobs when factories closed their doors. In South Gate, a working-class suburb of Los Angeles, for example, the giant Firestone tire factory shut down in 1980, only a few years after black and Latino workers had made their first breakthroughs in employment. When the national unemployment rate reached 8.9 percent at the end of 1981, the figure for blacks exceeded 20 percent. Nor did black workers share fully in the recovery that followed. Few had the education to take advantage of job openings in growing "knowledge-based" industries like technology and information services. Overall, during the 1980s black males fell farther than any other group in the population in terms of wages and jobs.

The Second Gilded Age

In retrospect, the 1980s, like the 1890s, would be widely remembered as a decade of misplaced values. Buying out companies generated more profits than running them; making deals, not making products, became the way to get rich. The merger of Nabisco and R. J. Reynolds Tobacco Company in 1988 produced close to $1 billion in fees for lawyers, economic advisers, and stockbrokers. "Greed is healthy," declared Wall Street financier Ivan Boesky (who ended up in prison for insider stock trading). "Yuppie"—the young urban professional who earned a high income working in a bank or stock brokerage firm and spent lavishly on designer clothing and other trappings of the good life—became a household word.

Taxpayers footed the bill for some of the consequences. The deregulation of savings and loan associations—banks that had generally confined themselves to financing home mortgages—allowed these institutions to invest in unsound real-estate ventures and corporate mergers. Losses piled up, and the Federal Savings and Loan Insurance Corporation, which insured depositors' accounts, faced bankruptcy. After Reagan left office, the federal government bailed out the savings and loan institutions, at a cost to taxpayers estimated at $250 billion.

Supply-side advocates insisted that lowering taxes would enlarge government revenue by stimulating economic activity. But spurred by large increases in funds for the military, federal spending far outstripped income, producing large budget deficits, despite assurances by supply-siders that this would not happen. During Reagan's presidency, the national debt tripled to $2.7 trillion. Nonetheless, Reagan remained immensely popular. He took credit for economic expansion while blaming congressional leaders for the ballooning federal deficit. He won a triumphant reelection in 1984. His opponent, Walter Mondale (best remembered for choosing Congresswoman Geraldine Ferraro of New York as his running mate, the first woman candidate on a major-party presidential ticket), carried only his home state of Minnesota and the District of Columbia.

Conservatives and Reagan

While he implemented their economic policies, Reagan in some ways disappointed ardent conservatives. The administration sharply reduced funding for Great Society antipoverty programs such as food stamps, school lunches, and federal financing of low-income housing. But it left intact core elements of the welfare state, such as Social Security, Medicare, and Medicaid, which many conservatives wished to curtail significantly or repeal. The Reagan era did little to advance the social agenda of the Christian Right. Abortion remained legal, women continued to enter the labor force in unprecedented numbers, and Reagan even appointed the first female member of the Supreme Court, Sandra Day O'Connor. In 1986, in *Bowers v. Hardwick*, in a rare victory for cultural conservatives, the Supreme Court did uphold the constitutionality of state laws outlawing homosexual acts. (In 2003, the justices would reverse the *Bowers* decision, declaring laws that criminalized homosexuality unconstitutional.)

Reagan gave verbal support to a proposed constitutional amendment restoring prayer in public schools but did little to promote its passage. The administration launched a "Just Say No" campaign against illegal drug use. But this failed to halt the

> *Reagan's social policies*

First lady Nancy Reagan promoting her "Just Say No" campaign against the use of drugs, in a photo from 1986.

spread in urban areas of crack, a potent, inexpensive form of cocaine that produced an upsurge of street crime and family breakdown. Reagan's Justice Department cut back on civil rights enforcement and worked to curtail affirmative action programs. But to the end of Reagan's presidency, the Supreme Court continued to approve plans by private employers and city and state governments to upgrade minority employment.

Reagan and the Cold War

In foreign policy, Reagan breathed new life into the rhetorical division of the world into a free West and unfree East. He resumed vigorous denunciation of the Soviet Union—calling it an "evil empire"—and sponsored the largest military buildup in American history, including new long-range bombers and missiles. In 1983, he proposed an entirely new strategy, the Strategic Defense Initiative, based on developing a space-based system to intercept and destroy enemy missiles. The idea was not remotely feasible technologically, and, if deployed, it would violate the Anti-Ballistic Missile Treaty of 1972. But it appealed to Reagan's desire to reassert America's worldwide power. He persuaded NATO, over much opposition, to introduce short-range nuclear weapons into Europe to counter Soviet forces. But the renewed arms race and Reagan's casual talk of winning a nuclear war caused widespread alarm at home and abroad. In the early 1980s, a movement for a nuclear freeze—a halt to the development of nuclear weapons—attracted millions of supporters in the United States and Europe. In 1983, half of the American population watched *The Day After*, a television program that unflinchingly depicted the devastation that would be caused by a nuclear war.

The Strategic Defense Initiative

Reagan came into office determined to overturn the "Vietnam syndrome"—as widespread public reluctance to commit American forces overseas was called. He sent American troops to the Caribbean island of Grenada to oust a pro-Cuban government. In 1982, Reagan dispatched marines as a peacekeeping force to

Troops overseas

Hollywood joined enthusiastically in the revived Cold War. The 1984 film *Red Dawn* depicted a Soviet invasion of the United States.

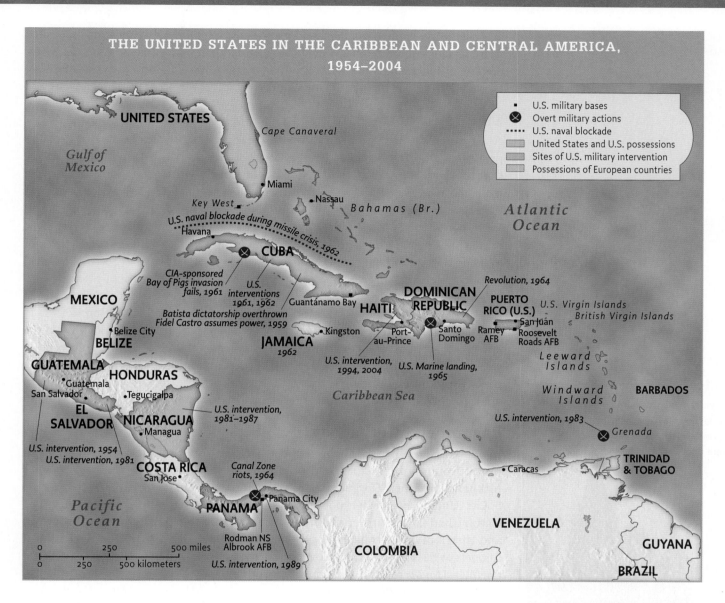

THE UNITED STATES IN THE CARIBBEAN AND CENTRAL AMERICA, 1954–2004

As in the first part of the twentieth century, the United States intervened frequently in Caribbean and Central American countries during and immediately after the Cold War.

Lebanon, where a civil war raged between the Christian government, supported by Israeli forces, and Muslim insurgents. But he quickly withdrew them after a bomb exploded at their barracks, killing 241 Americans. The public, Reagan realized, would support minor operations like Grenada but remained unwilling to sustain heavy casualties abroad.

Reagan generally relied on military aid rather than American troops to pursue his foreign policy objectives. Abandoning the Carter administration's emphasis on human rights, Reagan embraced the idea, advanced in 1979 by neoconservative writer Jeane Kirkpatrick, that the United States should oppose "totalitarian" communists but assist "authoritarian" noncommunist regimes. Kirkpatrick became the American ambassador to the United Nations, and the United States stepped up its alliances with Third World anticommunist dictatorships like the governments of Chile and South Africa. The administration poured in funds to combat insurgencies

Latin America

against the governments of El Salvador and Guatemala, whose armies and associated death squads committed flagrant abuses against their own citizens. When El Salvador's army massacred hundreds of civilians in the town of El Mozote in 1981, the State Department denied that the event, widely reported in the press, had taken place.

The Iran-Contra Affair

American involvement in Central America produced the greatest scandal of Reagan's presidency, the Iran-Contra affair. In 1984, Congress banned military aid to the Contras (derived from the Spanish word for "against") fighting the Sandinista government of Nicaragua, which, as noted earlier, had ousted the American-backed dictator Anastasio Somoza in 1979. In 1985, Reagan secretly authorized the sale of arms to Iran—now involved in a war with its neighbor, Iraq—in order to secure the release of a number of American hostages held by Islamic groups in the Middle East. CIA director William Casey and Lieutenant Colonel Oliver North of the National Security Council set up a system that diverted some of the proceeds to buy military supplies for the Contras in defiance of the congressional ban. The scheme continued for nearly two years.

Arms for hostages

In 1987, after a Middle Eastern newspaper leaked the story, Congress held televised hearings that revealed a pattern of official duplicity and violation of the law reminiscent of the Nixon era. Eleven members of the administration eventually were convicted of perjury or destroying documents, or pleaded guilty before being tried. Reagan denied knowledge of the illegal proceedings, but the Iran-Contra affair undermined confidence that he controlled his own administration.

Reagan and Gorbachev

In his second term, to the surprise of both his foes and supporters, Reagan softened his anticommunist rhetoric and established good relations with Soviet premier Mikhail Gorbachev. Gorbachev had come to power in 1985, bent on reforming the Soviet Union's repressive political system and reinvigorating its economy. The country had fallen further and further behind the United States in the production and distribution of consumer goods, and it relied increasingly on agricultural imports to feed itself. Gorbachev inaugurated policies known as *glasnost* (political openness) and *perestroika* (economic reform).

Gorbachev realized that significant change would be impossible without reducing his country's military budget. Reagan was ready to negotiate. A series of talks between 1985 and 1987 yielded more progress on arms control than in the entire postwar period to that point, including an agreement to eliminate intermediate- and short-range nuclear missiles in Europe. In 1988, Gorbachev began pulling Soviet troops out of Afghanistan. Having entered office as an ardent Cold Warrior, Reagan left with hostilities between the superpowers much diminished. He even repudiated his earlier comment that the Soviet Union was an "evil empire," saying that it referred to "another era."

Reagan's Legacy

Reagan's presidency revealed the contradictions at the heart of modern conservatism. In some ways, the Reagan Revolution undermined the very values and institutions conservatives held dear. Intended to discourage reliance on government handouts by rewarding honest work and business initiative, Reagan's policies

President Reagan visited Moscow in 1988, cementing his close relationship with Soviet leader Mikhail Gorbachev. They were photographed in Red Square.

inspired a speculative frenzy that enriched architects of corporate takeovers and investors in the stock market while leaving in their wake plant closings, job losses, and devastated communities. Nothing proved more threatening to local traditions or family stability than deindustrialization, insecurity about employment, and the relentless downward pressure on wages. Nothing did more to undermine a sense of common national purpose than the widening gap between rich and poor.

Because of the Iran-Contra scandal and the enormous deficits the government had accumulated, Reagan left the presidency with his reputation somewhat tarnished. Nonetheless, few figures have so successfully changed the landscape and language of politics. Reagan's vice president, George H. W. Bush, defeated Michael Dukakis, the governor of Massachusetts, in the 1988 election partly because Dukakis could not respond effectively to the charge that he was a "liberal"—now a term of political abuse. Conservative assumptions about the virtues of the free market and the evils of "big government" dominated the mass media and political debates. Those receiving public assistance had come to be seen not as citizens entitled to help in coping with economic misfortune, but as a drain on taxes. During the 1990s, these and other conservative ideas would be embraced almost as fully by President Bill Clinton, a Democrat, as by Reagan and the Republicans.

Reagan's impact

The Election of 1988

The 1988 election seemed to show politics sinking to new lows. Television advertisements and media exposés now dominated political campaigns. The race for the Democratic nomination had hardly begun before the front-runner, Senator Gary Hart of Colorado, withdrew after a newspaper reported that he had spent the night at his Washington town house with a woman other than his wife. Both parties ran negative campaigns. Democrats ridiculed the Republican vice-presidential nominee, Senator Dan Quayle of Indiana, for factual and linguistic mistakes. Republicans spread unfounded rumors that Michael Dukakis's wife had burned an American flag during the 1960s. The low point of the campaign came in a Republican television ad depicting the threatening image of Willie Horton, a black

A dismal campaign

Conservatives, including Karl Rove, seated at center, toast the inauguration of George H. W. Bush, January 1989.

murderer and rapist who had been furloughed from prison during Dukakis's term as governor of Massachusetts. Rarely in the modern era had a major party appealed so blatantly to racial fears. Before his death in 1991, Lee Atwater, who masterminded Bush's campaign, apologized for the Horton ad.

Although he did not match Reagan's landslide victory of 1984, Bush achieved a substantial majority, winning 54 percent of the popular vote. Democratic success in retaining control of Congress suggested that an electoral base existed for a comeback. But this would occur only if the party fashioned a new appeal to replace traditional liberalism, which had been eclipsed by the triumph of conservatism.

SUGGESTED READING

BOOKS

• Adler, William M. *Mollie's Job: A Story of Life and Work on the Global Assembly Line* (2000). Tracks how a manufacturing job moved from the North to the South and eventually out of the country, and what happened to the workers who held it.

• Allitt, Patrick. *Religion in America since 1945* (2003). A survey of the main trends of religious development since World War II.

• Anderson, Terry H. *The Pursuit of Fairness: A History of Affirmative Action* (2004). A careful study of the origins and development of affirmative action policies.

• Busch, Andrew E. *Ronald Reagan and the Politics of Freedom* (2001). Discusses how Ronald Reagan interpreted the idea of freedom and how it influenced his presidency.

• Greenberg, David. *Nixon's Shadow: The History of an Image* (2003). Explores how Nixon's supporters and enemies thought about him during his long political career.

• Himmelstein, Jerome L. *To the Right: The Transformation of American Conservatism* (1990). Studies the development of conservative ideas since World War II.

• Kruse, Kevin. *White Flight: Atlanta and the Making of Modern Conservatism* (2005). Explores how conservative politics took root in the predominantly white suburbs of Atlanta, with implications for similar communities across the country.

• Kutler, Stanley I. *The Wars of Watergate: The Last Crisis of Richard Nixon* (1990). The most thorough analysis of the Watergate scandal that brought down President Nixon.

• Luker, Kristin. *Abortion and the Politics of Motherhood* (1984). Describes how the abortion issue affected American politics and the ideas about gender relations that lay behind the debate.

• Martin, William. *With God on Our Side: The Rise of the Religious Right in America* (1996). Traces the development of religious conservatism and its impact on American society.

• Mathews, Donald G., and Jane S. De Hart. *Sex, Gender, and the Politics of ERA* (1990). An in-depth examination of the debate over the Equal Rights Amendment and why its opponents were successful.

• McGirr, Lisa. *Suburban Warriors: The Origins of the New American Right* (2001). An influential study of the rise of conservatism in Orange County, California, once one of its more powerful centers.

• Moyn, Samuel. *The Last Utopia: Human Rights in History* (2010). Traces the development of human rights consciousness, with special emphasis on the 1970s.

• Palermo, Joseph A. *The Eighties* (2012). A survey of political, social, and economic developments during Reagan's presidency.

• Schulman, Bruce J. *The Seventies: The Great Shift in American Culture, Society, and Politics* (2001). A survey of the numerous political, social, and economic changes that took place during the 1970s.

• Stein, Judith. *Pivotal Decade: How the United States Traded Factories for Finance in the Seventies* (2010). A careful analysis of the economic transformations of the 1970s.

• Wilentz, Sean. *The Age of Reagan: A History, 1974–2008* (2008). Explores how Ronald Reagan set the terms of public debate during and after his presidency.

WEBSITES

• China and the United States: From Hostility to Engagement: www.gwu.edu/~nsarchiv/NSAEBB/NSAEBB19/

• National Security Archive: www.gwu.edu/~nsarchiv/

CHAPTER REVIEW AND ONLINE RESOURCES

REVIEW QUESTIONS

1. Why were social issues associated with the sexual revolution so contested by all sides?

2. What were continuing challenges to the cohesiveness of the Democratic (New Deal) coalition? What were the consequences of those divisions?

3. What were the main features of Nixon's policy of "realism" in dealing with China and the Soviet Union?

4. Describe the basic events and the larger significance of the Watergate scandal.

5. What were the major causes for the decline of the U.S. economy in the 1970s?

6. What were the causes and consequences of the public's disillusionment with the federal government in the 1970s and 1980s?

7. Identify the groups and their agendas that combined to create the new conservative base in the 1970s and 1980s.

8. What impact did Ronald Reagan have on the American political scene?

9. Why was there growth in economic inequality in the 1980s?

10. How did various groups see the relationship between women's rights and freedom differently?

KEY TERMS

busing (p. 1012)

"reverse discrimination" (p. 1013)

affirmative action (p. 1013)

Title IX (p. 1014)

Strategic Arms Limitation Talks (p. 1015)

détente (p. 1015)

My Lai massacre (p. 1016)

War Powers Act (p. 1017)

Vietnam Syndrome (p. 1017)

Watergate (p. 1018)

oil embargo (p. 1020)

stagflation (p. 1020)

misery index (p. 1021)

Sunbelt (p. 1022)

Helsinki Accords (p. 1023)

Camp David Accords (p. 1026)

neoconservatives (p. 1028)

Reagan Revolution (p. 1033)

Reaganomics (p. 1037)

deregulation (p. 1038)

Iran-Contra affair (p. 1042)

wwnorton.com/studyspace

Visit StudySpace for these resources and more:

- **Author Videos**
- **A chapter outline**
- **A practice quiz**
- **Interactive maps**
- **Multimedia documents**

CHAPTER 27

GLOBALIZATION AND ITS DISCONTENTS

★

1989-2000

In December 1999, delegates from around the world gathered in Seattle for a meeting of the World Trade Organization (WTO), a 135-nation group created five years earlier to reduce barriers to international commerce and settle trade disputes. To the astonishment of residents of the city, more than 30,000 persons gathered to protest the meeting. Their marches and rallies brought together factory workers, who claimed that global free trade encouraged corporations to shift production to low-wage centers overseas, and "tree-huggers," as some reporters called environmentalists, who complained about the impact on the earth's ecology of unregulated economic development.

Some of the latter dressed in costumes representing endangered species—monarch butterflies whose habitats were disappearing because of the widespread destruction of forests by lumber companies, and sea turtles threatened by unrestricted ocean fishing. Protesters drew attention to the depletion of ozone in the atmosphere, which shields the earth from harmful solar radiation. The heightened use of aerosol sprays and refrigerants containing damaging chemicals had caused a large hole in the ozone layer. A handful of self-proclaimed anarchists embarked on a window-breaking spree at local stores. The police sealed off the downtown and made hundreds of arrests, and the WTO gathering disbanded.

Once a center of labor radicalism, the Seattle area in 1999 was best known as the home of Microsoft, developer of the Windows operating system used in most of the world's computers. The company's worldwide reach symbolized "globalization," the process by which people, investment, goods, information, and culture increasingly flowed across national boundaries. Globalization has been called "the concept of the 1990s." During that decade, the media resounded with announcements that a new era in human history had opened, with a borderless economy and a "global civilization" that would soon replace traditional cultures. Some commentators claimed that the nation-state itself had become obsolete in the globalized world.

Globalization, of course, was hardly a new phenomenon. The internationalization of commerce and culture and the reshuffling of the world's peoples had been going on since the explorations of the fifteenth century. But the scale and scope of late-twentieth-century globalization was unprecedented. Thanks to satellites and the Internet, information and popular culture flowed instantaneously to every corner of the world. Manufacturers and financial institutions scoured the world for profitable investment opportunities.

Perhaps most important, the collapse of communism between 1989 and 1991 opened the entire world to the spread of market capitalism and to the idea that government should interfere as little as possible with economic activity. The Free World triumphed over its communist rival, the free market over the idea of a planned economy, and the free individual over ideas of shared community and social citizenship. American politicians and social commentators increasingly criticized the regulation of wages and working conditions, assistance to the less fortunate, and environmental protections as burdens on international competitiveness. During the 1990s, presidents George H. W. Bush, a Republican, and Bill Clinton, a Democrat, both spoke of an American mission to create

FOCUS QUESTIONS

What were the major international initiatives of the Clinton administration in the aftermath of the Cold War? –p. 1049

What forces drove the economic resurgence of the 1990s? –p. 1057

What cultural conflicts emerged in the 1990s? –p. 1065

How did a divisive political partisanship affect the election of 2000? –p. 1079

What were the prevailing ideas of American freedom at the end of the century? –p. 1081

Demonstrators dancing atop the Berlin Wall on November 10, 1989. The next day, crowds began dismantling it, in the most dramatic moment of the collapse of communist rule in eastern Europe.

1989   Communism falls in eastern Europe

        U.S.-led Panamanian coup

1990   Americans with Disabilities Act

        Germany reunifies

1991   Gulf War

        Dissolution of the Soviet Union

1992   Los Angeles riots

        Casey v. Planned Parenthood of Pennsylvania

        Clinton elected president

1993   Israel and Palestinian Liberation Organization sign the Oslo Accords

        North American Free Trade Agreement approved

1994   Republicans win Congress; Contract with America

        Rwandan genocide

1995   Oklahoma City federal building bombed

1996   Clinton eliminates Aid to Families with Dependent Children

        Defense of Marriage Act

1998–1989 Clinton impeachment proceedings

        Kosovo War

1999   Protests in Seattle against the World Trade Organization

        Glass-Steagall Act repealed

2000   *Bush v. Gore*

a single global free market as the path to rising living standards, the spread of democracy, and greater worldwide freedom.

Similar demonstrations at economic summits overseas followed the Seattle protests. The media called the loose coalition of groups who organized the protests the "antiglobalization" movement. In fact, they challenged not globalization itself but its social consequences. Globalization, the demonstrators claimed, accelerated the worldwide creation of wealth but widened gaps between rich and poor countries and between haves and have-nots within societies. Decisions affecting the day-to-day lives of millions of people were made by institutions—the World Trade Organization, International Monetary Fund, World Bank, and multinational corporations—that operated without any democratic input. These international organizations required developing countries seeking financial aid to open their economies to penetration from abroad while reducing spending on domestic social concerns. Demonstrators demanded not an end to global trade and capital flows, but the establishment of international standards for wages, labor conditions, and the environment, and greater investment in health and education in poor countries.

The Battle of Seattle placed on the national and international agendas a question that promises to be among the most pressing concerns of the twenty-first century—the relationship between globalization, economic justice, and freedom.

THE POST–COLD WAR WORLD

The Crisis of Communism

The year 1989 was one of the most momentous of the twentieth century. In April, tens of thousands of student demonstrators occupied Tiananmen Square in the heart of Beijing, demanding greater democracy in China. Workers, teachers, and even some government officials joined them, until their numbers swelled to nearly 1 million. Both the reforms Mikhail Gorbachev had introduced in the Soviet Union and the example of American institutions inspired the protesters. The students erected a figure reminiscent of the Statue of Liberty, calling it "The Goddess of Democracy and Freedom." In June, Chinese troops crushed the protest, killing an unknown number of people, possibly thousands.

In the fall of 1989, pro-democracy demonstrations spread across eastern Europe. Gorbachev made it clear that unlike in the past, the Soviet Union would not intervene. The climactic event took place on November 9 when crowds breached the Berlin Wall, which since 1961 had stood as the Cold War's most prominent symbol. One by one, the region's communist governments agreed to give up power. In 1990, a reunified German nation absorbed East Germany. The remarkably swift and almost entirely peaceful collapse of communism in eastern Europe became known as the "velvet revolution."

Meanwhile, the Soviet Union itself slipped deeper and deeper into crisis. Gorbachev's attempts at economic reform produced only chaos, and his policy of political openness allowed long-suppressed national and ethnic tensions to rise to the surface. In August 1991, a group of military leaders attempted to seize power

Protesters dressed as sea turtles, an endangered species, at the demonstrations against the World Trade Organization in Seattle, December 1999.

to overturn the government's plan to give greater autonomy to the various parts of the Soviet Union. Russian president Boris Yeltsin mobilized crowds in Moscow that restored Gorbachev to office. Gorbachev then resigned from the Communist Party, ending its eighty-four-year rule. One after another, the republics of the Soviet Union declared themselves sovereign states. At the end of 1991, the Soviet Union ceased to exist; in its place were fifteen new independent nations.

The sudden and unexpected collapse of communism marked the end of the Cold War and a stunning victory for the United States and its allies. For the first time since 1917, there existed a truly worldwide capitalist system. Even China, while remaining under Communist Party rule, had already embarked on market reforms and rushed to attract foreign investment. Other events suggested that the 1990s would also be a "decade of democracy." In 1990, South Africa released Nelson Mandela, head of the African National Congress, from prison. Four years later, as a result of the first democratic elections in the country's history, Mandela became president, ending the system of state-sponsored racial inequality, known as "apartheid," and white minority government. Throughout Latin America and Africa, civilian governments replaced military rule.

A New World Order?

The sudden shift from a bipolar world to one of unquestioned American predominance promised to redefine the country's global role. President George H. W. Bush spoke of the coming of a "new world order." But no one knew what its characteristics would be.

Bush's first major foreign policy action was a throwback to the days of American interventionism in the Western Hemisphere. At the end of 1989, he dispatched troops to Panama to overthrow the government of General Manuel Antonio Noriega, a former ally of the United States who had become involved in the international drug trade. The United States installed a new government and flew Noriega to Florida, where he was tried and convicted on drug charges.

The Goddess of Democracy and Freedom, a statue reminiscent of the Statue of Liberty, was displayed by pro-democracy advocates during the 1989 demonstrations in Beijing's Tiananmen Square. After allowing it to continue for two months, the Chinese government sent troops to crush the peaceful occupation of the square.

EASTERN EUROPE AFTER THE COLD WAR

The end of the Cold War and breakup of the Soviet Union, Czechoslovakia, and Yugoslavia redrew the map of eastern Europe (compare this map with the map of Cold War Europe in Chapter 23). Two additional nations that emerged from the Soviet Union lie to the east and are not indicated here: Kyrgyzstan and Tajikistan.

Operation Desert Storm

The Gulf War

A far more serious crisis arose in 1990 when Iraq invaded and annexed Kuwait, an oil-rich sheikdom on the Persian Gulf. Fearing that Iraqi dictator Saddam Hussein might next attack Saudi Arabia, a longtime ally that supplied more oil to the United States than any other country, Bush rushed troops to defend the kingdom and warned Iraq to withdraw from Kuwait or face war. His policy aroused intense debate in the United States. But the Iraqi invasion so flagrantly violated international law that Bush succeeded in building a forty-nation coalition committed to restoring Kuwait's independence, secured the support of the United Nations, and sent half a million American troops along with a naval armada to the region.

In February 1991, the United States launched Operation Desert Storm, which quickly drove the Iraqi army from Kuwait. Tens of thousands of Iraqis and 184 Americans died in the conflict. The United Nations ordered Iraq to disarm and imposed economic sanctions that produced widespread civilian suffering for the rest of the decade. But Hussein remained in place. So did a large American military establishment in Saudi Arabia, to the outrage of Islamic fundamentalists who deemed its presence an affront to their faith.

The Gulf War was the first post–Cold War international crisis. Relying on high-tech weaponry like cruise missiles that reached Iraq from bases and aircraft

President Bush, with Defense Secretary Dick Cheney (*left*) and General Colin Powell (*right*), chair of the Joint Chiefs of Staff, at a meeting in January 1991, shortly before the beginning of the Gulf War. Cheney and Powell would play major roles in the administration of Bush's son, President George W. Bush.

carriers hundreds of miles away, the United States was able to prevail quickly and avoid the prolonged involvement and high casualties of Vietnam. The Soviet Union, in the process of disintegration, remained on the sidelines. In the war's immediate aftermath, Bush's public approval rating rose to an unprecedented 89 percent.

Visions of America's Role

In a speech to Congress, President Bush identified the Gulf War as the first step in the struggle to create a world rooted in democracy and global free trade. But it remained unclear how this broad vision would be translated into policy. Soon after the end of the war, General Colin Powell, chairman of the Joint Chiefs of Staff, and Dick Cheney, the secretary of defense, outlined different visions of the future. Powell predicted that the post–Cold War world would be a dangerous environment with conflicts popping up in unexpected places. To avoid being drawn into an unending role as global policeman, he insisted, the United States should not commit its troops abroad without clear objectives and a timetable for withdrawal. Cheney argued that with the demise of the Soviet Union, the United States possessed the power to reshape the world and prevent hostile states from achieving regional power. It must be willing to use force, independently if necessary, to maintain its strategic dominance. For the rest of the 1990s, it was not certain which definition of the American role in the post–Cold War world would predominate.

Powell and Cheney

The Election of Clinton

Had a presidential election been held in 1991, Bush would undoubtedly have been victorious. But in that year the economy slipped into recession. Despite victory in the Cold War and the Gulf, public-opinion polls showed that more and more Americans believed the country was on the wrong track. No one seized more effectively on the widespread sense of unease than Bill Clinton, a former governor of Arkansas. In 1992, Clinton won the Democratic nomination by combining social liberalism

Bill Clinton's appeal

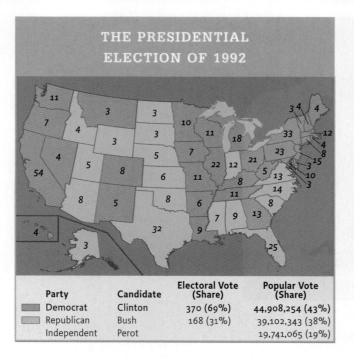

THE PRESIDENTIAL ELECTION OF 1992

Party	Candidate	Electoral Vote (Share)	Popular Vote (Share)
Democrat	Clinton	370 (69%)	44,908,254 (43%)
Republican	Bush	168 (31%)	39,102,343 (38%)
Independent	Perot		19,741,065 (19%)

(he supported abortion rights, gay rights, and affirmative action for racial minorities) with elements of conservatism (he pledged to reduce government bureaucracy and, borrowing a page from Republicans, promised to "end welfare as we know it"). A charismatic campaigner, Clinton conveyed sincere concern for voters' economic anxieties.

Bush, by contrast, seemed out of touch with the day-to-day lives of ordinary Americans. On the wall of Democratic headquarters, Clinton's campaign director posted the slogan, "It's the Economy, Stupid"—a reminder that the economic downturn was the Democrats' strongest card. Bush was further weakened when conservative leader Pat Buchanan delivered a fiery televised speech at the Republican national convention that declared cultural war against gays, feminists, and supporters of abortion rights. This seemed to confirm the Democratic portrait of Republicans as intolerant and divisive.

A third candidate, the eccentric Texas billionaire Ross Perot, also entered the fray. He attacked Bush and Clinton as lacking the economic know-how to deal with the recession and the ever-increasing national debt. That millions of Americans considered Perot a credible candidate—at one point, polls showed him leading both Clinton and Bush—testified to widespread dissatisfaction with the major parties. Perot's support faded as election day approached, but he still received 19 percent of the popular vote, the best result for a third-party candidate since Theodore Roosevelt in 1912. Clinton won by a substantial margin, a humiliating outcome for Bush, given his earlier popularity.

Clinton in Office

In his first two years in office, Clinton turned away from some of the social and economic policies of the Reagan and Bush years. He appointed several blacks and women to his cabinet, including Janet Reno, the first female attorney general, and named two supporters of abortion rights, Ruth Bader Ginsburg and Stephen Breyer, to the Supreme Court. He modified the military's strict ban on gay soldiers, instituting a "Don't ask, don't tell" policy by which officers would not seek out gays for dismissal from the armed forces. His first budget raised taxes on the wealthy and significantly expanded the Earned Income Tax Credit (EITC)—a cash payment for low-income workers begun during the Ford administration. The most effective antipoverty policy since the Great Society, the EITC raised more than 4 million Americans, half of them children, above the poverty line during Clinton's presidency.

Clinton shared his predecessor's passion for free trade. Despite strong opposition from unions and environmentalists, he obtained congressional approval in 1993 of the North American Free Trade Agreement (NAFTA), a treaty negotiated by Bush that created a free-trade zone consisting of Canada, Mexico, and the United States.

NAFTA

The major policy initiative of Clinton's first term was a plan devised by a panel headed by his wife, Hillary, a lawyer who had pursued an independent career after their marriage, to address the rising cost of health care and the increasing number of Americans who lacked health insurance. In Canada and western Europe, governments provided universal medical coverage. The United States had the world's most advanced medical technology and a woefully incomplete system of health insurance. The Great Society had provided coverage for the elderly and poor through the Medicare and Medicaid programs. Many employers offered health insurance to their workers. But tens of millions of Americans lacked any coverage at all. Beginning in the 1980s, moreover, businesses shifted their employees from individual doctors to health maintenance organizations (HMOs), which reduced costs by limiting physicians' fees and, critics charged, denying patients needed medical procedures.

Announced with great fanfare by Hillary Rodham Clinton at congressional hearings in 1993, Clinton's plan would have provided universal coverage through large groupings of organizations like the HMOs. Doctors and health insurance and drug companies attacked it vehemently, fearing government regulations that would limit reimbursement for medical procedures, insurance rates, and the price of drugs. Too complex to be easily understood by most voters, and vulnerable to criticism for further expanding the unpopular federal bureaucracy, the plan died in 1994. Nothing took its place. By 2008, some 50 million Americans, most of them persons who held full-time jobs, still lacked health insurance, meaning that illness could quickly become a financial disaster.

Edward Sorel's illustration for the cover of the *New Yorker* depicts Bill Clinton at his 1993 inauguration, flanked by some of his predecessors as president.

The "Freedom Revolution"

With the economy recovering slowly from the recession and Clinton's first two years in office seemingly lacking in significant accomplishments, voters in 1994 turned against the administration. For the first time since the 1950s, Republicans won control of both houses of Congress. They proclaimed their triumph the "Freedom Revolution." Newt Gingrich, a conservative congressman from Georgia who became the new Speaker of the House, masterminded their campaign. Gingrich had devised a platform called the "Contract with America," which promised to curtail the scope of government, cut back on taxes and economic and environmental regulations, overhaul the welfare system, and end affirmative action.

Newt Gingrich and the Contract with America

Viewing their electoral triumph as an endorsement of the contract, Republicans moved swiftly to implement its provisions. The House approved deep cuts in social, educational, and environmental programs, including the popular Medicare system. With the president and Congress unable to reach agreement on a budget, the government in December 1995 shut down all nonessential operations, including Washington, D.C., museums and national parks.

Gingrich had assumed that the public shared his intense ideological convictions. He discovered that in 1994 they had voted against Clinton, not for the full implementation of the Contract with America. Most Americans blamed Congress for the impasse, and Gingrich's popularity plummeted.

Clinton's Political Strategy

Like Truman after the Republican sweep of 1946, Clinton rebuilt his popularity by campaigning against a radical Congress. He opposed the most extreme parts of his opponents' program, while adopting others. In his state of the union address

Congressman Newt Gingrich of Georgia announcing the "Contract with America" on the steps of the Capitol in Washington. The Republican program for the congressional elections of 1994, the contract helped to produce a Republican sweep that resulted in Gingrich's selection as Speaker of the House.

of January 1996, he announced that "the era of big government is over," in effect turning his back on the tradition of Democratic Party liberalism and embracing the antigovernment outlook associated with Republicans since the days of Barry Goldwater.

In 1996, ignoring the protests of most Democrats, Clinton signed into law a Republican bill that abolished the program of Aid to Families with Dependent Children (AFDC), commonly known as "welfare." Grants of money to the states, with strict limits on how long recipients could receive payments, replaced it. At the time of its abolition, AFDC assisted 14 million individuals, 9 million of them children. Thanks to stringent new eligibility requirements imposed by the states and the economic boom of the late 1990s, welfare rolls plummeted. But the number of children living in poverty remained essentially unchanged. Nonetheless, Clinton had succeeded in one of his primary goals: by the late 1990s, welfare, a hotly contested issue for twenty years or more, had disappeared from political debate.

Ending AFDC

Commentators called Clinton's political strategy "triangulation." This meant embracing the most popular Republican policies, like welfare reform, while leaving his opponents with extreme positions unpopular among suburban middle-class voters, such as hostility to abortion rights and environmental protection. Clinton's strategy enabled him to neutralize Republican claims that Democrats were the party of high taxes and lavish spending on persons who preferred dependency to honest labor. Clinton's passion for free trade alienated many working-class Democrats but convinced middle-class voters that the party was not beholden to the unions.

Clinton's political strategy

Clinton easily defeated Republican Bob Dole in the presidential contest of 1996, becoming the first Democrat elected to two terms since FDR. Clinton had accomplished for Reaganism what Eisenhower had done for the New Deal, and Nixon for the Great Society—consolidating a basic shift in American politics by accepting many of the premises of his opponents.

Clinton and World Affairs

Like Jimmy Carter before him, Clinton's primary political interests concerned domestic, not international, affairs. But with the United States now indisputably the world's dominant power, Clinton, like Carter, took steps to encourage the settlement of long-standing international conflicts and tried to elevate support for human rights to a central place in international relations. He met only mixed success.

Clinton strongly supported a 1993 agreement, negotiated at Oslo, Norway, in which Israel for the first time recognized the legitimacy of the Palestine Liberation Organization. The Oslo Accords seemed to outline a road to Mideast peace. But neither side proved willing to implement them fully. Israeli governments continued to build Jewish settlements on Palestinian land in the West Bank—a part of Jordan that Israel had occupied during the 1967 Six-Day War. The new Palestinian Authority, which shared in governing parts of the West Bank as a stepping-stone to full statehood, proved to be corrupt, powerless, and unable to curb the growth of groups bent on violence against Israel. At the end of his presidency, Clinton brought Israeli and Palestinian leaders to Camp David to try to work out a final peace treaty. But the meeting failed, and violence soon resumed.

The Middle East

Like Carter, Clinton found it difficult to balance concern for human rights with strategic and economic interests and to formulate clear guidelines for humanitarian interventions overseas. For example, the United States did nothing in 1994 when tribal massacres racked Rwanda, in central Africa. More than 800,000 people were slaughtered, and 2 million refugees fled the country.

Massacres in Rwanda

The Balkan Crisis

The most complex foreign policy crisis of the Clinton years arose from the disintegration of Yugoslavia, a multiethnic state in southeastern Europe that had been carved from the old Austro-Hungarian empire after World War I. As in the rest of

Serbian refugees fleeing a Croat offensive during the 1990s. By the fall of 1995, the wars that followed the breakup of Yugoslavia and accompanying "ethnic cleansing" had displaced over 3 million people.

eastern Europe, the communist government that had ruled Yugoslavia since the 1940s collapsed in 1989. Within a few years, the country's six provinces dissolved into five new states. Ethnic conflict plagued several of these new nations. "Ethnic cleansing"—a terrible new term meaning the forcible expulsion from an area of a particular ethnic group—now entered the international vocabulary. By the end of 1993, more than 100,000 Bosnians, nearly all of them civilians, had perished.

Ethnic conflict

With the Cold War over, protection of human rights in the Balkans gave NATO a new purpose. After considerable indecision, NATO launched air strikes against Bosnian Serb forces, with American planes contributing. UN troops, including 20,000 Americans, arrived as peacekeepers. In 1998, ethnic cleansing again surfaced, this time by Yugoslavian troops and local Serbs against the Albanian population of Kosovo, a province of Serbia. More than 800,000 Albanians fled the region. To halt the bloodshed, NATO launched a two-month war in 1999 against Yugoslavia that led to the deployment of American and UN forces in Kosovo.

Human Rights

During Clinton's presidency, human rights played an increasingly important role in international affairs. Hundreds of nongovernmental agencies throughout the world defined themselves as protectors of human rights. During the 1990s, the agenda of international human rights organizations expanded to include access to health care, women's rights, and the rights of indigenous peoples like the Aborigines of Australia and the descendants of the original inhabitants of the Americas. Human rights emerged as a justification for interventions in matters once considered to be the internal affairs of sovereign nations. The United States dispatched the military to distant parts of the world to assist in international missions to protect civilians.

An expanding agenda

New institutions emerged that sought to punish violations of human rights. The Rwandan genocide produced a UN-sponsored war crimes court that sentenced the country's former prime minister to life in prison. An international tribunal put Yugoslav president Slobodan Milošević on trial for sponsoring the massacre of civilians. It remained to be seen whether these initiatives would grow into an effective international system of protecting human rights across national boundaries. Despite adopting human rights as a slogan, many governments continued to violate them in practice.

A NEW ECONOMY?

Clinton's popularity rested in part on the American economy's remarkable performance in the mid-and late 1990s. After recovery from the recession of 1990–1991, economic expansion continued for the rest of the decade. By 2000, unemployment stood below 4 percent, a figure not seen since the 1960s. The boom became the longest uninterrupted period of economic expansion in the nation's history. Because Reagan and Bush had left behind massive budget deficits, Clinton worked hard to balance the federal budget—a goal traditionally associated with fiscal conservatives. Since economic growth produced rising tax revenues, Clinton during his second term not only balanced the budget but actually produced budget surpluses.

Economic growth

The first Starbucks store, which opened in Seattle in 1971. By 2012, Starbucks had more than 17,000 such establishments in 55 countries around the globe.

The Computer Revolution

Many commentators spoke of the 1990s as the dawn of a "new economy," in which computers and the Internet would produce vast new efficiencies and the production and sale of information would occupy the central place once held by the manufacture of goods. Computers had first been developed during and after World War II to solve scientific problems and do calculations involving enormous amounts of data. The early ones were extremely large, expensive, and, by modern standards, slow. Research for the space program of the 1960s spurred the development of improved computer technology, notably the miniaturization of parts thanks to the development of the microchip on which circuits could be imprinted.

> *Origins of computers*

Microchips made possible the development of entirely new consumer products. Videocassette recorders, handheld video games, cellular phones, and digital cameras were mass-produced at affordable prices during the 1990s, mostly in Asia and Latin America rather than the United States. But it was the computer that transformed American life. Beginning in the 1980s, companies like Apple and IBM marketed computers for business and home use. As computers became smaller, faster, and less expensive, they found a place in businesses of every kind. In occupations as diverse as clerical work, banking, architectural design, medical diagnosis, and even factory production, they transformed the American workplace. They also changed private life. By the year 2000, nearly half of all American households owned a personal computer, used for entertainment, shopping, and sending and receiving electronic mail. Centers of computer technology, such as Silicon Valley south of San Francisco, the Seattle and Austin metropolitan areas, and lower Manhattan, boomed during the 1990s.

> *Computers in daily life*

The Internet, first developed as a high-speed military communications network, was simplified and opened to commercial and individual use through personal

> *The Internet*

Two architects of the computer revolution, Steve Jobs (on the left), the head of Apple Computer, and Bill Gates, founder of Microsoft, which makes the operating system used in most of the world's computers.

computers. The Internet expanded the flow of information and communications more radically than any invention since the printing press. At a time when the ownership of newspapers, television stations, and publishing houses was becoming concentrated in the hands of a few giant media conglomerates, the fact that anyone with a computer could post his or her ideas for worldwide circulation led "netizens" ("citizens" of the Internet) to hail the advent of a new, democratic public sphere in cyberspace.

The Stock Market Boom and Bust

Economic growth and talk of a new economy sparked a frenzied boom in the stock market that was reminiscent of the 1920s. Investors, large and small, poured funds into stocks, spurred by the rise of discount and online firms that advertised aggressively and charged lower fees than traditional brokers. By 2000, a majority of American households owned stocks directly or through investment in mutual funds and pension and retirement accounts.

Young people seemed to adapt to the computer revolution more readily than their elders. Here nine-year-old Anna Walter teaches several adults how to use the Internet in Wichita, Kansas.

Investors were especially attracted to the new "dot coms"—companies that conducted business via the Internet and seemed to symbolize the promise of the new economy. The NASDAQ, a stock exchange dominated by new technology companies, rose more than 500 percent from 1998 to 1999. Many of these "high-tech" companies never turned a profit. But economic journalists and stock brokers explained that the new economy had so revolutionized business that traditional methods of assessing a company's value no longer applied.

Inevitably, the bubble burst. On April 14, 2000, stocks suffered their largest one-day point drop in history. For the first time since the Depression, stock prices declined for three successive years (2000–2002), wiping out billions

Technicians at the offices of FHP Wireless in Belmont, California, one of numerous technology companies launched with great fanfare in the late 1990s. Unlike many, FHP survived. In 2002, *Fortune* magazine listed it as one of the country's "cool companies." It is now called Tropos Networks.

of dollars in Americans' net worth and pension funds. The value of NASDAQ stocks fell by nearly 80 percent between 2000 and 2002. Not until 2006 would the general stock index again reach the level of early 2000, while the NASDAQ still remains far below its record high. By 2001, the American economy had fallen into a recession. Talk of a new economy, it appeared, had been premature.

The Enron Syndrome

Only after the market dropped did it become apparent that the stock boom of the 1990s had been fueled in part by fraud. For a time in 2001 and 2002, Americans were treated almost daily to revelations of incredible greed and corruption on the part of respected brokerage firms, accountants, and company executives. During the late 1990s, accounting firms like Arthur Andersen, giant banks like JPMorgan Chase and Citigroup, and corporate lawyers pocketed extravagant fees for devising complex schemes to help push up companies' stock prices by hiding their true financial condition. Enron, a Houston-based energy company that epitomized the new economy—it bought and sold electricity rather than actually producing it—reported as profits billions of dollars in operating losses.

In the early twenty-first century, the bill came due for many corporate criminals. The founder of Adelphia Communications was convicted of misuse of company funds. A jury found

Cartoonist David Jacobson's comment on the Enron scandal.

"Let's say I was Enron, how would you do my taxes?"

the chairman of Tyco International guilty of looting the company of millions of dollars. A number of former chief executives faced long prison terms. Kenneth Lay and Jeffrey Skilling, chief officers of Enron, were convicted by a Texas jury of multiple counts of fraud. (Lay died before sentencing.) Even reputable firms like JPMorgan Chase and Citigroup agreed to pay billions of dollars to compensate investors on whom they had pushed worthless stocks.

Fruits of Deregulation

At the height of the 1990s boom, with globalization in full swing, stocks rising, and the economy expanding, the economic model of free trade and deregulation appeared unassailable. But the retreat from government economic regulation, a policy embraced by both the Republican Congress and President Clinton, left no one to represent the public interest.

The public interest

The sectors of the economy most affected by the scandals—energy, telecommunications, and stock trading—had all been subjects of deregulation. Enron could manipulate energy prices because Congress had granted it an exemption from laws regulating the price of natural gas and electricity.

Many stock frauds stemmed from the repeal in 1999 of the Glass-Steagall Act, a New Deal measure that had separated commercial banks, which accept deposits and make loans, from investment banks, which invest in stocks and real estate and take larger risks. The repeal made possible the emergence of "superbanks" that combined these two functions. Phil Gramm, the Texas congressman who wrote the repeal bill, which Clinton signed, explained his thinking in this way: "Glass-Steagall came at a time when the thinking was that government was the answer. In this era of economic prosperity, we have decided that freedom is the answer."

But banks took their new freedom as an invitation to engage in all sorts of misdeeds, knowing that they had become so big that if anything happened, the federal government would have no choice but to rescue them. Banks poured money into risky mortgages. When the housing bubble collapsed in 2007–2008, the banks suffered losses that threatened to bring down the entire financial system. The Bush and Obama administrations felt they had no choice but to expend hundreds of billions of dollars of taxpayer money to save the banks from their own misconduct.

The "Gini index" measures economic inequality; the higher the number, the more unequally income is distributed. As the graph shows, inequality peaked just before the Great Depression, fell dramatically during the New Deal, World War II, and the postwar economic boom, and then began a steady upward climb in the early 1970s.

Rising Inequality

The boom that began in 1995 benefited nearly all Americans. For the first time since the early 1970s, average real wages and family incomes began to grow significantly. Economic expansion at a time of low unemployment brought rapid increases in wages for families at all income levels. It aided low-skilled workers, especially non-whites, who had been left out of previous periods of growth. By 2000, the number of long-term unemployed, 2 million in 1993, had declined to around 700,000. Yet, despite these gains, average wages for nonsupervisory workers, adjusted for inflation, remained below the level of the 1970s. Overall, in the last two decades of the twentieth century, the poor and the middle class became worse off while the rich became significantly richer.

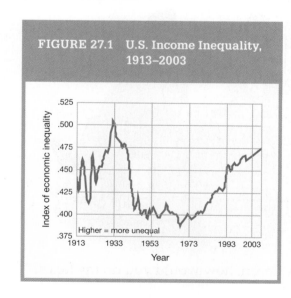

FIGURE 27.1 U.S. Income Inequality, 1913–2003

Index of economic inequality

Higher = more unequal

Year

A cartoonist offered this view in 1993 of the results of the North American Free Trade Agreement, suggesting that the United States was exporting manufacturing factories and jobs, and receiving immigrant workers in exchange.

Between 1977 and 1999, the average after-tax income of the poorest one-fifth of Americans fell 12 percent, and that of the middle one-fifth decreased by 3 percent. In contrast, thanks to the soaring stock market and increasingly generous pay for top executives, the income of the top one-fifth rose 38 percent. The wealth of the richest Americans exploded during the 1990s. Sales of luxury goods like yachts and mansions boomed. Bill Gates, head of Microsoft and the country's richest person, owned as much wealth as the bottom 40 percent of the American population put together.

> *Increasing inequality*

Dot-com millionaires and well-paid computer designers and programmers received much publicity. But companies continued to shift manufacturing jobs overseas. Thanks to NAFTA, a thriving industrial zone emerged just across the southern border of the United States, where American manufacturers built plants to take advantage of cheap labor and weak environmental and safety regulations. Business, moreover, increasingly relied for profits on financial operations rather than making things. The financial sector of the economy accounted for around 10 percent of total profits in 1950; by 2000 the figure was up to 40 percent. Companies like Ford and General Electric made more money from interest on loans to customers and other financial operations than selling their products.

The outsourcing of jobs soon moved from manufacturing to other areas, including accounting, legal services, banking, and other skilled jobs where companies could employ workers overseas for a fraction of their cost in the United States. All this lowered prices for consumers, but also threw millions of American workers into competition with those around the globe, producing a relentless downward pressure on American wages. In 2000, the United States no longer led

> *Outsourcing jobs*

VOICES OF FREEDOM

From BILL CLINTON,
SPEECH ON SIGNING OF NAFTA (1993)

The North American Free Trade Agreement was signed by President Bill Clinton early in his first term. It created a free-trade zone (an area where goods can travel freely without paying import duties) composed of Canada, the United States, and Mexico. Clinton asked Americans to accept economic globalization as an inevitable form of progress and the path to future prosperity. "There will be no job loss," he promised. Things did not entirely work out that way.

As President, it is my duty to speak frankly to the American people about the world in which we now live. Fifty years ago, at the end of World War II, an unchallenged America was protected by the oceans and by our technological superiority and, very frankly, by the economic devastation of the people who could otherwise have been our competitors. We chose then to try to help rebuild our former enemies and to create a world of free trade supported by institutions which would facilitate it. . . . As a result, jobs were created, and opportunity thrived all across the world. . . .

For the last 20 years, in all the wealthy countries of the world—because of changes in the global environment, because of the growth of technology, because of increasing competition—the middle class that was created and enlarged by the wise policies of expanding trade at the end of World War II has been under severe stress. Most Americans are working harder for less. They are vulnerable to the fear tactics and the averseness to change that are behind much of the opposition to NAFTA. But I want to say to my fellow Americans: When you live in a time of change, the only way to recover your security and to broaden your horizons is to adapt to the change—to embrace, to move forward. . . . The only way we can recover the fortunes of the middle class in this country so that people who work harder and smarter can, at least, prosper more, the only way we can pass on the American dream of the last 40 years to our children and their children for the next 40, is to adapt to the changes which are occurring.

In a fundamental sense, this debate about NAFTA is a debate about whether we will embrace these changes and create the jobs of tomorrow or try to resist these changes, hoping we can preserve the economic structures of yesterday. . . . I believe that NAFTA will create 1 million jobs in the first 5 years of its impact. . . . NAFTA will generate these jobs by fostering an export boom to Mexico by tearing down tariff walls. . . . There will be no job loss.

From GLOBAL EXCHANGE, SEATTLE, DECLARATION FOR GLOBAL DEMOCRACY (DECEMBER 1999)

The demonstrations that disrupted the December 1999 meeting of the World Trade Organization in Seattle brought to public attention a widespread dissatisfaction with the effects of economic "globalization." In this declaration, organizers of the protest offered their critique.

———————

As citizens of global society, recognizing that the World Trade Organization is unjustly dominated by corporate interests and run for the enrichment of the few at the expense of all others, we demand:

Representatives from all sectors of society must be included in all levels of trade policy formulations. All global citizens must be democratically represented in the formulation, implementation, and evaluation of all global social and economic policies.

Global trade and investment must not be ends in themselves, but rather the instruments for achieving equitable and sustainable development including protection for workers and the environment.

Global trade agreements must not undermine the ability of each nation-state or local community to meet its citizens' social, environmental, cultural or economic needs.

The World Trade Organization must be replaced by a democratic and transparent body accountable to citizens—not to corporations.

No globalization without representation!

QUESTIONS

1. *Why does Clinton feel that free trade is necessary to American prosperity?*

2. *Why do the Seattle protesters feel that the World Trade Organization is a threat to democracy?*

3. *How do these documents reflect contradictory arguments about the impact of globalization in the United States?*

Barbie's Liberty, a satirical work by the artist Hans Haacke, recasts the Barbie doll, one of America's most successful toys, in the image of the Statue of Liberty to comment on the loss of manufacturing jobs to low-wage areas overseas. Art © Hans Haacke/Artists Rights Society (ARS), New York/VG Bild-Kunst, Bonn.

A suburban nation

the world in the hourly wages of manufacturing workers, lagging behind several countries in Europe.

Overall, between 1990 and 2008, companies that did business in global markets contributed almost nothing to job growth in the United States. Those that did hire new workers tended to be those not facing global competition, such as health care, government agencies, retailers, and hotels and restaurants.

High-tech firms did not create enough high-paying jobs to compensate. Microsoft, symbol of the new economy, employed only 30,000 people. Apple, another highly successful company, whose computers, iPads, and iPhones were among the most ubiquitous consumer products of the early twenty-first century, in 2010 employed some 43,000 persons in the United States (the large majority a low-wage sales force in the company's stores). Its contractors, who made these products, had more than 700,000 employees, almost all of them overseas. In 1970, General Motors had been the country's largest corporate employer. In the early twenty-first century, it had been replaced by Wal-Mart, a giant discount retail chain that paid most of its 1.6 million workers slightly more than the minimum wage. Wal-Mart aggressively opposed efforts at collective bargaining. Not a single one of its employees belonged to a union. Thanks to NAFTA, which enabled American companies to expand their business in Mexico, by 2010 Wal-Mart was also the largest employer in Mexico.

In 2000, well over half of the labor force worked for less than fourteen dollars per hour, a wage on which families found it very difficult to make ends meet. Because of the decline in union membership and the spread of part-time employment, fewer and fewer workers enjoyed fringe benefits common in union contracts, such as employer-provided health insurance. In "dual cities" like Los Angeles and New York, high-tech computer companies and firms engaging in international finance coexisted with sweatshops reminiscent of the Progressive era, where workers toiled in overcrowded conditions for the minimum wage or less. Poverty was not limited to urban areas. The highest rates of poverty could be found in isolated rural regions that experienced the continuation of the long-term decline in family farming.

At the end of the twentieth century, the United States, more than ever before, was a suburban nation. Two-thirds of new jobs were created in the suburbs. Suburbs were no longer places from which people commuted to jobs in central cities—their office parks, industrial plants, and huge shopping malls employed many local residents. Nor were suburbs as racially segregated as in the past. In 2000, one-quarter of the suburban population was black, and Hispanics represented a majority of the population in the suburbs of Los Angeles and Miami. But suburbs remained divided by income—there were rich suburbs, middle-class suburbs, and poor suburbs, with little connection between them.

CULTURE WARS

The end of the Cold War ushered in hopes for a new era of global harmony. Instead, what one observer called a "rebellion of particularisms"—renewed emphasis on group identity and insistent demands for group recognition and power—racked the international arena during the 1990s. In the nineteenth and twentieth centuries, socialism and nationalism had united people of different backgrounds in pursuit of common goals. Now, in Africa, Asia, the Middle East, and parts of Europe, the waning of movements based on socialism and the declining power of nation-states arising from globalization seemed to unleash long-simmering ethnic and religious antagonisms. Partly in reaction to the global spread of a secular culture based on consumption and mass entertainment, intense religious movements attracted increasing numbers of followers—Hindu nationalism in India, orthodox Judaism in Israel, Islamic fundamentalism in much of the Muslim world, and evangelical Christianity in the United States. Like other nations, although in a far less extreme way and with little accompanying violence, the United States experienced divisions arising from the intensification of ethnic and racial identities and religious fundamentalism.

Recent immigrants reciting the Pledge of Allegiance during a naturalization ceremony.

The Newest Immigrants

Because of shifts in immigration, cultural and racial diversity became increasingly visible in the United States. Until the immigration law of 1965, the vast majority of twentieth-century newcomers had hailed from Europe. That measure, as noted in Chapter 25, sparked a wholesale shift in immigrants' origins. Between 1965 and 2010, nearly 38 million immigrants entered the United States, a number larger than the 27 million during the peak period of immigration between 1880 and 1924. About 50 percent came from Latin America and the Caribbean, 35 percent from Asia, and smaller numbers from the Middle East and Africa. Only 10 percent arrived from Europe, mostly from the war-torn Balkans and the former Soviet Union.

Increasing diversity

In 2010, the number of foreign-born persons living in the United States stood at more than 40 million, or 13 percent of the population. Although less than the peak proportion of 14 percent in 1910, in absolute numbers this represented the largest immigrant total in the nation's history. The immigrant influx changed the country's religious and racial map. By 2010, more than 4 million Muslims resided in the United States, and the combined population of Buddhists and Hindus exceeded 1 million.

TABLE 27.1	Immigration to the United States, 1960–2010				
DECADE	TOTAL	EUROPE	ASIA	WESTERN HEMISPHERE	OTHER AREAS
1961–1970	3,321,584	1,123,492	427,642	1,716,374	54,076
1971–1980	4,493,302	800,368	1,588,178	1,982,735	122,021
1981–1990	7,336,940	761,550	2,738,157	3,615,225	222,008
1991–2000	9,042,999	1,359,737	2,795,672	4,486,806	400,784
2001–2010	14,974,975	1,165,176	4,088,455	8,582,601	1,138,743

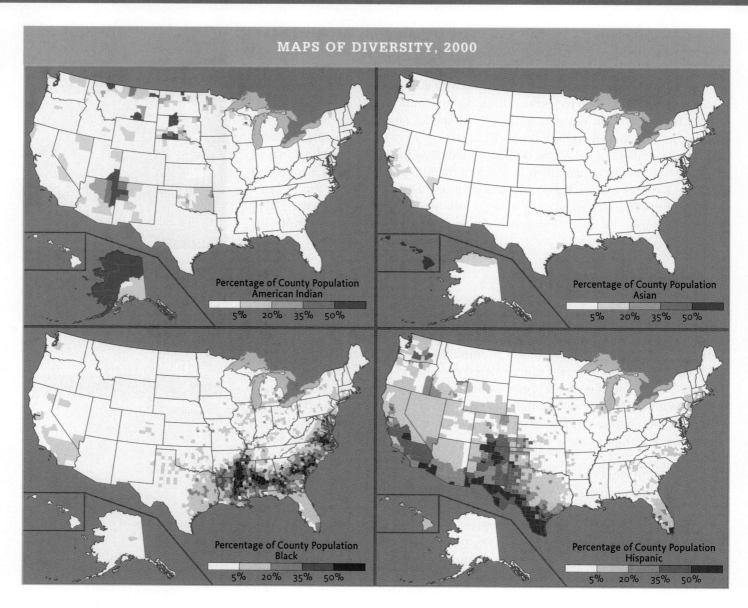

Percentage of County Population
American Indian

5% 20% 35% 50%

Percentage of County Population
Asian

5% 20% 35% 50%

Percentage of County Population
Black

5% 20% 35% 50%

Percentage of County Population
Hispanic

5% 20% 35% 50%

Based on the 2000 Census, these maps show that nearly every state has a significant non-white population.

Settlement patterns

As in the past, most immigrants became urban residents, with New York City, Los Angeles, Chicago, and Miami the most common destinations. New ethnic communities emerged, with homes, shops, restaurants, foreign-language newspapers, radio and television stations, and ethnic professionals like businessmen and lawyers. Unlike in the past, rather than being concentrated in one or two parts of city centers, immigrants quickly moved into outlying neighborhoods and older suburbs. The immigrant influx revitalized neighborhoods like New York City's Washington Heights (a Dominican enclave) and Flushing (a center for Asian newcomers). By the turn of the century, more than half of all Latinos lived in suburbs. Orange County, California, which had been a stronghold of suburban conservatism between 1960 and 1990, elected a Latina Democrat to Congress in the late 1990s. While most immigrants settled on the East and West Coasts, some

Latina nannies pushing baby carriages in Beverly Hills, California. In the 1990s, for the first time in American history, female immigrants outnumbered male immigrants.

moved to other parts of the country. They brought cultural and racial diversity to once-homogeneous communities in the American heartland.

Post-1965 immigration formed part of the worldwide uprooting of labor arising from globalization. In 2000, the global immigrant population was estimated at 100 million. Those who migrated to the United States came from a wide variety of backgrounds. They included poor, illiterate refugees from places of economic and political crisis—Central Americans escaping the region's civil wars and poverty, Haitians and Cambodians fleeing repressive governments. But many immigrants were well-educated professionals from countries like India and South Korea, where the availability of skilled jobs had not kept pace with the spread of higher education. In the year 2000, more than 40 percent of all immigrants to the United States had a college education.

For the first time in American history, women made up the majority of newcomers, reflecting the decline of manufacturing jobs that had previously absorbed immigrant men, as well as the spread of employment opportunities in traditionally female fields like care of children and the elderly and retail sales. Thanks to cheap global communications and jet travel, modern-day immigrants retained strong ties with their countries of origin, frequently phoning and visiting home.

The New Diversity

Latinos formed the largest single immigrant group. This term was invented in the United States and included people from quite different origins—Mexicans, Central and South Americans, and migrants from Spanish-speaking Caribbean islands

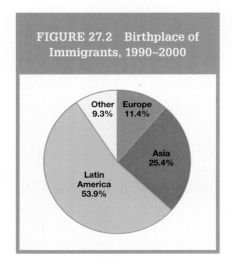

FIGURE 27.2 Birthplace of Immigrants, 1990–2000

Other 9.3%
Europe 11.4%
Asia 25.4%
Latin America 53.9%

During the 1990s, immigration from Latin America and Asia eclipsed immigration from Europe, traditionally the main source of newcomers to the United States.

The U.S. Border Patrol apprehending Mexicans who had entered the country in violation of immigration laws, near San Diego, California. In 1990, more than 1 million immigrants were arrested and deported after crossing the border illegally.

like Cuba, the Dominican Republic, and Puerto Rico (although the last group, of course, were American citizens, not immigrants). With 95 million people, Mexico in 2000 had become the world's largest Spanish-speaking nation. Its poverty, high birthrate, and proximity to the United States made it a source of massive legal and illegal immigration. In 2000, Mexican-Americans made up a majority of the Hispanic population of the United States and nearly half the residents of Los Angeles.

Latinos

Numbering around 50 million in 2010, Latinos had become the largest minority group in the United States. Between 1990 and 2010, 30 million Hispanics were added to the American population, half its total growth. Latinos were highly visible in entertainment, sports, and politics. Indeed, the Hispanic presence transformed American life. José was now the most common name for baby boys in Texas and the third most popular in California. Smith remained the most common American surname, but Garcia, Rodriguez, Gonzales, and other Hispanic names were all in the top fifty.

Poverty in Latino communities

Latino communities remained far poorer than the rest of the country. A flourishing middle class developed in Los Angeles, Miami, and other cities with large Spanish-speaking populations. But most immigrants from Mexico and Central America competed at the lowest levels of the job market. The influx of legal and illegal immigrants swelled the ranks of low-wage urban workers and agricultural laborers. Latinos lagged far behind other Americans in education. In 2010, their poverty rate stood at nearly double the national figure of 15 percent. Living and working conditions among predominantly Latino farm workers in the West fell back to levels as dire as when César Chavez established the United Farm Workers union in the 1960s.

Asian-Americans also became increasingly visible in the 1990s. There had long been a small population of Asian ancestry in California and New York City, but only after 1965 did immigration from Asia assume large proportions. Like Latinos,

Korean girls rehearsing a dance at the Veterans' Administration Medical Center in Columbia, South Carolina, an illustration of the growing diversity of American society.

Asian-Americans were a highly diverse population, including well-educated Koreans, Indians, and Japanese, as well as poor refugees from Cambodia, Vietnam, and China. Growing up in tight-knit communities that placed great emphasis on education, young Asian-Americans poured into American colleges and universities. Once subjected to harsh discrimination, Asian-Americans now achieved remarkable success. White Americans hailed them as a "model minority." By 2007, the median family income of Asian-Americans, $66,000, surpassed that of whites. But more than any other group, Asian-Americans clustered at opposite ends of the income spectrum. Large numbers earned either more than $75,000 per year (doctors, engineers, and entrepreneurs) or under $5,000 (unskilled laborers in sweatshops and restaurants).

Asian-Americans

The United States, of course, had long been a multiracial society. But for centuries race relations had been shaped by the black-white divide and the experience of slavery and segregation. The growing visibility of Latinos and Asians suggested that a two-race system no longer adequately described American life. Multiracial imagery filled television, films, and advertising. Interracial marriage, at one time banned in forty-two states, became more common and acceptable. Among Asian-Americans at the turn of the century, half of all marriages involved a non-Asian partner. The figure for Latinos was 30 percent. Some commentators spoke of the "end of racism" and the emergence of a truly color-blind society. Others argued that while Asians and some Latinos were being absorbed into an expanded category of "white" Americans, the black-white divide remained almost as impenetrable as ever.

One thing, however, seemed clear at the dawn of the twenty-first century: diversity was here to stay. In 2000, whites made up around 70 percent of the population, blacks and Hispanics around 13 percent each, and Asians 6 percent. Because the birthrate of racial minorities is higher than that of whites, the Census Bureau projected that by 2050, only 50 percent of the American population would be white, a little less than 25 percent would be Hispanic, and blacks and Asians would account for around 13 percent each.

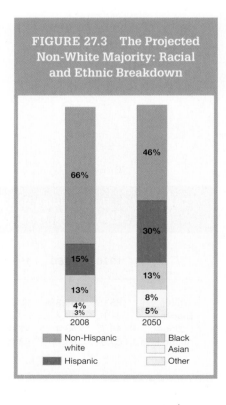

FIGURE 27.3 The Projected Non-White Majority: Racial and Ethnic Breakdown

2008: Non-Hispanic white 66%, Hispanic 15%, Black 13%, Asian 4%, Other 3%

2050: Non-Hispanic white 46%, Hispanic 30%, Black 13%, Asian 8%, Other 5%

Legend: Non-Hispanic white, Hispanic, Black, Asian, Other

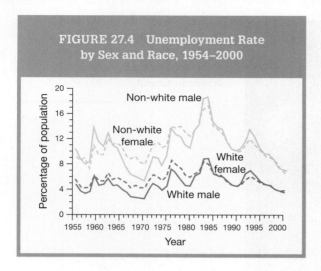

FIGURE 27.4 Unemployment Rate by Sex and Race, 1954–2000

Despite the ups and downs of unemployment, the rate for non-whites remains persistently higher than that for whites.

African immigration

TABLE 27.2 Home Ownership Rates by Group, 1970–2000

	1970	1980	1990	2000
Whites	65.0%	67.8%	68.2%	73.8%
Blacks	41.6	44.4	43.4	47.2
Latinos	43.7	43.4	42.4	46.3
All families	62.9	64.4	64.2	67.4

African-Americans in the 1990s

Compared with the situation in 1900 or 1950, the most dramatic change in American life at the turn of the century was the absence of legal segregation and the presence of blacks in areas of American life from which they had once been almost entirely excluded. Thanks to the decline in overt discrimination and the effectiveness of many affirmative action programs, blacks now worked in unprecedented numbers alongside whites in corporate board rooms, offices, and factories. The number of black policemen, for example, rose from 24,000 to 65,000 between 1970 and 2000, and in the latter year, 37 percent of the black population reported having attended college. The economic boom of the late 1990s aided black Americans enormously; the average income of black families rose more rapidly than that of whites.

One major change in black life was the growing visibility of Africans among the nation's immigrants. Between 1970 and 2000, twice as many Africans immigrated to the United States as had entered during the entire period of the Atlantic slave trade. For the first time, all the elements of the African diaspora—natives of Africa, Caribbeans, Central and South Americans of African descent, Europeans with African roots—could be found in the United States alongside the descendants of American slaves.

Nigeria, Ghana, and Ethiopia provided the largest number of African immigrants, and they settled overwhelmingly in urban areas, primarily in New York, California, Texas, and the District of Columbia. Some were impoverished refugees fleeing civil wars in Somalia, Sudan, and Ethiopia, but many more were professionals—more than half the African newcomers had college educations, the highest percentage for any immigrant group. Indeed, some African countries complained of a "brain drain" as physicians, teachers, and other highly skilled persons sought opportunities in the United States that did not exist in their own underdeveloped countries. While some prospered, others found it difficult to transfer their credentials to the United States and found jobs driving taxis and selling African crafts at street fairs.

Most African-Americans, nonetheless, remained in a more precarious situation than whites or many recent immigrants. The black unemployment rate remained double that of whites, and in 2007 their median family income of $34,000 and poverty rate of 25 percent put them behind whites, Asians, and Latinos. Half of all black children lived in poverty, two-thirds were born out of wedlock, and in every index of social well-being from health to quality of housing, blacks continued to lag. Despite the continued expansion of the black middle class, a far lower percentage of blacks than whites owned their homes or held professional and managerial jobs. Housing segregation remained pervasive. In 2000, more than one-third of the black population lived in suburbs, but mostly in predominantly black communities. The gap in wealth between blacks and whites remained enormous. In 2007, the total assets of the median white family (bank accounts, stocks, the value of a home, etc.) stood at $87,000. For black families, the figure was $5,400.

The Role of the Courts

As in the late nineteenth century, the Supreme Court in the last years of the twentieth century little by little retreated from the civil rights revolution. The justices made it increasingly difficult for victims of discrimination to win lawsuits and proved increasingly sympathetic to the pleas of whites that affirmative action plans discriminated against them. In *Patterson v. McLean Credit Union* (1989), the Court barred a black employee who suffered racial harassment while working from suing for damages under the Civil Rights Act of 1866. That law, the justices maintained, only prohibited discrimination at the moment of signing a contract, not on the job.

Despite the nation's growing racial diversity, school segregation—now resulting from housing patterns and the divide between urban and suburban school districts rather than laws requiring racial separation—was on the rise. Most city public school systems consisted overwhelmingly of minority students, large numbers of whom failed to receive an adequate education. The courts released more and more districts from desegregation orders. By 2000, the nation's black and Latino students were more isolated from white pupils than in 1970. Nearly 80 percent of white students attended schools where they encountered few if any pupils of another race. Since school funding rested on property taxes, poor communities continued to have less to spend on education than wealthy ones.

> *Housing patterns and school segregation*

The Spread of Imprisonment

During the 1960s, the nation's prison population had declined. But in the 1970s, with urban crime rates rising, politicians of both parties sought to convey the image of being "tough on crime." They insisted that the judicial system should focus on locking up criminals for long periods rather than rehabilitating them. They treated drug addiction as a violation of the law rather than as a disease. State governments greatly increased the penalties for crime and reduced the possibility of parole. Successive presidents launched "wars" on the use of illegal drugs. As a result, the number of Americans in prison rose dramatically, most of them incarcerated for nonviolent drug offenses.

A private, for-profit, maximum-security prison under construction in 1999 in California City, in the Mohave Desert, illustrates the expansion of the "prison-industrial complex."

During the 1990s, thanks to the waning of the "crack" epidemic and more effective urban police tactics, crime rates dropped dramatically across the country. But because of the sentencing laws of the previous two decades, this did nothing to stem the increase of the prison population. In 2008, it reached 2.3 million, ten times the figure of 1970. Several million more individuals were on parole, on probation, or under some other kind of criminal supervision. These figures dwarfed those of every other Western society.

As the prison population grew, a "prison-industrial complex" emerged. Struggling communities battered by deindustrialization saw prisons as a source of jobs and income. Between 1990 and 1995, the federal government and the states constructed more than 200 new prisons. In 2008, five states spent more money on their prison systems than on higher education. Convict labor, a practice the labor movement had managed to curtail in the late nineteenth century, revived in the late twentieth. Private companies in Oregon "leased" prisoners for three dollars per day. A call to Trans World Airlines for a flight reservation was likely to be answered by a California inmate.

The Burden of Imprisonment

Members of racial minorities experienced most strongly the paradox of growing islands of unfreedom in a nation that prided itself on liberty. In 1950, whites accounted for 70 percent of the nation's prison population and non-whites 30 percent. By 2010, these figures had been reversed. One reason was that severe penalties faced those convicted of using or selling crack, a particularly potent form of cocaine concentrated among the urban poor, while the use of powder cocaine, the drug of choice in suburban America, led to far lighter sentences.

The percentage of the black population in prison stood five times higher than the proportion for white Americans. More than one-quarter of all black men could expect to serve time in prison at some time during their lives. A criminal record made it very difficult for ex-prisoners to find jobs. Partly because so many young men were in prison, blacks had a significantly lower rate of marriage than other Americans. Their children became "prison orphans," forced to live with relatives or in foster homes.

Blacks convicted of crimes were also more likely than whites to receive the death penalty. In 1972, the Supreme Court had temporarily suspended states' use of this punishment. But the Court soon allowed it to resume, despite evidence of racial disparities in its application. Even as western Europe and other countries abolished the death penalty, the United States executed 598 persons between 1977 and 1999. In the 1830s, Alexis de Tocqueville had described executions as common in Europe but rare in America. At the close of the twentieth century, with more than 3,000 prisoners on death row, the United States ranked with China, Iran, and Saudi Arabia as the nations that most often executed their citizens. The 2.3 million Americans in prison in 2010 represented one-quarter of the entire world's inmates and far exceeded the number in any other country.

The continuing frustration of urban blacks exploded in 1992 when an all-white suburban jury found four Los Angeles police

The rising prison population

Racial minorities and incarceration

FIGURE 27.5 Institutional Inmates as a Percentage of the Population by Sex and Race, 1850–2010

officers not guilty in the beating of black motorist Rodney King, even though an onlooker had captured their assault on videotape. The deadliest urban uprising since the New York draft riots of 1863 followed. Some fifty-two people died, and property damage approached $1 billion. Many Latino youths, who shared blacks' resentment over mistreatment by the police, joined in the violence. The uprising suggested that despite the civil rights revolution, the nation had failed to address the plight of the urban poor.

The Continuing Rights Revolution

Reflecting the continued power of the rights revolution, the 1990s also witnessed the emergence of new movements for public recognition. In 1990, newly organized disabled Americans won passage of the Americans with Disabilities Act. This far-reaching measure prohibited discrimination in hiring and promotion against persons with disabilities and required that entrances to public buildings be redesigned so as to ensure access for the disabled.

The AIDS quilt, each square of which represents a person who died of AIDS, on display in Washington, D.C. The quilt was exhibited throughout the country, heightening public awareness of the AIDS epidemic.

Some movements that were descended from the late 1960s achieved their greatest visibility in the 1990s. Prominent among these was the campaign for gay rights, which in the last two decades of the century increasingly turned its attention to combating acquired immunodeficiency syndrome (AIDS), a fatal disease spread by sexual contact, drug use, and transfusions of contaminated blood. AIDS first emerged in the early 1980s. It quickly became epidemic among homosexual men. The gay movement mobilized to promote "safe sex," prevent discrimination against people suffering from AIDS, and press the federal government to devote greater resources to fighting the disease. By 2000, even though more than 400,000 Americans had died of AIDS, its spread among gays had been sharply curtailed. But in other parts of the world, such as Africa, the AIDS epidemic remained out of control.

Gay groups also played an increasing role in politics. In cities with large gay populations, such as New York and San Francisco, politicians vied to attract their votes. Overall, the growth of public tolerance of homosexuality was among the most striking changes in American social attitudes in the last two decades of the century.

Native Americans in 2000

Another social movement spawned by the 1960s that continued to flourish was the American Indian movement. The Indian population reached over 5 million (including people choosing more than one race) in the 2010 Census, a sign not only of population growth but also of a renewed sense of pride that led many Indians for the first time to identify themselves as such to census enumerators. Meanwhile, with the assistance of the Native American Rights Fund, established in 1971, some tribes embarked on a campaign for restitution for past injustices. In 2001, for example, a New York court awarded the Cayuga Nation $248 million for illegal land seizures two centuries earlier.

American Indian movement

The legal position of Indians as American citizens who enjoy a kind of quasi-sovereignty still survives in some cases. Notable examples are the lucrative Indian casinos now operating in states that otherwise prohibit gambling. Indian casinos take in around $15 billion each year, making some tribes very rich. One such group

This "public sculpture" by the Native American artist Lewis DeSoto links his own surname with more than four centuries of American history. The wall label invokes the depredations of the sixteenth-century Spanish conquistador Hernando de Soto. The car reminds the viewer that the Chrysler Corporation chose the name DeSoto for a now-defunct automobile. On the rear of the car is an insignia based on traditional Indian basket designs, encircled by the Latin word for smallpox, which the conquistadores transmitted to the Indian population.

Increasing tolerance

is the Pequot tribe of Connecticut. In 1637, as the result of a brief, bloody war, Puritan New Englanders exterminated or sold into slavery most of the tribe's members. The treaty that restored peace decreed that the tribe's name should be wiped from the historical record. Today, the few hundred members of the Pequot tribe operate Foxwoods, reputedly the world's largest casino.

Half of today's Indians live in five western states (California, Oklahoma, Arizona, New Mexico, and Washington). Although some tribes have reinvested casino profits in improved housing and health care and college scholarships for Native American students, most Indian casinos are marginal operations whose low-wage jobs as cashiers, waitresses, and the like have done little to relieve Indian poverty. Native Americans continue to occupy the lowest rung on the economic ladder. At least half of those living on reservations have incomes below the poverty line.

Multiculturalism

The new face of American society went hand in hand with one of the most striking developments of the 1990s—the celebration of group difference and demands for group recognition. "Multiculturalism" became the term for a new awareness of the diversity of American society, past and present, and for vocal demands that jobs, education, and politics reflect that diversity. As the numbers of minority and female students at the nation's colleges and universities rose, these institutions moved aggressively to diversify their faculties and revise the traditional curriculum.

One sign of multiculturalism could be seen in the spread of academic programs dealing with the experience of specific groups—Black Studies, Latino Studies, Women's Studies, and the like. Literature departments added the writings of female and minority authors to those of white men. Numerous scholars now taught and wrote history in ways that stressed the experiences of diverse groups of Americans, rather than a common national narrative.

At the same time, public-opinion polls revealed a remarkable growth of toleration. The number of respondents who accepted interracial dating without objection rose from 45 percent in 1987 to 78 percent in 2003. Those who believed gays should automatically be fired from teaching jobs fell from 50 to 35 percent over the same period. In addition, popular television shows portrayed gay characters in a sympathetic light.

The Identity Debate

Among some Americans, the heightened visibility of immigrants, racial minorities, and inheritors of the sexual revolution inspired not celebration of pluralism but alarm over perceived cultural fragmentation. Conservatives, and some traditional liberals as well, decried "identity politics" and multiculturalism for undermining a common sense of nationhood. As in the debates over the Alien Act of the 1790s, Irish immigration in the 1850s, and the "new immigrants" of the early twentieth century, the definition of American nationality again became a contentious political question. Bill Clinton's 1992 slogan, "It's the Economy, Stupid," was directed, in part, at members of the Democratic Party who preferred to focus on racial and gender issues rather than traditional economic concerns. Republicans appealed most directly to those alarmed by the influx of non-white immigrants and the decline of traditional "family values." But differences over diversity did not follow party lines.

Demonstrators for and against Proposition 187, with police separating them, at a rally in Los Angeles in August 1996. Approved by California voters two years earlier, the measure severely restricted the services available to undocumented immigrants.

Increased cultural diversity and changes in educational policy inspired harsh debates over whether immigrant children should be required to learn English and whether further immigration should be discouraged. These issues entered politics most dramatically in California, whose voters in 1994 approved Proposition 187, which denied illegal immigrants and their children access to welfare, education, and most health services. A federal judge soon barred implementation of the measure on the grounds that control over immigration policy rests with the federal government. But during the 1990s, California voters also approved measures banning bilingual education in public schools, and affirmative action in admission to public colleges and universities. By 2000, twenty-three states had passed laws establishing English as their official language (similar to measures enacted in the aftermath of World War I). The 1996 law that abolished welfare also barred most immigrants who had not become citizens from receiving food stamps.

But since 1900, the United States had become a far more tolerant society. Efforts to appeal to prejudice for political gain often backfired. In California, Republicans' anti-immigrant campaigns inspired minorities to mobilize politically and offended many white Americans. In 2000, Republican presidential candidate George W. Bush emphasized that his brand of conservatism was multicultural, not exclusionary.

Cultural Conservatism

Immigration occupied only one front in what came to be called the Culture Wars—battles over moral values that raged throughout the 1990s. The Christian Coalition, founded by evangelical minister Pat Robertson, became a major force in Republican politics. It launched crusades against gay rights, abortion, secularism in public schools, and government aid to the arts. Pat Buchanan's Republican convention speech of 1992 calling for a "religious war for the soul of America," mentioned earlier, alarmed many voters. But cultural conservatives hailed it as their new rallying cry.

> *The Culture Wars*

It sometimes appeared during the 1990s that the country was refighting old battles between traditional religion and modern secular culture. In an echo

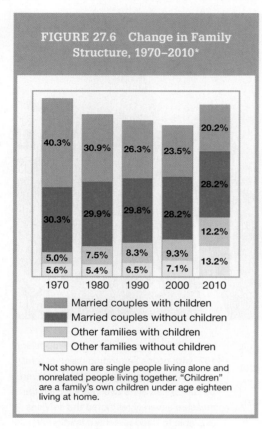

FIGURE 27.6 Change in Family Structure, 1970–2010*

	1970	1980	1990	2000	2010
Married couples with children	40.3%	30.9%	26.3%	23.5%	20.2%
Married couples without children	30.3%	29.9%	29.8%	28.2%	28.2%
Other families with children	5.0%	7.5%	8.3%	9.3%	12.2%
Other families without children	5.6%	5.4%	6.5%	7.1%	13.2%

Married couples with children
Married couples without children
Other families with children
Other families without children

*Not shown are single people living alone and nonrelated people living together. "Children" are a family's own children under age eighteen living at home.

At the beginning of the twenty-first century, less than one-quarter of American households consisted of a "traditional" family—a married couple living with their children.

Politics and women's lives

of the 1920s, a number of localities required the teaching of creationism, a religious alternative to Darwin's theory of evolution. The battles of the 1960s seemed to be forever unresolved. Many conservatives railed against the erosion of the nuclear family, the changing racial landscape produced by immigration, and what they considered a general decline of traditional values. Cultural conservatives were not satisfied with a few victories over what they considered immorality, such as the Defense of Marriage Act of 1996, which barred gay couples from spousal benefits provided by federal law.

"Family Values" in Retreat

The censuses of 2000 and 2010 showed "family values increasingly in disarray. Half of all marriages ended in divorce (70 percent on the West Coast). In 2010, more than 40 percent of births were to unmarried women, not only sexually active teenagers, but growing numbers of professional women in the thirties and forties as well. For the first time, fewer than half of all households consisted of married couples, and only one-fifth were "traditional" families—a wife, husband, and their children. More than half of all adults were single or divorced. Two-thirds of married women worked outside the home. The pay gap between men and women, although narrowing, persisted. In 2010, the weekly earnings of women with full-time jobs stood at 82 percent of those of men—up from 63 percent in 1980. In only two occupational categories did women earn more than men—postal service clerks and special education teachers.

Although dominated by conservatives, the Supreme Court, in *Casey v. Planned Parenthood of Pennsylvania* (1992), reaffirmed a woman's right to obtain an abortion. The decision allowed states to enact mandatory waiting periods and anti-abortion counseling, but it overturned a requirement that the husband be given notification before the procedure was undertaken. "At the heart of liberty," said the Court, "is the right to . . . make the most intimate and personal choices" without outside interference. In effect, *Casey* repudiated the centuries-old doctrine that a husband has a legal claim to control the body of his wife.

The narrowness of the 5-4 vote in *Casey* and the vehemence of the dissenters, including Chief Justice William Rehnquist, in insisting that *Roe v. Wade* must be reversed, left the legal status of abortion rights dependent on future changes in the Court's membership. As of 2000, however, although conservatives had controlled the presidency under Reagan and Bush, Congress after 1994, and the Supreme Court, they had not eliminated abortion rights, restored prayer to public schools, or persuaded women to abandon public aspirations and "go about the business of marrying and raising children," as Republican congressional leader Richard Armey indelicately demanded. Women did not listen to Armey. At the beginning of the twenty-first-century, women received more than 60 percent of all college degrees (as opposed to 35 percent in 1960) and over 40 percent of advanced law, medical, and business degrees (up from around 5 percent forty years earlier). The abortion rate declined throughout the 1990s, but this was mostly because teenagers had increasing access to contraception. The sexual revolution and feminism, it seemed, were here to stay.

The Antigovernment Extreme

At the radical fringe of conservatism, the belief that the federal government posed a threat to American freedom led to the creation of private militias who armed themselves to fend off oppressive authority. Groups like Aryan Nation, Posse Comitatus, and other self-proclaimed "Christian patriots" spread a mixture of racist, anti-Semitic, and antigovernment ideas. Private armies, like the Militia of Montana, vowed to resist enforcement of federal gun control laws. For millions of Americans, owning a gun became a prime symbol of liberty. "We're here because we love freedom," declared a participant in a 1995 Washington rally against proposed legislation banning semiautomatic assault weapons.

Many militia groups employed the symbolism and language of the American Revolution, sprinkling their appeals with warnings about the dangers of government tyranny drawn from the writings of Thomas Jefferson, Patrick Henry, and Thomas Paine. They warned that leaders of both major parties formed part of a conspiracy to surrender American sovereignty to the United Nations, or to some shadowy international conspiracy. Although such organizations had been growing for years, they burst into the national spotlight in 1995 when Timothy McVeigh, a member of the militant antigovernment movement, exploded a bomb at a federal office building in Oklahoma City. The blast killed 168 persons, including numerous children at a day-care center. McVeigh was captured, convicted, and executed. The bombing alerted the nation to the danger of violent antigovernment right-wing groups.

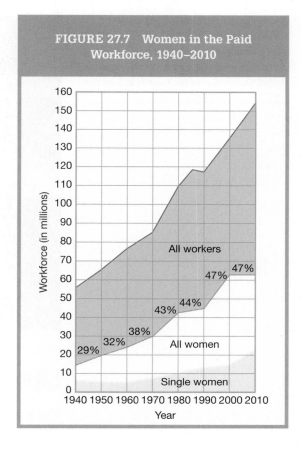

FIGURE 27.7 Women in the Paid Workforce, 1940–2010

By 2000, women represented nearly half of the American workforce, and unlike in the nineteenth century, a majority of women working outside the home were married.

Items on sale at Michigan's "Gun Stock '95," an antigovernment convention.

Rescue workers sifting the wreckage of a federal office building in Oklahoma City after it was heavily damaged by a bomb in 1995, the worst act of terrorism in the United States during the twentieth century.

IMPEACHMENT AND THE ELECTION OF 2000

The unusually intense partisanship of the 1990s seemed ironic, given Clinton's move toward the political center. Republicans' intense dislike of Clinton could only be explained by the fact that he seemed to symbolize everything conservatives hated about the 1960s. As a college student, the president had smoked marijuana and participated in antiwar demonstrations. He had married a feminist, made a point of leading a multicultural administration, and supported gay rights. Clinton's popularity puzzled and frustrated conservatives, reinforcing their conviction that something was deeply amiss in American life. From the very outset of his administration, Clinton's political opponents and scandal-hungry media stood ready to pounce. Clinton himself provided the ammunition.

Clinton and the right

The Impeachment of Clinton

Charges of sexual misconduct by public officials had a long history. But in the 1980s and 1990s, scrutiny of politicians' private lives became far more intense than in the past. Gary Hart, as noted in the previous chapter, had been driven from the 1988 campaign because of an extramarital liaison. In 1991, Senate hearings on the nomination to the Supreme Court of Clarence Thomas, a black conservative, became embroiled in dramatic charges of sexual harassment leveled against Thomas by law professor Anita Hill. To the outrage of feminists, the Senate narrowly confirmed him. Nonetheless, because of her testimony, Americans became more aware of the problem of sexual harassment in and out of the workplace, and complaints shot up across the country.

Sexual misconduct

From the day Clinton took office, charges of misconduct bedeviled him. In 1993, an investigation began of an Arkansas real-estate deal known as Whitewater, from which he and his wife had profited. The following year, an Arkansas woman, Paula Jones, filed a civil suit charging that Clinton had sexually harassed her while he served as governor of that state. In 1998, it became known that Clinton had carried on an affair with Monica Lewinsky, a White House intern. Kenneth Starr, the special counsel who had been appointed to investigate Whitewater, shifted his focus to Lewinsky. He issued a lengthy report containing almost pornographic details of Clinton's sexual acts with the young woman and accused the president of lying when he denied the affair in a deposition for the Jones lawsuit. In December 1998, the Republican-controlled House of Representatives voted to impeach Clinton for perjury and obstruction of justice. He became the second president to be tried before the Senate. Early in 1999, the vote took place. Neither charge mustered a simple majority, much less than the two-thirds required to remove Clinton from office.

Karl Marx once wrote that historical events occur twice—first as tragedy, the second time as farce. The impeachment of Andrew Johnson in 1868 had revolved around some of the most momentous questions in American history—the Reconstruction of the South, the rights of the former slaves, relations between the federal government and the states. Clinton's impeachment had to do with what many considered to be a juvenile escapade. Polls suggested that the obsession of Kenneth Starr and members of Congress with Clinton's sexual acts appalled Americans far more than the president's irresponsible behavior. Clinton's continuing popularity throughout the impeachment controversy demonstrated how profoundly traditional attitudes toward sexual morality had changed.

Herbert Block's 1998 cartoon comments humorously on Clinton's talent for political survival.

The Disputed Election

Had Clinton been eligible to run for reelection in 2000, he would probably have won. But after the death of FDR, the Constitution had been amended to limit presidents to two terms in office. Democrats nominated Vice President Al Gore to succeed Clinton (pairing him with Senator Joseph Lieberman of Connecticut, the first Jewish vice-presidential nominee). Republicans chose George W. Bush, the governor of Texas and son of Clinton's predecessor, as their candidate, with former secretary of defense Dick Cheney as his running mate.

A member of a Florida election board trying to determine a voter's intent during the recount of presidential ballots in November 2000. The U.S. Supreme Court eventually ordered the recount halted.

The election proved to be one of the closest in the nation's history. The outcome remained uncertain until a month after the ballots had been cast. Gore won the popular vote by a tiny margin—540,000 of 100 million cast, or one-half of 1 percent. Victory in the electoral college hinged on which candidate had carried Florida. There, amid widespread confusion at the polls and claims of irregularities in counting the ballots, Bush claimed a margin of a few hundred votes. In the days after the election, Democrats demanded a hand recount of the Florida ballots for which machines could not determine a voter's intent. The Florida Supreme Court ordered the recount to proceed.

As in the disputed election that ended Reconstruction (a contest in which Florida had also played a crucial role), it fell to Supreme Court justices to decide the outcome. On December 12, 2000, by a 5-4 vote, the Court ordered a halt to the recounting of Florida ballots, allowing the state's governor Jeb Bush (George W. Bush's brother) to certify that the Republican candidate had carried the state and had therefore won the presidency.

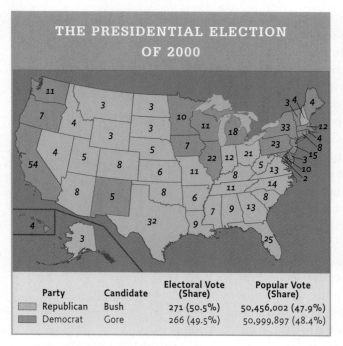

THE PRESIDENTIAL ELECTION OF 2000

Party	Candidate	Electoral Vote (Share)	Popular Vote (Share)
Republican	Bush	271 (50.5%)	50,456,002 (47.9%)
Democrat	Gore	266 (49.5%)	50,999,897 (48.4%)

A divided nation

The decision in *Bush v. Gore* was one of the oddest in Supreme Court history. In the late 1990s, the Court had reasserted the powers of the states within the federal system. Now, however, it overturned a decision of the Florida Supreme Court interpreting the state's election laws. Many observers did not expect the justices to consider the matter at all, since it did not seem to raise a federal constitutional question. They justified their decision by insisting that the "equal protection" clause of the Fourteenth Amendment required that all ballots within a state be counted in accordance with a single standard, something impossible given the wide variety of machines and paper ballots used in Florida. Perhaps recognizing that this new constitutional principle threatened to throw into question results throughout the country—since many states had voting systems as complex as Florida's—the Court added that it applied only in this single case.

The 2000 Result

The most remarkable thing about the election of 2000 was not so much its controversial ending as the even division of the country it revealed. Bush and Gore each received essentially half of the popular vote. The final count in the electoral college stood at 271-266, the narrowest margin since 1876. The Senate ended up divided 50-50 between the two parties. But these figures concealed deep political and social fissures. Bush carried the entire South and nearly all the states of the trans-Mississippi farm belt and Rockies. Gore won almost all the states of the Northeast, Old Northwest, and West Coast. Residents of urban areas voted overwhelmingly for Gore. Rural areas went just as solidly for Bush. Members of racial minorities gave Gore large majorities, while white voters preferred Bush. The results also revealed a significant "gender gap." Until the 1960s, women had tended to vote disproportionately Republican. In 2000, women favored Gore by 11 percent, while men preferred Bush by the same margin.

Democrats blamed the Supreme Court, Ralph Nader, and sheer bad luck for Bush's narrow victory. Running as the candidate of the environmentalist Green Party, Nader had won tens of thousands of votes in Florida that otherwise may have gone to Gore. In one county, a faulty ballot design led several thousand Gore voters accidentally to cast their votes for independent conservative candidate Pat Buchanan. Had their votes been counted for Gore, he would have been elected president.

A Challenged Democracy

Coming at the end of the "decade of democracy," the 2000 election revealed troubling features of the American political system at the close of the twentieth century. The electoral college, devised by the founders to enable the country's prominent men rather than ordinary voters to choose the president, gave the White House to a candidate who did not receive the most votes—an odd result in a political democracy. A country that prided itself on modern technology had a voting system in which citizens' choices could not be reliably determined. Counting both congressional and presidential races, the campaign cost more than $1.5 billion, mostly raised from wealthy individuals and corporate donors. This reinforced the widespread belief that money dominated the political system. The implications for democracy of the ever-closer connection between power in the economic marketplace and power in the marketplace of politics and ideas would be widely debated in the early twenty-first century.

Evidence abounded of a broad disengagement from public life. As governments at all levels competed to turn their activities over to private contractors, and millions of Americans walled themselves off from their fellow citizens by taking up residence in socially homogeneous gated communities, the very idea of a shared public sphere seemed to dissolve. Nearly half the eligible voters did not bother to go to the polls, and in state and local elections, turnouts typically ranged between only 20 and 30 percent. More people watched the televised Nixon-Kennedy debates of 1960 than the Bush-Gore debates of 2000, even though the population had risen by 100 million. Both candidates sought to occupy the political center and relied on public-opinion polls and media consultants to shape their messages. Major issues like health care, race relations, and economic inequality went virtually unmentioned during the campaign.

Another cartoon by Herbert Block, from 2000, suggests that democracy has been corrupted by the influence of "big money interests" on government.

FREEDOM AND THE NEW CENTURY

The century that ended with the 2000 election witnessed vast human progress and unimaginable human tragedy. It saw the decolonization of Asia and Africa, the emergence of women into full citizenship in most parts of the world, and amazing advances in science, medicine, and technology. Thanks to the spread of new products, available at ever-cheaper prices, it brought more improvement in the daily conditions of life to more human beings than any other century in history. Worldwide life expectancy in the twentieth century rose from forty to sixty-seven years, and the literacy rate increased from 25 percent to 80 percent. This was the first century in which the primary economic activity for most of mankind moved beyond the acquisition of basic food, clothing, and shelter. But the twentieth century also witnessed the death of uncounted millions in wars and genocides and the widespread degradation of the natural environment, the underside of progress.

Exceptional America

In the United States, people lived longer and healthier lives in 2000 compared to previous generations, and they enjoyed a level of material comfort unimagined a century before. In 1900, the average annual income was $3,000 in today's dollars. The typical American had no indoor plumbing, had no telephone or car, and had not graduated from high school. As late as 1940, one-third of American households did not have running water. In 2000, health conditions had improved so much that the average life expectancy for men had risen to seventy-four and for women to seventy-nine (from forty-six and forty-eight in

Broad social changes

At the beginning of the twenty-first century, more than 7 million American families lived in gated communities, where the wealthy, and some members of the middle class as well, walled themselves off from the rest of society. This one is in the Brentwood section of Los Angeles.

The social fabric

1900). More than 14 million Americans attended college in 2000, more than three times the figure for 1960.

In 2000, nearly one American in seven was older than sixty-five. Certain to continue rising in the twenty-first century, this figure sparked worries about the future cost of health care and the economic stability of the Social Security system. But it also suggested that people would enjoy far longer and more productive periods of retirement than in the past. On the other hand, poverty, income inequality, and infant mortality in the United States considerably exceeded that of other economically advanced countries, and fewer than 10 percent of workers in private firms belonged to unions, a figure not seen since the nineteenth century.

Many of the changes affecting American life, such as the transformed role of women, the better health and longer lifespan of the population, the spread of suburbanization, and the decline of industrial employment, have taken place in all economically advanced societies. In other ways, however, the United States at the dawn of the twenty-first century differed sharply from other developed countries. Prevailing ideas of freedom in the United States seemed more attuned to individual advancement than to broad social welfare. In 2003, when asked whether it was more important for the government to guarantee freedom from want or freedom to pursue individual goals, only 35 percent of Americans selected freedom from want, as opposed to 58 percent in Germany, 62 percent in France and Great Britain, and 65 percent in Italy. The United States was a far more religious country. Sixty percent of Americans agreed with the statement, "Religion plays a very important part in my life," while the comparable figure was 32 percent in Britain, 26 percent in Italy, and only 11 percent in France. One in three Americans said he or she believed in the literal truth of the Bible, and half that the United

States enjoys "special protection from God." Religion and nationalism reinforced one another far more powerfully in the United States than in the more secular nations of western Europe.

Other forms of American exceptionalism had a darker side. Among advanced countries, the United States has by far the highest rate of murder using guns. In 1998, the last year for which comparative statistics are available, there were 11,789 murders with guns in the United States, as opposed to 373 in Germany, 151 in Canada, 54 in Great Britain, and 19 in Japan. The United States continued to lag behind other countries in providing social rights to its citizens. In Europe, workers are guaranteed by law a paid vacation each year and a number of paid sick days. American employers are not required to offer either to their workers. Only four countries in the world have no national provision for paid maternity leave after a woman gives birth to a child: Liberia, Papua New Guinea, Swaziland, and the United States.

> *Global comparisons*

Varieties of Freedom

In a speech at midnight on January 1, 2000 (strictly speaking, a year before the twenty-first century actually began), President Clinton proclaimed, "The great story of the twentieth century is the triumph of freedom and free people." Freedom remained a crucial point of self-definition for individuals and society at large. When asked in a public-opinion survey what they were proudest of about America, 69 percent of respondents answered, "Freedom." Americans were increasingly tolerant of divergent personal lifestyles, cultural backgrounds, and religious persuasions. They enjoyed a degree of freedom of expression unmatched in virtually any country in the world. But their definition of freedom had changed markedly during the course of the twentieth century. Thanks to the rights revolution and the political ascendancy of antigovernment conservatives, the dominant definition of freedom stressed the capacity of individuals to realize their desires and fulfill their potential unrestricted by authority. Other American traditions—freedom as economic security, freedom as active participation in democratic government, freedom as social justice for those long disadvantaged—seemed to be in eclipse. Americans sought freedom within themselves, not through social institutions or public engagement.

It was an irony of late-twentieth-century life that Americans enjoyed more personal freedom than ever before but less of what earlier generations called "industrial freedom." Globalization—which treated workers at home and abroad as interchangeable factors of production, capable of being uprooted or dismissed without warning—seemed to render individual and even national sovereignty all but meaningless. Since economic liberty has long been associated with economic security, and rights have historically been linked to democratic participation and membership in a nation-state, these processes had ominous implications for traditional understandings of freedom. It remained to be seen whether a conception of freedom grounded in access to the consumer marketplace and the glorification of individual self-fulfillment unrestrained by government, social citizenship, or a common public culture could provide an adequate way of comprehending the world of the twenty-first century.

The approach of a new millennium inspired writers, artists, and politicians to reflect on the history and symbolism of freedom. In a work entitled *Chillin' with Liberty*, the artist Renée Cox poses herself atop the Statue of Liberty, audaciously staking her own claim to American freedom.

SUGGESTED READING

BOOKS

- Brands, H. W. *The Strange Death of American Liberalism* (2001). Explores how liberals' discrediting of the federal government through their criticisms of the Vietnam War and Watergate paved the way for the triumph of antigovernment conservatism.

- Cassidy, John. *Dot.con* (2002). Describes the rise and fall of the "new economy."

- Christianson, Scott. *With Liberty for Some: 500 Years of Imprisonment in America* (1998). A full-scale study of the history of imprisonment in the United States and its recent dramatic expansion.

- Foner, Nancy. *From Ellis Island to JFK: New York's Two Great Waves of Immigration* (2000). Studies the new immigration of the 1980s and 1990s and considers how it does and does not differ from earlier waves of newcomers.

- Friedman, Thomas L. *The Lexus and the Olive Tree* (1999). An influential account of globalization and its economic promise.

- Hodgson, Godfrey. *More Equal than Others: America from Nixon to the New Century* (2004). A survey of recent American history that identifies growing inequality as a major trend of these years.

- Johnson, Haynes. *The Best of Times: America in the Clinton Years* (2001). A sympathetic account of Clinton's presidency.

- Katz, Michael B. *The Price of Citizenship: Redefining the American Welfare State* (2001). Presents the history of welfare policy, with attention to the origins and impact of Clinton's welfare reform.

- Levitas, Daniel. *The Terrorist Next Door: The Militia Movement and the Radical Right* (2003). A careful study of right-wing extremism of the 1990s.

- Lichtenstein, Nelson. *The Retail Revolution: How Wal-Mart Created a Brave New World of Business* (2009). How Wal-Mart became the largest employer in the United States and one of the most profitable.

- Phillips, Kevin. *Wealth and Democracy* (2002). A critique of the influence of money on American politics.

- Power, Samantha. *A Problem from Hell: America and the Age of Genocide* (2002). Discusses genocides of the 1990s and the problem of the appropriate American response.

- Roberts, Sam. *Who We Are Now: The Changing Face of America in the Twenty-First Century* (2004). A social portrait of the American people based on the 2000 Census.

- Smelser, Neil J., and Jeffrey C. Alexander. *Diversity and Its Discontents: Cultural Conflict and Common Ground in Contemporary American Society* (1999). Describes the new social diversity of the 1990s and the cultural and political tensions arising from it.

- Spence, Michael. *The Next Convergence: The Future of Economic Growth in a Multispeed World* (2011). A Nobel Prize–winning economist examines the impact of globalization on jobs and incomes in the United States.

WEBSITES

- Global Exchange: www.globalexchange.org

- Making the Macintosh: Technology and Culture in Silicon Valley: http://library.stanford.edu/mac/

CHAPTER REVIEW AND ONLINE RESOURCES

REVIEW QUESTIONS

1. Why was the year 1989 one of the most momentous in the twentieth century?

2. Describe the different visions of the U.S. role in the post–Cold War world as identified by President George H. W. Bush and President Clinton.

3. Explain Clinton's political strategy of combining social liberalism with conservative economic ideas.

4. What are the causes and consequences of the growing "prison-industrial complex"?

5. Identify the factors that, in the midst of 1990s prosperity, increased the levels of inequality in the United States.

6. What are the similarities and differences between immigration patterns of the 1990s and earlier?

7. What main issues gave rise to the Culture Wars of the 1990s?

8. Assess the role of the Supreme Court in the presidential election of 2000.

9. What is globalization, and how did it affect the United States in the 1990s?

10. What is meant by "American exceptionalism"? In what ways is the United States different from the rest of the world and how is it similar?

KEY TERMS

globalization (p. 1047)

"new world order" (p. 1049)

Gulf War (p. 1050)

the Perot candidacy (p. 1052)

"don't ask, don't tell" (p. 1052)

North American Free Trade Agreement (p. 1052)

Contract with America (p. 1053)

welfare reform (p. 1054)

Oslo Accords (p. 1055)

Rwandan genocide (p. 1055)

Balkan crisis (p. 1055)

"ethnic cleansing" (p. 1056)

Patterson v. McLean Credit Union (p. 1071)

"tough on crime" movement (p. 1071)

"prison-industrial complex" (p. 1072)

Americans with Disabilities Act (p. 1073)

multiculturalism (p. 1074)

identity politics (p. 1075)

Culture Wars (p. 1075)

Defense of Marriage Act (p. 1076)

"family values" (p. 1076)

Clinton impeachment (p. 1078)

American exceptionalism (p. 1081)

wwnorton.com/studyspace

Visit StudySpace for these resources and more:

- **Author Videos**
- **A chapter outline**
- **A practice quiz**
- **Interactive maps**
- **Multimedia documents**

CHAPTER 28

A NEW CENTURY AND NEW CRISES

★

No member of the present generation will ever forget when he or she first learned of the events of September 11, 2001. That beautiful late-summer morning began with the sun rising over the East Coast of the United States in a crystal-clear sky. But September 11 soon became one of the most tragic dates in American history.

Around 8 AM, hijackers seized control of four jet airliners filled with passengers. They crashed two into the World Trade Center in New York City, igniting infernos that soon caused these buildings, which dominated the lower Manhattan skyline, to collapse. A third plane hit a wing of the Pentagon, the country's military headquarters, in Washington, D.C. On the fourth aircraft, passengers who had learned of these events via their cell phones overpowered the hijackers. The plane crashed in a field near Pittsburgh, killing all aboard. Counting the nineteen hijackers, the more than 200 passengers, pilots, and flight attendants, and the victims on the ground, around 3,000 people died on September 11. The victims included nearly 400 police and firefighters who had rushed to the World Trade Center in a rescue effort and perished when the "twin towers" collapsed. Relatives and friends desperately seeking information about the fate of those lost in the attacks printed thousands of "missing" posters. These remained in public places in New York and Washington for weeks, grim reminders of the lives extinguished on September 11.

The Bush administration quickly blamed Al Qaeda, a shadowy terrorist organization headed by Osama bin Laden, for the attacks. A wealthy Islamic fundamentalist from Saudi Arabia, bin Laden had joined the fight against the Soviet occupation of Afghanistan in the 1980s. He had developed a relationship with the Central Intelligence Agency and received American funds to help build his mountain bases. But after the Gulf War of 1991, his anger increasingly turned against the United States. Bin Laden was especially outraged by the presence of American military bases in Saudi Arabia and by American support for Israel in its ongoing conflict with the Palestinians. More generally, bin Laden and his followers saw the United States, with its religious pluralism, consumer culture, and open sexual mores, as the antithesis of the rigid values in which they believed. He feared that American influence was corrupting Saudi Arabia, Islam's spiritual home, and helping to keep the Saudi royal family, which failed to oppose this development, in power.

In the last three decades of the twentieth century, terrorist groups who held the United States and other Western countries responsible for the plight of the Palestinians had engaged in hijackings and murders. After the Gulf War, Osama bin Laden declared "war" on the United States. Terrorists associated with Al Qaeda exploded a truck-bomb at the World Trade Center in 1993, killing six persons, and set off blasts in 1998 at American embassies in Kenya and Tanzania, in which more than 200 persons, mostly African embassy workers, died. Thus, a rising terrorist threat was visible before September 11. Nonetheless, the attack came as a complete surprise. With the end of the Cold War in 1991, most Americans felt more secure, especially within their own borders, than they had for decades.

FOCUS QUESTIONS

What were the major policy elements of the war on terror in the wake of September 11, 2001? –p. 1089

How did the war in Iraq unfold in the wake of 9/11? –p. 1093

How did the war on terror affect the economy and American liberties? –p. 1097

What events eroded support for President Bush's policies during his second term? –p. 1103

What kinds of change did voters hope for when they elected Barack Obama? –p. 1117

What were the major challenges of Obama's first term? –p. 1121

Barack Obama and his family greet enthusiastic supporters at an outdoor celebration in Chicago on the night of his election as president on November 4, 2008.

1993   World Trade Center bombed

1997   Kyoto Protocol

1998   U.S. embassies in Kenya and Tanzania bombed

2001   9/11 attacks

       U.S. enters war in Afghanistan

       USA Patriot Act

2002   Bush identifies "axis of evil"

       Department of Homeland Security established

2003   Iraq War begins

       Supreme Court upholds affirmative action

       Lawrence v. Texas

2005   Hurricane Katrina hits the Gulf Coast

2006   Sadam Hussein executed

2007   Great Recession begins

2008   Federal bailout of banks and companies

       Barack Obama elected

2009   Federal stimulus package

       Tea Party movement develops

       Sonia Sotomayor named to Supreme Court

2010   Affordable Care Act

       Gulf oil spill

2011   Arab Spring

       Osama Bin Laden killed

       Occupy Wall Street movement

       U.S. troops withdrawn from Iraq

2012   Obama reelected

September 11 enveloped the country in a cloud of fear. In the months that followed, as the government periodically issued "alerts" concerning possible new attacks, national security remained at the forefront of Americans' consciousness, and fear of terrorism powerfully affected their daily lives.

In the immediate aftermath of September 11, the Bush administration announced a "war on terrorism." Over the next two years, the United States embarked on wars in Afghanistan and Iraq, the second with very limited international support. It created a new Department of Homeland Security to coordinate efforts to improve security at home, and it imposed severe limits on the civil liberties of those suspected of a connection with terrorism and, more generally, on immigrants from the Middle East.

The attacks of September 11, 2001, gave new prominence to ideas deeply embedded in the American past—that freedom was the central quality of American life, and that the United States had a mission to spread freedom throughout the world and to fight those it saw as freedom's enemies. The attacks and events that followed also lent new urgency to questions that had recurred many times in American history: Should the United States act in the world as a republic or an empire? What is the proper balance between liberty and security? Who deserves the full enjoyment of American freedom? None had an easy answer.

THE WAR ON TERRORISM

Bush before September 11

Before becoming president, George W. Bush had been an executive in the oil industry and had served as governor of Texas. He had worked to dissociate the Republican Party from the harsh anti-immigrant rhetoric of the mid-1990s and had proven himself an effective proponent of what he called "compassionate conservatism." Nonetheless, from the outset Bush pursued a strongly conservative agenda. In 2001, he persuaded Congress to enact the largest tax cut in American history. With the economy slowing, he promoted the plan as a way of stimulating renewed growth. In keeping with the "supply-side" economic outlook embraced twenty years earlier by Ronald Reagan, most of the tax cuts were directed toward the wealthiest Americans, on the assumption that they would invest the money they saved in taxes in economically productive activities.

In foreign policy, Bush emphasized American freedom of action, unrestrained by international treaties and institutions. To great controversy, the Bush administration announced that it would not abide by the Kyoto Protocol of 1997, which sought to combat global warming—a slow rise in the earth's temperature that scientists warned could have disastrous effects on the world's climate. Global warming is caused when gases released by burning fossil fuels such as coal and oil remain in the upper atmosphere, trapping heat reflected from the earth. Evidence of this development first surfaced in the 1990s, when scientists studying layers of ice in Greenland concluded that the earth's temperature had risen significantly during the past century.

Today, most scientists consider global warming a serious situation. Climate change threatens to disrupt long-established patterns of agriculture, and the melting of glaciers and the polar ice caps because of rising temperatures may raise ocean levels and flood coastal cities.

By the time Bush took office, some 180 nations, including the United States, had agreed to accept the goals set in the Kyoto Protocol for reducing the output of greenhouse gases from fossil fuels. Since the United States burns far more fossil fuel than any other nation, Bush's repudiation of the treaty, on the grounds that it would weaken the American economy, infuriated much of the world, as well as environmentalists at home.

"They Hate Freedom"

September 11 transformed the international situation, the domestic political environment, and the Bush presidency. An outpouring of popular patriotism followed the attacks, all the more impressive because it was spontaneous, not orchestrated by the government or private organizations. Throughout the country, people demonstrated their sense of resolve and their sympathy for the victims by displaying the American flag. Public trust in government rose dramatically, and public servants like firemen and policemen became national heroes. After two decades in which the dominant language of American politics centered on deregulation and individualism, the country experienced a renewed feeling of common social purpose. Americans of all backgrounds shared the sense of having lived through a traumatic experience.

The Bush administration benefited from this patriotism and identification with government. The president's popularity soared. Bush seized the opportunity to give his administration a new direction and purpose. Like presidents before him, he made freedom the rallying cry for a nation at war.

The twin towers of the World Trade Center after being struck by hijacked airplanes on September 11, 2001. Shortly after this photograph was taken, the towers collapsed.

A bystander gazes at some of the "missing" posters with photographs of those who died on September 11.

This photograph of three emergency-response workers at the World Trade Center site suggests that the composition of the construction industry labor force had become more diverse as a result of the civil rights movement.

On September 20, 2001, Bush addressed a joint session of Congress and a national television audience. His speech echoed the words of FDR, Truman, and Reagan: "Freedom and fear are at war. The advance of human freedom . . . now depends on us." The country's antagonists, Bush went on, "hate our freedoms, our freedom of religion, our freedom of speech, our freedom to assemble and disagree with each other." In later speeches, he repeated this theme. Why did terrorists attack the United States, the president repeatedly asked. His answer: "Because we love freedom, that's why. And they hate freedom."

The Bush Doctrine

A war on terrorism

Bush's speech announced a new foreign policy principle, which quickly became known as the Bush Doctrine. The United States would launch a war on terrorism. Unlike previous wars, this one had a vaguely defined enemy—terrorist groups around the world that might threaten the United States or its allies—and no predictable timetable for victory. The American administration would recognize no middle ground in the new war: "Either you are with us, or you are with the terrorists." Bush demanded that Afghanistan, ruled by a group of Islamic fundamentalists called the Taliban, surrender Osama bin Laden, who had established a base in the country. When the Taliban refused, the United States on October 7, 2001, launched air strikes against its strongholds.

Afghanistan

Bush gave the war in Afghanistan the name "Enduring Freedom." By the end of the year, the combination of American bombing and ground combat by the Northern Alliance (Afghans who had been fighting the Taliban for years) had driven the regime from power. A new government, friendly to and dependent on the United States, took its place. It repealed Taliban laws denying women the right to attend school and banning movies, music, and other expressions of Western culture but found it difficult to establish full control over the country. Bin Laden had not been found, and many Taliban supporters continued to pose a threat to the new government's stability. Indeed, by early 2007, the Taliban had reasserted their power in some parts of Afghanistan, and no end was in sight to the deployment of American troops there.

The "Axis of Evil"

Like the surprise attack on Pearl Harbor in 1941, September 11 not only plunged the United States into war but also transformed American foreign policy, inspiring a determination to reshape the world in terms of American ideals and interests. To facilitate further military action in the Middle East, the United States established military bases in Central Asia, including former republics of the Soviet Union like Kyrgyzstan, Uzbekistan, and Tajikistan. Such an action would have been inconceivable before the end of the Cold War.

Supporters of the Bush administration who turned out in Washington, D.C., late in 2001 to confront demonstrators opposed to the war in Afghanistan.

The toppling of the Taliban, Bush repeatedly insisted, marked only the beginning of the war on terrorism. In his State of the Union address of January 2002, the president accused Iraq, Iran, and North Korea of harboring terrorists and developing "weapons of mass destruction"—nuclear, chemical, and biological—that posed a potential threat to the United States. He called the three countries an "axis of evil," even though no evidence connected them with the attacks of September 11 and they had never cooperated with one another (Iraq and Iran, in fact, had fought a long and bloody war in the 1980s).

The National Security Strategy

In September 2002, one year after the September 11 attacks, the Bush administration released a document called the National Security Strategy. Like NSC-68 of 1950 (discussed in Chapter 23), the National Security Strategy outlined a fundamental shift in American foreign policy. And like NSC-68, it began with a discussion not of weaponry or military strategy, but of freedom.

The document defined freedom as consisting of political democracy, freedom of expression, religious toleration, free trade, and free markets. These, it proclaimed, were universal ideals, "right and true for every person, in every society." It went on to promise that the United States would "extend the benefits of freedom" by fighting not only "terrorists" but also "tyrants" around the world. And to replace the Cold War doctrine of deterrence, which assumed that the certainty of retaliation would prevent attacks on the United States and its allies, the National Security Strategy announced a new foreign policy principle—"preemptive" war. If the United States believed that a nation posed a possible future threat to its security, it had the right to attack before such a threat materialized.

Preemptive war

AN AMERICAN EMPIRE?

The "axis of evil" speech and National Security Strategy sent shock waves around the world. In the immediate aftermath of September 11, a wave of sympathy for the United States had swept across the globe. Most of the world supported the war in Afghanistan as a legitimate response to the terrorist attacks. By late 2002, however, many persons overseas feared that the United States was claiming the right to act as a world policeman in violation of international law.

The global response

Critics, including leaders of close American allies, wondered whether dividing the world into friends and enemies of freedom ran the danger of repeating some of the mistakes of the Cold War. Anti-Americanism in the Middle East, they argued, reached far beyond bin Laden's organization and stemmed not simply from dislike of American freedom but, rightly or wrongly, from opposition to specific American policies—toward Israel, the Palestinians, and the region's corrupt and undemocratic regimes.

Charges quickly arose that the United States was bent on establishing itself as a new global empire. Indeed, September 11 and its aftermath highlighted not only the vulnerability of the United States but also its overwhelming strength. In every index of power—military, economic, cultural—the United States far outpaced the rest of the world. It accounted for just under one-third of global economic output and more than one-third of global military spending. Its defense budget exceeded that of the next twenty powers combined. The United States maintained military bases throughout the world and deployed its navy on every ocean. It was not surprising that in such circumstances many American policymakers felt that the country had a responsibility to impose order in a dangerous world, even if this meant establishing its own rules of international conduct.

In public discussion in the United States after September 11, the word "empire," once a term of abuse, came back into widespread use. The need to "shoulder the burdens of empire" emerged as a common theme in discussions among foreign policy analysts and political commentators who embraced the new foreign policy.

Steve Benson's 2003 cartoon, which alters a renowned World War II photograph of soldiers raising an American flag, illustrates widespread skepticism about American motivations in the Iraq War.

Confronting Iraq

These tensions became starkly evident in the Bush administration's next initiative. The Iraqi dictatorship of Saddam Hussein had survived its defeat in the Gulf War of 1991. Hussein's opponents charged that he had flouted United Nations resolutions barring the regime from developing new weapons.

From the outset of the Bush administration, a group of conservative policymakers including Vice President Dick Cheney, Secretary of Defense Donald Rumsfeld, and Deputy Defense Secretary Paul D. Wolfowitz were determined to oust Hussein from power. They developed a military strategy to accomplish this—massive initial air strikes followed by invasion by a relatively small number of troops. They insisted that the oppressed Iraqi people would welcome an American army as liberators and quickly establish a democratic government, allowing for the early departure of American soldiers. This group seized on the opportunity presented by the attacks of September 11 to press their case, and President Bush adopted their outlook. Secretary of State Colin Powell, who believed the conquest and stabilization of Iraq would require hundreds of thousands of American soldiers and should not be undertaken without the support of America's allies, found himself marginalized in the administration.

Even though Hussein was not an Islamic fundamentalist, and no known evidence linked him to the terrorist attacks of September 11, the Bush administration in 2002 announced a goal of "regime change" in Iraq. Hussein, administration spokesmen insisted, must be ousted from power because he had developed an arsenal of chemical and bacterial "weapons of mass destruction" and was seeking to acquire nuclear arms. American newspaper and television journalists repeated these claims with almost no independent investigation. Early in 2003, despite his original misgivings, Secretary of State Powell delivered a speech before the UN outlining the administration's case. He claimed that Hussein possessed a mobile chemical weapons laboratory, had hidden weapons of mass destruction in his many palaces, and was seeking to acquire uranium in Africa to build nuclear weapons. (Every one of these assertions later turned out to be false.) Shortly after Powell's address, the president announced his intention to go to war with or without the approval of the United Nations. Congress passed a resolution authorizing the president to use force if he deemed it necessary.

> *Regime change in Iraq*

The Iraq War

The decision to go to war split the Western alliance and inspired a massive antiwar movement throughout the world. In February 2003, between 10 million and 15 million people across the globe demonstrated against the impending war. There were large-scale protests in the United States, which brought together veterans of the antiwar movement during the Vietnam era and a diverse group of young activists united in the belief that launching a war against a nation because it might pose a security threat in the future violated international law and the UN Charter.

Part of the massive crowd that gathered in New York City on February 15, 2003, a day of worldwide demonstrations against the impending war against Iraq.

Foreign policy "realists," including members of previous Republican administrations like Brent Scowcroft, the national security adviser under the first President Bush, warned that the administration's preoccupation with Iraq deflected attention from its real foe, Al Qaeda, which remained capable of launching terrorist attacks. They insisted that the United States could not unilaterally transform the Middle East into a bastion of democracy, as the administration claimed was its long-term aim.

Both traditional foes of the United States like Russia and China, and traditional allies like Germany and France, refused to support a "preemptive" strike against Iraq. Unable to obtain approval from the United Nations for attacking Iraq, the United States went to war anyway in March 2003, with Great Britain as its sole significant ally. President Bush called the war "Operation Iraqi Freedom." Its purpose, he declared, was to "defend our freedom" and "bring freedom to others." The Hussein regime proved no match for the American armed forces, with their precision bombing, satellite-guided missiles, and well-trained soldiers. Within a month, American troops occupied Baghdad. After hiding out for several months, Hussein was captured by American forces and subsequently put on trial before an Iraqi court. Late in 2006, he was found guilty of ordering the killing of many Iraqis during his reign, and was sentenced to death and executed.

VOICES OF FREEDOM

From THE NATIONAL SECURITY STRATEGY OF THE UNITED STATES (SEPTEMBER 2002)

The National Security Strategy, issued in 2002 by the Bush administration, outlined a new foreign and military policy for the United States in response to the terrorist attacks of September 11, 2001. It announced the doctrine of preemptive war—that the United States retained the right to use its military power against countries that might pose a threat in the future. But the document began with a statement of the administration's definition of freedom and its commitment to spreading freedom to the entire world.

The great struggles of the twentieth century between liberty and totalitarianism ended with a decisive victory for the forces of freedom—and a single sustainable model for national success: freedom, democracy, and free enterprise. . . . These values of freedom are right and true for every person, in every society. . . .

Today, the international community has the best chance since the rise of the nation-state in the seventeenth century to build a world where great powers compete in peace instead of continually prepare for war. . . . The United States will use this moment of opportunity to extend the benefits of freedom across the globe. We will actively work to bring the hope of democracy, development, free markets, and free trade to every corner of the world. . . .

In building a balance of power that favors freedom, the United States is guided by the conviction that all nations have important responsibilities. Nations that enjoy freedom must actively fight terror. Nations that depend on international stability must help prevent the spread of weapons of mass destruction. . . . Throughout history, freedom has been threatened by war and terror; it has been challenged by the clashing wills of powerful states and the evil designs of tyrants; and it has been tested by widespread poverty and disease. Today, humanity holds in its hands the opportunity to further freedom's triumph over all these foes. The United States welcomes our opportunity to lead in this great mission.

From PRESIDENT BARACK OBAMA, SPEECH ON THE MIDDLE EAST (2011)

In the wake of the Arab Spring of 2011, the United States found itself caught between its traditional alliances with dictatorial regimes throughout the Middle East and the principles of democracy and human rights. In May 2011, President Obama, in a speech at the State Department in Washington, announced what he called "a new chapter in American diplomacy," and sought to link the spring uprisings with the tradition of protest in the United States.

For six months, we have witnessed an extraordinary change taking place in the Middle East and North Africa. Square by square, town by town, country by country, the people have risen up to demand their basic human rights. . . .

The story of this revolution should not have come as a surprise. The nations of the Middle East and North Africa won their independence long ago, but in too many places their people did not. In too many countries, power has been concentrated in the hands of a few. . . .

But the events of the past six months show us that strategies of repression and strategies of diversion will not work anymore. Satellite television and the Internet provide a window into the wider world. Cell phones and social networks allow young people to connect and organize like never before. And so a new generation has emerged. And their voices tell us that change cannot be denied. . . .

The United States supports a set of universal rights. And these rights include free speech, the freedom of peaceful assembly, the freedom of religion, equality for men and women under the rule of law, and the right to choose your own leaders. . . .

History shows that countries are more prosperous and more peaceful when women are empowered. And that's why we will continue to insist that universal rights apply to women as well as men. . . .

For the American people, the scenes of upheaval in the region may be unsettling, but the forces driving it are not unfamiliar. Our own nation was founded through a rebellion against an empire. Our people fought a painful Civil War that extended freedom and dignity to those who were enslaved. And I would not be standing here today unless past generations turned to the moral force of nonviolence as a way to perfect our union—organizing, marching, protesting peacefully together to make real those words that declared our nation: "We hold these truths to be self-evident, that all men are created equal."

QUESTIONS

1. *How does the National Security Strategy define the global mission of the United States?*

2. *How does President Obama hope to change American diplomacy in the Middle East?*

3. *What are the areas of agreement and disagreement between these two statements about the role of the United States in the world?*

Another Vietnam?

Soon after the fall of Baghdad, a triumphant President Bush appeared in an air force flight suit on the deck of an aircraft carrier beneath a banner reading "Mission Accomplished." But after the fall of Hussein, everything seemed to go wrong. Rather than parades welcoming American liberators, looting and chaos followed the fall of the Iraqi regime. An insurgency quickly developed that targeted American soldiers and Iraqis cooperating with them. Sectarian violence soon swept throughout Iraq, with militias of Shiite and Sunni Muslims fighting each other. (Under Hussein, Sunnis, a minority of Iraq's population, had dominated the government and army; now, the Shiite majority sought to exercise power and exact revenge.) Despite holding a number of elections in Iraq, the United States found it impossible to create an Iraqi government strong enough to impose order on the country.

With no end in sight to the conflict, comparisons with the American experience in Vietnam became commonplace. In both wars, American policy was made by officials who had little or no knowledge of the countries to which they were sending troops and distrusted State Department experts on these regions, who tended be skeptical about the possibility of achieving quick military and long-term political success. Administration officials gave little thought to postwar planning.

The World and the War

The war marked a new departure in American foreign policy. The United States had frequently intervened unilaterally in the affairs of Latin American countries. But outside the Western Hemisphere it had previously been reluctant to use force except as part of an international coalition. And while the United States had exerted enormous influence in the Middle East since World War II, never before had it occupied a nation in the center of the world's most volatile region.

Sectarian conflict

President Bush standing on the deck of the aircraft carrier *Abraham Lincoln* on May 10, 2003, announcing the end of combat operations in Iraq. A banner proclaims, "Mission Accomplished." Unfortunately, the war was not in fact over.

In 2008, a church in Miami displayed nearly 4,500 small American flags in honor of each of the American soldiers who to that date had died in Afghanistan and Iraq.

Rarely in its history had the United States found itself so isolated from world public opinion. Initially, the war in Iraq proved to be popular in the United States. After all, unlike earlier wars, this one brought no calls for public sacrifice from the administration. There were no tax increases, and no reintroduction of the draft to augment the hard-pressed all-volunteer army. Many Americans believed the administration's claims that Saddam Hussein had something to do with September 11 and had stockpiled weapons of mass destruction. The realization that in fact Hussein had no such weapons discredited the administration's rationale for the war. By early 2007, polls showed that a large majority of Americans considered the invasion of Iraq a mistake, and the war a lost cause.

Much of the outside world now viewed the United States as a superpower unwilling to abide by the rules of international law.

An isolated position

THE AFTERMATH OF SEPTEMBER 11 AT HOME

Security and Liberty

Like earlier wars, the war on terrorism raised anew the problem of balancing security and liberty. In the immediate aftermath of the attacks, Congress rushed to pass the USA Patriot Act, a mammoth bill (it ran to more than 300 pages) that few members of the House or Senate had actually read. It conferred unprecedented powers on law-enforcement agencies charged with preventing the new, vaguely defined crime of "domestic terrorism," including the power to wiretap, spy on citizens, open letters, read e-mail, and obtain personal records from third parties like universities and libraries without the knowledge of a suspect. Unlike during World Wars I and II, with their campaigns of hatred against German-Americans

The USA Patriot Act

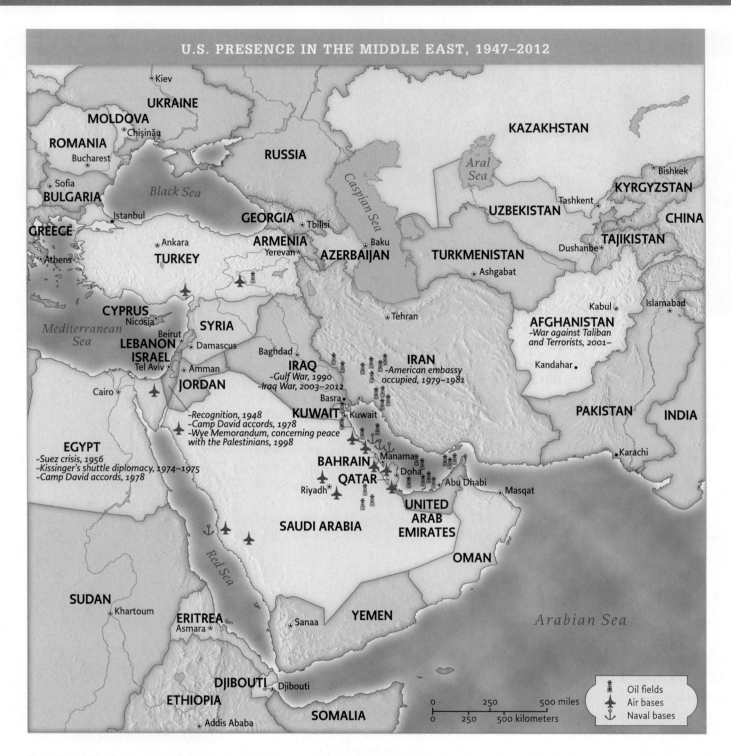

U.S. PRESENCE IN THE MIDDLE EAST, 1947–2012

IRAQ
-Gulf War, 1990
-Iraq War, 2003–2012

IRAN
-American embassy
occupied, 1979–1981

AFGHANISTAN
-War against Taliban
and Terrorists, 2001–

ISRAEL
-Recognition, 1948
-Camp David accords, 1978
-Wye Memorandum, concerning peace
with the Palestinians, 1998

EGYPT
-Suez crisis, 1956
-Kissinger's shuttle diplomacy, 1974–1975
-Camp David accords, 1978

	Oil fields
	Air bases
	Naval bases

0   250   500 miles
0   250   500 kilometers

Since World War II, the United States has become more and more deeply involved in the affairs of the Middle East, whose countries are together the world's largest exporter of oil.

and Japanese-Americans, the Bush administration made a point of discouraging anti-Arab and anti-Muslim sentiment. Nonetheless, at least 5,000 foreigners with Middle Eastern connections were rounded up, and more than 1,200 arrested. Many with no link to terrorism were held for months, without either a formal charge or a public notice of their fate. The administration also set up a detention camp at the U.S. naval base at Guantánamo Bay, Cuba, for persons captured in Afghanistan or otherwise accused of terrorism. More than 700 persons, the nationals of many foreign countries, were detained there.

In November 2001, the Bush administration issued an executive order authorizing the holding of secret military tribunals for noncitizens deemed to have assisted terrorism. In such trials, traditional constitutional protections, such as the right of the accused to choose a lawyer and see all the evidence, would not apply. A few months later, the Justice Department declared that American citizens could be held indefinitely without charge and not allowed to see a lawyer, if the government declared them to be "enemy combatants." The president's press secretary, Ari Fleischer, warned Americans to "watch what they say," and Attorney General John Ashcroft declared that criticism of administration policies aided the country's terrorist enemies.

The Power of the President

In the new atmosphere of heightened security, numerous court orders and regulations of the 1970s, inspired by abuses of the CIA, FBI, and local police forces, were rescinded, allowing these agencies to resume surveillance of Americans without evidence that a crime had been committed. Some

ISRAEL, THE WEST BANK, AND GAZA STRIP

- 1967 Cease-Fire line
- *Mediterranean Sea*
- Jordan River
- Nablus
- *West Bank*
- 1949 Armistice line
- Ramallah
- **ISRAEL**
- Jerusalem
- Bethlehem
- *Gaza Strip*
- Hebron
- *Dead Sea*
- 1950 Armistice line

- ▨ Territory under full Palestinian control
- ▢ Palestinian Authority responsible for social and civil services only
- ▢ Gaza Strip and West Bank territory under full Israeli control
- ▨ Jewish settlements
- ▨ Israeli military bases

Before the Cuban Revolution of 1959, Guantánamo Bay was mostly known as an American naval base where the families of servicemen enjoyed a slice of suburban life, as in this photograph from the 1950s. Today, Guantánamo is famous as the site of the world's most notorious prison.

of these measures were authorized by Congress, but the president implemented many of them unilaterally, claiming the authority to ignore laws that restricted his power as commander-in-chief in wartime. Thus, soon after September 11, President Bush authorized the National Security Agency (NSA) to eavesdrop on Americans' telephone conversations without a court warrant, a clear violation of a law limiting the NSA to foreign intelligence gathering.

Two centuries earlier, in the 1790s, James Madison had predicted that no nation could preserve its freedom "in the midst of continual warfare." Madison's remarkable warning about how presidents might seize the power afforded them in war to limit freedom has been borne out at many points in American history—from Lincoln's suspension of the writ of habeas corpus to Wilson's suppression of free speech and Franklin D. Roosevelt's internment of Japanese-Americans. The administration of George W. Bush was no exception.

The majority of Americans seemed willing to accept the administration's contention that restraints on time-honored liberties were necessary to fight terrorism. Others recalled previous times when wars produced limitations on civil liberties and public officials equated political dissent with lack of patriotism: the Alien and Sedition Acts during the "quasi-war" with France in 1798, the suspension of the writ of habeas corpus during the Civil War, the severe repression of free speech and persecution of German-Americans during World War I, Japanese-American internment in World War II, and McCarthyism during the Cold War. These episodes underscored the fragility of principles most Americans have learned to take for granted—civil liberties and the ideal of equality before the law, regardless of race and ethnicity. The debate over liberty and security seemed certain to last as long as the war on terrorism itself.

The Torture Controversy

Officials of the Bush administration also insisted in the aftermath of September 11 that the United States need not be bound by international law in pursuing the war on terrorism. They were especially eager to sidestep the Geneva Conventions and the International Convention against Torture, which regulate the treatment of prisoners of war and prohibit torture and other forms of physical and mental coercion. In January 2002, the Justice Department produced a memorandum stating that these rules did not apply to captured members of Al Qaeda as they were "unlawful combatants," not members of regularly constituted armies.

Amid strong protests from Secretary of State Powell and senior military officers who feared that the new policy would encourage the retaliatory mistreatment of American prisoners of war, in April 2003 the president prohibited the use of torture except where special permission had been granted. Nonetheless, the Defense Department approved methods of interrogation that most observers considered torture. In addition, the CIA set up a series of jails in foreign countries outside the traditional chain of military command and took part in the "rendition" of suspects—that is, kidnapping them and spiriting them to prisons in Egypt, Yemen, Syria, and former communist states of eastern Europe, where torture is practiced.

War and freedom

The United States and international law

In this atmosphere and lacking clear rules of behavior, some military personnel—in Afghanistan, at Abu Ghraib prison in Iraq, and at Guantánamo—beat prisoners who were being held for interrogation, subjected them to electric shocks, let them be attacked by dogs, and forced them to strip naked and lie atop other prisoners. Some prisoners in U.S. custody died from their maltreatment. Photographs of the maltreatment of prisoners, circulated by e-mail, became public. Their exposure around the world in newspapers, on television, and on the Internet undermined the reputation of the United States as a country that adheres to standards of civilized behavior and the rule of law.

Based on an infamous photograph, circulated around the world, of an Iraqi prisoner abused while in American custody, this 2004 cartoon suggests how such mistreatment damaged the image of the United States.

After much debate, Congress in 2005 inserted in the Defense Appropriations Act a measure sponsored by Senator John McCain of Arizona (a former prisoner of war in Vietnam) banning the use of torture. President Bush signed the bill but issued a "signing statement" reaffirming his right as commander-in-chief to set rules for the military by himself.

Late in 2008 and early the following year, previously secret government documents were released demonstrating that torture was the result not of missteps by a few "bad apples," as the administration had claimed, but decisions at the highest levels of government. Secretary of Defense Donald Rumsfeld, Attorney General Alberto Gonzales, and other officials had authorized the torture of persons captured in the war on terrorism, over the objections of many in the military. Ironically, some of the techniques used, especially water-boarding (simulated drowning), had been employed by the government during the Korean War to train soldiers how to withstand torture if captured by the enemy. No one in the administration seemed concerned about what these practices might do to the reputation of the United States as a law-abiding nation.

The Economy under Bush

During 2001, the economy slipped into a recession—that is, it contracted rather than grew. Growth resumed at the end of the year, but, with businesses reluctant to make new investments after the overexpansion of the 1990s, it failed to generate new jobs. Talk of "economic pain" reappeared in public discussions. The sectors that had expanded the most in the previous decade contracted rapidly. The computer industry slashed more than 40 percent of its jobs during the first two years of the Bush presidency. But 90 percent of the jobs lost during the recession of 2001–2002 were in manufacturing. Despite the renewed spirit of patriotism, deindustrialization continued. Textile firms closed southern plants and shifted production to cheap-labor factories in China and India. Maytag, a manufacturer

Recession

of washing machines, refrigerators, and other home appliances, announced plans to close its factory in Galesburg, Illinois, where wages averaged fifteen dollars per hour, to open a new one in Mexico, where workers earned less than one-seventh that amount.

A jobs loss

Even after economic recovery began, the problems of traditional industries continued. Employment in steel—520,000 in 1970—had dropped to 120,000 by 2004. Late in 2005, facing declining profits and sales, major companies moved to eliminate the remnants of the post–World War II "social contract," in which industries provided manufacturing workers with both high-paying jobs and the promise that they would be provided for in old age. Many eliminated or sharply reduced pensions and health benefits for retired workers. Bush became the first president since Herbert Hoover to see the economy lose jobs over the course of a four-year term.

Tax cuts

The Bush administration responded to economic difficulties by supporting the Federal Reserve Board's policy of reducing interest rates and by proposing another round of tax cuts. In 2003, the president signed into law a $320-billion tax reduction, one of the largest in American history. In accordance with supply-side theory, the cuts were again geared to reducing the tax burden on wealthy individuals and corporations. Left to future generations were the questions of how to deal with a rapidly mounting federal deficit (which exceeded $400 billion, a record, in 2004) and how to pay for the obligations of the federal government and the needs of American society.

THE WINDS OF CHANGE

The 2004 Election

John Kerry

With Bush's popularity sliding because of the war in Iraq and a widespread sense that many Americans were not benefiting from economic growth, Democrats in 2004 sensed a golden opportunity to retake the White House. They nominated as their candidate John Kerry, a senator from Massachusetts and the first Catholic to run for president since John F. Kennedy in 1960. A decorated combat veteran in Vietnam, Kerry had joined the antiwar movement after leaving the army. The party hoped that Kerry's military experience would insulate him from Republican charges that Democrats were too weak-willed to be trusted to protect the United States from further terrorist attacks, while his antiwar credentials in Vietnam would appeal to voters opposed to the invasion of Iraq.

Kerry proved a surprisingly ineffective candidate. An aloof man who lacked the common touch, he failed to generate the same degree of enthusiasm among his supporters as Bush did among his. Kerry's inability to explain why he voted in favor of the Iraq War in the Senate only to denounce it later as a major mistake enabled Republicans to portray him as lacking the kind of resolution necessary in dangerous times. Meanwhile, Karl Rove, Bush's chief political adviser, worked assiduously to mobilize the Republican Party's conservative base by having Republicans stress the president's stance on cultural issues—opposition to the extension of the right to marry to homosexuals (which the Supreme Court of Massachusetts had ruled must receive legal recognition in that state), opposition to abortion rights, and so on.

Throughout the campaign, polls predicted a very close election. Bush won a narrow victory, with a margin of 2 percent of the popular vote and thirty-four electoral votes. The results revealed a remarkable electoral stability. Both sides had spent tens of millions of dollars in advertising and had mobilized new voters—nearly 20 million since 2000. But in the end, only three states voted differently than four years earlier—New Hampshire, which Kerry carried, and Iowa and New Mexico, which swung to Bush.

Bush's Second Term

In his second inaugural address, in January 2005, Bush outlined a new American goal—"ending tyranny in the world." Striking a more conciliatory tone than during his first administration, he promised that the United States would not try to impose "our style of government" on others and that it would in the future seek the advice of allies. He said nothing specific about Iraq but tried to shore up falling support for the war by invoking the ideal of freedom: "The survival of liberty in our land increasingly depends on the success of liberty in other lands." In his first inaugural, in January 2001, Bush had used the words "freedom," "free," or "liberty" seven times. In his second, they appeared forty-nine times. Again and again, Bush insisted that the United States stands for the worldwide triumph of freedom.

A more conciliatory foreign policy

But the ongoing chaos in Iraq, coupled with a spate of corruption scandals surrounding Republicans in Congress and the White House, eroded Bush's standing. Vice President Cheney's chief of staff was convicted of perjury in connection with an investigation of the illegal "leak" to the press of the name of a CIA operative whose husband had criticized the manipulation of intelligence before the invasion of Iraq. He was the first White House official to be indicted while holding office since Orville Babcock, Grant's chief of staff, in 1875. A Texas grand jury indicted Tom DeLay, the House majority leader, for violating campaign finance laws. A "culture of corruption," Democrats charged, had overtaken the nation's capital. Bush's popularity continued to decline. At one point in 2006, his approval rating fell to 31 percent.

Domestic scandals

Hurricane Katrina

A further blow to the Bush administration's standing came in August 2005, when Hurricane Katrina slammed ashore near New Orleans. Situated below sea level between the Mississippi River and Lake Pontchartrain, New Orleans has always been vulnerable to flooding. For years, scientists had predicted a catastrophe if a hurricane hit the city. But requests to strengthen its levee system had been ignored by the federal government. When the storm hit on August 29 the levees broke, and nearly the entire city, with a population of half a million, was inundated. Nearby areas of the Louisiana and Mississippi Gulf Coast were also hard hit.

Disaster, natural and man-made

The natural disaster quickly became a man-made one, with ineptitude evident from local government to the White House. The mayor of New Orleans had been

A satellite photograph shows the immensity of Hurricane Katrina as its eye moved over New Orleans.

slow to order an evacuation, fearing this would damage the city's tourist trade. When he finally instructed residents to leave, a day before the storm's arrival, he neglected to provide for the thousands who did not own automobiles and were too poor to find other means of transportation. In November 2002, a new Department of Homeland Security had been created, absorbing many existing intelligence agencies, including the Federal Emergency Management Agency (FEMA), which is responsible for disaster planning and relief within the United States. FEMA was headed by Michael Brown, who lacked experience in disaster management and had apparently been appointed because he was a college friend of his predecessor in the office. Although warned of impending disaster by the National Weather Service, FEMA had done almost no preparation. Vacationing in Texas, the president announced that New Orleans had "dodged the bullet" when the storm veered away from a direct hit. When he finally visited the city, he seemed unaware of the scope of devastation. If the Bush administration had prided itself on anything, it was competence in dealing with disaster. Katrina shattered that image.

FEMA's inept response

The New Orleans Disaster

For days, vast numbers of people, most of them poor African-Americans, remained abandoned amid the floodwaters. Bodies floated in the streets and people died in city hospitals and nursing homes. By the time aid began to arrive, damage stood at $80 billion, the death toll was around 1,500, and two-thirds of the city's population had been displaced. The televised images of misery in the streets of New Orleans shocked the world and shamed the country.

The effects of Katrina

Hurricane Katrina shone a bright light on both the heroic and the less praiseworthy sides of American life. Where government failed, individual citizens stepped into the breach. People with boats rescued countless survivors from rooftops and attics, private donations flowed in to aid the victims, and neighboring states like Texas opened their doors to thousands of refugees. Like the publication of Jacob Riis's *How the Other Half Lives* (1890) and Michael Harrington's *The Other America* (1962), the hurricane's aftermath alerted Americans to the extent of poverty in the world's richest country. Generations of state and local policies pursuing economic growth via low-wage, nonunion employment and low investment in education, health, and social welfare had produced a large impoverished population in the South. Once a racially mixed city, New Orleans was now essentially segregated, with a population two-thirds black, surrounded by mostly white suburbs. Nearly 30 percent of New Orleans's population lived in poverty, and of these, seven-eighths were black.

Hurricane Katrina had another result as well. The shutting down of oil refining capacity on the Gulf Coast led to an immediate rise in the price of oil, and thus of gasoline for American drivers. With the rapidly growing economies of China and India needing more and more oil, and with instability in the Middle East threatening to affect oil production, prices remained at historic highs throughout 2006. Despite decades of talk about the need to develop alternative energy supplies, the United States remained as dependent as ever on imported oil and extremely vulnerable to potential disruptions of oil imports. Rising prices threatened to derail the economic recovery by dampening consumer spending on other goods. They also dealt yet another blow to American automobile manufacturers, who had staked their futures on sales of light trucks and sport utility vehicles (SUVs). These vehicles generated high profits for the car companies but achieved very low gas mileage. When gas prices rose, consumers shifted their purchasing to smaller cars with better fuel efficiency, most of which were produced by Japanese and other foreign automakers.

Residents of New Orleans, stranded on a rooftop days after flood waters engulfed the city, frantically attempt to attract the attention of rescue helicopters.

The Immigration Debate

In the spring of 2006, an issue as old as the American nation suddenly burst again onto the center stage of politics—immigration. As we have seen, the Hart-Celler Act of 1965 led to a radical shift in the origins of those entering the United States, and especially the rapid growth of the Hispanic population. Many of these newcomers were bypassing traditional immigrant destinations and heading for areas in the Midwest, small-town New England, and the Upper South. The city with the highest rate of growth of its immigrant population from 1990 to 2005 was Nashville, Tennessee. Racial and ethnic diversity was now a fact of life in the American heartland.

Alongside legal immigrants, undocumented newcomers made their way to the United States, mostly from Mexico. At the end of 2005, it was estimated, there were 11 million illegal aliens in the United States, 7 million of them members of the workforce. Economists disagree about their impact. It seems clear that the presence of large numbers of uneducated, low-skilled workers pushes down wages at the bottom of the economic ladder, especially affecting African-Americans. On the other hand,

Illegal aliens in the workforce

In April 2006, millions of people demonstrated for immigrant rights. This photograph shows part of the immense crowd in Chicago, bearing the flags of many nations.

immigrants both legal and illegal receive regular paychecks, spend money, and pay taxes. They fill jobs for which American workers seem to be unavailable because the wages are so low. It is estimated that more than one-fifth of construction workers, domestic workers, and agricultural workers are in the United States illegally.

Immigration politics

In 1986, the Reagan administration had granted amnesty—that is, the right to remain in the United States and become citizens—to 3 million illegal immigrants. During the 1990s, conservatives in states with significant populations of illegal immigrants, especially California, had called for a tough crackdown on their entry and rights within the United States. As governor of Texas, by contrast, George W. Bush had strived to win Hispanic support and downplayed the immigration issue. But in 2006, with many Americans convinced that the United States had lost control of its borders and that immigration was in part responsible for the stagnation of real wages, the House of Representatives approved a bill making it a felony to be in the country illegally and a crime to offer aid to illegal immigrants.

Demonstrations for immigrant rights

The response was utterly unexpected: a series of massive demonstrations in the spring of 2006 by immigrants—legal and illegal—and their supporters, demanding the right to remain in the country as citizens. In cities from New York to Chicago, Los Angeles, Phoenix, and Dallas, hundreds of thousands of protesters took to the streets. Nashville experienced the largest public demonstration in its history, a march of more than 10,000 mostly Hispanic immigrants. All Congress could agree on, however, was a measure to build a 700-mile wall along part of the U.S.-Mexico border. The immigration issue was at a stalemate, where it remains today, and its ultimate resolution impossible to predict.

Islam, America, and the "Clash of Civilizations"

The events of September 11, 2001 placed new pressures on religious liberty. Even before the terrorist attacks, the political scientist Samuel P. Huntington had published a widely noted book, *The Clash of Civilizations and the Remaking of the World*

Order (1996), which argued that with the Cold War over, a new global conflict impended between Western and Islamic "civilizations."

The idea of such a clash is fundamentally unhistorical, for it reduces politics and culture to a single characteristic—in this case, religion—that remains forever static, divorced from historical development. It denies the global exchange of ideas and the interpenetration of cultures that has been a feature of the modern world for centuries. It also makes it impossible to discuss divisions within these purported civilizations. ("Islam," for example, consists of well over a billion people, in very different countries ranging from South Asia to the Middle East, Africa, Europe, and the Americas.) Nonetheless, in the aftermath of September 11, Huntington's formula that pitted a freedom-loving United States against militant, authoritarian Muslims became widely popular as a way of making sense of the terrorist attacks.

A political cartoon comments on the spread of religious intolerance in the early twenty-first century.

What did this mean for the nearly 5 million Americans who practiced the Muslim religion? President Bush insisted that the war on terror was not a war against Islam. But many Americans found it difficult to separate the two, even though most American Muslims were as appalled by the terrorist attacks as their fellow countrymen. Some critics claimed that Islam was fundamentally incompatible with American life—a position reminiscent of prejudice in the nineteenth century against Catholics and Mormons. In a number of states, politicians appealed for votes by opposing the construction of new mosques and raising the nonexistent threat that courts would impose "sharia law"—the religious rules laid down in the Koran—on all Americans. Others complained when public schools and colleges made special accommodations for Muslims, such as setting aside time for students to conduct daily prayers.

In 2010, the issue of the place of Muslims in American life gained widespread attention in a heated debate over plans to build an Islamic Cultural Center near the site of the World Trade Center in New York. While the city's mayor, Michael Bloomberg, supported the project as an exercise of religious freedom, opponents vocally insisted that the center would be a "Trojan Horse" for terrorists, and that its presence would demean the memory of those who had died nearby. The city approved construction but as of 2012, it had yet to begin.

Demonstrators in New York City opposed to plans for an Islamic Cultural Center near the World Trade Center site.

The Constitution and Liberty

As in the 1980s and 1990s, conservatives proved far more successful in implementing their views in economic and foreign policy than in the ongoing culture wars. Two significant Supreme Court decisions in June 2003 revealed how the largely conservative justices had come to accept that the social revolution that began during the 1960s could not be undone.

In two cases arising from challenges to the admissions policies of the University of Michigan, the Supreme Court issued its most important rulings on affirmative action since the *Bakke* case twenty-five years earlier. A 5-4 majority upheld the right of colleges and universities to take race into account in admissions decisions. Writing for the majority, Justice Sandra Day O'Connor argued that such institutions have a legitimate interest in creating a "diverse" student body to enhance education. The Bush administration had urged the Court to reject affirmative action. But O'Connor was strongly influenced by briefs on its behalf filed by corporate executives and retired military officers. In today's world, they argued, the United States cannot compete in the global economy or maintain effective armed services without drawing its college-trained business and military leaders from a wide variety of racial and ethnic backgrounds.

Revisiting the Bakke *case*

Lawrence v. Texas

In the second decision, in *Lawrence v. Texas*, a 6-3 majority declared unconstitutional a Texas law making homosexual acts a crime. Written by Justice Anthony Kennedy, the majority opinion overturned the Court's 1986 ruling in *Bowers v. Hardwick*, which had upheld a similar Georgia law. Today, Kennedy insisted, the idea of liberty includes not only "freedom of thought, belief, [and] expression" but "intimate conduct" as well. The decision was a triumph for the feminist and gay movements, which had long campaigned to extend the idea of freedom into the most personal realms of life. And it repudiated the conservative view that constitutional interpretation must rest either on the "original intent" of the founding fathers or on a narrow reading of the document's text. Instead, Kennedy reaffirmed the liberal view of the Constitution as a living document whose protections expand as society changes. "Times can blind us to certain truths," he wrote, "and later generations can see that laws once thought necessary and proper in fact serve only to oppress. As the Constitution endures, persons in every generation can invoke its principles in their own search for greater freedom."

The Court and the President

Nor did the Supreme Court prove receptive to President Bush's claim of authority to disregard laws and treaties and to suspend constitutional protections of individual liberties. In a series of decisions, the Court reaffirmed the rule of law both for American citizens and for foreigners held prisoner by the United States.

The first cases were decided in 2004. In *Rasul v. Bush*, the Court allowed a British citizen held at Guantánamo Bay, Cuba, to challenge his incarceration in federal court. In *Hamdi v. Rumsfeld*, it considered the lawsuit of Yasir Hamdi, an American citizen who had moved to Saudi Arabia and been captured in Afghanistan. Hamdi was imprisoned in a military jail in South Carolina without charge or the right to see a lawyer. The Court ruled that he had a right to a judicial hearing. "A state of war," wrote Sandra Day O'Connor for the 8-1 majority, "is not a blank check for the president when it comes to the rights of the nation's citizens." Even Justice Antonin Scalia, the Court's most prominent conservative, rejected the president's claim of authority to imprison a citizen at will as antithetical to "the very core of liberty." After claiming in court that Hamdi was so dangerous that he could not even be allowed a hearing, the administration allowed him to return to Saudi Arabia on condition that he relinquish his American citizenship.

The rights of detainees

Freedom: Certain Restrictions Apply. This work by the artist George Mill includes language that parodies the small print in advertisements and consumer warranties. The disclaimer reads: "Certain restrictions apply. Subject to change without notice. The right of freedom is made available 'as is' and without warranty of any kind." This was part of a 2008 exhibit in which artists produced works on the theme "Thoughts on Freedom." Many of the works suggested that the policies of the Bush administration had made Americans' freedom more precarious.

By the time the next significant case, *Hamdan v. Rumsfeld*, came before the Court in 2006, President Bush had appointed two new justices—Chief Justice John Roberts, to replace William Rehnquist, who died in 2005, and Samuel Alito Jr., who succeeded the retiring Sandra Day O'Connor. The Court was clearly becoming more conservative. But in June 2006, by a 5-3 margin (with Roberts not participating because he had ruled on the case while serving on an appeals court), the justices offered a stinging rebuke to the key presumptions of the Bush administration— that the Geneva Conventions do not apply to prisoners captured in the war on terrorism, that the president can unilaterally set up secret military tribunals in which defendants have very few if any rights, and that the Constitution does not apply at Guantánamo. Congress, the majority noted, had never authorized such tribunals, and they clearly violated the protections afforded to prisoners of war by the Geneva Conventions, which, the Court declared, was the law of the land.

Like the Nixon tapes case of 1974, the decision was a striking illustration of the separation of powers envisioned by the Constitution's framers, an affirmation that the courts have the right and responsibility to oversee actions by the president. However, it was unusual that the decision came in wartime. The Court had upheld jailings under the Sedition Act in World War I, and Japanese internment in World War II. Previously, the Court had only exerted its oversight authority once peace arrived. But Bush's claims of presidential authority had been so sweeping that a judicial reaction was all but inevitable.

As the "war on terror" entered its sixth year later in 2006, the scope of the president's power to detain and punish suspects outside of normal legal procedures remained unresolved. In September 2006, in response to the *Hamdan* decision,

Hamdan v. Rumsfeld

Military tribunals

Congress enacted a bill authorizing the establishment of special military tribunals to try accused terrorists and giving the president the authority to jail without charge anyone he declared to be an "illegal enemy combatant." The measure authorized certain kinds of harsh treatment of prisoners, with evidence obtained during coercive interrogations usable in these new courts, and stripped detainees in military prisons of the right to challenge their detention in federal courts. Many military lawyers objected strongly to these provisions, as did other army officials, fearing that captured U.S. soldiers might be subjected to the same treatment. It remained to be seen whether the Supreme Court would allow Congress to override the Geneva Conventions and eliminate judicial oversight of the treatment of prisoners.

In June 2008, for the third time in four years, the Supreme Court rebuffed the Bush administration's strategy of denying detainees at Guantánamo Bay the normal protections guaranteed by the Constitution. Written by Justice Anthony Kennedy, the 5-4 decision in *Boumediene v. Bush* affirmed the detainees' right to challenge their detention in U.S. courts. "The laws and Constitution are designed," Kennedy wrote, "to survive, and remain in force, in extraordinary times." Security, he added, consists not simply in military might, but "in fidelity to freedom's first principles," including freedom from arbitrary arrest and the right of a person to go to court to challenge his or her imprisonment.

The Midterm Elections of 2006

With President Bush's popularity having plummeted because of the war in Iraq and the Hurricane Katrina disaster, Congress beset by scandal after scandal, and public-opinion polls revealing that a majority of Americans believed the country to be "on the wrong track," Democrats expected to reap major gains in the congressional elections of 2006. They were not disappointed. In a sweeping repudiation of the administration, voters gave Democrats control of both houses of Congress for the first time since the Republican sweep of 1994. In January 2007, Democrat Nancy Pelosi of California became the first female Speaker of the House in American history. No sooner had the votes been counted than political observers began to speculate about the presidential election of 2008—the first time since 1952 that the major party candidates for the highest office in the land would not include a sitting president or vice president.

Democratic majorities in Congress

As the end of his second term approached, Bush's popularity sank to historic lows. This occurred even though, in November 2008, the United States and Iraq approved an agreement providing for the withdrawal of all American troops by 2011—thus ensuring that one of the longest and most unpopular wars in American history would come to an end. By sending more troops to Iraq in 2007 (a step that Bush, mindful of memories of Vietnam, called a "surge" rather than an escalation) and by forging alliances with local tribal leaders anxious to end the bloodshed, the administration had achieved a significant decline in violence in Iraq, making American withdrawal seem possible. But no one could predict what a postwar Iraq would look like.

In January 2009, as Bush's presidency came to an end, only 22 percent of Americans approved of his performance in office—the lowest figure since such polls began in the mid-twentieth century. Indeed, it was difficult to think of many substantive achievements during Bush's eight years in office. His foreign policy

George W. Bush's legacy

alienated most of the world, leaving the United States militarily weakened and diplomatically isolated. Because of the tax cuts for the wealthy that he pushed through Congress during his first term, as well as the cost of the wars in Iraq and Afghanistan, the large budget surplus he had inherited was transformed into an immense deficit. The percentage of Americans living in poverty and those without health insurance rose substantially during Bush's presidency.

The Housing Bubble

At one point in his administration, Bush might have pointed to the economic recovery that began in 2001 as a major success. But late in 2007, the economy entered a recession. And in 2008, the American banking system suddenly found itself on the brink of collapse, threatening to drag the national and world economies into a repeat of the Great Depression.

The roots of the crisis of 2008 lay in a combination of public and private policies that favored economic speculation, free-wheeling spending, and get-rich-quick schemes over more traditional avenues to economic growth and personal advancement. For years, the Federal Reserve Bank kept interest rates at unprecedented low levels, first to help the economy recover from the bursting of the technology bubble in 2000 and then to enable more Americans to borrow money to purchase homes. The result was a new bubble, as housing prices rose rapidly. Consumer indebtedness also rose dramatically as people who owned houses took out second mortgages, or simply spent to the limits on their credit cards. In mid-2008, when the median family income was around $50,000, the average American family owed an $84,000 home mortgage, $14,000 in auto and student loans, $8,500 to credit card companies, and $10,000 in home equity loans.

All this borrowing fueled increased spending. An immense influx of cheap goods from China accelerated the loss of manufacturing jobs in the United States (which continued their decline despite the overall economic recovery) but also enabled Americans to keep buying, even though for most, household income stagnated during the Bush years. Indeed, China helped to finance the American

FIGURE 28.1   The Housing Bubble

Median home prices: Florida and the rest of the United States.

An Arizona house left unfinished when the housing bubble collapsed. When prices were at their peak, housing developers rushed to build new residences; many were abandoned when prices plunged.

spending spree by buying up hundreds of billions of dollars worth of federal bonds—in effect loaning money to the United States so that it could purchase Chinese-made goods. Banks and other lending institutions issued more and more "subprime" mortgages—risky loans to people who lacked the income to meet their monthly payments. The initially low interest rates on these loans were set to rise dramatically after a year or two. Banks assumed that home prices would keep rising, and if they had to foreclose, they could easily resell the property at a profit.

Wall Street bankers developed complex new ways of repackaging and selling these mortgages to investors. Insurance companies, including the world's largest, American International Group (AIG), insured these new financial products against future default. Credit rating agencies gave these securities their highest ratings, even though they were based on loans that clearly would never be repaid. Believing that the market must be left to regulate itself, the Federal Reserve Bank and other regulatory agencies did nothing to slow the speculative frenzy. Banks and investment firms reported billions of dollars in profits, and rewarded their executives with unheard-of bonuses.

Selling debt

The Great Recession

In 2006 and 2007, overbuilding had reached the point where home prices began to fall. More and more home owners found themselves owing more money than their homes were worth. As mortgage rates reset, increasing numbers of borrowers defaulted—that is, they could no longer meet their monthly mortgage payments. The value of the new mortgage-based securities fell precipitously. Banks suddenly found themselves with billions of dollars of worthless investments on their books. In 2008, the situation became a full-fledged crisis, as banks stopped making loans, business dried up, and the stock market collapsed. Once above 14,000, the Dow Jones Industrial Average plunged to around 8,000—the worst percentage decline since 1931. Some $7 trillion in shareholder wealth was wiped out. Lehman Brothers, a venerable investment house, recorded a $2.3 billion loss and went out of existence, in history's biggest bankruptcy. Leading banks seemed to be on the verge of failure.

With the value of their homes and stock market accounts in free fall, Americans cut back on spending, leading to business failures and a rapid rise in unemployment. By the end of 2008, 2.5 million jobs had been lost—the most in any year since the end of World War II. Unemployment was concentrated in manufacturing and construction, sectors dominated by men. As a result, by mid-2009, for the first time in American history, more women than men in the United States held paying jobs.

In the last three months of 2008, and again in the first three of 2009, the gross domestic product of the United States decreased by 6 percent—a remarkably steep contraction. Even worse than the economic meltdown was the meltdown of confidence as millions of Americans lost their jobs and/or their homes and saw their retirement savings and pensions, if invested in the stock market,

These graphs offer a vivid visual illustration of the steep decline in the American economy in 2008 and the first part of 2009, and the slow recovery to 2012.

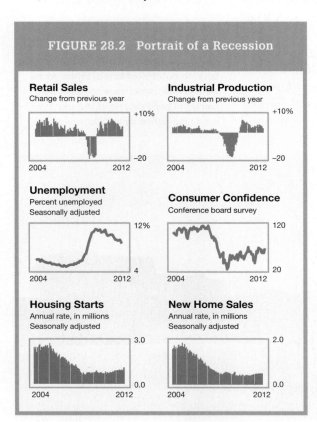

FIGURE 28.2 Portrait of a Recession

Retail Sales
Change from previous year

Industrial Production
Change from previous year

Unemployment
Percent unemployed
Seasonally adjusted

Consumer Confidence
Conference board survey

Housing Starts
Annual rate, in millions
Seasonally adjusted

New Home Sales
Annual rate, in millions
Seasonally adjusted

disappear. In April 2009, the recession that began in December 2007 became the longest since the Great Depression. In an era of globalization, economic crises inevitably spread worldwide. The decline in spending in the United States led to unemployment in China, and plunging car sales led to a sharp decline in oil prices and economic problems in oil-producing countries like Russia, Nigeria, and Saudi Arabia. Housing bubbles collapsed around the world, from Ireland to Dubai.

The mortgage crisis affected minorities the most. Many had been steered by banks into subprime mortgages even when they had the assets and income to qualify for more traditional, lower-cost loans. As a result, foreclosures were highest in minority areas, and the gains blacks, Asians, and Hispanics had made in home ownership between 1995 and 2004 now eroded. In 2012, Wells Fargo Bank, the nation's largest home mortgage lender, agreed to pay $175 million to settle claims that its brokers had charged higher fees to blacks and Hispanics who borrowed money to purchase homes during the housing bubble than to whites with comparable incomes, and pushed the minorities into risky subprime mortgages.

Effects of the crisis on minorities

"A Conspiracy against the Public"

In *The Wealth of Nations* (1776), Adam Smith wrote: "People of the same trade seldom meet together, even for merriment and diversion, but the conversation ends in a conspiracy against the public." This certainly seemed an apt description of the behavior of leading bankers and investment houses whose greed helped to bring down the American economy. Like the scandals of the 1920s and 1990s, those of the Bush era damaged confidence in the ethics of corporate leaders. Indeed, striking parallels existed between these three decades—the get-rich-quick ethos, the close connection between business and government, the passion for deregulation, and widespread corruption.

Damaged by revelations of corporate misdeeds, the reputation of stock brokers and bankers fell to lows last seen during the Great Depression. One poll showed that of various social groups, bankers ranked third from the bottom in public esteem—just above prostitutes and convicted felons. Resentment was fueled by the fact that Wall Street had long since abandoned the idea that pay should be linked to results. By the end of 2008, the worst year for the stock market since the Depression, Wall Street firms had fired 240,000 employees. But they also paid out $20 billion in bonuses to top executives. Even the executives of Lehman Brothers, a company that went bankrupt (and, it later turned out, had shortchanged New York City by hundreds of millions of dollars in corporate and other taxes), received $5.7 billion in bonuses in 2007 and 2008. In 2010, Goldman Sachs, the Wall Street banking and investment firm, paid a fine of half a billion dollars to settle charges that it had knowingly marketed to clients mortgage-based securities it knew were bound to fail, and then in effect bet on their failure. (This was like a real-estate agency selling an unsuspecting customer a house with faulty wiring and then taking out insurance so that the agency would be paid when the house burned down.) But no changes followed in management, and the fine represented only two weeks' profit for the mighty firm. Two years later, Barclays, one of the world's largest banks, paid a fine of similar size after admitting that it had provided false information to authorities so as to manipulate interest rates in a way that increased its profits.

Wall Street

It was also revealed that Bernard Madoff, a Wall Street investor who claimed to have made enormous profits for his clients, had in fact run a Ponzi scheme in which investors who wanted to retrieve their money were paid with funds from new participants. Madoff sent fictitious monthly financial statements to his clients but he never actually made stock purchases for them. When the scheme collapsed, Madoff's investors suffered losses amounting to around $50 billion. In 2009, Madoff pleaded guilty to fraud and was sentenced to 150 years in prison. In some ways, Madoff's scheme was a metaphor for the American economy at large over the previous decade. Its growth had been based on borrowing from others and spending money people did not have. The popular musical group Coldplay related what had happened:

The Bernard Madoff scandal ▶

> I used to rule the world. . . .
> I discovered that my castles stand
> On pillars of salt and pillars of sand.

The Collapse of Market Fundamentalism

The crisis exposed the dark side of market fundamentalism—the ethos of deregulation that had dominated world affairs for the preceding thirty years. Alan Greenspan, the head of the Federal Reserve Bank from 1987 to 2006, had steered the American economy through crises ranging from the stock market collapse of 1987 to the terrorist attacks of 2001. Greenspan had presided over much of the era of deregulation, artificially low interest rates, and excessive borrowing and spending. He and his successors had promoted the housing bubble and saw all sorts of speculative behavior flourish with no governmental intervention. In effect, they allowed securities firms to regulate themselves.

The Greenspan era ▶

This cartoon suggests that the near-collapse of the financial system in 2008 indicates the need for "a little more regulation."

In 2008, Greenspan admitted to Congress that there had been a "flaw" in his long-held conviction that free markets would automatically produce the best results for all and that regulation would damage banks, Wall Street, and the mortgage market. He himself, he said, was in a state of "shocked disbelief," as the crisis turned out to be "much broader than anything I could have imagined." Greenspan's testimony seemed to mark the end of an era. Every president from Ronald Reagan onward had lectured the rest of the world on the need to adopt the American model of unregulated economic competition, and berated countries like Japan and Germany for assisting failing businesses. Now, the American model lay in ruins and a new role for government in regulating economic activity seemed inevitable.

Bush and the Crisis

In the fall of 2008, with the presidential election campaign in full swing, the Bush administration seemed unable to come up with a response to the crisis. In keeping with the free market ethos, it allowed Lehman Brothers to fail. But this immediately created a domino effect, with the stock prices of other banks and investment houses collapsing, and the administration quickly reversed course. It persuaded a reluctant Congress to appropriate $700 billion dollars to bail out other floundering firms. Insurance companies like AIG, banks like Citigroup and Bank of America, and giant financial companies like the Federal Home Loan Mortgage Corporation (popularly known as Freddie Mac) and the Federal National Mortgage Association (Fannie Mae), which insured most mortgages in the country, were deemed "too big to fail"—that is, they were so interconnected with other institutions that their collapse would drive the economy into a full-fledged depression. Through the federal bailout, taxpayers in effect took temporary ownership of these companies, absorbing the massive losses created by their previous malfeasance. Most of this money was distributed with no requirements as to its use. Few of the rescued firms used the public funds to assist home owners threatened with foreclosure; indeed, since they pocketed lucrative fees from those who could not pay their mortgages, they had no incentive to help them keep their homes or sell them. Giant banks and investment houses that received public money redirected some of it to enormous bonuses to top employees. But despite the bailout, the health of the banking system remained fragile. Firms still had balance sheets weighed down with "toxic assets"—billions and billions of dollars in worthless loans.

"Too big to fail"

The crisis also revealed the limits of the American "safety net" compared with other industrialized countries. In western Europe, workers who lose their jobs typically receive many months of unemployment insurance amounting to a significant percentage of their lost wages. In the United States, only one-third of out-of-work persons even qualify for unemployment insurance, and it runs out after a few months. The abolition of "welfare" (the national obligation to assist the neediest Americans) during the Clinton administration left the American safety net a patchwork of a few national programs like food stamps, supplemented by locally administered aid. The poor were dependent on aid from the states, which found their budgets collapsing as revenues from property and sales taxes dried up. As the number of needy Americans rose, those receiving food stamps, a national program with uniform eligibility rules, skyrocketed, but welfare rolls did not

The limits of the American social safety net

A cartoon in the *Boston Globe* suggests the progress that has been made since Rosa Parks refused to give up her seat on a bus to a white passenger.

increase. Hard-pressed for cash, states used their ability to turn away applicants, greatly enhanced by the welfare reform of the 1990s, to save money. In 2012, only one in five poor children received cash aid, the lowest percentage in half a century.

THE RISE OF OBAMA

With the economy in crisis and President Bush's popularity at low ebb, the time was ripe for a Democratic victory in the election of 2008. To the surprise of nearly all political pundits, the long series of winter and spring caucuses and primary elections resulted in the nomination not of Hillary Rodham Clinton, the initial favorite, but Barack Obama, a relatively little-known forty-seven-year-old senator from Illinois when the campaign began. Obama was the first black candidate to win the nomination of a major party. His triumph was a tribute both to his own exceptional skills as a speaker and campaigner, and to how American politics had changed.

Obama's life story exemplified the enormous changes American society had undergone since 1960. Without the civil rights movement, his election would have been inconceivable. He was the product of an interracial marriage, which ended in divorce when he was two years old, between a Kenyan immigrant and a white American woman. When Obama was born in 1961, their marriage was still illegal in many states. He attended Columbia College and Harvard Law School, and worked in Chicago as a community organizer before going into politics. He also wrote two best-selling books about his upbringing in Indonesia (where his mother worked as an anthropologist) and Hawaii (where his maternal grandparents helped to raise him) and his search for a sense of identity given his complex background. Obama was elected to the U.S. Senate in 2004 and first gained national attention with an eloquent speech at the Democratic national convention that year.

The primary campaign

Clinton sought the Democratic nomination by emphasizing her political experience, both as First Lady and as a senator from New York. Obama realized that in 2008 people were hungry for change, not experience. Indeed, while Clinton's nomination would also have been pathbreaking—no woman has ever been the presidential candidate of a major party—Obama succeeded in making her seem a representative of the status quo. His early opposition to the Iraq War, for which Clinton had voted in the Senate, won the support of the party's large antiwar element; his race galvanized the support of black voters; and his youth and promise of change appealed to the young.

Obama recognized how the Internet had changed politics. He established an e-mail list containing the names of millions of voters with whom he could communicate instantaneously, and used web-based networks to raise enormous sums of money in small donations. His campaign put out videos on popular Internet sites. With its widespread use of modern technology and massive mobilization of new voters, Obama's was the first political campaign of the twenty-first century.

The 2008 Campaign

Having won the nomination, Obama faced Senator John McCain, the Republican nominee, in the general election. At age seventy-two, McCain was the oldest man ever to run for president, and he seemed even more a representative of the old politics than Clinton. Citing his willingness to break with his party on issues like campaign finance reform, McCain tried to portray himself not as part of the establishment but as a "maverick," or rebel. He surprised virtually everyone by choosing as his running mate Sarah Palin, the little-known governor of Alaska, in part as an attempt to woo Democratic women disappointed at their party's rejection of Hillary Clinton. Palin quickly went on the attack, accusing Democrats of being unpatriotic, lacking traditional values, and not representing the "real America." This proved extremely popular with the Republican Party's conservative base. But her performances in speeches and interviews soon made it clear that she lacked familiarity with many of the domestic and foreign issues a new administration would confront. Her selection raised questions among many Americans about McCain's judgment.

THE PRESIDENTIAL ELECTION OF 2008

Party	Candidate	Electoral Vote (Share)	Popular Vote (Share)
Democrat	Obama	365 (67.8%)	66,882,230 (53%)
Republican	McCain	173 (32.2%)	58,343,671 (46%)

But the main obstacles for the McCain campaign were President Bush's low popularity and the financial crisis that reached bottom in September and October. Obama's promise of change seemed more appealing than ever. On election day, he swept to victory with 53 percent of the popular vote and a large majority in the electoral college. His election redrew the nation's political map. Obama carried not only Democratic strongholds in New England, the mid-Atlantic states, the industrial Midwest, and the West Coast, but also states that had been reliably Republican for years. He cracked the solid South, winning Virginia, North Carolina, and Florida. He did extremely well in suburbs throughout the country. He even carried Indiana, where Bush had garnered 60 percent of the vote in 2004, but which now was hard hit by unemployment. Obama put together a real "rainbow" coalition, winning nearly the entire black vote and a large majority of Hispanics (who helped him to carry Colorado, Nevada, and Florida). He did exceptionally well among young voters. Obama carried every age group except persons over 65. Thus, he was elected even though he received only 43 percent of the nation's white vote.

Obama's victory

Obama's victory seemed to mark the end of a political era that began with Richard Nixon and his "southern strategy." Instead of using control of the South as the base to build a national majority, Republicans now ran the danger of becoming a regional and marginalized southern party. In the wake of the Iraq War, the economic meltdown, and the enthusiasm aroused by Obama's candidacy, Republican appeals to patriotism, low taxes, and resentment against the social changes sparked by the 1960s seemed oddly out of date. Democrats not only regained the presidency but ended up with 60 of the 100 seats in the Senate and a large majority in the House. The groups carried by Obama—young voters, Hispanics, suburbanites—represented the growing parts of the population, auguring well for future Democratic success. In an increasingly multiethnic, multiracial nation,

On inauguration day, January 20, 2009, a photograph of the outgoing president, George W. Bush, is replaced by one of Barack Obama at the headquarters of the U.S. Naval Station at Guantánamo, Cuba.

President Obama addressing an audience at Cairo University, Egypt, in June 2009. He called for a "new beginning between the United States and Muslims."

winning a majority of the white vote no longer translated into national victory. Republicans would have to find a way to appeal to the voters of the new America.

Obama's First Inauguration

Few presidents have come into office facing as serious a set of problems as Barack Obama. The economy was in crisis and the country involved in two wars. But Americans, including many who had not voted for him, viewed Obama's election as a cause for optimism. Two days after his victory, a poll found two-thirds of Americans describing themselves as proud of the result, and 60 percent excited at the prospect of an Obama administration.

On January 20, 2009, a day after the Martin Luther King Jr. holiday and more than forty-five years after King's "I Have a Dream" speech, Obama was inaugurated as president. More than 1 million people traveled to Washington to view the historic event. In his inaugural address (see the full text in the Appendix), Obama offered a stark rebuke to eight years of Bush policies and, more broadly, to the premises that had shaped government policy since the election of Reagan. He promised a foreign policy based on diplomacy rather than unilateral force, pledged to protect the environment, spoke of the need to combat income inequality and lack of access to health care, and blamed a culture of "greed and irresponsibility" for helping to bring on the economic crisis. He promised to renew respect for the Constitution. Unlike Bush, Obama said little about freedom in his speech, other than to note that the country could enjoy liberty and security at the same time rather than having to choose between them. Instead of freedom, he spoke of community and responsibility. His address harked back to the revolutionary-era ideal of putting the common good before individual self-interest.

Obama in Office

In many ways, Obama's first policy initiatives lived up to the promise of change. In his first three months, he announced plans to close the prison at Guantánamo Bay in Cuba, barred the use of torture, launched a diplomatic initiative to repair relations with the Muslim world, reversed the previous administration's executive orders limiting women's reproductive rights, and abandoned Bush's rhetoric about a God-given American mission to spread freedom throughout the world. When Supreme Court justice David Souter announced his retirement, Obama named Sonia Sotomayor, the first Hispanic and third woman in the Court's history, to replace him. The Senate confirmed her in August 2009.

Obama's first budget recalled the New Deal and Great Society. Breaking with the Reagan-era motto, "Government is the problem, not the solution," it anticipated active government support for health-care reform, clean energy, and public education, paid for in part by allowing Bush's tax cuts for the wealthy to expire in 2010. He pushed through Congress a "stimulus" package amounting to nearly $800 billion in new government spending—for construction projects, the extension of unemployment benefits, and aid to the states to enable them to balance their budgets. The largest single spending appropriation in American history, the bill was meant to pump money into the economy in order to save and create jobs and to ignite a resumption of economic activity.

A year into his presidency, in the spring of 2010, Obama had to deal with one of the worst environmental disasters in American history. An oil rig in the Gulf of Mexico owned by British Petroleum (BP) exploded, spewing millions of gallons of oil into the sea. The oil washed up on the beaches of Louisiana, Mississippi, Alabama, and Florida, killing marine life, birds, and other animals and devastating the Gulf tourist industry. It took months to stop the oil from rushing into the Gulf, and much longer to restore the beaches.

The disaster illustrated some of the downsides of globalization and deregulation. The government agency charged with inspections was so cozy with the oil industry that it allowed the companies to set their own safety standards and looked the other way in the face of BP's long record of cutting corners, safety violations, and accidents. The rig that exploded had been built in South Korea and was operated by a Swiss company under contract to BP. Primary responsibility for safety rested not with the United States but with the Republic of the Marshall Islands, a tiny, impoverished nation in the Pacific Ocean, where the rig was registered. Thus, BP enjoyed freedom from the effective oversight that might have prevented the disaster.

A marine bird soaked in oil from the damaged offshore drilling platform of British Petroleum in the Gulf of Mexico.

For most of Obama's first year in office, congressional debate revolved around a plan to restructure the nation's health-care system so as to provide insurance coverage to the millions of Americans who lacked it, and to end abusive practices by insurance companies, such as their refusal to cover patients with existing illnesses. After months of increasingly bitter debate, in March 2010, Congress passed a sweeping health-care bill that required all Americans to purchase health insurance and most businesses to provide it to their employees. It also offered subsidies to persons of modest incomes so they could afford insurance, and required insurance companies to accept all applicants. The measure aroused strong partisan opposition. Claiming that it amounted to a "government takeover" of the health-care industry (even though plans for a government-run insurance program had been dropped from the bill), every Republican in Congress voted against the bill.

Health care reform

Another significant measure, enacted in July 2010, was a financial regulatory reform law that sought to place under increased federal oversight many of the transactions that had helped create the economic crisis. Although the details remained to be worked out through specific regulations, the law represented a reversal of the policies of the past fifty years that had given banks a free hand in their operations. But it did not require a breakup of banks deemed "too big to fail," and left open the possibility of future taxpayer bailouts of these institutions.

Regulatory reform

Taken together, the measures of Obama's first year and a half in office saw the most dramatic domestic reform legislation since the Great Society of the 1960s. "Change"—the slogan of his election campaign—was significant, but did not go far enough for many of his supporters. The health-care bill failed to include a "public option," in which the government itself would offer medical insurance to those who desired it (much like Medicare for elderly Americans). Obama chose his economic advisers from Wall Street and continued the Bush administration policy of pouring taxpayer money into the banks and assuming responsibility for many of their debts. Little was done to help home owners facing foreclosure. During 2008 and 2009, the economy lost 8 million jobs. It would take a long time to recover them.

OBAMA'S FIRST TERM

The Continuing Economic Crisis

Although the recession officially ended in mid-2009, economic growth was so anemic that unemployment remained stubbornly high throughout Obama's first term in office. State and local governments, which account for nearly one-sixth of all jobs in the United States, cut back sharply on employment to save money. The poverty rate in 2011 exceeded 15 percent, its highest level in twenty years. With housing prices still falling, Americans found their net worth reduced by trillions of dollars from the height of the housing bubble. Thus, they cut back on borrowing and spending, adding to the economy's malaise.

A weak recovery

The deep recession and feeble recovery exacerbated structural trends long under way. Manufacturing employment, which once offered a route into the middle class for those (mostly men) with limited educations, rebounded from its low point of 2009 but remained several million jobs lower than in 2000. Job growth was concentrated either at the high or low end of the pay scale. The financial sector laid off hundreds of thousands of workers, but the incomes of those who kept their jobs remained extremely high. The fastest-growing job categories, however, were those that paid low wages. Indeed, the Bureau of Labor Statistics in 2012 projected that over the next decade, the largest areas of job growth would be in office work, sales, food preparation and service, child care, home health aides, and janitors—every one of which paid less than the median annual wage. All this strengthened the tendency toward economic inequality. The combined wealth of the family that owns Wal-Mart equals that of the bottom 150 million Americans. The median income of a male full-time worker in 2010 was lower, adjusted for inflation, than in 1973. Rising income inequality afflicted countries across the globe, but among industrialized nations the United States had the highest rate of all.

African-Americans and the recession

African-Americans suffered most severely from the recession. Unlike other Americans, blacks tended to own few if any stocks, so did not benefit when the stock market recovered many of its recession losses. All their family wealth was in their homes, and so the collapse of the housing bubble devastated their economic status. In 2011, the median family wealth of white families was $92,000, that of black only $4,900. Black unemployment remained nearly double that of whites, as did the poverty rate, which reached 27 percent among African-Americans. While the civil rights movement had produced a dramatic increase in the number of well-paid black professionals (like Obama himself, a lawyer), ordinary African-Americans had achieved economic gains by moving into jobs in manufacturing and government (the latter accounting for 20 percent of black employment), the two sectors hardest hit by the recession.

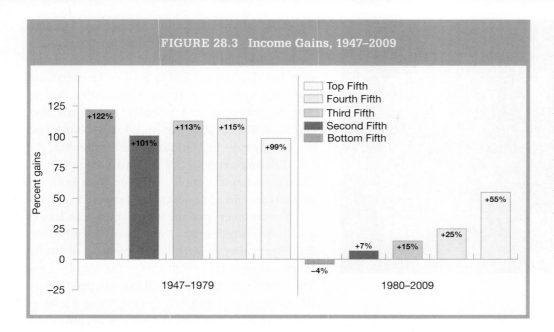

FIGURE 28.3 Income Gains, 1947–2009

Legend:
- Top Fifth
- Fourth Fifth
- Third Fifth
- Second Fifth
- Bottom Fifth

Percent gains

1947–1979: +122%, +101%, +113%, +115%, +99%

1980–2009: −4%, +7%, +15%, +25%, +55%

From 1947 to 1979, on a percentage basis, the bottom four fifths of the classes did better than the top fifth of earners. From 1980 to 2009, the poorest lost ground and income gains grew increasingly lopsided. The income ranges in 2009 dollars is: Bottom Fifth / $26,934 or less; Second Fifth / $26,935–$47,914; Third Fifth / $47,915–$73,338; Fourth Fifth / $73,339–$112,540; Top Fifth / $112,541 or more.

Obama and the World

The most dramatic achievement of Obama's presidency in foreign affairs was fulfillment of his campaign promise to end American involvement in the Iraq War. At the end of 2011, the last American soldiers came home. Nearly 5,000 Americans and, according to the estimates of U.S. and Iraqi analysts, hundreds of thousands of Iraqis, most of them civilians, had died during this eight-year conflict. The war had cost the United States nearly $2 trillion, an almost unimaginable sum. Whether it would produce a stable, democratic Iraq remained to be seen.

Iraq and Afghanistan

At the same time, Obama continued many of the policies of his predecessor. Obama dramatically increased the American troop presence in Afghanistan, while pledging to withdraw American forces by the end of 2014. Here again, the long-term outcome remained uncertain, given the Taliban's resurgence and the unpopularity of the corruption-plagued American-backed Afghan government. Indeed, by 2012, polls showed that a large majority of Americans felt the war was a mistake and wanted it to end.

Like many of his predecessors, Obama found that criticizing presidential power from outside is one thing, dismantling it another. As noted above, in his first weeks in office he banned the use of torture. But he reversed his previous promise to abolish the military tribunals Bush had established and to close the military prison at Guantánamo, Cuba. And in 2011 he signed a four-year extension of key provisions of the USA Patriot Act originally passed under Bush. In May 2011, to wide acclaim in the United States, Obama authorized an armed raid into Pakistan that resulted in the death of Osama bin Laden, who had been hiding there for years. More controversially, Obama claimed the right to order the assassination of American citizens in foreign countries if evidence indicated their connection with terrorism. And in 2011 he sent the air force to participate in a NATO campaign that assisted rebels who overthrew Libyan dictator Muammar

Fighting terrorism

Millions of Egyptians took part in the popular uprising of 2011 that overthrew the long-serving dictator Hosni Mubarak.

Gadhafi. Obama did not seek congressional approval of the action, deeming it unnecessary. In fact, by 2012, American troops or planes were involved in combat as part of an expanded war on terror not only in Afghanistan but in Yemen, Pakistan, and Somalia. American Special Forces were involved in efforts to suppress the drug trade in Honduras and Colombia. All told, Obama's conduct of foreign affairs proved to be considerably more bellicose than both his supporters and opponents had expected.

Events overseas presented new challenges and opportunities for the Obama administration. Beginning in 2011, to the surprise of almost everyone, popular revolts swept the Middle East. The uprisings brought millions of people into the streets, and toppled long-serving dictators in Tunisia, Egypt, and Libya. Freedom emerged as the rallying cry of those challenging autocratic governments. "I'm in Tahrir Square," one demonstrator yelled into his cell phone while standing at the epicenter of the Egyptian revolution. "In freedom, in freedom, in freedom." Once again, the tension between the ideals of freedom and democracy and American strategic interests posed a difficult challenge for policymakers. After some hesitation, the United States sided with those seeking the ouster of Hosni Mubarak, Egypt's long-serving dictator and a staunch American ally. It then stood on the sidelines throughout 2011 and 2012 as Egypt lurched from popular uprising to military rule, to electoral victory by the Muslim Brotherhood, a previously illegal Islamic group, with the final outcome of the revolution always in doubt. In Bahrain, an oil-rich principality in the Persian Gulf and home base of the American Fifth Fleet, the Obama administration looked the other way when the autocratic government suppressed popular discontent with force.

> *Freedom in Egypt*

The Republican Resurgence

In nearly all midterm elections in American history, the party in power has lost seats in Congress. But Democrats faced more serious difficulties than usual in the midterm elections of 2010. Grassroots Republicans were energized by hostility to Obama's sweeping legislative enactments. The Tea Party, named for the Boston Tea Party of the 1770s and inspired by its opposition to taxation by a far-away government, mobilized grassroots opposition to the administration. The Tea Party appealed to a long-established American fear of overbearing federal power, as well as to more recent anxieties, especially about immigration. Some supporters advocated repealing the provision of the Fourteenth Amendment granting automatic citizenship to all persons born in the United States. For a time, some activists denied that Obama was legally president at all, claiming that he had been born in Africa, not in the United States. (In fact, he was born in Hawaii.) With their opponents energized and their own supporters demoralized by the slow pace of economic recovery, Democrats suffered a severe reversal. Republicans swept to control of the House of Representatives and substantially reduced the Democratic majority in the

> *The Tea Party*

Senate. Republicans also captured numerous governorships, including in states crucial to Obama's prospects for reelection, such as Ohio, Pennsylvania, Michigan, and Wisconsin. The outcome at the national level was two years of political gridlock. Obama could no longer get significant legislation through Congress, but with the Senate still in Democratic hands, neither could Republicans.

But if Tea Party–inspired conservative Republicans could not get their way in Washington, their gains at the state level in 2010 unleashed a rash of new legislation. Several states moved to curtail abortion rights. In the name of combating a supposed epidemic of voting fraud, several states required voters to present a state-issued photo identification card such as a driver's license, an obstacle for poor Americans who did not own such a document, and restricted the ability of groups like the League of Women Voters to register new members of the electorate. Taken together, these measures represented the strongest effort to limit the right to vote since the early twentieth century. In Wisconsin, the legislature and Governor Scott Walker rescinded most of the bargaining rights of unions representing public employees. Workers and their supporters responded by occupying the state Capitol building for weeks, and then gathering petitions to force a recall election for Governor Walker in 2012, in which he succeeded in winning reelection. In Ohio, however, a similar anti-union law was repealed in a popular referendum.

New conservative legislatures also took aim at undocumented immigrants. Alabama, which has no land border with a foreign country and a small population of immigrants compared with other states, enacted the harshest measure, making it a crime for illegal immigrants to apply for a job, and for anyone to transport them, even to a church or hospital. During the contest for the Republican presidential nomination in early 2012, candidates vied with each other to demonstrate their determination to drive illegal immigrants from the country. Oddly, all this took place at a time when illegal immigration from Mexico, the largest source of undocumented workers, had ceased almost completely because of stricter controls at the border and the drying up of available jobs because of the recession. Despite the fact that the Obama administration had deported far more illegal immigrants than its predecessor, these measures associated the Republican Party with intense nativism in the minds of many Hispanic voters. In 2008, Obama had received around 70 percent of the Hispanic vote and in 2012 he seemed likely to come close to that figure again.

In the spring of 2009, Republicans and independents opposed to President Obama's "stimulus" plan held "tea parties" around the country, seeking to invoke the tradition of the Boston Tea Party and its opposition to taxation. In this demonstration in Austin, Texas, some participants wore hats reminiscent of the revolutionary era. One participant carries a sign urging the state to secede from the Union.

The immigration issue

The Occupy Movement

While most grassroots activism in 2011 and 2012 came from the right, these years also witnessed the emergence of a movement that targeted the depredations of Wall Street banks. On September 17, 2011, a few dozen young protesters

An Occupy Wall Street demonstrator expresses her concern about rising economic inequality.

Mitt Romney

unrolled sleeping bags in Zuccotti Park, in the heart of New York City's financial district. They vowed to remain—to Occupy Wall Street as they put it—as a protest against growing economic inequality, declining opportunity, and malfeasance by the banks.

Over the next few weeks, hundreds of people camped out in the park and thousands took part in rallies organized by the Occupy movement. Similar encampments sprang up in cities across the country. Using social media and the Internet, the Occupy movement spread its message far and wide. Although the technology was new, the movement bore some resemblance to previous efforts at social change, including the sit-down strikes of the 1930s and the civil disobedience of Henry David Thoreau and Martin Luther King Jr. In the spring of 2012, public authorities began to evict the protesters and the movement seemed to dissipate. But its language, especially the charge that "the one percent" (the very richest Americans) dominated political and economic life, had entered the political vocabulary. The Occupy movement tapped into a widespread feeling of alienation, especially among the young, a sense that society's rules have been fixed in favor of those at the top.

The 2012 Campaign

Despite the continuing economic crisis, sociocultural issues played a major role in the campaign for the Republican presidential nomination, as candidates vied to win the support of the evangelical Christians who formed a major part of the party's base. The front-runner was Mitt Romney, the former governor of Massachusetts. Romney had made a fortune directing Bain Capital, a firm that specialized in buying up other companies and then reselling them at a profit after restructuring them, which often involved firing large numbers of employees. But the party's powerful conservative wing disliked Romney because of his moderate record (as governor he had instituted a state health-care plan remarkably similar to Obama's 2011 legislation) and a distrust of his Mormon faith among many evangelical Christians. One after another, conservative champions rose and fell in the polls: Congresswoman Michele Bachmann of Minnesota, former Speaker of the House Newt Gingrich, Texas governor Rick Perry, African-American businessman Herman Cain, and former Pennsylvania Senator Rick Santorum. The emergence of Roman Catholics Gingrich and Santorum as heroes of the Protestant Republican right demonstrated how fully anti-Catholic prejudices have faded in the United States.

Romney spent the primary season attempting to demonstrate his conservative views and reaffirming his adherence to Christian beliefs. Issues long thought settled such as women's access to birth control suddenly roiled American politics. Eventually, using his personal fortune to outspend his rivals by an enormous amount, Romney emerged as the Republican candidate, the first Mormon to win a major party's nomination—a significant moment in the history of religious toleration in the United States. He chose as his running mate Congressman Paul D. Ryan of Wisconsin, a favorite of the Tea Party and a Roman Catholic. For the first time in its history, the Republican Party's ticket did not contain a traditional Protestant.

President Obama began the 2012 campaign with numerous liabilities. The enthusiasm that greeted his election had long since faded as the worst economic slump since the Great Depression dragged on, and voters became fed up with both the president and Congress because of the intensity of partisanship and legislative gridlock in Washington. The war in Afghanistan was increasingly unpopular and Obama's signature health-care law under ferocious assault by Republicans (although to the surprise of many observers, the Supreme Court in June 2012 held most of the law's provisions constitutional, with the conservative Chief Justice, John G. Roberts Jr., writing the opinion). Throughout 2012 Obama's approval ratings hovered below 50 percent—dangerous numbers for a president seeking reelection.

Nonetheless, after a heated campaign, Obama emerged victorious, winning 332 electoral votes to Romney's 206, and 51 percent of the popular vote to his opponent's 47 percent. Despite Obama's vulnerabilities—high unemployment, an anemic economic recovery, and vast sums of money poured into advertisements against him by conservative political action committees—the outcome was much the same as four years earlier. Only two states changed hands, Indiana and North Carolina, both of which Obama had carried by narrow margins in 2008 and now voted for Romney. But all the other "swing states," including such key battlegrounds as Ohio, Florida, Colorado, and Wisconsin, remained in Obama's column. At the same time, while Democrats gained a few seats in the House and Senate, the balance of power in Washington remained unchanged with a Democratic president and Senate and a Republican House. This set the stage for continued partisan infighting and political gridlock during Obama's second term.

Obama's victory stemmed from many causes, including an extremely efficient "get out the vote" organization on election day, and Romney's weaknesses as a campaigner. Romney never managed to shed the image of a millionaire who used loopholes to avoid paying taxes (his federal tax rate of 14 percent was lower than that of most working-class Americans) and who held ordinary people in contempt (an off-the-cuff remark that 47 percent of the people would not vote for him because they were "victims" dependent on government payments like Medicare and Social Security severely weakened his campaign). His effort to move to the political center after proclaiming himself a "severe conservative" in the primaries, left the impression that he lacked firm convictions. But more important, as in 2008, the result reflected the new diversity of the American population in the twenty-first century. Romney won 60 percent of the white vote, which in previous elections would have guaranteed victory. But Obama carried over 90 percent of the black vote and over 70 percent of Asians and Hispanics. In 1990, only 2 percent of the electorate was Hispanic. In 2012 that figure had risen to 10 percent, which gave Obama a margin of over 5 million votes. With the minority population on the increase, these figures heralded future difficulties for the Republican party unless it modified its strong anti-immigration rhetoric.

The 2012 election reflected the new diversity in other ways as well. Hawaii elected Tulsi Gabbard, the first Hindu to serve in Congress, and the first Buddhist, Mazie K. Hirono, to the Senate. And for the first time, popular referendums in Maine and Maryland registered approval of gay marriage, bringing to nine the number of states where such marriages were now lawful.

The design for World Trade Center One. The building illustrates the juxtaposition of optimism and fear a decade after the terrorist attacks of 2001. The soaring tower underscores Americans' capacity for recovery and regeneration. But at the insistence of the New York City police, the base consists of reinforced concrete, giving the building, at ground level, the appearance of a fortress. The two rectangles, planned as reflecting pools, mark the "footprints" of the original twin towers.

THE PRESIDENTIAL ELECTION OF 2012

Party	Candidate	Electoral Vote (Share)	Popular Vote (Share)
Democrat	Obama	332 (61.7%)	65,899,660 (51%)
Republican	Romney	206 (38.3%)	60,932,152 (47%)

An unstable world

But perhaps the most striking feature of the 2012 election was the unprecedented amount of money spent on the campaign. In 2010, in *Citizens United v. Federal Elections Commission*, the conservative majority on the Supreme Court had overturned federal restrictions on political contributions by corporations. At the same time, "political action committees" were allowed to spend as much money as they wished supporting or denigrating candidates for office so long as they did not coordinate their activities with the candidates' campaigns. Meanwhile, the Romney and Obama campaigns themselves raised and spent hundreds of millions of dollars from individual donors. All this resulted in an election that cost, taking presidential and congressional races combined, some $6 billion.

LEARNING FROM HISTORY

"The owl of Minerva takes flight at dusk." Minerva was the Roman goddess of wisdom, and this saying suggests that the meaning of events only becomes clear once they are over. It is still far too soon to assess the full impact of September 11 on American life and the long-term consequences of the changes at home and abroad it inspired.

As of the end of 2012, the world seemed far more unstable than anyone could have predicted when the Cold War ended twenty years earlier. An end to the war on terror seemed as remote as ever. The future of Iraq and Afghanistan remained uncertain, and Pakistan, traditionally the closest ally of the United States in that volatile region, experienced serious political instability. No settlement of the long-standing conflict between Israel and its Arab neighbors seemed in sight. Iran, its power in the region enhanced by the American removal of its chief rival, Saddam Hussein's regime in Iraq, appeared to be bent on acquiring nuclear weapons, which the United States vowed to prevent, raising the prospect of future conflict. Other regions of the world also presented daunting problems for American policymakers. North Korea had acquired nuclear weapons and refused international pressure to give them up. China's rapidly growing economic power posed a challenge to American predominance.

No one could predict how any of these crises, or others yet unimagined, would be resolved. But the United States, it seemed clear, would remain involved in the affairs of every region of the world. As of 2010, the country had more than 1,000 military bases of one kind or another around the globe, with at least some American soldiers stationed in 175 countries. A study by American intelligence agencies predicted that by 2025 the United States would remain the world's most powerful nation, but that its economic and military predominance would have declined significantly. A "multipolar world," with countries like China and India emerging as major powers, would succeed the era of unquestioned American

Seeking the lessons of history: a young visitor at the Civil Rights Memorial in Montgomery, Alabama.

dominance. How the continuing global financial crisis would affect these developments remained to be seen.

What *is* clear is that September 11 and its aftermath drew new attention to essential elements of the history of American freedom. As in the past, freedom is central to Americans' sense of themselves as individuals and as a nation. Americans continue to debate contemporary issues in a political landscape shaped by ideas of freedom. Indeed, freedom remains, as it has always been, an evolving concept, its definition open to disagreement, its boundaries never fixed or final. Freedom is neither self-enforcing nor self-correcting. It cannot be taken for granted, and its preservation requires eternal vigilance, especially in times of crisis.

An evolving concept of freedom

More than half a century ago, the African-American poet Langston Hughes urged Americans both to celebrate the freedoms they enjoy and to remember that freedom has always been incomplete:

> There are words like *Freedom*
> Sweet and wonderful to say.
> On my heartstrings freedom sings
> All day everyday.
>
> There are words like *Liberty*
> That almost make me cry.
> If you had known what I know
> You would know why.

SUGGESTED READING

BOOKS

- Bacevich, Andrew. *American Empire: The Realities and Consequences of U.S. Diplomacy* (2003). Examines how the idea of an American empire reemerged after September 11, and some of the results.

- Brinkley, Douglas. *The Great Deluge: Hurricane Katrina, New Orleans, and the Mississippi Gulf Coast* (2006). A scathing account of how government at all levels failed the people of New Orleans.

- Cole, David. *Terrorism and the Constitution* (rev. ed., 2006). Explores the constitutional issues raised by the war on terrorism.

- Gardner, Lloyd C. *The Long Road to Baghdad: A History of U.S. Foreign Policy from the 1970s to the Present* (2008). A careful study of recent American foreign policy and the origins of the Iraq War.

- Krugman, Paul. *The Return of Depression Economics and the Crisis of 2008* (2009). A leading economist explains the origins of the Great Recession.

- Lakoff, George. *Whose Freedom? The Battle over America's Most Important Idea* (2006). Describes how conservatives and liberals continue to interpret freedom in very different ways.

- Lansley, Stewart. *Divided We Stand: Why Inequality Keeps Rising* (2011). A prominent economist explains the reasons for rising economic inequality.

- Levitas, Mitchell, ed. *A Nation Challenged: A Visual History of 9/11 and Its Aftermath* (2002). Presents striking photographs of the terrorist attacks and the days that followed.

- Little, Douglas. *American Orientalism: The United States and the Middle East since 1945* (2003). A careful study of American relations with a volatile region since World War II.

- Nye, Joseph S., Jr. *The Paradox of American Power* (2002). An argument that despite its overwhelming power, the United States cannot do as it pleases in international affairs.

- Zakaria, Fareed. *The Future of Freedom: Illiberal Democracy at Home and Abroad* (2003). A foreign policy analyst discusses how the United States should respond to threats to freedom in the world.

WEBSITES

- September 11 Digital Archive: http://911digitalarchive.org

- The White House: www.whitehouse.gov

CHAPTER REVIEW AND ONLINE RESOURCES

REVIEW QUESTIONS

1. How did the foreign policy initiatives of the George W. Bush administration depart from the policies of other presidents since World War II?

2. How did the September 11 attacks transform Americans' understanding of their security? How did the response compare to that after Pearl Harbor?

3. What are the similarities and differences between America's involvement in Afghanistan and Iraq since 2001?

4. In what ways did American leaders and citizens draw lessons from Vietnam when considering U.S. involvement in Iraq?

5. What does the war on terrorism suggest about the tension between freedom and security as priorities of the United States?

6. What were the goals and impact of the Bush Administration's economic policies?

7. How did Supreme Court decisions since 2001 indicate that the rights revolution was here to stay?

8. What were the political and social effects of Hurricane Katrina? Which were lasting?

9. In what ways did the Obama Administration diverge from the policies of other recent administrations? In what ways was it similar?

10. How did the 2012 election reveal changes in American political and social practices? How did it represent continuities?

KEY TERMS

Kyoto Protocol (p. 1088)

the Bush Doctrine (p. 1090)

war in Afghanistan (p. 1090)

"war on terror" (p. 1090)

"axis of evil" (p. 1091)

Iraq War (p. 1092)

Arab Spring (p. 1095)

USA Patriot Act (p. 1097)

Guantánamo Bay detention camp (p. 1099)

"jobless" recovery (p. 1102)

Hurricane Katrina (p. 1103)

Lawrence v. Texas (p. 1108)

"housing bubble" (p. 1111)

Great Recession (p. 1112)

federal bailout (p. 1115)

Hillary Clinton (p. 1116)

Sonia Sotomayor (p. 1118)

"stimulus" package (p. 1118)

Gulf oil spill (p. 1119)

Tea Party (p. 1122)

Occupy Wall Street (p. 1123)

political action committees (p. 1126)

wwnorton.com/studyspace

Visit StudySpace for these resources and more:

- **Author Videos**
- **A chapter outline**
- **A practice quiz**
- **Interactive maps**
- **Multimedia documents**

APPENDIX

DOCUMENTS

The Declaration of Independence (1776)   A-2

The Constitution of the United States (1787)   A-5

From George Washington's Farewell Address (1796)   A-16

The Seneca Falls Declaration of Sentiments and Resolutions (1848)   A-21

From Frederick Douglass's "What, to the Slave, Is the Fourth of July?" Speech (1852)   A-24

The Gettysburg Address (1863)   A-27

Abraham Lincoln's Second Inaugural Address (1865)   A-28

The Populist Platform of 1892   A-29

Franklin D. Roosevelt's First Inaugural Address (1933)   A-32

From The Program for the March on Washington for Jobs and Freedom (1963)   A-35

Ronald Reagan's First Inaugural Address (1981)   A-36

Barack Obama's First Inaugural Address (2009)   A-39

TABLES AND FIGURES

Presidential Elections   A-42

Admission of States   A-50

Population of the United States   A-51

Historical Statistics of the United States:

Labor Force—Selected Characteristics Expressed as a Percentage of the Labor Force, 1800–2010   A-52

Immigration, by Origin   A-52

Unemployment Rate, 1890–2013   A-53

Union Membership as a Percentage of Nonagricultural Employment, 1880–2012   A-53

Voter Participation in Presidential Elections 1824–2012   A-53

Birthrate, 1820–2011   A-53

THE DECLARATION OF INDEPENDENCE (1776)

When in the course of human events, it becomes necessary for one people to dissolve the political bands which have connected them with another, and to assume among the Powers of the earth, the separate and equal station to which the Laws of Nature and of Nature's God entitle them, a decent respect to the opinions of mankind requires that they should declare the causes which impel them to the separation.

We hold these truths to be self-evident, that all men are created equal, that they are endowed by their Creator with certain unalienable rights, that among these are Life, Liberty, and the pursuit of Happiness. That to secure these rights, Governments are instituted among Men, deriving their just powers from the consent of the governed. That whenever any Form of Government becomes destructive of these ends, it is the Right of the People to alter or to abolish it, and to institute new Government, laying its foundation on such principles and organizing its powers in such form, as to them shall seem most likely to effect their Safety and Happiness. Prudence, indeed, will dictate that Governments long established should not be changed for light and transient causes; and accordingly all experience hath shown, that mankind are more disposed to suffer, while evils are sufferable, than to right themselves by abolishing the forms to which they are accustomed. But when a long train of abuses and usurpations, pursuing invariably the same Object evinces a design to reduce them under absolute Despotism, it is their right, it is their duty, to throw off such Government, and to provide new Guards for their future security.—Such has been the patient sufferance of these Colonies; and such is now the necessity which constrains them to alter their former Systems of Government. The history of the present King of Great Britain is a history of repeated injuries and usurpations, all having in direct object the establishment of an absolute Tyranny over these States. To prove this, let Facts be submitted to a candid world.

He has refused his Assent to Laws, the most wholesome and necessary for the public good.

He has forbidden his Governors to pass Laws of immediate and pressing importance, unless suspended in their operation till his Assent should be obtained; and when so suspended, he has utterly neglected to attend to them.

He has refused to pass other Laws for the accommodation of large districts of people, unless those people would relinquish the right of Representation in the Legislature, a right inestimable to them and formidable to tyrants only.

He has called together legislative bodies at places unusual, uncomfortable, and distant from the depository of their public Records, for the sole purpose of fatiguing them into compliance with his measures.

He has dissolved Representative Houses repeatedly, for opposing with manly firmness his invasions on the rights of the people.

He has refused for a long time, after such dissolutions, to cause others to be elected; whereby the Legislative powers, incapable of Annihilation, have returned to the People at large for their exercise; the State remaining in the mean time exposed to all dangers of invasion from without, and convulsions within.

He has endeavoured to prevent the population of these States; for that purpose obstructing the Laws of Naturalization of Foreigners; refusing to pass others to encourage their migrations hither, and raising the conditions of new Appropriations of Lands.

He has obstructed the Administration of Justice, by refusing his Assent to Laws for establishing Judiciary powers.

He has made Judges dependent on his Will alone, for the tenure of their offices, and the amount and payment of their salaries.

He has erected a multitude of New Offices, and sent hither swarms of Officers to harass our People, and eat out their substance.

He has kept among us, in times of peace, Standing Armies without the Consent of our legislatures.

He has affected to render the Military independent of and superior to the Civil Power.

He has combined with others to subject us to a jurisdiction foreign to our constitution, and unacknowledged by our laws; giving his Assent to their Acts of pretended Legislation:

For quartering large bodies of armed troops among us:

For protecting them, by a mock Trial, from Punishment for any Murders which they should commit on the Inhabitants of these States:

For cutting off our Trade with all parts of the world:

For imposing taxes on us without our Consent:

For depriving us of many cases, of the benefits of Trial by jury:

For transporting us beyond Seas to be tried for pretended offences:

For abolishing the free System of English Laws in a neighbouring Province, establishing therein an Arbitrary government, and enlarging its Boundaries so as to render it at once an example and fit instrument for introducing the same absolute rule into these Colonies:

For taking away our Charters, abolishing our most valuable Laws, and altering fundamentally the Forms of our Governments:

For suspending our own Legislatures, and declaring themselves invested with Power to legislate for us in all cases whatsoever.

He has abdicated Government here, by declaring us out of his Protection and waging War against us.

He has plundered our seas, ravaged our Coasts, burnt our towns, and destroyed the lives of our people.

He is at this time transporting large armies of foreign mercenaries to compleat the works of death, desolation, and tyranny, already begun with circumstances of Cruelty & perfidy scarcely paralleled in the most barbarous ages, and totally unworthy the Head of a civilized nation.

He has constrained our fellow Citizens taken Captive on the high Seas to bear Arms against their Country, to become the executioners of their friends and Brethren, or to fall themselves by their Hands.

He has excited domestic insurrections amongst us, and has endeavoured to bring on the inhabitants of our frontiers, the merciless Indian Savages, whose known rule of warfare, is an undistinguished destruction of all ages, sexes, and conditions.

In every stage of these Oppressions We have Petitioned for Redress in the most humble terms: Our repeated Petitions have been answered only by repeated injury. A Prince, whose character is thus marked by every act which may define a Tyrant, is unfit to be the ruler of a free people.

Nor have We been wanting in attention to our British brethren. We have warned them from time to time of attempts by their legislature to extend an unwarrantable jurisdiction over us. We have reminded them of the circumstances of our emigration and settlement here. We have appealed to their native justice and magnanimity, and we have conjured them by the ties of our common kindred to disavow these usurpations, which, would inevitably interrupt our connections and correspondence. They too must have been deaf to the voice of justice and of consanguinity. We must, therefore, acquiesce in the necessity, which denounces our Separation, and hold them, as we hold the rest of mankind, Enemies in War, in Peace Friends.

WE, THEREFORE, the Representatives of the UNITED STATES OF AMERICA, in General Congress, Assembled, appealing to the Supreme Judge of the world for the rectitude of our intentions, do, in the Name, and by Authority of the good People of these Colonies, solemnly publish and declare, That these United Colonies are, and of Right ought to be FREE AND INDEPENDENT STATES; that they are Absolved from all Allegiance to the British Crown, and that all political connection between them and the State of Great Britain, is and ought to be totally dissolved; and that as Free and Independent States, they have full Power to levy War, conclude Peace, contract Alliances, establish Commerce, and to do all other Acts and Things which Independent States may of right do. And for the support of this Declaration, with a firm reliance on the Protection of Divine Providence, we mutually pledge to each other our Lives, our Fortunes, and our sacred Honor.

The foregoing Declaration was, by order of Congress, engrossed, and signed by the following members:

John Hancock

NEW HAMPSHIRE
Josiah Bartlett
William Whipple
Matthew Thornton

MASSACHUSETTS BAY
Samuel Adams
John Adams
Robert Treat Paine
Elbridge Gerry

RHODE ISLAND
Stephen Hopkins
William Ellery

CONNECTICUT
Roger Sherman
Samuel Huntington
William Williams
Oliver Wolcott

NEW YORK
William Floyd
Philip Livingston
Francis Lewis
Lewis Morris

NEW JERSEY
Richard Stockton
John Witherspoon
Francis Hopkinson
John Hart
Abraham Clark

PENNSYLVANIA
Robert Morris
Benjamin Rush
Benjamin Franklin
John Morton
George Clymer
James Smith
George Taylor
James Wilson
George Ross

DELAWARE
Caesar Rodney
George Read
Thomas M'Kean

MARYLAND
Samuel Chase
William Paca
Thomas Stone
Charles Carroll, of Carrollton

VIRGINIA
George Wythe
Richard Henry Lee
Thomas Jefferson
Benjamin Harrison
Thomas Nelson, Jr.
Francis Lightfoot Lee
Carter Braxton

NORTH CAROLINA
William Hooper
Joseph Hewes
John Penn

SOUTH CAROLINA
Edward Rutledge
Thomas Heyward, Jr.
Thomas Lynch, Jr.
Arthur Middleton

GEORGIA
Button Gwinnett
Lyman Hall
George Walton

Resolved, That copies of the Declaration be sent to the several assemblies, conventions, and committees, or councils of safety, and to the several commanding officers of the continental troops; that it be proclaimed in each of the United States, at the head of the army.

THE CONSTITUTION OF THE UNITED STATES (1787)

We the People of the United States, in order to form a more perfect Union, establish Justice, insure domestic Tranquility, provide for the common defence, promote the general Welfare, and secure the Blessings of Liberty to ourselves and our Posterity, do ordain and establish this Constitution for the United States of America.

ARTICLE. I.

Section. 1. All legislative Powers herein granted shall be vested in a Congress of the United States, which shall consist of a Senate and House of Representatives.

Section. 2. The House of Representatives shall be composed of Members chosen every second Year by the People of the several States, and the Electors in each State shall have the Qualifications requisite for Electors of the most numerous Branch of the State Legislature.

No Person shall be a Representative who shall not have attained to the Age of twenty five Years, and been seven Years a Citizen of the United States, and who shall not, when elected, be an Inhabitant of that State in which he shall be chosen.

Representatives and direct Taxes shall be apportioned among the several States which may be included within this Union, according to their respective Numbers, which shall be determined by adding to the whole Number of free Persons, including those bound to Service for a Term of Years, and excluding Indians not taxed, three fifths of all other Persons. The actual Enumeration shall be made within three Years after the first Meeting of the Congress of the United States, and within every subsequent Term of ten Years, in such Manner as they shall by Law direct. The Number of Representatives shall not exceed one for every thirty Thousand, but each State shall have at Least one Representative; and until such enumeration shall be made, the State of New Hampshire shall be entitled to chuse three, Massachusetts eight, Rhode-Island and Providence Plantations one, Connecticut five, New York six, New Jersey four, Pennsylvania eight, Delaware one, Maryland six, Virginia ten, North Carolina five, South Carolina five, and Georgia three.

When vacancies happen in the Representation from any state, the Executive Authority thereof shall issue Writs of Election to fill such Vacancies.

The House of Representatives shall chuse their Speaker and other Officers; and shall have the sole Power of Impeachment.

Section. 3. The Senate of the United States shall be composed of two Senators from each State, chosen by the legislature thereof, for six Years; and each Senator shall have one Vote.

Immediately after they shall be assembled in Consequence of the first Election, they shall be divided as equally as may be into three Classes. The Seats of the Senators of the first Class shall be vacated at the Expiration of the second Year, of the second Class at the Expiration of the fourth Year, and of the third Class at the Expiration of the sixth Year, so that one third may be chosen every second Year; and if Vacancies happen by Resignation, or otherwise, during the Recess of the Legislature of any State, the Executive thereof may make temporary Appointments until the next Meeting of the Legislature, which shall then fill such Vacancies.

No Person shall be a Senator who shall not have attained to the Age of thirty Years, and been nine Years a Citizen of the United States, and who shall not, when elected, be an Inhabitant of that State for which he shall be chosen.

The Vice President of the United States shall be President of the Senate, but shall have no Vote, unless they be equally divided.

The Senate shall chuse their other Officers, and also a President pro tempore, in the Absence of the Vice President, or when he shall exercise the Office of President of the United States.

The Senate shall have the sole Power to try all Impeachments. When sitting for that Purpose, they shall be on Oath or Affirmation. When the President of the United States is tried, the Chief Justice shall preside: And no Person shall be convicted without the Concurrence of two thirds of the Members present.

Judgment in Cases of Impeachment shall not extend further than to removal from Office, and disqualification to hold and enjoy any Office of honor, Trust or Profit under the United States: but the Party convicted shall nevertheless be liable and subject to Indictment, Trial, Judgment and Punishment, according to Law.

Section. 4. The Times, Places and Manner of holding Elections for Senators and Representatives, shall be prescribed in each State by the Legislature thereof; but the Congress may at any time by Law make or alter such Regulations, except as to the Places of chusing Senators.

The Congress shall assemble at least once in every Year, and such Meeting shall be on the first Monday in December, unless they shall by Law appoint a different Day.

Section. 5. Each House shall be the Judge of the Elections, Returns and Qualifications of its own Members, and a Majority of each shall constitute a Quorum to do Business; but a smaller Number may adjourn from day to day, and may be authorized to compel the Attendance of absent Members, in such Manner, and under such Penalties as each House may provide.

Each House may determine the Rules of its Proceedings, punish its Members for disorderly Behaviour, and, with the Concurrence of two thirds, expel a Member.

Each House shall keep a Journal of its Proceedings, and from time to time publish the same, excepting such Parts as may in their Judgment require Secrecy; and the Yeas and Nays of the Members of either House on any question shall, at the Desire of one fifth of those Present, be entered on the Journal.

Neither House, during the Session of Congress, shall, without the Consent of the other, adjourn for more than three days, not to any other Place than that in which the two Houses shall be sitting.

Section. 6. The Senators and Representatives shall receive a Compensation for their Services, to be ascertained by Law, and paid out of the Treasury of the United States. They shall in all Cases, except Treason, Felony and Breach of the Peace, be privileged from Arrest during their Attendance at the Session of their respective Houses, and in going to and returning from the same; and for any Speech or Debate in either House, they shall not be questioned in any other Place.

No Senator or Representative shall, during the Time for which he was elected, be appointed to any civil Office under the Authority of the United States, which shall have been created, or the Emoluments whereof shall have been encreased during such time; and no Person holding any Office under the United States, shall be a Member of either House during his Continuance in Office.

Section. 7. All Bills for raising Revenue shall originate in the House of Representatives; but the Senate may propose or concur with Amendments as on other Bills.

Every Bill which shall have passed the House of Representatives and the Senate shall, before it become a Law, be presented to the President of the United States; If he approve he shall sign it, but if not he shall return it, with his Objections to that House in which it shall have originated, who shall enter the Objections at large on their Journal, and proceed to reconsider it. If after such Reconsideration two thirds of that House shall agree to pass the Bill, it shall be sent, together with the Objections, to the other House, by which it shall likewise be reconsidered, and if approved by two thirds of that House, it shall become a Law. But in all such Cases the Votes of both Houses shall be determined by Yeas and Nays, and the Names of the Persons voting for and against the Bill shall be entered on the Journal of each House respectively. If any Bill shall not be returned by the President within ten Days (Sundays excepted) after it shall have been presented to him, the Same shall be a Law, in like Manner as if he had signed it, unless the Congress by their Adjournment prevent its Return, in which Case it shall not be a Law.

Every Order, Resolution, or Vote to which the Concurrence of the Senate and House of Representatives may be necessary (except on a question of Adjournment) shall be presented to the President of the United States; and before the Same shall take Effect, shall be approved by him, or being disapproved by him, shall be repassed by two thirds of the Senate and House of Representatives, according to the Rules and Limitations prescribed in the Case of a Bill.

Section. 8. The Congress shall have Power To lay and collect Taxes, Duties, Imposts and Excises, to pay the Debts and provide for the common Defence and general Welfare of the United States; but all Duties, Imposts and Excises shall be uniform throughout the United States;

To borrow Money on the credit of the United States;

To regulate Commerce with foreign Nations, and among the several States, and with the Indian Tribes;

To establish an uniform Rule of Naturalization, and uniform Laws on the subject of Bankruptcies throughout the United States;

To coin Money, regulate the Value thereof, and of foreign Coin, and fix the Standard of Weights and Measures;

To provide for the Punishment of counterfeiting the Securities and current Coin of the United States;

To establish Post Offices and Post Roads;

To promote the Progress of Science and useful Arts, by securing for limited Times to Authors and Inventors the exclusive Right to their respective Writings and Discoveries;

To constitute Tribunals inferior to the supreme Court;

To define and punish Piracies and Felonies committed on the high Seas, and Offences against the Law of Nations;

To declare War, grant Letters of Marque and Reprisal, and make Rules concerning Captures on Land and Water;

To raise and support Armies, but no Appropriation of Money to that Use shall be for a longer Term than two Years;

To provide and maintain a Navy;

To make Rules for the Government and Regulation of the land and naval Forces;

To provide for calling forth the Militia to execute the Laws of the Union, suppress Insurrections and repel Invasions;

To provide for organizing, arming, and disciplining, the Militia, and for governing such Part of them as may be employed in the Service of the United States, reserving to the States respectively, the Appointment of the Officers, and the Authority of training the Militia according to the discipline prescribed by Congress;

To exercise exclusive Legislation in all Cases whatsoever, over such District (not exceeding ten Miles square) as may, by Cession of Particular States, and the Acceptance of Congress, become the Seat of the Government of the United States, and to exercise like Authority over all Places purchased by the Consent of the Legislature of the State in which the Same shall be, for the Erection of Forts, Magazines, Arsenals, dock-Yards, and other needful Buildings;—And

To make all Laws which shall be necessary and proper for carrying into Execution the foregoing Powers, and all other Powers vested by this Constitution in the Government of the United States, or in any Department or Officer thereof.

Section. 9. The Migration or Importation of such Persons as any of the States now existing shall think proper to admit, shall not be prohibited by the Congress prior to the Year one thousand eight hundred and eight, but a Tax or duty may be imposed on such Importation, not exceeding ten dollars for each Person.

The Privilege of the Writ of Habeas Corpus shall not be suspended, unless when in Cases of Rebellion or Invasion the public Safety may require it.

No Bill of Attainder or ex post facto Law shall be passed.

No Capitation, or other direct, Tax shall be laid, unless in Proportion to the Census or Enumeration herein before directed to be taken.

No Tax or Duty shall be laid on Articles exported from any State.

No Preference shall be given by any Regulation of Commerce or Revenue to the Ports of one State over those of another: nor shall Vessels bound to, or from, one State, be obliged to enter, clear, or pay Duties in another.

No Money shall be drawn from the Treasury, but in Consequence of Appropriations made by Law; and a regular Statement and Account of the Receipts and Expenditures of all public Money shall be published from time to time.

No Title of Nobility shall be granted by the United States: And no Person holding any Office of Profit or Trust under them, shall, without the Consent of the Congress, accept of any present, Emolument, Office, or Title, of any kind whatever, from any King, Prince, or foreign State.

Section. 10. No State shall enter into any Treaty, Alliance, or Confederation; grant Letters of Marque and Reprisal; coin Money; emit Bills of Credit; make any Thing but gold and silver Coin a Tender in Payment of Debts; pass any Bill of Attainder, ex post facto Law, or Law impairing the Obligation of Contracts, or grant any Title of Nobility.

No State shall, without the Consent of the Congress, lay any Imposts or Duties on Imports or Exports, except what may be absolutely necessary for executing its inspection Laws: and the net Produce of all Duties and Imposts, laid by any State on Imports or Exports, shall be for the Use of the Treasury of the United States; and all such Laws shall be subject to the Revision and Controul of the Congress.

No State shall, without the Consent of Congress, lay any Duty of Tonnage, keep Troops, or Ships of War in time of Peace, enter into any Agreement or Compact with another State, or with a foreign Power, or engage in War, unless actually invaded, or in such imminent Danger as will not admit of delay.

ARTICLE. II.

Section. 1. The executive Power shall be vested in a President of the United States of America. He shall hold his Office during the term of four Years, and, together with the Vice President, chosen for the same Term, be elected, as follows:

Each State shall appoint, in such Manner as the Legislature thereof may direct, a Number of Electors, equal to the whole Number of Senators and Representatives to which the State may be entitled in the Congress: but no Senator or Representative, or Person holding an Office of Trust or Profit under the United States, shall be appointed an Elector.

The Electors shall meet in their respective States, and vote by Ballot for two Persons, of whom one at least shall not be an Inhabitant of the same State with themselves. And they shall make a List of all the Persons voted for, and of the Number of Votes for each; which List they shall sign and certify, and transmit sealed to the Seat of the Government of the United States, directed to the President of the Senate. The President of the Senate shall, in the Presence of the Senate and House of Representatives, open all the Certificates, and the Votes shall then be counted. The Person having the greatest Number of Votes shall be the President, if such Number be a Majority of the whole Number of Electors appointed; and if there be more than one who have such Majority, and have an equal Number of Votes, then the House of Representatives shall immediately chuse by Ballot one of them for President; and if no Person have a Majority, then from the five highest on the List the said House shall in like Manner chuse the President. But in chusing the President, the Votes shall be taken by States, the Representation from each State having one Vote; A quorum for this Purpose shall consist of a Member or Members from two thirds of the States, and a Majority of all the States shall be necessary to a Choice. In every Case, after the Choice of the President, the Person having the greatest Number of Votes of the Electors shall be the Vice President. But if there should remain two or more who have equal Votes, the Senate shall chuse from them by Ballot the Vice President.

The Congress may determine the Time of chusing the Electors, and the Day on which they shall give their Votes; which Day shall be the same throughout the United States.

No Person except a natural born Citizen, or a Citizen of the United States, at the time of the Adoption of this Constitution, shall be eligible to the Office of President; neither shall any Person be eligible to that Office who shall not have attained to the Age of thirty five Years, and been fourteen Years a Resident within the United States.

In Case of the Removal of the President from Office, or of his Death, Resignation, or Inability to discharge the Powers and Duties of the said Office, the Same shall devolve on the Vice President, and the Congress may by Law provide for the Case of Removal, Death, Resignation or Inability, both of the President and Vice President, declaring what Officer shall then act as President, and such Officer shall act accordingly, until the Disability be removed, or a President shall be elected.

The President shall, at stated Times, receive for his Services, a Compensation, which shall neither be encreased or diminished during the Period for which he shall have been elected, and he shall not receive within that Period any other Emolument from the United States, or any of them.

Before he enters on the Execution of his Office, he shall take the following Oath or Affirmation:—"I do solemnly swear (or affirm) that I will faithfully execute the Office of President of the United States, and will to the best of my Ability, preserve, protect and defend the Constitution of the United States."

Section. 2. The President shall be Commander in Chief of the Army and Navy of the United States, and of the Militia of the several States, when called into the actual Service of the United States; he may require the Opinion, in writing, of the principal Officer in each of the executive Departments, upon any Subject relating to the Duties of their respective Offices, and he shall have Power to grant Reprieves and Pardons for Offences against the United States, except in Cases of Impeachment.

He shall have Power, by and with the Advice and Consent of the Senate, to make Treaties, provided two thirds of the Senators present concur; and he shall nominate, and by and with the Advice and Consent of the Senate, shall appoint Ambassadors, other public Ministers and Consuls, Judges of the supreme Court, and all other Officers of the United States, whose Appointments are not herein otherwise provided for, and which shall be established by Law: but the Congress may by Law vest the Appointment of such inferior Officers, as they think proper, in the President alone, in the Courts of Law, or in the Heads of Departments.

The President shall have Power to fill up all Vacancies that may happen during the Recess of the Senate, by granting Commissions which shall expire at the End of their next Session.

Section. 3. He shall from time to time give to the Congress Information of the State of the Union, and recommend to their Consideration such Measures as he shall judge necessary and expedient; he may, on extraordinary Occasions, convene both Houses, or either of them, and in Case of Disagreement between them, with Respect to the Time of Adjournment, he may adjourn them to such Time as he shall think proper; he shall receive Ambassadors and other public Ministers; he shall take Care that the Laws be faithfully executed, and shall Commission all the Officers of the United States.

Section. 4. The President, Vice President and all civil Officers of the United States, shall be removed from Office on Impeachment for, and Conviction of, Treason, Bribery, or other high Crimes and Misdemeanors.

ARTICLE. III.

Section. 1. The judicial Power of the United States, shall be vested in one supreme Court, and in such inferior Courts as the Congress may from time to time ordain and establish. The Judges, both of the supreme and inferior Courts, shall hold their Offices during good Behavior, and shall, at stated Times, receive for their Services, a Compensation, which shall not be diminished during their Continuance in Office.

Section. 2. The judicial Power shall extend to all Cases, in Law and Equity, arising under this Constitution, the Laws of the United States, and Treaties made, or which shall be made, under their Authority;—to all Cases affecting Ambassadors, other public Ministers and Consuls;—to all Cases of admiralty and maritime Jurisdiction;—the Controversies to which the United States shall be a Party;—to Controversies between two or more States;—between a State and Citizens of another State;—between Citizens of different States;—between Citizens of the same State claiming Lands under Grants of different States, and between a State, or the Citizens thereof, and foreign States, Citizens or Subjects.

In all cases affecting Ambassadors, other public Ministers and Consuls, and those in which a State shall be Party, the supreme Court shall have original Jurisdiction. In all the other Cases before mentioned, the supreme Court shall have appellate Jurisdiction, both as to Law and Fact, with such Exceptions, and under such Regulations as the Congress shall make.

The Trial of all Crimes, except in Cases of Impeachment, shall be by Jury; and such Trial shall be held in the State where the said Crimes shall have been committed; but when not committed within any State, the Trial shall be at such Place or Places as the Congress may by Law have directed.

Section. 3. Treason against the United States, shall consist only in levying War against them, or in adhering to their Enemies, giving them Aid and Comfort. No Person shall be convicted of Treason unless on the Testimony of two Witnesses to the same overt Act, or on Confession in open Court.

The Congress shall have Power to declare the Punishment of Treason, but no Attainder of Treason shall work Corruption of Blood, or Forfeiture except during the Life of the Person attainted.

ARTICLE. IV.

Section. 1. Full Faith and Credit shall be given in each State to the public Acts, Records, and judicial Proceedings of every other State. And the Congress may by general Laws prescribe the Manner in which such Acts, Records and Proceedings shall be proved, and the Effect thereof.

Section. 2. The Citizens of each State shall be entitled to all Privileges and Immunities of Citizens in the several States.

A Person charged in any State with Treason, Felony, or other Crime, who shall flee from Justice, and be found in another State, shall on Demand of the executive Authority of the State from which he fled, be delivered up, to be removed to the State having Jurisdiction of the Crime.

No Person held to Service or Labour in one State, under the Laws thereof, escaping into another, shall, in Consequence of any Law or Regulation therein, be discharged from such Service or Labour, but shall be delivered up on Claim of the Party to whom such Service or Labour may be due.

Section. 3. New States may be admitted by the Congress into this Union; but no new State shall be formed or erected within the Jurisdiction of any other State; nor any State be formed by the Junction of two or more States, or Parts of States, without the consent of the Legislatures of the States concerned as well as of the Congress.

The Congress shall have Power to dispose of and make all needful Rules and Regulations respecting the Territory or other Property belonging to the United States; and nothing in this Constitution shall be so construed as to Prejudice any Claims of the United States, or of any particular States.

Section. 4. The United States shall guarantee to every State in this Union a Republican Form of Government, and shall protect each of them against Invasion; and on Application of the Legislature, or of the Executive (when the Legislature cannot be convened) against domestic Violence.

ARTICLE. V.

The Congress, whenever two thirds of both Houses shall deem it necessary, shall propose Amendments to this Constitution, or, on the Application of the Legislatures of two thirds of the several States, shall call a Convention for proposing Amendments, which, in either Case, shall be valid to all Intents and Purposes, as Part of this Constitution, when ratified by the Legislatures of three fourths of the several States, or by Conventions in three fourths thereof, as the one or the other Mode of Ratification may be proposed by the Congress; Provided that no Amendment which may be made prior to the Year One thousand eight hundred and eight shall in any Manner affect the first and fourth Clauses in the Ninth Section of the first Article; and that no State, without its Consent, shall be deprived of its equal Suffrage in the Senate.

ARTICLE. VI.

All Debts contracted and Engagements entered into, before the Adoption of this Constitution, shall be as valid against the United States under this Constitution, as under the Confederation.

This Constitution, and the Laws of the United States which shall be made in Pursuance thereof; and all Treaties made, or which shall be made, under the Authority of the United States, shall be the supreme Law of the Land; and the Judges in every State shall be bound thereby, any Thing in the Constitution or Laws of any State to the Contrary notwithstanding.

The Senators and Representatives before mentioned, and the Members of the several State Legislatures, and all executive and judicial Officers, both of the United States and of the several States, shall be bound by Oath or Affirmation, to support this Constitution; but no religious Test shall ever be required as a Qualification to any Office or public Trust under the United States.

ARTICLE. VII.

The Ratification of the Conventions of nine States, shall be sufficient for the Establishment of this Constitution between the States so ratifying the Same.

Done in Convention by the Unanimous Consent of the States present the Seventeenth Day of September in the Year of our Lord one thousand seven hundred and Eighty seven and of the Independence of the United States of America the Twelfth. In witness thereof We have hereunto subscribed our Names,

G⁰. WASHINGTON—Presdᵗ.
and deputy from Virginia

NEW HAMPSHIRE
John Langdon
Nicholas Gilman

MASSACHUSETTS
Nathaniel Gorham
Rufus King

CONNECTICUT
Wᵐ Samˡ Johnson
Roger Sherman

NEW YORK
Alexander Hamilton

NEW JERSEY
Wil: Livingston
David A. Brearley
Wᵐ Paterson
Jona: Dayton

PENNSYLVANIA
B Franklin
Thomas Mifflin
Robᵗ Morris
Geo. Clymer
Thoˢ FitzSimons
Jared Ingersoll
James Wilson
Gouv Morris

DELAWARE
Geo: Read
Gunning Bedford jun
John Dickinson
Richard Bassett
Jaco: Broom

MARYLAND
James McHenry
Dan of Sᵗ Thoˢ Jenifer
Danˡ Carroll

VIRGINIA
John Blair—
James Madison Jr.

NORTH CAROLINA
Wᵐ Blount
Richᵈ Dobbs Spaight
Hu Williamson

SOUTH CAROLINA
J. Rutledge
Charles Cotesworth
  Pinckney
Charles Pinckney
Pierce Butler

GEORGIA
William Few
Abr Baldwin

AMENDMENTS TO THE CONSTITUTION

Articles in addition to, and Amendment of the Constitution of the United States of America, proposed by Congress, and ratified by the Legislatures of the several States, pursuant to the fifth Article of the original Constitution.

AMENDMENT I.*

Congress shall make no law respecting an establishment of religion, or prohibiting the free exercise thereof; or abridging the freedom of speech, or of the press; or the right of the people peaceably to assemble, and to petition the Government for a redress of grievances.

AMENDMENT II.

A well regulated Militia, being necessary to the security of a free State, the right of the people to keep and bear Arms, shall not be infringed.

AMENDMENT III.

No Soldier shall, in time of peace be quartered in any house, without the consent of the Owner, nor in time of war, but in a manner to be prescribed by law.

AMENDMENT IV.

The right of the people to be secure in their persons, houses, papers, and effects, against unreasonable searches and seizures, shall not be violated, and no Warrants shall issue, but upon probable cause, supported by Oath or affirmation, and particularly describing the place to be searched, and the persons or things to be seized.

AMENDMENT V.

No person shall be held to answer for a capital, or otherwise infamous crime, unless on a presentment or indictment of a Grand Jury, except in cases arising in the land or naval forces, or in the Militia, when in actual service in time of War or public danger; nor shall any person be subject for the same offence to be twice put in jeopardy of life or limb; nor shall be compelled in any criminal case to be a witness against himself, nor be deprived of life, liberty, or property, without due process of law; nor shall private property be taken for public use, without just compensation.

*The first ten Amendments (the Bill of Rights) were ratified in 1791.

AMENDMENT VI.

In all criminal prosecutions, the accused shall enjoy the right to a speedy and public trial, by an impartial jury of the State and district wherein the crime shall have been committed, which district shall have been previously ascertained by law, and to be informed of the nature and cause of the accusation; to be confronted with the witnesses against him; to have compulsory process for obtaining witnesses in his favor, and to have the Assistance of Counsel for his defence.

AMENDMENT VII.

In Suits at common law, where the value in controversy shall exceed twenty dollars, the right of trial by jury shall be preserved, and no fact tried by a jury, shall be otherwise re-examined in any Court of the United States, than according to the rules of the common law.

AMENDMENT VIII.

Excessive bail shall not be required, nor excessive fines imposed, nor cruel and unusual punishments inflicted.

AMENDMENT IX.

The enumeration in the Constitution, of certain rights, shall not be construed to deny or disparage others retained by the people.

AMENDMENT X.

The powers not delegated to the United States by the Constitution, nor prohibited by it to the States, are reserved to the States respectively, or to the people.

AMENDMENT XI.

The Judicial power of the United States shall not be construed to extend to any suit in law or equity, commenced or prosecuted against one of the United States by Citizens of another State, or by Citizens or Subjects of any Foreign State. [January 8, 1798]

AMENDMENT XII.

The Electors shall meet in their respective states, and vote by ballot for President and Vice-President, one of whom, at least, shall not be an inhabitant of the same state with themselves; they shall name in their ballots the person voted for as President, and in distinct ballots the person voted for as Vice-President, and they shall make distinct lists of all persons voted for as President, and of all persons voted for as Vice President, and of the number of votes for each, which lists they shall sign and certify, and transmit sealed to the seat of the government of the United States, directed to the President of the Senate;—The President of the Senate shall, in the presence of the Senate and House of Representatives, open all the certificates and the votes shall then be counted;—The person having the greatest number of votes for President, shall be the President, if such number be a majority of the whole number of Electors appointed; and if no person have such majority, then from the persons having the highest numbers not exceeding three on the list of those voted for as President, the House of Representatives shall choose immediately, by ballot, the President. But in choosing the President, the votes shall be taken by states, the representation from each state having one vote; a quorum for this purpose shall consist of a member or members from two-thirds of the states, and a majority of all the states shall be necessary to a choice. And if the House of Representatives shall not choose a President whenever the right of choice shall devolve upon them, before the fourth day of March next following, then the Vice-President shall act as President, as in the case of the death or other constitutional disability of the President.— The person having the greatest number of votes as Vice-President, shall be the Vice-President, if such number be a majority of the whole number of Electors appointed, and if no person have a majority, then from the two highest numbers on the list, the Senate shall choose the Vice-President; a quorum for the purpose shall consist of two-thirds of the whole number of Senators, and a majority of the whole number shall be necessary to a choice. But no person constitutionally ineligible to the office of President shall be eligible to that of Vice-President of the United States. [September 25, 1804]

AMENDMENT XIII.

Section 1. Neither slavery nor involuntary servitude, except as a punishment for crime whereof the party shall have been duly convicted, shall exist within the United States, or any place subject to their jurisdiction.

Section 2. Congress shall have power to enforce this article by appropriate legislation. [December 18, 1865]

AMENDMENT XIV.

Section 1. All persons born or naturalized in the United States, and subject to the jurisdiction thereof, are citizens of the United States and of the State wherein they reside. No State shall make or enforce any law which shall abridge the privileges or immunities of citizens of the United States; nor shall any State deprive any person of life, liberty, or property, without due process of law; nor deny to any person within its jurisdiction the equal protection of the laws.

Section 2. Representatives shall be apportioned among the several States according to their respective numbers, counting the whole number of persons in each State, excluding Indians not taxed. But when the right to vote at any election for the choice of electors for President and Vice President of the United States, Representatives in Congress, the Executive and Judicial officers of a State, or the members of the Legislature thereof, is denied to any of the male inhabitants of such State, being twenty-one years of age, and citizens of the United States, or in any way abridged, except for participation in rebellion, or other crime, the basis of representation therein shall be reduced in the proportion which the number of such male citizens shall bear to the whole number of male citizens twenty-one years of age in such State.

Section 3. No person shall be a Senator or Representative in Congress, or elector of President and Vice President, or hold any office, civil or military, under the United States, or under any State, who, having previously taken an oath, as a member of Congress, or as an officer of the United States, or as a member of any State legislature, or as an executive or judicial officer of any State, to support the Constitution of the United States, shall have engaged in insurrection or rebellion against the same, or given aid or comfort to the enemies thereof. But Congress may by a vote of two-thirds of each House, remove such disability.

Section 4. The validity of the public debt of the United States, authorized by law, including debts incurred for payment of pensions and bounties for services in suppressing insurrection or rebellion, shall not be questioned. But neither the United States nor any State shall assume or pay any debt or obligation incurred in aid of insurrection or rebellion against the United States, or any claim for the loss or emancipation of any slave; but all such debts, obligations and claims shall be held illegal and void.

Section 5. The Congress shall have power to enforce, by appropriate legislation, the provisions of this article. [July 28, 1868]

AMENDMENT XV.

Section 1. The right of citizens of the United States to vote shall not be denied or abridged by the United States or by any State on account of race, color, or previous condition of servitude—

Section 2. The Congress shall have power to enforce this article by appropriate legislation. [March 30, 1870]

AMENDMENT XVI.

The Congress shall have power to lay and collect taxes on incomes, from whatever source derived, without apportionment among the several States, and without regard to any census or enumeration. [February 25, 1913]

AMENDMENT XVII.

The Senate of the United States shall be composed of two senators from each State, elected by the people thereof, for six years; and each Senator shall have one vote. The electors in each State shall have the qualifications requisite for electors of the most numerous branch of the State legislatures.

When vacancies happen in the representation of any State in the Senate, the executive authority of such State shall issue writs of election to fill such vacancies: *Provided,* That the legislature of any State may empower the executive thereof to make temporary appointments until the people fill the vacancies by election as the legislature may direct.

This amendment shall not be so construed as to affect the election or term of any senator chosen before it becomes valid as part of the Constitution. [May 31, 1913]

AMENDMENT XVIII.

After one year from the ratification of this article, the manufacture, sale, or transportation of intoxicating liquors within, the importation thereof into, or the exportation thereof from the United States and all territory subject to the jurisdiction thereof for beverage purposes is hereby prohibited.

The Congress and the several States shall have concurrent power to enforce this article by appropriate legislation.

This article shall be inoperative unless it shall have been ratified as an amendment to the Constitution by the legislatures of the several States, as provided in the Constitution, within seven years from the date of the submission thereof to the States by Congress. [January 29, 1919]

AMENDMENT XIX.

The right of citizens of the United States to vote shall not be denied or abridged by the United States or by any State on account of sex.

The Congress shall have power by appropriate legislation to enforce the provisions of this article. [August 26, 1920]

AMENDMENT XX.

Section 1. The terms of the President and Vice-President shall end at noon on the twentieth day of January, and the terms of Senators and Representatives at noon on the third day of January, of the years in which such terms would have ended if this article had not been ratified; and the terms of their successors shall then begin.

Section 2. The Congress shall assemble at least once in every year, and such meeting shall begin at noon on the third day of January, unless they shall by law appoint a different day.

Section 3. If, at the time fixed for the beginning of the term of the President, the President-elect shall have died, the Vice-President-elect shall become President. If a President shall not have been chosen before the time fixed for the beginning of his term, or if the President-elect shall have failed to qualify, then the Vice-President-elect shall act as President until a President shall have qualified; and the Congress may by law provide for the case wherein neither a President-elect nor a Vice-President-elect shall have qualified, declaring who shall then act as President, or the manner in which one who is to act shall be selected, and such person shall act accordingly until a President or Vice-President shall have qualified.

Section 4. The Congress may by law provide for the case of the death of any of the persons from whom the House of Representatives may choose a President whenever the right of choice shall have devolved upon them, and for the case of the death of any of the persons from whom the Senate may choose a Vice-President whenever the right of choice shall have devolved upon them.

Section 5. Sections 1 and 2 shall take effect on the 15th day of October following the ratification of this article.

Section 6. This article shall be inoperative unless it shall have been ratified as an amendment to the Constitution by the legislatures of three-fourths of the several States within seven years from the date of its submission. [February 6, 1933]

AMENDMENT XXI.

Section 1. The eighteenth article of amendment to the Constitution of the United States is hereby repealed.

Section 2. The transportation or importation into any State, Territory or possession of the United States for delivery or use therein of intoxicating liquors, in violation of the laws thereof, is hereby prohibited.

Section 3. This article shall be inoperative unless it shall have been ratified as an amendment to the Constitution by convention in the several States, as provided in the Constitution, within seven years from the date of the submission thereof to the States by the Congress. [December 5, 1933]

AMENDMENT XXII.

Section 1. No person shall be elected to the office of the President more than twice, and no person who has held the office of President, or acted as President, for more than two years of a term to which some other person was elected President shall be elected to the office of the President more than once. But this Article shall not apply to any person holding the office of President when this Article was proposed by the Congress, and shall not prevent any person who may be holding the office of President, or acting as President, during the term within which this Article becomes operative from holding the office of President or acting as President during the remainder of such term.

Section 2. This article shall be inoperative unless it shall have been ratified as an amendment to the Constitution by the legislatures of three-fourths of the several States within seven years from the date of its submission to the States by the Congress. [February 27, 1951]

AMENDMENT XXIII.

Section 1. The District constituting the seat of government of the United States shall appoint in such manner as the Congress may direct:

A number of electors of President and Vice-President equal to the whole number of Senators and Representatives in Congress to which the District would be entitled if it were a State, but in no event more than the least populous State; they shall be in addition to those appointed by the States, but they shall be considered, for the purposes of the election of President and Vice-President, to be electors appointed by a State; and they shall meet in the District and perform such duties as provided by the twelfth article of amendment.

Section 2. The Congress shall have the power to enforce this article by appropriate legislation. [March 29, 1961]

AMENDMENT XXIV.

Section 1. The right of citizens of the United States to vote in any primary or other election for President or Vice President, for electors for President or Vice President, or for Senator or Representative in Congress, shall not be denied or abridged by the United States or any State by reason of failure to pay any poll tax or other tax.

Section 2. The Congress shall have power to enforce this article by appropriate legislation. [January 23, 1964]

AMENDMENT XXV.

Section 1. In case of the removal of the President from office or of his death or resignation, the Vice President shall become President.

Section 2. Whenever there is a vacancy in the office of Vice President, the President shall nominate a Vice President who shall take office upon confirmation by a majority vote of both Houses of Congress.

Section 3. Whenever the President transmits to the President pro tempore of the Senate and the Speaker of the House of Representatives his written declaration that he is unable to discharge the powers and duties of his office, and until he transmits to them a written declaration to the contrary, such powers and duties shall be discharged by the Vice President as Acting President.

Section 4. Whenever the Vice President and a majority of either the principal officers of the executive departments or of such other body as Congress may by law provide, transmit to the President pro tempore of the Senate and the Speaker of the House of Representatives their written declaration that the President is unable to discharge the powers and duties of his office, the Vice President shall immediately assume the powers and duties of the office as Acting President.

Thereafter, when the President transmits to the President pro tempore of the Senate and the Speaker of the House of Representatives his written declaration that no inability exists, he shall resume the powers and duties of his office unless the Vice President and a majority of either the principal officers of the executive departments or of such other body as Congress may by law provide, transmit within four days to the President pro tempore of the Senate and the Speaker of the House of Representatives their written declaration that the President is unable to discharge the powers and duties of his office. Thereupon Congress shall decide the issue, assembling within forty-eight hours for that purpose if not in session. If the Congress, within twenty-one days after receipt of the latter written declaration, or, if Congress is not in session, within twenty-one days after Congress is required to assemble, determines by two-thirds vote of both Houses that the President is unable to discharge the powers and duties of his office, the Vice-President shall continue to discharge the same as Acting President; otherwise, the President shall resume the powers and duties of his office. [February 10, 1967]

AMENDMENT XXVI.

Section 1. The right of citizens of the United States, who are eighteen years of age or older, to vote shall not be denied or abridged by the United States or by any State on account of age.

Section 2. The Congress shall have power to enforce this article by appropriate legislation. [June 30, 1971]

AMENDMENT XXVII.

No law, varying the compensation for the services of the Senators and Representatives shall take effect, until an election of Representatives shall have intervened. [May 8, 1992]

FROM GEORGE WASHINGTON'S FAREWELL ADDRESS (1796)

Friends and Citizens:

The period for a new election of a citizen to administer the executive government of the United States being not far distant, and the time actually arrived when your thoughts must be employed in designating the person who is to be clothed with that important trust, it appears to me proper, especially as it may conduce to a more distinct expression of the public voice, that I should now apprise you of the resolution I have formed, to decline being considered among the number of those out of whom a choice is to be made.

★ ★ ★

In looking forward to the moment which is intended to terminate the career of my public life, my feelings do not permit me to suspend the deep acknowledgment of that debt of gratitude which I owe to my beloved country for the many honors it has conferred upon me; still more for the steadfast confidence with which it has supported me; and for the opportunities I have thence enjoyed of manifesting my inviolable attachment, by services faithful and persevering, though in usefulness unequal to my zeal. If benefits have resulted to our country from these services, let it always be remembered to your praise, and as an instructive example in our annals, that under circumstances in which the passions, agitated in every direction, were liable to mislead, amidst appearances sometimes dubious, vicissitudes of fortune often discouraging, in situations in which not unfrequently want of success has countenanced the spirit of criticism, the constancy of your support was the essential prop of the efforts, and a guarantee of the plans by which they were effected. Profoundly penetrated with this idea, I shall carry it with me to my grave, as a strong incitement to unceasing vows that heaven may continue to you the choicest tokens of its beneficence; that your union and brotherly affection may be perpetual; that the free Constitution, which is the work of your hands, may be sacredly maintained; that its administration in every department may be stamped with wisdom and virtue; that, in fine, the happiness of the people of these States, under the auspices of liberty, may be made complete by so careful a preservation and so prudent a use of this blessing as will acquire to them the glory of recommending it to the applause, the affection, and adoption of every nation which is yet a stranger to it.

Here, perhaps, I ought to stop. But a solicitude for your welfare, which cannot end but with my life, and the apprehension of danger, natural to that solicitude, urge me, on an occasion like the present, to offer to your solemn contemplation, and to recommend to your frequent review, some sentiments which are the result of much reflection, of no inconsiderable observation, and which appear to me all-important to the permanency of your felicity as a people. These will be offered to you with the more freedom, as you can only see in them the disinterested warnings of a parting friend, who can possibly have no personal motive to bias his counsel. Nor can I forget, as an encouragement to it, your indulgent reception of my sentiments on a former and not dissimilar occasion.

Interwoven as is the love of liberty with every ligament of your hearts, no recommendation of mine is necessary to fortify or confirm the attachment.

The unity of government which constitutes you one people is also now dear to you. It is justly so, for it is a main pillar in the edifice of your real independence, the support of your tranquility at home, your peace abroad; of your safety; of your prosperity; of that very liberty which you so highly prize. But as it is easy to foresee that, from different causes and from different quarters, much pains will be taken, many artifices employed to weaken in your minds the conviction of this truth; as this is the point in your political fortress against which the batteries of internal and external enemies will be most constantly and actively (though often covertly and insidiously) directed, it is of infinite moment that you should properly estimate the immense value of your national union to your collective and individual happiness; that you should cherish a cordial, habitual, and immovable attachment to it; accustoming yourselves to think and speak of it as of the palladium of your political safety and prosperity; watching for its preservation with jealous anxiety; discountenancing whatever may suggest even a suspicion that it can in any event be abandoned; and indignantly frowning upon the first dawning of every attempt to alienate any portion of our country from the rest, or to enfeeble the sacred ties which now link together the various parts.

For this you have every inducement of sympathy and interest. Citizens, by birth or choice, of a common country, that country has a right to concentrate your affections. The name of American, which belongs to you in your national capacity, must always exalt the just pride of patriotism more than any appellation derived from local discriminations. With slight shades of difference, you have the same religion, manners, habits, and political principles. You have in a common cause fought and triumphed together; the independence and liberty you possess are the work of joint counsels, and joint efforts of common dangers, sufferings, and successes.

But these considerations, however powerfully they address themselves to your sensibility, are greatly outweighed by those which apply more immediately to your interest. Here every portion of our country finds the most commanding motives for carefully guarding and preserving the union of the whole.

The North, in an unrestrained intercourse with the South, protected by the equal laws of a common government, finds in the productions of the latter great additional resources of maritime and commercial enterprise and precious materials of manufacturing industry. The South, in the same intercourse, benefiting by the agency of the North, sees its agriculture grow and its commerce expand. Turning partly into its own channels the seamen of the North, it finds its particular navigation invigorated; and, while it contributes, in different ways, to nourish and increase the general mass of the national navigation, it looks forward to the protection of a maritime strength, to which itself is unequally adapted. The East, in a like intercourse with the West, already finds, and in the progressive improvement of interior communications by land and water, will more and more find a valuable vent for the commodities which it brings from abroad, or manufactures at home. The West derives from the East supplies requisite to its growth and comfort, and, what is perhaps of still greater consequence, it must of necessity owe the secure enjoyment of indispensable outlets for its own productions to the weight, influence, and the future maritime strength of the Atlantic side of the Union, directed by an indissoluble community of interest as one nation. Any other tenure by which the West can hold this essential advantage, whether derived from its own separate strength, or from an apostate and unnatural connection with any foreign power, must be intrinsically precarious.

While, then, every part of our country thus feels an immediate and particular interest in union, all the parts combined cannot fail to find in the united mass of means and efforts greater strength, greater resource, proportionably greater security from external danger, a less frequent interruption of their peace by foreign nations; and, what is of inestimable value, they must derive from union an exemption from those broils and wars between themselves, which so frequently afflict neighboring countries not tied together by the same governments, which their own rival ships alone would be sufficient to produce, but which opposite foreign alliances, attachments, and intrigues would stimulate and embitter. Hence, likewise, they will avoid the necessity of those overgrown military establishments which, under any form of government, are inauspicious to liberty, and which are to be regarded as particularly hostile to republican liberty. In this sense it is that your union ought to be considered as a main prop of your liberty, and that the love of the one ought to endear to you the preservation of the other.

These considerations speak a persuasive language to every reflecting and virtuous mind, and exhibit the continuance of the Union as a primary object of patriotic desire. Is there a doubt whether a common government can embrace so large a sphere? Let experience solve it. To listen to mere speculation in such a case were criminal. We are authorized to hope that a proper organization of the whole with the auxiliary agency of governments for the respective subdivisions, will afford a happy issue to the experiment. It is well worth a fair and full experiment. With such powerful and obvious motives to union, affecting all parts of our country, while experience shall not have demonstrated its impracticability, there will always be reason to distrust the patriotism of those who in any quarter may endeavor to weaken its bands.

★ ★ ★

To the efficacy and permanency of your Union, a government for the whole is indispensable. No alliance, however strict, between the parts can be an adequate substitute; they must inevitably experience the infractions and interruptions which all alliances in all times have experienced. Sensible of this momentous truth, you have improved upon your first essay, by the adoption of a constitution of government better calculated than your former for an intimate union, and for the efficacious management of your common concerns. This government, the offspring of our own choice, uninfluenced and unawed, adopted upon full investigation and mature deliberation, completely free in its principles, in the distribution of its powers, uniting security with energy, and containing within itself a provision for its own amendment, has a just claim to your confidence and your support. Respect for its authority, compliance with its laws, acquiescence in its measures, are duties enjoined by the fundamental maxims of true liberty. The basis of our political systems is the right of the people to make and to alter their constitutions of government. But the Constitution which at any time exists, till changed by an explicit and authentic act of the whole people, is sacredly obligatory upon all. The very idea of the power and the right of the people to establish government presupposes the duty of every individual to obey the established government.

★ ★ ★

I have already intimated to you the danger of parties in the State, with particular reference to the founding of them on geographical discriminations. Let me now take a more comprehensive view, and warn you in the most solemn manner against the baneful effects of the spirit of party generally.

This spirit, unfortunately, is inseparable from our nature, having its root in the strongest passions of the human mind. It exists under different shapes in all governments, more or less stifled, controlled, or repressed; but, in those of the popular form, it is seen in its greatest rankness, and is truly their worst enemy.

The alternate domination of one faction over another, sharpened by the spirit of revenge, natural to party dissension, which in different ages and countries has perpetrated the most horrid enormities, is itself a frightful despotism. But this leads at length to a more formal and permanent despotism. The disorders and miseries which result gradually incline the minds of men to seek security and repose in the absolute power of an individual; and sooner or later the chief of some prevailing faction, more able or more fortunate than his competitors, turns this disposition to the purposes of his own elevation, on the ruins of public liberty.

Without looking forward to an extremity of this kind (which nevertheless ought not to be entirely out of sight), the common and continual mischiefs of the spirit of party are sufficient to make it the interest and duty of a wise people to discourage and restrain it.

It serves always to distract the public councils and enfeeble the public administration. It agitates the community with ill-founded jealousies and false alarms, kindles the animosity of one part against another, foments occasionally riot and insurrection. It opens the door to foreign influence and corruption, which finds a facilitated access to the government itself through the channels of party passions. Thus the policy and the will of one country are subjected to the policy and will of another.

There is an opinion that parties in free countries are useful checks upon the administration of the government and serve to keep alive the spirit of liberty. This within certain limits is probably true; and in governments of a monarchical cast, patriotism may look with indulgence, if not with favor, upon the spirit of party. But in those of the popular character, in governments purely elective, it is a spirit not to be encouraged. From their natural tendency, it is certain there will always be enough of that spirit for every salutary purpose. And there being constant danger of excess, the effort ought to be by force of public opinion, to mitigate and assuage it. A fire not to be quenched, it demands a uniform vigilance to prevent its bursting into a flame, lest, instead of warming, it should consume.

It is important, likewise, that the habits of thinking in a free country should inspire caution in those entrusted with its administration, to confine themselves within their respective constitutional spheres, avoiding in the exercise of the powers of one department to encroach upon another. The spirit of encroachment tends to consolidate the powers of all the departments in one, and thus to create, whatever the form of government, a real despotism. A just estimate of that love of power, and proneness to abuse it, which predominates in the human heart, is sufficient to satisfy us of the truth of this position. The necessity of reciprocal checks in the exercise of political power, by dividing and distributing it into different depositaries, and constituting each the guardian of the public weal against invasions by the others, has been evinced by experiments ancient and modern; some of them in our country and under our own eyes. To preserve them must be as necessary as to institute them. If, in the opinion of the people, the distribution or modification of the constitutional powers be in any particular wrong, let it be corrected by an amendment in the way which the Constitution designates. But let there be no change by usurpation; for though this, in one instance, may be the instrument of good, it is the customary weapon by which free governments are destroyed. The precedent must always greatly overbalance in permanent evil any partial or transient benefit, which the use can at any time yield.

★ ★ ★

Observe good faith and justice towards all nations; cultivate peace and harmony with all. Religion and morality enjoin this conduct; and can it be, that good policy does not equally enjoin it? It will be worthy of a free, enlightened, and at no distant period, a great nation, to give to mankind the magnanimous and too novel example of a people always guided by an exalted justice and benevolence. Who can doubt that, in the course of time and things, the fruits of such a plan would richly repay any temporary advantages which might be lost by a steady adherence to it? Can it be that Providence has not connected the permanent felicity of a nation with its virtue? The experiment, at least, is recommended by every sentiment which ennobles human nature. Alas! is it rendered impossible by its vices?

In the execution of such a plan, nothing is more essential than that permanent, inveterate antipathies against particular nations, and passionate attachments for others, should be excluded; and that, in place of them, just and amicable feelings towards all should be cultivated. The nation which indulges towards another a habitual hatred or a habitual fondness is in some degree a slave. It is a slave to its animosity or to its affection, either of which is sufficient to lead it astray from its duty and its interest. Antipathy in one nation against another disposes each more readily to offer insult and injury, to lay hold of slight causes of umbrage, and to be haughty and intractable, when accidental or trifling occasions of dispute occur. Hence, frequent collisions, obstinate, envenomed, and bloody contests. The nation, prompted by ill-will and resentment, sometimes impels to war the government, contrary to the best calculations of policy. The government sometimes participates in the national propensity, and adopts through passion what reason would reject; at other times it makes the animosity of the nation subservient to projects of hostility instigated by pride, ambition, and other sinister and pernicious motives. The peace often, sometimes perhaps the liberty, of nations, has been the victim.

★ ★ ★

The great rule of conduct for us in regard to foreign nations is in extending our commercial relations, to have with them as little political connection as possible. So far as we have already formed engagements, let them be fulfilled with perfect good faith. Here let us stop. Europe has a set of primary interests which to us have none; or a very remote relation. Hence she must be engaged in frequent controversies, the causes of which are essentially foreign to our concerns. Hence, therefore, it must be unwise in us to implicate ourselves by artificial ties in the ordinary vicissitudes of her politics, or the ordinary combinations and collisions of her friendships or enmities.

Our detached and distant situation invites and enables us to pursue a different course. If we remain one people under an efficient government, the period is not far off when we may defy material injury from external annoyance; when we may take such an attitude as will cause the neutrality we may at any time resolve upon to be scrupulously respected; when belligerent nations, under the impossibility of making acquisitions upon us, will not lightly hazard the giving us provocation; when we may choose peace or war, as our interest, guided by justice, shall counsel.

Why forego the advantages of so peculiar a situation? Why quit our own to stand upon foreign ground? Why, by interweaving our destiny with that of any part of Europe, entangle our peace and prosperity in the toils of European ambition, rivalship, interest, humor or caprice?

It is our true policy to steer clear of permanent alliances with any portion of the foreign world; so far, I mean, as we are now at liberty to do it; for let me not be understood as capable of patronizing infidelity to existing engagements. I hold the maxim no less applicable to public than to private affairs, that honesty is always the best policy. I repeat it, therefore, let those engagements be observed in their genuine sense. But, in my opinion, it is unnecessary and would be unwise to extend them.

Taking care always to keep ourselves by suitable establishments on a respectable defensive posture, we may safely trust to temporary alliances for extraordinary emergencies.

Harmony, liberal intercourse with all nations, are recommended by policy, humanity, and interest. But even our commercial policy should hold an equal and impartial hand; neither seeking nor granting exclusive favors or preferences; consulting the natural course of things; diffusing and diversifying by gentle means the streams of commerce, but forcing nothing; establishing (with powers so disposed, in order to give trade a stable course, to define the rights of our merchants, and to enable the government to support them) conventional rules of intercourse, the best that present circumstances and mutual opinion will permit, but temporary, and liable to be from time to time abandoned or varied, as experience and circumstances shall dictate; constantly keeping in view that it is folly in one nation to look for disinterested favors from another; that it must pay with a portion of its independence for whatever it may accept under that character; that, by such acceptance, it may place itself in the condition of having given equivalents for nominal favors, and yet of being reproached with ingratitude for not giving more.

★ ★ ★

Relying on its kindness in this as in other things, and actuated by that fervent love towards it, which is so natural to a man who views in it the native soil of himself and his progenitors for several generations, I anticipate with pleasing expectation that retreat in which I promise myself to realize, without alloy, the sweet enjoyment of partaking, in the midst of my fellow-citizens, the benign influence of good laws under a free government, the ever-favorite object of my heart, and the happy reward, as I trust, of our mutual cares, labors, and dangers.

Geo. Washington

THE SENECA FALLS DECLARATION OF SENTIMENTS AND RESOLUTIONS (1848)

1. DECLARATION OF SENTIMENTS

When, in the course of human events, it becomes necessary for one portion of the family of man to assume among the people of the earth a position different from that which they have hitherto occupied, but one to which the laws of nature and of nature's God entitle them, a decent respect to the opinions of mankind requires that they should declare the causes that impel them to such a course.

We hold these truths to be self-evident: that all men and women are created equal; that they are endowed by their Creator with certain inalienable rights; that among these are life, liberty, and the pursuit of happiness; that to secure these rights governments are instituted, deriving their just powers from the consent of the governed. Whenever any form of government becomes destructive of these ends, it is the right of those who suffer from it to refuse allegiance to it, and to insist upon the institution of a new government, laying its foundation on such principles, and organizing its powers in such form, as to them shall seem most likely to effect their safety and happiness. Prudence, indeed, will dictate that governments long established should not be changed for light and transient causes; and accordingly all experience hath shown that mankind are more disposed to suffer, while evils are sufferable, than to right themselves by abolishing the forms to which they are accustomed. But when a long train of abuses and usurpations, pursuing invariably the same object, evinces a design to reduce them under absolute despotism, it is their duty to throw off such government, and to provide new guards for their future security. Such has been the patient sufferance of the women under this government, and such is now the necessity which constrains them to demand the equal station to which they are entitled. The history of mankind is a history of repeated injuries and usurpations on the part of man toward woman, having in direct object the establishment of an absolute tyranny over her. To prove this, let facts be submitted to a candid world.

He has never permitted her to exercise her inalienable right to the elective franchise.

He has compelled her to submit to laws, in the formation of which she had no voice.

He has withheld from her rights which are given to the most ignorant and degraded men—both natives and foreigners.

Having deprived her of this first right of a citizen, the elective franchise, thereby leaving her without representation in the halls of legislation, he has oppressed her on all sides.

He has made her, if married, in the eye of the law, civilly dead. He has taken from her all right in property, even to the wages she earns.

He has made her, morally, an irresponsible being, as she can commit many crimes with impunity, provided they be done in the presence of her husband.

In the covenant of marriage, she is compelled to promise obedience to her husband, he becoming, to all intents and purposes, her master—the law giving him power to deprive her of her liberty, and to administer chastisement.

He has so framed the laws of divorce, as to what shall be the proper causes, and in case of separation, to whom the guardianship of the children shall be given, as to be wholly regardless of the happiness of women—the law, in all cases, going upon a false supposition of the supremacy of man, and giving all power into his hands.

After depriving her of all rights as a married woman, if single, and the owner of property, he has taxed her to support a government which recognizes her only when her property can be made profitable to it.

He has monopolized nearly all the profitable employments, and from those she is permitted to follow, she receives but a scanty remuneration. He closes against her all the avenues to wealth and distinction which he considers most honorable to himself. As a teacher of theology, medicine, or law, she is not known.

He has denied her the facilities for obtaining a thorough education, all colleges being closed against her.

He allows her in Church, as well as State, but a subordinate position, claiming Apostolic authority for her exclusion from the ministry, and, with some exceptions, from any public participation in the affairs of the Church.

He has created a false public sentiment by giving to the world a different code of morals for men and women, by which moral delinquencies which exclude women from society, are not only tolerated, but deemed of little account in man.

He has usurped the prerogative of Jehovah himself, claiming it as his right to assign for her a sphere of action, when that belongs to her conscience and to her God.

He has endeavored, in every way that he could, to destroy her confidence in her own powers, to lessen her self-respect and to make her willing to lead a dependent and abject life.

Now, in view of this entire disfranchisement of one-half the people of this country, their social and religious degradation—in view of the unjust laws above mentioned, and because women do feel themselves aggrieved, oppressed, and fraudulently deprived of their most sacred rights, we insist that they have immediate admission to all the rights and privileges which belong to them as citizens of the United States.

In entering upon the great work before us, we anticipate no small amount of misconception, misrepresentation, and ridicule; but we shall use every instrumentality within our power to effect our object. We shall employ agents, circulate tracts, petition the State and National legislatures, and endeavor to enlist the pulpit and the press in our behalf. We hope this Convention will be followed by a series of Conventions embracing every part of the country.

2. RESOLUTIONS

WHEREAS, The great precept of nature is conceded to be, that "man shall pursue his own true and substantial happiness." Blackstone in his Commentaries remarks, that this law of Nature being coeval with mankind, and dictated by God himself, is of course superior in obligation to any other. It is binding over all the globe, in all countries and at all times; no human laws are of any validity if contrary to this, and such of them as are valid, derive all their force, and all their validity, and all their authority, mediately and immediately, from this original; therefore,

Resolved, That such laws as conflict, in any way, with the true and substantial happiness of woman, are contrary to the great precept of nature and of no validity, for this is "superior in obligation to any other."

Resolved, That all laws which prevent woman from occupying such a station in society as her conscience shall dictate, or which place her in a position inferior to that of man, are contrary to the great precept of nature, and therefore of no force or authority.

Resolved, That woman is man's equal—was intended to be so by the Creator, and the highest good of the race demands that she should be recognized as such.

Resolved, That the women of this country ought to be enlightened in regard to the laws under which they live, that they may no longer publish their degradation by declaring themselves satisfied with their present position, nor their ignorance, by asserting that they have all the rights they want.

Resolved, That inasmuch as man, while claiming for himself intellectual superiority, does accord to woman moral superiority, it is pre-eminently his duty to encourage her to speak and teach, as she has an opportunity, in all religious assemblies.

Resolved, That the same amount of virtue, delicacy, and refinement of behavior that is required of woman in the social state, should also be required of man, and the same transgressions should be visited with equal severity on both man and woman.

Resolved, That the objection of indelicacy and impropriety, which is so often brought against woman when she addresses a public audience, comes with a very ill-grace from those who encourage, by their attendance, her appearance on the stage, in the concert. Or in feats of the circus.

Resolved, That woman has too long rested satisfied in the circumscribed limits which corrupt customs and a perverted application of the Scriptures have marked out for her, and that it is time she should move in the enlarged sphere which her great Creator has assigned her.

Resolved, That it is the duty of the women of this country to secure to themselves their sacred right to the elective franchise.

Resolved, That the equality of human rights results necessarily from the fact of the identity of the race in capabilities and responsibilities.

Resolved, therefore, That, being invested by the Creator with the same capabilities, and the same consciousness of responsibility for their exercise, it is demonstrably the right and duty of woman, equally with man, to promote every righteous cause by every righteous means; and especially in regard to the great subjects of morals and religion, it is self-evidently her right to participate with her brother in teaching them, both in private and in public, by writing and by speaking, by any instrumentalities proper to be used, and in any assemblies proper to be held; and this being a self-evident truth growing out of the divinely implanted principles of human nature, any custom or authority adverse to it, whether modern or wearing the hoary sanction of antiquity, is to be regarded as a self-evident falsehood, and at war with mankind.

Resolved, That the speedy success of our cause depends upon the zealous and untiring efforts of both men and women, for the overthrow of the monopoly of the pulpit, and for the securing to women an equal participation with men in the various trades, professions, and commerce.

FROM FREDERICK DOUGLASS'S "WHAT, TO THE SLAVE, IS THE FOURTH OF JULY?" SPEECH (1852)

★ ★ ★

This, for the purpose of this celebration, is the Fourth of July. It is the birthday of your National Independence, and of your political freedom. This, to you, is what the Passover was to the emancipated people of God. It carries your minds back to the day, and to the act of your great deliverance; and to the signs and to the wonders associated with that act and that day. This celebration also marks the beginning of another year of your national life; and reminds you that the Republic of America is now seventy-six years old. I am glad, fellow citizens, that your nation is so young. Seventy-six years, though a good old age for a man, is but a mere speck in the life of a nation. Three score years and ten is the allotted time for individual men; but nations number their years by thousands. According to this fact, you are, even now, only in the beginning of your national career, still lingering in the period of childhood. I repeat, I am glad this is so. There is hope in the thought, and hope is much needed, under the dark clouds which lower above the horizon. The eye of the reformer is met with angry flashes, portending disastrous times; but his heart may well beat lighter at the thought that America is young, and that she is still in the impressible stage of her existence. May he not hope that high lessons of wisdom, of justice and of truth, will yet give direction to her destiny? Were the nation older, the patriot's heart might be sadder and the reformer's brow heavier. Its future might be shrouded in gloom and the hope of its prophets go out in sorrow. There is consolation in the thought that America is young. Great streams are not easily turned from channels worn deep in the course of ages. They may sometimes rise in quiet and stately majesty, and inundate the land, refreshing and fertilizing the earth with their mysterious properties. They may also rise in wrath and fury, and bear away on their angry waves the accumulated wealth of years of toil and hardship. They, however, gradually flow back to the same old channel and flow on as serenely as ever. But, while the river may not be turned aside, it may dry up and leave nothing behind but the withered branch and the unsightly rock, to howl in the abyss-sweeping wind, the sad tale of departed glory. As with rivers, so with nations.

Fellow citizens, I shall not presume to dwell at length on the associations that cluster about this day. The simple story of it is, that seventy-six years ago the people of this country were British subjects. The style and title of your "sovereign people" (in which you now glory) was not then born. You were under the British Crown. Your fathers esteemed the En glish government as the home government, and England as the fatherland. This home government, you know, although a considerable distance from your home, did, in the exercise of its parental prerogatives, impose upon its colonial children such restraints, burdens and limitations as, in its mature judgment, it deemed wise, right and proper.

★ ★ ★

Feeling themselves harshly and unjustly treated by the home government, your fathers, like men of honesty and men of spirit, earnestly sought redress. They petitioned and remonstrated, they did so in a decorous, respectful and loyal manner. Their conduct was wholly unexceptionable. This, however, did not answer the purpose. They saw themselves treated with sovereign indifference, coldness and scorn. Yet they persevered. They were not the men to look back.

★ ★ ★

Citizens, your fathers . . . succeeded; and today you reap the fruits of their success. The freedom gained is yours; and you, therefore, may properly celebrate this anniversary. The Fourth of July is the first great fact in your nation's history—the very ringbolt in the chain of your yet undeveloped destiny.

Pride and patriotism, not less than gratitude, prompt you to celebrate and to hold it in perpetual remembrance. I have said that the Declaration of Independence is the ringbolt to the chain of your nation's destiny; so, indeed, I regard it. The principles contained in that instrument are saving principles. Stand by those principles, be true to them on all occasions, in all places, against all foes, and at whatever cost.

★ ★ ★

[The fathers of this republic] were peace men, but they preferred revolution to peaceful submission to bondage. They were quiet men; but they did not shrink from agitating against oppression. They showed forbearance, but that they knew its limits. They believed in order, but not in the order of tyranny. With them, nothing was "settled" that was not right. With them, justice, liberty and humanity were "final," not slavery and oppression. You may well cherish the memory of such men. They were great in their day and generation. Their solid manhood stands out the more as we contrast it with these degenerate times.

* * *

Fellow citizens, pardon me, allow me to ask, why am I called upon to speak here today? What have I, or those I represent, to do with your national independence? Are the great principles of political freedom and of natural justice, embodied in that Declaration of Independence, extended to us? and am I, therefore, called upon to bring our humble offering to the national altar and to confess the benefits and express devout gratitude for the blessings resulting from your independence to us?

* * *

But such is not the state of the case. I say it with a sad sense of the disparity between us. I am not included within the pale of this glorious anniversary! Your high independence only reveals the immeasurable distance between us. The blessings in which you, this day, rejoice, are not enjoyed in common. The rich inheritance of justice, liberty, prosperity and independence, bequeathed by your fathers, is shared by you, not by me. The sunlight that brought light and healing to you, has brought stripes and death to me. This Fourth of July is *yours*, not *mine*. *You* may rejoice, *I* must mourn.

* * *

Fellow citizens, above your national, tumultuous joy I hear the mournful wail of millions! whose chains, heavy and grievous yesterday, are today rendered more intolerable by the jubilee shouts that reach them. If I do forget, if I do not faithfully remember those bleeding children of sorrow this day, "may my right hand forget her cunning, and may my tongue cleave to the roof of my mouth!" To forget them, to pass lightly over their wrongs and to chime in with the popular theme would be treason most scandalous and shocking and would make me a reproach before God and the world. My subject, then, fellow citizens, is American slavery. I shall see this day and its popular characteristics from the slave's point of view. Standing there identified with the American bondman, making his wrongs mine, I do not hesitate to declare, with all my soul, that the character and conduct of this nation never looked blacker to me than on this Fourth of July. Whether we turn to the declarations of the past or to the professions of the present, the conduct of the nation seems equally hideous and revolting. America is false to the past, false to the present, and solemnly binds herself to be false to the future.

* * *

For the present, it is enough to affirm the equal manhood of the Negro race. It is not astonishing that, while we are plowing, planting and reaping, using all kinds of mechanical tools, erecting houses, constructing bridges, building ships, working in metals of brass, iron, copper, silver and gold; that, while we are reading, writing and ciphering, acting as clerks, merchants and secretaries, having among us lawyers, doctors, ministers, poets, authors, editors, orators and teachers; that, while we are engaged in all manner of enterprises common to other men, digging gold in California, capturing the whale in the Pacific, feeding sheep and cattle on the hillside, living, moving, acting, thinking, planning, living in families as husbands, wives and children, and, above all, confessing and worshiping the Christian's God and looking hopefully for life and immortality beyond the grave, we are called upon to prove that we are men!

Would you have me argue that man is entitled to liberty? that he is the rightful owner of his own body? You have already declared it. Must I argue the wrongfulness of slavery? Is that a question for republicans? Is it to be settled by the rules of logic and argumentation, as a matter beset with great difficulty, involving a doubtful application of the principle of justice, hard to be understood? How should I look today, in the presence of Americans, dividing and subdividing a discourse, to show that men have a natural right to freedom, speaking of it relatively and positively, negatively and affirmatively? To do so would be to make myself ridiculous and to offer an insult to your understanding. There is not a man beneath the canopy of heaven that does not know that slavery is wrong *for him*.

* * *

What, to the American slave, is your Fourth of July? I answer: a day that reveals to him, more than all other days in the year, the gross injustice and cruelty to which he is the constant victim. To him, your celebration is a sham; your boasted liberty an unholy license; your national greatness swelling vanity; your sounds of rejoicing are empty and heartless; your denunciation of tyrants brass-fronted impudence; your shouts of liberty and equality hollow mockery; your prayers and hymns, your sermons and thanksgivings, with all your religious parade and solemnity, are to Him mere bombast, fraud, deception, impiety and hypocrisy—a thin veil to cover up crimes which would disgrace a nation of savages. There is not a nation on the earth guilty of practices more shocking and bloody than are the people of the United States at this very hour.

Go where you may, search where you will, roam through all the monarchies and despotisms of the Old World, travel through South America, search out every abuse, and when you have found the last, lay your facts by the side of the everyday practices of this nation, and you will say with me, that, for revolting barbarity and shameless hypocrisy, America reigns without a rival.

★ ★ ★

Americans! your republican politics, not less than your republican religion, are flagrantly inconsistent. You boast of your love of liberty, your superior civilization and your pure Christianity, while the whole political power of the nation (as embodied in the two great political parties) is solemnly pledged to support and perpetuate the enslavement of three millions of your countrymen. You hurl your anathemas at the crowned-headed tyrants of Russia and Austria and pride yourselves on your democratic institutions, while you yourselves consent to be the mere *tools* and *bodyguards* of the tyrants of Virginia and Carolina. You invite to your shores fugitives of oppression from abroad, honor them with banquets, greet them with ovations, cheer them, toast them, salute them, protect them, and pour out your money to them like water; but the fugitives from your own land you advertise, hunt, arrest, shoot and kill. You glory in your refinement and your universal education; yet you maintain a system as barbarous and dreadful as ever stained the character of a nation—a system begun in avarice, supported in pride, and perpetuated in cruelty. You shed tears over fallen Hungary, and make the sad story of her wrongs the theme of your poets, statesmen and orators, till your gallant sons are ready to fly to arms to vindicate her cause against the oppressor;* but, in regard to the ten thousand wrongs of the American slave, you would enforce the strictest silence and would hail him as an enemy of the nation who dares to make those wrongs the subject of public discourse! You are all on fire at the mention of liberty for France or for Ireland, but are as cold as an iceberg at the thought of liberty for the enslaved of America. You discourse eloquently on the dignity of labor; yet, you sustain a system which, in its very essence, casts a stigma upon labor. You can bare your bosom to the storm of British artillery to throw off a three-penny tax on tea, and yet wring the last hard-earned farthing from the grasp of the black laborers of your country. You profess to believe "that of one blood God made all nations of men to dwell on the face of all the earth"† and hath commanded all men, everywhere, to love one another; yet you notoriously hate (and glory in your hatred) all men whose skins are not colored like your own. You declare before the world, and are understood by the world to declare, that you *"hold these truths to be self-evident, that all men are created equal; and are endowed by their Creator with certain unalienable rights; and that among these are, life, liberty and the pursuit of happiness"*; and yet, you hold securely, in a bondage which, according to your own Thomas Jefferson, *"is worse than ages of that which your fathers rose in rebellion to oppose," a seventh part* of the inhabitants of your country.

Fellow citizens, I will not enlarge further on your national inconsistencies. The existence of slavery in this country brands your republicanism as a sham, your humanity as a base pretense, and your Christianity as a lie. It destroys your moral power abroad; it corrupts your politicians at home. It saps the foundation of religion; it makes your name a hissing and a byword to a mocking earth. It is the antagonistic force in your government, the only thing that seriously disturbs and endangers your union. It fetters your progress; it is the enemy of improvement; the deadly foe of education; it fosters pride; it breeds insolence; it promotes vice; it shelters crime; it is a curse to the earth that supports it; and yet you cling to it as if it were the sheet anchor of all your hopes.

★ ★ ★

Allow me to say, in conclusion, notwithstanding the dark picture I have this day presented, of the state of the nation, I do not despair of this country. There are forces in operation which must inevitably work the downfall of slavery.

★ ★ ★

---

*The fledgling Hungarian republic was invaded by Austria and Russia in 1849.
†Acts 17:26.

THE GETTYSBURG ADDRESS (1863)

Four score and seven years ago our fathers brought forth on this continent, a new nation, conceived in Liberty, and dedicated to the proposition that all men are created equal.

Now we are engaged in a great civil war, testing whether that nation, or any nation so conceived and so dedicated, can long endure. We are met on a great battle field of that war. We have come to dedicate a portion of that field, as a final resting place for those who here gave their lives that that nation might live. It is altogether fitting and proper that we should do this.

But, in a larger sense, we can not dedicate—we can not consecrate—we can not hallow—this ground. The brave men, living and dead, who struggled here, have consecrated it, far above our poor power to add or detract. The world will little note, nor long remember what we say here, but it can never forget what they did here. It is for us the living, rather, to be dedicated here to the unfinished work which they who fought here have thus far so nobly advanced. It is rather for us to be here dedicated to the great task remaining before us—that from these honored dead we take increased devotion to that cause for which they gave the last full measure of devotion—that we here highly resolve that these dead shall not have died in vain—that this nation, under God, shall have a new birth of freedom—and that government of the people, by the people, for the people, shall not perish from the earth.

Abraham Lincoln
November 19, 1863

ABRAHAM LINCOLN'S SECOND INAUGURAL ADDRESS (1865)

Fellow Countrymen:

At this second appearing to take the oath of the presidential office, there is less occasion for an extended address than there was at the first. Then a statement, somewhat in detail, of a course to be pursued, seemed fitting and proper. Now, at the expiration of four years, during which public declarations have been constantly called forth on every point and phase of the great contest which still absorbs the attention, and engrosses the energies of the nation, little that is new could be presented. The progress of our arms, upon which all else chiefly depends, is as well known to the public as to myself; and it is, I trust, reasonably satisfactory and encouraging to all. With high hope for the future, no prediction in regard to it is ventured.

On the occasion corresponding to this four years ago, all thoughts were anxiously directed to an impending civil war. All dreaded it—all sought to avert it. While the inaugural address was being delivered from this place, devoted altogether to *saving* the Union without war, insurgent agents were in the city seeking to *destroy* it without war—seeking to dissolve the Union, and divide effects, by negotiation. Both parties deprecated war; but one of them would *make* war rather than let the nation survive; and the other would *accept* war rather than let it perish. And the war came.

One eighth of the whole population were colored slaves, not distributed generally over the Union, but localized in the southern part of it. These slaves constituted a peculiar and powerful interest. All knew that this interest was, somehow, the cause of the war. To strengthen, perpetuate, and extend this interest was the object for which the insurgents would rend the Union, even by war; while the government claimed no right to do more than to restrict the territorial enlargement of it. Neither party expected for the war, the magnitude, or the duration, which it has already attained. Neither anticipated that the *cause* of the conflict might cease with, or even before, the conflict itself should cease. Each looked for an easier triumph, and a result less fundamental and astounding. Both read the same Bible, and pray to the same God; and each invokes His aid against the other. It may seem strange that any men should dare to ask a just God's assistance in wringing their bread from the sweat of other men's faces; but let us judge not that we be not judged. The prayers of both could not be answered; that of neither has been answered fully. The Almighty has His own purposes. "Woe unto the world because of offences! for it must needs be that offences come; but woe to that man by whom the offence cometh." If we shall suppose that American slavery is one of those offences which, in the providence of God, must needs come, but which, having continued through His appointed time, He now wills to remove, and that He gives to both North and South, this terrible war, as the woe due to those by whom the offence came, shall we discern therein any departure from those divine attributes which the believers in a living God always ascribe to Him? Fondly do we hope, fervently do we pray—that this mighty scourge of war may speedily pass away. Yet, if God wills that it continue until all the wealth piled by the bondsman's two hundred and fifty years of unrequited toil shall be sunk, and until every drop of blood drawn with the lash shall be paid by another drawn with the sword, as was said three thousand years ago, so still it must be said "the judgments of the Lord are true and righteous altogether."

With malice toward none; with charity for all; with firmness in the right as God gives us to see the right, let us strive on to finish the work we are in; to bind up the nation's wounds; to care for him who shall have borne the battle and for his widow and his orphan, to do all which may achieve and cherish a just and a lasting peace, among ourselves and with all nations.

THE POPULIST PLATFORM OF 1892

Assembled upon the 116th anniversary of the Declaration of Independence, the People's Party of America, in their first national convention, invoking upon their action the blessing of Almighty God, puts forth in the name and on behalf of the people of this country, the following preamble and declaration of principles:

PREAMBLE

The conditions which surround us best justify our co-operation; we meet in the midst of a nation brought to the verge of moral, political, and material ruin. Corruption dominates the ballot-box, the Legislatures, the Congress, and touches even the ermine of the bench. The people are demoralized; most of the States have been compelled to isolate the voters at the polling places to prevent universal intimidation and bribery. The newspapers are largely subsidized or muzzled, public opinion silenced, business prostrated, homes covered with mortgages, labor impoverished, and the land concentrating in the hands of the capitalists. The urban workmen are denied the right to organize for self-protection, imported pauperized labor beats down their wages, a hireling standing army, unrecognized by our laws, is established to shoot them down, and they are rapidly degenerating into European conditions. The fruits of the toil of millions are boldly stolen to build up the fortunes for a few, unprecedented in the history of mankind; and the possessors of these, in turn, despise the Republic and endanger liberty. From the same prolific womb of governmental injustice we breed the two great classes—tramps and millionaires.

The national power to create money is appropriated to enrich bondholders; a vast public debt, payable in legal tender currency, has been funded into gold-bearing bonds, thereby adding millions to the burdens of the people. Silver, which has been accepted as coin since the dawn of history, has been demonetized to add to the purchasing power of gold by decreasing the value of all forms of property as well as human labor, and the supply of currency is purposely abridged to fatten usurers, bankrupt enterprise, and enslave industry. A vast conspiracy against mankind has been organized on two continents, and it is rapidly taking possession of the world. If not met and overthrown at once it forebodes terrible social convulsions, the destruction of civilization, or the establishment of an absolute despotism.

We have witnessed for more than a quarter of a century the struggles of the two great political parties for power and plunder, while grievous wrongs have been inflicted upon the suffering people. We charge that the controlling influences dominating both these parties have permitted the existing dreadful conditions to develop without serious effort to prevent or restrain them. Neither do they now promise us any substantial reform. They have agreed together to ignore in the coming campaign every issue but one. They propose to drown the outcries of a plundered people with the uproar of a sham battle over the tariff, so that capitalists, corporations, national banks, rings, trusts, watered stock, the demonetization of silver, and the oppressions of the usurers may all be lost sight of. They propose to sacrifice our homes, lives, and children on the altar of mammon; to destroy the multitude in order to secure corruption funds from the millionaires.

Assembled on the anniversary of the birthday of the nation, and filled with the spirit of the grand general and chief who established our independence, we seek to restore the government of the Republic to the hands of "the plain people," with which class it originated. We assert our purpose to be identical with the purposes of the National Constitution, "to form a more perfect union and establish justice, insure domestic tranquility, provide for the common defense, promote the general welfare, and secure the blessings of liberty for ourselves and our posterity." We declare that this Republic can only endure as a free government while built upon the love of the whole people for each other and for the nation; that it cannot be pinned together by bayonets; that the civil war is over, and that every passion and resentment which grew out of it must die with it; and that we must be in fact, as we are in name, one united brotherhood of free men.

Our country finds itself confronted by conditions for which there is no precedent in the history of the world; our annual agricultural productions amount to billions of dollars in value, which must, within a few weeks or months, be exchanged for billions of dollars of commodities consumed in their production; the existing currency supply is wholly inadequate to make this exchange; the results are falling prices, the formation of combines and rings, the impoverishment of the producing class. We pledge ourselves, if given power, we will labor to correct these evils by wise and reasonable legislation, in accordance with the terms of our platform. We believe that the power of government—in other words, of the people—should be expanded (as in the case of the postal service) as rapidly and as far as the good sense of an intelligent people and the teaching of experience shall justify, to the end that oppression, injustice, and poverty shall eventually cease in the land.

While our sympathies as a party of reform are naturally upon the side of every proposition which will tend to make men intelligent, virtuous, and temperate, we nevertheless regard these questions—important as they are—as secondary to the great issues now pressing for solution, and upon which not only our individual prosperity but the very existence of free institutions depend; and we ask all men to first help us to determine whether we are to have a republic to administer before we differ as to the conditions upon which it is to be administered, believing that the forces of reform this day organized will never cease to move forward until every wrong is remedied, and equal rights and equal privileges securely established for all the men and women of this country.

PLATFORM

We declare, therefore—

First.—That the union of the labor forces of the United States this day consummated shall be permanent and perpetual; may its spirit enter into all hearts for the salvation of the Republic and the uplifting of mankind!

Second.—Wealth belongs to him who creates it, and every dollar taken from industry without an equivalent is rob-bery. "If any will not work, neither shall he eat." The interests of rural and civic labor are the same; their enemies are identical.

Third.—We believe that the time has come when the railroad corporations will either own the people or the people must own the railroads; and, should the government enter upon the work of owning and managing all railroads, we should favor an amendment to the Constitution by which all persons engaged in the government service shall be placed under a civil-service regulation of the most rigid character, so as to prevent the increase of the power of the national administration by the use of such additional government employees.

FINANCE.—We demand a national currency, safe, sound, and flexible, issued by the general government only, a full legal tender for all debts, public and private, and that without the use of banking corporations, a just, equitable, and efficient means of distribution direct to the people, at a tax not to exceed two per cent per annum, to be provided as set forth in the sub-treasury plan of the Farmers' Alliance, or a better system; also by payments in discharge of its obligations for public improvements.

1. We demand free and unlimited coinage of silver and gold at the present legal ratio of 16 to 1.

2. We demand that the amount of circulating medium be speedily increased to not less than $50 per capita.

3. We demand a graduated income tax.

4. We believe that the money of the country should be kept as much as possible in the hands of the people, and hence we demand that all State and national revenues shall be limited to the necessary expenses of the government, economically and honestly administered.

5. We demand that postal savings banks be established by the government for the safe deposit of the earnings of the people and to facilitate exchange.

TRANSPORTATION.—Transportation being a means of exchange and a public necessity, the government should own and operate the railroads in the interest of the people. The telegraph and telephone, like the post-office system, being a necessity for the transmission of news, should be owned and operated by the government in the interest of the people.

LAND.—The land, including all the natural sources of wealth, is the heritage of the people, and should not be monopolized for speculative purposes, and alien ownership of land should be prohibited. All land now held by railroads and other corporations in excess of their actual needs, and all lands now owned by aliens should be reclaimed by the government and held for actual settlers only.

EXPRESSION OF SENTIMENTS

Your committee on Platform and Resolutions beg leave unanimously to report the following:

Whereas, Other questions have been presented for our consideration, we hereby submit the following, not as a part of the Platform of the People's Party, but as resolutions expressive of the sentiment of this Convention:

1. *Resolved*, That we demand a free ballot and a fair count in all elections, and pledge ourselves to secure it to every legal voter without federal intervention, through the adoption by the States of the unperverted Australian or secret ballot system.

2. *Resolved*, That the revenue derived from a graduated income tax should be applied to the reduction of the burden of taxation now levied upon the domestic industries of this country.

3. *Resolved*, That we pledge our support to fair and liberal pensions to ex-Union soldiers and sailors.

4. *Resolved*, That we condemn the fallacy of protecting American labor under the present system, which opens our ports to the pauper and criminal classes of the world, and crowds out our wage-earners; and we denounce the present ineffective laws against contract labor, and demand the further restriction of undesirable emigration.

5. *Resolved*, that we cordially sympathize with the efforts of organized workingmen to shorten the hours of labor, and demand a rigid enforcement of the existing eight-hour law on Government work, and ask that a penalty clause be added to the said law.

6. *Resolved*, That we regard the maintenance of a large standing army of mercenaries, known as the Pinkerton system, as a menace to our liberties, and we demand its abolition; and we condemn the recent invasion of the Territory of Wyoming by the hired assassins of plutocracy, assisted by federal officers.

7. *Resolved*, That we commend to the favorable consideration of the people and the reform press the legislative system known as the initiative and referendum.

8. *Resolved*, That we favor a constitutional provision limiting the office of President and Vice-President to one term, and providing for the election of Senators of the United States by a direct vote of the people.

9. *Resolved*, That we oppose any subsidy or national aid to any private corporation for any purpose.

10. *Resolved*, That this convention sympathizes with the Knights of Labor and their righteous contest with the tyrannical combine of clothing manufacturers of Rochester, and declare it to be the duty of all who hate tyranny and oppression to refuse to purchase the goods made by the said manufacturers, or to patronize any merchants who sell such goods.

FRANKLIN D. ROOSEVELT'S FIRST INAUGURAL ADDRESS (1933)

I am certain that my fellow Americans expect that on my induction into the Presidency I will address them with a candor and a decision which the present situation of our Nation impels. This is preeminently the time to speak the truth, the whole truth, frankly and boldly. Nor need we shrink from honestly facing conditions in our country today. This great Nation will endure as it has endured, will revive and will prosper. So, first of all, let me assert my firm belief that the only thing we have to fear is fear itself—nameless, unreasoning, unjustified terror which paralyzes needed efforts to convert retreat into advance. In every dark hour of our national life a leadership of frankness and vigor has met with that understanding and support of the people themselves which is essential to victory. I am convinced that you will again give that support to leadership in these critical days.

In such a spirit on my part and on yours we face our common difficulties. They concern, thank God, only material things. Values have shrunken to fantastic levels; taxes have risen; our ability to pay has fallen; government of all kinds is faced by serious curtailment of income; the means of exchange are frozen in the currents of trade; the withered leaves of industrial enterprise lie on every side; farmers find no markets for their produce; the savings of many years in thousands of families are gone.

More important, a host of unemployed citizens face the grim problem of existence, and an equally great number toil with little return. Only a foolish optimist can deny the dark realities of the moment.

Yet our distress comes from no failure of substance. We are stricken by no plague of locusts. Compared with the perils which our forefathers conquered because they believed and were not afraid, we have still much to be thankful for. Nature still offers her bounty and human efforts have multiplied it. Plenty is at our doorstep, but a generous use of it languishes in the very sight of the supply. Primarily this is because the rulers of the exchange of mankind's goods have failed, through their own stubbornness and their own incompetence, have admitted their failure, and abdicated. Practices of the unscrupulous money changers stand indicted in the court of public opinion, rejected by the hearts and minds of men.

True they have tried, but their efforts have been cast in the pattern of an outworn tradition. Faced by failure of credit they have proposed only the lending of more money. Stripped of the lure of profit by which to induce our people to follow their false leadership, they have resorted to exhortations, pleading tearfully for restored confidence. They know only the rules of a generation of self-seekers. They have no vision, and when there is no vision the people perish.

The money changers have fled from their high seats in the temple of our civilization. We may now restore that temple to the ancient truths. The measure of the restoration lies in the extent to which we apply social values more noble than mere monetary profit.

Happiness lies not in the mere possession of money; it lies in the joy of achievement, in the thrill of creative effort. The joy and moral stimulation of work no longer must be forgotten in the mad chase of evanescent profits. These dark days will be worth all they cost us if they teach us that our true destiny is not to be ministered unto but to minister to ourselves and to our fellow men.

Recognition of the falsity of material wealth as the standard of success goes hand in hand with the abandonment of the false belief that public office and high political position are to be valued only by the standards of pride of place and personal profit; and there must be an end to a conduct in banking and in business which too often has given to a sacred trust the likeness of callous and selfish wrongdoing. Small wonder that confidence languishes, for it thrives only on honesty, on honor, on the sacredness of obligations, on faithful protection, on unselfish performance; without them it cannot live.

Restoration calls, however, not for changes in ethics alone. This Nation asks for action, and action now.

Our greatest primary task is to put people to work. This is no unsolvable problem if we face it wisely and courageously. It can be accomplished in part by direct recruiting by the Government itself, treating the task as we would treat the emergency of a war, but at the same time, through this employment, accomplishing greatly needed projects to stimulate and reorganize the use of our natural resources.

Hand in hand with this we must frankly recognize the overbalance of population in our industrial centers and, by engaging on a national scale in a redistribution, endeavor to provide a better use of the land for those best fitted for the land. The task can be helped by definite efforts to raise the values of agricultural products and with this the power to purchase the output of our cities. It can be helped by preventing realistically the tragedy of the growing loss through foreclosure of our small homes and our farms. It can be helped by insistence that the Federal, State, and local governments act forthwith on the demand that their cost be drastically reduced. It can be helped by the unifying of relief activities which today are often scattered, uneconomical, and unequal. It can be helped by national planning for and supervision of all forms of transportation and of communications and other utilities which have a definitely public character. There are many ways in which it can be helped, but it can never be helped merely by talking about it. We must act and act quickly.

Finally, in our progress toward a resumption of work we require two safeguards against a return of the evils of the old order; there must be a strict supervision of all banking and credits and investments; there must be an end to speculation with other people's money, and there must be provision for an adequate but sound currency.

There are the lines of attack. I shall presently urge upon a new Congress, in special session, detailed measures for their fulfillment, and I shall seek the immediate assistance of the several States.

Through this program of action we address ourselves to putting our own national house in order and making income balance outgo. Our international trade relations, though vastly important, are in point of time and necessity secondary to the establishment of a sound national economy. I favor as a practical policy the putting of first things first. I shall spare no effort to restore world trade by international economic readjustment, but the emergency at home cannot wait on that accomplishment.

The basic thought that guides these specific means of national recovery is not narrowly nationalistic. It is the insistence, as a first consideration, upon the interdependence of the various elements in all parts of the United States—a recognition of the old and permanently important manifestation of the American spirit of the pioneer. It is the way to recovery. It is the immediate way. It is the strongest assurance that the recovery will endure.

In the field of world policy I would dedicate this Nation to the policy of the good neighbor—the neighbor who resolutely respects himself and, because he does so, respects the rights of others—the neighbor who respects his obligations and respects the sanctity of his agreements in and with a world of neighbors.

If I read the temper of our people correctly, we now realize as we have never realized before our interdependence on each other; that we cannot merely take but we must give as well; that if we are to go forward, we must move as a trained and loyal army willing to sacrifice for the good of a common discipline, because without such discipline no progress is made, no leadership becomes effective. We are, I know, ready and willing to submit our lives and property to such discipline, because it makes possible a leadership which aims at a larger good. This I propose to offer, pledging that the larger purposes will bind upon us all as a sacred obligation with a unity of duty hitherto evoked only in time of armed strife.

With this pledge taken, I assume unhesitatingly the leadership of this great army of our people dedicated to a disciplined attack upon our common problems.

Action in this image and to this end is feasible under the form of government which we have inherited from our ancestors. Our Constitution is so simple and practical that it is possible always to meet extraordinary needs by changes in emphasis and arrangement without loss of essential form. That is why our constitutional system has proved itself the most superbly enduring political mechanism the modern world has produced. It has met every stress of vast expansion of territory, of foreign wars, of bitter internal strife, of world relations.

It is to be hoped that the normal balance of executive and legislative authority may be wholly adequate to meet the unprecedented task before us. But it may be that an unprecedented demand and need for undelayed action may call for temporary departure from that normal balance of public procedure.

I am prepared under my constitutional duty to recommend the measures that a stricken nation in the midst of a stricken world may require. These measures, or such other measures as the Congress may build out of its experience and wisdom, I shall seek, within my constitutional authority, to bring to speedy adoption.

But in the event that the Congress shall fail to take one of these two courses, and in the event that the national emergency is still critical, I shall not evade the clear course of duty that will then confront me. I shall ask the Congress for the one remaining instrument to meet the crisis—broad Executive power to wage a war against the emergency, as great as the power that would be given to me if we were in fact invaded by a foreign foe.

For the trust reposed in me I will return the courage and the devotion that befit the time. I can do no less.

We face the arduous days that lie before us in the warm courage of national unity; with the clear consciousness of seeking old and precious moral values; with the clean satisfaction that comes from the stern performance of duty by old and young alike. We aim at the assurance of a rounded and permanent national life.

We do not distrust the future of essential democracy. The people of the United States have not failed. In their need they have registered a mandate that they want direct, vigorous action. They have asked for discipline and direction under leadership. They have made me the present instrument of their wishes. In the spirit of the gift I take it.

In this dedication of a Nation we humbly ask the blessing of God. May He protect each and every one of us. May He guide me in the days to come.

FROM THE PROGRAM FOR THE MARCH ON WASHINGTON FOR JOBS AND FREEDOM (1963)

WHAT WE DEMAND*

1. Comprehensive and effective *civil rights legislation* from the present Congress—without compromise or filibuster—to guarantee all Americans

access to all public accommodations
decent housing
adequate and integrated education
the right to vote

2. Withholding of Federal funds from all programs in which discrimination exists.

3. *Desegregation of all school districts in 1963.*

4. Enforcement of the *Fourteenth Amendment*—reducing Congressional representation of states where citizens are disfranchised.

5. A new *Executive Order* banning discrimination in all housing supported by federal funds.

6. Authority for the Attorney General to institute *injunctive suits* when any constitutional right is violated.

7. A massive federal program to train and place all unemployed workers—Negro and white—on meaningful and dignified jobs at decent wages.

8. A national *minimum wage* act that will give all Americans a decent standard of living. (Government surveys show that anything less than $2.00 an hour fails to do this.)

9. A broadened *Fair Labor Standards Act* to include all areas of employment which are presently excluded.

10. A federal *Fair Employment Practices Act* barring discrimination by federal, state, and municipal governments, and by employers, contractors, employment agencies, and trade unions.

*Support of the March does not necessarily indicate endorsement of every demand listed. Some organizations have not had an opportunity to take an official position on all of the demands advocated here.

RONALD REAGAN'S FIRST INAUGURAL ADDRESS (1981)

WEST FRONT OF THE U.S. CAPITOL JANUARY 20, 1981

Senator Hatfield, Mr. Chief Justice, Mr. President, Vice President Bush, Vice President Mondale, Senator Baker, Speaker O'Neill, Reverend Moomaw, and my fellow citizens.

To a few of us here today this is a solemn and most momentous occasion, and yet in the history of our nation it is a commonplace occurrence. The orderly transfer of authority as called for in the Constitution routinely takes place, as it has for almost two centuries, and few of us stop to think how unique we really are. In the eyes of many in the world, this every-four-year ceremony we accept as normal is nothing less than a miracle.

Mr. President, I want our fellow citizens to know how much you did to carry on this tradition. By your gracious cooperation in the transition process, you have shown a watching world that we are a united people pledged to maintaining a political system which guarantees individual liberty to a greater degree than any other, and I thank you and your people for all your help in maintaining the continuity which is the bulwark of our republic. The business of our nation goes forward. These United States are confronted with an economic affliction of great proportions. We suffer from the longest and one of the worst sustained inflations in our national history. It distorts our economic decisions, penalizes thrift, and crushes the struggling young and the fixed-income elderly alike. It threatens to shatter the lives of millions of our people.

Idle industries have cast workers into unemployment, human misery, and personal indignity. Those who do work are denied a fair return for their labor by a tax system which penalizes successful achievement and keeps us from maintaining full productivity. But great as our tax burden is, it has not kept pace with public spending. For decades we have piled deficit upon deficit, mortgaging our future and our children's future for the temporary convenience of the present. To continue this long trend is to guarantee tremendous social, cultural, political, and economic upheavals.

You and I, as individuals, can, by borrowing, live beyond our means, but for only a limited period of time. Why, then, should we think that collectively, as a nation, we're not bound by that same limitation? We must act today in order to preserve tomorrow. And let there be no misunderstanding: We are going to begin to act, beginning today. The economic ills we suffer have come upon us over several decades. They will not go away in days, weeks, or months, but they will go away. They will go away because we as Americans have the capacity now, as we've had in the past, to do whatever needs to be done to preserve this last and greatest bastion of freedom.

In this present crisis, government is not the solution to our problem; government is the problem. From time to time we've been tempted to believe that society has become too complex to be managed by self-rule, that government by an elite group is superior to government for, by, and of the people. Well, if no one among us is capable of governing himself, then who among us has the capacity to govern someone else? All of us together, in and out of government, must bear the burden. The solutions we seek must be equitable, with no one group singled out to pay a higher price.

We hear much of special interest groups. Well, our concern must be for a special interest group that has been too long neglected. It knows no sectional boundaries or ethnic and racial divisions, and it crosses political party lines. It is made up of men and women who raise our food, patrol our streets, man our mines and factories, teach our children, keep our homes, and heal us when we're sick— professionals, industrialists, shopkeepers, clerks, cabbies, and truck drivers. They are, in short, "we the people," this breed called Americans.

Well, this administration's objective will be a healthy, vigorous, growing economy that provides equal opportunities for all Americans, with no barriers born of bigotry or discrimination. Putting America back to work means putting all Americans back to work. Ending inflation means freeing all Americans from the terror of runaway living costs. All must share in the productive work of this "new beginning," and all must share in the bounty of a revived economy. With the idealism and fair play which are the core of our system and our strength, we can have a strong and prosperous America, at peace with itself and the world.

So, as we begin, let us take inventory. We are a nation that has a government—not the other way around. And this makes us special among the nations of the Earth. Our government has no power except that granted it by the people. It is time to check and reverse the growth of government, which shows signs of having grown beyond the consent of the governed.

It is my intention to curb the size and influence of the federal establishment and to demand recognition of the distinction between the powers granted to the federal government and those reserved to the states or to the people. All of us need to be reminded that the federal government did not create the states; the states created the federal government.

Now, so there will be no misunderstanding, it's not my intention to do away with government. It is rather to make it work—work with us, not over us; to stand by our side, not ride on our back. Government can and must provide opportunity, not smother it; foster productivity, not stifle it.

If we look to the answer as to why for so many years we achieved so much, prospered as no other people on earth, it was because here in this land we unleashed the energy and individual genius of man to a greater extent than has ever been done before. Freedom and the dignity of the individual have been more available and assured here than in any other place on earth. The price for this freedom at times has been high, but we have never been unwilling to pay the price.

It is no coincidence that our present troubles parallel and are proportionate to the intervention and intrusion in our lives that result from unnecessary and excessive growth of government. It is time for us to realize that we're too great a nation to limit ourselves to small dreams. We're not, as some would have us believe, doomed to an inevitable decline. I do not believe in a fate that will fall on us no matter what we do. I do believe in a fate that will fall on us if we do nothing. So, with all the creative energy at our command, let us begin an era of national renewal. Let us renew our determination, our courage, and our strength. And let us renew our faith and our hope.

We have every right to dream heroic dreams. Those who say that we're in a time when there are no heroes, they just don't know where to look. You can see heroes every day going in and out of factory gates. Others, a handful in number, produce enough food to feed all of us and then the world beyond. You meet heroes across a counter, and they're on both sides of that counter. There are entrepreneurs with faith in themselves and faith in an idea who create new jobs, new wealth and opportunity. They're individuals and families whose taxes support the government and whose voluntary gifts support church, charity, culture, art, and education. Their patriotism is quiet, but deep. Their values sustain our national life.

Now, I have used the words "they" and "their" in speaking of these heroes. I could say "you" and "your," because I'm addressing the heroes of whom I speak—you, the citizens of this blessed land. Your dreams, your hopes, your goals are going to be the dreams, the hopes, and the goals of this administration, so help me God.

We shall reflect the compassion that is so much a part of your makeup. How can we love our country and not love our countrymen; and loving them, reach out a hand when they fall, heal them when they're sick, and provide opportunity to make them self-sufficient so they will be equal in fact and not just in theory?

Can we solve the problems confronting us? Well, the answer is an unequivocal and emphatic "yes." To paraphrase Winston Churchill, I did not take the oath I've just taken with the intention of presiding over the dissolution of the world's strongest economy.

In the days ahead I will propose removing the roadblocks that have slowed our economy and reduced productivity. Steps will be taken aimed at restoring the balance between the various levels of government. Progress may be slow, measured in inches and feet, not miles, but we will progress. It is time to reawaken this industrial giant, to get government back within its means, and to lighten our punitive tax burden. And these will be our first priorities, and on these principles there will be no compromise.

On the eve of our struggle for independence a man who might have been one of the greatest among the Founding Fathers, Dr. Joseph Warren, president of the Massachusetts Congress, said to his fellow Americans, "Our country is in danger, but not to be despaired of . . . On you depend the fortunes of America. You are to decide the important questions upon which rests the happiness and the liberty of millions yet unborn. Act worthy of yourselves." Well, I believe we, the Americans of today, are ready to act worthy of ourselves, ready to do what must be done to ensure happiness and liberty for ourselves, our children, and our children's children. And as we renew ourselves here in our own land, we will be seen as having greater strength throughout the world. We will again be the exemplar of freedom and a beacon of hope for those who do not now have freedom.

To those neighbors and allies who share our freedom, we will strengthen our historic ties and assure them of our support and firm commitment. We will match loyalty with loyalty. We will strive for mutually beneficial relations. We will not use our friendship to impose on their sovereignty, for our own sovereignty is not for sale. As for the enemies of freedom, those who are potential adversaries, they will be reminded that peace is the highest aspiration of the American people. We will negotiate for it, sacrifice for it; we will not surrender for it, now or ever.

Our forbearance should never be misunderstood. Our reluctance for conflict should not be misjudged as a failure of will. When action is required to preserve our national security, we will act. We will maintain sufficient strength to prevail if need be, knowing that if we do so we have the best chance of never having to use that strength. Above all, we must realize that no arsenal or no weapon in the arsenals of the world is so formidable as the will and moral courage of free men and women. It is a weapon our adversaries in today's world do not have. It is a weapon that we as Americans do have. Let that be understood by those who practice terrorism and prey upon their neighbors. I'm told that tens of thousands of prayer meetings are being held on this day, and for that I'm deeply grateful. We are a nation under God, and I believe God intended for us to be free. It would be fitting and good, I think, if on each Inaugural Day in future years it should be declared a day of prayer.

This is the first time in our history that this ceremony has been held, as you've been told, on the West Front of the Capitol. Standing here, one faces a magnificent vista, opening up on the city's special beauty and history. At the end of this open mall are those shrines to the giants on whose shoulders we stand.

Directly in front of me, the monument to a monumental man, George Washington, father of our country. A man of humility who came to greatness reluctantly. He led Americans out of revolutionary victory into infant nationhood. Off to one side, the stately memorial to Thomas Jefferson. The Declaration of Independence flames with his eloquence. And then, beyond the Reflecting Pool, the dignified columns of the Lincoln Memorial. Whoever would understand in his heart the meaning of America will find it in the life of Abraham Lincoln.

Beyond those monuments to heroism is the Potomac River, and on the far shore the sloping hills of Arlington National Cemetery, with its row upon row of simple white markers bearing crosses and Stars of David. They add up to only a tiny fraction of the price that has been paid for our freedom. Each one of those markers is a monument to the kind of hero I spoke of earlier. Their lives ended in places called Belleau Wood, the Argonne, Omaha Beach, Salerno, and halfway around the world on Guadalcanal, Tarawa, Pork Chop Hill, the Chosin Reservoir, and in a hundred rice paddies and jungles of a place called Vietnam.

Under one such marker lies a young man, Martin Treptow, who left his job in a small town barbershop in 1917 to go to France with the famed Rainbow Division. There, on the western front, he was killed trying to carry a message between battalions under heavy artillery fire.

We're told that on his body was found a diary. On the flyleaf under the heading "My Pledge," he had written these words: "America must win this war. Therefore I will work, I will save, I will sacrifice, I will endure, I will fight cheerfully and do my utmost, as if the issue of the whole struggle depended on me alone."

The crisis we are facing today does not require of us the kind of sacrifice that Martin Treptow and so many thousands of others were called upon to make. It does require, however, our best effort and our willingness to believe in ourselves and to believe in our capacity to perform great deeds, to believe that together with God's help we can and will resolve the problems which now confront us.

And after all, why shouldn't we believe that? We are Americans.

God bless you, and thank you.

BARACK OBAMA'S FIRST INAUGURAL ADDRESS (2009)

My fellow citizens: I stand here today humbled by the task before us, grateful for the trust you've bestowed, mindful of the sacrifices borne by our ancestors.

I thank President Bush for his service to our nation—(*applause*)—as well as the generosity and cooperation he has shown throughout this transition.

Forty-four Americans have now taken the presidential oath. The words have been spoken during rising tides of prosperity and the still waters of peace. Yet, every so often, the oath is taken amidst gathering clouds and raging storms. At these moments, America has carried on not simply because of the skill or vision of those in high office, but because we, the people, have remained faithful to the ideals of our forebears and true to our founding documents.

So it has been: so it must be with this generation of Americans.

That we are in the midst of crisis is now well understood. Our nation is at war against a far-reaching network of violence and hatred. Our economy is badly weakened, a consequence of greed and irresponsibility on the part of some, but also our collective failure to make hard choices and prepare the nation for a new age. Homes have been lost, jobs shed, businesses shuttered. Our health care is too costly, our schools fail too many—and each day brings further evidence that the ways we use energy strengthen our adversaries and threaten our planet.

These are the indicators of crisis, subject to data and statistics. Less measurable, but no less profound, is a sapping of confidence across our land; a nagging fear that America's decline is inevilable, that the next generation must lower its sights.

Today I say to you that the challenges we face are real. They are serious and they are many. They will not be met easily or in a short span of time. But know this America: They will be met. (*Applause*)

On this day, we gather because we have chosen hope over fear, unity of purpose over conflict and discord. On this day, we come to proclaim an end to the petty grievances and false promises, the recriminations and worn-out dogmas that for far too long have strangled our politics. We remain a young nation. But in the words of Scripture, the time has come to set aside childish things. The time has come to reaffirm our enduring spirit; to choose our better history; to carry forward that precious gift, that noble idea passed on from generation to generation; the God-given promise that all are equal, all are free, and all deserve a chance to pursue their full measure of happiness. (*Applause*)

In reaffirming the greatness of our nation we understand that greatness is never a given. It must be earned. Our journey has never been one of short-cuts or settling for less. It has not been the path for the faint-hearted, for those that prefer leisure over work, or seek only the pleasures of riches and fame. Rather, it has been the risk-takers, the doers, the makers of things—some celebrated, but more often men and women obscure in their labor—who have carried us up the long rugged path towards prosperity and freedom.

For us, they packed up their few worldly possessions and traveled across oceans in search of a new life. For us, they toiled in sweatshops, and settled the West, endured the lash of the whip, and plowed the hard earth. For us, they fought and died in places like Concord and Gettysburg, Normandy and Khe Sahn.

Time and again these men and women struggled and sacrificed and worked till their hands were raw so that we might live a better life. They saw America as bigger than the sum of our individual ambitions, greater than all the differences of birth or wealth or faction.

This is the journey we continue today. We remain the most prosperous, powerful nation on Earth. Our workers are no less productive than when this crisis began. Our minds are no less inventive, our goods and services no less needed than they were last week, or last month, or last year. Our capacity remains undiminished. But our time of standing pat, of protecting ffnarrow interests and putting off unpleasant decisions—that time has surely passed. Starting today, we must pick ourselves up, dust ourselves off, and begin again the work of remaking America. (*Applause*)

For everywhere we look, there is work to be done. The state of our economy calls for action, bold and swift. And we will act, not only to create new jobs, but to lay a new foundation for growth. We will build the roads and bridges, the electric grids and digital lines that feed our commerce and bind us together. We'll restore science to its rightful place, and wield technology's wonders to raise health care's quality and lower its cost. We will harness the sun and the winds and the soil to fuel our cars and run our factories. And we will transform our schools and colleges and universities to meet the demands of a new age. All this we can do. All this we will do.

Now, there are some who question the scale of our ambitions, who suggest that our system cannot tolerate too many big plans. Their memories are short, for they have forgotten what this country has already done, what free men and women can achieve when imagination is joined to common purpose, and necessity to courage. What the cynics fail to understand is that the ground has shifted beneath them, that the stale political arguments that have consumed us for so long no longer apply.

The question we ask today is not whether our government is too big or too small, but whether it works—whether it helps families find jobs at a decent wage, care they can afford, a retirement that is dignified. Where the answer is yes, we intend to move forward. Where the answer is no, programs will end. And those of us who manage the public's dollars will be held to account, to spend wisely, reform bad habits, and do our business in the light of day, because only then can we restore the vital trust between a people and their government.

Nor is the question before us whether the market is a force for good or ill. Its power to generate wealth and expand freedom is unmatched. But this crisis has reminded us that without a watchful eye, the market can spin out of control. The nation cannot prosper long when it favors only the prosperous. The success of our economy has always depended not just on the size of our gross domestic product, but on the reach of our prosperity, on the ability to extend opportunity to every willing heart—not out of charity, but because it is the surest route to our common good. (*Applause*)

As for our common defense, we reject as false the choice between our safety and our ideals. Our Founding Fathers—(*applause*)—our Founding Fathers, faced with perils that we can scarcely imagine, drafted a charter to assure the rule of law and the rights of man—a charter expanded by the blood of generations. Those ideals still light the world, and we will not give them up for expedience sake. (*Applause*)

And so, to all the other peoples and governments who are watching today, from the grandest capitals to the small village where my father was born, know that America is a friend of each nation, and every man, woman and child who seeks a future of peace and dignity. And we are ready to lead once more. (*Applause*)

Recall that earlier generations faced down fascism and communism not just with missiles and tanks, but with the sturdy alliances and enduring convictions. They understood that our power alone cannot protect us, nor does it entitle us to do as we please. Instead they knew that our power grows through its prudent use; our security emanates from the justness of our cause, the force of our example, the tempering qualities of humility and restraint.

We are the keepers of this legacy. Guided by these principles once more we can meet those new threats that demand even greater effort, even greater cooperation and understanding between nations. We will begin to responsibly leave Iraq to its people and forge a hard-earned peace in Afghanistan. With old friends and former foes, we'll work tirelessly to lessen the nuclear threat, and roll back the specter of a warming planet.

We will not apologize for our way of life, nor will we waver in its defense. And for those who seek to advance their aims by inducing terror and slaughtering innocents, we say to you now that our spirit is stronger and cannot be broken—you cannot outlast us, and we will defeat you. (*Applause*)

For we know that our patchwork heritage is a strength, not a weakness. We are a nation of Christians and Muslims, Jews and Hindus, and non-believers. We are shaped by every language and culture, drawn from every end of this Earth: and because we have tasted the bitter swill of civil war and segregation, and emerged from that dark chapter stronger and more united, we cannot help but believe that the old hatreds shall someday pass; that the lines of tribe shall soon dissolve; that as the world grows smaller, our common humanity shall reveal itself; and that America must play its role in ushering in a new era of peace.

To the Muslim world, we seek a new way forward, based on mutual interest and mutual respect. To those leaders around the globe who seek to sow conflict, or blame their society's ills on the West, know that your people will judge you on what you can build, not what you destroy. (*Applause*)

To those who cling to power through corruption and deceit and the silencing of dissent, know that you are on the wrong side of history, but that we will extend a hand if you are willing to unclench your fist. (*Applause*)

To the people of poor nations, we pledge to work alongside you to make your farms flourish and let clean waters flow; to nourish starved bodies and feed hungry minds. And to those nations like ours that enjoy relative plenty, we say we can no longer afford indifference to the suffering outside our borders, nor can we consume the world's resources without regard to effect. For the world has changed, and we must change with it.

As we consider the role that unfolds before us, we remember with humble gratitude those brave Americans who at this very hour patrol far-off deserts and distant mountains. They have something to tell us, just as the fallen heroes who lie in Arlington whisper through the ages.

We honor them not only because they are the guardians of our liberty, but because they embody the spirit of service—a willingness to find meaning in something greater than themselves.

And yet at this moment, a moment that will define a generation, it is precisely this spirit that must inhabit us all. For as much as government can do, and must do, it is ultimately the faith and determination of the American people upon which this nation relies. It is the kindness to take in a stranger when the levees break, the selflessness of workers who would rather cut their hours than see a friend lose their job which sees us through our darkest hours. It is the firefighter's courage to storm a stairway filled with smoke, but also a parent's willingness to nurture a child that finally decides our fate.

Our challenges may be new. The instruments with which we meet them may be new. But those values upon which our success depends—honesty and hard work, courage and fair play, tolerance and curiosity, loyalty and patriotism—these things are old. These things are true. They have been the quiet force of progress throughout our history.

What is demanded, then, is a return to these truths. What is required of us now is a new era of responsibility—a recognition on the part of every American that we have duties to ourselves, our nation and the world; duties that we do not grudgingly accept, but rather seize gladly, firm in the knowledge that there is nothing so satisfying to the spirit, so defining of our character than giving our all to a difficult task.

This is the price and the promise of citizenship. This is the source of our confidence—the knowledge that God calls on us to shape an uncertain destiny. This is the meaning of our liberty and our creed, why men and women and children of every race and every faith can join in celebration across this magnificent mall; and why a man whose father less than 60 years ago might not have been served in a local restaurant can now stand before you to take a most sacred oath. (*Applause*)

So let us mark this day with remembrance of who we are and how far we have traveled. In the year of America's birth, in the coldest of months, a small band of patriots huddled by dying campfires on the shores of an icy river. The capital was abandoned. The enemy was advancing. The snow was stained with blood. At the moment when the outcome of our revolution was most in doubt, the father of our nation ordered these words to be read to the people:

"Let it be told to the future world...that in the depth of winter, when nothing but hope and virtue could survive... that the city and the country, alarmed at one common danger, came forth to meet [it]."

America: In the face of our common dangers, in this winter of our hardship, let us remember these timeless words. With hope and virtue, let us brave once more the icy currents, and endure what storms may come. Let it be said by our children's children that when we were tested we refused to let this journey end, that we did not turn back nor did we falter; and with eyes fixed on the horizon and God's grace upon us, we carried forth that great gift of freedom and delivered it safely to future generations.

Thank you. God bless you. And God bless the United States of America. (*Applause*)

PRESIDENTIAL ELECTIONS

Year	Number of States	Candidates	Parties	Popular Vote	% of Popular Vote	Electoral Vote	% Voter Participation
1789	11	**GEORGE WASHINGTON**	NO PARTY			69	
		John Adams	DESIGNATIONS			34	
		Other candidates				35	
1792	15	**GEORGE WASHINGTON**	NO PARTY			132	
		John Adams	DESIGNATIONS			77	
		George Clinton				50	
		Other candidates				5	
1796	16	**JOHN ADAMS**	FEDERALIST			71	
		Thomas Jefferson	Republican			68	
		Thomas Pinckney	Federalist			59	
		Aaron Burr	Republican			30	
		Other candidates				48	
1800	16	**THOMAS JEFFERSON**	REPUBLICAN			73	
		Aaron Burr	Republican			73	
		John Adams	Federalist			65	
		Charles C. Pinckney	Federalist			64	
		John Jay	Federalist			1	
1804	17	**THOMAS JEFFERSON**	REPUBLICAN			162	
		Charles C. Pinckney	Federalist			14	
1808	17	**JAMES MADISON**	REPUBLICAN			122	
		Charles C. Pinckney	Federalist			47	
		George Clinton	Republican			6	
1812	18	**JAMES MADISON**	REPUBLICAN			128	
		DeWitt Clinton	Federalist			89	

Year	Number of States	Candidates	Parties	Popular Vote	% of Popular Vote	Electoral Vote	% Voter Participation
1816	19	**JAMES MONROE**	REPUBLICAN			183	
		Rufus King	Federalist			34	
1820	24	**JAMES MONROE**	REPUBLICAN			231	
		John Quincy Adams	Independent			1	
1824	24	**JOHN QUINCY ADAMS**	NO PARTY	108,740	31.0	84	26.9
		Andrew Jackson	DESIGNATIONS	153,544	43.0	99	
		William H. Crawford		46,618	13.0	41	
		Henry Clay		47,136	13.0	37	
1828	24	**ANDREW JACKSON**	DEMOCRAT	647,286	56.0	178	57.6
		John Quincy Adams	National Republican	508,064	44.0	83	
1832	24	**ANDREW JACKSON**	DEMOCRAT	687,502	54.5	219	55.4
		Henry Clay	National Republican	530,189	37.5	49	
		William Wirt	Anti-Masonic	101,051	8.0	7	
		John Floyd	Democrat			11	
1836	26	**MARTIN VAN BUREN**	DEMOCRAT	765,483	51.0	170	57.8
		William H. Harrison	Whig			73	
		Hugh L. White	Whig	739,795	49.0	26	
		Daniel Webster	Whig			14	
		William P. Mangum	Whig			11	
1840	26	**WILLIAM H. HARRISON**	WHIG	1,274,624	53.0	234	80.2
		Martin Van Buren	Democrat	1,127,781	47.0	60	

Year	Number of States	Candidates	Parties	Popular Vote	% of Popular Vote	Electoral Vote	% Voter Participation
1844	26	**JAMES K. POLK**	DEMOCRAT	1,338,464	50.0	170	78.9
		Henry Clay	Whig	1,300,097	48.0	105	
		James G. Birney	Liberty	62,300	2.0		
1848	30	**ZACHARY TAYLOR**	WHIG	1,360,967	47.5	163	72.7
		Lewis Cass	Democrat	1,222,342	42.5	127	
		Martin Van Buren	Free Soil	291,263	10.0		
1852	31	**FRANKLIN PIERCE**	DEMOCRAT	1,601,117	51.0	254	69.6
		Winfield Scott	Whig	1,385,453	44.0	42	
		John P. Hale	Free Soil	155,825	5.0		
1856	31	**JAMES BUCHANAN**	DEMOCRAT	1,832,955	45.0	174	78.9
		John C. Frémont	Republican	1,339,932	33.0	114	
		Millard Fillmore	American	871,731	22.0	8	
1860	33	**ABRAHAM LINCOLN**	REPUBLICAN	1,865,593	40.0	180	81.2
		Stephen A. Douglas	Northern Democrat	1,382,713	29.0	12	
		John C. Breckinridge	Southern Democrat	848,356	18.0	72	
		John Bell	Constitutional Union	592,906	13.0	39	
1864	36	**ABRAHAM LINCOLN**	REPUBLICAN	2,206,938	55.0	212	73.8
		George B. McClellan	Democrat	1,803,787	45.0	21	
1868	37	**ULYSSES S. GRANT**	REPUBLICAN	3,013,421	53.0	214	78.1
		Horatio Seymour	Democrat	2,706,829	47.0	80	

Year	Number of States	Candidates	Parties	Popular Vote	% of Popular Vote	Electoral Vote	% Voter Participation
1872	37	**ULYSSES S. GRANT**	REPUBLICAN	3,596,745	55.6	286	71.3
		Horace Greeley	Democrat	2,843,446	43.9	66	
1876	38	**RUTHERFORD B. HAYES**	REPUBLICAN	4,036,572	48.0	185	81.8
		Samuel J. Tilden	Democrat	4,284,020	51.0	184	
1880	38	**JAMES A. GARFIELD**	REPUBLICAN	4,453,295	48.4	214	79.4
		Winfield S. Hancock	Democrat	4,414,082	48.3	155	
		James B. Weaver	Greenback-Labor	308,578	3.5		
1884	38	**GROVER CLEVELAND**	DEMOCRAT	4,879,507	48.5	219	77.5
		James G. Blaine	Republican	4,850,293	48.2	182	
		Benjamin F. Butler	Greenback-Labor	175,370	1.8		
		John P. St. John	Prohibition	150,369	1.5		
1888	38	**BENJAMIN HARRISON**	REPUBLICAN	5,447,129	47.9	233	79.3
		Grover Cleveland	Democrat	5,537,857	48.6	168	
		Clinton B. Fisk	Prohibition	249,506	2.2		
		Anson J. Streeter	Union Labor	146,935	1.3		
1892	44	**GROVER CLEVELAND**	DEMOCRAT	5,555,426	46.1	277	74.7
		Benjamin Harrison	Republican	5,182,690	43.0	145	
		James B. Weaver	People's	1,029,846	8.5	22	
		John Bidwell	Prohibition	264,133	2.2		
1896	45	**WILLIAM McKINLEY**	REPUBLICAN	7,102,246	51.0	271	79.3
		William J. Bryan	Democrat	6,492,559	47.0	176	

Year	Number of States	Candidates	Parties	Popular Vote	% of Popular Vote	Electoral Vote	% Voter Participation
1900	45	**WILLIAM McKINLEY**	REPUBLICAN	7,218,491	52.0	292	73.2
		William J. Bryan	Democrat; Populist	6,356,734	46.0	155	
		John C. Wooley	Prohibition	208,914	1.5		
1904	45	THEODORE ROOSEVELT	REPUBLICAN	7,628,461	56.4	336	65.2
		Alton B. Parker	Democrat	5,084,223	37.6	140	
		Eugene V. Debs	Socialist	402,283	3.0		
		Silas C. Swallow	Prohibition	258,536	1.9		
1908	46	**WILLIAM H. TAFT**	REPUBLICAN	7,675,320	52.0	321	65.4
		William J. Bryan	Democrat	6,412,294	43.4	162	
		Eugene V. Debs	Socialist	420,793	2.8		
		Eugene W. Chafin	Prohibition	253,840	1.7		
1912	48	**WOODROW WILSON**	DEMOCRAT	6,296,547	41.9	435	58.8
		Theodore Roosevelt	Progressive	4,118,571	27.4	88	
		William H. Taft	Republican	3,486,720	23.2	8	
		Eugene V. Debs	Socialist	900,672	6.0		
		Eugene W. Chafin	Prohibition	206,275	1.4		
1916	48	**WOODROW WILSON**	DEMOCRAT	9,127,695	49.4	277	61.6
		Charles E. Hughes	Republican	8,533,507	46.2	254	
		A. L. Benson	Socialist	585,113	3.2		
		J. Frank Hanly	Prohibition	220,506	1.2		
1920	48	**WARREN G. HARDING**	REPUBLICAN	16,153,115	60.6	404	49.2
		James M. Cox	Democrat	9,133,092	34.3	127	
		Eugene V. Debs	Socialist	915,490	3.4		
		P. P. Christensen	Farmer-Labor	265,229	1.0		
1924	48	**CALVIN COOLIDGE**	REPUBLICAN	15,719,921	54.0	382	48.9
		John W. Davis	Democrat	8,386,704	29.0	136	
		Robert M. La Follette	Progressive	4,832,532	16.5	13	

Year	Number of States	Candidates	Parties	Popular Vote	% of Popular Vote	Electoral Vote	% Voter Participation
1928	48	**HERBERT C. HOOVER** Alfred E. Smith	REPUBLICAN Democrat	21,437,277 15,007,698	58.2 40.9	444 87	56.9
1932	48	**FRANKLIN D. ROOSEVELT** Herbert C. Hoover Norman Thomas	DEMOCRAT Republican Socialist	22,829,501 15,760,684 884,649	57.7 39.8 2.2	472 59	56.9
1936	48	**FRANKLIN D. ROOSEVELT** Alfred M. Landon William Lemke	DEMOCRAT Republican Union	27,757,333 16,684,231 892,267	60.8 36.6 2.0	523 8	61.0
1940	48	**FRANKLIN D. ROOSEVELT** Wendell L. Willkie	DEMOCRAT Republican	27,313,041 22,348,480	54.9 44.9	449 82	62.5
1944	48	**FRANKLIN D. ROOSEVELT** Thomas E. Dewey	DEMOCRAT Republican	25,612,610 22,017,617	53.5 46.0	432 99	55.9
1948	48	**HARRY S. TRUMAN** Thomas E. Dewey J. Strom Thurmond Henry A. Wallace	DEMOCRAT Republican States' Rights Progressive	24,179,345 21,991,291 1,176,125 1,157,326	49.7 45.3 2.4 2.4	303 189 39	53.0
1952	48	**DWIGHT D. EISENHOWER** Adlai E. Stevenson	REPUBLICAN Democrat	33,936,234 27,314,992	55.1 44.4	442 89	63.3

Year	Number of States	Candidates	Parties	Popular Vote	% of Popular Vote	Electoral Vote	% Voter Participation
1956	48	**DWIGHT D. EISENHOWER**	REPUBLICAN	35,590,472	57.6	457	60.6
		Adlai E. Stevenson	Democrat	26,022,752	42.1	73	
1960	50	**JOHN F. KENNEDY**	DEMOCRAT	34,226,731	49.7	303	62.8
		Richard M. Nixon	Republican	34,108,157	49.6	219	
1964	50	**LYNDON B. JOHNSON**	DEMOCRAT	43,129,566	61.0	486	61.9
		Barry M. Goldwater	Republican	27,178,188	38.4	52	
1968	50	**RICHARD M. NIXON**	REPUBLICAN	31,785,480	43.2	301	60.9
		Hubert H. Humphrey	Democrat	31,275,166	42.6	191	
		George C. Wallace	American Independent	9,906,473	12.9	46	
1972	50	**RICHARD M. NIXON**	REPUBLICAN	47,169,911	60.7	520	55.2
		George S. McGovern	Democrat	29,170,383	37.5	17	
		John G. Schmitz	American	1,099,482	1.4		
1976	50	**JIMMY CARTER**	DEMOCRAT	40,830,763	50.0	297	53.5
		Gerald R. Ford	Republican	39,147,793	48.0	240	
1980	50	**RONALD REAGAN**	REPUBLICAN	43,904,153	50.9	489	52.6
		Jimmy Carter	Democrat	35,483,883	41.1	49	
		John B. Anderson	Independent	5,720,060	6.6		
		Ed Clark	Libertarian	921,299	1.1		

Year	Number of States	Candidates	Parties	Popular Vote	% of Popular Vote	Electoral Vote	% Voter Participation
1984	50	**RONALD REAGAN** Walter F. Mondale	REPUBLICAN Democrat	54,455,075 37,577,185	58.8 40.5	525 13	53.1
1988	50	**GEORGE H. BUSH** Michael Dukakis	REPUBLICAN Democrat	48,886,097 41,809,074	53.4 45.6	426 111	50.1
1992	50	**BILL CLINTON** George H. Bush H. Ross Perot	DEMOCRAT Republican Independent	44,909,326 39,103,882 19,741,657	42.9 37.4 18.9	370 168	55.0
1996	50	**BILL CLINTON** Bob Dole H. Ross Perot	DEMOCRAT Republican Reform Party	47,402,357 39,198,755 8,085,402	49.2 40.7 8.4	379 159	49.0
2000	50	**GEORGE W. BUSH** Albert Gore Ralph Nader	REPUBLICAN Democrat Green Party	50,455,156 50,992,335 2,882,738	47.9 48.4 2.7	271 266	50.4
2004	50	**GEORGE W. BUSH** John F. Kerry	REPUBLICAN Democrat	62,040,610 59,028,111	50.7 48.3	286 251	56.2
2008	50	**Barack H. Obama** John S. McCain	DEMOCRAT Republican	66,882,230 58,343,671	53% 46%	365 173	56.8
2012	50	**Barack H. Obama** W. Mitt Romney	DEMOCRAT Republican	62,611,250 59,134,475	51 48	332 206	53.6

Candidates receiving less than 1 percent of the popular vote have been omitted. Thus, the percentage of popular vote given for any election year may not total 100 percent.

Before the passage of the Twelfth Amendment in 1804, the electoral college voted for two presidential candidates; the runner-up became vice president.

ADMISSION OF STATES

Order of Admission	State	Date of Admission	Order of Admission	State	Date of Admission
1	Delaware	December 7, 1787	26	Michigan	January 26, 1837
2	Pennsylvania	December 12, 1787	27	Florida	March 3, 1845
3	New Jersey	December 18, 1787	28	Texas	December 29, 1845
4	Georgia	January 2, 1788	29	Iowa	December 28, 1846
5	Connecticut	January 9, 1788	30	Wisconsin	May 29, 1848
6	Massachusetts	February 7, 1788	31	California	September 9, 1850
7	Maryland	April 28, 1788	32	Minnesota	May 11, 1858
8	South Carolina	May 23, 1788	33	Oregon	February 14, 1859
9	New Hampshire	June 21, 1788	34	Kansas	January 29, 1861
10	Virginia	June 25, 1788	35	West Virginia	June 30, 1863
11	New York	July 26, 1788	36	Nevada	October 31, 1864
12	North Carolina	November 21, 1789	37	Nebraska	March 1, 1867
13	Rhode Island	May 29, 1790	38	Colorado	August 1, 1876
14	Vermont	March 4, 1791	39	North Dakota	November 2, 1889
15	Kentucky	June 1, 1792	40	South Dakota	November 2, 1889
16	Tennessee	June 1, 1796	41	Montana	November 8, 1889
17	Ohio	March 1, 1803	42	Washington	November 11, 1889
18	Louisiana	April 30, 1812	43	Idaho	July 3, 1890
19	Indiana	December 11, 1816	44	Wyoming	July 10, 1890
20	Mississippi	December 10, 1817	45	Utah	January 4, 1896
21	Illinois	December 3, 1818	46	Oklahoma	November 16, 1907
22	Alabama	December 14, 1819	47	New Mexico	January 6, 1912
23	Maine	March 15, 1820	48	Arizona	February 14, 1912
24	Missouri	August 10, 1821	49	Alaska	January 3, 1959
25	Arkansas	June 15, 1836	50	Hawaii	August 21, 1959

POPULATION OF THE UNITED STATES

Year	Number of States	Population	% Increase	Population per Square Mile
1790	13	3,929,214		4.5
1800	16	5,308,483	35.1	6.1
1810	17	7,239,881	36.4	4.3
1820	23	9,638,453	33.1	5.5
1830	24	12,866,020	33.5	7.4
1840	26	17,069,453	32.7	9.8
1850	31	23,191,876	35.9	7.9
1860	33	31,443,321	35.6	10.6
1870	37	39,818,449	26.6	13.4
1880	38	50,155,783	26.0	16.9
1890	44	62,947,714	25.5	21.1
1900	45	75,994,575	20.7	25.6
1910	46	91,972,266	21.0	31.0
1920	48	105,710,620	14.9	35.6
1930	48	122,775,046	16.1	41.2
1940	48	131,669,275	7.2	44.2
1950	48	150,697,361	14.5	50.7
1960	50	179,323,175	19.0	50.6
1970	50	203,235,298	13.3	57.5
1980	50	226,504,825	11.4	64.0
1985	50	237,839,000	5.0	67.2
1990	50	250,122,000	5.2	70.6
1995	50	263,411,707	5.3	74.4
2000	50	281,421,906	6.8	77.0
2005	50	296,410,404	5.3	81.7
2010	50	308,745,538	4.2	87.4

HISTORICAL STATISTICS OF THE UNITED STATES

LABOR FORCE—SELECTED CHARACTERISTICS EXPRESSED AS A PERCENTAGE OF THE LABOR FORCE: 1800–2010

Year	Agriculture	Manufacturing	Domestic service	Clerical, sales, and service	Professions	Slave	Nonwhite	Foreign-born	Female
1800	74.4	—	2.4	—	—	30.2	32.6	—	21.4
1860	55.8	13.8	5.4	4.8[1]	3.0[1]	21.7	23.6	24.5[1]	19.6
1910	30.7	20.8	5.5	14.1	4.7	—	13.4	22.0	20.8
1950	12.0	26.4	2.5	27.3	8.9	—	10.0	8.7	27.9
2000	2.4	14.7	0.6	38.0[2]	15.6	—	16.5	10.3[2]	46.6
2010	1.6	10.1	1.6	40.2	22.2	—	18.7	15.8	46.7

[1]Values for 1870 are presented here because the available data for 1860 exclude slaves.
[2]1990.
Note: "Clerical, sales, and service" excludes domestic service.

IMMIGRATION, BY ORIGIN (in thousands)

Period	Europe	Americas	Asia
1820–30	106	12	—
1831–40	496	33	—
1841–50	1,597	62	—
1851–60	2,453	75	42
1861–70	2,065	167	65
1871–80	2,272	404	70
1881–90	4,735	427	70
1891–1900	3,555	39	75
1901–10	8,065	362	324
1911–20	4,322	1,144	247
1921–30	2,463	1,517	112
1931–40	348	160	16
1941–50	621	355	32
1951–60	1,326	997	150
1961–70	1,123	1,716	590
1971–80	800	1,983	1,588
1981–90	762	3,616	2,738
1991–2000	1,100	3,800	2,200

UNEMPLOYMENT RATE, 1890–2013

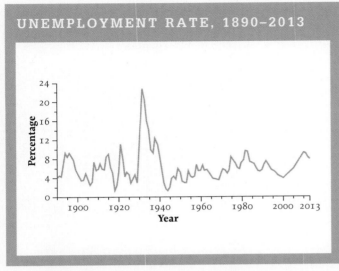

UNION MEMBERSHIP AS A PERCENTAGE OF NONAGRICULTURAL EMPLOYMENT, 1880–2012

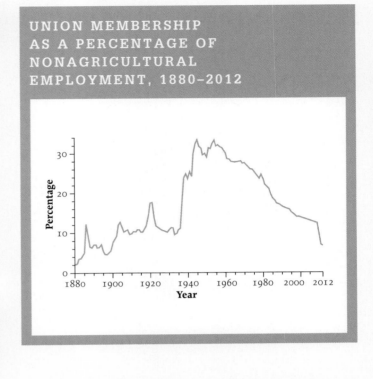

VOTER PARTICIPATION IN PRESIDENTIAL ELECTIONS, 1824–2012

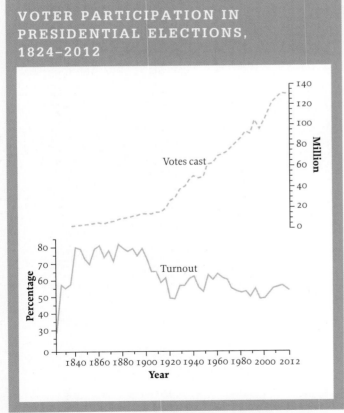

BIRTHRATE, 1820–2011

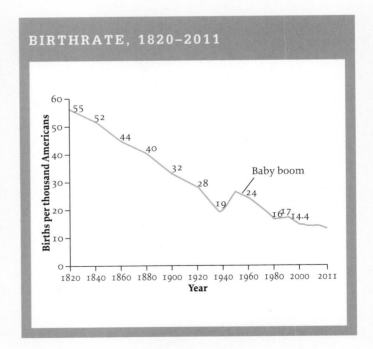

GLOSSARY

Abolitionism Social movement of the pre–Civil War era that advocated the immediate emancipation of the slaves and their incorporation into American society as equal citizens.

Affirmative action Policy efforts to promote greater employment opportunities for minorities.

Agricultural Adjustment Act (1933) New Deal legislation that established the Agricultural Adjustment Administration (AAA) to improve agricultural prices by limiting market supplies; declared unconstitutional in *United States v. Butler* (1936).

Aid to Families with Dependent Children Federal program, also known as "welfare," of financial assistance to needy American families; created in 1935 as part of the Social Security Act; abolished in 1996.

Alamo, Battle of the Siege in the Texas War for Independence, 1836, in which the San Antonio mission fell to the Mexicans.

Alien and Sedition Acts (1798) Four measures passed during the undeclared war with France that limited the freedoms of speech and press and restricted the liberty of noncitizens.

America First Committee Largely midwestern isolationist organization supported by many prominent citizens, 1940–1941.

American Civil Liberties Union Organization founded during World War I to protest the suppression of freedom of expression in wartime; played a major role in court cases that achieved judicial recognition of Americans' civil liberties.

American Colonization Society Organized in 1816 to encourage colonization of free blacks to Africa; West African nation of Liberia founded in 1822 to serve as a homeland for them.

"American exceptionalism" The belief that the United States has a special mission to serve as a refuge from tyranny, a symbol of freedom, and a model for the rest of the world.

American Federation of Labor Founded in 1881 as a federation of trade unions composed mostly of skilled, white, native-born workers; its long-term president was Samuel Gompers.

American System Program of internal improvements and protective tariffs promoted by Speaker of the House Henry Clay in his presidential campaign of 1824; his proposals formed the core of Whig ideology in the 1830s and 1840s.

Amistad Ship that transported slaves from one port in Cuba to another, seized by the slaves in 1839. They made their way northward to the United States, where the status of the slaves became the subject of a celebrated court case; eventually most were able to return to Africa.

Anarchism Belief that all institutions that exercise power over individuals, especially government, are illegitimate; it flourished among certain native-born individualists in the nineteenth century and radical immigrants in the early twentieth century.

Antietam, Battle of One of the bloodiest battles of the Civil War, fought to a standoff on September 17, 1862, in western Maryland.

Antifederalists Opponents of the Constitution who saw it as a limitation on individual and states' rights; their demands led to the addition of a Bill of Rights to the document.

Appomattox Courthouse, Virginia Site of the surrender of Confederate general Robert E. Lee to Union general Ulysses S. Grant on April 9, 1865, marking the end of the Civil War.

Arab Spring Revolutionary demonstrations and protests that swept the Middle East in 2011.

Army-McCarthy hearings Televised U.S. Senate hearings in 1954 on Senator Joseph McCarthy's charges of disloyalty in the army; his tactics contributed to his censure by the Senate.

Articles of Confederation First frame of government for the United States; in effect from 1781 to 1788, it provided for a weak central authority and was soon replaced by the Constitution.

Atlanta Compromise Speech to the Cotton States and International Exposition in 1895 by educator Booker T. Washington, the leading black spokesman of the day; black scholar W. E. B. Du Bois gave the speech its derisive name and criticized Washington for encouraging blacks to accommodate segregation and disenfranchisement.

Atlantic Charter Issued August 12, 1941, following meetings in Newfoundland between President Franklin D. Roosevelt and British prime minister Winston Churchill, the charter signaled the Allies' cooperation and stated their war aims.

Atlantic slave trade The systematic importation of African slaves from their native continent across the Atlantic Ocean to the New World, largely fuelled by rising demand for sugar, rice, coffee, and tobacco.

Atomic Energy Commission Created in 1946 to supervise peacetime uses of atomic energy.

Axis powers In World War II, the nations of Germany, Italy, and Japan.

Aztec Mesoamerican people who were conquered by the Spanish under Hernán Cortés, 1519–1528.

Baby boom Markedly higher birthrate in the years following World War II; led to the biggest demographic "bubble" in American history.

Bacon's Rebellion Unsuccessful 1676 revolt led by planter Nathaniel Bacon against Virginia governor William Berkeley's administration because of governmental corruption and because Berkeley had failed to protect settlers from Indian raids and did not allow them to occupy Indian lands.

Baker v. Carr **(1962)** U.S. Supreme Court decision that established the principle of "one man, one vote," that is, that legislative districts must be equal in population.

Bakke v. Regents of the University of California **(1978)** Case in which the U.S. Supreme Court ruled against the California university system's use of racial quotas in admissions but allowed the use of race as one factor in admissions decisions.

Balance of trade Ratio of imports to exports.

Bank of the United States Proposed by the first secretary of the treasury, Alexander Hamilton, the bank opened in 1791 and operated until 1811 to issue a uniform currency, make business loans, and collect tax monies. The Second Bank of the United States was chartered in 1816 but President Andrew Jackson vetoed the recharter bill in 1832.

Barbary pirates Plundering pirates off the Mediterranean coast of Africa; President Thomas Jefferson's refusal to pay them tribute to protect American ships sparked an undeclared naval war with North African nations, 1801–1805.

Barbed wire First practical fencing material for the Great Plains was invented in 1873 and rapidly spelled the end of the open range.

Bay of Pigs invasion Hoping to inspire a revolt against Fidel Castro, the CIA sent 1,500 Cuban exiles to invade their homeland on April 17, 1961, but the mission was a spectacular failure.

The Beats A term coined by Jack Kerouac for a small group of poets and writers who railed against 1950s mainstream culture.

Bill of Rights First ten amendments to the U.S. Constitution, adopted in 1791 to guarantee individual rights against infringement by the federal government.

Black Codes (1865–1866) Laws passed in southern states to restrict the rights of former slaves; to nullify the codes, Congress passed the Civil Rights Act of 1866 and the Fourteenth Amendment.

Black Legend Idea that the Spanish New World empire was more oppressive toward the Indians than other European empires; was used as a justification for English imperial expansion.

Black Power Post-1966 rallying cry of a more militant civil rights movement.

Bland-Allison Act (1878) Passed over President Rutherford B. Hayes's veto, the inflationary measure authorized the purchase each month of 2 to 4 million dollars' worth of silver for coinage.

"Bleeding Kansas" Violence between pro- and antislavery settlers in the Kansas Territory, 1856.

Boston Massacre Clash between British soldiers and a Boston mob, March 5, 1770, in which five colonists were killed.

Boston Tea Party On December 16, 1773, the Sons of Liberty, dressed as Indians, dumped hundreds of chests of tea into

Boston Harbor to protest the Tea Act of 1773, under which the British exported to the colonies millions of pounds of cheap—but still taxed—tea, thereby undercutting the price of smuggled tea and forcing payment of the tea duty.

Boxer Rebellion Chinese nationalist protest against Western commercial domination and cultural influence, 1900; a coalition of American, European, and Japanese forces put down the rebellion and reclaimed captured embassies in Peking (Beijing) within the year.

***Bracero* program** System agreed to by Mexican and American governments in 1942 under which tens of thousands of Mexicans entered the United States to work temporarily in agricultural jobs in the Southwest; lasted until 1964 and inhibited labor organization among farm workers since *braceros* could be deported at any time.

Brains trust Group of advisers—many of them academics—assembled by Franklin D. Roosevelt to recommend New Deal policies during the early months of his presidency.

Bretton Woods Town in New Hampshire and site of international agreement in 1944 by which the American dollar replaced the British pound as the most important international currency, and the World Bank and International Monetary Fund were created to promote rebuilding after World War II and to ensure that countries did not devalue their currencies.

Brook Farm Transcendentalist commune in West Roxbury, Massachusetts, populated from 1841 to 1847 principally by writers (Nathaniel Hawthorne, for one) and other intellectuals.

***Brown v. Board of Education of Topeka* (1954)** U.S. Supreme Court decision that struck down racial segregation in public education and declared "separate but equal" unconstitutional.

Bull Run, Battles of (First and Second Manassas) First land engagement of the Civil War took place on July 21, 1861, at Manassas Junction, Virginia, at which Union troops quickly retreated; one year later, on August 29–30, Confederates captured the federal supply depot and forced Union troops back to Washington.

Bunker Hill, Battle of First major battle of the Revolutionary War; it actually took place at nearby Breed's Hill, Massachusetts, on June 17, 1775.

"Burned-over district" Area of western New York strongly influenced by the revivalist fervor of the Second Great Awakening; Disciples of Christ and Mormons are among the many sects that trace their roots to the phenomenon.

Bush Doctrine President George W. Bush's foreign policy principle wherein the United States would launch a war on terrorism.

***Bush v. Gore* (2000)** U.S. Supreme Court case that determined the winner of the disputed 2000 presidential election.

Busing The means of transporting students via buses to achieve school integration in the 1970s.

Calvinism Doctrine of predestination expounded by Swiss theologian John Calvin in 1536; influenced the Puritan, Presbyterian, German and Dutch Reformed, and Huguenot churches in the colonies.

Camp David accords Peace agreement between the leaders of Israel and Egypt, brokered by President Jimmy Carter in 1978.

Caravel A fifteenth-century European ship capable of long-distance travel.

Carpetbaggers Derisive term for northern emigrants who participated in the Republican governments of the Reconstruction South.

Chancellorsville, Battle of Confederate general Robert E. Lee won his last major victory and General "Stonewall" Jackson died in this Civil War battle in northern Virginia on May 1–4, 1863.

Checks and balances A systematic balance to prevent any one branch of the national government from dominating the other two.

Chinese Exclusion Act (1882) Halted Chinese immigration to the United States.

Civil Rights Act of 1866 Along with the Fourteenth Amendment, guaranteed the rights of citizenship to former slaves.

Civil Rights Act of 1957 First federal civil rights law since Reconstruction; established the Civil Rights Commission and the Civil Rights Division of the Department of Justice.

Civil Rights Act of 1964 Outlawed discrimination in public accommodations and employment.

Civil Service Act of 1883 Established the Civil Service Commission and marked the end of the spoils system.

Closed shop Hiring requirement that all workers in a business must be union members.

Coercive Acts/Intolerable Acts (1774) Four parliamentary measures in reaction to the Boston Tea Party that forced payment for the tea, disallowed colonial trials of British soldiers, forced their quartering in private homes, and reduced the number of elected officials in Massachusetts.

Cold War Term for tensions, 1945–1989, between the Soviet Union and the United States, the two major world powers after World War II.

Collective bargaining The process of negotiations between an employer and a group of employees to regulate working conditions.

Columbian Exchange The transatlantic flow of goods and people that began with Columbus's voyages in 1492.

Common school Tax-supported state schools of the early nineteenth century open to all children.

Common Sense A pamphlet anonymously written by Thomas Paine in January 1776 that attacked the English principles of hereditary rule and monarchical government.

Commonwealth v. Hunt (1842) Landmark ruling of the Massachusetts Supreme Court establishing the legality of labor unions.

Communitarianism Social reform movement of the nineteenth century driven by the belief that by establishing small communities based on common ownership of property, a less competitive and individualistic society could be developed.

Compromise of 1850 Complex compromise devised by Senator Henry Clay that admitted California as a free state, included a stronger fugitive slave law, and delayed determination of the slave status of the New Mexico and Utah territories.

Compromise of 1877 Deal made by a Republican and Democratic special congressional commission to resolve the disputed presidential election of 1876; Republican Rutherford B. Hayes, who had lost the popular vote, was declared the winner in exchange for the withdrawal of federal troops from involvement in politics in the South, marking the end of Reconstruction.

Congress of Industrial Organizations (CIO) Umbrella organization of semiskilled industrial unions, formed in 1935 as the Committee for Industrial Organization and renamed in 1938.

Congress of Racial Equality (CORE) Civil rights organization started in 1942 and best known for its Freedom Rides, bus journeys challenging racial segregation in the South in 1961.

Conspicuous consumption Phrase referring to extravagant spending to raise social standing, coined by Thorstein Veblen in *The Theory of the Leisure Class* (1899).

Constitutional Convention Meeting in Philadelphia, May 25–September 17, 1787, of representatives from twelve colonies—excepting Rhode Island—to revise the existing Articles of Confederation; convention soon resolved to produce an entirely new constitution.

Containment General U.S. strategy in the Cold War that called for containing Soviet expansion; originally devised by U.S. diplomat George F. Kennan.

Continental army Army authorized by the Continental Congress in 1775 to fight the British; commanded by General George Washington.

Continental Congress Representatives of the colonies met first in Philadelphia in 1774 to formulate actions against British policies; the Second Continental Congress (1775–1789) conducted the war and adopted the Declaration of Independence and the Articles of Confederation.

Convict leasing System developed in the post–Civil War South that generated income for the states and satisfied planters' need for cheap labor by renting prisoners out; the convicts were often treated poorly.

Copperheads Republican term for northerners opposed to the Civil War; it derived from the name of a poisonous snake.

Coral Sea, Battle of the Fought on May 7–8, 1942, near the eastern coast of Australia, it was the first U.S. naval victory over Japan in World War II.

Cotton gin Invented by Eli Whitney in 1793, the machine separated cotton seed from cotton fiber, speeding cotton processing and making profitable the cultivation of the more hardy, but difficult to clean, short-staple cotton; led directly to the dramatic nineteenth-century expansion of slavery in the South.

Counterculture "Hippie" youth culture of the 1960s, which rejected the values of the dominant culture in favor of illicit drugs, communes, free sex, and rock music.

Court-packing plan President Franklin D. Roosevelt's failed 1937 attempt to increase the number of U.S. Supreme Court justices from nine to fifteen in order to save his Second New Deal programs from constitutional challenges.

Coverture Principle in English and American law that a married woman lost her legal identity, which became "covered" by that of her husband, who therefore controlled her person and the family's economic resources.

Crédit Mobilier scandal Millions of dollars in overcharges for building the Union Pacific Railroad were exposed; high officials of the Ulysses S. Grant administration were implicated but never charged.

Creoles (*Criollos* in Spanish) Persons born in the New World of European ancestry.

Cuban missile crisis Caused when the United States discovered Soviet offensive missile sites in Cuba in October 1962; the U.S.-Soviet confrontation was the Cold War's closest brush with nuclear war.

Cult of domesticity The nineteenth-century ideology of "virtue" and "modesty" as the qualities that were essential to proper womanhood.

Crop-lien system Merchants extended credit to tenants based on their future crops, but high interest rates and the uncertainties of farming often led to inescapable debts.

D-Day June 6, 1944, when an Allied amphibious assault landed on the Normandy coast and established a foothold in Europe, leading to the liberation of France from German occupation.

Dartmouth College v. Woodward (1819) U.S. Supreme Court upheld the original charter of the college against New Hampshire's attempt to alter the board of trustees; set precedent of support of contracts against state interference.

Dawes Act Law passed in 1887 meant to encourage adoption of white norms among Indians; broke up tribal holdings into small farms for Indian families, with the remainder sold to white purchasers.

Declaration of Independence Document adopted on July 4, 1776, that made the break with Britain official; drafted by a committee of the Second Continental Congress, including principal writer Thomas Jefferson.

Deindustrialization Term describing decline of manufacturing in old industrial areas in the late twentieth century as companies shifted production to low-wage centers in the South and West or in other countries.

Deism Enlightenment thought applied to religion; emphasized reason, morality, and natural law.

Democratic Party Established in 1828 and led by Andrew Jackson and Martin Van Buren, the party was a major opponent of the Whig Party until the Civil War; unlike the Whigs, Democrats believed government should adopt a hands-off approach toward the economy.

Democratic-Republican Societies Organizations created in the mid-1790s by opponents of the policies of the Washington administration and supporters of the French Revolution.

Department of Homeland Security Created to coordinate federal antiterrorist activity following the 2001 terrorist attacks on the World Trade Center and Pentagon.

Depression Period in which economic output declines sharply and unemployment rises; it applied especially to the Great Depression of the 1930s.

Depression of 1893 Worst depression of the nineteenth century, set off by a railroad failure, too much speculation on Wall Street, and low agricultural prices.

Disenfranchise To deprive of the right to vote; in the United States, exclusionary policies were used to deny groups, especially African-Americans and women, their voting rights.

Division of Powers The division of political power between the state and federal governments under the U.S. Constitution (also known as federalism).

Dixiecrats Deep South delegates who walked out of the 1948 Democratic National Convention in protest of the party's support for civil rights legislation and later formed the States' Rights Democratic (Dixiecrat) Party, which nominated Strom Thurmond of South Carolina for president.

Dollar Diplomacy A foreign policy initiative under President William Howard Taft that promoted the spread of American influence through loans and economic investments from American banks.

Dominion of New England Consolidation into a single colony of the New England colonies—and later New York and New Jersey—by royal governor Edmund Andros in 1686; dominion reverted to individual colonial governments three years later.

Dred Scott v. Sandford (1857) U.S. Supreme Court decision in which Chief Justice Roger B. Taney ruled that Congress could not prohibit slavery in the territories, on the grounds that such a prohibition would violate the Fifth Amendment rights of slaveholders, and that no black person could be a citizen of the United States.

Due-process clause Clause in the Fifth and the Fourteenth Amendments to the U.S. Constitution guaranteeing that states could not "deprive any person of life, liberty, or property, without due process of law."

Dust Bowl Great Plains counties where millions of tons of topsoil were blown away from parched farmland in the 1930s; massive migration of farm families followed.

Eighteenth Amendment (1919) Prohibition amendment that made illegal the manufacture, sale, or transportation of alcoholic beverages; repealed in 1933.

Ellis Island Reception center in New York Harbor through which most European immigrants to America were processed from 1892 to 1954.

Emancipation Proclamation (1863) President Abraham Lincoln issued a preliminary proclamation on September 22, 1862, freeing the slaves in areas under Confederate control as of January 1, 1863, the date of the final proclamation, which also authorized the enrollment of black soldiers into the Union army.

Embargo Act of 1807 Attempt to exert economic pressure by prohibiting all exports from the United States, instead of waging war in reaction to continued British impress-ment of American sailors; smugglers easily circumvented the embargo, and it was repealed two years later.

Emergency Banking Relief Act (1933) First New Deal measure that provided for reopening the banks under strict conditions and took the United States off the gold standard.

Emergency Immigration Act of 1921 Limited U.S. immigration to 3 percent of each foreign-born nationality in the 1910 census; three years later, Congress restricted immigration even further.

Encomienda System under which officers of the Spanish conquistadores gained ownership of Indian land.

Enlightenment Revolution in thought in the eighteenth century that emphasized reason and science over the authority of traditional religion.

Environmental Protection Agency (EPA) Created in 1970 during the first administration of President Richard M. Nixon to oversee federal pollution control efforts.

Equal Rights Amendment Amendment to guarantee equal rights for women, introduced in 1923 but not passed by Congress until 1972; it failed to be ratified by the states.

Era of Good Feelings Contemporary characterization of the administration of popular Republican president James Monroe, 1817–1825.

Erie Canal Most important and profitable of the canals of the 1820s and 1830s; stretched from Buffalo to Albany, New York, connecting the Great Lakes to the East Coast and making New York City the nation's largest port.

Espionage and Sedition Acts (1917–1918) Limited criticism of government leaders and policies by imposing fines and prison terms on those who opposed American participation in the First World War.

Eugenics "Science" of improving the human race by regulating who can bear children; flourished in early twentieth century and led to laws for involuntary sterilization of the "feeble-minded."

Ex parte Milligan (1866) Supreme Court case that declared it unconstitutional to bring accused persons before military tribunals where civil courts were operating.

Fair Deal Domestic reform proposals of the Truman administration; included civil rights legislation, national health insurance, and repeal of the Taft-Hartley Act, but only extensions of some New Deal programs were enacted.

Fair Employment Practices Commission Created in 1941 by executive order, the FEPC sought to eliminate racial discrimination in jobs; it possessed little power but represented a step toward civil rights for African-Americans.

Family wage Idea that male workers should earn a wage sufficient to enable them to support their entire family without their wives having to work outside the home.

Federalism A system of government in which power is divided between the central government and the states.

Federal Trade Commission Act (1914) Established the Federal Trade Commission to enforce existing antitrust laws that prohibited business combinations in restraint of trade.

The Federalist Collection of eighty-five essays that appeared in the New York press in 1787–1788 in support of the Constitution; written by Alexander Hamilton, James Madison, and John Jay and published under the pseudonym "Publius."

Federalist Party One of the two first national political parties; led by George Washington, John Adams, and Alexander Hamilton, it favored a strong central government.

Feminism Term that entered the lexicon in the early twentieth century to describe the movement for full equality for women, in political, social, and personal life.

Fifteenth Amendment Constitutional Amendment ratified in 1870, which prohibited states from discriminating in voting privileges on the basis of race.

"Fifty-four forty or fight" Democratic campaign slogan in the presidential election of 1844, urging that the northern border of Oregon be fixed at 54°40′ north latitude.

Filibuster In the nineteenth century, invasions of Central American countries launched privately by groups of Americans seeking to establish personal rule and spread slavery; in the twentieth century, term for the practice of members of the U.S. Senate delivering interminable speeches in order to prevent voting on legislation.

Fletcher v. Peck (1810) U.S. Supreme Court decision in which Chief Justice John Marshall upheld the initial fraudulent sale contracts in the Yazoo Fraud cases; it upheld the principle of sanctity of a contract.

Fordism Early twentieth-century term describing the economic system pioneered by Ford Motor Company based on high wages and mass consumption.

Fort McHenry Fort in Baltimore Harbor unsuccessfully bombarded by the British in September 1814; Francis Scott Key, a witness to the battle, was moved to write the words to "The Star-Spangled Banner."

Fort Sumter First battle of the Civil War, in which the federal fort in Charleston (South Carolina) Harbor was captured by the Confederates on April 14, 1861, after two days of shelling.

Four Freedoms Freedom of speech, freedom of worship, freedom from want, and freedom from fear.

Fourteen Points President Woodrow Wilson's 1918 plan for peace after World War I; at the Versailles peace conference, however, he failed to incorporate all of the points into the treaty.

Fourteenth Amendment (1868) Guaranteed rights of citizenship to former slaves, in words similar to those of the Civil Rights Act of 1866.

Franchise The right to vote.

"Free person of color" Negro or mulatto person not held in slavery; immediately before the Civil War, there were nearly a half million in the United States, split almost evenly between North and South.

Free Soil Party Formed in 1848 to oppose slavery in the territory acquired in the Mexican War; nominated Martin Van Buren for president in 1848. By 1854 most of the party's members had joined the Republican Party.

Free Speech Movement Founded in 1964 at the University of California at Berkeley by student radicals protesting restrictions on their right to distribute political publications.

Freedmen's Bureau Reconstruction agency established in 1865 to protect the legal rights of former slaves and to assist with their education, jobs, health care, and landowning.

Freedom Rides Bus journeys challenging racial segregation in the South in 1961.

French and Indian War Known in Europe as the Seven Years' War, the last (1755–1763) of four colonial wars fought between England and France for control of North America east of the Mississippi River.

Fugitive Slave Act of 1850 Gave federal government authority in cases involving runaway slaves; aroused considerable opposition in the North.

Fundamentalism Anti-modernist Protestant movement started in the early twentieth century that proclaimed the literal truth of the Bible; the name came from *The Fundamentals*, published by conservative leaders.

Gadsden Purchase (1853) Thirty thousand square miles in present-day Arizona and New Mexico bought by Congress from Mexico primarily for the Southern Pacific Railroad's transcontinental route.

Gag Rule Rule adopted by House of Representatives in 1836 prohibiting consideration of abolitionist petitions; opposition, led by former president John Quincy Adams, succeeded in having it repealed in 1844.

Geneva Accords (1954) A document that had promised elections to unify Vietnam and established the 17th Parallel demarcation line which divided North and South Vietnam.

Gentlemen's Agreement (1907) The United States would not exclude Japanese immigrants if Japan would voluntarily limit the number of immigrants coming to the United States.

Gettysburg, Battle of Fought in southern Pennsylvania, July 1–3, 1863; the Confederate defeat and the simultaneous loss at Vicksburg marked the military turning point of the Civil War.

Gibbons v. Ogden (1824) U.S. Supreme Court decision reinforcing the "commerce clause" (the federal government's right to regulate interstate commerce) of the Constitution; Chief Justice John Marshall ruled against the State of New York's granting of steamboat monopolies.

GI Bill of Rights (1944) The legislation that provided money for education and other benefits to military personnel returning from World War II.

Gideon v. Wainwright (1963) U.S. Supreme Court decision guaranteeing legal counsel for indigent felony defendants.

The Gilded Age Mark Twain and Charles Dudley Warner's 1873 novel, the title of which became the popular name for the period from the end of the Civil War to the turn of the century.

Glass-Steagall Act (Banking Act of 1933) Established the Federal Deposit Insurance Corporation and included banking reforms, some designed to control speculation. Repealed in 1999, opening the door to scandals involving banks and stock investment companies.

Globalization Term that became prominent in the 1990s to describe the rapid acceleration of international flows of commerce, financial resources, labor, and cultural products.

Glorious Revolution A coup in 1688 engineered by a small group of aristocrats that led to William of Orange taking the British throne in place of James II.

Gold standard Policy at various points in American history by which the value of a dollar is set at a fixed price in terms of gold (in the post–World War II era, for example, $35 per ounce of gold).

Good Neighbor Policy Proclaimed by President Franklin D. Roosevelt in his first inaugural address in 1933, it sought improved diplomatic relations between the United States and its Latin American neighbors.

Gospel of Wealth The idea proposed by Andrew Carnegie in 1889 that those who are wealthy have an obligation to use their resources to improve society.

Grandfather clause Loophole created by southern disfranchising legislatures of the 1890s for illiterate white males whose grandfathers had been eligible to vote in 1867.

Granger movement Political movement that grew out of the Patrons of Husbandry, an educational and social organization for farmers founded in 1867; the Grange had its greatest success in the Midwest of the 1870s, lobbying for government control of railroad and grain elevator rates and establishing farmers' cooperatives.

Great Awakening Fervent religious revival movement in the 1720s through the 1740s that was spread throughout the colonies by ministers like New England Congregationalist Jonathan Edwards and English revivalist George Whitefield.

Great Compromise (Connecticut Compromise) Settled the differences between the New Jersey and Virginia delegations to the Constitutional Convention by providing for a bicameral legislature, the upper house of which would have equal representation for each state and the lower house of which would be apportioned by population.

Great Depression Worst economic depression in American history; it was spurred by the stock market crash of 1929 and lasted until World War II.

Great Migration Large-scale migration of southern blacks during and after World War I to the North, where jobs had become available during the labor shortage of the war years.

Great Society Term coined by President Lyndon B. Johnson in his 1965 State of the Union address, in which he proposed legislation to address problems of voting rights, poverty, diseases, education, immigration, and the environment.

Greenback-Labor Party Formed in 1876 in reaction to economic depression, the party favored issuance of unsecured paper money to help farmers repay debts; the movement for free coinage of silver took the place of the greenback movement by the 1880s.

***Griswold v. Connecticut* (1965)** Supreme Court decision that, in overturning Connecticut law prohibiting the use of contraceptives, established a constitutional right to privacy.

Gulf of Tonkin resolution (1964) A resolution passed by Congress authorizing the president to take "all necessary measures to repel armed attack" in Vietnam.

Gulf War Military action in 1991 in which an international coalition led by the United States drove Iraq from Kuwait, which it had occupied the previous year.

Habeas corpus, Writ of An essential component of English common law and of the U.S. Constitution that guarantees that citizens may not be imprisoned without due process of law; literally means, "you may have the body"; suspended by President Lincoln during the Civil War and limited by President Bush after the attacks of September 11, 2001.

Hacienda Large-scale farm in the Spanish New World empire worked by Indian laborers.

Harlem Renaissance African-American literary and artistic movement of the 1920s centered in New York City's Harlem neighborhood; writers Langston Hughes, Jean Toomer, Zora Neale Hurston, and Countee Cullen were among those active in the movement.

Harpers Ferry, Virginia Site of abolitionist John Brown's failed raid on the federal arsenal, October 16–17, 1859; Brown became a martyr to his cause after his capture and execution.

Hart-Celler Act (1965) Eliminated the national origins quota system for immigration established by laws in 1921 and 1924; led to radical change in the origins of immigrants to the United States, with Asians and Latin Americans outnumbering Europeans.

Hartford Convention Meeting of New England Federalists on December 15, 1814, to protest the War of 1812; proposed seven constitutional amendments (limiting embargoes and changing requirements for officeholding, declaration of war, and admission of new states), but the war ended before Congress could respond.

Hawley-Smoot Tariff Act (1930) Raised tariffs to an unprecedented level and worsened the Great Depression by raising prices and discouraging foreign trade.

Haymarket affair Violence during an anarchist protest at Haymarket Square in Chicago on May 4, 1886; the deaths of eight, including seven policemen, led to the trial of eight anarchist leaders for conspiracy to commit murder.

Hessians German soldiers, most from Hesse-Cassel principality (hence, the name), paid to fight for the British in the Revolutionary War.

Holding company Investment company that holds controlling interest in the securities of other companies.

Homestead Act (1862) Authorized Congress to grant 160 acres of public land to a western settler, who had to live on the land for five years to establish title.

Homestead Strike Violent strike at the Carnegie Steel Company near Pittsburgh in 1892 that culminated in the defeat of the Amalgamated Association of Iron and Steel Workers, the first steelworkers' union.

House Un-American Activities Committee (HUAC) Formed in 1938 to investigate subversives in the government and holders of radical ideas more generally; best-known investigations were of Hollywood notables and of former State Department official Alger Hiss, who was accused in 1948 of espionage and Communist Party membership. Abolished in 1975.

Hundred Days Extraordinarily productive first three months of President Franklin D. Roosevelt's administration in which a special session of Congress enacted fifteen of his New Deal proposals.

Impeachment Bringing charges against a public official; for example, the House of Representatives can impeach a president for "treason, bribery, or other high crimes and misdemeanors" by majority vote, and after the trial the Senate can remove the president by a vote of two-thirds. Two presidents, Andrew Johnson and Bill Clinton, have been impeached and tried before the Senate; neither was convicted.

Implied powers Federal powers beyond those specifically enumerated in the U.S. Constitution; based on the "elastic clause" of Article I, Section 8, of the Constitution that allows Congress to enact laws that promote the "general welfare."

"In God We Trust" Phrase placed on all new U.S. currency as of 1954.

Indentured servant Settler who signed on for a temporary period of servitude to a master in exchange for passage to the New World; Virginia and Pennsylvania were largely peopled in the seventeenth and eighteenth centuries by English and German indentured servants.

Indian Removal Act (1830) Signed by President Andrew Jackson, the law permitted the negotiation of treaties to obtain the Indians' lands in exchange for their relocation to what would become Oklahoma.

Individualism Term that entered the language in the 1820s to describe the increasing emphasis on the pursuit of personal advancement and private fulfillment free of outside interference.

Industrial Workers of the World Radical union organized in Chicago in 1905 and nicknamed the Wobblies; its opposition to World War I led to its destruction by the federal government under the Espionage Act.

Inflation An economic condition in which prices rise continuously.

Insular Cases Series of cases between 1901 and 1904 in which the Supreme Court ruled that constitutional protection of individual rights did not fully apply to residents of "insular" territories acquired by the United States in the Spanish-American War, such as Puerto Rico and the Philippines.

Interstate Commerce Commission Reacting to the U.S. Supreme Court's ruling in *Wabash Railroad v. Illinois* (1886), Congress established the ICC to curb abuses in the railroad industry by regulating rates.

Iran-Contra affair Scandal of the second Reagan administration involving sales of arms to Iran in partial exchange for release of hostages in Lebanon and use of the arms money to aid the Contras in Nicaragua, which had been expressly forbidden by Congress.

Iraq War Military campaign in 2003 in which the United States, unable to gain approval by the United Nations, unilaterally occupied Iraq and removed dictator Saddam Hussein from power.

Iron Curtain Term coined by Winston Churchill to describe the Cold War divide between western Europe and the Soviet Union's eastern European satellites.

Isolationism The desire to avoid foreign entanglements that dominated the United States Congress in the 1930s; beginning in 1935, lawmakers passed a series of Neutrality Acts that banned travel on belligerents' ships and the sale of arms to countries at war.

Jamestown, Virginia Site in 1607 of the first permanent English settlement in the New World.

Japanese-American internment Policy adopted by the Roosevelt administration in 1942 under which 110,000 persons of Japanese descent, most of them American citizens, were removed from the West Coast and forced to spend most of World War II in internment camps; it was the largest violation of American civil liberties in the twentieth century.

Jay's Treaty Treaty with Britain negotiated in 1794 by Chief Justice John Jay; Britain agreed to vacate forts in the Northwest Territories, and festering disagreements (border with Canada, prewar debts, shipping claims) would be settled by commission.

Jim Crow Minstrel show character whose name became synonymous with racial segregation.

Kansas Exodus A migration in 1879 and 1880 by some 40,000–60,000 blacks to Kansas to escape the oppressive environment of the New South.

Kansas-Nebraska Act (1854) Law sponsored by Illinois senator Stephen A. Douglas to allow settlers in newly organized territories north of the Missouri border to decide the slavery issue for themselves; fury over the resulting repeal of the Missouri Compromise of 1820 led to violence in Kansas and to the formation of the Republican Party.

Kellogg-Briand Pact Representatives of sixty-two nations in 1928 signed the pact (also called the Pact of Paris) to outlaw war.

Keynesianism Economic theory derived from the writings of British economist John Maynard Keynes, which rejected the laissez-faire approach in favor of public spending to stimulate economic growth, even at the cost of federal deficits; dominated economic policies of administrations from the 1940s to the mid-1970s.

"King Cotton diplomacy" An attempt during the Civil War by the South to encourage British intervention by banning cotton exports.

King Philip's War Began in 1675 with an Indian uprising against white colonists. A multi-year conflict, the end result was broadened freedoms for white New Englanders and the dispossession of the region's Indians.

Knights of Labor Founded in 1869, the first national union lasted, under the leadership of Terence V. Powderly, only into the 1890s; supplanted by the American Federation of Labor.

Know-Nothing (American) Party Nativist, anti-Catholic third party organized in 1854 in reaction to large-scale German and Irish immigration; the party's only presidential candidate was Millard Fillmore in 1856.

Korean War Conflict touched off in 1950 when Communist North Korea invaded South Korea; fighting, largely by U.S. forces, continued until 1953.

Ku Klux Klan Organized in Pulaski, Tennessee, in 1866 to ffterrorize former slaves who voted and held political offices during Reconstruction; a revived organization in the 1910s and 1920s stressed white, Anglo-Saxon, fundamentalist Protestant supremacy; the Klan revived a third time to fight the civil rights movement of the 1950s and 1960s in the South.

Kyoto Protocol (1997) An international agreement that sought to combat global warming. To great controversy, the Bush administration announced in 2001 that it would not abide by the Kyoto Protocol.

Laissez-faire Term adopted from French, meaning "let people do as they choose," describing opposition to government action to regulate economic or personal behavior.

Land Ordinance of 1785 Directed surveying of the Northwest Territory into townships of thirty-six sections (square miles) each, the sale of the sixteenth section of which was to be used to finance public education.

League of Nations Organization of nations to mediate disputes and avoid war established after World War I as part of the Treaty of Versailles; President Woodrow Wilson's "Fourteen Points" speech to Congress in 1918 proposed the formation of the league, which the United States never joined.

Lend-Lease Act (1941) Permitted the United States to lend or lease arms and other supplies to the Allies, signifying increasing likelihood of American involvement in World War II.

Levittown Low-cost, mass-produced developments of suburban tract housing built by William Levitt after World War II on Long Island and elsewhere.

Lexington and Concord, Battle of The first shots fired in the Revolutionary War, on April 19, 1775, near Boston; approximately 100 minutemen and 250 British soldiers were killed.

Leyte Gulf, Battle of Largest sea battle in history, fought on October 25, 1944, and won by the United States off the Philippine island of Leyte; Japanese losses were so great that they could not rebound.

Liberalism Originally, political philosophy that emphasized the protection of liberty by limiting the power of government to interfere with the natural rights of citizens; in the twentieth century, belief in an activist government promoting greater social and economic equality.

Liberty Party Abolitionist political party that nominated James G. Birney for president in 1840 and 1844; merged with the Free Soil Party in 1848.

Lincoln-Douglas debates Series of senatorial campaign debates in 1858 focusing on the issue of slavery in the territories; held in Illinois between Republican Abraham Lincoln, who made a national reputation for himself, and incumbent Democratic senator Stephen A. Douglas, who managed to hold onto his seat.

Little Bighorn, Battle of Most famous battle of the Great Sioux War took place in 1876 in the Montana Territory; combined Sioux and Cheyenne warriors massacred a vastly outnumbered U.S. Cavalry commanded by Lieutenant Colonel George Armstrong Custer.

***Lochner v. New York* (1905)** Decision by Supreme Court overturning a New York law establishing a limit on the number of hours per week bakers could be compelled to work; "Lochnerism" became a way of describing the liberty of contract jurisprudence, which opposed all governmental intervention in the economy.

Long Telegram A telegram by American diplomat George Kennan in 1946 outlining his views of the Soviet Union that eventually inspired the policy of containment.

Louisiana Purchase President Thomas Jefferson's 1803 purchase from France of the important port of New Orleans and 828,000 square miles west of the Mississippi River to the Rocky Mountains; it more than doubled the territory of the United States at a cost of only $15 million.

Loyalists Colonists who remained loyal to Great Britain during the War of Independence.

Lusitania British passenger liner sunk by a German U-boat, May 7, 1915, creating a diplomatic crisis and public outrage at the loss of 128 Americans (roughly 10 percent of the total aboard); Germany agreed to pay reparations, and the United States waited two more years to enter World War I.

Lyceum movement Founded in 1826, the movement promoted adult public education through lectures and performances.

Lynching Practice, particularly widespread in the South between 1890 and 1940, in which persons (usually black) accused of a crime were murdered by mobs before standing trial. Lynchings often took place before large crowds, with law enforcement authorities not intervening.

Manhattan Project Secret American program during World War II to develop an atomic bomb; J. Robert Oppenheimer led the team of physicists at Los Alamos, New Mexico.

Manifest Destiny Phrase first used in 1845 to urge annexation of Texas; used thereafter to encourage American settlement of European colonial and Indian lands in the Great Plains and the West and, more generally, as a justification for American empire.

***Marbury v. Madison* (1803)** First U.S. Supreme Court decision to declare a federal law—the Judiciary Act of 1801—unconstitutional.

March on Washington Civil rights demonstration on August 28, 1963, where the Reverend Martin Luther King Jr., gave his "I Have a Dream" speech on the steps of the Lincoln Memorial.

Marshall Plan U.S. program for the reconstruction of post–World War II Europe through massive aid to former enemy nations as well as allies; proposed by General George C. Marshall in 1947.

Massive resistance In reaction to the *Brown* decision of 1954, effort by southern states to defy federally mandated school integration.

Maya Pre-Columbian society in Mesoamerica before about A.D. 900.

Mayflower Compact Signed in 1620 aboard the *Mayflower* before the Pilgrims landed at Plymouth, the document committed the group to majority-rule government.

McCarran Internal Security Act (1950) Passed over President Harry S. Truman's veto, the law required registration of American Communist Party members, denied them passports, and allowed them to be detained as suspected subversives.

McCarthyism Post–World War II Red Scare focused on the fear of Communists in U.S. government positions; peaked during the Korean War; most closely associated with Joseph McCarthy, a major instigator of the hysteria.

***McCulloch v. Maryland* (1819)** U.S. Supreme Court decision in which Chief Justice John Marshall, holding that Maryland could not tax the Second Bank of the United States, supported the authority of the federal government versus the states.

McNary-Haugen bill Vetoed by President Calvin Coolidge in 1927 and 1928, the bill to aid farmers would have artificially raised agricultural prices by selling surpluses overseas for low prices and selling the reduced supply in the United States for higher prices.

Meat Inspection Act (1906) Passed largely in reaction to Upton Sinclair's *The Jungle*, the law set strict standards of cleanliness in the meat packing industry.

Medicaid Great Society program established in 1965 that provided free medical care to the poor.

Medicare Key component of Great Society of Lyndon B. Johnson; government program created in 1965 to pay medical costs of elderly and disabled Americans.

Mercantilism Policy of Great Britain and other imperial ffpowers of regulating the economies of colonies to benefit the mother country.

Mestizo Spanish word for person of mixed Native American and European ancestry.

Mexican War Controversial war with Mexico for control of California and New Mexico, 1846–1848; the Treaty of Guadalupe Hidalgo fixed the border at the Rio Grande and extended the United States to the Pacific coast, annexing more than a half- million square miles of Mexican territory.

Midway, Battle of Decisive American victory near Midway Island in the South Pacific on June 4, 1942; the Japanese navy never recovered its superiority over the U.S. navy.

Military-industrial complex The concept of "an immense military establishment" combined with a "permanent arms industry," which President Eisenhower warned against in his 1961 Farewell Address.

Mill girls Women who worked at textile mills during the Industrial Revolution who were enjoyed new freedoms and independence not seen before.

Minstrel show Blackface vaudeville entertainment popular in the decades surrounding the Civil War.

***Miranda v. Arizona* (1966)** U.S. Supreme Court decision required police to advise persons in custody of their rights to legal counsel and against self-incrimination.

Missouri Compromise Deal proposed by Kentucky senator Henry Clay in 1820 to resolve the slave/free imbalance in Congress that would result from Missouri's admission as a slave state; Maine's admission as a free state offset Missouri, and slavery was prohibited in the remainder of the Louisiana Territory north of the southern border of Missouri.

Molly Maguires Secret organization of Irish coal miners that used violence to intimidate mine officials in the 1870s.

***Monitor* and *Merrimac*, Battle of the** First engagement between ironclad ships; fought at Hampton Roads, Virginia, on March 9, 1862.

Monroe Doctrine President James Monroe's declaration to Congress on December 2, 1823, that the American continents would be thenceforth closed to European colonization, and that the United States would not interfere in European affairs.

Montgomery bus boycott Sparked by Rosa Parks's arrest on December 1, 1955, for refusing to surrender her seat to a white passenger, a successful year-long boycott protesting segregation on city buses; led by the Reverend Martin Luther King Jr.

Moral Majority Televangelist Jerry Falwell's political lobbying organization, the name of which became synonymous with the Religious Right—conservative evangelical Protestants who helped ensure President Ronald Reagan's 1980 victory.

Mormons Founded in 1830 by Joseph Smith, the sect (officially, the Church of Jesus Christ of Latter-day Saints) was a product of the intense revivalism of the "burned-over district" of New York; Smith's successor Brigham Young led 15,000 followers to Utah in 1847 to escape persecution.

Muckrakers Writers who exposed corruption and abuses in politics, business, meatpacking, child labor, and more, primarily in the first decade of the twentieth century; their popular books and magazine articles spurred public interest in reform.

Mugwumps Reform wing of the Republican Party that supported Democrat Grover Cleveland for president in 1884 over Republican James G. Blaine, whose influence peddling had been revealed in the Mulligan letters of 1876.

Multiculturalism Term that became prominent in the 1990s to describe a growing emphasis on group racial and ethnic identity and demands that jobs, education, and politics reflect the increasingly diverse nature of American society.

***Munn v. Illinois* (1877)** U.S. Supreme Court ruling that upheld a Granger law allowing the state to regulate grain elevators.

NAFTA Approved in 1993, the North American Free Trade Agreement with Canada and Mexico allowed goods to travel across their borders free of tariffs; critics argued that American workers would lose their jobs to cheaper Mexican labor.

Nat Turner Rebellion Most important slave uprising in nineteenth-century America, led by a slave preacher who, with his followers, killed about sixty white persons in Southampton County, Virginia, in 1831.

National Association for the Advancement of Colored People (NAACP) Founded in 1910, this civil rights organization brought lawsuits against discriminatory practices and published *The Crisis*, a journal edited by African-American scholar W. E. B. Du Bois.

National Defense Education Act (1958) Passed in reaction to America's perceived inferiority in the space race; encouraged education in science and modern languages through student loans, university research grants, and aid to public schools.

National Industrial Recovery Act (1933) Passed on the last of the Hundred Days, it created public-works jobs through the Federal Emergency Relief Administration and established a system of self-regulation for industry through the National Recovery Administration, which was ruled unconstitutional in 1935.

National Organization for Women Founded in 1966 by writer Betty Friedan and other feminists, NOW pushed for abortion rights, nondiscrimination in the workplace, and other forms of equality for women.

National Road First federal interstate road, built between 1811 and 1838 and stretching from Cumberland, Maryland, to Vandalia, Illinois.

National Security Act (1947) Authorized the reorganization of government to coordinate military branches and security agencies; created the National Security Council, the Central Intelligence Agency, and the National Military Establishment (later renamed the Department of Defense).

National Youth Administration Created in 1935 as part of the Works Progress Administration, it employed millions of youths who had left school.

Nativism Anti-immigrant and anti-Catholic feeling especially prominent in the 1830s through the 1850s; the largest group was New York's Order of the Star-Spangled Banner, which expanded into the American (Know-Nothing) Party in 1854.

Naval stores Tar, pitch, and turpentine made from pine resin and used in shipbuilding; an important industry in the southern colonies, especially North Carolina.

Navigation Acts Passed by the English Parliament to control colonial trade and bolster the mercantile system, 1650–1775; enforcement of the acts led to growing resentment by colonists.

Neutrality Acts Series of laws passed between 1935 and 1939 to keep the United States from becoming involved in war by prohibiting American trade and travel to warring nations.

New Deal Franklin D. Roosevelt's campaign promise, in his speech to the Democratic National Convention of 1932, to combat the Great Depression with a "new deal for the American people"; the phrase became a catchword for his ambitious plan of economic programs.

New Freedom Democrat Woodrow Wilson's political slogan in the presidential campaign of 1912; Wilson wanted to improve the banking system, lower tariffs, and, by breaking up monopolies, give small businesses freedom to compete.

New Frontier John F. Kennedy's program, stymied by a Republican Congress and his abbreviated term; his successor Lyndon B. Johnson had greater success with many of the same concepts.

New Harmony Founded in Indiana by British industrialist Robert Owen in 1825, the short-lived New Harmony Community of Equality was one of the few nineteenth-century communal experiments not based on religious ideology.

New Left Radical youth protest movement of the 1960s, named by leader Tom Hayden to distinguish it from the Old (Marxist-Leninist) Left of the 1930s.

New Nationalism Platform of the Progressive Party and slogan of former president Theodore Roosevelt in the presidential campaign of 1912; stressed government activism, including regulation of trusts, conservation, and recall of state court decisions that had nullified progressive programs.

New Orleans, Battle of Last battle of the War of 1812, fought on January 8, 1815, weeks after the peace treaty was signed but prior to the news reaching America; General Andrew Jackson led the victorious American troops.

New South *Atlanta Constitution* editor Henry W. Grady's 1886 term for the prosperous post–Civil War South he envisioned: democratic, industrial, urban, and free of nostalgia for the defeated plantation South.

Nineteenth Amendment (1920) Granted women the right to vote.

Ninety-Five Theses The list of moral grievances against the Catholic Church by Martin Luther, a German priest, in 1517.

Nisei Japanese-Americans; literally, "second generation."

Normalcy Word coined by future president Warren G. Harding as part of a 1920 campaign speech—"not nostrums, but normalcy"—signifying public weariness with Woodrow Wilson's internationalism and domestic reforms.

North Atlantic Treaty Organization (NATO) Alliance founded in 1949 by ten western European nations, the United States, and Canada to deter Soviet expansion in Europe.

Northwest Ordinance of 1787 Created the Northwest Territory (area north of the Ohio River and west of Pennsylvania), established conditions for self-government and statehood, included a Bill of Rights, and permanently prohibited slavery.

Nullification Concept of invalidation of a federal law within the borders of a state; first expounded in Thomas Jefferson's draft of Kentucky resolution against Alien and Sedition Acts (1798); cited by South Carolina in its Ordinance of Nullification (1832) of the Tariff of Abominations, used by southern states to explain their secession from the Union (1861), and cited again by southern states to oppose the *Brown v. Board of Education* decision (1954).

Occupy Wall Street A grassroots movement in 2011 against growing economic inequality, declining opportunity, and the depredations of Wall Street banks.

Office of Price Administration Created in 1941 to control wartime inflation and price fixing resulting from shortages of many consumer goods, the OPA imposed wage and price freezes and administered a rationing system.

Okies Displaced farm families from the Oklahoma dust bowl who migrated to California during the 1930s in search of jobs.

Oneida Community Utopian community founded in 1848; the Perfectionist religious group practiced "complex marriage" under leader John Humphrey Noyes.

OPEC Organization of Petroleum Exporting Countries.

Open Door Policy In hopes of protecting the Chinese market for U.S. exports, Secretary of State John Hay demanded in 1899 that Chinese trade be open to all nations.

Open shop Situation in which union membership is not a condition of employment in a factory or other business.

Operation Dixie CIO's largely ineffective post–World War II campaign to unionize southern workers.

Oregon Trail Route of wagon trains bearing settlers from Independence, Missouri, to the Oregon Country in the 1840s through the 1860s.

Ostend Manifesto Memorandum written in 1854 from Ostend, Belgium, by the U.S. ministers to England, France, and Spain recommending purchase or seizure of Cuba in order to increase the United States' slaveholding territory.

Panic of 1819 Financial collapse brought on by sharply falling cotton prices, declining demand for American exports, and reckless western land speculation.

Panic of 1837 Beginning of major economic depression lasting about six years; touched off by a British financial crisis and made worse by falling cotton prices, credit and currency problems, and speculation in land, canals, and railroads.

Panic of 1857 Beginning of economic depression lasting about two years and brought on by falling grain prices and a weak financial system; the South was largely protected by international demand for its cotton.

Panic of 1873 Onset of severe six-year depression marked by bank failures and railroad and insurance bankruptcies.

Peace of Paris Signed on September 3, 1783, the treaty ending the Revolutionary War and recognizing American independence from Britain also established the border between Canada and the United States, fixed the western border at the Mississippi River, and ceded Florida to Spain.

Pendleton Civil Service Act (1883) Established the Civil Service Commission and marked the end of the spoils system.

Pentagon Papers Informal name for the Defense Department's secret history of the Vietnam conflict; leaked to the press by former official Daniel Ellsberg and published in the *New York Times* in 1971.

Pequot War An armed conflict in 1637 that led to the destruction of one of New England's most powerful Indian groups.

"Perfectionism" The idea that social ills once considered incurable could in fact be eliminated, popularized by the religious revivalism of the nineteenth century.

"Pet banks" Local banks that received deposits while the charter of the Bank of the United States was about to expire in 1836. The choice of these banks was influenced by political and personal connections.

Philippine War American military campaign that suppressed the movement for Philippine independence after the Spanish-American War; America's death toll was over 4,000 and the Philippines' was far higher.

Pilgrims Puritan Separatists who broke completely with the Church of England and sailed to the New World aboard the *Mayflower*, founding Plymouth Colony on Cape Cod in 1620.

Pinckney's Treaty Treaty with Spain negotiated by Thomas Pinckney in 1795; established United States boundaries at the Mississippi River and the thirty-first parallel and allowed open transportation on the Mississippi.

Plantation An early word for a colony, a settlement "planted" from abroad among an alien population in Ireland or the New World. Later, a large agricultural enterprise that used unfree labor to produce a crop for the world market.

Planter In the antebellum South, the owner of a large farm worked by twenty or more slaves.

Platt Amendment (1901) Amendment to Cuban constitution that reserved the United States' right to intervene in Cuban affairs and forced newly independent Cuba to host American naval bases on the island.

***Plessy v. Ferguson* (1896)** U.S. Supreme Court decision supporting the legality of Jim Crow laws that permitted or required "separate but equal" facilities for blacks and whites.

Poll tax Tax that must be paid in order to be eligible to vote; used as an effective means of disenfranchising black citizens after Reconstruction, since they often could not afford even a modest fee.

Popular Front A period during the mid-1930s when the Communist Party sought to ally itself with socialists and New Dealers in movements for social change, urging reform of the capitalist system rather than revolution.

Popular sovereignty Allowed settlers in a disputed territory to decide the slavery issue for themselves; program most closely associated with Senator Stephen A. Douglas of Illinois.

Populist Party Founded in 1892, it advocated a variety of reform issues, including free coinage of silver, income tax, postal savings, regulation of railroads, and direct election of U.S. senators.

Port Huron Statement (1962) A manifesto by Students for a Democratic Society that criticized institutions ranging from political parties to corporations, unions, and the military-industrial complex, while offering a new vision of social change.

Potsdam Conference Last meeting of the major Allied powers, the conference took place outside Berlin from July 17 to August 2, 1945; United States president Harry Truman, Soviet dictator Joseph Stalin, and British prime minister Clement Attlee finalized plans begun at Yalta.

Proclamation of Amnesty and Reconstruction President Lincoln's proposal for reconstruction, issued in 1863, allowed southern states to rejoin the Union if 10 percent of the 1860 electorate signed loyalty pledges, accepted emancipation, and had received presidential pardons.

Proclamation of 1763 Royal directive issued after the French and Indian War prohibiting settlement, surveys, and land grants west of the Appalachian Mountains; caused considerable resentment among colonists hoping to move west.

Progressive Party Created when former president Theodore Roosevelt broke away from the Republican Party to run for president again in 1912; the party supported progressive reforms similar to the Democrats but stopped short of seeking to eliminate trusts. Also the name of party backing Robert La Follette for president in 1924.

Progressivism Broad-based reform movement, 1900–1917, that sought governmental action in solving problems in many areas of American life, including education, public health, the economy, the environment, labor, transportation, and politics.

Proposition 13 Measure approved by California voters in 1978 prohibiting future increases in property taxes; marked beginning of "tax revolt" as major political impulse.

Public sphere The world of political organization and debate in private associations and publications outside the control of government.

Pueblo Revolt Uprising in 1680 in which Pueblo Indians temporarily drove Spanish colonists out of modern-day New Mexico.

Pullman Strike Strike against the Pullman Palace Car Company in the company town of Pullman, Illinois, on May 11, 1894, by the American Railway Union under Eugene V. Debs; the strike was crushed by court injunctions and federal troops two months later.

Pure Food and Drug Act (1906) First law to regulate manufacturing of food and medicines; prohibited dangerous additives and inaccurate labeling.

Puritans English religious group that sought to purify the Church of England; founded the Massachusetts Bay Colony under John Winthrop in 1630.

Quakers (Society of Friends) Religious group in England and America whose members believed all persons possessed the "inner light" or spirit of God; they were early proponents of abolition of slavery and equal rights for women.

Radical Republicans Group within the Republican Party in the 1850s and 1860s that advocated strong resistance to the expansion of slavery, opposition to compromise with the South in the secession crisis of 1860–1861, emancipation and arming of black soldiers during the Civil War, and equal civil and political rights for blacks during Reconstruction.

Railroad Strike of 1877 Interstate strike, crushed by federal troops, which resulted in extensive property damage and many deaths.

Reaganomics Popular name for President Ronald Reagan's philosophy of "supply side" economics, which combined tax cuts with an unregulated marketplace.

Reconquista The "reconquest" of Spain from the Moors completed by King Ferdinand and Queen Isabella in 1492.

Reconstruction Act (1867) Established temporary military governments in ten Confederate states—excepting Tennessee—and required that the states ratify the Fourteenth Amendment and permit freedmen to vote.

Reconstruction Finance Corporation Federal program established in 1932 under President Herbert Hoover to loan money to banks and other institutions to help them avert bankruptcy.

Red Scare Fear among many Americans after World War I of Communists in particular and noncitizens in general, a reaction to the Russian Revolution, mail bombs, strikes, and riots.

Redeemers Conservative white Democrats, many of them planters or businessmen, who reclaimed control of the South following the end of Reconstruction.

Regulators Groups of backcountry Carolina settlers who protested colonial policies.

Republican motherhood The ideology that emerged as a result of American independence where women played an indispensible role by training future citizens.

Republican Party Organized in 1854 by antislavery Whigs, Democrats, and Free Soilers in response to the passage of the Kansas-Nebraska Act; nominated John C. Frémont for president in 1856 and Abraham Lincoln in 1860; also the name of the party formed by Thomas Jefferson and James Madison in the 1790s.

Republicanism Political theory in eighteenth-century England and America that celebrated active participation in public life by economically independent citizens as central to freedom.

Revolution of 1800 First time that an American political party surrendered power to the opposition party; Jefferson, a Republican, had defeated incumbent Adams, a Federalist, for president.

Right-to-work State laws enacted to prevent imposition of the closed shop; any worker, whether or not a union member, could be hired.

Roe v. Wade **(1973)** U.S. Supreme Court decision requiring states to permit first-trimester abortions.

Roosevelt Corollary (1904) President Theodore Roosevelt announced in what was essentially a corollary to the Monroe Doctrine that the United States could intervene militarily to prevent interference from European powers in the Western Hemisphere.

Rough Riders The first U.S. Volunteer Cavalry, led in battle in the Spanish- American War by Theodore Roosevelt; they were victorious in their only battle near Santiago, Cuba, and Roosevelt used the notoriety to aid his political career.

Sacco-Vanzetti case A case held during the 1920s in which two Italian-American anarchists were found guilty and executed for a crime in which there was very little evidence linking them to the particular crime.

Salem witch trials A crisis of trials and executions in Salem, Massachusetts in 1692 that resulted from anxiety over witchcraft.

Santa Fe Trail Beginning in the 1820s, a major trade route from St. Louis, Missouri, to Santa Fe, New Mexico Territory.

Saratoga, Battle of Major defeat of British general John Burgoyne and more than 5,000 British troops at Saratoga, New York, on October 17, 1777.

Scalawags Southern white Republicans—some former Unionists—who supported Reconstruction governments.

Schenck v. U.S. **(1919)** U.S. Supreme Court decision upholding the wartime Espionage and Sedition Acts; in the opinion he wrote for the case, Justice Oliver Wendell Holmes set the now-familiar "clear and present danger" standard.

Scientific management Management campaign to improve worker efficiency using measurements like "time and motion" studies to achieve greater productivity; introduced by Frederick Winslow Taylor in 1911.

Scopes trial (1925) Trial of John Scopes, Tennessee teacher accused of violating state law prohibiting teaching of the theory of evolution; it became a nationally celebrated confrontation between religious fundamentalism and civil liberties.

Scottsboro case (1931) In overturning verdicts against nine black youths accused of raping two white women, the U.S. Supreme Court established precedents in *Powell v. Alabama* (1932), that adequate counsel must be appointed in capital cases, and in *Norris v. Alabama* (1935), that African-Americans cannot be excluded from juries.

Second American Revolution The transformation of American government and society brought about by the Civil War.

Second Great Awakening Religious revival movement of the early decades of the nineteenth century, in reaction to the growth of secularism and rationalist religion; began the predominance of the Baptist and Methodist churches.

Second Great Migration The movement of black migrants from the rural South to the cities of the North and West, which occurred from 1941 through World War II, that dwarfed the Great Migration of World War I.

Segregation Policy of separating persons on the basis of race in schools, transportation, and other public facilities; *de facto* segregation refers to social customs that accomplish this, *de jure* segregation to laws requiring it.

Seneca Falls Convention First women's rights meeting and the genesis of the women's suffrage movement; held in July 1848 in a church in Seneca Falls, New York, organized by Elizabeth Cady Stanton and Lucretia Coffin Mott.

"Separate but equal" Principle underlying legal racial segregation, upheld in *Plessy v. Ferguson* (1896) and struck down in *Brown v. Board of Education* (1954).

Separation of Powers Feature of the U.S. Constitution, sometimes called "checks and balances," in which power is divided between executive, legislative, and judicial branches of the national government so that no one can dominate the other two and endanger citizens' liberties.

Servicemen's Readjustment Act (1944) The "GI Bill of Rights" provided money for education and other benefits to military personnel returning from World War II.

Settlement houses Late-nineteenth-century movement to offer a broad array of social services in urban immigrant neighborhoods; Chicago's Hull House was one of hundreds of settlement houses that operated by the early twentieth century.

Seventeenth Amendment (1913) Progressive reform that required U.S. senators to be elected directly by voters; previously, senators were chosen by state legislatures.

Shakers Founded by Mother Ann Lee in England, the United Society of Believers in Christ's Second Appearing settled in Watervliet, New York, in 1774 and subsequently established eighteen additional communes in the Northeast, Indiana, and Kentucky.

Sharecropping Type of farm tenancy that developed after the Civil War in which landless workers—often former slaves—farmed land in exchange for farm supplies and a share of the crop.

Shays's Rebellion (1787) Massachusetts farmer Daniel Shays and 1,200 compatriots, seeking debt relief through issuance of paper currency and lower taxes, attempted to prevent courts from seizing property from indebted farmers.

Sherman Antitrust Act (1890) First law to restrict monopolistic trusts and business combinations; extended by the Clayton Antitrust Act of 1914.

Sherman Silver Purchase Act (1890) In replacing and extending the provisions of the Bland-Allison Act of 1878, it increased the amount of silver periodically bought for coinage.

Single tax Concept of taxing only landowners as a remedy for poverty, promulgated by Henry George in *Progress and Poverty* (1879).

Sit-down strikes Tactic adopted by labor unions in the mid- and late 1930s, whereby striking workers refused to leave factories, making production impossible; proved highly effective in the organizing drive of the Congress of Industrial Organizations.

Sit-ins Tactic adopted by young civil rights activists, beginning in 1960, of demanding service at lunch counters or public accommodations and refusing to leave if denied access; marked the beginning of the most militant phase of the civil rights struggle.

Sixteenth Amendment (1913) Legalized the federal income tax.

***Smith v. Allwright* (1944)** U.S. Supreme Court decision that outlawed all-white Democratic Party primaries in Texas.

"Social contract" In leading industries, labor and management hammered out what has been called a new "social contract." Unions signed long-term agreements that left decisions regarding capital investment, plant location, and output in management's hands, and they agreed to try to prevent unauthorized "wildcat" strikes.

Social Darwinism Application of Charles Darwin's theory of natural selection to society; used the concept of the "survival of the fittest" to justify class distinctions and to explain poverty.

Social Gospel Preached by liberal Protestant clergymen in the late nineteenth and early twentieth centuries; advocated the application of Christian principles to social problems generated by industrialization.

Social Security Act (1935) Created the Social Security system with provisions for a retirement pension, unemployment insurance, disability insurance, and public assistance (welfare).

Socialist Party Political party demanding public ownership of major economic enterprises in the United States as well as reforms like recognition of labor unions and women's suffrage; reached peak of influence in 1912 when presidential candidate Eugene V. Debs received over 900,000 votes.

Sons of Liberty Organizations formed by Samuel Adams, John Hancock, and other radicals in response to the Stamp Act.

South Carolina Exposition and Protest Written in 1828 by Vice-President John C. Calhoun of South Carolina to protest the so-called Tariff of Abominations, which seemed to favor northern industry; introduced the concept of state interposition and became the basis for South Carolina's Nullification Doctrine of 1833.

Southeast Asia Treaty Organization (SEATO) Pact among mostly Western nations signed in 1954; designed to deter Communist expansion and cited as a justification for U.S. involvement in Vietnam.

Southern Christian Leadership Conference (SCLC) Civil rights organization founded in 1957 by the Reverend Martin Luther King Jr., and other civil rights leaders.

"Southern Manifesto" (1956) A document that repudiated the Supreme Court decision in *Brown v. Board of Education* and supported the campaign against racial integration in public places.

Spoils system The term—meaning the filling of federal government jobs with persons loyal to the party of the president—originated in Andrew Jackson's first term.

Sputnik First artificial satellite to orbit the earth; launched October 4, 1957, by the Soviet Union.

Stagflation A combination of stagnant economic growth and high inflation present during the 1970s.

Stalwarts Conservative Republican Party faction during the presidency of Rutherford B. Hayes, 1877–1881; led by Senator Roscoe B. Conkling of New York, Stalwarts opposed civil service reform and favored a third term for President Ulysses S. Grant.

Stamp Act (1765) Parliament required that revenue stamps be affixed to all colonial printed matter, documents, and playing cards; the Stamp Act Congress met to formulate a response, and the act was repealed the following year.

Standard Oil Company Founded in 1870 by John D. Rockefeller in Cleveland, Ohio, it soon grew into the nation's first industry-dominating trust; the Sherman Antitrust Act (1890) was enacted in part to combat abuses by Standard Oil.

Staple crop Important cash crop, for example, cotton or tobacco.

Steamboats Paddlewheelers that could travel both up- and down-river in deep or shallow waters; they became commercially viable early in the nineteenth century and soon developed into America's first inland freight and passenger service network.

Stono Rebellion A slave uprising in 1739 in South Carolina that led to a severe tightening of the slave code and the temporary imposition of a prohibitive tax on imported slaves.

Strategic Defense Initiative ("Star Wars") Defense Department's plan during the Reagan administration to build a system to destroy incoming missiles in space.

Student Nonviolent Coordinating Committee (SNCC) Founded in 1960 to coordinate civil rights sit-ins and other forms of grassroots protest.

Students for a Democratic Society (SDS) Major organization of the New Left, founded at the University of Michigan in 1960 by Tom Hayden and Al Haber.

Sugar Act (Revenue Act of 1764) Parliament's tax on refined sugar and many other colonial products.

Taft-Hartley Act (1947) Passed over President Harry Truman's veto, the law contained a number of provisions to weaken labor unions, including the banning of closed shops.

Tariff Federal tax on imported goods.

Tariff of Abominations (Tariff of 1828) Taxed imported goods at a very high rate; aroused strong opposition in the South.

Tariff of 1816 First true protective tariff, intended to protect certain American goods against foreign competition.

Tax Reform Act (1986) Lowered federal income tax rates to 1920s levels and eliminated many loopholes.

Tea Party A grassroots Republican movement, named for the Boston Tea Party of the 1770s and developed in 2009, that opposed the Obama administration's sweeping legislative enactments and advocated for a more stringent immigration policy.

Teapot Dome Harding administration scandal in which Secretary of the Interior Albert B. Fall profited from secret leasing to private oil companies of government oil reserves at Teapot Dome, Wyoming, and Elk Hills, California.

Tennessee Valley Authority Created in 1933 to control flooding in the Tennessee River valley, provide work for the region's unemployed, and produce inexpensive electric power for the region.

Tenure of Office Act (1867) Required the president to obtain Senate approval to remove any official whose appointment had also required Senate approval; President Andrew Johnson's violation of the law by firing Secretary of War Edwin Stanton led to Johnson's impeachment.

Tet Offensive Surprise attack by the Viet Cong and North Vietnamese during the Vietnamese New Year of 1968; turned American public opinion strongly against the war in Vietnam.

Thirteenth Amendment Constitutional amendment adopted in 1865 that irrevocably abolished slavery throughout the United States.

Three-fifths clause A provision signed into the Constitution in 1787 that three-fifths of the slave population would be counted in determining each state's representation in the House of Representatives and its electoral votes for president.

Three Mile Island Nuclear power plant near Harrisburg, Pennsylvania, site of 1979 accident that released radioactive steam into the air; public reaction ended the nuclear power industry's expansion.

Title IX Part of the Educational Amendments Act of 1972 that banned gender discrimination in higher education.

Tonkin Gulf Resolution (1964) Passed by Congress in reaction to supposedly unprovoked attacks on American warships off the coast of North Vietnam; it gave the president unlimited authority to defend U.S. forces and members of SEATO.

Totalitarianism The term which described aggressive, ideologically driven states that sought to subdue all of civil society to their control, thus leaving no room for individual rights or alternative values.

Townshend Acts (1767) Parliamentary measures (named for the chancellor of the Exchequer) that taxed tea and other commodities, and established a Board of Customs Commissioners and colonial vice-admiralty courts.

Trail of Tears Cherokees' own term for their forced removal, 1838–1839, from the Southeast to Indian lands (later Oklahoma); of 15,000 forced to march, 4,000 died on the way.

Transcendentalism Philosophy of a small group of mid-nineteenth-century New England writers and thinkers, including Ralph Waldo Emerson, Henry David Thoreau, and Margaret Fuller; they stressed personal and intellectual self-reliance.

Transcontinental railroad First line across the continent from Omaha, Nebraska, to Sacramento, California, established in 1869 with the linkage of the Union Pacific and Central Pacific railroads at Promontory, Utah.

Truman Doctrine President Harry S. Truman's program announced in 1947 of aid to European countries—particularly Greece and Turkey—threatened by communism.

Trust Companies combined to limit competition.

Twenty-first Amendment (1933) Repealed the prohibition of the manufacture, sale, and transportation of alcoholic beverages, effectively nullifying the Eighteenth Amendment.

Twenty-second Amendment (1951) Limited presidents to two full terms of office or two terms plus two years of an assumed term; passed in reaction to President Franklin D. Roosevelt's unprecedented four elected terms.

Twenty-sixth Amendment (1971) Lowered the voting age from twenty-one to eighteen.

U.S.S. *Maine* Battleship that exploded in Havana Harbor on February 15, 1898, resulting in 266 deaths; the American public, assuming that the Spanish had mined the ship, clamored for war, and the Spanish-American War was declared two months later.

Uncle Tom's Cabin Harriet Beecher Stowe's 1852 antislavery novel popularized the abolitionist position.

Underground Railroad Operating in the decades before the Civil War, the "railroad" was a clandestine system of routes and safehouses through which slaves were led to freedom in the North.

Understanding clause Added to southern state constitutions in the late nineteenth century, it allowed illiterate whites to circumvent literacy tests for voting by demonstrating that they understood a passage in the Constitution; black citizens would be judged by white registrars to have failed.

Unitarianism Late-eighteenth-century liberal offshoot of the New England Congregationalist Church; rejecting the Trinity,

Unitarianism professed the oneness of God and the goodness of rational man.

United Farm Workers Union for the predominantly Mexican-American migrant laborers of the Southwest, organized by César Chavez in 1962.

United Nations Organization of nations to maintain world peace, established in 1945 and headquartered in New York.

Universal Negro Improvement Association Black nationalist movement active in the United States from 1916 to 1923, led by Marcus Garvey.

USA Patriot Act (2001) A mammoth bill that conferred unprecedented powers on law-enforcement agencies charged with preventing domestic terrorism, including the power to wiretap, read private messages, and spy on citizens.

V-E Day May 8, 1945, the day World War II officially ended in Europe.

Versailles Treaty The treaty signed at the Versailles peace conference after World War I which established President Woodrow Wilson's vision of an international regulating body, redrew parts of Europe and the Middle East, and assigned economically crippling war reparations to Germany, but failed to incorporate all of Wilson's Fourteen Points.

Vertical integration Company's avoidance of middlemen by producing its own supplies and providing for distribution of its product.

Veto President's constitutional power to reject legislation passed by Congress; a two-thirds vote in both houses of Congress can override a veto.

Vicksburg, Battle of The fall of Vicksburg, Mississippi, to General Ulysses S. Grant's army on July 4, 1863, after two months of siege was a turning point in the war because it gave the Union control of the Mississippi River.

Vietnam War Longest war in which the United States has been involved; began with giving American financial assistance to France, who sought to maintain control over Vietnam colony; moved to dispatching advisers to bolster the government of South Vietnam; and finally sent over 500,000 American

soldiers by the mid-1960s; resulted in massive antiwar movement, eventual American withdrawal, and communist victory in 1975; only war the United States has lost.

Virginia and Kentucky Resolutions (1798–1799) Passed by the Virginia and the Kentucky legislatures; written by James Madison and Thomas Jefferson in response to the Alien and Sedition Acts, the resolutions advanced the state-compact theory of the Constitution. Virginia's resolution called on the federal courts to protect free speech. Jefferson's draft for Kentucky stated that a state could nullify federal law, but this was deleted.

Virginia and New Jersey Plans Differing opinions of delegations to the Constitutional Convention: New Jersey wanted one legislative body with equal representation for each state; Virginia's plan called for a strong central government and a two-house legislature apportioned by population.

Volstead Act (1919) Enforced the Prohibition amendment, beginning January 1920.

Voting Rights Act of 1965 Passed in the wake of Martin Luther King Jr.'s, Selma to Montgomery March, it authorized federal protection of the right to vote and permitted federal enforcement of minority voting rights in individual counties, mostly in the South.

***Wabash Railroad v. Illinois* (1886)** Reversing the U.S. Supreme Court's ruling in *Munn v. Illinois*, the decision disallowed state regulation of interstate commerce.

Wade-Davis bill (1864) Radical Republicans' plan for reconstruction that required loyalty oaths, abolition of slavery, repudiation of war debts, and denial of political rights to high-ranking Confederate officials; President Lincoln refused to sign the bill.

Wagner Act (National Labor Relations Act of 1935) Established the National Labor Relations Board and facilitated unionization by regulating employment and bargaining practices.

War Industries Board Run by financier Bernard Baruch, the board planned production and allocation of war materiel, supervised purchasing, and fixed prices, 1917–1919.

War of 1812 Fought with Britain, 1812–1814, over issues that included impressment of American sailors, interference with shipping, and collusion with Northwest Territory Indians; settled by the Treaty of Ghent in 1814.

War on Poverty Announced by President Lyndon B. Johnson in his 1964 State of the Union address; under the Economic Opportunity Bill signed later that year, Head Start, VISTA, and the Jobs Corps were created, and programs were created for students, farmers, and businesses in efforts to eliminate poverty.

War Powers Act Law passed in 1973, reflecting growing opposition to American involvement in Vietnam War; required congressional approval before president sent troops abroad.

War Production Board Created in 1942 to coordinate industrial efforts in World War II; similar to the War Industries Board in World War I.

Warren Court The U.S. Supreme Court under Chief Justice Earl Warren, 1953–1969, decided such landmark cases as *Brown v. Board of Education* (school desegregation), *Baker v. Carr* (legislative redistricting), and *Gideon v. Wainwright* and *Miranda v. Arizona* (rights of criminal defendants).

Washington Armaments Conference Leaders of nine world powers met in 1921–1922 to discuss the naval race; resulting treaties limited to a specific ratio the carrier and battleship tonnage of each nation (Five-Power Naval Treaty), formally ratified the Open Door to China (Nine-Power Treaty), and agreed to respect each other's Pacific territories (Four-Power Treaty).

Watergate Washington office and apartment complex that lent its name to the 1972–1974 scandal of the Nixon administration; when his knowledge of the break-in at the Watergate and subsequent coverup was revealed, Nixon resigned the presidency under threat of impeachment.

Webster-Hayne debate U.S. Senate debate of January 1830 between Daniel Webster of Massachusetts and Robert Hayne of South Carolina over nullification and states' rights.

Welfare state A term that originated in Britain during World War II to refer to a system of income assistance, health coverage, and social services for all citizens.

Whig Party Founded in 1834 to unite factions opposed to President Andrew Jackson, the party favored federal responsibility for internal improvements; the party ceased to exist by the late 1850s, when party members divided over the slavery issue.

Whiskey Rebellion Violent protest by western Pennsylvania farmers against the federal excise tax on whiskey, 1794.

Wilmot Proviso Proposal to prohibit slavery in any land acquired in the Mexican War, but southern senators, led by John C. Calhoun of South Carolina, defeated the measure in 1846 and 1847.

Women's Christian Temperance Union Largest female reform society of the late nineteenth century; it moved from opposing sale of liquor to demanding the right to vote for women.

Works Progress Administration (WPA) Part of the Second New Deal, it provided jobs for millions of the unemployed on construction and arts projects.

Wounded Knee, Battle of Last incident of the Indian Wars took place in 1890 in the Dakota Territory, where the U.S. Cavalry killed over 200 Sioux men, women, and children.

Writs of assistance One of the colonies' main complaints against Britain, the writs allowed unlimited search warrants without cause to look for evidence of smuggling.

XYZ affair French foreign minister Tallyrand's three anonymous agents demanded payments to stop French plundering of American ships in 1797; refusal to pay the bribe was followed by two years of undeclared sea war with France (1798–1800).

Yalta conference Meeting of Franklin D. Roosevelt, Winston Churchill, and Joseph Stalin at a Crimean resort to discuss the postwar world on February 4–11, 1945; Joseph Stalin claimed large areas in eastern Europe for Soviet domination.

Yellow journalism Sensationalism in newspaper publishing that reached a peak in the circulation war between Joseph Pulitzer's *New York World* and William Randolph Hearst's *New York Journal* in the 1890s; the papers' accounts of events in Havana Harbor in 1898 led directly to the Spanish-American War.

Yeoman farmers Small landowners (the majority of white families in the Old South) who farmed their own land and usually did not own slaves.

Yick Wo v. Hopkins Supreme Court decision in 1886 overturning San Francisco law that, as enforced, discriminated against Chinese-owned laundries; established principle that equal protection of the law embodied in Fourteenth Amendment applied to all Americans, not just former slaves.

Yorktown, Battle of Last battle of the Revolutionary War; General Lord Charles Cornwallis along with over 7,000 British troops surrendered at Yorktown, Virginia, on October 17, 1781.

Young Americans for Freedom Organization of conservative students founded in 1960; played major role in 1964 presidential campaign of Barry Goldwater and in rebirth of conservatism in the 1960s.

Zimmermann Telegram From the German foreign secretary to the German minister in Mexico, February 1917, instructing him to offer to recover Texas, New Mexico, and Arizona for Mexico if it would fight the United States to divert attention from Germany in the event that the United States joined the war.

CREDITS

PHOTOS

iii Lady Liberty: Library of Congress; **iv** Celebrating the Constitution: Granger Collection; **vii** Author portrait: © Flynn Larsen; **xxxix** Eastman Johnson (American, 1824–1906) *A Ride for Liberty—The Fugitive Slaves*, ca. 1862. Oil on paper board, 21 15/16 × 26 1/8 in. (55.8 × 66.4 cm). Brooklyn Museum, Gift of Gwendolyn O. L. Conkling, 40.59a-b; **1** Lady Liberty: Library of Congress; **2 (top)** Bridgeman Art Library; **2 (bottom)** Self-Portrait, by Thomas Smith, 1948.19, Worcester Art Museum, Worcester, Massachusetts; **3 (top)** Unidentified artist, British, 18th century or first quarter 19th century; *Quaker Meeting*; Museum of Fine Arts, Boston; Bequest of Maxim Karolik; 64.456; **3 (bottom)** Granger Collection; **4** Collection du monastère des Ursulines de Québec, Musée des Ursulines de Québec (1997.1017); **8** Library of Congress; **9** Photo Courtesy of Edward E. Ayer Collection, The Newberry Library, Chicago; **10 (top)** National Park Service, Chaco Culture National Historic Park, Chaco Archive neg. no. 25462; **10 (bottom)** Timothy O'Sullivan, Ancient Ruins in the Canon de Chelle, N.M. in a Niche 50 Feet above Present Canon Bed, albumen silver print, 1873; Amon Carter Museum, Fort Worth, Texas P1982.27.38; **12** Bridgeman Art Library; **13** Library of Congress; **14** Bridgeman Art Library; **15 (top)** Courtesy Lilly Library, Indiana University, Bloomington, IN; **15 (bottom)** Library of Congress; **20 (top)** Ellen Mack/Getty Images; **20 (bottom)** Granger Collection; **21** Granger Collection; **23** Granger Collection; **24** akg-images; **26** The Art Archive at Art Resource, NY; **27** Courtesy of the Library of Congress; **28 (top)** Bridgeman Art Library; **28 (bottom)** Museo de la Basilica de Guadalupe, Mexico City; **29** Rare Books Division, The New York Public Library, Astor, Lenox, and Tilden Foundations; **30 (top)** Library of Congress; **30 (bottom)** Museo Naval, Madrid; **34** Library of Congress; **35** National Museum of American History, Smithsonian Institution, Behring Center; **38** History Collection, Nova Scotia Library; **40** Bettmann/Corbis; **42** GLC03582 Novi Belgi Novaeque Angliae (New Netherland and New England) by Nicholas Visscher, 1682/Courtesy of The Gilder Lehrman Institute of American History; **43** Museum of the City of New York/Bridgeman Art Library; **44** The Colonial Williamsburg Foundation; **48** Granger Collection; **51** Woburn Abbey, Bedfordshire, UK/The Bridgeman Art Library; **52** The John Carter Brown Library at Brown University; **54** Granger Collection—**55** GLC 4110. Document signed: contracts relating to the indenture of James Mahony, 31 March 1773. The Gilder Lehrman Collection, courtesy of the Gilder Lehrman Institute of American History, New York; **56** The London Art Archive/Alamy; **57** Museum of Art, Rhode Island School of Design. Gift of Robert Winthrop. Photography by Erik Gould; **59 (top)** Corbis; **59 (bottom)** National Portrait Gallery, Smithsonian Institution/Art Resource, NY; **60** Granger Collection; **61 (top)** Library of Congress; **61 (bottom)** George Arents

Collection, New York Public Library; **62** Mary Evans Picture Library/Alamy; **63** Corbis; **65** Library of Congress; **66** American Antiquarian Society; **67 (top)** Courtesy of the John Carter Brown Library at Brown University; **67 (bottom)** Courtesy of the Massachusetts Archives; **68** Worcester Art Museum, Worcester, Massachusetts, Gift of William A. Savage; **69** Massachusetts Historical Society; **71** The New York Public Library/Art Resource, NY; **76 (top)** Annenberg Rare Book and Manuscript Library, Van Pelt-Dietrich Library Center, U Penn; **76 (bottom)** Library of Congress; **78** Self-Portrait, by Thomas Smith, 1948.19, Worcester Art Museum, Worcester, Massachusetts; **79** *Mrs. Elizabeth Freake and Baby Mary*, unknown artist, 1963.134, Worcester Art Museum, Worcester, Massachusetts; **80** Historical Picture Archive/Corbis; **81** World History Archive/Alamy; **82 (top)** Private Collection/Bridgeman Art Library; **82 (bottom)** By permission of the British Library; **83** The Cromwell Museum, Huntingdon; **86** Art Resource, NY; **91** Library of Congress; **92** Historical Society of Pennsylvania; **93** Germantown Historical Society, Philadelphia, PA; **94** Unidentified artist, British, 18th century or first quarter 19th century; *Quaker Meeting*; Museum of Fine Arts, Boston; Bequest of Maxim Karolik; 64.456; **96** © British Library Board. All Rights Reserved/The Bridgeman Art Library; **97** Private Collection/Bridgeman Art Library; **98** Colonial Williamsburg Foundation; **100** National Maritime Museum, London; **102** The John Carter Brown Library at Brown University; **103** Springhill, County Londonderry, Northern Ireland, National Trust Photographic Library/Derrick E. Witty/Bridgeman Art Library; **105** Rare Books Division, The New York Public Library, Astor, Lenox, and Tilden Foundations; **109** Emmet Collection, Miriam and Ira D. Wallach Division of Art, Prints and Photographs, The New York Public Library, Astor, Lenox, and Tilden Foundations; **111** The Historical Society of Pennsylvania; **114** Benjamin West, Pennsylvania Academy of the Fine Arts; Joseph and Sarah Harrison Collection; **115** The Library Company of Philadelphia; **116** Winterthur Museum; **117** The Colonial Williamsburg Foundation; **118** Photograph © 2010 Museum of Fine Arts, Boston; **119** Geoffrey Clements/Corbis; **120** Carter's Grove. Aug 1995. Photo by Melissa Wilkins. http://creativecommons.org/licenses/by-sa/2.0/deed.en; **120** Virginia Historical Society, Richmond; **121** Fenimore Art Museum, Cooperstown, New York; **122** Gift of Edgar William and Bernice Chrysler Garbisch, Image © 2006 Board of Trustees, National Gallery of Art, Washington; **126** Granger Collection; **130 (top)** The John Carter Library at Brown University; **130 (bottom)** Library of Congress; **132** © Musée d'histoire de Nantes–Château des ducs de Bretagne/Alain Guillard; **133** Courtesy of the Maryland Historical Society; **134 (top)** Granger Collection; **134 (bottom)** Library of Congress; **137** Abby Aldrich Rockefeller Folk Art

Museum, Colonial Williamsburg Foundation, Williamsburg, VA; **139** Charleston Library Society; **141** Chicago Historical Society; **142** By courtesy of the Trustees of Sir John Soane's Museum; **143 (top)** Library of Congress; **143 (bottom)** © National Portrait Gallery, London; **145** The Library Company of Philadelphia; **147** This item is reproduced by permission of The Huntington Library, San Marino, California; **149** Library of Congress; **150 (top)** Portrait of Benjamin Franklin, Mason Chamberlin, 1762, Philadelphia Museum of Art: Gift of Mr. and Mrs. Wharton Sinkler, 1956; **151** National Portrait Gallery, London; **152** Courtesy of the John Carter Brown Library at Brown University; **154** Courtesy of the Bancroft Library, University of California, Berkeley; **155** Benard de la Harpe, "Carte Nouvelle de la Partie de l'Ouest de la Province de la Louisiane" [map], 1720, Louisiana Research Collection, Tulane University; **157** Granger Collection; **158** Library of Congress; **164** Library of Congress; **167 (both)** Library of Congress; **168 (top)** Granger Collection; **168 (bottom)** Chicago Historical Society; **169 (top)** © New Bedford Whaling Museum; **169 (bottom)** Private Collection/The Bridgeman Art Library; **171** Library of Congress; **173** By permission of the Houghton Library, Harvard University; **174** Library of Congress; **175 (top)** Corbis; **175 (bottom)** The Colonial Williamsburg Foundation; **176** Kunhardt/Picture History; **177** Library of Congress; **180 (top)** Library of Congress; **180 (bottom)** Michael Nicholson/Corbis; **181** Library of Congress; **182** Library of Congress; **183** Special Collections Research Center, University of Chicago Library; **184** Miriam and Ira D. Wallach Division of Art, Prints and Photographs, New York Public Library; **185** Chicago Historical Society; **186** National Portrait Gallery, London; **187** American Philosophical Society; **190** Library of Congress; **191** American Antiquarian Society; **192** Sid Lapidus Collection. Department of Rare Books and Special Collections. Princeton University Library; **193** Yale University, Lewis Walpole Library, Print Collection; **194** Anne S.K. Brown Military Collection, Brown University; **195** Morristown National Historic Park; **199** American Antiquarian Society/Bridgeman Art Library; **200 (top)** Library of Congress; **200 (bottom)** *George Washington's War in Caricature and Print*. Kenneth Baker, Grub Street Publishing; **204** Library Company of Philadelphia. Gift of the artist, 1792; **207** National Gallery of Art, Washington, Gift of Mrs. Robert Homans; **208** Gianni Dagli Orti/The Art Archive at Art Resource, NY; **209** Historical Society of Pennsylvania; **210** Courtesy of the Beinecke Rare Book and Manuscript Library, Yale University; **211** Courtesy of the New-York Historical Society; **212** *North Eastern view, Watertown, CT.* 1836 John Warner Barber/The Connecticut Historical Society, Hartford CT; **213** York County Historical Society, USA/The Bridgeman Art Library; **215** American Antiquarian Society; **216** Bettmann/Corbis; **217** Reproduced by permission of the

Huntington Library, San Marino, California; **219** Library of Congress; **223** Corbis; **225** American Antiquarian Society; **226** Library of Congress; **227** National Archives, London; **228** Collection of The New-York Historical Society; **229** Museum of Art, Rhode Island School of Design; Gift of Miss Lucy Truman Aldrich; **232** Picture History; **233 (top)** Southern Historical Collection, Wilson Library, The University of North Carolina at Chapel Hill; **233 (bottom)** Courtesy, Winterthur Museum, gift of Henry Francis du Pont; **234 (top)** Charles Wilson Peale, Portrait of John and Elizabeth Lloyd Cadwalader, and their daughter Anne, Philadelphia Museum of Art: Purchased from the Cadwalader Collection with funds contributed by the Myrin Trust and the gift of an anonymous donor; **235** Library of Congress; **238** Collection of the New-York Historical Society/Bridgeman Art Library; **243** American Antiquarian Society; **245** Print Collection, Miriam and Ira D. Wallach Division of Art, Prints, and Photographs, The New York Public Library; Astor, Lenox, and Tilden Foundations; **247 (top)** Library of Congress; **247 (bottom)** Independence National Historical Park; **249** Library of Congress; **251** Library of Virginia; **252** From the collection of the National Constitution Center, Philadelphia, gift of Robert L. McNeil Jr.; **253** MPI/Getty Images; **254** Library of Congress; **255** Granger Collection; **256** Courtesy of the New-York Historical Society; **257** Granger Collection; **258** Collection of The New-York Historical Society; **259** Library of Congress; **263** The Buffalo and Erie County Historical Society; **265** Chicago Historical Society; **266** Unidentified artist, circa 1805, *Benjamin Hawkins and the Creek Indian*, circa 1805, Greenville County Museum of Art, Greenville, SC; **268** Granger Collection; **269** Virginia Historical Society, Richmond/Bridgeman Art Library; **272** National Portrait Gallery, Washington D.C. Photograph copyright Nicholas S. West; **275 (top)** Chicago Historical Society; **275 (bottom)** Fenimore Art Museum, Cooperstown, New York. Photo by Richard Walker; **276 (top)** Courtesy of the Maryland Historical Society; **276 (bottom)** Library of Congress; **277** Library of Congress; **278** Courtesy, Winterthur Museum, bequest of Henry F. DuPont; **279** Print Collection, Miriam and Ira D. Wallach Division of Art, Prints, and Photographs, The New York Public Library; Astor, Lenox, and Tilden Foundations; **280** Chicago Historical Society; **281** © National Portrait Gallery, London; **284** Museum of Early Southern Decorative Arts, Winston-Salem, NC; **285** Library of Congress; **286** Library of Congress; **288** National Museum of American History, Smithsonian Institution, Behring Center; **289** Photos 12/Alamy; **291** I.N. Stokes Collection, Miriam and Ira D. Wallach Division of Art, Prints, and Photographs, The New York Public Library; Astor, Lenox, and Tilden Foundations; **292** Private Collection; **294** Missouri Historical Society, St. Louis; **295** GLC07730 The attack made on Tripoli on the 3d. August 1804, by John Guerrazzi, August 23rd. 1852/Courtesy of The Gilder Lehrman Institute of American History; **296** Courtesy of the New-York Historical Society; **298** Royal Ontario Museum; **299 (top)** National Portrait Gallery, Smithsonian Institution/Art Resource, NY; **299 (bottom)** Photo by Mark Sexton. © Peabody Essex Museum, 2003, all rights reserved; **302** American Antiquarian Society, Massachusetts/Bridgeman Art Library; **303** Photography by Erik Ameson copyright Nicholas S. West; **306** I.N. Phelps Stokes Collection, Miriam and Ira D. Wallach Division of Art, Prints, and Photographs, The New York Public Library, Astor, Lenox, and Tilden Foundations; **309 (top)** I.N. Stokes Collection, Miriam and Ira D. Wallach Division of Art, Prints, and Photographs, The New York Public Library; Astor, Lenox, and Tilden Foundations; **309 (bottom)** Courtesy University of Michigan Library's Making of America; **311** Chicago Historical Society; **312** Courtesy of the Maryland Historical Society; **315** Edwin Whitefield, Minnesota Historical Society; **317** Abby Aldrich Rockefeller Folk Art Museum, Colonial Williamsburg Foundation, Williamsburg, VA; **318** Cincinnati Museum Center/Getty Images; **319** Courtesy, The Winterthur Library: Joseph Downs Collection of Manuscripts and Printed Ephemera; **322** Library of Congress; **323 (top)** Granger Collection; **323 (bottom)** Barfoot, American, Progress of Cotton, Reeding or Drawing In, No. 9, Mabel Brady Garvan Collection, Yale University Art Gallery; **324 (top)** Courtesy of the Manchester (N.H.) Historic Association; **324 (bottom)** Granger Collection; **325** Bishop Hill State Historic Site/Illinois Historic Preservation Agency; **326** Historical Society of Pennsylvania, medium graphics collection, H. Bucholzer; **327** Granger Collection; **330** Corbis; **331 (left)** Granger Collection; **331 (right)** Corbis; **334** © New Bedford Whaling Museum; **335** Library of Congress; **337 (top)** Church Archives of The Church of Jesus-Christ of Latter-day Saints; **337 (bottom)** John Neagle, American, 1796–1865; *Pat Lyon at the Forge*, 1826–27; Museum of Fine Arts, Boston; Henry H. and Zoe Oliver Sherman Fund; 1975.806; **338** Library of Congress; **339** Courtesy, American Antiquarian Society; **340 (top)** Library of Congress; **340 (bottom)** Gift of Edgar William and Bernice Chrysler Garbisch, Image © 2006 Board of Trustees, National Gallery of Art, Washington; **342** Edwin Kilroe Collection, Butler Library, Columbia University; **343** Library of Congress; **346** Gift of Stephen C. Clark, Fenimore Art Museum, Cooperstown, New York. Photo by Milo Stewart; **349 (top)** Library of Congress; **349 (bottom)** Courtesy the Rhode Island Historical Society, Dorr Liberation Society, Rhode Island, 1844, engraving, Rhi X3 6692; **350** Historical Society of Pennsylvania, large graphics collection, John Lewis Krimmel; **351** Library of Congress; **352** Library of Congress; **354** Library of Congress; **355** The Corcoran Gallery of Art/Corbis; **361** Huntington Library, San Marino, California; **365** Bettmann/Corbis; **366** Library of Congress; **367** Private Collection/The Bridgeman Art Library; **368** Joseph Yeager, *The Procession of Victuallers*, 1821, Philadelphia Museum of Art: Gift of the Estate of Charles M. B. Cadwalader; **370** Saint Louis Art Museum, Missouri, USA/Gift of Bank of America/The Bridgeman Art Library; **372** Library of Congress; **373** Library of Congress; **374 (top)** Granger Collection; **374 (bottom)** Library of Congress; **376** Charles Deas, *The Trapper and His Family*, © Museum of Fine Arts, Boston; **377** Smithsonian American Art Museum, Washington, D.C./Art Resource, NY; **378** Library of Congress; **380** Library of Congress; **381** Library of Congress; **385** Bettmann/Corbis; **386 (top)** Hulton Archive/Getty Images; **386 (bottom)** Chicago History Museum; **387 (top)** Collection of Dr. and Mrs. John Livingston and Mrs. Elizabeth Livingston Jaeger, Photo: Hearts and Hands Media Arts. Photography courtesy of Hearts & Hands Media Arts, from the book and film *Hearts and Hands: A Social History of 19th Century Women and Their Quilts* (New Day Films); **387 (bottom)** Fine Arts Museums of San Francisco, Gift of Joseph Martin Jr., 1994.120.4; **388** Hirshhorn Museum & Sculpture Garden, Washington D.C./Bridgeman Art Library; **391 (top)** Samuel J. Miller, *Frederick Douglass*, 1847–52, Major Acquisitions Centennial Endowment, The Art Institute of Chicago; **391 (bottom)** Universal Images Group/Art Resource, NY; **393** Library of Congress; **394** Hulton Archive/Getty Images; **395** Library of Congress; **396** Library of Congress; **398 (top)** Library of Congress; **398 (bottom)** LSU Museum of Art 87.23 Gift of the Friends of LSU Museum of Art and Mrs. Ben Hamilton in memory of her mother, Mrs. Tela Meir © David Humphreys 2004; **399** Merseyside Maritime Museum, Liverpool; **401** Granger Collection; **402 (top)** Chicago Historical Society; **402 (bottom)** New Hampshire Historical Society; **403** Courtesy of South Caroliniana Library, University of South Carolina, Columbia; **408** Courtesy of the Maryland Historical Society; **410** Library of Congress; **411 (top)** Library of Congress; **411 (bottom)** Chicago Historical Society; **412** North Carolina Museum of Art, Raleigh, Purchased with funds from the State of North Carolina; **413** Abby Aldrich Rockefeller Folk Art Museum, Colonial Williamsburg Foundation, Williamsburg, VA; **414** provided courtesy © HarpWeek., LLC; **415** Historic New Orleans Collection 1960.46; **418** GLC07238 $2,500 Reward! Mississippi Co., Missouri broadside advertising runaway slaves, August 23, 1852/Courtesy of The Gilder Lehrman Institute of American History; **419** akg-images/British Library; **421** Library of Congress; **424** Courtesy of the Massachusetts Historical Society. Banner, William Lloyd Garrison (1805–1879) "Proclaim Liberty Throughout all the Land unto all the inhabitants thereof." MHS image #332; **427** Library of Congress; **429** Bibliotheque Nationale, Paris, France/Archives Charmet/The Bridgeman Art Library; **430** Library of Congress; **431** Library of Congress; **432** Corbis; **433** Courtesy of the New-York Historical Society; **434** Collection of the New-York Historical Society, Neg no. 35903; **435** Library of Congress; **436 (both)** Library of Congress; **437 (top)** Bettmann/Corbis; **437 (bottom)** Library of Congress; **438** The Boston Athenaeum, TBMR VEP.An 847. The Anti-Slavery Alphabet, a children's book (1847); **439** Library of Congress; **440** Madison County Historical Society, Oneida, NY; **441 (both)** Chicago Historical Society; **442** Library of Congress; **443** Library of Congress; **444 (top)** Library of Congress; **444 (bottom)** American Antiquarian Society, Massachusetts/Bridgeman Art Library; **445** *Destruction by Fire of Pennsylvania Hall, on the Night of the 17th May, 1838* by J.C. Wild, printed by J.T. Bowen. The Library Company of Philadelphia; **446** Collection of Dr. and Mrs. John Livingston and Mrs. Elizabeth Livingston Jaeger, Photo: Hearts and Hands Media Arts. Photography courtesy of Hearts & Hands Media Arts, from the book and film *Hearts and Hands: A Social History of 19th Century Women and Their Quilts* (New Day Films); **448** Library of Congress; **449** Bettmann/Corbis; **452 (both)** Bettmann/Corbis; **453** Bettmann/Corbis; **455** Library of Congress; **458** John Perry Newell, Lazell, Perkins & Co. Bridgewater,

Mass., ca. 1860. Yale University Art Gallery, Mabel Brady Garvan Collection; **461 (left)** Library of Congress; **461 (right)** Architect of the Capitol; **461 (bottom)** Christie's Images/Corbis; **463** Courtesy of the State Preservation Board, Austin, Texas, Photographer F. Thomson, Post 1990, CHA 1989.68, post conservation; **464** Bettmann/Corbis; **465** From Rafael Barajas's La historia de un país en caricatura. Caricatura mexicana de combate 1829–1872 (2000) Consejo Nacional para la Cultura y las Artes, Direccion General de Publicaciones, México. p. 157; **466** Granger Collection; **468** Ferdinand Deppe (Germany, Berlin, 1794–1861) San Gabriel Mission, c. 1832 Laguna Art Museum Collection, Gift of Nancy Dustin Wall Moure 1994.083; **471 (top)** Yale Collection of Western Americana, Beinecke Rare Book and Manuscript Library; **471 (bottom)** Image copyright © The Metropolitan Museum of Art/Art Resource, NY; **475** © The Metropolitan Museum of Art/Art Resource, NY; **477** Corbis; **479** Chicago Historical Society; **481** Library of Congress; **482 (top)** Library of Congress; **482 (bottom)** Courtesy of Mrs. Screven Lorillard. Photo by Tyler Anbinder; **483** Chicago Historical Society; **484** Bettmann/Corbis; **485** Courtesy of the New-York Historical Society; **486** Bettmann/Corbis; **488 (left)** Chicago Historical Society; **488 (right)** George Eastman House; **489** Collection of The New-York Historical Society; **492** Courtesy of the Maryland Historical Society; **495** Library of Congress; **497** Fotosearch/Getty Images; **498** Library of Congress; **499** Chicago Historical Society; **502** Museum of Fine Arts, Boston/M. and M. Karolik Collection of American Watercolors and/Drawings, 1800–75/The Bridgeman Art Library; **506 (both)** Library of Congress; **507 (top)** Newark Museum/Art Resource, NY; **507 (bottom)** Library of Congress; **508 (top)** Chicago Historical Society; **508 (bottom)** Library of Congress; **511** Edward Owen/Art Resource, NY; **513** Slave Reward Advertisement, page 179, in the Manigault Family Papers #484, Southern Historical Collection, Wilson Library, University of North Carolina at Chapel Hill; **514** Chicago Historical Society; **516** Chicago History Museum; **517** Chicago Historical Society; **518** Chicago History Museum; **519 (top)** Library of Congress; **519 (bottom)** GLC00968 Unknown (Civil War Songbook). November 24, 1862, p. 4/Courtesy of The Gilder Lehrman Institute of American History; **520 (top)** Library of Congress; **520 (bottom)** Wadsworth Atheneum Museum of Art/Art Resource, NY; **521** Library of Congress; **522** National Archives; **523** Library of Congress; **524 (both)** Chicago Historical Society; **525 (top)** Granger Collection; **525 (bottom)** National Archives; **528** Chicago Historical Society; **529 (top)** U.S. Army Military History Institute; **529 (bottom)** Chicago Historical Society; **530 (top)** Library of Congress; **530 (bottom)** Granger Collection; **532 (both)** Louisiana State University Special Collections from the U.S. Civil War Center exhibit Beyond Face Value, courtesy of Jules d'Hemecourt; **533** From the Collections of the South Carolina Historical Society; **534** Provided courtesy © HarpWeek., LLC; **537 (both)** Library of Congress; **538 (both)** Library of Congress; **539** National Archives; **540** Friends Freedmen's Association teachers in a school in Norfolk, 1863. Collection Number 950, Haverford College Special Collections; **541** National Archives; **543 (top)** Library

of Congress; **543 (bottom)** Provided courtesy © Harp-Week LLC; **545** © The Metropolitan Museum of Art/Art Resource, NY; **548** Chicago Historical Society; **551 (top)** Library of Congress; **551 (bottom)** National Museum of American History, Smithsonian Institution; **552 (top)** Library of Congress; **552 (bottom)** Granger Collection; **554** Smithsonian American Art Museum, Washington, D.C./Art Resource, NY; **555 (both)** Library of Congress; **556 (top)** Courtesy of the New-York Historical Society; **556 (bottom)** Cook Collection, Valentine Richmond History Center; **558** Library of Congress; **559** Kemper Leila Williams Foundation/The Historic New Orleans Collection; **564 (both)** Library of Congress; **565** Ed Sullivan Collection, Special Collections, University of Hartford; **566** Library of Congress; **567** Manuscripts, Archives, & Rare Books Division, Schomburg Center for Research in Black Culture, The New York Public Library, Astor, Lenox, and Tilden Foundations; **568** Library of Congress; **569** Library of Congress; **570** Library of Congress; **572** Library of Congress; **573** Library of Congress; **574 (top)** Library of Congress; **574 (bottom)** Granger Collection; **575** Library of Congress; **576** Clements Library Collection, University of Michigan; **577** Granger Collection; **579 (top)** Greg French Early Photography; **579 (bottom)** Fine Arts Museums of San Francisco, Gift of Joseph Martin Jr., 1994.120.4; **580 (both)** Library of Congress; **582** Granger Collection; **583** Library of Congress; **586 (top)** Library of Congress; **587 (top)** Private Collection, Museum of American Folk Art, NY; **587 (bottom)** Library of Congress; **588** © The Metropolitan Museum of Art. Image source: Art Resource, NY; **591** © Deutsches Historiches Museum, Unter den Linden 2, 0-1086 Berlin; **593 (left)** Chicago History Museum/Getty Images; **593 (right)** Granger Collection; **594** The Art Archive/Art Resource; **595 (both)** Granger Collection; **597 (both)** Library of Congress; **598** Library of Congress; **599** Museum of the City of New York, The Jacob Riis Collection; **600 (top)** Bettmann/Corbis; **600 (bottom)** Private Collection/The Bridgeman Art Library; **601** Solomon Butcher Collection. Nebraska State Historical Society; **602** Courtesy of the California History Room, California State Library, Sacramento, California; **603** Courtesy of the author; **604** Granger Collection; **608** Image copyright © The Metropolitan Museum of Art/Art Resource, NY; **609 (top)** Bettmann/Corbis; **609 (bottom)** Library of Congress; **610** Smithsonian Institution, National Anthropological Archives; **612 (top)** Private Collection, Museum of American Folk Art, NY; **612 (bottom)** Photography Collection. Miriam and Ira D. Wallach Division of Art, Prints, and Photographs, The New York Public Library, Astor, Lenox, and Tilden Foundations; **613 (both)** Smithsonian Institution, National Anthropological Archives; **614 (both)** Library of Congress; **616** Library of Congress; **618** The Ohio State University Billy Ireland Cartoon Library & Museum; **619** Museum of the City of New York/The Art Archive at Art Resource, NY; **621** Thomas Pollock Anshutz, *The Ironworker's Noontime*, 1880, Fine Arts Museum of San Francisco, Gift of Mr. and Mrs. John D. Rockefeller 3rd, 1979.7.4; **623** Image copyright © The Metropolitan Museum of Art/Art Resource, NY; **625 (bottom)** Corbis; **626** Bettmann/Corbis; **628** Bettmann/Corbis; **630** Bettmann/Corbis; **631** State Historical Society of

Wisconsin; **634** Hawai'i State Archives. Honolulu, Hawai'i. Kahn Collection [37/36]; **637 (top)** Library of Congress; **637 (bottom)** Kansas State Historical Society; **638** Ed Sullivan Collection, Special Collections, University of Hartford; **641 (top)** Library of Congress; **641 (bottom)** Picture History; **643 (top)** Library of Congress; **643 (bottom)** National Museum of American History, Smithsonian Institution, Behring Center; **645** Florida State Archives; **646 (both)** Library of Congress; **647 (both)** Library of Congress; **650 (both)** Library of Congress; **651** Library of Congress; **652** Courtesy of the Tennessee State Museum; **654** The Denver Public Library, Western History Collection, X-21518; **655** University of Washington Libraries, Special Collections, #1678; **656** Library of Congress; **657** Library of Congress; **658** Library of Congress; **661** Courtesy of the Bernice Pauahi Bishop Museum Archives; **662** Library of Congress; **664** Frederic Remington Art Museum; **666 (top)** Granger Collection; **666 (bottom)** National Archives; **667 (top)** W.C. Brown Photograph Collection, U.S. Army Military History Institute; **667 (bottom)** Library of Congress; **671** North Wind Picture Archives/Alamy; **672 (top)** Library of Congress; **672 (bottom)** National Portrait Gallery, Smithsonian Institution/Art Resource, NY; **673** David J. & Janice L. Frent Collection/Corbis; **676** John Sloan (1871–1951) © Artist Rights Society, (ARS) NY, *Sixth Avenue and Thirtieth Street, New York City*, Philadelphia Museum of Art, Gift of Meyer P. Potamkin and Vivian O. Potamkin, 2000; **679 (top)** Library of Congress; **679 (bottom)** Museum of the City of New York, The Byron Collection; **680 (top)** The J. Paul Getty Museum, Los Angeles, © Estate of Georgia O'Keeffe, © 2013 The Georgia O'Keeffe Foundation/Artists Rights Society (ARS), New York; **680 (bottom)** Bettmann/Corbis; **683** Library of Congress; **684 (bottom)** Library of Congress; **685** Courtesy of the author; **686** California Museum of Photography, Keystone-Mast Collection, University of California, Riverside; **687 (top)** John Sloan © 2013 Delaware Art Museum/Artists Rights Society (ARS), New York. Granger Collection; **687 (bottom)** Library of Congress; **688** Image Courtesy of The Advertising Archives; **689** Corbis; **691** Walter P. Reuther Library, Wayne State University; **694** Brown Brothers; **695** From the Albert R. Stone Negative Collection, Rochester Museum & Science Center Rochester, N.Y.; **696 (top)** Sam DeVincent Collection of Illustrated Sheet Music, Archives Center, National Museum of American History, Behring Center, Smithsonian Institution; **696 (bottom)** Library of Congress; **697 (top)** Bettmann/Corbis; **697 (bottom)** Department of Special Collections, Davidson Library, University of California, Santa Barbara; **698** Reprinted with permission from Planned Parenthood® Federation of America, Inc. © 2004 PPFA. All rights reserved; **700** Museum of the City of New York, The Byron Collection; **701** University of Illinois at Chicago, the University Library, Jane Addams Memorial Collection; **702** Museum of the City of New York, Long-term loan from the Visiting Nurse Service of New York; **703** Nebraska State Historical Society; **704 (bottom)** Bettmann/Corbis; **706 (top)** Hulton Archive/Getty Images; **706 (bottom)** provided courtesy © HarpWeek LLC; **707 (top)** Purchase, Jim and Carol Kautz, class of 1955, in honor of Richard and Ronay Menschel/Francis Lehman Loeb Art Center, Vassar

College; **707 (bottom)** Library of Congress; **709** Courtesy of Debs Collection, Cunningham Memorial Library, Indiana State University; **714** Library of Congress; **717** Paris Pierce/Alamy; **719** Library of Congress; **721** Arizona Historical Society; **722** Smithsonian/National Air and Space Museum; **723** Private Collection/Chris Deakes/The Art Archive; **724 (top)** Bettmann/Corbis; **724 (bottom)** Albin Egger-Lienz, Nordfrankreich, 1917/Photo by Ji-Elle. 2012; http://creativecommons.org/licenses/by-sa/3.0/deed .en; **726** The U.S. Army Military History Institute; **727 (top)** Eileen Tweedy/The Art Archive at Art Resource, NY; **727 (bottom)** Library of Congress; **728** National Archives; **729 (left)** National Archives; **729 (right)** Library of Congress; **730 (top)** Library of Congress; **730 (bottom)** Cover of *Union Signal*, Jan 27, 1916, Frances E. Willard Memorial Library and Archives; **732** Granger Collection; **734** Arizona State Library, Archives and Public Records, History and Archives Division, Phoenix, #01-3116; **735** Collection of Robert MacKay; **738 (top)** Wisconsin Historical Society; **738 (bottom)** Library of Congress; **741** St. Louis Post-Dispatch, 17 April 1906; **742** Photographs and Prints Division, Schomburg Center for Research in Black Culture, The New York Public Library, Astor, Lenox, and Tilden Foundations; **743** Library of Congress; **744** Tulsa Historical Society; **745** Library of Congress; **747** Courtesy of the author; **748** Bettmann/Corbis; **749** National Archives; **752** Bettmann Corbis; **756 (top)** Honolulu Academy of Arts: Gift of Philip H. Roach, Jr., 2001; **756 (bottom)** Library of Congress; **757 (top)** Library of Congress; **757 (bottom)** Cover to the propaganda comic book, Catechetical Guild "Is This Tomorrow" http://en.wikipedia.org/wiki/Public_domain; **758** Thomas Hart Benton, *City Activities with Dance Hall, from America Today*, 1930; Art: The Metropolitan Museum of Art, Gift of AXA Equitable, 2012 (2012.478a-j) Image © The Metropolitan Museum of Art, Art Resource. **761 (both)** Library of Congress; **762** George Eastman House/Getty Images; **763** Corbis; **764** Minnesota Historical Society; **765** Charles Sheeler (1883–1965) *River Rouge Plant*, 1932. Whitney Museum of American Art, New York; Purchase 32.43. Photography copyright © 1996 Whitney Museum; **767 (top)** Honolulu Academy of Arts: Gift of Philip H. Roach, Jr., 2001; **767 (bottom)** Library of Congress; **768 (left)** Legacy Tobacco Documents Library, University of California, San Francisco; **768 (right)** Procter & Gamble; **769** The Art Archive/Culver Pictures; **770** Library of Congress; **771** Granger Collection; **774** Courtesy of the Drew University Library; **778 (top)** San Diego Museum of Art; **778 (bottom)** The Denver Public Library, Western History Collection, Rh-1158; **779** Bettmann/Corbis; **780** Smithsonian Institutions Archives; **781** Washington State Historical Society; **783** Granger Collection; **784** Los Angeles Public Library Photo Collection; **785** Nebraska State Historical Society; **786** Photographs and Prints Division, Schomburg Center for Research in Black Culture, The New York Public Library, Astor, Lenox, and Tilden Foundations; **787** Library of Congress; **788** Scurlock Studio Records, Archives Center, National Museum of American History, Smithsonian Institution; **789 (top)** Collection of David J. and Janice L. Frent; **789 (bottom)** Library of Congress; **790** Courtesy of author; **791 (top)**

Library of Congress; **791 (bottom)** National Archives; **792 (both)** National Archives; **793** Robert F. Wagner Labor Archives, New York University, Charles Rivers Collection, photograph by Charles Rivers; **794** Museum of History & Industry/Corbis; **795** AP Photo; **798** Smithsonian American Art Museum/Art Resource. See end of credits for the full image; **802** Granger Collection; **803** Bettmann/Corbis; **804** Library of Congress; **805** National Archives; **806** David Rumsey Map Collection; **808** Kansas State Historical Society; **809** Library of Congress; **810 (top)** Library of Congress; **810 (bottom)** Punch Limited; **811** Library of Congress; **812** Highlander Research and Educational Center; **813** Bettmann/Corbis; **814** Library of Congress; **815** Billy Graham Center Archives, Wheaton College, Wheaton, IL; **816** Library of Congress; **817** National Archives; **818** Library of Congress; **819** Franklin D. Roosevelt Library; **822** Granger Collection; **823** Franklin D. Roosevelt Library; **825** Bettmann/Corbis; **828** Herald-Examiner Collection/Los Angeles Public Library; **829** Photograph © Morgan and Marvin Smith; **830** HOLC Residential Security Map, Federal Home Loan Bank Board, Records of the City Survey Program," RG 195, 450/68/03/02, National Archives II, College Park, MD; **832** Special Collections, University of Hartford; **833 (top)** Franklin D. Roosevelt Presidential Library; **833 (bottom)** Library of Congress; **834** © Barbara Morgan, Barbara Morgan Archive; **835** Brown Brothers; **840** Used with permission of Joshua Brown; **843** Library of Congress; **844** The Wiener Library, Institute of Contemporary History, UK; **845** Washington Star; **846** Andreas Feninger/George Eastman House/Getty Images; **847** National Archive; **848 (top)** Bettmann/Corbis; **848 (bottom)** National Archives; **850 (top)** Bettmann/Corbis; **850 (bottom)** National Archives; **852** AP/Wide World Photo; **853** Library of Congress; **855** Library of Congress; **856 (top)** Library of Congress; **856 (bottom)** Courtesy of the Bard Graduate Center for Studies in the Decorative Arts Design and Culture, New York, Photographer: Bruce White; **857 (left)** Courtesy Herb Friedman, retired U.S. Army Sergeant Major/ www.psywarrior.com; **857 (right)** Courtesy Northwestern University Library; **858** Library of Congress; **859 (top)** McCall's Magazine Collection, California Lutheran University; **859 (bottom)** Library of Congress; **860** Library of Congress; **861** National Archives; **862** Art © Estate of Ben Shahn/Licensed by VAGA, New York, NY; Photo: Library of Congress, Prints & Photographs Division, LC-U57ZW-4730; **864** *Detroit Free Press*; **866** National Archives; **867** AP Photo; **869** Library of Congress; **870** Library of Congress; **871** National Archives; **874** AP Photo; **875** National Archives; **877** Unidentified Photographer, (Interior damage to steel frame of Honkawa Grammar School Auditorium, Hiroshima), November 8, 1945, International Center of Photography, Purchase, with funds provided by the ICP Acquisitions Committee, 2006; **879** Library of Congress; **881** Courtesy of *Chicago Defender*; **884** Cover to the propaganda comic book, Catechetical Guild "Is This Tomorrow" http://en.wikipedia.org/wiki/Public_domain; **887** The Lincoln Highway National Museum & Archives; **888 (top)** Bettmann/Corbis; **888 (bottom)** Library of Congress; **889** Bettmann/Corbis; **890** AP Photo; **893**

AP Photo; **895** AP Photo; **897** Michael Barson Collection; **898** Photopat/Alamy; **899** Derso and Kelen Collection. Public Policy Papers Division, Department of Rare Books and Special Collections, Princeton University Library; **901** Bettmann/Corbis; **903 (top)** Library of Congress, Visual Materials from the NAACP Records, LC-USZ62-84483; **903 (bottom)** © Hy Peskin; **906** Vintage Vegas; **907** Bettmann/Corbis; **908** Elliott Erwitt/Magnum Photos; **909 (top)** Office of the Historian of the U.S. Senate; **909 (bottom)** © 1949 Herbert Block; **915** Bettmann/Corbis; **922** Courtesy of Hagley Museum and Library; **925** Howard Sochurek/Time Life Pictures/Getty Images; **926 (top)** Bettmann/Corbis; **926 (bottom)** California Historical Society, Ticor Title Insurance Collection, USC Library; **927** Hulton Archive/Getty Images; **928 (top)** Bettmann/Corbis; **928 (bottom)** Used with the permission of Pinnacle Foods Corporation, Swanson ® is a registered trademark of CSC Brands, Inc; **929** Bettmann/Corbis; **931 (top)** Jack Gould photograph, courtesy of the Fogg Art Museum, Harvard University Art Museums, on deposit from the Carpenter Center for the Visual Arts. Photo by Allan Macintyre. © 2004 President and Fellows of Harvard College; **932 (top)** Advertising Archive; **932 (bottom)** Elliott Erwitt/Magnum Photos; **933 (top)** Courtesy of University of Southern California, on behalf of the USC Specialized Libraries and Archival Collections; **933 (bottom)** LaGuardia Community College, Laguardia and Wagner Archives, J146 © NYCHA #02.015.15473; **934** Bettmann/Corbis; **935 (top)** American Economic Foundation, "Man's Belief in God Is Personal," CU Libraries Exhibitions, accessed February 22, 2013, https://exhibitions.cul.columbia .edu/items/show/2829; **935 (bottom)** National Postal Museum, Smithsonian Institution; **936** Cornell Capa/Magnum Photos; **938** Dwight D. Eisenhower Presidential Library; **940** © The New Yorker Collection 1958, Alan Dunn from the cartoonbank.com. All rights reserved; **942** Corbis; **943** Bettmann/Corbis; **944** Harry S. Truman Library; **945 (top)** AP Photo; **945 (bottom)** © 1948 Herbert Block; **947 (top)** Dan Weiner/Time Life Pictures/Getty Images; **947 (bottom)** Bruce Davidson/Magnum Photos; **948 (top)** Frank Driggs Collection; **948 (bottom)** Cal Bernstein/LOOK Magazine; **952** Ed Clark/Time Life Pictures/Getty Images; **953** Carl/Wasaki/Time Life Pictures/Getty Images; **954** AP Photo; **955** Don Cravens/Time & Life Pictures/Getty Images; **957 (top)** Collection of Civil Rights Archive, CADVC-UMBC, Baltimore, MD, 2005.183. On Center for Art, Design, and Visual Culture, University of MD Baltimore County website: http://www.umbc.edu/cadvc/foralltheworld/section3 /context.php; **957 (bottom)** Bettmann/Corbis; **958** Collection of the Norman Rockwell Museum, Stockbridge, Massachusetts; **959** Time & Life Pictures/Getty Images; **960** Bettmann/Corbis; **961** Bettmann/Corbis; **964** National Archives; **967 (top)** Image courtesy of the Raleigh City Museum; **967 (bottom)** © Cecil Williams; **968 (top)** Ed Jones/The Birmingham News/Landov; **968 (bottom)** Bettmann/Corbis; **969** © Walter P. Reuther Library, Wayne State University; **971** Ed Meek/University of Mississippi; **972 (top)** Photo by Carl Mydans/Time Life Pictures/Getty Images; **972 (bottom)** Cecil Stoughton, White House/John Fitzgerald

Kennedy Library, Boston; **973** AP Photo; **975** Bettmann/Corbis; **976** Bruce Davidson/Magnum Photos; **977** LBJ Library photo by Cecil Stoughton; **979** George Meany Memorial Archives; **980** Bettmann/Corbis; **981** Scurlock Studio Records, Archives Center, National Museum of American History, Smithsonian Institution; **982** University of California, Berkeley Art Museum; purchased with the aid of funds from the National Endowment for the Arts (selected by the Committee for the Acquisition of Afro-American Art); **983** Photo by C. Clark Kissinger; **984** Lon Wilson/UC Berkeley, University Archives; **986** Photograph by Yoichi Okamoto, courtesy of the Lyndon Baines Johnson Library; **990 (top)** Larry Burrows/Time Life Pictures/Getty Images; **990 (bottom)** Library of Congress **991 (top)** © Lisa Law; **991 (bottom)** © Gene Anthony; **992** Getty Images; **993 (top)** Courtesy Wheaton College Archives and Special Collections; **993 (bottom)** Ralph Crane/Time Life Pictures/Getty Images; **995** Boston Globe via Getty Images; **996** Bettmann/Corbis; **997 (top)** JP Laffont/Sygma/Corbis; **997 (bottom)** George Meany Memorial Archives/Eisenberg photo; **998** AP Photo; **1000** Billy Ireland Cartoon Library & Museum, Ohio State University; **1001 (top)** © Grey Villet; **1001 (bottom)** © 1963 Herbert Block; **1002** Danny Lyon, NOW, ca.1968 International Center of Photography, Purchase, with funds provided by the ICP Acquisitions Committee, 2001; **1003** Copyrighted photo by Richard Copley; **1004** Frederick Douglass mural on the "Solidarity Wall," Falls Road, Belfast; http://en.wikipedia.org/wiki/GNU_Free_Documentation_License; **1005** © Robert Rauschenberg/Licensed by VAGA, New York, NY; **1008** Courtesy Ronald Reagan Library; **1012** National Archives; **1014** © Co Rentmeester; **1015** Photo by Ollie Atkins/Time Life Pictures/Getty Images; **1016** May 4 Collection. Kent State University Libraries, Special Collections and Archives; **1017** Leonard Freed/Magnum; **1018** David Fenton/Getty Images; **1019** © 1973 Herbert Block; **1021** Bob Kreisel/Alamy; **1022** AP Photo; **1023** Courtesy Gerald R. Ford Library; **1024** Fox Photos/Getty Images; **1025** J. L. Atlas/Corbis/Sygma; **1026** AP Photo; **1027** Bettmann/Corbis; **1029** Bettmann/Corbis; **1030** © 1982 Doug Marlette; **1031 (top)** Bettmann/Corbis; **1031 (bottom)** Mark Meyer/Time & Life Pictures/Getty Images; **1033 (top)** Time Life Pictures/Getty Images; **1033 (bottom)** University of Southern California; **1037** Library of Congress; **1038** © Mary Ellen Mark; **1039** Ronald Reagan Presidential Library; **1040** Photofest; **1042** AP Photo; **1043** © 2001 Susanna Raab, all rights reserved; **1046** AP Photo; **1049 (top)** Patrick Hagerty/Corbis Sygma; **1049 (bottom)** Peter Turnley/Corbis; **1051** AP Photo; **1053** Courtesy of Edward Sorel, published as the cover of The New Yorker; **1054** Erik Freeland/Corbis; **1055** Peter Turnely/Corbis; **1057** Wolfgang Kaehler/Corbis; **1058 (top)** Photo by Joi Ito; http://creativecommons.org/licenses/by/2.0/deed.en; **1058 (bottom)** AP Photo; **1059 (top)** © 2004 Bob Sacha; **1059 (bottom)** Reprinted with permission of David Jacobson; **1061** Copyright 1993 Robert Ariail/The State; **1064** Hans Haacke © 2004 Artists Rights Society (ARS), New York/ VG Bild-Kunst, Bonn; **1065** Gilles Mingasson/Getty Images; **1067** Catherine Karnow/Corbis; **1068** Stephanie Maze/Corbis; **1069**

Takaaki Iwabu KRT/Newscom; **1071** AP Photo; **1073** Reuters/Corbis; **1074** The Aldrich Contemporary Art Museum; **1075** AP Photo; **1077** Jetta Fraser; **1078** Ralf-Finn Hestoft/Corbis; **1079 (top)** © 1998 Herbert Block; **1079 (bottom)** Reuters/Corbis; **1081** © 2000 Herbert Block; **1082** A. Ramey/Woodfin Camp and Associates; **1083** © Renee Cox; **1086** Ralf-Finn Hestoft/Corbis; **1089 (top)** Steve Ludlum/The New York Times/Redux; **1089 (bottom)** Lionel Hahn/Abaca USA; **1090** Earl Dotter; www.earldotter.com; **1091** Serge J-F. Levy; **1092** Steve Benson/Creators Syndicate; **1093** Mario Tama/Getty Images; **1096** AP Photo; **1097** Joe Raedle/Getty Images; **1099** Hank Walker/Getty Images; **1101** Michael Ramirez/Creators Syndicate; **1104** NOAA; **1105** AP Photo; **1106** AP Photo; **1107 (top)** © Angelo Lopez; **1107 (bottom)** Mark Peterson/Redux; **1109** Author: George Mill. Title: Freedom: Certain Restrictions Apply; **1111** Joshua Lott/The New York Times/Redux; **1114** AUTH © 2009 The Philadelphia Inquirer. Reprinted with permission of UNIVERSAL UCLICK. All rights reserved; **1116** © Tribune Media Services, Inc. All Rights Reserved. Reprinted with permission; **1118 (top)** AP Photo; **1118 (bottom)** Official White House Photo by Chuck Kennedy; **1119** Win McNamee/Getty Images; **1122** Monique Jacques/Corbis; **1123** AP Photo; **1124** Spencer Platt/Getty Images; **1125** AP Photo/Port Authority of NY & NJ, Durst Organization; **1127** Eli Reed/Magnum Photos.

TEXT, TABLES, AND FIGURES

36 Bartolomé de las Casas: *History of the Indies*, translated and edited by Andrée Collard (New York: Harper & Row, 1971), pp. 82, 112–115. Copyright © 1971 by Andrée M. Collard, renewed © 1999 by Joyce J. Contrucci. Reprinted by permission of Joyce J. Contrucci; **74** Thomas Hutchinson: "The Examination of Mrs. Anne Hutchinson at the Court of Newtown." Reprinted by permission of the publisher from *The History of the Colony and Province of Massachusetts Bay, Vol. II* by Thomas Hutchinson, edited by Lawrence Shaw Mayo, pp. 366–391, Cambridge, Mass.: Harvard University Press, Copyright © 1963 by the President and Fellows of Harvard College. Copyright © renewed 1964 by Lawrence Shaw Mayo; **107** (Table 3.1) Aaron S. Fogleman, "From Slaves, Convicts, and Servants to Free Passengers: The Transformation of Immigration in the Era of the American Revolution," Journal of American History 85 (June 1998) 43–76; **112** Johannes Hanner: Letter by an Immigrant to Pennsylvania, 1769, *Unpublished Documents on Emigration from the Archives of Switzerland*, Albert B. Faust, *Deutsch-Amerikanische Geschichtsblätter*, Vol. 18–19, pp. 37–39. Translation by Volker Berghahn. Reprinted by permission of Volker Berghahn; **135** (Table 4.1) Ira Berlin, *Many Thousands Gone: The First Two Centuries of Slavery in North America* (Cambridge, Mass.: Harvard University Press, 1998) 369–70; **230** Abigail Adams: "Abigail Adams to John Adams, 31 March 1776." Reprinted by permission of the publisher from *The Adams Papers: Adams Family Correspondence, Volume I: December 1761–May 1776*, edited by L.H. Butterfield, Cambridge, Mass.: The Belknap Press of Harvard University Press, Copyright © 1963 by the Massachusetts Historical Soci-

ety; **267** (Table 7.1) U.S. Bureau of the Census, *A Century of Population Growth* (Washington, D.C., 1900), 47, 57; **282** Democratic-Republican Society of Pennsylvania: Excerpt from minutes of The Democratic Society of Pennsylvania, December 18, 1794. The Historical Society of Pennsylvania (HSP), Collection # Am. 315/3150. Reprinted with permission; **315** (Table 9.1) U.S. Bureau of the Census, *Historical Statistics of the United States* (Washington, D.C., 1975), 24–36; **393** (Table 11.1) U.S. Bureau of the Census, *A Century of Population Growth* (Washington, D.C., 1900) 133; **394** (Table 11.2) Census of 1850; **404** Joseph Taper: Excerpts from "Letter from Joseph Taper to Joseph Long, November 11, 1840" in the Joseph Long Papers located in the Rare Book, Manuscript, and Special Collections Library, Duke University. Reprinted by permission; **407** (Table 11.3) Census of 1860; **590** (Table 16.1) U.S. Bureau of the Census, *Historical Statistics of the United States* (Washington D.C., 1975), 134; **652** (Table 17.1) Arwin D. Smallwood, *The Atlas of African-American History and Politics* (New York, 1998), 106; **681** (Table 18.1) U.S. Bureau of the Census, *Historical Statistics of the United States* (Washington D.C., 1975), 11–12; **683** (Table 18.2) Census of 1920; **684** (Table 18.3) U.S. Bureau of the Census, *Historical Statistics of the United States* (Washington D.C., 1975), 131; **685** (Table 18.4) U.S. Bureau of the Census, *Historical Statistics of the United States* (Washington D.C., 1975), 139; **686** (Table 18.5) U.S. Bureau of the Census, *Historical Statistics of the United States* (Washington D.C., 1975), 716; **737** W.E.B. Du Bois: "Returning Soldiers." W. W. Norton & Co. wishes to thank the Crisis Publishing Co., Inc., the publisher of the magazine of the National Association for the Advancement of Colored People, for the use of this material first published in the May 1919 issue of Crisis Magazine; **744** (Table 19.1) Robert B. Grant, *The Black Man Comes to the City* (Chicago, 1972) 28–30; **782** (Table 20.1) Mae M. Ngai, "The Architecture of Race in American Immigration Law: A Reexamination of the Immigration Act of 1924," *Journal of History* 86 (June 1999), 25; **821** John Steinbeck: Excerpt from *The Harvest Gypsies* by John Steinbeck. Copyright © 1936 by *The San Francisco News*. Reprinted by permission of Heyday Books, Berkeley, California; **855** (Table 22.1) U.S. Bureau of the Census, *Historical Statistics of the United States, Colonial Times to 1970* (Washington D.C., 1970), 176–77; **872** Henry R. Luce: "The American Century," *Time*, February 7, 1941, pp. 22–31. Copyright 1941 Life Inc. Reprinted with permission. All rights reserved; **873** Charles Wesley: "The Negro Has Always Wanted the Four Freedoms," from *What the Negro Wants* edited by Rayford W. Logan. Copyright © 1944 by the University of North Carolina Press, renewed 1972 by Rayford W. Logan. Used by permission of the publisher; **912** Will Herberg: From *Protestant, Catholic, Jew: An Essay in American Religious Sociology* by Will Herberg. Copyright © 1955, 1960 by Will Herberg. Used by permission of Doubleday, a division of Random House, Inc. For on-line information about other Random House, Inc. books and authors, see the Internet website at http://www.random-house.com; **913** Henry S. Commager: "Who Is Loyal to America?" Harper's Magazine, September 1947, p. 143. Reprinted by permission of the Estate of Henry S. Commager; **950** Martin Luther King Jr.: "Meeting at Holt Street Church," Reprinted by arrangement with The Heirs to the Estate of Martin Luther King Jr., c/o Writers house as agent for the proprietor, New York, NY. Copyright © 1963 Martin Luther King Jr.; Copyright © renewed 1991 Coretta Scott King; **978** (Figure 25.1) *Congressional Quarterly, Civil Rights: A Progress Report* (1971), 46; **988** Young Americans for Freedom: The Sharon Statement, *National Review*, September 24, 1960. Reprinted by permission of Young Americans for Freedom/YAF Foundation; **989** Students for a Democratic Society: The Port Huron Statement, 1964, pp. 3–8. Reprinted by permission of Tom Hayden; **1014** (Table 26.1) U.S. Bureau of the Census, *Statistical Abstract of the United States* (Washington D.C., 1982); **1034** Redstockings of the Women's Liberation Movement: The Redstockings Manifesto was issued in New York City on July 7, 1969. It first appeared as a mimeographed flyer, designed for distribution at women's liberation events. Further information about the Manifesto and other materials from the 1960s rebirth years of feminism is available from the Redstockings Women's Liberation Archives for Action at www.redstockings.org. Reprinted with permission; **1035** Jerry Falwell: From *Listen, America!* by Jerry Falwell, copyright © 1980 by Jerry Falwell. Used by permission of Doubleday, a division of Random House, Inc.* For on-line information about other Random House, Inc. books and authors, see the Internet web site at http://www.randomhouse.com; **1063** Global Exchange: "Declaration for Global Democracy," from Global Exchange, Seattle, December 1999. Reprinted by permission; **1070** (Figure 27.4) U.S. Census Bureau; **1070** (Table 27.2) Lizabeth Cohen, *A Consumer's Republic: The Politics of Mass Consumption in Postwar America* (New York, 2003) 222; **A-35** John Lewis: "Patience Is a Nasty and Dirty Word," Speech at March on Washington, 1963. Reprinted with the permission of Simon & Schuster, Inc., from *Walking with the Wind: A Memoir of the Movement* by John Lewis and Michael D'Orso. Copyright © 1998 by John Lewis. All rights reserved; **A-53** U.S. National Archives and Records Administration; **A-54** Historical Statistics of the United States (1975); Statistical Abstract of the United States (1991, 1996); Population Estimates Program, Population Division, U.S. Census Bureau. Every effort has been made to contact the copyright holder of each of the selections. Rights holders of any selections not credited should contact Permissions Department, W. W. Norton & Company, Inc., 500 Fifth Avenue, New York, NY 10110, in order for a correction to be made in the next reprint.

INDEX

Page numbers in *italics* refer to illustrations.

AAA, *see* Agricultural Adjustment Act
Abe Lincoln's Last Card, 514
Abilene, Kans., 604
abolition movement, 129, 134, 207, 224–26, *225*, 339, 385, 390, *425*, 436–46, *437*, *438*, *439*, *443*, *444*, *445*, 454–55, 475, 516, 573, 656, 732, 736, 900, 983, 995, *1004*
Abby Kelley and, *425*
Abraham Lincoln and, 487–88
African-Americans and, 389, *391*, 416–22, 435, 436, 441–43
British, 226–28
in Civil War, 514, 540
colonization and, 435–36
in early U.S., 167, 226–29, *288*, 358
Frederick Douglass and, 389, *391*
John Brown and, 489–92
The Liberator newspaper for, 351, *455*
obstacles to, in early U.S., 224–25
pacifism and, 439
rise in militant form of, 436
after Turner's rebellion, 421–22
U.S. Constitution and, 256
in Virginia, 421
women's rights linked to, 446, 447, 454–55
Aborigines, 601, 1056
abortion, 1014, 1029, *1031*, 1054, 1076, 1103
Clinton and, 1052
conservatism and, 920, 1029, 1030–31
feminists and, 996, 1004, 1030–31
religious right and, 1029, 1040, 1075
Supreme Court and, 921, 1002, 1029
Tea Party and, 1123
Abraham Lincoln (aircraft carrier), *1096*
Abraham Lincoln Brigade, 845
Abrams, Jacob (1886–1953), 776
Abu Ghraib (prison), 1101, *1101*
abuse, domestic, 702, 730
Acadians, 158
Acheson, Dean (1893–1971), 887, 915
ACLU, *see* American Civil Liberties Union
Acoma pueblo, 33–34, *34*
acquired immunodeficiency syndrome (AIDS), 1073, *1073*
Across the Continent (Palmer), *600*
Act Concerning Religion (1649), 83
activism, in "The Sixties," 994–1005
Act of Union (1707), 127
Adamic, Louis (1899–1951), 833
Adams, Abigail (1744–1818), 205, *207*, 217, 232, 234
letters to John Adams by, 205, 230, 234
Adams, Brooks (1848–1927), 672

Adams, Charles Francis (1807–1886), 473
Adams, Hannah, 281
Adams, Henry (b. 1843), 550
Adams, John (1735–1826), 173, 217, 224, 239, *288*, 291, 358, 361, 711
Abigail Adams's letters to, 205, 230, 234
Boston Massacre and, 180
Constitutional Convention and, 247
education and, 215
in election of 1796, 284
in election of 1800, 287–88
expansion of navy by, 295
in First Continental Congress, 182–83
Fries's Rebellion and, 285
and Native Americans, 377
presidency of, 285–90, *285*
religion and, 212
on the right to vote, 208, 209
in Second Continental Congress, 185
selected vice president, 273
on the Stamp Act, 176
Thomas Paine and, 186
Treaty of Paris and, 200
on women's rights, 232, 234
XYZ affair and, 285, *285*
Adams, John Quincy (1767–1848), 276, 347, 356, 358, 360, *361*, 444, 473, 672
in *Amistad* case, 419
in election of 1824, 361–65, *365*
in election of 1828, 366
views on federal power, 365
Adams, Samuel (1722–1803), 182–83, 246, 256
Adamson Act (1916), 711
Adams-Onís Treaty (1819), 314
Addams, Jane (1860–1935), 701–2, *701*, 741, 768, 771
Addison County society, 280
Address at Sanitary Fair, Baltimore (Lincoln), 527
Address to the Slaves, 436
Adelphia Communications, 1059
Adenauer, Konrad (1876–1967), 940
Adventures of Ozzie and Harriet, The (TV show), 929
advertising, 761, 763, 764, 767–68, *768*, 857–59, *858*, 860, *942*, 947, 1069
consumerism and, *687*, *688*, 760, *761*, 928, 929
corporate, 936
family life in, 931, *932*
political, 905, 1043–44, 1103
television and, 928, 929, *936*, 939
women and, *768*
Advertising Council, 936

AFDC, *see* Aid to Families with Dependent Children
affirmative action, 980, 1012, 1013, 1032, 1038, 1040, 1052, 1053, 1070, 1071, 1075, 1108
Affluent Society, The (Galbraith), 947
Afghanistan, 1027, 1042, 1087, 1090–91, *1091*, 1092, *1097*, 1099, 1101, 1108, 1111, 1126
U.S. presence increased in, 1121
U.S. war on, 1088
war on terror in, 1122
AFL, *see* American Federation of Labor
Africa, 2, 3, 5, 6, 18–21, *19*, *20*, 24, 88, 127, 715, 752, 873, 874, 875–76, 881, 897, 943, 1049, 1065, 1066, 1081, 1095
AIDS and, 1073
immigrants from, 1070
African-Americans, 352–53, 631, *645*, *646*, 657, 673, 832, *832*, 833, 834, 836, 881, *915*, 934, 961, 1069–70, 1080, 1116, 1117, 1127
in abolition movement, 389, *391*, 416–22, 435, 441–43
as Afro-Americans, 982
in American Revolution, 193–94, *194*
in arts, 787–88
barred from Missouri, 358
barred from Progressive Party convention, 741
barred from public land, 339
Birmingham campaign and, 966–67, *968*
and Black Codes, 563–64, 565
black internationalism and, 873, 875–76
Booker T. Washington and, 656
Carter and, 1024
citizenship and, 440, 571, 572, 782, 783
civil rights and, 834–35, 870–76, *875*, 965–69, *967*, 978, 979–82
in Civil War, 517–19, *518*, *519*, 539–40, 544–45, *548*
in Clinton administration, 1052
Constitution and, 266–68, 1016
as cowboys, 604
decline in economic status of, 339
decolonization and, 896
as Democrats, 757, 800
early emancipation struggles of, 226, 234–36
education and, 645, 646
entertainment of, 767
as Ethiopian Regiment, 194
as excluded from Rough Riders, 663
and FDR, 823
feminists and, 766

as First Rhode Island Regiment, *194*
free blacks, 97–98, 133, 229–32, 403–7, *407*, 435
Freedom's Journal newspaper for, 351, 443
Freedom Train and, 885–86
ghetto uprisings and, 979–80
in gold rush, 470
Great Society and, 978–79
Hurricane Katrina and, 1104–5, *1104*
immigrants vs., 483
IQ tests and, 739
Jefferson on, 268–69
and jobs in New York City, 339
juries and, 835
Knights of Labor and, 625, *625*
and Ku Klux Klan, *see* Ku Klux Klan
labor and, 339, 835, 949, 968, *1090*
LBJ and, 972–74
loss of freedom of, 587, 1016
loss of voting rights of, 587, 648–49, 701, 742, 743, 826, 829–30, 835, 873, 957–58, 973, 976, 979
in Louisiana, 294–95
March on Washington and, 870, 968–69, *969*
market revolution and, 339, 343
in Maryland colony, 97
naturalization of, 782
New Deal and, 826–27, 828–30
Nixon and, 1012
northern migration of, 586, 647–48, 743–44, *744*, 783, *786*, 869, 949
as part of society, 438, 440
Plessy v. Ferguson and, 650–51, *650*
in politics, 573–74, 648
population of, *267*, *786*
prison population of, 1072
Progressives and, 741
progressivism and, 741–43
in Quaker society, 93
Reagan and, 1038
recession and, 1120
in Reconstruction, 386–87, 558–59, 565–67, *566*, 568–71, *569*, 572–74, 645, 649, 651–52, 741, 757, 842, 902
religion of, 413–14, *414*
and segregation, *see* segregation
Selma campaign and, 952, 976, *976*
in Seminole War, 376
sit-ins and, 965
slavery and, *121*
as soldiers for Confederacy, 535
in South, 636, 646–47, 743, 870, 873
in suburbs, 932, 1064, 1071
as troops in Philippines, 670
Truman and, 902–5

African-Americans (*continued*)
    unemployment and, 829, *829*, 980, 982, 1070, 1120
    as viewed by Jackson, 367
    voting rights of, 144, 347, 348–49, 351, 352, 654, *874*
    wages and, 339, 540, 740, 787, 1038, 1105
    welfare and, 1010
    westward expansion and, 317
    women, *646*, 647, 648, 684, 741, 870, *982*
    women's movement neglect of, 741
    World War I and, 737, 743, *743*
    World War II and, 757, 842, 864, 866, 869–76, *869*, *875*
    see also civil rights movement; Great Migration; slavery; slaves
African Chief, The, 281
African Methodist Episcopal Church, *338*, 339, 420
African National Congress, 1049
African religion, in American colonies, 136–37
Age of Jackson, 210, 349, 366, 367–77, 382, 435, 439, 477
Age of Revolution, 167
Agitator, 571
Agnew, Samuel (1833–1902), 554
Agnew, Spiro T. (1918–1996), 1019, 1023
Agreement of the People, 81, 148
Agricultural Adjustment Act (AAA), 807, 810, 830
agriculture, 5, 10, 20, 25, 121, 154, 155, 168, 266, 275, *276*, 278, 307, 380, 395–96, 602–4, *602*, *604*, 618, 678–79, 683, 711, 828, 830, 854, 865
    African-Americans and, 740, 826
    American Revolution and, 217
    bonanza farms and, 603–4, *603*
    in Civil War, 524
    Democratic Party and, 369, 789
    Eisenhower and, 940
    and farm populations, 925
    and foreclosures, 763, 790
    Great Depression and, 790, 792
    and immigration, 109–10
    Indian, 57–58
    industrial revolution and, 479, 589–90
    invention of, 6
    Jamestown and, 58, 59
    Jefferson's views on, 294, 354
    market revolution and, 307, 318
    migrant workers and, 682, 821, 828, 833, 997–98
    New Deal and, 757, 799, 807, *809*, 816, *816*, 818, 823, 826, 837, 940
    in 1920s, 763–64, *764*, 772
    in Panic of 1837, 380
    Populists and, 587, 636–37, 638
    post-World War II, 925
    in Progressive era, 680
    promotion by J. Q. Adams of, 365
    Pueblo Indians and, 10, 14
    railroads and, *602*, 636
    Southern expansion of, 645–46
    technology and, 978

tobacco and, 61, 114
    women and, 14, 15, 122–23
"Agrippa," 261
Aguinaldo, Emilio (1869–1964), 666, *666*, 669, 670
AIDS, *see* acquired immunodeficiency syndrome
Aid to Dependent Children, 818
Aid to Families with Dependent Children (AFDC), 1010, 1054
aircraft, *see* aviation and aircraft
Air Force, U.S., segregation in, 869
Air Force (movie), 864
airplanes, 722
Alabama, 156, 312, 314, 374, 834, 836, 1000, 1123
    black voting in, 903
    BP oil spill and, 1119
    Confederate flag and, 957
    lynchings in, 775
    women's groups in, 702
Alabama, University of, segregation at, 958
Al-Ahram, 750
Alamance, Battle of, 177
Alamo, 462
Alaska, 986, 1021
    acquisition from Russia of, 467
    corporate mining in, 604
    pipeline, 1021
    purchase of, 660
    Russian fur traders in, 154
Albania, 1056
Albany, Ga., 966
Albany, N.Y., 41, 309
Albany Plan of Union (1754), 164
Albuquerque, N.Mex., 152, *612*, 927
Alcatraz Island, 998, *998*
Alcoa Presents (TV show), 929
alcohol, banning of, *see* Prohibition
Alcorn, James L. (1816–1894), 575
Aldrich, Winthrop W. (1885–1974), 885
Alexander I, czar of Russia (1777–1825), 512
Alexander VI, Pope (1431?–1503), 28
Alger, John B., 400
Algonquian Indians, 45
Alien Act (1798), 285–87, 327, 732, 1075, 1100
Alito, Samuel, Jr. (1950–), 1109
Allen, Ethan (1738–1789), 178, 185
Allen, Joseph, 184
Allen, Richard (1760–1831), 339
Allende, Salvador (1908–1973), 1015
Alliance for Progress, 970
Allies:
    in World War I, 721, 724, *725*, 726, 746, 752
    in World War II, 757, 850, *850*, 874, 876, 878–81, 899
Al Qaeda, 1087, 1093, 1100
Altgeld, John Peter (1847–1902), 630
Amalgamated Association, 635, 747
Amazon, 26
America, democracy in, 346–84
America First Committee, 846
America in the War, 860
American Anti-Slavery Society, 438, *439*, 441, 454, 568

American Ballet Caravan, 844
American Bible Society, 432
American Century, The (Luce), 860–61, 872, 896
American Civil Liberties Union (ACLU), 776, 779, 835, 910
American colonies, 3, 49, 53–54
    African religion in, 136–37
    Anglicization of, 119
    artisans of, 115–16
    assemblies in, 146
    cities of, 115–16
    diversity of, 6, 107, 123
    election campaigns in, 207
    elite class in, 118
    and English Civil War, 82
    expansion of, 3, 127
    expansion of England's, 88–94
    Glorious Revolution in, 103–4
    government in, 145–46
    hierarchical structure in, 119–22
    Islam in, 136–37
    liberties in, 55–56
    literacy in, 147
    maps of, *108*, *153*
    middle class in, 121–22
    politics in, 143–44
    population of, 3, 61–62, 106–7, 132
    poverty in, 120–21
    Protestantism in, 42, 64, 82, 91, 101, 103–4, 107, 109, 110
    reduced death rate in, 122
    as refuge, 52–53
    relationship with Indians in, 91–92
    salutary neglect and, 145
    society of, 114–15, 118–23
    voting rights in, 144, 207–8
    western frontier of, 156–57
    women's role in, 122–23
    see also American Revolution
American Colonization Society, 269, 435, *435*, 436, 441
American Creed, 874, 897
American Crisis, The (Paine), 195
American Dictionary (Webster), 343, 350
American Dilemma, An (Myrdal), 874, 949
American Document, 834, *834*
American Economic Foundation, 935
"American Economic System," 936
American Enterprise Institute, 1028
American Federation of Labor (AFL), 656–57, 688, 689, 691, 726, 727, 733, 746–47, 771, 812, 813, 834, 871, 901, 902, 941
American Flag, The, 520
American Foot Soldiers, Yorktown Campaign, *194*
American Freedom and Catholic Power (Blanshard), 959
American Heritage Foundation, 885–86
American Husbandry (Anon.), 121
American identity, 734–35
American Indian Movement, 998, 1073
American Individualism (Hoover), 788
American International Group (AIG), 1112, 1115

Americanism, 780, 832, 834, 897, 913, 977
    vs. racism, 834, 863
Americanization, 773, 780–86, 932
    Catholics and, 785, 834
    of immigrants, 734, 735, *735*, 738, *738*, 780, 831, 864–65
    see also Americanism; assimilation
Americanization of the World, The; or, the Trend of the Twentieth Century (Stead), 715
American Jewish Committee, 834, 868, 871
American League, 705
American Legion, 910
American Liberty League, 819
American Magazine, The, *158*
American Medical Association, 705, 818, 898
American National Exhibition, 923, *925*
American National Red Cross, 530
American Party, *see* Know-Nothing Party
American Philosophical Society, 147
American Progress (Gast), *461*
American Protective League (APL), 733
American Psychiatric Association, 1014
American Railway Union, 641
American Revolution, 170–203, *192*, 224, 233, 279, 290, 307, 387, 390, 437, 517, 620, *832*, 857, 861, *887*, 891, 898, 899, 904, 983, 1077
    American advantages in, 193
    American mutinies in, 199
    Andrew Jackson in, 347
    Articles of Confederation and, 240
    background of, 171–82
    battles of, 194–200
    black soldiers in, 193–94, *194*
    British advantages in, 193
    casualties in, 193, 506
    creation of national identity and, 263
    debt created by, 274
    democracy and, 168, 206–10, 284
    early battles of, 184–85, 194–99
    economic effect of, 217–18, 245–46
    equality and, 205
    family life and, 234
    force strength in, 193
    French assistance in, 193, *200*
    indentured servitude and, 193, 205, 216, 234
    Indians and, 205, 221–23, 235
    low point of, 195
    Loyalists in, 218–21, *220*
    map of battles in, *196*
    Paine's view of, 186–87, 188
    religious freedom and, 210–15
    slavery and, 167, 205, 223–32, 234, 235, 415, 435
    in South, 197–99, *198*
    Spanish help in, 197
    views of elite on, 207–8
    voting rights and, 209–10
    women and, 179, 232, *233*

"American Scholar, The" (Emerson), 330, 332

American Standard, 455

Americans with Disabilities Act (1990), 1073

American System, 353–55, 364, 369, 382

American Telephone and Telegraph (AT&T), 1014

American Temperance Society, 431

American Tobacco, 708

American Tract Society, 432–33

American University, 971

American Way, 999

American Woman's Home, The (Beecher and Beecher Stowe), *351*

American Woman Suffrage Association, 571

America Triumphant and Britannia in Distress, 235

Ames, Adelbert (1835–1933), 582

Am I Not a Man and a Brother?, 442, *443*

Am I Not a Woman and a Sister? (Bourne), *453*

Amistad, 419

Amity and Commerce, Treaty of (1778), 197

Amnesty International, 1025

Amsterdam, 41

Anabaptists, 110

anarchism, 625, 629, 733, 739, 759, 777

Ancona, Victor, *870*

Anderson, John (1922–), 1033

Anderson, Marian (1897–1993), 829

Anderson, Sherwood (1876–1941), 788

Andersonville, Ga., Confederate prison at, 506, 564

Andes Mountains, 8, 25, 31

And Not This Man (Nast), *580*

Andrews, Sidney (1837–1880), 551, 554

Andros, Edmund (1637–1714), 90–91, 103–4

Angel Island, 681

Anglican Church, 41, 71, 80, 81, 83, 102–3, 104, 110, 118, 181

    American Revolution and, 211–12, 214, 219

    creation of, 50

    Dissenters and, 83, 102–3, 210

    Puritans and, 64–66

Anglo-Dutch war, 88

Anglo-Iranian Oil Company, 944

Angola, 943

    as source of slaves, 98

Ann Arbor, Mich., Beats in, 948

Anniston, Ala., 966

"annuity" system (for Native Americans), 265

Anshutz, Thomas (1891–1912), *621*

Anthony, Saint, *35*

Anthony, Susan B. (1820–1906), 454, *570*, 571, *658*

Anti-Ballistic Missile Treaty (1972), 1015, 1040

anti-Catholicism, 935, 959–60, *959*

Anti-Defamation League of B'nai B'rith, 785

Antietam, Battle of, 507, 510, *511*, 515

Anti-Evolution League, 779

Anti-Federalists, 256, 257, 258, 261

Antigua, *96*

Anti-Imperialist League, 671

Antinomianism, 73

anti-Semitism, 785, 815, 864, 935, 1009, 1077

    see also Jews

antiwar movement, Vietnam era, 990–91, 1002–4, 1016, *1017*, 1093, 1102

Antrobus, John (1837–1907), *415*

Antwerp, *44*

Apaches, 34, 35, 153, 460, 609

apartheid, 992, 1049

Apess, William (1798–1839), 222, 376–77

Appalachia, *977*, 978

Appalachian Mountains, 242, 243, 264, 308

    crossing of, 312

    population west of, 314

Appeal in Favor of That Class of Americans Called Africans, An (Child), 440

Appeal of the Independent Democrats, 478

Appeal to Reason, 691

Appeal to the Coloured Citizens of the World, An (Walker), 436, *436*, 442

appeasement, 844

Apple Computers, 1057, *1058*, 1064

appliances, household, *see* consumerism, and household appliances; *specific appliances*

Appomattox Courthouse, 542, 563

aqueducts, 708

Arabella, 68

Arabs, 751, 753, 1020

    and Arab Spring, 1095

    nationalism and, 944–45, 1027

Arab Spring, 1095

Aragon, 21

Arapahos, 525

Arbenz Guzmán, Jacobo (1913–1971), 944, 946

Arbuckle, Fatty (1887–1933), 775

Argentina, 506, 604, 1025–26

Aristotle (384–322 B.C.E.), 17, 207

    on democracy, 349

Arizona, 10, *10*, 467, 990, 1074, *1111*

    agriculture in, 679, 925

Arkansas, 312, 648, 1051

    enters Union, 337

    lynchings in, 775

Arlington, Vt., 841

Armada Portrait (Gower), *51*

armed forces, U.S., *see* military, U.S.

Armey, Richard (1940–), 1076

Arminianism, 149–50

armistice, Korean War, 893

Armory show, 696

Armour, Philip D. (1832–1901), 528

Armstrong, Louis, 952

Armstrong, Samuel (1839–1893), 656

Army, U.S., 876

    African-Americans in, 353, 517–19

    desegregation in, 874

    fear of standing, 275

Army-McCarthy hearings, 909–10, *909*, 929

Army of Northern Virginia, Confederate, 509

Army of the Potomac, Union, 509, 510, 536, 537

Arnold, Benedict (1741–1801), 185, 199, 211, *235*

Arthur, Chester A. (1829–1886), 617

Arthur Andersen Company, 1059

Articles of Confederation (1781), 240–47, *241*, 249, 250, 254, 274

    weaknesses of, 245–46

artisans, 319, 339

    African-Americans as, 339

    Second New Deal and, 816

    see also craftsmen

arts:

    African-Americans in, 787–88

    during Cold War, 897

    Second New Deal and, 816, *817*

Aryan Nation, 1077

Aryans, as "master race," 784, 863, 902

Ashanti people, 130, 136

Ashcan School, *677*

Ashcroft, John (1942–), 1099

Asia, 2, 18, *19*, 664–65, 715, 752, 873, 874, 886, 897, 943, 945, 1057, 1065, 1066, 1081

    and Native Americans, 6

    pre-World War II, 844

    sea route to, 2

Asian immigrants, 680–81, *682*, 740, 782, 865, 921, 976–77, *1067*, 1068–69, 1070

    affirmative action and, 1013

    naturalization of, 782

    World War II and, 866–69

asiento, 128

assemblies, colonial, 146

    governor vs., 146

    Parliament vs., 173

    rise of, 146

assembly lines, 686, 811, 855, *928*

assimilation, 784, 831, 864–65, 935

associational action, 788, 793

Astor, John Jacob (1763–1848), 338

Astor House, 338

asylum of liberty, U.S. as, 167, 187, 191, 214, 268, 520, 783

asylums, 433, 645, 739

AT&T (American Telephone and Telegraph), 1014

Atkinson, Edward (1827–1905), 620

Atlanta, Ga., Sherman's capture of, 537, 538

Atlanta Cotton Exposition, 656

Atlanta University, 742

Atlantic, Battle of the, 849

Atlantic and Pacific Tea Company, 592

Atlantic cable, 592

Atlantic Charter, 880, *881*, 899

Atlantic City, N.J., 973, 974

Atlantic Monthly, 772

Atlantic trade, of New England colonies, 128–29, *129*

atomic bomb, 877–78, *877*, 880, 886, 908, 941

    of Soviet Union, 891

    see also hydrogen bomb; nuclear weapons

Atomic Energy Commission, 889, 936

Attack Made on Tripoli, 295

Attlee, Clement (1883–1967), 878

Attucks, Crispus (ca. 1723–1770), 180, 552

Atwater, Lee (1951–1991), 1044

Augusta County, Va., 121

Austin, Moses (1761–1821), 460

Austin, Stephen (1793–1836), 460–61

Austin, Tex., 1057

Australia, 604, 752

    in World War II, 849

Austria, 158, 749, 844

Austro-Hungarian Empire, 721, 750, *750*, 1055

    immigrants from, 654, 680

Autobiography (Franklin), 147, *147*

Autobiography of Malcolm X (Malcolm X), 981

automobiles, 688, 760, 763, *765*, 768, 772, 790, 852, *853*, 919, 923, 924, 926, 927, 929–31, *929*, 1105

    Detroit and, 929

    Ford and, 685–86, *686*

    highways and, 940

    Japanese, 1105

    Japanese production of, 1021

    in Los Angeles, 764

    manufacturers of, 929–30, *929*

    pollution and, 961, 1010

aviation and aircraft, 722, 762, 763, 853, 859, 870, 871, 906, 924, 1024, *1024*

Avilés, Pedro Menéndez de, *see* Menéndez de Avilés, Pedro

Axis of Evil, 1091, 1092

Axis powers, 845, 848, 856, 866, 870

Azikiwe, Nnamdi (1904–1996), 876

Azores, 20

Aztecs, 8, *9*, 23–24, *23*, 25, 27, 390

    smallpox epidemic and, 24

Babcock, Orville (1835–1884), 1103

baby boom, 919, 925, 931, *931*

Bacall, Lauren (1924–), *907*

Bache, Sarah Franklin (1743–1808), 232

Bachelor Girls Social Club, 685

Bachmann, Michele (1956), 1124

Backus, Isaac (1724–1806), 152, 212

Bacon, Nathaniel (1647–1676), 100

Bacon's Rebellion, 99–101, *100*, 161

Baghdad, 1093, 1096

Bahamas, 21

Bahrain, 1122

Bailey v. Alabama, 742

Bain Capital, Mitt Romney and, 1124

Baker, Ella (1903–1986), 966, 969, 995

Baker v. Carr, 1001

Balanchine, George (1904–1983), 897

Balboa, Vasco Núñez de (1475–1519), *8, 22, 23*

Baldwin, James (1924–1987), 965, 983

Balkans, 1055–56

"Ballad for Americans," 834

Ballinger, Richard A. (1858–1922), 709

balloons, hot air, 504

Ballou's Magazine, 391

Baltimore, Md., *938*
Baltimore and Ohio (B&O), 311, *312*
Bandung Conference, 943
Bank of America, 1115
Bank of England, 140, 380
Bank of Pennsylvania, *276*
Bank of the United States, 274, 299, 353, 370, *378*
  battle with Jackson of, 377–79
  Congress and, 378–79
  Second, 355, *378*
bankruptcy, 342
Bankruptcy Scene, A, 245
banks, 369, 396, 558, 618, 619, 636, 644, 711, 717, 718, 720, 763, 815, 915, 1038, 1060
  British, 715
  failure of, 790, 804
  in financial crisis of 2008, 1111–12, 1113, 1115, 1119
  and foreclosures, 763, 790, 794, 808, 809
  in Great Depression, 790, 791, 794, 803–4, *803*, 808, 809, 826
  national, 169, 275, 354–56, 528; *see also* Bank of the United States
  New Deal and, 757, 837
  Socialist party and, 709
  Southern, 393
  in Soviet Union, 746
  suburbs and, 932
  2008 financial crisis and, 1060
  World War I and, 723, 845
"Banned in Boston," 775
Banneker, Benjamin (1731–1806), 268, 276
Banner of the Society of Pewterers, 239
Baptists, *111*, 151, 152, 955, 1023
  African-American, 413, 551
  in American colonies, 144
  Free-Will, 214
  in Gabriel's Rebellion, 289
  in Great Awakening, 151, 152
  in Massachusetts colony, 82, 211
  Prohibition and, 730
  racial division among, 653
  in Second Great Awakening, 334, 413
  Seventh Day, 110
  slavery and, 473
Barbados, 96, 127, 133, 717
  as founder of Carolina colony, 92
  population of, 97
Barbary Coast, 95, 295
Barbary Wars, 295–96, *295*
Barbie doll, *1064*
Barbie's Liberty (Haacke), *1064*
Barclays bank, 1113
Bargain of 1877, 582–83
Barlow, Joel (1754–1812), 268
Barnett, Ross (1898–1987), 966
Barrow plantation, maps of, *553*
Bart, Lily, 599
Barton, Bruce (1886–1967), 764
Barton, Clara (1821–1912), 529, 530
Baruch, Bernard (1870–1965), 726
baseball, 705–6
Bataan, 848
  death march in, 848, *866*

Bataan (movie), 864
Batista, Fulgencio (1901–1973), 844, 970
Baton Rouge, La., 155, 314
"Battle Hymn of the Republic" (Howe), 520
Battle of Antietam, The (Hope), *511*
Baum, L. Frank (1856–1919), 644
Bavaria, 746
Baxter Street Court, *599*
Bay of Pigs invasion, 970
Beard, Charles (1874–1948), 764, 795
Beats, 948–49, *948*, 949
  Buddhism and, 993
Beaufort, South Carolina, *137*
Beauregard, P. G. T. (1818–1893), 504
Becker, Carl (1873–1945), 728
Beebe, Abner, 219
Beecher, Catharine (1800–1878), 351, *351*, 448
Beecher, Lyman (1775–1863), 327
Begin, Menachem (1913–1992), *1026*
Beijing, 1015, 1048, *1049*
Belfast, 746, *1004*
Belgium, *44*, 721, 845
Bell, John (1797–1869), 494–95
Bellamy, Edward (1850–1898), 626, 627–28, *628*, 689, 698
Bellows, George (1882–1925), 680, *778*
Belmont, Alva (1853–1933), 677
Belmont, Calif., *1059*
Beloved (Morrison), 477
Benedict, Ruth (1887–1948), 784, 864
Benét, Stephen Vincent (1898–1943), 856
Ben Hur (movie), 934
Benin, 20
Benito Cereno (Melville), 352
Benjamin Hawkins Trading with the Creek Indians, 266
Bennett, Thomas, Jr. (1781–1865), 420
Benson, Steve, *1092*
Bentham, Jeremy, 235
Benton, Thomas Hart (1782–1858), 374, *758*
Bergdorf Goodman department store, *679*
Berger, Victor (1860–1929), 689, 748
Bering Strait, 6
Berkeley, John (1602–1678), 93
Berkeley, William (1606–1677), 99–100, *100*, 103
Berlin, 891, 1040
  airlift, 891
  blockade, 890–91, *890*
  occupation of, 890–91
Berlin Congress of 1884–1885, 659
Berlin Wall, 970, *1047*, 1048
Bernard, Francis (1712–1779), 174–75
Bernays, Edward (1891–1995), 728, 768
Bethune, Mary McLeod (1875–1955), 829
Better America League, 910
Beveridge, Albert (1862–1927), 672
Beverly Hills, Calif., *1067*
Bible, 2, 28, 65, *67*, 68–70, 71, 73, *76*, 130, *142*, 150, 152, 413–14, 420, 432, *643*, 772, 778, *780*, 956, 1001, 1035, 1082

Book of Exodus of, 647
  interpretation of, 779–80, *780*
  Jefferson's version of, 212
  slavery in, 398, 405
  see also New Testament
Bible Belt, 628
Bible Commonwealth, 70, 71, 77, 104
Biddle, Nicholas (1786–1844), 377–79, *378*
Bierstadt, Albert, *608*
Big Minstrel Jubilee, *662*
Bilbo, Theodore (1877–1947), 831
bilingual education, 1075
Bill of Rights (American), 256, 257–63, 373, 566, 569, 777, 855, *856*, 910, 913, *1000*, 1002, 1036
Bill of Rights (English), 102, 259, 263
"Bill of Rights for the Disadvantaged," 980
Biloxi, Miss., 966
Bingham, George Caleb (1811–1879), *367*, *370*
bin Laden, Osama (1957–2011), 1087, 1090–91, 1092
  death of, 1121
Birch, William Russell, *292*
Birmingham, Ala., *874*, 885–86, 949
  church bombing in, 967
  civil rights campaign in, 966–67, *968*
  Freedom Rides in, 966
  manufacturing in, 645, 901
Birney, James G. (1825–1864), 444, 455, 464
birth control, 697, *698*, 730, 768, 775, 994, 1002, 1014
  in 2012 election and campaign, 1124
Birth of a Nation (movie), 741
birthrate:
  decline in U.S., 340, 791
  infant mortality and, 1082
  in Mexico, 1068
  minority, 1069
Bisbee, Ariz., strikes in, 733
Bishop Hill, Ill., *325*
Bismarck, Otto von (1815–1898), 520
Bisno, Abraham (1866–1929), 685
Black, Hugo (1886–1971), 868
black Americans, *see* African-Americans
Blackbirds (Broadway show), 787
Blackboard Jungle (movie), 947
Black Codes, 563–64, *564*, 565
Black Hawk (1767–1838), 13, *374*, 374
Black Hawk and His Son, Whirling Thunder (Jarvis), 374
Black Hawk War, *374*
Black Hills, 609
black internationalism, 873, 875–76
Black Legend, *30*, 31, 35, 36, 44
blacklisting:
  in Hollywood, 908
  of union organizers, 817
Black Muslims, 981
Black Panther Party, 982, 998, 1003
Black Pioneers, 228
Black Power, 976, 981–82, *982*, 997, 1016
Black Sea, 888

Blackstone, William (1723–1780), 179
Black Studies, 1074
Black Sunday, *808*
"black supremacy," 577
Black Tuesday, 790
Blackwell, Henry (1825?–1909), 453
Blaine, James G. (1830–1893), 617, *618*, 654, 661
Blair, Francis P., Jr. (1821–1875), *567*, 568
Blanchard, Jonathan (1811–1892), 336
Blanshard, Paul (1892–1980), 959
Blatch, Harriot Stanton (1856–1940), 766
"Bleeding Kansas," 484–85
Blithedale Romance, The (Hawthorne), 429
blitzkrieg, 845
Block, Herbert (1909–2001), *909*, 945, *1001*, *1019*, *1079*, *1081*
"blockbusting," 934
Bloomberg, Michael (1942–), in Islamic Cultural Center debate, 1107
Bloomer, Amelia (1818–1894), 452
Blue Eagle, 804
Blue Ridge Mountains, 212
Boardman, Elijah (1760–1823), *119*
Board of Trade (English), 172
Boas, Franz (1858–1942), 784
Bock, Vera (1905–), *816*
Body of Liberties (1641), 70, 77–78
Boesky, Ivan (1937–), 1038
Bogart, Humphrey (1899–1957), *907*
bohemians, 696, 983, 992, 1014
Bombardment of Fort Sumter (Currier and Ives), *499*
bomb shelters, 942, *943*
bonanza farms, 603–4, *603*
Bonneville Power Authority, 799
bonus marchers, 792
Book of Mormon, The, 336–37
Book of Negroes, 227
Booth, John Wilkes (1838–1865), 326, 542
Booth, Junius Brutus, 326
bootleggers, 779
Border Patrol, U.S., 783, *784*, 865, *1067*
border states:
  in Civil War, 513, 514
  Emancipation Proclamation and, 516
Bosch, Juan (1909–2001), 986
Bosnia, 1033, 1055–56
Bosnia-Herzegovina, 721
Bosses of the Senate, The, 616
Boston, Mass., 115, 147, 173, *309*
  integration in, 1012
  police strike in, 747
  population of, 115
  poverty in, 120–21
  Puritans in, 78–79
  religious tolerance in, 211
  Townshend boycott in, 178–79
  Washington's army abandons, 194
Boston Almanack, *175*
Boston Associates, 321
Boston Gazette, 141
Boston Globe, 1116
Boston Guardian, 741

Bostonians Paying the Excise-Man, The, 181
Boston Marathon, *995*
Boston Massacre, 179–80, *180*, 552
Boston Massacre, The (Revere), *180*
Boston News-Letter, 147
Boston Tea Party, 181, *181*
Boulevard Houses, *933*
Boumediene v. Bush, 1110
Bourke-White, Margaret (1906–1971), 764
Bourne, Randolph (1886–1918), 699, 700, 726, 731–32, 735
Boutwell, George S. (1818–1905), 672
Bow, Clara (1905–1965), 768
Bowdoin, James (1726–1790), 246
Bowers v. Hardwick, 1039, 1108
Bowser, David B., *520*
Bowser, Mary Elizabeth (b. 1840s), 534
boycotts, 703, 902, 954–56, *955*, 956, 997–98, *997*
Boy Scouts, *856*
bracero program, 865, 866
Braddock, Edward (1695–1755), 158
Bradford, William (1590–1657), 77
Bradwell, Myra (1831–1894), 571
Brady, Mathew (1823?–1896), 507, *522*, *530*
Bragg, Braxton (1817–1876), 554
"brains trust," 802
Brandeis, Louis D. (1856–1941), 689, 704–5, *704*, 710, 776–77, 802
Brant, Joseph (c. 1742–1807), 222
Braun, Carol Moseley (1947–), 573
Brazil, 23, 28, 43, 96, 128, *131*, 132, 506, 636
   abolition of slavery in, 511
   Dutch control of, 41
   slavery in, 137, 402–3, 411, 416, 511
Breckinridge, John C. (1821–1875), 329, 493–94
Breed's Hill, Battle of, 185
Brent, Margaret (1601–1670?), 63
Brentwood, Calif., *1082*
Brer Rabbit stories, 415
Bretton Woods, N.H., conference at, 879, 1020
Brewer, David J. (1837–1910), 655
Breyer, Stephen (1938–), 1052
Brezhnev, Leonid (1906–1982), 1015
Bridges, Harry (1901–1990), 811
Bridges, Ruby (1954–), *958*
Bridgewater, Mass., *459*
brinksmanship, 942
Bristol, England, 129
Britain, Battle of, 846
British Americans, *864*
   pride in, 185
   World War I and, 722
British colonies, *see* American colonies
British Empire, 81, 95–97, 186, 314, 659, 715, 746, 750, 752, 879, 887, 889, 896
   abolition of slavery in, 511
   American vs. British view of, 174–75
   expansion of, 88–94
British liberty, *see* English liberty
British navy, 296
British Petroleum (BP), and Gulf of Mexico oil spill, 1119, *1119*

Britton, Nan (1896–1991), 770
Broadway theater, 787
bronze, 20
Brooke, Edward W. (1919–), 573
Brook Farm, 429
Brooklyn, N.Y., 591, 697, *698*, 810, *933*
Brooklyn Dodgers, 903–4, *903*
Brooks, Preston (1819–1857), 484, *484*
Brotherhood of Sleeping Car Porters, 870
Broun, Heywood (1888–1939), 759
Browder, Earl (1891–1973), 832
Brown, Henry "Box" (b. 1816), 418
Brown, John (1800–1859), 442, 489–92, *489*, *490*, *568*
Brown, Joseph E. (1821–1894), 394, 532
Brown, Linda (1942–), *953*
Brown, Matt, 558
Brown, Michael, 1104
Brown, Oliver (1918–1961), 953
Brown, Olympia, 571
Brown Fellowship Society, 407
Brownson, Orestes (1803–1876), 343
Brown v. Board of Education, 570, 919, 951, 953–54, *953*, 956, 958, 965, 976
Broz, Josip (Tito; 1892–1980), 879
Bruce, Blanche K. (1841–1898), 573
Bryan, George (1731–1791), 257, 260
Bryan, William Jennings (1860–1925), 642–43, *643*, 672, 708, 719, 722, 779, *780*
   "cross of gold" speech of, 642, *643*
Bryant, Anita (1940–), 1029
Bryant, William Cullen (1794–1878), *331*
Bryn Mawr, 1014
Buchanan, James (1791–1868), 485, 487, 496
   and Mormons, 605
Buchanan, Pat (1938–), 1052, 1075, 1080
Buchanan administration, 487
Buck, Pearl (1892–1973), 864
Buckley, William F. (1925–), 975
Buck v. Bell, 739
Buddhism, Buddhists:
   Beats and, 993
   as immigrants, 1066
   Mazie k. Hirono and, 1125
   in Vietnam, 946, 985–86
Buena Vista, Battle of, 466
buffalo, 10, 31, 613
   hunting of, 608, *609*, *612*
Buffalo, N.Y., 706
Buffalo Bill's Wild West Show, 610
Buffalo Chase over Prairie Bluffs (Catlin), *377*
Bulgaria, 887
Bulge, Battle of the, 876
Bulger, Andrew (1789–1858), *298*
Bull Run, First Battle of, 509
Bull Run, Second Battle of, 509
Bulosan, Carlos (1913–1956), 856–57
Bunau-Varilla, Philippe (1859–1940), 717
Bunker Hill, Battle of, 185, 364
Bureau of Indian Affairs, U.S., 611, 698
Bureau of Intelligence, U.S., 870

Bureau of Labor Statistics, 620, 1120
Bureau of Land Management, 1032
Burger, Warren (1907–1995), 1012
Burger Court, 1012–13
Burgoyne, John (1722–1792), 195, 219
Burk, John D. (1776?–1808), 281
Burke, Edmund (1729–1797), 164, 224, 415
Burma, 848
Burns, Anthony (1829–1862), *477*
Burnside, Ambrose E. (1824–1881), 510, 536
Burr, Aaron (1756–1836), 284, 287
Burris, Roland, 573
Burwell, Carter (1716–1756), *120*
Bush, George H. W. (1924–), 1043–44, 1047, 1049, 1056, 1076, 1093
   in election of 1992, 1051–52
   Gulf War and, 1050, 1051, *1051*
   inauguration of, *1043*
   NAFTA and, 1052
Bush, George W. (1946–), 921, *1051*, 1075, 1088–92, 1094, 1102, 1116, 1117, *1118*
   affirmative action and, 1108
   background of, 1088–89
   civil liberties and, 1097–1101, *1109*
   debates with Gore, 1081
   economy under, 1101–2, 1111–12, 1113, 1115
   in election of 2000, 1079, 1080
   foreign policy of, 1088–89, 1090–91, 1093, 1094, 1101, 1110–11
   and Hurricane Katrina, 1103–4, 1110
   Iraq War and, 1093, 1096, *1096*, 1110
   Islam and, 1107
   and Latinos, 1106
   and Supreme Court, 1108–10
   unemployment and, 1101–2
Bush, Jeb (1953–), 1079
Bush (George W.) administration, 1087, 1088–92, *1091*, 1092–93, 1094, 1096, 1098, 1100, 1101, 1103–4, 1108, 1109, *1109*, 1110–11, 1115, 1118, 1119
   2008 financial crisis and, 1060
Bush Doctrine, 1090–91
Bushnell, Horace (1802–1876), 328
Bush v. Gore, 1080
business:
   and government, 769–74, 860
   horizontal expansion of, 597
   rise of, 594–97
   vertically integrated, 595, 597
   see also corporations
busing, desegregation of schools and, 1012, 1032
Bute, Lord, *182*
Butler, Andrew P. (1796–1857), *484*
Butler, Benjamin F. (1818–1893), 513, 517
Butte, Mont., 733
Byllesby, Langdon (1803–1890), 343
Byrd, William, III (1728–1777), 119

Cabeza de Vaca, Álvar Núñez (ca. 1490–1557?), 31
Cable Act (1922), 782

Cabot, John (ca. 1450–ca. 1499), 22, 23, 50
Cabral, Pedro (1467–1520), 22, 23
Cabrillo, Juan Rodriguez (d. 1543), 31
Cadillac, *853*, *929*
Cadwalader family, *234*
Caesar (former slave), *228*
Caesar's Column (Donnelly), 626
Cage, John (1912–1992), 897
Cahokia, 9
Cain, Herman (1945–), 1124
Cairo University (Egypt), *1118*
Caitlin, George, 377
Cajuns, 158
Calhoun, Floride (1792–1866), 372
Calhoun, John C. (1782–1850), *355*, 363, 475
   American System and, 354–55, *355*
   annexation of Texas and, 463
   compact theory of, 371–73
   concurrent majority theory of, 373
   death of, 477
   Declaration of Independence as viewed by, 400
   Democratic Party and, 382
   Missouri Controversy and, 356
   nationalism and, 371–72
   nullification crisis and, 371–73, *372*
   sectionalism and, 372
   slavery as viewed by, 398, 400
   states' rights and, 371–73
   as vice president, 372
   as War Hawk, 297
California, 464–65, 467, *468*, 602, 604–5, *604*, 681, 700, 704, 775, 777, 783, *784*, 790, 807, 828, 835, 854, 910, 924, *933*, 1068, 1070, 1074, 1075, *1075*
   agriculture in, 679, 925
   Asian-Americans in, 740, 1068
   boycott of grapes from, 997–98, *997*
   constitution of, 470
   enters Union, 475
   gold rush in, 469–70, *470*, *471*, 493, 601
   immigrants in, 654, *654*, 1075, *1075*, 1106
   Indian forced labor in, 601
   Japanese-Americans in, 867
   migration to, 459, 764
   1934 election in, 814
   1964 election in, 974–75
   oil spill off coast of, 999
   population of, 154, 460, 469, 470, 471
   prisons in, 1072
   Reagan as governor of, 1033
   Spanish settlements in, 154–55, *154*
   suburbs in, 926–27, *926*
   tax law in, 1032
   woman suffrage in, 640
California, University of, 928
   at Berkeley, 984–85, *984*, 1016
   at Davis, 1013
California City, *1071*
"California Harvest Scene—Dr. Glenn's Farm in Colusa County," *603*
California Supreme Court, 655
   segregation and, 953

California Trail, 608

Californios, 155, 460, *468*

Call, The, 697

Calley, William (1943–), 1016–17

Calvert, Cecilius, Lord Baltimore (1605–1675), 64, 83

Calvert, Charles, Lord Baltimore (1637–1715), 101, 104

Calvin, John (1509–1564), 65

Calvinists, 41, 104

Cambodia, 848, 1016, 1069
  immigrants from, 1067

Cambridge, Mass., 69, *748*
  first American printing press in, *65*, 69

camera, handheld, 592

Campbell, Helen, 703

Camp David, 943, 1026, 1055

Camp of Thirty-first Pennsylvania Infantry, Near Washington, D.C., *530*

Canada, 9, 10, 87, 155, 164, 174, 221, 300, 365, 610, 783, 799, 1062, 1083
  border with United States, 365
  ceded to Great Britain, 158
  D-Day and, 850
  draft dodgers' flight to, 992
  French, 38–40
  Great Britain and, 466
  lynching in, 652
  NAFTA and, 1052
  Native Americans in, 87
  as slave refuge, 416, 418, 477
  U.S. invasion of, 300, 376
  War Hawks' plan for annexation of, 297
  see also French Canada

Canadians, Canadian immigrants, 602

canals, 168, *307*, 309–11, *310*, 354, 355, 379
  plan of Gallatin for, 354

Canal Zone, 717, *717*

Canary Islands, 20, 21

cancer, skin, 961

Cannery and Agricultural Workers union, 834

Cantino, Alberto, *20*

Cantino World Map, *20*

Canyon de Chelly, *10*

Cape Breton Island, 158

Cape Cod, 66, *67*

Cape Henry, 49

Cape of Good Hope, 20

Cape Verde Islands, 20

Capital and Labor, *623*

capitalism, 788, 802, 860, 861, 862, 889, 937
  communism vs., *630*
  consumerism and, 684
  development of, 41
  free market, 943
  "golden age" of, 924–38
  industrial, 688
  international, 1047, 1049
  labor vs., 620, 624–32
  modern, 923, 924
  people's, 936–37
  revolution vs. reform of, 832
  Ronald Reagan and, 1033
  Socialist Party vs., 709, 832

as threat to freedom, 275
  as "welfare capitalism," 766
  women and, 340–41

Capitalism and Freedom (Friedman), 937

Capitol, *1017*

"captains of industry," 528, 594–97

caravels, 19

Care, Henry (1646–1688), 81

Carey, Henry (1793–1879), 337

Caribbean, 25, 26, 31, 127, 128–29, 285, *718*, 740, 875, 977, 1040, *1041*
  free blacks in, 407
  French, 158
  immigrants from, 1066, 1068–69, 1070
  influence on New Orleans of, 393
  as part of slave empire, 492
  U.S. troops in, 586, 716
  see also West Indies

Carleton, Guy, 227

Carlisle, *613*

Carmichael, Stokely (1941–1998), 981

Carnegie, Andrew (1835–1919), 528, 594–95, 606, 635, *637*

Carolina (1669), 143

Carolina colony, 101, 103
  founding of, 92
  fur trade in, 133
  hierarchical society of, 92
  Indians in, 92

Caroline, Fort, 33

carpetbaggers, 574–75

Carroll, James, 211

Carson, Ann Baker, 234

Carson, Rachel (1907–1964), 983, 999

Carswell, G. Harold (1920–1992), 1011

Carter, Jimmy (1924–), 718, 920, 1023, *1026*, 1032, 1055
  economic crisis and, 1024
  in election of 1980, 1033
  human rights and, 1025–26, 1028, 1041
  Iran hostage crisis and, 1026–27
  Nobel Peace Prize of, 1033

Carter, Landon (1710–1778), 133

Carter, Robert, III (1728–1804), 152, 228

Carter, Robert "King" (1663–1732), 119, 152

Carter administration, 1023–27, *1027*, 1041

Carter Doctrine, 1027

Carter family, 156

Carter's Grove, *120*

Cartwright, John (1740–1824), *192*

Caruso, Enrico (1873–1921), 762

Casey, William (1913–1987), 1042

Casey v. Planned Parenthood of Pennsylvania, 1076

Casino Grounds, *598*

casinos, gambling, Native Americans and, 1073–74

Cass, Lewis (1782–1866), 473

Castile, 21

Castillo Armas, Carlos (1914–1957), *945*

Castleman, Peggy, *284*

Castro, Fidel (1926–), 970–71

Catawba Indians, *13*, 111

Catcher in the Rye (Salinger), 947

Catechetical Guild Education Society of St. Paul, Minnesota, *885*

Catherine of Aragon (1485–1536), 50

Catholic Holy Name Society, 785

Catholics, Catholicism, 21, 23, 40, 52, 65, 76, 102–4, 140, 141, 154, 164, 182, *182*, 210–11, 326, *326*, *327*, 460, 469, 481–82, *482*, 494, 617, 629, 642, 649, 667, 688, 775, 777, 789, 823, 934–35, *935*, 1004, *1004*
  and abortion, 996, 1004, 1030
  in American colonies, 110, 144, 210–11, 213
  and Americanization, 785, 834
  anticommunism of, 910
  banned in Ireland, 83
  Church of England and, 65, 80, 102
  Civil War and, *522*
  counterculture and, 992
  as Democrats, 370
  in FDR administration, 831
  and freeing of slaves, 97
  French and, 164
  Germans as, 109
  immigrants and, 683
  JFK as, 959–60, *959*, 1102
  John Kerry as, 1102
  Know-Nothing Party vs., 481–82
  Ku Klux Klan and, 781
  liberties of, 213
  in Maryland colony, 64, 83, 104
  Native Americans and, 3, 28–30, *29*, 34–35, 39–41
  in New Netherland, 43
  Newt Gingrich and, 1124
  in 1960 campaign, 959–60, *959*
  Paul D. Ryan and, 1124
  in Pennsylvania colony, 110
  prejudice against, 785, 1107
  slavery and, 137
  Spanish colonies and, 25, 28–30, *29*, 34–35, 44–45
  temperance movement and, 432
  in Vietnam, 946

Catlin, George (1796–1872), *482*

Cato's Letters (Trenchard and Gordon), 142, 148

Catskill Mountains, *331*

Catt, Carrie Chapman (1859–1947), 659

cattle drives, 604

Caucasian Race—Equal Privileges resolution, 866

Cayugas, 12, 1073

CCC (Civilian Conservation Corps), 805, *805*, 826, 830, 855

Celia (slave; d. 1855), 402

censorship, 777
  anticommunism and, 910
  Hollywood and, 775
  sex and, 775, 777

census, federal, 412, 738, *1066*, 1069, 1073

Census Bureau, 590

CENTO, 895

Central America, 7, 8, 31, *32*, 844, *1041*, 1042, 1049
  immigrants from, 1067, 1068, 1070
  Spain in, 155

Theodore Roosevelt's policies in, 718
  U.S. troops in, 586

Central High School, Ark., segregation at, *957*, 958

Central Intelligence Agency (CIA), 889, 944, *945*, 1015, 1019, 1087, 1099, 1100, 1103
  Bay of Pigs Invasion and, 970
  support of arts by, 897

Central Pacific, 524

Central Powers (World War I), 721

Cermak, Anton (1873–1933), 791

Chaco Canyon, 10, *10*

Chain of Friendship, 93, 111

Challenge to Liberty, The (Hoover), 822

Chalmers, James (1727–1806), 189

Chamberlain, Mason, *150*

Chamberlain, Neville (1869–1940), 844

Chamber of Commerce, U.S., 819

Chambers, Whittaker (1901–1961), 908

Champlain, Samuel de (1567–1635), 38–40, *40*, *49*

Chancellorsville, Battle of, 536

Chaney, James (1943–1964), 973

Chaplin, Charlie (1889–1977), 762

Charge of the Rough Riders at San Juan Hill (Remington), *644*

Chariot of Liberty, A, 183

Charles I, king of England (1600–1649), 64, 65, 80, *81*, 82–83, *82*, *83*, 141

Charles II, king of England (1630–1685), 80, 82, 88, 90, 91, 102, 103

Charleston, S.C., 115, 119, *134*, 138, 199, 226, 228
  black community in, 407, 418
  demands return of slaves, 227
  slave trade in, 92

Charleston (dance), 768

Charleston Harbor, 386

Charles Town Harbor (Roberts), *117*

Charter of Liberties and Privileges (1683), 91

Charter of Liberty (1682), 93

Chartist movement, 326, 474–75

Chase, Salmon P. (1808–1873), 478

Chase Manhattan Bank, 885

Chavez, César (1927–1993), 997, *997*, 1068

Chavez Ravine, 933

Checkers speech, 939

checks and balances, 250–51, 254

Cheney, Dick (1941–), 1051, *1051*, 1079, 1092, 1103

Cherokee Nation v. Georgia, 374

Cherokee Phoenix, 351

Cherokees, 12, 111, 156, 222, 242, *266*, 298, 300, 374–76, *374*, 525
  Constitution of, 374, 375

Chesapeake, 296

Chesapeake Bay, 49, 199

Chesapeake region, 42, 54, 58, *58*, 61–62, 67–68, 77–78, 98–101, 107, 109, 128
  boycott in, 179
  Great Awakening in, 152
  indentured servants in, 132, 133
  as runaway slave refuge, 138

settlement of, 58–64
slavery in, 132–33, 134, 137–38
society in, 133
tenant farmers in, 133
tobacco in, *58*, 61, *61*, *63*, 94, 98–99,
  98, 107, 109, 117, 123, 132–33
Chevalier, Michel (1806–1879), 329
Cheves, Langdon, III, *533*
Chevrolet, 929
Chevrolet Corvair, 999
Cheyennes, 525–28, 608, 609
Chicago, Ill., 319, 322, *786*, *947*, 1022,
  1066, *1087*, *1106*, 1116
  African-Americans in, 786, 932
  alleged voter fraud in, 960
  in Great Depression, 791
  Haymarket affair in, 629–31
  immigrants to, 682
  "lyrical left" in, 696
  as manufacturing center, 479–81
  manufacturing in, 591
  1968 Democratic convention
    in, 1003
  population of, 591
  race riot in, 744
  World's Fair in, *595*
Chicago Defender, *881*
Chicago Freedom Movement, 980
Chicago Gospel Tabernacle, *815*
Chicago Sanitary Fair, *529*
Chicago *Times*, 598
Chicago Tribune, 520, 753, 780
Chicanos, 997, 998
  culture of, 865
  see also Latinos
Chickasaws, 12, 156, 242, 374
Child, Lydia Maria (1802–1880), 341,
  351, 440, 449
child labor, 680, *680*, 700, 702, 710,
  711, 767, 771, 823, 824
Children's Bureau, 702
Chile, 772, 1015, 1041
Chillin' with Liberty (Cox), *1083*
China, 18, 20, 24, 472, 506, 604,
  664–65, 750, 802, 844, 876, 891,
  986, 1010, 1015, *1015*, *1049*, 1069,
  1072, 1111, 1113, 1126
  Iraq War and, 1093
  jobs exported to, 1102
  Korean War and, 891–95
  Lend-Lease and, 846
  loss of U.S. jobs to, 1102
  market reforms in, 1049
  and oil, 1105
  rise of communists in, 891
  Tiananmen Square protest in, 589,
    1048, *1049*
  in U.N., 880
Chinese, Chinese immigrants, 470, 524,
  559, 570, 601, 604, 651, 654–56,
  654, 673, 680, 681, 738, 903
  in Hawaii, 661
  in IWW, 691
  World War II and, 866
  see also Asian immigrants
chinos, *28*
Chivington, John (1821–1894), 525
chlorofluorocarbons, 961
Choate, J. H. (1848–1902), *613*

Choctaws, 12, 222, 223, 242, *266*, 374
Chou En-lai (1898–1976), *1015*
Christian Coalition, 1075
Christianity, 12, 15, 16–17, 21, 27, *27*,
  29–30, *59*, 60, 71, 76, 214–15, 296,
  628–29, *643*, 760, 937, 956, 974,
  1028–29, 1065
  in Balkans, 1056
  "Christian lobby" and, 628
  "Christian patriots" and, 1077
  Civil War and, 522
  Filipinos and, 667
  and free exercise of religion, 83, 93
  fundamentalism and, 777–79,
    1028–29
  Great Awakening and, 150–52
  growth of, in U.S., 334–35
  imperialism and, 659
  liberty and, 432
  media and, 815
  modernism in, 777, 778–79
  Native Americans and, 12, 33, 36, 37,
    52, 87, 154–55, 610
  in New World, 45
  and Republican Party (modern),
    1009, 1035, 1075–76
  Second Great Awakening, 334–36
  sects of, 110
  slavery and, 99, 136–37, 152, 413–14,
    446
  in 2012 election and campaign, 1123
  see also specific denominations
"Christian liberty," 17
"Christian lobby," 628
Christian Republicanism, 215
Christian Right, 920, 1033, 1039
  see also religious right
"Christian Sparta," America as, 215
Chrysler, 763, 929, *1074*
Church, Frank (1924–1984), 1019
church and state, separation of, 212,
  214–15, 779, 1001
Church Committee, 1019
churches, tax support of, 110, 151,
  211–12, 213, 214
Churchill, Winston (1871–1947), 788,
  846, 878, 879, *879*, 880, *881*, 887,
  940
Church of England, *see* Anglican
  Church
Church of Jesus Christ of Latter-day
  Saints, *see* Mormons
Church of Latter-Day Saints, *see*
  Mormons
CIA, *see* Central Intelligence Agency
Cibola, seven golden cities of, 31
cigarettes, marketing to women of,
  768, *768*
Cincinnati, Ohio, *318*, 319, 323
  race riots in, 338
CIO, *see* Congress of Industrial
  Organizations
cities, growth of, 319, *320*
Citigroup, 1059, 1115
Citizens Alliance, 811
Citizens Committee, 650
citizenship, 565, 569, 572, 650, 670, 829
  of African-Americans, 440, 572,
    782, 783, 800

of Asian-Americans, 570
Chinese immigrants and, 655
economic, 705
expansion of, 781–82
Fourteenth Amendment and, 440,
  570, 572
Hawaii and, 670
Native Americans and, 263, 265,
  612–14
Puerto Rico and, 670, 740
restrictions on, 587
second-class, *see* segregation
social, 978, 982, 1047
voting rights and, 701
welfare state and, 705
of women, 781–82
*Citizens United v. Federal Elections
  Commission*, 1126
City Activities with Dance Hall (Benton),
  758
City of Ambition (Stieglitz), *680*
"City Slave Girls" (Cusack), 598
City University of New York, 1022
civic nationalism, 263
Civil and Political Rights, 900
civil disobedience, 1124
Civilian Conservation Corps (CCC),
  805, *805*, 826, 830, 855
Civil Liberties Bureau, *see* American
  Civil Liberties Union (ACLU)
Civil Rights Act (1866), 1071
Civil Rights Act (1875), *548*, 580, 650
Civil Rights Act (1964), 919, 968,
  972–73, 974, 995
civil rights and liberties, 732, 733,
  748, 774–77, 795, 831, 834–35,
  875, 885, 886, 914, 915, 949–59,
  1000–1001, 1028, 1036, 1040,
  1073, 1088, *1090*, 1099–1100
  abuses of, 258
  Adlai Stevenson and, 915
  Alien and Sedition Acts and,
    285–87, 327
  in American colonies, 49–50, 55,
    144, 206, 207–8
  American Revolution and, 209–10,
    211–15
  A. Mitchell Palmer and, 748
  anticommunism and, 910, 911
  Baldwin on, 965
  Bush administration and, 1097–
    1101, 1108–10, *1109*
  Civil War and, 523
  Cold War and, 914, 915
  Eleanor Roosevelt and, 825
  in England, 80–81
  FDR and, 829–30
  in Great Depression, 795, 832
  Iraq War and, 921
  and Japanese-Americans, 867–69
  Japanese internment and, 867–69
  labor and, 695, 835–36
  legislation on, 575
  New Deal and, 835–36
  new movements in, 994–1005
  post-World War II, 862, 902–4,
    903, 915
  revolution in, 1000–1001
  Scottsboro case and, 834

security vs., 921
September 11 terrorist attacks and,
  1099–1100
in Soviet Union, 898, 900
suspension of, 1108
Truman and, 902–5
violations as federal offenses, 578
Woodrow Wilson and, 732
World War II and, 842, 866, 949,
  954
see also Bill of Rights (American);
  civil rights movement;
  constitutional amendments, U.S.;
  freedom; McCarthy era; women's
  rights
Civil Rights Bill (1866), 565, 566
Civil Rights Cases, 650
Civil Rights Memorial, *1127*
civil rights movement, 949–59, *957*,
  958, 977–78, 979–82, *979*, 1028,
  1038, 1116
  backlash against, 920, 976, 1032
  Birmingham campaign and,
    966–67, *968*
  birth of, 870–76, *874*, *875*
  FBI and, 1019
  freedom and, 954–56
  JFK and, 971–72
  LBJ and, 972–74
  March on Washington and, 968–69,
    969
  Montgomery bus boycott and,
    954–56
  1964 election and, 973–75
  radicalization of, 981
  Selma campaign and, 976
  in South, 919, 965–69, *967*, *968*
  television and, 967, *968*, 976
  "wade-ins" and, 966
  women and, 994–96
Civil Service Act (1883), 618
Civil War, U.S., 385, 386–87, 395,
  459, *499*, 502–47, *503*, *548*, 549,
  551, 589, 609, 616, 619, 620–21,
  630–31, 636, 721, 727, 731, 783,
  819, 885, 1005, 1095, 1100
  agriculture in, 524
  beginning of, 498–99
  black soldiers in, 517–19, *519*
  blockade in, 508, 533
  campaigns of, *510*, *512*, *536*
  casualties in, 503, 505–6, 507, 510,
    511, 518, 523, 537, *538*, 553
  civil liberties and, 523
  Confederate advantages in, 504
  draft in, 504, 528, 531, 533
  draft riots in, 533
  emancipation and, 385, 386, 503,
    511–19, *515*, 518, 520, 540, 544–45,
    548–57
  end of, 541–42
  financing of, 528
  as first modern war, 503–11
  industry in, 524
  message to Congress, 512
  photography in, 507
  propaganda in, 506–7
  religion and, 522–23, *522*
  resources for, *506*

Civil War (*continued*)
   as Second American Revolution, 519–31
   Sherman's March to the Sea in, *542*
   songs of, *524*
   technology of, 504–6, *507*
   transportation in, 507, *508*
   Union advantages in, 504
   West in, 511, *512*, 537
   women in, 528–30, *529*
Civil Works Administration (CWA), 806
Clarendon County, S.C., 953
Clark, Kenneth (1914–2005), 954
Clark, Mamie (1917–1983), 954
Clark, Tom C. (1899–1977), 886
Clark, William (1770–1838), 294, *294*, 608
Clark University, 696
Clash of Civilizations and the Remaking of World Order, The (Huntington), 1106–7
class:
   in American Society, 338, 341, *351*, 352–53, 371, 620
   development of, 341
   education and, 434
   race and, 352–53, *352*
   see also middle class
Clay, Henry (1777–1852), 315, *378*, 382, 416
   American Colonization Society and, 435
   American System and, 354
   annexation of Texas and, 463–64
   Compromise of 1850 and, 475
   death of, 477
   in duel with Randolph, 397
   election of 1824 and, 361–64
   election of 1828 and, 366
   in election of 1832, 379
   Missouri Controversy and, 356, 358
   nickname of, 367
   nullification crisis and, 373
   on slavery, 391
   as War Hawk, 297
Clayton Act (1914), 711
Clean Air Act (1970), 999, 1010
Clean Water Act (1972), 999
Clemenceau, Georges (1841–1929), 749
Clermont, 309
Cleveland, Grover (1837–1908), 617, 641, 643, 654, 661, 793
cliff dwellings, *10*
climate change, 1098
   see also global warming
Clinton, Bill (1946–), 827, 869, *958*, 1043, 1047, 1048, 1051–56, *1053*, 1060, 1062, 1075, 1078–79, *1079*, 1083, 1115
   Balkan crisis and, 1055–56
   budget and, 1056
   Contract with America and, 1053
   in election of 1992, 1051–52
   foreign policy of, 1055–56
   impeachment of, 1078–79
   national health care plan of, 1053
   sexual misconduct and, 1078–79
   Whitewater and, 1078

Clinton, De Witt (1769–1828), 303, 309
Clinton, George (1739–1812), 164, 277
Clinton, Henry (1738–1795), 197, 227
Clinton, Hillary Rodham (1947–), 1052, 1116, 1117
   as feminist, 1078
Clinton administration, 1051–56, 1115
   women in, 1052
Close, Gilbert (1906–1952), 750
closed shops, 902
Close the Gate, 739
Cloud, N. B. (1809–1875), *578*
coal, 524, *646*, 901, 1021, 1088
   mining, *646*, 707, 747, *825*
   strikes, 706–7
Coast Guard. U.S., *848*
Coats, William, *115*
Cobb, Howell (1815–1868), 536
Coca-Cola, 762, 928
Cochise, 609
"code-talkers," 866
Coercive Acts, *see* Intolerable Acts
Coeur d'Alene, Idaho, 641
coffee, 115, 128
coinage, 146, 273, *275*
Cold Harbor, Battle of, 537
Coldplay, 1114
Cold War, 728, 756, 757, 880, 884–917, *885*, *892*, 918, 919, 921, 937, 984, 989, 990, 991, 994, 1015, 1019, 1026, 1027–28, *1040*, *1041*, 1091–92, 1100, 1126
   Beats and, 949
   Berlin blockade in, 890–91, *890*
   big business and, 935
   Carter and, 1025
   consumerism and, 923, 924
   cultural, 897, *898*
   Eisenhower and, 941–43
   end of, 1048, *1050*, 1051, 1056, 1064
   end of ideology and, *934*, 935, *935*
   family life and, 931–32
   freedom and, 895, 896–900, *898*, 906–7, *909*, 935, 946
   free enterprise and, 940, 946
   highways and, 906, 940
   human rights and, 898–900
   Iran and, 887
   JFK and, 969–71
   Khrushchev and, 943
   Korean War and, 891–95
   and Middle East oil, 887, 888
   "missile gap," 960
   national exhibitions and, 923
   in 1960 election, 960
   organized labor and, 914
   origins of, 886–96
   political debate and, 946
   Reagan and, 1040–41, 1042
   religion and, 912, 934–35
   September 11 attacks and, 1087–88
   in Third World, 943–45
   Vietnam War and, 919–20
Cole, Thomas (1801–1848), *331*
Coles, Edward (1786–1868), 269
Colfax, La., massacre in, 578, 582
Colfax, Schuyler (1823–1885), *568*, 616
Collier, John (1789–1883), 827
Colman, Lucy (1817–1906), 446

Colombia, 717, *717*
   drug trade in, 1122
colonialization:
   decolonization and, 896, 943–44
   international, 659
   of slaves, 435–36, 514, 517
Colorado, 703, 807, 1117
   entrance into Union of, 610
   woman suffrage in, 640, 703
Colorado Fuel and Iron Company, 695
Colored Farmers' Alliance, 639
   see also Farmers' Alliance
Colored Rule in a Reconstructed (?) State (Nast), *580*
Colossus of Rhodes, 589
Columbia, S.C., *1069*
Columbia College, 1116
Columbian Exchange, 24, *24*
Columbian Magazine, 215, *216*
Columbia River, 10, 799, *799*, 801, 827
Columbia University, 775, 795, 802, 1003, 1016
Columbus, Christopher (1451–1506), 5, 18, 20–23
   voyages of, 20–23, *21*, *22*, 24
Columbus, N.Mex., 721
Columbus's Landfall, 21
Comanches, 153, 460, 608, 609
Come and Join Us Brothers, *518*
"comity," 358
Commager, Henry Steele (1902–1998), 911, 913
Commissioner of Indian Affairs, 827
Commission of Public Safety, 733
Commission on Civil Rights, 904
Commission on Immigration, 911
Commission on Industrial Relations, 679, 695
Committee of Correspondence, 175, 225, 232
Committee of Safety, 104, 183, 218
Committee on Public Information (CPI), 727–28, 735, 764
common law, development of English, 80
Common Sense (Paine), 186–87, *187*, 188, 191, 207, 235
"Commonwealth and Free State", England as, 80
Commonwealth v. Hunt, 328
communication, 168, 239, 308
communism, 426, 709, 757, 771, 777, 780, 811, 812, 831–32, 836, 844, 845, 871, 879, *885*, 886, 887, 888, 889, 891, *892*, 897, 898, 902, 906–8, *907*, *908*, 918, 943, 944, 945, 969, 975, 988, 999, 1004, 1014–15, 1017, 1023, 1025, 1041, 1056
   capitalism vs., *630*, 943
   in China, 891, *893*
   civil rights movement and, 971
   collapse of, 1047, *1047*, 1048–49
   crusade against, 906–15, *909*, 919–20, 934–35, *935*, 937, 939, 985, 1000
   flag of, 733
   Henry Wallace and, 905
   immigration and, 977

refugees from, 906
religion and, 912
rise of, 724
in Soviet Union, 923
Truman Doctrine and, 889
in Vietnam, 985
women and, 931
Communist Labor Party, 777
Communist Party, 748, 792, *793*, 814, 831–32, 834, 836, 868, *885*, 905, 908, 910, 942, 982
   Americanization and, *832*
   in China, 1049
Communist Party Congress, 942
communitarians, 430
Company of New France, 38
company unions, 766
compass, 19
"Composite Nation" (Douglass), 570
Compromise of 1850, 475, *476*, 477
computers, 853, 906, 1057–58, 1061, 1101
   see also Internet
concentration camps, 844, 850, *850*, 865
   see also Japanese immigrants, Japanese Americans, World War II internment of
Concord, Battle of, 184, *184*, *185*, *196*, 216, 280
"Concord Hymn" (Emerson), *184*
concurrent majority theory, 373
Conestoga Indians, massacre of, 161
Coney Island, *947*
Confederate Constitution, 525–28
Confederate States of America, 386, 497–98, 526, 531–35, 540, *542*, 608, 630
   black soldiers and, 535
   currency of, *532*
   division among, 533
   economic problems of, 533–34
   government of, 531
   Senate of, 535
   states' rights and, 532
   Union sympathizers in, 534
   women and, 534–35
Conference on Home Building and Home Ownership, 808
Confidence Man, The (Melville), 355
Congregationalists, 65, 69, 110, 150, 211, *212*, 446, 660
   American Revolution and, 214
   Half-Way Covenant and, 79
   in Massachusetts, 213
Congress, U.S., 374, 617, 662, 803–4, 818, 862, *888*, 939, 1012, 1019, 1023, 1031, 1076, 1100, 1109–10, 1111
   African-Americans in, 648
   anticommunism and, 911
   apologizes for Japanese-American internment, 869
   under Articles of Confederation, 240–42
   authority of, 356, 372
   Bank of the United States and, 378–79

Civil Rights Act (1964) and, 968
civil rights and, 958
and coinage, 273, 275
under Constitution, 249–51
and currency, 217, 528
Deborah Sampson pensioned by, 232
in elections of 1946, 902
Equal Pay Act and, 995
FDR and, 823
federal bailouts and, 1115
Greenspan's testimony to, 1115
health care bill passed by, 1119
immigration restriction and, 655, 739, 782–83, 866
Independent Treasury policy and, 381
isolationism and, 845
and League of Nations, 753
Missouri Compromise and, 358
National Road authorized by, 309, 354
and Native American treaty system, 610
New Deal and, 803–4, 805, 861
oaths of allegiance and, 219
petitioned for emancipation, 288
political parties in, 273
presidential veto and, 379, 565–66, 902, 911
Reagan's defiance of, 1042
Reconstruction policies of, 563
slavery and, 288, 474
"stimulus" package passed by, 1118
Truman Doctrine and, 888–89
Universal Declaration of Human Rights and, 900
Voting Rights Act passed by, 976
and wage and price controls, 218
World War II and, 848
see also House of Representatives, U.S.; Senate, U.S.
Congressional Medal of Honor, 518, 741
"Congressional Pugilists," 286
Congress of Industrial Organizations (CIO), 812–13, 815, 826, 832, 834, 835, 837, 862, 871, 901, 902, 914, 941
Congress of Racial Equality (CORE), 871, 956, 966, 973, 982
Connecticut, 240, 254
slavery in, 229
Connecticut colony, 72, 116, 151
government in, 144
militia of, 185
in Pequot War, 76–77
slavery in, 135
women in, 123
Connecticut River valley, settlement of, 77
Connor, Eugene "Bull" (1897–1973), 967, 1028
conquistadores, 9, 23–24, 25, 30, 1074
Conscience of a Conservative, The (Goldwater), 974
conservationism, 587, 707–8, 707, 708, 999, 1028

conservatism, 863, 920, 937–38, 943, 974–76, 1000, 1008–45, 1009, 1018, 1043, 1066, 1074, 1075–76, 1107–8, 1117
abortion and, 920, 1029, 1030–31
anti-Semitism and, 1009
Clinton and, 1052
colleges and, 982
libertarians and, 937
neoconservatism and, 1027
New Deal and, 860
Nixon and, 1005, 1009, 1010–11
radical, 975, 988, 1077
Reagan and, 1039–40
Tea Party and, 1123
"conspicuous consumption," 599
constitution:
of California, 470
Cherokee, 374, 375
English, 140–41, 186
of Texas, 469
Constitution, U.S., 168, 247–63, 259, 282, 364, 391, 695, 731, 736, 766, 773, 823, 885, 912, 951, 1000–1001, 1002, 1013, 1029, 1036, 1079, 1107–8, 1109, 1110, 1118
African-Americans and, 549, 570, 1016
American System and, 354
Andrew Jackson and, 349
Calhoun's view of, 372
celebration pageants for, 239
checks and balances in, 250–51, 254
compact theory of, 371–73
Confederate constitution and, 497
free blacks and, 266–67
Garrison's suggested abrogation of, 437
J. Q. Adams and, 365
Louisiana Purchase and, 292
map of ratification of, 262
Marbury v. Madison in, 291
Missouri Compromise and, 358
national bank and, 356
Native Americans and, 263, 265
political parties and, 273
powers granted under, 250–51
preamble to, 252, 253
ratification of, 239, 239, 254–63, 254, 256
signing of, 255
slavery and, 251–52, 251, 263, 440–41, 474, 486
state vs. federal powers in, 259
strict constructionism and, 275, 354, 355, 356, 365
tariffs in, 253
and territories acquired, 670
three-fifths clause of, 251, 252, 288, 303
trade in, 253
Webster's view of, 372
women's rights and, 281, 571
see also Constitutional Convention
Constitution, USS, 299, 300
constitutional amendments, U.S., 35
First, 258, 259, 263, 286, 775, 776, 856, 908, 1000, 1001
Second, 258

Eighth, 259
Ninth, 259
Tenth, 259
Twelfth, 287
Thirteenth, 541, 565, 885
Fourteenth, 440, 566, 570, 571–72, 581, 623, 649, 650, 650, 655, 742, 773, 777, 786, 885, 951, 954, 1013, 1080
Fifteenth, 568, 568, 571–72, 648–49, 742, 766, 885
Sixteenth, 709
Seventeenth, 489, 700
Eighteenth, 731, 731
Nineteenth, 729
Twentieth, 823
Twenty-first, 809
Twenty-fourth, 976
Constitutional Convention (1787), 247–53, 249, 253
Constitutional Union Party, 494
Constitution Hall, 829
constitutions, state, 208–9
consumerism, 683, 684, 919, 923, 927–28, 1087
advertising and, 687, 688, 760, 761, 928, 929
in American National Exhibition, 923
automobiles and, 929–31, 929
capitalism and, 684
economy and, 762–63, 764
and household appliances, 762, 763, 768, 860, 919, 923–24, 925, 1030, 1102
suburbia and, 932
television and, 928–29
unionization and, 686–87
wages and, 684, 687, 703, 764
containment, 757, 887, 888–89, 891, 893, 895, 907, 942, 943, 944, 985
double, 891
Continental Army, 170, 187, 193, 194, 216
demoralization of, 195
strength of, 193–94
Continental Association, 183
Continental Congress, see First Continental Congress; Second Continental Congress
contracts, labor, 622–23, 624–25, 657
"yellow dog," 624
contracts, "liberty of contract" doctrine and, 705
"Contract with America," 1053, 1054
Contras, 1042, 1043
Coolidge, Calvin (1872–1933), 747, 756, 760, 769, 770–71, 772, 783, 789
Coolidge administration, 772
"coolies," 524
cooling off periods, 902
Cooper, Gary (1901–1961), 908
Cooper, Mary, 123
Cooper, Thomas (1759–1839), 286
Cooperative Commonwealth, The (Gronlund), 625, 627, 628
Cooper Union, 696
Coote, Richard (1636–1701), 115
Copely, John Singleton (1738–1815), 268

copper, 597, 604, 772
Copperheads, 530
Coral Sea, Battle of, 849, 849
CORE (Congress of Racial Equality), 871, 956, 966, 973, 982
Cornish, Samuel (ca. 1795–1858), 443
Cornwallis, Lord Charles (1738–1805), 199–200, 200
Coronado, Francisco Vásquez de (1510–1554), 31
Coronation of Louis XVI, 208
corporations, 638, 657, 700, 706, 802, 831, 924, 936, 936, 984, 1058–60, 1102
absentee, 670
automobile, 929
Bush era scandals in, 1113
and conformity, 946
corporate advertising and, 936
corruption of, 615
economic control of countries by, 944
farms owned by, 828, 961
Federal Trade Commission and, 711
free enterprise and, 935–36
Ku Klux Klan and, 781
multinational, 1048
"new despotism" of, 823
in 1920s, 765
power and, 700, 944, 1080
and profits, 763, 816, 837, 853, 855, 1022, 1031, 1036, 1037, 1038
and public relations, 766
rise of, 586
and rise of West, 604–5
Social Darwinist view of, 621–22
states and, 709
taxes on, 816
television sponsorship and, 929
Theodore Roosevelt and, 706
and white collar jobs, 925
in World War II, 853
see also specific corporations
Corregidor Island, 848
corruption:
of corporations, 615
of politics, 615–16
Cortés, Hernán (1485–1547), 9, 22, 23–24, 23, 27, 390, 721
Cortland family, 178
Cosby, William (1690–1736), 148
Cosmopolitan, 996
Costa Rica, 718
cost of living wage increases, 914, 941
cotton, 316, 321, 356, 380, 385, 390–91, 409, 531–32, 557, 558–59, 558, 637, 645, 646, 684, 830, 835, 889, 925
compressing of, 391
exporting of, 392
market revolution and, 312, 316
in New Orleans, 394
and North, 392, 492
and Northern textile industry, 385
plantations, see planters, plantations, cotton
and wealth in South, 481
see also Cotton Kingdom
Cotton, John (1584–1652), 73
Cotton Belt, 409, 557

Cotton Club, 787
cotton gin, 315, 317
cotton industry and strikes, *812*
Cotton Kingdom, 312, 315–17, *316*, 347, 356, 391, 393, 412, 496, 531–32
Cotton Pressing in Lousiana, 391
Couch, W. T. (1901–1988), 873
Coughlin, Charles E. (1891–1979), 815, 846
Council of the Indies, 25
Council on African Affairs, 876
counterculture, 991–92, 1013, *991*
    Catholics and, 992
    cults and, 993–94
    Hinduism and, 993
    religion and, 992–94, *993*
    yoga and, 993, *993*
Country Party, 142
County Election (Bingham), *370*
Court of Common Pleas, The, 80
"court packing," 823, *823*, 837
"cousinocracy," 118
Covenant Chain, 90–91
coverture, 17, 233
cowboys, 604–5
Cowpens, S.C., American victory at, 199
Cox, Archibald (1912–2004), 1018–19
Cox, James (1870–1957), 800
Cox, Renée (1960–), *1083*
Coxey, Jacob (1854–1951), 641
Coxey's Army, 641, *641*, 642
coyotes, *28*
crack cocaine, 1040, 1072
Craft, Ellen (1826?–1891), 418
Craft, William (1824–1900), 418
craftsmen, 319, 323, 324, 325, 342
    African-Americans as, 339, 389, 407, 459
    see also artisans
Crawford, Thomas (1813?–1857), 459, *461*
Crawford, William H. (1732–1782), 361–64
Crazy Horse (1842?–1877), 609
creationism, 779, 1076
    see also fundamentalism
Crédit Mobilier, 616, 617
Creek Confederacy, 111
Creek Indians, 92, 111, 133, 222, 223, *266*, 298, 300, 361, 374, 376
Creel, George (1876–1953), 727–28
Creole, 419
Creoles, 136
Crèvecoeur, Hector St. John de (1735–1813), 267, 834
cricket, 140
crime, 1072
criollos, 25
Crisis, The, 429, *737, 742, 743, 752*, 870, 871
Crittenden, John J. (1786–1863), 496, 497, 513
Croatia, *1055*
"Croaton," 51
Croly, Herbert (1869–1930), 706, 726
Cromwell, Oliver (1599–1658), 80, 82–83, *83*, 88
crop rotation, 53

"cross of gold" speech, 642, *643*
Crowe, Eyre (1824–1910), *389*
Crow Indians, 608
Cruikshank, U.S. v., 582
Cuba, 21, 30, 33, 36, 158, 359, 361, 365, 492–93, 496, *635*, 660, 661, 662, 663, 664, *664, 672*, 843, 844, 1099, *1099*
    Bay of Pigs invasion in, 970
    Guantánamo Bay, 1099, *1099*, 1101, 1108, 1109, 1118, *1118*
    immigrants from, 1068
    Missile Crisis in, 970–71
    slavery in, 137
    U.S. intervention in, 718
Cullen, Countee (1903?–1946), 787
"cult of domesticity," 339–40, *339*, 454
cultural pluralism, 784
currency, 146, 172, *183*, 217, 246, *248*, 250, 274, 275, *324*, 355, 369, 378, 379, 381, 528, 618, 642, 643
    Confederate, 532, 533
    Federal Reserve System and, 711
    for international trade, 879–80
    lack of uniform, 354
    reform, 625
Currency Act (1764), 173, 175
Currier, Nathaniel (1813–1888), *311, 499, 565, 579*
Curtis, Charles (1860–1936), *789*
Curtis, George William (1824–1892), 519
Cusack, Nell, 598
Custer, George A. (1839–1876), 609, *610*
Customs Service, 775
Cutting Sugar Cane, 96
Cuttyhunk Island, *67*
Cuzco, *30*
CWA (Civil Works Administration), 806
Czakalinski, Steve, *923*
Czechoslovakia, 749, 753, 844, 1004
    breakup of, *1050*
Czolgosz, Leon (1873–1901), 706

Dade County, Fla., 1029
Dahl, Michael (1659–1743), *143*
Dahomey people, 130
Dakota Territory, 609
    gold in, 604, 609
Daley, Richard J. (1902–1976), 980
Dallas, Tex., 972, *972*
Dallas (TV show), 1039
dams, 827, 828
    Columbia River, 799, *799*
Dana, Richard Henry, 460
"Dandy Jim," 352
Daniels, John Daniel, *408*
Darnall, Henry, III (1702–ca. 1787), *133*
Darrow, Clarence (1857–1938), 691, 695, 779, *780*, 788, 805
Dartmouth College v. Woodward, 328
Darwin, Charles (1809–1882), 621–22, 756, 779, 1076
Darwinism, *see* evolution
Daugherty, Harry (1860–1941), 770
Daughters of Liberty, 179
Daughters of the American Revolution, 829, 910

David (Indian), *57*
Davis, "Cyclone" (1854–1940), 638
Davis, David (1815–1886), 523
Davis, James J. (1873–1947), 783
Davis, Jefferson (1808–1889), 459, *461*, 497, 498, 531–32, 534, 540
    Abraham Lincoln compared to, 531, 532
Davis, John W. (1873–1955), 771
Davis, Joseph (1784–1870), 540
Davis, Pauline (1813–1876), 452
Davis, Sammy, Jr. (1925–1990), 952
Dawes, Henry L. (1816–1903), 611
Dawes Act (1887), 611–12, *614*, 827
Day After, The (movie), 1040
D-Day, 510, *850*
DDT, 999
Dean, James (1931–1955), 947
Deas, Charles, *376*
Death and Life of Great American Cities, The (Jacobs), 983
death march, in Bataan, 848, *866*
death penalty, 1072
De Bow's Review, 405
de Bry, Theodor (1528–1598), *15, 30, 52, 61*
Debs, Eugene V. (1855–1926), 642, 690–91, 709, *709*, 732, 736, 776
debt, imprisonment for, 342
Declaration for Global Democracy, 1063
Declaration of Independence (1776), 187–90, *190*, 191–92, 214, 235, 239, *249*, 258, 259, 400, 670, 693, 742, 834, 885, 896, 913, 944
    ideas of equality in, 206
    Lincoln's views on, 489
    Native Americans and, 222–23
    rewritten by Federated Trades of the Pacific Coast, 625
    Robert Livingston and, 219
    slavery and, 190, 225, 268, 270, 420, 436, 441
"Declaration of Josephe" (Josephe), 37
Declaration of Principles (1905), 742
Declaration of Sentiments, 448, 449
Declaration of the Immediate Causes of Secession, 496
Declaratory Act (1766), 176
decolonization, African-Americans and, 896
Dedham, Mass., *761*
de Diego, José (1866–1918), 740
Deep South, 315, 317, 347, 390, 396, 418, 492, 493, 496, 497, 575, 646, 966, 974, 976
Deere, John (1804–1886), 319
Deer Island, 87
Defense Appropriations Act, 1101
Defense Department, U.S., 897, 960, *986*, 1017, 1079, 1100, 1101
    McCarthy and, 909
Defense of Marriage Act, 1076
deference, tradition of, 145
deficit, federal, *see* national debt
de Gaulle, Charles (1890–1970), 940
deindustrialization, 1037, *1037*
de Islas, Andrés, *28*
deism, 149–50, 151
    in Second Great Awakening, 335

separation of church and state and, 212, 215
DeLancey family, 118, 145, 176, 207, 221
Delany, Martin, 875
Delany, Martin R. (1812–1885), 442, *568*
Delaware colony, 92
Delaware Indians, 156, 158, 161
DeLay, Tom (1947–), 1103
Delegation of Advocates of Women's Suffrage Addressing the House Judiciary Committee, A, 570
de Lesseps, Ferdinand (1805–1894), 717
Delta Council, 915
demobilization, of U.S. military, 886, 901
democracy, in America, 346–84
Democracy in America (Tocqueville), 307, 349
Democratic Party, 169, 368–69, *370*, 373, 380–82, *381*, 386, 463–64, 466, 473, 477–79, 483, 485, 487, 489, 490, 503, 515, 523, 617, 618, 639, 642–43, 644, 709, 711, 757, 778, 789–91, 813, 814, 822, 833, 855, 857, 887, 911, 915, 939, 941, 974, 976, 978, 981, 990, 1003, 1024, 1028, 1033, 1036, 1043–44, 1047, 1054, 1066, 1075, 1080, 1102–3, 1110, 1116, 1117
    African-Americans and, 830, 949
    anti-Redeemers in, 648
    and Bank of the United States, 378–79, *378*
    in campaign of 1960, 959, 960
    civil rights movement and, 973–74
    in the Civil War, 530–31
    creation of, 364
    decolonization and, 896
    economic policies of, 861, 1023
    1860 convention of, 493–94
    in election of 1900, 672
    in election of 1920, 800
    in election of 1924, 771, 789
    in election of 1928, 789
    in election of 1932, 801–2
    in election of 1946, 902
    in election of 1948, 904–6, *915*
    in election of 1952, 939, *939*
    in election of 1954, 939
    in election of 1972, 1018
    in election of 1992, 1052
    in election of 2000, 1079
    FDR's transformation of, 800
    Fifteenth amendment and, 568
    Great Society and, 977, 978
    high tariff opposed by, 618
    HUAC and, 836
    Irish and, 327
    John C. Calhoun and, 382
    left wing of, 836
    liberalism and, 911
    and New Deal coalition, 823, 1010, 1012, 1028
    1964 national convention of, 973–74, *973*
    Nixon and, 1009–10
    nomination of Buchanan and, 485
    press of, 369, 382, 523

in Reconstruction, 566, *566*, 575, 577, 578, 579–82, *582*
South and, 645, 648–49, 826, 836–37
Truman Doctrine and, 888
views on freedom of, 369–70
welfare and, 1054
see also specific elections and campaigns
Democratic-Republican societies, 280, 281, 282, 284
Federalist Party views on, 280
Democratic Review, 469
Dempsey, Jack (1895–1983), 762
Denmark, 139, 715
in the West Indies, 96
Dennett, Mary Ware (1872–1947), 777
Dennis v. United States, 910
Department of Female Nurses, 529
Departure of the 7th Regiment, 503
depression, economic:
agricultural, 764
of early 1840s, 474
of 1819, 341, 356
of 1837, 311, 341, 380, *380*, 453, 459
of 1857, 479
of 1873, 580, 594, 595, 597, 603, 622
of 1893, 594, 597, 603, 622, 641, 642, 661, 679
of 1929, *see* Great Depression
deregulation, 1024, *1024*, 1031, 1038, 1054, 1060, 1089, 1119
financial crisis of 2008 and, 1113, 1114, *1114*
Deseret, Mormons and, 605
de Soto, Hernando (1496–1542), 31–33, *1074*
deSoto, Lewis, *1074*
Destruction by Fire of Pennsylvania Hall, *445*
détente, 1014–15, 1023, 1027
Detroit, Mich., 160, 699, 788, *852*, *853*, 869, 929, 1022
breadlines in, 791
riot in, 979
Detroit Free Press, 864
Dew, Thomas R. (1802–1846), 421
Dewey, George (1837–1917), 662, 666
Dewey, John (1859–1952), 590, 699, 726, 771, 795
Dewey, Thomas E. (1902–1917), 876, 905
De Witt, Benjamin P., 678
Dial, 449
Dias, Bartholomeu (1450–1500), 20
Díaz, Porfirio (1830–1915), 720
Dickinson, John (1731–1808), 178–79, 187, *208*
dictators, dictatorships, 757, 843–44, 845, 863, 895, 921, 970, 1015, 1025, 1056
FDR and, 843–44
U.S. support of, 1042
see also Hitler, Adolf; Mussolini, Benito; Saddam Hussein; Stalin, Joseph; totalitarianism
Dictionary of Races of People, 734
Diego, Juan, 27
Dies Irae (Rosenberg), *791*
Diggers, 81

Dingley Tariff (1897), 644
Dinwiddie, Robert (1693–1770), 156
Discourse Concerning Western Planting, A (Hakluyt), *52*
discrimination:
reverse, 979
see also segregation
diseases:
Africans and, 94, 131
in Civil War, 506
Indians and, 2, 3, 5, 24, 27, 32, 40, 54, 58, 73, 76, 87, 96, 106, 155
in Jamestown, 58
Pilgrims and, 67
Disney, Walt (1901–1966), 908
"Disquistion on Government, A" (Calhoun), 363
Dissenters, 71, 83, 102, 110, 144, 151, 181, 210–11
diversity, *211*, 784, 834, 863–64, *1066*, 1067–69, *1069*, 1074–75, 1076, 1078
see also pluralism
division of powers, in U.S. Constitution, 250–51, 254
divorce, 1013, *1014*, 1029, 1076
Dix, Dorothea (1802–1887), 446
Dix, Fort, 728
Dixiecrats, 904–5
Dixie to Broadway (Broadway show), 787
Dixon, Frank (1892–1965), 871
Dodge, Mabel (1879–1962), 696
Dodge City, Kans., 604
Dole, Bob (1923–), 1054
Dollar Diplomacy, 719
domestic abuse, 702, 730
domestic terrorism, 1097
Dominican Republic, 21, 660, 718, 719, 720, 844, 986, 991
immigrants from, 1066, 1068
Dominion of New England, 103
Donelson, Fort, 511
Donnelly, Ignatius (1831–1901), 626, 638
"Don't Buy Where You Can't Work" campaign, 829, *829*
Doolittle, Amos (1754–1832), *184*, *285*
Dorr, Thomas (1805–1854), 348–49, *349*
Dorr Liberation Stock, *349*
Dorr War, 348–49, *349*
Dos Passos, John (1896–1970), 759
dot coms, 1058, 1061
double-V, 871
Douglas, Helen Gahagan (1900–1980), 939
Douglas, Stephen A. (1813–1861), 477–79, 485, 486–89, *488*, 490–91, 493–94, 495
Douglas, William O. (1898–1980), 1002
Douglass, Frederick (1817–1895), 390, *391*, 403, *440*, 446, 514, *568*, 874, 956, *1004*
on abolition, 545, 551
autobiography of, 442
biography of, 389
on black soldiers, 519
"Composite Nation" speech of, 570
on the Constitution, 441

death of, 656
Independence Day speech of, 443
on plantations, 395
on slavery, 403, 410, 415, 418, 446, 451, 520
Dow, Neal (1804–1897), 617
"dower rights," 62, 63
Dow Jones Industrial Average, 1112
Downfall of Mother Bank, The, *378*
draft:
in Civil War, 504, 528, 531, 533
Puerto Ricans and, 740
in Vietnam War, 990, 1016, 1017, 1026
in World War I, 726, 733, 738
in World War II, 846, 869
Drayton, William Henry (1742–1779), 222
Dred Scott case, *485*, 485–86, 488, 494, 569, 624
Dreiser, Theodore (1871–1945), 680, 775
Dresden, 878
Drew, Charles, 869
Drift and Mastery (Lippmann), 701
drugs, 949, 991, *991*, 992, 994, 1039–40, 1071, 1122
Noriega and, 1049
Vietnam War and, 1016
see also crack cocaine
Drunkard's Progress, The, *430*
Dubious, 643
Du Bois, W. E. B. (1868–1963), 737, 742–43, *742*, 745, 751, 752, 783, 787, 829, 874, 876, 914, 956
Dubuclet, Antoine (1810–1887), 407
Duchess County, N.Y., 800
dueling, 397
Dukakis, Michael (1933–), 1043, 1044
Dulles, John Foster (1888–1959), *899*, 900, 942, 943
Dumbarton Oaks, conference at, 880
Duncan, Isadora (1877?–1927), 696, *696*
Dunkers, 109, 110
Dunmore, John Murray, earl of (1732–1809), 186, 193, 221, 226, 228, 290
Dunn, Alan (1980–), *940*
DuPont, *923*
Duquesne, Fort, 158
Duquesne, Pa., 811
Durand, Asher B. (1796–1886), *331*
Durant, Will (author; 1885–1981), 856
Durant, William C. (GM founder; 1861–1947), 790
Dust Bowl, 807, *808*
Dutch East India Company, 41
Dutch East Indies, 848, 896
see also Indonesia
Dutch Empire, 41, 90, 128
see also Netherlands
Dutch Reformed Church, 41
Dutch West India Company, 41, 43, *43*
Dyer, Mary (d. 1660), 82
Dylan, Bob (1941–), 992
Dynasty (TV show), 1039

Eagle's Nest, The, *521*
Earned Income Tax Credit (EITC), 1052

Earth Day, 999
East, 319
East Anglia, England, 77
Eastern Bank of Alabama, *532*
Easter Rebellion, 722
East Germany:
absorption of, 1048
creation of, 891
East Harlem, 933, *934*
East India Company, 181
East Indies, 18, 23
Eastman, Crystal (1881–1928), 696
East St. Louis, Ill., race riot in, 744, *745*
East Village, N.Y., 992
Eaton, Peggy (1799?–1879), 372
Economic, Social, and Cultural Rights, 900
Economic Bill of Rights, 862–63, 900
economic citizenship, 705
economic freedom:
American Revolution and, 215–18
hoarding and, 217
monopolies and, 217
price controls and, 217–18, *217*
economy:
Bush and, 1101–2
Clinton and, 1056
of Confederate States of America, 533–34
early U.S., 215–18, 239, 242, 245–46
financial crisis of 2008 and, 1111–16, *1112*, *1114*, 1117, 1119
government and, 168–69
growth in South of, 854, *854*
growth of, 586, 615, 617, 760
G. W. Bush and, 1101–2, 1111–16
housing bubble crisis and, 1111–12, *1111*, 1114
indicators of change in, *590*
of New England colonies, 77–78
1819 downturn of, 341, 355–56
Northern vs. Southern, 216
rise of corporations in, 594–97
slavery and, 225
U.S. and new, 1056–64
of West Indies, 96–97
see also depression, economic; market economy; market revolution; recessions
Economy Act (1932), 805, 825
Ecuador, 359
Eden, Richard (1521?–1576), 16
Edict of Nantes (1598), 38
Edison, Thomas A. (1847–1931), 593, *594*, 789
Edison Illuminating Company, 685
Edisto Island, S.C., 560
education:
civil rights and, 966, *971*, 979
of freed slaves, 539–40, 551, *551*, *553*, 556
higher, 906, 941, 994, 996, 1014, 1067
individualism and, 434
and literacy, 1081
Native Americans and, 998
in New World, 25

education (continued)
  public, 208, 215, 342, 433–35, *434*,
    575, *576*, *577*, 619, 650–51, 689,
    699, 702, 703, 780, 814, 836, 861,
    862, 901, 904, 924, 934, 1071,
    1075, 1118
  reform, 425
  slaves barred from, 401
  social classes and, 434
  women and, 281, 283, 702, 705, 729,
    1076
Edwards, Jonathan (1703–1758), 150,
  150
Edward VI, king of England (1537–
  1853), 50
Egerton, John (1935–), 952
Egypt, 636, 750, 1020, 1026, *1026*, 1100
  Obama's speech to Islamic world
    in, *1118*
  in Suez fiasco, 944
  uprising in, 1122, *1122*
Ehrlichman, John (1925–1999), 1019
Eickemeyer, Rudolph (1831–1895), *551*
Eighteenth Amendment, 731, *731*
Eighth Amendment, 259
Einstein, Albert (1879–1955), 876, 877
Eisenhower, Dwight D. (1890–1960),
    912, 946, 953, 958, 959, 1010,
    1054
  atomic bomb and, 878
  civil rights and, 952, 958
  Cold War and, 941–43
  D-Day and, 850
  Farewell Address of, 960
  inaugural address of, 942
  Little Rock and, 958
  "military-industrial complex" and,
    842
  Modern Republicanism and,
    940–41
  1952 campaign and, 909, 938–40,
    938, *939*
  Suez fiasco and, 944
Eisenhower, Mamie (1896–1979), 960
Eisenhower administration, 938–49,
    945, 952, 954, 985
  and Cuba, 970
  Native Americans and, 998
Eisenhower Doctrine, 944
EITC, *see* Earned Income Tax Credit
Electioneering in the South, 572
elections and campaigns:
  of 1789, 273
  of 1792, 284
  of 1796, 284–85
  of 1800, 287–88, *287*
  of 1804, 297
  of 1808, 297
  of 1816, 356
  of 1820, 356
  of 1824, 361–64, *364*, 366
  of 1828, 365, 366, *366*
  of 1836, 380–81
  of 1840, 381–82, *381*, *382*
  of 1844, 463–64
  of 1848, 473
  of 1852, 477
  of 1856, 483–85, *483*, *485*
  of 1858, 486–89

  of 1860, *486*, 494–95, *494*
  of 1862, 515
  of 1864, 537
  of 1868, 567, *567*, *569*, 617
  of 1872, 580
  of 1876, *581*, 582, *582*, 617
  of 1880, 617
  of 1884, 617
  of 1888, 617
  of 1892, 617, 640, *640*
  of 1896, 643–44, *644*
  of 1900, 672, *673*
  of 1912, 709–10, *709*, *710*, 802
  of 1916, 723, *724*
  of 1920, 800
  of 1924, 770–71
  of 1928, 788–89, *790*
  of 1932, 801–2, *802*
  of 1934, 815
  of 1936, 822–23, *832*
  of 1938, 863
  of 1940, 846, 874
  of 1944, 862, *862*, 876, 888
  of 1946, 902
  of 1948, 904–6, *905*, 939, 974
  of 1952, 938–40, *939*
  of 1960, 959–60, *960*, 971, 1009
  of 1964, 973–75, *973*, *974*, 1009
  of 1968, *1004*
  of 1972, 1018
  of 1976, 1023, *1023*
  of 1980, 1032, *1032*, 1033
  of 1984, 1039
  of 1988, 1043–44
  of 1992, 1051–52, *1052*, *1053*
  of 1996, 1054
  of 2000, 1079–80, *1079*, *1081*
  of 2004, 1102–3
  of 2006, 1110
  of 2008, *1087*, 1110, 1116–18, *1117*
  of 2012, 1124–26
  in Middle Colonies, 144
  in New England colonies, 144–45
  third parties in, 619
Electoral College, 250, 251, 252, 285,
    288, 297, 366, *366*, 617, 723, 1033,
    1079, 1080, 1103
  Twelfth Amendment and voting
    by, 287
  as undemocratic, 349
Electoral Commission (1877), 582
electrical industry, 688, 772
Electric Auto-Lite, 811
electricity, 592, 799, 837, 924, 1059,
    1060
Eliot, John (1604–1690), *76*
Elizabeth I, queen of England (1533–
    1603), 49–50, *51*, 52, 53
Elk, John, 613
Elk v. Wilkins, 613
Elliott, Robert B. (1842–1884), *548*
Ellis Island, 681
Ellison, Ralph (1914–1994), 954
Ellsberg, Daniel (1931–), 1018
El Mozote, El Salvador, massacre in,
    1042
El Salvador, 1026, 1042
e-mail, 1057, 1116
Emancipation, 575

Emancipation Proclamation (1862),
    386, 503, *515*, 516–19, *517*, 524,
    560, 841, 885
Emancipation Proclamation,
    Preliminary (1862), *514*, 515
Embargo (1807), 296–97, *296*, 321
Emergency Banking Act (1933), 803,
    804
Emerson, John (d. 1843), 485
Emerson, Ralph Waldo (1803–1882),
    184, 185, 330, *330*, 332, 343, 352,
    369–70, 425, 455, 473, 476
empire, U.S., 586, 664–65, *665*, 670–73,
    921
enclosure movement, 53
encomienda system, 31
Endangered Species Act (1973), 999,
    1010
End Poverty in California, 814
Enforcement Acts (1870–71), 578, 582
engagés, 38
England, 49, 127, 760
  Civil War of, 80–81, *81*, 82, 102, 140,
    144, 148
  and colonization of America, 48–85
  as "Commonwealth and Free State,"
    80
  debate over freedom in, 80–81
  emigration from, 3, 54–55
  empire expansion by, 88–94
  Glorious Revolution of, 102–3, 140
  as haven for former slaves, 227, 228
  Ireland conquered by, 50–51
  justification for colonization by, 3,
    15, 52–54, 81
  political upheavals of, 80–81
  poor economic conditions in, 53–54
  population of, 53, 54
  prejudice in, 94–95
  Protestantism in, 50, 51, 81, 83, 140
  Reformation in, 50
  War of Jenkins' Ear and, 139
  in West Indies, 96
  see also British Empire; Great Britain
England, Church of, *see* Anglican
    Church
English, as official language, 1075
English colonies, *see* American
    Colonies
English common law, development
    of, 80
English Country Party, 146
*English Liberties, or, The Free-Born
    Subject's Inheritance* (Care), 81
English liberty, 3, 79–80, *80*, 81, 91,
    100, 135, 141, 171, 172, 173, 175, 184
English Toleration Act (1690), 104
Enlightenment, 149, 178, 212, 898
  American, 149–50
  religion and, 150
Enron, 1059–60, *1059*
entail, 217
environmentalism, 983, 998–1000,
    1024, 1031, 1036, 1047, 1052,
    1053, 1054, 1089
  see also pollution
Environmental Protection Agency,
    1010
Episcopalians, *212*, 1028

Equal Credit Opportunity Act (1972),
    1014
Equal Employment Opportunity
    Commission, 977, 995
Equal Pay Act (1963), 995
Equal Rights Amendment (ERA),
    766, 1029–30, *1029*, *1030*, 1032,
    1035
Equiano, Olaudah (1745–1797), 127, *130*,
    131, 162
ERA, *see* Equal Rights Amendment
"Era of Good Feelings," 357
Erie, Lake, 300
Erie Canal, 307, *307*, 309–11, 392
Erwitt, Elliot (1928–), *932*
Espionage Act (1917), 732, 736, 776
Essex County, Mass., 121
Estonia, 749, 879
Ethiopia, 844, 1070
Ethiopian Regiment, of Lord
    Dunmore, 193
ethnic cleansing, *1055*
ethnic nationalism, 259
eugenics, 428, 734
Europe, European powers, 2, 5, *19*, 279,
    290, 748–52, *750*, *751*, 788, 886,
    889, 891, 893, 1020, 1065
  Eastern, 918
  Enlightenment in, 149
  expansion of, 6–9, 18–21
  hierarchical society of, 17
  Hitler's conquest of, 757
  immigration from, 976, 1065
  negative views of Indians in, 15
  New World rivalry of, 127–28,
    152–56
  post–World War II, 924
  pre–World War II, 844
  social status in, 17
  speed of American exploration by,
    23–24
  Western, 5
  see also specific countries
European Court of Human Rights,
    1056
Evans, George Henry (1805–1856), 474
Evers, Medgar (1925–1963), 967
evolution, 621, 756, 779, 1076
executive branch, U.S. government, 291
Executive Order 8802, 870
Executive Order 9066, 867
Exodus, book of, 414, 647–48, *647*
Ex parte Milligan, 523
Exposition and Protest, 372
extraterritoriality, 252

factories, 684, 760, 764, *765*, 925, 1047
  automobile, 760
  New Deal and, 799, 812
  pollution and, 1010
  in Soviet Exhibition, 923
  system, 319–23
  during World War II, 855
Factories in the Field (McWilliams), 828
Fairbanks, Douglas (1883–1939), *728*
Fair Deal, 901
Fair Employment Practices
    Commission (FEPC), 866, 870,
    885

Fair Labor Standards Act (1938), 800, 830
Fair Labor Standards Bill, 824
Fall, Albert (1861–1944), 770
Fallen Timbers, Battle of, 265
Fall In!, 823
Falmouth, Maine, 187
Falwell, Jerry (1933–2007), 1029, 1035
Family Assistance Plan, 1010
family life, 996, 1001, 1002, 1033
    Cold War and, 931–32
    consumerism and, 919
    "family values" and, 1076, *1076*
    and nuclear family, 1076
Family Record, 551
Farmers' Alliance, 636–37
    Colored, 639
Farmer's and Mechanics Almanac, 243
Farmington, Conn., 182
farms, *see* agriculture
Farragut, David G. (1801–1870), 511
Farrell, Frank J., 625
fascism, 815, 816, 844, 845, 846, 857, 863, 897
    Mussolini as founder of, 844
"Father Was Killed by a Pinkerton Man" (song), 635
Faubus, Orval (1910–1994), 958
FBI, *see* Federal Bureau of Investigation
FCC, *see* Federal Communications Commission
FDIC, *see* Federal Deposit Insurance Corporation
Federal Art Project, *816, 833*
Federal Bureau of Investigation (FBI), 748, 886, 910, 971, 982, 1019, 1099
Federal Communications Commission (FCC), 809
Federal Dance Project, 816
Federal Deposit Insurance Corporation (FDIC), 803
Federal Emergency Management Agency (FEMA), 1104
Federal Emergency Relief Administration, 805
Federal Hall, 273
Federal Home Loan Bank System, 794
Federal Home Loan Mortgage Corporation (Freddie Mac), 1115
Federal Housing Administration (FHA), 809, 830
federalism, 250, *254*
Federalist, The (Hamilton, Madison, and Jay), 254–55, 294
Federalist Party, 277, 279, 284, 299, 356, 371
    in election of 1800, 287, 288
    in election of 1804, 297
    in election of 1824, 364
    elimination of, 303
    in Missouri Compromise, 358
    and national bank, 169
    platform of, 277–78
    views on Democratic-Republican societies of, 280
    views on press of, 286
Federal Music Project, 816, 833

Federal National Mortgage Association (Fannie Mae), 1115
Federal Reserve Bank, 355, 1111, 1112, 1114
Federal Reserve Board, 770, 1102
Federal Reserve System, 711, 1024
Federal Savings and Loan Insurance Corporation, 1038
Federal Theater Project, 816, 837
Federal Trade Commission, 711, 770
Federated Trades of the Pacific Coast, 625
Felton, Rebecca, 741
FEMA, *see* Federal Emergency Management Agency
Female Anti-Slavery Society, 425
Female Moral Reform Society, 447
Feminine Mystique, The (Friedan), 994–95
feminism, 446–55, 779, 911, 932, 965, 994–96, *995*, 1004, 1052, 1076, 1078, 1108
    African-Americans and, 766
    Hillary Clinton and, 1078
    Ku Klux Klan and, 781
    Latino activism vs., 998
    in middle class, 994, 995
    new, 695–96
    radical, 996, 1034
    reproductive rights and, 996, 1002, 1004
    second-wave, 1030
    World War I and, 722
    see also gender relations; women; women's rights
Feminist Alliance, 695
femme sole (unmarried woman), 63
FEPC, *see* Fair Employment Practices Commission
Ferdinand, king of Spain (1452–1516), 21, *21*
Ferraro, Geraldine (1935–), 1039
feudalism, 92, 123
FHA, *see* Federal Housing Administration
FHP Wireless, *1059*
field labor, 61–62
Fields, J. D., 636
Fifteenth Amendment, 568, *568*, 571–72, 648–49, 742, 766, 885
    Native Americans and, 613
Fifth Freedom, 858–59
Fifty-fourth Massachusetts Volunteers, 518
Fight for Freedom rally, *846*, 847
Filene, Edward (1860–1937), 686
Filipinos, 666–67, *666, 667*, 848, 856, 925
    atrocities by U.S. against, 666
    Christianity and, 667
    immigration quota on, 783
    see also Philippines
Filling Cartridges at the U.S. Arsenal of Watertown, Massachusetts, 528
Fillmore, Millard (1800–1874), 472, 475, 485
financial crisis of 2008, 1111–16, *1112, 1114*, 1117
Finland, 749

Finney, Charles Grandison (1792–1875), 334, 335–36, 438
"fire-eaters," 493
Fire Next Time, The (Baldwin), 983
fireside chats, 819, *819*, 820
Firestone, 871, 1038
First Amendment, 258, 259, 286, 775, 776, 856, 908, 1000, 1001
    Holmes doctrine and, 776
First Continental Congress (1775), 182–83, 211
First Rhode Island Regiment, *194*
First Seminole War, 376
First South Carolina Volunteers, 515
First Vote, The, *573*
fish, 128–29
Fisher, Sidney George, 570
Fisher Body Plant, 812
Fisk University, 551, 742
Fitzgerald, F. Scott (1896–1940), 776
Fitzhugh, George (1806–1881), 397, 400–401, 488, 496
Five Civilized Tribes, 374, *375*
Five Generations of a Black Family, 552
Five Iroquois Nations, 90–91, *91*
Five Points (Catlin), *482*
Flag Day, 661
Flanders, 192
flappers, 760, 768
Fleischer, Ari (1960–), 1099
Fletcher v. Peck, 292
Flint, Michigan, 790, 812, *813*
Florentine Codex, 23
Florida, *15*, 25, 26, 31, 91–92, 139, 147, 197, 314, 374, 376, 790, 902, 1117
    BP oil spill and, 1119
    ceded to Great Britain, 158
    colonization of, 33
    in election of 2000, 1079–80, *1079*, 1080
    as haven for fleeing slaves, 138
    lynchings in, 775
    Noriega in, 1049
    population of, 152
    prison labor and, *645*
    Seminoles in, 376
    Supreme Court of, 1079–80
    U.S. acquisition of, 317, 365
    War Hawks' plan for conquest of, 297
Flushing, N.Y., 1066
FOIA (Freedom of Information Act) (1966), 1019
Fong Yue Ting, 655
Food Administration, 727, 731
food stamps, 978, 1010, 1039, 1075
Foraker Act (1900), 670
Forbes, Charles (1880–1954), 770
Force Bill, 373
Ford, Gerald (1913–2006), 1023, *1023*, 1028, 1031, 1033
    Nixon pardoned by, 1023
Ford, Henry (1863–1947), 685–86, 760, 761, 764, *765*, 772, 790, 813, 845, 846
Ford, James, *832*
Ford administration, 1052
Fordism, 685–86

Ford Motor Company, 685–86, *686*, 735, 760, 763, 845, 929, *936*, 1064
    assembly lines and, 686
    and German slave labor, 845
Fordney-McCumber Tariff (1922), 772
Foreign Anti-Slavery Society, 454
Foreign Trade, 88
Forest Service, U.S., 708
Forging the Shaft (Weir), *589*
Forrest, Nathan B. (1821–1877), 519
Fort Caroline, 33
Fort Dix, 728
Fort Donelson, 511
Fort Duquesne, 158
Forten, Charlotte (1837–1914), 540
Forten, James (1766–1842), 441
Fort George, 177
Fort Gibson, *810*
Fort Henry, 511
Fort Hood, 903
Fort Knox, 355
Fort Louisbourg, 158
Fort McHenry, 300
Fort McIntosh, 242
Fort Necessity, 158
Fort Orange, 41
Fort Pillow, 519, 545
Fort Stanwix, 242
Fort Sumter, 386, 498–99, *499*, 508, 520
Fort Ticonderoga, 158, 185
Fortune, 793, 819, 856, *858*, 937, *1059*
Fort Wagner, 518
Fort Washington, 194
"47 percent" remark, in 2012 election and campaign, 1125
Fosdick, Harry Emerson (1878–1969), 777–78
Foster, Stephen S. (1809–1881), 425
Founding Fathers:
    as slaveholders, 224, 225, 227, 229, 251, 269
    western land speculation of, 221
Four Freedoms, 757, 841–42, *843*, 855–57, 860, 863, 871, 873, 880–81, 885, 889, 899, 936
Four Freedoms Show, 841
Fourier, Charles (1772–1837), 429
Four Racial Groups (de Islas), *28*
Fourteen Points, 724–25, 746, 748–49, 750, *750*
Fourteenth Amendment, 440, 566, 570, 571–72, 581, 623, 649, 650, *650*, 655, 742, 773, 777, 786, 885, 951, 954, 1013, 1080
    Native Americans and, 613
    Tea Party and, 1122
Fox, Ebenezer (1763–1843), 216
Foxwoods casino, 1074
Fragment on Government (Bentham), 235
Frame of Government, 93
France, 23, 35, 38–41, 52, 104, 111, 139, 140, 141, 157–58, 187, 239, 493, 589, 746, 772, 844–45, 876, 879, 880, *889*, 890–91, 940, 944, 1082, 1100
    American Revolution and, 193, 197, *200, 208*, 211
    Catholicism and, 164

France (*continued*)
  change of government in, 474–75
  communist party in, 889
  declares war on Germany, 845
  designs on Cuba by, 361
  in Great Depression, 790, 802
  industry in, 590
  Iraq War and, 1093
  justification for colonization by, 3, 15
  Louisiana Purchase and, 292–94, *293*
  male suffrage in, 615
  New World exploration of, 35, 38–40
  1968 strike in, 1004
  occupation of Germany of, 890–91
  population compared to England, 54
  progressivism in, 699
  seizure of American ships by, 285
  socialism in, 691
  in Suez fiasco, 944
  trade with, 285
  in U.N., 880
  U.S. Civil War and, 509
  in wars with American colonists, 127
  in wars with Great Britain, 276, 280, 296–97
  welfare state and, 940
  in West Indies, 96
  in World War I, 721, 722
  see also French Empire
Franciscans, 34, *35*
Franco, Francisco (1892–1975), 844, 845
Frank, Leo (1884–1915), 781
Frankfurter, Felix (1882–1965), 759
Frank Leslie's Illustrated Newspaper, *343*, *564*, *570*, *625*, *626*
Franklin, Benjamin (1706–1790), 147, *147*, 148, 149, 150, *150*, 151, 164, *164*, *183*, 232, 243, 267, 736
  at Constitutional Convention, 248, 253
  as deist, 150
  as head of Pennsylvania Abolition Society, 288
  Stamp Act and, 178
  Treaty of Amity and Commerce and, 197
  Treaty of Paris and, 200
  writings of, 116, 142, 147, 149
Franklin, James (1697–1735), 148
Franz Ferdinand, archduke of Austria (1863–1914), 721
Frazier, Garrison (b. 1797), 549
Freake, Elizabeth (1642–1713), *79*
Freake, John (1635–1675), *79*
Frederick, Va., *284*
Fredericksburg, Va., *127*
Fredericksburg, Battle of, 510
free blacks:
  in Caribbean, 407
  as laborers, 408
  in New Orleans, 407
  population of, *406*, 407
  see also African-Americans; slaves, emancipated

"freeborn Englishman," 80, 127
Freedmen's Bureau, 551, 555–56, 565, *566*, 575, 608
Freedmen's Bureau, The, 555
Freedmen's Bureau Bill (1866), 566
freedom, 126–66, *331*, 587, 673, 874, 885, 899, 918, 919, 921, 1001–2, 1082, 1083, 1100, 1110, 1118
  African-Americans and, 1016
  in Age of Jackson, 369–70
  American National Exhibition and, 923
  American Revolution and, 168, 171, 206, 207–8, 235–36
  of assembly, 835, *856*, 1095
  Bellamy's view of, 627–28
  Black Power and, 981
  Chief Joseph on, 609
  civil rights movement and, 915, 949–59, *957*
  Civil War and, 385, 520, 523
  Cold War and, 893, 895, 896–900, *898*, 907, 910, 935, 946, 965
  conservatism and, 937–38
  consumerism and, 683, 684, 919, 927–28, 930–31
  counterculture and, 991, 992
  Debs's view of, 642
  degradation of, 775–76
  Democratic vs. Whig view of, 369
  desire of slaves for, 101, 138–39, 226, 231, 415–16
  economic, 53–54
  employer vs. employee, 635–36
  European idea of, 15–18
  expansion of, 127
  of expression, 148, 208, 219, 257, 258, 259–63, 282, 286–87, 290, 392, 445–46, 696–97, 698, 731, 733, 736, 775, 776, 779, 835–36, 841, 855, *856*, 873, 881, 899, 908, 910, 923, 936, 985, 1083, 1090, 1091, 1095, 1100, 1108
  FDR and, 818–22
  feminism and, 449
  frozen meals and, 932
  in Gilded Age, 620–24
  in Great Depression, 795
  Great Society and, 978–79
  guns and, 1077
  immigration and, 682–83
  Indians and, 15–16, 221–23, 266, 610–14
  individualism and, 330–31, 336
  as inducement to English colonization, 53–54
  industrialization and, 323
  Iraq War and, 1093, 1094, 1103
  land possession and, 178
  left wing groups and, 831–32
  Lincoln's views of, 520–21, 527
  Locke on, 268
  market revolution and, 336
  Marshall Plan and, 889
  New Deal and, 757, 804, 818–22
  New Left's definition of, 983
  in New Netherland, 41–45
  in 1964 election, 1009

political power vs., 146
  post-World War II, 860–63
  of the press, 148, 217, 257, 258, 259, 290, 392, 445, 736, 775, 777, 1000, 1017
  Prohibition and, 778–79
  Ralph Waldo Emerson and, 332
  Reagan and, 920, 1036
  in Reconstruction, 550–51
  Red Scare and, 759
  reform and, 432–33
  religious, *see* religious freedom
  September 11 terrorist attacks and, 1127
  slaveholders' views of, 385
  Social Darwinists view of, 622
  of speech, *see* freedom, of expression
  Stamp Act and, 171, 174
  Statue of Liberty and, 589
  suburbia and, 932
  Thurmond and, 904–5, 906
  Truman Doctrine and, 888–89
  U.S. foreign policy and, 716
  in utopian societies, 430
  from want, 856–57, *856*
  after War of 1812, 307
  war on terror and, 1088, 1090, 1091, 1094, *1109*
  Webster's definition of, 343
  Whig views of, 370–71
  white vs. Indian, 221–23
  women and, 685, 692, 766–68, *768*, 859–60, *861*, 994–96
  of workers, 597–99
  World War I and, 728, 732
  World War II and, 757, 842, *843*, 855–57, *856*, *861*, *864*, 880–81
  see also Four Freedoms; religious freedom
Freedom Award, 976
Freedom Budget, *979*, 980
Freedom: Certain Restrictions Apply, *1109*
freedom dues, 55
Freedom House, 847, 900
Freedom in the Modern World, 795
Freedom of Information Act (FOIA) (1966), 1019
Freedom of Speech (Rockwell), 842
Freedom of Worship (Rockwell), *864*
Freedom Pledge, 885
Freedom Revolution, 1053
Freedom Rides, 965, 966
"Freedoms and Exemptions," 43
Freedom Scroll, 885
Freedom's Journal, 351, 443
Freedom Summer, 973–74
Freedom to the Slave, 517
Freedom Tower, *1125*
Freedom Train, 885–86, *887*
Freed Slaves Celebrating President Lincoln's Decree of Emancipation, *516*
free enterprise, 757, 858, *858*, 895, 936–37, 940, 946, 1030
"free labor," 483–84, 513, *623*
freemen, in Pennsylvania, 94
Free Soil Party, 474, 483
Free Speech Movement, *984*, 985
free trade, 218, 772, 1051, 1052, 1054, 1060, 1062, 1091, 1094

  see also NAFTA (North American Free Trade Agreement)
freeways, 927
Free Woman, 449
Free World, 895, 896, 936, 937
  U.S. president as leader of, 888–89
Free World Association, 846, 861
Frelinghuysen, Theodore (1817–1885), 150
Frémont, John C. (1813–1890), 466, *483*, 485, 514, 539
French Americans, *864*
French and Indian War, *see* Seven Years' War
French Canada, 38–40
French Empire, 3, 25, 26, 35, 38–41, *44*, 49, 97, 152, *153*, 156–57, 659, 715, 751
  end of, *159*
  Vietnam and, 945
French Indochina, 848, 896, 984
French Revolution, 160, 236, 276–77, 279, 280, 898, 899
Freud, Sigmund (1856–1939), 696, 769
Frick, Henry Clay (1849–1919), 635
Friedan, Betty (1921–2006), 994–95
Friedman, Milton (1912–2006), 937
Fries, John (1750–1818), 285
Fries's Rebellion, 285
From Factory Life as It Is., 333
Frugal Housewife, The (Child), 341
Fuel Agency, 727
Fugitive Slave Act (1850), 475–77, *477*
fugitive slaves, 288, 376, 475–77, 513, *513*
  Abraham Lincoln and, 487, 496
  as contraband in Civil War, 513, 516
  in U.S. Constitution, 288
Full Employment Bill, 863
Fuller, Margaret (1810–1850), 449, *449*
Fulton, Mo., "iron curtain" speech at, 887
Fulton, Robert (1765–1815), 309
Fundamental Constitutions of Carolina (1669), 92, 143
fundamentalism, 777–80, 1027, 1028–29, 1065
  Islamic, 1027, 1050, 1065, 1090, 1093
  radio broadcasts and, 815
  religious freedom vs., 779
  Saddam Hussein and, 1093
  see also creationism
Fundamental Orders (1639), 72
fur trade, 38, 56–58, 117, 123
  animal populations and, 58
  Carolina colony and, 133
  Five Iroquois Nations and, 91
  in New France, 38
  of Pequots, 76
  Russian, 154
  Treaty of Paris and, 160

Gabbard, Tulsi (1981–), 1125
Gabel, Hortense (1912–1990), 915
Gabriel (slave; 1776–1800), 289–90, 419, 421
Gabriel's Rebellion, 289–90

Gadhafi, Muammar (1942–2011), over-
throw of, 1121–22
Gadsden Purchase, 467, 472
Gaffney, Mary (b. 1846), 556
Gage, Thomas (1721–1787), 193
gag rule, regarding abolition, 444, 445
Gaines, Lloyd (1913?-1939), 953
Galbraith, John Kenneth (1908–2006),
947
Gales, Joseph (1786–1860), 281
Galesburg, Ill., Maytag factory in,
1102
Gallatin, Albert (1761–1849), 354
Galloway, Joseph (1731–1803), 186
Gallup poll, 1014
Gama, Vasco da (1460–1524), 20
Gandhi, Mahatma (1869–1948), 752
Gandhi, Mohandas (Mahatma; 1869–
1948), 881, 956
Gardner, Alexander (1821–1882), 544
Garfield, James A. (1831–1881), 550, 617
assassination of, 617, 618
Garland, Hamlin (1860–1940), 635
Garner, John Nance (1868–1967), 861
Garner, Margaret, 477
Garnet, Henry Highland (1815–1882),
436, 442
Garrison, William Lloyd (1805–1879),
421, 437, 437, 439, 441, 442, 444,
446, 455, 568, 736
Garvey, Marcus (1887–1940), 745
Garveyism, 745, 875
Garvey movement, 787
Gast, John, 461
Gates, Bill (1955–), 1058, 1061
GATT, see General Agreement on
Tariffs and Trade
Gaumont film company, 762
Gay Liberation Day, 997
gay rights, 697, 907–8, 911, 919, 921,
965, 998, 1014, 1029, 1039, 1052,
1073, 1074, 1075, 1076, 1078,
1108
gay marriage and, 1103, 1125
McCarthyism and, 907–8, 997
military and, 1052
see also homosexuals, homosexuality
Gaza Strip, 1099
GE, see General Electric
"gender gap", electoral, 1080
gender relations:
European, 15
Native American, 14
World War II and, 842
see also women; women's rights
General Agreement on Tariffs and
Trade (GATT), 890
General Assembly, U.N., 880, 899
General Court (Conn.), 76
General Court (Mass.), 69, 75, 78, 103,
104
General Electric (GE), 593, 1033
General Electric Theater, The (TV show),
929
General History of Virginia (Smith), 60
General Motors, 760, 763, 790, 812–13,
813, 814, 835, 853, 940, 961, 1000,
1061
General Slocum, 677

General Theory of Employment, Interest,
and Money (Keynes), 824
Genet, Edmond (1763–1834), 277
Geneva:
summit conference in, 942
Vietnam peace conference in, 946
Geneva Accords (1954), 984
Geneva Conventions:
First, 530, 1100, 1109–10
as obsolete, 1100
Genoa, 20, 23
Gentlemen's Agreement (1907), 740
George, David Lloyd (1863–1945), 749
George, Fort, 177
George, Henry (1839–1897), 626, 629,
631, 687–88, 698
George, Lloyd (1863–1945), 749
George III, king of England (1738–
1820), 170, 171, 186, 190, 191
Georgia, 288, 315, 374–76, 560, 645,
646, 836, 1023, 1108
Confederate flag and, 957
government in, 209
Ku Klux Klan in, 781
population of slaves in, 135
slavery in, 252
textiles in, 645
Trail of Tears in, 376
voting rights in, 352
Georgia colony, 33, 144
in American Revolution, 194, 199
creation of, 134–35
Declaration of Independence and,
190
French in, 156
Loyalists in, 219
rice plantations in, 133
slavery in, 133, 138, 227
German-Americans, 110, 156, 324–26,
370, 602, 654, 689, 784, 864
Prohibition and, 730
World War I and, 722, 738, 1098,
1100
World War II and, 844, 867
German Beer Garden on Sunday Evening,
A, 432
Germans, German immigrants, 109,
110, 111, 112, 156, 324–26, 432, 432
as Democrats, 370
English liberty and, 184
"German triangle," 325
Germany, 749, 750, 752, 764, 772, 772,
850, 850, 878, 880, 897, 1020,
1023, 1082, 1083, 1115
aggression by, 844, 845
as Axis power, 845
D-Day and, 850
declaration of war against U.S. of,
848
division of, 888, 890–91
empire of, 715
in Great Depression, 790
industry in, 590
invasion of Poland by, 845
invasion of Soviet Union by, 846,
887
Iraq War and, 1093
occupation of, 890–91
post-Cold War, 1048

progressivism in, 699
rise of Hitler in, 802, 844, 844, 845
socialism in, 691
Soviet Union invasion of, 876
submarine war and, 849, 850
Venezuela crisis and, 718
in World War I, 721–24
in World War II, 757, 840, 845–47,
850, 867, 874, 876, 878, 879
see also East Germany; West
Germany
Geronimo (1829–1909), 609
Gettysburg, Battle of, 536, 536
Gettysburg Address, The, 521, 616,
834, 885
Ghana, 943, 1070
Ghent, Treaty of (1814), 300
Ghost Dance, 613–14, 614
Gibbons v. Ogden, 328
GI Bill of Rights (1944), 862, 866, 870,
901, 901, 936
Giddings, Joshua (1795–1864), 478
Gideon's Band, 540
Gifford, Abigail, 71
Gilbert, Humphrey (1539–1583), 51
Gilded Age, 387, 588–633, 598, 623,
688, 689, 691, 699, 703
and Andrew Carnegie, 606
corruption of politics in, 615–16
courts in, 623–24
economy in, 617–18
elections in, 617, 617
freedom in, 620–24
labor in, 624–31, 626
liberty of contract in, 622–23
political parties in, 617
politics in, 615–20
Social Darwinism, 621–22
social reform in, 628
state governments in, 619, 620
Gilded Age, The (Twain and Warner),
615
Gilman, Charlotte Perkins (1860–
1935), 685, 692, 726
Gingrich, Newt (1943–), 1053, 1054,
1124
Gini index, 1060
Gin Lane (Hogarth), 53
Ginsberg, Allen (1926–1997), 949
Ginsburg, Ruth Bader (1933–), 1052
Gitlow, Benjamin (1891–1965), 776
Glacier Point, Calif., 707, 708
Gladden, Washington (1836–1918), 629
Glasgow, 746
glasnost, 1042
Glass-Steagall Act (1932), 803, 1060
"Gleaner, The," 281
Gleason, Jackie (1916–1987), 929
Gliddon, George R. (1809–1857), 442
globalization, 921, 1047–48, 1057,
1060, 1062, 1063, 1065, 1067,
1083, 1113, 1119
global warming, 961, 1088–89
see also climate change
Glorious Revolution, 102–3, 103
Glory, 518
GNP, see gross national product
Goddess of Democracy and Freedom,
1048, 1049

Goddess of Liberty, 307, 329
Godkin, E. L. (1831–1902), 579, 671
"God Save the King," 140
gold, 19, 24, 25, 29, 33, 35, 49, 53, 54, 58,
59, 88, 97, 106, 380, 1020
in California gold rush, 381, 469–70,
470, 471, 493
Chinese immigrants and, 654
coinage, 146
corporate mining of, 604
currency and, 355, 378, 379
as inducement to exploration, 2, 19,
31, 33, 35
tobacco as substitute for, 61
Goldbergs, The (TV show), 929
Gold Coast, 896, 943
Golden Anniversary of the Festival of
Lights, 789
"golden door," 781–83
Goldman, Emma (1869–1940), 697,
697, 733, 748
Goldman Sachs, 1113
gold rush, California, 601
gold standard, 618, 643, 790, 804, 879,
1020
Gold Standard Act (1900), 644
Goldwater, Barry (1909–1998), 974–76,
1009, 1033, 1054
Gompers, Samuel (1850–1924), 657,
688, 691, 726
Gonzales, Alberto (1955–), 1101
Goodell, William (1792–1878), 440
Goodman, Andrew (1949–1964),
973
Good Neighbor Policy, 842–44, 866
Goodrich, Samuel (1793–1860), 288
Gorbachev, Mikhail (1931–), 1042,
1042, 1048–49
Gordon, Thomas (d. 1750), 143, 148
Gore, Albert (1907–1998), 957
Gore, Albert, Jr. (1948–), 1079–81
Gorgas, Josiah (1818–1883), 508
Gosnold, Bartholomew (1572–1607), 67
"gospel of wealth," of Andrew
Carnegie, 608
Gould, Jack, 931
Gould, Jay (1836–1892), 528, 629
government, U.S.:
business and, 769–74, 860
Constitutional debate over, 168,
248, 261
corruption in, 770
debt of, see national debt
economy and, 168–69
employment discrimination, 830
housing discrimination by, 830, 830
labor and, 641
regulatory powers of, 706–7, 770,
803–4, 824, 837, 977, 978
in Second New Deal, 817–18
society and, 256
structure of, 248–49
workforce size of, 617
see also specific branches
Grady, Henry (1850–1889), 645
Graham, Billy (1918–), 935
Graham, Martha (1894–1991), 834, 834
grain, 128–29, 275, 317, 408
Gramm, Phil, 1060

Grand Coulee Dam, 799, *799, 801, 806,* 827

Grand Council of the Five Iroquois Nations, *91*

"grandees," 100, 119

grandfather clause, voting rights and, 649

Grand Federal Procession, 239, *239, 256, 258*

Grand Rapids, Mich., manufacturing in, 591

Grand Review of the Union armies, 544–45

Grange, 619

Grant, Madison (1865–1932), 734

Grant, Ulysses S. (1822–1885), 511, 537, *537,* 540, *542, 568,* 578, 579, 660
  background of, 511
  in election of 1868, 567, *569*
  Indian policy of, 608, 616
  Ku Klux Klan and, 578
  Lee's surrender to, 542
  on Mexican War, 465
  at Petersburg, 541
  scandals under, 577
  Southern violence and, 581–82

Grapes of Wrath, The (Steinbeck), 807, 821

Gray, Simon, 408

Great Awakening, 110, 138, 150–52, *150, 151*
  impact of, 151–52
  individualism and, 335
  slavery and, 152, 413

Great Awakening, Second, 334–36, *335,* 385, 431, 437

Great Awakening, Third, 1029

Great Britain, 2–3, *22,* 23, 115, 221–22, 239, 364, 365, 493, 746, 757, 772, 817, 844–46, 873, 888, 940, 959, 1004, 1032, 1082, 1083
  American boycott of, 183
  Canada and, 466
  Chartist movement in, 474
  creation of, 127
  D-Day and, 850
  declares war on Germany, 845
  empire of, 25, 26, 157–58
  in Great Depression, 790, 802
  immigrants from, 602
  industry in, 590
  Iraq War and, 921, 1093
  Lend-Lease and, 846
  as obstacle to westward expansion, 329
  occupation of Germany by, 890–91
  Oregon Territory and, 459, *462,* 464–65
  patriotism of, 140
  progressivism in, 699
  regulation of American trade with, 117
  seizure of American ships by, 285
  submarine war and, 850
  in Suez fiasco, 944
  suffrage in, 615, 729
  and Third World, 943
  trade with, 285
  in U.N., 880
  unemployment in, 764
  U.S. Civil War and, 509
  Venezuela and, 718
  war debt of, 172–73
  in war with France, 276, 280, 296–97
  welfare state and, 940
  in World War I, 721–24
  see also British Empire; England

Great Council, 12

Great Depression, 756, 757, 788–95, *791, 794,* 799–800, *799,* 802, *809,* 813, 815, 821, *822,* 853, 856, 858, 861, 865, 879, 880, 889, 1020, 1031, 1058, 1111, 1113, 1125
  Dust Bowl and, 807
  economic inequality in, *1060*
  Eisenhower and, 940
  homelessness and, 791, *794,* 821
  housing and, 808–9
  minorities and, 826–31, *829*
  socialist view of, 832
  wages in, 791, 793
  women and, 825
  World War II and, 837, 841, *852*
  see also New Deal

Greatest Department Store on Earth, The, 715

Great Famine, as cause of Irish immigration, 325

Great Labor Parade of September 1, 626

Great Labor Question from a Southern Point of View, The (Homer), *555*

Great Lakes, 40, 307, 354

Great Lakes region, 91, 155, 160

Great League of Peace, 12

Great Migration, 67, 79, 648, 743–44, *744,* 783, *786, 788,* 869

Great Plains, 10, 31, 601, 603, 604, 610, 638, 679
  women in, 603

Great Railroad Strike of 1877, 591, *624, 625*

Great Salt Lake Valley, Mormons in, 605

Great Society, 555, 734, 831, 875, 920, 977–79, 990, 1005, 1010, 1039, 1052, 1054, 1118, 1119
  see also Johnson, Lyndon

Great Steel Strike, 747, *747,* 813

"Great Sun," 13

Great Triumvirate, 477

Great War, *see* World War I

Greece, ancient, slavery in, 398

Greece, rebellion in, 888

Greeley, Horace (1811–1872), 579–80

Green, James K. (1823–1891), 573

Greenback-Labor Theory, 617, 619

Greene, Nathanael (1742–1786), 199

Greenglass, David (1922–), 908

Greenhow, Rose, 535

Greenland, 21, 1088

Green Mountain Boys, 178, 185

Green Party, 1080

Greensboro, N.C., 965
  sit-in at, 965

Greenspan, Alan (1926–), 1023, 1114–15

Greenville, Treaty of (1795), 265, *265,* 298

Greenwich Village, N.Y., 696, 697
  Stonewall Bar raid in, 997

Grenada, 1040, 1041

Grenville, George (1712–1770), 173, *177*

Grier, Robert C. (1794–1870), 486

Griffith, D. W. (1875–1948), 741

Griggs v. Duke Power Company, 1013

Grimké, Angelina (1805–1879), 441, 447–48, 450

Grimké, Sarah (1792–1873), 447–48

Griswold, Roger (1762–1812), *286*

Griswold v. Connecticut, 1002

Gromyko, Andrey (1909–1989), 1023

Gronlund, Laurence (1846–1899), 626, 627

Gropper, William, *799, 822*

gross national product (GNP), 841, 848, 852, 924, *925*

Grotius, Hugo (1583–1645), 27

Gruening, Ernest (1887–1974), 986

Guadalcanal, 849

Guadalupe Hidalgo, Treaty of (1848), 467, 468

Guadeloupe, 106, 158
  slave uprising in, 139

Guale Indians, 33

Guam, 664, 670
  in World War II, 848, 876

Guantánamo Bay, 1099, *1099,* 1101, 1108, 1109, 1110, 1118, *1118,* 1121

Guatemala, 944, *945,* 946, 991, 1026, 1042

Guerriere, 300

Guilford Courthouse, N.C., American victory at, 199

"Gulf Between, The" (Siegfried), 772

Gulf Coast, 31, 155
  Hurricane Katrina and, 1103–5, *1104*

Gulf of Mexico, *9,* 10, 38
  BP oil spill in, 1119, *1119*

Gulf of Tonkin resolution, 986

Gulf War, 1050–51, *1051,* 1052, 1087, 1092
  casualties in, 1050

Gullah Jack, 420

Gullah language, 138

Gulliver's Travels (Swift), *822*

guns, 130
  and gun control, 1077, *1077*
  murder rate and, 1083

Gutenberg, Johannes (1390–1468), 23

Guthrie, Tex., *558*

Guthrie, Woody (1912–1967), 799

Guyana, 994

Gypsies, Nazi extermination of, 850

Haacke, Hans (1936–), *1064*

Haas, Ernst (1921–1986), *927*

"habeas corpus," 80, 867, 1100

Habitat for Humanity, 1033

haciendas, 25

Haight-Ashbury, Calif., 992

Hair (musical), 994

Haiti, 21, 97, 288–89, 416, 420, 514, 720–21, 843, 959, 1033
  creation of, 289
  immigrants from, 1067

Haitian Revolution, 288–89, *444*

Hakluyt, Richard (1552?–1616), 52–53

Haldeman, H. R. (1926–1993), 1019

Hale, Edward Everett (1822–1909), 522

Half-Way Covenant (1662), 78–79

Hamdan v. Rumsfeld, 1109

Hamdi, Yasir, 1108

Hamdi v. Rumsfeld, 1108

Hamer, Fannie Lou (1917–1977), 973, *973,* 995

Hamilton, Alexander (1757?–1804), 247, *247,* 248, 254, 267, 270, 287
  centralized state sought by, 290–91
  French Revolution as viewed by, 276
  proposes standing army, 274
  religion and, 212
  selected as head of Treasury Department, 274
  social hierarchy as viewed by, 278
  Treasury program of, 274, *276, 278*
  war with France desired by, 285

Hamilton, Andrew (ca. 1676–1741), 148

Hamilton, Walton H. (1881–1998), 795

Hammond, James Henry (1807–1864), *372, 393,* 416

Hampton, Wade (1818–1902), 582

Hampton Institute, 656

Hampton University, 551

Hancock, John (1737–1793), 179, 191, 226, 256

Hancock, Winfield Scott (1824–1886), 617

Handsome Lake, 298

Hanna, Mark (1837–1904), 644, 691

Hanna, Tom, 631

Hänner, Johannes, 112

Hansford, Charles (1735?–1815), 136

Hardenbroeck, Margaret (d. ca. 1690), 42

Harding, Warren G. (1865–1923), 732, 753, 756, 770, *770, 771,* 772, 783
  death of, 760

Harding, William L. (1877–1934), 738

Harlan, John Marshall (1833–1911), 626, 650, 1036

Harlem, N.Y., 786–88, 829, *829,* 834
  race riots in, 865, 979

Harlem Renaissance, 787–88

Harmony community, 429

Harper, Frances Ellen Watkins (1825–1911), 572

Harpers Ferry, 489–92, *490*

Harper's Magazine, 427, 913

Harper's Monthly, 452

Harper's Weekly, 414, 432, 448, 519, *528, 538, 555, 572, 573, 580, 582, 583, 614*

Harrington, Michael (1928–1989), 977–78, 983, 1105

Harris, Townsend (1804–1878), 472

Harrison, Benjamin (1833–1901), 617, 661

Harrison, William Henry (1773–1841), 299, 300, *381,* 382

Harrison administration, 661

Hart, Gary (1936–), 1043, 1078

Hart-Celler Act (1965), 976, 1105

Harte, Bret (1839–1902), 545

Hartford, Conn., 72

Hartford Convention, 303

Harvard College, 69, *69,* 281, 332

Harvard Law School, 1116

Harvard University, 742, 759, 800, 992
  Marshall Plan announced at, 889
*Harvest Gypsies, The: On the Road to the
  Grapes of Wrath* (Steinbeck), 821
Hassam, Childe, *595*
Hat Act (1732), 172
Havana, Cuba, 33
Havana Harbor, 662
Havemeyer, Louisine (1855–1929), *704*
Havens, Richie (1941–), 992
Hawaii, *635*, 667, 670, 681, 783, 786,
  1116
  acquisition of, *661*, 664
Hawkins, Benjamin (1754–1818), *266*,
  298
Hawkins, Eric, *834*
Hawley, Joseph (1723–1788), 187
Hawley-Smoot Tariff (1930), 794
Hawthorne, Nathaniel (1804–1864),
  309, 429
Hay, Harry (1912–2002), 997
Hay, John (1838–1905), 662, 665
Hayashida, Fumiko (1911–), *867*
Hayden, Tom (1939–), 989, 1003
Hayek, Friedrich A. (1899–1992), 863
Hayes, Max (1866–1945), 691
Hayes, Rutherford B. (1822–1893),
  582–83, 609, 617, 625
Haymarket affair, 629–31
Hayne, Robert Y. (1791–1839), 372,
  372, 420
Haynes, Lemuel (1753–1833), 226, *229*
Haynsworth, Clement (1912–1989),
  1011
Hays code, 775
Haywood, William "Big Bill" (1869–
  1928), 691, 694
Head Start, 978
health care, national, 861, 862, 898,
  901, 904, 914, 1053
Health Maintenance Organizations
  (HMOs), 1053
Hearst, William Randolph (1863–1951),
  661, *664*
Heaten, John, *121*
Helsinki Accords, 1023
Hemings, Sally (1773–1835), 269
Hemingway, Ernest (1899–1961), 775,
  776
Henderson, Alex, *923*
Henry, Fort, 511
Henry, Patrick (1736–1799), 175, 183,
  252, 256–57, 290, 1077
  as slaveholder, 227
  western land speculation of, 221
Henry VII, king of England (1457–
  1509), 50
Henry VIII, king of England (1491–
  1547), 50, 53
Henson, Josiah (1789–1883), 410, 441
Hepburn Act (1906), 707
Herald Of Freedom, *455*
Herberg, Will (1901–1977), 912, 935
Hercules, *175*
Heritage Foundation, 1028
Herndon, Angelo (1913–1997), 836
Heroes of America, 534
Hersey, John (1914–1993), 878
Hessians, 193, 195

Heterodoxy, 696
Hewitt, Abram (1822–1903), 621, 631
Hidden Persuaders, The (Packard), 947
Higginson, Martha, 446
Higginson, Thomas Wentworth
  (1823–1911), 517
Highlander School, 955
Highland Park, Mich., Ford plant at,
  685–86, *686*
Highland Scots, 219
highways, 927, 936
  building of, 906, *930*, 940
Hill, Anita (1956–), 1078
Hill, Israel, 407
Hillman, Sidney (1887–1946), 747
Hilton, David, *601*
Hinduism:
  counterculture and, 993
  Tulsi Gabbard and, 1125
Hindus, 1065
  as immigrants, 1066
Hine, Lewis (1874–1940), *646*, 680,
  680, *762*, 764
Hirohito, emperor of Japan (1901–
  1989), 878
Hirono, Mazie K. (1947–), 1125
Hiroshima:
  atomic bombing of, 877, 942
  population of, *877*
Hiroshima (Hersey), 878
Hispanics, *see* Latinos
Hispaniola, 21, 24, 32, 36
Hiss, Alger (1904–1996), 908, 909, 939
History of Southern Illinois, *833*
History of the American Revolution, The
  (Ramsay), 260
History of the Indies (Las Casas), 36
History of the Standard Oil Company
  (Tarbell), 680
Hitler, Adolf (1889–1945), 753, 757, 802,
  844–46, *844*, *845*, 876, 877, 885,
  886, 902, 905
  "final solution" of, 850, 865
  and nonaggression pact, 845, 846
Hitler Youth, *844*
HMOs, *see* Health Maintenance
  Organizations
hoarding, to fix prices, 217
Ho Chi Minh (1890–1969), 751, 752,
  944, 945
Hodges, Willis A. (1815–1890), 408
Hoffman, Abbie (1936–1989), 992, 1003
Hoffman, Julius (1896–1983), 1003
Hogarth, William (1697–1764), *53*,
  142, *180*
Holland, *see* Netherlands
Hollywood, 764, 775
  blacklisting in, 908
  communism and, 897, *897*, *907*,
  908, *1040*
  image of America and, 764
  racism and, 897
  rise of, 762
  sexually charged films from, 768
  strikes in, 901
  World War II and, 859, 864
  see also motion pictures
Hollywood Ten, 908
Holmes, John Hayes (1879–1964), 776

Holmes, Oliver Wendell (1841–1935),
  739, 776
Holmes doctrine, 776
Holocaust, 850, 864
Holy Experiment, Pennsylvania
  colony's, 161
Holy Trinity, 83
Home, Sweet Home (song), 808
Homeland Security Department, U.S.,
  1088, 1104
homelessness, 1038, *1038*
  Great Depression and, 791, *794*, 821
home ownership, *1070*, 1071, 1112, 1113
  middle class and, 808, 823
  post-World War II, 862, 901
Home Owners' Loan Corporation,
  808, 809, *830*
Home Protection movement, 658
Homer, Winslow (1836–1910), *545*,
  554, *555*
Homestead, Pa., Carnegie's factories
  in, 595, *637*, 656, 747, 813
Homestead Act (1862), 245, 524, 565,
  602, 603, 679
Home to Harlem (McKay), 787
homosexuals, homosexuality, 697, 837,
  907–8, 910, 911, 919, 948, 965,
  1014, 1035, 1039, 1074, 1075,
  1076, 1103, 1108
  and AIDS, 1073
  Nazi extermination of, 850
  see also gay rights
Honduras, 718, 719
  drug trade in, 1122
Hone, Philip (1780–1851), 347
Honeymooners, The (TV show), 929
"Honor America," *1012*
Hooker, "Fighting Joe" (1814–1879), 536
Hooker, Thomas (1586–1647), 72
Hoover, Herbert (1874–1964), 747, 764,
  788–89, *789*, 801, *802*, 808, 842,
  1102
  background of, 788
  Depression and, 792–94, *792*
  Eisenhower and, 940
  in election of 1928, 788–89
  as Food Administration director,
  727
  New Deal and, 822
  as Secretary of Commerce, 770
Hoover, J. Edgar (1895–1972), 748,
  910, 971
Hooverville, 791, *794*
Hope, James, *511*
Hopis, 10
Hopkins, Harry (1890–1946), 802,
  815, 816
Horne, Lena (1917–2010), 952
horses, 8, 10, 608
Horseshoe Bend, Battle of, 300
Horton, Willie, 1043–44
Hose, Sam (d. 1899), 651
hospitals, 1038
House Beautiful, 928
House of Burgesses, Va., 59, 99, 101,
  118, 145, 175, 213
House of Commons, British, 18, 80, 83,
  140, 142, 146, *174*, 175, 615
  see also Parliament, British

House of Lords, British, 80–81, 140,
  615
  see also Parliament, British
House of Mirth, The (Wharton), 599
House of Representatives, U.S., 249,
  287, 347, 391, *564*, 566, 580, 616,
  642, 951, 1053, *1054*, 1097, 1106,
  1110
  abolition and, 444
  African-Americans in, 573
  Clinton's impeachment and, 1079
  creation of, 249
  in election of 1824, 364
  Johnson's impeachment and, 567–68
  Judiciary Committee of, 1019
  Un-American Activities Committee
  (HUAC) of, 836, *907*, 908, 910,
  939, 1000
  World War I and, 724
Housing Act (1949), 933
Housing and Urban Development
  Department, U.S., 977
housing bubble, 1111–12, *1111*, 1114, 1120
Houston, Charles H. (1895–1950), 834
Houston, Sam (1793–1863), 462
Houston, Tex., 927
  population of, 854
Houston, Ulysses S. (b. 1825), 549
Howard, Merrimon (b. 1821), 552
Howard, O. O. (1830–1909), 555, 556,
  560, 608
Howard University, 551, *981*
Howe, Julia Ward (1819–1910), 520
Howe, Samuel Gridley (1801–1876),
  454
Howe, Timothy (1816–1883), 572
Howe, William (1729–1814), 185,
  194–95, *195*
Howells, William Dean (1837–1920),
  671
Howl (Ginsberg), 949
How the Other Half Lives (Riis), 600, 1105
HUAC, *see* House of Representatives,
  U.S., Un-American Activities
  Committee of
Hubenthal, Karl (1917–1998), *1000*
Hudson, Henry (d. 1611), 41, 49
Hudson-Bank Gymnasium, *700*
Hudson River, 115, 307, 309
Hudson River school, *331*, 680
Hudson Valley, 43, 45, 123, 135, 257
huelga, 997
Huerta, Victoriano (1854–1916), 721
Huexotzinco, *27*
Huexotzinco Codex, 27
Hughes, Charles Evans (1862–1948),
  723, 770, 823–24
Hughes, John (1797–1864), 326, 432
Hughes, Langston (1902–1967), 787,
  885, 1127
Huguenots, *15*, 33, 38, 41
  see also Christianity
Hull House, 701–2, *701*, 703, 735, 802
Human Be-In, *991*, 992
human rights, 1041, 1055, 1056, 1095
  ambiguities of, 899–900
  rise of, 898–900, 904
Human Rights Commission, U.N., *899*
Hume, David (1711–1776), 179

Humphrey, Hubert (1911–1978), 904, 959, 960, 974, 1003, 1005
Hundred Days, 804, 805, 806
Hungary, 746, 749, 943
Hunt, Thomas, 67
Hunter, Robert (1666–1734), 145
hunting, 57–58, 114, 154
Huntington, Samuel P. (1927–2008), 1106–7
Hurons, 40, 160
Hurwitz, Ben, 840
Hutchinson, Anne (1591–1643), 72–73, 78, 82
Hutchinson, Thomas (1711–1780), 171, 173, 176
Hyannisport, Mass., 960
Hyde Park, 800
hydrogen bomb, 941
    see also atomic bomb; nuclear weapons

Iberian Peninsula, 18, 21
IBM, 1057
Ibo people, 136
ICBMs, see intercontinental ballistic missiles
Ice Age, 6
"I Choose Exile" (Wright), 1016
Ickes, Harold (1874–1952), 802, 806, 829
Idaho, 609, 703, 1019
    corporate mining in, 605
    entrance into union of, 610
    mining strike in, 690
    socialism in, 690
    woman suffrage in, 640, 703
Ideas Have Consequences (Weaver), 937
identity politics, 1075
"If We Must Die" (McKay), 787
"I Have a Dream" (King), 956
Illegal Act, The, 810
Illinois, 312, 930, 1029, 1033
    Black Hawk War in, 374
    black rights in, 353
    blacks barred from, 339
    Lincoln-Douglas campaign in, 486–89
    38th Infantry of, 506
    woman suffrage in, 704
Illinois, University of, 933
Illinois Central Railroad, 479, 487
Illinois Federal Art Project, 833
Illinois Supreme Court, 623
Illustrated London News, 530
I Married a Communist (movie), 897
"Immediate Emancipation Illustrated," 444
immigrants, immigration, 2, 3, 5, 106–7, 107, 324–26, 324, 325, 326, 482, 589, 590, 601, 604, 636, 661, 671, 679, 679, 681, 682, 701, 702, 734, 735–38, 757, 808, 821, 831, 834, 864–65, 931, 1061, 1065–69, 1065, 1067, 1068, 1069, 1074, 1075, 1075, 1076, 1088, 1105–6
    Abraham Lincoln and, 494
    AFL and, 657
    from Africa, 1070
    African-Americans vs., 483

Americanization and, 734, 735, 738, 738, 780, 831, 864–65
Asian, 680–81, 682, 740, 782, 783, 865, 921, 976–77, 1067, 1068–69, 1070
from China, 604, 654–56, 654
to cities, 680–82
Cold War and, 906
Congress and, 911
from England, 49–50, 53–55, 61–62, 66–67, 107
from France, 38
freedom and, 682–83, 685
from Germany, 156, 324–26, 432, 689
global, 680–82
"golden door" and, 781–83
growth of, 324, 586
G. W. Bush and, 1088, 1110
illegal, 1105–6
from India, 1067, 1069
IQ tests and, 739
from Ireland, 324–26, 432
from Japan, 604
Know-Nothings and, 483
Ku Klux Klan, 781
from Latin America, 921, 977, 1066, 1067–68, 1067, 1070
from Mexico, 601, 695, 783, 828, 828, 865–66, 977, 1067–68, 1068, 1105, 1123
from Middle East, 1099
to New York, 679, 700
numbers of, 324, 324
population of, 324
prejudice and, 587, 759
progressivism and, 701, 702
quotas, 976–77
reform of 1965, 976–77
religion and, 777
Republicans as anti-immigration, 1075, 1123
restrictions on, 653, 654–56, 739, 739, 781–86, 782, 783, 811, 831, 865, 866, 921
rights, 1106, 1106
from Russia, 722
from Scandinavia, 326
of Scotch-Irish, 109, 156
to South Carolina, 134
from Spain, 26–27
from Sweden, 325
Tea Party and, 1122
Texas and, 1106
volume of, 680–82, 683
wages and, 683
and West, 601, 602
from Western Hemisphere, 783
women and, 684–85, 1067, 1067
World War I and, 586, 648, 743
World War II and, 842
    see also specific nationalities
Immigration Act (1924), 783
Immigration Commission, U.S., 734
Immigration Restriction League, 654, 759
impeachment:
    of Andrew Johnson, 567–68
    of Clinton, 1078–79

imperialism, 694, 873, 889
    Christianity and, 659
    decolonization and, 896, 943–44
    international, 659
    moral, 719–20
    as "New Imperialism," 659
    U.S., 659–73, 673, 861
impressment, 141, 277, 296–97, 300
Inauguration of Mr. Lincoln, 498
Incas, 8, 24, 32
Inchon, South Korea, 893, 894
income:
    gains in, 1121
    inequality in, 1120
income taxes, see taxes, income
indentured servitude, 6, 38, 55, 55, 61–62, 63, 64, 96–97, 229, 339
    American Revolution and, 167, 193, 205, 216, 234
    in Carolina, 92
    decline of, 216
    in New England, 77–78, 135
    in Pennsylvania, 135
    slavery compared with, 94
    in Virginia, 97, 98–99, 100, 132, 133
Independence Day Celebration in Centre Square (Krimmel), 350
Independence Hall, 249
Independent Monitor, 578
Independent Treasury, 381
India, 18, 20, 20, 24, 158, 174, 181, 604, 636, 746, 751, 876, 879, 881, 896, 943, 959, 993, 1065, 1126
    immigrants from, 681, 1067, 1069
    jobs exported to, 1102
    loss of U.S. jobs to, 1102
    and oil, 1105
Indiana, 9, 312, 974, 983, 1117
    anticommunist law in, 910
    blacks barred from, 339
    in election of 1858, 489
    Ku Klux Klan, 781
Indian Affairs Committee, 612
"Indian country," 114
"Indian New Deal," 827
Indian radicalism, 698
Indian removal, 374–77, 375, 601
    Missouri and, 374
    slavery as motive for, 374
    see also Native Americans
Indian Removal Act (1830), 374
Indian Reorganization Act (1934), 827
"Indians of All Tribes," 998, 998
indigo, 128, 134
individualism, 330–31, 627, 687, 934, 937, 1089
    education and, 434
    freedom and, 330–31, 336
    market revolution and, 328–37
    reform and, 432
    Second Great Awakening and, 335
    in Utopian societies, 430
Indonesia, 20, 848, 896, 943, 1116
industrial production, 824
industrial revolution, 315, 319–23, 321, 390, 479, 503, 590
    "second," 586, 589–600

Industrial Workers of the World (IWW), 691–94, 691, 695, 697, 727, 733, 747, 748, 775, 811, 812
industry, 459, 528, 528, 863, 865, 866
    African-Americans in, 835, 870
    in California, 764
    child labor and, 680
    in Civil War, 524, 528
    decline in, 1022
    Depression and, 826
    factory system and, 319–23
    Fordism and, 685–86
    freedom and, 688–89
    immigration and, 682, 783
    law and, 327–28
    New Deal and, 837
    in New York, 677
    Populists and, 641
    post-World War I, 747
    post-World War II, 924, 929
    in Progressive era, 677, 678, 680, 699
    rise of, 586, 715
    scientific management in, 688
    in South, 645, 826, 854, 941
    women in, 859, 860
    workers' life and, 323–24, 324
    World War II and, 757, 852, 852, 853–54, 858–60
    see also manufacturing; market revolution; specific industries
Infant Liberty Nursed by Mother Mob, 277
infant mortality, 1082
inflation, 217–18, 889, 902, 1012, 1020, 1021, 1021, 1022, 1023, 1024, 1027, 1032, 1036, 1037, 1038
Influence of Sea Power Upon History, The (McMahon), 661
influenza, 24, 721, 746
information revolution, 350–51
Ingersoll, Robert G. (1833–1899), 617, 618
innovations, technological, 592–93
In re Debs, 642
In Side of the Old Lutheran Church in 1800, York, Pa., 213
Insular Cases, 670
insurance:
    national health, 818, 837, 861, 898, 901, 904, 914, 977, 1053, 1102, 1119
    unemployment, 817, 826, 830, 940, 1115
    unions and, 914, 941, 1064
integration, labor and, 625, 646
    see also race, racism, integration and
intercontinental ballistic missiles (ICBMs), 960
Interior Department, U.S., 799, 806
Interior of New York City's First Infant School, 434
International Church of the Foresquare Gospel, 815
International Convention Against Torture, 1100
International Harvester, 594
internationalism, black, 873, 875–76
International Labor Defense, 834–35

International Ladies' Garment
    Workers Union, 677
International League for Human
    Rights, 1025
International Longshoremen's
    Association, 811
International Monetary Fund, 879,
    1048
Internet, 815, 1047, 1057–58, *1058*, 1101,
    1116, 1124
    Middle East and, 1095
Interrupting the Ceremony, 753
Interstate Commerce Act (1887), 624
Interstate Commerce Commission
    (ICC), 618, 707, 966
Interstate Highway System, *930*
intervention, era of U.S., 716–21
Intolerable Acts (1774), 181–82, 185
Iowa, 738, 788, 1103
    blacks barred from, 339
IQ tests, 739, 769
Iran, 887, 944, *944*, 946, 991, 1015,
    1021, 1024, 1026, 1042, 1072,
    1091, 1126
    American hostages in, 1026–27,
    1027
    television and American hostages
    in, *1027*
Iran-Contra affair, 1042, 1043
Iraq, 752, 1042, 1091, 1092–93, 1126
    economic sanctions on, 1050
    in Gulf War, 1050
    militias in, 1096
Iraq War, 506, 728, 921, 1088, 1092–97,
    1092, *1096*, 1102, 1103, 1110, 1116,
    1117
    casualties in, *1097*, 1110, 1121
    financial cost of, 1097
    Obama and end of, 1121
    protests against, *1093*
Ireland, 3, 50–51, 52, 61, 94, 109, 604,
    751, 752, 753, *1004*
    conquered by England, 50–51
    emigration to North America from,
    55
    English control over, 83
    English immigration to, 54
Ireton, Henry (1611–1651), 144
Irish, Irish immigrants, 324–26, 432,
    432, 617, 631, 654, 685, 722, 784,
    864, 1075
    integration and, 1012
    World War II and, 845
Irish-Americans, 3, 324–26, 370, 482,
    483
Irish Free State, 752
Iron Act (1750), 172
ironclads, 504
"iron curtain," 887
iron industry, 604, 645–46
Ironworkers' Noontime, The (Anshutz),
    621
Iroquois, 12, 15, *15*, 40, 87, 156, *157*,
    222–23, 298
    relations with New York colony, 87
    in World War II, 866
Iroquois Confederacy, 45, 90–91, 222
Isabella, queen of Spain (1451–1504),
    21

Islam, *20*, 150
    in American colonies, 136–37
    in America today, 1106–7, *1107*
    in Balkans, 1056
    and fundamentalism, 1065, 1090,
    1092
    Gulf War and, 1050
    Iran and, 1026–27
    Middle East, 1042
    Nation of, 981
    Obama's speech to repair relations
    with, *1118*
    radicals and, 946
    Saudi Arabia and, 981, 1087
Islamic Cultural Center debate, 1107,
    1107
isolationism, 757, 772, 844–45, 886,
    938
Israel, 753, 944, 1020, 1026, *1026*, 1041,
    1055, 1065, 1087, 1092, *1099*, 1126
issei, 867
Is This a Republican Form of Government?
    (Nast), *583*
Italians, Italian-Americans, 680, 681,
    683, 734, 759, 831
    in East Harlem, 933, *934*
    in Hollywood, 833
    World War II and, 845, *864*, 865,
    867
Italy, 604, 772, *840*, 845, 867, 897,
    1004, 1082
    as Axis power, 845
    communist party in, 889
    liberation of, 850
    rise of Mussolini in, 844
    Venezuela and, 718
It Can't Happen Here (Lewis), 816
"It's Fun to be Free," *846*, 847
Ives, James (1824–1895), *499*, *565*, *579*
Ivory soap, 592
IWW, *see* Industrial Workers of the
    World

Jackson, Andrew (1767–1845), 210, 307,
    365, *366*, *372*, 444, 463, 475
    American Colonization Society
    and, 435
    annexation of Texas and, 462
    in battle with Bank of the United
    States, 377–79, *378*
    defies Supreme Court, 375
    dubbed "King Andrew," 347, *349*
    in election of 1824, 361–64
    in election of 1828, 366, *366*
    inauguration of, 347
    Indians and, 347, 367, 374–76
    Indian wars of, 314
    Kitchen Cabinet of, 369
    nickname of, 367
    in nullification crisis, 374
    "pet banks" and, 379
    rise of democracy and, 347, 351
    as slaveholder (1767–1845), 300
    state banks and, 379
    veto power and, 379, 565
    views of blacks of, 367
    in War of 1812, 300–302
Jackson, Blyden (1910–2000), 652
Jackson, Rachel (1767–1828), 366

Jackson, Robert H. (1892–1954), 868
Jackson, Thomas "Stonewall" (1824–
    1863), 505, 536, 653
Jackson State University, 1016
Jacksonville, Fla., 33
Jacobin clubs, 280
Jacobs, Jane, 983
Jacobson, David, *1059*
Jamaica, 26, 36, 119, 138, 139, 416, 786
    free blacks in, 407
    seizure by England of, 83
    slave uprisings in, 139
James, duke of York (1633–1701), *see*
    James II, king of England
James, Thomas, 176
James I, king of England (1566–1625),
    49–50, 60, 61, 80
James II, king of England (1633–1701),
    90, 91, 93, 102, 103, 104
James River, 49
Jamestown, Va., 49, 58–61, *58*, 100
    death rate at, 58–59
    difficult beginnings of, 58–59
    founding of, 49–50
    Indian conflicts in, 60–61
    Indian relations with, 60–61
    Indian uprising of 1622, 60–61, *61*
    typhoid fever in, 58
Japan, 471–72, 664, *719*, 740, 746, 750,
    752, 772, 783, 802, 844, 848–49,
    849, 853, 877–78, 880, 891, 895,
    1020–21, 1083, 1115
    automobiles from, 1105
    as Axis power, 845
    economic reconstruction of, 890
    expulsion from Vietnam of, 945
    immigrants from, 604, 681
    invasion of Manchuria by, 844
    post-World War II, 924
    progressivism in, 698
    trade with, 845, 846
    U.S. declaration of war against, 848
    U.S. oil and, 845, 846
    in World War I, 721
    in World War II, 757, 845–49,
    848, 857, *857*, 866–67, 871, 876,
    877–78, *877*
    World War II surrender of, 877
Japanese immigrants, Japanese-
    Americans, 866–69, 1069, 1099
    in Hawaii, 661
    World War II internment of, 258,
    757, 842, 867–69, *867*, *868*, 953,
    1100, 1109
Jarvis, John Wesley (1780–1840), *374*
Jay, John (1745–1829), 200, 229, 252,
    254, 267, 274, 277
Jay, William (1792–1837), 445
Jay's Treaty (1795), 277
jazz, 787, 897
Jazz Age, 760
Jefferson, Thomas (1743–1826), 118, 145,
    222, 246, 247, 279, 317, *361*, 364,
    365, 449, 638, 736, 1077
    on African-Americans, 268–69
    agriculture and, *276*
    on Alien and Sedition Acts, 286
    Bible version by, 212
    campaign portrait of, *288*

Declaration of Independence and,
    187–90, *190*, 191–92, 206, 213–14,
    221, 225, 235, 258
    in election of 1796, 284
    in election of 1800, 287–88
    in election of 1804, 297
    and elimination of Federalist Party,
    303
    embargo of, *296*
    "empire of liberty" and, 239, 245
    foreign policy of, 295
    freedom and, 217
    French Revolution and, 276
    Haiti and, 289
    inauguration of, 290
    Indian policies of, 297–98
    Louisiana Purchase and, 292–94
    on Missouri Compromise, 358
    national bank opposed by, 275
    on Native Americans, 222, 266
    Ordinance of 1784 and, 243
    public schools and, 215
    religion and, 150, 212
    selected secretary of state, 273–74
    on Shays's rebellion, 246
    as slaveholder, 227, 251, *269*
    slavery and, 225, *269*
    strong local self-government sought
    by, 290
    trade as viewed by, 296
    western land speculation of, 221
    writings of, 184, 212
Jeffersonian, 732
Jehovah's Witnesses, 856
Jemison, Edwin Francis (d. 1862), *506*
Jennings, Samuel (1755?–1834?), *205*, 232
jeremiads, 79
Jerry (slave), 477
Jesuits, *15*, 40, *91*
Jesus, *27*, 34, *35*, 37, 83, 93, 215, 414, 421,
    427, 643, *652*, 653, 764, 811
    Jefferson's life of, 212
    Mormons and, 336–37
Jesus People, 993
Jews, 41, 116, 140, 649, 689, 690, 735,
    738, 752, 777, 781, 784, 815, 823,
    864–65, 881, 908, 934–35, *935*,
    1065, 1079
    in American colonies, 110, 144, 211
    Book of Exodus and, 647
    in colonial Maryland, 83
    in colonial Pennsylvania, 93, 110
    in colonial Rhode Island, 71
    in FDR administration, 831
    in flight from Russia, 683, *684*
    Hasidic, 150
    in Hollywood, 833, 864
    Holocaust and, 850, *850*, 864
    Ku Klux Klan and, 781
    lynching of, 781
    in Nazi Germany, 802, 844
    in New Amsterdam, 43
    prejudice against, 785
    in Spain, 21, 26, 28
    on television, 929
    U.S. population of, 503
    voting rights and, 213
    World War I and, 722
    see also anti-Semitism

Jim Crow, 885, 919, 952, 954, 956, 969, 1001, 1038
Jobs, Steve (1955–2011), *1058*
John, king of England (1166–1216), 79
"John Brown's Body" song, *519*
John Quincy Adams, 354
Johnson, Andrew (1808–1875), 386, 394, 560, 1079
  background of, 562
  emancipation and, 563
  impeachment of, 567–68
  Reconstruction policies of, 556, 560, 562–66, *565*, 570
Johnson, Anthony (d. 1670), 98
Johnson, Hiram (1866–1945), 700
Johnson, Hugh S. (1871–1938), 804
Johnson, Lady Bird (1912–2007), *972*
Johnson, Lyndon (1908–1973), 920, 957, 972–79, *972*, 977, 1003, 1010, 1012, 1016, 1036
  in campaign of 1960, 959
  civil rights and, 972–74, 977–78, 979
  Dominican Republic and, 986, 991
  in election of 1964, 974, 975
  Great Society and, 977–79
  Native Americans and, 998
  Vietnam and, 984, 986–90
Johnson, Richard M., 300
Johnson, Samuel (1709–1784), 160, 224
Johnson, William (1715–1774), 407
Johnston, Joseph E. (1807–1891), 509
"Join, or Die," *164*
Joint Chiefs of Staff, 1051, *1051*
joint stock company, 41
Joliet, Louis (1645–1700), 38
Jones, Charles C., 396, 414
Jones, Jim (1931–197), People's Temple and, 993–94
Jones, Mary "Mother" (1830–1930), 695
Jones, Paula (1966–), 1079
Jones, Samuel "Golden Rule" (1846–1904), 699
Jones v. Alfred H. Mayer Co., 1001
Joplin, Janice (1943–1970), *1005*
Joseph, Chief (1840–1904), 609
Josephe, 37
Journal of Commerce, 370
Joyce, James (1882–1941), 775, 777
J.P. Morgan Chase, 1060
Jubilee of Liberty, 307
Judeo-Christian heritage, 935, *935*
Judge, 643, 653, 672, 719
judicial review, 291–92
Judiciary Act of 1789, 291
Julius Caesar (Shakespeare), 205
Jungle, The (Sinclair), 680
Junto (club), 147
juries, African-Americans and, 835
Justice Department, U.S., 733, 885, 1036, 1099, 1100
  Civil Liberties Unit, 836
  civil rights and, 1040
  Radical Division of, 748
Just Say No campaign, 1039, *1039*
juvenile delinquency, 947

Kaiser Aluminum & Chemical Corporation, 1013

Kallen, Horace (1882–1974), 784, 795, 834
Kansas, 478, 487, 493, 602, *1014*
  black migration to, *646*, 647–48, *647*
  in Dust Bowl, 807, *808*
  population of, 679
  Populist Party in, *637*
  violence in, 484–85
  woman suffrage in, 640
Kansas City, Mo., 631
Kansas-Nebraska Act (1854), 478–79, *478*, 481, 485, 486, 487
Kansas Pacific Railroad, 604, *609*
Katrina, Hurricane, 1103–5, *1104*, 1110
  and African-Americans, 1104–5, *1104*
  death toll from, 1104
Kaufman, Irving (1910–1992), 908
Kaufmann, Theodore (1910–1986), *574*
Kearney, Stephen W. (1794–1848), 466
Keating-Owen Act (1916), 711
Keep Within Compass, 233
Kefauver, Estes (1903–1963), 957
Kelley, Abby (1810–1887), 425, 426, *440*, 449, 454, 571, 995
Kelley, Florence (1859–1932), 702–3, 726, 770
Kelley, William D. (1814–1890), 703
Kemmelmayer, Frederick (ca. 1760–ca. 1821), *278*
Kendall, Amos (1789–1869), 444
Kennan, George (1904–2005), 887, 895
Kennedy, Anthony (1936–), 1108, 1110
Kennedy, Jacqueline (1929–1994), 960, *960, 972*
Kennedy, John F. (1917–1963), 960, 969–72, 977, *986*, 1001, *1005*, 1102
  assassination of, 972, *972*, 986
  in campaign of 1960, 959–60, *959*, 1009
  civil rights and, 971–72
  Cuban Missile Crisis and, 970–71
  in debates with Nixon, 960, 1081
  desegregation and, 966, 967
  inaugural address of, 969
  Native Americans and, 998
  space race and, 960
  Vietnam and, 985–86
Kennedy, Robert F. (1925–1968), 971, *1005*
  assassination of, 1003
Kennedy administration, *968*, 969–72
Kent State University, 1016, *1016*
Kentucky, 242
  creation of, 284
  in Panic of 1819, 356
  resolution in legislature of, 286–87, 372
  voting rights in, 352
Kenya, 943
  terrorist attack in, 1087
Kenyatta, Jomo (1894–1978), 876
Kerner, Otto (1908–1976), 979
Kerner Report, 979
Kerouac, Jack (1922–1969), 948, 949
Kerr, Clark (1911–2003), 928
Kerry, John (1943–), 1102–3
Key, David M. (1824–1900), 582
Key, Francis Scott (1779–1843), 300

Keynes, John Maynard (1883–1946), 788, 802, 824, 861
Keynesian economics, 824, 861–62, 1027
Key of Liberty, The (Manning), 280
Khmer Rouge, 1016
Khomeini, Ayatollah (1900–1989), 946, 1026–27
Khrushchev, Nikita (1894–1971), 923–24, *925*, 942, 970
Kieft, William (1597–1647), 45
Kindred Spirits (Durand), *331*
King, Charles Bird (1785–1862), *299, 355*
King, Martin Luther, Jr. (1929–1968), 466, 640, 949, 950, 956, *979*, 980, 990, 997, 1024, 1118, 1124
  assassination of, 1003, *1003, 1005*
  Birmingham campaign and, 967
  FBI wiretaps on, 971
  Malcolm X and, 980
  March on Washington and, 968
  Montgomery boycott and, 955, 956
  Poor People's March and, *1003*
  Selma campaign of, 976
King, Rodney (1965–), 1073
King, Rufus (1755–1827), 278, 356
"King Andrew," 347, *349*
King George's War, 157
King Philip's War, 87, 101
Kiowas, 608
Kipling, Rudyard (1865–1936), 670, *671*
Kirk, Russell (1918–1994), 937
Kirkpatrick, Jeane (1926–2006), 1041
Kissinger, Henry (1923–), 1014, 1015, 1023
Kitchen Ball at White Sulphur Springs, Virginia (Mayr), *412*
Kitchen Cabinet, 368
kitchen debate, 923, *925*, 937
kivas, 35
Kiyoshi, Kobayakawa, *767*
Kleindeutschland, 325
Knights of Labor, 625–26, *625*, 629, 631, 637, 645, 656, 687, 871
Know-Nothing (American) Party, 481–82, 485, 494, 631
Knox, Fort, 355
Knox, Henry (1750–1806), 185, 232, 266
Knox, Lucy (1754–1824), 232
Koehler, Karl, *870*
Koehler, Robert (1850–1917), *591*
Koehn, Daryl (1955–), *1014*
Kongo, 139
Korea, 751, 891–95
  immigrants from, 866, 1069, *1069*
  see also North Korea; South Korea
Korean War, 891–95, *894, 895*, 904, 909, 939, 945, 1101
  armistice in, 941, 942
  casualties in, 893
Korematsu, Fred (1919–2005), 868, 869
Korematsu v. United States, 868
Kosciuszko, Tadeusz (1746–1817), 269
Kosovo, 1056
Krans, Olof, *325*
Kremlin, 891
Krimmel, John Lewis (1786–1821), *350*

Kroc, Ray (1902–1984), 930
Kroeber, Alfred (1876–1960), 784
Kühn, Justus Engelhardt (d. 1717), *133*
Ku Klux Klan, 578, *578, 579*, 582, 631, 650, 741, *781*, 785, 789, 966, 973
  reemergence of, 780–81
Kursk, Russia, 850
Kuwait, 1050
Kyoto Protocol (1997), 1088, 1089
Kyrgyzstan, *1050*, 1091

La Bahia, N.Mex., 153
labor, 624–31, *631*, 810–14, *816*, 885, 941
  African-Americans and, 339, 835, 952, 968, *1090*
  agricultural, 325, 828, 941, 978
  capitalism vs., 624–32
  capital vs., 620
  civil liberties and, 695, 835–36
  contracts, 622–23, 625, 941, 952
  costs, 319
  "cross of gold" speech and, 642
  decline of, 765–66
  demand for, 324
  dignity of, *621*
  Fordism and, 685–86
  free blacks as unskilled, 407
  gang, 408–10
  in Gilded Age, 624–31, *626*
  globalization and, 1067
  government and, 641
  New Deal and, 804, 860, 861
  Philadelphia Mechanic's Advocate newspaper for, 351
  and politics, 813–14
  Populist Party and, 638
  prisoners as, 645, *645*
  and Prohibition, 730
  racially integrated, 625, *646*
  radicals, 831, 833, 835–36
  railroads and, 641–42
  Reagan and, 1037
  reform, 710
  Republican Party (modern) and free, 483
  rise of free, 215–16
  segregation and, 647
  unemployment and, 380, 709, 710, 762–63, 790–91, *792*, 793, *795*, 802, 805, 814, 815, 817, 818, 824, *824*, 825, 826, 829, *829*, 830, 836, 924, 980, 1021, 1070, *1070*, 1101–2, 1112
  as wage earners, 216, 323
  in West, 329
  women and, 339–41, 452–53, 625, 700, 704–5, 740, 841, 1076, *1077*, 1112
  and work hours, 323, *323*, 342, 343, 598, 620, 622, 683, 699, 704–5, 728, 740, 811, 824, 863
  working conditions and, 689, 702, 703, 704–5, 727, 740, 766
  and working hours, 608
  workmen's compensation and, 705
  and World War II, 852, *852*, 855, 901
  see also child labor; unions
Labor Department, U.S., 811, 825, 826, 831, 1012

"Laboring Classes, The" (Brownson), 343

labor movement, 343, 434, 439, 474, 531, 689, *704*, 800
  decline of, 1037
  early nineteenth century, 341–42, *342*
  in Panic of 1837, 380
  World War I and, 722
  see also unions

Laboulaye, Édouard de (1811–1883), 589

Labour Party (Great Britain), 878

Ladies' Association, 232

Lady's Magazine and Repository of Entertaining Knowledge, 280

Lafayette, Marquis de (1757–1834), 199, 307–8

La Follette, Robert M. (1855–1925), 700, 701, 771, 835

Lagonda Agricultural Works, 481

La Guardia, Fiorello (1882–1947), 831

La Isabella, 21

laissez-faire economics, 629, 631, 708, 819, 863

Lakin, A. S. (1810–1890), *578*

Lakotas, *613*

Lancaster, Pa., massacre of Indians at, 161

Land Commission, 576

Land Grant College Act (1862), 524

land grants, 2, 146, 177

Land of the Free (MacLeish), 819

Landon, Alfred (1887–1987), 823

Lange, Dorothea (1895–1965), 833, *833*

L'Anse aux Meadows, 21

Lansing, Robert (1864–1928), 750–51

Laos, 848, 1019

Larcom, Lucy (1824–1893), 323–24

Lardner, Ring, Jr. (1915–2000), 908

La Salle, René-Robert Cavelier, Sieur de (1643–1687), 38

Las Casas, Bartolomé de (1474–1566), 29–31, 36, 52, 59–60

"Las Siete Partidas," 97

Las Vegas, Nev.:
  nuclear tests in, *906*
  segregation in, 952

Lathrop, Julia (1858–1932), 702

Latin America, 772, 842–44, 874, 887, 986, 1025, 1049, 1057, 1096
  JFK and, 970
  Liberation theology and, 993

Latinos, 919, 925, 934, 1012–13, 1038, 1066, 1070, 1073, 1080, 1117, 1118
  activism among, 997–98, *997*
  affirmative action and, 1013
  and feminism, 998
  G. W. Bush and, 1106
  immigrant rights movement and, 1106
  as immigrants, 921, 977, 1066, 1067–68, *1067*, 1069
  nativism and, 1123
  population growth, 1105
  in suburbs, 1064
  in 2012 election and campaign, 1125

Latino Studies, 1074

Latrobe, Benjamin (1764–1820), *127*, *276*

Latvia, 749, 879

Laurens, Henry (1724–1792), 228, 885

Laurens, John (1754–1782), 228

law, corporate, 328

Lawrence, D. H. (1885–1930), 775

Lawrence, Mass., strike in, 694

Lawrence v. Texas, 1108

Lay, Kenneth (1942–2006), 1060

Laying Tracks at Union Square for a Railroad, 619

Lazarus, Emma (1849–1887), 589

League for Industrial Democracy, 984

League of Nations, 725, 749, 750, 752, 753, *753*, 757, 772, 880, 900
  Congress and, 753

League of United Latin American Citizens (LULAC), 953

League of Women Voters, 767
  Tea Party and, 1123

Leary, Timothy (1920–1996), *991*, 992

Lease, Mary Elizabeth (1853–1933), 639–40

Leave It to Beaver (TV show), 929

Lebanon, 752, *899*, 944, 1041

Lecompton Constitution, 487, 493

Lee, Ann (1736–1784), 427

Lee, Richard Henry (1732–1794), 183

Lee, Robert E. (1807–1870), 489, 508, 509, 510, 535, 537, *537*, 541, *542*, 652, 653

Lee, Russell (1903–1986), *810*

Lee family, 118, 156

Left-wing Manifesto (Gitlow), 776

Le Havre, *889*

Lehman Brothers, 1112, 1113, 1115

Leisler, Jacob (ca. 1640–1691), 104–5, 143

Lely, Peter (1618–1680), *83*, *100*

Le Monde Illustré, 516

Lend-Lease Act (1941), 846

L'Enfant, Pierre Charles (1754–1825), 275, 290, *291*

Lenin, Vladimir I. (1870–1924), 724, 746, 752

Lenni Lanapes, 114

Leopard, 296

Leo XIII, Pope (1810–1903), 687

"Letter from Birmingham Jail" (King), 967

Letters from a Farmer in Pennsylvania (Dickinson), 178, 187

Letters from an American Farmer (Crèvecoeur), 267

Letters on the Equality of the Sexes (Sarah Grimké), 448

Levellers, 81, *82*, 148

Levi's, 928

Levitt, Alfred (1912–1966), 926

Levitt, William (1907–1994), 926, 932–33

Levittown, N.Y., 926, *926*

Lewelling, Lorenzo, 640

Lewinsky, Monica (1973–), 1079

Lewis, John L. (1880–1969), 812, 969

Lewis, Meriwether (1774–1809), 294, *294*, 608

Lewis, Sinclair (1885–1951), 816

Lewis and Clark expedition, 294, *294*
  Native-Americans and, 294

Lexington, Battle of, 184, *185*, *196*, 216

Leyte Gulf, 876

Libby Prison, 534

libel, 148–49

liberalism, 142–43, 795, 800, 832, 834, 861, 871, 875, 901, 910, 911, 937–38, 974, 982, 985, 1005, 1009, 1018, 1028, 1031, 1036, 1043, 1044, 1074
  Clinton and, 1052, 1054
  Democratic Party and, 911
  FDR and, 819
  Great Society and, 920
  New Deal and, 905, 965
  New Left and, 982, 991
  1968 election and, 1005
  Nixon's welfare plan and, 1011
  Watergate and, 1019–20

Liberal Republican Party, 579–80, 621

Liberation of Aunt Jemima, The (Saar), *982*

Liberation theology, 993

Liberator, 351, 421, 437, *437*, 439, 441, 450, *453*, 455

Liberia, 435, *435*, 719, 1083

libertarianism, 937–38, 1033

Liberty, 179

Liberty, Miss., 869

Liberty and Washington, 275

Liberty Bell, *425*, 441, 728, 936, *944*

Liberty Bonds, 727, 728, 747

Liberty Displaying the Arts and Sciences (Jennings), *205*, 232

Liberty Enlightening the World, 589

Liberty Hall, 175

Liberty Island, 589

Liberty Loans, 733

Liberty Motors and Engineering Corporation, 858

liberty of contract, 587, 705, 756, 810, 819, 823, 836

Liberty Party, 455, *455*, 464

Liberty Pole, 175, 278, 286

Liberty Tracts, 671

Liberty Tree, 175, *181*, 185, *185*

libraries, public, 147, 149

Library Company of Philadelphia, 147

Libya, 1040
  uprising in, 1122

Lieber, Francis (ca. 1798–1872), 370, 521

Lieberman, Joseph (1942–), 1079

Liebknecht, Karl (1871–1919), 732

Liebowitz, Sam (1893–1978), *835*

Life, 872, 934, 937, 946, *952*

Life in California (Robinson), 460

light bulb, 593, 790

Lilienthal, David E. (1899–1981), 936

Liliuokalani, queen of Hawaii (1838–1917), 661

Lima, *130*

Lima, Peru, 25

Lincoln, Abraham (1809–1865), 263, 386, 389, 401, 403, *486*, *488*, 490–91, *497*, 509, 512, *520*, 541–44, 562, *568*, 575, 589, *616*, 736, *738*, 772, 800, 820, 830, *832*, 857, *857*, 1100

Address at Sanitary Fair of, 527
assassination of, 542, *545*
in Black Hawk War, 374
and black suffrage, 519
Civil War message to Congress, 512
in 1858 Senate campaign, 487–89
elected president, 494–95, *495*
in election of 1860, 494–95
emergence of, 485–95
inaugural address of, 497
and Jefferson Davis compared, 531, 532
market revolution and, 308
and Mexican War, 466
parents of, 242
plans for reconstruction of, 540
second inaugural address, 541
slavery as viewed by, 487–88
Southern secession and, 497
and suspension of habeas corpus, 523
war planning and, 508
see also Emancipation Proclamation

Lincoln, Benjamin (1733–1810), 246

Lincoln, James (d. 1791), 256

Lincoln administration, 495, 514, 517, 523, 530, 531

Lincoln and the Female Slave (Bowser), *520*

Lincoln Memorial, 829, 991
  King's speech in front of, 968, *969*

Lindbergh, Charles (1902–1974), 762, 846

Lippmann, Walter (1889–1974), 687, 701, 710, 726, 733, 746, 769, 803, 818, 880, 984
  on Cold War, 895–96

Listen America! (Falwell), 1035

literacy, in America, 1081

"Literacy, Land, and Liberation," 572

Lithuania, 749, 879

Little, Frank (1880–1917), 733

Little, Malcolm, *see* Malcolm X

Little Bighorn, Battle of, 609, *610*

Little Gray Home in the West, The (song), 808

Little Rock, Ark., integration in, 949, *957*, 958

Little Turtle (1752–1812), 265

Livermore, Mary (1820–1905), 530, 571

Liverpool, 129

livestock, 6, 25, 43, 58, 128, 134, 135, 266, 319

Livingston, Robert (1746–1814), 90, 219

Livingston family, 118, 145, 176, 178, 207, 219

Living Wage, A (Ryan), 687

Lloyd, Henry Demarest (1847–1903), 597

Lloyd's of London, 792

lobbies:
  business, 769–70, 862
  special interest, 616

"Lochnerism," 625

Lochner v. New York, 624, 704

Locke, Alaine (1885–1954), 744

Locke, John (1632–1704), 143, *143*, 149, 184, 191, 224, 268

Lockheed, 871

Lodge, Henry Cabot (1902–1985), 753
Logan, James (1674–1751), 114
London, *53*, 140, 876, 878
London, Meyer (1871–1926), 689
Lonely Crowd, The (Riesman), 947
Long, Huey (1893–1935), 814, *814*, 816
Long, Joseph, 404
Longfellow, Henry Wadsworth (1807–1882), 498–99
Long Island, N.Y., 43, 91, 926, 933
Long Telegram, 887, 895
Long Walk, Navajo's, *see* Trail of Tears
Look, 931, *958*
Looking Backward (Bellamy), 626, 628, *628*, 629
"Lords of the Lash," 392
"Lords of the Loom," 392
Lords of Trade, 103, 133
Los Adaes, N.Mex., 153
Los Alamos, N.Mex., 908
Los Angeles, Calif., 154, *828*, 834, 854, *926*, *927*, *961*, 1064, 1066, 1068, *1075*, *1082*
   homelessness in, 1038, *1038*
   Mexicans in, 1068
   1992 riots in, 1072–73
   oil discovered in, 604
   pollution in, 961
   population of, 764
   water needs of, 708
   Watts riot in, 979, *980*
   zoot suit riots in, 865–66
Los Angeles Dodgers, 933
Los Angeles Herald Examiner, *1000*
Lossing, Benson, *427*
Lost Cause mythology, 652–53, *652*
Lost Generation, 776
Louisbourg, Fort, 158
Louisiana, 292, *292*, 312, 540, 814, *814*
   BP oil spill and, 1119
   Gulf Coast of, 1103
   illiteracy in, 645
   obtained by Spanish, 152
   Plessy v. Ferguson and, 650–51, *650*
   2nd Regiment of, *506*
   voting rights in, 649
Louisiana Purchase (1803), *273*, 292–94, *293*, 298, 354, 357, *357*, 358, 365, 473, 477
   Texas and, 464
Louisiana Purchase Exposition (1904), *667*
Louisiana Territory, 158, 159, 294–95
   population of, 155
   slave uprising in, 139
Louis XVI, king of France (1754–1793), 276
Lovejoy, Elijah P. (1802–1837), 444, 445
Loving, Richard and Mildred, 1001, *1001*
Loving v. Virginia, 1001, *1001*
Lowell, Abbott Lawrence (1856–1943), 759
Lowell, Mass., 322, 323, *323*, 325, 333, 342
Loyalists, 199, 200, 207, 218–21, *219*, *220*, 234, 235
Loyal Nine, 171

Loyal Publication Society, 727
loyalty, 913
   oaths, 219, 221, 733, 869, 910
   program (review system), 907–8, 911, 914
Loyalty Day, 738
LSD, *991*, 992
Luce, Henry (1898–1967), 860–61, 872, 896
Lucky Strike, *768*
Lucy, Autherine, 958
Ludlow, Colo., strike in, 695
Ludlow Massacre, 695, 764
Luke, William (1831–1870), 578
LULAC (League of United Latin American Citizens), 953
lumber, 604, 700, 707, 763, 854, 1047
Lumberton, N.C., *812*
Lundeen, Ernest (1878–1940), 826
Lusitania, 722, 723
Luther, Martin (1483–1546), 28
Lutherans, 109, 110
Lynch, James D. (1839–1872), 549, 572
lynchings, 651–52, *651*, 733, 741, *741*, 742, 743, 744, 775, 781, 829, 831, 869, *870*, 871, 903, 904, 956
   antilynching legislation and, 830, 831, 835, 870, 874, 903, 904
   in Canada, 652
   of Jews, 781
Lynd, Helen (1896–1982), 769
Lynd, Robert (1892–1970), 769
Lyon, Matthew (1749–1822), 286, *286*
Lyon, Pat, *337*
lyrical left, 696

MacArthur, Douglas (1880–1964), 792, 890, 891–93, *894*, 938
Macbeth (Shakespeare), 816
machismo, 998
Mackintosh, Ebenezer (1737–1816), 171
MacLeish, Archibald (1892–1982), 819, 898
Macmillan, Harold (1894–1986), 943
Macon's Bill No. 2, 297
Macy's, 927
MAD (mutual assured destruction), 942
Madame Butterfly (Puccini), 472
Madeira, 20
Madero, Francisco (1873–1913), 720
Madison, James (1751–1836), 191, 246, *247*, 279, 299, 365, 910, 1100
   agriculture and, *276*
   Alien and Sedition Acts as viewed by, 286
   American System plan of, 354, 355
   Bank of the United States opposed by, 275
   Bill of Rights and, 257–58, 259
   church-state separation and, 214
   colonization and, 435
   at Constitutional Convention, 248–50
   elected president, 297
   elimination of Federalist Party and, 303
   Federalist and, 254–56
   in *Marbury v. Madison*, 291

   religion and, 212, 214
   as slaveholder, 227, 251
   trade policy of, 297
   Virginia Plan and, 248
   on war, 299
Madison, Wis., Beats in, 948
Madison Square Garden, *846*, 847
Madoff, Bernard (1938–), 1114
Magazine of Wall Street, The, *790*
Magellan, Ferdinand (1480–1521), 22, 23
Magna Carta (1215), 79–80, 841
Mahan, Alfred T. (1840–1914), 661
Mahoney, James, *55*
Maiden Tribute of Modern Babylon (Stead), 715
Maine, 312, 823
   entrance into union of, 358
   gay marriage in, 1125
   voting rights in, 352
Maine, 662, *662*
Maine Bank of Portland, 379
malaria, 134, 717
Malaya, 896
Malaysia, 943
Malcolm X (1925–1965), 981
Mali, 19
Malik, Charles (1906–1987), *899*
Malvern Hill, Battle of, *506*
Manchuria, 844, 877
Mandela, Nelson (1918–), 1049
Manhattan Island, 41
Manhattan Project, 877
manifest destiny, 329, 459–72, *461*, 660
Manigault, Louis, *513*
Manila, 25
Manila Bay, 662, 666
Mann, Horace (1796–1859), 434
Mann Act (1910), 629
Manning, Richard I. (1859–1931), 699
Manning, William (1747–1814), 280
Man Nobody Knows, The (Sheeler), 764
Manon, 155
Mansfield, Lord, *182*
Man's Most Dangerous Myth: The Fallacy of Race (Montagu), 864
manufacturing, 679, 682, 924, 931, 978, 1021–22, 1047, 1067, 1102
   decline of, 1020, 1037–38, *1037*, 1043, 1061–64, *1061*, 1101–2, 1111
   in early nineteenth century, 319–23, *319*
   J. Q. Adams's promotion of, 365
   in Mexico, 1061
   rebound in, 1120
   unions and, 1037
   see also industry
"Man Without a Country, The" (Hale), 522
Mao Zedong (1893–1976), 891, *893*
Mapuche, 601
Marbury, William, 291
Marbury v. Madison, 291
March on Washington, 870, 968–69, *969*
March to the Sea, *541*
Marie Antoinette, queen of France (1755–1793), 599

Marine Corps, U.S., 296, *848*
   segregation in, 869
Marion, Francis (1732?–1795), 199
market economy:
   capitalism and, 1047
   and "captains of industry," 594–97
   competition in, 594, 595–97
   expansion of, 592
   rich and poor in, 599–600, *600*
   workers' freedom and, 597–99
market fundamentalism, 1114–15
market revolution, 306–45, *310*, *313*, 348, 351, 369, 394, 488
   abolition and, 439
   Abraham Lincoln and, 308
   African-Americans and, 339
   agriculture and, 307, 318
   canals and, 168, 309–11, *310*, 354, 355
   cotton and, 312, *316*
   freedom and, 336, 341
   individual and, 328–37
   manufacturing and, 319–23
   middle class created by, 338, 341
   prosperity and, 337–43, *337*
   railroads and, 168, 308, 311, 319
   Republicans and, 479
   rise of banks in, 355, 377
   roads and, 308, *310*
   rural areas and, 318
   Second Great Awakening and, 336
   society and, 318–28
   technology and, 315, 319–23, *321*, *481*
   textile mills and, 321–24, *321*, *323*
   transportation and, 307, 308, 319, 328
   urban areas and, 319, *320*
   water power and, *321*, 322
   women and, 339–41
Marlette, Douglas (1949–2007), *1030*
"maroons," 139
Marquette, Jacques (1637–1675), 38
marriage, 1013, *1014*, 1076, *1076*, *1077*
   see also Defense of Marriage Act; divorce; gay rights
"Married" (lithograph), *339*
Marshall, George C. (1880–1959), 889
Marshall, John (1755–1835), 247, 328, 371
   American Colonization Society and, 435
   death of, 379
   French Revolution as viewed by, 276
   Missouri Controversy and, 357
   nationalism and, 357
   Native Americans and, 374–75
   strong Supreme Court favored by, 291
   see also Supreme Court, U.S.
Marshall, Thurgood (1908–1993), 953–54
Marshall Court, 291, 328, 371
Marshall Island, and BP oil rig, 1119
Marshall Plan, *888*, 889–90, *889*, 970
Martí, José (1853–1895), 664
Martin, Bradley (1841–1913), 599
Martin, James (b. 1753), 234
Martin, Luther (1748–1826), 251
Martin (slave), 289

Martineau, Harriet (1802–1876), 328, 435

Martinique, 106, 158

Marx, Karl (1818–1883), 517, 627, 722, 937, 1079

Mary I, queen of England (1516–1568), 50

Mary II, queen of England (1662–1694), 102

Maryland, 275, 974, 1001, 1019
constitution of, 209, 213
free blacks in, 408
gay marriage in, 1125
settlement of, 58
slave trade in, 317
uprising in, 103–4
voting rights in, 209, 352

Maryland colony, 2, 54, 63–64, 91, 103–4, 117–18
close ties to Britain of, 132–33
as feudal domain, 64
free blacks in, 98
government of, 64, 144
indentured servitude in, 64
"plundering time" in, 83
religion in, 64, 82–83
tobacco in, 63–64

Mashpees, 223

Mason, George (1725–1792), 132, 247, 248

Mason-Dixon Line, 390

Massachuset language, 76

Massachusetts, 234, 341, 364, 770, 1018, 1124
constitution of, 210, 213, 223
government in, 209
legislature, 328
Shays's rebellion in, 246
Supreme Court of, 1103
U.S. Constitution and, 257
war debt and, 275

Massachusetts Bay Company, 66–67, 69

Massachusetts Charter (1629), 82, 182

Massachusetts colony, 56, 66–71, 66, 72–73, 77–78, 104–5, 119, 173, 173, 211, 221
assembly in, 146
General Court of, 69, 78, 103
government of, 68–70
and King Philips War, 87
in Pequot War, 76–77
population of, 67
Quakers in, 82
repeals economic regulations, 78
seal of, 67
self-governing towns in, 69
slave trade in, 128
uprising in, 171
views on independence of, 185

Massachusetts Magazine, 281

Massachusetts Spy, The, 225

Massasoit (ca. 1590–1661), 67

Masses, The, 685, 732

"massive retaliation," 941–42

"masterless men," 53–54, 107

"master race," 863, 902

maternalist reform, 704–5, 766, 817

Mather, Cotton (1663–1728), 140

Mather, Increase (1639–1723), 106

Matlack, Timothy (1736?–1829), 207

Mattachine Society, 997

May Day, 629

Mayflower, 66

Mayflower Compact (1620), 66, 885

Mayr, Christian (ca. 1805–1851), 412

May Session of the Woman's Rights Convention, The, 448

Maytag, 1102

Mazzini, Giuseppe (1805–1872), 520

McCain, John (1936–), 990, 1101, 1117

McCall's, 859

McCarran Internal Security Act (1950), 898, 911

McCarran Internal Security Bill, 911

McCarran-Walter Act (1952), 911

McCarthy, Eugene (1916–2005), 1003

McCarthy, Joseph R. (1908–1957), 907, 909, 909, 910–11

McCarthy era, 258, 731, 907–8, 909–10, 914, 935, 946, 949, 1000

McCarthyism, 907–8, 909–10, 914, 935, 946, 949, 1100
and homosexuality, 907–8, 997

McClellan, George B. (1826–1885), 509, 510, 539

McClure's Magazine, 680, 709

McCormick, Cyrus (1809–1884), 319

McCormick Company, 629

McCulloch v. Maryland, 356

McDonald's, 930

McGovern, George (1922–), 1018

McHenry, Fort, 300

McIlvaine, Samuel (1824–1863), 503

McIntosh, Fort, 242

McKay, Claude (1890–1948), 787–88

McKinley, William (1843–1901), 643–44, 661, 662, 663, 669, 672, 691
assassination of, 706
Philippines and, 664, 667, 673

McKinley administration, 667

McKinley Tariff (1890), 643

McNamara, Robert (1916–), 986, 1017–18

McNary-Haugen Bill, 771

McNeill, George E. (1837–1906), 625, 671

McPherson, Aimee Semple (1890–1944), 815

McRea, Ed, 835

McReynolds, James C. (1862–1946), 773

McVeigh, Timothy (1968–2001), 1077

McWilliams, Carey (1905–1980), 828

Meade, George G. (1815–1872), 536

measles, 24, 131

Meat Inspection Act (1906), 680, 707

Mecca, 896

Medicaid, 977, 1031, 1039, 1053

Medicare, 977, 1039, 1053, 1054

medicine men, 12

Mediterranean Sea, 20, 888

Meeting of the General Council of the Army at Putney, 82

Mellon, Andrew (1855–1937), 792

Melting Pot, The (Zangwill), 735

"melting pot," U.S. as, 267, 735, 740, 864, 934

Melville, Herman (1819–1891), 335, 343, 352, 355, 465

Membertou, 38

Memphis, Tenn., 835, 885, 965, 1003, 1003
Reconstruction riot in, 567

Memphis Free Press, 652

Mencken, H. L. (1880–1956), 701

Mendez v. Westminster, 953

Menéndez de Avilés, Pedro (1519–1574), 33

Mennonites, 109, 110, 219

mercantilism, 78, 88, 90, 132

Mercedes, 685

Meredith, James (1933–), 966, 971

Meridian, Miss., 578

Merrimac, 504

Merrimack River, 322

Merryman, John (1824–1881), 523

Meschianza, 197

message to Congress, 354, 362, 365, 512
see also State of the Union Address

mestizos, 27, 28, 34, 106

Metacom (King Philip; d. 1676), 87, 376

Methodism, 150

Methodists, 110, 376, 413, 664
African-American, 413, 551
Gabriel's Rebellion and, 289
in Great Awakening, 151, 152
Prohibition and, 730
racial division among, 653
in Second Great Awakening, 334–35, 413
slavery and, 473

metis (French-Indian children), 40

Meuse-Argonne campaign, 725

Mexican Cession, 467, 468

Mexicans, Mexican immigrants, 601, 604, 681, 683, 685, 740, 783, 830, 834, 972, 977, 1012, 1067–68, 1068, 1105
activism among, 997–98, 997
as cowboys, 604
New Deal and, 828
Operation Wetback and, 911
and wages, 998, 1105
World War II and, 865–66

Mexican War, 386, 463, 465–69, 465, 467, 475, 605, 721, 724, 736, 855

Mexico, 8, 10, 23, 24, 25, 27, 28, 31, 32, 33, 106, 314, 365, 468–69, 492, 493, 496, 609, 721, 723, 783, 784, 828–29, 865
abolition of slavery in, 461, 469
border wall with, 1106
California gold rush and, 471
conquering of, 24
Cortés's exploration of, 23
frontier of, 460
immigration from, 1123
independence of, 155, 359, 460
invention of agriculture in, 6
jobs exported to, 1102
loss of U.S. jobs to, 1102
NAFTA and, 1052, 1062, 1064
as obstacle to westward expansion, 329
population decline of, 24
slaves bound for, 98

Texas revolt and, 460–62
Wilson and, 720–21

Mexico City, Mexico, 25, 26, 27, 34, 35, 37, 147, 467
Olympics at, 1004
population of, 115

Meyer v. Nebraska, 773, 785, 786

MFDP, see Mississippi Freedom Democratic Party

Miami, Fla., 33, 1064, 1066, 1068, 1097

Miami Confederacy, 265

Michigan, 312, 685, 686, 700, 852, 1077

Michigan, University of, affirmative action and, 1108

microchip, 1057

Microcosm of London, The, 80

Microsoft, 1047, 1058, 1061, 1064

Middle Ages, 18, 20

Middle Border, 602–3

middle class, 924, 928, 929, 931, 932, 1038, 1060, 1062, 1070
created by market revolution, 338, 341
feminism in, 994, 995
growth of, 586
home ownership and, 808, 823
market revolution and, 341
materialism of, 949
poverty invisible to, 978
reformers, 626
socialism and, 627
women in, 351, 947

Middle Colonies, 54, 114, 118, 120, 128–29
in election of 1800, 287
elections in, 145
slavery in, 135, 138

Middle East, 721, 750, 752, 753, 888, 895, 921, 944–45, 945, 1020, 1026–27, 1065, 1066, 1088, 1091, 1092, 1093, 1095, 1098, 1099, 1105
Islam and, 1042
uprisings in, 1122
U.S. presence in, 1093, 1098
see also Gulf War; Iraq War; Israel

middle ground, 156–57

Middle Passage, 132

Middle States, 275
construction of roads in, 309

Middletown (Lynd and Lynd), 769

Midgley, Thomas (1889–1944), 961

"midnight judges," 291

Midway Island, Battle of, 849, 849

migrant farm workers, 681, 821, 828–29, 831, 833, 925, 997–98

Militant Liberty, 897

military, U.S.:
desegregation of, 904
gays in, 1052
and Operation Wetback, 911
post-World War II demobilization of, 886, 901
prisons, 1100–1101, 1101, 1108, 1110, 1118
Reagan and build-up of, 1040
segregation in, 743, 869–70, 871
spending on, 920, 940, 942, 1092
tribunals, 1099, 1109–10, 1121

military bases, *854*
military-industrial complex, 842, 853, 906, 960, 984, 1020
military spending, 920, 940, 942
Militia of Montana, 1077
militias:
  blacks in, 353
  Connecticut colony and, 185
  in Iraq, 1096
  New York and, *503*
  radical conservative, 1077
Mill, George, *1109*
Millay, Edna St. Vincent (1892–1950), 759
Miller, Lewis (1796–1882), *317*
Milliken v. Bradley, 1013
Millionaire's Row, 679
Mill on the Brandywine, 322
Mills, C. Wright (1916–1962), 946
Mills, Florence (1895–1927), 787
Milošević, Slobodan (1941–2006), 1056
Milton, John (1608–1674), 80–81, *119*
Milwaukee, Wis., 682
Minerva, *175*
minimum wage, 705, 709, 727, 770, *770*, 810, 823, 824, 830, 863, 901, 937, 941, 968, 1064, 1102
mining, 605, 682, 683, 710, 763, 854
  coal, 645, *646*, 707, 747, *825*
  in national parks, 708
  strikes and, 642, 733
  United Mine Workers and, 693
Minneapolis, Minn., 766, 811, 904
Minnesota, 9, 602, *764*, 826, 1003, 1039
minorities:
  home ownership and, 1113
  "subprime" mortgages and, 1113
Miracle, The (movie), 775
Miranda v. Arizona, 1001
misery index, 1021, *1021*
Miss America pageant, protest at, 996
missiles, 1040, 1042
  and Cold War "missile gap," 960
  cruise, 1050
  and Cuba, 970–71
  Jupiter, 970
  see also nuclear weapons
missionaries, 34–35, 58, 156, 266, 460, 739
  in Hawaii, 670
  Jesuit, 40
  Spanish, 28–29, *29*, *30*, 33, 147, 154–55, *154*
Mississippi, 156, 292, 312, 374, 830, 831, 900, 915, *958*, 981
  black voting in, 903
  BP oil spill and, 1119
  "freedom schools" in, 955
  Gulf Coast of, 1103
  Senate, *574*
  voter registration drive in, 973
Mississippi, University of, 966, 971, *971*
Mississippi Freedom Democratic Party (MFDP), 973–74, *973*
Mississippi River, 38, 49, 155, *159*, 292, 307, 309, 312, *313*, 354, 1103
Mississippi Valley, 9, 153, 155, 299, 311, 540

Missouri, 312
  constitution of, 358
  entrance into union of, 356–58, 435
  legislature, *367*
Missouri, University of, segregation at, 953
Missouri Compromise (1820), 356–58, *357*, 366, 371, 420, 473, 474, 478, *478*, 485–86, 496
Missouri Territory, slave population of, 357
Mitchell, John N. (1913–1988), 1019
Mitchell, John P. (1870–1919), 624, 693
Mitred Minuet, The, *182*
Mobile, Ala., 155, 317, *534*
Moby Dick (Melville), 352
Model A, 760
Model T, 685–86, 760
modernism, 778–79
Modern Republicanism, 940–41
Modern Times, N.Y., 430
Modern Woman: The Lost Sex, 932
Moga, 767
Mohave Desert, *1071*
Mohawks, 12, 222, 266
Mohicans, 299
Molasses Act (1733), 172, 173
monarchy, U.S. rejection of, 206, 208
Mondale, Walter (1928–), 1039
Monitor, 504
monopolies, 217, 328, 597, *616*, 629
  Federal Trade Commission and, 711
  "natural," 699
  Theodore Roosevelt and, 706
  see also trusts, business
Monroe, James (1758–1831), 289, 356, 362
  Era of Good Feelings under, 357
  Monrovia named for, 435
Monroe Doctrine, 360–61, 362, 364, 660, 716, 717–18
  American foreign policy and, 360–61
  nationalism and, 361
  neutrality and, 361
Monrovia, Liberia, 435
Montagu, Ashley (1905–1999), 864
Montana, 763, 1077
  entrance into Union of, 610
  socialism in, 690
Monterey, Calif., 154
Montesquieu, Baron (1689–1755), 140, 179
Montezuma, Carlos, 698
Montgomery, Ala., 954, *954*
  bus boycott in, 919, 949, 954–56, *955*, 956
  Civil Rights Memorial in, *1127*
Montgomery Court Square, 955
Montgomery Ward, 592, 855
Montreal, surrender of, 158
moon landing, 970, *1005*
Moore, Joshua B., 533
Moors, 21, 26, 51
Moral Majority, 1029, 1035
Moravian Brethren, 109, 110, 214, 219
Moravian Indians, 164
More, Thomas (1478–1535), 53, 426
Morgan, Barbara, *834*

Morgan, Daniel (1736–1802), 199
Morgan, J. P. (1837–1913), 528, 594, 679, 691, 706, 711, 769
Morgenthau, Hans (1904–1980), 947
Morgues, Jacques Le Moyne de (d. 1588), *15*
Mormons, 336–37, *337*, *462*, 703
  Deseret and, 605
  in Great Salt Lake Valley, 605
  and James Buchanan, 605
  and Jesus, 336–37
  Mitt Romney and, 1124
  Mountain Meadows Massacre and, 605
  polygamy and, 337, 605
  prejudice against, 1107
  in Utah, 605
  see also Christianity
Morris, Gouverneur (1752–1816), 251, 253
Morris, Robert (1734–1806), 218
Morrison, Toni (1931–), 477
Morse, Samuel F. B. (1791–1872), 311
Morse, Wayne (1900–1974), 986
Morton, Sarah W., 281
Moscow, 896, 898, 919, 942, 944, 1017, 1027, *1042*, 1049
  Nixon and Khrushchev in, 923, *925*, 937, 995
Moses, Robert (1888–1981), 965
Mossadegh, Mohammed (1882–1967), 944, *944*, 946
Mother and Daughter Reading, Mt. Meigs, Alabama (Eickemeyer), *551*
motion pictures, 593, 715, 756, 760, 762, 764, 768, 775, 784, 831, 832, 833, 857, 864, 923, 1069
  family life in, 931
  in World War I, 727
  see also Hollywood
Mott, Lucretia (1793–1880), 448, 571
"mound builders," 9, 13
Mountain Meadows Massacre, 605
Movie, 5 Cents (Sloan), *687*
Mozambique, 943
Mr. Deeds Goes to Town (movie), 833
Mr. Smith Goes to Washington (movie), 833
Mubarak, Hosni (1928–), uprising against, 1122, *1122*
Müch, Karl, 738
muckrakers, 680
Muir, John (1838–1914), 707, *707*
mulattos, 138
Muller v. Oregon, 704, 770
multiculturalism, 1074–75
  see also diversity; pluralism
Muncie, Ind., 769
Munich conference, 844
Munn v. Illinois, 623
Murphy, Frank (1890–1949), 812, 836
Murray, Judith Sargent (1751–1820), 281, 283
Museum of Modern Art, 897, *898*
music, *137*, *524*, 833
Muslim Brotherhood, 1122
Muslims, 19, 20, 21, 28, 150, *295*, 296, 943, 1026, 1041, 1065, 1087, 1096, 1098, 1118

in Afghanistan, 1027, 1090
in Balkans, 1056
Black, 981
in Bosnia, 1033
fundamentalism and, 1027, 1050
Gulf War and, 1050
as immigrants, 1066
Malcolm X and, 981
Obama's speech to repair relations with, *1118*
in Pennsylvania colony, 110
prejudice against, 1107, *1107*
September 11 and, 1099
Shiite, 921, 1096
Sunni, 921, 1096
Mussolini, Benito (1883–1945), 844, 850
"mustee," *139*
mutual assured destruction (MAD), 942
Myanmar, *see* Burma
My Bondage and My Freedom (Douglass), 451
Myers, Myer, 116
My Lai massacre, 1016
Myrdal, Gunnar, 874, 949
Mystic, Conn., 76–77
Mystic River, *76*

NAACP, *see* National Association for the Advancement of Colored People
NAACP v. Alabama, 1000
Nabisco, 1038
Nader, Ralph (1934–), 1000, 1080
NAFTA (North American Free Trade Agreement), 1052, 1061, *1061*, 1062, 1064
Nagasaki, atomic bombing of, 877, 942
Nanjing, 844
napalm, 990
Napoleon I, emperor of France (1769–1821), 292, 293, 296, 300, 302
Napoleon III, emperor of France, 475
Narragansett Indians, *57*, *76*, 299
NASDAQ, 1058–59
Nash-Kelvinator Corporation, 859
Nashville, Tenn., 1105, 1106
Nasser, Gamal Abdel (1918–1970), 944–45
Nast, Thomas (1840–1902), *569*, *580*, *583*
Natchez, Miss., 317
Natchez Indians, 13, 139
Nation, The, 579, 620, 671, 775, 861
National American Woman Suffrage Association, *658*, 659, 703
National Archives, 885
National Association for the Advancement of Colored People (NAACP), 737, 741, 742, *742*, 826, 829, 834, 868, *869*, 870, 871, 900, 903, *903*, 914, 949, 953, 954, 957, 967, 973
National Association of Colored Women, The, 648
National Association of Manufacturers, 858, 910, 941
National Catholic Welfare Conference, 819

National Catholic Welfare Council, 785
National Civic Federation, 691
National Committee for a Sane
    Nuclear Policy, 943
National Conference of Christians and
    Jews, 834
National Consumer's League, 703
national debt, 274, 370, 618, 1039, 1052,
    1102
National Defense Education Act, 941
National Endowment for the Arts,
    977, 1076
National Endowment for the
    Humanities, 977
National Equal Rights League, 741
National Farmer's Holiday
    Association, 792
National Guard, 746, 747, 811, 958, 979,
    1016, *1016*
National Indian Youth Council, 998
National Industrial Recovery Act
    (1935), 804, 811
nationalists, nationalism, 246–47, *248*,
    297, 353–58, *355*, 1065, 1082
    Arab, 943–44, 1027
    Civil War, 521
    John C. Calhoun and, 371–72
    Monroe Doctrine and, 361
    and "New Nationalism," 710, 711,
        726
    R.F.K. assassination and
        Palestinian, 1003
    socialism as, 628
    South and rise of, 490–91
    World War I and, 722
National Labor Relations Board, 816
National League, 706
National Liberation Front, 946
National Organization for Women
    (NOW), 995–96
national parks, 707–8, *707*, 999
National Police Gazette, 657
National Recovery Administration
    (NRA), 804–5, *804*, 810, *810*
National Reform Association, 628
National Resources Planning Board
    (NRPB), 827, 861–62
National Review, 976
National Security Agency (NSA), 986,
    1100
National Security Council, 889, 891,
    893, 945, 986, 1042
National Security Strategy of the
    United States (2002), 1091, 1092
National Transportation Safety Board,
    1010
National War Labor Board, 874
National Weather Service, 1104
National Woman Suffrage Association,
    571
National Women's Party, 729, 766
National Youth Administration, 816,
    855
Nation of Islam, 981
Native American Rights Fund, 1073
Native Americans, 2, 3, 8, *12, 15, 21, 56,*
    106, 111, 114, *114,* 122, 134, 139,
    154, 263–66, 314, 610–14, 673,
    919, 1073–74, *1074*

affirmative action and, 1013
in alliance with French, 39, 104, 127
American Revolution and, 205,
    221–23, 235
in attempted conversion to
    Catholicism, 3, 28–29, *29,* 34,
    39–41
in battles with Spanish, 31–32, 33–35
buffalo and, 600, 608
California gold rush and, 470, *471*
in Carolina, 92
as casino operators, 1073, 1074
Cherokee Phoenix newspaper for, 351
Christianity and, 12, 33, 36, 37, 52,
    87, 154–55, 610
citizenship and, 782
citizenship (U.S.) and, 612–14, 1073
civil rights movement and, 998, *998*
cliff dwellings of, *10*
coastal tribes of, 76
colonial assemblies and, 147
conflicts with colonists, 57
conflict with Jamestown of, 60–61
Constitution and, 613
crafts by, *612*
Declaration of Independence and,
    222–23
displacing of, 56–57
diverse societies of, 10–13
of eastern North America, 10–12
economy of, 12–13
English relations with, 54, 56–57,
    300
epidemics and, 2, 3, 5, 24, 27, 32, 40,
    49, 54, 58, 73, 76, 87, 96, 106, 155
Europeans' negative views of, 15, 38
European trade with, 57–58, 66–67,
    92, 156
execution of, *525*
forced labor of, 6, 16, 25, 29–31, 33,
    34, 52, 92, 133, 155, 601
freedom and, 15–16, 221–23, 266
gender relations of, 14
George Washington and, 222
government of, 10, 12, 16
government treatment of, 610–14
intermixing with Europeans by,
    27, *28,* 56
Irish compared with, 51
Jackson and, 314, 347, 367, 374–76
Jamestown and, 60–61
Jefferson's policies on, 297–98
John Adams and, 377
lack of technologies of, 34
land as viewed by, 12–13, *13*
Lewis and Clark expedition and,
    294
loss of Southern land of, 317
maps of tribes of, *11, 264*
matrilineal societies of, 14
in Mexican Cession, 468, 469
New Deal and, 827–28
of New England, 13
New England and, *57*
New France and, 38–41
New York colony and, 90–91
as "noble savages," 14
origins of, 6
pan-Indian identity of, 160

and Pennsylvania colony, 161
Pilgrims and, 66–67
poverty and, 1074
progressivism and, 698
Puritans and, 73, 76–77, 87, 1074
railroads and, 524
religion of, 136
religions of, 12, *12,* 14, *15*
removal of, 374–77, *375,* 459, 590,
    708, 834, 897
as Rough Riders, 663
Seven Years' War and, 156–58
sexual division of labor of, 14, *15*
slavery and, 6, 16, 25, 29–31, 87,
    94–95, *121,* 470, 601, 1074
societies of, 2, 6
Spanish and, 106
"termination" and, 998
trade among, 9–10, 13, *13*
treaty system and, 610
tribalism attacked, 611–14
uprisings of, 34–35, 87, 92, 160,
    221–23
U.S. treaties with, 242, 265
in Virginia, 99–100, 111
voting rights and, 144
war atrocities against, 222–23
War of 1812 and, 300
in West, 377, *608*
of western North America, 9–10
westward expansion of U.S. and,
    242–43, 297–98, 329, 459, 601–2
women's roles among, 14
World War II and, 865, 866
see also Indian removal
Native Americans, population of, 8,
    242, 374, 600
    in California, 154, 470
    decline of, 10, 24, 25, 29, 34
    in Florida, 154
    in New England, 73
nativism, 326–27, 481, 783, 789, 864,
    1123
NATO, *see* North Atlantic Treaty
    Organization
Nat Turner's Rebellion, 420–22
Naturalization Act (1790), 268, 782
Naturalization Act (1798), 285
Nauvoo, Ill., 337, *337*
Navajos, 34, 35, 460, 525, 827
    "code-talkers" of, 866
Navajos' Long Walk, *see* Trail of Tears
Naval Academy, U.S., 1023
Navigation Acts, 83, 88, 103, 117, *117,*
    172, 173, 186, 218
Navy, U.S., *848*
    African-Americans in, 353, 517, 874
    in Mexican War, 466
    segregation, 743, 869
    at Tripoli, *295,* 296
Nazi Party, 802, 844, *844,* 845, 856,
    857, 863, 864, 866, 869, 870,
    870, 874, 876, 878, 880, 881, 886,
    897, 899
NBC Symphony Orchestra, 844
Nebraska, 478, *601,* 602, 613, *703,* 770,
    773, 785
    entrance into Union of, 610
    population of, 679

Necessity, Fort, 158
Negro Leagues, 904
Nehru, Jawaharlal (1889–1964), 943
neoconservatives, 1028
Neolin, 160, 163, 299, 613
Netherlands, 38, 41, 83, 88, 364, 845
    in Anglo-Dutch war, 88
    colonization and, 2, 15, 35, 66
    freedom in, 41
    see also Dutch Empire
Neue Jerusalem, Das, 335
Neutrality Acts, 845
Nevada, 467, 906, 1117
    Sagebrush Rebellion and, 1032
Nevis, Spanish attack on, 96
New Amsterdam, 41, *42,* 43, 90
    role of women in, 90
Newark, N.J., riot in, 979
Newcastle, duke of, 145, 157
New Deal, 555, 643, 748, 757, 798–840,
    822, 842, 846, 860, 861, 863, 875,
    880, 905, 936, 940, 965, 975, 982,
    1005, 1024, 1060, *1060,* 1118
    African-Americans and, 826–27,
        828–30, 978
    agriculture and, 807, *809,* 826, 828,
        830
    economic inequality in, *1060*
    Eisenhower and, 940, 941, 1010,
        1054
    end of, 836–37, 855
    Father Coughlin and, 815
    First, 800–810
    Goldwater and, 974
    Great Society and, 977, 978
    housing and, 808–9, *810*
    Johnson and, 972
    legacy of, 800, 836–37
    libertarians and, 937
    McCarthyism and, 911
    Mexican immigrants and, 828, *828*
    OWI and, 857–58
    Popular Front and, 832, 833, 834
    Progressivism and, 734
    Reagan and, 1033
    roads in, 805, 806, *806*
    Second, 815–18, 824, 853
    in South, 826
    Supreme Court and, 810, *810,* 824
    Theodore Bilbo and, 831
    Truman and, 901, 911
    wages and, 814
    West and, 806, 807, 827–29
    women and, 825–26
    work projects in, 799, *799,* 805–6,
        806, 837
"New Deal coalition," 823, 1010, 1012,
    1028
New Democracy, The (Weyl), 740
New Democrats, 1024
New Display of the United States, A
    (Doolittle), *285*
New Empire, The (Brooks Adams), 672
New England, *49,* 275, *321,* 392
    building of roads in, 309
    deindustrialization in, 763
    Dominion of, 103
    in election of 1796, 284
    in election of 1800, 287

New England (*continued*)
  in election of 1804, 297
  in election of 1824, 361, 364
  Indian of, *57*
  inducement to settle, 54
  industrialization of, 321–22
  industrial revolution in, 590
  Puritan emigration to, 66, 1074
  shipbuilding in, 88
  strikes in, 811
  trade with West Indies, 78
  voting rights in, 353
New England colonies, 2, 54, 64–71,
    103, 104, 110, 123, 156, 164, 194,
    226
  Atlantic trade of, 128–29, *129*
  division in, 70–79
  economy of, 77–78
  elections in, 144–45
  hierarchical society of, 69–70
  map of, *72*
  Native Americans in, 13
  population growth of, 120
  population of, 87
  slavery in, 135
  social equality in, 77
  triangular trade of, 130–31
New England Courant, 147
New Federalism, 1010
Newfoundland, 21, 23, 38, 51, 159
New France, 35, 38–41, *39*, 106, 147
  Indians and, 38–41
  population of, 38
New Freedom, 710, 711
New Hampshire, 1003, 1103
New Hampshire colony, 116, 178
  chartering of, 78
New Harmony, Ind., 429, 992
New Haven, Conn., 72
New Jersey, 710
  constitution of, 209–10, 228
  election of 1796 and, 284
  slaves in, 229
  voting rights in, 351
New Jersey colony, 54, 93, 110, 114–15
  slaves in, 135
  Washington's army in, 194, *196*
New Jersey Dutch Reformed, 150
New Jersey Plan, 249
New Lanark, Scotland, 429
New Laws, 30–31
New Left, 965, 982–83, 991, 993,
    994
New Lights, 151
New Madrid County, Mo., *809*
New Mexico, 10, *10*, 33–35, *35*, 37, 40,
    49, 147, 152, 153, 467, 469, 605,
    877, *991*, 1074, 1103
  population of, 460
New Nationalism, 710, 711, 726, 741
"New Negro," 787
New Negro, The (Locke), 744
New Netherland, 35, *39*, 49, 88, 90
  freedom in, 41–45
  population of, 42
  religious freedom in, 42
  seal of, *43*
  slavery in, 42
  uprisings in, 45

New Orleans, La., 155, *155*, 292, 294,
    350, 353–54, *394*, 575, 766, 854,
    958
  battle of, 301, *350*, 361
  black community in, 407, 418, 541
  Caribbean heritage of, 393
  in Civil War, 511, *512*
  cotton trade in, 393, *394*
  French heritage of, 393
  and Hurricane Katrina, 1103–5, *1104*
  population of, 295, 393, 854
  Reconstruction riot in, 567
  slave auctions in, 391
  slave rebellion in, 419–20
  slave trade in, 317
  sugar trade in, 393
Newport, R.I., 119, *598*, 599
New Republic, 688, 706, 726, 733, 822,
    863, 885
New Rochelle, N.Y., *932*
New School for Social Research, *758*,
    795
News from America, 76
New South, 645–46, 647, 652
New Spain, *32*
newspapers, *see* press
New Sweden, 44
Newsweek, 923
New Testament, 16, 17
Newton, Isaac (1642–1727), 150, 218
New World, 4–47, 52
  commerce in, 83, 88
  conquering of, 23–24
  dangers of, 54
  education in, 25
  peoples of, 8–16, 23–24
  settling of, 7
  slavery in, 3, 5, 25, 94–97, 130–32
  women and, 27, 38, 40
New York, 10, 12, 41, 158, 242, 287, *440*,
    823, 926, 996, 997, 1033, 1034,
    1070, 1116
  Al Smith as governor of, 789
  constitution of, 213
  demands return of slaves, 227
  election of 1796 and, 284
  homelessness in, 1038
  legislature, 328
  map of, *157*
  militia, *503*
  Mormons in, 336, 337
  population of, 358
  religious liberty in, 213
  slavery in, *228*
  Theodore Roosevelt as governor
    of, 663
  U.S. Constitution and, 257, *259*
  voting rights in, 209, 353
New York, N.Y., 73, 90–91, 115, 116, 139,
    211, 227, 281, 309, *311*, *319*, 325,
    392, *680*, *689*, 702, *704*, 738, *758*,
    768, 778, *793*, *803*, 806, *806*, 813,
    817, 836, *840*, 841, *846*, 847, *898*,
    927, *972*, 998, 1057, 1064, 1066,
    1068, 1073, *1089*, *1093*, 1113, *1125*
  African-Americans in, 339, 786–88
  antiwar demonstration in, 1012
  Beats in, 948
  boycotts of Britain in, 179

  as capital of U.S., 273
  as country's financial center, 481
  draft riots in, 1073
  fiscal crisis in, 1022
  garment strike in, 677, 691–95, *694*
  Gay Liberation Day in, *997*
  immigration to, *679*, 681–82, 689
  Islamic Cultural Center debate in,
    1107, *1107*
  "lyrical left" in, 696
  manufacturing in, 591, 677
  Occupy Movement in, 1123–24, *1124*
  population of, 115
  population of slaves in, 135, 229
  Puerto Ricans in, 933
  religious diversity in, *211*, 1107, *1107*
  September 11 attacks in, 1087, *1089*
  slave uprising in, 138–39
  socialism and, 689, 690
  Statue of Liberty in, 589
  World Trade Center in, 1022, *1022*
New York colony, 2, 54, 87, 90–91, 103,
    104, 110, 147–48, 156, *170*
  African-Americans lose jobs in, 90
  American Revolution and, 207
  anti-British rebellion in, 104
  assembly in, 146
  British boycott in, 183
  growth of, 114–15
  Howe's army occupies, *195*
  Loyalists in, 219, *220*, 221
  Native Americans and, 87, 90–91
  politics in, 143–44
  population of, 90
  slavery in, 135, 138–39
  slave trade in, 129
  Stamp Act Congress and, 175
  Vermont split from, 178
  views on independence of, 186
  Washington's army in, 194, *196*
New York Consumers' League, 802
New York Court of Appeals, 624
New Yorker, *940*, *1053*
New York Evening Post, 445
New York Harbor, 41, 129
New York Herald, *350*, 351, 352
New York House of Refuge, The, *433*
New York Illustrated, *534*
New York Journal, 661, *664*
New York school (of painting), 897,
    898
New York State Committee Against
    Discrimination in Housing, 915
New York Stock Exchange, 792, 992
  explosion at, 748
New York Sun, 350
New York Times, 324, 523, 625, 822,
    1016–17, 1018
New York Times v. Sullivan, 1000
New York Tribune, 449, 579, 747
New York University Law School, 696
New York World, 661
New York Zoological Society, 734
New Zealand, 347
Next!, 597
Nez Percés, 608–9
Ngo Dinh Diem (1901–1963), 946, 985
Nguyen That Thanh, *see* Ho Chi Minh
Niagara Falls, 742

Nicaragua, 493, 718, 719, 772, *772*, 843,
    1026, 1042
Niebuhr, Reinhold (1892–1971), 766
Nigeria, 896, 943, 1070
Nineteenth Amendment, 729
Ninety-Five Theses (Luther), 28
Ninigret II, *57*
Ninth Amendment, 259
nisei, 867
Nixon, E. D. (1899–1987), 956
Nixon, Pat (1912–1993), 960
Nixon, Richard (1913–1994), 908, 999,
    1009–20, *1012*, 1028, 1032, 1042,
    1054, 1109, 1117
  African-Americans and,
    1011–12
  in China, 1014–15, *1015*
  in debates with JFK, 960, 1081
  détente and, 1014–15, 1023
  in election of 1968, 1005
  in Moscow, 923, *925*, 937, 995
  New Federalism of, 1010
  in 1952 campaign, 939–40
  in 1960 campaign, 959, 960, 1009
  pardoned by Ford, 1023
  Pentagon Papers and, 1018
  resignation of, 1019
  Supreme Court and, 1011–13
  tape recordings of, 1109
  Vietnam War and, 1016–18
  Watergate scandal and, 1018–19
  welfare and, 1010
Nixon administration, 1005,
    1009–20
Nkrumah, Kwame (1909–1972), 876,
    943
Nobel Peace Prize, 717
*No More Grinding the Poor—But Liberty
    and the Rights of Man*, 342
nonaggression pact, 845
"Non-Freeholders," 348
Non-Intercourse Act (1809), 297
Norfolk, Va., 187
Noriega, Manuel Antonio (1934–),
    1049
Normandy, France, 850
*Norman's Chart of the Lower Mississippi
    River* (1858), *396*
Norris, George T. (1861–1944), 770
North, in election of 1824, 361
North, Frederick (1732–1792), 181,
    182
North, Oliver (1943–), 1042
North Africa, *840*, 845, 849–50
North America, 2, 6, 7, 8, 9, *44*, 51,
    89, 201
  Dutch in, 43–44
  early population of, 24, 31–33
  English colonization of, 48–85
  exploration of, 31–33
  Indians of, 9–14, *11*
  Irish emigration to, *55*
  map of, *153*
  map of east coast of, *108*
North American Free Trade
    Agreement (NAFTA), 1052, 1061,
    1061, 1062, 1064
North American Review, 608, 669
Northampton County, Pa., 184

North Atlantic Treaty Organization (NATO), 891, 895, 938, 1040, 1056
  Muammar Gadhafi overthrow and, 1121–22
North Briton, 180
North Carolina, 51, 144, 240, 288, 374, 902, 1012, 1117
  "second Reconstruction" in, 639
  textiles in, 645
  U.S. Constitution and, 257, *259*
  voting rights in, 210, 348, 353
North Carolina Agricultural and Technical State University, 965
North Carolina colony, 114, 134
  in American Revolution, 199
  French in, 156
  Loyalists in, 219, *220*
  Moravian Brethren in, 214
  Regulators in, 177
North Dakota, 602
  corporate mining in, 604
  entrance into Union of, 610
  population of, 679
Northern Alliance, 1090
Northern Ireland, 753, 1004, *1004*
Northern Pacific Railroad, 707
Northern Securities Company, 706
North Korea, 891–93, 1091, 1126
  creation of, 891–93
Northup, Solomon (1808–1863?), 409, 415, 418
North Vietnam, 986, 990, 1002, 1015, 1016
Northwest Ordinance (1787), 245, 358, 474, 485
Northwest Passage, 35, 41, 294
Notes on the State of Virginia (Jefferson), 212, 268
Nott, Josiah C. (1804–1873), *442*
Nova Scotia, 38, *38*, 158
  as haven for former slaves, 227, 228
NOW, *see* National Organization for Women
Noyes, John Humphrey (1811–1886), 427–28
NRA, *see* National Recovery Administration
NRPB, *see* National Resources Planning Board
NSC-68, 891, 1091
nuclear energy, 1024
nuclear weapons, 941–42, *942*, 1026, 1040, 1042, 1091, 1092, 1093, 1126
  cessation of tests of, 943, 971
  proposed international control of, 905
  Reagan and, 1040
  tests of, 906, *906*
  U.S. arsenal of, 942
  use in Vietnam of, 946
  U.S.-Soviet treaty on, 971
  see also atomic bomb; hydrogen bomb; missiles
Nueces River, 465
nullification crisis, *355*, 371–74, *372*, 375, 381
Nuremberg, Nazi trials at, 899

nurses, in Civil war, 529, *529*
Nye, Gerald P. (1892–1971), 845

Oakland, Calif., 875, 982
Oath of a Freeman, 70
Obama, Barack (1961–), 573, 1116–26, *1116, 1118, 1123*
  background of, 1115
  campaign spending of, 1126
  health-care law and, 1125
  Iraq War end and, 1121
  and Osama bin Laden's death, 1121
  speech to Middle East, 1095
  in 2008 election and campaign, *1087*, 1116–18
Obama administration, 1118–22
  and Afghanistan, 1121, 1125
  and Taliban, 1121
  torture banned by, 1121
  2008 financial crisis and, 1060
Obamacare:
  opposition to, 1125
  Supreme Court upholding of, 1125
Occupational Safety and Health Administration, 1010
Occupy Movement, 1123–24, *1124*
O'Connor, Sandra Day (1930–), 1039, 1108, 1109
Of Course He Wants to Vote the Democratic Ticket, 582
Office of Economic Opportunity, 978, 1010
Office of Price Administration, 852
Office of War Information (OWI), *843*, 857–58, *857*, 859, 864
Oglesby, Carl (1935–), 990
Oglethorpe, James (1696–1785), 134
O-Grab-Me, or, the American Snapping-Turtle, 296
Ohio, 242, 312, 1123
  120th Infantry of, 503
  population of, 315
  Supreme Court of, 994
Ohio Company (1750s), 156, 158
Ohio Company (1780s), 245
Ohio River, 38, 156, 307, *318*, 354
Ohio River Valley, 9, 91, 156, *157*, 222, 245, 265, 294, 311
  Indians of, 160
oil, 597, 604, 710, 715, 761, 764, 772, 814, 848, 854, 944, *945*, 1024, 1037, 1088, 1105, 1113
  Arab embargo on, 1021, *1021*
  BP Gulf of Mexico spill, 1119, *1119*
  Cold War and, 887, 888
  environment and, 999
  Gulf War and, 1050
  G. W. Bush and, 1088
  highways and, 929, 941
  in Iran, 943, 946
  Japan and U.S., 845, 846
  -producing regions, 772, *1098*
  and Teapot Dome scandal, 770
  see also Standard Oil Company
Oklahoma, 609, 612, 613, 1074
  in Dust Bowl, 807
  Indians removed to, 609
  population of, 679

socialism in, 690
  Trail of Tears in, 376
Oklahoma City, Okla., terrorist attack in, 748, 1077, *1078*
Old Left, 982–83
Old Lights, 151
Old Northwest, 312, 374
Old Plantation Home, The (Currier and Ives), *579*
Old Southwest, 313
Old State House Bell, *425*, 441
Olive Branch Petition (1775), 186
Oliver, Andrew (1706–1774), 171, 175
Oliver, James (1725–1783), *175*, 748
Oliver family, *118*
Olmsted, Frederick Law (1822–1903), 416
Olney, Richard (1835–1917), 641
Olympic Games, 1004, 1027
Oñate, Juan de (ca. 1551–ca. 1626), 33–34
"On Civil Disobedience" (Thoreau), 466
One Big Union, 691
Oneida community, 427–28
Oneida County, New York, 334
Oneidas, 12, 222
O'Neill, John, 689
"one percent, the," power of, 1124
One World (Willkie), 874, 895
Only Way to Handle It, The, 783
Onondagas, 12
Ontario, 40
"On the Equality of the Sexes" (Murray), 281
On the Origin of Species (Darwin), 621
On the Road (Kerouac), 949
OPEC (Organization of Petroleum Exporting Countries), 1021
Opechancanough, 60
Open Door policy, 665
Open Housing Act (1968), 1003
Operation Desert Storm, 1050
Operation Dixie, 901
Operation Iraqi Freedom, 1093
  see also Iraq War
Operation Wetback, 911
Orange, Fort, 41
Orangeburg, S.C., *967*
Orange County, Calif., 953, 975, 1066
oranges, 925
Oration on the Beauties of Liberty (Allen), 183–84
Ordinance of 1784, 243
Ordnance Bureau, Confederate, 508
Oregon, 608, 609, 780, 785, 799, 986
  Ku Klux Klan in, 781
  prisoners in, 1072
  women's rights in, 704
Oregon Territory, 294, 314
  blacks barred from, 339
  Great Britain and, 459, *462*
  migration to, 459, *462*
  U.S.-British dispute over, 464–65
Oregon Trail, 608
Organization Man, The (White), 947
Organization of African American Unity, 981
Organization of Petroleum Exporting Countries (OPEC), 1021

Osceola, 376
Oslo, Norway, accords in, 1055
Ostend Manifesto, 493
O'Sullivan, John L. (1813–1895), 329, 469
Oswald, Lee Harvey (1939–1963), 972
Other America, The (Harrington), 977, 983, 1105
Otis, Harrison James (1725–1783), 173, 224, 232, 287
Otis, James (1725–1783), *175*, 748
Ottawa Indians, 160
Ottoman Empire, in World War I, 721, 750, 752
Our Bodies, Ourselves, 1004
Our Country (Strong), 660
Our Friend (Shahn), 862
Our Lady of Guadalupe, 997
Outdoor Recreation League, 700
Outer Banks, N.C., *12*
"outwork" system, 321
Ovando, Nicolás de (ca. 1451–ca. 1511), 21
Overseas Highway, 806, *806*
Overseer Doing His Duty, An, 127
overtime pay, 824
Owen, Robert (1771–1858), 429, *429*, 447
Owen, Robert Dale (1801–1877), *429*
Owenites, 429–30
Owens Valley, Calif., aqueduct at, 708
Oxford, Miss., 966
Oxford University, *1014*
ozone layer, 961
  depletion of, 1047

Pacific islands, 906
  and Native Americans, 6
Pacific Northwest, 799
Pacific Ocean, 23, 24–25, 35, 294
pacifism:
  abolitionists and, 439
  Quaker, 93
  World War I and, 722
  World War II and, 845
Packard, Vance (1914–1996), 947
PACs (political action committees), 1126
Padmore, George (1903–1959), 875–76
Page, Horace (1833–1890), 654–55
Paine, Thomas (1737–1809), 167, *186*, *191*, 195, 206, 207, 208, 209, 224, 280, 732, 736, 1033, 1036, 1077
  Common Sense and, 186–87, 188, 191
Pakistan, 896, 943, 1126
  Osama bin Laden killed in, 1121
  war on terror in, 1122
Pale, 51
Palestine, 752, 1003, 1055, 1087, 1092
  terrorism and, 1087
Palestine Liberation Organization, 1055
Palestinian Authority, 1055
Palin, Sarah (1964–), 1117
Palmer, A. Mitchell (1872–1936), 746, 748
Palmer, Frances F. (1812–1876), (1812–1876), *600*
Palmer Raids, 748

Palmerston, Henry John Temple, Viscount, 532
Pan-African Conference, 751
Pan-African Congress, 875
Panama, 23, 717, *717*, 1049
Panama Canal, 715, 717, *717*, 1026
  construction of, 717
Panama Canal Company, 717
Pan-American Exposition, 706
Panic of 1819, 355–56
Panic of 1837, 380
Panic of 1907, 711
Papacy, 50, 52
Papua New Guinea, 1083
Paradise Lost (Milton), *119*
Paraguay, 506
Paris, 1003, 1004
  African-Americans in, 1016
  German occupation of, 845
  liberation of, 850
  Vietnam peace agreement in, 1017
Paris, Treaty of (1763), 158
Paris, Treaty of (1783), 200, 221, 222
Paris Commune, 506
Park Forest, Ill., *947*
Parks, Rosa (1913–2005), 950, 954, *954*, 955, *1116*
Parliament, British, 49, 80, 103, 109, 140, 148, *192*, 259
  army of, 82
  Bill of Rights and, 102
  Charles I's conflict with, 80
  colonists' desire for representation in, 173, 224
  first Navigation Act and, 83
  forces in Maryland colony, 82–83
  taxation on America by, 171, 172–76, *174*, 187–90
  see also House of Commons, British; House of Lords, British
Parsons, Albert (1849–1887), 630
Parsons, Lucy (1853?–1942), 631
parties, political, 366, 367–69, 477–79
  newspapers and, 368, 369
  origins of U.S., 273, 277–78
  patronage and, 368
  spoils system and, 368
  views of Van Buren of, 365–66
  see also specific parties
Passing of Great Race, The (Grant), 734
PATCO, 1037
Paterson, N.J.:
  industrial city planned for, 274
  manufacturing in, 591, 1022
  strike in, 694
  Thomas Rodgers and, 338
Pathé film company, 762
Pat Lyon at the Forge, *337*
patronage, political parties and, 368
Patrons of Husbandry, *see* Grange
"patroons," 43
Patten, Simon (1852–1922), 653, 688
Patterson v. McLean Credit Union, 1071
Patuxet Indians, 67
Paul, Alice (1885–1977), 729, 766–67, 1029
Paul III, Pope (1468–1549), 29
Pawtucket, R.I., 319, 322

Paxton Boys, march on Philadelphia by, 161
Payne-Aldrich Tariff (1909), 709
Peabody Conservatory of Music, *787*
Peace Corps, 969, 978
Peace of Paris (1763), *159*, 160
Peale, Charles Willson (1741–1827), *234*, *247*
Pearl Harbor, 510, 661
  Japanese attack on, 757, 847–48, *847*, 857, 865, 867, 972, 1091
Pearson, Levi, 953
Peckham, Rufus (1838–1909), 624
Pelosi, Nancy, 1110
Pemberton, John C. (1814–1881), 537
Pendergast, Tom (1872–1945), 888
penicillin, 931
peninsulares, 26
Penn, William (1644–1718), 92–94, *92*, *93*, 111, *114*, 161
Penn family, *114*, 118, 146
Penn school, 540
Pennsylvania, 12, 229, 616, 1024, *1025*
  coat of arms of, *210*
  constitution of, 208, *208*, 209, 215
  and election of 1796, 284
  in election of 1858, 489
  religious laws in, 371
  voting rights in, 353
  Whiskey Rebellion and, 278
Pennsylvania, University of, 441
Pennsylvania Abolition Society, 288
Pennsylvania Assembly, *150*
Pennsylvania colony, 2, 110, 111, *111*, 112, 114, 118, 135, 138, 156, 158, *158*, 161
  American Revolution and, 207–8, 219
  assembly in, 146
  elections in, *145*
  establishment of, *93*
  freemen in, 94
  government in, 93–94, 144
  Holy Experiment in, 161
  immigration to, 54, 110
  Loyalists in, 219
  Native Americans and, 161
  population of, 114
  religious freedom in, 102, 110, 210
  social order in, 93
  standard of living in, 116
  views on independence of, 186
Pennsylvania Gazette, 147
Pennsylvania Magazine, *191*
Pennsylvania Railroad, 594
Pennsylvania Steelworkers outside the Local Headquarters of the Steel Workers Organizing Committee (Rothstein), *811*
"penny press," 350
Pentagon, 991
  September 11 attack on, 1087
Pentagon Papers, 1017, 1018, 1019
"peonage" laws, 742
People's Convention, 348
People's Party, *see* Populist Party
People's Party Paper, 638, *639*
People's Temple cult, 993–94
People the Best Governors, The (anon.), 208

Pequot Indians, 76–77, *76*, 222, 299, 1074
Pequot War, 76–77
perestroika, 1042
perfectionism, 433
Perkins, Frances (1882–1965), 802, 811, 818, 825, 826, 831, 847
Perkins, George (1862–1920), 691
Perot, Ross (1930–), 1052
Perry, Matthew (1794–1858), 472
Perry, Oliver H. (1785–1819), 300
Perry, Rick (1950–), 1124
Persac, Marie Adrien (1823–1873), *398*
Pershing, John J. (1860–1948), 725
Persian Gulf, 1050
  Carter Doctrine and, 1027
Peru, 8, 24, 25, *30*, 31, 33, *130*, 359
Pesotta, Rose (1896–1965), 834
"pet banks," 379, 381
Petersburg, Battle of, 537, 541
Petitions of Slaves to the Massachusetts Legislature, 231
Phantom Public, The (Lippmann), 769
Philadelphia, Miss., 973, 1032
Philadelphia, Pa., 10, 115–16, *115*, 158, 218, 322, 341, *368*, 830
  in American Revolution, 195–97
  boycott of Britain in, 179, 183
  Constitutional celebrations in, 239
  Constitution ratified in, 239
  Freedom Train in, 885
  population of, 116
  shipbuilding in, 239
  skilled workers of, 116
  slaves in, 135
  trade with West Indies, 116
Philadelphia Mechanic's Advocate, 351
Philadelphia Plan, 1012
Philadelphia Society for the Promotion of Agriculture, *276*
Philadelphia State House, *249*
Philip, King (Wampanoag chief; d. 1676), 87, 376
Philip II, king of Spain (1556–1598), 33
Philippines, 23, 25, 662, 670, 672, 708, 1015, 1026
  immigrants from, 604, 661, 783, 866
  independence of, 896
  returned to Spain, 158
  U.S. acquisition of, *635*, 636, 664–69, 715
  in World War II, 848, *848*, 876
  see also Filipinos
Philippine War, 666–67, 672, 732
Philipse, Frederick (1626–1702), 90
Philipse family, 178, 221
Phillips, Wendell (1811–1884), 445, 545, 736
Phillipsburgh Proclamation, 226–27
Phillips County, Ark., race riot in, 744
Phoenix, Ariz., 927, 1022
phonograph, 593, 762
photography:
  in Civil War, 507
  in Great Depression, 833
  in Second New Deal, 819
Picasso, Pablo (1881–1973), 696
Pickett, George E. (1825–1875), 537
Pickford, Mary (1893–1979), 775

Piedmont, 132
Pierce, Franklin (1804–1869), 477, 479, 484, 493
Pierce, George (1811–1884), 522
Pietists, 110
Pike, James, *185*
Pike, James S. (1811–1882), 580
Pilgrims, 41, 66–67, *67*
Pillow, Fort, 519, 545
Pinchback, Pinckney B. S. (1837–1921), 573
Pinchot, Gifford (1865–1946), 708, 709
Pinckney, Charles C. (1746–1825), 252, 297
Pinckney, Thomas (1750–1823), 284
Pinckney's Treaty (Treaty of San Lorenzo) (1795), 293
Pingree, Hazen (1840–1901), 699–700
Pinkerton Detective Agency, 635
Pinochet, Augusto (1915–2006), 1015
pirates, 33, 38
  Barbary Coast, 95
Pitt, William (1708–1778), 158, 160
Pittsburgh, Pa.:
  manufacturing in, 591
  September 11 terrorist attack in, 1087
Pittsburgh Courier, 826, 871, 876
Pius IX, Pope (1792–1878), *482*
Pizarro, Francisco (ca. 1475–1541), 24
Plains Indians, 605–8, 610
Plains of Abraham, 158
Plain Truth (Chalmers), 189
Plantation Burial (Antrobus), *415*
Planter, 574
planter class, 395–96
planters, plantations, 51, 83, 118, *137*, 139, *292*, 317, 347, 395–96, 408, 409, 474, 540, 572, 575, *579*, 645, 646
  in California, 604
  in Caribbean, 666
  cotton, 317, *410*, 463, 540
  as dominating South, 393, 394
  emancipated slaves and, *553*
  in Hawaii, 670, 783
  and national affairs, 385
  post-Civil War, 554, 555, 556
  Protestants and, 83
  rice, 409
  slavery on, 6, 20, 92–93, 118, 133
  sugar, 96–97, *96*, 132, *398*, 409, 419, 473, 667, 681
  tobacco, 118, 132–33
  of the West Indies, 106
Planters Bank of Savannah, 379
Platt, Orville H. (1827–1905), 664
Platt Amendment (1901), 664, 843
Playboy, 948, 996
Pleasants, John H. (1797–1846), 397
Pledge of Allegiance, 661, 898, 934, *1065*
Plessy, Homer (1858?–1925), 650
Plessy v. Ferguson, 650, *650*, 951, 953
PLO, *see* Palestine Liberation Organization
"plumbers" unit, Nixon's, 1018
plumbing, indoor, 924
Plumer, William (1759–1850), 356

"plundering time", in Maryland colony, 83
pluralism, 834, 864, 865–66, 897, 977
    see also diversity
Plymouth Colony, 66–67, 68, 104
Plymouth Harbor, 49
Pocahontas (ca. 1596–1617), 56, 59–60, 59
Pocanets, 299
Poems on Slavery (Longfellow), 498
Poinier, Arthur, 864
Poland, 749, 879, 887
    German invasion of, 845
    immigrants from, 680
Polish-Americans, 683, 747, 785, 864, 864, 910
political action committee (PACs), 1126
Political Chart of the United States, 483
Polk, James K. (1795–1849), 381, 416, 463–66, 485
    as slaveholder, 463
Polling, The (Hogarth), 142
Pollock, Jackson (1912–1956), 897, 898
pollution, 961, 1010
    see also environmentalism
polygamy, in Utah, 605, 703
Ponce de León, Juan (1460–1521), 31
Pontchartrain, Lake, 1103
Pontiac (ca. 1720–1769), 160, 163
Pontiac's Rebellion, 160, 161, 163
Ponzi schemes, 1114
Poor People's March, 1003
Poor Richard's Almanack, 149
Pope, John (1822–1892), 509
Popé (d. 1688), 34, 35
"popery," see Catholics, Catholicism
"Popery Truly Displayed" (Las Casas), 52
Popular Front, 832, 834, 835, 863, 911
popular sovereignty, 473, 487
population:
    of African-Americans, 232, 267, 786
    of aging in America, 1082
    in agriculture, 925
    in American colonies, 2–3, 61–62, 106–7, 132
    of Barbados, 96
    black, of English Caribbean, 96
    of Boston, 115
    of buffalo, 608
    of California, 154, 460, 469, 470, 471
    of Chicago, 591
    of Civil War border states, 513
    of Confederacy, 504
    of early South America, 24, 31
    of England, 53, 54
    of Florida, 154
    of France compared with England, 54
    of free blacks, 406, 407, 407
    growth of, 1022
    of Hiroshima, 877
    of Houston, 854
    of immigrants, 324
    of Indians, 24, 25, 111
    of Indians, decline in, 10, 24, 29, 34
    of Jews in America, 503
    of London, 140
    of Los Angeles, 155, 764

    of Louisiana, 155
    of Massachusetts, 67
    of Mexican Cession, 468
    of Mexico, 24, 31
    of Mexico City, Mexico, 115
    of Middle Border, 602
    of Native Americans, 600
    of New England, 87, 121
    of New England Indians, 73
    of New France, 38
    of New Mexico, 34, 35, 153, 460
    of New Netherland, 44
    of New Orleans, 294, 393, 854
    of New York, 90, 358
    of New York City, 115
    of Pennsylvania, 114
    of Philadelphia, 116
    rise of, 678
    of San Francisco, 470
    of slaves, 101, 132, 135, 154, 223, 229, 232, 239, 289, 294, 357, 372, 385, 390, 392, 393, 516
    of Southern Indians, 374
    of Spanish America, 26
    of Texas, 153–54, 460
    of Union, 504
    of United States, 239, 307, 315, 931, 931, 1011
    of urban centers, 319
    of Virginia, 62, 358
    of West, 298
    in Western states, 315
    West Indies English, 96
    west of Appalachian Mountains, 315
    world, 31
Populist movement, 257, 636–44, 687, 792, 814
    agriculture and, 587, 636–37
Populist (People's) Party, 637–44, 637, 638, 639, 640, 648–49, 656, 689, 711
    Bryan in, 643
    depression of 1893 and, 641
    election of 1892 and, 640
    election of 1896 and, 644
    industrial workers and, 636, 637, 641–43
    labor and, 638
    platform of 1892 of, 638
    Pullman strike and, 641
    racial alliances of, 638
    supporters of, 637
    woman suffrage and, 703
    women in, 639–40
Porter, James (b. 1828), 549
Port Huron, Mich., 984, 989
Port Huron Statement, 975, 984, 989
Portia (Abigail Adams), 205
Portland, Oreg., 799, 854
Portrait of John and Elizabeth Lloyd Cadwalader and Their Daughter Anne (Peale), 234
Port Royal, S.C., 139
Portsmouth, N.H., 78
Portugal, 19, 20, 22, 28, 49, 97, 943
    loses Brazil to Dutch, 41
    navigation of, 18–19, 19
    and West Africa, 19–20
Posse Comitatus, 1077

Post, Louis (1849–1928), 748
Postal Service, U.S., 775
Potomac River, 991
Potsdam conference, 878, 942
poultry, 925
Poverty Point, 9
poverty rate, 924, 978, 1022
    of African-Americans, 1120
    of Native Americans, 1074
Powderly, Terence V. (1849–1924), 625, 625
Powell, Colin (1937–), 1051, 1051, 1092–93, 1100
Powell, John Wesley, 603
Powell, Lewis F. (1907–1998), 1013
Powhatan (ca. 1550–1618), 59–60, 60, 76
Poyntz, Juliet Stuart (1886–1937?), 766
preemptive war principle, 1091
Presbyterians, 109, 110, 211, 777, 1028
    American Revolution and, 214
    in Great Awakening, 150, 151
Presidential Citizens Medal, 958
Presidential Medal of Freedom, 869
Presidential Reconstruction, 563
presidents, presidency, U.S., 248, 249–50
    expansion of powers of, 804, 809, 1099–1100, 1109
    as "Free World" leader, 888–89
    veto power of, 379, 565–66, 902, 911
    see also specific presidents
President's Daughter, The (Britton), 770
presidios, 153
Presley, Elvis (1935–1977), 948, 948
press, 279, 466, 468, 554, 654, 769, 770, 855, 858, 869, 870, 886, 904, 1000, 1043–44, 1058, 1101
    African-American, 826, 869, 870, 876, 881, 886, 954
    "alternative," 351
    attack on Washington by, 280
    circulation of, 350
    in Civil War, 507, 509, 520, 523
    colonial, 147
    Democratic, 369, 382, 523
    in election of 1830, 368
    in election of 1928, 790
    in election of 1936, 822, 823
    and FDR, 823
    in Great Depression, 793
    growth of, 280, 350
    Iraq War and, 1093
    Philippine War and, 666
    politics and, 368, 369
    during Reconstruction, 579–80
    Republican (Jeffersonian), 280, 286
    Republican (modern), 509, 523, 631
    rise of, 350
    and Sea Islands, 539
    Sedition Act and, 732
    sensationalism in, 350
    as sexist, 994
    slavery and antislavery, 401, 420, 421, 441, 443, 444, 452, 473
    on tolerance, 785
    Underground, 992
    women's rights and, 449, 452
    in World War I, 727

    as "yellow press," 661, 662
    see also freedom, of the press
"Price of Free World Victory, The" (Wallace), 861
prices, control of, 217–18, 217
primogeniture, 122–23, 217
Prince Edwards County, Va., desegregation in, 957
printing press, 65, 69
Prioleau, George W., 670
prisons, 433, 1071–73, 1071, 1072
    African-Americans in, 1072
    debt and, 342
    labor from, 645, 645
    population of, 1071–72, 1072
privacy, right to, 776, 786, 1002
private property, 426
    shunned by Shakers, 427
    in Utopian societies, 429
Problem We All Live With, The (Rockwell), 958
Procession of Victuallers, 368
Proclamation of 1763, 160–61, 173, 221
Procter & Gamble, 768
profits, see corporations, and profits
Progress and Poverty (George), 626, 627
Progressive era, 676–713, 700, 704
    women in, 730
Progressive Movement, The (DeWitt), 678
Progressive Party, 709, 771, 817, 905
    African-Americans barred from convention by, 741
    social agenda of, 710
progressivism, 387, 587, 677–78, 795, 999, 1024, 1033, 1036, 1064
    ACLU and, 776
    and African-Americans, 741, 742
    Alfred Landon and, 823
    civil liberties and, 733
    consumerism and, 683, 684
    disintegration of, 769, 770
    FDR and, 802
    Harding and, 753, 770
    Herbert Hoover and, 788
    immigration and, 679, 679, 680, 734, 735–38, 739, 783–84
    as international movement, 698–99
    Native Americans and, 698
    politics in, 698–705
    presidents in, 706–12
    Prohibition and, 730–31
    race and, 734
    Simon Patten and, 688
    socialism and, 689, 690, 691
    varieties of, 688–89
    women's rights in, 695–97
    World War I and, 725, 726–32, 748, 753, 756, 772
Progress of the Century, The, 595
Prohibition, 629, 730–31, 730, 731, 756, 760, 762, 770, 778–79, 778, 785, 789, 801, 809
    see also temperance
Prohibitionist Party, 617
propaganda, in World War I, 727, 728, 738
Propagation Society, The - More Free than Welcome, 482
Prophetstown, 299

Proposition 13, 1032
Proposition 14, 974–75
Proposition 187, 1075, *1075*
proprietorship, 2, 69, 92, 103, 104, 118,
    134, 135
    Maryland as, 64
Prospective Scene in the City of Oaks, A,
    578
Prostrate State, The (Pike), 580
Protestant Association, 104
Protestant-Catholic-Jew (Herberg), 912,
    935
Protestants, *30*, 150, 164, 370, 429,
    432, 446, 469, 629, 707, 739, 780,
    784, 823, 908, 934, *935*, 959, 960,
    1028, 1030
    and Al Smith, 789
    in American colonies, 101, 104, 107,
        109, 110
    in Amsterdam, 41
    Dissenters, and, 71, 102
    in England, 50–51, 81, 83, 140
    evangelical, 482, 1028, 1030
    French, 33, 38
    fundamentalist, 777–79
    immigration to South Carolina
        of, 134
    Indians and, 3, 28
    and Irish immigrants, 326
    in Maryland colony, 64, 83, 101, 104
    modernism and, 777, 778–79
    in New York colony, 42–43, 91
    planter class, 83
    Prohibition and, 730
    slavery and, 137
    social reform and, 628–29
    and spread of Protestantism, 52
    tax support of, 213
    voting rights and, 210–11
    women preachers allowed by, *338*
    see also Christianity; *specific*
        denominations
protests, against Vietnam War, 920
Providence, R.I., 682
Prussia, 158, 364
PTAs (parent-teacher associations),
    1081
public housing, 933, *933*
Publick Occurrences, Both Foreign and
    Domestick, 147
public opinion, opinion polls, 906,
    937, 1014, 1030, 1074, 1079, 1081,
    1083, 1097, 1103, 1110, 1113
    public relations and, 769, 857, 870,
        871
Public Opinion (Lippmann), 769
public relations, 728, 738, 766
    and public opinion, 769, 857, 870,
        871
    see also Bernays, Edward
Public Utilities Act, 700
Public Whipping of Slaves in Lexington,
    Missouri, in 1856, A, 411
Public Works Administration (PWA),
    806, *806*
"Publius," 254
Puccini, Giacomo (1858–1924), 472
Puck, 597, 616, 635, 661, 715
Pueblo Bonita, 10, *10*

Pueblo Indians, 10, 14, 34–35, 101, 123,
    153, 460
Pueblo Revolt, 34–35, *35*, 37
pueblos, 10
Puerto Rico, 31, *635*, 662, 667, 670, 672,
    740, 998
    as commonwealth, 670
    migration from, 933–34, *934*, 1068
    U.S. acquisition of, *635*, 636, 661,
        664, 666, 715
Pujo, Arsène (1861–1939), 765
Pulitzer, Joseph (1847–1911), 661
Pullman, Ill., strike in, 641, *641*, 656,
    690
Punch, 514
Pure Food and Drug Act (1906), 680,
    707
Puritans, Puritanism, 43, 53, 66–67,
    104–5, 172, 432
    beliefs of, 65–66, 68–70
    emigration to New England, 65–66
    families of, 68, *68*
    Indians and, 73, 76, 87, 1074
    intolerance in, 70–71, 82
    liberties of, 70
    rise of, 64–66
    sermons of, 65
    slavery and, 70, 1074
    women's role in, 68, 77
    worldly success as viewed by, 65, 79
Putting the Screws on Him, 706
PWA, *see* Public Works
    Administration
pyramids, Egyptian, 9

quadrant, 19
Quaker Meeting, A, 94
Quaker Oats Company, 592, *982*
Quakers, 82, 92–94, *94*, 105, 110, 129–
    30, 144, 161, 219, 225, 233
    Gabriel's Rebellion and, 289
    liberty of, 93–94
    as pacifists, 93
    in Pennsylvania Assembly, 146
    slavery repudiated by, 93, 435, 446,
        447
"qualified Monarchy," 81
Quayle, Dan (1947–), 1043
Quebec, 38, 49, 158, 174, *174*
Quebec Act (1774), 182, *182*, 211
Queen Anne's War, 157
Quicksilver Messenger Service, *991*
Quincy, Edmund (1808–1877), 442
Quito, Ecuador, 25
"quitrents," 64

Rabelais, François (ca. 1494–1553?), 775
race, racism, 834, 864, 865, 870, 874,
    875–76, 897, 900, 904, 907, *968*,
    969, 976, 982, 994, 1044, 1077,
    1105
    Americanism vs., 834, 863, 977
    Andrew Johnson and, 563
    and class, 352–53
    Hollywood and, 897
    integration and, *574*
    and Japanese-Americans, 757,
        866–67, *866*, 867–68
    lack of opportunities and, 338–39

law and, 783–84
    Nixon and, 1011–12
    as pillar of slavery, 398
    and post-World War II civil rights,
        903–4
    progressivism and, 734
    as "race problem," 734, 740
    Reconstruction and, 577
    riots and, 338, 648, *655*, 865, 869,
        979–80, *980*, 1073
    social construction of, 784
    in South Africa, 896
    theories of, 468–69
    by U.S. government, 830
    see also segregation
Races and Racism (Benedict), 864
radar, 853, 924
radiation, 877, 906, *906*, 943
Radical Division, Justice Department,
    748
Radical Reconstruction, 562–76
Radical Republicans, 514, 538, 541,
    564–65, *564*, 566–67, 579, 638
radio, 756, 760, 762, 763, *763*, 779, 857,
    858
    fundamentalism on, 815
    religion and, 815, *815*, 935
Railroad Administration, 726
railroads, 168, 308, 311, 319, 325, 379,
    396, 408, *459*, *479*, *480*, 558, 591,
    593, 594, 602, 616, 649, 683, 686,
    689, 700, 709, 710, 711, 771
    agriculture and, 603, 636
    Chinese immigrants and, 654
    in Civil War, 504, 507, 524, 531
    Great Depression and, 794
    Indians and, 611
    labor and, 641–42
    land granted to, 590, 602, *602*
    lobbyists of, 616
    and mileage built, *591*
    network of, *592*
    in Northwest, 479
    Populists and, 638
    prison labor and, 645
    protests against, 618
    rate discrimination and, 623
    rates regulated, 707
    in Reconstruction, 575
    segregation and, 649
    Socialist party and, 709
    Southern, 393, 395
    strikes, *591*, 624–25, *625*, 629, 770,
        902
    transcontinental, 477, 494, 524,
        582, 591
    trusts, 594, 706
    westward expansion and, 604–5,
        604, 610
"Railsplitter, The," *468*
Rainsborough, Thomas (ca. 1610–
    1648), 81
Raleigh, N.C., 965, *967*
Raleigh, Walter (1554–1618), *12*, 51, 52
Ramsay, David (1749–1815), 260
Randolph, A. Philip (1889–1979), 870,
    915, 968, *979*, 980
Randolph, Edmund (1753–1813),
    267

Randolph, John (1773–1833), 187, 297,
    397
Randolph, Richard, 228, 407
Rankin, Jeanette (1880–1973), 729, 847
Rapidan River, *508*
Rapp, George (1757–1847), 429
Rapp-Coudert Committee, 836
Rasul v. Bush, 1108
Rauschenbusch, Walter (1861–1918),
    629
RCA Victor, 762
Readjustor movement, 648
"re-Africanization," 136
Reagan, Nancy (1921–), 1033, *1039*
Reagan, Ronald (1911–2004), 864,
    908, *1009*, 1027, 1033–44, *1033*,
    1052, 1056, 1076, 1088, 1090,
    1106, 1118
    background of, 1033, 1036
    Cold War and, 1040–41, 1042
    conservatives and, 1039–40
    in election of 1980, 920, 1032, 1033
    Gorbachev and, 1042, *1042*
    as host of *General Electric Theater*, 929
    inequality under, 1037–38, 1043
    Iran-Contra affair and, 1042, 1043
    labor and, 1037
    legacy of, 1042–43
Reaganomics, 1037
Reagan Revolution, 1033–44
real estate:
    deals, 1038
    speculation, 1038
reaper, 319, *481*
Reason, Charles L. (1818–1893), 443
Reasonableness of Christianity, The
    (Locke), 149
Rebel without a Cause (movie), 947
recessions:
    of 1974–75, 1022
    of 1991, 1051, 1052, 1059
    of 2001, 1083, 1101–2
    of 2007, 1111, 1112–13, *1112*, 1120
    African-Americans and, 1120
    Reaganomics and, 1037
reconquista, 21
Reconstruction, 386–87, 389, 416, 518,
    540–41, 545, 548–85, *548*, *551*,
    559, *581*, 586, 609, 621, 638, 1079
    African-Americans in, 386–87, 548–
        57, 558–59, 565–67, *566*, 568–71,
        569, 572–74, 645, 646, 648, 649,
        651–52, 741, 757, 842, 902
    battle over, 563
    black officeholders during, 573–74
    "black supremacy" during, 577
    Johnson's policies in, 556, 562–66,
        565, 566–67
    Ku Klux Klan in, 650, 741, 781
    overthrow of, 577–83, *832*
    public schools in, 575, *576*, 577
    radical, 562–76
    railroads built in, 575
    Redeemers and, 645
    segregation in, 649–51
    violence in, 577–78
    white farmers in, 557–59, *558*
    women's rights and, 570–71
    see also Presidential Reconstruction;

Radical Reconstruction; Second Reconstruction
Reconstruction Act (1867), 566–67, 572
Reconstruction Finance Corporation, 794
Red Cross, 869, *869*
Red Dawn (movie), *1040*
Redeemers, 582, 645
redemptioners, 110
   see also indentured servitude
Red Horse, *610*
Red Jacket (1750–1830), *263*
Red Line Agreement, 772
redlining, *830*
Red Menace, The (movie), 897, *897*
Red Monday, 1000
Red Power, 998
Red Scare, 258, 748, 759, 789, 913
Red Square, *1042*
Red Sticks (Creeks), 300, 376
Redstockings Manifesto, 1034
Reed, Esther (1746–1780), 232
Reed, Joseph (1741–1785), 232
Reed, Philip, 459
Reeder, Andrew H. (1807–1864), 484
Reedy, William M., 696
reform, 424–57, 564, 702–3, *704*, 710, 836–37
   freedom and, 432–33
   in Gilded Age, 618–22, 628
   and immigrants, 739–40, *739*
   maternalist, 704–5, 766, 817
   middle class and, 626
   and Prohibition, 730–31, *730*
   Protestants and, 628–29
   religion and, 430–31, 628–29
   segregation and, 741
   sexual freedom and, 768
   temperance and, 431, 628
   utopian communities and, 426–30
   World War I and, 723
Reform Act (1884), 615
Reformation, 28, 50, 52, 65
Reform Bureau, 628
reform schools, *433*
Regents of the University of California v. Bakke, 1013, 1108
Regulators, 176–77, 199
regulatory power, 770
   rise of U.S. government, 706–7, 803–4, 824, 837, 977, 978
Rehnquist, William (1924–2005), 1076, 1109
Reid, Wallace (1892–1923), 775
religion, 715, 756, 1075–76, 1082, 1087
   African, 136–37
   of African-Americans, rise in, 550–51, *553*
   and attempted conversions of Indians, 3, 12, 28–31, *29*, 33, 34, 40–41
   Bible and, 28, 65, 68, 70–71
   Bible Commonwealth and, 70, 71, 77, 104
   Civil War and, 522–23, *522*
   Cold War and, 912, 934–35
   communism and, 912
   as conflict source, 1106–7, *1107*
   counterculture and, 992–94, *993*

divisiveness of, 1106–7, *1107*
Enlightenment and, 149, 150
and founding of Connecticut, 72
fundamentalist, 777–79
in Maryland, 64, 83
media and, 815, *815*
missionaries and, 28–30, *29*, *30*, 33, 34–35, 40–41, 58, 147, 154–55, 156, 266
Native American, 12, 14, *15*, 136
and Prohibition, 730
radio and, 815, *815*
reform and, 430–31
Salem witch trials and, 105–6
and separation of church and state, 110, 167, 212–15
social reform and, 628–29
temperance and, 628
Thomas Jefferson and, 150, 212, 213–14
witchcraft and, 70, 105–6
   see also Great Awakening, Great Awakening, Second; *specific denominations*
Religious Camp Meeting, 334
religious freedom, 257, 258, 873, 1095
   in American colonies, 2, 3, 103, 110
   in Carolina, 92
   communism and, 934–35
   in early U.S., 150, 210–15, 324
   in England, 80–81
   First Amendment and, 257, *259*
   Four Freedoms and, 841, 855, 881
   Fourteenth Amendment and, 786
   fundamentalism vs., 779
   in Maryland colony, 64, 104
   Muslims and, 1107, *1107*
   in New England colonies, 2, 104
   in New Netherland, 42–43
   in New York City, *211*
   in New York colony, 90, 91
   in Pennsylvania, 208
   in Pennsylvania colony, 93
   in Rhode Island, 72
   September 11 terrorist attacks and, 1090, 1091
   Universal Declaration of Human Rights and, 900
   voting rights and, 211–14
   see also diversity; pluralism
religious right, 1028–29, 1033, 1043
   see also Christian Right
"Remember the Maine," *662*
Remington, Frederic (1861–1909), *614*, *664*
Reno, Janet (1938–), 1052
Reno, Milo, 792
repartimiento system, 31
"Report on Economic Conditions in the South," 836
Report on Manufactures (Hamilton), 274
reproductive rights, 996, 1002, 1004, 1118
republicanism, 141–42, 143
Republicanism, Christian, 215
"republican motherhood," 339–40

Republican Party (Jeffersonian), 277–78, 280, 284, 287, 299, 354, 357, 366
   in election of, 1824, 364
   in Missouri Compromise, 358
   and national bank, 169
   platform of, 279
   press of, 280, 286
Republican Party (modern), 386–87, 486–92, 496–92, 515, 530, 531, 615, 616, *618*, 627, 639, 642, 643–44, 769–70, 783, 831, 834, 837, 846, 855, 891, 905, 909, 911, 938, 940–41, 973, 976, 986, 990, 1010, 1024, 1043, 1047, 1054, 1060, 1075, 1102–3, 1110, 1117, 1118, 1119, 1122–23, *1123*
   as anti-immigrant, 1075, 1088
   as antislavery, 483–84
   black members of, 648
   black voters and, 572–73
   in campaign of 1960, 959, 960
   Christianity aligned with, 1009, 1035, 1075–76
   Clinton and, 1052
   conservatives in, 943
   Contract with America, 1053, *1054*
   corruption in, 616
   Eisenhower and, 938–41
   in election of 1896, 643, *644*
   in election of 1900, *673*
   in election of 1928, 789
   in election of 1936, 823
   in election of 1946, 902
   in election of 1952, 938, 939, *939*
   in election of 1968, 1005
   in election of 1972, 1018
   in election of 1992, 1052
   in election of 2000, 1079
   and Equal Rights Amendment, 1032
   high tariff supported by, 618
   Indians and, 611
   industrialists and, 625
   Johnson's impeachment and, 567–68
   Ku Klux Klan and, 781
   Liberal, 579–80, 621
   liberal reformers' split from, 621
   and Lincoln's nomination, 494
   in 1916 elections, 723
   in 1920s, 769–70
   1964 convention of, 974, 1033
   1984 convention of, *1009*, *1033*
   1992 convention of, 1052, 1075
   North and, 643–44
   press of, 509, 523, 631
   in Reconstruction, 554, 562–68, 572–73, 575–76, 577, 579, 580–82
   rise of, 479–85, 631
   South and, 648–49
   Soviet Union and, 842
   and Supreme Court, 810
   Taft and, 708–9
   Truman Doctrine and, 888
   YAF and, 976
   see also Radical Republicans; *specific elections and campaigns*
Republic Steel, 813
Rerum Novarum, 687

reservations, Indian, 609, 610–14, *611*, *614*, 698, 782, 827, 866, 998
Return from Toil, The (Sloan), *685*
Revels, Hiram (1822–1901), *568*, 573, *574*
Revenue Act (1767), 173
Revere, Paul (1735–1818), *141*, 180, *180*, 184
reverse discrimination, 979
"Revolution of 1800," 289
Rhineland, 749, 844
Rhine River, 109, 876
Rhode Island, 247, *349*
   Dorr War in, 348
   Narragansetts of, *57*
   U.S. Constitution and, 257, *259*
   voting rights in, 348
Rhode Island colony, 71, 82, 103, 110, 194, 210, 216
   government in, 144
   religious freedom in, 71
   slavery in, 135
   slave trade in, 128
Rhodes Scholar, *1014*
rice, 128, *409*, 646
   slavery and, 133–35, 138
   in Southern colonies, 92, 118, 132, 133–35
Richardson, Elliot (1920–1999), 1019
Richmond, Va., 289, 508, 509, 534, 541–42, *541*, *544*
   population of slaves in, 289
Richmond *Enquirer*, 401
Richmond Times-Dispatch, 823
Richmond Whig, 397
Rickey, Branch (1881–1965), 903–4
Ridge, Major (ca. 1771–1839), 298
Riesman, David (1909–2002), 947
rifles, in Civil War, 505, 509
"rights of Englishmen," 79–80
Rights of Man (Paine), 280
right to work laws, 902
Riis, Jacob (1849–1914), *599*, 600, 1105
Rindisbacher, Peter (1806–1834), *298*
Rio Grande, 106, 153, 465
riots:
   draft, *530*, 533, 1073
   race, 339, 648, *655*, 744–45, *744*, *745*, 865, 869, 979–80, *980*, 1073
   Reconstruction, 567
   zoot suit, 865–66
Riots in New York, The: The Mob Lynching a Negro in Clarkson Street, *530*
Ritchie, Thomas (1778–1854), 366
"River, The," 1022
River Rouge Plant (Sheeler), *765*
Riverside Church, 778
R.J. Reynolds Tobacco Company, 1038
roads, 309, *310*, 354, 355, 760, 805, 806, *806*, 814
   toll, 309
Road to Serfdom, The (Hayek), 863
Roanoke Island, Va., 51
Roaring Twenties, 760
robber barons, 597, 936
Roberts, Bishop, *117*
Roberts, John (1955–), 1109
Roberts, John G., Jr. (1955–), 1125
Roberts, Lemuel (b. 1751), 185

Robertson, Pat (1930–), 1075
Robeson, Paul (1898–1976), 834, 875, *875*, 876, 914
Robin Hood, 910
Robinson, Alfred (1806–1895), 460
Robinson, Earl (1910–1991), 834
Robinson, Jackie (1919–1972), 903–4, *903*
Robinson, Jo Ann (1912–1992), 954, 969
Rochester, N.Y., 309
rock-and-roll, 948, 992
Rockefeller, John D. (1839–1937), 528, 597, 660, 680, 695, 708, 764, 778
Rockefeller, Nelson (1908–1979), 844, 1023
Rockwell, Norman (1894–1978), 841, 842, *843*, 856–57, 859, 860, 864, 897, *958*
Rocky Mountains, Lander's Peak (Bierstadt), *608*
Rödel, Peter, 343
Rodgers, Thomas (1792–1856), 338
Roe v. Wade, 1002, 1030, *1031*, 1076
Rogers, Will (1879–1935), 771
Rolfe, John (1585–1622), 56, 60, 61
"Roll on, Columbia" (Guthrie), 799
Romania, 887
Rome, ancient, 25, *91*
  slavery in, 95, 398, 459, *461*
Rommel, Erwin (1891–1944), 849–50
Romney, Mitt (1947–):
  Bain Capital and, 1124
  "47 percent" remark by, 1125
  Massachusetts health-care plan and, 1124
  in 2012 election and campaign, 1124–26
Romney campaign spending, 1126
Roosevelt, Eleanor (1884–1962), 825, *825*, 829, 899, *899*, 900
Roosevelt, Franklin D. (1882–1945), 646, 677, 748, 757, *802*, 815, *819*, 820, 826, 831, 833, 842–44, 847, 852, 853, 870, 875, 878–79, *879*, *881*, 886, 888, 904, 911, 920, 978, 1009, 1036, 1054, 1079, 1090
  antilynching law and, 830, 831
  Atlantic Charter and, 880
  background of, 800–801
  black voters and, 823
  "court packing" by, 823, *823*, 837
  death of, 876
  Economic Bill of Rights and, 862–63
  First New Deal and, 803–10, *810*
  Four Freedoms and, 757, 841, *843*, 855–57, 880–81, 936
  freedom and, 818–22, 841, *843*, 869, 885
  Hitler and, 844, 846, 865
  on housing, 809
  Japanese American internment and, 867, 1100
  pluralism and, 864
  and polio, 801–2
  Second New Deal and, 815–18
  on Social Security, 817–18
  and South, 836
  U.S.-Soviet relations and, 887

  and West, 799
  see also New Deal
Roosevelt, Theodore (1858–1919), 631, 701, *706*, 719, 726, 800, 823, 1052
  African-Americans and, 741
  Asian-Americans and, 740
  as conservationist, *707*, 709
  and corporations, 706
  Panama Canal and, 717, *717*
  as Progressive candidate, 709, 802
  as Progressive president, 587, 706–12, *706*
  as Rough Rider, 662–63, *664*
  U.S. government regulatory power and, 706–7
  World War I and, 722
Roosevelt Corollary, 718–19
Rose, Ernestine (1810–1892), 453
Rose, John (1752/1753–1820), *137*
rosemary, 19
Rosenberg, Ethel (1915–1953), 908, *908*
Rosenberg, James N. (1874–1970), *791*
Rosenberg, Julius (1918–1953), 908, *908*
Rosie the Riveter, 859
Ross, Frederick (1796–1883), 401
Ross, John (1790–1866), 298, 375
Ross, Thomas J., 561
Rossiter, Thomas Pritchard (1818–1871), *253*
Rothstein, Arnold (ca. 1882–1928), *811*
Rough Riders, 662–63, *664*
Rove, Karl (1950–), 1102
Rowlandson, Mary (1637?–1711), 76
Royal Africa Company, 88, 101, 143
Royal Air Force, 846
Royal Army, 194
Royal Navy, 117, 127, 141
Royal Society, *150*
Royal University of Mexico, 69
rubber, 657, 761, 853, 930
Ruef, Abraham (1864–1936), 700
Ruins of the Pittsburgh Round House, 625
"Rule Britannia," 140
Rumsfeld, Donald, 1092, 1101, 1108
Rural Electrification Agency, 816
Rush, Benjamin (1745–1813), 186, 207, 225, 234, 239, 253
  public schools and, 215
Russia, 31, 158, 361, 364, 683, *684*, *750*
  Alaskan fur traders from, 154
  Iraq War and, 1093
  U.S. acquires Alaska from, 467
  in World War I, 721, 722
  see also Soviet Union
Russian immigrants, 654, 680, *682*
Russian Revolution, 724, 733, 746, 747, 748
Russo-Japanese War, 717
Russwurm, John B. (1799–1851), 443
Rustin, Bayard (1910–1987), 980
Ruth, Babe (1895–1948), 762
Rwanda, genocide in, 1055, 1056
Ryan, John A. (1869–1945), 687–88, 819
Ryan, Martha, *233*
Ryan, Paul D. (1970–), 1124

Saar, Betye (1926–), *982*
Saar Basin, 749
Sacajawea (ca. 1786–ca. 1812), 294

Sacco, Nicola (1891–1927), 759, *761*
Sadat, Anwar (1918–1981), *1026*
Saddam Hussein (1937–2006), 921, 1050, 1092–93, 1094, 1097, 1126
  and weapons of mass destruction, 1092, 1093, 1097
Sagebrush Rebellion, 1032
Saginaw, Mich., 835
Sahara Desert, 19
St. Augustine, Fla., 33, 139, 152
St. Clair, Arthur (1736–1818), 265
Saint Domingue, 97, 106, 228, 289, *289*, 292, 293
St. Helena Island, 540
St. John Baker, Anthony (1784–1854), *361*
St. John Plantation (Persac), *398*
St. Lawrence River, 38, 49, 158
St. Lawrence valley, 106, 155
St. Louis, Mo., 9, 222, 319, *667*
St. Louis Post-Dispatch, 635, *741*
Salem, Mass., 105–6
Salinger, J. D. (1919–), 947
SALT (Strategic Arms Limitations Talks), 1016, 1026
Salt Lake City, Utah, 462
"salutary neglect," 145
Sambo (slave), 401
Sampson, Deborah (1760–1827), 232
San Antonio, N.Mex., 152, 153
San Antonio, Tex., *464*
San Antonio Independent School District v. Rodriguez, 1012
San Bernardino Valley, Calif, 927
San Carlos Mission, *30*
San Diego, Calif., 154, *1068*
Sandinistas, 772, 1026, 1042
Sandino, Augusto César (1895–1934), 772
Sandwich, Mass., *309*
Sandy (Jefferson's slave), *269*
San Fernando Valley, Calif., 927
Sanford, Maine, *324*
San Francisco, Calif., 154, 470, 599, 700, *792*, 854, 871, 992, 997, 1057, 1073
  Beats in, 948, *948*, 949
  immigration to, 682
  manufacturing and trading in, 604
  population of, 470
  strike in, 811
  U.N. conference in, 880
  water needs of, 708
San Francisco Bay, 998, *998*
San Francisco Chronicle, 889
San Francisco Mission, *154*
Sanger, Margaret (1883–1966), 697, *698*, 730
Sanitary Fairs, 527, 529, *529*, 530
San Jacinto, Battle of, 462, *463*
San Jose, Calif., 1022
San Juan, P.R., 36, 934
San Juan Hill, 662, 663, *664*, 670
San Juan Pueblo, 34
Sankore University, *20*
San Lorenzo, Treaty of (Pinckney's Treaty) (1795), 293
San Salvador, 21

Santa Anna, Antonio López de, 461–62, 466
Santa Barbara, Calif., 154
Santa Fe, N.Mex., 34–35, 49, 152
Santa Fe Trail, 460, 466
Santiago, Cuba, 662
Santorum, Rick (1958), 1124
Sarajevo, Serbia, 721
Saratoga, Battle of, 195–97, *196*
Saturday Evening Post, 841, 856
Saturday Night Massacre, 1019
Saudi Arabia, 981, 1050, 1072, 1087, 1108
Sauk Indians, 374
Savage, Edward (1761–1817), *68*
Savage Family, The (Savage), *68*
Savannah, Ga., *134*, 135, 138, 199, 223, 228, *495*
  return of slaves demanded by, 227
"Save the Holy Places" (Block), *945*
savings and loans associations, 1038
Savio, Mario (1942–1996), 984, *985*
scabs, *689*
scalawags, 575–76
Scalia, Antonin (1936–), 1108
Scandinavia, 845
  socialism in, 691
Scandinavian immigrants, 326, 602, 654, *864*
Schaff, Philip (1819–1893), 432
Schechter Poultry Company, 810
Schenck, Charles T., 776
Schenck v. United States, 777
Schlafly, Phyllis (1924–), *1029*, 1030
school prayer, *1001*
school prayer, proposed amendment regarding, 1039
Schultz, George (1920–), 1012
Schurz, Carl (1829–1906), 555, 569
Schuylkill River, *111*
Schwerner, Michael (1939–1964), 973
Scopes, John (1900–1970), 779–80
Scopes Trial, 779–80, *779*
Scotch-Irish, 109, 111, 156, 161, 211
  as immigrants to America, 109, 111, 156, 161
Scotland, 3, 109, 127
Scott, Dred (ca. 1800–1858), 485–86, *485*, 488, 494
Scott, Harriet (d. ca. 1859), 486
Scott, Thomas A. (1823–1881), 594
Scott, Winfield (1786–1866), 466, 477, 721
Scottish immigrants, 219
Scottsboro, Ala., trial in, 834, *835*, 954
Scourge of Aristocracy, The (Lyon), 286
Scowcroft, Brent (1925–), 1093
Screen Actors Guild, 1033
Scribner's Magazine, 625
SDS, *see* Students for a Democratic Society
Sea Islands, 33, *139*, 517, 539–40, *539*, 556, 574
  Special Field Order 15 and, 549
Seale, Bobby (1936–), 1003
Sears, Roebuck & Co., 592, *593*
SEATO, 895

Seattle, Wash., 766, *794*, 854, 1057, *1057*, 1063
  anti-Chinese riot in, *655*
  government contracts and, 924
  strike in, 747
  WTO meeting in, 1047, 1048, *1049*
Seattle Post-Intelligencer, 867
secession, 495–97, *505*
  see also South
Second Amendment, 258
"Second American Revolution," 519–31
Second Confiscation Act, 514
Second Continental Congress, 184, 185, 186, 187, 195, 205, 207, 211, 230
Second Emancipation, 743
Second Great Awakening, *see* Great Awakening, Second
"second industrial revolution," *see* industrial revolution, "second"
Second New Deal, *see* New Deal, Second
Second Reconstruction, 639, 659
  civil rights movement as, 583
Second Seminole War, 376
Second Vatican Council, social activism and, 992–93
sectionalism:
  Calhoun and, 372
  fear of political, 366
Securities and Exchange Commission, 809
Security Council, U.N., 880, 891, 893, 1093
Sedgwick, Catharine Maria (1789–1867), 351
Sedition Act (1798), 285–87, *286*, 290, 732, 1000, 1100
Sedition Act (1918), 732, 776, 1109
seditious libel, 148–49
segregation, 575, 649–51, 673, 741, 742, *788*, 829, *830*, 857, 864, 865, 866, 869–70, *869*, 870, 871, 873, 874–75, 885–86, *903*, 904, 907, 915, 932–33, 949–54, 958, 966, 979, 1011–13, 1036, 1069, 1070–71, 1105
  Birmingham campaign and, 968–69
  Booker T. Washington on, 656
  Brown v. Board of Education and, 919
  courts and, 951, 952–54, 957–58, *957*, *958*
  dismantling of, 919, 951, 954, 957–58, *957*, *958*, 976, 980, 1011–13
  diversity vs., 833–35
  education and, 655, 1011–13
  federal government and, 969
  in federal housing, 830, *830*
  in Greensboro, N.C., 965
  JFK and, 970
  labor and, 647
  laws, 649–51
  railroads and, 649
  reformers and, 741
  "separate but equal" principle and, 650–51, *650*, 951, 953–54
  South and, 645–53
  in Southwest, 739–40
  in Spanish-American War, 663
  suburbia and, 932–34, *933*, 1064

in U.S. military, 743, 869–70, 871
  see also race, racism; South, segregation in
Seidel, Emil (1864–1947), 689
seigneuries, 38
Seine River, 309
Selective Service Act (1917), 726
Self, The, 215
"self-made" man, *337*, 338, 389
  Andrew Jackson as, 347
  Frederick Douglass as, 389
Selling a Freeman to Pay His Fine at Monticello, Florida, 564
Selling of Joseph, The, (Sewall), 225
Selma, Ala., 949, 976, *976*
Seminoles, 314, 361, 374
  fugitive slaves and, 376
Seminole War:
  First, 376
  Second, 376
Senate, U.S., 249, 347, 617, 660, 661, 814, 817, 880, 951, 1078, 1080, 1097, 1101, 1102, 1116, 1118
  African-Americans in, 573–74
  comic book hearings of, 947
  creation of, 249
  and Johnson's impeachment, 567–68
  LBJ in, 972
  McCarthy and, 909–10
  popular vote and, 700
  World War I and, 724
  see also Congress, U.S.
Seneca Falls Convention, *446*, 448, 449, 452, 890
Seneca Falls Declaration of Sentiments, 448, 449
Seneca Indians, 12, *263*, 298
Senegal, 959
Seoul, South Korea, *895*
"separate but equal" principle, 650–51, *650*, 951, 953–54
separation of powers, in U.S. Constitution, 250–51
separatists, 66
September 11, 2001, terrorist attacks of, 510, 731, 921, 972, 1022, 1087, 1088, 1089, *1089*, *1090*, 1091, 1092, 1094, 1097, 1106–7, 1114, *1125*, 1126, 1127
  Cold War and, 1087–88
Sequoia, *374*
Serbia, 721, 1033, 1055–56, *1055*
serfs, 92
Serra, Junípero (1713–1784), 154
Servicemen's Readjustment Act, 862
settlement houses, *701*, 702, 710
Seven Days' Campaign, 509
Seventeenth Amendment, 489, 700
Seventh Day Baptists, 110
Seven Years' War, 127, 156–58, *159*, 163, 185, 193, 197, 221, 267, 292
  effects of, 160, 161, 164, 171–72, 173
Sewall, Samuel (1652–1730), 225
Seward, William H. (1801–1872), 473, 475, 484, 494, 515, 660
"Seward's icebox," 660
sex:
  Beats and, 949
  censorship and, 775, 777

and public officials, 1078–79
  women's rights and, 453, 697, 756, 766–68, 932, 994, 996
sexism, 996
Sex Side of Life, The (Dennett), 777
sexual harassment, 1078
sexual politics, 996
sexual revolution, 920, 992, 1002, 1013–14, *1014*, 1028, 1074, 1076
Seymour, Horatio (1810–1886), 567, *567*
Shackle Broken-by the Genius of Freedom, The, 548
Shahn, Ben (1898–1969), *862*
Shakers, 426–27, *427*, 429
Shakespeare, William (1564–1616), *119*, 179
shamans, 12
Shame of the Cities, The (Steffens), 680
"shape up" system, 811
sharecropping, 387, 557, *557*, 561, 575, 636, 744, *809*, 819, 830, 833, *833*, 925, *958*
Share Our Wealth, 814, 816
sharia law, in Koran, 1107
Sharon, Conn., 975
Sharon Statement, 975, 988
Shaw, Lemuel (1781–1861), 328
Shaw, Robert Gould (1837–1863), 518
Shawnees, 156, 298
Shays, Daniel (1747?–1825), 246
Shays's Rebellion, 246, *254*, 274
Sheeler, Charles (1883–1965), 764, *765*
Sheen, Fulton J. (1895–1979), 935
sheep farming, 605
Shenandoah Valley, 114, 121
Sheppard-Towner Act (1921), 767
Sheridan, Philip H. (1831–1888), 608
Sherman, William T. (1820–1891), 533, 537, 538, *541*, 549, 555, 573, 969
  March to the Sea of, *541*
Sherman Antitrust Act (1890), 618, 624, 706, 708
  see also monopolies; trusts, business
Shiite Muslims, 921, 1096
Shiloh, Battle of, 511, *512*
shipbuilding:
  European, 940
  in New England, 88
  in Philadelphia, 239
  in South, 924
  in World War II, 859
Shoemakers' Strike in Lynn-Procession in the Midst of a Snow-Storm, of Eight Hundred Women Operatives, The, 343
shopping, 927
Shoshones, 294
"shunpikes," 309
Siam, *see* Thailand
Sicily, invasion of, 850
Sickles, Daniel E. (1819–1914), 513
Siegfried, André (1875–1959), 762, 772
Sierra Club, 707, 999
Sierra Leone, as haven for former slaves, *227*, 228
"Significance of the Frontier in American History, The" (F.J. Turner), 600

Signing of the Constitution, The (Rossiter), 253
Silent Protest Parade, 745
Silent Spring (Carson), 983, 999
Silicon Valley, 1057
silver, 24, 25, 29, 33, 53, 54, 58, 88, 97, 106, 380
  coinage, 146
  corporate mining of, 604–5
  as currency, 642–43, *643*
  currency and, 355, 378, 379
Simmons, Isaac (d. 1944), 869
Sinclair, Upton (1878–1968), 680, 726, 775, 814
Singer Sewing Machines, 660
Singleton, Benjamin "Pap" (1809–1892), 647, *647*
Sinners in the Hands of an Angry God (Edwards), 150–51
Sioux, 525, 608, 609, 610, *610*, *612*, *614*
Sioux Dakotas, execution of, *525*
Sirica, John J. (1904–1992), 1018
Sister Carrie (Dreiser), 680
Sisterhood is Powerful!, 996
sit-down strike, 812, *813*
sit-ins, 965, 966, *967*, 970, 980
Sitting Bull (ca. 1831–1890), 608, 609, *609*, 610
Six-Day War, 1055
Sixteenth Amendment, 709
Sixth Avenue and Thirtieth Street (Sloan), 677
"Sixties, The," 983, 997, 999, 1002
  activism in, 994–96
  legacy of, 1005
Skilling, Jeffrey, 1060
slacker raids, 733
Slater, Samuel (1768–1835), 319, 321
Slaughterhouse Cases (1873), 581
Slave Auction, The (Crowe), *389*
Slave Market of America, 439
Slave Power, 483, 487, 626
slavery, 6, 94–101, *205*, 234–36, *269*, 281, 366, 388–423, 429, *579*, 874, 876, 900, 1069, 1095
  abolished in Mexico, 461, 469
  American, origins of, 94–101
  American Revolution and, 167, 205, 223–32, 234, 235, 415, 435
  in ancient Greece, 398
  in ancient Rome, 95, 398, 459, *461*
  arguments in favor of, 398–99, 621
  bank financing of, 355
  Biblical passages as justification for, 398, 405
  in Brazil, *see* Brazil, slavery in
  and Catholic Church, 97, 137
  in Chesapeake region, 132–33, 134, 137–38
  Christianity and, 99, 136–37, 152, 413–14, 446, 473
  in cities, 410
  Civil War and, 511–19
  Congress and, 473
  Constitution and, 251–52, *251*, 263
  cotton gin and, 317
  in Cuba, 137
  Democratic Party and, 369
  divisiveness of, 288–89

slavery (*continued*)

Dred Scott decision and, 485–86

English Liberty vs., 141

in Europe, 20, 95

expansion of, 127, 169

federal government and, 372

Free Soil position and, 474

gender roles in, 413

in Georgia, 252

in Georgia colony, 134–35, 138

growth of, 134

history of, 95

indentured servitude vs., 94

Indian, abolition of, 30–31

Indians and, 6, 16, 25, 29–31, 87, 94, *121*, 470, 601, 1074

law and, 421

Levellers opposed to, 81

in Lincoln-Douglas campaign, 488–89

Lincoln's views of, 487–88

Locke and, 143

in Louisiana, 294–95

in Mediterranean, 95

in Middle Colonies, 132, 135

in Missouri Territory, 356–58

in New England, 77, 132, 135

in New Netherland, 42

newspapers and, 401, 420, 421, 441, 443, 444, *452*, 473

in New World, 3, 5, 25, 29–31, 94–97, *129*, 132

in New York, *228*

North as affected by, 393

in Northern colonies, 135

Northern vs. Southern, 135

party politics and, 477–79

paternalist ethos and, 396, *398*

perceived advantages of, 94

planter class and, 395–96

Puritanism and, 70

Quaker repudiation of, 93

racism as justification for, 396

Republican Party (modern) opposed to, 483–84

on rice plantations, 118, 133–35

Seward's views on, 484

slave resistance to, 138–39, 416–22, *417*

South as affected by, 393, 652–53

in Southern colonies, 132–33, 215–16

strengthening of, 493

in Texas, 462

on tobacco plantations, 118, 132–33

United States as center of, 390

in Virginia colony, 59, 98, 100–101, 132, 133

after War of 1812, 307

in West, 601

in West Indies, 25, 31, 87, 92, 96, 128, *131*, 132, 133

westward expansion and, 243, 317, 358, 374, 385, 386, 390, 470, 473, 474, 483–84

Wilmot proviso and, 473, 474

see also abolition movement

Slavery As It Is (Weld), 438

slaves, 32, 55, 59, *63*, *97*, 120, 121, *121*, *134*, 144, 227, *409*, *410*, *411*

in Antigua, *96*

barred from education, 401

bound for Mexico, 98

in Carolina colony, 92

and Christianity, 413–14

Civil War and, 535

colonization of, 435–36, 514, 517

culture of, 136–39, *137*, 385, 411–16

death rate of, 100, 132

diet and health of, 402

disciplining of, 410–11

emancipated, 228, 511–19, *517*, 544–45

family life of, *412*

folk tales of, 415

freedom desired by, 101, 138–39, 226, 231, 415–16, 435

fugitive, 288, 376, 418, *418*, 475–77, 487, 496, 513, *513*, 514, 516

gang labor and, 408–10

harbored by Seminoles, 376

holdings, *397*

importation from Africa of, 95–96, 252

labor of, 408

law and, 401–2

Native Americans as, 87, *121*, 470

New York uprising of, 138–39

population of, 134, *135*, 289, 357, 385, 516

prices of, 395

prohibition on importation of, 390

religion and, 413–14, *414*

revolts, 289–90, 419–20, 439

rights of, 97–98

runaway, advertisement for, 418, *418*

tax on importation of, 134

women as, *98*

slaves, emancipated, 548–57, *551*, *556*, *575*

Andrew Johnson and, 563

Second New Deal and, 816

suffrage and, 549, 551, 567, 568

slaves, population of:

in British colonies, 132

in colonies, 224

in Florida, 154

in Missouri Territory, 356–58

in New York City, 135, 229

in 1776, 223

in South Carolina, 371

in U.S., 239, 390, *392*, *393*

slave ships, *132*

slave trade, 20, *20*, 42, 88, 94, 116–17, 127–35, *130*, 132, 223, *223*, *389*, 391–92, *393*, 492, 876

abolished in Washington, D.C., 475

advertisement for, *411*

and Africa, 5, 20

Atlantic, 128–30

auctions in, 391, *393*

in Charleston, S.C., 92

Congressional prohibition on, 391

Constitution and, 251–52, *251*

cotton plantations and, 317

families and, 412

Middle Passage of, 130–32, 136

in New Orleans, 317, 391

in original Declaration of Independence, 190

prohibition of, 251, 317

reopening of, 317

statistics on, 391

within U.S., 317

Slave Trader, Sold to Tennessee (Miller), 317

"slavocracy", Southern planters as, 394

Slavs, Nazi extermination of, 850

Sloan, John (1871–1951), *677*, 680, *685*, 687

smallpox, 24, *24*, 40, 66, 131, *1074*

Smalls, Robert (1837–1915), 574

Smith, Adam (1723–1790), 5, 18, 218, 235

Smith, Adams (1723–1790), 1113

Smith, Alfred E. (1873–1974), 789

Protestants and, 789

Smith, Henry (d. 1893), *651*

Smith, John (1580–1631), 49–50, 54, 58–59, *59*, *60*

Smith, Joseph (1805–1844), 336

Smith, Matthew (1810–1879), 599, *600*

Smith, Melancton (1744–1798), 256

Smith, Thomas, *78*

Smith Act (1940), 836

Smithsonian Institute, 608

Smith v. Allwright, 874

SNCC, *see* Student Non-Violent Coordinating Committee

Snell, Hannah (1723–1792), *232*

social contract, 143

Social Darwinism, 621–22, 625, 629, 631

Social Gospel, 629, 643, 668, 993

socialism, 426, 689–90, 691, 694, 697, 771, 775, 777, 779, 792, 802, 811, 814, 900, 911, 943, 983, 1004, 1027, 1065

capitalism vs., 709, 832

in Chicago, 629

Communist Party and, 831–32

Espionage Act and, 732

European vs. American view of, 627

Friedrich Hayek and, 863

in Gilded Age, 625, 627–28

Henry Wallace and, 905

immigrants and, 739, 766

middle class and, 627

as nationalism, 628

woman suffrage and, 703

World War I and, 722, 734

Socialist Party, 689, *690*, 697, 709, *709*, 727, 736, 748, 766

capitalism vs., 709, 832

Social Security, 814, 815, *818*, 823, 826, 837, 875, 937, 974, 1010, 1039, 1082

African-Americans and, 827, 830, 978

creation of, 817–18

Eisenhower and, 940

FDR on, 817–18

freedom and, 824

NRPB and, 861

taxes support for, 818, 826, 827

Truman and, 901, 905, 911

in World War II, 855

Social Security Act (1935), 800, 817–18, 826, 828

Social Security Bill, 818

Society in America (Martineau), 435

Society of American Indians, 698

Society of Friends, *see* Quakers

Society of Pennsylvania, 282

Solomon (slave), 290

Solomon Islands, 849

Somalia, 1070

war on terror in, 1122

Somerset case, 252

Somoza, Anastasio (1925–1980), 772, 843–44, 1026, 1042

Son of the Forest, A, 376

Sonoma, Calif., 154

Sons of Italy, 759

Sons of Liberty, 176, *176*, 178, 180, 207, 223

Sorel, Edward (1929–), *1053*

Sotomayor, Sonia (1954–), 1118

Soule, George (1887–1970), 822

Soulé, Pierre (1801–1870), 492

Souls of Black Folks, The (Du Bois), 742, 752

Souter, David (1939–), 1118

South, 275, 617, 618, *731*, 743, 763, 841, *854*, 870, 966–67, 1009, 1018, 1080, 1117

African-Americans in, 646–47, 743, 766, 786, *786*, 865, 870, 873, 915, 973, 979

agriculture in, 925

black migration from, 934, 949

cotton crop in, 317

Democratic Party and, 645, 789

desegregation in, 871, 951, 954, 957–58, *958*, 980

economy of, 393–96

election of 1796 and, 285

in election of 1824, 364

in election of 1948, 905

in election of 1964, 974

factory production in, 323

family life in antebellum, *395*

Freedom Rides in, 966

fundamentalists in, 779

illiteracy in, 394

industry in, 826, 854, 924, 941

Jim Crow and, 952

libertarianism in, 937

New, *see* New South

New Deal and, 826

Nixon and, 1011–12

Operation Dixie in, 901

People's Party in, 637

political influence of, 358

population growth and, 1022

poverty in, 836, 1105

religion in, 756

secession of, 495–97

segregation in, 636, 645–53, 865, 873, *952*, 953, 965, 966–67, 1011–13

sit-ins in, 965, *967*

slavery and, 391, 393

slave trade in, 317

society in, 396

strikes in, 811

urban areas of, 558–59
voting in, 769, 903, 973
see also Confederate States of
America
South Africa, 752, 896, 1015, 1041,
1049
apartheid in, 991
South America, 2, 6, *7*, 8, 23, 25–26, *32*,
106, 155, 604, 844
early population of, 24, 31
immigrants from, *682*, 1067, 1070
South Braintree, Mass., Sacco and
Vanzetti in, 759
South Carolina, 219, 240, 288, 347, 366,
367, 376, 560, 645, 646, 699, 1108
Confederate flag and, 957
at Constitutional Convention, 251
constitution of, 209, 210
in nullification crisis, 371–74, *372*
Reconstruction in, 575–76, 580
secession of, 496
slavery in, 252, 372
slave trade in, 317
textiles in, 645
upcountry of, 317
voting rights in, 352, 366
South Carolina Canal and Railroad, 311
South Carolina colony, 33, 111, 114, *117*,
139, 144, 145, 156, 183
in American Revolution, 194, 199,
222
assembly in, 146
Declaration of Independence and,
190
elite class in, 119–20
Indians in, 111
Loyalists in, 219, *220*
planters in, 119
population of slaves in, 134
Regulators in, 177
rice plantations in, 133–34
slavery in, 133–34, *137*, 139, 190, 224,
226, 227, 252
task system, 134
South Carolina Gazette, *139*
South Dakota, 602, *612*
corporate mining in, 605
entrance into Union of, 610
population of, 679
Wounded Knee massacre in, 613
Southern Christian Leadership
Conference, 956
Southern Conference for Human
Welfare, 836, 914
Southern Manifesto, 951, 957
Southern Pacific Railroad, *602*, 604,
700
Southern Tenant Farmers Union, 835
Southern veto, 826–27
South Gate, Calif., 1038
South Korea, 1020, 1026
and BP oil rig, 1119
creation of, 891–93
immigrants from, 1067
South Vietnam, 984, 986, 990, *990*,
1002, 1016
Sovereignty and Goodness of God, The
(Rowlandson), 76
Soviet Exhibition, 923

Soviet Union, 746, 756, 757, 791, 802,
832, 842, 845, 850, 877, 878, 879,
886–87, 888, 898, 900, 905, 908,
914, 938, 947, 982, 1010, 1015,
1024, 1026, 1042, 1066
Afghanistan invasion by, 1027
American National Exhibition and,
923, *925*
atomic bomb of, 891
Berlin occupation by, 890–91
breakup of, 1049, *1050*, 1051
Cold War and, 895–96
collapse of communism in, 918,
1048–49
Cuban Missile Crisis and, 970–71
Czechoslovakia invasion by, 1004
Eastern Europe occupation by,
878–79, 880, 886, 890, 891
Eisenhower and, 942–43
European empires and, 943
German invasion of, 846, 850, *851*,
886
Gulf War and, 1051
hydrogen bomb and, 942
invasion of Germany by, 876
Korean War and, 891–95
Lend-Lease and, 846
Manchuria invasion by, 877
Reagan and, 1040
reforms in, 1048
space exploration and, *940*, 941,
960, 970
spying of, 910
support of the arts by, 897
in U.N., 880
Universal Declaration of Human
Rights and, 900
Vietnam and, 984, 1015
weapons tests of, 906
see also Cold War
soybean, 925
Spain, *15*, 21–27, *22*, *23*, 28–31, *44*, 49,
52, 53, 54, 111, 157, 158, 187, 239,
365, 492, 661–65, 746, 910
American Revolution and, 197
and Catholicism, 52
Columbus sponsored by, 21
loses Jamaica to England, 83
Louisiana Territory and, 293
as refuge for Huguenots, 38
rise of Franco in, 844
slavery in, 20
in War of Jenkins' Ear, 139
Spanish America, 3, 21–35, *29*, 36, *44*,
49, 51, 52, 56, 133–34, 314
beginnings of, 21
boundaries of, 152
in Florida, 25, 31, 91, 147, 152
government of, 25
immigrants to, 26–27
independence of, 359, *360*
Indians and, 31–37, 92, 106
interracial mixing in, 27, *28*
justification for conquest of, 3, 15,
27–28, 30
in Louisiana, 294–95
map of, *153*
in New Mexico, 33–35, 49, 152
in North America, 152–55, 287

as obstacle to westward expansion,
329
population of, 25
Pueblo Indians and, 10, 34–35, 101
size of, 25
in Texas, 152
women in, 27
Spanish-American War, 586, 661–62,
663, 664–65, *664*, *665*, 670, *672*,
708, 783
acquisition of empire and, *635*, 715
Battle of San Juan Hill in, 662, 663
casualties in, 662
causes of, 661–62
effects of, 667
naval battle at Manila Bay in, 662
see also Philippine War
Spanish Armada, *51*, 52
Spanish Civil War, 845, 910
Spanish Inquisition, 34
Sparkman, John (1899–1985), 915
speakeasies, 760, 779, 787
Special Field Order 15, 549
special interests, 708
lobbying by, 616, 769–70, 862
specie, 355
Specie Circular, 380
Spencer, Lilly M. (1822–1902), *507*
Spiegel, Marcus M. (1829–1864), 503
Spirit of the New Deal, The, *804*
spoils system, 368
see also parties, political; patronage
Spokane, Wash., 695
Spotswood, Alexander (1676–1740),
101
Spotsylvania, Battle of, 537
Spotsylvania, Va., *538*
Sprigs, Elizabeth, 55
Springfield, Mo., *741*
Springsteen, Bruce (1949–), 1022
Sputnik, 941, 960
Squanto (d. 1622), 67
Square Deal, 706
squatters, 312, *315*
stagflation, 1020–21, 1031, 1032
Stalin, Joseph (1879–1953), 802, 832,
845, 878–79, *879*, 886, 888, 891,
895, 905, 911, 942
death of, 942
and nonaggression pact, 845
Stalingrad, 850
Stamp Act (1765), 171, *176*, 223
repeal of, 177, *177*
resistance to, 173–76, 178, 226
teapot, *175*
Stamp Act Congress (1765), 175
Standard Oil Company, 594, 597, *597*,
660, 680, 706, 708
Stanford University, 739
Stanton, Edwin M. (1814–1869), 549,
567
Stanton, Elizabeth Cady (1815–1902),
448, 452, 453, 570, *570*, 571, *658*,
736, 766
Stanton, Frederick (1794–1859), 395
Stanwix, Fort, 242
Starbucks, *1057*
Star of Empire, *461*
Starr, Kenneth (1947–), 1079

"Star-Spangled Banner, The" (Key),
300, 661
"starving time," 59
state-church separation, 212–15, 779,
1001
State Department, U.S., 887, 908, 942,
958, 984, 1024, 1042, 1092–93,
1096
McCarthy and, 908, 909
State of the Union Address (1815), 354
State of the Union Address (1825), 365
State of the Union Address (1941), 841
State of the Union Address (1996),
1053–54
State of the Union Address (2002),
1091
states' rights, 370, 372, 904, 1032
Andrew Johnson's views of, 562
Calhoun and, 371–73
Confederacy and, 532
in Constitution, 259
nullification and, 371
States' Rights Democratic Party, 904,
905
Statue of Freedom, 459, *461*
Statue of Liberty, 589, 629, 631, 686,
687, 722, 728, *738*, 741, *741*, *856*,
864, *909*, 936, *996*, *1000*, 1048,
1049, *1064*, *1083*
Stead, W. T. (1849–1912), 715
steamboats, 168, 307, 309, *318*, 328, *593*
steamships, 594
steel industry, 595, *597*, 635, 646, 657,
686, 688, 715, 747, 760, 770, 811,
811, 813, 854, 901, 924, 930, 940,
941, 1020, 1037, 1102
Steel Workers Organizing Committee,
811, 813
Steffens, Lincoln (1866–1936), 680, 762
Stegner, Wallace (1913–1993), 329
Steichen, Edward (1879–1973), 680
Stein, Gertrude (1874–1946), 776
Steinbeck, John (1902–1968), 807, 821
Stennis, John C. (1901–1995), 1018
Stephens, Alexander (1812–1883), 497,
508, 526
sterilization, involuntary, 739
Stevens, Thaddeus (1792–1868), 353,
514, 564–65, *564*, 566, 579
Stevenson, Adlai (1900–1965), 915, 939
Steward, Ira (1831–1883), 607
Stewart, Alexander T. (1803–1876),
600
Stewart, Maria (1803–1879), 447, 448
Stewart, William (1827–1909), 564
Stieglitz, Alfred (1864–1946), 680, *680*
Stiles, Ezra (1727–1795), *210*, 235
Stimson, Henry (1867–1950), 853, 874,
876
Stockbridge Indians, 221
stock market, 760, 765, *765*, *791*, 803,
1037, 1058–59, 1061, 1112, 1113,
1114
New Deal and, 757
Stone, Lucy (1818–1893), 425, 453,
454, 571
Stonewall Bar, police raid on, 997
Stono, S.C., 139
Stono Rebellion, 139

Story, Joseph (1779–1845), 347
Story, Moorfield (1845–1929), 742
Stowe, Harriet Beecher (1811–1896), *351, 441, 442*
Strategic Arms Limitations Talks (SALT), 1015
Strategic Bombing Survey, *877*
Strategic Defense Initiative, 1040
Straus, Jack (1900–1985), 927
strict constructionism, 275, 354–55, 356, 365
Stride Toward Freedom (King), 956
Strike, The (Koehler), *591*
strikes, 328, 342, *343*, 380, 573, 619, 624–25, 689, 691–95, 746–47, 766, 901–2, 1003, *1003*, 1037
of air traffic controllers, 1037
in Arizona, 733, *734*
in Boston, Mass., 747, 770
in California, 836
in colleges, 1016
of cowboys, 604
in Depression, 811–13, *813*
in Detroit, Mich., 869
in France, 1004
in Homestead, Pa., 635–36, 657
in Idaho, 690
in Lawrence, Mass., 694
in Ludlow, Colo., 695
McCormick Company and, 629
in Memphis, Tenn., 871
mining and, 642, 733
in New Orleans, La., 694
in New York, N.Y., 677, 691–95, *694*
in 1934, 811
in Paterson, N.J., 694
in Pennsylvania, 706
Pullman, 641–42, 657
railroad, *591*, 624–25, *625*, 629, 770
rights and, 711
scabs and, *689*
in Seattle, Wash., 747
sit-down, 812, *813*
steel, 747, *747*, 941
suppression of, 770
wildcat, 941
women and, *343*
in World War II, 855
in W.Va., 706
Strong, Josiah (1847–1916), 660, 668
Stuart, Gilbert (1755–1828), *207*
Stuart kings, 80
Student Non-Violent Coordinating Committee (SNCC), 966, 969, 973, 978, 981, 982, 990, 995, 998, *1002*
students, as activists, 966
Students for a Democratic Society (SDS), *983*, 984–85, 989, 990, 996, 997, 998, 1003
Stump Speaking (Bingham), *367*
Stuyvesant, Peter (1610?–1672), 43
submarines:
construction of, 924
in World War I, 721, 722, 723, *723*
in World War II, 849, 850
"subprime" mortgages, 1112, 1113
minorities and, 1113
subtreasury plan, 637, 642

Suburban Gardens, *788*
suburbs, 947, *947*, 961, 994, 1013, 1028, 1033, 1067, 1082, 1117
African-Americans in, 1064, 1071
"blockbusting" and, 934
highways and, *930*, 940
Latinos in, 1064, 1067
rise of, 760, 918, 925–27, *926*, 930, *930*
as segregated, 932–33, *933*, 952, 1064
Sudan, 1070
Sudbury, Mass., 78
Sudetenland, 844
Suez Canal, 943
Suffolk Resolves (1775), 182, 183
suffrage, *see* voting rights
sugar, 20, 77, 83, 88, *96*, 116, 117, 128, 308, *409*
in Caribbean, 717
in Cuba, 970
in Hawaii, 661
as most profitable crop, 97
plantations, *see* planters, plantations, sugar
in Puerto Rico, 933
trade in New Orleans, 393
Sugar Act (1764), 173, 174, 175, 176
suicide rate, Great Depression and, 791
Sullivan, John (1741–1795), 222
Summary View of the Rights of British America, A (Jefferson), 184
Sumner, Charles (1811–1874), 484, *484*, 564–65, 569, 570, *570*, 736
Sumner, William Graham (1840–1910), 622
Sumter, Fort, 386, 498, *499*, 508, 520
Sunday, Billy (1862–1935), 778, *778*
Sunni Muslims, 921, 1096
Sun of Liberty, 286
Sunshine and Shadow in New York (Smith), 599, *600*
Sun Yat-Sen, 698
Superman, 947
supply and demand, law of, 218, 620
supply-side economics, 1024, 1038, 1039, 1088
Suppressed Book about Slavery, The, 411
Supreme Court, U.S., 249, 274, 276, 291, 347, 356, 357, 371, 374–75, 570, 571, 581, 582, 613, 623, 642, 649, 650, 655, 670, 689, 704, *704*, 706, 708, 759, 770, *770*, 773, 776–77, 784, 785, 910, *1001*, 1019, 1029, 1036, 1072, 1107–8
abortion and, 921, 1002, 1030, *1031*, 1076
affirmative action and, 1013, 1071
African-American rights and, 742, 874
Amistad and, 419
Brown v. Board of Education and, 919, 951, 953, *953*, 956
and campaign contributions, 1126
civil liberties and, 776–77, 836, 919, 956–57
civil rights and, 1001–2, *1001*, 1004, 1011–13, 1071
in Civil War, 523

Clinton's appointments to, 1052
"court packing" and, 823, *823*
Dred Scott decision of, *485*, 485–86, 569
FDR and, 802, 823–24, *823*, 837
First Amendment and, 856
G. W. Bush and, 1108–10
homosexuals and, 1039
housing segregation and, 932
Jackson's defiance of, 375
Japanese-American internment and, 868
and judicial review power, 291–92
New Deal and, 810, *810*
Obama and, 1118
Obamacare upheld by, 1125
Plessy v. Ferguson and, 650–51, *650*, 951, 953
right to privacy and, 1002
sanctions involuntary sterilization, 739
Scottsboro case and, 835
"separate but equal" ruling of, 650–51, *650*
and 2000 election, 1079–80, *1079*
as undemocratic, 349
see also Burger Court; Marshall Court; Warren Court
surgeon's kit, Civil War, *508*
Susquehanna Indians, 114
Sutherland, George (1862–1942), *770*
Sutter, Johann A. (1803–1880), 469
Swann v. Charlotte-Mecklenburg Board of Education, 1012
Swanson, *928*
Swaziland, 1083
sweatshops, 677, 703
Sweatt, Heman (1912–1982), 953
Swedish immigrants, *325*
Sweet, Henry O. (ca. 1905–1940), 788
Swift, Jonathan (1667–1745), 822
Switzer, Katherine, *995*
Switzerland, male suffrage in, 615
Syria, 752, 1020, 1100

Taft, Robert (1889–1953), 819, 868, 938
Taft, William Howard (1857–1930), 587, 667, *667*, 706, 708–9, 711, 770
inaugural address of, 708
Latin America and, 718
Taft-Hartley Act (1947), 902, 904, 914, 941
Taiping Rebellion, 506
Taiwan, 891, 1015, 1020
Tajikistan, *1050*, 1091
Taliban, 1027, 1090–91, 1121
Tallmadge, James (1778–1853), 357
Tammany Hall, 789
Taney, Roger B. (1777–1864), 328, 379, 486, 523
tanks (military), 852, *852*
Tanzania, 943
terrorist attack in, 1087
Tape, Joseph and Mary, 655
Taper, Joseph, 404, 416
Tape v. Hurley, 655
Tappan, Arthur (1786–1865), 438
Tappan, Lewis (1788–1873), 438
Tarbell, Ida (1857–1944), 680

"tariff of abominations," 371
tariffs, 169, 245, 247, 275, 354, 355, 369, 382, 494, 528, 590, 618, *618*, 642, 643, 644, 661, 709, 711, 769, 794
in Constitution, 253
of 1828, 371
of 1832, 373
J. Q. Adams and, 365
lowered by Democrats, 370
Polk and, 464
Tarkington, Booth (1869–1946), 856
Tarleton, Banastre (1754–1833), 199
Tartarus of Maids, The (Melville), 343
taxes, 61, 103, 179, *254*, 355, 710, 772, 814, 902, 936, 937, 1028, 1036, 1038, 1052, 1071, 1102, *1123*
under Articles of Confederation, 240
in Civil War, 528, 533
corporate, 855
on corporations, 816
demands for lowering, 1031–32
dispute over, 167, 205
Gingrich and, 1053
in Great Britain, 80, 1032
Great Depression and, 794
G. W. Bush's cuts in, 1088, 1102, 1111, 1118
on imported slaves, 134, 139
imposed by British Parliament, 171, 172–76, *174*, 187–90
income, 528, 638, 707, 709, 711, 727, 769, 852, 974, 977
inheritance, 707
Jefferson's abolition of, 290
John Adams and, 205
in Massachusetts colony, 70
New Deal and, 826, 827
poll, 98, 649, 741, 904, 976
property, 699, 1012
Reagan's cuts in, 920
and representation, 174–75
right to consent to, 91
single, 627
Social Security, 818, 826, 827
to support churches, 110, 151, 211–12, 213, 214
on tea, 181
in Virginia colony, 99–100
on whiskey, 274, 275
on women, 98
World War I and, 727
World War II and, 852
Tax Reform Act (1986), 1036
Taylor, Frederick W. (1856–1915), 688
Taylor, Zachary (1784–1850), 473, 475
as Mexican War general, 465
tea, 115, 181, 308
Tea Act (1773), 181
Teachers in the Freedmen's School in Norfolk, 1861, 540
Tea Party, *1123*
agenda of, 1122–23
Paul D. Ryan and, 1124
Teapot Dome scandal, 770
technology, 57
agriculture and, 315, 319, *481*
in Civil War, 504–6, *507*
effects of, on exploration, 18–20

innovations in, 592–93
manufacturing and, 319–23
market revolution and, 315, 319–23, *321*, *481*
Native American, 34
in World War I, 721
Tecumseh (1768–1813), 298–99, 300
teenagers, 947, *947*, *948*
Tehran, 878, *879*, 1027
Tejanos, 460–62
telegraph, 309, 311
in Civil War, 504
transatlantic, 592
telephones, 592, 761, 762, *762*
television, 919, 923, 924, 925, 928–29, *928*, *929*, 1004, 1035, 1040, 1042, 1058, 1069, 1074, 1101
civil rights movement and, 967, *968*, 976
family life on, 929, 931
Iran hostage crisis and, *1027*
Middle East and, 1095
in 1960 campaign, 960
politics and, 939–40, 1043–44
religion and, 815, 935
religious programing and, 1029
Vietnam War and, 1003
Teller, Henry (1830–1914), 662
Teller Amendment, 662
temperance, 370, 426, *430*, 431, *431*, 628, *656*, 657–58
see also Prohibition
"Temperance diagram" (Franklin), *147*
Tenant uprising, 178
Ten Commandments, 841
Ten Commandments, The (movie), 934
Tennent, Gilbert (1703–1764), 150
Tennent, William (1673–1746), 150
Tennessee, 242, 367, 648
creation of, 284
Ku Klux Klan founded in, 578
prison labor in, 645
Scopes trial in, 779–80, *779*
Tennessee (ship), *847*
Tennessee River, 806
Tennessee Valley Authority (TVA), 806, *807*
Tenochtitlán, 8, *9*, 23–24, *23*, 25
Ten-Percent Plan of Reconstruction, 541
Tenskwatawa (1775–1836), 298, *299*, 613
Tenth Amendment, 259
Tenure of Office Act (1867), 567
Ten Views in Antigua, *96*
Terman, Lewis (1877–1956), 739
"termination", and Native Americans, 998
terrorism, 1041, 1087
domestic, 1097
in Oklahoma City, 748, 1077, *1078*
September 11 attacks, 731, 921, 972, 1022, 1087, 1088, 1089, *1089*, *1090*, 1091, 1092, 1094, 1097, 1106–7, 1114, *1125*, 1126, 1127
war on, 1088, 1089–91, 1092, 1094, 1097–1101, 1107, 1109–10, 1122, 1127
Terry, Eli (1772–1852), 322

Tesla, Nikola (1856–1943), 593
Tet offensive, 1002
Texas, 152, 153, 314, 460, *859*, 866, 902, *903*, 1033, *1033*, 1068, 1070, 1108
agriculture in, 925
annexation of, 467, 469
in Dust Bowl, 807
G. W. Bush and, 1088
Hurricane Katrina victims and, 1105
immigration and, 1106
independence from Mexico of, 462
population of, 460, 679
Populist Party in, 636
Republic of, 462
revolt in, 460–62
segregation in, 830
slavery in, 462
U.S. annexation of, *464*
Texas, University of, segregation at, 953
Texas and Pacific Railroad, 582
textile industry, 130
and child labor, 702
during Civil War, 524
and cotton, 385
decline of, 924
and immigration, 325
and market revolution, 321–24, *321*, *323*
plant closings in, 1101
in South, 645
strikes in, 766, 811, 901
Thailand, 848
Thames, Battle of, 300
Thanksgiving, 67
Thatcher, Margaret (1925–), 1032
Theory of the Leisure Class, The (Veblen), 599
Thind, Bhagat Singh (1892–1967), 784
Third Great Awakening, 1028
third parties, in U.S. elections, 619
Third World, 943–45, 949, 984, 998, 1014, 1026, 1041
Cold War in, 943–45
Thirteenth Amendment, 541, 565, 885
This Hand Guides the Reich, 844
This Is the Army (movie), 864
This Is the Enemy (Ancona and Koehler), 870
Thomas, Clarence (1948–), 1078
Thomas, Jesse (1777–1853), 357, 358
Thomas, Lorenzo (1804–1875), 518
Thoreau, Henry David (1817–1862), 330–31, *331*, 466, 489, 707, 956, 1124
Thoughts on African Colonization, 437
Thoughts on Government (J. Adams), 208
three-fifths clause of U.S. Constitution, 251, 252, 288, 303
Three Mile Island, 1024, *1025*
Thurmond, Strom (1902–2003), 904–5, 906, *915*, 976
Tiananmen Square, protests in, 589, 1048, *1049*
Tibet, 993
Ticonderoga, Fort, 158, 185
Tidewater, Va., 132
Tilden, Samuel J. (1814–1886), 582

Till, Emmett (1941–1955), 954
Tillman, Juliann Jane, *338*
Timbuktu, Mali, *20*
Time, 832, 872, 896, 908, 947, 954, 999
Times, The, *380*
Times Square, *845*
"Times They Are A-Changin', The" (Dylan), 992
Tippecanoe, Battle of, 299
Tipsy (Kiyoshi), *767*
Titanic, 715
Title IX, 1014
Tito, *see* Broz, Josip
Tituba, 106
tobacco, 88, 128, 172, 275, 317, 407, *409*, 557, 646
in the backcountry, 114
in Chesapeake region, 54, *58*, 61, *61*, 63–64, *63*, 94, 98, *98*, 107, 109, 117, 123, 132–33
health effects of, 61
in New England, 77
in Northern colonies, 135
plantations, 118, 132–33
as substitute for gold, 61
and workers' death rate, 97
Tobacco Belt, 557
"tobacco brides," 62
Tocqueville, Alexis de (1805–1859), 307, 328, 330, 335, 349, 351, 352, 395, 425, 445, 621, 1072
Tokyo, Japan, 878
Tokyo Harbor, 472
Toledo, Ohio, 699, 811
Toleration Act (British; 1689), 102–3
Toleration Act (Maryland; 1649), as repealed, 83
tolls, 309
"too big to fail" financial institutions, 1115, 1119
Topeka, Kans., *953*
torture, 1100–1101, 1118
banned, 1121
To Secure These Rights, 904
totalitarianism, 897–98, 1042
see also dictators, dictatorships
Tourgée, Albion W. (1838–1905), 650
Toussaint L'Ouverture, François Dominique (1744–1803), 289, *289*
Towne, Laura M. (1825–1901), 540
Townsend, Francis (1867–1960), 814
Townsend Clubs, 814
Townshend, Charles (1725–1767), 178
Townshend Acts, repeal of, 180
Townshend crisis, 178–79
Toynbee Hall, 702
trade, 20–21, 35, 38–41, 64, 114–15, 294
in British-French war, 296–97
in Constitution, 253
of Dutch Empire, 35
in early U.S., 308
English mercantilism and, 88
European, with Africa, 19, 20
European, with Asia, 18, 19, *19*
European, with Indians, 57–58, 66–67, 92, 156, *158*
expansion of, 844
free, 218

fur, 38, 40, 43, 57–58, 76, 91, 117, 123, 133, 154, 160
among Indians, 9–10, 13, *13*
in Jefferson's inaugural address, 290
Navigation Acts and, 88
New England and, 77
regulations of, 104
of Rhode Island, 247
routes of, 18, *19*
transatlantic, 2, 5, 115–17, 127
in World War II, 845, 846, 856
see also free trade; slave trade
Trail of Tears, 376, 525
transcendentalism, 330, 429, 449, 707
"Trans-National America" (Bourne), 735
transportation, 168, 239, 307, 308, *311*, 328, 354, 355, 699
in Europe, 940
market revolution and, 307, 308, 318, 328
in Northwest, 318
public, 927
in South, 318
see also canals; railroads
Transportation Department, U.S., 977
Transportation of Cargo by Westerners at the Port of Yokohama (Utagawa), *471*
Trans World Airline, 1072
Trapper and His Family, The (Deas), 376
Travis, James W., *506*
Treasury Department, U.S., 381
Treaty of Amity and Commerce (1778), 891
Treaty of Ghent (1814), 300
Treaty of Greenville (1795), 265, *265*, 298
Treaty of Guadalupe Hidalgo (1848), 467, 468
Treaty of Paris (1763), 158, 160
Treaty of Paris (1783), 200, *210*, 221, 222
Treaty of San Lorenzo (Pinckney's Treaty) (1795), 293
Treaty of Utrecht (1713), 128
treaty system, 265
elimination of, 610
Tree of Liberty, 286
Trelawny, Edward (1792–1881), 138
Trenchard, John (1662–1723), 143, 148
Trenton, Battle of, 195
Triangle Shirtwaist Company, fire at, 677, 684, 789, 802
triangular trade, of New England colonies, 130–31
"triangulation," 1054
tribalism, attack on Native American, 611–14
Triborough Bridge, 806, *806*
trickle-down economics, *see* supply-side economics
Trifle Embarrassed, A, 535
Tripoli, 295, 296
Triumphant Entry of the Royal Troops into New York, 195
Tropos Networks, *1059*

Trotter, William Monroe (1872–1934), 741, 743

Troubles, The, 1004

Troy, N.Y., manufacturing in, 591

"True Sons of Freedom," 743

Trujillo Molina, Rafael (1891–1961), 843–44

Truman, Harry S. (1884–1972), 862, 876, 878, 880, 885, 886, 887–89, 888, 1053, 1090
  African-Americans and, 902–5
  anticommunism and, 911, 915
  Berlin airlift and, 891
  in campaign of 1948, 904–6
  civil rights and, 902–5, 952, 958
  communist China and, 891
  decolonization and, 896, 898
  Fair Deal and, 901
  Korean War and, 891–93
  presidency of, 901–6, 938
  strikes and, 901–2
  Vietnam and, 943, 945

Truman administration, 885, 886, 887, 891, 893, 895, 901–6, 908, 909, 914, 915, 940, 984
  Native Americans and, 998

Truman Doctrine, 887–89, 888, 907, 915, 936

Trumbo, Dalton (1905–1976), 908

Trumbull, Lyman (1813–1896), 565, 579

trusts, business, 594, 706, 706, 708, 711, 727, 764, 863
  and antitrust laws, 711, 863
  see also monopolies; Sherman Antitrust Act (1890)

Truth, Sojourner (1799–1883), 452

Tryon, William (1729–1788), 157

Tubman, Harriet (1820–1913), 418

Tucker, George (1775–1861), 290

Tufts, Joshua, 151

Tulsa, Okla., 744

Tulsa, Okla., race riot in, 744, 745

Tunisia, uprising in, 1122

Turkey, 659, 721, 888, 970
  missiles removed from, 970

Turner, Frederick Jackson, 600

Turner, Nat (1800–1831), 420–22, 421, 439

Tuskegee Institute, 656

TVA, see Tennessee Valley Authority

TV dinner, 928–29, 928

Twain, Mark (1835–1910), 615, 666

Tweed, "Boss" William M. (1823–1878), 616

Tweed Ring, 577, 616

Twelfth Amendment, 287

Twentieth Amendment, 823

Twenty-first Amendment, 809

Twenty-fourth Amendment, 976

Two Great Missionaries of Civilization, The, 672

Two Treatises on Government (Locke), 143, 143

Two Years Before the Mast (Dana), 460

Tyco International, 1060

Tyler, John (1790–1862), 349, 382, 419, 463

Tyler administration, 419, 463

Types of Mankind (Nott and Gliddon), 442

typewriter, 592

typhoid fever, in Jamestown, 58

U-2 spy plane, 942

UAW, see United Auto Workers

UFW, see United Farm Workers

Ulysses (Joyce), 777

Uncle Sam, 569, 653, 715, 747, 804, 810, 822, 845, 858

Uncle Sam's Thanksgiving Dinner (Nast), 569

Uncle Tom's Cabin (Stowe), 441, 442

Underground Railroad, 418

Underhill, John (1609–1672), 76

Underwood Tariff (1913), 711

unemployment, 380, 689, 709, 710, 762–63, 824, 825, 826, 834, 841, 852, 924, 933–34, 967, 968, 978, 1021, 1024, 1038, 1060, 1061–64, 1070, 1112, 1117, 1120
  of African-Americans, 980, 982, 1120
  African-Americans and, 829, 829, 980, 982, 1070
  Great Depression and, 790–91, 792, 793, 795, 805, 814, 820
  insurance, 817, 826, 830, 1115
  of Latinos, 998
  in 1990s, 1056
  public spending to combat, 824
  Second New Deal and, 815, 818, 824, 836, 837
  in Soviet Union, 802
  in 2001, 1101–2

Union League, 573, 574, 727

Union of Soviet Socialist Republics, see Soviet Union

Union Pacific Railroad, 524, 616

unions, 342, 426, 587, 629–30, 643, 657, 694, 746–47, 747, 766, 770, 775, 792, 810–13, 831, 834, 835, 870, 885, 911, 924, 936, 937, 984, 1022, 1037, 1082
  African-Americans and, 740, 744, 834–35, 870, 871, 949, 968
  blacklisting organizers of, 817
  Brandeis and, 689
  Clinton and, 1054
  company unions vs., 766
  consumerism and, 687
  counterculture and, 991
  discrimination by, 994
  in election of 1936, 823
  emergence of, 379, 812
  Ford and, 687
  in Great Britain, 1032
  in Great Depression, 810–13, 812
  highways and, 941
  Homestead strike and, 635–36
  industrialism and, 597
  Ku Klux Klan and, 781
  Latinos and, 997–98
  membership in, 813, 855, 855, 1064
  NAFTA and, 1052
  New Deal and, 757, 804–5, 836, 837
  in 1950s, 941
  Nixon and, 1012

open shop policies and, 804
Operation Dixie and, 901
Reagan and, 1033, 1036, 1037
restrictions on, 1123
scabs and, 689
supported by left, 831–32
Supreme Court and, 624
Taft-Hartley Act and, 902, 914
Tweed and, 616
Wal-Mart and, 1064
War Labor Board and, 727
War on Poverty and, 978
women and, 860
in World War II, 855
see also labor; labor movement; specific unions

United Auto Workers (UAW), 812–13, 814, 826, 859

United Electric Worker's union, 994

United Farm Workers union (UFW), 997–98, 997, 1068

United Fruit Company, 718, 943

United Labor Party, 631

United Mine Workers of America, 693, 695, 812

United Nations, 757, 886, 891, 893, 895, 899, 899, 900, 921, 1015, 1024, 1041, 1050, 1056, 1077, 1093
  in Balkans, 1056
  Charter of, 943, 1093
  creation of, 880
  Iraq War and, 1093
  see also General Assembly, U.N.; Security Council, U.N..

United States Housing Act, 824

United States Magazine and Democratic Review, 351

United States Sanitary Commission, 529
  see also nurses

United States v. Butler, 810

United States v. Cruikshank, 581

United States v. E. C. Knight Co., 624

United States v. Wong Kim Ark, 655

United Steelworkers of America, 812–13

United Steelworkers of America v. Weber, 1013

United Textile Workers, 811

Universal Declaration of Human Rights, 900

Universalists, 214

Universal Negro Improvement Association, 745

universal suffrage, 569, 571

University of North Carolina Press, 873

Unmarried Woman, An (movie), 1013

Unsafe at Any Speed (Nader), 1000

Uprising of the 20,000, 677, 691

urbanization, 678–88
  rise of cities, 681

Urban League, 826, 914

urban renewal, 933

Ursuline Convent, 327

Uruguay, 506

USA Patriot Act, 1097
  extension of, 1121

U.S. Steel, 594, 596, 706, 790, 813

Utagawa Sadahide (1807–1873), 471

Utah, 337, 467, 658, 703
  Mormons in, 605
  polygamy in, 605, 703
  woman suffrage in, 703

Utes, 460

utilities, 699, 710

Utopia, Ohio, 430

Utopia (More), 53, 426

utopian communities, 426–30, 428

Utrecht, Treaty of (1713), 128

Uzbekistan, 1091

"vagrants," 53

Valentino, Rudolph (1895–1926), 768

Vallandigham, Clement C. (1820–1871), 523

Valley Forge, Pa., 197

Valley of Mexico, 27

Van Bergen, Marten, 121

Van Bergen Overmantel (Heaten), 121

Van Buren, Martin (1782–1862), 375–76, 378, 462
  Amistad and, 419
  and annexation of Texas, 463–64
  background of, 365–66
  and depression of 1837, 380–82
  and election of 1828, 366
  Free Soil Party and, 474
  as Jackson's Secretary of State, 372
  nickname of, 367
  sectionalism and, 366

Vance, Cyrus (1917–2002), 986

van de Passe, Simon, 59

Vanderberg, Arthur (1884–1951), 888

Vanderbilt, Cornelius, II (1794–1877), 679

Vanderbilt, William (1821–1885), 677

Van Lew, Elizabeth (1818–1900), 534

Van Rensselaer, Kiliaen, 43

Van Rensselaer family, 118

Vanzetti, Bartolomeo (1888–1927), 759, 761

Vassa, Gustavus, see Equiano, Olaudah

vaudeville, 684

Veblen, Thorstein (1857–1929), 599

V-E Day, 876

velvet revolution, 1048

Venerate the Plough, 276

Venezuela, 359, 718, 772

Vera Cruz, Mexico, 466, 721

Verdun, Battle of, 721

Vermont, 823
  colony of, 178
  constitution of, 209, 228
  creation of, 284
  government in, 209
  2nd Vermont Volunteers of, 511

Verrazano, Giovanni da (ca. 1480–1527?), 14, 16, 66

Versailles conference, 746, 788

Versailles Treaty, 749, 749, 750, 752, 752, 753, 788, 844
  Senate debate on, 753

vertical integration, 595, 596, 597

Very Brief Account of the Destruction of the Indies, A (Las Casas), 29

Vesey, Denmark (1767?–1822), 420

Vespucci, Amerigo (1454–1512), 22, 23

Veteran in a New Field, The (Homer), 545
Veterans' Administration, 809
Veterans' Administration Medical
  Center, *1069*
Veterans' Bureau, 770
veto, presidential, 379, 565–66, 902, 911
veto, Southern, 826–27
vice presidency, U.S., 250
Vicksburg, Battle of, *507, 536*, 537, 540
Viet Cong, 985, 990, 1002, 1017
Vietnam, 751, 848, 943, 1069, 1096
  see also North Vietnam; South
    Vietnam
Vietnamization, 1016
Vietnam War, 729, 919–20, 960, 982–
    94, *986, 987, 1017, 1018*, 1019,
    1020, 1024, 1051, 1102, 1110
  and antiwar movement, 990–91,
    990, 1002–4, 1016, *1017*
  casualties in, 1016, 1017
  draft resisters of, 991, 1026
  My Lai massacre in, 1016
  Nixon and, 1016–18
  origins of, 945–46, 984–85
  Paris peace agreement and, 1017
  protests against, 990–91, 1009, 1093
  television and, 1003
  Tet offensive in, 1002
  troop numbers in, *986*, 1003
View from Bushongo Tavern, 216
Vikings, 21, 50
Villa, "Pancho" (1878–1923), 721
Village of Secoton, The (White), *12*
Vindication of the Rights of Woman, A
    (Wollstonecraft), 281, *281*, 453
Vinland, 21
Vinson, Fred (1890–1953), 953
Virginia, 217, 224, 240, 275, 1001, *1001*,
    1117
  desegregation in, 957
  domination of federal government
    by, 303
  Gabriel's Rebellion in, 289–90
  government of, 209, 214
  population of, 358
  religious freedom in, 211
  resolution in legislature of, 286–87,
    372
  slavery in, 391, *413*
  slave trade in, 317
  U.S. Constitution ratified by, 257
  voting rights in, 209, 348, 352
Virginia, University of, 214
*Virginia Bill for Establishing Religious
    Freedom*, 213
Virginia colony, *13*, 49–50, *52*, 54, *54,
    56*, 59–60, *59*, 60–61, *61*, 64, 66,
    103, 111, 118–19, 127, 144, 145,
    156, 179
  assembly in, 146
  Bacon's rebellion and, 99–100
  black population of, 101
  Britain's close ties to, 132
  Dissenter persecution in, 83
  elite class in, 118–19
  as first royal colony, 61
  free blacks in, 98, 99, 133, 144
  independence as viewed by, 185
  Indians in, 99–100, 111

population of, 62
poverty in, 99, 121
settlement of, *58*
sides with Charles I, 82
slavery in, 98, 100–101, 132, 133, *251*
Stamp Act and, 175
status of children in, 99
white society of, 61–62
women's role in, 62–63
Virginia Company, 2, 49–50, 59, 61
Virginia Luxuries, *413*
Virginia Plan, 248
Virgin Islands, 715
  slave uprising in, 139
Virgin Mary, 27, *27*, 35, 37, 38
Virgin of Guadalupe, 27, *28*
"virtual representation", in British
    Parliament, 173, *174*
Vishinsky, Andrei Y. (1883–1954), *899*
Visit from the Old Mistress, A (Homer),
    554
visiting nurse, *702*
VISTA, 978
Voice of America, McCarthy and, 909
Volga River, 850
voting rights, 211–14, 224, 350, 351–52,
    483, 687, 701, 954, 1080
  African-American loss of, 587, 649,
    701, 742, 743, 826, 829–30, 835,
    873, 957–58, 973, 976, 979
  for African-Americans, 403, 519,
    567, 568, 570, *874*
  in American colonies, 144, 207–8
  citizenship and, 701
  criminal records and, 1080
  emancipated slaves and, 549, 551,
    567, 568
  grandfather clause and, 649
  for Japanese women, 890
  literacy tests and, 649, 701
  Loyalists and, 221
  of Native Americans, 782
  photo I.D., and, 1123
  property qualifications and, 168,
    208, 209, 348, 349
  Puerto Ricans and, 740
  registration and black, 648–49,
    701
  religious freedom and, 211–14
  Tea Party and, 1123
  universal, *569*, 571
  in U.S., 169, 207–8
  Voting Rights Act and, 919, 976
  for women, 144, 351, 352, 448, 449,
    568, *569*, 570–71, 587, 640, 654,
    658–59, 678, 701, 703, *703, 704*,
    723, 728–29, *729, 730*, 766, 770
Voting Rights Act (1965), 352, 919,
    976, 980

Wabash v. Illinois, 623
Wade, Benjamin F., 567
Wade-Davis Bill, 541
"wade-ins," 966
wages, 216, 217–18, *318*, 325, 342, 343,
    439, 473, 747, 831, 1120
  African-Americans and, 339, 540,
    740, 787, 1038, 1105
  agricultural work for, 603

consumerism and, 684, 687, 703,
    764
cost of living increases in, 914, 941
cowboys and, 604
decline in real, 379, 1022, *1022*, 1024,
    1038, 1043, 1060, 1061
equal pay for equal work and, 448,
    1030, *1030*
Fordism and, 686
Great Depression and, 791, 793
hourly, 323, 1064
immigrants and, 683
inflation and increasing, 762
international standards for,
    1047–48
"living wage" and, 710, 728, 818, 825
and Mexican immigrants, 998, 1105
migrant farm workers and, 998
minimum, 705, 709, 770, *770*, 810,
    823, 824, 941, 1064, 1102
New Deal and, 814
overtime and, 824
and Prohibition, 730
and right to vote, 348
rising, 924
slavery compared with working for,
    343, *343*, 439
Social Security tax on, 818, 826,
    827
in South, 762
stagnation of, 1106
strike for higher, 328, 342, 573,
    604
tax brackets and, 1030, 1032, 1036
in U.S. compared with Europe, 598
and wage-earning poor, 329
women and, 340, 449, 453, 657, 740,
    860, 994, 1030, *1030*, 1076
in World War I, 727
in World War II, 852, 855, 860
Wagner, Fort, 518
Wagner, Robert (1877–1953), 817
Wagner Act (1935), 811, 816–17, 823,
    828, 885
Wahhabbism, 150
Wahunsonacock, 59
Waite, Davis (1825–1901), 642
Walden (Thoreau), 331
  title page of, *331*
Waldorf-Astoria Hotel, 599
Waldseemüller, Martin (1475–1522), *8*
Walker, David, 875
Walker, David (1796?–1830), 436, *436*,
    442
Walker, Francis Amasa (1840–1897),
    654
Walker, Scott (1967–), 1123
Walker, William (1824–1860), 493
Walking Purchase (1737), 111, 114
Wallace, George (1919–1998), 974, 976,
    1005, *1012*, 1028
Wallace, Henry (1888–1965), 861, 862,
    887, 905, 906
Wall Street, 678, 765, 771, 815, 846,
    905, 937, 1060, 1112, 1113, 1114,
    1115, 1119
  in depression, 792
  Occupy Movement and, 1123–24,
    1124

Wall Street Journal, 770
Wal-Mart, 1064
  and owners' wealth, 1120
Walt Disney, *846*
Walter, Anna, *1058*
Waltham, Mass., 321–22
Wampanoags, 87
wampum, *91*
War Advertising Council, 858
war bonds, 727, *728*, 852, 858, 869
War Department, U.S., 853, 874, 876
Warehouse Act (1916), 711
War Hawks, 297
War Industries Board, 726, 804
War Labor Board, 727
War Manpower Commission, 852
Warner, Charles Dudley (1829–1900),
    615
War News from Mexico (Woodville), *466*
War of 1812, 296, *298*, 299–302, *299,
    303*, 321, *350*, 353, 354, 355, 376,
    382, 552, 736, 847
  causes of, 297, 299
War of Independence, *see* American
    Revolution
War of Jenkins' Ear, 139
War of the Spanish Succession, 157
War of Triple Alliance, 506
War on Poverty, 977–78, *977*, 982, 998,
    1010
War on Terrorism, 921, 1088, 1089–91,
    1092, 1094, 1097–1101, 1109,
    1122, 1127
War Party at Fort Douglas
    (Rindisbacher), *298*
War Powers Act (1973), 1017
War Production Board, 852
Warren, Earl (1891–1974), 919, 953, 954,
    1000, 1002, 1012
Warren, James (1726–1808), 232
Warren, Josiah, 430
Warren, Mercy Otis (1728–1814), 232
Warren Court, 954, 1000–2, 1005
Warrior, Clyde (1939–1968), 998
Warsaw Pact, 891
War Spirit at Home (Spencer), *507*
washing machines, 762, 763, 928
Washington, 799, 823, 1074
  entrance into union of, 610
Washington, Augustus, *489*
Washington, Booker T. (1856?–1915),
    656, *656*, 657, 659, 741, 742, 829
Washington, D.C., 290, *291, 292*, 792,
    829, *908, 909, 981, 1003, 1031*,
    1032, 1039, 1070, *1073, 1091*, 1118
  British invasion of, 300
  march on, 968–69, *969*
  segregation in, 954
  September 11 attacks on, 1087
  Vietnam protests in, 991
Washington, Fort, 194
Washington, George (1732–1799),
    118–19, 156, 161, 179, 185, 193, *200*,
    290, 307, *350*, 356, 485, *658*, 736,
    846, 960
  in battle against French and
    Indians, 158
  cabinet of, 273
  Constitutional Convention and, 247

Washington, George (*continued*)
  at Constitution signing, *253*
  in Continental Congress, 183
  death of, 269, *275*
  Delaware crossing of, 195
  and exclusion of blacks from
    military, 193, 517
  executes mutineers, 199
  Farewell Address of, 284
  inauguration of, 273
  Native Americans and, 222, 265, 266
  re-election of, 284
  Republican press abuse of, 280
  and return of slaves, 227
  as slaveholder, *227, 228, 269*
  war strategy of, 194
  western land speculation of, 221
  Whiskey Rebellion and, 278–79, *278*
  at Yorktown, 199
Washington, Harry, 228
Washington, Lund (1737–1796), 193
Washington, Madison, 419
Washington, Martha (1732–1802), 269
Washington Heights, N.Y., 1066
Washington Naval Arms Conference,
  772
Washington Post, 1018
Washington Society, 431
Washington Star, 804
Wassaja newspaper, 698
Watch and Ward Committee, 775
water:
  conservation of, 708
  needs of Los Angeles and San
    Francisco, 708
  Owens Valley and, 708
water-boarding, 1101
Watergate scandal, 1018–19, *1019*, 1023,
  1024
water power, *321, 322*, 328
Waters, Ethel (1896–1977), 787
Watertown, Conn., *212*
Watling Island, 21
Watson, Tom (1854–1934), *638, 639,*
  649
Watson , Tom, 732
Watts, Calif., riot in, 979, *980*
Waud, William (1832–1878), *538*
Wayne, Anthony (1745–1796), 265, *265*
Wayne State University, 933
WCTU, *see* Women's Christian
  Temperance Union
Wealth Against Commonwealth (Lloyd),
  597
Wealth of Nations, The (Smith), 5, 218,
  235, 1113
weapons of mass destruction, 1091
  long-range bombers and, 942
  Saddam Hussein and, 1092, 1093,
    1097
  tests of, 906, *906*, 971
Weaver, James B. (1833–1912), 617,
  640, 656
Weaver, Richard (1910–1963), 937
Webster, Daniel (1782–1852), 368, *378,*
  736
  American Colonization Society
    and, 435
  Compromise of 1850 and, 475, *475*

death of, 477
  nullification crisis and, 372
Webster, Noah (1758–1843), 217, 343,
  350
Weekly Journal, 147, *149*
Weir, John F. (1841–1926), *589*
Welch, Joseph (1805–1891), 909, *909*
Weld, Theodore (1803–1895), 438,
  444, 445
welfare, 705, 710, 817–18, 823, 827,
  831, 836, 905, 911, 940, 974, 976,
  1028, 1032, 1039, 1052, 1053,
  1054, 1075, 1082, 1115–16
  expansion of, 861
  Nixon and, 1010–11
  Reagan and, 1032, 1036, 1039
  stigma of, 827
"welfare capitalism," 766
Welles, Gideon (1802–1878), 517
Wells, H. G. (1866–1946), 706
Wells, Ida B. (1862–1931), 652
Wells Fargo Bank, 1113
Wentworth, John (1737–1820), 221
"We Shall Overcome," 976
Wesley, Charles H., 873
West, *325*, 604, 605, 618, 619, 620, 636,
  731, 841, *854, 859*, 1009, 1030,
  1032
  African-Americans in, 830, 869
  cattle drives in, 604
  economic development of, 806, 807
  in election of 1824, 364
  fundamentalists in, 779
  government contracts and, 924
  immigrants and, 601, 602
  libertarianism in, 937
  manifest destiny and, 329
  Native Americans in, *377, 608*
  New Deal and, 806, 807, 827–29
  People's Party in, 637
  political corruption in, 616
  population growth in, 298, 1022
  religion in, 756
  rise of, 312–15
  rural migration to, 808, *810*
  as "safety valve," 600
  slavery in, 601
  transformation of, 600–615
  war production in, 853
West, Benjamin (1730–1813), *114*
West, William H. (1788–1857), *662*
West, woman suffrage in, *730*
West Bank, 1055
West Berlin, 1040
Westchester, Calif., *926*
Western Hemisphere, *44*
Western Ordinances, *244*
West Germany, 940
  creation of, 891
West India Company, 41, 43–44, *43*
West Indies, 5, 24, 42, 51, 106, *115*, 117,
  139, 173, 174, 245, *247*, 277, 492,
  786
  American embargo of, 183
  in American Revolution, 197
  economy of, 96–97
  English population of, 96
  European owners of, 96
  immigration to, 38, 54, 221

New England trade with, 78
  Philadelphia's trade with, 116
  slavery in, 25, 31, 87, 92, 95–97,
    128, *131*, 132, 133, 228, 396, 402,
    403–4, 412, 416, 443
  tobacco in, 61
West Jersey Concessions (1677), 93
West Memphis, Ark., *952*
Westo Indians, 101
West Point, N.Y., 199
West Side Story (musical), 933
West Virginia, *825*
  coal strike in, 706
  in 1960 election, 960
West Virginia (ship), *847*
westward expansion of U.S., 167, 221,
  240–45, *241*, 356, *472*, 591
  African-Americans and, 317
  Civil War and, 511, *512*
  Confederation government and, 242
  Douglas's views on, 477–79
  Jefferson's views on, 274
  Madison's views on, 255–56, 274
  market revolution and, 168, 308,
    312–15, *313*, 328–29, 348
  Mexican War and, 386
  Native Americans and, 242, 263,
    297–98
  of the North, 318
  numbers of people in, 459
  Ordinance of 1784 and, 243
  slavery and, 243, 317, 374, 385, 386,
    390, 470, 473, 474, 483–84
  of the South, 317
Weyl, Walter (1873–1919), 688, 740
Wharton, Edith (1862–1937), 599, 696
"What Every Girl Should Know," 697
"What Freedom Means to Us" (Nixon),
  923
What Social Classes Owe to Each Other
  (Sumner), 622
What the Negro Wants, 873
wheat, 319, 602
Wheatley, Phillis (1753?–1784), 226, *226*
Wheeling, W.Va., McCarthy speech
  at, 909
Whig Party, *367*, 368–69, 373, 380,
  381–82, *381*, 434, 463, 464, 466,
  485, 580, 631
  Abraham Lincoln as member of,
    487
  beliefs of, 369, 370–71
  collapse of, 479
  creation of, 364
  division between Democrats and,
    169, 369
  in election of 1836, 380
  in election of 1840, 381–82
  in election of 1848, 473
  freedom as viewed by, 370
  origin of name of, 347
  presidential veto and, 379
  and westward expansion of slavery,
    386
Whirling Thunder, *374*
Whiskey Rebellion, 278–79, *278*, 280,
  284
Whiskey Ring, 577, 616
White, Garland H. (1829–1894), 541

White, Horace (1834–1916), 623
White, John, 732
White, John (1540–1593), *12, 14*
White, Theodore (1915–1986), 1009
White, Walter (1893–1955), 830
White, William Allen (1868–1944), 846
white-collar jobs:
  corporations and, 925
  minorities and, 933–34
Whitefield, Edwin, *315*
Whitefield, George (1714–1770), 151, *151*
White Hall Plantation, 292
White House, The, *361*
White-Jacket (Melville), 465
"white man's burden," 670, 671, *671*
Whitewater, 1078
Whitman, Walt (1819–1892), 307, 600,
  808
Whitney, Anita (1867–1955), 777
Whitney, Asa (1791–1874), 524
Whitney, Eli (1765–1825), 315–17, 322
Whitney, Richard (1888–1974), 792
Whittier, John Greenleaf (1807–1892),
  454
"Who is Loyal to America?"
  (Commager), 913
*Whole Book of Psalms Faithfully Translated
  into English Metre, The*, 65
Whom Shall We Welcome, 911
Whyte, William (1917–1999), 947
Wichita, Kans., 604, *1058*
wildcat strikes, 941
Wilder, L. Douglas (b. 1931), 574
Wilderness, Battle of the, 537
Wilhelm II, emperor of Germany
  (1859–1941), 726, 728
Wilkes, John (1727–1797), *180*, 181
Willard, Frances (1839–1898), 658
William III, king of England (1650–
  1702), 102, *103*, 104
William Penn's Treaty with the Indians, 114
Williams, Roger (1820–1910), 13, 71,
  73, 82
Williamsburg, Va., *120*
Willkie, Wendell (1892–1944), 846,
  874, 895
Wilmington, Del., 44
  race riot in, 648
Wilmot, David (1814–1868), 473, 474
Wilmot Proviso, 473, 474, 475
Wilson, Charles (1890–1961), 940
Wilson, Edith (1872–1961), 753
Wilson, Edmund (1895–1972), 759
Wilson, Fred M. Huntington, 771
Wilson, James (1742–1798), *253*
Wilson, Woodrow (1856–1924), 586,
  587, 689, *704*, 706, 709–11, 719,
  721, 724, 732, 746, 747, 749–52,
  749, 752–53, 802, 912, 1100
  African-Americans and, 741, 743
  civil liberties and, 732
  Debs and, 732
  first term of, 710–11
  foreign policy of, 716, 720–21
  Fourteen Points and, 724–25
  immigrants and, 735–38, 739
  and League of Nations, 753
  Mexican policy of, 720–21
  New Freedom of, 710

Soviet Union and, 746
stroke of, 753
at Versailles, 748–49
woman suffrage and, 728–29
World War I and, 723, 726, 845
Wilson administration, 727, 729, 732,
743, 748, 845, 864
Wilsonism, 753
Winnipeg, 746
Winstanley, Gerard (1609?–1660), 81
Winthrop, John (1588–1649), 53, 66, 68,
70, 75, 432, 992
Anne Hutchinson and, 73
liberty as viewed by, 66, 68
Roger Williams and, 71
Speech to Massachusetts General
Court of, 75
Winthrop, John, II (1606–1676), 57
Wirz, Henry (1823–1865), 564
Wisconsin, 312, 700, 771, 907, 909,
974, 1123
Wisconsin, University of, 700
Wisconsin Idea, 700
Wisconsin Territory, 485
Wise, Henry A. (1806–1876), 489
witchcraft, 70
in New England, 105–6
"witch doctors," 15
Wolfe, James (1727–1759), 127
Wolfe, Tom (1931–), 1014
Wolfowitz, Paul D. (1943–), 1092
Wollaston, John (ca. 1642–1749), 151
Wollstonecraft, Mary (1759–1797), 281,
281, 453
Woman in the Nineteenth Century, 449
Woman Rebel, 697
Woman's Emancipation, 452
"Woman's Liquor Raid, A," 657
women, 677–78, 680, 756, 947, 1076
advertising and, 768, 860
affirmative action and, 1014
African-American, 646, 647, 648,
684, 741, 870, 982
agriculture and, 14, 15, 122–23
and American Revolution, 179,
232–35
capitalism and, 340–41
changing role of, 685, 685, 766–68,
859–60, 861
citizenship and, 781–82
and Civil War, 528–30, 529, 729
in Clinton administration, 1052
colonial roles of, 122–23
Confederacy and, 534–35
and "cult of domesticity," 339, 340,
340, 454
Daughters of Liberty, 179, 232–36
and decline in birthrate, 340
education and, 281, 283, 702, 705,
729, 1076
freedom and, 684–85, 692, 766–68,
768, 859–60
free speech and, 447–48
in gold rush, 470
in Great Plains, 603
Great Society and, 831
as immigrants, 1067, 1067
industrialization and, 323–24, 324
in kitchen debate, 923

Knights of Labor and, 625
labor and, 340–41, 625
market revolution and, 339–41, 343
maternalist reform and, 704–5,
766, 817
middle class, 351, 947
minimum wage and, 770, 770, 810
Native American, 14
in New Amsterdam, 90
New Deal and, 825–26
in New Netherland, 42
in New World, 27, 38, 40
in New York colony, 90
of planter class, 395
politics and, 232–34, 702, 703
poll tax on, 98
in Progressive era, 730
as Protestant preachers, 338
and "republican motherhood,"
339–40
right to vote for Japanese, 890
rise of feminism and, 657–59
role of, 233
as slaves, 98
strikes and, 343
subservience of European, 15, 17
Supreme Court and, 1076
and traditional homemaker role,
919, 920, 923, 931–32, 932, 961,
1030, 1076, 1076
in Virginia colony, 62–63
and wages, 449, 453, 657, 740, 860,
994, 1076
in the work force, 339–41, 452–53,
599, 625, 684–85, 684, 685, 692,
700, 702, 702, 841, 859, 860,
860, 931–32, 1014, 1039, 1076,
1077, 1112
working hours and, 704–5, 740
and World War I, 722
and World War II, 841, 842, 856,
859–60
see also gender relations; women's
rights
Women and Economics (Perkins), 685,
692
Women's Christian Temperance Union
(WCTU), 628, 658
Home Protection movement of,
658, 730
Women's Party, 1029
women's rights, 17, 169, 210, 280, 281,
340, 385, 425, 426, 446–55,
448, 587, 648, 657–59, 700, 756,
766–68, 781–82, 890, 919, 965,
994–96, 995, 998, 1004, 1005,
1034, 1081, 1118
Abigail Adams and, 205
American Revolution and, 167, 205,
232–35
antislavery movement and, 385
Declaration of Sentiments and,
448, 449
and education, 281, 283, 702, 705,
729
equal pay for equal work and, 448
families and, 454
Frederick Douglass and, 389
John Locke and, 143

Latinos and, 998
in Louisiana, 294–95
Lydia Maria Child and, 341
marriage and, 696
in Middle East, 1095
newspapers and, 449, 452
Owenites and, 429
post-World War II, 932
in Progressive era, 695–97, 703–5
Prohibition and, 730, 730
in Quaker society, 93, 94
quilt, 446
Reconstruction and, 568, 570–71
Seneca Falls Convention and, 446,
448, 452
sex and, 453, 697, 756, 766–68
and suffrage, 144, 351, 352, 448, 449,
529, 568, 570, 571, 587, 640, 654,
658–59, 678, 696, 701, 702, 703,
703, 704, 723, 728–29, 729, 730,
766, 770
in Utopian societies, 426, 430
see also abortion; gender relations;
women
Women's Studies, 1074
Women's Trade Union League, 677,
767
Wonderful Wizard of Oz, The (Baum), 644
Woodbury, Levi (1789–1851), 379
Woodside, John Archibald (1781–1853),
303
Woodstock, 992, 992
Woodville, Richard D. (1825–1855), 466
Wool Act (1699), 172
Woolman, John (1720–1772), 129–30
Woolworth's, sit-in at, 965
Worcester v. Georgia, 375
Workingman's Advocate, 341
*Workingman's Conception of Industrial
Liberty, The* (J.P. Mitchell), 693
Workingmen's Parties, 342
workmen's compensation, 705, 710
Works Progress Administration
(WPA), 799, 816, 816, 817, 824,
855
World Anti-Slavery Convention, 448
World Bank, 879, 886, 921, 1048
World's Constable, The, 719
World Series, 706
World's Fair, 595
World Trade Center, 1022, 1022, 1087,
1089, 1090, 1125
Islamic Cultural Center debate and,
1107, 1107
World Trade Organization (WTO), 921,
1047, 1048, 1049, 1063
World War I, 586, 721–34, 732, 750,
756, 757, 764, 772, 776, 783, 784,
785, 795, 804, 857, 1109
African-Americans and, 743, 869
agriculture in, 763
aircraft in, 722
casualties in, 721, 726
causes of, 721
divisiveness of, 856
effects of, 753, 772, 862
freedom and, 728, 731–32
Hoover's relief program in, 788
idealism and, 766

immigration and, 586, 648, 743,
842, 864–65
Jeanette Rankin and, 729, 847–48
Meuse-Argonne campaign in, 725
mobilization in, 841
Nye and, 845
patriotism in, 733–34
Progressives and, 724, 726–32
propaganda in, 727, 738
revolutions and, 746
technology in, 721
U.S. view of, 587, 716, 722
western front, 725
woman suffrage and, 728–29
women and, 722
World War II, 684, 728, 756, 799,
801, 840–83, 843, 845, 851, 856,
863–64, 864, 874, 875, 896, 935,
938, 1057, 1092, 1096, 1098
African-Americans and, 757, 842,
864, 865, 866, 869–76, 869, 874,
875, 949
British welfare state and, 817
casualties in, 847, 848–49, 850, 876,
878, 886
causes of, 757, 844
civil rights and, 842, 866, 949, 954
economic inequality in, 1060
effects of, 757, 880, 886
European theater of, 850, 851
freedom and, 757, 842, 843, 856,
857–58, 861, 864, 880–81
as Good War, 855
Great Depression and, 837
home front during, 852–60, 854
industry and, 852, 853–54, 853,
859, 860
Japanese-Americans and, 757, 842,
866–69, 867, 868, 953, 1099, 1100,
1109
Pearl Harbor and, 847–48
and post-war freedom, 860–63
Rosenbergs and, 908
unions in, 855
U.S. entry into, 837, 847–48
women and, 842, 859–60, 859
see also Four Freedoms
Wounded Knee Creek, Indian massacre at, 613–14
Wright, Frances (1795–1852), 447, 448
Wright, Jonathan (1840–1887), 574
Wright, Orville (1871–1948), 722
Wright, Wilbur (1867–1912), 722
WTO, *see* World Trade Organization
Wyatt, Francis (c. 1575–1644), 60
Wyoming, 658, 1021
entrance into union of, 610
woman suffrage in, 703
Yellowstone in, 707, 707, 708

XYZ affair, 285

YAF, *see* Young Americans for
Freedom
Yalta, conference at, 878–79, 887
Yamasee Indians, 92
Yazoo-Mississippi Delta, 974
yellow fever, 717
yellow press, 661, 662, 664

Yellowstone National Park, 707, *707*, 708
Yeltsin, Boris (1931–2007), 1049
Yemen, 1100
    war on terror in, 1122
Yick Wo v. Hopkins, 655
yippies, 992
yoga, counterculture and, 993, *993*
Yoga Journal, 993
Yom Kippur War, 1020

York, Pa., *213*, 216
Yorktown, Battle of, *198*, 200, *200*
Yoruba people, 136
Yosemite National Park, *707*, 708, *805*
Young, Andrew (1932–), 1024
Young, Brigham (1801–1877), 337, 605
Young, Thomas, 207
Young Americans for Freedom (YAF), 975–76, *975*, 988

Young Lady's Book, 340
Young Lords Organization, 998
Youth International Party, 992
Yugoslavia, 749, 753, 879, 1055–56, *1055*
    breakup of, *1050*
yuppies, 1038

Zangwill, Israel, 735, 740
Zenger, John Peter (1697–1746), 148–49, *149*

Zheng, Admiral, 18
Zimmermann, Arthur (1864–1940), 723
Zimmermann Telegram, 723
Zoar, 426
"zoot suit" riots, 865–66
Zulu, 601
Zuni Indians, 10

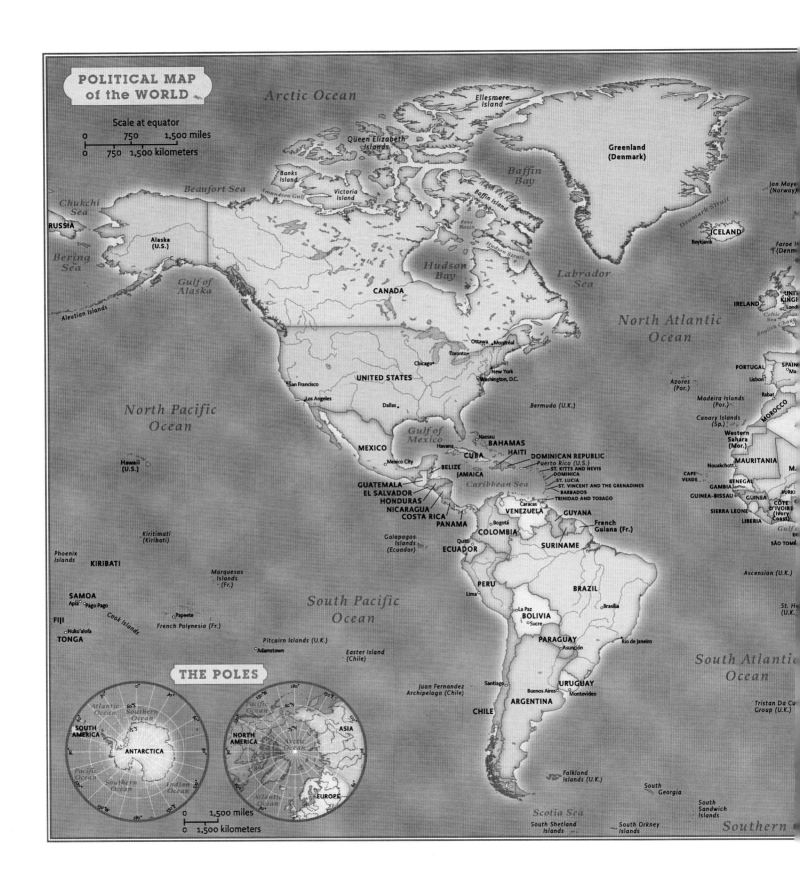

POLITICAL MAP of the WORLD

Scale at equator

0 — 750 — 1,500 miles

0 — 750 — 1,500 kilometers

Arctic Ocean

Ellesmere Island

Queen Elizabeth Islands

Greenland (Denmark)

Baffin Bay

Jan Maye (Norway)

Banks Island

Beaufort Sea

Amundsen Gulf

Victoria Island

Baffin Island

Denmark Strait

ICELAND

Chukchi Sea

RUSSIA

Alaska (U.S.)

Foxe Basin

Reykjavík

Faroe I (Denm

Bering Sea

Gulf of Alaska

Hudson Strait

Hudson Bay

Labrador Sea

North Atlantic Ocean

IRELAND

UNIT KINGI Lond

Aleutian Islands

CANADA

Celtic Sea

English Chan

Ottawa Montréal

Toronto

Chicago

New York

Washington, D.C.

PORTUGAL

SPAIN Ma

North Pacific Ocean

San Francisco

UNITED STATES

Azores (Por.)

Lisbon

Rabat

MOROCCO

Los Angeles

Dallas

Bermuda (U.K.)

Madeira Islands (Por.)

Canary Islands (Sp.)

Western Sahara (Mor.)

Hawaii (U.S.)

MEXICO

Gulf of Mexico

Nassau

Havana

BAHAMAS

CUBA

HAITI

DOMINICAN REPUBLIC

Puerto Rico (U.S.)

ST. KITTS AND NEVIS

DOMINICA

MAURITANIA

Nouakchott

M

Mexico City

BELIZE

JAMAICA

Caribbean Sea

ST. LUCIA

ST. VINCENT AND THE GRENADINES

BARBADOS

TRINIDAD AND TOBAGO

CAPE VERDE

SENEGAL

GAMBIA

BURKI

GUATEMALA

EL SALVADOR

HONDURAS

NICARAGUA

COSTA RICA

PANAMA

Caracas

VENEZUELA

GUYANA

French Guiana (Fr.)

GUINEA-BISSAU

GUINEA

SIERRA LEONE

LIBERIA

CÔTE D'IVOIRE (Ivory Coast)

Gulf En

SÃO TOMÉ

Kiritimati (Kiribati)

Galapagos Islands (Ecuador)

Bogotá

COLOMBIA

Quito

ECUADOR

SURINAME

Phoenix Islands

KIRIBATI

Marquesas Islands (Fr.)

PERU

Lima

BRAZIL

Brasília

Ascension (U.K.)

SAMOA

Apia Pago Pago

FIJI

Nuku'alofa

TONGA

Cook Islands

Papeete

French Polynesia (Fr.)

South Pacific Ocean

La Paz

BOLIVIA

Sucre

St. He (U.K.

PARAGUAY

Asunción

Rio de Janeiro

South Atlantic Ocean

Pitcairn Islands (U.K.)

Adamstown

Easter Island (Chile)

Santiago

Buenos Aires

URUGUAY

Montevideo

Tristan Da Cu Group (U.K.)

Juan Fernandez Archipelago (Chile)

ARGENTINA

CHILE

THE POLES

Atlantic Ocean

Southern Ocean

SOUTH AMERICA

60°S

75°S

ANTARCTICA

Pacific Ocean

Southern Ocean

Indian Ocean

Pacific Ocean

180°

150°W

60°N

75°N

Arctic Ocean

NORTH AMERICA

ASIA

Atlantic Ocean

EUROPE

0 — 1,500 miles

0 — 1,500 kilometers

Falkland Islands (U.K.)

South Georgia

South Sandwich Islands

Scotia Sea

South Shetland Islands

South Orkney Islands

Southern O